MARQUEE SERIES

Using Computers in the Medical Office

Microsoft® Word | Excel PowerPoint

2016

Workbook

Audrey Roggenkamp
Pierce College Puyallup
Puyallup, Washington

PARADIGM
EDUCATION SOLUTIONS

St. Paul

Division President	Linda Hein
Vice President, Content Strategy	Christine Hurney
Managing Editor	Cheryl Drivdahl
Developmental Editor	Jennifer Gehlhar
Assistant Developmental Editor	Mamie Clark
Tester	Janet Blum
Director of Production	Timothy W. Larson
Production Editor	Jen Weaverling
Senior Design and Production Specialist	Jaana Bykonich
Copy Editor	Sarah Kearin
Proofreader	Shannon Kottke
Indexer	Terry Casey
Vice President, Digital Solutions	Chuck Bratton
Digital Projects Manager	Tom Modl
Digital Solutions Manager	Gerry Yumul
Digital Production Manager	Aaron Esnough
Vice President Sales and Marketing	Scott Burns
Director of Marketing	Lara Weber McLellan

Care has been taken to verify the accuracy of information presented in this book. However, the authors, editors, and publisher cannot accept responsibility for web, email, newsgroup, or chat room subject matter or content, or for consequences from the application of the information in this book, and make no warranty, expressed or implied, with respect to its content.

Trademarks: Microsoft is a trademark or registered trademark of Microsoft Corporation in the United States and/or other countries. Some of the product names and company names included in this book have been used for identification purposes only and may be trademarks or registered trade names of their respective manufacturers and sellers. The authors, editors, and publisher disclaim any affiliation, association, or connection with, or sponsorship or endorsement by, such owners.

Paradigm Publishing, Inc., is independent from Microsoft Corporation and not affiliated with Microsoft in any manner.

Cover & Title Page Photo Credits: © Dutko/iStock.com, © yumiyum/iStock.com

We have made every effort to trace the ownership of all copyrighted material and to secure permission from copyright holders. In the event of any question arising as to the use of any material, we will be pleased to make the necessary corrections in future printings. Duplication of this content is permitted for internal distribution to staff or students using *Using Computers in the Medical Office*, for classroom use only and not for resale. No other use is permitted without written permission from the publisher.

ISBN 978-0-76388-045-3 (print)
ISBN 978-0-76387-834-4 (digital)

© 2018 by Paradigm Publishing, Inc.
875 Montreal Way
St. Paul, MN 55102
Email: CustomerService@ParadigmEducation.com
Website: ParadigmEducation.com

Printed in the United States of America

26 25 24 23 22 21 20 19   2 3 4 5 6 7 8 9 10

Contents

Information Technology Essentials   ITE-1

WORD 2016

Section 1 Creating and Editing a Document   1

Section 2 Formatting Characters and Paragraphs   9

Section 3 Formatting and Enhancing a Document   17

Section 4 Formatting with Special Features   29

EXCEL 2016

Section 1 Analyzing Data Using Excel   43

Section 2 Editing and Formatting Worksheets   51

Section 3 Using Functions, Adding Visual Elements, Printing,
and Working with Tables   59

Integrating Programs: Word and Excel   69

POWERPOINT 2016

Section 1 Preparing a Presentation   71

Section 2 Editing Slides and Slide Elements   79

Integrating Programs: Word, Excel, and PowerPoint   93

Workbook
Information Technology Essentials

Knowledge Check

Complete the Knowledge Check to assess your comprehension and recall of application features, technology, and functions.

Recheck

Check your understanding by taking this quiz.

Study Tools

Study tools include In Brief steps and medical resources. Use the study tools to help you further develop and review skills learned in this section.

Knowledge Check

Complete the Knowledge Check to assess your comprehension and recall of application features, technology, and functions.

Recheck

Check your understanding by taking this quiz.

Skills Review

 Columbia River General Hospital

Review 1 Moving the Insertion Point, Scrolling, and Inserting Text

 **Data File**

1. Open **CRGHConsult.docx** and save it with the name **1-CRGHConsult**.
2. Using the mouse pointer and/or keyboard, practice moving the insertion point by completing the following steps:
   a. Move the insertion point to the end of the document.
   b. Move the insertion point back to the beginning of the document.
   c. Scroll to the end of the document.
   d. Scroll back to the beginning of the document.
   e. Move the insertion point to the beginning of the second page.
   f. Move the insertion point to the beginning of the document.
3. Move the insertion point to the beginning of the date *06/25/2019* near the beginning of the document, type Date of Admission:, and then press the spacebar.
4. Move the insertion point to the beginning of the date *04/05/1939*, type Date of Birth:, and then press the spacebar.
5. Save **1-CRGHConsult.docx**.

Columbia River General Hospital **Review 2** Selecting and Deleting Text; Using Undo and Redo

1. With **1-CRGHConsult.docx** open, select and then delete the words *as well* located at the end of the second sentence in the *HISTORY* section. (Make sure the period that ends the sentence is positioned immediately to the right of the word *area*.)
2. Select and then delete the words *was brought to the Emergency Room by her husband and* from the fourth sentence in the *HISTORY* section.
3. Use the selection bar to select the line containing the sentence *Review of systems is unremarkable* in the second paragraph in the *HISTORY* section and then delete the line. ***Note: Make sure no extra space displays above the EXAMINATION heading.***

4. Undo the deletion.
5. Redo the deletion.
6. Select and then delete the last sentence in the *HISTORY* section. (*The rest of her social and family history is noted on the admission report.*).
7. Undo the deletion.
8. Deselect the text.
9. Save **1-CRGHConsult.docx**.

Columbia River General Hospital **Review 3** Checking the Spelling and Grammar in a Document

1. With **1-CRGHConsult.docx** open, move the insertion point to the beginning of the document.
2. Complete a spelling and grammar check on the document. ***Note: The medical term* nontender *is spelled correctly.***
3. Save **1-CRGHConsult.docx**.

Columbia River General Hospital **Review 4** Creating an AutoCorrect Entry and Using the Thesaurus

1. With **1-CRGHConsult.docx** open, add the following entries to the AutoCorrect dialog box:
   a. Insert *ic* in the *Replace* text box and *intertrochanteric* in the *With* text box.
   b. Insert *tr* in the *Replace* text box and *trochanter* in the *With* text box.
2. Move the insertion point to the blank line above the *RECOMMENDATIONS* heading (below the *EXAMINATION* section) and then type the text shown in Figure WB-1.1. ***Hint: Press Shift + Enter after typing* X-RAY *and after typing* IMPRESSION.**
3. Use the Thesaurus to make the following changes:
   a. In the first sentence of the *EXAMINATION* section, change *aware* to *alert*.
   b. At the end of the *HISTORY* section, change *unidentified* to *unknown*.
4. Delete the AutoCorrect entries for *ic* and *tr*.
5. Save, print, and then close **1-CRGHConsult.docx**.

Figure WB-1.1 Review 4, Step 2

X-RAY
Review of x-rays demonstrates a comminuted right ic hip fracture with comminution of the greater tr, as well as lesser tr.

IMPRESSION
Right comminuted ic hip fracture, noninsulin dependent diabetes mellitus, and hypercholesterolemia.

 **Review 5** Creating a Fax Using a Template

1. Click the File tab and then click the *New* option.
2. At the New backstage area, click in the search text box, type equity fax, and then press the Enter key.
3. Click the *Fax (Equity theme)* template and then click the Create button. (If this template is not available, use ***EquityFax.docx*** in the WordMedS1 folder.)
4. Insert the following information in the specified locations:
   a. *[Type the recipient name]* = Andres Diaz
   b. Select the text after the *From:* heading and then type your first and last names.
   c. *[Type the recipient fax number]* = (503) 555-0988
   d. *[Type number of pages]* = Cover page plus 1 page
   e. *[Type the recipient phone number]* = (503) 555-0900
   f. *[Pick the date]* = 5.30.2019
   g. *[Type text]* (located after *Re:*) = Interpreting Services and Fees
   h. *[Type text]* (located after *CC:*) = Greg Gordon
   i. Click in the square immediately to the left of *Please Comment* and then type the letter X.
   j. *[Type comments]* = Interpreting services and fees are shown on the following document.
5. Save the completed fax and name it **1-Fax**.
6. Print and then close **1-Fax.docx**.

Skills Assessment

 **Assessment 1** Inserting Text in a Document

1. Open **NSMCNotice.docx** and save it with the name **1-NSMCNotice**.
2. In the first paragraph of text, make the following changes:
   a. Change the day from *Thursday* to *Wednesday*.
   b. Change the date from *24* to *23*.
   c. Change the time from *7:30 to 9:00* to *7:00 to 8:30*.
3. Press Ctrl + End to move the insertion point to the end of the document and then type the information shown in Figure WB-1.2.
4. Save, print, and then close **1-NSMCNotice.docx**.

Figure WB-1.2 Assessment 1, Step 3

The presentation will include information on the prevalence of diabetes among people of different age and ethnic groups, health complications related to diabetes, and treatment and prevention of diabetes. For more information on the presentation, please contact Lee Elliott.

Assessment 2 Preparing a Memo

1. Open **CVPMemoForm.docx** and save it with the name **1-CVPMemoForm**.
2. Insert the following information after the specified heading:

To:	All Front Office Staff
From:	Sydney Larsen, Office Manager
Date:	(Insert current date)
Re:	Well-child Checkup Appointments

3. Move the insertion point below the *Re:* heading and then write the body of the memo using the following information (write the information in paragraph form—do not use bullets):
   - With the recent hiring of Dr. Joseph Yarborough, pediatric specialist, we will be scheduling additional well-child checkup appointments.
   - Schedule appointments at the ages of 2 weeks and 2, 4, 6, 12, 18, and 24 months.
   - Appointment length is generally 20 minutes.
   - Schedule well-child checkup appointments for Dr. Yarborough on Tuesdays and Thursdays.
   - Evening hours for appointments with Dr. Yarborough will be added next month.
4. Complete a spelling and grammar check on the memo.
5. Save, print, and then close **1-CVPMemoForm.docx**.

Assessment 3 Adding Text to a Scheduling Information Document

1. Open **CVPApptSched.docx** and save it with the name **1-CVPApptSched**.
2. Create an AutoCorrect entry that inserts *Appointments* when you type *Aps*.
3. Insert the following text in the document:
   a. Move the insertion point to the beginning of the second paragraph (begins with *These are short visits*), type Acute Illness Aps (20 minutes), and then press Shift + Enter. (The AutoCorrect feature will insert *Appointments* when you press the spacebar after typing *Aps*.)
   b. Move the insertion point to the beginning of the paragraph that begins *These appointments, available within one week*, type Routine Aps (20 minutes), and then press Shift + Enter.
   c. Move the insertion point to the beginning of the paragraph that begins *Physical examination appointments are usually*, type Physical Examination Aps (30 minutes), and then press Shift + Enter.
   d. Move the insertion point to the beginning of the paragraph that begins *All children should be seen*, type Well-child Checkup Aps (20 minutes), and then press Shift + Enter.
4. Complete a spelling and grammar check on the document.
5. Delete the AutoCorrect entry *Aps*.
6. Save, print, and then close **1-CVPApptSched.docx**.

Assessment 4   Locating Information about Word 2016 Features

1. At a blank document, display the Help task pane, click the <u>More</u> hyperlink, click the *Get started* option, and then click the <u>What's new in Word 2016</u> hyperlink.
2. Read about the new features in Word 2016.
3. Using the information you learn, prepare a memo to your instructor describing at least three new Word 2016 features.
4. Save the memo and name it **1-NewFeatures**.
5. Print and then close **1-NewFeatures.docx**.

Assessment 5   Researching a Medical Spelling Dictionary

1. As you learned in Activity 1.5, the standard spelling dictionary in Word does not contain all medical terms. Most offices, clinics, and hospitals that prepare medical documents and forms add a supplemental medical spelling dictionary to their Word software. One of the most popular is *Stedman's Medical Dictionary*. As the medical office assistant at North Shore Medical Clinic, your supervisor has asked you to locate information about the Stedman's medical spelling dictionary. Using the Internet, go to the Stedman's home page at www.stedmans.com. (If this website is not available, search for another company that sells a medical spelling dictionary and visit their home page.)
2. After looking at the information at the Stedman's website, prepare a memo to your supervisor, Lee Elliott, Office Manager. Include information on the medical spelling dictionary, including its web address, price, features, and how to order it.
3. Save the completed memo and name it **1-Dictionary**.
4. Print and then close **1-Dictionary.docx**.

Marquee Challenge

Challenge 1   Preparing a Presurgery Letter to a Doctor

1. Open **NSMCLtrhd.docx** and then save it with the name **1-NSMCInfoLtr**.
2. Type the letter as shown in Figure WB-1.3.
3. Remove the hyperlink from the email address (displays in underlined blue font) by right-clicking the email address and then clicking *Remove Hyperlink* at the shortcut menu.
4. Save, print, and then close **1-NSMCInfoLtr.docx**.

Challenge 2   Preparing Patient Chart Notes

1. Open **NSMCLtrhd.docx** and then save it with the name **1-NSMCNote**.
2. Type the chart notes as shown in Figure WB-1.4.
3. Save, print, and then close **1-NSMCNote.docx**.

Figure WB-1.3 Challenge 1, Step 2

North Shore
Medical Clinic

Date: _____

Dear Doctor _____:

Our mutual patient _____, D.O.B. _____, is scheduled for
surgery on _____. Please assist us by providing the following information:

      Pathology report
      Copy of most recent EKG
      New lab work (Basic Metabolic Panel, HCT/Hemoglobin, Protime/INR, K+)
      Clearance for surgery

The surgeon would like the patient to stop taking Coumadin as soon as possible prior to surgery. Please
let us know if instructing the patient to do so is safe and how long the patient can be off the medication.

Please fax or email requested information to us as soon as possible. Our fax number is (503) 555-2335
and our email address is http://ppi-edu.net/nsmc. If you have any questions, please call the clinic at
(503) 555-2330.

Sincerely,

Darrin Lancaster, CMA
Medical Assistant

1-NSMCInfoLtr.docx

7450 Meridian Street, Suite 150
Portland, OR 97202
(503) 555-2330
http://ppi-edu.net/nsmc

Figure WB-1.4 Challenge 2, Step 2

North Shore
Medical Clinic

PATIENT: Grace Montgomery
DATE OF VISIT: 04/18/2019

SUBJECTIVE
Patient is complaining of itching and a rash that began about three weeks ago, starting on the hands and arms and spreading to the chest and back. She is currently taking Benadryl at bedtime with little relief. She stated that she tried a new perfume after her shower three or four days before the rash appeared.

OBJECTIVE
GENERAL APPEARANCE: Normal.
VITAL SIGNS: Temperature 98.6 degrees, blood pressure 140/74, weight 145, height 5 feet 6 inches, heart rate 74, respirations 22.
SKIN: Patient has a smooth, erythematous rash over her neck extending over her trunk and back. She has a confluent, erythematous rash extending to fingertips on her upper extremities. Wheals with patechiae are noted in the antecubital fossae bilaterally.

ASSESSMENT
Contact dermatitis, secondary to allergy to perfume.

PLAN
Avoid use of any perfume or perfumed soap.
Wash or dry-clean all clothing and linens exposed to suspected perfume.
Take diphenhydramine (Benadryl) 25 mg q6 h x 3 days.

_____

Jonathon Melina, MD

JM:SN

7450 Meridian Street, Suite 150
Portland, OR 97202
(503) 555-2330
http://ppi-edu.net/nsmc

Study Tools

Study tools include In Brief steps and medical resources. Use the study tools to help you further develop and review skills learned in this section.

Knowledge Check

Complete the Knowledge Check to assess your comprehension and recall of application features, technology, and functions.

Recheck

Check your understanding by taking this quiz.

Skills Review

Review 1   Applying Fonts; Using the Format Painter; Using the Repeat Command

Data File

1. Open **CVPWell-Child.docx** and save it with the name **2-CVPWell-Child**.
2. Select the entire document and then change the font to Constantia.
3. Select the title, *WELL-CHILD APPOINTMENTS*, change the font to 16-point Candara, apply bold formatting, and then deselect the text.
4. Select the heading *Appointment Recommendations*, change the font to 14-point Candara, apply bold formatting, and then deselect the heading.
5. Using Format Painter, apply the same formatting you applied in Step 4 to the remaining headings (*Appointment Services*, *Appointment Suggestions*, *Immunizations*, and *Child Development Assessment*).
6. Select the last paragraph of text in the document (the text in parentheses), change the font size to 10 points, and then apply small caps formatting. ***Hint: The* Small caps *check box is located in the* Effects *section on the Font tab of the Font dialog box.***
7. Select *WELL-CHILD APPOINTMENTS* and then apply the shadow option in the first column, first row in the *Outer* section from the *Shadow* side menu of the Text Effects and Typography button drop-down list.
8. Select the heading *Appointment Recommendations* and then apply the shadow option in the first column, first row in the *Outer* section from the *Shadow* side menu of the Text Effects and Typography button drop-down list.
9. Use the Repeat command to apply the text effect from Step 8 to the remaining headings in the document (*Appointment Services*, *Appointment Suggestions*, *Immunizations*, and *Child Development Assessment*).
10. Save **2-CVPWell-Child.docx**.

Review 2 Aligning and Indenting Text; Changing Line and Paragraph Spacing; Inserting Bullets and Numbering

1. With **2-CVPWell-Child.docx** open, position the insertion point anywhere in the paragraph below the heading *Appointment Recommendations*, change the paragraph alignment to justify, and then indent the paragraph 0.25 inch from the left margin.
2. Position the insertion point anywhere in the last paragraph of text in the document (the text in parentheses) and then change the paragraph alignment to center.
3. Select the entire document and then change the line spacing to 1.15.
4. Click anywhere in the heading *Appointment Recommendations* and then change the spacing after paragraphs to 6 points.
5. Use the Repeat command to change the paragraph spacing after the remaining headings (*Appointment Services*, *Appointment Suggestions*, *Immunizations*, and *Child Development Assessment*) to 6 points.
6. Select the seven lines of text below the *Appointment Services* heading and then insert bullets.
7. Select the paragraphs of text below the heading *Appointment Suggestions* and then insert numbering.
8. Move the insertion point to the end of the second numbered paragraph, press the Enter key, and then type Bring snacks for young children in case you have to wait for your appointment.
9. Save **2-CVPWell-Child.docx**.

Review 3 Setting Tabs; Adding Borders, Shading, and Symbols

1. With **2-CVPWell-Child.docx** open, position the insertion point at the end of the paragraph that begins *Cascade View Pediatrics' schedule for immunizations*, press the Enter key two times, and then create the tabbed text shown in Figure WB-2.1 with the following specifications:
   a. Set a left tab at the 1.5-inch mark on the horizontal ruler.
   b. Set a right tab at the 5-inch mark on the horizontal ruler.
   c. Type the column headings (*Vaccine* and *Shots/Doses*) with bold and underline formatting at the appropriate tabs.
   d. Before typing the column entries, display the Tabs dialog box and add leaders to the right tab as shown in the figure.
   e. Type the remainder of the text as shown in the figure.
2. Select the tabbed text you just typed (including the blank line above the column headings, the sentences after the asterisks, and the blank line below the sentences) and then apply a border and shading of your choosing.
3. Click anywhere in the title *WELL-CHILD APPOINTMENTS* and then apply shading of your choosing. (The shading will span from the left to the right margin.)
4. Apply a page border of your choosing to the document. (If possible, match the color of the page border with the colors in the letterhead and/or title shading.)
5. Position the insertion point in the heading *Immunizations* and then keep the heading with the paragraph of text located on the next page. ***Hint: Use the* Keep with next *check box in the Paragraph dialog box.***
6. Move the insertion point to the end of the document.

Figure WB-2.1 Review 3

Vaccine	Shots/Doses
Hepatitis B	3 shots
DTaP	5 shots
Hib	4 shots
Pneumococcal (PCV)	4 shots
Polio	4 shots
Measles-Mumps-Rubella	2 shots
Varicella (chickenpox)	1 shot
Influenza*	1 or 2 doses
Hepatitis A**	2 shots

*Two doses are recommended for children receiving the influenza vaccine for the first time.
**The hepatitis A vaccine is recommended only in certain areas where infection rates are highest.

7. Change the font to Candara, the line spacing to single, and the spacing after paragraphs to 0. Type the following text at the left margin:
   ®2019 Cascade View Pediatrics
   Raphaël Severin, MD
8. Save, print, and then close **2-CVPWell-Child.docx**.

North Shore Medical Clinic

Review 4   Applying Styles and a Theme; Inserting the Date, Time, and Quick Parts

Data File

1. Open **CysticFibrosis.docx** and save it with the name **2-CysticFibrosis**.
2. Apply the Heading 1 style to the title *Cystic Fibrosis* and apply the Heading 2 style to the headings *Cause, Diagnosis,* and *Symptoms of Cystic Fibrosis*.
3. Apply the Lines (Simple) style set to the document.
4. Apply the Depth theme.
5. Apply the Slipstream theme colors.
6. Apply the Cambria theme fonts.
7. Change the paragraph spacing to Tight. ***Hint: Use the Paragraph Spacing button in the Document Formatting group on the Design tab.***
8. Move the insertion point to the end of the document, insert the current date (you choose the format), press Shift + Enter, and then insert the current time (you choose the format).
9. Insert the Sideline cover page. ***Hint: Choose the Sideline cover page at the Building Blocks Organizer dialog box.***
10. Click the *[Company name]* placeholder and then type North Shore Medical Clinic.
11. Click the *[Document title]* placeholder and then type Cystic Fibrosis.
12. Delete the *[Document subtitle]* placeholder.
13. Select the name displayed toward the bottom of the cover page and then type your first and last name.
14. Insert the current date in the *[Date]* placeholder.
15. Save, print, and then close **2-CysticFibrosis.docx**.

Skills Assessment

North Shore Medical Clinic

Assessment 1 Changing Fonts; Aligning and Indenting Text; Changing Paragraph Spacing

Data File

1. Open **NSMCRequest.docx** and save it with the name **2-NSMCRequest**.
2. Select the entire document and then change the font to Cambria and the font size to 12 points.
3. Set the title, *MEDICAL RECORDS*, in 14-point Constantia and then apply bold formatting.
4. Set the heading *How to Request a Copy of Your Medical Records* in 12-point Constantia, apply bold formatting, add a shadow text effect, and then change the spacing after the paragraph to 6 points.
5. Use Format Painter to apply the same formatting you applied in Step 4 to the following headings in the document:
   Information from Your Medical Records
   Submitting a Request
   Additional Information about Medical Records
   Mailing Medical Records
   Reproduction Charges
   Sending Records to Another Medical Facility
   Processing Time
   Picking Up Medical Records
6. Select the title, *MEDICAL RECORDS*, center the text, and then apply paragraph shading of your choosing.
7. Select the four lines of text below the paragraph in the *How to Request a Copy of Your Medical Records* section (*AIDS/HIV* through *Fertility treatment*) and then apply bullets.
8. Select all the text in the *Submitting a Request* section *except* the first paragraph (the paragraph that begins *Once you have completed*) and then indent it 0.5 inch from the left margin.
9. Move the insertion point to the end of the document and then type the following text at the left margin (press Shift + Enter after typing the first line of text):
   ®2019 North Shore Medical Clinic
   Maria Cárdenas, MD
10. Save and then print **2-NSMCRequest.docx**.
11. Apply the Heading 1 style to the title, *MEDICAL RECORDS*, and apply the Heading 2 style to the headings (*How to Request a Copy of Your Medical Records, Information from Your Medical Records, Submitting a Request, Additional Information about Medical Records, Mailing Medical Records, Reproduction Charges, Sending Records to Another Medical Facility, Processing Time,* and *Picking Up Medical Records*).
12. Apply the Basic (Elegant) style set, apply the Frame theme, and then change the theme colors to Violet.
13. Save, print, and then close **2-NSMCRequest.docx**.

Assessment 2   Preparing and Formatting a Letter

1. Open **NSMCLtrhd.docx** and save it with the name **2-NSMCLetter**.
2. Click the *No Spacing* style. (This removes the 8 points of spacing after paragraphs and changes the line spacing to single.)
3. You have been asked by your supervisor to send a letter to the local community college indicating that a medical office assistant internship is available. Send the letter to Mrs. Janae Meyers, Medical Assistant Program, Columbia River Community College, Third Avenue North, Portland, OR 97301, and include the following information:
    - In the first paragraph, tell Mrs. Meyers that your clinic has an opening for a medical office assistant intern for 15 hours a week. Note that the position pays minimum wage and has flexible hours.
    - In the second paragraph, tell Mrs. Meyers that the intern will be trained in specific areas and then include the following in a numbered list: registering patients, typing memos and correspondence, filing correspondence and some medical records, making photocopies, and scheduling appointments.
    - In the third paragraph, tell Mrs. Meyers that she can contact Lee Elliott at the clinic. Provide the clinic name, address, telephone number, and web address. *Hint: This information can be found in the letterhead.*
    - End the letter with the complimentary close *Sincerely,* and then type your name four lines below it.
4. After typing the letter, select the text and then change the font to a font other than Calibri.
5. Change the numbered list to a bulleted list.
6. Save, print, and then close **2-NSMCLetter.docx**.

Assessment 3   Setting Leader Tabs

1. Open **CVPLtrhd.docx** and save it with the name **2-CVPHours**.
2. Type the text shown in Figure WB-2.2. *Hint: Make sure to apply bold formatting to the title,* **CLINIC HOURS.**
3. After typing the text, select the document and then change the font to Candara.
4. Save, print, and then close **2-CVPHours.docx**.

Assessment 4   Finding Information on Controlling Page Breaks

1. Your supervisor at North Shore Medical Clinic, Lee Elliott, has asked you to learn about how to prevent page breaks between paragraphs and how to make sure that at least two lines of a paragraph appear at the top or bottom of a page to prevent widows (when the last line of a paragraph appears by itself at the top of a page) and orphans (when the first line of a paragraph appears by itself at the bottom of a page). Use the Help task pane in Word to locate the necessary information.
2. Your supervisor would like you to prepare a memo to all medical office staff about the information you have found. To do so, complete the following steps:
    a. Open **NSMCMemoForm.docx** and save it with the name **2-NSMCMemo**.
    b. Create an appropriate subject for the memo.
    c. Write a paragraph discussing how to prevent page breaks between paragraphs in Word and list the steps required to complete the task.

Figure WB-2.2 Assessment 3

CLINIC HOURS

Monday .... 8:00 a.m. to 7:00 p.m.

Tuesday .... 8:00 a.m. to 5:00 p.m.

Wednesday .... 8:00 a.m. to 7:00 p.m.

Thursday .... 8:00 a.m. to 5:00 p.m.

Friday .... 8:00 a.m. to 3:00 p.m.

Saturday .... 9:00 a.m. to 1:00 p.m.

Sunday .... CLOSED

---

    d.   Write a paragraph discussing how to keep selected paragraphs together on a single page and list the steps required to complete the task.

    e.   Write a paragraph discussing how to prevent widows and orphans and list the steps required to complete the task.

3. Save, print, and then close **2-NSMCMemo.docx**.

Assessment 5   Locating Information and Writing a Memo

1. Visit the website of the American Association of Medical Assistants (AAMA) at www.aama-ntl.org. At the website, find the following information:
   - Mission of the AAMA
   - Administrative duties of a medical assistant
   - Salaries and benefits of a medical assistant
   - Any other information you find interesting

2. Using one of Word's memo templates, create a memo to your instructor explaining the information you found at the website.

3. Save the completed memo with the name **2-AAMAMemo**.

4. Print and then close **2-AAMAMemo.docx**.

Marquee Challenge

Challenge 1   Preparing a Job Announcement

1. Open **NSMCLtrhd.docx** and save it with the name **2-NSMCAnnouncement**.

2. Click the *No Spacing* style, change the font to 12-point Cambria, and then type the job announcement shown in Figure WB-2.3. Change the font size of the title to 14 points and apply paragraph shading as shown. ***Hint: Display the Colors dialog box to locate the purple shading color.***

3. Save, print, and then close **2-NSMCAnnouncement.docx**.

JOB ANNOUNCEMENT

JOB TITLE .... Medical Office Assistant
STATUS .... Full-time employment
SALARY .... Depending on experience
CLOSING DATE .... March 1, 2019

JOB SUMMARY
- Register new patients; assist with form completion
- Retrieve charts
- Enter patient data into computer database
- Maintain and file medical records
- Schedule patients
- Call patients with appointment reminders
- Answer telephones and route messages
- Call and/or fax pharmacy for prescription order refills
- Mail lab test results to patients
- Perform other clerical duties as required

REQUIRED SKILLS
- Keyboarding (35+ wpm)
- Knowledge of Microsoft Word, Excel, and PowerPoint
- Thorough understanding of medical terms
- Excellent grammar and spelling skills
- Excellent customer service skills

EDUCATION
- High school diploma
- Post-secondary training as a medical office assistant, CMA or RMA preferred
- CPR certification

For further information, contact Lee Elliott at (503) 555-2330.

7450 Meridian Street, Suite 150
Portland, OR 97202
(503) 555-2330
http://ppi-edu.net/nsmc

 **North Shore Medical Clinic** **Challenge 2** Preparing a Flyer for a Diabetes Presentation

1. At a blank document, remove the spacing after paragraphs, change the font to Constantia, and then create the flyer shown in Figure WB-2.4.
2. Save the completed flyer with the name **2-Flyer**.
3. Print and then close **2-Flyer.docx**.

Figure WB-2.4 Challenge 2

Understanding

DIABETES

Please join Dr. Kári St. Claire from North Shore Medical Clinic as she presents *Understanding Diabetes*. At this informative presentation, she will discuss:

- Types of diabetes
- Statistics on diabetes
- Complications of diabetes
- Living with diabetes
- Developing self-management skills

When .... Wednesday, October 16
Time ....7:00 p.m. to 8:30 p.m.
Where .... Columbia River General Hospital
Location .... Room 224
Cost .... FREE!

Sponsored by the
Greater Portland Healthcare Workers Association

Study Tools

Study tools include In Brief steps and medical resources. Use the study tools to help you further develop and review skills learned in this section.

Knowledge Check

Complete the Knowledge Check to assess your comprehension and recall of application features, technology, and functions.

Recheck

Check your understanding by taking this quiz.

Skills Review

Review 1   Finding and Replacing Text; Cutting and Pasting Text

1. Open **CRGHMedRecs.docx** and then save it with the name **3-CRGHMedRecs**.
2. Find every occurrence of *crgh* and replace it with *Columbia River General Hospital*.
3. Select the heading *Modifying Medical Records*, the paragraph of text below it, and the blank line below the paragraph and then move the selected text to the end of the document.
4. Save **3-CRGHMedRecs.docx**.

Review 2   Copying and Pasting Text

1. With **3-CRGHMedRecs.docx** open, open **CRGHRecMaint.docx**.
2. Display the Clipboard task pane and make sure it is empty.
3. At **CRGHRecMaint.docx**, select and then copy text from the beginning of the heading *Storage and Security* to the blank line just above the heading *Creating a Patient Profile*.
4. Select and then copy text from the beginning of the heading *Creating a Patient Profile* to the blank line just above the heading *Creating Progress Notes*.
5. Select and then copy text from the heading *Creating Progress Notes* to the end of the document.
6. Make **3-CRGHMedRecs.docx** the active document.
7. Display the Clipboard task pane.
8. Move the insertion point to the end of the document and then paste the text (merge formatting) that begins with the heading *Creating Progress Notes*.
9. With the insertion point positioned at the end of the document, paste the text (merge formatting) that begins with the heading *Creating a Patient Profile*.

10. With the insertion point positioned at the end of the document, paste the text (merge formatting) that begins with the heading *Storage and Security*.
11. Clear the contents of the Clipboard task pane and then close the task pane.
12. Save **3-CRGHMedRecs.docx**.
13. Make **CRGHRecMaint.docx** the active document and then close it.

 **Review 3** Inserting Page Numbers; Changing Margins; Changing Page Orientation

1. With **3-CRGHMedRecs.docx** open, insert page numbers that print at the bottom of each page using the *Plain Number 2* option.
2. Change the page orientation to landscape.
3. Change the top and bottom margins to 1.5 inches.
4. Save and then print **3-CRGHMedRecs.docx**.

 **Review 4** Inserting a Footer; Applying a Theme

1. With **3-CRGHMedRecs.docx** open, change the page orientation to portrait and then change the left and right margins to 1 inch.
2. Remove the page numbering. ***Hint: Do this with the* Remove Page Numbers *option at the Page Number button drop-down list.***
3. Insert the Ion (Dark) footer. When the footer is inserted in the document, click the *[DOCUMENT TITLE]* placeholder text and then type Creating and Maintaining Medical Records. Type your first and last names in the *[AUTHOR NAME]* placeholder and then double-click in the document to make it active.
4. Apply the Heading 1 style to the title *COLUMBIA RIVER GENERAL HOSPITAL* and then apply the Heading 2 style to the following headings: *Legal Department, Creating and Maintaining Medical Records, Creating Medical Records, Modifying Medical Records, Creating Progress Notes, Creating a Patient Profile,* and *Storage and Security.*
5. Apply the Lines (Simple) style set to the document.
6. Apply the Organic theme to the document.
7. Change the theme colors to Blue.
8. Save **3-CRGHMedRecs.docx**.

 **Review 5** Inserting WordArt; Drawing a Shape; Inserting a Text Box

1. With **3-CRGHMedRecs.docx** open, move the insertion point to the beginning of the document, press the Enter key two times, move the insertion point back to the beginning of the document, and then click the Clear All Formatting button in the Font group.
2. Insert the WordArt shown in Figure WB-3.1. ***Hint: Click the* Blue Outline *option in the fourth column, second row of the drop-down gallery.***
3. With the WordArt selected, type 0.6 in the *Shape Height* measurement box, type 6 in the *Shape Width* measurement box, and then press the Enter key. Apply the Square text effect. (Find this effect by clicking the Text Effects button on the Drawing Tools Format tab and then pointing to *Transform.*) Move the WordArt so it is positioned as shown in Figure WB-3.1.
4. Change the paragraph alignment to center for the headings *COLUMBIA RIVER GENERAL HOSPITAL* and *Legal Department.*

5. Move the insertion point to the end of the document and then draw a Bevel shape (use the shape option in the first column, third row of the *Basic Shapes* section) as shown in Figure WB-3.2. Change the height of the shape to 1.5 inches and the width to 4 inches and then apply the blue shape style in the second column, fourth row in the *Theme Styles* section.
6. With the shape selected, type the text shown in Figure WB-3.2. Select the text and then change the font size to 13 points. If necessary, move the shape so it is centered between the left and right margins.
7. Press Ctrl + Home to move the insertion point to the beginning of the document and then insert the *Grid Quote* text box.
8. With the text box selected, type A patient's medical record is a legal document that records events and decisions that help physicians manage patient care.
9. Change the width of the text box to 2.3 inches and then change the position of the text box to Position in Middle Right with Square Text Wrapping.
10. Save **3-CRGHMedRecs.docx**.

 Columbia River General Hospital

Review 6   Formatting Text in Columns

1. With **3-CRGHMedRecs.docx** open, move the insertion point to the blank line below the last paragraph of text (above the shape) and then insert a continuous section break.
2. Move the insertion point to the beginning of the first paragraph of text (the text that begins *At Columbia River General Hospital, physicians are*) and then insert a continuous section break.
3. Format text into two columns with a line and 0.4-inch spacing between them.
4. Press Ctrl + End to move the insertion point to the end of the document and then insert a continuous section break.
5. Scroll through the document, making sure to keep headings with paragraphs of text. If necessary, move the shape at the end of the document so it does not overlap any text.
6. Save, print, and then close **3-CRGHMedRecs.docx**.

Figure WB-3.1 WordArt for Review 5

Figure WB-3.2 Shape for Review 5

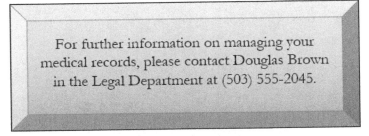

North Shore
Medical Clinic

Review 7   Inserting and Formatting an Image

Data File

1. Open **NSMCPreCare.docx** and then save it with the name **3-NSMCPreCare**.
2. Insert the image *pregnancy.png* from the WordMedS3 folder on your storage medium. Change the text wrapping for the image to *Tight*, change the height of the image to 2.5 inches, and then apply the Drop Shadow Rectangle picture style to the image. (This style is the fourth thumbnail in the Picture Styles group on the Picture Tools Format tab.) Position the image as shown in Figure WB-3.3.
3. Save, print, and then close **3-NSMCPreCare.docx**.

North Shore
Medical Clinic

Review 8   Preparing an Envelope

1. At a blank document, prepare an envelope with the return and delivery addresses shown in Figure WB-3.4 and add the envelope to the document.
2. Save the document with the name **3-NSMCEnv**.
3. Print and then close **3-NSMCEnv.docx**. (You may need to manually feed the envelope into the printer.)

Figure WB-3.3 Review 7

North Shore
Medical Clinic

TAKING CARE OF YOURSELF

Prenatal Care Guidelines

- Stop smoking and avoid consistent or prolonged exposure to second-hand smoke.
- Stop all alcohol and recreational drug use.
- Limit your caffeine intake to the equivalent of one cup of coffee a day.
- Eat a healthy, well-balanced diet.
- Drink approximately eight glasses of water daily.
- Participate in moderate exercise regularly.
- Sleep seven to eight hours a night.
- Take your prenatal vitamins daily.
- Avoid taking any over-the-counter or prescribed medication unless your physician knows you are taking them.
- Avoid contact with noxious chemicals such as household cleaners, paint, varnish, and hair dye.
- Avoid changing kitty litter and wear gloves when gardening to decrease exposure to infections that may be present in cat litter and soil.
- All meat, poultry, fish, and seafood should be well cooked.
- Limit your intake of fish purchased in stores and restaurants to six to twelve ounces per week.

7450 Meridian Street, Suite 150
Portland, OR 97202
(503) 555-2330
http://ppi-edu.net/nsmc

Figure WB-3.4 Review 8

North Shore Medical Clinic
7450 Meridian Street
Suite 150
Portland, OR 97202

Jennifer Cruz
Women's Health Center
142 Southeast Powell Boulevard
Portland, OR 97334

Review 9   Preparing Mailing Labels

1. At a blank document, prepare a sheet of return-address mailing labels for the following name and address using the Avery US Letter 5160 Easy Peel Address Labels:

   North Shore Medical Clinic
   7450 Meridian Street
   Suite 150
   Portland, OR 97202

2. Save the mailing label document with the name **3-NSMCLabel**.
3. Print and then close **3-NSMCLabel.docx**.

Skills Assessment

Data File

Assessment 1   Formatting a Document on Fibromyalgia

1. Open **Fibromyalgia.docx** and then save it with the name **3-Fibromyalgia**.
2. Open **FM.docx** and then individually copy the three sections (*Triggers and Metabolism*, *Symptoms*, and *Diagnosing Fm*), including the blank line below each section, to the Clipboard task pane.
3. Make **3-Fibromyalgia.docx** the active document and then paste the sections from **FM.docx** into **3-Fibromyalgia.docx**, merging the formatting so the sections are in the following order: *What Is Fibromyalgia?*, *Symptoms*, *Diagnosing Fm*, *Causes of Fm*, *Triggers and Metabolism*, and *Treatment*.
4. Make **FM.docx** the active document and then close it.
5. With **3-Fibromyalgia.docx** the active document, search for all occurrences of *fm* and replace them with *fibromyalgia*. (Make sure the *Match case* check box at the expanded Find and Replace dialog box does not contain a check mark.)
6. Select the heading *What Is Fibromyalgia?*, apply bold formatting, and then change the spacing after paragraphs to 6 points.
7. Use Format Painter to apply bold formatting and 6 points of space after paragraphs to the remaining headings: *Symptoms*, *Diagnosing Fibromyalgia*, *Causes of Fibromyalgia*, *Triggers and Metabolism*, and *Treatment*.

8. Search for all occurrences of 11-point Candara bold formatting and replace them with 12-point Corbel bold formatting.
9. Change the left and right margins to 1.5 inches.
10. Delete the title *FACTS ABOUT FIBROMYALGIA* and then create the title *Facts about Fibromyalgia* as WordArt with the following specifications: use the orange outline WordArt option in the fourth column, third row, change the text wrapping to *Top and Bottom*, change the width to 5.7 inches, apply the Wave: Down transform effect, and center the WordArt between the left and right margins.
11. Insert the Integral footer and then type your first and last names in the *Author* placeholder.
12. Move the insertion point to the end of the document and then insert a continuous section break.
13. Move the insertion point to the beginning of the heading *What Is Fibromyalgia?* and then insert a continuous section break.
14. Format the text into two columns with a line and 0.3-inch spacing between them.
15. Save, print, and then close **3-Fibromyalgia.docx**.

Assessment 2   Creating an Announcement

Data File

1. Open **CVPLtrhd.docx** and then save it with the name **3-CVPEOTM**.
2. Draw a shape of your choosing in the middle of the document and then insert the following information inside the shape (you determine the font type, font size, and font color of the text):

Congratulations!
Lindsay Levy
Employee of the Month

3. Apply a shape style to the shape that is complementary to the letterhead image.
4. Save, print, and then close **3-CVPEOTM.docx**.

Assessment 3   Preparing a Notice

Data File

1. Open **CVPLtrhd.docx** and then save it with the name **3-CVPSupport**.
2. Use the information in Figure WB-3.5 to create a notice of a support group with the following specifications:
   a. Set the text in a font type and font color that is complementary to the font style and color in the letterhead.
   b. To make it stand out, format the heading *Support Group for New Moms* differently than the paragraph that follows it.
   c. Set the text regarding dates, times, and location in tabbed columns. Consider using leaders to make the information more readable.
   d. Insert a clip art image related to mothers and babies. If you cannot locate an image in the Insert Pictures window, use ***mother.png*** in the WordMedS3 folder.
3. Save, print, and then close **3-CVPSupport.docx**.

Figure WB-3.5 Assessment 3

Support Group for New Moms

You and your baby are invited to meet other new moms and learn about parenting your newborn. Discussion topics include infant feeding, sleep patterns, newborn personalities, and child development. Support activities and educational sessions are coordinated by Deanna Reynolds, Child Development Specialist at Cascade View Pediatrics. The support group for new moms will provide you with opportunities to meet other new moms while sharing the joys, frustrations, successes, and challenges of motherhood. Join us weekly until your baby is six months old.

> When: Monday evenings
> Time: 7:00 p.m. to 8:30 p.m.
> Location: Cascade View Pediatrics
> Room: Conference Room 3B
> Cost: $25 per month

Assessment 4   Preparing Mailing Labels

1. Prepare return-address mailing labels with the following information:
   Columbia River General Hospital
   Education Department
   4550 Fremont Street
   Portland, OR 97045
2. Save the labels document with the name **3-CRGHLabel**.
3. Print and then close **3-CRGHLabel.docx**.

Assessment 5   Finding Information on Flipping and Copying Objects

1. Use Word's Help feature to learn how to flip and copy objects.
2. At a blank document, re-create the content of Figure WB-3.6. Create the arrow at the left by clicking the Shapes button and then clicking the arrow option in the fifth column, second row in the *Block Arrows* section. Format the arrow with dark red fill as shown. Copy and flip the arrow to create the arrow at the right side. Create the text in a text box. ***Hint: Use the*** **Draw Text Box** ***option at the Text Box button drop-down list, and make sure to remove the shape fill and shape outline from the text box.***
3. Save the completed document with the name **3-NSMCClose**.
4. Print and then close **3-NSMCClose.docx**.

Figure WB-3.6 Assessment 5

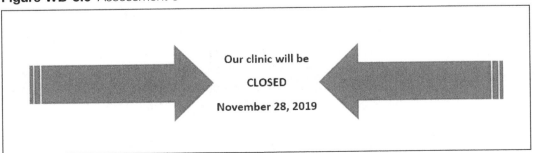

Our clinic will be

CLOSED

November 28, 2019

Assessment 6   Locating Information and Creating a Banner

1. Using the Internet, search for a hospital near you. When you find the website for the hospital, locate the hospital address and telephone number.
2. Create a banner using a shape and insert the hospital name, address, and telephone number inside the banner.
3. Save the banner document with the name **3-Banner**.
4. Print and then close **3-Banner.docx**.

Assessment 7   Locating Information on Chickenpox

1. Using the Internet, search for information on chickenpox. Find information on the symptoms, treatment, incubation period, and infectious period of chickenpox.
2. Using the information you find, create a document that contains information on the four areas listed above: symptoms, treatment, incubation period, and infectious period.
3. Add any enhancements you feel will improve the appearance of the document. You might include an image, WordArt, or a shape.
4. Save the document with the name **3-Chickenpox**.
5. Print and then close **3-Chickenpox.docx**.

Marquee Challenge

Challenge 1   Preparing a Class Announcement Document

1. Open **CVPLtrhd.docx** and then save it with the name **3-CVPBabyCare**.
2. Create the class announcement shown in Figure WB-3.7. Set the text in 12-point Constantia and the title in 18-point Constantia. Use the *father.png* image in the WordMedS3 folder.
3. Save, print, and then close **3-CVPBabyCare.docx**.

Challenge 2   Preparing a Fact Sheet on Fifth Disease

1. Open **FifthDisease.docx** and then save it with the name **3-FifthDisease**.
2. Format the document so it appears as shown in Figure WB-3.8. Insert the page border, the WordArt (blue outline option in the fourth column, second row with the Gold, Accent 4, Lighter 80% text fill applied), and the image *hands.png* from the WordMedS3 folder.
3. Save, print, and then close **3-FifthDisease.docx**.

Challenge 3   Preparing a Cascade View Pediatrics Newsletter

1. Open **CVPNewsltr.docx** and then save it with the name **3-CVPJanNews**.
2. Format the document so it appears as shown in Figure WB-3.9 on page WB-27. Use the *pediatrician1.png* and *pediatrician2.png* images from the WordMedS3 folder. The page border option is the third from the bottom in the *Style* section of the Borders and Shading dialog box with the Page Border tab selected. Change the page border color to a blue color. Make sure the contents of the document all display on the first page.
3. Save, print, and then close **3-CVPJanNews.docx**.

Cascade View
Pediatrics

350 North Skagit ⋎ Portland, OR 97505 ⋎ (503) 555-7700 ⋎ http://ppi-edu.net/cvp

BABY CARE CLASS

Deanna Reynolds, Child Development Specialist for Cascade View Pediatrics, is offering a one-day class on basic baby care. This five-hour class offers basic survival techniques to care for your newborn. During this informative class, you will learn about newborn characteristics, infant milestones, bathing and hygiene, diapering, crying and comforting, sleeping, and recognizing signs of illness in your newborn. This class is ideal for first-time parents.

Date...Saturday, April 6

Time ....9:oo a.m. to 2:oo p.m.

Location ....Cascade View Pediatrics

Room.................................... Conference Room 2

Cost $70

**For more information, contact
Deanna Reynolds at (5o3) 555-77o5**

Fifth Disease

Fifth disease (also called *erythema infectiosum*) is an infection common in children between the ages of 5 and 15. It produces a red rash on the face that spreads to the trunk, arms, and legs. Fifth disease is actually a viral illness caused by a virus called parvovirus B19. Most children recover from Fifth disease in a short time with no complications.

Symptoms

Fifth disease begins with a low-grade fever, headache, body aches, and mild cold-like symptoms such as a stuffy or runny nose. These symptoms pass and the illness seems to be gone but, in 7 to 10 days, a red rash on the cheeks appears, making the face look like it has been slapped. (This is why the disease is also called *slapped cheek syndrome.*) The rash spreads to other parts of the body and red blotches expand down the trunk, arms, and legs. The rash may last from one to three weeks and may recur over weeks to months.

Contagiousness

A person with Fifth disease is most contagious before the rash appears and probably no longer contagious after the rash begins. Fifth disease spreads easily from person to person in fluids from the nose, mouth, and throat of someone with the infection and especially through large droplets from coughs and sneezes. It can also spread through sharing a drinking glass and from mother to fetus. Once someone is infected with the virus, they develop immunity to it and more than likely will not become infected again.

Treatment

Since a virus causes Fifth disease, it cannot be treated with antibiotics. Antiviral medicines do exist but none that will treat Fifth disease. No specific medication or vaccine is available and treatment is limited to relieving the symptoms.

Complications

Most children with Fifth disease recover without any complications and usually feel well by the time the rash appears. The infection, however, is more serious for children with HIV or blood disorders such as sickle cell anemia or hemolytic anemia. The virus can temporarily slow down or stop the body's production of the oxygen-carrying red blood cells, causing anemia.

Prevention

To help prevent your child from being infected with the virus, encourage your child to use good hygiene including frequent hand washing, disposing of tissues, and not sharing eating utensils with a sick person.

Figure WB-3.9 Challenge 3

Cascade View Pediatrics

January 2019 Newsletter

Pediatrician Joins CVP

We are pleased to announce that Dr. Joseph Yarborough, Pediatric Specialist, has joined our clinic. With the addition of Dr. Yarborough to our staff, we are able to accommodate additional

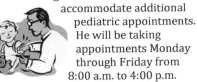

pediatric appointments. He will be taking appointments Monday through Friday from 8:00 a.m. to 4:00 p.m. Tuesdays and Thursdays have been reserved for well-child checkup appointments. Evening hours for well-child checkup appointments with Dr. Yarborough will be available next month.

Bring Your Insurance Card

At CVP, we deal with over 25 different insurance plans! No insurance plan is the same as the other and each has different co-pays, allowables, and deductibles. We do our best to assist you with insurance questions but you are responsible for knowing what your insurance covers. To help us with insurance issues, please bring your insurance card with you every time you visit the clinic. This may seem inconvenient but when we do not check insurance coverage with every visit, our billing accuracy declines by 10 percent.

Benefits of Lycopene

Lycopene is an antioxidant that is abundant in red tomatoes and processed tomato products. Antioxidants like lycopene neutralize free radicals, which can damage cells in the body. Research has shown that lycopene may help prevent macular degeneration (a common cause of blindness in the elderly), prostate cancer and some other forms of cancer, and heart disease.* To consume the recommended amount of at least 5 to 10 mg of lycopene per day, consider eating the following foods:

- Spaghetti sauce, ½ cup, approximately 28.1 mg of lycopene
- Tomato juice, 1 cup, approximately 25.0 mg of lycopene
- Tomato paste, 2 tablespoons, approximately 13.8 mg of lycopene
- Tomato soup, 1 cup, approximately 9.7 mg of lycopene

Other foods to consider that contain lycopene include watermelon, pink grapefruit, chili sauce, seafood sauce, and ketchup.

*Discuss medical conditions or problems with your doctor. Good nutrition is not a substitute for medical treatment and a doctor's care.

Well-Child Appointments

When you bring your child for a well-child checkup appointment, the doctor will be checking your child's progress and growth. During the visit, your doctor will weigh your child, measure his or her length and head circumference, and plot the information on your child's own growth chart. The doctor will perform a physical examination, paying special attention to any previous problems. You will be able to ask your doctor questions about how you are doing with your child and to seek advice on what to expect during the coming months. Your child will receive immunizations during some visits.

> **Study Tools**

Study tools include In Brief steps and medical resources. Use the study tools to help you further develop and review skills learned in this section.

> **Knowledge Check**

Complete the Knowledge Check to assess your comprehension and recall of application features, technology, and functions.

> **Recheck**

Check your understanding by taking this quiz.

Skills Review

Columbia River
General Hospital

Review 1 Creating and Merging Letters

1. Use the Mail Merge feature to prepare six letters using the information shown in Figures WB-4.1 and WB-4.2. When completing the steps, consider the following:
    a. Create a data source using the information shown in Figure WB-4.1. (Enter the records in this order—*Watanabe, Reeves, Torres, Wickstrom, O'Leary,* and *Fuentes.*) Save the data source document in the WordMedS4 folder on your storage medium and name it **4-CRGHEdList**.
    b. Type the letter shown in Figure WB-4.2, using your initials in place of the *xx*. Insert a fill-in field for the *(School)* field. (You determine the prompt message.) ***Hint: Remove the hyperlink from the web address by right-clicking the web address and then clicking* Remove Hyperlink *at the shortcut menu.***
    c. Click the Finish & Merge button and then click *Edit Individual Documents* at the drop-down list.
    d. At the Merge to New Document dialog box, make sure *All* is selected and then click the OK button.
    e. When merging the letters, type the following in each specific record:
Record 1	Jefferson Elementary School
Record 2	Jefferson Elementary School
Record 3	Evergreen Elementary School
Record 4	Jefferson Elementary School
Record 5	Evergreen Elementary School
Record 6	Jefferson Elementary School
2. Save the merged letters in the normal manner in the WordMedS4 folder on your storage medium and name the document **4-CRGHEdLtrs**.

Figure WB-4.1 Review 1 Data Source

Mr. Paul Watanabe Division Street Clinic 5330 Division Street Portland, OR 97255	Ms. Nora Reeves Community Counseling 1235 North 122nd Avenue Portland, OR 97230
Mr. Ramon Torres Youth and Family Services 8904 McLoughlin Boulevard Oak Grove, OR 97267	Dr. Thomas Wickstrom Columbia Mental Health Center 550 Columbia Street Portland, OR 97305
Ms. Suzanna O'Leary Family Counseling Center 100 Center Street Oak Grove, OR 97268	Dr. Christina Fuentes Parenting Services 210 Martin Luther King Way Portland, OR 97403

Figure WB-4.2 Review 1 Letter

February 4, 2019

«AddressBlock»

«GreetingLine»

The staff in the Education Department at Columbia River General Hospital have prepared parent education classes designed for parents of children between the ages of 5 and 10. Classes focus on a commonsense approach to parenting and provide parents with practical ideas about setting limits and teaching children to make responsible choices. Parents are given ideas and techniques that can be used at home to help children develop decision-making and problem-solving skills.

Qualified family counselors will teach the classes, which will occur every Monday and Wednesday evening, beginning Monday, March 4, and ending Wednesday, Friday, April 10. Classes will be held from 7:00 to 8:30 p.m. at (School). Cost for the classes is based on a sliding-fee scale. For more information on these parenting classes and how parents can register, as well as directions to the school, please visit us online at http://ppi-edu.net/crgh or call me at (503) 555-2500.

Sincerely,

Laura Latterell
Education Director

xx
CRGHEdLtrs.docx

3. Print and then close **4-CRGHEdLtrs.docx**. (This document will print six letters.)
4. Save the main document in the normal manner in the WordMedS4 folder on your storage medium and name it **4-CRGHEdMainDoc**.
5. Close **4-CRGHEdMainDoc.docx**.

Review 2 Preparing Envelopes

1. Use the Mail Merge feature to prepare envelopes for the letters created in Review 1.
2. Specify **4-CRGHEdList.mdb** as the data source file.
3. Save the merged envelope document in the WordMedS4 folder on your storage medium and name the document **4-CRGHEdEnvs**.
4. Print and then close **4-CRGHEdEnvs.docx**. (Manual feed may be required when printing.)
5. Close the envelope main document without saving it.

Review 3 Creating Chart Notes Using a Table

1. Open **NSMCLtrhd.docx** and then save it with the name **4-NSMCNotes**. (If necessary, change the zoom to *100%*.)
2. Click the *No Spacing* style, change the font to Constantia, and then add 12 points of spacing before paragraphs. ***Hint: Add 12 points of spacing before paragraphs by clicking the Line and Paragraph Spacing button in the Paragraph group on the Home tab and then clicking* Add Space Before Paragraph *at the drop-down list.***
3. Create a table with 2 columns and 19 rows.
4. Select and then merge each row (individually) as shown in Figure WB-4.3. ***Hint: To merge cells, select the cells and then click the Merge Cells button in the Merge group on the Table Tools Layout tab.***
5. Type the text in the cells as shown in Figure WB-4.3.
6. Select the title, *CHART NOTES*, change the font size to 16 points, apply bold formatting, and then change the paragraph alignment to center.
7. Apply Gold, Accent 4, Lighter 60% shading to the top row. ***Hint: Do this with the Shading button in the Table Styles group on the Table Tools Design tab.***
8. Save, print, and then close **4-NSMCNotes.docx**.

CHART NOTES

NAME	DOB
DATE	AGE
Reason for visit:	
B/P	PULSE
SHEENT	
Neck	
Lungs	
Cardiovascular	
Abdomen	
Genitourinary	
Musculoskeletal	
Neurologic/Psychiatric	
Lab/X-rays	
Impressions:	
Plan:	

7450 Meridian Street, Suite 150
Portland, OR 97202
(503) 555-2330
http://ppi-edu.net/nsmc

Columbia River
General Hospital

Data File

Review 4 Preparing a Form

1. Create the form shown in Figure W-4.4 as a template. Begin by opening **CRGHSecPayerForm.docx** from the WordMedS4 folder on your storage medium. With the document open, press the F12 key to display the Save As dialog box, type XXX-CRGHSPFormTemplate in the *File name* text box (type your initials in place of the *XXX*), change the *Save as type* option to *Word Template (*.dotx),* and then click the Save button.

2. Insert the plain text content controls and check box content controls as shown in Figure WB-4.4. For the *Name of Insurance Company:* cell, insert a drop-down list content control with the following options: *Assure Medical*, *Premiere Group*, *Sound Medical*, *Health Plus*, and *First Choice*.

3. Protect the template document to only allow filling in the form.

4. Save and then close **XXX-CRGHSPFormTemplate.dotx**.

5. Create a form document from the **XXX-CRGHSPFormTemplate** template. Begin by clicking the File tab, clicking the *New* option, clicking the *PERSONAL* option, and then clicking the ***XXX-CRGHSPFormTemplate.dotx*** thumbnail.

6. Insert the following data in the specified fields:

Patient Name:	Wyatt Johnston
Patient Number:	839488
Address:	3107 North Cedar Street
City:	Portland
State:	OR
Zip:	97429
Telephone:	(503) 555-4775
Date of Birth:	05/15/1975

    Insert a check mark in the *Yes* check box for the first question and insert a check mark in the *No* check box for questions 2 through 6.

Name of Insurance Company:	Choose *Health Plus* from the drop-down list.
Telephone Number:	1-800-555-3995
Name of Policy Holder:	Wyatt Johnston
Policy Number:	RT-90338

7. Save the document with the name **4-CRGHPayer**.

8. Print and then close **4-CRGHPayer.docx**.

Figure WB-4.4 Review 4

Columbia River
General Hospital

SECONDARY PAYER FORM

Patient Name: Click or tap here to enter text.	**Patient Number:** Click or tap here to enter text.

Address: Click or tap here to enter text.	**City:** Click or tap here to enter text.	**State:** Click or tap here to enter text.	**Zip:** Click or tap here to enter text.

Telephone: Click or tap here to enter text.	**Date of Birth:** Click or tap here to enter text.

Please answer the following questions related to your illness or injury:

Yes	No	
☐	☐	Is illness/injury due to an automobile accident?
☐	☐	Is illness/injury due to an accident covered by Workers' Compensation?
☐	☐	Does the Black Lung Program cover this illness?
☐	☐	Are you eligible for coverage under the Veterans Administration?
☐	☐	If under 65, do you have Medicare coverage due to a disability?
☐	☐	Do you have coverage under a spouse's health insurance plan?

Name of Insurance Company: Choose an item.	**Telephone Number:** Click or tap here to enter text.
Name of Policy Holder: Click or tap here to enter text.	**Policy Number:** Click or tap here to enter text.

Skills Assessment

North Shore
Medical Clinic

Data File

Assessment 1   Creating and Merging Letters

1. Use the Mail Merge feature to create the letter shown in Figure WB-4.5 and merge it with the **NSMCPatientsDS.mdb** data source file with the following specifications:
   a. Browse to the WordMedS4 folder and then double-click **NSMCPatientsDS.mdb**. Display the Mail Merge Recipients dialog box by clicking the Edit Recipient List button and then add the following record:

Title:	Mrs.
First Name:	Lola
Last Name:	Solberg
Address Line 1:	23100 North Tillicum
Address Line 2:	(leave blank)
City:	Portland
State:	OR
ZIP Code:	97402
Home Phone:	(503) 555-3437
Specialty:	Obstetrics

   b. With the Mail Merge Recipients dialog box displayed, identify only those records containing a specialty of *Obstetrics*.
   c. Type the letter shown in Figure WB-4.5. (Use your initials in place of the *xx*.)
   d. Click the Finish & Merge button and then click *Edit Individual Documents* at the drop-down list.
   e. At the Merge to New Document dialog box, make sure *All* is selected and then click OK.
2. Save the merged letters in the normal manner in the WordMedS4 folder on your storage medium and name the document **4-NSMCClassLtrs**.
3. Print and then close **4-NSMCClassLtrs.docx**. (Three letters should print.)
4. Save the main document in the normal manner in the WordMedS4 folder on your storage medium and name the document **4-NSMCClassMainDoc**.
5. Close **4-NSMCClassMainDoc.docx**.

Figure WB-4.5 Assessment 1

October 18, 2019

«AddressBlock»

«GreetingLine»

North Shore Medical Clinic is partnering with the Education Department at Columbia River General Hospital and offering childbirth education classes. A certified nurse practitioner teaches the classes at various times during the year. Participants in the class meet once a week for six weeks.

You can register for the classes directly with Columbia River General Hospital by calling the Education Department at (503) 555-2500 or by contacting us at (503) 555-2330. The fee for the classes is $75 payable directly to Columbia River General Hospital.

Sincerely,

Lee Elliot
Office Manager

xx
NSMCClassLtrs.docx

Assessment 2   Modifying and Formatting a Calendar

Data File

1. Open **CVPCalendar.docx** and then save it with the name **4-CVPCalendar**.
2. Delete one of the middle rows in the calendar. (Do not delete the first or last row because the table border may get deleted.)
3. Select the entire table and then change the font to 10-point Candara.
4. With the table still selected, change the row height to 1.2 inches. ***Hint: Do this with the* Table Row Height** *measurement box in the Cell Size group on the Table Tools Layout tab.*
5. Position the insertion point in any cell in the second row and then change the row height to 0.2 inches.
6. Merge the cells in the top row.
7. With the top row selected (one cell), change the font size to 26 points, turn on bold formatting, click the Align Center button in the Alignment group on the Table Tools Layout tab, apply Gold, Accent 4, Lighter 60% shading, and then type the text shown in the cell in Figure WB-4.6. ***Hint: Press the Enter key after typing the word* Classes.**

8. Select the second row, change the font size to 11 points, turn on bold formatting, click the Align Center button in the Alignment group on the Table Tools Layout tab, apply Gold, Accent 4, Lighter 80% shading, and then type the text shown in the second row in Figure WB-4.6.

9. Type the text in each cell as shown in Figure WB-4.6. (Make sure to center-align the text as shown.)

10. Save, print, and then close **4-CVPCalendar.docx**.

Figure WB-4.6 Assessment 2

Cascade View Pediatrics

350 North Skagit ✶ Portland, OR 97505 ✶ (503) 555-7700 ✶ http://ppi-edu.net/cvp

Parenting Classes
April 2019

Sunday	Monday	Tuesday	Wednesday	Thursday	Friday	Saturday
	1 Basic Parenting 7:00 to 8:30 p.m.	2	3 Basic Parenting 7:00 to 8:30 p.m.	4	5 Mom & Baby 9:30 to 11:00 a.m.	6
7	8 Basic Parenting 7:00 to 8:30 p.m.	9	10 Basic Parenting 7:00 to 8:30 p.m.	11	12 Mom & Baby 9:30 to 11:00 a.m.	13
14	15 Basic Parenting 7:00 to 8:30 p.m.	16	17 Basic Parenting 7:00 to 8:30 p.m.	18	19 Mom & Baby 9:30 to 11:00 a.m.	20
21	22 Basic Parenting 7:00 to 8:30 p.m.	23	24 Basic Parenting 7:00 to 8:30 p.m.	25	26 Mom & Baby 9:30 to 11:00 a.m.	27
28	29 Basic Parenting 7:00 to 8:30 p.m.	30				

North Shore Medical Clinic

Data File

Assessment 3 Formatting and Filling in a Medical History Questionnaire

1. Create the form shown in Figure WB-4.7 as a template. Begin by opening **NSMCMedHistory.docx** from the WordMedS4 folder on your storage medium. With the document open, press the F12 key to display the Save As dialog box, type XXX-NSMCMedHistoryTemplate in the *File name* text box (typing your initials in place of the *XXX*), change the *Save as type* option to *Word Template (*.dotx)*, and then click the Save button.

2. Press Ctrl + End and then create the fourth table in the medical history document as shown in Figure WB-4.7. Use the second and third tables in the document as a guideline for formatting the fourth table. After creating the table, insert the content controls in all four tables as shown in the figure.

3. Protect the document.

4. Save and then close **XXX-NSMCMedHistoryTemplate.dotx**.

5. Create a form document from **XXX-NSMCMedHistoryTemplate.dotx**. Begin by clicking the File tab, clicking the *New* option, clicking the *PERSONAL* option, and then clicking the ***XXX-NSMCMedHistoryTemplate.dotx*** thumbnail.

6. Fill in the first table with the following information:
   a. Patient's name is Camilla Galetti, her patient ID number is 5423, and her insurance is Premiere Group. Insert the current date in the *Date:* content control.
   b. Click the *Yes* check box after the *Prior operations?* question and then type Appendectomy, 2012 in the *Specify:* content control.
   c. Click the *No* check box for the next two questions.
   d. Click the *Yes* check box after the *Current medications?* question and then type Prilosec, Tylenol in the *List:* content control.

7. Fill in the second table with the following information:
   a. In the *Mother* column, click the check boxes for *Asthma* and *Eczema/dermatitis*.
   b. In the *Father* column, click the check box for *High blood pressure*.
   c. In the *Relative* column, click the check boxes for *Arthritis*, *Cancer*, *Heart disease*, and *High blood pressure*.

8. Fill in the third table with the following information:
   a. Click the *Yes* check box after the *Currently employed?* question and then type Firefighter in the *Occupation:* content control.
   b. Click the *No* check box for the next three questions.
   c. Click the *Yes* check box after the *Married?* question.

9. Save the document with the name **4-MedHistory**.

10. Print and then close **4-MedHistory.docx**.

Figure WB-4.7 Assessment 3

MEDICAL HISTORY QUESTIONNAIRE

Patient Name: Click or tap here to enter text.	Patient ID#: Click or tap here to enter text.
Insurance: Click or tap here to enter text.	Date: Click or tap here to enter text.

PAST MEDICAL HISTORY

	Yes	No	
Prior operations?	☐	☐	Specify: Click or tap here to enter text.
Prior major illness?	☐	☐	Specify: Click or tap here to enter text.
Allergies to medications?	☐	☐	List: Click or tap here to enter text.
Current medications?	☐	☐	List: Click or tap here to enter text.

FAMILY HISTORY

	Mother	Father	Relative
Allergies	☐	☐	☐
Arthritis	☐	☐	☐
Asthma	☐	☐	☐
Cancer	☐	☐	☐
Diabetes	☐	☐	☐
Eczema/dermatitis	☐	☐	☐
Heart disease	☐	☐	☐
High blood pressure	☐	☐	☐
Lung disease	☐	☐	☐
Other:	☐	☐	☐

SOCIAL HISTORY

	Yes	No	
Currently employed?	☐	☐	Occupation: Click or tap here to enter text.
Pregnant?	☐	☐	
Smoke tobacco?	☐	☐	Daily quantity: Click or tap here to enter text.
Drink alcohol?	☐	☐	Daily quantity: Click or tap here to enter text.
Married?	☐	☐	

Assessment 4   Converting a Table to Text

1. Use Word's Help feature to learn how to convert a table to text.
2. Open **Table.docx** and save it with the name **4-Table**.
3. Convert the table to text, separating the text with tabs.
4. Save, print, and then close **4-Table.docx**.

Assessment 5   Locating Information and Writing a Memo

1. Two doctors from the clinic are traveling to Chicago for a medical conference. Lee Elliott has asked you to find information on round-trip airfare from Portland to Chicago. For the departure date, use the first Monday of the next month and for the return date, use the first Saturday after the departure date. Use an Internet travel company (such as Expedia or Travelocity) to search for flights. The doctors want to leave sometime between 9:00 a.m. and noon and return sometime between noon and 3:00 p.m.
2. Open **NSMCMemoForm.docx**. Using the flight information you found, write a memo to Lee Elliott that includes a table containing information such as airline names, flight numbers, times, and costs. Format and modify the table so the information is attractive and easy to read.
3. Save the completed memo and name it **4-Conference**.
4. Print and then close **4-Conference.docx**.

Marquee Challenge

Challenge 1   Preparing a Treadmill Exercise Test Form

1. Open **NSMCLtrhd.docx** and then save it with the name **4-Treadmill**.
2. Change the spacing after paragraphs to 0 points.
3. Create the document shown in Figure WB-4.8.
4. Save, print, and then close **4-Treadmill.docx**.

Challenge 2   Preparing a Pre-operative Questions Form

1. Open **NSMCPreOpQuestions.docx** from the WordMedS4 folder on your storage medium and then save it as a template with the name **XXX-NSMCPreOpQuestionsTemplate**. *Hint: Do this at the Save As dialog box.*
2. Insert data in the table, format the table, and insert text content controls and check box content controls so your form appears the same as shown in Figure WB-4.9 on page WB-42.
3. Protect the template document and only allow filling in the form.
4. Save and then close **XXX-NSMCPreOpQuestionsTemplate.dotx**.
5. Create a form document from **NSMCPreOpQuestionsTemplate.dotx**. You determine the information to insert in the form.
6. Save the document with the name **4-PreOp**.
7. Print and then close **4-PreOp.docx**.

TREADMILL EXERCISE TEST

EXERCISE					
Stage (mph – grade)	Blood Pressure	Heart Rate	Premature Beats	ST mm	ST slope
AT REST					
Stage 1/2 (1.7 mph – 5%)					
Stage I (1.7 mph – 10%)					
Stage II (2.5 mph – 12%)					
Stage III (3.4 mph – 14%)					
Stage IV (4.2 mph – 16%)					
Stage V (5.0 mph – 18%)					
Stage VI (5.5 mph – 22%)					
Stage VII (6.0 mph – 22%)					

RECOVERY					
RECOVERY	Blood Pressure	Heart Rate	Premature Beats	ST mm	ST slope
IMMEDIATE					
1 Minute					
3 Minutes					
5 Minutes					
7 Minutes					

7450 Meridian Street, Suite 150
Portland, OR 97202
(503) 555-2330
http://ppi-edu.net/nsmc

PRE-OPERATIVE QUESTIONS

Patient Name: Click or tap here to enter text.   **Patient ID#:** Click or tap here to enter text.

Birth Date: Click or tap here to enter text.   **Surgery Date:** Click or tap here to enter text.

Do you now have or have you ever had:

	Yes	No	
Anesthesia	☐	☐	When? Click or tap here to enter text.
Difficulty with anesthesia	☐	☐	What? Click or tap here to enter text.
A relative who has difficulty with anesthesia	☐	☐	What? Click or tap here to enter text.
Asthma, bronchitis, or other lung problems	☐	☐	
Abnormal chest x-ray	☐	☐	
Hypertension, chest pain, irregular heart beat	☐	☐	What? Click or tap here to enter text.
Heart attack, heart murmur, abnormal EKG	☐	☐	What? Click or tap here to enter text.
Bleeding or clotting problems	☐	☐	
Convulsions or seizures	☐	☐	
Stroke, muscle weakness, numbness	☐	☐	
Hepatitis or jaundice	☐	☐	
Diabetes	☐	☐	
Kidney problems or blood in your urine	☐	☐	
Cortisone pills or injections	☐	☐	
Taking aspirin, ibuprofen, or blood thinners	☐	☐	
Taking prescription drugs	☐	☐	List: Click or tap here to enter text.
Smoke tobacco	☐	☐	

> **Study Tools**

Study tools include In Brief steps and medical resources. Use the study tools to help you further develop and review skills learned in this section.

> **Knowledge Check**

Complete the Knowledge Check to assess your comprehension and recall of application features, technology, and functions.

> **Recheck**

Check your understanding by taking this quiz.

Skills Review

Note: If you submit your work in hard copy, check with your instructor before completing these reviews to find out if you need to print two copies of each worksheet with one of the copies showing the cell formulas instead of the calculated results.

North Shore Medical Clinic

Review 1 Entering Labels and Values; Formatting Cells

1. Create a new workbook using the Blank workbook template.
2. Enter the labels and data shown in Figure WB-1.1. Use the fill handle whenever possible to facilitate data entry. Do not format the cells.
3. Select the range G12:G20 and then apply the Accounting format.
4. Deselect the range and then save the workbook with the name **1-NSMCPOtoMedCare**.

North Shore Medical Clinic

Review 2 Entering and Copying Formulas; Using AutoSum

1. With **1-NSMCPOtoMedCare.xlsx** open, enter the following labels and create the following formulas by typing them into the Formula bar or the cell, using the pointing method, or clicking the AutoSum button:
    a. In cell H11, type the label Line Total.
    b. In cell H12, multiply the order quantity by the price by entering =e12*g12.
    c. Use the fill handle to copy the formula to cells H13:H20.
    d. In cell F22, type the label Subtotal.
    e. In cell H22, use a Sum function to add the range H12:H20.
    f. In cell F23, type the label Shipping.
    g. In cell H23, type the value 25.
    h. In cell F24, type the label Order Total.
    i. In cell H24, calculate the purchase order total by entering =h22+h23.

Figure WB-1.1 Review 1 Worksheet

▲	A	B	C	D	E	F	G
1	North Shore Medical Clinic						
2	Purchase Order						
3							
4	Vendor:						
5	Medcare Medical Supplies			Telephone		Fax	
6	1913 NE 7th Avenue			(503) 555-4589		(800) 555-6315	
7	Portland, OR 97212-3906						
8							
9							
10							
11	Item				Order Qty	Unit	Price
12	Disposable shoe cover				1	per 300	38.15
13	Disposable bouffant cap				1	per 100	7.91
14	Disposable examination table paper				8	per roll	9.1
15	Disposable patient gown				8	per doz.	8.25
16	Disposable patient slippers				8	per doz.	4.35
17	Disposable skin staple remover				8	per doz.	35.9
18	Disposable skin stapler				8	per doz.	42.55
19	Disposable thermometer tips				8	per 100	5.13
20	Disposable earloop mask				8	per 50	6.48
21							

2. Apply the Accounting format to cell H23.
3. Save **1-NSMCPOtoMedCare.xlsx**.

North Shore
Medical Clinic

Review 3   Improving the Appearance of the Worksheet; Previewing and Printing

1. With **1-NSMCPOtoMedCare.xlsx** open, select cells A1:H1 and then click the Merge & Center button.
2. Merge and center cells A2:H2.
3. Select the range E11:H11 and then apply center alignment.
4. Select the range E12:E20 and then apply center alignment.
5. Make cell A9 the active cell, type the following label, and then press the Enter key:
   Terms: 1%/10, net 30 days. No substitutions.
6. Display the worksheet in the Print backstage area. Preview and then print the worksheet.
7. Save **1-NSMCPOtoMedCare.xlsx**.

North Shore
Medical Clinic

Review 4   Using Help

1. With **1-NSMCPOtoMedCare.xlsx** open, display the Help task pane, type How do I add a background color? in the search box, and then press the Enter key.
2. Click the Add or change the background color of cells hyperlink.
3. Read the information displayed in the Help task pane about filling cells with color.
4. Close the Help task pane.
5. Select the range A11:H11 and then apply the Blue, Accent 5, Lighter 60% fill color (ninth column, third row in the *Theme Colors* section) using the Fill color button in the Font group, as you learned in the Help task pane.

6. Select the range A1:A2 and then apply the Blue, Accent 5, Lighter 40% fill color (ninth column, fourth row in the *Theme Colors* section).
7. Deselect cells A1:A2.
8. Save, print, and then close **1-NSMCPOtoMedCare.xlsx**.

Skills Assessment

Note: If you submit your work in hard copy, check with your instructor before completing these assessments to find out if you need to print two copies of each worksheet with one of the copies showing the cell formulas instead of the calculated results.

 **Assessment 1**   Adding Values and Formulas to a Worksheet

1. Open **CVPTravelExpenses.xlsx** and save it with the name **1-CVPTravelExpenses**.
2. You have been asked by Sydney Larsen, office manager at Cascade View Pediatrics, to calculate the estimated travel expenses for the American Academy of Pediatrics members who will be attending the International Pediatric Medical Conference in Toronto, Ontario, Canada, May 20 to 24. Sydney has already received quotes for airfare, hotel, and airport transfers. This information is summarized below.
   - Return airfare from Portland to Toronto is $566.00 per person.
   - Sydney has negotiated a hotel rate of $536.75 per room for the duration, with two persons per room.
   - Airport Transfer Limousine Service charges a flat rate of $75.00 in Toronto and $55.00 in Portland for all travelers.
   - All of the above prices include taxes and fees and are quoted in U.S. dollars.
   - Members attending the conference include:
        Dr. Raphaël Severin
        Dr. Joseph Yarborough
        Dr. Beth Delaney
        Deanna Reynolds, Child Development Specialist
3. Cascade View Pediatrics reimburses all traveling employees for food expenses at the rate of $70.00 per day.
4. Enter the appropriate values and formulas to complete the worksheet.
5. Make any formatting changes you think would improve the appearance of the worksheet.
6. Save, print, and then close **1-CVPTravelExpenses.xlsx**.

Assessment 2   Creating a New Workbook for a Seminar

1. Sydney Larsen, office manager of Cascade View Pediatrics, has asked you to prepare a cost estimate for a seminar on ADHD treatment strategies that Dr. Beth Delaney is hosting for the local chapter of the American Academy of Pediatrics. Using the following information, create a worksheet that will calculate the total seminar costs and the registration fee that needs to be charged to each member in order to cover these costs.
   a. Create a new workbook using the Blank workbook template and then create a worksheet to summarize the seminar costs for 75 members using the following prices:
        - Rental fee for the meeting room at the Hilton Portland & Executive Tower is $50.00.

- Rental fee for the audio-visual equipment Dr. Delaney needs for her presentation is $45.00 for the day.
- Handouts, name badges, and other materials have been estimated at $23.95 (for all supplies).
- Morning coffee and refreshments are quoted at $2.17 per person.
- Lunch is quoted at $7.90 per person.

   b. Calculate the total cost.

   c. In a separate row below the total cost, calculate the cost per member.

2. Make any formatting changes you think would improve the appearance of the worksheet.
3. Save the workbook and name it **1-CVPADHDSeminar**.
4. Print and then close **1-CVPADHDSeminar.xlsx**.

Columbia River General Hospital Assessment 3   Creating a New Workbook to Estimate Funds Needed

1. Laura Latterell, education director at Columbia River General Hospital, has asked you to prepare an estimate of the funds needed in the professional development budget for 2020. Professional development funding includes in-service sessions, continuing education course fees, and conference registration fees. All other related costs such as travel expenses are funded directly from each medical professional's department budget. Create a new workbook to calculate the total 2020 professional development budget. Include a subtotal for each category of funded professional development.
2. A survey of the department managers has provided the following information:
   - There are in-service training requests for 15 sessions throughout the year. Sessions are run by consultants Laura hires at the rate of $60.00 per session.
   - There are the following requests for continuing education courses:

     18 requests for doctors at $350.00 per course

     30 requests for nurses at $295.00 per course

     12 requests for respiratory therapists at $185.00 per course

     14 requests for anesthesiologists at $192.00 per course

     11 requests for radiologists at $195.00 per course

     10 requests for physical therapists at $160.00 per course

     10 requests for management staff at $150.00 per course

     10 requests for support staff at $135.00 per course

3. The hospital buys block registrations for the following conferences:

   American Medical Association national annual conference.........$6,500.00

   American Academy of Nursing annual conference.....................$5,750.00

   International Respiratory Congress...$4,100.00

   Radiological Society of North America annual meeting..............$2,250.00

   American Society of Anesthesiologists annual conference..........$3,700.00

   American Physical Therapy Association annual conference........$1,775.00

   American Hospital Association annual meeting..........................$1,950.00

4. Make any formatting changes you think would improve the appearance of the workbook.
5. Save the workbook with the name **1-CRGHPDBudget**.
6. Print and then close **1-CRGHPDBudget.xlsx**.

North Shore
Medical Clinic   Assessment 4   Experimenting with Hiding Zero Values

Data File

1. Open **NSMCSupplies.xlsx** and then save it with the name **1-NSMCSupplies**.
2. Open the Excel Options dialog box and then click *Advanced* in the left pane. Scroll down to the section titled *Display options for this worksheet*.
3. Click the *Show a zero in cells that have zero value* check box to remove the check mark and then click OK. Notice that all cells in the worksheet that had a zero value now display as blank cells.
4. Display the Print backstage area and then change the page orientation to landscape.
5. Print page 1 of the worksheet.
6. Save and then close **1-NSMCSupplies.xlsx**.

Assessment 5   Creating a School Budget

WWW

1. Create a worksheet to calculate the estimated total cost of completing your diploma or certificate. You determine the items that need to be included in the worksheet. You might include tuition fees, textbooks, supplies, accommodation costs, transportation, telephone, food, and entertainment. Use the Internet to find reasonable cost estimates if you do not want to use your own personal data. Arrange the labels and values by quarter, semester, or academic year according to your preference. Make sure to include a cell that shows the total cost of your education.
2. Save the worksheet with the name **1-SchoolBudget**.
3. Apply alignment and formatting options as necessary to improve the appearance of the worksheet.
4. If necessary, change the page orientation to landscape and then print the worksheet.
5. Save and then close **1-SchoolBudget.xlsx**.

Marquee Challenge

Columbia River
General Hospital   Challenge 1   Preparing a Surgery Average Cost Report

1. At a blank workbook, enter the data shown in Figure WB-1.2.
2. Use the following information to complete the worksheet:
   a. Total average cost in column K is the sum of items starting with column F (*Ward*) and ending with column J (*Pharmacy*).
   b. Total cost of all cases in column L is column K (*Total Avg Cost*) times column D (*Cases*).
3. Apply the Accounting format to the values in columns K and L.
4. Add a grand total for all cases at the bottom of column L. Label the value appropriately.
5. Save the workbook with the name **1-CRGHAvgCostAnalysis**.
6. At the Print backstage area, change the page orientation to landscape and then print the worksheet.
7. Close **1-CRGHAvgCostAnalysis.xlsx**.

Figure WB-1.2 Challenge 1

	A	B	C	D	E	F	G	H	I	J	K	L	M
1			Columbia River General Hospital Average Cost Analysis Per Physician Service										
2													
3	Physician Service:			Cases		Ward	OR & Periop	Lab Fees	X-Ray Imaging	Pharmacy	Total Avg Cost	Total All Cases	
4	Cardiac Surgery			1233		4129	5211	1102	388	1146			
5	Cardiology			3765		2276	332	532	361	774			
6	Gastroenterology			633		4621	128	544	441	944			
7	General Surgery			3129		3566	1298	442	573	1125			
8	Nephrology			524		5578	336	988	499	2187			
9	Neurosurgery			1187		6155	2367	687	876	2174			
10	Obstetrics and Gynecology			3897		2355	431	321	165	213			
11	Ophthalmology			223		1123	1765	142	0	126			
12	Orthopedic Surgery			3859		3566	3211	453	765	542			
13	Otolaryngology			554		2215	3125	431	112	389			
14	Pediatrics			2139		2754	1187	541	422	228			
15	Plastic Surgery			668		3127	2122	422	133	551			
16	Psychiatry			1127		6744	0	233	0	1128			
17													

North Shore Medical Clinic **Challenge 2** **Completing an Invoice**

1. Use a template to create the worksheet shown in Figure WB-1.3. At the New backstage area, click in the *Search for online templates* text box and then type invoice with tax.
2. Double-click the *Service invoice with tax calculation* template. (If this template is not available, display the ExcelMedS1 folder on your storage medium and then double-click *ServiceInvoice.xtlx*.)
3. Enter the information and data shown in Figure WB-1.3, letting the formulas calculate the amount, subtotal, sales tax, and total.
4. Save the workbook with the name **1-NSMCInvToCRGH**.
5. Print and then close **1-NSMCInvToCRGH.xlsx**.

North Shore Medical Clinic

INVOICE

7450 Meridian Street, Suite 150
Portland, OR 97202
Phone (503) 555-2330

DATE: (use current date)
INVOICE # A-128

BILL TO:
Laura Latterell, Education Director
Columbia River General Hospital
4550 Fremont Street
Portland, OR 97045
(503) 555-2000 ext. 2347

FOR: Educational Services

DESCRIPTION	HOURS	RATE	AMOUNT
In-Service Training Session	2.00	$60.00	$ 120.00

SUBTOTAL	$ 120.00
TAX RATE	10.00%
SALES TAX	12.00
OTHER	
TOTAL	$ 132.00

Make all checks payable to North Shore Medical Clinic
Total due in 15 days. Overdue accounts subject to a service charge of 1% per month.

THANK YOU FOR YOUR BUSINESS!

Study Tools

Study tools include In Brief steps and medical resources. Use the study tools to help you further develop and review skills learned in this section.

Knowledge Check

Complete the Knowledge Check to assess your comprehension and recall of application features, technology, and functions.

Recheck

Check your understanding by taking this quiz.

Skills Review

Review 1   Inserting an Image; Editing and Clearing Cells; Deleting Columns and Rows

Data File

1. Open **CRGHLabReqRpt.xlsx** and save it with the name **2-CRGHLabReqRpt**.
2. With cell A1 the active cell, insert **CRGHLogo.jpg**.
3. Resize and move the image so that it is positioned at the right side of cell A1.
4. Change the value in cell E30 from *17.87* to *16.55*.
5. Clear the contents and formatting of the range A3:A4.
6. Clear the contents of the range J40:P40.
7. Change the label in cell A26 from *Other* to *Immunology*.
8. Make cell B6 the active cell and then type 12 hr fast.
9. Make cell B24 the active cell and then type 30 min rest.
10. Delete row 3 and column C.
11. Save **2-CRGHLabReqRpt.xlsx**.

Review 2   Moving and Copying Cells; Inserting and Deleting Rows; Freezing Panes

1. With **2-CRGHLabReqRpt.xlsx** open, move the contents of cell A2 to cell A3 and then merge and center the range A3:F3.
2. Move the contents of cell E44 to cell A44.
3. Make cell G5 the active cell and then freeze panes.
4. Copy the formula in cell F44 and then paste it into cells I44, K44, M44, and N44.
5. Delete row 2.
6. Delete the row for which no requisitions were ordered in January (*Other Swabs*).

7. Insert a new row between *Other Tests* and *HDL & LDL* and then type Antiphospholipid Antibodies in column A of the new row.

8. Add the following data for Antiphospholipid Antibodies:

Lab Code:	29011	Fee:	38.57
Reqs:	2	Insured Reqs:	0
Third Party Bill Reqs:	0	Patient Direct Bill Reqs:	2

9. Enter the formulas required to finish the total calculations for antiphospholipid antibodies requisitions.

10. Unfreeze the panes.

11. Save **2-CRGHLabReqRpt.xlsx**.

 **Review 3** Adjusting Column Width; Replacing Data; Formatting Numbers; Indenting Text

1. With **2-CRGHLabReqRpt.xlsx** open, AutoFit columns A, B, and C.

2. Change the width of column G to *1.00 (16 pixels)*.

3. Select columns E, H, J, and L and then change the width to *6.00 (61 pixels)*.

4. Use the Replace feature to replace all occurrences of the value *15.45* with *16.25*.

5. Apply the Comma format to the values in columns I, K, M, and N.

6. Apply the Accounting format to the values in column F.

7. Format the values in column O to display with two decimal places.

8. Select the ranges A4:A15, A18:A22, A25:A29, A32:A36, and A39:A41 and then click the Increase Indent button.

9. Save **2-CRGHLabReqRpt.xlsx**.

 **Review 4** Changing Font, Font Attributes, and Alignment; Applying Cell Styles; Adding Borders and Fill Color; Using Format Painter

1. With **2-CRGHLabReqRpt.xlsx** open, change the font in cell A1 to 36-point Candara. *Note: If necessary, substitute another font, such as Corbel.*

2. Change the fill color in cell A1 to *Blue, Accent 1, Lighter 60%* (fifth column, third row in the *Theme Colors* section).

3. If necessary, move the logo image to the right border of cell A1.

4. Center the labels in the range C3:O3 both horizontally and vertically.

5. Center horizontally the labels in the ranges C17:D17, C24:D24, C31:D31, and C38:D38.

6. Select the range A2:O2, apply bold formatting, and then change the fill color to *Blue, Accent 1, Lighter 80%* (fifth column, second row in the *Theme Colors* section).

7. Select the range C3:O3 and then apply the Accent1 cell style.

8. Make cell A3 the active cell and then apply the Accent3 cell style. Use Format Painter to copy the formatting from cell A3 to cells A17, A24, A31, and A38.

9. Add a top and bottom border to the range A3:O3.

10. Add a top and double bottom border to cells F43, I43, K43, M43, and N43.

11. Make cell B3 the active cell and then type Comments. Use Format Painter to copy the formatting from cell C3 to cell B3.

12. Save **2-CRGHLabReqRpt.xlsx**.

Review 5   Inserting Comments; Changing the Zoom

1. With **2-CRGHLabReqRpt.xlsx** open, make cell O6 the active cell and then insert the following comment:

    Check billings. Two extra reqs have been added to Insured, Third Party, or Patient Direct.

2. Make cell O14 the active cell and then add the same comment text as in Step 1.
3. Display the worksheet in the Print backstage area. Notice the worksheet will print on two pages.
4. Click the Back button to close the Print backstage area.
5. Change the zoom to *80%*.
6. Click the Page Layout tab and then change the orientation to landscape.
7. In the Scale to Fit group, change the width to *1 page*.
8. In the Scale to Fit group, change the height to *1 page*.
9. Change the zoom to *100%*.
10. Print the worksheet. ***Note: Check with your instructor if you submit your work in hard copy to see if you need to print two copies of this worksheet with one of the copies showing the cell formulas instead of the calculated results.***
11. Save and then close **2-CRGHLabReqRpt.xlsx**.

Skills Assessment

Assessment 1   Changing Zoom; Adjusting Column Width; Changing Font Color and Fill Color

Data File

1. Tracy Fitzgerald, manager of support services at Columbia River General Hospital, has asked you to make changes to a worksheet containing recent Canadian healthcare statistical data. Tracy, along with Michelle Tan, CEO, will be presenting at a medical conference in Vancouver, British Columbia. Their presentation on the differences between patient costs and outcomes in the United States and Canada will rely heavily on the data in this worksheet. To begin, open **CRGHCdnHealthStats.xlsx**.
2. Save the workbook with the name **2-CRGHCdnHealthStats.xlsx**.
3. Make the following changes:
    a. Change the zoom so you can view as much of the worksheet as possible to minimize horizontal scrolling. Make sure the cells are still readable. ***Note: Depending on your monitor size and resolution settings, change the zoom to a value between 70% and 90%.***
    b. AutoFit all column widths to the length of the longest entry.
    c. Change the fill color behind the title *Total Healthcare Costs in Canada* (currently displays with an orange fill color). You determine the color.
    d. Change the font color and fill color for *Breakdown of Healthcare Costs by Procedures in Canada* and *Mortality Rates by Age/Sex in Canada by 100,000*. You determine the colors.
    e. Change the font color and fill color for *Leading Causes of Death in Canada 2018* and *Physical activity by age group and sex in Canada 2018*. You determine the colors.
4. Change the page orientation to landscape.
5. Save **2-CRGHCdnHealthStats.xlsx**.

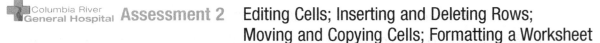
1. There is still work to be done on the Canadian healthcare statistical data worksheet before Tracy and Michelle can prepare the presentation for the conference in Vancouver. With **2-CRGHCdnHealthStats.xlsx** open, edit the worksheet using the following information:

   a. In the *Total Healthcare Costs in Canada* section, for the year 2016, *Hospitals* should be *15326* instead of *14175.2*.

   b. In the *Total Healthcare Costs in Canada* section of the worksheet, insert a new column before *2015* and then enter the data as follows:

	2014
Hospitals:	10299
Other institutions:	8204.7
Physicians:	21992
Other professionals:	21584.1
Drugs:	34669.8
Other:	15792.5

   c. AutoFit column Q to the longest entry and then clear the formatting in cell Q1.

   d. The formula to sum total healthcare costs for each year is missing. Enter the correct formula for the first year, 2014 (Q10) and then copy the formula to cells R10, S10, T10, and U10. **Hint: Be careful to sum the correct range**.

   e. Apply the Comma format with no decimal places to the numeric cells in the *Total Healthcare Costs in Canada* section of the worksheet.

   f. Type in millions of dollars in cell P2 and then apply bold and italic formatting.

   g. Merge and center cells A1, A25, I1, I29, and P1 over the columns in the respective sections.

   h. Change the alignment of any headings in the worksheet whose appearance could be improved.

   i. Move the contents of the range P1:U10 (*Total Healthcare Costs in Canada* section) to the range I58:N67. Adjust the column widths as necessary after moving the cells.

   j. Apply font, border, and color formatting to enhance the appearance of the worksheet.

2. Save **2-CRGHCdnHealthStats.xlsx**.

1. Tracy has reviewed the latest copy of the Canadian healthcare statistical data worksheet and noted the following changes to be made. With **2-CRGHCdnHealthStats.xlsx** open, complete the worksheet using the following information:

   a. Type the following label in cell A60:

   Source: Statistics Canada, http://www.statcan.ca

b. Cancer and cardiac disease are the two leading causes of death in Canada in 2018. In cell G3, create a formula to sum the male deaths from cancer and cardiac disease in the *Leading Causes of Death in Canada* section. In cell H3, create a formula to sum the female deaths from cancer and cardiac disease in the *Leading Causes of Death in Canada* section. In cell F3, calculate the total of cells G3 and H3 (male and female cardiac and cancer cases) as a percentage of cell E18.

c. Apply the Percent format with one decimal place to cell F3.

d. Enter a formula in cell B20 that will calculate the total deaths by psychoses and suicide as a percentage of cell E18. Format the result using the Percent format with one decimal place.

e. Enter a formula in cell B21 that will calculate the increase in total deaths by psychoses and suicide in the next year using the percent value in cell D21 as the increase percentage on the current total. Format the result using the Comma format.

2. Save **2-CRGHCdnHealthStats.xlsx**.

Columbia River General Hospital Assessment 4   **Performing a Spelling Check; Adjusting Column Widths; Editing and Clearing Cells; Using Replace**

1. Further research at the Statistics Canada website has revealed that some input errors exist in the Canadian healthcare statistics worksheet. With **2-CRGHCdnHealthStats.xlsx** open, make the following corrections:

a. Make cell A1 the active cell. Perform a spelling check and correct any errors.

b. AutoFit all column widths except column F, whose width should be set to *8*.

c. Correct the following data entry errors in the *Physical activity by age group and sex in Canada 2018* section:

15–19 years, Females, Physically active:	430,212
20–24 years, Males, Physically inactive:	392,789
25–34 years, Males, Physically active:	472,345
35–44 years, Females, Physically inactive:	1,567,954

d. Clear the contents of the range I4:N4.

e. Make cell N5 the active cell and then type the formula that will calculate the overall average from 2015 to 2018 for major surgery healthcare costs: =sum(j5:m5)/4. Copy this formula to the remaining rows in the section. If necessary, format the values to one decimal place.

f. Replace all occurrences of *Disease* with *Illness*. ***Note: Do not use Replace All. Do not replace the text in cells in which other word forms of Disease (such as Diseases) exist.***

g. Make cell A62 active, type Date:, and then type today's date.

2. Click the Page Layout tab and then change the *Width* option in the Scale to Fit group to *1 page*.

3. Print **2-CRGHCdnHealthStats.xlsx**. ***Note: Check with your instructor if you submit your work in hard copy to see if you need to print two copies of this worksheet with one of the copies showing the cell formulas instead of the calculated results.***

4. Save and then close **2-CRGHCdnHealthStats.xlsx**.

 **Assessment 5** Finding Information on Dates

1. Use Excel's Help feature to find more information on how Excel stores dates and how they can be used in formulas.
2. Open **2-CRGHCdnHealthStats.xlsx**.
3. Add the label *Presentation Date:* to cell A63.
4. Enter the date *April 18, 2019* in cell B63.
5. Add the label *Final Preparation Date:* to cell A64.
6. Create a formula in cell B64 that will subtract 5 days from the presentation date.
7. Save the workbook with the name **2-CRGHCdnHealthStatsDates.xlsx**.
8. Print and then close **2-CRGHCdnHealthStatsDates.xlsx**. *Note: Check with your instructor if you submit your work in hard copy to see if you need to print two copies of this worksheet with one of the copies showing the cell formulas instead of the calculated results.*

 **Assessment 6** Locating Information on U.S. Healthcare Costs

1. Tracy Fitzgerald has asked you to research healthcare costs in the United States for the presentation in Vancouver. Search the Internet for healthcare cost statistics for the United States. Consider narrowing your search to one area of focus, such as cancer or cardiac costs.
2. Create a workbook that summarizes the information you found.
3. Insert related online images.
4. Create a formula that includes an absolute cell reference.
5. Include the sources for your data in the workbook.
6. Save the workbook with the name **2-USHealthStats**.
7. Display formulas in the worksheet, print, and then close **2-USHealthStats.xlsx**.

Marquee Challenge

 **Challenge 1** Preparing a Weekly Staffing Schedule for Neurology

Data File

1. Create the worksheet shown in Figure WB-2.1, including all formatting options. The worksheet shown has the Circuit theme applied. Use your best judgment to determine font type, font size, font and fill colors, column widths, and/or row heights.
2. Insert **CRGHLogo.jpg** into the worksheet and then size and position it as desired.
3. Change the page orientation to landscape.
4. Save the workbook with the name **2-NeurologyStaffing**.
5. Print and then close **2-NeurologyStaffing.xlsx**.

 **Challenge 2** Preparing a Radiology Requisition Form

Data File

1. Open **CRGHRadiologyReq.xlsx**.
2. Edit and format the worksheet as shown in Figure WB-2.2, including performing a spelling check. Use your best judgment to match as closely as possible the colors and fonts shown. The worksheet shown has the Circuit theme applied.
3. Save the workbook with the name **2-CRGHRadiologyReq**.
4. Print and then close **2-CRGHRadiologyReq.xlsx**.

Figure WB-2.1 Challenge 1

	A	B	C	D	E	F	G	H	I
1			Columbia River General Hospital					Columbia River General Hospital	
2					Neurology Staffing Worksheet				
3	Beds:	6	Shift 1:	7am- 7pm		Rotation			
4			Shift 2:	7pm- 7am		2 days followed by 2 nights; 4 on followed by 5 off			
5	Bed	Shift	Mon	Tue	Wed	Thu	Fri	Sat	Sun
6	1	1	McAllister	McAllister	Keller	Keller	Rashmi	Rashmi	Hillman
7	1	2	Yoshiko	Yoshiko	McAllister	McAllister	Huang	Huang	Baird
8	2	1	Hillman	Graham	Johan	Johan	McKenna	Petrovic	Zukic
9	2	2	Baird	Hillman	Hillman	Zukic	Zukic	Graham	Graham
10	3	1	Graham	Baird	Santos	Santos	Bernis	McKenna	Huang
11	3	2	Santos	Santos	Bernis	Bernis	Anatolius	Alvarez	Alvarez
12	4	1	Jorgensen	Jorgensen	Wei	Wei	Vezina	Zukic	Petrovic
13	4	2	McKenna	Wells	Wells	Jenkins	Johan	Johan	McKenna
14	5	1	Alvarez	Alvarez	Yoshiko	Yoshiko	Orlowski	Bernis	Jenkins
15	5	2	Petrovic	Petrovic	Jorgensen	Jorgensen	Jenkins	Anatolius	Lind
16	6	1	Huang	Biorje	Baird	Wells	Wells	Tomasz	Anatolius
17	6	2	Keller	Keller	Rashmi	Rashmi	Wei	Wei	Tomasz
18									

Figure WB-2.2 Challenge 2

	A	B	C	D	E
1	Columbia River General Hospital				
2	Radiology Requisition				
3	Patient Last Name		Date		
4	Patient First Name		Office use only		
5	Chart Number		Dept Charge Code		
6	Physician		Amount		
7	Technician			Left	Right
8	Esophagus		Ribs		
9	Upper G.I. Series		Sternoclavicular Joints		
10	Small Bowel		Clavicle		
11	Barium Enema		Shoulder		
12			A.C. Joints		
13	Acute Abdomen		Scapula		
14	Chest		Humerus		
15	Sternum		Elbow		
16	Facial Bones		Forearm		
17	Mandible		Write		
18	Nasal Bones		Hand		
19	Skull		Finger or Thumb		
20	Sinuses		Hip		
21	T.M. Joints		Femur		
22	Cervical Spine		Knee		
23	Thoracic Spine		Tibia and Fibula		
24	Lumbosacral Spine		Ankle		
25	Pelvis		Heel		
26	Sacrum and Coccyx		Foot		
27			Toe		
28	*Esophagus, Stomach, or Small Bowel		**Mammogram		
29	*Nothing to eat or drink after midnight prior to examination.				
30	**Wear separate blouse with skirt or slacks. No deodorant or talc.				
31					

Study Tools

Study tools include In Brief steps and medical resources. Use the study tools to help you further develop and review skills learned in this section.

Knowledge Check

Complete the Knowledge Check to assess your comprehension and recall of application features, technology, and functions.

Recheck

Check your understanding by taking this quiz.

Skills Review

Review 1   Inserting Statistical Functions

Data File

1. Open **CVPOpExp.xlsx** and then save it with the name **3-CVPOpExp**.
2. Make cell A15 the active cell.
3. Type Average Expense and then press the Enter key.
4. Type Maximum Expense and then press the Enter key.
5. Type Minimum Expense and then press the Enter key.
6. Make cell B15 the active cell and then create the formula that will calculate the average of the expense values in the range B4:B9.
7. Make cell B16 the active cell and then create the formula that will return the maximum expense value within the range B4:B9.
8. Make cell B17 the active cell and then create the formula that will return the minimum expense value within the range B4:B9.
9. Copy the formulas in the range B15:B17 to the range C15:F17.
10. Apply the Comma format with zero decimal places to the range B15:F17.
11. Save **3-CVPOpExp.xlsx**.

Review 2   Inserting Date Functions

1. With **3-CVPOpExp.xlsx** open, make cell A19 the active cell.
2. Type Date Created: and then press the Right Arrow key.
3. With cell B19 the active cell, use the DATE function to insert the current date.
   Note: You do not want to use the TODAY function, because you do not want the date to update each time you open the file.
4. Make cell A20 the active cell.

5. Type Next Revision Date: and then press the Right Arrow key.
6. With cell B20 the active cell, type the formula =b19+360 and then press the Enter key.
7. Save **3-CVPOpExp.xlsx**.

Review 3   Naming Ranges; Using the IF Function

1. With **3-CVPOpExp.xlsx** open, insert three rows above row 19.
2. Make cell A19 the active cell, type Current Target, and then press the Enter key.
3. With cell A20 the active cell, type Expense Over Target and then press the Enter key.
4. Sydney Larsen has set a quarterly target of $960,000 for total expenses. Make cell B19 the active cell and then type 960. Apply the Comma format with no decimal places to cell B19 and then name the cell *Target*.
5. Sydney wants you to insert a formula that, when applicable, will show the amount by which a quarter's total expenses have been exceeded. Make cell B20 the active cell and then enter the following IF function using the Function Arguments dialog box or by typing the formula directly into the cell: =if(b11>target,b11-target,0)
6. Drag the fill handle from cell B20 to the range C20:E20.
7. In the space provided below, write the values displayed in the cells indicated.

   B20: _____
   C20: _____
   D20: _____
   E20: _____

8. In the space provided, write in your own words a brief explanation of the IF function you entered in cell B20.

   _____
   _____
   _____

9. Change the value in cell B19 from 960 to 955.
10. Save **3-CVPOpExp.xlsx**.

Review 4   Inserting an Image; Sorting a List; Setting Print Options

Data File

1. With **3-CVPOpExp.xlsx** open, change the height of row 1 to 60.00 (100 pixels).
2. Select the range A1:F1 and then change the fill color to White, Background 1 (first column, first row in the *Theme Colors* section).
3. Make cell A1 the active cell and then insert **CVPLogo.jpg** from your ExcelMedS3 folder.
4. Adjust the size and position of the logo until it is centered over columns A through F in row 1.
5. Select the range A3:F9 and then sort the range in ascending order. Click in any cell to deselect the range.
6. Change the top margin to 2 inches.
7. Create a header that will print your first and last names in the left header box and the current date and time (separated by one space) in the right header box.
8. Create a footer that will print the word *Page* followed by the page number (separated by one space) in the center footer box.
9. Save, print, and then close **3-CVPOpExp.xlsx**. ***Note: If you submit your work in hard copy, check with your instructor to see if you need to print two copies of this worksheet with one of the copies showing the cell formulas instead of the calculated results.***

Cascade View
Pediatrics

Review 5 Creating and Modifying a Chart; Drawing an Arrow and Text Box; Formatting a Table

Data File

1. Open **CVPRent&Maint.xlsx** and then save it with the name **3-CVPRent&Maint**.
2. Select the range A3:E10 and then create a 3-D Clustered Column chart. Apply the third quick layout (third column, first row), change the chart title to *Rent and Maintenance Costs*, and then move the chart to a new sheet titled *ColumnChart*.
3. With ColumnChart the active sheet, draw an arrow pointing to the column in the chart representing clinic cleaning for the fourth quarter. Draw a text box at the end of the arrow and then type the following text inside the box: Includes price increase from new contractor Universal Cleaning Corporation.
4. Change the font of the text in the text box to 10-point Candara and then apply a dark red shape outline to the text box.
5. Apply a dark red shape outline to the arrow.
6. Display Sheet1 and then select the range A3:F10. Format the range as a table using the yellow table style in the fifth column, third row in the *Light* section. Band the columns instead of the rows. Click the Home tab, click the Sort & Filter button in the Editing group, and then click *Filter* at the drop-down list to remove the filter arrows from the labels in row 3.
7. Save **3-CVPRent&Maint.xlsx**.
8. Print the entire workbook (the *Sheet1* worksheet and the *ColumnChart* worksheet) and then close **3-CVPRent&Maint.xlsx**.

Skills Assessment

Note: If you submit your work in hard copy, check with your instructor before completing these assessments to find out if you need to print two copies of each worksheet with one of the copies showing the cell formulas instead of the calculated results.

North Shore
Medical Clinic

Assessment 1   Using Statistical and IF Functions

Data File

1. Lee Elliott, Office Manager, has started a worksheet that includes the clinic's 15 most frequent medical supply purchases. Lee wants to calculate purchase quantity discounts from the clinic's two preferred medical supply vendors. Both vendors charge the same unit price, but each offers a discount plan with different percentages and quantity levels. Lee has asked for your help in writing the correct formulas to calculate the savings from each vendor. Specifically, Lee wants to know which supplier provides the better offer. To begin, open **NSMC15Supplies.xlsx**.
2. Save the workbook with the name **3-NSMC15Supplies**.
3. In cell E4, create a formula to calculate the discount from AllCare Medical Supplies using the following criteria:
   - AllCare offers a 1.75% discount on the product's unit price for zero to four units ordered.
   - The discount rises to 2.5% when five or more units are ordered.
   - Create appropriate range names to reference the percentage values in cells B21 and B22 within your IF statement.

4. In cell F4, create a formula to calculate the discount from BestCare Health Supply using the following criteria:
   - BestCare offers a 1.8% discount on the product's unit price for zero to five units ordered.
   - The discount rises to 2.25% when six or more units are ordered.
   - Create appropriate range names to reference the percentage values in cells B23 and B24 within your IF statement.
5. Copy the formulas to the remaining rows in columns E and F.
6. Calculate the total discount value for all 15 supplies in cells E19 and F19.
7. Apply formatting options as needed.
8. Enter an appropriate label and create a formula to calculate the average discount below the total row for each vendor.
9. Print the worksheet in landscape orientation, centered horizontally.
10. Save and then close **3-NSMC15Supplies.xlsx**.

Assessment 2   Changing Print Options; Using Date and IF Functions

Data File

1. Darrin Lancaster, CMA, has asked you to finish the worksheet he started in order to track Dr. Hydall's dermatology patient records. To begin, open **NSMCDermPatients.xlsx**.
2. Save the workbook with the name **3-NSMCDermPatients**.
3. Medical records are completed on the system 12 days after Dr. Hydall's report has been mailed to the referring physician. Create a formula in cell H4 that calculates the date the system report should be filed.
4. Copy the formula to the remaining rows in column H.
5. Create a formula for a recall date in column I using the following information:
   - If *Repeat Assessment* contains *Y* for Yes, then calculate the recall date 45 days from the date of the consultation visit.
   - If *Repeat Assessment* does not contain *Y*, instruct Excel to place the words *Not required* in the cell. ***Hint: Use quotation marks before and after a text entry in an IF statement. For example, =IF(G4="Y",…).***
   - Format the column to display the date in the same format as other dates within the worksheet.
   - Expand the column width as necessary.
6. Set the following print options:
   a. Change the orientation to landscape.
   b. Change the top margin to 1.75 inches and center the worksheet horizontally.
   c. Create a header that will print your name in the left header box and the current date in the right header box.
   d. Scale the worksheet to fit on one page.
7. Apply any other formatting changes to improve the worksheet's appearance.
8. Save, print, and then close **3-NSMCDermPatients.xlsx**.

Assessment 3 **Creating and Formatting Charts; Drawing an Arrow and a Text Box**

Data File

1. Dr. Hydall has asked you to create charts from the dermatology patient analysis report for a presentation to the local members of the American Academy of Dermatology. Dr. Hydall has specifically requested a column chart depicting the patient numbers for all diagnoses by age group and a pie chart summarizing all of the diagnoses by total patients. To begin, open **NSMCDermStats.xlsx**.
2. Save the workbook with the name **3-NSMCDermStats**.
3. On a new sheet labeled *ColumnChart*, create a column chart that will display the values for patients aged 0–12 through 51+ for each diagnosis. Include an appropriate chart title. Include any other chart elements that will make the chart data easier to interpret.
4. Create a 3-D pie chart that will display the number of patients in each age group as a percentage of 100. ***Hint: Select the ranges B3:G3 and B9:G9 before selecting the 3-D pie option.*** Include an appropriate chart title and display percentages as the data labels. Place the pie chart at the bottom of the worksheet starting in row 12 and resize the chart so that its width extends from the left edge of column A to the right edge of column H.
5. Draw an arrow pointing to the 13–20 age group slice in the pie chart. Create a text box at the end of the arrow containing the text *This age group growing 10% per year!*
6. If necessary, move and/or resize the arrow and text box. Change the font color of the text inside the text box and the outline color of the text box to a color complementary to the chart.
7. Change the line color of the arrow to the same color you used for the text box.
8. Center the worksheet horizontally.
9. Print the entire workbook. (Make sure the text box created in Step 5 fits on the first page of the worksheet.)
10. Save and then close **3-NSMCDermStats.xlsx**.

Assessment 4 **Working with Tables**

Data File

1. Laura Latterell, Education Director, has started a worksheet in which she tracks professional development completion for full-time nursing staff. Laura assists nurses with selection of professional development activities and plans workshops throughout the year to provide in-service training. Laura would like the worksheet to be used to provide printouts she needs for planning upcoming workshops. To begin, open **CRGHNursePD.xlsx**.
2. Save the workbook with the name **3-CRGHNursePD**.
3. Format the range A4:H32 as a table. You determine the table style.
4. Filter the table to obtain a list of nurses who are RNs and work in the ICU unit.
5. Sort the list in ascending order by last name.
6. Print the filtered list, changing print options as necessary to fit the printout on one page.

7. Redisplay all records.
8. Filter the list to obtain a list of nurses working in the PreOp unit who are not current with professional development (PD) activities.
9. Sort the list in ascending order by last name.
10. Print the filtered list.
11. Redisplay all records.
12. Sort the entire list first by *PD Current?*, then by *Years Experience*, and then by *Employee Last Name*, all in ascending order.
13. Print the sorted list.
14. Save and then close **3-CRGHNursePD.xlsx**.

Assessment 5 Finding Information on Inserting, Renaming, and Deleting Worksheets

1. Use the Help feature to learn how to insert, rename, and delete worksheets.
2. Open **3-NSMCDermStats.xlsx** and then save it with the name **3-NSMCDermStats_A5**.
3. Change the name of the *ColumnChart* sheet to *AgeStatsChart*.
4. Change the name of the *Sheet1* sheet to *DiagnosisByAgeGroup*.
5. Create a footer on each sheet that prints the file name followed by the sheet name, separated by a comma and one space in the center footer box. ***Hint: Use the Page Setup dialog box to create a footer in a chart sheet.***
6. Print the entire workbook.
7. Save and then close **3-NSMCDermStats_A5.xlsx**.

Assessment 6 Researching and Calculating Conference Costs

1. Visit the website for the American Association of Medical Assistants (AAMA) and find the dates and location for the upcoming annual convention.
2. The local chapter of the AAMA is willing to sponsor a student to attend the conference. As part of the application for sponsorship, you need to submit a detailed expense estimate.
3. Use the Internet to research airfare, hotel accommodations, conference registration fees, and any other expenses related to attending the conference.
4. Create an Excel worksheet that summarizes the cost of the conference.
5. Apply formatting enhancements to produce a professional quality worksheet.
6. Preview the worksheet and then adjust print options as necessary to improve the printed appearance and minimize paper usage.
7. Save the workbook and name it **3-AAMAConference**.
8. Print and then close **3-AAMAConference.xlsx**.

Marquee Challenge

 **Challenge 1**   Preparing a Patient Cost Record

1. Create the worksheet shown in Figure WB-3.1, including all formatting options. Use your best judgment to determine font, font size, font color, fill color, column widths, and/or row heights. Also note the following specifications:
   a. For all date entries, use a DATE function.
   b. Use a formula to calculate Length of Stay.
   c. Use a formula to calculate Direct Overhead at 15% of Total Direct Charges.
   d. Use a formula to calculate Indirect Overhead at 10% of Total Direct Charges.
   e. Use a formula to calculate TOTAL COST as the sum of Total Direct Charges, Direct Overhead, and Indirect Overhead.
2. Center the worksheet horizontally.
3. Create a header that will print your name in the left header box and the current date in the right header box.
4. Create a footer that will print the file name in the center footer box.
5. Make any other required changes to page layout options to ensure the cost report will print on one page.
6. Save the workbook and name it **3-CRGHCost70176345**.
7. Print and then close **3-CRGHCost70176345.xlsx**.

Challenge 2   Charting 10-Year New Cancer Rate Statistics

Data File

1. Open **USCancerStats.xlsx** and then save it with the name **3-USCancerStats**.
2. Using the data in the worksheet, create the chart shown in Figure WB-3.2 on page WB-67 in its own sheet, including all formatting options and drawn objects. Use your best judgment to determine colors and chart style.
3. Using the Page Setup dialog box, create a header that will print your name in the left header box and the current date in the right header box, and then create a footer that will print the file name in the center footer box.
4. Save **3-USCancerStats.xlsx**.
5. Print only the chart worksheet and then close **3-USCancerStats.xlsx**.

Figure WB-3.1 Challenge 1

Columbia River General Hospital
Patient Cost Record

Date of Cost Report	2/25/2019		TOTAL COST			$ 27,143.53
Patient Chart #	70176345		Attending Physician			Dr. Ruby Priyanka
PIN #	2365		Diagnosis/ Principal Procedure			Hip Replacement
Patient Last Name	**Nguyen**		Admit Date		2/8/2019	
Date of Birth	Mary		Disharge Date		2/12/2019	
	10/22/1976		Length of Stay		4	

Department	Dept Code	Service Code	Description		Charges
Patient Registration	521	13	IP Registration	$	65.15
Health Records	534	17	Clerical		187.50
Food Services	341	67	Patient Meals		375.15
Nursing	122	27	Orthopaedics		4,576.12
Operating Room	431	26	OR		6,548.55
Operating Room	431	31	Respiratory Therapy		235.00
Recovery Room	658	87	Recovery Level 4		678.23
Laboratory Services	377	18	Lab Requisitions		349.00
General Radiology	876	35	HIP LT AP		134.66
General Radiology	876	44	Pelvis & HIP LT		175.33
General Radiology	876	64	Ultrasound		133.28
Pharmacy	912	38	Inpatient Drugs		873.44
Physiotherapy	765	29	Physiotherapy		673.44
Occupational Therapy	844	28	Occupational Therapy		534.22
Physician Service	115	34	OR Surgeon		3,587.75
Inpatient Ward	239	12	General Ward		2,588.00
			Total Direct Charges	$	21,714.82
			Direct Overhead	$	3,257.22
			Indirect Overhead	$	2,171.48

Figure WB-3.2 Challenge 2

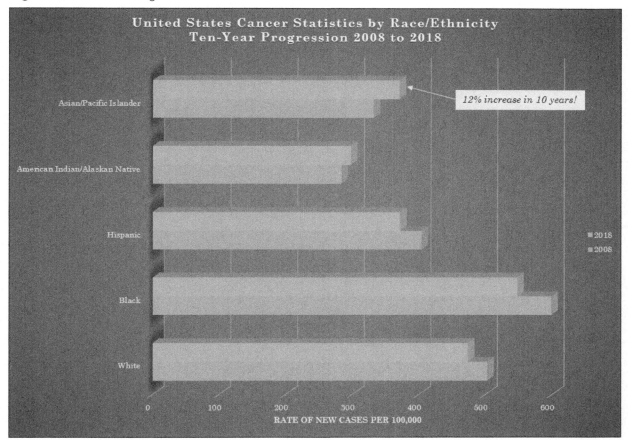

> **Study Tools**

Study tools include In Brief steps and medical resources. Use the study tools to help you further develop and review skills learned in this section.

> **Recheck**

Check your understanding by taking this quiz.

Skills Review

Review 1 Copying and Pasting Data

> **Data Files**

1. Make Excel active and then open **CRGHVolunteers.xlsx**.
2. Make Word active and then open **CRGHVolPost.docx**.
3. Save the document with the name **1-CRGHVolPost**.
4. Make Excel active, select the range C7:F28 and then click the Copy button in the Clipboard group on the Home tab.
5. Make Word active and then press Ctrl + End to move the insertion point to the end of the document.
6. Paste the table into the Word document.
7. Select the table, display the Table Properties dialog box, center the table between the left and right margins, and then deselect the table.
8. View the document at the Print backstage area.
9. Click the Back button to return to the document.
10. Save, print, and then close **1-CRGHVolPost.docx**.
11. Make Excel active, remove the marquee, and then deselect the range.
12. Close **CRGHVolunteers.xlsx**.

Review 2 Linking an Object

> **Data Files**

1. Make Word active and then open **CRGH4thQtrFees.docx**.
2. Save the document with the name **1-CRGH4thQtrFees**.
3. Make Excel active and then open **CRGHQtrlyBilling.xlsx**.
4. Save the workbook with the name **1-CRGHQtrlyBilling**.
5. Select the range A7:G16 and then link the cells to the end of the Word document **1-CRGH4thQtrFees.docx**.
6. Save, print, and then close **1-CRGH4thQtrFees.docx**.
7. Make Excel active, remove the marquee, and then deselect the range.
8. Close **1-CRGHQtrlyBilling.xlsx**.

Review 3   Creating and Linking a Chart

1. With Excel active, open **1-CRGHQtrlyBilling.xlsx**.
2. Make Word active and then open **1-CRGH4thQtrFees.docx**. Click No when prompted to update links.
3. Make Excel active and then select the ranges A7:A15 and G7:G15.
4. Create a 3-D pie chart with the following options:
   a. Insert *Fourth Quarter Tuition by Course* as the chart title.
   b. Apply the Style 3 chart style.
   c. Position the chart below the worksheet, starting in cell A18.
5. With the chart selected, copy and then link the chart to the Word document **1-CRGH4thQtrFees.docx**. Insert a triple space below the linked worksheet. If necessary, make changes to the chart or page layout options to fit the document on one page.
6. Save, print, and then close **1-CRGH4thQtrFees.docx**.
7. Make Excel active and then click any cell to deselect the chart.
8. Save, print, and then close **1-CRGHQtrlyBilling.xlsx**.

Review 4   Editing Linked Objects

1. With Excel active, open **1-CRGHQtrlyBilling.xlsx**.
2. Make the following changes to the data in the specified cells:

B10:	575
D10:	1125
E10:	850
C14:	225
C15:	1175

3. Save, print, and then close **1-CRGHQtrlyBilling.xlsx**.
4. Make Word active and then open **1-CRGH4thQtrFees.docx**. Click Yes when prompted to update linked data.
5. Save, print, and then close **1-CRGH4thQtrFees.docx**.

Review 5   Embedding and Editing an Object

Data Files

1. With Word active, open **CRGHFoundation.docx**.
2. Save the document with the name **1-CRGHFoundation**.
3. Make Excel active and then open **CRGHFactSheet.xlsx**.
4. Select the range A6:H23 and then embed the cells at the end of the Word document **1-CRGHFoundation.docx**.
5. Make Excel active, remove the marquee, click any cell to deselect the range, and then close **CRGHFactSheet.xlsx**.
6. Close Excel.
7. Double-click the embedded object in **1-CRGHFoundation.docx**.
8. Select the range A7:H23 and then apply Blue, Accent 1, Lighter 80% fill color (fifth column, second row in the *Theme Colors* section).
9. Change the value for *Volunteer & Auxiliary Members* to *812*.
10. Click outside the embedded object.
11. Save, print, and then close **1-CRGHFoundation.docx**.
12. Close Word.

> **Study Tools**

Study tools include In Brief steps and medical resources. Use the study tools to help you further develop and review skills learned in this section.

> **Knowledge Check**

Complete the Knowledge Check to assess your comprehension and recall of application features, technology, and functions.

> **Recheck**

Check your understanding by taking this quiz.

Skills Review

 Columbia River General Hospital

Review 1   Applying a Design Theme and Creating Slides

1. With a blank presentation open in PowerPoint, click the Design tab, click the More Themes button at the right of the theme thumbnails in the Themes group, and then click the *Basis* option.
2. Click the third variant in the Variants group (white with an orange border).
3. Type the title and subtitle for Slide 1 as shown in Figure WB-1.1.
4. Click the Home tab and then click the New Slide button in the Slides group.
5. Apply the Title Slide layout. (You will arrange the text in the placeholder in the next review activity.)
6. Type the text in Slide 2 as shown in Figure WB-1.1.
7. Continue creating the slides for the presentation, using the text shown in Figure WB-1.1.
8. Save the presentation and name it **1-Fibromyalgia**.

Figure WB-1.1 Review 1

| Slide 1 | Title | Columbia River General Hospital |
| | Subtitle | Facts about Fibromyalgia |

Slide 2   Title   What is Fibromyalgia?
            Subtitle   Fibromyalgia is an arthritis-related condition characterized by generalized muscular pain and fatigue.

Slide 3   Title   Treatments for Fibromyalgia
            Bullets
- Medication to diminish pain and improve sleep
- Exercise programs that stretch muscles
- Relaxation techniques
- Education programs to help understand the disorder

Slide 4   Title   Who is Affected by Fibromyalgia?
            Bullets
- Approximately 1 in 50 Americans may be affected
- Mostly women but men and children can also have the disorder
- People with certain diseases such as rheumatoid arthritis, lupus, and spinal arthritis
- People with a family member with fibromyalgia may be more likely to be diagnosed with the disorder

 **Review 2** **Inserting a Slide; Changing the Slide Layout; Rearranging Slides; Moving a Placeholder**

1. With **1-Fibromyalgia.pptx** open, insert a new Slide 4 between the current Slides 3 and 4 and type the text shown in Figure WB-1.2.
2. Click the Slide Sorter button in the view area on the Status bar.
3. Move Slide 5 (*Who is Affected by Fibromyalgia?*) to the left of Slide 3 (*Treatments for Fibromyalgia*).
4. Move Slide 5 (*Causes of Fibromyalgia*) to the left of Slide 4 (*Treatments for Fibromyalgia*).
5. Click the Normal button in the view area on the Status bar.
6. Display Slide 2 in the slide pane and then change the slide layout to *Title Only*.
7. Click in the text containing the description of fibromyalgia and then move the placeholder so it is centered horizontally and vertically on the slide.
8. Display Slide 4 in the slide pane, click in the bulleted text to select the placeholder, and then decrease the right side of the placeholder by dragging the middle right sizing handle to the left. (Do not decrease the width of the placeholder so much that the bulleted text has to wrap.)
9. Position the placeholder so that the bulleted text is centered on the slide.
10. Save **1-Fibromyalgia.pptx**.

Figure WB-1.2 Review 2

Slide 4	Title Bullets	Causes of Fibromyalgia • Infectious illness • Physical and/or emotional trauma • Muscle abnormalities • Hormonal changes • Repetitive injuries

Review 3   Adding Transitions and Transition Sounds; Running a Slide Show; Printing a Presentation

1. With **1-Fibromyalgia.pptx** open, click the Transitions tab.
2. Click the More Transitions button at the right side of the transition thumbnails in the Transition to This Slide group and then click a transition of your choosing.
3. Click the *Sound* option box arrow and then click a transition sound of your choosing.
4. Apply the transition and transition sound to all slides in the presentation.
5. Make Slide 1 the active slide and then run the slide show.
6. Print the presentation as an outline.
7. Print the presentation with all five slides displayed horizontally on the page.
8. Save and then close **1-Fibromyalgia.pptx**.

Skills Assessment

Assessment 1   Preparing a Presentation for Columbia River General Hospital

1. Prepare a presentation for Columbia River General Hospital with the information shown in Figure WB-1.3. (You determine the design template.)
2. Add a transition and transition sound of your choosing to all slides in the presentation.
3. Run the slide show.
4. Print the presentation with all five slides displayed horizontally on one page.
5. Save the presentation and name it **1-CRGHInfo**.
6. Close **1-CRGHInfo.pptx**.

Figure WB-1.3 Assessment 1

Slide 1	Title Subtitle	Columbia River General Hospital Our mission is to provide comprehensive and high-quality care for all of our patients.
Slide 2	Title Bullets	Hospital Directives • Highest-quality patient care • Exceptional customer services • Fully trained and qualified staff • Delivery of first-class health education
Slide 3	Title Bullets	Facilities • 400 licensed beds • Level II adult trauma system • 14 operating rooms • 25-bed adult intensive care unit • Level III neonatal intensive care unit • 24-hour emergency services
Slide 4	Title Bullets	Physicians Clinics • Division Street • Lake Oswego • Fremont Center • Oak Grove
Slide 5	Title Subtitle	Health Foundation Columbia River General Hospital's Health Foundation is a nonprofit organization that promotes the well-being of adults and families served by the hospital.

 **Assessment 2** Preparing a Presentation for Cascade View Pediatrics

1. Prepare a presentation for Cascade View Pediatrics with the information shown in Figure WB-1.4. (You determine the design theme.)
2. Add a transition and transition sound of your choosing to all slides in the presentation.
3. Run the slide show.
4. Print the presentation with all five slides displayed horizontally on one page.
5. Save the presentation and name it **1-CVPInfo**.
6. Close **1-CVPInfo.pptx**.

Figure WB-1.4 Assessment 2

Slide 1	Title Subtitle	Cascade View Pediatrics 350 North Skagit Portland, OR 97505 (503) 555-7700
Slide 2	Title Bullets	Doctor Consultations • By appointment only • Monday through Friday, 9:00 a.m. to 5:30 p.m. • Monday and Wednesday, 6:30 to 8:00 p.m. • Saturday, 9:00 a.m. to noon
Slide 3	Title Bullets	Nurse Consultations • By appointment only • Tuesday and Thursday, 2:00 to 4:30 p.m. • Monday and Wednesday, 6:30 to 8:00 p.m.
Slide 4	Title Bullets	Accepted Insurance Plans • Premiere Group • Health Plus America • Madison Health • Healthwise Cooperative • Uniform Medical
Slide 5	Title Bullets	Education Programs • Child development and therapy • Asthma education • Diabetes education • Positive parenting • Grandparents' workshop • First aid

 **Assessment 3** Finding Information on the Undo Button

1. Open **1-CVPInfo.pptx** and then use the Help feature to learn how to undo an action.
2. After learning how to undo an action, make Slide 1 the active slide.
3. In the slide pane, click immediately right of the telephone number *(503) 555-7700* and then press the Enter key.
4. Type the email address CVP@ppi.cvpediatrics.com and then press the Enter key. (PowerPoint converts the email address to a hyperlink [changes the color and underlines the text].)
5. Undo the action that converted the text to a hyperlink.
6. Type Website: http://ppi-edu.net/cvp.

7. Press the Enter key. (This converts the website to a hyperlink.)
8. Undo the action that converted the text to a hyperlink.
9. If necessary, increase the size of the placeholder to better accommodate the new text.
10. Print only Slide 1.
11. Save and then close **1-CVPInfo.pptx**.

 **Assessment 4**   Finding Information on Setting Slide Show Timings

1. Open **1-CVPInfo.pptx**.
2. Use the Help feature or experiment with the options on the Transitions tab to learn how to set slide show timings manually.
3. Set up the presentation so that, when running the slide show, each slide advances after three seconds.
4. Run the slide show.
5. Save and then close **1-CVPInfo.pptx**.

 **Assessment 5**   Locating Information and Preparing a
                                    Presentation on Chickenpox

1. You need to prepare a presentation on chickenpox that includes information such as symptoms, treatment, incubation period, and infectious period. Use the information you prepared for **3-Chickenpox.docx** and research additional information on the Internet.
2. Using PowerPoint, create a presentation about chickenpox that contains a title slide with Cascade View Pediatrics and the name you choose for your presentation. Include additional slides that cover a description of chickenpox and its symptoms, treatments, and incubation and infectious periods.
3. Run the slide show.
4. Print all of the slides displayed horizontally on one page.
5. Save the presentation and name it **1-Chickenpox**.
6. Close **1-Chickenpox.pptx**.

Marquee Challenge

 **Challenge 1**   Preparing a Presentation on Cystic Fibrosis

1. Prepare the presentation shown in Figure WB-1.5 using the Berlin design theme.
2. Save the completed presentation and name it **1-CysticFibrosis**.
3. Apply a transition and transition sound to all slides and then run the slide show.
4. Print the presentation as a handout with all six slides displayed horizontally on one page.
5. Save and then close **1-CysticFibrosis.pptx**.

Figure WB-1.5 Challenge 1

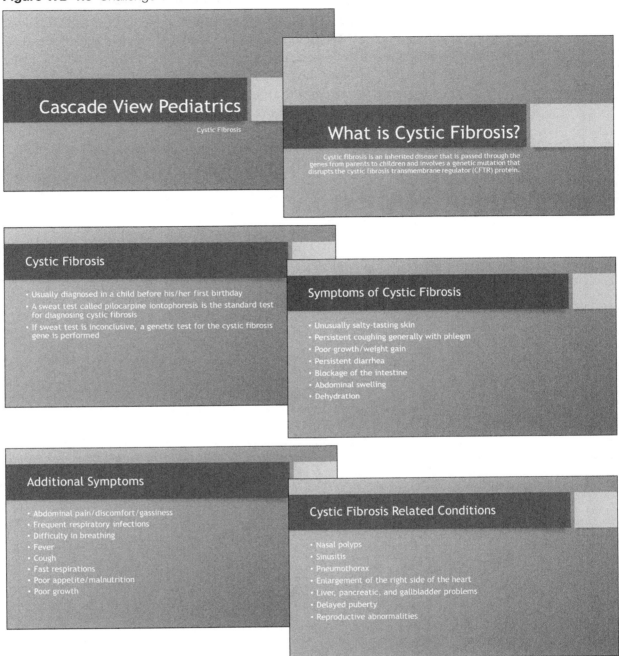

Challenge 2   Editing a Presentation on Clinic Services

1. Open **NSMCServices.pptx** and then save it with the name **1-NSMCServices**.
2. Apply the Parallax design theme, change the slide layout for the second slide (allow the subtitle text to automatically wrap as you decrease the size of the placeholder), and then size and move the placeholders as shown in Figure WB-1.6.
   Hint: Increase the size of the subtitle placeholder in Slide 8 to automatically increase the size of the text in the placeholder.
3. Run the slide show.
4. Print the presentation as a handout with four slides displayed horizontally per page.
5. Save and then close **1-NSMCServices.pptx**.

Figure WB-1.6 Challenge 2

Study Tools

Study tools include In Brief steps and medical resources. Use the study tools to help you further develop and review skills learned in this section.

Knowledge Check

Complete the Knowledge Check to assess your comprehension and recall of application features, technology, and functions.

Recheck

Check your understanding by taking this quiz.

Skills Review

Data File

Review 1   Decreasing and Increasing Indents; Copying and Pasting Text

1. Open **CRGHComEd.pptx** and then save it with the name **2-CRGHComEd**.
2. Make Slide 4 (*Childbirth Preparation Refresher*) the active slide.
3. Increase the indent of the bulleted text *Breathing and relaxation* to the next list level.
4. Increase the indent of the bulleted text *Coach's role* to the next list level.
5. Make Slide 6 active and then decrease the indent of the bulleted text *Designed for boys and girls 11 to 13* to the previous list level.
6. Make Slide 3 (*Childbirth Preparation*) the active slide.
7. Select the text *Cost:* (including the space after the colon) and then click the Copy button.
8. Make Slide 4 (*Childbirth Preparation Refresher*) the active slide.
9. Position the insertion point immediately left of the dollar sign in the last bulleted item and then click the Paste button.
10. Make Slide 5 (*Bringing up Baby*) the active slide, position the insertion point immediately left of the dollar sign, and then click the Paste button.
11. Make Slide 6 (*Babysitting*) the active slide, position the insertion point immediately left of the dollar sign, and then click the Paste button.
12. Make Slide 7 (*Support Groups*) the active slide, position the insertion point immediately left of the *F* in *Free*, and then click the Paste button.
13. Save **2-CRGHComEd.pptx**.

1. With **2-CRGHComEd.pptx** open, make Slide 1 the active slide and then click the Design tab.
2. Click the More Variants button in the Variants group, point to *Colors*, and then click *Blue Warm* at the side menu.
3. Click the More Variants button in the Variants group, point to *Fonts*, and then click *Calibri Light-Constantia* at the side menu.
4. Click the More Variants button in the Variants group, point to *Background Styles*, and then click the option in the first column, first row of the side menu.
5. With Slide 1 active, select the text *Columbia River General Hospital*, change the font to 72-point Candara, change the font color to Blue, Accent 2, Darker 50%, and then apply bold formatting.
6. Make Slide 2 active, select the text *Community Education*, change the font to Candara, change the font color to Blue, Accent 2, Darker 50%, and then apply bold formatting.
7. Select the text *Class Offerings* and then change the font size to 32 points.
8. Make Slide 3 active, select the heading *Childbirth Preparation*, change the font to Candara, change the font color to Teal, Accent 5, Darker 25%, and then apply bold formatting.
9. Using Format Painter, apply the same formatting to the titles in Slides 4, 5, 6, 7, 9, and 10. (Skip Slide 8.)
10. Make Slide 2 active, click any character in the title *Community Education*, and then click the Format Painter button. Make Slide 8 active and then select *Professional Education*.
11. Select the subtitle text in Slide 8 and then change the font size to 32 points.
12. Make Slide 1 the active slide.
13. Click anywhere in the title and then click the Center button.
14. Make Slide 2 active and then center the title and subtitle.
15. Make Slide 8 active and then center the title and subtitle.
16. Make Slide 3 active, select the bulleted text, and then change the line spacing to 1.5.
17. Make Slide 4 active, select the bulleted text, and then change the line spacing to 1.5.
18. Make Slide 9 active, select the bulleted text, and then change the spacing after paragraphs to 12 points.
19. Make Slide 10 active, select the bulleted text, and then change the spacing before paragraphs to 18 points.
20. Print Slide 1.
21. Save **2-CRGHComEd.pptx**.

Review 3 Inserting and Formatting Images

1. With **2-CRGHComEd.pptx** open, delete Slide 1.
2. At the beginning of the presentation, insert a new slide with the Blank layout. *Hint: To insert a new slide at the beginning of the presentation, click immediately above the Slide 1 thumbnail in the slide thumbnails pane and then click the New Slide button arrow.*
3. Use the Pictures button in the Images group on the Insert tab to insert **CRGHLogo.jpg** and then size and move the image so it displays as shown in Figure WB-2.1.
4. Make Slide 3 active, insert **pregnancy.jpg**, and then size and move the image so it displays as shown in Figure WB-2.2. *Hint: Apply the Center Shadow Rectangle picture style.*
5. Make Slide 6 active, insert **toddler.png**, and then size and move the image so it displays as shown in Figure WB-2.3. Change the color of the image to the teal color in the sixth column, third row in the *Recolor* section of the Color button drop-down gallery.
6. Make Slide 9 active and then insert **nurse.jpg**. You determine the formatting, color, size, and positioning of the image.
7. Save **2-CRGHComEd.pptx**.

Figure WB-2.1 Review 3, Slide 1

Figure WB-2.2 Review 3, Slide 3

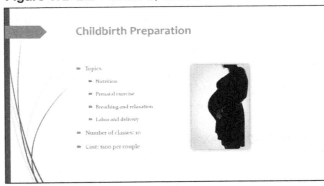

Figure WB-2.3 Review 3, Slide 6

 **Review 4**   Creating and Formatting SmartArt Graphics

1. With **2-CRGHComEd.pptx** open, make Slide 10 active and then insert a new slide with the Blank layout.

2. Insert the SmartArt graphic shown in Figure WB-2.4 with the following specifications:
   - Click the *Hierarchy* option in the left panel at the Choose a SmartArt Graphic dialog box and then double-click the *Hierarchy* option in the middle panel.
   - To create the boxes in the order shown in the figure, click the outside border of the white inside box of the third box in the third row and then press the Delete key. Press the Delete key a second time, and your boxes should display in the same order as the boxes in Figure WB-2.4.
   - With the SmartArt Tools Design tab selected, change the colors to the third option in the *Colorful* section and then apply the Polished SmartArt style.
   - Type the text in the boxes as shown in Figure WB-2.4.

3. With Slide 11 active, insert a new slide with the Title Only layout. Click in the *Click to add title* placeholder and then type Health Philosophy. Select *Health Philosophy*, change the font to Candara, change the font color to Teal, Accent 5, Darker 25%, and then apply bold formatting.

4. Insert the SmartArt graphic shown in Figure WB-2.5 with the following specifications:
   - Click the *Relationship* option in the left panel at the Choose a SmartArt Graphic dialog box and then double-click the *Basic Venn* option in the middle panel.
   - With the SmartArt Tools Design tab selected, change the colors to the fourth option in the *Colorful* section and then apply the Polished SmartArt style.
   - Type the text in the graphic as shown in Figure WB-2.5.
   - Decrease the size and then position the graphic so it displays as shown in Figure WB-2.5.

5. Save **2-CRGHComEd.pptx**.

Figure WB-2.4 Review 4, Slide 11

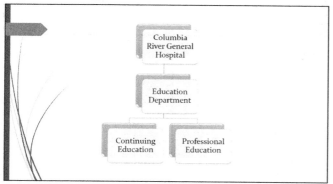

Figure WB-2.5 Review 4, Slide 12

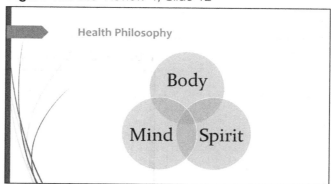

Review 5 Creating and Formatting WordArt; Applying Animation Schemes

1. With **2-CRGHComEd.pptx** open, make the last slide in the presentation active, and then insert a new slide with the Blank layout.
2. Insert the WordArt shown in Figure WB-2.6 with the following specifications:
   - Click the blue WordArt option in the third column, first row of the drop-down list.
   - Type the text shown in Figure WB-2.6.
   - Apply the Blue, Accent 3, Darker 50% text outline color. *Hint: Use the Text Outline button in the WordArt Styles group on the Drawing Tools Format tab.*
   - Click the Text Effects button on the Drawing Tools Format tab, point to *Transform*, and then click the option in the first column, seventh row in the *Warp* section.
   - Increase the shape height to 4 inches and the shape width to 8.5 inches.
   - Position the WordArt as shown in Figure WB-2.6.
3. Make Slide 11 active and then animate the hierarchy graphic using options on the Animations tab. (You determine the type of animation.)
4. Make Slide 9 active and then animate the bulleted items using options on the Animations tab. (You determine the type of animation.)
5. Make Slide 1 active and then run the slide show.
6. Delete Slide 5.
7. Print the presentation as a handout with six slides displayed horizontally per page.
8. Save and then close **2-CRGHComEd.pptx**.

Figure WB-2.6 Review 5, Slide 13

Skills Assessment

Assessment 1   Formatting a Presentation for Columbia River General Hospital

Data File

1. Open **CRGHCCPlan.pptx** and then save it with the name **2-CRGHCCPlan**.
2. Apply the Parallax theme and then change the theme colors to Blue and the theme fonts to Garamond-TrebuchetMS. Apply the background style in the first column, first row of the *Background Styles* side menu.
3. Make Slide 1 active and then center the title *"Community Commitment" Reorganization Plan*.
4. With Slide 1 active, insert **CRGHLogo.jpg**. *Hint: Do this with the Pictures button on the Insert tab.* Change the shape width to 5 inches and then center the logo below the slide title.
5. Make Slide 4 active and then demote (increase the indent of) the text *Medicare cost-cutting among doctors and hospitals* to the next list level.
6. Make Slide 5 active and then promote (decrease the indent of) the text *Reconfigure lobby and registration areas* to the previous list level.
7. Make Slide 3 active, select the bulleted text, and then change the line spacing to 1.5.
8. Make Slide 4 active, select the bulleted text, and then change the line spacing before paragraphs to 12 points.
9. Make Slide 7 active, select the bulleted text, and then change the line spacing to 1.5.
10. Insert a new slide after Slide 1 (the new slide will be Slide 2) with the Blank slide layout. Using the Text Box button on the Insert tab, draw a text box in the slide and then type the text shown in Figure WB-2.7. Change the font size to 28 points, justify the paragraph alignment of text, and right-align the name and title as shown in the figure.
11. Insert a new slide at the end of the presentation and then insert the Basic Target SmartArt graphic (located in the *Relationship* category) as shown in Figure WB-2.8. Add a shape to the graphic, change the colors to the third option in the *Accent 1* section, and then apply the Cartoon SmartArt style. Type the text as shown in Figure WB-2.8 and then size and position the graphic as shown in the figure.
12. Insert a new blank slide at the end of the presentation and then insert WordArt that contains the text *Plan Completion* on one line and *April 2020* on the next line. You determine the style, shape, size, and position of the WordArt.
13. Print the presentation as handouts with six slides displayed horizontally per page.
14. Run the slide show.
15. Save and then close **2-CRGHCCPlan.pptx**.

Figure WB-2.7 Assessment 1, Slide 2

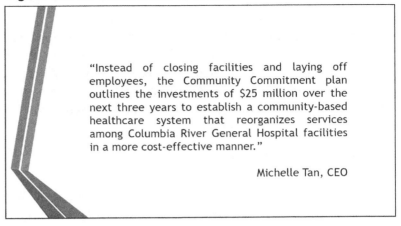

Figure WB-2.8 Assessment 1, Slide 9

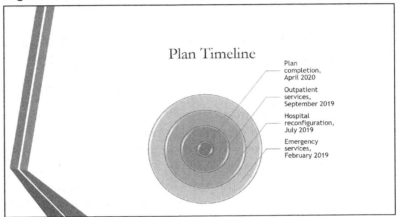

Columbia River
General Hospital

Assessment 2 Formatting a Presentation on Sickle Cell Anemia

Data File

1. Open **SickleCell.pptx** and then save it with the name **2-SickleCell**.
2. Apply any formatting you feel is necessary to improve the appearance of each slide. Insert at least one online image in the presentation or use the images **sick.jpg** and/or **glass.png** from the PowerPointMedS2 folder.
3. Insert a new blank slide at the end of the presentation and then insert WordArt text that reads *Thank you!* You determine the formatting, size, and positioning of the WordArt.
4. Apply animations of your choosing to the bulleted text in at least two of the slides in the presentation.
5. Run the slide show.
6. Print the presentation as handouts with six slides displayed horizontally per page.
7. Save and then close **2-SickleCell.pptx**.

Assessment 3 — Drawing a Shape and Changing the Shape

1. Open **2-SickleCell.pptx**.
2. Make Slide 9 active and then insert a new blank slide. Draw a shape of your choosing in the slide and then insert the following information in the shape. You determine the formatting, size, and positioning of the text and shape. *Hint: Use the Symbol button on the Insert tab to insert the á symbol and make sure the Font option is set to* (normal text) *in the Symbol dialog box.*

   > Dr. Maria Cárdenas
   > North Shore Medical Clinic
   > 7450 Meridian Street, Suite 150
   > Portland, OR 97202
   > (503) 555-2330

3. Save **2-SickleCell.pptx** and then print only Slide 10.
4. Use the Help feature to learn how to change a shape into another shape.
5. After learning how to change a shape, change the shape you created in Slide 10 to another shape of your choosing.
6. Save **2-SickleCell.pptx** and then print only Slide 10.
7. Run the slide show and then close **2-SickleCell.pptx**.

Assessment 4 — Using an Office.com Design Theme Template

1. Office.com provides a number of design theme templates you can apply to a PowerPoint presentation. You decide to search for a design theme template related to healthcare. To do this, click the File tab and then click the *New* option. At the New backstage area, type medical in the search text box and then press the Enter key. Double-click the *Medical design presentation (widescreen)* template. *Note: If this template is not available, open medical.potx from the PowerPointMedS2 folder.*
2. Select and then delete all the slides in the slide thumbnails pane. (Only one gray, blank slide should display in the slide pane.)
3. Import a presentation into the blank design theme template. Begin by clicking the Home tab, clicking the New Slide button arrow, and then clicking *Reuse slides* at the drop-down list.
4. At the Reuse Slides task pane, click the Browse button and then click *Browse File* at the drop-down list.
5. At the Browse dialog box, navigate to the PowerPointMedS2 folder on your storage medium and then double-click **2-CRGHCCPlan.pptx**.
6. Click each slide thumbnail in the Reuse Slides task pane, beginning with Slide 1, and then close the task pane.
7. Make Slide 1 active and then delete the hospital logo.
8. Check each slide and make any adjustments needed to make the presentation more attractive and easy to read.
9. Run the slide show.
10. Save the presentation with the name **2-CRGHMedical.pptx**.
11. Print the presentation as handouts with six slides displayed horizontally per page and then close the presentation.

 **Assessment 5** Locating Information on Support Groups

1. Using the Internet, search for support groups in your town or county for each of the following diseases and conditions: Alzheimer's, breast cancer, depression, diabetes, eating disorders, fibromyalgia, heart disease, and multiple sclerosis.
2. When you have gathered the information, prepare a presentation. Include your name and the name of the presentation on the first slide, and then prepare a specific slide for each support group that contains the name of the group and any other information you gathered, such as meeting dates and times, locations, telephone numbers, contacts, and so on.
3. On the final slide in the presentation, include the words *Thank you* as WordArt.
4. Apply animations of your choosing to all slides in the presentation.
5. Save the presentation with the name **2-Support**.
6. Run the slide show.
7. Print the slides as handouts with six slides displayed horizontally per page.
8. Save and then close **2-Support.pptx**.

 **Assessment 6** Locating Information on Medical Front-Office Jobs

1. Using your local newspapers, employment agencies, and/or the Internet, locate information on medical front-office jobs such as medical office assistant positions.
2. Prepare a presentation with the information you find, and include at least the following information: job titles, average wages, education requirements, required experience, and required knowledge of or training in specific software (if any).
3. Apply any formatting or enhancements you feel will improve the appearance of the presentation.
4. Save the presentation with the name **2-Job**.
5. Run the slide show.
6. Print the slides as handouts with six slides displayed horizontally per page.
7. Save and then close **2-Job.pptx**.

Marquee Challenge

Challenge 1   Preparing a Presentation on Cholesterol

1. Prepare the presentation shown in Figure WB-2.9 with the following specifications:
   - Apply the Gallery theme and the second option in the Variants group.
   - Change the theme colors to Violet.
   - Size and position the placeholders as shown in Figure WB-2.9.
   - Insert, size, and format the images **treadmill.png** and **medicine.png** as shown in the figure.
   - Decrease the size of the title placeholder in Slide 1 so the title displays as shown in the figure.
   - Apply bold formatting to the titles in Slides 3 through 7.
   - Insert **NSMCLogo.jpg** in Slide 1 and then size and position the logo as shown in the figure. Apply a transparent background color to the logo. To do this, click the Color button in the Adjust group on the Picture Tools Format tab and then click *Set Transparent Color* at the drop-down gallery. Position the mouse pointer on any white color in the logo background and then click the left mouse button.
   - Apply the Blank layout to Slide 2 and then create a text box for the title and another text box for the description. Make sure the font of the title is Century Gothic, change the font size to 36 points, change the font color to Lavender, Accent 2, Darker 25%, and then apply bold formatting. Increase the size of the font in the description to 20 points and change the alignment to center.
   - Add 18 points of spacing before the bulleted text in Slides 3 through 7.
   - Apply the Blank layout to Slide 8 and then create a text box for the title. Apply the title formatting from Slide 2 to the title in Slide 8. Use WordArt to insert the telephone number (apply the transform text effect in the third column, fourth row of the *Warp* section to the WordArt).
2. Save the completed presentation with the name **2-NSMCCholesterol**.
3. Print the presentation as handouts with four slides displayed horizontally per page.
4. Close **2-NSMCCholesterol.pptx**.

Figure WB-2.9 Challenge 1

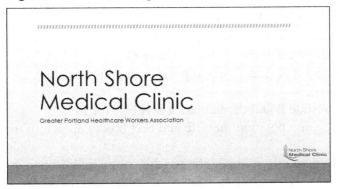

North Shore
Medical Clinic

Greater Portland Healthcare Workers Association

North Shore
Medical Clinic

Type of Cholesterol

- Low-density lipoproteins (LDL) – Deliver cholesterol to the body. About 70% of cholesterol is transported as LDL. Too much LDL is harmful to the body.

- High-density lipoproteins (HDL) – Removes cholesterol from the bloodstream. About 20% of cholesterol is transported as HDL.

HDL Cholesterol Levels

- Less than 40 means higher risk for heart disease
- 60 or higher reduces the risk of heart disease

Cholesterol Medications

- Statins (also called HMG-CoA reductase inhibitors)
- Resins (also called bile acid sequestrants)
- Fibrates (also called fibric acid derivatives)
- Niacin (also called nicotinic acid)
- Ezetimibe

What is Cholesterol?

Cholesterol is a type of fat (lipid) that is made by the body. Cholesterol is essential for good health and is found in every cell in the body. Too much cholesterol in the blood can raise the risk of heart attack or stroke.

LDL Cholesterol Levels

- Less than 130 is best
- Between 130 to 159 is borderline
- 160 or more means higher risk for heart disease

Improve Cholesterol Levels

- Do not smoke.
- Eat a healthy, low-fat diet that includes lots of fruits and vegetables.
- Exercise regularly.
- Limit alcohol consumption.
- Take medication.

Cholesterol Screening Call
for an Appointment

503-555-2330

Columbia River
General Hospital **Challenge 2** Preparing a Hospital Center Presentation

1. Prepare the presentation shown in Figure WB-2.10 with the following specifications:
   - Apply the Facet theme and change the theme colors to Blue Green.
   - Insert **CRGHLogo.jpg** in Slide 1 and then size and position the logo as shown in the figure.
   - Apply the Title Only layout to Slide 2 and then create a text box for the description of the disorder. Size and position the title and text box as shown in the figure.
   - Insert a Basic Venn SmartArt graphic in Slide 3, change the colors to the first option in the *Colorful* section, apply the Polished SmartArt style, and then size and position the SmartArt as shown in the figure.
   - In Slide 5, insert the image **doctorbag.png** from the PowerPointMedS2 folder. Change the color of the picture to Blue, Accent color 6, Light and then size and position the image as shown in the figure.
   - Insert an Organization Chart SmartArt graphic in Slide 6, change the colors to the first option in the *Colorful* section, apply the Polished SmartArt style, and then size and position the SmartArt as shown in the figure.
2. Save the completed presentation with the name **2-EatingDisorder**.
3. Print the presentation as handouts with six slides displayed horizontally on one page.
4. Close **2-EatingDisorder.pptx**.

Figure WB-2.10 Challenge 2

> **Study Tools**

Study tools include In Brief steps and medical resources. Use the study tools to help you further develop and review skills learned in this section.

> **Recheck**

Check your understanding by taking this quiz.

Skills Review

Review 1   Exporting a PowerPoint Presentation to Word

Columbia River
General Hospital

Data Files

1. Open PowerPoint.
2. Open **CRGHCCRPlan.pptx** and then save it with the name **2-CRGHCCRPlan**.
3. Export the PowerPoint data to Word as slides with blank lines next to them. Click the *Blank lines next to slides* option and the *Paste link* option at the Send to Microsoft Word dialog box.
4. Save the Word document and name it **2-CRGHComPlan**.
5. Print and then close **2-CRGHComPlan.docx**.
6. Click the PowerPoint button on the taskbar.
7. Make Slide 5 active and then delete the second bulleted item.
8. Make Slide 6 active and then insert a new bullet after (but at the same level as) the *Expand fitness center* bulleted item that reads *Implement community health education plan*.
9. Save and then print the presentation as handouts with four slides displayed horizontally per page.
10. Make Word active, open **2-CRGHComPlan.docx**, and then click the Yes button at the message asking if you want to update the link.
11. Save, print, and then close the document.
12. Make PowerPoint active and then close **2-CRGHCCRPlan.pptx**.

Review 2   Linking and Editing an Excel Chart in a PowerPoint Slide

Columbia River
General Hospital

Data Files

1. Make sure PowerPoint is open and then open Excel.
2. Make PowerPoint active and then open **CRGHEdDept.pptx**.
3. Save the presentation with the name **2-CRGHEdDept**.
4. Make Slide 6 active.
5. Make Excel active and then open **CRGHChart01.xlsx**. Save the workbook with the name **2-CRGHChart01**.
6. Click the chart once to select it (make sure you select the entire chart and not just a chart element) and then copy and link the chart to Slide 6 in **2-CRGHEdDept.pptx**. (Be sure to use the Paste Special dialog box to link the chart.)

7. Increase the size of the chart to better fill the slide and then center the chart on the slide.
8. Click outside the chart to deselect it.
9. Save the presentation with the same name (**2-CRGHEdDept.pptx**).
10. Print only Slide 6 of the presentation and then close **2-CRGHEdDept.pptx**.
11. Click the button on the taskbar representing the Excel workbook **2-CRGHChart01.xlsx**.
12. Click outside the chart to deselect it.
13. Insert another department in the worksheet (and chart) by making cell A6 active, clicking the Insert button arrow in the Cells group on the Home tab, and then clicking *Insert Sheet Rows* at the drop-down list. (This creates a new row 6.) Type the following text in the specified cells:

    A6: CPR   C7: 105
    B6: 85   D7: 134

14. Click in cell A3.
15. Save, print, and close **2-CRGHChart01.xlsx** and then close Excel.
16. Click the PowerPoint button on the taskbar and then open **2-CRGHEdDept.pptx**. At the message telling you that the presentation contains links, click the Update Links button. Display Slide 6 and then notice the change to the chart.
17. Save **2-CRGHEdDept.pptx** and then print only Slide 6.
18. Close **2-CRGHEdDept.pptx**.

Review 3   Embedding and Editing a Word Table in a PowerPoint Slide

Data Files

1. With Word and PowerPoint open, make PowerPoint active and then open **2-CRGHEdDept.pptx**. At the message telling you that the presentation contains links, click the Update Links button.
2. Make Slide 7 active.
3. Make Word active and then open **CRGHContacts.docx**.
4. Select the table and then copy and embed it in Slide 7 in **2-CRGHEdDept.pptx**. (Make sure you use the Paste Special dialog box.)
5. With the table selected in the slide, use the sizing handles to increase the size and change the position of the table so it better fills the slide.
6. Click outside the table to deselect it and then save **2-CRGHEdDept.pptx**.
7. Double-click the table and then click in the text *Christina Fuentes*.
8. Insert a row below by clicking the Table Tools Layout tab and then clicking the Insert Below button.
9. In the new row, type John Shapiro in the *Contact* column, type Sterling Health Services in the *Agency* column, and then type (503) 555-4220 in the *Telephone* column.
10. Click outside the table to deselect it.
11. Print Slide 7 of the presentation.
12. Apply a transition and transition sound of your choosing to all slides in the presentation.
13. Run the slide show.
14. Save and then close **2-CRGHEdDept.pptx** and then close PowerPoint.
15. Close the Word document **CRGHContacts.docx** and then close Word.

BRIEF CONTENTS

CHAPTER 1
A Human Perspective 1

PART I

Human Organization 13

CHAPTER 2
Chemistry of Life 13

CHAPTER 3
Cell Structure and Function 35

CHAPTER 4
Organization and Regulation of Body Systems 55

PART II

Maintenance of the Human Body 77

CHAPTER 5
Cardiovascular System: Heart and Blood Vessels 77

CHAPTER 6
Cardiovascular System: Blood 97

CHAPTER 7
Digestive System and Nutrition 115

CHAPTER 8
Respiratory System 141

CHAPTER 9
Urinary System and Excretion 159

PART III

Movement and Support in Humans 177

CHAPTER 10
Skeletal System 177

CHAPTER 11
Muscular System 197

PART IV

Integration and Coordination in Humans 217

CHAPTER 12
Nervous System 217

CHAPTER 13
Senses 243

CHAPTER 14
Endocrine System 265

PART V

Reproduction in Humans 289

CHAPTER 15
Reproductive System 289

CHAPTER 16
Development and Aging 309

PART VI

Human Genetics 333

CHAPTER 17
Cell Division and the Human Life Cycle 333

CHAPTER 18
Patterns of Inheritance 351

CHAPTER 19
DNA Biology and Technology 367

CHAPTER 20
Genetic Counseling 389

PART VII

Human Disease 413

CHAPTER 21
Defenses Against Disease 413

CHAPTER 22
Parasites and Pathogens 431

CHAPTER 23
Sexually Transmitted Diseases 453

CHAPTER 24
Cancer 471

PART VIII

Human Evolution and Ecology 487

CHAPTER 25
Human Evolution 487

CHAPTER 26
Global Ecology 505

CHAPTER 27
Human Population, Planetary Resources, and Conservation 521

CONTENTS

Readings   *vii*
Preface   *viii*
Guided Tour   *xv*

C H A P T E R   1

A Human Perspective   1

1.1   Biologically Speaking 2
1.2   The Process of Science 6
1.3   Science and Social Responsibility 9

P A R T   I

Human Organization   13

C H A P T E R   2

Chemistry of Life   13

2.1   Basic Chemistry 14
2.2   Water and Living Things 18
2.3   Molecules of Life 22
2.4   Carbohydrates 22
2.5   Lipids 24
2.6   Proteins 26
2.7   Nucleic Acids 29

C H A P T E R   3

Cell Structure and Function   35

3.1   What Is a Cell? 36
3.2   Cellular Organization 38
3.3   Cellular Metabolism 48

C H A P T E R   4

Organization and Regulation of Body Systems   55

4.1   Types of Tissues 56
4.2   Integumentary System 64
4.3   Organ Systems 66
4.4   Homeostasis 70

P A R T   II

Maintenance of the Human Body   77

C H A P T E R   5

Cardiovascular System: Heart and Blood Vessels   77

5.1   Overview of the Cardiovascular System 78
5.2   The Blood Vessels 79
5.3   The Heart 80
5.4   Features of the Cardiovascular System 84
5.5   The Cardiovascular Pathways 86
5.6   Cardiovascular Disorders 88
5.7   The Lymphatic System Helps the Cardiovascular System 92

C H A P T E R   6

Cardiovascular System: Blood   97

6.1   Blood: An Overview 99
6.2   Composition of Blood 99
6.3   Blood Clotting 104
6.4   Blood Typing 106
6.5   Capillary Exchange 108
6.6   Homeostasis 110

C H A P T E R   7

Digestive System and Nutrition   115

7.1   The Digestive Tract 116
7.2   Three Accessory Organs 124
7.3   Digestive Enzymes 126
7.4   Nutrition 128

C H A P T E R   8

Respiratory System   141

8.1   The Respiratory System 142
8.2   Mechanism of Breathing 146
8.3   Gas Exchanges in the Body 150
8.4   Respiration and Health 152

C H A P T E R   9

Urinary System and Excretion   159

9.1   Urinary System 160
9.2   Kidney Structure 163
9.3   Urine Formation 167
9.4   Regulatory Functions of the Kidneys 168
9.5   Problems with Kidney Function 171
9.6   Homeostasis 172

PART **III**

Movement and Support in Humans 177

CHAPTER 10

Skeletal System 177

10.1 Tissues of the Skeletal System 178

10.2 Bone Growth, Remodeling, and Repair 180

10.3 Bones of the Skeleton 185

10.4 Articulations 192

CHAPTER 11

Muscular System 197

11.1 Types and Functions of Muscles 198

11.2 Mechanism of Skeletal Muscle Fiber Contraction 202

11.3 Whole Muscle Contraction 206

11.4 Energy for Muscle Contraction 208

11.5 Muscular Disorders 210

11.6 Homeostasis 212

PART **IV**

Integration and Coordination in Humans 217

CHAPTER 12

Nervous System 217

12.1 Nervous Tissue 218

12.2 The Central Nervous System 224

12.3 The Limbic System and Higher Mental Functions 230

12.4 The Peripheral Nervous System 232

12.5 Drug Abuse 237

CHAPTER 13

Senses 243

13.1 Sensory Receptors and Sensations 244

13.2 Proprioceptors and Cutaneous Receptors 246

13.3 Senses of Taste and Smell 248

13.4 Sense of Vision 250

13.5 Sense of Hearing 256

13.6 Sense of Equilibrium 261

CHAPTER 14

Endocrine System 265

14.1 Endocrine Glands 266

14.2 Hypothalamus and Pituitary Gland 270

14.3 Thyroid and Parathyroid Glands 273

14.4 Adrenal Glands 275

14.5 Pancreas 278

14.6 Other Endocrine Glands 280

14.7 Homeostasis 284

PART **V**

Reproduction in Humans 289

CHAPTER 15

Reproductive System 289

15.1 Male Reproductive System 290

15.2 Female Reproductive System 294

15.3 Female Hormone Levels 297

15.4 Control of Reproduction 301

CHAPTER 16

Development and Aging 309

16.1 Fertilization 310

16.2 Development Before Birth 311

16.3 Pregnancy and Birth 324

16.4 Development After Birth 326

PART **VI**

Human Genetics 333

CHAPTER 17

Cell Division and the Human Life Cycle 333

17.1 Cell Increase and Decrease 334

17.2 Mitosis 337

17.3 Meiosis 340

17.4 Comparison of Meiosis with Mitosis 344

17.5 The Human Life Cycle 346

CHAPTER 18

Patterns of Inheritance 351

18.1 Genotype and Phenotype 352

18.2 One- and Two-Trait Inheritance 353

18.3 Beyond Simple Inheritance Patterns 359

18.4 Sex-Linked Inheritance 362

CHAPTER 19

DNA Biology and Technology 367

19.1 DNA and RNA Structure and Function 368

19.2 Gene Expression 371

19.3 Genomics 378

19.4 DNA Technology 380

CHAPTER 20

Genetic Counseling 389

20.1 Counseling for Chromosomal
     Disorders 390
20.2 Counseling for Genetic Disorders:
     The Present 398
20.3 Counseling for Genetic Disorders:
     The Future 406

PART **VII**

Human Disease 413

CHAPTER 21

Defenses Against
Disease 413

21.1 Organs, Tissues, and Cells of the
     Immune System 414
21.2 Nonspecific and Specific Defenses 417
21.3 Acquired Immunity 424
21.4 Immunity Side Effects 426

CHAPTER 22

Parasites and
Pathogens 431

22.1 Microbes and You 432
22.2 Viruses as Infectious Agents 436
22.3 Bacteria as Infectious Agents 441
22.4 Other Infectious Agents 446

CHAPTER 23

Sexually Transmitted
Diseases 453

23.1 Bacterial Infections 454
23.2 Viral Infections 457
23.3 Other Infections 459
23.4 AIDS (Acquired Immunodeficiency
     Syndrome) 460

CHAPTER 24

Cancer 471

24.1 Cancer Cells 472
24.2 Causes of Cancer 476
24.3 Diagnosis and Treatment 479

PART **VIII**

Human Evolution and
Ecology 487

CHAPTER 25

Human Evolution 487

25.1 Origin of Life 488
25.2 Biological Evolution 489
25.3 Humans Are Primates 493
25.4 Evolution of Australopithecines 496
25.5 Evolution of Humans 497

CHAPTER 26

Global Ecology 505

26.1 The Scope of Ecology 506
26.2 Energy Flow 509
26.3 Global Biogeochemical Cycles 510
26.4 Global Ecosystems 514

CHAPTER 27

Human Population,
Planetary Resources, and
Conservation 521

27.1 Human Population Growth 522
27.2 Human Use of Resources and
     Pollution 524
27.3 Biodiversity 531
27.4 Working Toward a Sustainable
     Society 537

APPENDIX:
Answer Key A–1

Glossary G–1
Credits C–1
Index I–1

READINGS

Bioethical Focus

Fertilization with 20-Year-Old Sperm 10
Genetically Modified Foods 31
Stem Cell Research 51
Paying for an Unhealthy Lifestyle 93
Bans on Smoking 156
Performance-Enhancing Drugs 211
Hormone Replacement Therapy 283

Designer Children 305
Maternal Health Habits 329
Genetic Testing for Cancer Genes 348
Choosing Gender 363
DNA Fingerprinting and the Criminal
    Justice System 386
Genetic Profiling 409

Growth Promoters 449
Providing Access to HIV/AIDS
    Medications 467
Tobacco and Alcohol Use 484
The Theory of Evolution 501
Oil Drilling in the Arctic 517
Cyanide Fishing and Coral Reefs 536

Ecology Focus

Ecosystems 5
The Harm Done by Acid Rain 21
Fish: The Good News and the
    Bad News 105

Photochemical Smog Can Kill 147
Endocrine-Disrupting
    Contaminants 303

Pesticide: An Asset and a
    Liability 421

Health Focus

A Balanced Diet 28
Nerve Regeneration 61
Do You Have Diabetes? 69
Prevention of Cardiovascular Disease 90
Artificial Blood 102
Very Low Carbohydrate Diets 131
The Most Often Asked Questions About
    Tobacco and Health 155
Urinary Tract Infections Require
    Attention 162
You Can Avoid Osteoporosis 184

Exercise, Exercise, Exercise 207
Degenerative Brain Disorders 236
Hearing Loss 258
Melatonin 281
Reproductive and Therapeutic
    Cloning 314
Preventing Birth Defects 322
Chromosome Organization 336
Are Genetically Engineered Foods
    Safe? 385

Living with Klinefelter Syndrome 395
New Cures on the Horizon 407
Preventing Asthma 427
BioDefense 433
Emerging Viral Pathogens 440
Antibiotics 445
Preventing Transmission of STDs 463
Prevention of Cancer 478
Shower Check for Cancer 480

Visual Focus

Types of Simple Epithelia 63
External and Internal Respiration 151
Processes in Urine Formation 166
Anatomy of a Muscle Fiber 203

Autonomic System Structure and
    Function 234
Mechanoreceptors for Equilibrium 260
Hypothalamus and the Pituitary 271

Ovarian Cycle 296
Polypeptide Structure 375
Inflammatory Reaction 416

PREFACE

When I was teaching general biology, it became apparent to me that students were very interested in how their bodies worked, how to keep them healthy, and how they can occasionally malfunction. Students also found environmental concepts intriguing. I decided it would be possible to write a text and develop a course for nonmajors that built on these interests while teaching biological concepts and how scientists think and carry out research.

The application of biological principles to practical human concerns is now widely accepted as a beneficial approach to the study of biology. Students should leave college with a firm grasp of how their bodies normally function and how the human population can become more fully integrated into the biosphere. We are frequently called upon to make health and environmental decisions. Wise decisions require adequate knowledge and can help ensure our continued survival as individuals and as a species.

In this edition, as in previous editions, *Human Biology* introduces students to the anatomy and physiology of the human body. All systems of the body are represented, and each system has its own chapter. The text also helps students understand that humans are a part of the biosphere, and that human activities can have environmental consequences.

Each chapter in *Human Biology* presents concepts clearly, simply, and distinctly so that students will feel capable of achieving an adult level of understanding. Detailed, high-level scientific data and terminology are not included because I believe true knowledge consists of having a working understanding of concepts rather than technical facility.

This Edition

This ninth edition of *Human Biology* continues to stress relevancy and student interest. Some of the highlights of the ninth edition include:

- **System chapters in Part II have been reorganized.**
  Part II "Maintenance of the Human Body" has been reorganized to better emphasize the importance of the cardiovascular system to homeostasis and the importance of blood to the cardiovascular system. The first chapter in Part II is now entitled "Cardiovascular System: Heart and Blood Vessels." This reorganization is consistent with the recognition that blood and tissue fluid make up the internal environment of humans.

- **New chapter added to Part VI "Human Genetics."**
  Chapter 20 "Genetic Counseling" is new and serves as the pinnacle of the student's study of genetics, because it covers all aspects of chromosomal and genetic diseases and ends with a discussion of how genomics may lead to better therapy for such disorders.

- **Existing chapters in Part VI have been reorganized and rewritten.**
  Chapter 17 "Cell Division and the Human Life Cycle" offers a much improved discussion of mitosis and meiosis (with new illustrations) and relates these two types of cell division to the human life cycle. Chapter 18 "Patterns of Inheritance" presents the basic principles of particulate inheritance in a way that leads to student understanding of both one-trait and two-trait autosomal crosses. The chapter also includes sex-linked inheritance. Chapter 19 "DNA Biology and Technology" is a more in-depth, but student-friendly, examination of DNA/RNA structure and function. This material serves as a necessary background to an appreciation of modern-day utilization of DNA technology. The discussion of genomics and related fields helps students have a current understanding of genetics in the 21st century.

- **Part VIII "Human Evolution and Ecology" has been reorganized into three chapters.**
  Chapter 27 "Human Population, Planetary Resources, and Conservation" combines Chapters 26 and 27 from the eighth edition and shows the relationship between consumption of resources and pollution, and their effects on biodiversity.

- **Homeostasis is emphasized through new illustrations.**
  The **Human Systems Work Together** illustrations have been newly designed and revised to more efficiently highlight how body systems work together to achieve homeostasis. Each illustration outlines the functions of the various systems with brief, concise statements, and the accompanying human figure provides a visual of each system. On the facing page of the illustration, a full page of text discusses homeostasis in the context of that chapter, and features a possible event in the student's everyday life.

The **Human Systems Work Together** illustrations appear in:
- Chapter 4 "Organization and Regulation of Body Systems," along with the in-depth discussion on homeostasis.
- Chapter 6 "Cardiovascular System: Blood," after the entire cardiovascular system has been covered.
- Chapter 9 "Urinary System and Excretion," after the digestive, respiratory, and urinary systems have been covered.
- Chapter 11 "Muscular System," after the skeletal and muscular systems have been covered.
- Chapter 14 "Endocrine System," after the nervous and endocrine systems have been covered.

- **New set of end-of-chapter questions has been added to each chapter.**
  A set of questions entitled "Thinking Critically About the Concepts" has been added to the end of each chapter. These questions refer students back to the chapter's opening story and encourage students to apply the concepts they've just studied to the real-life story.
- Many **new or revised vignettes, readings, illustrations, and portions of text** have been developed to increase student appeal.

OVERVIEW OF CHANGES TO *Human Biology*, Ninth Edition

Part II Reorganized

Part II "Maintenance of the Human Body" emphasizes the importance of the cardiovascular system to homeostasis and the importance of blood to the cardiovascular system.

New Chapter Added to Part VI "Human Genetics"

Chapter 20 "Genetic Counseling" is new and serves as the pinnacle of the student's study of genetics.

Part VI Reorganized

Chapter 17 offers an improved discussion of mitosis and meiosis (with new illustrations). Chapter 18 clearly presents the basic principles of particulate inheritance. Chapter 19 is an in-depth, student-friendly examination of DNA/RNA structure and function.

Part VIII Reorganized

Chapter 27 "Human Population, Planetary Resources, and Conservation" combines Chapters 26 and 27 from the eighth edition and shows the relationship between consumption of resources and pollution, and their effects on biodiversity.

Greater Emphasis on Homeostasis

The **Human Systems Work Together** illustrations have been newly designed and revised. Each illustration outlines the functions of the systems with concise statements, and a figure provides a visual of each system. On the facing page of the illustration, a full page of text discusses homeostasis in the context of that chapter, and features a possible event in the student's everyday life.

New Set of Questions Added

"Thinking Critically About the Concepts" questions have been added at the end of each chapter. These questions refer students back to the chapter's opening story, encouraging students to apply the concepts they've just studied to the real-life story.

New Vignettes and Boxed Readings

This edition includes many new vignettes and boxed readings to capture students' interest.

ACKNOWLEDGMENTS

To produce *Human Biology* requires the constant and concerted effort of many, and it is a pleasure to thank everyone who made this edition so special. First, I want to thank the dedicated professionals I work with at McGraw-Hill. Michael Lange, Editor-in-Chief, and Kent Peterson, Editorial Director, have long given me support and encouragement. My editor Tom Lyon, marketing manager Tamara Maury, and developmental editor Rose Koos worked tirelessly to help me bring you a text and ancillaries that will serve your needs in every way. They planned well and supplied creativity, advice, and support whenever it was needed. Jayne Klein, my project manager, ushered the book through production, never failing to keep everyone on track.

Laurie Janssen was the designer who chose everything from the different type styles, to the colors of the opening pages, to the cover of the book. Also, Laurie is always willing to lend a hand at designing illustrations that delight and please the viewer. Lori Hancock and Connie Mueller found just the right photographs and micrographs for the many illustrations in the text.

In my office, Beth Butler proved that she was capable of shouldering the load, from preparing illustration grid sheets to paging the book. I would be remiss if I did not also take this opportunity to thank my husband and children for their continued patience and encouragement. Their interest in my work has always touched me greatly.

Reviewers and Contributors

As with previous editions, many instructors contributed creative ideas, corrections, and suggestions for improvement. I am extremely thankful to each one, for they have all worked diligently to remain true to our calling—to provide a product that will be the most useful to our students. With appreciation, I acknowledge the help of the following reviewers of the ninth edition.

Michael Adams
Pasco-Hernando Community College

Joseph F. Antognini
University of California–Davis

Marilynn R. Bartels
Black Hawk College

Carolyn L. Bessette
Trocaire College

Joanna D. Borucinska
University of Hartford

Hessel Bouma III
Calvin College

Jane Bradley
Des Moines Area Community College

Ellen Brisch
Minnesota State University–Moorhead

Mike Bumbulis
Baldwin-Wallace College

Christy A. Carello
The Metropolitan State College of Denver

Robert H. Chesney
William Paterson University

Mary C. Colavito
Santa Monica College

Barbara J. Cole
Phoenix College

Dawn Colomb-Lippa
Quinnipiac University

Victoria P. Connaughton
American University

Richard Connett
Monroe Community College

Mary L. Crooks
Community College of Southern Nevada

Susan L. Devlin
Lewis Clark State College

Charles J. Dick
Pasco-Hernando Community College

Robert S. Dill
Bergen Community College

Alison Brown Dixon
Wingate University

Lynn Dreese
Saint Paul College

John A. Drew
Concord Academy

JodyLee Estrada Duek
Pima Community College

Willo Faye Edberg
Gulf Coast Community College

David K. Ferris
University of South Carolina–Spartanburg

Maria Florez-Duquet
California Polytechnic State University

Heidi L. Forman
SUNY College at Buffalo

David E. Fulford
Edinboro University of Pennsylvania

Marie Gabbard
Boise State University

Catherine Tiene Gleason
Hudson Valley Community College

Kevin Gribbins
Wittenberg University

Dennis C. Haney
Furman University

Craig Hanke
University of Wisconsin–Green Bay

Clare Hays
Metropolitan State College of Denver

John B. Hess
Central Missousi State University

Mark F. Hoover
Penn State Altoona

Ali M. Jafri
Malcolm X College

Laura Jaquish
Northwestern Michigan College

Mark Kaelin
Bellarmine University

Mary Kind Kananen
Penn State Altoona

Mark D. Kirk
University of Missouri–Columbia

Margaret M. Klindworth
Minnesota State University–Moorhead

Johanna Kruckeberg
Kirkwood Community College

E. Ray Latham
San Joaquin Delta College

Monica LeClerc
Jefferson Community College

Aimee T. Lee
University of Southern Mississippi

Craig Longtine
North Hennepin Community College

Deborah J. McCool
Penn State Altoona

Cherie McKeever
MSU College of Technology

Jacqueline S. McLaughlin
Penn State Berks–Lehigh Valley College

William J. Mackay
Edinboro University of Pennsylvania

Richard Maloof
County College of Morris

Bruce Maring
Daytona Beach Community College

Joel Maruniak
University of Missouri

Patricia Matthews
Grand Valley State University

Rey D. Morales
Evergreen Valley Community College

Lance Myler
SUNY College of Technology at Canton

Melanie O'Brien
DeAnza Community College

Robert K. Okazaki
Weber State University

Robin Pals-Rylaarsdam
Trinity Christian College

Jeanie S. Payne
Bergen Community College

Linda S. W. Pezzolesi
Hudson Valley Community College

Joel B. Piperberg
Millersville University of Pennsylvania

Darrell L. Ray
The University of Tennessee at Martin

Jill D. Reid
Virginia Commonwealth University

Katherine N. Schick
San Joaquin Delta Community College

Barkur S. Shastry
Oakland University

Marilyn L. Shaver
ACTC

Stephanie R. Songer
Concord College

Lei Lani Stelle
Rochester Institute of Technology

Judith Stewart
Community College of Southern Nevada

Pamela Tabery
Northampton Community College

Mary L. Talbot
San Jose City College

R. Brent Thomas
University of South Carolina–Spartanburg

Kent R. Thomas
Wichita State University

William L. Trotter
Des Moines Area Community College

Mary Walkinshaw
Pima College

Rod Waltermyer
York College of Pennsylvania

Robert P. West
Lee University

Robert J. Wiggers
Stephen F. Austin State University

Anne Zayaitz
Kutztown University of Pennsylvania

Ted Zerucha
Keene State College

Scott Zimmerman
University of Wisconsin

I am also grateful to the following, who made significant contributions to this edition of *Human Biology*:

JodyLee Estrada Duek
Pima Community College

Patrick Galliart
North Iowa Area Community College

Kimberly G. Lyle-Ippilito
Anderson University

Joel Maruniak
University of Missouri

William D. Rogers
Ball State University

Stephanie R. Songer
Concord College

Mary L. Talbot
San Jose City College

Michael W. Thompson
Middle Tennessee State University

McGraw-Hill offers a variety of tools and technology products to support the ninth edition of *Human Biology*. Instructors can obtain teaching aids by calling the Customer Service Department at (800) 338-3987 or by contacting their local McGraw-Hill sales representative.

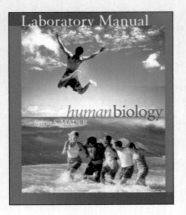

Human Biology Laboratory Manual

The *Human Biology Laboratory Manual*, ninth edition, was written by Dr. Sylvia Mader. With few exceptions, each chapter in the text has an accompanying laboratory exercise in the manual. Every laboratory has been written to help students learn the fundamental concepts of human biology and the specific content of the chapter to which the lab relates, as well as gain a better understanding of the scientific method. ISBN 0-07-285799-4

Digital Content Manager

This collection of multimedia resources provides tools for rich visual support of your lectures. You can utilize artwork from the text in multiple formats to create customized classroom presentations, visually based tests and quizzes, dynamic course website content, or attractive printed support materials. The following assets are grouped by chapter on this cross-platform CD-ROM:

- **Art** Full-color digital files of all illustrations in the book, plus the same art saved in an unlabeled version, can be readily incorporated into lecture presentations, exams, or custom-made classroom materials.

- **TextEdit Art** Every line art figure is placed into a PowerPoint slide that allows the user to revise, move, or delete labels and leader lines as desired for creation of customized presentations and/or for testing purposes.

- **Photos** All photos from the text are available in color, and photos with labels are also available unlabeled. A separate folder contains hundreds of additional photos relative to the study of human biology.

- **Tables** Every table that appears in the text is provided in electronic format.

Animations Full-color presentations of key biological processes have been brought to life via animation. These animations offer flexibility for instructors and were designed to be used in lecture. Many of the animations are also available with Spanish narration and audio.

Active Art Illustrations depicting key processes have been converted to a format that allows the artwork to be edited inside of PowerPoint. Each piece can be broken down to its core elements, grouped or ungrouped, and edited to create customized illustrations.

PowerPoint Lecture Outlines A ready-made presentation that combines lecture notes, art, and animations is written for each chapter. They can be used as they are, or the instructor can customize them to preferred lecture topics and sequences.

PowerPoint Art Slides Art, photographs, and tables from each chapter have been pre-inserted into blank PowerPoint slides to which you can add your own notes.

Instructor's Testing and Resource CD-ROM

This cross-platform CD-ROM provides these resources for the instructor:

Computerized Test Bank utilizing McGraw-Hill's EZ Test, a flexible and easy-to-use electronic testing program. The program allows instructors to create tests from book-specific items. It accommodates a wide range of question types, and instructors may add their own questions. Multiple versions of the test can be created, and any test can be exported for use with course management systems such as WebCT, BlackBoard, or PageOut. The program is available for Windows and Macintosh environments. Word files of the test bank are included for those who prefer to work outside of the test-generator software.

Instructor's Manual provides behavioral objectives, extended lecture outlines, and student activities. In addition, there is an explanation of text changes and reorganization as well as information on new and revised illustrations and tables.

Transparencies

This set of overhead transparencies includes all line art from the textbook plus tables. Images are printed with better visibility and contrast than ever before, and labels are large and bold for clear projection. ISBN 0-07-284189-3

Biology Digitized Video Clips

McGraw-Hill is pleased to offer adopting instructors a new presentation tool—digitized biology video clips on DVD! Licensed from some of the highest-quality science video producers in the world, these brief segments range from 15 seconds to just over two minutes in length and cover all areas of general biology from cells to ecosystems. Engaging and informative, McGraw-Hill's digitized biology video clips will help capture students' interest while illustrating key biological concepts and processes, such as how cilia and flagella work and how the stages of mitosis appear when viewed through a microscope. ISBN 007-312155-X

eInstruction Classroom Performance System (CPS)

Wireless technology brings interactivity into the classroom or lecture hall. Instructors and students receive immediate feedback through wireless response pads that are easy to use and engage students. eInstruction can be used by instructors to:

- Take attendance
- Administer quizzes and tests
- Create a lecture with intermittent questions
- Manage lectures and student comprehension through use of the CPS grade book
- Integrate interactivity into their PowerPoint presentations

Online Learning Center

The *Human Biology* Online Learning Center (OLC) at www.mhhe.com/maderhuman9 offers access to a vast array of premium online content to fortify the learning and teaching experience for students and instructors.

In addition to all of the resources for students, the Instructor Edition of the Online Learning Center has these assets:

- **eInstruction Classroom Performance System (CPS) Question Bank** A set of questions for use with the CPS is provided for every textbook chapter. The questions are tied to the main concepts in each

chapter to assist instructors in quickly assessing student comprehension of the concepts.
- **Laboratory Resource Guide** A preparation guide that provides set-up instructions, sources for materials and supplies, time estimates, special requirements, and suggested answers to all questions in the laboratory manual.
- **PageOut** McGraw-Hill's exclusive tool for creating your own website for your general biology course. It requires no knowledge of coding and is hosted by McGraw-Hill.
- **Course Management System** OLC content is readily compatible with online course management software such as WebCT and Blackboard. Contact your local McGraw-Hill sales representative for details.

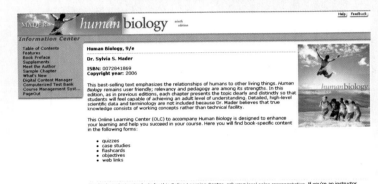

Mader Micrograph Slides

This set contains one hundred 35mm slides of many of the photomicrographs and electron micrographs in the text. ISBN 0-07-239977-5

Life Science Animations Library 3.0 CD-ROM

This CD-ROM contains over 600 full-color animations of biological concepts and processes. Harness the visual impact of processes in motion by importing these files into classroom presentations or online course materials. ISBN 0-07-248438-1

Students can order the following supplemental study materials by contacting the McGraw-Hill Customer Service Department at (800) 338-3987.

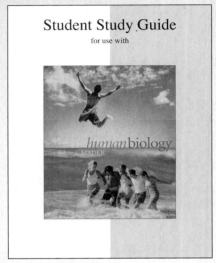

Student Study Guide

To ensure close coordination with the text, Dr. Sylvia Mader has written the *Student Study Guide* that accompanies the text. Each text chapter has a corresponding study guide chapter that includes a listing of objectives, study questions, and a chapter test. Answers to the study questions and the chapter tests are provided to give students immediate feedback.

The concepts in the study guide are the same as those in the text, and the questions in the study guide are sequenced according to those concepts. Instructors who make their choice of concepts known to the students can thereby direct student learning in an efficient manner. Students who make use of the *Student Study Guide* should find that performance increases dramatically. ISBN 0-07-293615-0

Student Interactive CD-ROM

This CD includes chapter-based quizzes, animations of complex processes, and PowerPoints of all the images found in the textbook. It is organized chapter-by-chapter and provides a link directly to the text's Online Learning Center. This Interactive CD-ROM offers an indispensable resource for enhancing topics covered within the text.

Online Learning Center

The *Human Biology* Online Learning Center (OLC) at www.mhhe.com/maderhuman9 offers access to a vast array of premium online content.

The Student Edition of the OLC features a wide variety of tools to help students learn biological concepts and to reinforce their knowledge.

e-Learning Connection Online study aids are organized according to the major sections of each chapter. **Practice quizzes, interactive activities, animations, labeling exercises, flashcards,** and much more will complement the learning and understanding of human biology.

Online Tutoring This tutorial service is moderated by qualified instructors. Help with difficult concepts is only an e-mail away!

Essential Study Partner This collection of interactive study modules contains hundreds of animations, learning activities, and quizzes designed to help students grasp complex concepts.

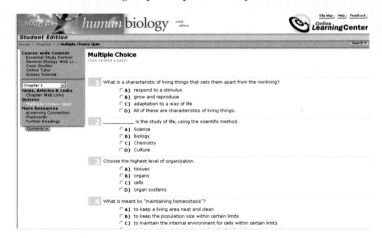

Student Study Art Notebook

This Art Notebook, which includes every piece of line art from the textbook, is designed for students to take notes during lecture. Ample space around the figures makes taking notes an easier process. ISBN 0-07-310659-3

Significant Changes to *Human Biology*, Ninth Edition!

PART II REORGANIZED

Part II "Maintenance of the Human Body" has been reorganized to better emphasize the importance of the cardiovascular system to homeostasis and the importance of blood to the cardiovascular system.

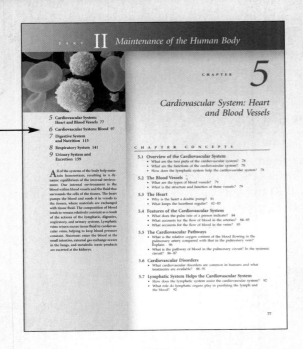

PART II *Maintenance of the Human Body*

5 Cardiovascular System: Heart and Blood Vessels 77
6 Cardiovascular System: Blood 97
7 Digestive System and Nutrition 115
8 Respiratory System 141
9 Urinary System and Excretion 159

CHAPTER 5

Cardiovascular System: Heart and Blood Vessels

CHAPTER CONCEPTS

5.1 Overview of the Cardiovascular System
• What are the two parts of the cardiovascular system? 78
• What are the functions of the cardiovascular system? 78
• How does the lymphatic system help the cardiovascular system? 78

5.2 The Blood Vessels
• What are the types of blood vessels? 79
• What is the structure and function of these vessels? 79

5.3 The Heart
• Why is the heart a double pump? 81
• What keeps the heartbeat regular? 82–83

5.4 Features of the Cardiovascular System
• What does the pulse rate of a person indicate? 84
• What accounts for the flow of blood in the arteries? 84–85
• What accounts for the flow of blood in the veins? 85

5.5 The Cardiovascular Pathways
• What is the relative oxygen content of the blood flowing in the pulmonary artery compared with that in the pulmonary vein? Explain. 86
• What is the pathway of blood in the pulmonary circuit? In the systemic circuit? 86–87

5.6 Cardiovascular Disorders
• What cardiovascular disorders are common in humans and what treatments are available? 88–91

5.7 Lymphatic System Helps the Cardiovascular System
• How does the lymphatic system assist the cardiovascular system? 92
• What role do lymphatic organs play in purifying the lymph and the blood? 92

77

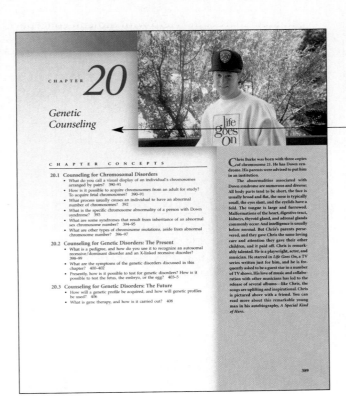

CHAPTER 20

Genetic Counseling

CHAPTER CONCEPTS

20.1 Counseling for Chromosomal Disorders
• What do you call a visual display of an individual's chromosomes arranged by pairs? 390–91
• How is it possible to acquire chromosomes from an adult for study? To acquire fetal chromosomes? 390–91
• What process usually causes an individual to have an abnormal number of chromosomes? 392
• What is the specific chromosome abnormality of a person with Down syndrome? 393
• What are some syndromes that result from inheritance of an abnormal sex chromosome number? 394–95
• What are other types of chromosome mutations, aside from abnormal chromosome number? 396–97

20.2 Counseling for Genetic Disorders: The Present
• What is a pedigree, and how do you use it to recognize an autosomal recessive/dominant disorder and an X-linked recessive disorder? 398–99
• What are the symptoms of the genetic disorders discussed in this chapter? 400–402
• Presently, how is it possible to test for genetic disorders? How is it possible to test the fetus, the embryo, or the egg? 403–5

20.3 Counseling for Genetic Disorders: The Future
• How will a genetic profile be acquired, and how will genetic profiles be used? 406
• What is gene therapy, and how is it carried out? 408

Chris Burke was born with three copies of chromosome 21. He has Down syndrome. His parents were advised to put him in an institution.

The abnormalities associated with Down syndrome are numerous and diverse. All body parts tend to be short, the face is usually broad and flat, the nose is typically small, the eyes slant, and the eyelids have a fold. The tongue is large and furrowed. Malformations of the heart, digestive tract, kidneys, thyroid gland, and adrenal glands commonly occur. And intelligence is usually below normal. But Chris's parents persevered, and they gave Chris the same loving care and attention they gave their other children, and it paid off. Chris is remarkably talented. He is a playwright, actor, and musician. He starred in *Life Goes On*, a TV series written just for him, and he is frequently asked to be a guest star in a number of TV shows. His love of music and collaboration with other musicians has led to the release of several albums—like Chris, the songs are uplifting and inspirational. Chris is pictured above with a friend. You can read more about this remarkable young man in his autobiography, *A Special Kind of Hero*.

389

NEW CHAPTER IN THE GENETICS SECTION

Chapter 20 "Genetic Counseling" is new and serves as the pinnacle of the student's study of genetics, because it covers all aspects of chromosomal and genetic diseases, including gene therapy.

In addition, Chapters 17–19 in the Genetics section have been revised to improve clarity and student appeal, so students can more easily understand the concepts.

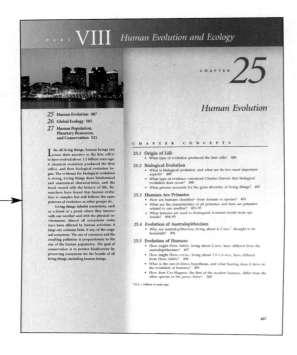

PART VIII *Human Evolution and Ecology*

25 Human Evolution 487
26 Global Ecology 505
27 Human Population, Planetary Resources, and Conservation 521

CHAPTER 25

Human Evolution

CHAPTER CONCEPTS

25.1 Origin of Life
• What type of evolution produced the first cells? 488

25.2 Biological Evolution
• What is biological evolution, and what are its two most important aspects? 489
• What type of evidence convinced Charles Darwin that biological evolution does occur? 490
• What process accounts for the great diversity of living things? 492

25.3 Humans Are Primates
• How are humans classified—from domain to species? 493
• What are the characteristics of all primates, and how are primates related to one another? 493–95
• What features are used to distinguish hominid fossils from ape fossils? 494–95

25.4 Evolution of Australopithecines
• Why are australopithecines, living about 4–3 MYA¹, thought to be hominids? 496

25.5 Evolution of Humans
• How might *Homo habilis*, living about 2 MYA, have differed from the australopithecines? 497
• How might *Homo erectus*, living about 1.9–1.6 MYA, have differed from *Homo habilis*? 498
• What is the out-of-Africa hypothesis, and what bearing does it have on the evolution of humans? 499
• How does Cro-Magnon, the first of the modern humans, differ from the other species in the genus *Homo*? 500

¹MYA = millions of years ago

487

PART VIII SIGNIFICANTLY REVISED

In Part VIII "Human Evolution and Ecology" Chapters 26 and 27 of the eighth edition have been combined into one chapter (Chapter 27). Chapter 27 now discusses the relationship between consumption of resources and pollution, and their effects on biodiversity.

Vivid Illustrations Created for Clarity

VISUAL FOCUS ART

These illustrations provide a conceptual overview that relates structure to function. Step-by-step descriptions take a concept that could be difficult to understand and turn it into one that students can readily grasp.

Visual Focus

Injured tissue cells and mast cells release inflammatory chemicals (e.g., histamine) that dilate capillaries, bringing blood to the scene. Redness and heat result.

histamine

free nerve ending (pain)

Mast cell

Monocytes

Permeability of capillary causes a local accumulation of tissue fluid. Swelling stimulates free nerve endings, resulting in pain

Neutrophils and monocytes squeeze through the capillary wall and begin to phagocytize pathogens

Macrophage

Blood clots wall off capillary, preventing blood loss

Dendritic cell

Macrophages in most tissues

Neutrophil

pathogens

Dendritic cells in skin, lungs, intestines

Dendritic cells and macrophages phagocytize pathogens and stimulate the immune response

Figure 21.2 Inflammatory reaction.
When a blood vessel is injured, mast cells, a type of white blood cell found in tissue around blood vessels, release substances, such as histamine. Histamine dilates blood vessels and increases permeability so that tissue fluid leaks from the vessel. Swelling in the area stimulates pain receptors (free nerve endings). Neutrophils and monocytes squeeze through the capillary wall. These white blood cells begin to phagocytize pathogens (e.g., disease-causing viruses and bacteria). Dendritic cells and macrophages are even better at phagocytizing pathogens, and these cells go on to stimulate other immune cells. Blood clotting seals off the capillary, preventing blood loss and pathogen spread.

416

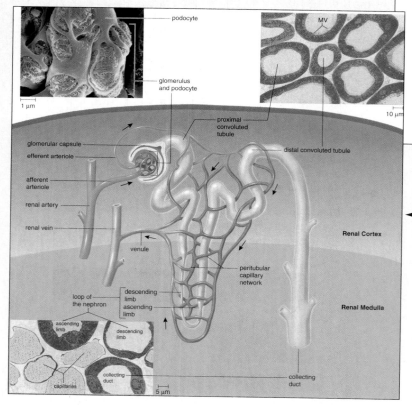

podocyte

MV

glomerulus and podocyte

1 μm

10 μm

proximal convoluted tubule

glomerular capsule

efferent arteriole

distal convoluted tubule

afferent arteriole

renal artery

renal vein

Renal Cortex

venule

peritubular capillary network

loop of the nephron

descending limb

ascending limb

Renal Medulla

ascending limb

descending limb

capillaries

collecting duct

collecting duct

5 μm

COMBINATION ART

Drawings of structures are paired with micrographs to provide students with two perspectives: the explanatory clarity of line drawings and the realism of photos.

ICONS

Icons orient students to the whole structure or process, by providing small drawings that help students visualize how a particular structure is part of a larger one.

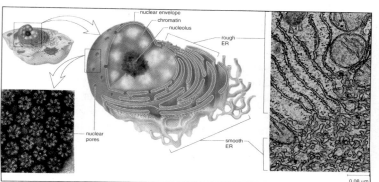

nuclear envelope

chromatin

nucleolus

rough ER

nuclear pores

smooth ER

0.08 μm

MACROSCOPIC TO MICROSCOPIC ART

Such illustrations guide students from the more intuitive macroscopic level of learning to the functional foundations revealed through microscopic images.

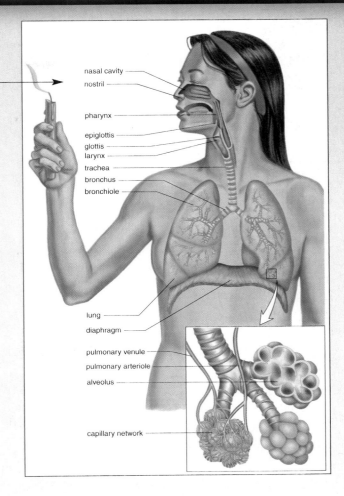

nasal cavity
nostril
pharynx
epiglottis
glottis
larynx
trachea
bronchus
bronchiole
lung
diaphragm
pulmonary venule
pulmonary arteriole
alveolus
capillary network

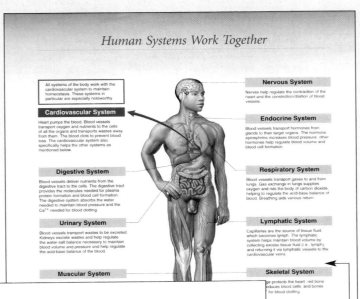

Human Systems Work Together

All systems of the body work with the cardiovascular system to maintain homeostasis. These systems in particular are especially noteworthy.

Cardiovascular System

Heart pumps the blood. Blood vessels transport oxygen and nutrients to the cells of all the organs and transports wastes away from them. The blood clots to prevent blood loss. The cardiovascular system also specifically helps the other systems as mentioned below.

Digestive System

Blood vessels deliver nutrients from the digestive tract to the cells. The digestive tract provides the molecules needed for plasma protein formation and blood cell formation. The digestive system absorbs the water needed to maintain blood pressure and the Ca^{2+} needed for blood clotting.

Urinary System

Blood vessels transport wastes to be excreted. Kidneys excrete wastes and help regulate the water-salt balance necessary to maintain blood volume and pressure and help regulate the acid-base balance of the blood.

Muscular System

Nervous System

Nerves help regulate the contraction of the heart and the constriction/dilation of blood vessels.

Endocrine System

Blood vessels transport hormones from glands to their target organs. The hormone epinephrine increases blood pressure, other hormones help regulate blood volume and blood cell formation.

Respiratory System

Blood vessels transport gases to and from lungs. Gas exchange in lungs supplies oxygen and rids the body of carbon dioxide, helping to regulate the acid-base balance of blood. Breathing aids venous return.

Lymphatic System

Capillaries are the source of tissue fluid which becomes lymph. The lymphatic system helps maintain blood volume by collecting excess tissue fluid (i.e., lymph), and returning it via lymphatic vessels to the cardiovascular veins.

Skeletal System

...ge protects the heart, red bone ...oduces blood cells, and bones ...for blood clotting.

---

110   Part II   Maintenance of the Human Body

6.6 Homeostasis

In Chapter 4, you learned that the body's internal environment contains blood and tissue fluid. In this chapter, you saw that tissue fluid actually originates from blood. In fact, it is very similar to the plasma component of blood, except that it contains no plasma proteins. Tissue fluid is taken up from the space between the tissue cells by lymphatic capillaries, after which it is referred to as lymph. The lymph courses through lymphatic vessels and is eventually returned to the venous system. Thus, the cardiovascular and lymphatic systems are intimately linked. Fluid cycles continuously through blood plasma, tissue fluid, and lymph, and back to blood plasma again.

Homeostasis is possible only if: (1) the cardiovascular system delivers oxygen and nutrients to, and takes away metabolic wastes from, the tissue fluid that surrounds cells, and (2) the lymphatic system returns tissue fluid to the bloodstream. Homeostasis can be disturbed if the cardiovascular or lymphatic system is impaired. For instance, if the heart is unable to pump the blood or if lymphatic vessels are blocked or damaged, blood pressure can become inadequate to move the blood. The presence of edema (swelling) indicates that tissue fluid is building up. This can happen due to tumors, infection, accidental injury, or surgical removal of lymphatic vessels. Sometimes, in breast cancer surgery, the underarm lymph nodes adjacent to the cancerous breast are also removed. The result is edema localized to the underarm region, which usually subsides over time.

Just think of how important it is to homeostasis for all the human systems to work together. For example, imagine what must be one of a student's worst nightmares. You slowly open your eyes in the morning, blearily gaze at your alarm clock, and realize that you've overslept. In fact, it's just a few minutes before class begins. Then, you snap wide awake as you remember why you were up so late the night before—you were studying for the final exam! Most likely, your heart starts beating faster, stimulated by your stressed nervous system. The resulting rise in blood pressure rises to help prepare the body for action. Hormones, such as epinephrine (adrenaline) from the adrenal glands, pour into the bloodstream to prolong your body's physical response to stress.

Frantic, you throw on your clothes and sprint to the bus (Fig. 6.11). As you run, your muscles require more oxygen to support their activity. Your breathing and heart rate increase, in order to deal with the demand. The hard-working muscles generate carbon dioxide, wastes, and heat. Carbon dioxide is carried via the blood to the lungs so it can be expelled, and nitrogenous wastes will eventually be excreted by the kidneys. To keep you from overheating, you not only sweat, but blood flow to your skin increases so that heat radiates away.

The nightmare continues. In your mad dash, you trip on the steps as you board the bus, and fall, skinning your knee. At first, blood flows from the wound, but a clot will soon form to seal off the injured area and allow a scab to form, so

Figure 6.11   Human systems work together.
How many human systems participate in helping you get through an emergency situation?

that healing can begin. Any injury that breaks the skin can allow harmful bacteria into the body, but the immune system usually deals with them in short order. Later, you might notice that your knee is not only skinned, but also black and blue. The bruise is where blood leaked out of damaged vessels underneath the skin, and then clotted.

You make it to class just in time to get your exam from the instructor. As you settle down to take the exam, your heartbeat and breathing gradually slow, since the need of your muscles is not as great. Now that you are in thinking mode, blood flow increases in certain highly active parts of your brain. The brain is a very demanding organ in terms of both oxygen and glucose.

You start to feel hungry. Since there is little glucose in your bloodstream to provide fuel for your body's cells, glycogen stored in the liver is broken down to make glucose available to the blood. Finally, you hand in the exam and go to the dining hall for breakfast. When most of the nutrients from your meal are absorbed from the digestive tract, they enter the bloodstream. However, the lipoproteins enter lacteals, which are vessels of the lymphatic system, for transport to the blood.

Notice in this scenario how many organ systems had to interact with the cardiovascular system. The nervous, endocrine, respiratory, muscular, and lymphatic systems helped to serve the cells' needs. Throughout all of the challenges to homeostasis described above, the lymphatic system was busy taking up excess tissue fluid and protecting the body from disease. No organ system works alone, where homeostasis is concerned! Human Systems Work Together on the next page summarizes how the cardiovascular and lymphatic systems cooperate with the other systems of the body to maintain homeostasis.

111

Revised

HUMAN SYSTEMS WORK TOGETHER

These revised and newly designed illustrations make it easier for students to understand how body systems work together to achieve homeostasis.

Strategically placed throughout the book, each illustration uses **brief, concise statements** to outline the functions of the body systems, while the accompanying figure provides a **visual representation** of each system.

A full page of text discussing homeostasis in the context of that chapter, and featuring a possible event in the student's everyday life, also accompanies each illustration.

Proven Pedagogical Features

CHAPTER CONCEPTS

The chapter outline contains questions, encouraging students to study the chapter for answers.

OPENING VIGNETTE

A short, thought-provoking vignette applies chapter material to a real-life situation. Many of the vignettes have been revised for great student appeal.

CHAPTER

8

*Respiratory
System*

CHAPTER CONCEPTS

8.1 The Respiratory System
- What events are required in order to supply cells with oxygen and rid them of carbon dioxide? 142
- How is air that is inhaled or exhaled modified by respiratory surfaces? 142
- What is the path of air, and what are the functions of the organs along that path? 143–45

8.2 Mechanism of Breathing
- Why do physicians measure our ability to move air into and out of the lungs? What measurements do they take? 146
- How is breathing achieved? Is pressure within the lungs greatest during inspiration or expiration? 148–49
- What controls the breathing rate? 149

8.3 Gas Exchanges in the Body
- What are the differences between external respiration and internal respiration? 150–51
- What respiratory pigment is found in human red blood cells? How does it function in the transport of oxygen; carbon dioxide? 150–51

8.4 Respiration and Health
- What are some common respiratory infections and disorders of the upper respiratory tract? Of the lower respiratory tract? 152–54
- What are three respiratory disorders commonly associated with smoking tobacco? 153–54

Just before winning a gold metal for the 400-m race at the 2004 Olympic games, Jeremy Wariner of the United States warmed up by stretching, sprinting, and jogging. Onlookers may have thought he was trying to prevent an injury when he ran the race. Maybe, but this type of warmup can also help a runner win the race, primarily because it causes an increase in blood flow to the leg muscles. A good warmup can increase the number of open capillary beds in the region as much as 1,000%. More blood flow brings the fuel and oxygen a runner's working muscles will need, and it also removes the waste products they generate during the race. When muscles contract, lots of CO_2, H^+, and lactic acid enters the bloodstream, and so does heat.

Hemoglobin, the respiratory pigment that carries oxygen, is well adapted to these conditions. As acidity and temperature rise, hemoglobin tends to release more oxygen than otherwise. In distance runners, the body temperature can rise from 98.6°F to 102°F, and pH can be reduced from 7.4 to 6.9, greatly facilitating the release of extra O_2 (20% or more) into the runner's exercising leg muscles.

World-class athletes, such as Jeremy Wariner, need every advantage in order to win a race. Therefore, a prerace warmup is critical, so that the cardiovascular and respiratory systems are ready to perform, even from the moment the race begins. Only if these systems are ready can an athlete hope to win a gold medal at the Olympic games. Even though you may not be a world-class athlete, your cardiovascular and respiratory systems still need to perform optimally when you exercise. Therefore, a warmup is essential for you also, regardless of your chosen sport.

141

Chapter 3 Cell Structure and Function   45

The Endomembrane System

The **endomembrane system** consists of the nuclear envelope, the endoplasmic reticulum, the Golgi apparatus, lysosomes, and **vesicles** (tiny membranous sacs) (Fig. 3.12).

The Endoplasmic Reticulum

The endoplasmic reticulum has two portions. Rough ER is studded with ribosomes on the side of the membrane that faces the cytoplasm. Here, proteins are synthesized and enter the ER interior, where processing and modification begin. Some of these proteins are incorporated into membrane, and some are for export. Smooth ER, which is continuous with rough ER, does not have attached ribosomes. Smooth ER synthesizes the phospholipids that occur in membranes and has various other functions, depending on the particular cell. In the testes, it produces testosterone, and in the liver it helps detoxify drugs.

The ER forms vesicles in which large molecules are transported to other parts of the cell. Often, these vesicles are on their way to the plasma membrane or the Golgi apparatus.

The Golgi Apparatus

The **Golgi apparatus** is named for Camillo Golgi, who discovered its presence in cells in 1898. The Golgi apparatus consists of a stack of slightly curved saccules, whose appearance can be compared to a stack of pancakes. Here, proteins and lipids received from the ER are modified. For example, a chain of sugars may be added to them, thereby making them glycoproteins and glycolipids, which are molecules found in the plasma membrane.

The vesicles that leave the Golgi apparatus move to other parts of the cell. Some vesicles proceed to the plasma membrane, where they discharge their contents. Altogether, the Golgi apparatus is involved in processing, packaging, and secretion. Other vesicles that leave the Golgi apparatus are lysosomes.

Lysosomes

Lysosomes, membranous sacs produced by the Golgi apparatus, contain *hydrolytic enzymes.* When a lysosome fuses with such an endocytic vesicle, its contents are digested by lysosomal enzymes into simpler subunits that then enter the cytoplasm. Even parts of a cell are digested by its own lysosomes (called autodigestion). Normal cell rejuvenation most likely takes place in this manner, but autodigestion is also important during development. For

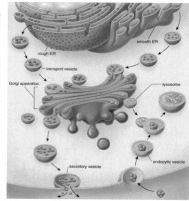

Figure 3.12 Endomembrane system.
The organelles in the endomembrane system work together to produce, modify, secrete, and digest proteins and lipids.

example, when a tadpole becomes a frog, lysosomes digest away the cells of the tail. The fingers of a human embryo are at first webbed, but they are freed from one another as a result of lysosomal action.

The organelles of the endomembrane system are as follows.
Endoplasmic reticulum (ER): series of saccules (flattened) and tubules
  Rough ER: ribosomes present
  Smooth ER: ribosomes not present
Golgi apparatus: stack of flattened and curved saccules
Lysosomes: specialized vesicles
Vesicles: membranous sacs

INTERNAL SUMMARY STATEMENTS

A summary statement appears at the end of each major section of the chapter to help students focus on the key concepts.

---

30   Part I   Human Organization

The nucleotides in DNA contain the sugar d and the nucleotides in RNA contain the sugar difference accounts for their respective names There are four different types of bases in DN **(A), thymine (T), guanine (G), and cytosine (C** can have two rings (adenine or guanine) o (thymine or cytosine). In RNA, the base **uracil (** the base thymine. These structures are called ba their presence raises the pH of a solution.

The nucleotides form a linear molecule call which has a backbone made up of phosp phosphate-sugar, with the bases projecting to the backbone. Since the nucleotides occur in a de so do the bases. After many years of work, rese know the sequence of the bases in human human genome. This breakthrough is expected improved genetic counseling, gene therapy, an to treat the causes of many human illnesses.

DNA is double-stranded, with the two stra about each other in the form of a *double helix* (see In DNA, the two strands are held together by bonds between the bases. When unwound, DNA a stepladder. The uprights (sides) of the ladde entirely of phosphate and sugar molecules, and the ladder are made only of complementary p Thymine always pairs with adenine, and guar pairs with cytosine. Complementary bases have fit together.

Complementary base pairing allows DNA to a way that ensures the sequence of bases will same. This sequence of the DNA bases contains specifies the sequence of amino acids in the proteins of the cell. RNA is single-stranded, and when it forms, complementary base pairing with one DNA strand passes this information on to RNA.

such as carbohydrates and proteins. In muscle cells, the energy is used for muscle contraction, and in nerve cells, it is used for the conduction of nerve impulses. After ATP breaks down, it is rebuilt by the addition of Ⓟ to ADP. Notice in Figure 2.18 that an input of energy is required to re-form ATP.

DNA has a structure like a twisted ladder: Sugar and phosphate molecules make up the uprights of the ladder, and hydrogen-bonded bases make up the rungs.

ATP is a high-energy molecule. ATP breaks down to ADP + Ⓟ, releasing energy, which is used for all metabolic work done in a cell.

Adenosine triphosphate (ATP)   Adenosine diphosphate (ADP)   Phosphate

Figure 2.18 ATP reaction.
ATP, the universal energy currency of cells, is composed of adenosine and three phosphate groups (called a triphosphate). When cells require energy, ATP undergoes hydrolysis, producing ADP + Ⓟ, with a release of energy.

READINGS

Human Biology offers three types of boxed readings that put the chapter concepts in the context of modern-day issues:

- **Health Focus** readings review procedures and technology that can contribute to our well-being.
- **Ecology Focus** readings show how the concepts of the chapter can be applied to ecological concerns and preserving the biosphere.
- **Bioethical Focus** readings describe modern situations that call for value judgments and challenge students to develop a point of view.

Health Focus

Very Low Carbohydrate Diets

People following a low-carbohydrate diet seem to think that weight gain is caused by carbohydrates, an idea that cannot be supported scientifically. Weight gain is caused by consuming too many calories, whether they are from carbohydrate, protein, or fat. Logically, you are more likely to gain weight because...

is better to be protective of one's kidneys rather than to stress them.

Usually, a very low carbohydrate diet includes a higher amount of saturated fat than usual, if only because meat is usually high in saturated fats. As you know, a diet high in...

Ecology Focus

Fish: The Good News and the Bad News

"I thought fish was good for me!" "Do I have to give up tuna?" Fish is good for you! It contains high-quality protein and omega-3 fatty acids, which prevent blood from clotting and help maintain a regular heartbeat. The American Heart Association guidelines recommend eating fish twice a week to maintain...

methylmercury by bacteria and taken up by the bacteria and plankton in the water. Fish consume the bacteria and the plankton, and the methylmercury accumulates in their tissues. These fish are eaten by larger fish that accumulate more mercury in their tissues where it can, in turn, eventually be con-...

Bioethical Focus

Bans on Smoking

In 1964, the surgeon general of the United States made it known to the general public that smoking was hazardous to our health and thereafter, a health warning was placed on packs of cigarettes. At that time, 40.4% of adults smoked, but by 1990, only 26% of adults smoked. In the meantime, however, the public became aware that passive smoking—that is, just being in the vicinity of someone who is smoking, can also lead to cancer and other health problems. By now, many state and local governments have passed legislation that bans smoking in public places such as restaurants, elevators, public meeting rooms, and in the workplace.

Is legislation that restricts the freedom to smoke ethical? Or is such legislation akin to racism and creating a population of second-class citizens who are segregated from the majority on the basis of a habit? Are the desires of nonsmokers being allowed to infringe on the rights of smokers? Or is this legislation one way to help smokers become nonsmokers? One study showed that workplace bans on smoking reduce the daily consumption of cigarettes among smokers by 10%.

Is legislation that disallows smoking in family-style restaurants fair, especially if bars and restaurants associated with casinos are not included in the ban on smoking? The selling of tobacco and even the increased need for health care it generates helps the economy. One smoker writes, "Smoking causes...

people to drink more, eat more, and leave larger tips. Smoking also powers the economy of Wall Street." Is this a reason to allow smoking to continue? Or should we simply require all places of business to put in improved air filtration systems? Would that do away with the dangers of passive smoking?

Does legislation that bans smoking in certain areas represent government invasion of our privacy? If yes, is reducing the chance of cancer a good enough reason to allow the government to invade our privacy? Some people are prone to cancer more than others. Should we all be regulated by the same legislation? Are we our brother's keeper, meaning that we have to look out for one another?

Decide Your Opinion

1. Is legislation that bans smoking in public places creating a group of second-class citizens whose rights are being denied?
2. Should we be concerned about passing and following legislation that possibly puts a damper on the economy even if it does improve the health of people?
3. Are bans on smoking an invasion of our privacy? If so, is prevention of cancer in certain persons a good enough reason to risk a possible invasion of our privacy?

---

364 Part VI Human Genetics

Summarizing the Concepts

18.1 Genotype and Phenotype
It is customary to use letters to represent the genotypes of individuals. Homozygous dominant (two capital letters) and heterozygous (a capital letter and a lowercase letter) exhibit the dominant phenotype. Homozygous recessive (two lowercase letters) exhibits the recessive phenotype.

18.2 One- and Two-Trait Inheritance
Whereas the individual has two alleles (copies of a gene) for each trait, the gametes have only one allele for each trait. A Punnett square can help determine the phenotypic ratio among offspring because it gives the results when all possible sperm types are given an equal chance to fertilize all possible egg types, for a particular cross. When a heterozygous individual reproduces with another heterozygote, there is a 75% chance the child will have the dominant phenotype and a 25% chance the child will have the recessive phenotype. When a heterozygous individual reproduces with a pure recessive, the offspring has a 50% chance of having either phenotype.

It is impossible to determine, by inspection, if a person with the dominant phenotype is homozygous or heterozygous. But when a cross with a pure recessive results in a phenotypic ratio of 1:1, the person has to be heterozygous. Each child from such a cross has a 50% chance of having the recessive phenotype and a 50% chance of having the dominant phenotype.

Because of meiosis, the gametes have only one of each pair of homologous chromosomes/alleles and in all possible combinations. Therefore, individuals heterozygous for two traits can form four types of gametes, and the phenotypic ratio for a dihybrid cross is 9:3:3:1; ⁹⁄₁₆ of the offspring have the two dominant traits, ³⁄₁₆ have one of the dominant traits with one of the recessive traits, ³⁄₁₆ have the other dominant trait with the other recessive trait, and ¹⁄₁₆ have both recessive traits. It is impossible to determine, by inspection, if a person with the dominant phenotype for two traits is homozygous or heterozygous for each trait. But when a cross with a pure recessive results in a phenotypic ratio of 1:1:1:1, the person has to be heterozygous in both traits. Each child from such a cross has a 25% chance for each possible phenotype.

18.3 Beyond Simple Inheritance Patterns
There are many types of inheritance beyond simple dominant/recessive patterns. They are multifactorial inheritance (skin color), degrees of dominance (curly hair), and multiple alleles (ABO blood type).

For multifactorial traits, several genes each contribute to the overall phenotype in equal, small degrees. The environment plays a role in the continuously varying expression that follows a bell-shaped curve. Twin studies have allowed investigators to determine that behavioral traits are most likely multifactorial ones.

18.4 Sex-Linked Inheritance
Some traits are sex-linked, meaning that although they do not determine gender, they are carried on the sex chromosomes. Most of the alleles for these traits are carried on the X chromosome, and the Y is blank. It is customary to show an X-linked allele as a superscript on the X chromosome; for example X^B. The phenotypic results of crosses are given for females and males separately.

An X-linked recessive allele is always expressed in males because it is the only allele a son receives for an X-linked trait. Also, notice that the recessive allele has to have come from his

mother because a father does not pass on an allele for an X-linked trait to a son.

Studying the Concepts

1. What is the difference between the genotype and the phenotype of an individual? For which phenotype—dominant or recessive—are there two possible genotypes? 352
2. Why do the gametes have only one allele for each trait? Explain why *Aa* is genotype for an individual and not a gamete. 353
3. What is the chance of producing a child with the dominant phenotype from each of the following crosses? 354–55
   AA × AA
   Aa × AA
   Aa × Aa
   aa × aa
4. Which of the crosses in question 3 can result in an offspring with the recessive phenotype? Explain. 354–55
5. What does the phrase "chance has no memory" mean? 354
6. What is the genotype of a heterozygote with a widow's peak and short fingers? Give all possible gametes for this individual. 356
7. What are the expected results of the following crosses? 354–358
   monohybrid × monohybrid
   monohybrid × recessive
   dihybrid × dihybrid
   dihybrid × recessive in both traits
8. Which of these crosses would best allow you to determine that an individual with the dominant phenotype is homozygous or heterozygous? 354–358
9. Show the events of meiosis, also explain why all possible combinations of alleles occur in the gametes. 356
10. Give examples of these patterns of inheritance: multifactorial inheritance, incomplete dominance/codominance, and multiple alleles. 359–61
11. If a trait is on an autosome, how do you give the genotype for a homozygous dominant female? If a trait is on an X chromosome, how do you give the genotype for a homozygous dominant female? 362
12. What phenotypic ratio is expected when a woman who is a carrier for color blindness reproduces with a man who has normal vision? 362
13. How do you give the genotype for a woman who is homozygous dominant for widow's peak and is color-blind? 363

Thinking Critically About the Concepts

Refer to the opening vignette on page 351, and then answer these questions.

1. Of all the patterns of inheritance discussed in this chapter, which most likely governs cleft chin?
2. What would be the genotype and phenotype of their children if Michael Douglas is homozygous dominant for cleft chin and homozygous recessive for type of hairline; his wife, Catherine Zeta Jones, is homozygous recessive for type of chin and homozygous recessive for type of hairline?
3. Suppose crossing-over occurred between the nonsister chromatids in Michael Douglas, with regard to cleft chin. What would be the genotypes and phenotypes of their children?

SUMMARIZING THE CONCEPTS

The summary is organized according to the major sections in the chapter and helps students review the important topics and concepts.

STUDYING THE CONCEPTS

This page-referenced question set follows the sequence of the chapter and reviews the concepts that are presented.

THINKING CRITICALLY ABOUT THE CONCEPTS

This new set of chapter questions encourages students to apply what they've just learned to the real-life story that opened the chapter.

TESTING YOUR KNOWLEDGE OF THE CONCEPTS

These objective questions allow students to check their knowledge of the chapter concepts. Answers are provided in the Appendix.

Testing Your Knowledge of the Concepts

Choose the best answer for each question. Assume simple dominance unless told otherwise.

1. Which of these is a correct statement?
   a. Each gamete contains two alleles for each trait.
   b. Each individual has one allele for each trait.
   c. Fertilization gives each new individual one allele for each trait.
   d. All of these are correct.
   e. None of these is correct.

2. Which of the following indicates a heterozygous individual?
   a. AB c. Aa
   b. AA d. aa

3. Which of these could be a normal gamete?
   a. A
   b. Aa
   c. AA
   d. None of these is correct.

4. List the gametes produced by $AaBb$.
   a. Aa, Bb c. AB, ab
   b. A, a, B, b d. AB, Ab, aB, ab

5. Homologous chromosomes have
   a. genes for the same traits.
   b. the same shape and size.
   c. DNA base sequences.
   d. All of these are correct.

6. In humans, pointed eyebrows (P) are dominant over smooth eyebrows (p). Mary's father has pointed eyebrows, but she and her mother have smooth. What is the genotype of the father?
   a. pp
   b. Pp
   c. $PPpp$
   d. pp
   e. Any one of these are correct.

7. The genotypic ratio from a monohybrid cross is
   a. 1:1.   d. 9:3:3:1.
   b. 3:1.   e. 1:1:1:1.
   c. 1:2:1.

8. A straight hairline is recessive. If two parents with a widow's peak have a child with a straight hairline, then what is the chance that their next child will have a straight hairline?
   a. no chance   d. 1/2
   b. 1/4   e. 1/16
   c. 3/16

9. What is the chance that an Aa individual will be produced from an $Aa \times Aa$ cross.
   a. 50%   d. 25%
   b. 75%   e. 100%
   c. 0%

10. The genotype of an individual, with the dominant phenotype, can be determined best by reproduction with
    a. the recessive genotype or phenotype.
    b. a heterozygote.
    c. the dominant phenotype.
    d. the homozygous dominant.
    e. Both a and b are correct.

11. Using the diagram below, show how four types of gametes (SW, sw, Sw, sW) are produced from the dihybrid individual represented in the top circle.

one pair   one pair
either   or
Meiosis I
Meiosis II

12. Because the homologous chromosome align independently at the equator during meiosis
    a. all possible combinations of alleles can occur in the gametes.
    b. only the parental combinations of gametes can occur in the gametes.
    c. only the nonparental combinations of gametes can occur in the gametes.

13. What is the chance that a dihybrid cross will produce a homozygous recessive in both traits.
    a. 9/16   d. 3/16
    b. 1/4   e. 1/8
    c. 1/16

14. Which of the following is not a feature of multifactorial inheritance?
    a. Effects of dominant alleles are additive.
    b. Genes affecting the trait may be on multiple chromosomes.
    c. Environment influences phenotype.
    d. Recessive alleles are harmful.

15. The ABO blood system exhibits
    a. codominance.
    b. dominance.
    c. multiple alleles.
    d. All of these are correct.
    e. None of these is correct.

For questions 16–19, match the cross type with the expected ratios in the key. Each answer can be used more than once.

Key:
a. 3:1   c. 9:3:3:1
b. 1:1   d. 1:1:1:1

16. Phenotypic ratio, when a dihybrid reproduces with a dihybrid.

17. Phenotypic ratio, when a monohybrid reproduces with a monohybrid.

---

18. Phenotypic ratio, when a dihybrid reproduces with the homozygous recessive in both traits.

19. Phenotypic ratio, when a monohybrid reproduces with a homozygous recessive for the trait.

20. The occurrence of the blood type AB shows that two alleles involved in determining blood type are
    a. completely dominant.
    b. incompletely dominant.
    c. codominant.

21. Assume two normal parents have a color-blind son. Which parent is responsible for color blindness in the son?
    a. the mother
    b. the father
    c. either parent
    d. None of these is correct—two normal parents cannot have a color-blind son.

22. If a child has type O blood and the mother has type A, then which of the following could be the blood type of the child's father?
    a. A only   d. A or O
    b. B only   e. A, B, or O
    c. O only

23. Cleft chin is a dominant trait. A man without a cleft chin marries a woman with a cleft whose mother lacked the cleft. What proportion of their children would lack the cleft chin?
    a. 1/4
    b. 1/2
    c. 3/4
    d. All of these are correct.
    e. None of these is correct.

24. A researcher does a statistical study of a population and finds that the phenotypes for a particular trait follow a bell-shaped curve. He concludes rightly that the trait is governed by
    a. codominant genes.
    b. simple dominance.
    c. an X-linked gene.
    d. multifactorial genes, plus the environment.

25. Alice and Henry are at the opposite extremes for a multifactorial trait. Their children will
    a. be bell-shaped.
    b. be a phenotype typical of a 3:1 ratio.
    c. have the middle phenotype between their two parents.
    d. look like one parent or the other.

26. A woman with very light skin has medium-brown parents. If this woman reproduces with a light-skinned man, what is the darkest skin color possible for their children?
    a. dark skin
    b. light skin
    c. medium-brown skin
    d. Any one of these may occur.

27. A woman is color-blind, and her spouse has normal vision. What are the chances of a color-blind son, daughter?
    a. 0% for son, 100% for daughter
    b. 100% for son, 0% for daughter
    c. 50% for son, 50% for daughter
    d. 75% for son, 25% for daughter

28. Two wavy-haired individuals (neither curly hair nor straight hair are completely dominant) reproduce. What are the chances that their children will have wavy hair?
    a. 0%   c. 50%
    b. 25%   d. 100%

Understanding Key Terms

allele 352
autosome 362
codominance 360
dihybrid 357
dominant allele 352
genotype 352
heterozygous 352
homozygous dominant 352
homozygous recessive 352
incomplete dominance 360
locus (pl., loci) 352
monohybrid 354
multifactorial inheritance 359
multiple allele 361
phenotype 352
Punnett square 354
recessive allele 352
sex chromosome 362
sex-linked 362
X-linked 362

Match the key terms to these definitions.

Match the terms to these definitions:
a. _____ Grid-like device used to calculate the expected results of simple genetic crosses.
b. _____ Alternative forms of a gene that occur at the same locus on homologous chromosomes.
c. _____ Allele that exerts its phenotypic effect in the heterozygote; it masks the expression of the recessive allele.
d. _____ Particular site where a gene is found on a chromosome.
e. _____ Alleles of an individual for a particular trait or traits such as BB or Aa or $BBAa$

Online Learning Center

www.mhhe.com/maderhuman9

The Online Learning Center provides a wealth of information fully organized and integrated by chapter. You will find practice quizzes, interactive activities, labeling exercises, flashcards, and much more that will complement your learning and understanding of human biology.

Looking at Both Sides

Each day, the Internet, media, and other people present you with opposing viewpoints on a wide range of subjects. Your ability to develop an informed opinion on an issue, and talk to others about it, is extremely important.

To expand and enhance your knowledge of a highly relevant bioethical issue, visit the "Student Edition" of the Online Learning Center. Under "Course-Wide Content," select "Looking at Both Sides." Once there, you will be asked to complete activities that will increase your understanding of a current bioethical issue related to this chapter and allow you to defend your opinion.

UNDERSTANDING KEY TERMS

The boldface terms in the chapter are page referenced, and a matching exercise allows students to test their knowledge of the terms.

WEBSITE REMINDER

Located at the end of each chapter is this reminder that quiz questions and additional learning activities are on the Online Learning Center at www.mhhe.com/maderhuman9.

LOOKING AT BOTH SIDES

This pedagogical tool directs students to the Online Learning Center where they are invited to expand their knowledge of highly relevant bioethical issues. Through this tool, students are encouraged to consider opposing viewpoints on an issue, synthesize the information, and develop an informed opinion. Such skills are critical to society, and also help students relate to the chapter concepts.

CHAPTER

1

A Human Perspective

CHAPTER CONCEPTS

1.1 Biologically Speaking
- How are humans organized biologically? 2
- What is homeostasis and how do various organ systems contribute to homeostasis? 2
- The life of a human being includes what developmental stages? 2
- By what processes are humans related to all other living things? 2–3
- What evidence can you give that humans are members of the biosphere? 4

1.2 The Process of Science
- What steps do biologists follow to gather information and come to conclusions about the natural world? 6–7
- Why do laboratory studies have a control group? 8–9

1.3 Science and Social Responsibility
- Who is responsible for deciding how to use new emerging scientific information and discoveries? 9

Looking at the sonogram, April exclaimed gleefully, "Twin boys! Look, there's a hand, and a foot, and another hand, and another one! We're going to be parents!"

April and her husband are excited and hopeful for the future, but becoming pregnant wasn't an easy task for them. After two years of trying to become pregnant, April realized that something was wrong. She was diagnosed as infertile, and her doctor prescribed fertility drugs. Within weeks, she had become pregnant with twins. Multiple births are not uncommon among women using fertility drugs. April and her husband will face many trials and tribulations in the coming years, but they are optimistic.

Despite her excitement, April knows that more growth and development are required before the twins will be ready to be born. We share this and many other characteristics with other animals. We have many of the same tissues and organs, we have similar energy and nutritional needs, and we are adapted to a land environment. But many things make us distinctly human—such as very highly developed brains, the ability to use tools and alter our environment, and distinct social and cultural orders that set us apart from other organisms.

The science of biology is the study of living organisms. This text approaches biology from a human perspective: the composition of our bodies, how we are organized, how our various body organs and tissues regulate themselves, and how we interact with our environment. The following chapter will introduce you to concepts of human biology.

1.1 Biologically Speaking

Biology is the study of life. You are about to begin your study of human biology in which you will learn how the human body works and how human beings relate to other living things. Before you begin, it is appropriate to take a look at who humans are and how they fit into the world at large.

Who Are We?

Certain characteristics tell us who human beings are biologically speaking.

Human Beings Are Highly Organized

A **cell** is the basic unit of life, and human beings are multicellular because they are composed of many types of cells. Like cells form **tissues,** and several tissues make up an **organ,** a structure that performs a specific function in the body. Each organ belongs to an organ system. The organs of an organ system work together to accomplish a common purpose. Together, the organ systems maintain **homeostasis,** an internal environment for cells that usually varies only within certain limits. For example, body temperature stays close to 37°C (98.6°F) but lowers slightly at night and rises during the day. This text emphasizes how all the systems of the human body help maintain homeostasis. The digestive system takes in nutrients, and the respiratory system exchanges gases with the environment. The cardiovascular system distributes nutrients and oxygen to the cells and picks up their wastes. The metabolic waste products of cells are excreted by the urinary system. The work of the nervous and endocrine systems is critical because they coordinate the functions of the other systems.

Homeostasis would be impossible without the ability of the body to respond to internal stimuli. Sensory receptors detect a change in the internal environment, and the nervous system brings about a response. For example, should blood pressure fall, the nervous system causes blood vessels to constrict and the blood pressure rises again. Response to external stimuli is more apparent to us because it involves the muscular and skeletal systems, as when we quickly remove a hand from a hot stove.

Human Beings Reproduce, Grow, and Develop

Reproduction and growth are fundamental characteristics of all living things. Just as cells come only from preexisting cells, living things have parents. When living things **reproduce,** they create a copy of themselves and ensure the continuance of their own kind. Human reproduction requires that a sperm contributed by a male fertilize an egg contributed by a female. Growth occurs as the resulting cell develops into the newborn. Development includes all the changes that occur from the time the egg is fertilized until death and, therefore, all the changes that occur during childhood, adolescence, and adulthood.

Human Beings Have a Cultural Heritage

We are born without knowledge of an accepted way to behave but we gradually acquire this knowledge by adult instruction and imitation of role models. The previous generation passes on their beliefs, values, and skills to the next generation. Many of the skills involve tool use, which can vary from how to hunt in the wild to how to use a computer. Human skills have also produced a rich heritage in the arts. Collectively called **culture,** customs and skills can vary greatly between groups of people. The culture of highly civilized people, in particular, gives us the impression we are separate from other animals and makes us think we are not a part of nature. But actually we are a product of **evolution,** a process of change that has resulted in the diversity of life, and we are a part of the **biosphere,** a network of life that spans the surface of the Earth.

How Do We Fit In?

Certain characteristics tell us how human beings fit into the world of living things.

Human Beings Are a Product of an Evolutionary Process

Life has a history that began with the evolution of the first cell(s) about 3.5 billion years ago. It is possible to trace human ancestry from the first cell, through a series of increasingly complex organisms, before arriving at our direct prehistoric ancestors and the evolution of modern-day humans. The presence of the same types of chemicals tells us that human beings are related to all other living things. DNA is the genetic material, and ATP is the energy currency in all cells, including human cells. It is even possible to do research with bacteria, the simplest of organisms, and apply the results to human beings.

The classification of living things mirrors their evolutionary relationships. We now classify living things into three **domains** (Fig 1.1*a*). Of these, domain Eukarya contains four **kingdoms,** and humans are vertebrates in the kingdom Animalia. Figure 1.1*b* shows representatives of other types of vertebrates. **Vertebrates** have a nerve cord that is protected by a vertebral column whose repeating units (the vertebrae) indicate that we and other vertebrates are segmented animals. Among the vertebrates, we are most closely related to the apes, specifically the chimpanzee, from whom we are distinguished by our highly developed brains, completely upright stance, power of creative language, and ability to use a wide variety of tools.

Human beings did not evolve from apes. Rather, humans and apes evolved from a common apelike ancestor. Today's apes are our evolutionary cousins, and we couldn't have evolved from our cousins because we are contemporaries—living on Earth at the same time. Our relationship to apes is analogous to you and your first cousin being descended from your grandparents.

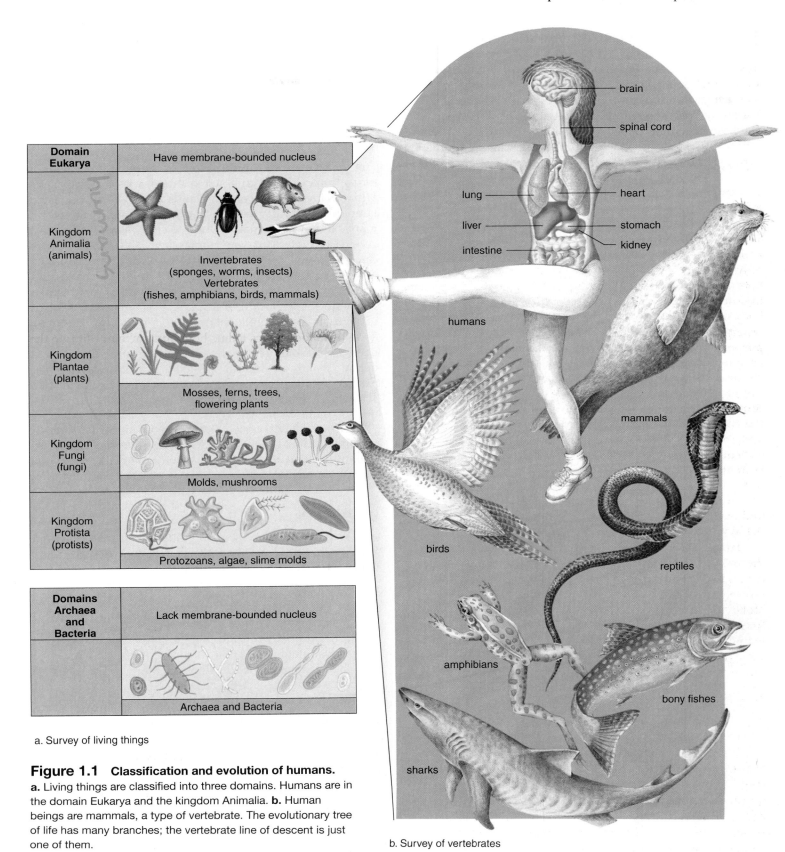

Domain Eukarya	Have membrane-bounded nucleus		
Kingdom Animalia (animals)	Invertebrates (sponges, worms, insects) Vertebrates (fishes, amphibians, birds, mammals)		
Kingdom Plantae (plants)	Mosses, ferns, trees, flowering plants		
Kingdom Fungi (fungi)	Molds, mushrooms		
Kingdom Protista (protists)	Protozoans, algae, slime molds		

Domains Archaea and Bacteria	Lack membrane-bounded nucleus
	Archaea and Bacteria

brain
spinal cord
lung
heart
liver
stomach
intestine
kidney
humans
mammals
birds
reptiles
amphibians
bony fishes
sharks

a. Survey of living things

b. Survey of vertebrates

Figure 1.1   Classification and evolution of humans.
a. Living things are classified into three domains. Humans are in the domain Eukarya and the kingdom Animalia. **b.** Human beings are mammals, a type of vertebrate. The evolutionary tree of life has many branches; the vertebrate line of descent is just one of them.

Human Beings Are Members of the Biosphere

All living things on Earth are part of the biosphere, a living network that spans the surface of the Earth into the atmosphere and down into the soil and seas. In one area, such as a forest or a pond, each organism belongs to a population[1] within an ecosystem. As discussed in the Ecology Focus on the next page, the various populations of an ecosystem interact with one another and with the physical environment.

The role a population plays in an ecosystem is very much dependent on how its members get their food. All organisms, including humans, require a supply of nutrients from the environment (Fig. 1.2). Nutrients supply humans with energy and also with the chemical building blocks they need to repair tissues, grow, and develop. In ecosystems, human beings are consumers; they take in preformed food. As such, they are dependent on the ability of plants to produce food. Human beings either eat plants directly or they feed on animals that have eaten plants.

Although humans can grow a large portion of their food and raise farm animals, they still depend on the environment for innumerable services. We dump millions of tons of waste material into natural ecosystems each year and if it were not for microorganisms that decompose it, waste would soon cover the entire surface of the Earth. The populations of natural ecosystems are also capable of breaking down and immobilizing pollutants, such as heavy metals and pesticides. Aside from supplying us with fish as a food source, freshwater ecosystems, such as rivers and lakes, provide us with drinking water and water to irrigate crops. The

Figure 1.2   Acquiring nutrient materials and energy.
a. A lion is a carnivorous consumer on the plains of Africa.
b. Humans are omnivorous consumers that feed often on plants and animals they raise in an area that was formerly an unaltered ecosystem.

water-holding capacity of forests prevents flooding, and the ability of forests and other ecosystems to retain soil prevents soil erosion. Most of our crops and prescription drugs were originally derived from plants that grew wild in an ecosystem. Some human populations around the globe still depend on wild animals as a food source. And we must not forget that almost everyone prefers to vacation in the natural beauty of an ecosystem.

Humans Threaten the Biosphere   The human population tends to modify existing ecosystems for its own purposes. Humans clear forests or grasslands in order to grow crops; later, they build houses on what was once farmland; and finally, they convert small towns into cities. Almost all natural ecosystems are altered by human activities, which also reduce biodiversity. The present **biodiversity** of our planet has been estimated to be as high as 15 million species, and so far, under 2 million have been identified and named. **Extinction** is the death of a species[2] or larger group of organisms. It is estimated that presently we are losing as many as 400 species per day due to human activities. Many biologists are alarmed about the present rate of extinction and believe it may eventually rival the rates of the five mass extinctions that have occurred during our planet's history. The dinosaurs became extinct during the last mass extinction, 65 million years ago.

One of the major bioethical issues of our time is preservation of ecosystems and biodiversity. If we adopt a conservation ethic that preserves the biosphere and biodiversity, we are helping to ensure the continued existence of our species.

Summary

As a summary to our discussion thus far, consider that aside from our cultural heritage, these characteristics of human beings are shared by all other living things:

1. Living things are organized; their organs are specialized for specific purposes.
2. Living things are homeostatic; they stay just about the same internally despite changes in the external environment.
3. Living things respond to stimuli; they react to internal and external changes.
4. Living things reproduce; they produce offspring that resemble themselves.
5. Living things grow and develop; during their lives they change, sometimes undergoing various stages from fertilization to death.
6. Living things are adapted; they have modifications that make them suited to a particular way of life.
7. Living things take materials and energy from the environment; they interact with other species in the biosphere.

[1]A population includes the members of the same species in a particular area.
[2]A species is a group of organisms that are anatomically similar and can interbreed.

Ecosystems

Ecologists (scientists who study the workings of the biosphere) have a saying that "everything is connected to everything else." Though it is not always apparent to us, humans are also connected to everything else in the natural world.

How Ecosystems Work

Let's examine the grassland ecosystem in Figure 1A to see that an ecosystem is characterized by energy flow and chemical cycling. **Producers** are organisms, such as plants, that are able to absorb solar energy and use it to carry on photosynthesis, the process that begins with inorganic nutrients (carbon dioxide and water) and ends with organic nutrients (e.g., sugar). Organic nutrients serve as food for producers and all the other populations in an ecosystem. This occurs because producers are the start of food chains in which one population feeds on another. Organisms use food as a source of chemical building blocks and energy.

Rabbits, mice, snakes, and hawks are **consumers.** Rabbits and mice feed directly on plant material and they serve as food for snakes. All of these animals are food for hawks.

In any case, you can trace the consumption of organic food from producers through all consumers. Therefore, it is possible to trace the path of chemicals and energy from one population to the next. Whenever food is used as an energy source by organisms, some of it is dispersed into the environment as heat.

Decomposers are microorganisms that break down organic matter consisting of wastes and dead organisms. Once the process of decomposition is finished, inorganic nutrients become available to producers once more. However, the energy originally available in organic nutrients has all been dispersed into the environment as heat. Therefore, chemicals cycle in ecosystems but energy flows out of ecosystems. And all living things are dependent on the continuous supply of solar energy.

How Humans Affect Ecosystems

The ecosystem we have just described is self-sustaining as long as solar energy is available. Humans affect ecosystems in a way that makes them unsustainable. Humans consume other resources than food. We use environmental sources of energy and materials to produce goods and for transportation purposes. Our "throwaway" society is characterized by a high output of waste materials that are often pollutants. **Pollution** is any alteration of the environment that is detrimental to wildlife and also to humans and their crops and farm animals. The gases given off when we burn fossil fuels (coal, oil, and gasoline) lead to the death of forests and lakes. Yet humans use forests as a source of wood and they use lakes as a source of fish. In this way, we see that everything *is* connected to everything else. And the damage we do to ecosystems will eventually be detrimental to ourselves, also.

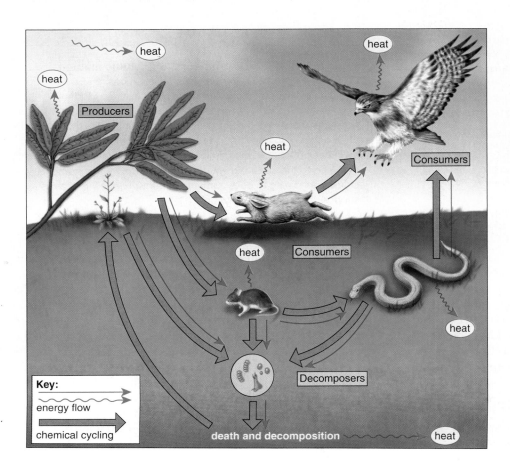

Figure 1A A simplified ecosystem.
The populations of an ecosystem are categorized as producers (produce food), consumers (consume food), and decomposers (break down wastes and organic matter to inorganic nutrients for producers). Solar energy is required to sustain an ecosystem because, while chemicals cycle as food passes from one population to the next, energy is given off as heat.

Key:
energy flow
chemical cycling

death and decomposition

1.2 The Process of Science

Science is a way of knowing about the natural world. Science aims to be objective rather than subjective, even though it is very difficult to make objective observations and to come to objective conclusions because we are often influenced by our own particular prejudices. Still, scientists strive for objective observations and conclusions. We should also keep in mind that scientific conclusions are subject to change whenever new findings so dictate. Quite often in science, new studies, which might utilize new techniques and equipment, tell us when previous conclusions need to be modified or changed entirely.

Scientific Theories in Biology

Science is not just a pile of facts. The ultimate goal of science is to understand the natural world in terms of **scientific theories,** concepts that tell us about the order and the patterns within the natural world; in other words, how the natural world is organized. For example, these are some of the basic theories of biology.

Theory	Concept
Cell	All organisms are composed of cells and new cells only come from pre-existing cells.
Homeostasis	The internal environment of an organism stays relatively constant.
Gene	Organisms contain coded information that dictates their form, function, and behavior.
Ecosystem	Populations of organisms interact with each other and the physical environment.
Evolution	All living things have a common ancestor, but each is adapted to a particular way of life.

Evolution is the unifying concept of biology because it makes sense of what we know about living things. For example, the theory of evolution enables scientists to understand the variety of living things, and the anatomy, physiology, and development of organisms—even their behavior. Because the theory of evolution has been supported by so many observations and experiments for over a hundred years, some biologists refer to the **principle** of evolution. This term is preferred terminology for theories that are generally accepted as valid by an overwhelming number of scientists.

The Scientific Method Has Steps

Unlike other types of information available to us, scientific information is acquired by a process known as the **scientific method.** The approach of individual scientists to their work is as varied as they themselves; still, for the sake of discussion, it is possible to speak of the scientific method as consisting of certain steps (Fig. 1.3).

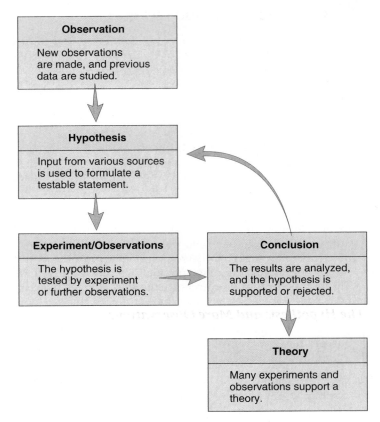

Figure 1.3   Flow diagram for the scientific method.
On the basis of new and/or previous observations, a scientist formulates a hypothesis. The hypothesis is tested by further observations and/or experiments, and new data either support or do not support the hypothesis. The return arrow indicates that a scientist often chooses to retest the same hypothesis or to test a related hypothesis. Conclusions from many different but related experiments may lead to the development of a scientific theory. For example, studies pertaining to development, anatomy, and fossil remains all support the theory of evolution.

After making initial observations, a scientist will, most likely, study any previous **data,** which are facts pertinent to the matter at hand. Imagination and creative thinking also help a scientist formulate a **hypothesis** that becomes the basis for more observation and/or experimentation. The new data help a scientist come to a **conclusion** that either supports or does not support the hypothesis. Because hypotheses are always subject to modification, they can never be proven true; however, they can be proven untrue. When the hypothesis is not supported by the data, it must be rejected; therefore, some think of the body of science as what is left after alternative hypotheses have been rejected.

Science is different from other ways of knowing by its use of the scientific method to examine a phenomenon. Any suggestions about the natural world that are not based on data gathered by employing the scientific method cannot be accepted as within the realm of science. Scientific theories are concepts based on a wide range of observations and experiments.

The Discovery of Lyme Disease

In order to examine the scientific method in more detail, we will relate how scientists discovered the cause of Lyme disease, a debilitating illness that affects the whole body.

Observation

When Allen C. Steere began his work on Lyme disease in 1975, a number of adults and children in the city of Lyme, Connecticut, had been mistakenly diagnosed as having rheumatoid arthritis. Steere knew that children rarely get rheumatoid arthritis, so this made him suspicious, and he began to make observations. He found that (1) most victims lived in heavily wooded areas, (2) the disease was not contagious—that is, whole groups of people did not come down with Lyme disease, (3) symptoms first appeared in the summer, and (4) several victims remembered a strange bull's-eye rash occurring several weeks before the onset of symptoms.

The Hypothesis and More Observations

Inductive reasoning occurs when you generalize from assorted facts. Steere used inductive reasoning—that is, he put the pieces together to formulate the hypothesis that Lyme disease was caused by a pathogen most likely transmitted by the bite of an insect (Fig. 1.4).

   Deductive reasoning helps scientists decide what further observations and experimentations they will make to test the hypothesis. Deductive reasoning utilizes an "if . . . then" statement: If Lyme disease is caused by the bite of a tick, then it should be possible to show that a tick carries the pathogen (disease-causing agent) and that the pathogen is in the blood of those who have the disease. With the tests that Steere used he was unable to find the presence of an infectious microbe in the blood of Lyme disease victims. Finally, in 1977, one victim saved the tick that had bitten him, and it was identified as *Ixodes dammini*, the deer tick. Then, Willy Burgdorfer, an authority on tick-borne diseases, was able to isolate a spirochete (spiral bacterium) from deer ticks, and he also found this microbe in the blood of Lyme disease victims. The new spirochete was named *Borrelia burgdorferi*, after Burgdorfer.

The Conclusion

The new data collected when Burgdorfer applied deductive reasoning supported the hypothesis and allowed scientists to conclude that Lyme disease is caused by the bacterium *Borrelia burgdorferi* transmitted by the bite of the deer tick.

Even though the scientific method is quite variable, it is possible to point out certain steps that characterize it: making observations, formulating a hypothesis, testing it, and coming to a conclusion.

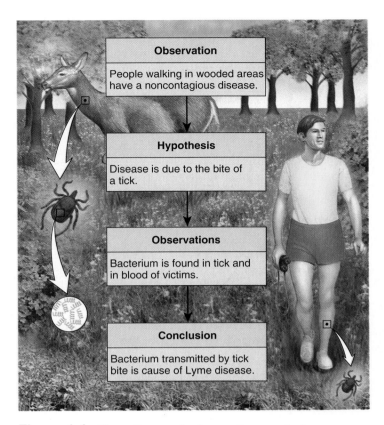

Figure 1.4   Flow diagram for Lyme disease study.
These steps allowed scientists to conclude that Lyme disease is caused by a bacterium transmitted by a tick.

Where Scientific Information Is Found

It is customary to report findings in a scientific journal so that the design and the results of the experiment are available to all. When you are looking for scientific information about a topic you will want to be sure to consult one of the many scientific magazines found online, in your school, or in your town library. For example, data about tick-borne diseases are often reported in the journal *Clinical Microbiology Review*. For a study to be accepted as scientific, it is necessary to give details on how the study was conducted because other scientists using the same procedures must also get the same results. Otherwise, the hypothesis is no longer supported, and the conclusion may be incorrect.

   The authors of a report may suggest or the reader may think of other types of experiments that could be done to expand the study. In our example, it was later found that the bull's-eye rash often observed in persons with Lyme disease is due to the presence of the causative spirochete.

Observations and the results of experiments are published in a journal, where they can be examined. These results are expected to be repeatable—that is, they will be obtained by anyone following the same procedure.

A Controlled Laboratory Study

When researchers are doing a study, they often perform an **experiment,** a series of procedures performed to test a hypothesis. When experiments are done in a laboratory, all conditions can be kept constant except for the **experimental variable,** which is deliberately changed. A **control group** is not exposed to the experimental variable but one or more **test groups** are exposed to the experimental variable. If by chance the control group shows the same results as a test group, the experimenter knows the results are invalid. Let us take an example.

The Experiment

In the experiment under discussion, the experimental variable is sweetener S. On the basis of available information, researchers formulated a hypothesis that sweetener S is a safe food additive, even if the diet is 1/3 sweetener S. In other words, 2/3 of the diet contains no sweetener S and 1/3 is nothing but sweetener S.

HYPOTHESIS: Sweetener S is a safe food additive.

To test the hypothesis, the scientists decide on the following experimental design. They intend to make use of a test group and a control group. The test group and the control group are treated similarly except that the control group is not exposed to sweetener S.

Test groups: Diet contains 1/3 sweetener S.

Control group: Diet contains no sweetener S.

To help ensure that the test groups and the control group are genetically similar, the researchers place a large number of randomly chosen inbred mice into the various groups. If any of the mice are genetically different, it is hoped that random selection has distributed them evenly among the two groups. The researchers also make sure that conditions, such as availability of water, cage setup, and temperature of the surroundings, are constant for both groups. The food for each group is exactly the same except for the amount of sweetener S, the experimental variable.

After several weeks, both groups of mice are examined for bladder cancer. Let's suppose that the majority of the mice in the test group are found to have bladder cancer, while none in the control group have bladder cancer (Fig. 1.5).

The results of this experiment do not support the hypothesis that sweetener S is a safe food additive.

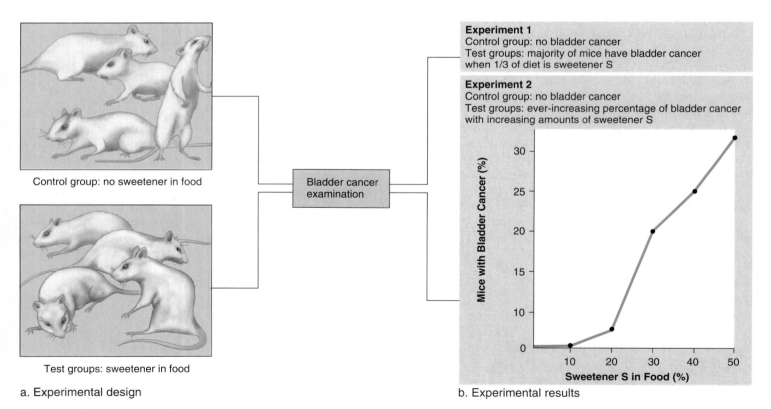

Control group: no sweetener in food

Test groups: sweetener in food

a. Experimental design

Bladder cancer examination

Experiment 1
Control group: no bladder cancer
Test groups: majority of mice have bladder cancer when 1/3 of diet is sweetener S

Experiment 2
Control group: no bladder cancer
Test groups: ever-increasing percentage of bladder cancer with increasing amounts of sweetener S

(Graph: y-axis "Mice with Bladder Cancer (%)" from 0 to 30; x-axis "Sweetener S in Food (%)" from 10 to 50.)

b. Experimental results

Figure 1.5   **A controlled laboratory experiment.**
For both experiment 1 and experiment 2, genetically similar mice are randomly divided into a control group and test group(s) that contain 100 mice each. **a.** The test groups are exposed to sweetener S but the control group is not subjected to sweetener S in their food. Otherwise, the conditions for all groups are the same. At the end of the experiment, all mice are examined for bladder cancer. **b.** The results of experiment 1 and experiment 2, which are described in the text, are shown on the far right.

CONCLUSION: The hypothesis is not supported. Sweetener S is not a safe food additive when the diet is 1/3 sweetener S.

These results cause the scientists to believe that sweetener S may be less harmful if the diet contains a lesser amount. So, they decide to do another experiment.

The Next Experiment

After analyzing the results of the first experiment, the researchers decide to hypothesize that sweetener S is safe if the diet contains a limited amount of sweetener S. They think it may be possible to determine the amount of sweetener S that is safe in the diet.

HYPOTHESIS: Sweetener S is a safe food additive if the diet contains a limited amount.

In this second study, the researchers feed sweetener S to test groups of mice at ever-decreasing amounts of sweetener S. A control group received no sweetener S.

Test groups: The diet ranges from 1/3 to 1/10 sweetener S.

After keeping careful records for several weeks, the researchers present their data in the form of a graph. The mice in the control group have no bladder cancer. But the incidence of bladder cancer among the experimental groups increases sharply when a diet is more than 1/10 sweetener S (Fig. 1.5b). The researchers statistically analyze their data to determine if the differences in the number of cases of bladder cancer among the various experimental groups are significant and not due to simple chance. The researchers conclude that they can now make a recommendation concerning the intake of sweetener S. They suggest that an intake of sweetener S up to 1/10 of the diet is relatively safe, but thereafter you would expect to see an ever-greater incidence of bladder cancer.

CONCLUSION: The hypothesis is supported. Sweetener S is safe if the diet contains a limited amount.

It's possible that data gathered by doing experiments in mice would not be the same if the experiment had been done using humans. However, when it is not possible to perform a similar experiment in humans, it is possible, tentatively, to use the results in laboratory animals.

Some biological studies are conducted in the field, and some are done in the laboratory. In an experiment, conditions are kept constant, except for the experimental variable. The experiment tests the hypothesis, which is accepted or rejected based on the results.

1.3 Science and Social Responsibility

Many scientists work in the field or laboratory collecting data and coming to conclusions that sometimes seem remote from our everyday lives. Other scientists are interested in using the findings of past and present scientists to produce a product or develop a technique that does affect our lives. The application of scientific knowledge for a practical purpose is called **technology.** For example, virology, the study of viruses and molecular chemistry, led to the discovery of new drugs that extend the life span of people who have AIDS. And cell biology research discovers the causes of cancer and has allowed physicians to develop various cancer treatments.

Most technologies have benefits but also drawbacks. Research has led to modern agricultural practices that are helping to feed the burgeoning world population. However, the use of nitrogen fertilizers leads to water pollution, and the use of pesticides, as you may know, kills not only pests but also other types of organisms. The book *Silent Spring* was written to make the public aware of the harmful environmental effects of pesticide use.

Who should decide how, and even whether, a technology should be put to use? Making value judgments is not a part of science. Ethical and moral decisions must be made by all people. Therefore, the responsibility for how to use the fruits of science must reside with people from all walks of life, not with scientists alone. Scientists should provide the public with as much information as possible, but all citizens, including scientists, should make decisions about the use of technologies.

Presently, we need to decide if we want to stop producing bioengineered organisms, which could possibly be harmful to the environment. Also, through gene therapy, we are developing the ability to cure diseases and to alter the genes of our offspring. Perhaps one day we might even be able to clone ourselves. Should we do these things? So far, as a society, we continue to believe that life is precious, and therefore we have passed laws against doing research with fetal tissues or using fetal tissues to cure human ills. Even if the procedure is perfected, we may also continue to rule against human cloning. The bioethical issue for this chapter asks if it is ethical, because of possible complications, to use indefinitely frozen sperm to fertilize an egg.

Technology provides products and develops techniques that sometimes have drawbacks. We all must decide if the benefits of any particular product or procedure are worth the possible disadvantages.

Bioethical Focus

Fertilization with 20-Year-Old Sperm

People in today's society generally find in vitro fertilization (fertilization in laboratory glassware) an acceptable way for couples to reproduce (Fig 1B). Recently, however, in vitro fertilization was done using sperm that had been frozen for over 20 years! This sparked a new debate about the ethics of assisted reproductive technologies and the various dilemmas surrounding the practice. In this particular instance, a young man had a supply of his sperm frozen because treatment for testicular cancer would leave him sterile. His cancer was successfully treated, and 20 years later, he and his new wife desired to have children. They had the 20-year-old sperm thawed and used to fertilize eggs that were placed in his wife's uterus. After multiple attempts, the wife conceived, and gave birth to a healthy baby boy. While the couple has remained anonymous, they wanted the case publicized to encourage future cancer patients to remain hopeful about the future.

The case drew media attention because the sperm had remained frozen for such a long time. In the past, sperm, eggs, and embryos, stored at extremely low temperatures (called cryopreservation), have been used only within short amounts of time. A recent study performed at the Mayo Clinic in Minnesota tells us that no difference was found between in vitro fertilization success rates performed with fresh or frozen sperm. However, we know that repeated freezing and thawing of sperm can damage DNA and, therefore, it seems that the DNA of sperm stored for a long period could suffer damage. Not in this instance, however, because the baby boy born to this couple was normal. "This case provides evidence that long-term freezing can successfully preserve sperm quality and fertility," stated Greg Horne, a British embryologist who worked with the couple, "Even after 21 years of storage, the percentage of motile sperm after thawing was high."

While, in general, the use of frozen sperm to preserve the reproductive ability of men undergoing cancer treatment is considered ethical, questions still remain about the particulars. For example, should men who are very old or sick and may not live long enough to see a child grow be allowed to reproduce by using sperm frozen in the past? Suppose there is a risk of DNA damage and, therefore, the birth of a child with a birth defect or other genetic disorders.

Long-term storage of sperm even makes it possible for a dead man to father a child. A British judge recently denied a widow access to her late husband's frozen sperm, because he said the man had not given permission before his death. The American Society for Reproductive Medicine disagreed, insisting that access to the sperm in this case was acceptable because "a spousal relationship existed when the sperm were

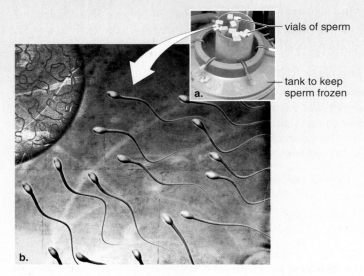

Figure 1B **Use of frozen sperm.**
a. Sperm can be preserved by freezing them. **b.** Thawed sperm can be used to fertilize an egg.

preserved." Knowing that access could be a problem, a man could state in his will that a widow, or even a friend, should be given access to his sperm—for how long? Should there be a time limit—if so, what should the time limit be? Would it be acceptable to freeze the sperm of famous actors, visionary leaders, and great thinkers, for use by anyone at any time in the future? Would the child belong to the dead man; be legally his and have the right of inheritance?

Decide Your Opinion

1. In the near future, it will be possible to preserve eggs in the same manner as sperm. Would you find the postmortem use of these eggs by a widower and a surrogate mother to be unethical? Why or why not?
2. Do you think that the use of frozen sperm to preserve a family line, even after the death of the last male family member, is ethical? What would you think if this was done more than 20 or 30 years after the death of this male?
3. Should geniuses be allowed to freeze their sperm for use by anyone at any time in the future? What restrictions should be imposed?
4. Do you believe that it is cruel to deny a child born of sperm from a deceased father the right to meet and know his father? Why or why not?

Summarizing the Concepts

1.1 Biologically Speaking
Human beings, like other living things, are highly organized. Cells form tissues, which form organs that function in organ systems. The organ systems maintain homeostasis, the relative constancy of the internal environment. Human beings come into existence through reproduction, growth, and development.

Unlike other living things, human beings have a cultural heritage that sometimes hinders the realization that they are the product of an evolutionary process. Human beings are vertebrates closely related to the apes. Human beings are also a part of the biosphere, where populations interact with the physical environment and with one another. Human activities threaten the existence of ecosystems to their own detriment. Biodiversity is now being reduced at a rapid rate.

1.2 The Process of Science
When studying the world of living things, biologists, like other scientists, use the scientific method, which consists of these steps: making an observation, formulating a hypothesis, carrying out an experiment or simply making further observations, and coming to a conclusion. The scientific method results in scientific theories, concepts that tell us how the natural world works.

1.3 Science and Social Responsibility
It is the responsibility of all to make ethical and moral decisions about how best to use the results of scientific investigations.

Studying the Concepts

1. Name seven characteristics of human beings, and discuss each one. 2–4
2. What is homeostasis, and how is it maintained? Choose one organ system, and tell how it helps maintain homeostasis. 2
3. Give evidence that human beings are related to all other living things. 2–3
4. What are the four kingdoms in the domain Eukarya, and which one includes humans? 2–3
5. Human beings depend on what services performed by plants? 4
6. Discuss the importance of a scientific theory, and name several theories that are basic to understanding biological principles. 6
7. Name the steps of the scientific method, and discuss each one. 6–7
8. How do you recognize a control group, and what is its purpose in an experiment? 8–9
9. What is our social responsibility, in regard to scientific findings? 9

Thinking Critically About the Concepts

Refer to the opening vignette on page 1, and then answer these questions.

1. The early developmental stages of humans resemble those of other animals, but the later stages are distinctly human. Explain.
2. All animals that live on land share some of the same adaptations. What are some of these adaptations?
3. Describe some ways humans are specifically adapted to a terrestrial environment.
4. What are some ways that humans are different from all other organisms on planet Earth?

Testing Your Knowledge of the Concepts

Choose the best answer for each question.
In questions 1–4, match each description with a human characteristic in the key.

Key:
a. Human beings are organized.
b. Human beings reproduce and grow.
c. Human beings have a cultural heritage.
d. Human beings are the product of an evolutionary process.
e. Human beings are a part of an ecosystem.

1. Humans are related to all other living things.
2. The human population encroaches on natural habitats.
3. Like cells form tissues in the human body.
4. We learn how to behave from our elders.
5. Which of these associations is mismatched?
   a. Kingdom Protista—small, flagellated plants and animals
   b. Kingdom Fungi—molds and mushrooms
   c. Kingdom Plantae—woody and nonwoody flowering plants
   d. Kingdom Animalia—fishes, reptiles, birds, humans
6. The level of organization that includes cells of the same structure and function would be a(n)
   a. organ.   c. organ system.
   b. tissue.   d. organism.
7. The level of organization most responsible for the maintenance of homeostasis is the
   a. cellular level.
   b. organ level.
   c. organ system level.
   d. tissue level.
8. Human beings differ from other living things in
   a. having a cultural heritage.
   b. maintaining homeostasis.
   c. being separate from nature.
   d. being products of evolution.
9. Which best describes the evolutionary relationship between humans and apes?
   a. Humans evolved from apes.
   b. Humans and chimpanzees evolved from apes.
   c. Humans and apes evolved from a common apelike ancestor.
   d. Chimpanzees evolved from humans.
10. The kingdom that contains humans is the kingdom
   a. Animalia.   c. Plantae.
   b. Fungi.   d. Protista.

11. The level of organization that includes all the populations in a given area along with the physical environment would be a(n)
    a. community.
    b. ecosystem.
    c. biosphere.
    d. tribe.

12. Energy is brought into ecosystems by which of the following?
    a. fungi and other decomposers
    b. cows and other animals that graze on grass
    c. meat-eating animals
    d. organisms that photosynthesize, such as plants

13. An example of chemical cycling occurs when
    a. plants absorb solar energy and make their own food.
    b. energy flows through an ecosystem and becomes heat.
    c. hawks soar and nest in trees.
    d. death and decay make inorganic nutrients available to plants.

14. A principle differs from a theory in that it
    a. has not yet been tested by experimentation.
    b. is generally accepted as valid by most scientists.
    c. is supported by experiments and observations.
    d. has been tested by experimentation, but the results were not conclusive.

15. Science always studies a phenomenon that
    a. has previously been published.
    b. lends itself to experimentation.
    c. is observable with the eye or with instruments.
    d. fits in with an already existing theory.
    e. Both b and c are correct.

In questions 16–18, match the explanation with a theory in the key.

Key:

    a. homeostasis   c. evolution
    b. cell   d. gene

16. All living things share a common ancestor.

17. The internal environment remains relatively stable.

18. Organisms contain coded information that dictates form and function.

In questions 19–23, match each description with a step in the process of science from the key.

Key:

    a. conclusion
    b. experiment
    c. hypothesis
    d. observation
    e. theory

19. Rejection or acceptance of a hypothesis.

20. Statement to be tested.

21. Procedure designed to test a hypothesis.

22. Hypothesis supported by many studies.

23. Fact that may lead to the development of a hypothesis.

Understanding Key Terms

biodiversity 4
biology 2
biosphere 2
cell 2
conclusion 6
consumer 5
control group 8
culture 2
data 6
decomposer 5
domain 2
ecologist 5
evolution 2
experiment 8
experimental variable 8
extinction 4

homeostasis 2
hypothesis 6
kingdom 2
organ 2
pollution 5
principle 6
producer 5
reproduce 2
science 6
scientific method 6
scientific theory 6
technology 9
test group 8
tissue 2
vertebrate 2

Match the key terms to these definitions.

a. _____ Zone of air, land, and water at the surface of the Earth in which living organisms are found.

b. _Cell_ Smallest unit of a human being and all living things.

c. _____ Concept supported by a broad range of observations, experiments, and conclusions.

d. _____ An internal environment that normally varies only within certain limits.

e. _Domain_ The most inclusive category used to classify organisms.

Online Learning Center

www.mhhe.com/maderhuman9

The Online Learning Center provides a wealth of information fully organized and integrated by chapter. You will find practice quizzes, interactive activities, labeling exercises, flashcards, and much more that will complement your learning and understanding of human biology.

Looking at Both Sides

Each day, the Internet, media, and other people present you with opposing viewpoints on a wide range of subjects. Your ability to develop an informed opinion on an issue, and talk to others about it, is extremely important.

To expand and enhance your knowledge of a highly relevant bioethical issue, visit the "Student Edition" of the Online Learning Center. Under "Course-Wide Content," select "Looking at Both Sides." Once there, you will be asked to complete activities that will increase your understanding of a current bioethical issue related to this chapter and allow you to defend your opinion.

2 Chemistry of Life 13

3 Cell Structure and Function 35

4 Organization and Regulation of Body Systems 55

The human body is composed of cells, the smallest units of life. An understanding of cell structure, physiology, and biochemistry serves as a foundation for understanding how the human body functions.

In Part I, we first discuss the principles of inorganic and organic chemistry, and then undertake a study of cell structure. The human cell is bounded by a membrane and contains organelles, many of which are also membranous. A plasma membrane regulates the entrance and exit of molecules into the cell, and the membrane also helps cellular organelles carry out their functions.

The many cells of the body are specialized into tissues that are found within the organs of the various systems of the body. Normal chemical conditions exist in each cell because all body systems help maintain homeostasis, a dynamic equilibrium of the internal environment, which consists of blood and tissue fluid.

C H A P T E R

2

Chemistry of Life

C H A P T E R C O N C E P T S

2.1 Basic Chemistry
- How is an atom organized? 14
- What are radioactive isotopes, and how can they be used for the biological benefit of humans? 15
- What are the two basic types of bondings between atoms? 16–17

2.2 Water and Living Things
- What characteristics of water help support life? 18–19
- How does the hydrogen ion concentration change among water, acids, and bases? 20

2.3 Molecules of Life
- What are the four classes of molecules unique to cells? 22
- What individual subunits make up carbohydrates, fats, proteins, and nucleic acids? 22

2.4 Carbohydrates
- What is a usual function of carbohydrates in organisms? 22
- What are some examples of different types of carbohydrates? 22–23

2.5 Lipids
- What is the function of fats and oils, and of what are they composed? 24
- What are the uses of steroids in the body? 25

2.6 Proteins
- What are the major functions of proteins in organisms? 26
- How do proteins illustrate the principle that the shape of a molecule influences its function? 26

2.7 Nucleic Acids
- What is the function of DNA in cells? 29
- How is the function of RNA related to the function of DNA? 29
- What does it mean to say that DNA is a double helix? 29–30

Joel just talked to his doctor about the results of his annual physical exam, and he has reason to be concerned. The doctor told him that the level of cholesterol, a type of lipid molecule, in his blood was abnormally high.

Cholesterol is a necessary component of the plasma membrane, the boundary of cells. It is used to produce the sex hormones and also bile, which helps us break down fats in our digestive system. However, excess cholesterol in the blood gives one an increased risk of stroke or heart attack.

In order to bring Joel's cholesterol level down, his doctor may recommend dietary changes. However, dietary cholesterol is only a small portion of the total cholesterol level, because most cholesterol is made in the body. So Joel's doctor may also prescribe a type of drug called a statin. Statin drugs are chemicals that interfere with the body's cholesterol production.

Like every living thing, Joel is made up of a complex mixture of chemicals, each of which must be present in just the right amount. Physicians are acutely aware that the chemicals making up our bodies need to be in balance if we are to remain healthy. An imbalance in the amount of any chemical, such as cholesterol, can lead to serious consequences.

2.1 Basic Chemistry

All matter, be it ourselves or anything we touch, is composed of basic substances called **elements**. It's quite remarkable

that there are only 92 naturally occurring elements. It is even more surprising that over 90% of the human body is composed of just four elements: carbon, nitrogen, oxygen, and hydrogen.

Every element has a name and a symbol; for example, carbon has been assigned the atomic symbol C (Fig. 2.1a). Some of the symbols we use for elements are derived from Latin. For example, the symbol for sodium is Na because *natrium* in Latin means sodium.

Atoms

An **atom** is the smallest unit of an element that still retains the chemical and physical properties of the element. While it is possible to split an atom by physical means, an atom is the smallest unit to enter into chemical reactions. For our purposes, it is satisfactory to think of each atom as having a central nucleus and pathways about the nucleus called shells. The subatomic particles called **protons** and **neutrons** are located in the nucleus, and **electrons** orbit about the nucleus in the shells (Fig. 2.1b). Most of an atom is empty space. If we could draw an atom the size of a football stadium, the nucleus would be like a gumball in the center of the field, and the electrons would be tiny specks whirling about in the upper stands.

Protons carry a positive (+) charge, and electrons have a negative (−) charge. The **atomic number** of an atom tells you how many protons, and therefore how many electrons, an atom has when it is electrically neutral. For example, the atomic number of carbon is six; therefore, when carbon is neutral, it has six protons and six electrons. How many electrons are there in each shell of an atom? The inner shell has the lowest energy level and can hold only two electrons; after that, each shell for the atoms noted in Figure 2.1a can hold up to eight electrons. Using this information, calculation determines that carbon has two shells and the outer shell has four electrons. As we shall see, an atom is most stable when the outer shell has eight electrons. (Hydrogen, with only one shell, is an exception to this statement. Atoms with only one shell are stable when this shell contains two electrons.)

The subatomic particles are so light that their weight is indicated by special designations called atomic mass units. Protons and neutrons each have a weight of one atomic mass unit, and electrons have almost no mass. Therefore, the **atomic weight** of an atom generally tells you the number of protons plus the number of neutrons. How could you calculate that carbon (C) has six neutrons? Carbon's atomic weight is 12, and you know from its atomic number that it has six protons. Therefore, carbon has six neutrons (Fig. 2.1b).

As shown in Figure 2.1b, the atomic number of an atom is often written as a subscript to the lower left of the atomic symbol. The atomic weight is often written as a superscript to the upper left of the atomic symbol. Therefore, carbon can be designated in this way: $^{12}_{6}C$

Common Elements in Living Things				
Element	Atomic Symbol	Atomic Number	Atomic Weight	Comment
hydrogen	H	1	1	These
carbon	C	6	12	elements
nitrogen	N	7	14	make up
oxygen	O	8	16	most
phosphorus	P	15	31	biological
sulfur	S	16	32	molecules.
sodium	Na	11	23	These
magnesium	Mg	12	24	elements
chlorine	Cl	17	35	occur mainly
potassium	K	19	39	as dissolved
calcium	Ca	20	40	salts.

a.

p = protons
n = neutrons
● = electrons

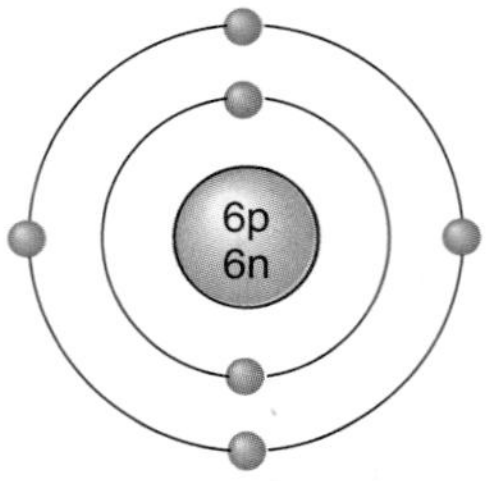

Carbon
$^{12}_{6}C$

b.

Figure 2.1   Elements and atoms.

a. The atomic symbol, atomic number, and atomic weight are given for the common elements in living things. The atomic symbol for carbon is C, the atomic number is 6, and the atomic weight is 12. **b.** An atom contains the subatomic particles called protons (p) and neutrons (n) in the nucleus (colored pink) and electrons (colored blue) in shells about the nucleus.

Isotopes

Isotopes of the same type of atom differ in the number of neutrons and, therefore, the weight. For example, the element carbon has three naturally occurring isotopes:

$$^{12}_{6}C \qquad ^{13}_{6}C \qquad ^{14}_{6}C^{*}$$

*radioactive

Carbon 12 has six neutrons, carbon 13 has seven neutrons, and carbon 14 has eight neutrons. Unlike the other two isotopes of carbon, carbon 14 is unstable and breaks down over time. As carbon 14 decays, it releases various types of energy in the form of rays and subatomic particles, and therefore it is a **radioactive isotope.** The radiation given off by radioactive isotopes can be detected in various ways. You may be familiar with the use of a Geiger counter to detect radiation.

Low Levels of Radiation

The importance of chemistry to biology and medicine is nowhere more evident than in the many uses of radioactive isotopes. A radioactive isotope behaves the same as do the stable isotopes of an element. This means that you can put a small amount of radioactive isotope in a sample and it becomes a **tracer,** by which to detect molecular changes.

Specific tracers are used in imaging the body's organs and tissues. For example, after a patient drinks a solution containing a minute amount of ^{131}I (iodine 131), it becomes concentrated in the thyroid—the only organ to take it up to make the hormone thyroxine. A subsequent image of the thyroid indicates whether it is healthy in structure and function (Fig. 2.2). Positron-emission tomography (PET) is a way to determine the comparative activity of tissues. Radioactively labeled glucose, which emits a subatomic particle known as a positron, can be injected into the body. The radiation given off is detected by sensors and analyzed by a computer. The result is a color image that shows which tissues took up glucose and are metabolically active (Fig. 2.3). A PET scan of the brain can help diagnose a brain tumor, Alzheimer disease, epilepsy, or whether a stroke has occurred.

High Levels of Radiation

Radioactive substances in the environment can harm cells, damage DNA, and cause cancer. The release of radioactive particles following a nuclear power plant accident can have far-reaching and long-lasting effects on human health. The harmful effects of radiation can also be put to good use, however. Radiation from radioactive isotopes has been used for many years to sterilize medical and dental products. Now the possibility exists that it can be used to sterilize the U.S. mail to free it of possible pathogens, such as anthrax spores.

The ability of radiation to kill cells is often applied to cancer cells. Radioisotopes can be introduced into the body in a way that allows radiation to destroy only cancer cells, with little risk to the rest of the body.

An atom has an atomic symbol, atomic number (number of protons), and atomic weight (protons plus neutrons). Isotopes have the same atomic number but differ in the number of neutrons and the weight. Radioactive isotopes have the potential to do harm, but also have many beneficial uses.

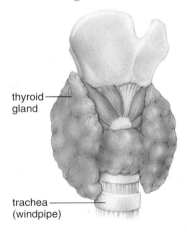
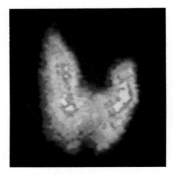

thyroid gland

trachea (windpipe)

Figure 2.2 **Use of radiation to aid a diagnosis.**
After the administration of radioactive iodine, a scan reveals pathology because a portion of the thyroid is missing.

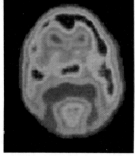

Figure 2.3 **Use of radiation to study the brain.**
After the administration of radioactively labeled glucose, a PET scan reveals which portions of the brain are most active.

Molecules and Compounds

Atoms often bond with one another to form a chemical unit called a **molecule.** A molecule can contain atoms of the same kind, as when an oxygen atom joins with another oxygen atom to form oxygen gas. Or the atoms can be different, as when an oxygen atom joins with two hydrogen atoms to form water. When the atoms are different, a **compound** is present.

Two types of bonds join atoms: the ionic bond and the covalent bond.

Ionic Bonding

Recall that atoms with more than one shell are most stable when the outer shell contains eight electrons. During an ionic reaction, atoms give up or take on an electron(s) in order to achieve a stable outer shell.

Figure 2.4 depicts a reaction between a sodium (Na) atom and a chlorine (Cl) atom. Sodium, with one electron in the outer shell, reacts with a single chlorine atom. Why? Because once the reaction is finished and sodium loses one electron to chlorine, its outer shell will have eight electrons. Similarly, a chlorine atom, which has seven electrons already, needs only to acquire one more electron to have a stable outer shell.

Ions are particles that carry either a positive (+) or negative (−) charge. When the reaction between sodium and chlorine is finished, the sodium ion carries a positive charge because it now has one more proton than electrons, and the chloride ion carries a negative charge because it now has one less proton than electrons:

Sodium Ion	Chloride Ion
11 protons (+)	17 protons (+)
10 electrons (−)	18 electrons (−)
One (+) charge	One (−) charge

The attraction between oppositely charged sodium ions and chloride ions forms an **ionic bond.** The resulting compound, sodium chloride, is table salt, which we use to enliven the taste of foods.

In contrast to sodium, why would calcium, with two electrons in the outer shell, react with two chlorine atoms? Because, whereas calcium needs to lose two electrons, each chlorine, with seven electrons already, requires only one more electron to have a stable outer shell. The resulting salt ($CaCl_2$) is called calcium chloride.

The balance of various ions in the body is important to our health. Too much sodium in the blood can contribute to high blood pressure; not enough calcium leads to rickets (a bowing of the legs) in children; too much or too little potassium results in heartbeat irregularities. Bicarbonate, hydrogen, and hydroxide ions are all involved in maintaining the acid-base balance of the body (see page 21).

An atom becomes an ion when it gains or loses one or more electrons. An ionic bond is the attraction between oppositely charged ions.

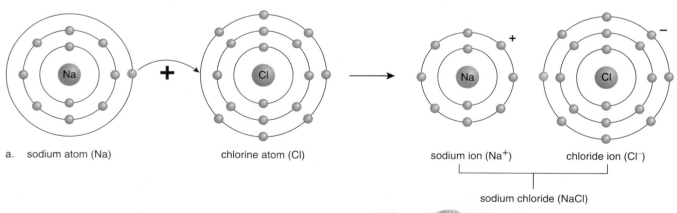

a.   sodium atom (Na)   chlorine atom (Cl)   sodium ion (Na⁺)   chloride ion (Cl⁻)

sodium chloride (NaCl)

Figure 2.4   Ionic bonding.

a. During the formation of sodium chloride, an electron is transferred from the sodium atom to the chlorine atom. At the completion of the reaction, each atom has eight electrons in the outer shell, but each also carries a charge as shown. **b.** In a sodium chloride crystal, ionic bonding between Na⁺ and Cl⁻ causes the ions to form a three-dimensional lattice configuration in which each sodium ion is surrounded by six chloride ions, and each chloride ion is surrounded by six sodium ions.

b. 1 mm

Covalent Bonding

Atoms share electrons in **covalent bonds.** The overlapping outermost shells in Figure 2.5 indicate that the atoms are sharing electrons. Just as two hands participate in a handshake, each atom contributes one electron to the pair that is shared. These electrons spend part of their time in the outer shell of each atom; therefore, they are counted as belonging to both bonded atoms.

Covalent bonds can be represented in a number of ways. In contrast to the diagrams in Figure 2.5, structural formulas use straight lines to show the covalent bonds between the atoms. Each line represents a pair of shared electrons. Molecular formulas indicate only the number of each type of atom making up a molecule. A comparison follows:

Structural formula: Cl—Cl

Molecular formula: Cl_2

Double and Triple Bonds Besides a single bond, in which atoms share only a pair of electrons, a double or a triple bond can form. In a double bond, atoms share two pairs of electrons, and in a triple bond, atoms share three pairs of

electrons between them. For example, in Figure 2.5, each nitrogen atom (N) requires three electrons to achieve a total of eight electrons in the outer shell. Notice that six electrons are placed in the outer overlapping shells in the diagram and that three straight lines are in the structural formula for nitrogen gas (N_2).

What would be the structural and molecular formulas for carbon dioxide? Carbon, with four electrons in the outer shell, requires four more electrons to complete its outer shell. Each oxygen, with six electrons in the outer shell, needs only two electrons to complete its outer shell. Therefore, carbon shares two pairs of electrons with each oxygen atom, and the formulas are as follows:

Structural formula: O=C=O

Molecular formula: CO_2

A covalent bond arises when atoms share a pair of electrons. Double and triple covalent bonds are also possible.

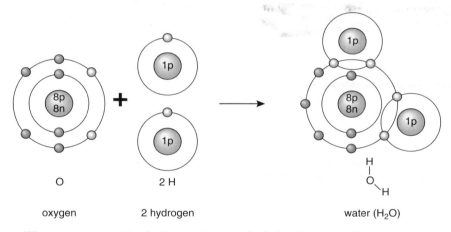

a. When an oxygen and two hydrogen atoms covalently bond, water results.

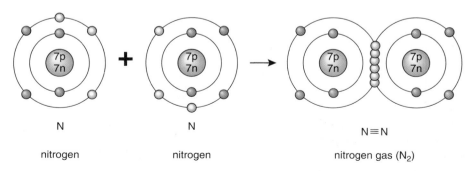

b. When two nitrogen atoms covalently bond, nitrogen gas results.

Figure 2.5 **Covalent bonding.**
An atom can fill its outer shell by sharing electrons. To determine this, it is necessary to count the shared electrons as belonging to both bonded atoms. Hydrogen is most stable with two electrons in the outer shell; oxygen and nitrogen are most stable with eight electrons in the outer shell. Therefore, the molecular formula for water is (**a**) H_2O and for nitrogen gas it is (**b**) N_2.

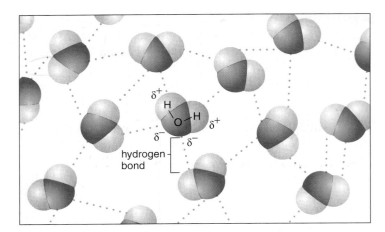

Figure 2.6   Hydrogen bonding between water molecules.
The polarity of the water molecules allows hydrogen bonds (dotted lines) to form between the molecules.

2.2 Water and Living Things

Water is the most abundant molecule in living organisms, usually making up about 60–70% of the total body weight. Further, the physical and chemical properties of water make life as we know it possible.

In water, the electrons spend more time circling the oxygen (O) atom than the hydrogens because oxygen, the larger atom, has a greater ability to attract electrons than do the smaller hydrogen (H) atoms. Because the negatively charged electrons are closer to the oxygen atom, the oxygen atom becomes slightly negative and the hydrogens, in turn, are slightly positive. Therefore, water is a **polar** molecule; the oxygen end of the molecule has a slight negative charge (δ^-), and the hydrogen end has a slight positive charge (δ^+):

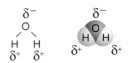

The diagram on the left shows the structural formula of water, and the one on the right is called a space-filling model.

Hydrogen Bonds

A **hydrogen bond** occurs whenever a covalently bonded hydrogen is slightly positive and attracted to a negatively charged atom some distance away. A hydrogen bond is represented by a dotted line because it is relatively weak and can be broken rather easily.

In Figure 2.6, you can see that each hydrogen atom, being slightly positive, bonds to the slightly negative oxygen atom of another water molecule.

Properties of Water

Because of their polarity and hydrogen bonding, water molecules are cohesive, meaning that they cling together. Polarity and hydrogen bonding cause water to have many characteristics beneficial to life.

1. Water is a liquid at room temperature. Therefore, we are able to drink it, cook with it, and bathe in it.

Compounds with a low molecular weight are usually gases at room temperature. For example, oxygen (O_2), with a molecular weight of 32, is a gas, but water, with a molecular weight of 18, is a liquid. The hydrogen bonding between water molecules keeps water a liquid and not a gas at room temperature. Water does not boil and become a gas until 100°C, one of the reference points for the Celsius temperature scale (see inside back cover). Without hydrogen bonding between water molecules, our body fluids—and indeed our bodies—would be gaseous!

2. The temperature of liquid water rises and falls slowly, preventing sudden or drastic changes.

The many hydrogen bonds that link water molecules cause water to absorb a great deal of heat before it boils (Fig. 2.7a). A **calorie** of heat energy raises the temperature of one gram of water 1°C. This is about twice the amount of heat required for other covalently bonded liquids. On the other hand, water holds heat, and its temperature falls slowly. Therefore, water protects us and other organisms from rapid temperature changes and helps us maintain our normal internal temperature. This property also allows great bodies of water, such as oceans, to maintain a relatively constant temperature. Water is a good temperature buffer.

3. Water has a high heat of vaporization, keeping the body from overheating.

It takes a large amount of heat to change water to steam (Fig. 2.7a). (Converting one gram of the hottest water to steam requires an input of 540 calories of heat energy.) This property of water helps moderate the Earth's temperature so that life can continue to exist. Also, in a hot environment, most mammals sweat and the body cools as body heat is used to evaporate sweat, which is mostly liquid water (Fig. 2.7b).

4. Frozen water is less dense than liquid water, so that ice floats on water.

As water cools, the molecules come closer together. They are densest at 4°C, but they are still moving about. At temperatures below 4°C, there is only vibrational movement, and hydrogen bonding becomes more rigid, but also more open. This makes ice less dense. Bodies of water always freeze from the top down, making skate sailing possible (Fig. 2.7c). When a body of water freezes on the surface, the ice acts as an insulator to prevent the water below it from

a.   b.   c.

Figure 2.7 Characteristics of water.

a. Water boils at 100°C. If it boiled and was a gas at a lower temperature, life could not exist. **b.** It takes much body heat to vaporize sweat, which is mostly liquid water, and this helps keep bodies cool when the temperature rises. **c.** Ice is less dense than liquid water, and it forms on top of water, making skate sailing possible. It also allows aquatic organisms to survive the winter in the liquid water beneath the ice.

freezing. Thus, aquatic organisms are protected and have a better chance of surviving the winter.

5. Water molecules are cohesive, and therefore liquids fill vessels, such as blood vessels.

Water molecules cling together because of hydrogen bonding, and yet, water flows freely. This property allows dissolved and suspended molecules to be evenly distributed throughout a system. Therefore, water is an excellent transport medium. Within our bodies, the blood that fills our arteries and veins is 92% water. Blood transports oxygen and nutrients to the cells and removes wastes, such as carbon dioxide, from cells.

6. Water is a solvent for polar (charged) molecules, and thereby facilitates chemical reactions both outside and within our bodies.

When ions and molecules disperse in water, they move about and collide, allowing reactions to occur. Therefore, water is a solvent that facilitates chemical reactions. For example, when a salt such as sodium chloride (NaCl) is put into water, the negative ends of the water molecules are attracted to the sodium ions, and the positive ends of the water molecules are attracted to the chloride ions. This causes the sodium ions and the chloride ions to separate and to dissolve in water:

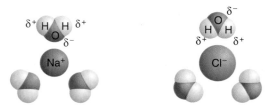

The salt NaCl dissolves in water.

Ions and molecules that interact with water are said to be **hydrophilic.** Nonionized and nonpolar molecules that do not interact with water are said to be **hydrophobic.**

Because of its polarity and hydrogen bonding, water has many characteristics that benefit life.

Acids and Bases

When water molecules dissociate (break up), they release an equal number of hydrogen ions (H^+) and hydroxide ions (OH^-):

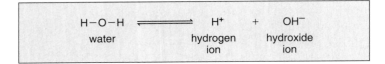

Only a few water molecules at a time dissociate, and the actual number of H^+ and OH^- is 10^{-7} moles/liter. A mole is a unit of scientific measurement for atoms, ions, and molecules.[2]

Acidic Solutions (High H^+ Concentrations)

Lemon juice, vinegar, tomatoes, and coffee are all acidic solutions. What do they have in common? **Acids** are substances that dissociate in water, releasing hydrogen ions (H^+). For example, an important inorganic acid is hydrochloric acid (HCl), which dissociates in this manner:

$$HCl \longrightarrow H^+ + Cl^-$$

Dissociation is almost complete; therefore, HCl is called a strong acid. If hydrochloric acid is added to a beaker of water, the number of hydrogen ions (H^+) increases greatly.

Basic Solutions (Low H^+ Concentrations)

Milk of magnesia and ammonia are commonly known basic substances. **Bases** are substances that either take up hydrogen ions (H^+) or release hydroxide ions (OH^-). For example, an important inorganic base is sodium hydroxide (NaOH), which dissociates in this manner:

$$NaOH \longrightarrow Na^+ + OH^-$$

Dissociation is almost complete; therefore, sodium hydroxide is called a strong base. If sodium hydroxide is added to a beaker of water, the number of hydroxide ions increases.

pH Scale

The **pH scale**[3] is used to indicate the acidity and basicity (alkalinity) of a solution. Pure water with an equal number of hydrogen ions (H^+) and hydroxide ions (OH^-) has a pH of exactly 7.

The pH scale was devised to simplify discussion of the hydrogen ion concentration [H^+] and consequently of the hydroxide ion concentration [OH^-]; it eliminates the use of cumbersome numbers. In order to understand the relationship between hydrogen ion concentration and pH, consider the following:

	[H⁺] (moles per liter)	pH
0.000001	$= 1 \times 10^{-6}$	6
0.0000001	$= 1 \times 10^{-7}$	7
0.00000001	$= 1 \times 10^{-8}$	8

Of the two values above and below pH 7, which one indicates a higher hydrogen ion concentration than pH 7 and therefore refers to an acidic solution? A number with a smaller negative exponent indicates a greater quantity of hydrogen ions (H^+) than one with a larger negative exponent. Therefore, the pH 6 solution is an acidic solution.

Bases add hydroxide ions (OH^-) to solutions and increase the hydroxide ion concentration [OH^-] of water. Basic solutions have fewer hydrogen ions (H^+) compared with hydroxide ions. Of the three values, the pH 8 solution is a basic solution because it indicates a lower hydrogen ion concentration [H^+] (greater hydroxide ion concentration) than the pH 7 solution.

The pH scale (Fig. 2.8) ranges from 0 to 14. As we move toward a higher pH, each unit has 10 times the basicity of the previous unit, and as we move toward a lower pH, each unit has 10 times the acidity of the previous unit. The Ecology Focus on page 21 describes some detrimental environmental consequences to nonliving and living things as rain and snow have become more acidic.

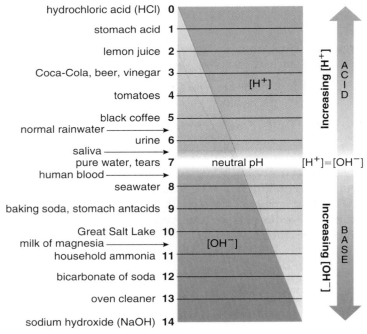

Figure 2.8   The pH scale.
The proportionate amount of hydrogen ions to hydroxide ions is indicated by the diagonal line. Any solution with a pH above 7 is basic, while any solution with a pH below 7 is acidic.

---

[2]In chemistry, a mole is defined as the amount of matter that contains as many objects (atoms, molecules, ions) as the number of atoms in exactly 12 grams of ^{12}C.

[3]pH is defined as the negative log of the hydrogen ion concentration [H^+]. A log is the power to which 10 must be raised to produce a given number.

Ecology Focus

The Harm Done by Acid Rain

Very strong evidence tells us that an observed increase in rainwater acidity is a result of the burning of fossil fuels such as coal, oil, and gasoline derived from oil. When fossil fuels are burned, sulfur dioxide and nitrogen oxides are produced, and they combine with water vapor in the atmosphere to form sulfuric and nitric acids. These acids return to Earth dissolved in rain or snow, a process properly called wet deposition, but more often called acid rain. Dry particles of sulfate and nitrate salts descend from the atmosphere during dry deposition.

The use of tall smokestacks to reduce local air pollution only causes pollutants to be carried far away. For example, acid rain in southeastern Canada results from the burning of fossil fuels in factories and power plants in the Midwest. Acid rain not only causes lakes to become more acidic, it also causes them to accumulate toxic substances by leaching aluminum from the soil, carrying aluminum into the lakes, and by converting mercury deposits in lake bottom sediments to soluble and toxic methyl mercury. The increasing deterioration of thousands of lakes and rivers in southern Norway and Sweden during the past two decades has been attributed to acid rain. Some lakes contain no fish, and others have decreasing numbers of fish. The same phenomenon has been observed in Canada and the United States (mostly in the Northeast and upper Midwest).

In forests, acid rain weakens trees because it leaches away nutrients and releases aluminum. By 1988, most spruce, fir, and other conifer trees atop North Carolina's Mt. Mitchell were dead from being bathed in ozone and acid fog for years. The soil was so acidic that new seedlings could not survive. Many countries in northern Europe have also reported woodland and forest damage most likely due to acid rain (Fig. 2A).

Lake and forest deterioration aren't the only effects of acid rain. Reduction of agricultural yields, damage to marble and limestone monuments and buildings, and even illnesses in humans have been reported. Acid rain has been implicated in the increased incidence of lung cancer and possibly colon cancer in residents of the U.S. East Coast. Tom McMillan, former Canadian Minister of the Environment, says that acid rain is "destroying our lakes, killing our fish, undermining our tourism, retarding our forests, harming our agriculture, devastating our heritage, and threatening our health."

a.

b.

Figure 2A   **Effects of acid rain.**
The burning of gasoline derived from oil, a fossil fuel, leads to acid rain, which causes (**a**) statues to deteriorate and (**b**) trees to die.

Buffers

In living things, the pH of body fluids needs to be maintained within a narrow range, or else health suffers. Normally, pH stability is possible because the body has built-in mechanisms to prevent pH changes. Buffers are the most important of these mechanisms. **Buffers** help keep the pH within normal limits because they are chemicals or combinations of chemicals that take up excess hydrogen ions (H^+) or hydroxide ions (OH^-). For example, carbonic acid (H_2CO_3) is a weak acid that minimally dissociates and then re-forms in the following manner:

H_2CO_3	$\xrightleftharpoons[\text{re-forms}]{\text{dissociates}}$	H^+	+	HCO_3^-
carbonic acid		hydrogen ion		bicarbonate ion

The pH of our blood when we are healthy is always about 7.4—that is, just slightly basic (alkaline). Blood always contains a combination of some carbonic acid and some bicarbonate ions. When hydrogen ions (H^+) are added to blood, the following reaction occurs:

$$H^+ + HCO_3^- \longrightarrow H_2CO_3$$

When hydroxide ions (OH^-) are added to blood, this reaction occurs:

$$OH^- + H_2CO_3 \longrightarrow HCO_3^- + H_2O$$

These reactions prevent any significant change in blood pH.

A pH value is the hydrogen ion concentration [H^+] of a solution. Buffers act to keep the pH within normal limits.

2.3 Molecules of Life

Four categories of molecules, called carbohydrates, lipids, proteins, and nucleic acids, are unique to cells. In each category, the molecules are composed of more than one subunit:

Category	Example	Subunits
Lipids	Fat	Glycerol and fatty acids
Carbohydrates	Polysaccharide	Monosaccharide
Proteins	Polypeptide	Amino Acid
Nucleic acids	DNA, RNA	Nucleotide

When a cell constructs a **macromolecule,** a molecule that contains many subunits, it uses a **dehydration reaction.** During a dehydration reaction, an —OH (hydroxyl group) and an —H (hydrogen atom), the equivalent of a water molecule, are removed as the molecule forms (Fig. 2.9*a*). The reaction is reminiscent of a train whose length is determined by how many boxcars it has hitched together. To degrade macromolecules, the cell uses a **hydrolysis reaction** in which the components of water are added (Fig. 2.9*b*).

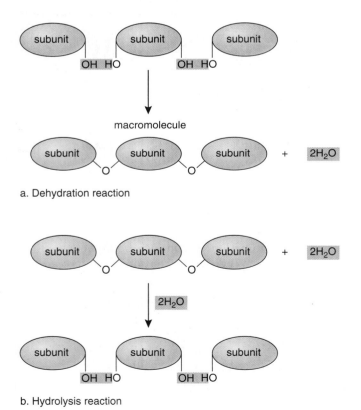

a. Dehydration reaction

b. Hydrolysis reaction

Figure 2.9 **Synthesis and degradation of macromolecules.**
a. In cells, synthesis often occurs when subunits bond following a dehydration reaction (removal of H_2O). **b.** Degradation occurs when the subunits in a macromolecule separate after the addition of H_2O.

2.4 Carbohydrates

Carbohydrates, like all **organic molecules,** always contain carbon (C) and hydrogen (H) atoms. However, carbohydrate molecules are characterized by the presence of the atomic grouping H—C—OH, in which the ratio of hydrogen atoms (H) to oxygen atoms (O) is approximately 2:1. Since this ratio is the same as the ratio in water, the name "hydrates of carbon" seems appropriate. **Carbohydrates** first and foremost function for quick and short-term energy storage in all organisms, including humans. Figure 2.10 shows some foods that are rich in carbohydrates.

Simple Carbohydrates

If the number of carbon atoms in a carbohydrate is low (from three to seven), it is called a simple sugar, or **monosaccharide.** The designation **pentose** means a 5-carbon sugar, and the designation **hexose** means a 6-carbon sugar. **Glucose,** the hexose our bodies use as an immediate source of energy, can be written in any one of these ways:

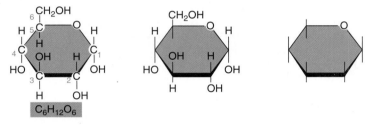

$C_6H_{12}O_6$

Other common hexoses are fructose, found in fruits, and galactose, a constituent of milk.

Figure 2.10 **Common foods.**
Carbohydrates such as bread and pasta are digested to sugars; lipids such as oils are digested to glycerol and fatty acids; and proteins such as meat are digested to amino acids. Cells use these subunit molecules to build their own macromolecules.

A **disaccharide** (*di,* two; *saccharide,* sugar) is made by joining only two monosaccharides together by a dehydration reaction (see Fig. 2.9a). Maltose is a disaccharide that contains two glucose molecules:

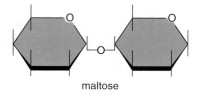

maltose

When glucose and fructose join, the disaccharide sucrose forms. Sucrose, which is ordinarily derived from sugarcane and sugar beets, is commonly known as table sugar.

Complex Carbohydrates (Polysaccharides)

Macromolecules such as starch, glycogen, and cellulose are **polysaccharides** that contain many glucose units.

Starch and Glycogen

Starch and **glycogen** are readily stored forms of glucose in plants and animals, respectively. Some of the macromolecules in starch are long chains of up to 4,000 glucose units. Starch has fewer side branches, or chains of glucose that branch off from the main chain, than does glycogen, as

shown in Figures 2.11 and 2.12. Flour, which we usually acquire by grinding wheat and use for baking, is high in starch, and so are potatoes.

After we eat starchy foods, such as potatoes, bread, and cake, glucose enters the bloodstream, and normally the liver stores glucose as glycogen. In between eating, the liver releases glucose so that the blood glucose concentration is always about 0.1%.

Cellulose

The polysaccharide **cellulose** is found in plant cell walls. In cellulose, the glucose units are joined by a slightly different type of linkage than that in starch or glycogen. While this might seem to be a technicality, actually it is important because we are unable to digest foods containing this type of linkage; therefore, cellulose largely passes through our digestive tract as fiber, or roughage. It is believed that fiber in the diet is necessary to good health, and some have suggested it may even help prevent colon cancer.

Cells usually use the monosaccharide glucose as an energy source. The polysaccharides starch and glycogen are storage compounds in plant and animal cells, respectively, and the polysaccharide cellulose found in plant cell walls is dietary fiber.

Figure 2.11   Starch structure and function.
Starch has straight chains of glucose molecules. Some chains are also branched, as indicated. The electron micrograph shows starch granules in potato cells. Starch is the storage form of glucose in plants.

potato cells

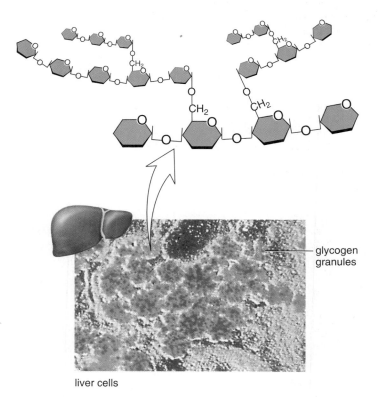

liver cells

Figure 2.12   Glycogen structure and function.
Glycogen is more branched than starch. The electron micrograph shows glycogen granules in liver cells. Glycogen is the storage form of glucose in humans.

2.5 Lipids

Lipids contain more energy per gram than other biological molecules, and some function well as energy storage molecules in organisms. Others form a membrane so that the cell is separated from its environment and has inner compartments as well. Steroids are a large class of lipids that includes, among other molecules, the sex hormones.

Lipids are diverse in structure and function, but they have a common characteristic: They do not dissolve in water. Their low solubility in water is due to an absence of polar groups. They contain little oxygen and consist mostly of carbon and hydrogen atoms.

Fats and Oils

The most familiar lipids are those found in fats and oils. **Fats,** which are usually of animal origin (e.g., lard and butter), are solid at room temperature. **Oils,** which are usually of plant origin (e.g., corn oil and soybean oil), are liquid at room temperature. Fat has several functions in the body: It is used for long-term energy storage, it insulates against heat loss, and it forms a protective cushion around major organs.

Fats and oils form when one glycerol molecule reacts with three fatty acid molecules (Fig. 2.13). A fat is sometimes called a **triglyceride** because of its three-part structure, or the term neutral fat can be used because the molecule is nonpolar and carries no charges.

Emulsification

Emulsifiers can cause fats to mix with water. They contain molecules with a nonpolar end and a polar end. The molecules position themselves about an oil droplet so that their polar ends project outward. Now the droplet disperses in water, which means that **emulsification** has occurred.

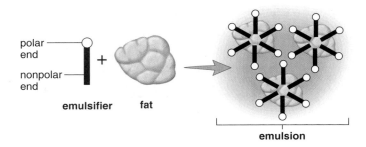

emulsifier   fat

emulsion

Emulsification takes place when dirty clothes are washed with soaps or detergents. Also, prior to the digestion of fatty foods, fats are emulsified by bile. The gallbladder stores bile for emulsifying fats prior to the digestive process.

Saturated and Unsaturated Fatty Acids

A **fatty acid** is a carbon–hydrogen chain that ends with the acidic group —COOH (Fig. 2.13). Most of the fatty acids in cells contain 16 or 18 carbon atoms per molecule, although smaller ones with fewer carbons are also known.

Fatty acids are either saturated or unsaturated. **Saturated fatty acids** have only single covalent bonds because the carbon chain is saturated, so to speak, with all the hydrogens it can hold. Saturated fatty acids account for the solid nature of fats, such as lard and butter at room temperature. **Unsaturated fatty acids** have double bonds between carbon atoms wherever fewer than two hydrogens are bonded to a carbon atom. Unsaturated fatty acids account for the liquid nature of vegetable oils at room temperature. Hydrogenation of vegetable oils can convert them to so-called *trans fats,* often found in processed foods.

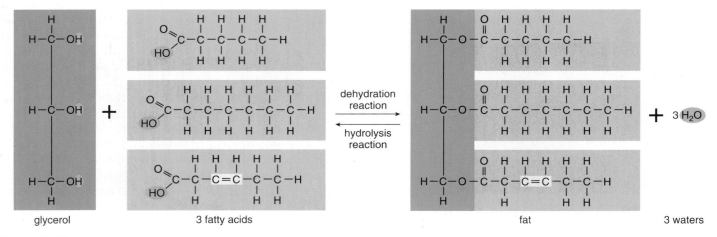

Figure 2.13 Synthesis and degradation of a fat molecule.
Fatty acids can be saturated (no double bonds between carbon atoms) or unsaturated (have double bonds, colored yellow, between carbon atoms). When a fat molecule forms, three fatty acids combine with glycerol, and three water molecules are produced. The carbon chains of the fatty acids are longer than those here and usually have 16–18 carbons.

Phospholipids

Phospholipids have a phosphate group (Fig. 2.14). Essentially, they are constructed like fats, except that in place of the third fatty acid, there is a phosphate group or a grouping that contains both phosphate and nitrogen. These molecules are not electrically neutral, as are fats, because the phosphate and nitrogen-containing groups are ionized. They form the so-called polar head of the molecule, while the rest of the molecule becomes the hydrophobic tails. Phospholipids are the primary components of cellular membranes; they spontaneously form a bilayer in which the hydrophilic heads face outward toward watery solutions and the tails form the hydrophobic interior.

a. Testosterone
b. Estrogen

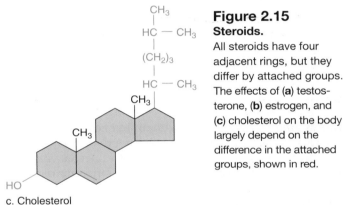

c. Cholesterol

Figure 2.15
Steroids.

All steroids have four adjacent rings, but they differ by attached groups. The effects of (**a**) testosterone, (**b**) estrogen, and (**c**) cholesterol on the body largely depend on the difference in the attached groups, shown in red.

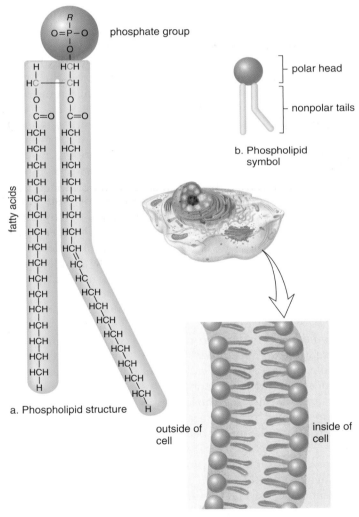

phosphate group

polar head

nonpolar tails

b. Phospholipid symbol

fatty acids

a. Phospholipid structure

outside of cell

inside of cell

c. Membrane structure

Figure 2.14 Phospholipid structure and function.
a. Phospholipids are structured like fats—the three carbons of glycerol are highlighted—but one fatty acid is replaced by a polar phosphate group. **b.** Therefore, the head is polar, while the tails are nonpolar. **c.** This causes the molecules to arrange themselves as shown when exposed to water.

Steroids

Steroids are lipids that have an entirely different structure from those of fats. Steroid molecules have a backbone of four fused carbon rings. Each one differs primarily by the functional groups attached to the rings.

Cholesterol is a component of an animal cell's plasma membrane and is the precursor of several other steroids, such as the sex hormones estrogen and testosterone. The male sex hormone, testosterone, is formed primarily in the testes, and the female sex hormone, estrogen, is formed primarily in the ovaries. Testosterone and estrogen differ only by the functional groups attached to the same carbon backbone, yet they have a profound effect on the body and the sexuality of an animal (Fig. 2.15).

We now know that a diet high in saturated fats, trans fats, and cholesterol can cause fatty material to accumulate inside the lining of blood vessels, thereby reducing blood flow. The Health Focus on page 28 discusses which types of carbohydrates, fats, and protein sources are recommended for inclusion in the diet.

Lipids include fats and oils, phospholipids, and steroids. Phospholipids, unlike other lipids, are soluble in water because they have a hydrophilic group.

2.6 Proteins

Proteins perform many functions. Proteins such as keratin, which makes up hair and nails; and collagen, which lends support to ligaments, tendons, and skin, are structural proteins. The proteins actin and myosin account for the movement of cells and the ability of our muscles to contract. Many hormones, which are messengers that influence cellular activity, are also proteins. Some proteins transport molecules in the blood; hemoglobin is a complex protein in our blood that transports oxygen. Antibodies in blood and other body fluids are proteins that combine with foreign substances, preventing them from destroying cells and upsetting homeostasis.

Enzymes are proteins that control nearly all the chemical reactions in the body because they allow reactions to occur under relatively mild conditions. Without enzymes, most reactions wouldn't occur in the body. In the next section, we will stress that genes govern the production of proteins; in this way, genes control all the processes of the body.

Amino Acids

Proteins are macromolecules with amino acid subunits. An **amino acid** has a central carbon atom bonded to a hydrogen atom and three groups. The name of the molecule is appropriate because one of these groups is an amino group ($-NH_2$) and another is an acidic group ($-COOH$). The third group is called an R group because it is the *Remainder* of the molecule.

Amino acids differ from one another by their R group; the R group varies from having a single carbon to being a complicated ring structure.

Levels of Protein Organization

The structure of a protein has at least three levels of organization and can have four levels (Fig. 2.16). The first level, called the *primary structure*, is the linear sequence of the amino acids joined by peptide bonds. Polypeptides can be quite different from one another. If you likened a polysaccharide to a necklace that contains a single type of "bead," namely glucose, then polypeptides make use of 20 different possible types of "beads," namely amino acids. Each particular polypeptide has its own sequence of amino acids.

A bond that joins any two amino acids is called a **peptide bond** (Fig. 2.16, *top*). A **polypeptide** is a single chain of amino acids. The atoms associated with the peptide bond—oxygen (O), carbon (C), nitrogen (N), and hydrogen (H)—

share electrons in such a way that the oxygen has a slight negative charge and the hydrogen has a slight positive charge:

δ^- = slightly negative
δ^+ = slightly positive

Therefore, the peptide bond is polar, and hydrogen bonding is possible between the $C=O$ of one amino acid and the $N-H$ of another amino acid in a polypeptide.

The *secondary structure* of a protein comes about when the polypeptide takes on a certain orientation in space. A coiling of the chain results in a helix, or a right-handed spiral, and a folding of the chain results in a pleated sheet. Hydrogen bonding between peptide bonds holds the shape in place.

The *tertiary structure* of a protein is its final three-dimensional shape. In muscles, myosin molecules have a rod shape ending in globular (globe-shaped) heads. In enzymes, the polypeptide bends and twists in different ways. Invariably, the hydrophobic portions are packed mostly on the inside, and the hydrophilic portions are on the outside, where they can make contact with water. The tertiary shape of a polypeptide is maintained by various types of bonding between the R groups; covalent, ionic, and hydrogen bonding all occur.

Some proteins have only one polypeptide, and others have more than one polypeptide, each with its own primary, secondary, and tertiary structures. These separate polypeptides are arranged to give some proteins a fourth level of structure, termed the *quaternary structure*. Hemoglobin is a complex protein having a quaternary structure; most enzymes also have a quaternary structure.

The final shape of a protein is very important to its function. As we will discuss in Chapter 3, enzymes cannot function unless they have their usual shape. When proteins are exposed to extremes in heat and pH, they undergo an irreversible change in shape called **denaturation.** For example, we are all aware that the addition of acid to milk causes curdling and that heating causes egg white, which contains a protein called albumin, to coagulate. Denaturation occurs because the normal bonding between the R groups has been disturbed. Once a protein loses its normal shape, it is no longer able to perform its usual function. Researchers hypothesize that an alteration in protein organization has occurred when Alzheimer disease and Creutzfeldt-Jakob disease (the human form of mad cow disease) develop.

Proteins, which have levels of organization, are important in the structure and the function of cells. Some proteins are enzymes, which allow reactions to occur in the relatively mild conditions of cells.

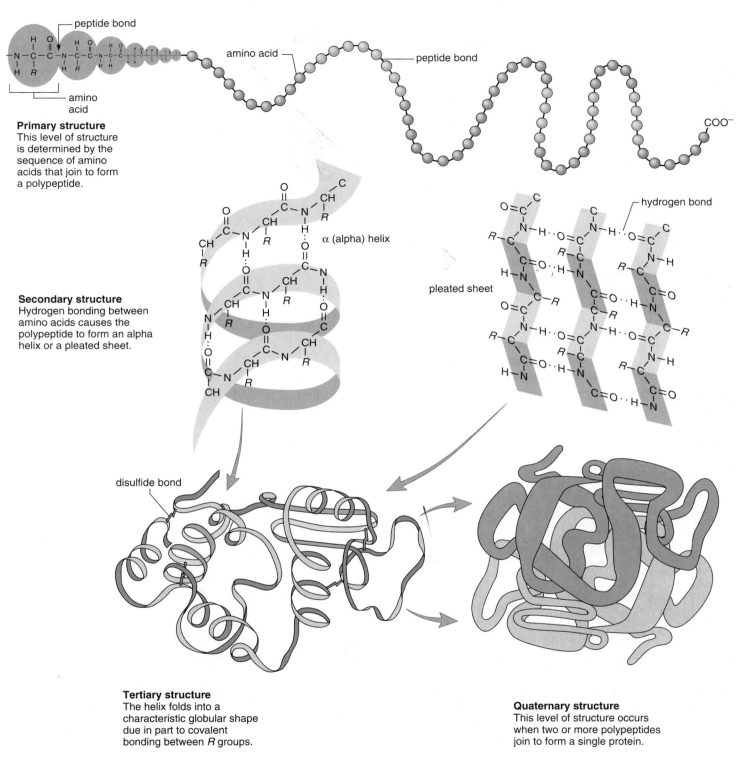

Primary structure
This level of structure is determined by the sequence of amino acids that join to form a polypeptide.

Secondary structure
Hydrogen bonding between amino acids causes the polypeptide to form an alpha helix or a pleated sheet.

α (alpha) helix

pleated sheet

hydrogen bond

peptide bond

amino acid

peptide bond

amino acid

COO⁻

disulfide bond

Tertiary structure
The helix folds into a characteristic globular shape due in part to covalent bonding between *R* groups.

Quaternary structure
This level of structure occurs when two or more polypeptides join to form a single protein.

Figure 2.16   Levels of protein organization.

A Balanced Diet

Everyone agrees that we should eat a balanced diet, but just what is a balanced diet? The food pyramid advocated by the U.S. Department of Agriculture (USDA) since 1992 (Fig. 2Ba) has now come under criticism because it promotes the consumption of all types of complex carbohydrates and a limited intake of all types of fats and oils. Nutritionists at Harvard Medical School have offered a new pyramid (Fig. 2Bb) that they believe will better promote our health and a new USDA pyramid soon to be released is expected to be similar to this one.

Carbohydrates

Carbohydrates are the quickest, most readily available source of energy for the body. Certainly, so-called complex carbohydrates, such as those in whole-grain breads and cereals are preferable to candy and ice cream, containing simple carbohydrates. Foods rich in complex carbohydrates contain not only starch but also dietary fiber (*nondigestible* plant material), plus vitamins and minerals. Insoluble fiber has a laxative effect, and soluble fiber combines with the cholesterol in food and prevents cholesterol from entering the body proper. In contrast, researchers have found that the starch in potatoes and processed foods, such as white bread and white rice, leads to a high blood glucose level just like simple carbohydrates do. Researchers ask themselves, Is this why many adults are now coming down with adult-onset diabetes?

Fats

We have known for many years now that saturated fats in animal products contribute to the formation of deposits called plaque, which clog arteries, leading to high blood pressure and heart attacks. Processed foods often contain "trans-unsaturated fatty acids," which are especially capable of causing cardiovascular disease. Trans fats are oils that have been hydrogenated to solidify them.

Notice that the new pyramid (Fig. 2Bb), unlike the old one, advocates an intake of certain liquid oils. These oils contain monounsaturated and polyunsaturated fatty acids, which researchers have found are protective against the development of cardiovascular disease.

Other

Red meat is rich in protein, but it is usually also high in saturated fat; therefore, fish and chicken are preferred sources of protein. Also, a combination of legumes and rice can provide all of the various amino acids you need to build cellular proteins. *Legume* is a botanical term that includes peas and beans.

Nutritionists agree that the eating of fruits and vegetables is beneficial. The new USDA guidelines recommend eating nine servings of fruit and vegetables a day. At the very least, they provide us with vitamins we need in our diet.

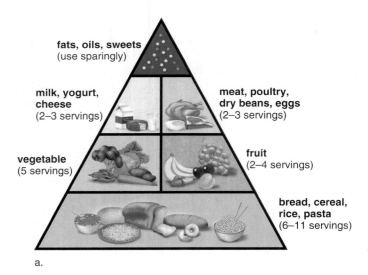

a.

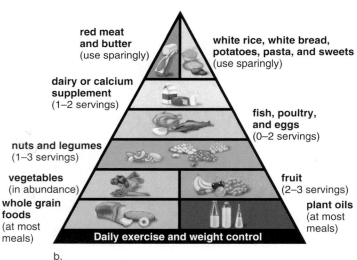

b.

Figure 2B Food guide pyramids.

a. The U.S. Department of Agriculture has advocated this pyramid for many years. It emphasizes the importance of including grains, fruits, and vegetables in the diet but makes no distinctions between types of carbohydrates and fats. All but simple carbohydrates are encouraged and all fats and oils are to be used sparingly. **b.** A new pyramid suggested by nutritionists at Harvard Medical School differs from the pyramid shown in **(a)** by recommending the inclusion of certain oils in the diet and the restriction of all but complex carbohydrates.

2.7 Nucleic Acids

The two types of nucleic acids are **DNA (deoxyribonucleic acid)** and **RNA (ribonucleic acid).** The discovery of the structure of DNA has had an enormous influence on biology and on society in general. DNA stores genetic information in the cell and in the organism. Further, it replicates and transmits this information when a cell reproduces and when an organism reproduces. We now know not only how genes work, but we can manipulate them. The science of biotechnology is largely devoted to altering the genes in living organisms.

DNA codes for the order in which amino acids are to be joined to form a protein. RNA is an intermediary that conveys DNA's instructions regarding the amino acid sequence in a protein.

Structure of DNA and RNA

Both DNA and RNA are polymers of nucleotides (Fig. 2.17). Every **nucleotide** is a molecular complex of three types of subunit molecules—phosphate (phosphoric acid), a pentose sugar, and a nitrogen-containing base:

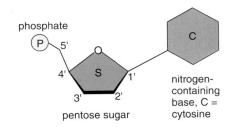

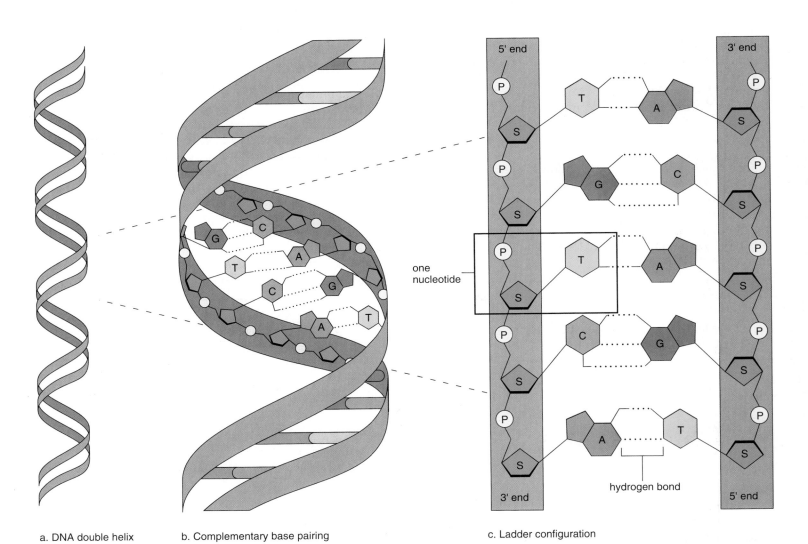

a. DNA double helix   b. Complementary base pairing   c. Ladder configuration

Figure 2.17 Overview of DNA structure.
a. Double helix. **b.** Complementary base pairing between strands. **c.** Ladder configuration. Notice that the uprights are composed of phosphate and sugar molecules and that the rungs are complementary paired bases.

The nucleotides in DNA contain the sugar deoxyribose, and the nucleotides in RNA contain the sugar ribose; this difference accounts for their respective names (Table 2.1). There are four different types of bases in DNA: **adenine (A), thymine (T), guanine (G),** and **cytosine (C).** The base can have two rings (adenine or guanine) or one ring (thymine or cytosine). In RNA, the base **uracil (U)** replaces the base thymine. These structures are called bases because their presence raises the pH of a solution.

The nucleotides form a linear molecule called a strand, which has a backbone made up of phosphate-sugar-phosphate-sugar, with the bases projecting to one side of the backbone. Since the nucleotides occur in a definite order, so do the bases. After many years of work, researchers now know the sequence of the bases in human DNA—the human genome. This breakthrough is expected to lead to improved genetic counseling, gene therapy, and medicines to treat the causes of many human illnesses.

DNA is double-stranded, with the two strands twisted about each other in the form of a *double helix* (see Fig. 2.17a,b). In DNA, the two strands are held together by hydrogen bonds between the bases. When unwound, DNA resembles a stepladder. The uprights (sides) of the ladder are made entirely of phosphate and sugar molecules, and the rungs of the ladder are made only of complementary paired bases. Thymine always pairs with adenine, and guanine always pairs with cytosine. Complementary bases have shapes that fit together.

Complementary base pairing allows DNA to replicate in a way that ensures the sequence of bases will remain the same. This sequence of the DNA bases contains a code that specifies the sequence of amino acids in the proteins of the cell. RNA is single-stranded, and when it forms, complementary base pairing with one DNA strand passes this information on to RNA.

DNA has a structure like a twisted ladder: Sugar and phosphate molecules make up the uprights of the ladder, and hydrogen-bonded bases make up the rungs.

Table 2.1	DNA Structure Compared to RNA Structure	
	DNA	**RNA**
Sugar	Deoxyribose	Ribose
Bases	Adenine, guanine, thymine, cytosine	Adenine, guanine uracil, cytosine
Strands	Double-stranded with base pairing	Single-stranded
Helix	Yes	No

ATP (Adenosine Triphosphate)

In addition to being the monomers of nucleic acids, nucleotides have other metabolic functions in cells. When adenosine (adenine plus ribose) is modified by the addition of three phosphate groups instead of one, it becomes **ATP (adenosine triphosphate),** an energy carrier in cells. A glucose molecule contains too much energy to be used as a direct energy source in cellular reactions. Instead, the energy of glucose is converted to that of ATP molecules. ATP contains an amount of energy that makes it usable to supply energy for chemical reactions in cells.

ATP is a high-energy molecule because the last two phosphate bonds are unstable and easily broken. Usually in cells, the terminal phosphate bond is hydrolyzed, leaving the molecule **ADP (adenosine diphosphate)** and a molecule of inorganic phosphate (P) (Fig. 2.18). The energy released by ATP breakdown is used by the cell to synthesize macromolecules such as carbohydrates and proteins. In muscle cells, the energy is used for muscle contraction, and in nerve cells, it is used for the conduction of nerve impulses. After ATP breaks down, it is rebuilt by the addition of (P) to ADP. Notice in Figure 2.18 that an input of energy is required to re-form ATP.

ATP is a high-energy molecule. ATP breaks down to ADP + (P), releasing energy, which is used for all metabolic work done in a cell.

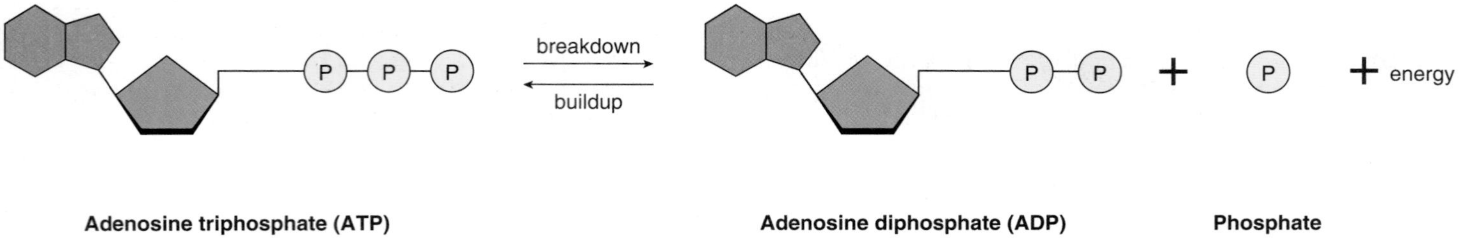

Adenosine triphosphate (ATP)   **Adenosine diphosphate (ADP)**   **Phosphate**

Figure 2.18   ATP reaction.
ATP, the universal energy currency of cells, is composed of adenosine and three phosphate groups (called a triphosphate). When cells require energy, ATP undergoes hydrolysis, producing ADP + (P), with a release of energy.

Bioethical Focus

Genetically Modified Foods

There's nothing quite like the taste of a juicy, red, vine-ripened tomato fresh from the garden in the summertime. Tomatoes have become a staple of our Western diets, and demand for them has never been greater. However, bringing them to market has never been easy. If allowed to ripen naturally, tomatoes become mushy and mealy, and often do not survive shipment. Thus, they are picked while still green, shipped to market, and ripened artificially using ethylene gas. While this causes the tomato to appear ripened at the surface, it remains mostly unripe. As anyone who has eaten a store-bought tomato can confirm, the flavor and texture are usually not as appealing as that of vine-ripened tomatoes. New biotechnology techniques are being utilized to address this problem and many others, attracting both praise and scorn alike, and igniting a national discussion on the future of genetically altered foods.

Tomatoes become mushy and mealy mostly after pectin, a complex carbohydrate that gives tomatoes their firmness, breaks down. When tomatoes ripen, they make an enzyme that degrades pectin in the tomato, causing the tomato to become soft and mushy. To solve these problems, scientists produced a genetically altered tomato lacking the enzyme. As a result, the bioengineered tomatoes could be allowed to ripen on the vine before being picked, packaged, and shipped to market.

In 1994, the genetically altered tomato received FDA approval. Many scientists and consumers alike praised the tomato for its quality and hardiness, and embraced the technology behind it. The tomatoes initially sold well in the marketplace, indicating acceptance by the general population. Although the flavor was not quite as good as that of tomatoes fresh from the garden, it was close.

However, not everyone has embraced genetically modified foods. Consumer advocacy groups and environmental groups have questioned the safety of such foods. In particular, questions remain regarding the stability of the genetically modified crops, the possible accumulation of toxins in the modified tomatoes, and the potential of foreign proteins in these crops to induce allergies in some individuals. Many also questioned whether environmental damage would result from the accidental transfer of genetic alterations to native plants and animals, primarily because some plants are both pest- and herbicide-resistant. Critics derided the tomato and other genetically modified crops as dangerous to our health (Fig. 2C).

The genetically altered tomato was eventually pulled from supermarket shelves because of a disagreement with tomato growers. Tepid sales were also blamed, having fallen off after the initial consumer exuberance. Despite the failure of the bioengineered tomato, the technology used to produce it has led to the development of many other genetically modified crops that have weathered the marketplace and have found their way to our dinner tables. However, many consumer advocates, government entities, and scientists remain wary of the long-term effects of these modifications on our health and on the environment.

Figure 2C   Regulation of transgenic plants.
Activists protest the present regulation of transgenic plants, which they believe to be too permissive.

Decide Your Opinion

1. Despite the promises of higher crop yields, tastier foods, and improved nutritional value, much fear and skepticism remains. Do you think that this fear is justified? Why or why not?
2. Do you believe that it is possible that the changes in genetically altered crops may be transferred to other organisms? How do you think that this might occur?
3. Is the fear of increased allergic reactions to genetically modified foods justified? Why or why not?
4. How should genetically modified foods be labeled in supermarkets? Should producers be required to disclose the presence of genetically modified food ingredients on food labels?
5. What steps could corporations take to increase public acceptance of genetically modified foods?

Summarizing the Concepts

2.1 Basic Chemistry

All matter is composed of 92 naturally occurring elements. Each element is made up of just one type of atom. An atom has a weight, which is dependent on the number of protons and neutrons in the nucleus, and its chemical properties depend on the number of electrons in the outer shell. Atoms react with one another by forming ionic bonds or covalent bonds. Ionic bonds are an attraction between charged ions. In covalent bonds, which can be single, double, or triple bonds, atoms share electrons.

2.2 Water and Living Things

Water, acids, and bases are important inorganic molecules. The polarity of water accounts for its being the universal solvent; hydrogen bonding accounts for it boiling at 100°C and freezing at 0°C. Because it is slow to heat up and slow to freeze, water is liquid at the temperature of living things.

Pure water has a neutral pH; acids increase the hydrogen ion concentration [H$^+$] but decrease the pH of water, and bases decrease the hydrogen ion concentration [H$^+$] but increase the pH.

2.3 Molecules of Life

Carbohydrates, lipids, proteins, and nucleic acids are macromolecules with specific functions in cells (Table 2.2). Dehydration reactions between subunits result in these macromolecules. Hydrolysis reactions result in their breakdown.

Table 2.2	Organic Molecules	
Macromolecule	**Monomer**	**Function**
Proteins	Amino acids	Enzymes speed up chemical reactions; structural components (e.g., muscle proteins)
Carbohydrates		
Starch	Glucose	Energy storage in plants
Glycogen	Glucose	Energy storage in animals
Cellulose	Glucose	Plant cell walls
Lipids		
Fats and oils	Glycerol, 3 fatty acids	Long-term energy source
Phospholipids	Glycerol, 2 fatty acids, phosphate group	Cell membrane structure
Nucleic Acids		
DNA	Nucleotides with deoxyribose sugar	Genetic material
RNA	Nucleotides with ribose sugar	Protein synthesis

2.4 Carbohydrates

Glucose is the 6-carbon sugar most utilized by cells for "quick" energy. Plants store glucose as starch, and animals store glucose as glycogen. Humans cannot digest cellulose, which forms plant cell walls.

2.5 Lipids

Lipids are varied in structure and function. Fats and oils, which function in long-term energy storage, contain glycerol and three fatty acids. Fatty acids can be saturated or unsaturated. Plasma membranes contain phospholipids that have a polarized end. The sex hormones, testosterone and estrogen, are steroids.

2.6 Proteins

Proteins have numerous functions in cells; some are enzymes that speed chemical reactions. The primary structure of a polypeptide is its own particular sequence of the possible 20 types of amino acids. The secondary structure is a helix or pleated sheet. The tertiary structure occurs when a polypeptide bends and twists into a three-dimensional shape. A protein can contain several polypeptides, and this accounts for a possible quaternary structure.

2.7 Nucleic Acids

Nucleic acids are macromolecules composed of nucleotides. Each nucleotide has three components: a sugar, a base, and a phosphate. DNA, which contains the sugar deoxyribose, is the genetic material that stores information for its own replication and for the order in which amino acids are to be sequenced in proteins. DNA, with the help of RNA (which contains ribose), specifies protein synthesis.

ATP, with its unstable phosphate bonds, is the energy currency of cells. Hydrolysis of ATP to ADP + ⓟ releases energy that is used by the cell to do metabolic work.

Studying the Concepts

1. Name the subatomic particles of the atom; describe their charge, atomic mass unit, and location in the atom. 14
2. Give an example of ionic bonding, and explain it. 16
3. Diagram the atomic structure of calcium, and explain how it can react with two chlorine atoms. 16
4. Give an example of covalent bonding between carbon and hydrogen atoms. Explain the molecule. 17
5. Relate the characteristics of water to its polarity and hydrogen bonding between water molecules. 18–19
6. On the pH scale, which numbers indicate a basic solution? An acidic solution? Why? 20
7. What are buffers, and why are they important to life? 21
8. Name the four categories of molecules unique to cells. 22
9. Name some monosaccharides, disaccharides, and polysaccharides, and state some general functions for each. What is the most common subunit for polysaccharides? 22–23
10. What are the subunits of a triglyceride? What is a saturated fatty acid? An unsaturated fatty acid? What is the function of fats? 24
11. Relate the structure of a phospholipid to that of a neutral fat. What is the function of a phospholipid? 25
12. Name two steroids that function as sex hormones in humans. 25
13. What are some functions of proteins? What is a peptide bond and a polypeptide? 26
14. Discuss the primary, secondary, and tertiary structures of proteins. 26–27
15. Discuss the structure and function of the nucleic acids DNA and RNA. 29–30

Thinking Critically About the Concepts

Refer to the opening vignette on page 14, and then answer these questions.

1. Cholesterol is an organic compound. What evidence does the text give that inorganic acids and bases need to be balanced for our health and the health of the environment?
2. How do the molecules derived from cholesterol show how the diversity of organic compounds is achieved?
3. Cholesterol is found in animal cells. What types of organic molecules studied in the chapter are found in both plant and animal cells?

Testing Your Knowledge of the Concepts

Choose the best answer for each question.

1. The atomic number tells you the
   a. number of neutrons in the nucleus.
   b. number of protons in the nucleus.
   c. weight of the atom.
   d. number of protons in the outer shell.

2. Isotopes differ in their
   a. number of protons.   c. number of neutrons.
   b. atomic number.   d. number of electrons.

3. Which type of bond results from the sharing of electrons between atoms?
   a. covalent   c. hydrogen
   b. ionic   d. neutral

4. In the molecule CH_4,
   a. all atoms have eight electrons in the outer shell.
   b. all atoms are sharing electrons.
   c. carbon could accept more hydrogen atoms.
   d. All of these are correct.

5. Which of these properties of water is not due to hydrogen bonding between water molecules?
   a. Water stabilizes the temperature inside and outside a cell.
   b. In water, molecules are cohesive.
   c. Water is a solvent for polar molecules.
   d. Ice floats on water.

6. If a chemical accepted H^+ from the surrounding solution, the chemical could be considered
   a. a base.
   b. an acid.
   c. a buffer.
   d. None of these is correct.
   e. Both a and c are correct.

7. Which of these statements best describes the changes that occur when a solution goes from pH 5 to pH 8?
   a. The hydrogen ion concentration decreases as the solution goes from acidic to basic.
   b. The hydrogen ion concentration increases as the solution goes from basic to acidic.
   c. The hydrogen ion concentration decreases as the solution goes from basic to acidic.

In questions 8–11, match each subunit with a molecule in the key.

Key:
   a. fat   c. polypeptide
   b. polysaccharide   d. DNA, RNA

8. Monosaccharide

9. Nucleotide

10. Glycerol and fatty acids

11. Amino acid

In questions 12–15, match the molecular category with a molecule in the preceding key.

12. Lipids

13. Proteins

14. Nucleic acids

15. Carbohydrates

16. Which of these molecules contain nitrogen (N)?
   a. glucose and fatty acids
   b. amino acids and ATP
   c. nucleotides and steroids
   d. cellulose and starch

17. An example of a polysaccharide used for energy storage is
   a. cellulose.   c. cholesterol.
   b. glycogen.   d. glucose.

18. Saturated fatty acids and unsaturated fatty acids differ in
   a. the number of carbon-to-carbon double bonds.
   b. the consistency at room temperature.
   c. the number of hydrogen atoms present.
   d. All of these are correct.

19. The difference between one amino acid and another is found in the
   a. amino group.   c. *R* group.
   b. carboxyl group.   d. peptide bond.

20. An RNA nucleotide and not a DNA nucleotide
   a. contains the sugar ribose.
   b. contains a nitrogen-containing base.
   c. contains a phosphate molecule.
   d. becomes bonded to other nucleotides by dehydration.

21. The joining of two adjacent amino acids involves
   a. a peptide bond.
   b. a dehydration reaction.
   c. a covalent bond.
   d. All of these are correct.

22. A hydrophilic group is
   a. attracted to water.
   b. a polar and/or ionized group.
   c. found in phospholipids.
   d. the opposite of a hydrophobic group.
   e. All of these are correct.

23. An example of a hydrolysis reaction is
    a. amino acid + amino acid ⟶ dipeptide + H₂O.
    b. dipeptide + H₂O ⟶ amino acid + amino acid.
    c. denaturation of a polypeptide.
    d. Both a and b are correct.
    e. Both b and c are correct.

24. Cellulose is nondigestible by humans because
    a. it contains glucose subunits.
    b. it is a fibrous protein.
    c. of the linkage between the glucose molecules.
    d. of the peptide linkage between the amino acid molecules.
    e. the carboxyl groups ionize.

25. The linear sequence of amino acids in a protein is its
    a. secondary structure.   c. primary structure.
    b. tertiary structure.   d. quaternary structure.

26. Which of the following is not a protein?
    a. collagen   d. hemoglobin
    b. myosin   e. glycogen
    c. actin

27. ATP
    a. is an amino acid.
    b. has a helical structure.
    c. is a high-energy molecule that can break down to ADP and phosphate.
    d. provides enzymes for metabolism.
    e. is most energetic when in the ADP state.

28. Label this diagram using these terms: dehydration reaction, hydrolysis reaction, subunits, macromolecule.

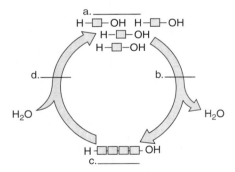

Understanding Key Terms

acid 20
adenine (A) 30
ADP (adenosine
  diphosphate) 30
amino acid 26
atom 14
atomic number 14
atomic weight 14
ATP (adenosine
  triphosphate) 30
base 20
buffer 21
calorie 18
carbohydrate 22

cellulose 23
compound 16
covalent bond 17
cytosine (C) 30
dehydration reaction 22
denaturation 26
disaccharide 23
DNA (deoxyribonucleic
  acid) 29
electron 14
element 14
emulsification 24
enzyme 26
fat 24

fatty acid 24
glucose 22
glycogen 23
guanine (G) 30
hexose 22
hydrogen bond 18
hydrolysis reaction 22
hydrophilic 19
hydrophobic 19
ion 16
ionic bond 16
isotope 15
lipid 24
macromolecule 22
molecule 16
monosaccharide 22
neutron 14
nucleotide 29
oil 24
organic molecule 22

pentose 22
peptide bond 26
pH scale 20
phospholipid 25
polar 18
polypeptide 26
polysaccharide 23
protein 26
proton 14
radioactive isotope 15
RNA (ribonucleic acid) 29
saturated fatty acid 24
starch 23
steroid 25
thymine (T) 30
tracer 15
triglyceride 24
unsaturated fatty acid 24
uracil (U) 30

Match the key terms to these definitions.

a. _____ Breaking up of fat globules into smaller droplets by the action of bile salts or any other emulsifier.

b. _____ Charged particle that carries a negative or positive charge.

c. _____ Chemical bond in which atoms share one pair of electrons.

d. _____ Type of molecule that interacts with water by dissolving in water and/or forming hydrogen bonds with water molecules.

e. _____ Weak bond that arises between a slightly positive hydrogen atom of one molecule and a slightly negative atom of another molecule or between parts of the same molecule.

Online Learning Center

www.mhhe.com/maderhuman9

The Online Learning Center provides a wealth of information fully organized and integrated by chapter. You will find practice quizzes, interactive activities, labeling exercises, flashcards, and much more that will complement your learning and understanding of human biology.

Looking at Both Sides

Each day, the Internet, media, and other people present you with opposing viewpoints on a wide range of subjects. Your ability to develop an informed opinion on an issue, and talk to others about it, is extremely important.

To expand and enhance your knowledge of a highly relevant bioethical issue, visit the "Student Edition" of the Online Learning Center. Under "Course-Wide Content," select "Looking at Both Sides." Once there, you will be asked to complete activities that will increase your understanding of a current bioethical issue related to this chapter and allow you to defend your opinion.

CHAPTER 3

Cell Structure and Function

CHAPTER CONCEPTS

3.1 What Is a Cell?
- What does the cell theory state? 36
- Why are cells so tiny? 36
- How do the micrographs produced by three of the most common types of microscopes differ? 37

3.2 Cellular Organization
- What is an organelle? 38
- What is the structure and function of the plasma membrane? 40
- What types of fibers are in the cytoskeleton and what do they do? 43
- Why is a nucleus indispensable to cells? 44
- What role does each member of the endomembrane system play in cells? 45
- How do you know that cilia and flagella are essential to human cells? 46
- What is the structure and function of a mitochondrion? 47

3.3 Cellular Metabolism
- How does the process of cellular respiration exemplify cellular metabolism? 48–50

Helen is nervous. But when she hops on her bike at the start of the race, her organs answer the challenge. Her brain sends messages along nerves to her skeletal muscles, which contract, moving her bones. The energy to power her muscles comes from sugars absorbed by her digestive tract. Oxygen, needed to release energy from sugars, is absorbed by her lungs. Sugar and oxygen molecules are delivered to her muscles by blood vessels.

But consider that these organs are composed of cells. Helen can win the race because the cells of each organ have done their jobs to keep her legs moving. It's hard to imagine that organs are composed of cells because it takes a microscope to see cells. The electron microscope, developed in the twentieth century, further reveals that cells contain organelles, little bodies that are specialized in structure to carry out particular functions. Helen trained for many months to increase her endurance, and her muscle cells have more mitochondria than those of people who have not trained. This will help her win the race.

This chapter discusses the generalized structure of cells. It also describes the structure and function of the various organelles that carry on the activities of a cell. The chapter ends by describing the cellular reactions that provide energy for Helen's muscles.

3.1 What Is a Cell?

Organisms, including humans, are composed of cells, a fact which isn't apparent until you compare unicellular organisms with the tissues of multicellular ones under the microscope. The cell theory, one of the fundamental principles of modern biology, wasn't formulated until the invention of the microscope in the seventeenth century.

Most cells are quite small and can only be seen under a microscope. The small size of cells means that they are usually measured in units of the metric system, which may seem foreign to you. In everyday language, you are not apt to hear that something is about 1 to 100 micrometers (μm). But these units, which are explained on the inside back cover, are common to people who use microscopes professionally.

The Cell Theory

As stated by the **cell theory,** *a cell is the basic unit of life.* Nothing smaller than a cell is alive. A unicellular organism exhibits the seven characteristics of life we discussed in the first chapter. There is no smaller unit of life that is able to reproduce, respond to stimuli, remain homeostatic, grow and develop, take in and use materials from the environment, and become adapted to the environment. In short, life has a cellular nature.

All living things are made up of cells. While it may be apparent that a unicellular organism is necessarily a cell, what about multicellular ones? Humans are multicellular. Is there any tissue in the human body that is not composed of cells? At first, you might be inclined to say that bone is not composed of cells. But, if you were to examine bone tissue under the microscope, you would be able to see that it, too, is composed of cells surrounded by material they have deposited. Cells look quite different—a blood cell looks quite different from a nerve cell and they both look quite different from a cartilage cell (Fig. 3.1a). Cells in a multicellular organism are specialized in structure and function but they all have certain parts in common. This chapter discusses what these parts are.

New cells arise only from preexisting cells. This statement also requires some understanding, since it certainly wasn't readily apparent to early investigators who believed that organisms could arise from dirty rags, for example. Today, we know you can't arrive, say at a new mouse, without there being preexisting mice. When mice or humans reproduce, a sperm cell joins with an egg cell to form a zygote, which is the first cell of a new multicellular organism. Parents pass a copy of their genes onto their offspring, and the genes contain the instructions that allow the zygote to grow and develop into the full-blown organism.

The cell theory states that: (1) cells are the basic units of life, (2) all living things are made up of cells, and (3) new cells arise only from preexisting cells.

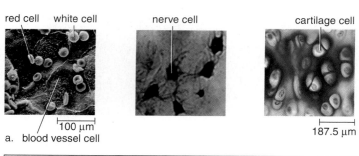

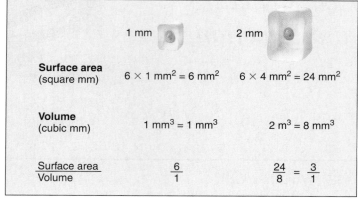

a. blood vessel cell

b.

Figure 3.1   Cells.
a. Cells vary in structure and function but they all exchange substances with their environment. **b.** As the volume of a cell increases from 1 mm³ to 2 mm³, the surface-area-to-volume ratio decreases.

Cell Size

A few cells, such as a hen's egg or a frog's egg, are large enough to be seen by the naked eye, but most are not. The small size of cells is explained by considering the surface-area-to-volume ratio of cells. Nutrients enter a cell, and wastes exit a cell at its surface; therefore, the greater the amount of surface, the greater the ability to get material in and out of the cell. A large cell requires more nutrients and produces more wastes than a small cell. In other words, the volume represents the needs of the cell. Yet, as cells get larger in volume, the proportionate amount of surface area actually decreases, as you can see by comparing the two cubes in Figure 3.1b.

We would expect, then, that there would be a limit to how large an actively metabolizing cell can become. Once a hen's egg is fertilized and starts metabolizing, it divides repeatedly without growth. Cell division restores the amount of surface area needed for adequate exchange of materials. Also important is the decrease in the distance a substance must travel to reach a destination, when a cell is small compared with one that is large.

A cell needs a surface area that suits its need to exchange materials with the environment. This explains why cells stay small.

Microscopy and Cell Structure

Micrographs are photographs of objects most often obtained by using the compound light microscope, the transmission electron microscope, and the scanning electron microscope (Fig. 3.2).

A compound light microscope uses a set of glass lenses and light rays passing through the object to produce an image that can be viewed by the human eye. The human eye can't see electrons, therefore, the transmission electron microscope uses a set of magnetic lenses and electrons passing through the object to produce an image that is projected onto a fluorescent screen or photographic film.

The magnification produced by a transmission electron microscope is much higher than that of a light microscope. Also, the ability of this microscope to make out detail in enlarged images is much greater. In other words, the transmission electron microscope has a higher resolving power—that is, the ability to distinguish between two adjacent points. Following is a comparison of the resolving power of the eye, the light microscope, and the transmission electron microscope:

Eye:	0.2 mm	= 200 μm	= 200,000 nm
Light microscope: (1,000×)	0.0002 mm	= 0.200 μm	= 200 nm
Transmission electron microscope: (50,000×)	0.00001 mm	= 0.01 μm	= 10 nm

A scanning electron microscope provides a three-dimensional view of the surface of an object. A narrow beam of electrons is scanned over the surface of the specimen, which has been coated with a thin layer of metal. The metal gives off secondary electrons, which are collected to produce a television-type picture of the specimen's surface on a screen.

As you no doubt will discover in the laboratory, the light microscope has the ability to view living specimens—this is not true of the electron microscope. Because electrons cannot travel very far in air, a strong vacuum must be maintained along the entire path of the electron beam. Usually for light microscopy and always for electron microscopy, cells are fixed so that they do not decompose, and are embedded into a matrix that allows the specimen to be thinly sliced. Cells are ordinarily transparent; therefore, sections are often stained with colored dyes before they are viewed by a light microscope. Certain components take up the dye more than other components, therefore contrast is enhanced.

The application of electron-dense metals provides contrast with electron microscopy. The latter provides no color, so electron micrographs are colored after the micrograph is obtained. The micrographs are said to be falsely colored because the colors used are not at all related to the color of the contents.

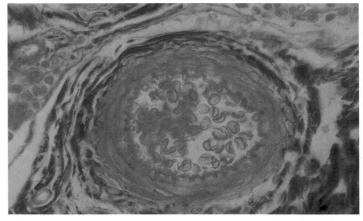

a. Photomicrograph

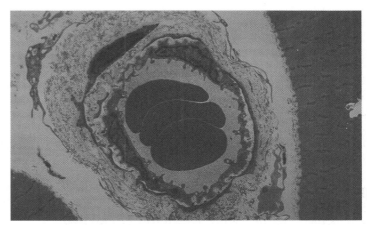

b. Transmission electron micrograph

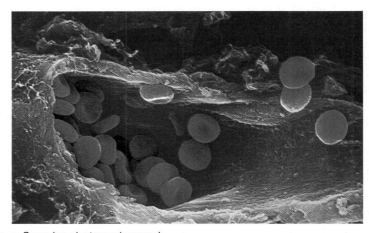

c. Scanning electron micrograph

Figure 3.2   Micrographs of blood vessels and red blood cells.
a. Photomicrograph from a compound light microscope.
b. Transmission electron micrograph. **c.** Scanning electron micrograph.

3.2 Cellular Organization

How cells are organized wasn't apparent to the first microscopists. Only the advent of the electron microscope allowed biologists to determine the internal organization of a cell.

Today, we know that a **plasma membrane** surrounds the cell, keeps it intact, and regulates what enters and exits a cell. The plasma membrane is a phospholipid bilayer that is said to be selectively permeable because it allows certain molecules, but not others, to enter the cell. Proteins present in the plasma membrane play important roles in allowing substances to enter the cell.

The **nucleus** is a large, often centrally located structure that can often be seen with a light microscope. The nucleus contains the chromosomes and is the control center of the cell. It controls the metabolic functioning and structural characteristics of the cell. The **nucleolus** is a region inside the nucleus.

The **cytoplasm** is the portion of the cell between the nucleus and the plasma membrane. The matrix of the cytoplasm is a semifluid medium that contains water and various types of molecules suspended or dissolved in the medium. The presence of proteins accounts for the semifluid nature of the cytoplasm.

The cytoplasm contains various **organelles.** Organelles are small, often membranous, structures that can usually only be seen with an electron microscope. Each type of organelle has a specific function. One type of organelle transports substances, for example, and another type produces ATP for the cell. Since many organelles are composed of membrane, we can say that membrane compartmentalizes the cell, keeping the various cellular activities separated from one another (Table 3.1 and Fig. 3.3).

Cells also have a **cytoskeleton,** a network of interconnected filaments and microtubules in the cytoplasm. The name *cytoskeleton* is convenient in that it allows us to compare the cytoskeleton to the bones and muscles of an animal. Bones and muscles give an animal structure and produce movement. Similarly, the elements of the cytoskeleton maintain cell shape and allow the cell and its contents to move. Some cells move by using cilia and flagella, which contain microtubules, as does the cytoskeleton.

The human cell has a central nucleus and an outer plasma membrane. Various organelles are found within the cytoplasm, the portion of the cell between the nucleus and the plasma membrane.

Table 3.1	Structures in Animal Cells	
Name	**Composition**	**Function**
Plasma membrane	Phospholipid bilayer with embedded proteins	Selective passage of molecules into and out of cell
Nucleus	Nuclear envelope surrounding nucleoplasm, chromatin, and nucleolus	Storage of genetic information
Nucleolus	Concentrated area of chromatin, RNA, and proteins	Ribosomal formation
Ribosome	Protein and RNA in two subunits	Protein synthesis
Endoplasmic reticulum (ER)	Membranous saccules and canals	Synthesis and/or modification of proteins and other substances, and transport by vesicle formation
Rough ER	Studded with ribosomes	Protein synthesis
Smooth ER	Having no ribosomes	Various; lipid synthesis in some cells
Golgi apparatus	Stack of membranous saccules	Processing, packaging, and distribution of molecules
Vacuole and vesicle	Membranous sacs	Storage and transport of substances
Lysosome	Membranous vesicle containing digestive enzymes	Intracellular digestion
Mitochondrion	Inner membrane (with cristae) within outer membrane	Cellular respiration
Cytoskeleton	Microtubules, actin filaments, and intermediate filaments	Shape of cell and movement of its parts
Cilia and flagella	9 + 2 pattern of microtubules	Movement of cell
Centriole	9 + 0 pattern of microtubules	Formation of basal bodies

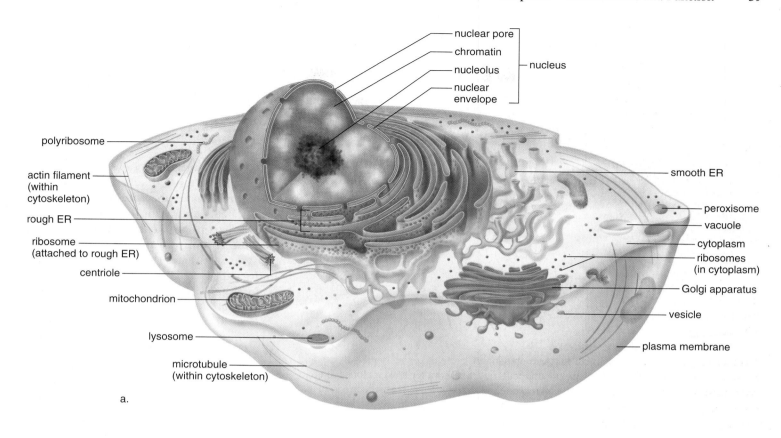

nuclear pore
chromatin
nucleolus — nucleus
nuclear envelope

polyribosome

actin filament (within cytoskeleton)

rough ER

ribosome (attached to rough ER)

centriole

mitochondrion

lysosome

microtubule (within cytoskeleton)

smooth ER

peroxisome

vacuole

cytoplasm

ribosomes (in cytoplasm)

Golgi apparatus

vesicle

plasma membrane

a.

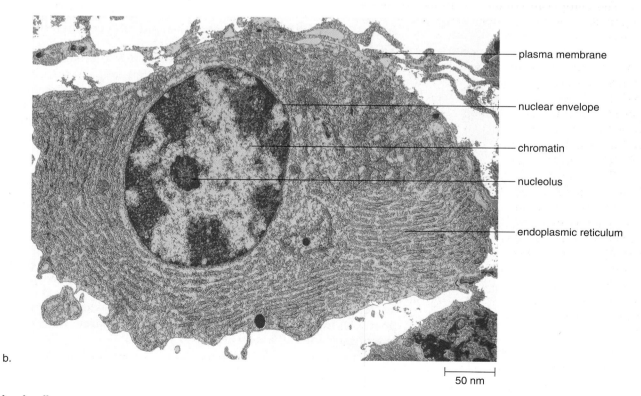

plasma membrane

nuclear envelope

chromatin

nucleolus

endoplasmic reticulum

50 nm

b.

Figure 3.3 **Animal cell.**

a. Generalized drawing. **b.** Transmission electron micrograph. See Table 3.1 for a description of these structures, along with a listing of their functions.

The Plasma Membrane

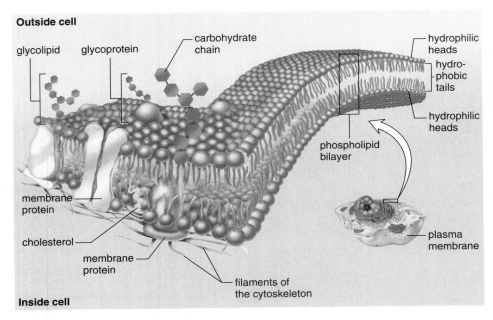

Figure 3.4   **The plasma membrane.**
The membrane is a phospholipid bilayer. Also present are proteins, cholesterol (yellow), and carbohydrate chains (green). Some proteins function as receptors for chemical messengers, as conductors of molecules through the membrane, or as enzymes in metabolic reactions.

A human cell, like all cells, is surrounded by an outer plasma membrane (Fig. 3.4). The plasma membrane marks the boundary between the outside and the inside of the cell. Plasma membrane integrity and function are necessary to the life of the cell.

The plasma membrane is a phospholipid bilayer with attached or embedded proteins. A phospholipid molecule has a polar head and nonpolar tails (see Fig. 2.14). The polar heads, being charged, are hydrophilic (water-loving) and face outward, toward the cytoplasm on one side and the tissue fluid on the other side, where they will encounter a watery environment. The nonpolar tails are hydrophobic (not attracted to water) and face inward toward one another, where there is no water. When phospholipids are placed in water, they naturally form a spherical bilayer because of the chemical properties of the heads and the tails. At body temperature, the phospholipid bilayer is a liquid; it has the consistency of olive oil, and the proteins are able to change their position by moving laterally. The fluid-mosaic model, a working description of membrane structure, says that the protein molecules form a shifting pattern within the fluid phospholipid bilayer. Cholesterol lends support to the membrane.

Short chains of sugars are attached to the outer surface of some protein and lipid molecules (called glycoproteins and glycolipids, respectively). It is believed that these carbohydrate chains, specific to each cell, help mark it as belonging to a particular individual. They account for why people have different blood types, for example. Other glycoproteins have a special configuration that allows them to act as a receptor for a chemical messenger, such as a hormone. Some plasma membrane proteins form channels through which certain substances can enter cells; others are enzymes that catalyze reactions or carriers involved in the passage of molecules through the membrane.

Plasma Membrane Functions

The plasma membrane keeps a cell intact. It allows only certain molecules and ions to enter and exit the cytoplasm freely; therefore, the plasma membrane is said to be **selectively permeable** (Fig. 3.5). Small molecules that are lipid-soluble, such as oxygen and carbon dioxide, can pass through the membrane easily. Certain other small molecules, such as water, are not lipid-soluble, but they still freely cross the membrane. Ions and large molecules cannot cross the membrane without assistance.

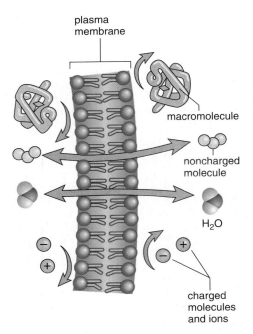

Figure 3.5   **Selective permeability.**
Gases and small, nonpolar molecules can cross the plasma membrane, but ions and large molecules cannot.

The plasma membrane, composed of phospholipid and protein molecules, is selectively permeable and regulates the entrance and exit of molecules and ions into and out of the cell.

Diffusion **Diffusion** is the random movement of molecules from the area of higher concentration to the area of lower concentration, until they are equally distributed. Diffusion is a passive way for molecules to enter or exit a cell, meaning that no cellular energy is needed to bring it about.

To illustrate diffusion, a perfume bottle may be opened in the corner of a room. The smell of the perfume soon permeates the room because the molecules that make up the perfume move from where they are concentrated to all parts of the room. When equally distributed, the molecules will still be moving randomly in all directions.

The molecules that can freely cross the plasma membrane do so by diffusion. If there are molecules of a substance on both sides of the membrane, which way will they go? The molecules will move in both directions, but the *net movement* will be from the region of higher concentration to the region of lower concentration until equilibrium is achieved. At equilibrium, as many molecules of the substance will be entering as leaving the cell (Fig. 3.6). Oxygen diffuses across the plasma membrane and the net movement is toward the inside of the cell because a cell uses oxygen when it produces ATP molecules for energy purposes.

Osmosis **Osmosis** is the diffusion of water across a plasma membrane. Osmosis involves water and a solute (dissolved substance) that cannot readily cross the plasma membrane. **Tonicity** is simply the concentration of the solute in a solution versus the concentration of the water. As the amount of salt or sugar, for example, increases, the amount of water in a solution decreases. Normally, body fluids are isotonic to cells (Fig. 3.7a)—that is, there is the same concentration of nondiffusible solutes and water on both

sides of the plasma membrane, and cells maintain their usual size and shape. Intravenous solutions medically administered are usually isotonic.

Solutions that cause cells to swell or even to burst due to an intake of water are said to be hypotonic. If red blood cells are placed in a hypotonic solution, which has a lower concentration of solute and a higher concentration of water than do the cells, water enters the cells and they swell to bursting (Fig. 3.7b). The term *lysis* is used to refer to disrupted cells; hemolysis, then, means disrupted red blood cells.

Solutions that cause cells to shrink or shrivel due to a loss of water are said to be hypertonic. If red blood cells are placed in a hypertonic solution, which has a higher concentration of solute and a lower concentration of water than do the cells, water leaves the cells and they shrink (Fig. 3.7c). The term *crenation* refers to red blood cells in this condition.

These changes have occurred due to osmotic pressure. Osmotic pressure is the force exerted on a selectively permeable membrane because water has moved from the area of higher to lower concentration of water (higher concentration of solute).

In an isotonic solution, a cell neither gains nor loses water. In a hypotonic solution, a cell gains water. In a hypertonic solution, a cell loses water and the cytoplasm shrinks.

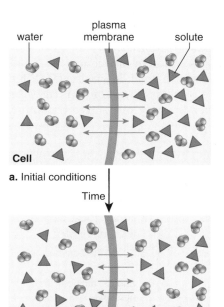

Figure 3.6 **Net movement.**
a. When a substance can diffuse across the plasma membrane it will move back and forth across the membrane, but the net movement will be toward the region of lower concentration. **b.** At equilibrium, an equal number of molecules cross in both directions.

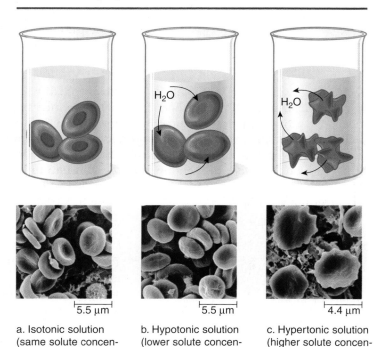

a. Isotonic solution (same solute concentration as in cell) b. Hypotonic solution (lower solute concentration than in cell) c. Hypertonic solution (higher solute concentration than in cell)

Figure 3.7 **Effect of tonicity on red blood cells.**
a. In an isotonic solution, red blood cells remain the same. **b.** In a hypotonic solution, red blood cells gain water and may burst (lysis). **c.** In a hypertonic solution, red blood cells lose water and shrink (crenation). Arrows show the net movement of water in (**b**) and (**c**).

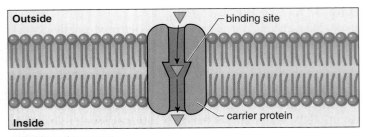

a. Facilitated transport

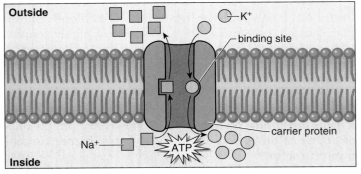

b. Active transport

Figure 3.8   **Transport by carriers.**
a. In facilitated transport, a molecule diffuses faster than usual due to the action of a carrier protein that binds to the molecule and transports it across the membrane. **b.** Active transport requires energy, as well as a carrier protein. The sodium-potassium pump transports sodium to the outside and potassium to the inside by binding first to ATP and Na$^+$ ions, and then later to K$^+$ ions.

Facilitated Transport   Many solutes do not simply diffuse across a plasma membrane; rather, they are transported by means of protein carriers within the membrane. During **facilitated transport,** a molecule is transported at a rate higher than otherwise across the plasma membrane from the side of higher concentration to the side of lower concentration (Fig. 3.8*a*). This is a passive means of transport because the cell does not need to expend energy to move a substance

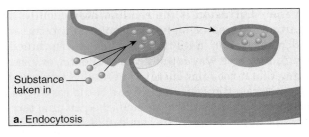

a. Endocytosis

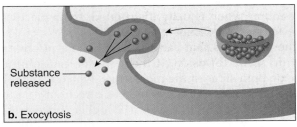

b. Exocytosis

Figure 3.9   **Endocytosis and exocytosis.**
a. During endocytosis, a substance and fluid are enclosed within a small portion of the plasma membrane, which pinches off to form an endocytic vesicle. **b.** During exocytosis, a vesicle fuses with the plasma membrane, thereby releasing its contents to the exterior of the cell.

down its concentration gradient. Each protein carrier, sometimes called a transporter, binds only to a particular molecule, such as glucose. Diabetes type 2 results when cells lack a sufficient number of transporters.

Active Transport   During **active transport,** a molecule is moving contrary to the normal direction—that is, from lower to higher concentration. For example, iodine collects in the cells of the thyroid gland; sugar is completely absorbed from the gut by cells that line the digestive tract; and sodium (Na$^+$) is sometimes almost completely withdrawn from urine by cells lining kidney tubules.

Active transport requires a protein carrier and the use of cellular energy obtained from the breakdown of ATP. When ATP is broken down, energy is released, and in this case, the energy is used by a carrier to carry out active transport.

Table 3.2	Passage of Molecules into and out of Cells			
	Name	**Direction**	**Requirement**	**Examples**
PASSIVE MECHANISMS	Diffusion	Toward lower concentration	Concentration gradient	Lipid-soluble molecules, water, and gases
	Facilitated transport	Toward lower concentration	Carrier and concentration gradient	Sugars and amino acids
ACTIVE MECHANISMS	Active transport	Toward higher concentration	Carrier plus energy	Sugars, amino acids, and ions
	Endocytosis	Toward inside the cell	Vesicle formation	Macromolecules
	Exocytosis	Toward outside the cell	Vesicle fuses with plasma membrane	Macromolecules

Proteins involved in active transport often are called pumps, because just as a water pump uses energy to move water against the force of gravity, proteins use energy to move substances against their concentration gradients. One type of pump that is active in all cells, but is especially associated with nerve and muscle cells, moves sodium ions (Na^+) to the outside and potassium ions (K^+) to inside the cell (Fig. 3.8*b*).

The passage of salt (NaCl) across a plasma membrane is of primary importance in cells. First, sodium ions are pumped across a membrane; then, chloride ions simply diffuse through channels that allow their passage. Chloride ion channels malfunction in persons with cystic fibrosis, and this leads to the symptoms of this inherited (genetic) disorder.

Endocytosis and Exocytosis   During endocytosis, a portion of the plasma membrane invaginates, or forms a pouch, to envelop a substance and fluid. Then, the membrane pinches off to form an endocytic vesicle inside the cell (Fig. 3.9*a*). Some white blood cells are able to take up pathogens (disease-causing agents) by endocytosis, and the process is given a special name: *phagocytosis*. Usually, cells take up molecules and fluid and then the process is called *pinocytosis*. An inherited form of cardiovascular disease occurs when cells fail to take up a combined lipoprotein and cholesterol molecule from the blood by pinocytosis.

During exocytosis, a vesicle fuses with the plasma membrane as secretion occurs (Fig. 3.9*b*). Later in the chapter we will see that a steady stream of vesicles move between certain organelles before finally fusing with the plasma membrane. This is the way insulin leaves insulin-secreting cells, for instance.

Table 3.2 summarizes the various ways molecules get into and out of cells. Molecules pass through the membrane by passive mechanisms (diffusion and facilitated transport), which do not require energy, and active mechanisms, which do (active transport, endocytosis, and exocytosis).

The Cytoskeleton

It took a high-powered electron microscope to discover that the cytoplasm of the cell is criss-crossed by several types of protein fibers collectively called the **cytoskeleton.** The cytoskeleton helps maintain a cell's shape and either anchors the organelles or assists their movement, as appropriate. The cytoskeleton includes microtubules, intermediate filaments, and actin filaments (Fig. 3.10*a*). Fluorescence microscopy is another way to make these protein fibers visible (Fig. 3.10*b*).

Microtubules are much larger than actin filaments. Each is a cylinder that contains 13 longitudinal rows of a protein called tubulin. Remarkably, microtubules can assemble and disassemble. The regulation of microtubule assembly is under the control of a microtubule organizing center called the **centrosome.** Microtubules begin to assemble in the centrosome, and then they grow outward, extending through the entire cytoplasm.

Microtubules help maintain the shape of the cell and act as tracks along which organelles move. During cell division, microtubules form spindle fibers, which assist the movement of chromosomes.

Actin filaments, made of a protein called actin, are long, extremely thin fibers that usually occur in bundles or other groupings. Actin filaments have been isolated from various types of cells, especially those in which movement occurs. Microvilli, which project from certain cells and can shorten and extend, contain actin filaments. Actin filaments, like microtubules, can assemble and disassemble.

Intermediate filaments, as their name implies, are intermediate in size between microtubules and actin filaments. Their structure and function are different according to the type of the cell.

The cytoskeleton is a network of microtubules and filaments that gives cells their shape and gives organelles the capacity to move about in the cell.

Figure 3.10   **Cytoskeleton.**
a. The electron microscope reveals the presence of the cytoskeleton, which contains three types of fibers called microtubules, intermediate filaments, and actin filaments. **b.** Fluorescence microscopy can also detect these fibers at a much lower magnification.

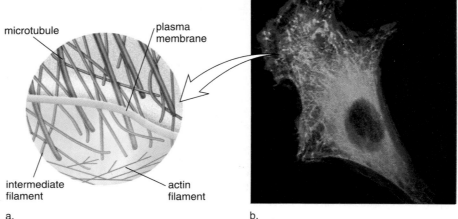

microtubule

plasma membrane

intermediate filament

actin filament

a.

b.

The Nucleus and Ribosomes

The nucleus and the ribosomes work together to bring about protein synthesis.

The Nucleus

The **nucleus,** a prominent structure in cells, stores genetic information (Fig. 3.11). Every cell contains the same genes, but each type has certain genes, or segments of DNA, turned on, and others turned off. Activated DNA, with RNA acting as an intermediary, specifies the proteins in a cell. Proteins determine a cell's structure and functions, particularly because the cell's enzymes are protein.

When you look at the nucleus, even in an electron micrograph, you cannot see DNA molecules, but you can see **chromatin.** Chromatin undergoes coiling into rodlike structures called chromosomes just before the cell divides. Each **chromosome** contains a specific DNA molecule and its associated proteins. Chromatin is immersed in a semifluid medium called the **nucleoplasm.** A difference in pH suggests that nucleoplasm has a different composition from cytoplasm.

When you look at an electron micrograph of a nucleus, you will see one or more dark regions of the chromatin. These are nucleoli (sing., **nucleolus**), where another type of RNA, called ribosomal RNA (rRNA), is produced, and where rRNA joins with proteins to form the subunits of ribosomes.

The nucleus is separated from the cytoplasm by a double membrane known as the **nuclear envelope,** which is continuous with the **endoplasmic reticulum (ER),** a membranous system of saccules and channels discussed in the next section. The nuclear envelope has **nuclear pores** of sufficient size to permit the passage of proteins into the nucleus and ribosomal subunits out of the nucleus.

Ribosomes

Ribosomes are organelles composed of proteins and rRNA. Protein synthesis occurs at the ribosomes. Ribosomes are often attached to the endoplasmic reticulum; they also occur free within the cytoplasm, either singly or in groups called **polyribosomes.**

Proteins synthesized by cytoplasmic ribosomes are used inside the cell for various purposes. Those produced by ribosomes attached to endoplasmic reticulum may eventually be secreted from the cell or become part of the plasma membrane.

The nucleus, surrounded by a nuclear envelope and containing the nucleolus, is the control center of the cell, because it houses genetic information. Ribosomes are small organelles, where protein synthesis takes place. Ribosomes may be attached to the endoplasmic reticulum, but they also occur in the cytoplasm both singly and in groups (i.e., polyribosomes).

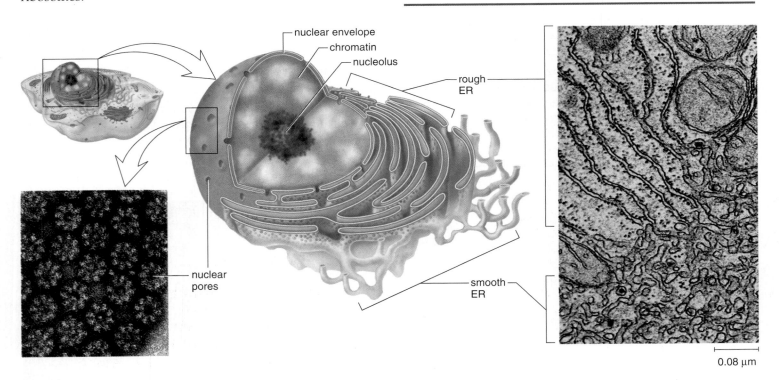

0.08 μm

Figure 3.11   **The nucleus and the ribosomes.**
The nucleus contains chromatin. Chromatin has a special region called the nucleolus, which is where rRNA is produced and ribosomes are assembled. The nuclear envelope contains pores that allow substances to enter and exit the nucleus to and from the cytoplasm. The nuclear envelope is attached to the endoplasmic reticulum, which often has attached ribosomes where protein synthesis occurs.

The Endomembrane System

The **endomembrane system** consists of the nuclear envelope, the endoplasmic reticulum, the Golgi apparatus, lysosomes, and **vesicles** (tiny membranous sacs) (Fig. 3.12).

The Endoplasmic Reticulum

The endoplasmic reticulum has two portions. Rough ER is studded with ribosomes on the side of the membrane that faces the cytoplasm. Here, proteins are synthesized and enter the ER interior, where processing and modification begin. Some of these proteins are incorporated into membrane, and some are for export. Smooth ER, which is continuous with rough ER, does not have attached ribosomes. Smooth ER synthesizes the phospholipids that occur in membranes and has various other functions, depending on the particular cell. In the testes, it produces testosterone, and in the liver it helps detoxify drugs.

The ER forms vesicles in which large molecules are transported to other parts of the cell. Often, these vesicles are on their way to the plasma membrane or the Golgi apparatus.

The Golgi Apparatus

The **Golgi apparatus** is named for Camillo Golgi, who discovered its presence in cells in 1898. The Golgi apparatus consists of a stack of slightly curved saccules, whose appearance can be compared to a stack of pancakes. Here, proteins and lipids received from the ER are modified. For example, a chain of sugars may be added to them, thereby making them glycoproteins and glycolipids, which are molecules found in the plasma membrane.

The vesicles that leave the Golgi apparatus move to other parts of the cell. Some vesicles proceed to the plasma membrane, where they discharge their contents. Altogether, the Golgi apparatus is involved in processing, packaging, and secretion. Other vesicles that leave the Golgi apparatus are lysosomes.

Lysosomes

Lysosomes, membranous sacs produced by the Golgi apparatus, contain *hydrolytic enzymes.* When a lysosome fuses with such an endocytic vesicle, its contents are digested by lysosomal enzymes into simpler subunits that then enter the cytoplasm. Even parts of a cell are digested by its own lysosomes (called autodigestion). Normal cell rejuvenation most likely takes place in this manner, but autodigestion is also important during development. For

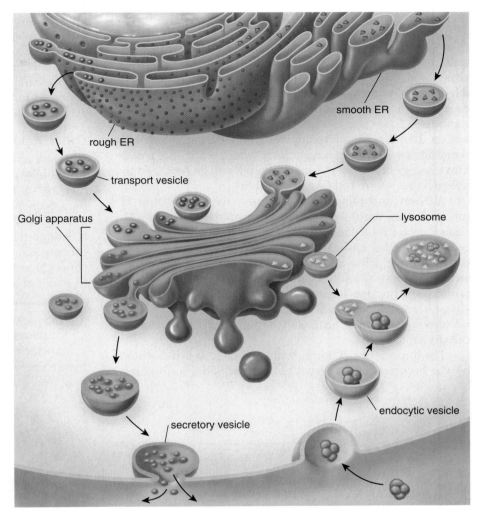

Figure 3.12 **Endomembrane system.**
The organelles in the endomembrane system work together to produce, modify, secrete, and digest proteins and lipids.

example, when a tadpole becomes a frog, lysosomes digest away the cells of the tail. The fingers of a human embryo are at first webbed, but they are freed from one another as a result of lysosomal action.

The organelles of the endomembrane system are as follows.

Endoplasmic reticulum (ER): series of saccules (flattened) and tubules
  Rough ER: ribosomes present
  Smooth ER: ribosomes not present

Golgi apparatus: stack of flattened and curved saccules

Lysosomes: specialized vesicles

Vesicles: membranous sacs

Cilia and Flagella

Cilia and flagella (sing., **cilium, flagellum**) are projections of cells that can move both in an undulating fashion, like a whip, or stiffly, like an oar. Cilia are short (2–10 μm), while flagella are longer (usually no more than 200 μm). Ciliated cells are critical to our respiratory health and to the ability to reproduce. The ciliated cells that line our respiratory tract sweep debris trapped within mucus back up the throat, which helps keep the lungs clean. Similarly, ciliated cells move an egg along the oviduct, where it will be fertilized by a flagellated sperm cell (Fig. 3.13).

A cilium and a flagellum have the same organization of microtubules within a plasma membrane covering. Attached motor molecules, powered by ATP, allow the microtubules in cilia and flagella to interact and bend, and thereby move. Cilia and flagella grow from **basal bodies,** structures that have the same organization as centrioles, which are structures located in centrosomes outside the nucleus. A possible relationship between centrioles and microtubules is mentioned again in Chapter 17, which concerns cell division.

The importance of normal cilia and flagella is illustrated by the occurrence of a genetic disorder. Some individuals have an inherited genetic defect that leads to malformed microtubules in cilia and flagella. Not surprisingly, they suffer from recurrent and severe respiratory infections, because the ciliated cells lining respiratory passages fail to keep their lungs clean. They also are infertile—due to the lack of ciliary action to move the egg in a female, or the lack of flagella action by sperm in a male.

Other Types of Cell Movements

We have already mentioned that the presence of actin filaments allows microvilli, short projections of some cells, to increase or decrease in size as they assemble and disassemble. Actin filaments can also allow some types of human cells to crawl. White blood cells can move out of a blood vessel into the tissues, where they help defend us against disease-causing agents. Then too, actin filaments are necessary to the contraction of muscle cells that allow all of us to have the freedom of locomotion.

Movement of cells is dependent on the organization of microtubules in cilia and flagella or on the presence of actin filaments.

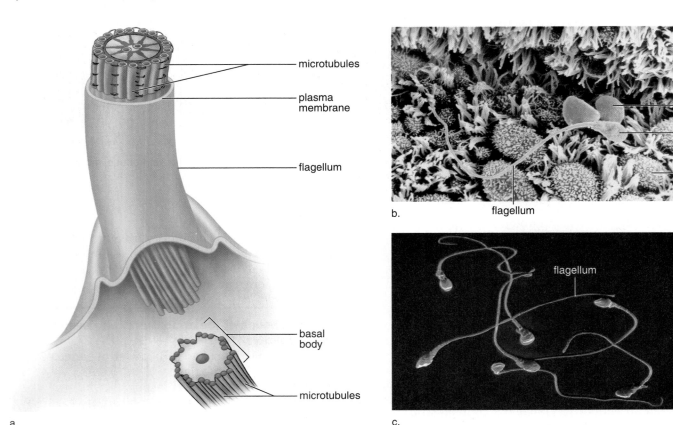

a.

b.

c.

Figure 3.13   **Cilia and flagella.**
a. Both cilia and flagella have an inner core of microtubules within a covering of plasma membrane. **b.** Ciliated cells within the oviduct move the egg to where it is fertilized by a flagellated sperm. **c.** Human reproduction is dependent on the normal activity of cilia and flagella.

Mitochondria

Mitochondria (sing., **mitochondrion**) are often called the powerhouses of the cell—just as a powerhouse burns fuel to produce electricity, the mitochondria convert the chemical energy of glucose products into the chemical energy of ATP molecules. In the process, mitochondria use up oxygen and give off carbon dioxide and water. The oxygen you breathe in enters cells and then mitochondria; the carbon dioxide you breathe out is released by mitochondria. Because oxygen is involved, we say that mitochondria carry on cellular respiration (Fig. 3.14a). Cellular respiration is a very important part of cellular metabolism as discussed on pages 48–50.

Mitochondria are bounded by a double membrane. The inner membrane is folded to form little shelves called cristae, which project into the matrix, an inner space filled with a gel-like fluid (Fig. 3.14b). The matrix of a mitochondrion contains enzymes for breaking down glucose products. ATP production then occurs at the cristae. The protein complexes that aid in the conversion of energy are located in an assembly-line fashion on these membranous shelves.

Every cell uses a certain amount of ATP energy to synthesize molecules, but many cells use ATP to carry out their specialized functions. For example, muscle cells use ATP for muscle contraction, which produces movement, and nerve cells use it for the conduction of nerve impulses, which make us aware of our environment.

Mitochondria are involved in cellular respiration, a process that provides ATP molecules to the cell.

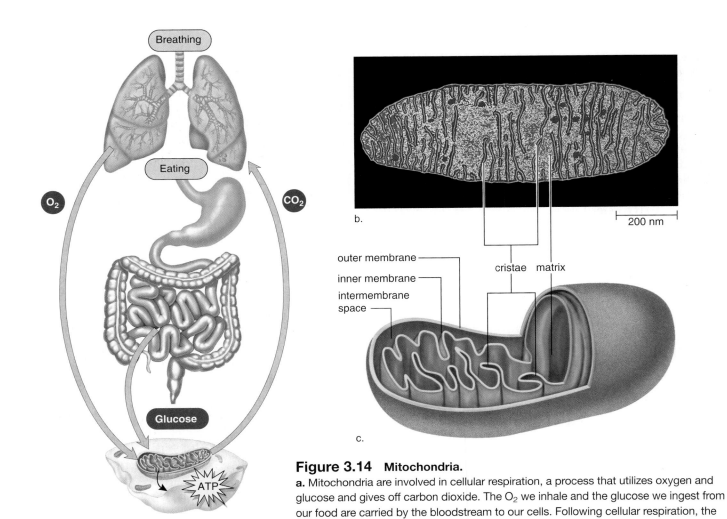

Figure 3.14 **Mitochondria.**
a. Mitochondria are involved in cellular respiration, a process that utilizes oxygen and glucose and gives off carbon dioxide. The O_2 we inhale and the glucose we ingest from our food are carried by the bloodstream to our cells. Following cellular respiration, the ATP stays in the cell, but the CO_2 is carried to the lungs for exhalation. **b.** Electron micrograph of a mitochondrion. **c.** Generalized drawing in which the outer membrane and portions of the inner membrane have been cut away to reveal the cristae.

3.3 Cellular Metabolism

Cellular **metabolism** includes all the chemical reactions that occur in a cell. Quite often metabolic pathways are carried out by enzymes located within membranes to ensure that the reactions occur in the correct order:

$$\overset{1}{A} \rightarrow \overset{2}{B} \rightarrow \overset{3}{C} \rightarrow \overset{4}{D} \rightarrow \overset{5}{E} \rightarrow \overset{6}{F} \rightarrow G$$

The letters, except A and G, are **products** of the previous reaction and the **reactants** for the next reaction. A represents the beginning reactant(s), and G represents the end product(s). The numbers in the pathway refer to different enzymes. *Each reaction in a metabolic pathway requires a specific enzyme.* In effect, no reaction in the pathway occurs unless its enzyme is present. For example, if enzyme 2 in the diagram is missing, the pathway cannot function; it will stop at B. Since enzymes are so necessary in cells, their mechanism of action has been studied extensively.

Most metabolic pathways are regulated by feedback inhibition: The end product of the pathway binds to a special site on the first enzyme of the pathway. This binding shuts down the pathway, and no more product is produced.

Enzymes and Coenzymes

When an enzyme speeds up a reaction, the reactant that participates in the reaction is called the enzyme's **substrate;** there can be more than one reactant and more than one substrate. Enzymes are often named for their substrates. For example, lipids are broken down by lipase, maltose by maltase, and lactose by lactase. Enzymes have a specific region, called an **active site,** where the substrates are brought together so that they can react. An enzyme's specificity is caused by the shape of the active site, where the enzyme and its substrate(s) fit together in a specific way, much as the pieces of a jigsaw puzzle fit together (Fig. 3.15). After one reaction is complete, the product or products are released, and the enzyme is ready to be used again. Therefore, a cell only requires a small amount of a particular enzyme to carry out a reaction, which can be summarized in the following manner:

$$E + S \rightarrow ES \rightarrow E + P$$

(where E = enzyme, S = substrate, ES = enzyme-substrate complex, and P = product). An enzyme can be used over and over again.

Many enzymes require cofactors. Some cofactors are inorganic, such as copper, zinc, or iron. Other cofactors are organic, nonprotein molecules called **coenzymes.** These cofactors assist the enzyme and may even accept or contribute atoms to the reaction. It is interesting that vitamins are often components of coenzymes. The vitamin niacin is a part of the coenzyme **NAD (nicotinamide adenine dinucleotide),** which carries hydrogen (H) atoms after an enzyme called a **dehydrogenase** removes them from a substrate. Hydrogen atoms are sometimes removed by NAD as molecules are broken down. NAD that is carrying hydrogen atoms is written as $NADH_2$ because NAD removes two hydrogen atoms at a time. As we shall see, the removal of hydrogen atoms releases energy that can be used for ATP buildup.

Metabolic pathways contain many enzymes that speed their reactions by forming an enzyme-substrate complex.

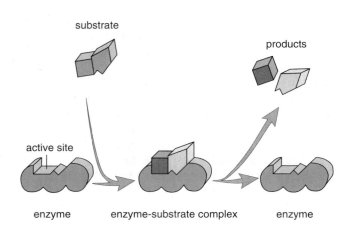

a. Degradation

b. Synthesis

Figure 3.15   Enzymatic action.
An enzyme has an active site, where the substrates and enzyme fit together in such a way that the substrates are oriented to react. Following the reaction, the products are released, and the enzyme is free to act again. **a.** Some enzymes carry out degradation; the substrate is broken down to smaller products. **b.** Other enzymes carry out synthesis; the substrates are combined to produce a larger product.

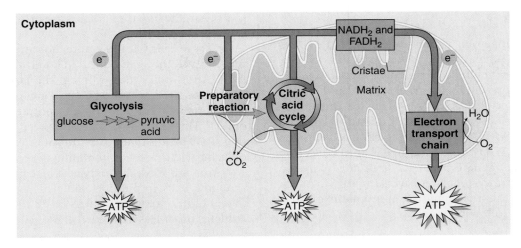

Figure 3.16   **The four phases of complete cellular respiration.**
The overall reaction (*top, left*) actually requires four phases: glycolysis, the preparatory reaction, the citric acid cycle, and the electron transport chain. As reactions occur, a number of hydrogen (H) atoms and carbon dioxide (CO_2) molecules are removed from the various substrates. The coenzymes NAD and FAD carry hydrogen atoms to the electron transport chain. At the end of this chain, oxygen (O_2) acts as the final acceptor for hydrogen atoms and becomes water (H_2O).

Cellular Respiration

Even though it is possible to write an overall equation for **cellular respiration,** glucose breakdown requires four phases: glycolysis, the preparatory reaction, the citric acid cycle, and the electron transport chain (Fig. 3.16). It's possible to associate the reactants and the products of the overall equation with these phases, in this manner:

1. Glucose, a 6-carbon molecule, is associated with **glycolysis,** the breakdown of glucose to two molecules of pyruvic acid, a 3-carbon molecule. During glycolysis, which occurs in the cytoplasm, energy is released as hydrogen (H) atoms are removed and added to NAD, forming $NADH_2$. This energy is used to form two ATP molecules (Fig. 3.16).

> As a result of glycolysis per glucose molecule:
> 2 C_3 molecules, 2 $NADH_2$, 2 ATP

2. Carbon dioxide (CO_2) is associated with the **preparatory reaction** and the citric acid cycle, both of which occur in the matrix of the mitochondria. During the preparatory reaction, pyruvic acid is converted to a 2-carbon acetyl group after CO_2 comes off. Because the preparatory reaction occurs twice per glucose molecule, two molecules of CO_2 are released. Hydrogen (H) atoms are also removed at this time.

> As a result of the preparatory reaction:
> 2 C_2, 2 CO_2, 2 $NADH_2$

The acetyl group enters the **citric acid cycle,** a cyclical series of reactions that gives off two CO_2

molecules and produces one ATP molecule. Since the citric acid cycle occurs twice per glucose molecule, altogether four CO_2 and two ATP are produced per glucose molecule. Hydrogen (H) atoms are removed from the substrates and added to the coenzyme NAD or to flavinadenine dinucleotide (FAD), another dehydrogenase coenzyme, forming $NADH_2$ and $FADH_2$ as the citric acid cycle occurs.

> As a result of the citric acid cycle:
> 4 CO_2, 2 ATP, 6 $NADH_2$, 2 $FADH_2$

3. Oxygen (O_2) and water (H_2O) are associated with the electron transport chain, which is located in the cristae of a mitochondrion. The **electron transport chain,** which usually begins with $NADH_2$ but can begin with $FADH_2$, consists of molecules that carry electrons. High-energy electrons (e^-) are removed from the hydrogen atoms, leaving behind hydrogen ions (H^+), and then the electrons are passed from one molecule to another until the electrons are received by an oxygen atom. At this point, 2 H^+ combine with each oxygen, and water results.

    Certain molecules of the electron transport chain pump the hydrogen ions left behind in the matrix across the inner membrane into the intermembrane space. When these hydrogens flow down their concentration gradient through a channel protein, an associated ATPase forms ATP.

> As a result of the electron transport chain:
> 6 H_2O, about 32 ATP, 10 NAD, 2 FAD

4. Altogether, about 36 ATP molecules, or so, result from the breakdown of one glucose molecule.

Fermentation

Fermentation is an anaerobic process, meaning that it does not require oxygen. When oxygen is not available to cells, the electron transport chain soon becomes inoperative because oxygen is not present to accept electrons. In this case, most cells have a safety valve so that some ATP can still be produced. Glycolysis operates as long as it is supplied with "free" NAD—that is, NAD that can pick up hydrogen atoms. Normally, $NADH_2$ takes hydrogens to the electron transport chain, and thereby becomes "free" of hydrogen atoms. However, if the system is not working due to a lack of oxygen, $NADH_2$ passes its hydrogen atoms to pyruvic acid as shown in the following reaction:

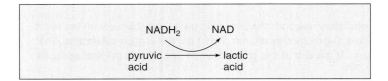

The citric acid cycle and the electron transport chain do not function as part of fermentation. When oxygen is available again, lactic acid can be converted back to pyruvic acid, and metabolism can proceed as usual.

Fermentation takes less time than cellular respiration, but since glycolysis alone is occurring, it produces only two ATP per glucose molecule. Also, fermentation results in the buildup of lactic acid. Lactic acid is toxic to cells and causes muscles to cramp and fatigue. If fermentation continues for any length of time, death follows.

It is of interest to know that fermentation takes its name from yeast fermentation. Yeast fermentation produces alcohol and carbon dioxide (instead of lactic acid). When yeast is used to leaven bread, carbon dioxide production makes the bread rise. When yeast is used to produce alcoholic beverages, it is the alcohol that humans make use of.

Lactic Acid and the Athlete

Exercise is a dramatic test of homeostatic mechanisms. During exercise, the mitochondria of our muscle cells require much oxygen (O_2), and they produce an increased amount of carbon dioxide (CO_2). No doubt, if you run as fast as you can, even for a short time, you notice that you get out of breath. You are in oxygen deficit—your muscles have run out of oxygen and have started fermenting instead. Aerobic exercise occurs when you can manage to get a steady supply of oxygen to your muscle cells so that oxygen deficit does not occur. Athletes are better at this than nonathletes. Why?

First off, the number of mitochondria is higher in the muscles of persons who train. Therefore, an athlete is more likely to rely on the citric acid cycle and the electron transport chain to generate ATP. The citric acid cycle can be powered by fatty acids, instead of glucose; therefore, the level of glucose in the blood remains at a normal level, even though exercise is occurring.

Muscle cells with few mitochondria don't start consuming O_2 until they are out of ATP and ADP concentration is high. After endurance training, the large number of mitochondria start consuming O_2 as soon as the ADP concentration starts rising due to muscle contraction and breakdown of ATP. This faster rise in O_2 uptake at the onset of exercise (Fig. 3.17) means that the O_2 deficit is less, and the formation of lactic acid due to fermentation is less.

As mentioned, the body is able to process lactic acid and change it back to pyruvic acid. This is the oxygen deficit—the amount of oxygen it takes to rid the body of lactic acid. Athletes incur less of an oxygen deficit than nonathletes do.

Fermentation is an anaerobic process that does not require oxygen, produces very little ATP per glucose molecule, and results in the buildup of lactic acid in humans. Athletes ferment less than those who do not train.

Figure 3.17   Training reduces fermentation.
In athletes, there is an increase in fat metabolism that keeps blood glucose at a normal level; a smaller O_2 deficit due to a more rapid increase in O_2 uptake at the onset of work; a reduction in lactic acid formation; and an increase in lactic acid removal.

Bioethical Focus

Stem Cell Research

Some human illnesses, such as diabetes type 1, Alzheimer disease, and Parkinson disease, are clearly due to a loss of specialized cells. In diabetes type 1, there is a loss of insulin-secreting cells in the pancreas, and in Alzheimer disease and Parkinson disease there is a loss of brain cells. Specific types of cells are needed to cure these conditions.

Stem cells are cells that continuously divide to produce new cells that go on to become specialized cells. The bone marrow of adults and the umbilical cord of infants (Fig. 3A) contain stem cells for each type of blood cell in the body. It is relatively easy to retrieve blood stem cells from either of these sources. Researchers report that they have injected blood stem cells into the heart and liver only to find that they became cardiac cells and liver cells, respectively! The skin, gastrointestinal lining, and the brain also have stem cells, but the technology to retrieve them has not been perfected. Also, it has not been possible to change adult stem cells into a fully developed specific type of cell outside the body. If the technique is perfected, it might be possible to, say, change a brain stem cell into the dopamine-secreting cell needed by a Parkinson patient. But the fact the brain is not now doing it—or else the patient wouldn't have Parkinson disease—makes us less hopeful.

Today, young, relatively infertile couples seek assistance in achieving pregnancy and having children. During in vitro fertilization, several eggs and sperm are placed in laboratory glass, where fertilization occurs and development begins. A physician places two or three embryos in the woman's uterus for further development, but may hold back some in case these fail to take hold. Embryos that are never used remain frozen indefinitely unless they are made available to researchers. Each cell of an embryo is called an embryonic stem cell because it can become any kind of specialized cell in the body. Researchers have already used nonhuman embryonic cells to create supplies of nonhuman specialized cells. Therefore, they think the same will hold true with human embryonic stem cells. If so, medicine would undergo an advancement of enormous proportions.

Even so, there is a down side. What about the embryos that have been forced to give up a chance of becoming an adult in order to extend the health span of those already living? Would this be ethical? In Great Britain, researchers can work with embryos that are 14 days or younger because embryos usually implant in the uterus around day 14. Robert George of Princeton University doesn't agree with this solution to the problem. He says, "I believe that all human beings are equal, and ought not to be harmed or considered to be less than human on the basis of age or size or stage of development or condition of dependency." He believes that embryos should not be used as a means to an end, even good ends, such as a cure for diseases or to save another human life. President George W. Bush agrees and signed an executive

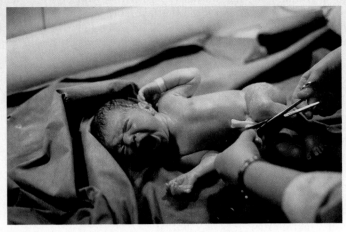

Figure 3A   Umbilical cords are valuable.
The blood from a baby's umbilical cord can be banked, and then used as a source of blood stem cells. Investigators are hopeful they will be able to convert blood stem cells to various types of mature cells.

order that forbids the use of federal funds for the purpose of creating new cell lines derived from embryos in the United States. The order does not affect any embryonic stem cell lines previously established nor any work with adult stem cells. Nevertheless, some researchers have left the United States to work in countries where stem cell research is freely allowed without governmental restrictions.

Michael Sandel of Harvard University offers a way out of the bioethical dilemma. He says that to think in dualistic terms is not helpful—it isn't that an embryo is a human being or is not a human being—it's that a fully developed human being comes about gradually. He offers this situation to illustrate his point. What would you do if there was a fire in a fertility clinic and you were faced with the choice of saving a five year-old girl or a tray of 10 embryos? Which would you choose? He still believes that "life is a gift that commands our reverence and restricts our use." While he believes that stem cell research is ethical, he does not believe that humans should be cloned.

Decide Your Opinion

1. Should researchers have access to embryonic stem cells or only adult stem cells? What is your reasoning?
2. Do you believe, as Sandel does, that while it is ethical to do research with embryonic stem cells to cure human ills, it is not ethical to clone humans? What is your reasoning?
3. Some researchers are mixing nonhuman with human embryonic stem cells in order to study developmental differences. Is this ethical? Why or why not?

Summarizing the Concepts

3.1 What Is a Cell?
Cells are quite small, and it usually takes a microscope to see them. Small cubes, like cells, have a more favorable surface-to-volume ratio than do large cubes. Only eggs are large enough to be seen by the naked eye; once development begins, cell division results in small-sized cells.

3.2 Cellular Organization
A cell is surrounded by a plasma membrane, which regulates the entrance and exit of molecules and ions. Some molecules, such as water and gases, diffuse through the membrane. The direction in which water diffuses is dependent on its concentration within the cell, relative to outside the cell. Transport by carriers also allows substances to cross the plasma membrane, as do endocytosis and exocytosis. Diffusion and facilitated transport are passive ways to cross the plasma membrane; active transport, endocytosis, and exocytosis are active ways to cross the plasma membrane.

The cytoskeleton, consisting of microtubules, intermediate filaments, and actin filaments, provides a scaffolding inside the cytoplasm that allows organelles to travel within the cell. Each organelle in a cell has specific functions. The nucleus is of primary importance because it controls the rest of the cell. Within the nucleus lies the chromatin, which condenses to become chromosomes during cell division.

Within the endomembrane system, proteins are made at the rough ER before being modified and packaged by the Golgi apparatus into vesicles for secretion. During secretion, a vesicle discharges its contents at the plasma membrane. Golgi-derived lysosomes fuse with incoming vesicles to digest any material enclosed within, and lysosomes also carry out autodigestion of old parts of cells.

Cilia and flagella, which contain microtubules, allow a cell to move. Their function is critical, as witnessed by a genetic disorder that leads to respiratory infections and infertility when microtubules are malformed.

Mitochondria, which take in oxygen and glucose and give off carbon dioxide, are the powerhouses of the cell. During the process of cellular respiration, mitochondria convert carbohydrate energy to ATP energy.

3.3 Cellular Metabolism
Cellular metabolism is the sum of all the biochemical pathways of the cell. In a pathway, a series of reactions proceeds in an orderly, step-by-step manner. Each of these reactions requires a specific enzyme. Sometimes enzymes require coenzymes, nonprotein molecules that participate in the reaction. NAD is a coenzyme.

Cellular respiration (the breakdown of glucose to carbon dioxide and water) includes four pathways: glycolysis, the preparatory reaction, the citric acid cycle, and the electron transport chain. If oxygen is not available in cells, the electron transport chain is inoperative, and fermentation (an anaerobic process) occurs. Fermentation makes use of glycolysis only, plus one more reaction. In humans, pyruvic acid is reduced to lactic acid.

Studying the Concepts

1. Explain the two tenets of the cell theory. 36
2. Contrast and compare the compound light microscope, the transmission electron microscope, and the scanning electron microscope. 37
3. Describe the overall organization of a cell. 38–39
4. Describe the structure and function of a plasma membrane. 40
5. Describe two passive mechanisms and three active mechanisms by which substances either enter or exit cells. Define isotonic, hypotonic, and hypertonic solutions. 41–43
6. Describe the structure and function of the cytoskeleton. 43
7. Describe the nucleus and its contents, including the terms DNA and RNA in your description. 44
8. Describe the endomembrane system, including the structure and function of the organelles that make up the system. 45
9. Describe the structure of cilia and flagella and give examples of human cells that have these structures. 46
10. Describe the structure of mitochondria, and relate this structure to the pathways of cellular respiration. 47, 49
11. Draw and discuss a diagram for a metabolic pathway. Discuss and give a generalized reaction to describe how enzymes speed reactions. Define coenzyme. 48
12. Name and describe the events within the three subpathways that make up cellular respiration. Why is fermentation necessary but potentially harmful to the human body? 49–50

Thinking Critically About the Concepts

Refer to the opening vignette on page 35, and then answer these questions.

1. How many different types of cells must perform well for Helen to be able to race her bicycle?
2. How are cellular respiration and lung respiration (see Chapter 8) related?
3. Besides an increase in the number of mitochondria, what other changes occur in muscle cells due to exercise?
4. If exercise is good for you, why do you think some people have fatal heart attacks during exercise?

Testing Your Knowledge of the Concepts

Choose the best answer for each question.

1. The cell theory states:
   a. Cells form as organelles, and molecules become grouped together in an organized manner.
   b. The normal functioning of an organism does not depend on its individual cells.
   c. The cell is the basic unit of life for all living things.
   d. Only mammalian organisms are made of cells.

2. The small size of cells is best correlated with
   a. the fact that they are self-reproducing.
   b. an adequate surface area for exchange of materials.
   c. their vast versatility.
   d. All of these are correct.

In questions 3–6, match each function to an organelle in the key.

Key:

    a. mitochondrion   c. Golgi apparatus

    b. nucleus   d. rough ER

3. Packaging and secretion.

4. Powerhouse of cell.

5. Protein synthesis.

6. Control center for cell.

7. Vesicles carrying proteins for secretion move between the ER and the
   a. smooth ER.
   b. lysosomes.
   c. Golgi apparatus.
   d. plasma membranes of adjoining cells.

8. Lysosomes function in
   a. protein synthesis.
   b. processing and packaging.
   c. intracellular digestion.
   d. lipid synthesis.
   e. All of these are correct.

9. Mitochondria
   a. are involved in cellular respiration.
   b. break down ATP to release energy for cells.
   c. contain hemoglobin and cristae.
   d. have a convoluted outer membrane.
   e. All of these are correct.

10. Which of the following is a component of the cytoskeleton?
    a. flagella
    b. centrioles
    c. microtubules
    d. microvilli

11. Cilia and flagella
    a. move by different mechanisms.
    b. contain microtubules.
    c. are of the same length.
    d. Both a and c are correct.

12. Which of the following organelles produces ATP?
    a. Golgi apparatus
    b. mitochondrion
    c. lysosome
    d. ribosome
    e. Both b and c are correct.

13. A phospholipid molecule has a head and two tails. The tails are found
    a. at the surfaces of the membrane.
    b. in the interior of the membrane.
    c. spanning the membrane.
    d. where the environment is hydrophilic.
    e. Both a and b are correct.

14. When a cell is placed in a hypotonic solution,
    a. solute exits the cell to equalize the concentration on both sides of the membrane.
    b. water exits the cell toward the area of lower solute concentration.

c. water enters the cell toward the area of higher solute concentration.
d. solute exits and water enters the cell.

15. Use these terms to label the following diagram of the plasma membrane: carbohydrate chain, cholesterol, filaments of the cytoskeleton, glycolipid, glycoprotein, hydrophilic head, hydrophobic tails, membrane protein (used twice), phospholipid bilayer.

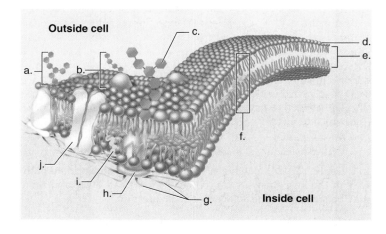

16. The metabolic process that produces the most ATP molecules is
    a. glycolysis.
    b. the citric acid cycle.
    c. the electron transport chain.
    d. fermentation.

17. Facilitated transport differs from diffusion in that facilitated transport
    a. involves the use of a carrier protein.
    b. moves molecules from a high to low concentration.
    c. moves a molecule down a concentration gradient.
    d. is a passive process.
    e. involves the use of ATP molecules.

18. Which of these utilizes ATP?
    a. synthesis of molecules in cells
    b. active transport of molecules across the plasma membrane
    c. muscle contraction
    d. nerve conduction
    e. All of these are correct.

19. The active site of an enzyme
    a. is identical to that of any other enzyme.
    b. is the part of the enzyme where its substrate can fit.
    c. can be used over and over again.
    d. is not affected by environmental factors, such as pH and temperature.
    e. Both b and c are correct.

20. Coenzymes
    a. assist enzymes in functioning.
    b. have an active site just as enzymes do.
    c. can be a carrier for proteins.
    d. always have a phosphate group.
    e. are not used in cellular respiration.

21. Use these terms to label the following diagram: substrates, enzyme (used twice), active site, product, and enzyme-substrate complex. Explain the importance of an enzyme's shape to its activity.

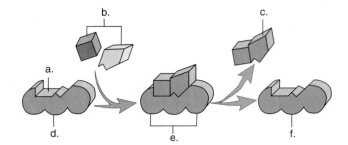

22. The oxygen required by cellular respiration becomes part of which molecule?
    a. ATP
    b. H_2O
    c. pyruvic acid
    d. CO_2

In questions 23–25, match each molecule to the appropriate pathway in the key. Answers can be used more than once, and there may be more than one answer for each question.

Key:
    a. glycolysis
    b. citric acid cycle
    c. electron transport chain
    d. preparatory reaction

23. $NADH_2 \rightarrow NAD$

24. CO_2

25. O_2

In questions 26–28, match each pathway to a location in the key. Answers may be used more than once or not at all.

Key:
    a. matrix of the mitochondrion
    b. cristae of the mitochondrion
    c. in the cytoplasm
    d. None of these is correct.

26. Electron transport chain

27. Preparatory reaction

28. Citric acid cycle

29. Which of the following is not true of fermentation? Fermentation
    a. has a net gain of only two ATP.
    b. occurs in the cytoplasm.
    c. donates electrons to the electron transport chain.
    d. begins with glucose.
    e. occurs in the absence of oxygen.

Understanding Key Terms

actin filaments 43
active site 48
active transport 42
basal body 46
cell theory 36

cellular respiration 49
centrosome 43
chromatin 44
chromosome 44
cilium 46

citric acid cycle 49
coenzyme 48
cytoplasm 38
cytoskeleton 38, 43
dehydrogenase 48
diffusion 41
electron transport chain 49
endomembrane system 45
endoplasmic reticulum
    (ER) 44
facilitated transport 42
fermentation 50
flagellum 46
glycolysis 49
Golgi apparatus 45
intermediate filament 43
lysosome 45
metabolism 48
microtubule 43
mitochondrion 47

NAD (nicotinamide adenine
    dinucleotide) 48
nuclear envelope 44
nuclear pore 44
nucleolus 38, 44
nucleoplasm 44
nucleus 38, 44
organelle 38
osmosis 41
plasma membrane 38
polyribosome 44
preparatory reaction 49
product 48
reactant 48
ribosome 44
selectively permeable 40
substrate 48
tonicity 41
vesicles 45

Match the key terms to these definitions.

a. _____ Nonprotein organic molecule that aids the action of the enzyme to which it is loosely bound.

b. _____ Diffusion of water through a selectively permeable membrane.

c. _____ Having degrees of permeability; the cell is impermeable to some substances and allows others to pass through at varying rates.

d. _____ Anaerobic breakdown of glucose that results in a gain of two ATP and end products, such as alcohol and lactic acid.

e. _____ Metabolic pathways that use the energy from carbohydrate breakdown to produce ATP molecules.

Online Learning Center

www.mhhe.com/maderhuman9

The Online Learning Center provides a wealth of information fully organized and integrated by chapter. You will find practice quizzes, interactive activities, labeling exercises, flashcards, and much more that will complement your learning and understanding of human biology.

Looking at Both Sides

Each day, the Internet, media, and other people present you with opposing viewpoints on a wide range of subjects. Your ability to develop an informed opinion on an issue, and talk to others about it, is extremely important.

To expand and enhance your knowledge of a highly relevant bioethical issue, visit the "Student Edition" of the Online Learning Center. Under "Course-Wide Content," select "Looking at Both Sides." Once there, you will be asked to complete activities that will increase your understanding of a current bioethical issue related to this chapter and allow you to defend your opinion.

CHAPTER

4

Organization and
Regulation of
Body Systems

C H A P T E R   C O N C E P T S

4.1 Types of Tissues

- What are the four major tissue types found in the human body?   56
- What tissue type binds and supports other body tissues? What are some examples of this type of tissue?   56–58
- Which tissue type is responsible for body movements? What are some examples of this type of tissue?   59
- Which tissue type coordinates the activities of the other tissue types in the body?   60
- How is epithelial tissue classified? Where do you find epithelial tissues, and what are their functions?   62–63

4.2 Integumentary System

- What is the integumentary system?   64–65

4.3 Organ Systems

- What is the overall function of each of the body systems?   66–67
- What are the two major body cavities? What two cavities are in each of these?   68
- What are four types of body membranes?   68

4.4 Homeostasis

- What is homeostasis, and why is it important to body function?   70
- How do body systems contribute to homeostasis?   70–71
- How do negative feedback and positive feedback contribute to homeostasis?   72–73

The hot July sun blazed high in a cloudless sky—perfect for an afternoon at the beach. As Olivia packed towels and sunglasses into her tote, her mother called out, "Don't forget your sunblock and be sure to take plenty of water with you."

Because our bodies are well-equipped to endure many different environmental conditions, it is easy to overlook taking steps to ensure that the internal environment of the body remains fairly constant. When we go to the beach, our bodies continue to regulate the internal temperature, maintain water balance, and prevent radiation damage.

As the heat from the July sun bore down on Olivia, thousands of tiny sweat glands in her skin released water, thereby helping regulate her internal body temperature. The melanin granules forming in her skin cells give her skin a golden-brown color, which helps protect it from damage due to the sun's radiation. Olivia's nervous system is also at work, as when it instructs the pupils to constrict, in order to avoid overloading her eyes with too much light.

Using sunscreen and drinking water are two obvious ways we can help our bodies cope with the environment. As you read this chapter, keep this scenario in mind as a backdrop to learning about the various tissues and organs of the human body, how they are organized, and how these tissues and organs interact with one another and with the outside world.

4.1 Types of Tissues

Recall the biological levels of organization. Cells are composed of molecules; a tissue has like cells; an organ contains several types of tissues; and several organs are found in an organ system. In this chapter, we consider the tissue, organ, and organ system levels of organization.

A **tissue** is composed of specialized cells of the same type that perform a common function in the body. The tissues of the human body can be categorized into four major types:

> *Connective tissue* binds and supports body parts.
> *Muscular tissue* moves the body and its parts.
> *Nervous tissue* receives stimuli and conducts nerve
>   impulses.
> *Epithelial tissue* covers body surfaces and lines body
>   cavities.

Cancers are classified according to the type of tissue from which they arise. Sarcomas are cancers arising in muscle or connective tissue (especially bone or cartilage); leukemias are cancers of the blood; lymphomas are cancers of lymphoid tissue, and **carcinomas,** the most common type, are cancers of epithelial tissue. The chance of developing cancer in a particular tissue shows a positive correlation to the rate of cell division; epithelial cells reproduce at a high rate, and 2,500,000 new blood cells appear each second. Thus, carcinomas and leukemias are common types of cancers.

Connective Tissue

Connective tissue is quite diverse in structure and function, but, even so, all types have three components: specialized cells, ground substance, and protein fibers (Fig. 4.1). The term **matrix** includes ground substance and fibers. The ground substance is a noncellular material that separates the cells and varies in con-

sistency from solid to semifluid to fluid. The fibers are of three possible types. White **collagen fibers** contain collagen, a protein that gives them flexibility and strength. **Reticular fibers** are very thin collagen fibers that are highly branched and form delicate supporting networks. Yellow **elastic fibers** contain elastin, a protein that is not as strong as collagen but is more elastic.

Fibrous Connective Tissue

Both loose fibrous and dense fibrous connective tissues have cells called **fibroblasts** that are located some distance from one another and are separated by a jelly-like matrix containing white collagen fibers and yellow elastic fibers.

Loose fibrous connective tissue supports epithelium and also many internal organs (Fig. 4.2a). Its presence in lungs, arteries, and the urinary bladder allows these organs to expand. It forms a protective covering enclosing many internal organs, such as muscles, blood vessels, and nerves.

Adipose tissue (Fig. 4.2b) is a special type of loose connective tissue in which the cells enlarge and store fat. The body uses this stored fat for energy, insulation, and organ protection. Adipose tissue is found beneath the skin, around the kidneys, and on the surface of the heart.

Dense fibrous connective tissue contains many collagen fibers that are packed together. This type of tissue has more specific functions than does loose connective tissue. For example, dense fibrous connective tissue is found in **tendons,** which connect muscles to bones, and in **ligaments,** which connect bones to other bones at joints.

Supportive Connective Tissue

In **cartilage,** the cells lie in small chambers called lacunae (sing., **lacuna**), separated by a matrix that is solid yet flexible. Unfortunately, because this tissue lacks a direct blood supply, it heals very slowly. There are three types of cartilage, distinguished by the type of fiber in the matrix.

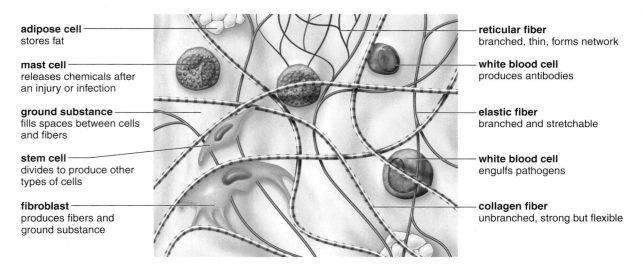

adipose cell
stores fat

mast cell
releases chemicals after
an injury or infection

ground substance
fills spaces between cells
and fibers

stem cell
divides to produce other
types of cells

fibroblast
produces fibers and
ground substance

reticular fiber
branched, thin, forms network

white blood cell
produces antibodies

elastic fiber
branched and stretchable

white blood cell
engulfs pathogens

collagen fiber
unbranched, strong but flexible

Figure 4.1   **Diagram of fibrous connective tissue.**

Hyaline cartilage (Fig. 4.2c), the most common type of cartilage, contains only very fine collagen fibers. The matrix has a glassy, translucent appearance. Hyaline cartilage is found in the nose and at the ends of the long bones and the ribs, and it forms rings in the walls of respiratory passages. The fetal skeleton also is made of this type of cartilage. Later, the cartilaginous fetal skeleton is replaced by bone.

Elastic cartilage has more elastic fibers than hyaline cartilage. For this reason, it is more flexible and is found, for example, in the framework of the outer ear.

Fibrocartilage has a matrix containing strong collagen fibers. Fibrocartilage is found in structures that withstand tension and pressure, such as the pads between the vertebrae in the backbone and the wedges in the knee joint.

Bone

Bone is the most rigid connective tissue. It consists of an extremely hard matrix of inorganic salts, notably calcium salts, deposited around protein fibers, especially collagen fibers. The inorganic salts give bone rigidity, and the protein fibers provide elasticity and strength, much as steel rods do in reinforced concrete.

Compact bone makes up the shaft of a long bone (Fig. 4.2d). It consists of cylindrical structural units called osteons (Haversian systems). The central canal of each osteon is surrounded by rings of hard matrix. Bone cells are located in spaces called lacunae between the rings of matrix. Blood vessels in the central canal carry nutrients that allow bone to renew itself. Thin extensions of bone cells within canaliculi (minute canals) connect the cells to each other and to the central canal.

The ends of a long bone contain spongy bone, which has an entirely different structure. **Spongy bone** contains numerous bony bars and plates, separated by irregular spaces. Although lighter than compact bone, spongy bone is still designed for strength. Just as braces are used for support in buildings, the solid portions of spongy bone follow lines of stress.

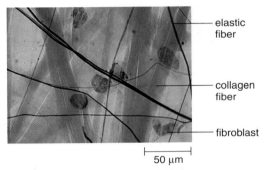

⊢ 50 μm ⊣

a. **Loose fibrous connective tissue**
- has space between components.
- occurs beneath skin and most epithelial layers.
- functions in support and binds organs.

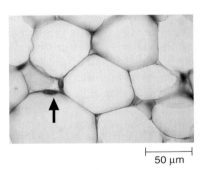

⊢ 50 μm ⊣

b. **Adipose tissue**
- cells are filled with fat.
- occurs beneath skin, around organs and heart.
- functions in insulation, stores fat.

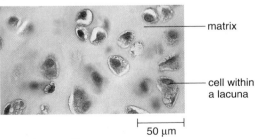

⊢ 50 μm ⊣

c. **Hyaline cartilage**
- has cells in lacunae.
- occurs in nose and walls of respiratory passages; at ends of bones including ribs.
- functions in support and protection.

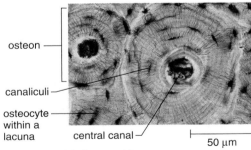

⊢ 50 μm ⊣

d. **Compact bone**
- has cells in concentric rings.
- occurs in bones of skeleton.
- functions in support and protection.

Figure 4.2   Connective tissue examples.
a. In loose fibrous connective tissue, cells called fibroblasts are separated by a jelly-like matrix, which contains both collagen and elastic fibers. **b.** Adipose tissue cells have nuclei (see arrow) pushed to one side because the cells are filled with fat. **c.** In hyaline cartilage, the flexible matrix has a glassy, translucent appearance. **d.** In compact bone, the hard matrix contains calcium salts. Concentric rings of matrix, separated by cells in lacunae, form an elongated cylinder called an osteon (Haversian system). An osteon has a central canal that contains blood vessels and nerve fibers.

Fluid Connective Tissues

Blood, which consists of formed elements (Fig. 4.3) and plasma, is a fluid connective tissue located in blood vessels. Some people do not classify blood as connective tissue; instead, they suggest a separate tissue category called vascular tissue.

The internal environment of the body consists of blood and **tissue fluid.** The systems of the body help keep blood composition and chemistry within normal limits, and blood in turn creates tissue fluid. Blood transports nutrients and oxygen to tissue fluid and removes carbon dioxide and other wastes. It helps distribute heat and also plays a role in fluid, ion, and pH balance. The formed elements, discussed below, each have specific functions.

The **red blood cells** are small, biconcave, disk-shaped cells without nuclei. The presence of the red pigment hemoglobin makes the cells red, and in turn, makes the blood red. Hemoglobin is composed of four units; each unit is composed of the protein globin and a complex iron-containing structure called heme. The iron forms a loose association with oxygen, and in this way red blood cells transport oxygen.

White blood cells may be distinguished from red blood cells by the fact that they are usually larger, have a nucleus, and without staining would appear translucent. White blood cells characteristically look bluish because they have been stained that color. White blood cells fight infection, primarily in two ways. Some white blood cells are phagocytic and engulf infectious **pathogens.** Other white blood cells either produce antibodies, molecules that combine with foreign substances to inactivate them, or they kill cells outright.

Platelets are not complete cells; rather, they are fragments of giant cells present only in bone marrow. When a blood vessel is damaged, platelets form a plug that seals the vessel, and injured tissues release molecules that help the clotting process.

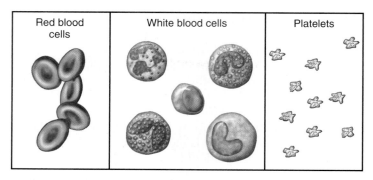

Figure 4.3   Formed elements in blood.
Red blood cells, which lack a nucleus, transport oxygen. Each type of white blood cell has a particular way to fight infections. Platelets, which are fragments of a particular cell, function in blood clotting.

Lymph is a fluid, derived from blood, which is located in lymphatic vessels. Lymphatic vessels absorb excess tissue fluid and various dissolved solutes in the tissues and transport them to particular vessels of the cardiovascular system. Special lymphatic capillaries, called lacteals, absorb fat molecules from the small intestine. Lymph nodes, composed of fibrous connective tissue, occur along the length of lymphatic vessels. Lymph is cleansed as it passes through lymph nodes in particular because white blood cells congregate there. Lymphatic nodes enlarge when you have an infection.

Connective tissue is classified into three types: fibrous, supportive, and fluid connective tissue (Fig. 4.4). Fibrous connective tissue forms the structural framework, binds organs, and stores fat. Supportive connective tissue supports, protects, and is involved in movement of the body. Fluid connective tissue transports and fights infections.

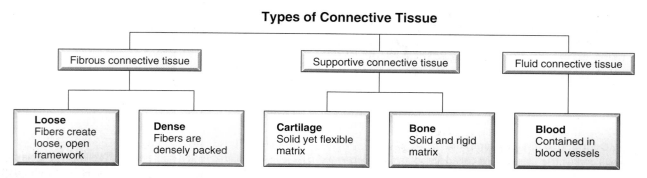

Figure 4.4   Types of connective tissue.

Muscular Tissue

Muscular (contractile) tissue is composed of cells called muscle fibers. Muscle fibers contain protein filaments, called actin and myosin filaments, whose interaction accounts for movement. The three types of vertebrate muscular tissue are skeletal, smooth, and cardiac.

Skeletal muscle, also called voluntary muscle (Fig. 4.5*a*), is attached by tendons to the bones of the skeleton, and when it contracts, body parts move. Contraction of skeletal muscle is under voluntary control and occurs faster than in the other muscle types. Skeletal muscle fibers are cylindrical and quite long—sometimes they run the length of the muscle. They arise during development when several cells fuse, resulting in one fiber with multiple nuclei. The nuclei are located at the periphery of the cell, just inside the plasma membrane. The fibers have alternating light and dark bands that give them a **striated,** or striped, appearance. These bands are due to the placement of actin filaments and myosin filaments in the cell.

Smooth (visceral) muscle is so named because the cells lack striations. The spindle-shaped cells form layers in which the thick middle portion of one cell is opposite the thin ends of adjacent cells. Consequently, the nuclei form an irregular pattern in the tissue (Fig. 4.5*b*). Smooth muscle is not under voluntary control, and therefore is said to be involuntary. Smooth muscle, found in the walls of viscera (intestine, stomach, and other internal organs) and blood vessels, contracts more slowly than skeletal muscle but can remain contracted for a longer time. When the smooth muscle of the intestine contracts, food moves along its lumen (central cavity). When the smooth muscle of the blood vessels contracts, blood vessels constrict, helping to raise blood pressure.

Cardiac muscle (Fig. 4.5*c*) is found only in the walls of the heart. Its contraction pumps blood and accounts for the heartbeat. Cardiac muscle combines features of both smooth and skeletal muscle. Like skeletal muscle, it has striations, but the contraction of the heart is involuntary for the most part. Cardiac muscle cells also differ from skeletal muscle cells in that they usually have a single, centrally placed nucleus. The cells are branched and seemingly fused one with another, and the heart appears to be composed of one large interconnecting mass of muscle cells. Actually, cardiac muscle cells are separate and individual, but they are bound end to end at **intercalated disks,** areas where folded plasma membranes between two cells contain adhesion junctions and gap junctions.

All muscular tissue contains both actin and myosin filaments; these form a striated pattern in skeletal and cardiac muscle, but not in smooth muscle.

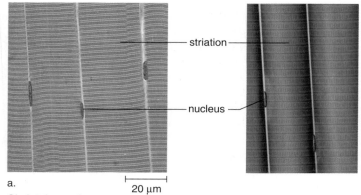

a.   20 μm

Skeletal muscle
• has striated cells with multiple nuclei.
• occurs in muscles attached to skeleton.
• functions in voluntary movement of body.
• is voluntary.

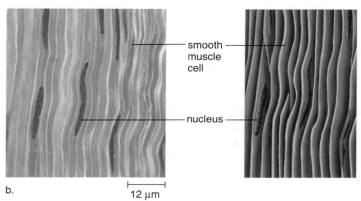

b.   12 μm

Smooth muscle
• has spindle-shaped cells, each with a single nucleus.
• cells have no striations.
• functions in movement of substances in lumens of body.
• is involuntary.

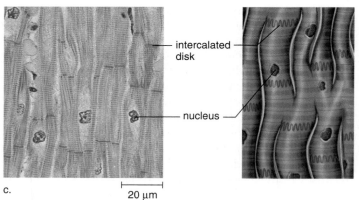

c.   20 μm

Cardiac muscle
• has branching striated cells, each with a single nucleus.
• occurs in the wall of the heart.
• functions in the pumping of blood.
• is involuntary.

Figure 4.5 Muscular tissue.

a. Skeletal muscle is voluntary and striated. **b.** Smooth muscle is involuntary and nonstriated. **c.** Cardiac muscle is involuntary and striated. Cardiac muscle cells branch and fit together at intercalated disks.

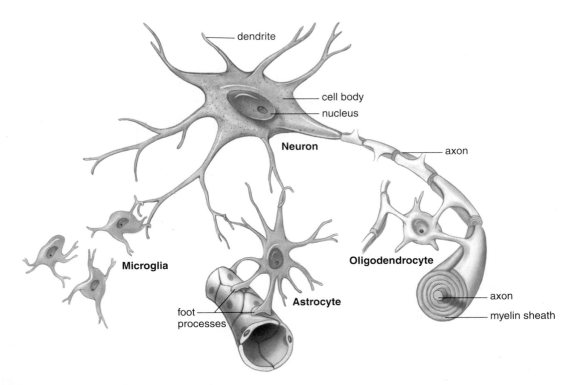

Figure 4.6 **A neuron and some types of neuroglia.**
Neurons conduct nerve impulses, while neuroglia primarily support and nourish neurons. Microglia are a type of neuroglia that become mobile in response to inflammation and phagocytize debris. Astrocytes lie between neurons and a capillary; therefore, substances entering neurons from the blood must first pass through astrocytes. Oligodendrocytes form the myelin sheaths around fibers in the brain and spinal cord.

Nervous Tissue

Nervous tissue, which contains nerve cells called neurons, is present in the brain and spinal cord. A **neuron** is a specialized cell that has three parts: dendrites, a cell body, and an axon (Fig. 4.6, *top*). A dendrite is an extension that receives signals from sensory receptors or other neurons. The cell body contains the major concentration of the cytoplasm and the nucleus of the neuron. An axon is an extension that conducts nerve impulses. Long axons are covered by myelin, a white fatty substance. The term *fiber*[1] is used here to refer to an axon along with its myelin sheath, if it has one. Outside the brain and spinal cord, fibers bound by connective tissue form **nerves.**

The nervous system has just three functions: sensory input, integration of data, and motor output. Nerves conduct impulses from sensory receptors to the spinal cord and the brain, where integration occurs. The phenomenon called sensation occurs only in the brain, however. Nerves also conduct nerve impulses away from the spinal cord and brain to the muscles and glands, causing them to contract and secrete, respectively. In this way, a coordinated response to the stimulus is achieved.

Neuroglia

In addition to neurons, nervous tissue contains neuroglia. **Neuroglia** are cells that outnumber neurons nine to one and take up more than half the volume of the brain. Although the primary function of neuroglia is to support and nourish neurons, research is currently being conducted to determine how much they directly contribute to brain function. Types of neuroglia found in the brain are, for example, microglia, astrocytes, and oligodendrocytes (Fig. 4.6, *bottom*). Microglia, in addition to supporting neurons, engulf bacterial and cellular debris. Astrocytes provide nutrients to neurons and produce a hormone known as glia-derived growth factor, which someday might be used as a cure for Parkinson disease and other diseases caused by neuron degeneration. Oligodendrocytes form myelin. Neuroglia don't have a long extension, but even so, researchers are now beginning to gather evidence that they do communicate among themselves and with neurons!

Nerve cells, called neurons, have processes called axons and dendrites. In general, neuroglia support and service neurons.

---

[1]In connective tissue, a fiber is a component of the matrix; in muscle tissue, a fiber is a muscle cell; in nervous tissue, a fiber is an axon.

Health Focus

Nerve Regeneration

In humans, axons outside the brain and spinal cord can regenerate, but not those inside these organs. After injury, axons in the human central nervous system (CNS) degenerate, resulting in permanent loss of nervous function. Not so in cold-water fishes and amphibians, where axon regeneration in the CNS does occur. So far, investigators have identified several proteins that seem to be necessary to axon regeneration in the CNS of these animals (Fig. 4A), but it may be a long time before biochemistry can offer a way to bring about axon regeneration in the human CNS. It's possible, though, that one day these proteins will become drugs or that gene therapy might be used to cause humans to produce the same proteins when CNS injuries occur.

In the meantime, some accident victims are trying other ways to bring about a cure. In 1995, Christopher Reeve, best known for his acting role as "Superman," was thrown head-first from his horse, crushing the spinal cord just below the neck's top two vertebrae. Immediately, his brain lost almost all communication with the portion of his body below the site of damage and he could not move his arms and legs. Many years later, Reeve could move his left index finger slightly and could take tiny steps while being held upright in a pool. He had sensation throughout his body and could feel his wife's touch.

Reeve's improvement was not the result of cutting-edge drugs or gene therapy—it was due to exercise (Fig. 4B)! Reeve exercised as much as five hours a day, especially using

Figure 4B Treatment today for spinal cord injuries.
a. Reeve suffered a spinal cord injury when horseback riding in 1995. **b.** He exercised many hours a day. Here he receives aqua therapy. Reeve died in 2004.

a.

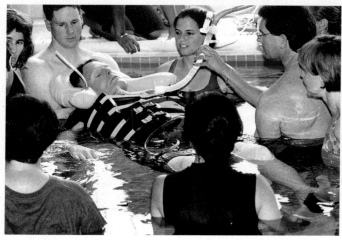

b.

a.

Figure 4A Researchers at work.
a. Some researches are studying the activity of proteins that allow cold-bodied animals to regenerate axons in the CNS. **b.** Others are doing stem cell research. Stem cells might one day be used to cure people with spinal cord injuries.

b.

a recumbent bike outfitted with electrodes that made his leg muscles contract and relax. The bike cost him $16,000. It could cost less if commonly used by spinal cord injury patients in their own homes. Reeve, who was an activist for the disabled, was pleased that insurance would pay for the bike about 50% of the time.

It's possible that Reeve's advances were the result of improved strength and bone density, which lead to stronger nerve signals. Normally, nerve cells are constantly signaling one another, but after a spinal cord injury, the signals cease. Perhaps Reeve's intensive exercise brought back some of the normal communication between nerves. Reeve's physician, John McDonald, a neurologist at Washington University in St. Louis, is convinced that his axons were regenerating. Fred Gage, a neuroscientist at the Salk Institute in La Jolla, California, has shown that exercise does enhance the growth of new cells in adult brains.

For himself, Reeve was convinced that stem cell therapy would one day allow him to be off his ventilator and functioning normally; however, Reeve died in 2004. So far, researchers have shown that both embryonic stem cells and bone marrow stem cells can differentiate into neurons in the laboratory. Bone marrow stem cells apparently can also become neurons when injected into the body (see page 408).

Epithelial Tissue

Epithelial tissue, also called epithelium (pl., epithelia), consists of tightly packed cells that form a continuous layer. Epithelial tissue covers surfaces and lines body cavities. Usually, it has a protective function, but it can also be modified to carry out secretion, absorption, excretion, and filtration.

Epithelial cells may be connected to one another by three types of junctions composed of proteins (Fig. 4.7). Regions where proteins join them together are called tight junctions. In the digestive tract, digestive juices stay within the intestine, and in the kidneys, the urine stays within kidney tubules because epithelial cells are joined by tight junctions. Adhesion junctions, for example in the skin, allow epithelial cells to stretch and bend, while gap junctions are protein channels that permit the passage of molecules between two adjacent cells.

Epithelial cells are exposed to the environment on one side, but on the other side they have a so-called **basement membrane.** The basement membrane should not be confused with the plasma membrane or the body membranes we will be discussing. It is simply a thin layer of various types of proteins that anchors the epithelium to underlying connective tissue.

Simple Epithelia

Epithelial tissue is either simple or stratified. Simple epithelia have only a single layer of cells (Fig. 4.8) and are classified according to cell type. **Squamous epithelium,** which is composed of flattened cells, is found lining the air sacs of lungs and walls of blood vessels. **Cuboidal epithelium** contains cube-shaped cells and is found lining the kidney tubules and various glands. **Columnar epithelium** has cells resembling rectangular pillars or columns, with nuclei usually located near the bottom of each cell. This epithelium is found lining the digestive tract, where it efficiently absorbs nutrients from the small intestine because of minute cellular extensions called microvilli. Ciliated columnar epithelium is found lining the oviducts, where it propels the egg toward the uterus, or womb.

When an epithelium is pseudostratified, it appears to be layered, but true layers do not exist because each cell touches the baseline. The lining of the windpipe, or trachea, is pseudostratified ciliated columnar epithelium. A secreted covering of mucus traps foreign particles, and the upward motion of the cilia carries the mucus to the back of the throat, where it may either be swallowed or expectorated. Smoking can cause a change in mucus secretion and inhibit ciliary action, resulting in a chronic inflammatory condition called bronchitis.

Stratified Epithelia

Stratified epithelia have layers of cells piled one on top of the other. Only the bottom layer touches the basement membrane. The nose, mouth, esophagus, anal canal, and vagina are all lined with stratified squamous epithelium. As we shall see, the outer layer of skin is also stratified squamous epithelium, but the cells have been reinforced by keratin, a protein that provides strength. Stratified cuboidal and stratified columnar epithelia also occur in the body.

Glandular Epithelia

When an epithelium secretes a product, it is said to be glandular. A **gland** can be a single epithelial cell, as in the case of mucus-secreting goblet cells within the columnar epithelium lining the digestive tract, or a gland can contain many cells. Glands that secrete their product into ducts are called exocrine glands, and those that secrete their product directly into the bloodstream are called endocrine glands. The pancreas is both an exocrine and an endocrine gland; it secretes digestive juices into the small intestine via ducts, and it secretes insulin into the bloodstream.

Epithelial tissue is named according to the shape of the cell. These tightly packed protective cells can occur in more than one layer, and the cells lining a cavity can be ciliated and/or glandular.

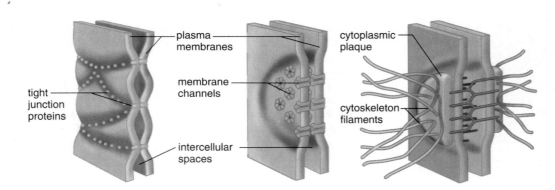

Figure 4.7 Junctions between epithelial cells.
Junctions between cells are composed of protein molecules. **a.** Tight junctions hold epithelial cells close together. **b.** Gap junctions allow materials to pass from cell to cell. **c.** Adhesion junctions allow them to stretch.

plasma membranes

cytoplasmic plaque

tight junction proteins

membrane channels

cytoskeleton filaments

intercellular spaces

a. Tight junction   b. Gap junction   c. Adhesion junction

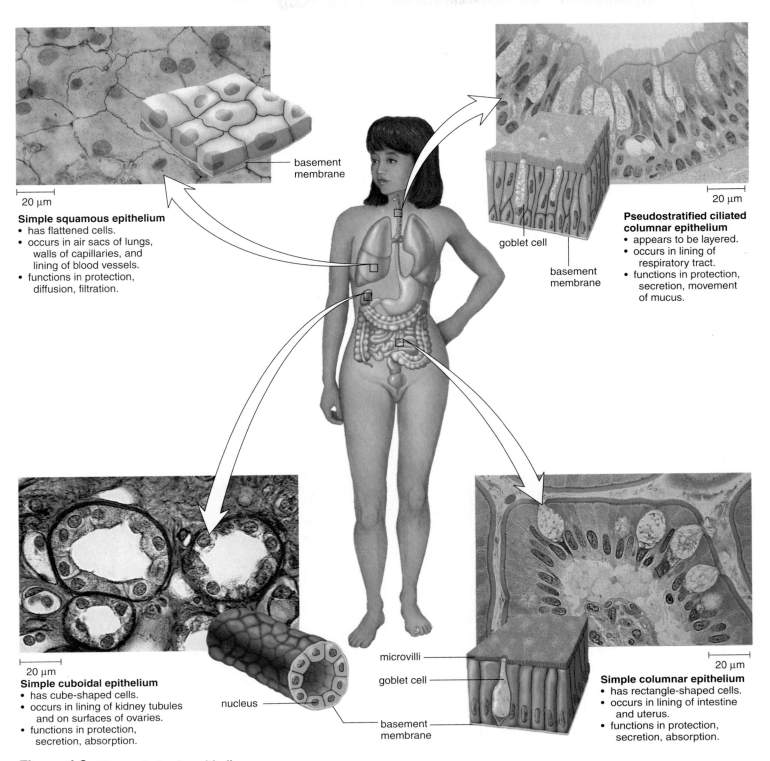

basement membrane

Simple squamous epithelium
- has flattened cells.
- occurs in air sacs of lungs, walls of capillaries, and lining of blood vessels.
- functions in protection, diffusion, filtration.

20 μm

goblet cell

basement membrane

Pseudostratified ciliated columnar epithelium
- appears to be layered.
- occurs in lining of respiratory tract.
- functions in protection, secretion, movement of mucus.

20 μm

20 μm

Simple cuboidal epithelium
- has cube-shaped cells.
- occurs in lining of kidney tubules and on surfaces of ovaries.
- functions in protection, secretion, absorption.

nucleus

microvilli

goblet cell

basement membrane

Simple columnar epithelium
- has rectangle-shaped cells.
- occurs in lining of intestine and uterus.
- functions in protection, secretion, absorption.

20 μm

Figure 4.8 Types of simple epithelia.
Simple epithelia—squamous, cuboidal, and columnar—are named for the shapes of their cells. They all have a protective function, as well as the other functions noted.

4.2 Integumentary System

The skin and its accessory organs (hair, nails, sweat glands, and sebaceous glands) are collectively called the **integumentary system.** Skin covers the body, protecting underlying tissues from physical trauma, pathogen invasion, and water loss; it also helps regulate body temperature. Therefore, skin plays a significant role in homeostasis. The skin even synthesizes certain chemicals that affect the rest of the body. Because skin contains sensory receptors, skin also helps us to be aware of our surroundings and to communicate through touch.

Regions of the Skin

The **skin** has two regions: the epidermis and the dermis (Fig. 4.9). A **subcutaneous layer** is found between the skin and any underlying structures, such as muscle or bone.

The Epidermis

The **epidermis** is made up of stratified squamous epithelium. New cells derived from stem (basal) cells become flattened and hardened as they push to the surface (Fig. 4.10*a*). Hardening takes place because the cells produce keratin, a waterproof protein. Dandruff occurs when the rate of keratinization in the skin of the scalp is two or three times the normal rate. A thick layer of dead keratinized cells, arranged in spiral and concentric patterns, forms fingerprints and footprints.

Specialized cells in epidermis called **melanocytes** produce melanin, the main pigment responsible for skin color. Melanocytes proliferate and move to the surface, producing a tan when a light-skinned person is exposed to sunlight. While we tend to associate a tan with health, actually it signifies that the body is trying to protect itself from the dangerous rays of the sun. Some ultraviolet radiation does serve a purpose, however. Certain cells in the epidermis convert a steroid related to cholesterol into **vitamin D** only with the aid of ultraviolet radiation. Vitamin D is required for proper bone growth.

Too much ultraviolet radiation is dangerous and can lead to skin cancer. Basal cell carcinoma (Fig. 4.10*b*), derived from stem cells gone awry, is the more common type of skin cancer and the most curable. Melanoma (Fig. 4.10*c*), the type of skin cancer derived from melanocytes, is extremely serious.

The Dermis

The **dermis** is a region of dense fibrous connective tissue beneath the epidermis. The dermis contains collagen and

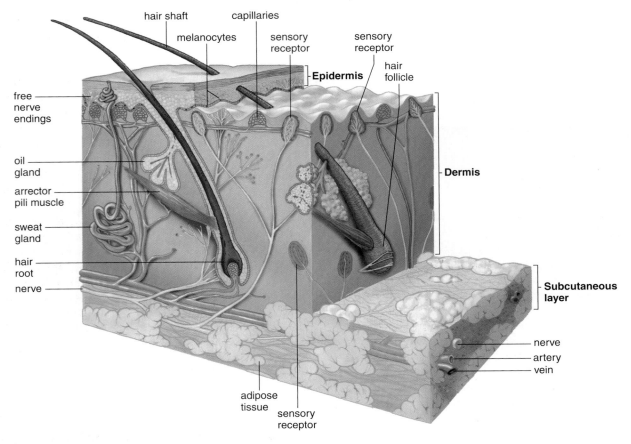

Figure 4.9   Human skin anatomy.
Skin consists of two regions: the epidermis and the dermis. A subcutaneous layer lies below the dermis.

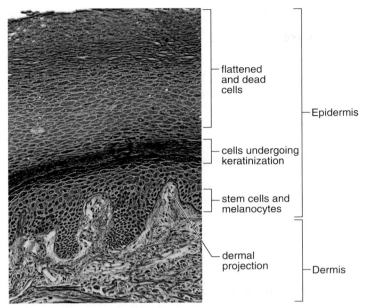

a. Photomicrograph of skin

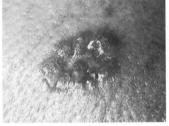

b. Basal cell carcinoma

c. Melanoma

Figure 4.10   The epidermis.
a. Epidermal ridges following dermal projections are clearly visible. Stem cells and melanocytes are in this region. **b.** Basal cell carcinoma derived from stem cells and melanoma (**c**) derived from melanocytes are types of skin cancer.

elastic fibers. The collagen fibers are flexible but offer great resistance to overstretching; they prevent the skin from being torn. The elastic fibers maintain normal skin tension but also stretch to allow movement of underlying muscles and joints. (The number of collagen and elastic fibers decreases with age and with exposure to the sun, causing the skin to become less supple and more prone to wrinkling.) The dermis also contains blood vessels that nourish the skin. When blood rushes into these vessels, a person blushes, and when blood is minimal in them, a person turns "blue."

Sensory receptors are specialized nerve endings in the dermis that respond to external stimuli. There are sensory receptors for touch, pressure, pain, and temperature. The fingertips contain the most touch receptors, and these add to our ability to use our fingers for delicate tasks.

The Subcutaneous Layer

Technically speaking, the subcutaneous layer beneath the dermis is not a part of skin. It is composed of loose con-

nective tissue and adipose tissue, which stores fat. Fat is a stored source of energy in the body. Adipose tissue helps to thermally insulate the body from either gaining heat from the outside or losing heat from the inside. A well-developed subcutaneous layer gives the body a rounded appearance and provides protective padding against external assaults. Excessive development of the subcutaneous layer accompanies obesity.

Accessory Organs of the Skin

Nails, hair, and glands are structures of epidermal origin, even though some parts of hair and glands are largely found in the dermis.

Nails are a protective covering of the distal part of fingers and toes, collectively called digits. Nails grow from special epithelial cells at the base of the nail in the portion called the nail root. The cuticle is a fold of skin that hides the nail root. The whitish color of the half-moon-shaped base, or lunula, results from the thick layer of cells in this area. The cells of a nail become keratinized as they grow out over the nail bed.

Hair follicles begin in the dermis and continue through the epidermis where the hair shaft extends beyond the skin. Contraction of the arrector pili muscles attached to hair follicles causes the hairs to "stand on end" and goose bumps to develop. Epidermal cells form the root of a hair, and their division causes a hair to grow. The cells become keratinized and die as they are pushed farther from the root.

Each hair follicle has one or more **oil glands,** also called sebaceous glands, which secrete sebum, an oily substance that lubricates the hair within the follicle and the skin itself. If the sebaceous glands fail to discharge, the secretions collect and form "whiteheads" or "blackheads." The color of blackheads is due to oxidized sebum. Acne is an inflammation of the sebaceous glands that most often occurs during adolescence due to hormonal changes.

Sweat glands, also called sudoriferous glands, are quite numerous and are present in all regions of skin. A sweat gland is a tubule that begins in the dermis and either opens into a hair follicle, or more often opens onto the surface of the skin. Sweat glands play a role in modifying body temperature. When body temperature starts to rise, sweat glands become active. Sweat absorbs body heat as it evaporates. Once body temperature lowers, sweat glands are no longer active.

Skin has two regions: the epidermis and the dermis. A subcutaneous layer lies beneath the skin. The accessory organs of the skin—nails, hair, and glands are of epidermal origin—even those portions located in the dermis.

4.3 Organ Systems

It should be emphasized that just as organs work together in an organ system, so do organ systems work together in the body. This text has several Human Systems Work Together illustrations, such as the one on page 71, that show how the various systems cooperate to maintain homeostasis, the relative constancy of the internal environment. In one sense, it is arbitrary to assign a particular organ to one system when it also assists the functioning of many other systems. The functions of the various systems of the body are listed in Figure 4.11.

Integumentary System

The integumentary system, which was discussed in the previous section, contains skin and also includes nails, located at the ends of digits; hairs; muscles that move hairs; the oil and sweat glands; blood vessels; and nerves leading to sensory receptors. It is clear that the skin has a protective function. It also synthesizes vitamin D, collects sensory data, and helps regulate body temperature.

Cardiovascular System

In the **cardiovascular system,** the heart pumps blood and sends it out under pressure into the blood vessels. In humans, the blood is always contained in blood vessels and never runs free unless the body suffers an injury.

While blood is moving throughout the body, it distributes heat produced by the muscles. Blood transports nutrients and oxygen to the cells and removes their waste molecules, including carbon dioxide. Despite the movement of molecules into and out of the blood, it has a fairly constant volume and pH, particularly due to exchanges in the lungs, the digestive tract, and the kidneys. The red blood cells in blood transport oxygen while the white blood cells fight infections. Platelets are involved in blood clotting.

Lymphatic and Immune Systems

The **lymphatic system** consists of lymphatic vessels, which transport lymph, lymph nodes, and other lymphatic organs. This system absorbs fat from the digestive tract and collects excess tissue fluid and takes them to cardiovascular veins. It also protects the body from disease by purifying lymph and storing lymphocytes, the white blood cells that produce antibodies.

The **immune system** consists of all the cells in the body that protect us from disease. The lymphocytes, in particular, belong to this system.

Digestive System

The **digestive system** consists of the mouth, esophagus, stomach, small intestine, and large intestine (colon), along with these associated organs: teeth, tongue, salivary glands, liver, gallbladder, and pancreas. This system receives food and digests it into nutrient molecules, which can enter the cells of the body. The nondigested remains are eventually eliminated.

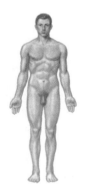 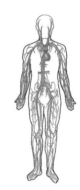 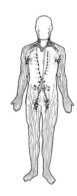 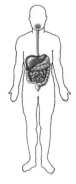 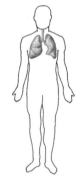 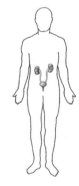

Integumentary system
• protects body.
• receives sensory input.
• helps control temperature.
• synthesizes vitamin D.

Cardiovascular system
• transports blood, nutrients, gases, and wastes.
• defends against disease.
• helps control temperature, fluid, and pH balance.

Lymphatic and immune systems
• help control fluid balance.
• absorb fats.
• defend against disease.

Digestive system
• ingests food.
• digests food.
• absorbs nutrients.
• eliminates waste.

Respiratory system
• maintains breathing.
• exchanges gases at lungs and tissues.
• helps control pH balance.

Urinary system
• excretes metabolic wastes.
• helps control fluid balance.
• helps control pH balance.

Figure 4.11   Organ systems of the body.

Respiratory System

The **respiratory system** consists of the lungs and the tubes that take air to and from them. The respiratory system brings oxygen into the body and removes carbon dioxide from the body at the lungs, restoring pH.

Urinary System

The **urinary system** contains the kidneys, the urinary bladder, and the tubes that carry urine. This system rids the body of metabolic wastes, particularly nitrogenous wastes, and helps regulate the fluid balance and pH of the blood.

Skeletal System

The bones of the **skeletal system** protect body parts. For example, the skull forms a protective encasement for the brain, as does the rib cage for the heart and lungs. The skeleton helps move the body because it serves as a place of attachment for the skeletal muscles.

The skeletal system also stores minerals, notably calcium, and it produces blood cells within red bone marrow.

Muscular System

In the **muscular system,** skeletal muscle contraction maintains posture and accounts for the movement of the body and its parts. Cardiac muscle contraction results in the heartbeat. The walls of internal organs contract due to the presence of smooth muscle.

Nervous System

The **nervous system** consists of the brain, spinal cord, and associated nerves. The nerves conduct nerve impulses from sensory receptors to the brain and spinal cord where integration occurs. Nerves also conduct nerve impulses from the brain and spinal cord to the muscles and glands, allowing us to respond to both external and internal stimuli.

Endocrine System

The **endocrine system** consists of the hormonal glands, which secrete chemical messengers, called hormones. Hormones have a wide range of effects, including regulation of cellular metabolism, regulation of fluid and pH balance, and helping us respond to stress. Both the nervous and endocrine systems coordinate and regulate the functioning of the body's other systems. The endocrine system also helps maintain the functioning of the male and female reproductive organs.

Reproductive System

The **reproductive system** has different organs in the male and female. The male reproductive system consists of the testes, other glands, and various ducts that conduct semen to and through the penis. The testes produce sex cells called sperm. The female reproductive system consists of the ovaries, oviducts, uterus, vagina, and external genitals. The ovaries produce sex cells called eggs. When a sperm fertilizes an egg, an offspring begins development.

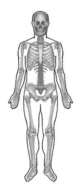 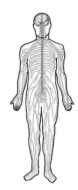 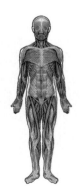 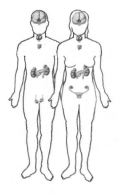 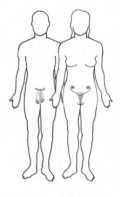

Skeletal system
• supports the body.
• protects body parts.
• helps move the body.
• stores minerals.
• produces blood cells.

Muscular system
• maintains posture.
• moves body and internal organs.
• produces heat.

Nervous system
• receives sensory input.
• integrates and stores input.
• initiates motor output.
• helps coordinate organ systems.

Endocrine system
• produces hormones.
• helps coordinate organ systems.
• responds to stress.
• helps regulate fluid and pH balance.
• helps regulate metabolism.

Reproductive system
• produces gametes.
• transports gametes.
• produces sex hormones.
• nurtures and gives birth to offspring in females.

Figure 4.11 **Organ systems of the body—continued.**

Body Cavities

The human body is divided into two main categories: the ventral cavity and the dorsal cavity (Fig. 4.12*a*). The ventral cavity, which is called a **coelom** during development, becomes divided into the thoracic and abdominal cavities. The thoracic cavity contains the right and left lungs, and the heart. The thoracic cavity is separated from the abdominal cavity by a horizontal muscle called the **diaphragm.** The stomach, liver, spleen, gallbladder, and most of the small and large intestines are in the upper portion of the abdominal cavity. The lower portion contains the rectum, the urinary bladder, the internal reproductive organs, and the rest of the large intestine. Males have an external extension of the abdominal wall, called the scrotum, containing the testes.

The dorsal cavity also has two parts: The cranial cavity within the skull contains the brain; the vertebral canal, formed by the vertebrae, contains the spinal cord.

Body membranes line cavities and the internal spaces of organs and tubes that open to the outside.

Mucous membranes line the tubes of the digestive, respiratory, urinary, and reproductive systems. They are composed of an epithelium overlying a loose fibrous connective tissue layer. The epithelium contains goblet cells that secrete mucus. This mucus ordinarily protects the body from invasion by bacteria and viruses; hence, more mucus is secreted and expelled when a person has a cold and has to blow her/his nose. In addition, mucus usually protects the walls of the stomach and small intestine from digestive juices, but this protection breaks down when a person develops an ulcer.

Serous membranes, which line the thoracic and abdominal cavities and cover the organs they contain, are also composed of epithelium and loose fibrous connective tissue (Fig. 4.12*b*). They secrete a watery fluid that keeps the membranes lubricated. Serous membranes support the internal organs and compartmentalize the large thoracic and abdominal cavities.

Serous membranes have specific names according to their location. The pleurae (sing., **pleura**) line the thoracic cavity and cover the lungs; the pericardium forms the pericardial sac and covers the heart; the peritoneum lines the abdominal cavity and covers its organs. A double layer of peritoneum, called mesentery, supports the abdominal organs and attaches them to the abdominal wall. **Peritonitis** is a life-threatening infection of the peritoneum that may occur if an inflamed appendix bursts before it is removed.

Synovial membranes composed only of loose connective tissue line the cavities of freely movable joints. They secrete synovial fluid into the joint cavity; this fluid lubricates the ends of the bones so that they can move freely. In rheumatoid arthritis, the synovial membrane becomes inflamed and grows thicker, restricting movement.

The **meninges** are membranes found within the dorsal cavity. They are composed only of connective tissue and serve as a protective covering for the brain and spinal cord. **Meningitis** is a life-threatening infection of the meninges.

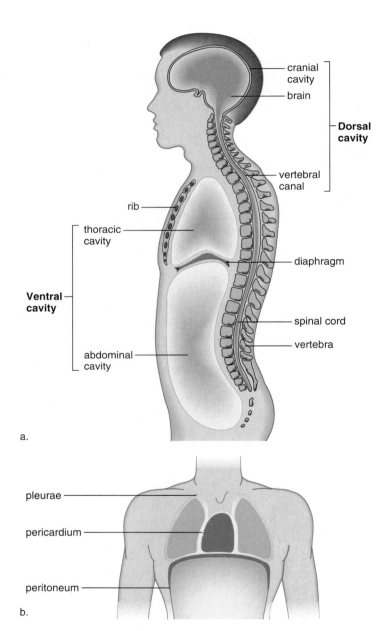

Figure 4.12   Human body cavities.
a. Side view. The dorsal (toward the back) cavity contains the cranial cavity and the vertebral canal. The brain is in the cranial cavity, and the spinal cord is in the vertebral canal. The well-developed ventral (toward the front) cavity is divided by the diaphragm into the thoracic cavity and the abdominal cavity. The heart and lungs are in the thoracic cavity, and most other internal organs are in the abdominal cavity. **b.** Serous membranes.

Health Focus

Do You Have Diabetes?

The world is experiencing a diabetes epidemic—more and more people are being diagnosed with the condition. In the United States, 18 million people now have either diabetes mellitus type 1 or diabetes type 2. The number of those with diabetes type 2, in particular, is expected to rise at an alarming rate. By 2025, the incidence of diabetes type 2 is expected to double over what it is now.

People with diabetes have to check their blood sugar level, usually before meals and at bedtime. Today, automatic lances prick the finger and computerized devices can record readings automatically (Fig. 4C). Normally, the device records a blood sugar level between 70 and 110 mg/dL (milligrams per deciliter). In diabetics, the blood sugar level is more than 140 mg/dL. What's wrong? In the non-diabetic, the hormone insulin secreted by the pancreas causes tissue cells (particularly fat, muscle, and liver cells) to take up glucose so that the blood sugar level remains within the normal range. In diabetes type 1, the pancreas fails to secrete insulin—the cells that make insulin have died off! In diabetes type 2, the pancreas usually fails to secrete enough insulin, but the real problem is that the cells are resistant to insulin. Receptors in the plasma membrane don't bind insulin properly, and then the plasma membrane doesn't have enough transporters to transport the glucose into the cell.

Most people don't have a means to check their blood glucose level, so how do they become aware that they have diabetes? These symptoms can help you decide if a physician should check you out:

- Frequent urination, especially at night
- Unusual hunger and/or thirst
- Unexplained change of weight
- Blurred vision
- Sores that do not heal
- Excessive fatigue

A physician has a number of other ways to diagnose diabetes. One of the most common is to test for sugar in the urine. When the blood sugar level is high, the kidneys excrete sugar, and a lab test can detect its presence in the urine. Excessive thirst accompanies untreated diabetes because the kidneys use large amounts of water to flush the excess glucose out of the body. Hunger and exhaustion occur because the cells are starving for glucose in the midst of plenty. Without glucose, cells cannot produce ATP, the energy currency of cells.

Diabetes type 1 usually occurs after a viral infection. The immune system gears up to fight the infection by killing off cells that are harboring the virus. When the infection is over, the immune system keeps on killing cells—this time the pancreatic cells that produce insulin. Diabetes type 1 is clearly a self-inflicted disease, but in another way so is diabetes type 2. Diabetes type 2 used to be thought of as an adult-onset disorder. Now more and more children have it. The risk factors for getting diabetes type 2 are excessive food

Figure 4C   Testing the blood sugar level.
Diabetics have to test their blood sugar level during the day and just before retiring to make sure their treatment is keeping it within the normal range.

intake leading to obesity, especially fat located in the abdominal region, and physical inactivity. Those with diabetes type 1 must have insulin injections, but those with diabetes type 2 usually receive metformin, a medication that makes cells more open to the presence of insulin. A healthy diet and exercise are emphasized as an important part of their regimen. Even limited weight loss can often lead to better blood glucose regulation. Some intake of sugars with meals is fine, but these must be substituted for other carbohydrates, not added on. Foods rich in complex carbohydrates, including dietary fiber, are preferred over easily digested foods such as many junk foods (for example, potato chips). Building up the muscles and using them regularly by, say, walking, riding a bike, or dancing uses up glucose and improves insulin efficiency. All diabetics must work closely with a physician to tailor the correct regimen of medications, diet, and exercise for them.

Diabetes is associated with the possibility of blindness, cardiovascular diseases, and kidney disease. Nerve deterioration can lead to an inability to feel pain, particularly in the hands and feet. If so, treatment of an infection may be delayed to the point that limb amputation is required. Diabetes is definitely a disorder to avoid if at all possible. The very best course of action is to adopt a healthy lifestyle—the younger the better—in order to keep this condition at bay. This is the way you can help your body maintain homeostasis, the relative constancy of the internal environment; in this case, a normal blood glucose level.

4.4 Homeostasis

Homeostasis is the relative constancy of the body's internal environment. Even though external conditions may change dramatically, internal conditions usually stay within a narrow range of normality. For example, blood glucose, pH levels, and body temperature typically fluctuate during the day, but not greatly. If internal conditions should change to any great degree, illness results. As discussed in the Health Focus on page 69, diabetes results when the blood glucose level is too high.

The Internal Environment

The internal environment has two parts: blood and tissue fluid. Blood delivers oxygen and nutrients to the tissues and carries carbon dioxide and wastes away. Tissue fluid, not blood, actually bathes all of the body's cells. Therefore, tissue fluid is the medium through which substances are exchanged between cells and blood. Oxygen and nutrients pass through tissue fluid on their way to the cells, and then carbon dioxide and wastes pass through tissue fluid on their way to the blood and tissue cells. The cooperation of body systems is required to keep these substances within the range of normality in blood and tissue fluid.

The Body Systems and Homeostasis

The nervous and endocrine systems are particularly important in coordinating the activities of all the other organ systems as they function to maintain homeostasis. The nervous system is able to bring about rapid responses to any changes in the internal environment. It issues commands by electrochemical signals that are rapidly transmitted to effector organs, which can be muscles, such as skeletal muscles, or glands, such as sweat and salivary glands. The endocrine system brings about responses that are slower to occur but generally have more lasting effects. Glands of the endocrine system, such as the pancreas or the thyroid, release hormones. Hormones, such as insulin from the pancreas, are chemical messengers that must travel through the blood and tissue fluid in order to reach their targets.

The nervous and endocrine systems together direct numerous activities that maintain homeostasis, but all the organ systems must do their part in order to keep us alive and healthy. Picture what would happen if, say, the cardiovascular, respiratory, digestive, or urinary system failed (Fig. 4.13). If someone is having a heart attack, the heart is unable to pump the blood to supply cells with oxygen. Or think of a person who is choking. Since the trachea (or windpipe) is blocked, no air can reach the lungs for uptake by the blood. Unless the obstruction is removed quickly, cells will begin to die as the blood's supply of oxygen is depleted. When the lining of the digestive tract is damaged, as in a severe bacterial infection, nutrient absorption is impaired and cells face an energy crisis. It is important not only to maintain adequate

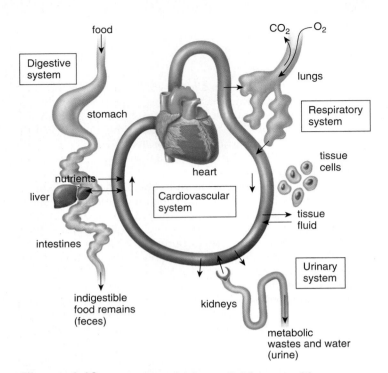

Figure 4.13   Regulation of tissue fluid composition.
Cells are surrounded by tissue fluid (blue), which is continually refreshed by exchanges with blood. Blood is renewed by exchanges with other systems of the body.

nutrient levels in the blood, but also to eliminate wastes and toxins. The liver makes urea, a nitrogenous end product of protein metabolism, but urea and other metabolic wastes are excreted by the kidneys, the urine-producing organs of the body. The kidneys rid the body of nitrogenous wastes and also help to adjust the blood's water-salt and acid-base balances.

A closer examination of how the blood glucose level is maintained helps us understand homeostatic mechanisms. When a healthy person consumes a meal and glucose enters the blood, the pancreas secretes the hormone insulin. Now glucose is removed from the blood as cells take it up. In the liver, glucose is stored in the form of glycogen. This storage is beneficial because later, if blood glucose levels drop, glycogen can be broken down to ensure that the blood level remains constant. As discussed in the Health Focus on page 69, in diabetes mellitus, the pancreas cannot produce enough insulin, or the body cells cannot respond appropriately to it. Therefore glucose does not enter the cells and they must turn to other molecules, such as fats and proteins, in order to survive. This along with too much glucose in the blood leads to the numerous complications of diabetes mellitus.

All systems of the body contribute to homeostasis—that is, maintaining the relative constancy of the internal environment, blood, and tissue fluid.

Human Systems Work Together

All systems of the body contribute to maintain homeostasis. These systems in particular are especially noteworthy.

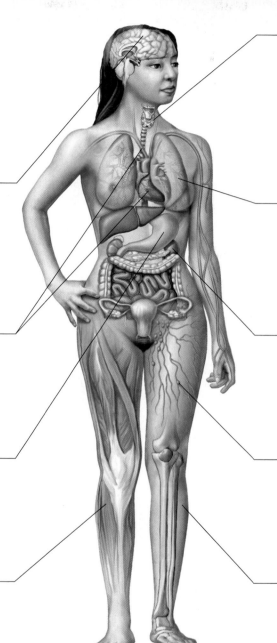

Endocrine System

Endocrine glands secrete hormones, which also regulate and coordinate the activities of other systems. Works more slowly than the nervous system.

Nervous System

Regulates and coordinates the activities of all the other systems. It responds quickly to internal and external stimuli.

Respiratory System

Supplies blood with oxygen for tissue cells and rids blood of carbon dioxide. Helps regulate the acid-base balance of the blood.

Cardiovascular System

Transports oxygen and nutrients to tissue cells and transports wastes away from cells. Also transports hormones secreted by the endocrine glands.

Urinary System

Excretes nitrogenous and other wastes. Regulates water-salt balance of the blood. Helps regulate the acid-base balance of the blood.

Digestive System

Supplies blood with nutrients and water for tissue cells. Rids the body of nondigestible remains.

Lymphatic System

Helps maintain blood volume by collecting excess tissue fluid and returning it via lymphatic vessels to the cardiovascular veins.

Muscular System

Produces heat that maintains body temperature. Protects and supports internal organs.

Integumentary System

Helps maintain body temperature and protects internal organs.

Negative Feedback

Negative feedback is the primary homeostatic mechanism that keeps a variable, such as the blood glucose level, close to a particular value, or set point. A homeostatic mechanism has at least two components: a sensor and a control center (Fig. 4.14). The sensor detects a change in the internal environment; the control center then brings about an effect to bring conditions back to normal again. Now, the sensor is no longer activated. In other words, a negative feedback mechanism is present when the output of the system dampens the original stimulus. For example, when the pancreas detects that the blood glucose level is too high, it secretes insulin, the hormone that causes cells to take up glucose. Now, the blood sugar level returns to normal, and the pancreas is no longer stimulated to secrete insulin.

Mechanical Example

A home heating system is often used to illustrate how a more complicated negative feedback mechanism works (Fig. 4.15). You set the thermostat at, say, 68°F. This is the *set point*. The thermostat contains a thermometer, a sensor that detects when the room temperature is above or below the set point. The thermostat also contains a control center; it turns the furnace off when the room is warm and turns it on when the room is cool. When the furnace is off, the room cools a bit, and when the furnace is on, the room warms a bit. In other words, typical of negative feedback mechanisms, there is a fluctuation above and below normal.

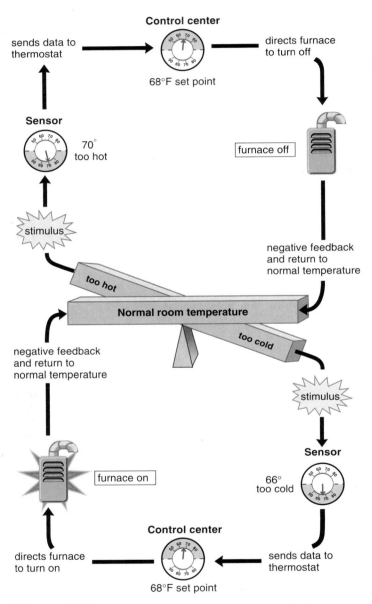

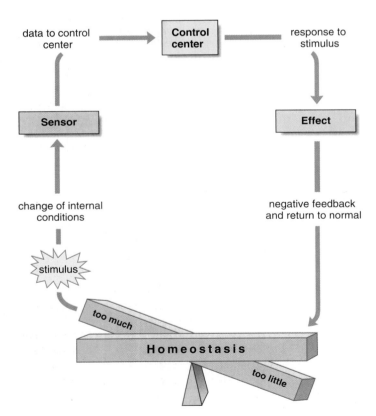

Figure 4.14   Negative feedback mechanism.
This diagram shows how the basic elements of a feedback mechanism work. A sensor detects the stimulus and a control center brings about an effect that dampens the stimulus.

Figure 4.15   Complex negative feedback mechanism.
This diagram shows how room temperature is returned to normal when the room becomes too hot (*above*) or too cold (*below*). The thermostat contains both the sensory and the control center. *Above:* The sensor detects that the room is too hot, and the control center turns the furnace off. The stimulus is no longer present when the temperature returns to normal. *Below:* The sensor detects that the room is too cold, and the control center turns the furnace on. The stimulus is no longer present when the temperature returns to normal.

Human Example: Regulation of Body Temperature

The sensor and control center for body temperature is located in a part of the brain called the hypothalamus. Notice that a negative feedback mechanism prevents change in the same direction; body temperature does not get warmer and warmer because warmth brings about a change toward a lower body temperature. Also, body temperature does not get colder and colder because a body temperature below normal brings about a change toward a warmer body temperature.

Above Normal Temperature When the body temperature is above normal, the control center directs the blood vessels of the skin to dilate. This allows more blood to flow near the surface of the body, where heat can be lost to the environment. In addition, the nervous system activates the sweat glands, and the evaporation of sweat helps lower body temperature. Gradually, body temperature decreases to 98.6°F.

Below Normal Temperature When the body temperature falls below normal, the control center directs (via nerve impulses) the blood vessels of the skin to constrict (Fig. 4.16). This conserves heat. If body temperature falls even lower, the control center sends nerve impulses to the skeletal muscles, and shivering occurs. Shivering generates heat, and gradually body temperature rises to 98.6°F. When the temperature rises to normal, the control center is inactivated.

Positive Feedback

Positive feedback is a mechanism that brings about an ever greater change in the same direction. When a woman is giving birth, the head of the baby begins to press against the cervix, stimulating sensory receptors there. When nerve impulses reach the brain, the brain causes the pituitary gland to secrete the hormone oxytocin. Oxytocin travels in the blood and causes the uterus to contract. As labor continues, the cervix is ever more stimulated and uterine contractions become ever stronger until birth occurs.

A positive feedback mechanism can be harmful, as when a fever causes metabolic changes that push the fever still higher. Death occurs at a body temperature of 113°F because cellular proteins denature at this temperature and metabolism stops. Still, positive feedback loops such as those involved in childbirth, blood clotting, and the stomach's digestion of protein assist the body in completing a process that has a definite cut-off point.

Negative feedback mechanisms keep conditions within the range of normality; in contrast positive feedback allows rapid change in one direction and does not achieve relative stability.

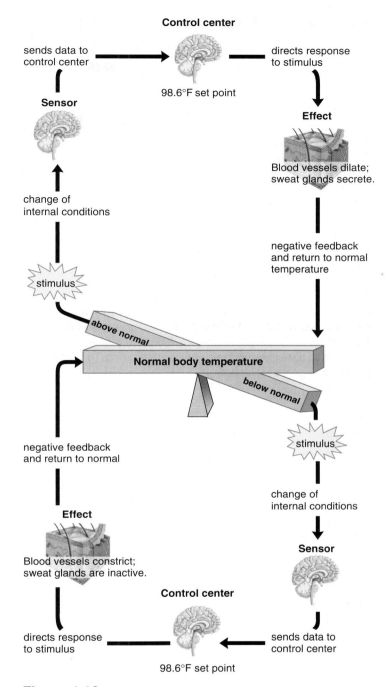

Figure 4.16 Regulation of body temperature.
Above: When body temperature rises above normal, the hypothalamus senses the change and causes blood vessels to dilate and sweat glands to secrete so that temperature returns to normal. *Below:* When body temperature falls below normal, the hypothalamus senses the change and causes blood vessels to constrict. In addition, shivering may occur to bring temperature back to normal. In this way, the original stimulus was removed.

Summarizing the Concepts

4.1 Types of Tissues

Human tissues are categorized into four groups. In connective tissues, cells are separated by a matrix, composed of ground substance and fibers. The proportion of collagen, elastic, and reticular fibers varies according to the tissue. Loose fibrous connective tissue supports epithelium and encloses organs. Adipose tissue, a type of loose connective tissue, stores fat. Dense fibrous connective tissue, such as that of tendons and ligaments, contains closely packed collagen fibers.

Cartilage and bone are supportive connective tissues. In both lie cells within lacunae, but the matrix for cartilage is more flexible than that for bone, which contains calcium salts. Blood is a fluid connective tissue composed of formed elements and plasma.

Muscular tissue is of three types. Both skeletal and cardiac muscle are striated; both cardiac and smooth muscle are involuntary. Skeletal muscle is found in muscles attached to bones, and smooth muscle is found in internal organs. Cardiac muscle makes up the heart.

Nervous tissue has one main type of conducting cell, the neuron, and several types of neuroglia. Each neuron has dendrites, a cell body, and an axon. Axons are specialized to conduct nerve impulses.

Epithelial tissue covers the body and lines its cavities. There are three different types of simple epithelia: squamous, cuboidal, and columnar. Certain of these may have cilia or microvilli. Stratified epithelia have many layers of cells—only the bottom layer touches basement membrane. Epithelial cells sometimes form glands that secrete either into ducts or into the blood.

4.2 Integumentary System

Skin has two regions. The epidermis contains stem cells, which produce new epithelial cells that become keratinized as they move toward the surface. The dermis, a dense fibrous connective tissue, contains epidermally derived glands and hair follicles, nerve endings, and blood vessels. Sensory receptors for touch, pressure, temperature, and pain are also present in the dermis. A subcutaneous layer, made up of loose fibrous connective tissue containing adipose cells, lies beneath the skin. Skin and its accessory organs comprise the integumentary system.

4.3 Organ Systems

Each organ system functions to help maintain homeostasis. The digestive, cardiovascular, lymphatic, respiratory, and urinary systems perform processing and transporting functions. The skeletal and muscular systems support the body and permit movement. The nervous system receives sensory input from sensory receptors and directs the muscles and glands to respond to outside stimuli. The endocrine system produces hormones, some of which influence the functioning of the reproductive system, which allows humans to make more of their own kind.

The internal organs occur within cavities. The thoracic cavity contains the heart and lungs; the abdominal cavity contains organs of the digestive, urinary, and reproductive systems, among others. Membranes line body cavities and the internal spaces of organs. Mucous membrane lines the tubes of the digestive system, while serous membrane lines the thoracic and abdominal cavities and covers the organs they contain.

4.4 Homeostasis

Homeostasis is the relative constancy of the internal environment. The internal environment consists of blood and tissue fluid. The cardiovascular, respiratory, digestive, and urinary systems directly regulate the amount of gases, nutrients, and wastes in the blood. The contributions of these and other systems are described in the Human Systems Work Together illustration on page 71.

Negative feedback mechanisms keep the environment relatively stable. When a sensor detects a change above or below a set point, a control center brings about an effect that reverses the change and brings conditions back to normal again. For example, when the temperature lowers, a control center in the brain brings about constriction of blood vessels in the skin and shivering if necessary. Now, the control center is no longer activated.

In contrast, a positive feedback mechanism brings about rapid change in the same direction as the stimulus. Still, positive feedback mechanisms are useful under certain conditions, such as during birth.

Studying the Concepts

1. Name the four major types of tissues. 56
2. What are the functions of connective tissue and how are they categorized? Name the different kinds, and give one location for each. 56–58
3. What are the functions of muscular tissue? State the characteristics and give a location for each type. 59
4. Nervous tissue contains what types of cells? Which organs in the body are made up of nervous tissue? 60
5. Name the different kinds of simple epithelial tissue, and give a location and function for each. What is stratified epithelium? 62
6. What is the makeup of the integumentary system? State at least two functions of skin, and describe its structure. 64–65
7. Name the organ systems and list their major functions. 66–67
8. In what body cavities are the major organs located? 68
9. Distinguish between the terms plasma membrane and body membrane. What two types of tissue are in a body membrane? 68
10. After consulting Human Systems Work Together on page 71, explain how body systems contribute to homeostasis. 70–71
11. Give a mechanical and a biological example of a negative feedback mechanism. Give an example of a positive feedback mechanism. 72–73

Thinking Critically About the Concepts

Refer to the opening vignette on page 55, and then answer these questions.

1. What are the consequences of major water loss for the body?
2. Why do you think it is important to maintain a constant internal body temperature?
3. Melanin production (tanning) is one of our body's defenses against ultraviolet radiation. How else can the body/we defend ourselves against ultraviolet radiation?
4. Organs have more than one cell type within them. What would be the advantage of having these multiple cell types? What disadvantages might this have?

Testing Your Knowledge of the Concepts

Choose the best answer for each question.

1. The tissue that contains a fluid ground substance is
   a. epithelial.
   b. classified as nervous.
   c. muscle.
   d. blood.

2. _____ glands secrete directly into the _____.
   a. Exocrine, blood
   b. Exocrine, arteries
   c. Endocrine, urine
   d. Endocrine, blood

3. Without the contribution from the connective tissue, the basement membrane would lack
   a. glycoprotein.
   b. fibers.
   c. muscle cells.
   d. All of these are correct.

4. Tight junctions are associated with
   a. connective tissue.
   b. adipose.
   c. cartilage.
   d. epithelium.

5. The loss of _____ will prevent proper blood clotting.
   a. red blood cells
   b. white blood cells
   c. platelets
   d. oxygen

6. Blood is a(n) _____ tissue because it has a _____.
   a. connective, gap junction
   b. muscle, ground substance
   c. epithelial, gap junction
   d. connective, ground substance

7. Skeletal muscle is
   a. striated.
   b. under voluntary control.
   c. multinucleated.
   d. All of these are correct.

8. A reduction in red blood cells would cause problems with
   a. fighting infection.
   b. carrying oxygen.
   c. blood clotting.
   d. None of these is correct.

9. Fluid balance is a primary goal of which system?
   a. cardiovascular
   b. lymphatic
   c. digestive
   d. integumentary

10. A thoracic surgeon would be experienced in medicine pertaining to the
    a. heart.
    b. lungs.
    c. bladder.
    d. Both a and b are correct.

11. Which choice is true of both cardiac and skeletal muscle?
    a. striated
    b. single nucleus per cell
    c. multinucleated cells
    d. involuntary control

12. The skeletal system functions in
    a. blood cell production.
    b. mineral storage.
    c. movement.
    d. All of these are correct.

13. Which of these is involved in storing energy?
    a. epidermis of skin
    b. dermis of skin
    c. subcutaneous layer beneath skin
    d. None of these is correct.

14. The correct order for homeostatic processing is
    a. sensory detection, control center, effect brings about change.
    b. control center, sensory detection, effect brings about change in environment.
    c. sensory detection, control center, effect causes no change in environment.
    d. None of these is correct.

15. Which allows rapid change in one direction and does not achieve stability?
    a. homeostasis
    b. positive feedback
    c. negative feedback
    d. All of these are correct.

16. Without melanocytes, skin would
    a. be too thin.
    b. lack nerves.
    c. lack color.
    d. None of these is correct.

17. Which of these correctly describes a layer of the skin?
    a. The epidermis is simple squamous epithelium in which hair follicles develop and blood vessels expand when we are hot.
    b. The subcutaneous layer lies between the epidermis and the dermis. It contains adipose tissue, which keeps us warm.
    c. The dermis is a region of connective tissue that contains sensory receptors, nerve endings, and blood vessels.
    d. The skin has a special layer, still unnamed, in which there are all the accessory structures such as nails, hair, and various glands.

18. Which of the following is an example of negative feedback?
    a. Air conditioning goes off when room temperature lowers.
    b. Insulin decreases blood sugar levels after eating a meal.
    c. Heart rate increases when blood pressure drops.
    d. All of these are examples of negative feedback.

19. Label the following diagram of body cavities.

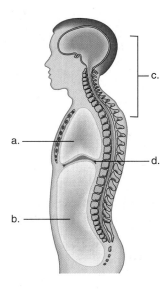

20. Which of the following is a function of skin?
    a. temperature regulation
    b. manufacture of vitamin D
    c. collection of sensory input
    d. protection from invading pathogens
    e. All of these are correct.

21. Which of these is not a type of epithelial tissue?
    a. simple cuboidal and stratified columnar
    b. bone and cartilage
    c. stratified squamous and simple squamous
    d. pseudostratified
    e. All of these are epithelial tissue.

Understanding Key Terms

adipose tissue 56
basement membrane 62
blood 58
bone 57
carcinoma 56
cardiac muscle 59
cardiovascular system 66
cartilage 56
coelom 68
collagen fiber 56
columnar epithelium 62
compact bone 57

connective tissue 56
cuboidal epithelium 62
dense fibrous connective
    tissue 56
dermis 64
diaphragm 68
digestive system 66
elastic cartilage 57
elastic fiber 56
endocrine system 67
epidermis 64
epithelial tissue 62

fibroblast 56
fibrocartilage 57
gland 62
hair follicle 65
homeostasis 70
hyaline cartilage 57
immune system 66
integumentary system 64
intercalated disks 59
lacuna 56
ligament 56
loose fibrous connective
    tissue 56
lymph 58
lymphatic system 66
matrix 56
melanocyte 64
meninges 68
meningitis 68
mucous membrane 68
muscular system 67
muscular (contractile) tissue 59
nail 65
negative feedback 72
nerve 60
nervous system 67
nervous tissue 60
neuroglia 60

neuron 60
oil gland 65
pathogen 58
peritonitis 68
platelet 58
pleura 68
positive feedback 73
red blood cell 58
reproductive system 67
respiratory system 67
reticular fiber 56
serous membrane 68
skeletal muscle 59
skeletal system 67
skin 64
smooth (visceral) muscle 59
spongy bone 57
squamous epithelium 62
striated 59
subcutaneous layer 64
sweat gland 65
synovial membrane 68
tendon 56
tissue 56
tissue fluid 58
urinary system 67
vitamin D 64
white blood cell 58

Match the key terms to these definitions.

a. _____ Dense fibrous connective tissue that joins bone to bone at a joint.

b. _____ Outer region of the skin composed of stratified squamous epithelium.

c. _____ Having bands, such as in cardiac and skeletal muscle.

d. _____ Relative constancy of the body's internal environment.

e. _____ Porous bone found at the ends of long bones where blood cells are formed.

Online Learning Center

www.mhhe.com/maderhuman9

The Online Learning Center provides a wealth of information fully organized and integrated by chapter. You will find practice quizzes, interactive activities, labeling exercises, flashcards, and much more that will complement your learning and understanding of human biology.

5 Cardiovascular System:
Heart and Blood Vessels 77

6 Cardiovascular System: Blood 97

7 Digestive System
and Nutrition 115

8 Respiratory System 141

9 Urinary System and
Excretion 159

All of the systems of the body help maintain homeostasis, resulting in a dynamic equilibrium of the internal environment. Our internal environment is the blood within blood vessels and the fluid that surrounds the cells of the tissues. The heart pumps the blood and sends it in vessels to the tissues, where materials are exchanged with tissue fluid. The composition of blood tends to remain relatively constant as a result of the actions of the lymphatic, digestive, respiratory, and urinary systems. Lymphatic vessels return excess tissue fluid to cardiovascular veins, helping to keep blood pressure constant. Nutrients enter the blood at the small intestine, external gas exchange occurs in the lungs, and metabolic waste products are excreted at the kidneys.

CHAPTER 5

Cardiovascular System: Heart and Blood Vessels

CHAPTER CONCEPTS

5.1 Overview of the Cardiovascular System
- What are the two parts of the cardiovascular system? 78
- What are the functions of the cardiovascular system? 78
- How does the lymphatic system help the cardiovascular system? 78

5.2 The Blood Vessels
- What are the types of blood vessels? 79
- What is the structure and function of these vessels? 79

5.3 The Heart
- Why is the heart a double pump? 81
- What keeps the heartbeat regular? 82–83

5.4 Features of the Cardiovascular System
- What does the pulse rate of a person indicate? 84
- What accounts for the flow of blood in the arteries? 84–85
- What accounts for the flow of blood in the veins? 85

5.5 The Cardiovascular Pathways
- What is the relative oxygen content of the blood flowing in the pulmonary artery compared with that in the pulmonary vein? Explain. 86
- What is the pathway of blood in the pulmonary circuit? In the systemic circuit? 86–87

5.6 Cardiovascular Disorders
- What cardiovascular disorders are common in humans and what treatments are available? 88–91

5.7 The Lymphatic System Helps the Cardiovascular System
- How does the lymphatic system assist the cardiovascular system? 92
- What role do lymphatic organs play in purifying the lymph and the blood? 92

Charles drove his father immediately to the emergency room because his father seemed confused and was having trouble speaking. The physician in charge ordered an angiogram, a photo of the cardiovascular system using low-level radiation. "Your father has suffered a minor stroke," said Dr. Garcia as he pointed to a black area of the photo. "An obstruction in an artery has caused this area of his brain to become deprived of oxygen. After we administer a clot-busting drug called t-PA to clear the blockage, he should improve. It's good you knew something was wrong and you brought your father to the hospital as soon as you did. If he had arrived even fifteen minutes later, he might have not survived."

Cardiovascular disease is treatable today in ways that were not thought possible even a few decades ago. Ever newer drugs and surgical techniques for cardiovascular disease are being developed. Also, some studies are helping investigators understand what dietary and lifestyle changes are needed to help prevent cardiovascular disease in the first place. As you read the following chapter, you will learn how the cardiovascular system works, and how to protect yourself from cardiovascular disease.

5.1 Overview of the Cardiovascular System

The cardiovascular system consists of two components: (1) the heart, which pumps blood, and (2) the blood vessels, through which the blood flows. The blood vessels form two closed pathways: the flow of blood through the lungs is called the **pulmonary circuit** and the flow though the rest of the body is called the **systemic circuit** (Fig. 5.1). In both circuits, vessels called **arteries** take blood away from the heart, and others called **veins** take blood to the heart. Exchange occurs across the thin walls of the smallest blood vessels, called **capillaries:** Gas exchange occurs in pulmonary capillaries, and tissue fluid is refreshed at tissue capillaries.

The lymphatic system is a one-way system of vessels that works closely with the cardiovascular system. Excess tissue fluid enters lymphatic capillaries and lymphatic vessels return this fluid to cardiovascular veins.

Functions of the Cardiovascular System

In this chapter, we will see that:

1. Contractions of the heart generate blood pressure and blood pressure moves blood through the two circuits.
2. The heart and the blood vessels keep O_2-rich blood separated from O_2-poor blood.
3. Valves in the heart and veins keep the blood flowing in one direction.
4. The heart and blood vessels regulate blood flow according to the needs of the body.
5. Exchange across capillary walls refreshes blood and tissue fluid.

Exchange in Lungs

Gas exchange occurs in the lungs. Carbon dioxide diffuses from the blood into the lungs, and oxygen diffuses from the lungs into the blood at the pulmonary capillaries.

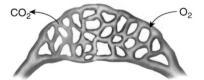

Exchange in Tissues

Exchange also occurs in the tissue capillaries. Oxygen and nutrients, such as glucose and amino acids, diffuse from the blood into tissue fluid. Carbon dioxide and other wastes diffuse into blood from tissue fluid. In this way, tissue fluid is refreshed and the needs of cells are met.

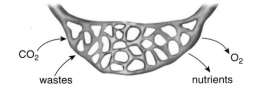

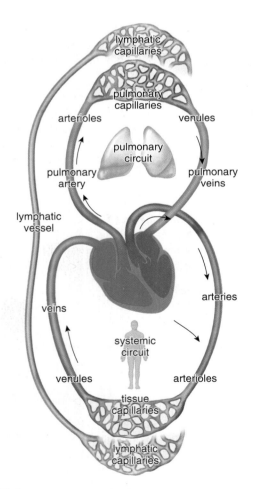

Figure 5.1 The cardiovascular system.
The cardiovascular system consists of the heart and blood vessels arranged in two circuits: the pulmonary circuit and the systemic circuit.

5.2 The Blood Vessels

The structure of the three types of blood vessels (arteries, capillaries, and veins) is appropriate to their function (Fig. 5.2).

The Arteries

The arterial wall has three layers. The innermost layer is simple squamous epithelium called endothelium, the middle layer is a relatively thick layer of smooth muscle and elastic tissue, while the outer layer is connective tissue. The strong walls of an artery give it support when blood enters under pressure; the elastic tissue allows an artery to expand to absorb the pressure. **Arterioles** are small arteries just visible to the naked eye. The middle layer of arterioles has some elastic tissue but is composed mostly of smooth muscle, whose fibers encircle the arteriole. When these muscle fibers contract, the vessel constricts; when these muscle fibers relax, the vessel dilates. Whether arterioles are constricted or dilated affects blood pressure. The greater the number of vessels dilated, the lower the blood pressure.

The Capillaries

Arterioles branch into capillaries. Each capillary is an extremely narrow, microscopic tube with one-cell-thick walls composed only of endothelium with a basement membrane. Although each capillary is small, their total surface area in humans is about 6,300 square meters. Capillary beds (networks of many capillaries) are present in all regions of the body, so no cell is far from a capillary. In the tissues, only certain capillaries are open at any given time. For example, after eating, the capillaries that serve the digestive system are open, and those that serve the muscles are closed. When a capillary bed is closed, the precapillary sphincters contract, and the blood moves from arteriole to venule by way of an arteriovenous shunt.

The Veins

Venules are small veins that drain blood from the capillaries and then join to form a vein. The walls of venules (and veins) have the same three layers as arteries, but there is less smooth muscle in the middle layer and less connective tissue in the outer layer. Therefore, the wall of a vein is thinner than that of an artery.

Veins often have **valves,** which allow blood to flow only toward the heart when open and prevent the backward flow of blood when closed. Valves are found in the veins that carry blood against the force of gravity, especially the veins of the lower extremities.

Since the walls of veins are thinner, they can expand to a greater extent. At any one time, about 70% of the blood is in the veins. In this way, the veins act as a blood reservoir. If blood is lost due to hemorrhaging, nervous stimulation causes the veins to constrict, providing more blood to the rest of the body.

Arteries and arterioles help regulate blood pressure; capillaries allow exchange to take place; venules and veins can act as blood reservoirs.

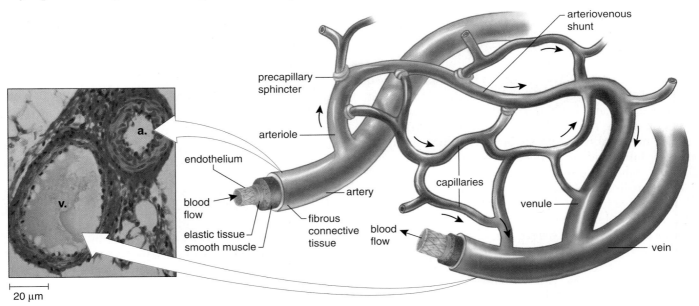

Figure 5.2 Anatomy of a capillary bed.
A capillary bed forms a maze of capillary vessels that lies between an arteriole and a venule. When sphincter muscles are relaxed, the capillary bed is open, and blood flows through the capillaries. When sphincter muscles are contracted, blood flows through a shunt that carries blood directly from an arteriole to a venule. As blood passes through a capillary in the tissues, it gives up its oxygen (O_2). Therefore, blood goes from being O_2-rich in the arteriole (red color) to being O_2-poor in the vein (blue color). In the photomicrograph, a.=artery; v.=vein.

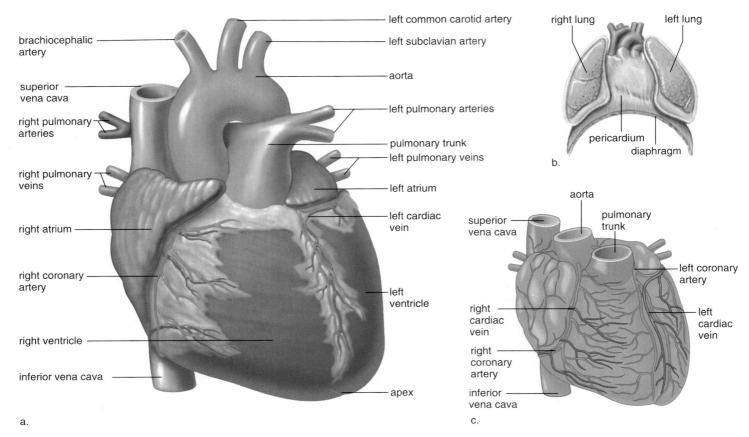

Figure 5.3 **External heart anatomy.**
a. The superior vena cava and the pulmonary trunk are attached to the right side of the heart. (The right side of the heart means how the heart is positioned in the body, not the right side of the diagram.) The aorta and pulmonary veins are attached to the left side of the heart. **b.** The heart lies within a two-layered pericardium. The layers are separated by a fluid that reduces friction between them as the heart moves. **c.** The coronary arteries and cardiac veins pervade cardiac muscle. The coronary arteries bring oxygen and nutrients to cardiac cells.

5.3 The Heart

The **heart** is a cone-shaped, muscular organ about the size of a fist. It is located between the lungs directly behind the sternum (breastbone) and is tilted so that the apex (the pointed end) is oriented to the left. The major portion of the heart, called the **myocardium,** consists largely of cardiac muscle tissue. The muscle fibers of the myocardium are branched and tightly joined to one another. The heart is surrounded by the **pericardium,** a thick, membranous sac that secretes a small quantity of lubricating liquid. The inner surface of the heart is lined with endocardium, which consists of connective tissue and endothelial tissue.

The heart has four chambers. The two upper, thin-walled atria (sing., **atrium**) have wrinkled, protruding appendages called auricles. The two lower chambers are the thick-walled **ventricles,** which pump the blood (Fig. 5.3).

Internally, a wall called the **septum** separates the heart into a right side and a left side (Fig. 5.4*a*). The heart has four valves, which direct the flow of blood and prevent its backward movement. The two valves that lie between the atria

and the ventricles are called the **atrioventricular valves.** These valves are supported by strong fibrous strings called **chordae tendineae.** The chordae, which are attached to muscular projections of the ventricular walls, support the valves and prevent them from inverting when the heart contracts. The atrioventricular valve on the right side is called the tricuspid valve because it has three flaps, or cusps. The atrioventricular valve on the left side is called the bicuspid (or mitral) valve because it has two flaps. The remaining two valves are the **semilunar valves,** whose flaps resemble half-moons, between the ventricles and their attached vessels. The pulmonary semilunar valve lies between the right ventricle and the pulmonary trunk. The aortic semilunar valve lies between the left ventricle and the aorta.

Humans have a four-chambered heart (two atria and two ventricles). A septum separates the right side from the left side.

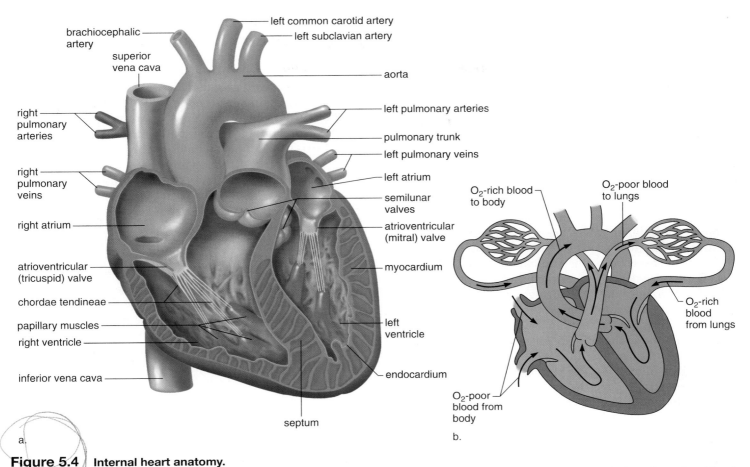

Figure 5.4 **Internal heart anatomy.**
a. The heart has four valves. Each side has an atrioventricular valve and each side has a semilunar valve. The atrioventricular valves allow blood to pass from the atria to the ventricles, and the semilunar valves allow blood to pass out of the heart. **b.** This diagrammatic representation of the heart allows you to trace the path of the blood through the heart.

Passage of Blood Through the Heart

We can trace the path of blood through the heart (Fig. 5.4b) in the following manner:

- The superior vena cava and the inferior vena cava, which carry O_2-poor blood, enter the right atrium.
- The right atrium sends blood through an atrioventricular valve (the tricuspid valve) to the right ventricle.
- The right ventricle sends blood through the pulmonary semilunar valve into the pulmonary trunk. The pulmonary trunk divides into two **pulmonary arteries,** which go to the lungs.
- Four **pulmonary veins,** which carry O_2-rich blood, enter the left atrium.
- The left atrium sends blood through an atrioventricular valve (the bicuspid, or mitral, valve) to the left ventricle.
- The left ventricle sends blood through the aortic semilunar valve into the aorta to the body proper.

From this description, you can see that O_2-poor blood never mixes with O_2-rich blood and that blood must go through the lungs in order to pass from the right side to the left side of the heart. In fact, the heart is a double pump because the right ventricle of the heart sends blood through the lungs, and the left ventricle sends blood throughout the body. Since the left ventricle has the harder job of pumping blood to the entire body, its walls are thicker than those of the right ventricle, which pumps blood a relatively short distance to the lungs.

The pumping of the heart sends blood out under pressure into the arteries. Because the left side of the heart is the stronger pump, blood pressure is greatest in the aorta. Blood pressure then decreases as the total cross-sectional area of arteries and then arterioles increases (see Fig. 5.9).

The right side of the heart pumps blood to the lungs, and the left side of the heart pumps blood throughout the body.

The Heartbeat

Each heartbeat is called a **cardiac cycle** (Fig. 5.5). When the heart beats, first the two atria contract at the same time; then the two ventricles contract at the same time. Then all chambers relax. **Systole,** the working phase, refers to contraction of the chambers, and the word **diastole,** the resting phase, refers to relaxation of the chambers. The heart contracts, or beats, about 70 times a minute, and each heartbeat lasts about 0.85 seconds. A normal adult rate at rest can vary from 60 to 80 beats per minute.

When the atria are in systole, the ventricles are in diastole and vice versa. When the atria are in systole, the atrioventricular valves are open, and when the ventricles are in systole, the semilunar valves are open. Study Figure 5.5 to determine when the various valves are open or closed.

When the heart beats, the familiar "lub-dup" sound occurs. The longer and lower-pitched "lub" is caused by vibrations occurring when the atrioventricular valves close due to ventricular contraction. The shorter and sharper "dup" is heard when the semilunar valves close due to back pressure of blood in the arteries. A heart murmur, or a slight swishing sound after the "lub," is often due to ineffective valves, which allow blood to pass back into the atria after the atrioventricular valves have closed. Rheumatic fever resulting from a bacterial infection is one possible cause of a faulty valve, particularly the bicuspid valve. Faulty valves can be surgically corrected.

Intrinsic Control of Heartbeat

The rhythmical contraction of the atria and ventricles is due to the intrinsic conduction system of the heart. Nodal tissue, which has both muscular and nervous characteristics, is a unique type of cardiac muscle located in two regions of the heart. The **SA (sinoatrial) node** is located in the upper dorsal wall of the right atrium; the **AV (atrioventricular) node** is located in the base of the right atrium very near the septum (Fig. 5.6*a*). The SA node initiates the heartbeat and automatically sends out an excitation impulse every 0.85 second; this causes the atria to contract. When impulses reach the AV node, there is a slight delay that allows the atria to finish their contraction before the ventricles begin their contraction. The signal for the ventricles to contract travels from the AV node through the two branches of the **atrioventricular bundle** (AV bundle) before reaching the numerous and smaller **Purkinje fibers.** The AV bundle, its branches, and the Purkinje fibers consist of specialized cardiac muscle fibers that efficiently cause the ventricles to contract.

The SA node is called the **pacemaker** because it usually keeps the heartbeat regular. If the SA node fails to work properly, the heart still beats due to impulses generated by the AV node. But the beat is slower (40 to 60 beats per minute). To correct this condition, it is possible to implant an artificial pacemaker, which automatically gives an electrical stimulus to the heart every 0.85 second.

> The intrinsic conduction system of the heart consists of the SA node, the AV node, the atrioventricular bundle, and the Purkinje fibers.

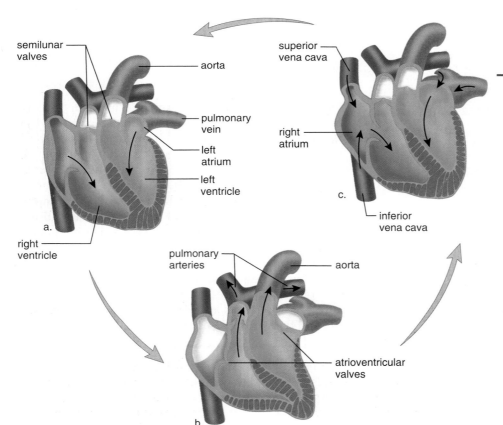

Figure 5.5   Stages in the cardiac cycle.
a. When the atria contract, the ventricles are relaxed and filling with blood. The atrioventricular valves are open and the semilunar valves are closed. **b.** When the ventricles contract, the atrioventricular valves are closed, the semilunar valves are open, and the blood is pumped into the pulmonary trunk and aorta. **c.** When the heart is relaxed, both the atria and the ventricles are filling with blood. The atrioventricular valves are open and the semilunar valves are closed.

Extrinsic Control of Heartbeat

The body has an extrinsic way to regulate the heartbeat. A cardiac control center in the medulla oblongata, a portion of the brain that controls internal organs, can alter the beat of the heart by way of the autonomic system, a portion of the nervous system. The autonomic system has two subdivisions: the parasympathetic division, which promotes those functions we tend to associate with a resting state, and the sympathetic division, which brings about those responses we associate with increased activity and/or stress. The parasympathetic division decreases SA and AV nodal activity when we are inactive, and the sympathetic division increases SA and AV nodal activity when we are active or excited.

The hormones epinephrine and norepinephrine, which are released by the adrenal medulla, also stimulate the heart. During exercise, for example, the heart pumps faster and stronger due to sympathetic stimulation and due to the release of epinephrine and norepinephrine.

The body has an extrinsic way to regulate the heartbeat. The autonomic system and hormones can modify the heartbeat rate.

The Electrocardiogram

An **electrocardiogram (ECG)** is a recording of the electrical changes that occur in myocardium during a cardiac cycle. Body fluids contain ions that conduct electric currents, and therefore the electrical changes in myocardium can be detected on the skin's surface. When an ECG is being taken, electrodes placed on the skin are connected by wires to an instrument that detects the myocardium's electrical changes. Thereafter, a pen rises or falls on a moving strip of paper. Figure 5.6*b* depicts the pen's movements during a normal cardiac cycle.

When the SA node triggers an impulse, the atrial fibers produce an electrical change that is called the P wave. The P wave indicates that the atria are about to contract. After that, the QRS complex signals that the ventricles are about to contract. The electrical changes that occur as the ventricular muscle fibers recover produce the T wave.

Various types of abnormalities can be detected by an ECG. One of these, called ventricular fibrillation, is an uncoordinated contraction of the ventricles (Fig. 5.6*c*). Ventricular fibrillation is of special interest because it can be caused by an injury or drug overdose. It is the most common cause of sudden cardiac death in a seemingly healthy person over age 35. Once the ventricles are fibrillating, they have to be defibrillated by applying a strong electric current for a short period of time. Then the SA node may be able to reestablish a coordinated beat.

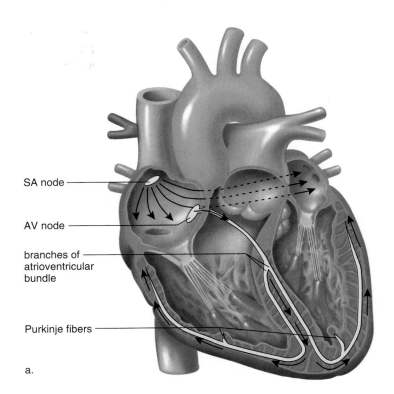

SA node

AV node

branches of atrioventricular bundle

Purkinje fibers

a.

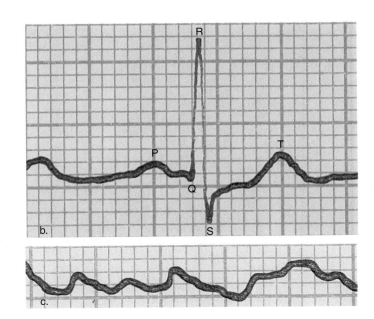

b.

c.

Figure 5.6   **Conduction system of the heart.**
a. The SA node sends out a stimulus, which causes the atria to contract. When this stimulus reaches the AV node, it signals the ventricles to contract. Impulses pass down the two branches of the atrioventricular bundle to the Purkinje fibers, and thereafter the ventricles contract. **b.** A normal ECG indicates that the heart is functioning properly. The P wave occurs just prior to atrial contraction; the QRS complex occurs just prior to ventricular contraction; and the T wave occurs when the ventricles are recovering from contraction. **c.** Ventricular fibrillation produces an irregular electrocardiogram due to irregular stimulation of the ventricles.

5.4 Features of the Cardiovascular System

When the left ventricle contracts, blood is sent out into the aorta under pressure. A progressive decrease in pressure occurs as blood moves through the arteries, arterioles, capillaries, venules, and finally the veins. Blood pressure is highest in the aorta and lowest in the venae cavae, which enter the right atrium.

Pulse

The surge of blood entering the arteries causes their elastic walls to stretch, but then they almost immediately recoil. This rhythmic expansion and recoil of an arterial wall can be felt as a **pulse** in any artery that runs close to the body's surface. It is customary to feel the pulse by placing several fingers on the radial artery, which lies near the outer border of the palm side of a wrist (Fig. 5.7). A carotid artery, on either side of the trachea in the neck, is another accessible location for feeling the pulse. Normally, the pulse rate indicates the rate of the heartbeat because the arterial walls pulse whenever the left ventricle contracts. The pulse rate is usually 70 beats per minute but can vary between 60 and 80 beats per minute.

Blood Flow

The beating of the heart is necessary to homeostasis because it creates the pressure that propels blood in the arteries and the arterioles. Arterioles lead to the capillaries where exchange with tissue fluid takes place.

Blood Flow in Arteries

Blood pressure is the pressure of blood against the wall of a blood vessel. A sphygmomanometer (blood pressure instrument) can be used to measure blood pressure, usually in the brachial artery of the arm (Fig. 5.8). The highest arterial pressure, called the **systolic pressure,** is reached during ejection of blood from the heart. The lowest arterial pressure, called the **diastolic pressure,** occurs while the heart ventricles are relaxing. Normal resting blood pressure for a young adult is said to be 120 mm mercury (Hg) over 80 mm Hg, or simply 120/80. The higher number is the systolic pressure, and the lower number is the diastolic pressure. Actually, blood pressure varies throughout the body. As already stated, blood pressure is highest in the aorta and lowest in the venae cavae. It is customary, however, to take the blood pressure in the brachial artery of the arm, where it is usually 120/80.

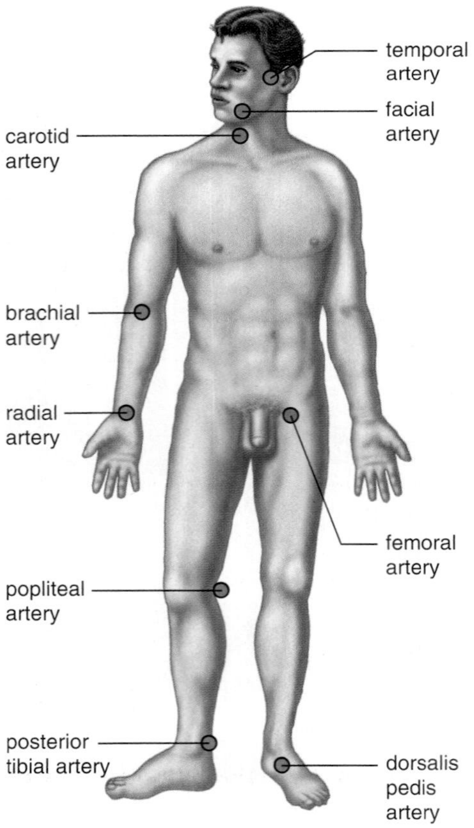

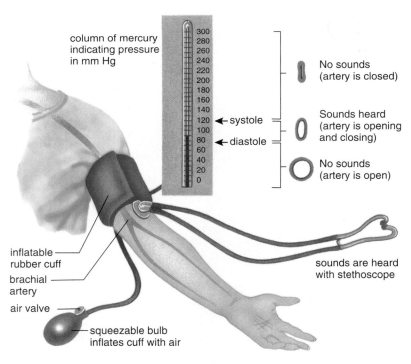

Figure 5.7   Pulse points.
The pulse can be taken at these arterial sites.

Figure 5.8   Use of a sphygmomanometer.
The technician inflates the cuff with air, gradually reduces the pressure, and listens with a stethoscope for the sounds that indicate blood is moving past the cuff in an artery. This is systolic blood pressure. The pressure in the cuff is further reduced until no sound is heard, indicating that blood is flowing freely through the artery. This is diastolic pressure.

Both systolic and diastolic blood pressure decrease with distance from the left ventricle because the total cross-sectional area of the blood vessels increases—there are more arterioles than arteries. The decrease in blood pressure causes the blood velocity to gradually decrease as it flows toward the capillaries.

Blood Flow in Capillaries

There are many more capillaries than arterioles, and blood moves slowly through the capillaries (Fig. 5.9). This is important because the slow progress allows time for the exchange of substances between the blood in the capillaries and the surrounding tissues.

Blood Flow in Veins

Blood pressure is minimal in venules and veins (20–0 mm Hg). Instead of blood pressure, venous return is dependent upon three factors: skeletal muscle contraction, the presence of valves in veins, and respiratory movements. When the skeletal muscles contract, they compress the weak walls of the veins. This causes blood to move past the next valve. Once past the valve, blood cannot flow backward (Fig. 5.10). The importance of muscle contraction in moving blood in the venous vessels can be demonstrated by forcing a person to stand rigidly still for an hour or so. Frequently, fainting occurs because blood collects in the limbs, depriving the brain of needed blood flow and oxygen. In this case, fainting is beneficial because the resulting horizontal position aids in getting blood to the head.

When inhalation occurs, the thoracic pressure falls and abdominal pressure rises as the chest expands. This also aids the flow of venous blood back to the heart because blood flows in the direction of reduced pressure. Blood velocity increases slightly in the venous vessels due to a progressive reduction in the cross-sectional area as small venules join to form veins.

Blood pressure accounts for the flow of blood in the arteries and the arterioles. Skeletal muscle contraction, valves in veins, and respiratory movements account for the flow of blood in the venules and the veins.

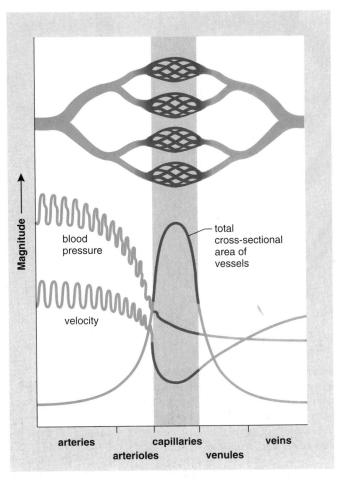

Figure 5.9   **Cross-sectional area as it relates to blood pressure and blood velocity.**

Blood pressure and blood velocity drop off in capillaries because capillaries have a greater cross-sectional area than arterioles.

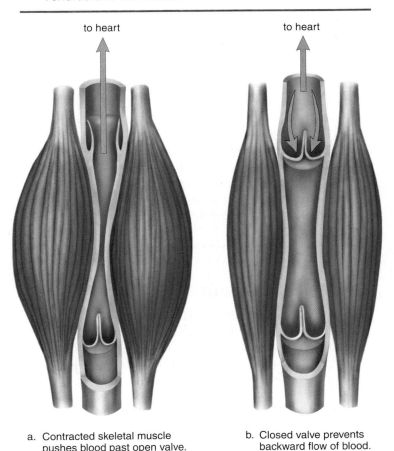

a. Contracted skeletal muscle pushes blood past open valve.

b. Closed valve prevents backward flow of blood.

Figure 5.10   **Skeletal muscle contraction moves blood in veins.**

a. Muscle contraction exerts pressure against the vein, and blood moves past the valve. **b.** Blood cannot flow back once it has moved past the valve.

5.5 The Cardiovascular Pathways

As mentioned, the blood flows in two circuits: the pulmonary circuit, which circulates blood through the lungs, and the systemic circuit, which serves the needs of body tissues (Fig. 5.11). Both circuits, as we shall see, are necessary to homeostasis.

The Pulmonary Circuit

The path of blood through the lungs can be traced as follows: Blood from all regions of the body first collects in the right atrium and then passes into the right ventricle, which pumps it into the pulmonary trunk. The pulmonary trunk divides into the right and left pulmonary arteries, which branch as they approach the lungs. The arterioles take blood to the pulmonary capillaries, where carbon dioxide is given off and oxygen is picked up. Blood then passes through the pulmonary venules, which lead to the four pulmonary veins that enter the left atrium. Since blood in the pulmonary arteries is O₂-poor but blood in the pulmonary veins is O₂-rich, it is not correct to say that all arteries carry blood that is high in oxygen and all veins carry blood that is low in oxygen (as people tend to believe). Just the reverse is true in the pulmonary circuit.

The pulmonary arteries take O_2-poor blood to the lungs, and the pulmonary veins return blood that is O_2-rich to the heart.

The Systemic Circuit

The systemic circuit includes all of the arteries and veins shown in Figure 5.12. The largest artery in the systemic circuit is the **aorta,** and the largest veins are the **superior** and **inferior venae cavae.** The superior vena cava collects blood from the head, the chest, and the arms, and the inferior vena cava collects blood from the lower body regions. Both enter the right atrium. The aorta and the venae cavae serve as the major pathways for blood in the systemic circuit.

The path of systemic blood to any organ in the body begins in the left ventricle, which pumps blood into the aorta. Branches from the aorta go to the organs and major body

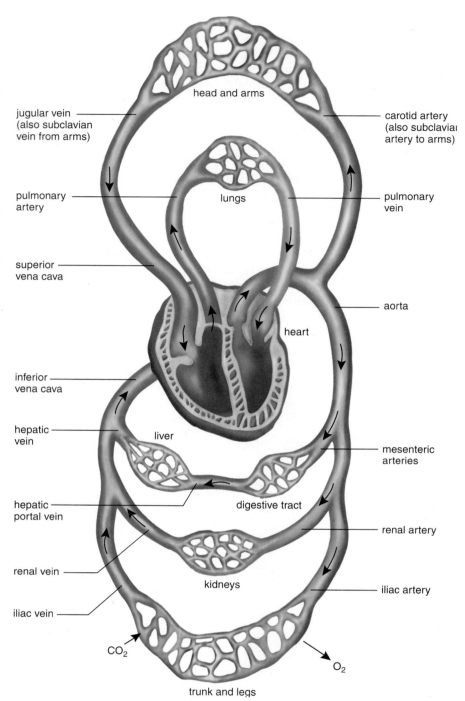

Figure 5.11   Cardiovascular system diagram.
The blue-colored vessels carry blood high in carbon dioxide, and the red-colored vessels carry blood high in oxygen; the arrows indicate the flow of blood. Compare this diagram, useful for learning to trace the path of blood, with Figure 5.13 to realize that arteries and veins go to all parts of the body. Also, there are capillaries in all parts of the body. No cell is located far from a capillary.

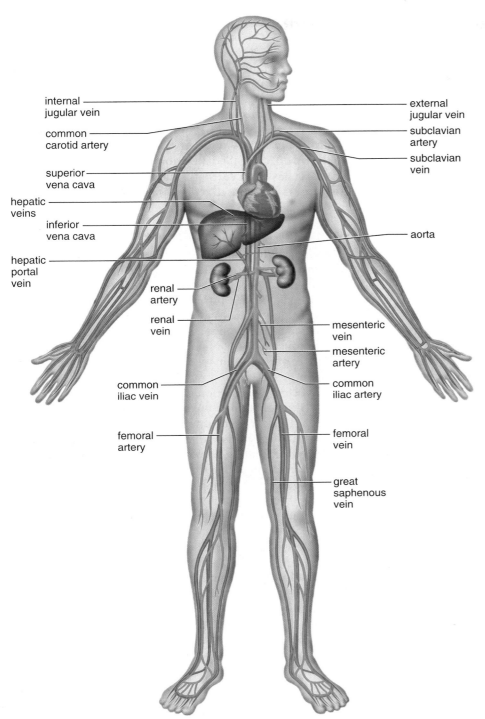

internal jugular vein

common carotid artery

superior vena cava

hepatic veins

inferior vena cava

hepatic portal vein

renal artery

renal vein

common iliac vein

femoral artery

external jugular vein

subclavian artery

subclavian vein

aorta

mesenteric vein

mesenteric artery

common iliac artery

femoral vein

great saphenous vein

Figure 5.12 **Major arteries and veins of the systemic circuit.**
A realistic representation of major blood vessels of the systemic circuit shows how the systemic arteries and veins are actually arranged in the body. The superior and inferior venae cavae take their names from their relationship to which organ?

regions. For example, this is the path of blood to and from the lower legs:

> left ventricle—aorta—common iliac artery—femoral artery—lower leg capillaries—femoral vein—common iliac vein—inferior vena cava—right atrium

Notice that, when tracing blood, you need only mention the aorta, the proper branch of the aorta, the region, and the vein returning blood to the vena cava. In most instances, the artery and the vein that serve the same region are given the same name (Fig. 5.12). What happens when the blood reaches a particular region? Capillary exchange takes place, refreshing tissue fluid so that its composition stays relatively constant.

The **coronary arteries** (see Fig. 5.3) serve the heart muscle itself. (The heart is not nourished by the blood in its chambers.) The coronary arteries are the first branches off the aorta. They originate just above the aortic semilunar valve, and they lie on the exterior surface of the heart, where they divide into diverse arterioles. Because they have a very small diameter, the coronary arteries may become clogged, as discussed in the Health Focus on page 90. The coronary capillary beds join to form venules. The venules converge to form the cardiac veins, which empty into the right atrium.

A portal system begins and ends in capillaries. The body has a portal system called the **hepatic portal system,** which is associated with the liver. In this instance, the first set of capillaries occurs at the villi of the small intestine, and the second occurs in the liver. Blood passes from the capillaries of the intestinal villi into venules that join to form the **hepatic portal vein.** The hepatic portal vein connects the villi of the intestine with the liver, an organ that monitors the chemical makeup of the blood. The **hepatic vein** leaves the liver and enters the inferior vena cava. While Figure 5.11 is helpful in tracing the path of blood, remember that all parts of the body receive both arteries and veins, as illustrated in Figure 5.12.

The systemic circuit takes blood from the left ventricle of the heart through the body proper, and back to the right atrium of the heart.

5.6 Cardiovascular Disorders

Cardiovascular disease (CVD) is the leading cause of untimely death in the Western countries. Modern research efforts have resulted in improved diagnosis, treatment, and prevention. This section discusses the range of advances that have been made, first in correcting vascular disorders, and then in correcting heart disorders. The Health Focus on page 90 emphasizes how to prevent CVD from developing in the first place.

Disorders of the Blood Vessels

Hypertension and atherosclerosis lead, most often, to stroke due to an artery blocked by a blood clot, or a heart attack due to a coronary artery clogged by plaque. Treatment involves doing away with the blood clot or prying open the coronary artery. Another possible outcome is an aneurysm, in which a burst blood vessel must be replaced.

Hypertension and Atherosclerosis

Hypertension occurs when blood moves through the arteries at a higher pressure than normal. Also called high blood pressure, hypertension is sometimes called a silent killer because it may not be detected until it has caused a heart attack, stroke, or even kidney failure. Hypertension is present when the systolic blood pressure is 140 or greater or the diastolic blood pressure is 90 or greater. While both systolic and diastolic pressures are considered important, it is the diastolic pressure that is emphasized when medical treatment is being considered.

The best safeguard against developing hypertension is regular blood pressure checks and a lifestyle that lowers the risk of CVD. If already present, a physician can prescribe various drugs that help lower blood pressure. Diuretics cause the kidneys to excrete water; beta blockers and angiotensin-converting enzyme (ACE) inhibitors counteract hormones that tend to raise the blood pressure.

It has long been thought that genetic makeup might account for the development of hypertension because the condition runs in families. Knowing you have a propensity to the condition is helpful if it causes you to adopt a lifestyle that will prevent it from developing. Researchers have discovered genes that may be involved in some individuals. Therefore, the possibility exists that persons with hypertension might one day be cured by gene therapy.

Hypertension is often seen in individuals who have **atherosclerosis,** an accumulation of soft masses of fatty materials including cholesterol, beneath the inner linings of arteries. Such deposits are called **plaque.** As it develops, plaque tends to protrude into the lumen of the vessel and interfere with the flow of blood (see Fig. 5A). In most instances, atherosclerosis begins in early adulthood and develops progressively through middle age, but symptoms may not appear until an individual is 50 or older. To prevent the onset and development of plaque, the American Heart Association and other organizations recommend a diet low in saturated fat and cholesterol but rich in omega-3 polyunsaturated fatty acids, as discussed in the Health Focus on page 90.

Plaque can cause a clot to form on the irregular arterial wall. As long as the clot remains stationary, it is called a **thrombus,** but when and if it dislodges and moves along with the blood, it is called an **embolus.** If **thromboembolism** (a clot that has been carried in the bloodstream but is now stationary) is not treated, complications can arise, as mentioned in the following section.

Stroke, Heart Attack, and Aneurysm

Stroke, heart attack, and aneurysm are associated with hypertension and atherosclerosis. A cerebrovascular accident (CVA), also called a **stroke,** often results when a small cranial arteriole bursts or is blocked by an embolus. A lack of oxygen causes a portion of the brain to die, and paralysis or death can result. A person is sometimes forewarned of a stroke by a feeling of numbness in the hands or the face, difficulty in speaking, or temporary blindness in one eye.

A myocardial infarction (MI), also called a **heart attack,** occurs when a portion of the heart muscle dies due to a lack of oxygen. If a coronary artery becomes partially blocked, the individual may then suffer from **angina pectoris,** characterized by a radiating pain in the left arm. Nitroglycerin or related drugs dilate blood vessels and help relieve the pain. When a coronary artery is completely blocked, perhaps because of thromboembolism, a heart attack occurs.

An **aneurysm** is a ballooning of a blood vessel, most often the abdominal artery or the arteries leading to the brain. Atherosclerosis and hypertension can weaken the wall of an artery to the point that an aneurysm develops. If a major vessel such as the aorta should burst, death is likely. It is possible to replace a damaged or diseased portion of a vessel, such as an artery, with a plastic tube. Cardiovascular function is preserved, because exchange with tissue cells can still take place at the capillaries. In the future, it may be possible to use vessels made by injecting a patient's cells inside an inert mold.

Dilated and Inflamed Veins

Varicose veins develop when the valves of veins become weak and ineffective due to the backward pressure of blood. Abnormal and irregular dilations are particularly apparent in the superficial (near the surface) veins of the lower legs. Crossing the legs or sitting in a chair so that its edge presses against the back of the knees can contribute to the development of varicose veins. Varicose veins also occur in the rectum, where they are called piles, or more properly, **hemorrhoids.**

Phlebitis, or inflammation of a vein, is a more serious condition, particularly when a deep vein is involved. Blood in an unbroken but inflamed vessel may clot, and the clot may be carried in the bloodstream until it lodges in a small vessel. If a blood clot blocks a pulmonary vessel, death can result.

Dissolving Blood Clots

Medical treatment for thromboembolism includes the use of t-PA, a biotechnology drug. This drug converts plasminogen, a molecule found in blood, into plasmin, an enzyme that dissolves blood clots. In fact, t-PA, which stands for tissue plasminogen activator, is the body's own way of converting plasminogen to plasmin. t-PA is also being used for thrombolytic stroke patients but with limited success because some patients experience life-threatening bleeding in the brain. A better treatment might be new biotechnology drugs that act on the plasma membrane to prevent brain cells from releasing and/or receiving toxic chemicals caused by the stroke.

If a person has symptoms of angina or a stroke, aspirin may be prescribed. Aspirin reduces the stickiness of platelets, and thereby lowers the probability that a clot will form. There is evidence that aspirin protects against first heart attacks, but there is no clear support for taking aspirin every day to prevent strokes in symptom-free people. Physicians warn that long-term use of aspirin might have harmful effects, including bleeding in the brain.

Treating Clogged Arteries

Cardiovascular disease used to require open-heart surgery, and therefore a long recuperation time and a long unsightly scar that could occasionally ache. Now, bypass surgery can be accomplished by using robotic technology (Fig. 5.13a). A video camera and instruments are inserted through small cuts, while the surgeon sits at a console and manipulates interchangeable grippers, cutters, and other tools attached to movable arms above the operating table. Looking through two eyepieces, the surgeon gets a 3-D view of the operating field. Robotic surgery also has been used in many valve repairs and other heart procedures.

One way to treat an artery clogged with plaque is a **coronary bypass operation,** during which a surgeon takes a blood vessel—usually a vein from the leg—and stitches one end to the aorta and the other end to a coronary artery past the point of obstruction. Figure 5.13b shows a triple bypass in which three blood vessel segments have been used to allow blood to flow freely from the aorta to cardiac muscle by way of the coronary artery. Instead of coronary bypass, gene therapy has been used since 1997 to grow new blood vessels that will carry blood to cardiac muscle. The surgeon need only make a small incision and inject many copies of the gene that codes for VEGF (vascular endothelial growth factor) between the ribs directly into the area of the heart that most needs improved blood flow. VEGF encourages new blood vessels to sprout out of an artery. If collateral blood vessels do form, they

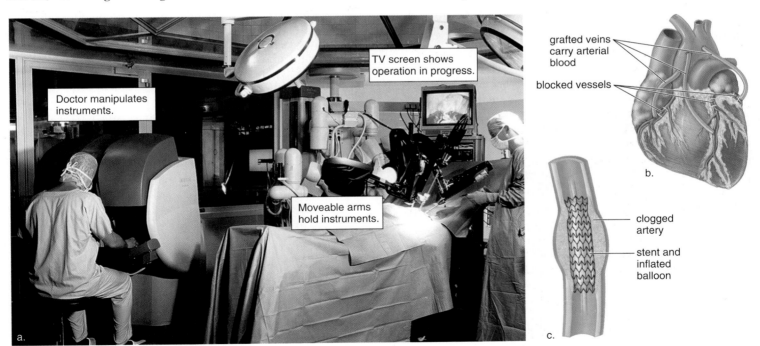

Figure 5.13   Treatment for clogged coronary arteries.
a. Many heart procedures, such as coronary bypass and stent insertion, can be performed using robotic surgery techniques. **b.** During a coronary bypass operation, blood vessels (usually veins from the leg) are stitched to the heart, taking blood past the region of obstruction. **c.** During stenting, a cylinder of expandable metal mesh is positioned inside the coronary artery by using a catheter. Then, a balloon is inflated so that the stent expands and opens the artery.

Prevention of Cardiovascular Disease

Certain genetic factors predispose an individual to cardiovascular disease, such as family history of heart attack under age 55, male gender, and ethnicity (African Americans are at greater risk). Those with one or more of these risk factors need not despair, however. It only means that they should pay particular attention to the following guidelines for a heart-healthy lifestyle.

The Don'ts

Smoking

When a person smokes, the drug nicotine, present in cigarette smoke, enters the bloodstream. Nicotine causes the arterioles to constrict and the blood pressure to rise. Restricted blood flow and cold hands are associated with smoking in most people. More serious is the need for the heart to pump harder to propel the blood through the lungs at a time when the blood's oxygen-carrying capacity is reduced.

Drug Abuse

Stimulants, such as cocaine and amphetamines, can cause an irregular heartbeat and lead to heart attacks in people who are using drugs even for the first time. Intravenous drug use may also result in a cerebral blood clot and stroke.

Too much alcohol can destroy just about every organ in the body, the heart included. But investigators have discovered that people who take an occasional drink have a 20% lower risk of heart disease than do teetotalers. Two to four drinks a week is the recommended limit for men, one to three drinks for women.

Weight Gain

Hypertension (high blood pressure) is prevalent in persons who are more than 20% above the recommended weight for their height. More tissues require servicing, and the heart sends the blood out under greater pressure in those who are overweight. It may be harder to lose weight once it is gained, and therefore it is recommended that weight control be a lifelong endeavor. Even a slight decrease in weight can bring with it a reduction in hypertension.

Being overweight increases the risk of diabetes type 2 in which glucose damages blood vessels and makes them prone to the development of plaque (Fig. 5A). Diabetics especially need to follow the diet discussed next.

The Do's

Healthy Diet

A diet low in saturated fats and cholesterol is protective against cardiovascular disease. Cholesterol is ferried in the blood by two types of plasma proteins, called LDL (low-density lipoprotein) and HDL (high-density lipoprotein). LDL (called "bad" lipoprotein) takes cholesterol from the liver to the tissues, and HDL (called "good" lipoprotein) transports cholesterol out of the tissues to the liver. When the LDL level in blood is abnormally high or the HDL level is abnormally low, cholesterol accumulates in the cells. When cholesterol-laden cells line the arteries, plaque develops, which interferes with circulation (Fig. 5A).

It is recommended that everyone know his or her blood cholesterol level. Individuals with a high blood cholesterol level (200 mg/100 mL) should be further tested to determine their LDL-cholesterol level. The LDL-cholesterol level, together with other risk factors such as age, family history, presence of diabetes, and whether the patient smokes, will determine who needs dietary therapy to lower their LDL. Eating foods high in saturated fat (red meat, cream, and butter) and foods containing so-called trans-fats (margarine, commercially baked goods, and deep-fried foods) raises the LDL-cholesterol level. Unsaturated fatty acids in olive and canola oils, most nuts, and cold-water fish tend to lower LDL-cholesterol levels. Cold-water fish (e.g., halibut, sardines, tuna, and salmon) contain polyunsaturated fatty acids and especially omega-3 polyunsaturated fatty acids that can reduce plaque. If dietary changes are not sufficient, drugs called statins can be used to lower the LDL level.

Exercise

People who exercise are less apt to have cardiovascular disease. One study found that moderately active men who spent an average of 48 minutes a day on a leisure-time activity, such as gardening, bowling, or dancing, had one-third fewer heart attacks than peers who spent an average of only 16 minutes each day on such activities. Exercise, which helps keep weight under control, may also help minimize stress and reduce hypertension.

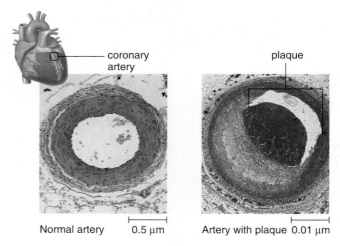

Normal artery   0.5 μm   Artery with plaque 0.01 μm

Figure 5A   Coronary arteries and plaque.
When plaque is present in a coronary artery, a heart attack is more apt to occur because of restricted blood flow.

transport blood past clogged arteries, making bypass surgery unnecessary. About 60% of all patients who undergo the procedure do show signs of vessel growth within two to four weeks.

Another alternative to bypass surgery is available; namely, the stent (Fig. 5.13c). A stent is a small metal mesh cylinder that holds a coronary artery open after a blockage has been cleared. Until a couple of years ago, stenting was a second step following angioplasty. During **angioplasty,** a plastic tube is inserted into an artery of an arm or a leg and then guided through a major blood vessel toward the heart. When the tube reaches the region of plaque in an artery, a balloon attached to the end of the tube is inflated, forcing the vessel open. Now, instead of the long balloon, a stent plus an inner balloon is pushed into the blocked area. When the balloon inside the stent is inflated, it expands, locking itself in place. Some patients go home the same day; at most after an overnight stay. The stent is more successful when it is coated with a drug that seeps into the artery lining and discourages cell growth. Uncoated stents can close back up in a few months but not ones coated with a drug that discourages closure. Because blood clotting might occur, recipients have to take anti-clotting medications.

Disorders of the Heart

When a person has **heart failure,** the heart no longer pumps as it should. Heart failure is a growing problem because people who used to die from heart attacks now survive, but are left with damaged hearts. Often, the heart is oversized not because the cardiac wall is stronger but because it is sagging and swollen. One idea is to wrap the heart in a fabric sheath to prevent it from getting too big and to allow better pumping,

similar to the way a weightlifter's belt restricts and reinforces stomach muscles. But a failing heart can have other problems, such as an abnormal heart rhythm. To counter that condition, it's possible to implant a cardioverter-defibrillator (ICD) just beneath the skin of the chest. These devices can sense both an abnormally slow and an abnormally fast heartbeat. If the former, they generate the missing beat like a pacemaker does. If the latter, they send the heart a sharp jolt of electricity to slow it down. If the heart rhythm should become erratic, it sends an even stronger shock like a defibrillator does.

Although heart transplants are now generally successful, many more people are waiting for new hearts than there are organs available. Today, only about 2,200 heart transplants are done annually, while many more thousands could use one. Because of the shortage of human hearts, genetically altered pigs may one day be used as a source of hearts. Also, bone marrow stem cells have been injected into the heart and researchers report that they apparently become cardiac muscle!

Today, a left ventricular assist device (LVAD), implanted in the abdomen, is an alternative to a heart transplant. A tube passes blood from the left ventricle to the device, which pumps it on to the aorta. A cable passes from the device through the skin to an external battery the patient must tote around. Soon, as many as 20,000 people a year may be outfitted with an LVAD. Instead of an LVAD, a few pioneers have volunteered to receive a Jarvik 2000, a pump that is inserted inside the left ventricle. The Jarvik is powered by an external battery no larger than a C-size battery.

Fewer patients still have received a so-called **total artificial heart (TAH).** The only model now available to patients is the AbioCor model (Fig. 5.14), which has no wires or tubes protruding from the chest. An internal battery and controller regulate the pumping speed, and an external battery powers the device by passing electricity through the skin via external and internal coils. A rotating centrifugal pump moves silicon hydraulic fluid between left and right sacs to force blood out of the heart into the pulmonary trunk and the aorta. This TAH is made mainly of titanium and a kind of polyurethane plastic called Angioflex. The valves and membranes inside the ventricles are made of the plastic, which has held up to beating 100,000 times a day for years. All recipients, thus far, have been near death and most have lived for only a short time. It's possible that once healthier patients receive an AbioCor, survival rate will improve. Different types of TAHs are being investigated in animals, however.

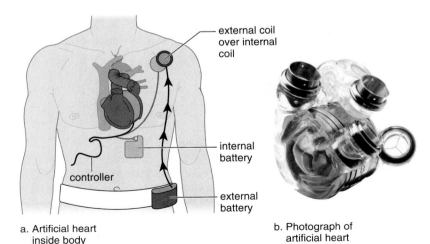

Figure 5.14   Total artificial heart.
The AbioCor is a quiet, pulsatile device that moves the blood in the same manner as a natural heart. It is powered by an external battery pack that is small and portable so the recipient can be fairly active.

Hypertension and atherosclerosis often lead to stroke, heart attack, or an aneurysm. The end result of CVD is heart failure, which can also be treated.

5.7 The Lymphatic System Helps the Cardiovascular System

The **lymphatic system** consists of lymphatic vessels and the lymphatic organs (Fig. 5.15). This system, which is closely associated with the cardiovascular system, has three main functions that contribute to homeostasis: (1) Lymphatic capillaries take up excess tissue fluid and return it to the bloodstream; (2) lacteals receive fat molecules at the intestinal villi and transport them to the bloodstream (see Fig. 7.6); and (3) the lymphatic system helps defend the body against disease.

Lymphatic Pathways

The **lymphatic vessels** carry **lymph,** which has the same composition as tissue fluid. Tissue fluid forms when capillary exchange occurs in the tissues (see page 109). Any excess tissue fluid, which contains not only water but also solutes that have diffused from a blood capillary, is taken up by lymphatic capillaries lying near blood capillaries. Once tissue fluid is absorbed by lymphatic capillaries, it is called lymph.

The lymphatic capillaries join to form larger lymphatic vessels, which have a structure comparable to that of cardiovascular veins, including the presence of valves (Fig. 5.15). Like cardiovascular veins, movement within lymphatic vessels is dependent upon skeletal muscle contraction, respiratory movements, and valves that prevent backward flow.

The lymphatic vessels merge before entering one of two ducts: the thoracic duct or the right lymphatic duct. The lymphatic ducts enter the subclavian veins, which are cardiovascular veins in the thoracic region.

Lymphatic Organs

The lymphatic organs play a critical role in keeping us free of disease; therefore, they are discussed in more detail in Chapter 21, which pertains to immunity. In the meantime, we will note that **lymph nodes** are small ovoid or round structures that cleanse the lymph of debris and pathogens. White blood cells are produced in the red bone marrow, which is located at the ends of long bones and an assortment of other bones, including the ribs and vertebrae. Certain white blood cells mature in the bone marrow, while others mature in the thymus, a gland located in the neck. The various types of white blood cells are described in the next chapter. Some white blood cells phagocytize pathogens, such as viruses and bacteria. Others kill infected cells outright or produce antibodies that combine with disease-causing agents. The **spleen,** located in the upper abdominal cavity, is about the size of a fist. The spleen cleanses blood in much the same way as lymph nodes cleanse lymph.

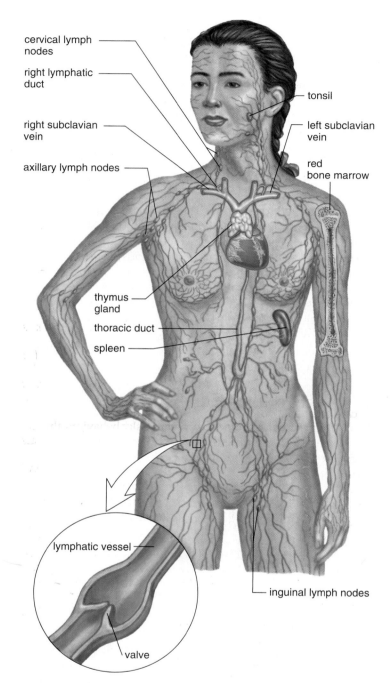

cervical lymph nodes

right lymphatic duct

tonsil

right subclavian vein

left subclavian vein

axillary lymph nodes

red bone marrow

thymus gland

thoracic duct

spleen

lymphatic vessel

inguinal lymph nodes

valve

Figure 5.15   Lymphatic system.
Lymphatic vessels drain excess fluid from the tissues and return it to the cardiovascular system. The enlargement shows that lymphatic vessels, like cardiovascular veins, have valves to prevent backward flow. The lymph nodes, the tonsils, the thymus, the red bone marrow, and the spleen are all lymphatic organs.

The lymphatic system consists of the one-way lymphatic vessels and the lymphatic organs, which have various functions to avoid infections.

Bioethical Focus

Paying for an Unhealthy Lifestyle

Cardiovascular disease is not only the number one killer in the United States today, it is also one of the most expensive. This disorder now accounts for more than $360 billion annually in spending on treatment and research, according to the American Heart Association and the National Heart, Lung, and Blood Institute (NHLBI). However, most cases of cardiovascular disease are preventable. Many well-known risk factors put an individual at high risk for developing cardiovascular disease. Among these are a sedentary lifestyle, obesity, smoking, and poor dietary habits. With few exceptions, these risk factors are largely a matter of choice. As treatment costs and insurance premiums continue to climb at an unprecedented rate, public debate has raged: Should individuals suffering from cardiovascular disease receive the benefits of treatment at public expense? As the cost of health care soars, patients now rely much more on third-party payers to cover the cost of treatment than in the past. With much of the population covered by some type of health insurance, the risk is spread out over most of the population. This has created a system under which everyone, healthy or not, pays in part for treatment of the unhealthy. Under this system, everyone who pays into this system has a vested interest in ensuring that others avoid risky behaviors that contribute to rising health-care costs (Fig. 5B).

To an extent, people who practice risky behaviors already pay more for their habits. For example, unhealthy individuals often pay more for life or health insurance than healthy individuals. Taxes on risky behaviors, such as smoking and drinking alcohol, used to help defray health-care costs, are commonplace. Despite these policies, most studies show that ultimately, we all pay for the treatment of cardiovascular disease. For example, insurance companies may refuse to cover pre-existing conditions, including cardiovascular disease. Furthermore, more than 40 million people in the United States, many of them elderly and at risk for developing cardiovascular disease, do not have health insurance. In both cases, treatment costs are usually borne by the government. This creates an incentive, both within government and within the general public, to either ensure that such individuals adopt healthy lifestyle practices, or bear more of the cost for their own treatment if they refuse to do so.

Since obesity is a major cardiovascular disease risk factor, several organizations, including the Center for Science in the Public Interest (CSPI) and the World Health Organization (WHO), have pushed for the adoption of a "fat tax." This tax would be levied on foods with high fat content and/or poor nutritional value to pay, in part, for treatment of obesity-related diseases, including heart disease. Although taxing unhealthy behaviors to help defray treatment costs are generally popular with the public, the "fat tax" has proved surprisingly unpopular with voters. Thus, this measure seems unlikely to ever become public policy in the United States.

An alternative approach being employed is prevention. Senator Tom Harkin recently introduced the Help America Act, which emphasizes healthy lifestyles and prevention. Smoking, one of the largest risk factors for cardiovascular

Figure 5B   Unhealthy lifestyle.
An unhealthy lifestyle contributes to the development of cardiovascular disease.

disease, would be taxed to help pay for the program. Many studies show that every dollar invested in cardiovascular disease prevention results in a three-dollar savings in long-term health-care costs. With this in mind, many medical associations have endorsed this bill or other similar approaches to health care.

However, not everyone agrees that cardiovascular disease is as rampant as reports indicate, or that the current public policy initiatives are the proper approach. One such critic points out that throughout the 1990s, despite large increases in obesity and marginal declines in risky behaviors, such as smoking, the incidence of cardiovascular disease has declined nearly 25%. Other critics insist that such intervention programs, while well intentioned, infringe on individual freedom, and that rewarding healthy behaviors and penalizing risky behaviors are beyond the scope of government and public policy.

Regardless of whether or not you agree with shifting more of the cost of treatment to the unhealthy, it is up to individuals to adopt healthy practices that minimize the risk of cardiovascular disease. The ultimate human cost greatly outweighs the financial costs.

Decide Your Opinion

1. Would you support charging higher insurance premiums or taxes on people who do not practice a healthy lifestyle?
2. Do you support the use of public money for prevention programs targeted toward unhealthy people, if there is the possibility of saving money in the future?
3. Since the public does subsidize health care that disproportionately benefits the less healthy, do you believe that financial interests trump personal freedom in this matter? Why or why not?

Summarizing the Concepts

5.1 Overview of the Cardiovascular System
The heart pumps blood into the pulmonary circuit (through the lungs) and the systemic circuit (through the rest of the body). Exchanges occur at the capillaries; gas exchange occurs in the lungs; and tissue fluid is refreshed at the tissue capillaries.

5.2 The Blood Vessels
Blood vessels include arteries (and arterioles) that take blood away from the heart; capillaries, where exchange of substances occurs; and veins (and venules) that take blood to the heart. Arteries have the thickest walls, which allows them to withstand blood pressure; capillaries have thin walls that allow exchange to take place; and veins have relatively weak walls with valves that keep the blood flowing in one direction.

5.3 The Heart
The heart has a right and left side and four chambers. On the right side, an atrium receives O_2-poor blood from the body, and a ventricle pumps it into the pulmonary circuit. On the left side, an atrium receives O_2-rich blood from the lungs, and a ventricle pumps it into the systemic circuit. During the cardiac cycle, the SA node (pacemaker) initiates the heartbeat by causing the atria to contract. The AV node conveys the stimulus to the ventricles, causing them to contract. The heart sounds, "lub-dup," are due to the closing of the atrioventricular valves, followed by the closing of the semilunar valves.

5.4 Features of the Cardiovascular System
The pulse rate indicates the heartbeat rate. Blood pressure caused by the beating of the heart accounts for the flow of blood in the arteries, but because blood pressure drops off after the capillaries, it cannot cause blood flow in the veins. Skeletal muscle contraction, the presence of valves, and respiratory movements account for blood flow in veins. The reduced velocity of blood flow in capillaries facilitates exchange of nutrients and wastes in the tissues.

5.5 The Cardiovascular Pathways
The cardiovascular system is divided into the pulmonary circuit and the systemic circuit. In the pulmonary circuit, the pulmonary trunk from the right ventricle and the two pulmonary arteries take O_2-poor blood to the lungs, and four pulmonary veins return O_2-rich blood to the left atrium. To trace the path of blood in the systemic circuit, start with the aorta from the left ventricle. Follow its path until it branches to an artery going to a specific organ. It can be assumed that the artery divides into arterioles and capillaries, and that the capillaries lead to venules. The vein that takes blood to the vena cava, most likely, has the same name as the artery that delivered blood to the organ. In the adult systemic circuit, unlike the pulmonary circuit, the arteries carry O_2-rich blood, and the veins carry O_2-poor blood.

5.6 Cardiovascular Disorders
Hypertension and atherosclerosis are two cardiovascular disorders that can lead to stroke, heart attack, and aneurysm. Procedures are available for dissolving clots and opening vessels clogged with plaque. Heart failure can be treated today; usually by a left ventricle assist device; infrequently by a heart transplant; and rarely by receiving a total artificial heart. Medical and surgical procedures are available to control cardiovascular disease, but the best policy is prevention by following a heart-healthy diet, getting regular exercise, maintaining a proper weight, and not smoking.

5.7 The Lymphatic System Helps the Cardiovascular System
The lymphatic system is a one-way system taking excess tissue fluid (lymph) to the subclavian veins. The lymphatic vessels are constructed similarly to the cardiovascular veins and contain valves to keep lymph moving from the tissues to the veins. The lacteals are lymphatic vessels in the intestinal villi that absorb the products of fat digestion. Lymph nodes occur along the length of the lymphatic vessels, and these filter the lymph and store lymphocytes to fight infection. The other lymphatic organs are the red bone marrow, the spleen, and the thymus.

Studying the Concepts

1. How is the cardiovascular system organized? 78
2. What are the types of blood vessels? Discuss their structure and function. 79
3. Trace the path of blood through the heart, mentioning the vessels attached to, and the valves within, the heart. 81
4. Describe the cardiac cycle (using the terms *systole* and *diastole*), and explain the heart sounds. 82
5. Describe the cardiac conduction system and an ECG. Explain how an ECG is related to the cardiac cycle. 83
6. In what vessel is blood pressure highest? Lowest? Why is the slow movement of blood in capillaries beneficial? 84–85
7. What factors assist venous return of blood? 85
8. Trace the path of blood in the pulmonary circuit as it travels from and returns to the heart. 86
9. Trace the path of blood to and from the kidneys in the systemic circuit. 86–87
10. What is atherosclerosis? Name two illnesses associated with hypertension and thromboembolism. 88
11. Discuss the medical and surgical treatment for arterial disorders and disorders of the heart. 88–89, 91
12. List three functions of the lymphatic system, and tell how these functions are carried out. How is a lymphatic vessel like a cardiovascular vein? 92

Thinking Critically About the Concepts

Refer to the opening vignette on page 78, and then answer these questions.

1. With this scenario in mind, what other dietary and lifestyle changes should Charles' father make?
2. What are some of the major risk factors that may have contributed to his stroke?
3. When the stroke occurred, what were some of the responses and reactions that would have happened to other organs of the cardiovascular system and to other organs of the body?
4. Knowing what you do about the function of blood, what events do you think occurred in this tissue?
5. What cardiovascular disease risk factors could have contributed directly to this?

Testing Your Knowledge of the Concepts

Choose the best answer for each question.

In questions 1–4, match the descriptions to the circuit in the key. Answers may be used more than once.

Key:

    a. pulmonary circuit
    b. systemic circuit
    c. both pulmonary and systemic

1. Arteries carry O_2-rich blood.

2. Carbon dioxide leaves the capillaries, and oxygen enters the capillaries.

3. Arteries carry blood away from the heart, and veins carry blood toward the heart.

4. This contains the renal arteries and veins.

In questions 5–10, match the descriptions to the blood vessel in the key. Answers may be used more than once.

Key:

    a. venules   d. arteries
    b. veins   e. arterioles
    c. capillaries

5. Drain blood from capillaries

6. Smallest blood vessels

7. May contain valves

8. Take blood to the heart

9. Sites for exchange of substances between blood and tissue fluid

10. Rate of blood flow is lowest

11. During ventricular diastole,
    a. blood flows into the aorta.
    b. atrioventricular valves are closed.
    c. semilunar valves are closed.
    d. Both a and b are correct.

12. If a person's blood pressure is 120 mm Hg over 80 mm Hg, the 80 represents
    a. systolic pressure.
    b. diastolic pressure.
    c. pressure during ventricular relaxation.
    d. Both b and c are correct.

13. Heart valves located at the bases of the pulmonary trunk and aorta are called
    a. atrioventricular valves.
    b. semilunar valves.
    c. mitral valves.
    d. chordae tendineae.

14. When the atria contract, the blood flows
    a. into the attached blood vessels.
    b. into the ventricles.
    c. through the atrioventricular valves.
    d. to the lungs.
    e. Both b and c are correct.

15. The pulmonary trunk and the aorta
    a. are attached to the atria.
    b. are attached to the ventricles.
    c. start at the semilunar valves.
    d. start at the atrioventricular valves.
    e. Both b and c are correct.

16. Which of these associations is mismatched?
    a. left ventricle—aorta
    b. right ventricle—pulmonary trunk
    c. right atrium—vena cava
    d. left atrium—pulmonary artery
    e. Both b and c are incorrectly matched.

17. Accumulation of plaque in an artery wall is
    a. an aneurysm.
    b. an angina pectoris.
    c. atherosclerosis.
    d. hypertension.
    e. a thromboembolism.

18. Where would you find the Purkinje fibers?
    a. at the entrance to the heart
    b. in the walls of the atria
    c. in the walls of the ventricles
    d. at the region of the atrioventricular valves
    e. at the region of the semilunar valves

19. Which statement is not correct concerning the heartbeat?
    a. The atria contract at the same time.
    b. The ventricles relax at the same time.
    c. The atrioventricular valves open at the same time.
    d. The semilunar valves open at the same time.
    e. First the right side contracts, and then the left side contracts.

20. When the ventricles contract, the blood flows
    a. into the attached blood vessels.
    b. into the atria.
    c. through the atrioventricular valves.
    d. to the lungs and the body.
    e. Both a and d are correct.

21. Which of the following is not a function of the lymphatic system?
    a. Transports carbon dioxide from the tissues.
    b. Returns excess fluid to the blood.
    c. Transports lipids absorbed from the digestive system.
    d. Defends the body against pathogens.

22. What structural similarities do veins and lymphatic vessels have in common?
    a. Both have thick walls of smooth muscle.
    b. Both contain valves for one-way flow of fluids.
    c. Both empty directly into the heart.
    d. Both are fed fluids from arterioles.

23. Label the following diagram of the cardiovascular system using this alphabetized list:

aorta
carotid artery
hepatic portal vein
hepatic vein
iliac artery
iliac vein
inferior vena cava

jugular vein
mesenteric arteries
pulmonary artery
pulmonary vein
renal artery
renal vein
superior vena cava

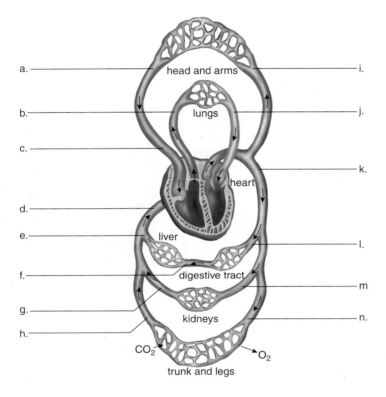

a.

b.

c.

d.

e.

f.

g.

h.

head and arms

lungs

heart

liver

digestive tract

kidneys

CO_2 O_2

trunk and legs

i.

j.

k.

l.

m.

n.

Understanding Key Terms

aneurysm 88
angina pectoris 88
angioplasty 91
aorta 86
arteriole 79
artery 78
atherosclerosis 88
atrioventricular bundle 82
atrioventricular valve 80
atrium 80
AV (atrioventricular) node 82
blood pressure 84

capillary 78
cardiac cycle 82
chordae tendineae 80
coronary artery 87
coronary bypass operation 89
diastole 82
diastolic pressure 84
electrocardiogram (ECG) 83
embolus 88
heart 80
heart attack 88
heart failure 91

hemorrhoids 88
hepatic portal system 87
hepatic portal vein 87
hepatic vein 87
hypertension 88
inferior vena cava 86
lymph 92
lymphatic system 92
lymphatic vessels 92
lymph node 92
myocardium 80
pacemaker 82
pericardium 80
phlebitis 89
plaque 88
pulmonary artery 81
pulmonary circuit 78
pulmonary vein 81
pulse 84

Purkinje fibers 82
SA (sinoatrial) node 82
semilunar valve 80
septum 80
spleen 92
stroke 88
superior vena cava 86
systemic circuit 78
systole 82
systolic pressure 84
thromboembolism 88
thrombus 88
total artificial heart (TAH) 91
valve 79
varicose vein 88
vein 78
ventricle 80
venule 79

Match the key terms to these definitions.

a. _____ Relaxation of a heart chamber.

b. _____ Large systemic vein that returns blood from body areas below the diaphragm.

c. _____ Rhythmic expansion and recoil of arteries resulting from heart contraction; can be felt from outside the body.

d. _____ Vessel that takes blood from capillaries to a vein.

e. _____ That part of the cardiovascular system that serves body parts and does not include the gas-exchanging surfaces in the lungs.

Online Learning Center

www.mhhe.com/maderhuman9

The Online Learning Center provides a wealth of information fully organized and integrated by chapter. You will find practice quizzes, interactive activities, labeling exercises, flashcards, and much more that will complement your learning and understanding of human biology.

Looking at Both Sides

Each day, the Internet, media, and other people present you with opposing viewpoints on a wide range of subjects. Your ability to develop an informed opinion on an issue, and talk to others about it, is extremely important.

To expand and enhance your knowledge of a highly relevant bioethical issue, visit the "Student Edition" of the Online Learning Center. Under "Course-Wide Content," select "Looking at Both Sides." Once there, you will be asked to complete activities that will increase your understanding of a current bioethical issue related to this chapter and allow you to defend your opinion.

CHAPTER

6

Cardiovascular System: Blood

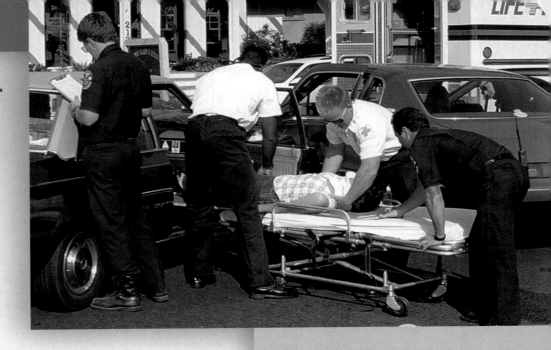

CHAPTER CONCEPTS

6.1 Blood: An Overview
- What are the functions of blood and what are its two main portions?   98–99

6.2 Composition of Blood
- What is the composition of plasma, and what are the functions of the plasma proteins?   99
- What substance allows red blood cells to transport oxygen?   100
- What are the formed elements?   100
- What events comprise the life cycle of red blood cells?   101
- What are the different types of white blood cells?   103
- What is the structure and function of each type of white blood cell?   103

6.3 Blood Clotting
- What are the participants in blood clotting, and what are their functions?   104

6.4 Blood Typing
- What are the different types of blood, and how is blood typed?   106–7

6.5 Capillary Exchange
- How does the structure of a capillary suit its function?   108
- How does exchange of materials take place across a capillary wall in the tissues?   108–9
- What happens to excess tissue fluid created by capillary exchange?   109

6.6 Homeostasis
- How does the cardiovascular system work with the other systems of the body to maintain homeostasis?   110–11

The paramedics arrived on the scene of the automobile accident within minutes. Henry realized that Alice was quickly losing blood and would need to be taken to the hospital immediately. The paramedics quickly checked her vital signs and medical history. "Type A negative," Henry barked to the paramedics without having to be asked. On the way to the hospital she was given a potentially life-saving blood transfusion to replace the fluid that had been lost.

Incidents like this remind us of how very vital our blood is to the function of our bodies. Without its life-giving oxygen transport functions, Alice would have lost consciousness very quickly, with more severe complications possible. Besides transporting oxygen, our blood carries out many other vital functions, such as transporting nutrients, carrying signals between organs, removing metabolic wastes from our cells, and fighting off potentially deadly pathogens. Various salts and proteins in our blood also help us to sustain proper body temperature and water balance, as well as to maintain the integrity of our cardiovascular system. Because of these vital functions, excessive blood loss can be fatal.

The blood coursing through our arteries and veins is subjected to many everyday stresses, including numerous cuts and scrapes to our skin, toxins in our environment, and pathogens that we encounter. The components of blood, the various functions associated with each component, and how these components interact with one another and with the other organs of our bodies will be discussed in this chapter.

FORMED ELEMENTS	Function and Description	Source
Red Blood Cells (erythrocytes) 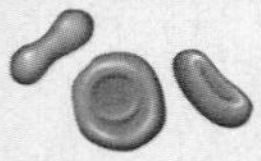 4 million–6 million per mm³ blood	Transport O_2 and help transport CO_2 7–8 µm in diameter Bright-red to dark-purple biconcave disks without nuclei	Red bone marrow
White Blood Cells (leukocytes) 5,000–11,000 per mm³ blood	Fight infection	Red bone marrow
Granular leukocytes		
*Neutrophils 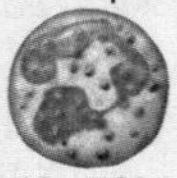 40–70%	10–14 µm in diameter Spherical cells with multilobed nuclei; fine, pink granules in cytoplasm; phagocytize pathogens	
*Eosinophils 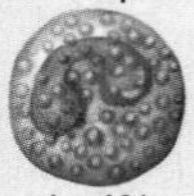 1–4%	10–14 µm in diameter Spherical cells with bilobed nuclei; coarse, deep-red, uniformly sized granules in cytoplasm; phagocytize antigen-antibody complexes and allergens	
*Basophils  0–1%	10–12 µm in diameter Spherical cells with lobed nuclei; large, irregularly shaped, deep-blue granules in cytoplasm; release histamine, which promotes blood flow to injured tissues	
Agranular leukocytes		
*Lymphocytes  20–45%	5–17 µm in diameter (average 9–10 µm) Spherical cells with large round nuclei; responsible for specific immunity	
*Monocytes 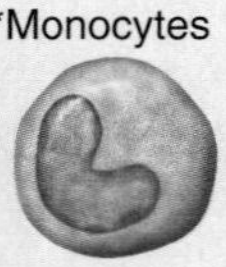 4–8%	10–24 µm in diameter Large spherical cells with kidney-shaped, round, or lobed nuclei; become macrophages that phagocytize pathogens and cellular debris	
Platelets (thrombocytes)  150,000–300,000 per mm³ blood	Aid clotting 2–4 µm in diameter Disk-shaped cell fragments with no nuclei; purple granules in cytoplasm	Red bone marrow

PLASMA	Function	Source
Water (90–92% of plasma)	Maintains blood volume; transports molecules	Absorbed from intestine
Plasma proteins (7–8% of plasma)	Maintain blood osmotic pressure and pH	Liver
Albumins	Maintain blood volume and pressure	
Globulins	Transport; fight infection	
Fibrinogen	Clotting	
Salts (less than 1% of plasma)	Maintain blood osmotic pressure and pH; aid metabolism	Absorbed from intestine
Gases		
Oxygen Carbon dioxide	Cellular respiration End product of metabolism	Lungs Tissues
Nutrients	Food for cells	Absorbed from intestine
Lipids Glucose Amino acids		
Nitrogenous wastes	Excretion by kidneys	Liver
Urea Uric acid		
Other		
Hormones, vitamins, etc.	Aid metabolism	Varied

Plasma 55%

Formed elements 45%

*These cells have been stained with Wright's stain.

Figure 6.1   Composition of blood.

When blood is transferred to a test tube and prevented from clotting, it forms two layers. The transparent, yellow top layer is plasma, the liquid portion of blood. The formed elements are in the bottom layer. This table describes the formed elements and the contents of plasma in detail.

6.1 Blood: An Overview

In Chapter 5, we learned that the cardiovascular system consists of the heart, which pumps the blood, and the blood vessels that conduct blood around the body. In this chapter, we learn about the functions and composition of blood.

Portions of Blood

If blood is transferred from a person's vein to a test tube and is prevented from clotting, it separates into two layers (Fig. 6.1). The lower layer consists of red blood cells, white blood cells, and blood platelets, which are derived from cells. Collectively, these are called the **formed elements,** which can be defined as the portion of blood that is cellular or derived from a cell. Formed elements make up about 45% of the total volume of whole blood. The upper layer is **plasma,** a liquid that contains a variety of inorganic and organic molecules dissolved or suspended in water. Plasma accounts for about 55% of the total volume of whole blood.

Functions of Blood

The functions of blood fall into three categories: transport, defense, and regulation.

Blood is the primary transport medium. Blood delivers oxygen from the lungs and nutrients from the digestive tract to the tissues, where an exchange takes place. It picks up and transports carbon dioxide and wastes away from the tissues to exchange surfaces in the lungs and kidneys, respectively. In this way, capillary exchanges keep the composition of tissue fluid within normal limits.

Various organs and tissues secrete hormones into the blood, and blood transports these to other organs and tissues, where they serve as signals that influence cellular metabolism.

Blood defends the body against invasion by pathogens in several ways. Certain blood cells are capable of engulfing and destroying pathogens, and others produce and secrete antibodies into the blood. Antibodies incapacitate pathogens, making them subject to destruction, sometimes by white blood cells.

When an injury occurs, blood clots, and so prevents blood loss. Blood clotting involves platelets and a plasma protein, fibrinogen. Without blood clotting, we could bleed to death even from a small cut.

Blood has regulatory functions. Blood helps regulate body temperature by picking up heat, mostly from active muscles, and transporting it about the body. If the blood is too warm, the heat dissipates from dilated blood vessels in the skin.

The salts and plasma proteins in blood act to keep the liquid content of blood high. In this way, blood plays a role in helping to maintain its own water-salt balance.

Because blood contains buffers, it helps regulate body pH and keep it relatively constant.

6.2 Composition of Blood

Plasma is the liquid portion of blood, and about 92% of plasma is water. The remaining 8% of plasma consists of various salts (ions) and organic molecules (Table 6.1). The salts, which are simply dissolved in plasma, help maintain the pH of the blood. Small organic molecules such as glucose, amino acids, and urea can also dissolve in plasma. Glucose and amino acids are nutrients for cells; urea is a nitrogenous waste product on its way to the kidneys for excretion. The large organic molecules in plasma include hormones and the plasma proteins.

The Plasma Proteins

Three major types of plasma proteins are the albumins, globulins, and fibrinogen. Most plasma proteins are made in the liver. An exception is the antibodies produced by B lymphocytes, which function in immunity.

The plasma proteins have many functions that help maintain homeostasis. They are able to take up and release hydrogen ions; therefore, the plasma proteins help buffer the blood and keep its pH around 7.4. **Osmotic pressure** is a force caused by a difference in solute concentration on either side of a membrane. The plasma proteins, particularly the **albumins,** contribute to the osmotic pressure that pulls water into the blood and helps keep it there.

Certain plasma proteins combine with and transport large organic molecules. For example, an albumin transports the molecule bilirubin, a breakdown product of hemoglobin. Lipoproteins, whose protein portion is a globulin, transport cholesterol.

Antibodies, which help fight infections by combining with antigens, are a type of plasma protein called gamma globulins. Other plasma proteins also have specific functions. Fibrinogen is necessary to blood clotting, for example.

The functions of blood and plasma proteins contribute to maintaining homeostasis.

Table 6.1	Blood Plasma Solutes
Plasma proteins	Albumin, globulins, fibrinogen
Inorganic ions (salts)	Na^+, Ca^{2+}, K^+, Mg^{2+}, Cl^-, HCO_3^-, HPO_4^{2-}, SO_4^{2-}
Gases	O_2, CO_2
Organic nutrients	Glucose, fats, phospholipids, amino acids, etc.
Nitrogenous waste products	Urea, ammonia, uric acid
Regulatory substances	Hormones, enzymes

The Formed Elements

The formed elements are red blood cells, white blood cells, and platelets.

Red Blood Cells

Red blood cells (erythrocytes) are small, biconcave disks that lack a nucleus when mature. They occur in great quantity; there are 4–6 million red blood cells per mm³ of whole blood.

Red blood cells transport oxygen because they contain **hemoglobin (Hb),** the respiratory pigment that gives them their red color. In hemoglobin, each of four polypeptide chains making up globin has an iron-containing heme group in the center. Oxygen combines loosely with iron when hemoglobin is oxygenated.

Hemoglobin, combined with oxygen, is called oxyhemoglobin. Oxyhemoglobin forms in the lungs and has a bright red color. Hemoglobin, which is not combined with oxygen, is called deoxyhemoglobin. Deoxyhemoglobin is a dark maroon color. Unfortunately, carbon monoxide combines with hemoglobin more readily than does oxygen, and it stays combined for several hours, making hemoglobin unavailable for oxygen transport.

A red blood cell contains about 200 million hemoglobin molecules. If this much hemoglobin were suspended within the plasma rather than enclosed within the cells, blood would be so viscous that the heart would have difficulty pumping it. Still, as discussed in the Health Focus on page 102, most types of artificial blood are solutions of hemoglobin.

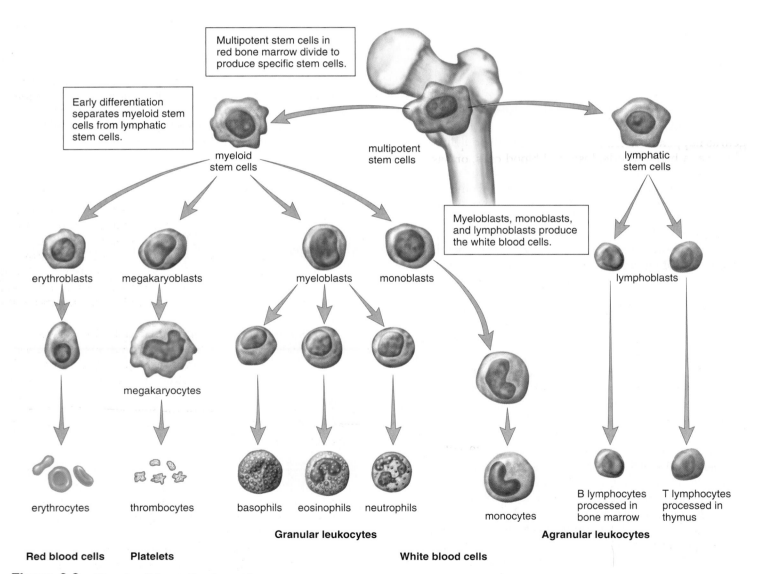

Figure 6.2   Blood cell formation in red bone marrow.
Multipotent stem cells give rise to two specialized stem cells. The myeloid stem cell gives rise to still other cells, which become red blood cells, platelets, and all the white blood cells except lymphocytes. The lymphatic stem cell gives rise to lymphoblasts, which become lymphocytes.

Production of Red Blood Cells All blood cells, including erythrocytes, are formed from special red bone marrow cells called stem cells (Fig. 6.2). A **stem cell** is ever capable of dividing and producing new cells that differentiate into specific types of cells. Now, it's been discovered that red bone marrow stem cells are, most likely, capable of becoming cardiac and nerve cells, in addition to blood cells. There is great interest in possibly using red bone marrow stem cells to cure various human ills because they are a relatively accessible source of stem cells from an adult body. Other investigators still believe that embryonic stem cells derived from leftover embryos at fertility clinics are the best source of stem cells, see the Bioethical Focus on page 51.

As red blood cells mature, they lose their nucleus and acquire hemoglobin. Possibly because they lack a nucleus, red blood cells live only about 120 days. As they age, red blood cells are destroyed in the liver and spleen, where they are engulfed by macrophages. It is estimated that about 2 million red blood cells are destroyed per second, and therefore an equal number must be produced to keep the red blood cell count in balance.

Whenever blood carries a reduced amount of oxygen, as happens when an individual first takes up residence at a high altitude, loses red blood cells, or has impaired lung function, the kidneys accelerate their release of **erythropoietin** (Fig. 6.3). This hormone speeds up the maturation of cells that are in the process of becoming red blood cells. The liver and other tissues also produce erythropoietin. Erythropoietin, now mass-produced through biotechnology, is sometimes abused by athletes in order to raise their red blood cell counts, and thereby increase the oxygen-carrying capacity of their blood.

Destruction of Red Blood Cells When red blood cells are broken down, hemoglobin is released. The globin portion of hemoglobin is broken down into its component amino acids, which are recycled by the body. The iron is recovered and returned to the bone marrow for reuse. The heme portion of the molecule undergoes chemical degradation and is excreted as bile pigments by the liver into the bile. These are the bile pigments bilirubin and biliverdin, which contribute to the color of feces. Chemical breakdown of heme is also what causes a bruise of the skin to change color from red/purple to blue to green to yellow.

Anemia

When there is an insufficient number of red blood cells or the cells do not have enough hemoglobin, the individual suffers from **anemia** and has a tired, run-down feeling. Iron, the B vitamin folic acid, and vitamin B_{12} are necessary for the production of red blood cells. When the diet does not contain enough of these substances, anemia can develop. Iron deficiency anemia is well known, but folic

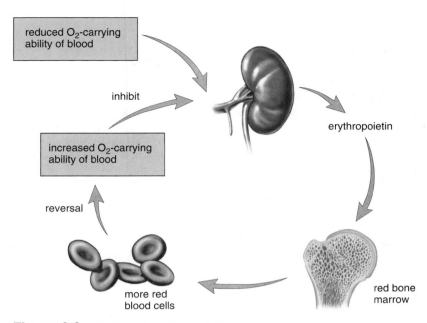

Figure 6.3 **Action of erythropoietin.**
The kidneys release increased amounts of erythropoietin whenever the oxygen capacity of the blood is reduced. Erythropoietin stimulates the red bone marrow to speed up its production of red blood cells, which carry oxygen. Once the oxygen-carrying capacity of the blood is sufficient to support normal cellular activity, the kidneys cut back on their production of erythropoietin.

acid anemia also occurs. Pernicious anemia occurs when the digestive tract is unable to absorb enough vitamin B_{12}, which is found in dairy products, fish, eggs, and poultry. Without adequate amounts of iron, folic acid, and vitamin B_{12}, immature red blood cells tend to accumulate in the bone marrow in large quantities. A special diet and administration of these substances are effective treatments for anemia.

Hemolysis is the rupturing of red blood cells. In hemolytic anemia, the rate of red blood cell destruction increases. **Sickle-cell disease** is a hereditary condition in which the individual has sickle-shaped red blood cells that tend to rupture as they pass through the narrow capillaries. Hemolytic disease of the newborn, which is discussed on page 107 of this chapter, is also a type of hemolytic anemia.

Red blood cells are produced from stem cells in red bone marrow. As red blood cells mature, they lose a nucleus and gain hemoglobin, a molecule that transports oxygen. Red blood cells live only about 120 days and are destroyed by phagocytic cells in the liver and spleen. Anemia results when the blood has too few red blood cells and/or not enough hemoglobin.

Health Focus

Artificial Blood

As any doctor or nurse can attest, hospitals always have a dire need for a large supply of blood. Blood is needed for treating patients who are seriously injured, undergoing major surgery, or have other chronic medical problems. Constant calls for blood donations by the American Red Cross remind us that, today, all types of blood must be donated by others. Even when blood is properly matched, receiving a transfusion always carries a small but significant risk. Because blood is a tissue, transfusion is in effect a "tissue transplant." If the patient's immune system detects that the glycoproteins on the red blood cell membrane are foreign, the transfused cells will be rejected. Such a rejection, called a transfusion reaction, can be fatal. Then too, donor blood may be infected with viruses that will cause illness in the recipient.

As a possible solution to many of these problems, researchers are experimenting with artificial blood. For artificial blood to be an effective substitute, it must: be cheap to produce, possess a longer shelf life than whole blood, and be accepted by anyone without untoward effects. Most of the blood substitutes formulated are solutions of hemoglobin, the protein in red blood cells that is responsible for oxygen transport (Fig. 6A). Some researchers attempted to bypass the need for human hemoglobin by using blood from other animals, such as pigs. Animal hemoglobin, while similar to our own, is different enough that is has the potential to cause severe allergic reactions and other complications. It must be carefully screened for potentially lethal pathogens. Furthermore, growing the animals to produce the blood needed was neither economical nor fast. Researchers have sidestepped this obstacle through the use of biotechnology, using bacteria to produce human hemoglobin.

Human hemoglobin introduced into the bloodstream breaks down immediately into smaller molecules that are toxic, especially to nerve cells, the liver, and kidneys. However, hemoglobin that is first chemically modified to prevent it from breaking down can be safely transfused. Once in the cardiovascular system, the hemoglobin will transport oxygen in much the same way that it does inside intact red blood cells. The modified hemoglobin is slowly broken down, and eliminated from the body, without harming the patient's liver or kidneys.

Hemoglobin-based blood substitutes have several benefits. They are better oxygen transporters than whole blood, although they remain in the patient's body for only a few days. Unlike whole blood, blood substitutes are free of disease-causing contaminants and can be stored for months at room temperature. Moreover, blood substitutes cannot cause a transfusion reaction because they lack the membrane proteins of a red blood cell. This makes them the perfect "one-size-fits-all" substance for transfusion, and perhaps the ideal solution for critical-care emergencies. Blood substitutes are currently in widespread clinical trials in South Africa, where the AIDS outbreak has caused a critical shortage of available donors of whole blood. Other clinical trials are under way in the United States and Europe.

While blood substitutes have improved greatly in the last few years, they are still not without side effects. One problem is that some patients experience increased levels of bilirubin, a breakdown product of hemoglobin, which can lead to jaundice. Despite improved consistency, some patients still experience high blood pressure after treatment, for reasons that are unknown. Iron toxicity has also been described as a result of hemoglobin breakdown over time. Biotechnology may, once again, come to the rescue. Researchers are hopeful they can develop a hemoglobin with improved stability and ability to transport oxygen, through manipulation of the hemoglobin gene.

Even so, there are still other obstacles to be overcome. Without the essential clotting components of whole blood, these blood substitutes are ineffective in treating patients with clotting disorders. They are ineffective in treating infection, because these products lack the normal immune component of whole blood. Current blood substitute products have shown promise in many cases, especially for the treatment of trauma patients; they are constantly improving, and may be coming soon to an emergency room near you.

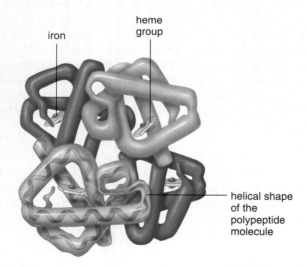

iron

heme group

helical shape of the polypeptide molecule

Figure 6A **Hemoglobin contains four polypeptide chains (blue).**
There is an iron-containing heme group in the center of each chain. Oxygen combines loosely with iron when hemoglobin is oxygenated. Oxyhemoglobin is bright red, and deoxyhemoglobin is a dark maroon color.

The White Blood Cells

White blood cells (leukocytes) differ from red blood cells in that they are usually larger, have a nucleus, lack hemoglobin, and are translucent unless stained. White blood cells are not as numerous as red blood cells; there are only 5,000–11,000 per mm^3 of blood. White blood cells fight infection and in this way are important contributors to homeostasis. This function of white blood cells is discussed at greater length in Chapter 21, which concerns immunity.

White blood cells are derived from stem cells in the red bone marrow, and they, too, undergo several maturation stages. **Colony-stimulating factors (CSFs)** are proteins that help regulate the production of white blood cells. Researchers have shown that there is a different CSF for the production of white blood cells derived from specific stem cells (see Fig. 6.2).

White blood cells are able to squeeze through pores in the capillary wall, and therefore they are found in tissue fluid and lymph (Fig. 6.4). **Lymph** is tissue fluid within lymphatic vessels (see Fig. 6.10). When there is an infection, white blood cells greatly increase in number. Many white blood cells live only a few days—they probably die while engaging pathogens. Others live for months or even years.

White blood cells fight infection. They defend us against pathogens that have invaded the body.

Types of White Blood Cells

White blood cells are classified into the **granular leukocytes** and the **agranular leukocytes.** Both types of cells have granules in the cytoplasm surrounding the nucleus, but the granules are more visible upon staining in granular leukocytes. The granules contain various enzymes and proteins, which help white blood cells defend the body. There are three types of granular leukocytes and two types of agranular leukocytes. They differ somewhat by the size of the cell and the shape of the nucleus (see Fig. 6.1), and they also differ in their functions.

Among granular leukocytes, **neutrophils** are the most abundant of the white blood cells. They have a multilobed nucleus joined by nuclear threads; therefore, they are also called polymorphonuclear. They have granules that do not significantly take up the stain eosin, a pink to red acidic stain, or a basic stain that is blue to purple. (This accounts for their name, neutrophil.) Neutrophils are the first type of white blood cell to respond to an infection, and they engulf pathogens during **phagocytosis.**

Eosinophils have a bilobed nucleus, and their large, abundant granules take up eosin and become a red color. (This accounts for their name, eosinophil.) Not much is known specifically about the function of eosinophils, but they increase in number in the event of a parasitic worm infection or an allergic reaction.

Basophils have a U-shaped or lobed nucleus. Their granules take up the basic stain and become a dark blue

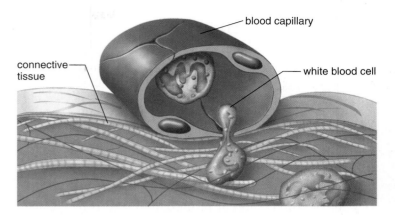

Figure 6.4 Mobility of white blood cells.
White blood cells can squeeze between the cells of a capillary wall and enter the tissues of the body.

color. (This accounts for their name, basophil.) In the connective tissues, basophils, and also similar type cells called mast cells, release histamine associated with allergic reactions. Histamine dilates blood vessels, but constricts the air tubes that lead to the lungs.

The agranular leukocytes include monocytes, which have a kidney-shaped nucleus, and lymphocytes, which have a spherical nucleus. Lymphocytes are responsible for specific immunity to particular pathogens and their toxins (poisonous substances). Pathogens have surface molecules called **antigens** that allow the immune system to recognize them as foreign.

Monocytes are the largest of the white blood cells, and after taking up residence in the tissues, they differentiate into even larger macrophages. Macrophages phagocytize pathogens, old cells, and cellular debris. They also stimulate other white blood cells, including lymphocytes, to defend the body.

The **lymphocytes** are of two types, B cells and T cells. B cell descendants (plasma cells) protect us by producing **antibodies** that combine with antigens and thereby target pathogens for destruction. Some T cells (cytotoxic T cells) directly destroy any cell that has foreign antigens. B lymphocytes and T lymphocytes are discussed more fully in Chapter 21.

The Platelets

Platelets (thrombocytes) result from fragmentation of certain large cells, called **megakaryocytes,** in the red bone marrow. Platelets are produced at a rate of 200 billion a day, and the blood contains 150,000–300,000 per mm^3. These formed elements are involved in the process of blood **clotting,** or coagulation.

When a blood vessel in the body is damaged, platelets clump at the site of the puncture and seal the break, if it is not too extensive. A large break may also require a blood clot to stop the bleeding.

6.3 Blood Clotting

When the lining of a blood vessel breaks, platelets adhere to exposed collagen fibers and release a substance that promotes platelet aggregation, so that a so-called platelet plug forms. Thereafter, at least 12 clotting factors participate in the formation of a blood clot. Each clotting factor has a very specific job to do, and we will discuss the roles played by fibrinogen, prothrombin, and thrombin. **Fibrinogen** and **prothrombin** are proteins manufactured and deposited in blood by the liver. Vitamin K, found in green vegetables and also formed by intestinal bacteria, is necessary for the production of prothrombin, and if by chance this vitamin is missing from the diet, hemorrhagic disorders develop.

A break in a blood vessel causes damaged tissue to release tissue thromboplastin, a blood clotting factor that initiates a series of reactions involving several clotting factors and calcium ions (Ca^{2+}). These reactions lead to production of **prothrombin activator,** which converts prothrombin to thrombin. This reaction also requires Ca^{2+}. **Thrombin,** in turn, acts as an enzyme that severs two short amino acid chains from each fibrinogen molecule. These activated fragments then join end to end, forming long threads of **fibrin.** Fibrin threads wind around the platelet plug in the damaged area of the blood vessel and provide the framework for the clot. Red blood cells also are trapped within the fibrin threads; these cells make a clot appear red (Fig. 6.5). A fibrin clot is present only temporarily. As soon as blood vessel repair is initiated, an enzyme called plasmin destroys the fibrin network and restores the fluidity of plasma.

After blood clots, a yellowish fluid escapes from the clot. This fluid is called **serum,** and it contains all the components of plasma except fibrinogen and prothrombin. Table 6.2

Table 6.2	Body Fluids Related to Blood
Name	**Composition**
Blood	Formed elements and plasma
Plasma	Liquid portion of blood
Serum	Plasma minus fibrinogen and prothrombin
Tissue fluid	Plasma minus most proteins
Lymph	Tissue fluid within lymphatic vessels

reviews the different terms we have used to refer to various body fluids related to blood.

Disorders Related to Blood Clotting

Thrombocytopenia, a low platelet count can be due to any impairment of the red bone marrow. Thrombocytopenia can result in the inability of blood to clot. On the other hand, sometimes a clot forms in an unbroken blood vessel. Such a clot is called a thrombus if it remains stationary. Should the clot dislodge, and travel in the blood, it is called an embolus. If thromboembolism is not treated, a heart attack can occur, as discussed in Chapter 5.

Hemophilia is an inherited clotting disorder due to a deficiency in a clotting factor. The slightest bump can cause bleeding into the joints. Cartilage degeneration in the joints and resorption of underlying bone can follow. Bleeding into muscles can lead to nerve damage and muscular atrophy. The most frequent cause of death is bleeding into the brain with accompanying neurological damage. Hemophilia A, due to the lack of clotting factor VIII, is more apt to be inherited by boys than girls (see page 402).

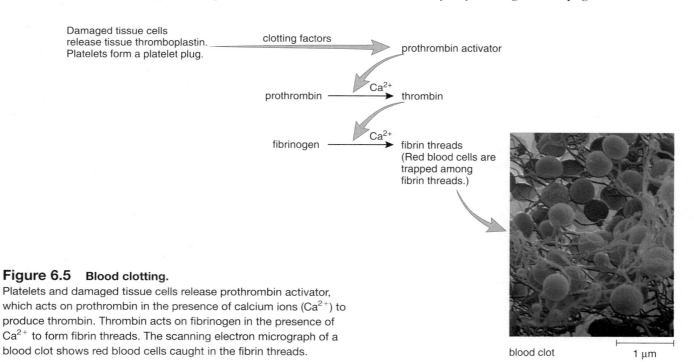

Figure 6.5 **Blood clotting.**
Platelets and damaged tissue cells release prothrombin activator, which acts on prothrombin in the presence of calcium ions (Ca^{2+}) to produce thrombin. Thrombin acts on fibrinogen in the presence of Ca^{2+} to form fibrin threads. The scanning electron micrograph of a blood clot shows red blood cells caught in the fibrin threads.

Damaged tissue cells release tissue thromboplastin. Platelets form a platelet plug.
clotting factors → prothrombin activator
prothrombin → Ca^{2+} → thrombin
fibrinogen → Ca^{2+} → fibrin threads (Red blood cells are trapped among fibrin threads.)
blood clot   1 μm

Ecology Focus

Fish: The Good News and the Bad News

"I thought fish was good for me!" "Do I have to give up tuna?" Fish is good for you! It contains high-quality protein and omega-3 fatty acids, which prevent blood from clotting and help maintain a regular heartbeat. The American Heart Association guidelines recommend eating fish twice a week to maintain a healthy heart, but recent advisories have people concerned about the safety of eating fish. Due to the amount of mercury present in some fish, in January 2001, the U.S. Food and Drug Administration (FDA) advised that pregnant women (or those who might become pregnant), nursing mothers, and young children should avoid certain types of fish. Fish on the "avoid altogether" list include swordfish, king mackerel, shark, and tilefish. These groups of people should also limit the amount of other types of fish, such as tuna, halibut, sea bass, cod, and pollock.

The FDA, which regulates commercially sold fish, considers up to 1 part per million (ppm) mercury to be safe. They report that fish sold in the United States, on average, contains less than 0.3 ppm mercury. However, the FDA stopped testing for mercury in fish in 1998 and allows the fish industry to police itself. States issue fish advisories for fish caught in their waters. In 2001, 44 states issued fish advisories for particular bodies of water within their borders because levels of methylmercury in the water exceeded the limit of 1 ppm.

Ecologists know that "everything is connected to everything else." Mercury enters our atmosphere by the combustion of fossil fuels containing mercury and human uses of mercury in various products (e.g., thermometers, thermostats, and mercury vapor lamps) and in industry. From there, it enters streams, rivers, lakes, and the ocean, where it is converted into methylmercury by bacteria and taken up by the bacteria and plankton in the water. Fish consume the bacteria and the plankton, and the methylmercury accumulates in their tissues. These fish are eaten by larger fish that accumulate more mercury in their tissues where it can, in turn, eventually be consumed by humans. Methylmercury levels are typically 100,000 times higher in certain predatory fish than in the surrounding water.

The fetus and children being nursed are especially vulnerable, since methylmercury passes through the mother's blood and breast milk. Small children are more vulnerable due to their smaller size. After digestion, methylmercury is absorbed into the blood, and then distributed throughout the body. It concentrates in the hair, and mercury levels can be determined from hair or blood samples. The Environmental Protection Agency (EPA) has determined that approximately 2% of women of childbearing age have a blood mercury concentration greater than 5.8 parts per billion (ppb) and 8% have a concentration of 7.0 ppb or higher (Fig. 6B). The children of these women have an increased risk of adverse health effects.

The effects of methylmercury are often neurological in these children: delayed development, reduced attention spans, altered muscle tone and tendon reflexes, loss of fine muscle control, and depressed intelligence or even mental retardation. There is also evidence that methylmercury affects the cardiovascular, immune, and reproductive systems of these children.

Adults who consume an excessive amount of mercury-contaminated fish may experience numbness or tingling in the extremities and loss of coordination. Over time, the human body is able to rid itself of some of the mercury by metabolism and excretion, but this process is fairly slow.

Therefore, it is recommended that the general public consume no more than one 7-ounce serving per week of any species that has been listed in a fish advisory, and no more than 14 ounces per week of other types of fish. The FDA recommendation is not to give up eating fish, but to eat safer types of fish, to fish only in safe areas, and to eat various types of fish in moderation.

And what about giving up tuna? The FDA did not put tuna on the "avoid altogether" list because they did not believe that it presented a health risk. However, the Center for Policy Research recommends eating only canned light tuna, which contains much less mercury than fresh tuna and canned white tuna. They also recommend eating only smaller fish, such as salmon, flounder, and haddock, as well as farmed trout and catfish.

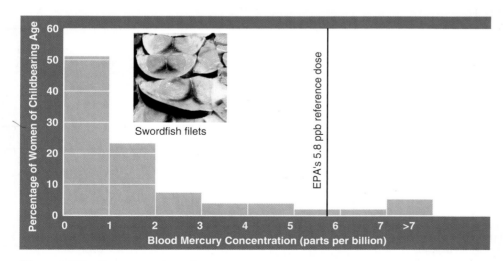

Figure 6B Concentration of mercury in blood of women of childbearing age.
Mercury enters ecosystems due to the combustion of fossil fuels and the production of such products as thermometers, thermostats, and mercury vapor lamps. The result can be children with neuromuscular impairments.

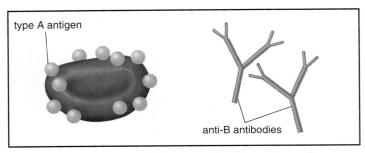

Type A blood. Red blood cells have type A surface antigens. Plasma has anti-B antibodies.

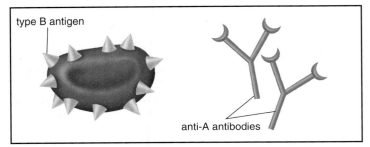

Type B blood. Red blood cells have type B surface antigens. Plasma has anti-A antibodies.

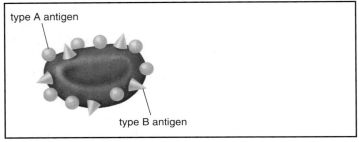

Type AB blood. Red blood cells have type A and type B surface antigens. Plasma has neither anti-A nor anti-B antibodies.

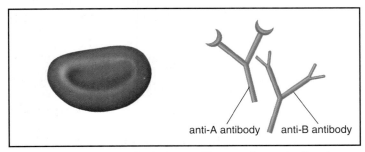

Type O blood. Red blood cells have neither type A nor type B surface antigens. Plasma has both anti-A and anti-B antibodies.

Figure 6.6 Types of blood.
In the ABO system, blood type depends on the presence or absence of antigens A and B on the surface of red blood cells. In these drawings, A and B antigens are represented by different shapes on the red blood cells. The possible anti-A and anti-B antibodies in the plasma are shown for each blood type. Notice that an anti-B antibody cannot bind to an A antigen, and vice versa.

6.4 Blood Typing

A **blood transfusion** is the transfer of blood from one individual into the blood of another. In order for transfusions to be safely done, it is necessary for blood to be typed so that **agglutination** (clumping of red blood cells) does not occur. Blood typing usually involves determining the ABO blood group and whether the individual is Rh^- (negative) or Rh^+ (positive).

ABO Blood Groups

Only certain types of blood transfusions are safe because the plasma membranes of red blood cells carry glycoproteins that can be antigens to others. ABO blood typing is based on the presence or absence of two possible antigens, called type A antigen and type B antigen. Whether these antigens are present or not depends on the particular inheritance of the individual.

A person with type A antigen on the surface of the red blood cells has type A blood; one with type B blood has type B antigen on the surface of the red blood cells. What antigens would be present on the surface of red blood cells if the person has type AB blood or type O blood? Notice in Figure 6.6 that a person with type AB blood has both antigens, and a person with type O blood has neither antigen on the surface of the red blood cells.

It so happens that an individual with type A blood has anti-B antibodies in the plasma; a person with type B blood has anti-A antibodies in the plasma; and a person with type O blood has both antibodies in the plasma (Fig. 6.6). These antibodies are not present at birth, but they appear over the course of several months after birth. The presence of these antibodies can cause agglutination.

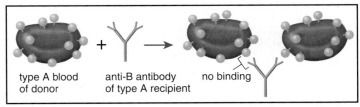

a. No agglutination

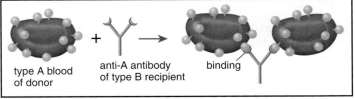

b. Agglutination

Figure 6.7 Blood transfusions.
No agglutination (**a**) versus agglutination (**b**) is determined by whether antibodies are present that can combine with antigens.

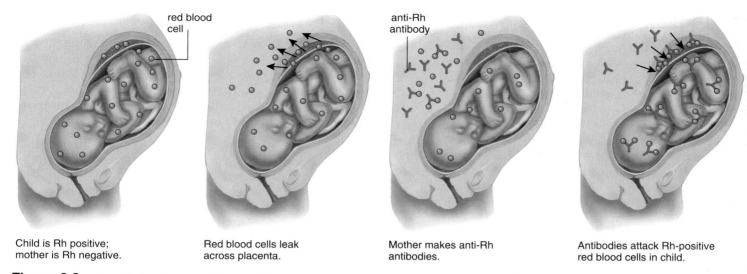

Child is Rh positive; mother is Rh negative.

Red blood cells leak across placenta.

Mother makes anti-Rh antibodies.

Antibodies attack Rh-positive red blood cells in child.

Figure 6.8 **Hemolytic disease of the newborn.**
Due to a pregnancy in which the child is Rh-positive, an Rh-negative mother can begin to produce antibodies against Rh-positive red blood cells. Usually in a subsequent pregnancy, these antibodies can cross the placenta and cause hemolysis of an Rh-positive child's red blood cells.

Blood Compatibility

Blood compatibility is very important when transfusions are done. The antibodies in the plasma must not combine with the antigens on the surface of the red blood cells, or else agglutination occurs. With agglutination, anti-A antibodies have combined with type A antigens, or anti-B antibodies have combined with type B antigens, or both types of binding have occurred. Therefore, agglutination is expected if the donor has type A blood and the recipient has type B blood (Fig. 6.7). What about other combinations of blood types? Try out all other possible donors and recipients to see if agglutination will occur.

Type O blood is sometimes called the universal donor because it has neither type A nor type B antigens on the red blood cells, and type AB blood is sometimes called the universal recipient because this blood type has neither anti-A nor anti-B antibodies in the plasma. In practice, however, there are other possible blood groups, aside from ABO blood groups, so it is necessary to physically put the donor's blood on a slide with the recipient's blood and observe whether agglutination occurs before blood can be safely given from one person to another. This procedure, called blood-type matching, is done before a blood transfusion is performed.

As explained in the Health Focus on page 102, the use of blood substitutes does away with the problems of matching blood types.

For the purpose of blood transfusions, the donor's blood must be compatible with the recipient's blood. The ABO system is used to determine the general compatibility of donor's and recipient's blood.

Rh Blood Groups

The designation of blood type usually also includes whether the person has or does not have the Rh factor on the red blood cell. Rh$^-$ individuals normally do not have antibodies to the Rh factor, but they make them when exposed to the Rh factor.

If a mother is Rh$^-$ and the father is Rh$^+$, a child can be Rh$^+$. During a pregnancy, Rh$^+$ can leak across the placenta into the mother's bloodstream. The presence of these Rh$^+$ antigens causes the mother to produce anti-Rh antibodies (Fig. 6.8). Usually in a subsequent pregnancy with another Rh$^+$ baby, the anti-Rh antibodies may cross the placenta and destroy the child's red blood cells. This is called hemolytic disease of the newborn (HDN) because hemolysis continues after the baby is born. Due to red blood cell destruction, excess bilirubin in the blood can lead to brain damage and mental retardation or even death.

The Rh problem is prevented by giving Rh$^-$ women an Rh immunoglobulin injection no later than 72 hours after giving birth to an Rh$^+$ child. This injection contains anti-Rh antibodies that attack any of the baby's red blood cells in the mother's blood before these cells can stimulate her immune system to produce her own antibodies. This injection is not beneficial if the woman has already begun to produce antibodies; therefore, the timing of the injection is most important.

The possibility of hemolytic disease of the newborn exists when the mother is Rh$^-$ and the father is Rh$^+$.

6.5 Capillary Exchange

The pumping of the heart sends blood by way of arteries to the capillaries where exchange takes place across thin capillary walls. Blood that has passed through capillaries returns to the heart via veins. Capillary walls are largely one layer of epithelial cells, therefore, they are extremely thin.

In the tissues of the body, metabolically active cells require oxygen and nutrients and give off wastes, including carbon dioxide. Capillaries are extremely numerous—the body most likely contains a billion, and their total surface area is estimated at 6,300 m². Therefore, most cells of the body are near a capillary. During capillary exchange—not including the gas-exchanging surfaces of the lungs—oxygen and nutrients leave a capillary, and cellular wastes, including carbon dioxide, enter a capillary (Fig. 6.9). Certainly, arterial blood contains more oxygen and nutrients than venous blood, and venous blood contains more wastes than arterial blood.

The internal environment of the body consists of blood and tissue fluid. **Tissue fluid** is simply the fluid that surrounds the cells of the body. In other words, substances that leave a capillary pass through tissue fluid before entering the body's cells, and substances that leave the body's cells pass through tissue fluid before entering a capillary. The composition of tissue fluid stays relatively constant because of capillary exchange. Tissue fluid is mainly water. Any excess tissue fluid is collected by lymphatic capillaries, which are always found near blood capillaries.

Blood Capillaries

Water and other small molecules can cross through the cells of a capillary wall or through tiny clefts that occur between the cells. Large molecules in plasma, like the plasma proteins, are too large to pass through capillary walls.

Three processes influence capillary exchange: blood pressure, diffusion, and osmotic pressure:

Blood pressure, which is created by the pumping of the heart, is the pressure of blood against a vessel's (e.g., capillary) walls.
Diffusion, as you know, is simply the movement of substances from the area of higher to the area of lower concentration.
Osmotic pressure is a force caused by a difference in solute concentration on either side of a membrane.

To understand osmotic pressure, consider that water will cross a membrane toward the side that has the greater concentration of solutes, and the accumulation of this water results in a pressure. The presence of the plasma proteins, and also salts to some degree, means that blood has a greater osmotic pressure than does tissue fluid. Therefore, the osmotic pressure of blood pulls water into and retains water inside a capillary.

Notice in Figure 6.9 that a capillary has an arterial end (contains arterial blood) and a venous end (contains venous blood). In between, a capillary has a midsection. We will now consider the exchange of molecules across capillary walls at each of these locations.

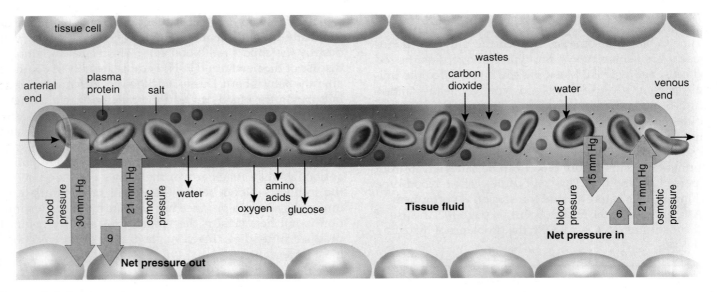

Figure 6.9   Capillary exchange in the tissues.
At the arterial end of a tissue capillary, blood pressure is higher than osmotic pressure; therefore, water tends to leave the bloodstream. In the midsection, small molecules follow their concentration gradients: Oxygen and nutrients leave a capillary, while wastes, including carbon dioxide, enter a capillary. At the venous end of a capillary, osmotic pressure is higher than blood pressure; therefore, water tends to enter the bloodstream.

Arterial End of Capillary

When arterial blood enters tissue capillaries, it is bright red because the hemoglobin in red blood cells is carrying oxygen. Blood is also rich in nutrients, which are dissolved in plasma.

At the arterial end of a capillary, blood pressure, an outward force, is higher than osmotic pressure, an inward force. Pressure is measured in terms of mm Hg (mercury); in this case, blood pressure is 30 mm Hg, and osmotic pressure is 21 mm Hg. Because blood pressure is higher than osmotic pressure at the arterial end of a capillary, water and other small molecules exit a capillary at its arterial end.

Red blood cells and a large proportion of the plasma proteins generally remain in a capillary because they are too large to pass through its wall. The exit of water and other small molecules from a capillary creates tissue fluid. Therefore, tissue fluid consists of all the components of plasma except it contains fewer plasma proteins.

Midsection of Capillary

Diffusion takes place along the length of the capillary, as small molecules follow their concentration gradient by moving from the area of higher to the area of lower concentration. In the tissues, the area of higher concentration of oxygen and nutrients is always blood, because after these molecules have passed into tissue fluid, they are taken up and metabolized by cells. The cells use oxygen and glucose in the process of cellular respiration, and they use amino acids for protein synthesis.

As a result of metabolism, tissue cells give off carbon dioxide and other wastes. Because tissue fluid is always the area of greater concentration for waste materials, they diffuse into a capillary.

Venous End of Capillary

At the venous end of the capillary, blood pressure is much reduced to only about 15 mm Hg, as shown in Figure 6.9. Blood pressure is reduced at the venous end because capillaries have a greater cross-sectional area at their venous end than their arterial end. However, there is no reduction in osmotic pressure, which remains at 21 mm Hg and is now higher than blood pressure. Therefore, water tends to enter a capillary at the venous end. As water enters a capillary, it brings with it additional waste molecules. Blood that leaves the capillaries is deep maroon in color because red blood cells now contain reduced hemoglobin—hemoglobin that has given up its oxygen and taken on hydrogen ions.

In the end, about 85% of the water that left a capillary at the arterial end returns to it at the venous end. Therefore, retrieving fluid by means of osmotic pressure is not completely effective. The body has an auxiliary means of collecting tissue fluid; any excess usually enters lymphatic capillaries.

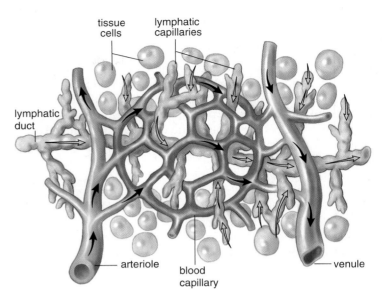

Figure 6.10   Lymphatic capillaries.
Lymphatic capillaries lie near blood capillaries. The black arrows show the flow of blood. The yellow arrows show that lymph is formed when lymphatic capillaries take up excess tissue fluid.

Lymphatic Capillaries

Lymphatic vessels begin as lymphatic capillaries whose blind ends lie near blood capillaries (Fig. 6.10). Larger lymphatic vessels have a structure similar to that of cardiovascular veins, except that their walls are thinner and they have more valves. The valves prevent the backward flow of lymph as lymph flows toward the thoracic cavity. Lymphatic capillaries join to form larger vessels that merge into the lymphatic ducts. Lymphatic ducts empty into cardiovascular veins within the thoracic cavity.

Lymph, the fluid carried by lymphatic vessels, has the same composition as tissue fluid. Why? Because lymphatic capillaries absorb excess tissue fluid at the blood capillaries. The lymphatic system contributes to homeostasis in several ways. One way is to maintain normal blood volume and pressure by returning excess tissue fluid to the blood.

Edema

Edema is swelling that occurs when tissue fluid is not collected by the lymphatic capillaries. Edema can be due to many causes including blocked lymphatic vessels. One dramatic cause of a blockage is a parasitic infection of lymphatic vessels by a small worm. An affected leg can become so large that the disease is called elephantiasis.

Exchange of nutrients for wastes occurs at the capillaries. Here, lymphatic capillaries also collect excess tissue fluid.

6.6 Homeostasis

In Chapter 4, you learned that the body's internal environment contains blood and tissue fluid. In this chapter, you saw that tissue fluid actually originates from blood. In fact, it is very similar to the plasma component of blood, except that it contains no plasma proteins. Tissue fluid is taken up from the space between the tissue cells by lymphatic capillaries, after which it is referred to as lymph. The lymph courses through lymphatic vessels and is eventually returned to the venous system. Thus, the cardiovascular and lymphatic systems are intimately linked. Fluid cycles continuously through blood plasma, tissue fluid, and lymph, and back to blood plasma again.

Homeostasis is possible only if: (1) the cardiovascular system delivers oxygen and nutrients to, and takes away metabolic wastes from, the tissue fluid that surrounds cells, and (2) the lymphatic system returns tissue fluid to the bloodstream. Homeostasis can be disturbed if the cardiovascular or lymphatic system is impaired. For instance, if the heart is unable to pump the blood or if lymphatic vessels are blocked or damaged, blood pressure can become inadequate to move the blood. The presence of edema (swelling) indicates that tissue fluid is building up. This can happen due to tumors, infection, accidental injury, or surgical removal of lymphatic vessels. Sometimes, in breast cancer surgery, the underarm lymph nodes adjacent to the cancerous breast are also removed. The result is edema localized to the underarm region, which usually subsides over time.

Just think of how important it is to homeostasis for all the human systems to work together. For example, imagine what must be one of a student's worst nightmares. You slowly open your eyes in the morning, blearily gaze at your alarm clock, and realize that you've overslept. In fact, it's just a few minutes before class begins. Then, you snap wide awake as you remember why you were up so late the night before—you were studying for the final exam! Most likely, your heart starts beating faster, stimulated by your stressed nervous system. The resulting rise in blood pressure rises to help prepare the body for action. Hormones, such as epinephrine (adrenaline) from the adrenal glands, pour into the bloodstream to prolong your body's physical response to stress.

Frantic, you throw on your clothes and sprint to the bus (Fig. 6.11). As you run, your muscles require more oxygen to support their activity. Your breathing and heart rate increase, in order to deal with the demand. The hard-working muscles generate carbon dioxide, wastes, and heat. Carbon dioxide is carried via the blood to the lungs so it can be expelled, and nitrogenous wastes will eventually be excreted by the kidneys. To keep you from overheating, you not only sweat, but blood flow to your skin increases so that heat radiates away.

The nightmare continues. In your mad dash, you trip on the steps as you board the bus, and fall, skinning your knee. At first, blood flows from the wound, but a clot will soon form to seal off the injured area and allow a scab to form, so

Figure 6.11   Human systems work together.
How many human systems participate in helping you get through an emergency situation?

that healing can begin. Any injury that breaks the skin can allow harmful bacteria into the body, but the immune system usually deals with them in short order. Later, you might notice that your knee is not only skinned, but also black and blue. The bruise is where blood leaked out of damaged vessels underneath the skin, and then clotted.

You make it to class just in time to get your exam from the instructor. As you settle down to take the exam, your heartbeat and breathing gradually slow, since the need of your muscles is not as great. Now that you are in thinking mode, blood flow increases in certain highly active parts of your brain. The brain is a very demanding organ in terms of both oxygen and glucose.

You start to feel hungry. Since there is little glucose in your bloodstream to provide fuel for your body's cells, glycogen stored in the liver is broken down to make glucose available to the blood. Finally, you hand in the exam and go to the dining hall for breakfast. When most of the nutrients from your meal are absorbed from the digestive tract, they enter the bloodstream. However, the lipoproteins enter lacteals, which are vessels of the lymphatic system, for transport to the blood.

Notice in this scenario how many organ systems had to interact with the cardiovascular system. The nervous, endocrine, respiratory, muscular, and lymphatic systems helped to serve the cells' needs. Throughout all of the challenges to homeostasis described above, the lymphatic system was busy taking up excess tissue fluid and protecting the body from disease. No organ system works alone, where homeostasis is concerned! Human Systems Work Together on the next page summarizes how the cardiovascular and lymphatic systems cooperate with the other systems of the body to maintain homeostasis.

Human Systems Work Together

All systems of the body work with the cardiovascular system to maintain homeostasis. These systems in particular are especially noteworthy.

Cardiovascular System

Heart pumps the blood. Blood vessels transport oxygen and nutrients to the cells of all the organs and transports wastes away from them. The blood clots to prevent blood loss. The cardiovascular system also specifically helps the other systems as mentioned below.

Digestive System

Blood vessels deliver nutrients from the digestive tract to the cells. The digestive tract provides the molecules needed for plasma protein formation and blood cell formation. The digestive system absorbs the water needed to maintain blood pressure and the Ca^{2+} needed for blood clotting.

Urinary System

Blood vessels transport wastes to be excreted. Kidneys excrete wastes and help regulate the water-salt balance necessary to maintain blood volume and pressure and help regulate the acid-base balance of the blood.

Muscular System

Muscle contraction keeps blood moving through the heart and in the blood vessels, particularly the veins.

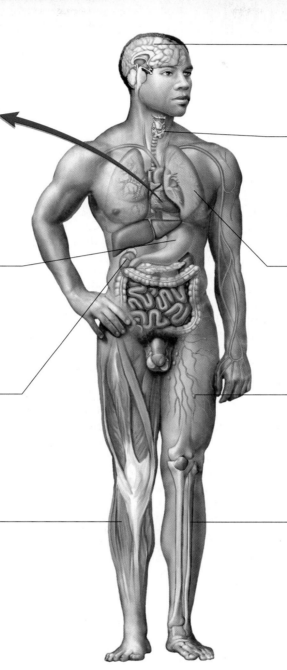

Nervous System

Nerves help regulate the contraction of the heart and the constriction/dilation of blood vessels.

Endocrine System

Blood vessels transport hormones from glands to their target organs. The hormone epinephrine increases blood pressure; other hormones help regulate blood volume and blood cell formation.

Respiratory System

Blood vessels transport gases to and from lungs. Gas exchange in lungs supplies oxygen and rids the body of carbon dioxide, helping to regulate the acid-base balance of blood. Breathing aids venous return.

Lymphatic System

Capillaries are the source of tissue fluid, which becomes lymph. The lymphatic system helps maintain blood volume by collecting excess tissue fluid (i.e., lymph), and returning it via lymphatic vessels to the cardiovascular veins.

Skeletal System

The rib cage protects the heart, red bone marrow produces blood cells, and bones store Ca^{2+} for blood clotting.

Summarizing the Concepts

6.1 Blood: An Overview
Blood, which contains formed elements and plasma, has several functions. It transports hormones, oxygen, and nutrients to the cells, and carbon dioxide and other wastes away from the cells. It fights infections and has various regulatory functions. It maintains blood pressure, regulates body temperature, and keeps the pH of body fluids within normal limits. All of these functions help maintain homeostasis.

6.2 Composition of Blood
Small organic molecules, such as glucose and amino acids, are dissolved in plasma and serve as nutrients for cells; oxygen gas is needed for cellular respiration, and carbon dioxide is a waste product of this process.

Plasma is mostly water (92%) and plasma proteins (8%). The plasma proteins, most of which are produced by the liver, occur in three categories: albumins, globulins, and fibrinogen. The plasma proteins maintain osmotic pressure, help regulate pH, and transport molecules. Some plasma proteins have specific functions: The gamma globulins, which are antibodies produced by plasma cells, function in immunity, and fibrinogen is necessary to blood clotting.

Red blood cells are small, biconcave disks that lack a nucleus. Red blood cells contain hemoglobin, the respiratory pigment, which combines with oxygen and transports it to the tissues. All blood cells, including red blood cells, are produced within red bone marrow from stem cells, which are ever capable of dividing and producing new cells. They live about 120 days and are destroyed in the liver and spleen when they are old or abnormal. The production of red blood cells is controlled by the oxygen concentration of the blood. When the oxygen concentration decreases, the kidneys increase their production of erythropoietin, and more red blood cells are produced.

White blood cells are larger than red blood cells, have a nucleus, and are translucent unless stained. Like red blood cells, they are produced in the red bone marrow. White blood cells are divided into the granular leukocytes and the agranular leukocytes. The granular leukocytes have conspicuous granules: In eosinophils, granules are red when stained with eosin, and in basophils, granules are blue when stained with a basic dye. The granules in neutrophils don't take up either dye significantly. Neutrophils are the most plentiful of the white blood cells, and they are able to phagocytize pathogens. Many neutrophils die within a few days when they are fighting an infection. The agranulocytes include the lymphocytes and the monocytes, which function in specific immunity. On occasion, the monocytes become large phagocytic cells of great significance. They engulf worn-out red blood cells and pathogens at a ferocious rate.

6.3 Blood Clotting
When there is a break in a blood vessel, the platelets clump to form a plug. Blood clotting itself requires a series of enzymatic reactions involving blood platelets, prothrombin, and fibrinogen. In the final reaction, fibrinogen becomes fibrin threads, entrapping cells. The fluid that escapes from a clot is called serum and consists of plasma minus fibrinogen and prothrombin.

6.4 Blood Typing
The red blood cells of an individual are not necessarily received without difficulty by another individual. For example, the plasma membranes of red blood cells may contain type A and/or B antigens, or neither antigen. In the plasma, there are two possible antibodies: anti-A or anti-B. If the corresponding antigen and antibody are put together, clumping, or agglutination, occurs; in this way, the blood type of an individual may be determined in the laboratory. It is possible to decide who can give blood to whom. For this, it is necessary to consider the donor's antigens and the recipient's antibodies.

Another important antigen is the Rh antigen. This particular antigen must also be considered in transfusing blood, and it is important during pregnancy because an Rh$^-$ mother may form antibodies to the Rh antigen while carrying or after the birth of an Rh$^+$ child. These antibodies can cross the placenta to destroy the red blood cells of any subsequent Rh$^+$ child.

6.5 Capillary Exchange
This discussion pertains to capillary exchange in tissues of body parts—not including the gas-exchanging surfaces of the lungs. At the arterial end of a cardiovascular capillary, blood pressure is greater than osmotic pressure; therefore, water leaves the capillary. In the midsection, oxygen and nutrients diffuse out of the capillary, while carbon dioxide and other wastes diffuse into the capillary. At the venous end, osmotic pressure created by the presence of proteins exceeds blood pressure, causing water to enter the capillary.

Retrieving fluid by means of a higher osmotic pressure is not completely effective. There is always some fluid that is not picked up at the venous end of the cardiovascular capillary. This excess tissue fluid enters the lymphatic capillaries. Lymph is tissue fluid contained within lymphatic vessels. The lymphatic system is a one-way system, and lymph is returned to blood by way of a cardiovascular vein.

6.6 Homeostasis
Homeostasis is absolutely dependent upon the cardiovascular system because it serves the needs of the cells. However, several other body systems are critical to the functioning of the cardiovascular system. The digestive system supplies nutrients, and the respiratory system supplies oxygen and removes carbon dioxide from the blood. Like the heart, the nervous and endocrine systems are involved in maintaining the blood pressure that moves blood in the arteries and arterioles. The lymphatic system returns tissue fluid to the veins where blood is mainly propelled by skeletal muscle contraction and breathing movements.

Studying the Concepts

1. State the two main components of blood, and give the functions of blood. 98–99
2. List and discuss the major components of plasma. Name several plasma proteins, and give a function for each. 99
3. What is hemoglobin, and how does it function? 100
4. Describe the life cycle of red blood cells, and tell how the production of red blood cells is regulated. 101
5. Name the five types of white blood cells; describe the structure and give a function for each type. 103

6. Name the steps that take place when blood clots. Which substances are present in blood at all times, and which appear during the clotting process? 104
7. Define blood, plasma, serum, tissue fluid, and lymph. 104
8. What are the four ABO blood types? For each, state the antigen(s) on the red blood cells and the antibody(ies) in the plasma. 106
9. Explain why a person with type O blood cannot receive a transfusion of type A blood. 106–7
10. Problems can arise if a mother is which Rh type and the father is which Rh type? Explain why this is so. 107
11. What forces operate to facilitate exchange of molecules across the capillary wall? 108–9

Thinking Critically About the Concepts

Refer to the opening vignette on page 97, and then answer these questions.

1. With your knowledge of the composition and functions of blood, what kinds of complications might have resulted if Alice's blood loss had not been treated quickly?
2. What precautions should she take to minimize long-term problems that might result?
3. What would have resulted from Alice receiving the wrong blood type from her transfusion?
4. What other problems can result from a blood transfusion?

Testing Your Knowledge of the Concepts

Choose the best answer for each question.

In questions 1–5, match each description with a component of blood in the key. Answers can be used more than once.

Key:

a. red blood cells
b. white blood cells
c. red and white blood cells and platelets
d. plasma

1. Antigens in plasma membrane determine blood type
2. Transports oxygen
3. Includes monocytes
4. Contains fibrinogen
5. Formed elements

In questions 6–9, match each statement with a factor in the key.

Key:

a. prothrombin activator
b. prothrombin
c. fibrinogen
d. thromboplastin
e. thrombin

6. Enzyme that severs amino acid chains from fibrinogen
7. Becomes fibrin

8. Initiates a series of reactions
9. Converts prothrombin to thrombin

In questions 10–14, match each statement with the name of a fluid in the key.

Key:

a. blood
b. plasma
c. serum
d. tissue fluid
e. lymph

10. Tissue fluid within lymphatic vessels
11. Liquid portion of blood
12. Plasma minus fibrinogen and prothrombin
13. Formed elements and plasma
14. Plasma minus most proteins

In questions 15–17, match each statement with the name of a plasma protein in the key.

Key:

a. albumin
b. fibrinogen
c. globulin

15. Antibodies that fight infection
16. Necessary to blood clot formation
17. Transport bilirubin

In questions 18–20, match each description with a phrase in the key.

Key:

a. blood pressure
b. diffusion
c. osmotic pressure

18. Occurs along the entire length of the capillary
19. Greater at the arterial end of the capillary
20. Responsible for the movement of fluid into the venous end of the capillary

21. Which hemoglobin component is recovered for reuse following red blood cell destruction?
a. heme
b. globin
c. iron
d. polypeptide

22. Theoretically, a person with type AB blood should be able to receive
a. type B blood and type AB blood.
b. type O blood and type B blood.
c. type A blood and type O blood.
d. All of these are correct.

23. Stem cells are responsible for
a. red blood cell production.
b. white blood cell production.
c. platelet production.
d. the production of all formed elements.

24. Megakaryocytes give rise to
    a. basophils.
    b. lymphocytes.
    c. monocytes.
    d. platelets.

25. Which of the following is in the correct sequence for blood clotting?
    a. thromboplastin, prothrombin, fibrinogen
    b. prothrombin activator, thrombin, fibrin threads
    c. thrombin, prothrombin activator, fibrin threads
    d. prothrombin, thromboplastin, fibrinogen
    e. Both a and b are correct.

26. When the oxygen capacity of the blood is reduced,
    a. the liver produces more bile.
    b. the kidneys release erythropoietin.
    c. the bone marrow produces more red blood cells.
    d. sickle-cell disease occurs.
    e. Both b and c are correct.

27. If a person has type B⁻ blood, the minus sign means there are
    a. anti-A antibodies in the plasma.
    b. no B antigens on the red blood cells.
    c. Rh antigens on the red blood cells.
    d. no Rh antigens on the red blood cells.
    e. Both a and d are correct.

28. Which of the following conditions can cause anemia?
    a. lack of iron, folic acid, or vitamin B_{12} in the diet
    b. red blood cell destruction
    c. lack of hemoglobin
    d. All of these are correct.
    e. All but a are correct.

29. Capillaries
    a. have thin walls.
    b. are quite extensive.
    c. are located between arterial blood and venule blood.
    d. are where gas exchange occurs.
    e. All of these are correct.

30. Which of the following is not a formed element of blood?
    a. leukocyte
    b. eosinophil
    c. fibrinogen
    d. platelet

31. Which of the plasma proteins contributes most to osmotic pressure?
    a. albumin
    b. sodium
    c. globulins
    d. erythrocytes
    e. fibrin

32. Which of the following stem cells give rise to granular leukocytes?
    a. myeloblasts
    b. erythroblasts
    c. lymphoblasts
    d. megakaryoblasts

33. Label arrows a–d as either blood pressure or osmotic pressure.

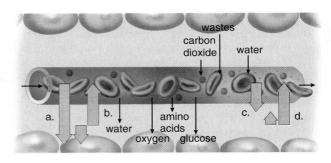

Understanding Key Terms

agglutination 106
agranular leukocyte 103
albumin 99
anemia 101
antibody 103
antigen 103
basophil 103
blood transfusion 106
clotting 103
colony-stimulating factor (CSF) 103
edema 109
eosinophil 103
erythropoietin 101
fibrin 104
fibrinogen 104
formed element 99
granular leukocyte 103
hemoglobin (Hb) 100
hemolysis 101

hemophilia 104
lymph 103
lymphocyte 103
megakaryocyte 103
monocyte 103
neutrophil 103
osmotic pressure 99
phagocytosis 103
plasma 99
platelet (thrombocyte) 103
prothrombin 104
prothrombin activator 104
red blood cell (erythrocyte) 100
serum 104
sickle-cell disease 101
stem cell 101
thrombin 104
tissue fluid 108
white blood cell (leukocyte) 103

Match the key terms to these definitions.

a. _____ Iron-containing protein in red blood cells that combines with and transports oxygen.

b. _____ Component of blood that is either cellular or derived from a cell.

c. _____ Liquid portion of blood.

d. _____ The force that causes capillaries to reabsorb water.

e. _____ Plasma protein that is converted to thrombin during the steps of blood clotting.

Online Learning Center

www.mhhe.com/maderhuman9

The Online Learning Center provides a wealth of information fully organized and integrated by chapter. You will find practice quizzes, interactive activities, labeling exercises, flashcards, and much more that will complement your learning and understanding of human biology.

CHAPTER

7

Digestive System and Nutrition

CHAPTER CONCEPTS

7.1 The Digestive Tract
- What is the general structure of the digestive tract and what are its functions? 116
- The path of food involves what organs of the digestive system? What are their respective special features and functions? 116–22
- How does the structure of the small intestine facilitate absorption of nutrients? 121, 127
- How are digestive secretions regulated? 122
- What happens to indigestible materials? 122

7.2 Three Accessory Organs
- What are the three main accessory organs that assist with the digestive process? 124–25
- How does each accessory organ contribute to the digestion of food? 124–25

7.3 Digestive Enzymes
- What nutrient molecules are absorbed following the digestion of carbohydrates? Of proteins? Of lipids? 126–27
- What are the main digestive enzymes, and what factors affect how they function? 126–27

7.4 Nutrition
- Five classes of nutrients make what specific contributions to nutrition? 128–35
- What health problems can arise from a diet high in proteins and lipids? 129–30
- What are the characteristics of three main eating disorders? 136–37

Now weighing more than 350 pounds, seventeen-year-old Monica sat on the edge of her bed, staring blankly at her reflection in the mirror on the wall. Disgusted with what she saw, she mulled her options silently in her head. She had tried dieting—Jenny Craig, Weight Watchers, the Atkins diet, and many others—and had lost a few pounds here and there, but the weight loss never seemed to last. She had even consulted a nutritionist, to no avail. Unable to control her weight by any other means, she decided to ask her doctor about surgical remedies.

Monica is considering bariatric surgery, a term used to describe several procedures that are performed on the digestive system to promote weight loss. One common procedure is known as "stomach stapling." In this procedure, the stomach is reduced to the size of a golf ball, and the digestive tract is rerouted so that food bypasses the first two feet of the intestine. Bariatric surgery compels patients to eat less because they become very ill if they overeat. After bariatric surgery is performed, patients remain at a lifelong risk of nutritional deficiencies.

With nearly two thirds of Americans overweight and one third obese, we are mired in an obesity epidemic. Bariatric surgery is becoming more widely used, and an increasing number of obese teens, like Monica, are asking for these procedures. As you read the following chapter, you will learn how the digestive system is organized, how it ordinarily works, and how its function is regulated by other organs of the body.

7.1 The Digestive Tract

Digestion takes place within a tube called the digestive tract, which begins with the mouth and ends with the anus (Fig. 7.1). The functions of the digestive system are to ingest food, digest it to nutrients that can cross plasma membranes, absorb nutrients, and eliminate indigestible remains.

Digestion involves two main processes that occur simultaneously. During mechanical digestion, large pieces of food become smaller pieces, readying them for chemical digestion. Mechanical digestion begins with the chewing of the food in the mouth and continues with the churning and mixing of food that occurs in the stomach. Parts of the digestive tract produce digestive enzymes. During chemical digestion, many different enzymes break down macromolecules to small organic molecules that can be absorbed. Each enzyme has a particular job to do.

The Mouth

The mouth, which receives food, is bounded externally by the lips and cheeks. The lips extend from the base of the nose to the start of the chin. The red portion of the lips is poorly keratinized, and this allows blood to show through.

Most people enjoy eating food largely because they like its texture and taste. Sensory receptors called taste buds occur primarily on the tongue, and when these are activated by the presence of food, nerve impulses travel by way of cranial nerves to the brain. The tongue is composed of skeletal muscle, whose contraction changes the shape of the tongue. Muscles exterior to the tongue cause it to move about. A fold of mucous membrane on the underside of the tongue attaches it to the floor of the oral cavity.

The roof of the mouth separates the nasal cavities from the oral cavity. The roof has two parts: an anterior (toward the front) **hard palate** and a posterior (toward the back) **soft palate** (Fig. 7.2a). The hard palate contains several bones, but the soft palate is composed entirely of muscle. The soft palate ends in a finger-shaped projection called the uvula. The tonsils are in the back of the mouth, on either side of the tongue and in the nasopharynx (called adenoids). The tonsils help protect the body against infections. If the tonsils become inflamed, the person has **tonsillitis.** The infection can spread to the middle ears. If tonsillitis recurs repeatedly, the tonsils may be surgically removed (called a tonsillectomy).

Three pairs of **salivary glands** send juices (saliva) by way of ducts to the mouth. One pair of salivary glands lies at the sides of the face immediately below and in front of the ears. These glands swell when a person has the mumps, a disease caused by a viral infection. Salivary glands have ducts that open on the inner surface of the cheek at the location of the second upper molar. Another pair of salivary glands lies beneath the tongue, and still another pair lies beneath the floor of the oral cavity. The ducts from these salivary glands open under the tongue. You can locate the openings if you use your tongue to feel for small flaps on the inside of your cheek and under your tongue. Saliva contains an enzyme called **salivary amylase** that begins the process of digesting starch.

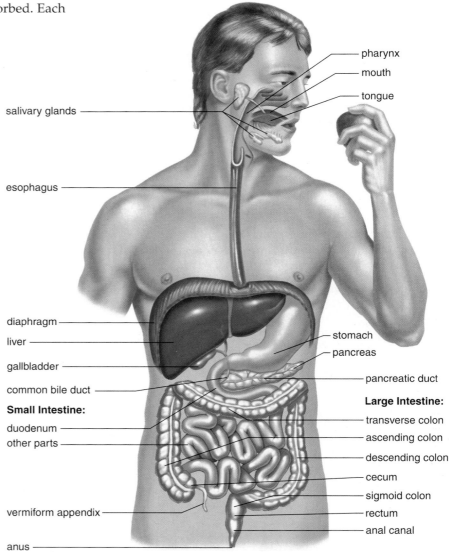

Figure 7.1   Digestive system.
Trace the path of food from the mouth to the anus. The large intestine consists of the cecum, the colon (composed of the ascending, transverse, descending, and sigmoid colon), and the rectum and anal canal. Note also the location of the accessory organs of digestion: the pancreas, the liver, and the gallbladder.

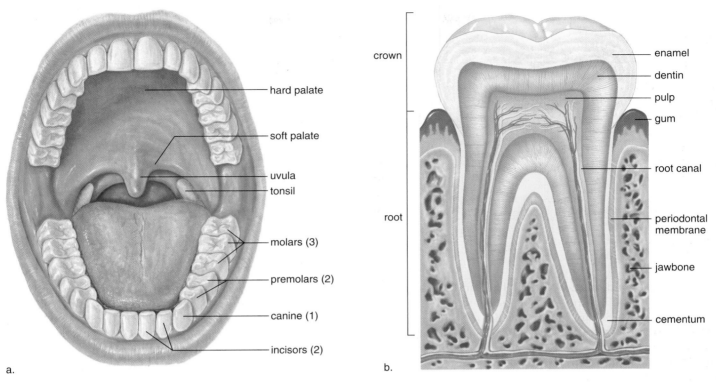

Figure 7.2 Adult mouth and teeth.
a. The chisel-shaped incisors bite; the pointed canines tear; the fairly flat premolars grind; and the flattened molars crush food. The last molar, called a wisdom tooth, may fail to erupt, or if it does, it is sometimes crooked and useless. Often dentists recommend the extraction of the wisdom teeth. **b.** Longitudinal section of a tooth. The crown is the portion that projects above the gum line and can be replaced by a dentist if damaged. When a "root canal" is done, the nerves are removed. When the periodontal membrane is inflamed, the teeth can loosen.

The Teeth

With our teeth, we chew food into pieces convenient for swallowing. During the first two years of life, the 20 smaller deciduous, or baby, teeth appear. These are eventually replaced by 32 adult teeth (Fig. 7.2a). The third pair of molars, called the wisdom teeth, sometimes fail to erupt. If they push on the other teeth and/or cause pain, they can be removed by a dentist or oral surgeon.

Each tooth has two main divisions: a crown and a root (Fig. 7.2b). The crown has a layer of enamel, an extremely hard outer covering of calcium compounds; dentin, a thick layer of bonelike material; and an inner pulp, which contains the nerves and the blood vessels. Dentin and pulp are also found in the root.

Tooth decay, called **dental caries,** or cavities, occurs when bacteria within the mouth metabolize sugar and give off acids, which erode teeth. Two measures can prevent tooth decay: eating a limited amount of sweets, and daily brushing and flossing of teeth. Fluoride treatments, particularly in children, can make the enamel stronger and more resistant to decay. Gum disease is more apt to occur with aging. Inflammation of the gums (gingivitis) can spread to the periodontal membrane, which lines the tooth socket. A person then has periodontitis, characterized by a loss of

bone and loosening of the teeth so that extensive dental work may be required. Stimulation of the gums in a manner advised by your dentist is helpful in controlling this condition. Medications are also available.

The tongue mixes the chewed food with saliva. It then forms this mixture into a mass called a bolus in preparation for swallowing.

The salivary glands send saliva into the mouth, where the teeth chew the food and the tongue forms it into a bolus for swallowing.

The Pharynx

The **pharynx** is a region that receives air from the nasal cavities and food from the mouth. The soft palate has a projection called the uvula, which projects into the pharynx and that people often confuse with the tonsils. The tonsils, however, are embedded in the mucous membrane of the pharynx.

Table 7.1 traces the path of food. From the mouth, food passes through the pharynx and esophagus to the stomach,

Table 7.1	Path of Food			
Organ	**Function of Organ**	**Special Feature(s)**	**Function of Special Feature(s)**	
Mouth	Receives food; starts digestion of starch	Teeth Tongue	Chew food Forms bolus	
Pharynx	Passageway	——	——	
Esophagus	Passageway	——	——	
Stomach	Storage of food; acidity kills bacteria; starts digestion of protein	Gastric glands	Release gastric juices	
Small intestine	Digestion of all foods; absorption of nutrients	Intestinal glands Villi	Release intestinal juices Absorb nutrients	
Large intestine	Absorption of water; storage of indigestible remains	——	——	

small intestine, and large intestine. The food passage and air passage cross in the pharynx because the trachea (windpipe) is anterior to (in front of) the esophagus, a long muscular tube that takes food to the stomach. Swallowing, a process that occurs in the pharynx (Fig. 7.3), is a **reflex action** performed automatically, without conscious thought. Usually during swallowing, the soft palate moves back to close off the **nasopharynx,** and the trachea moves up

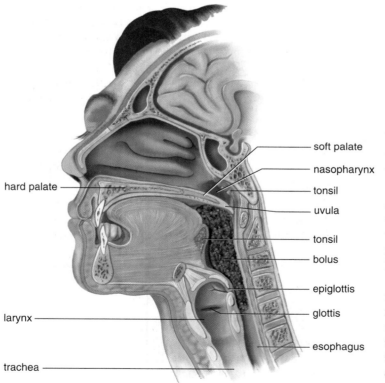

hard palate

larynx

trachea

soft palate
nasopharynx
tonsil
uvula
tonsil
bolus
epiglottis
glottis
esophagus

Figure 7.3   Swallowing.
When food is swallowed, the soft palate closes off the nasopharynx, and the epiglottis covers the glottis, forcing the bolus to pass down the esophagus. Therefore, a person does not breathe while swallowing.

under the **epiglottis** to cover the glottis. The **glottis** is the opening to the larynx (voice box), and therefore the air passage. During swallowing, food normally enters the esophagus because the air passages are blocked. We do not breathe when we swallow.

Unfortunately, we have all had the unpleasant experience of having food "go the wrong way." The wrong way may be either into the nasal cavities or into the trachea. If it is the latter, coughing will most likely force the food up out of the trachea and into the pharynx again. The up-and-down movement of the Adam's apple, the front part of the larynx, is easy to observe when a person swallows.

The Esophagus

The **esophagus** is a muscular tube that passes from the pharynx through the thoracic cavity and diaphragm into the abdominal cavity, where it joins the stomach. The esophagus is ordinarily collapsed, but it opens and receives the bolus when swallowing occurs.

A rhythmic contraction called **peristalsis** pushes the food along the digestive tract. Peristalsis begins in the esophagus and continues in all the organs of the digestive tract. Occasionally, peristalsis begins even though there is no food in the esophagus. This produces the sensation of a lump in the throat.

The esophagus plays no role in the chemical digestion of food. Its sole purpose is to move the food bolus from the mouth to the stomach. **Sphincters** are muscles that encircle tubes and act as valves; tubes close when sphincters contract, and they open when sphincters relax. The entrance of the esophagus to the stomach is marked by a constriction, often called a gastroesophageal sphincter, although the muscle is not as developed as in a true sphincter. Relaxation of the sphincter allows food to pass into the stomach, while contraction prevents the acidic contents of the stomach from backing up into the esophagus. When food or saliva is swallowed, the sphincter relaxes for a few seconds to allow the food or saliva to pass from the esophagus into the stomach, and then it closes again. It is common for acid contents of the stomach to occasionally back up, or reflux, into the esophagus. Ordinarily this causes little difficulty because saliva, which is basic, can neutralize any acid from the stomach.

Acid Reflux

Acid reflux is apparent when refluxed stomach acid touches the lining of the esophagus and causes a burning sensation in the chest or throat called **heartburn.** The fluid may even be tasted in the back of the mouth, and this is called acid indigestion. Heartburn that occurs more than twice a week may be considered acid reflux disease, more properly called gastroesophageal reflux disease. Nausea and vomiting may occur. When vomiting occurs, a contraction of the abdominal muscles and diaphragm propels the contents of the stomach upward through the esophagus.

Acid reflux can be a serious problem during pregnancy. The elevated hormone levels of pregnancy probably cause reflux by lowering the pressure in the lower esophageal sphincter. At the same time, the growing fetus increases the pressure in the abdomen. Both of these effects would be expected to increase reflux.

Various medications—nonprescription and prescription drugs—are available to counter acid reflux. If these fail, surgery is also an option.

The air passage and food passage cross in the pharynx. The esophagus conducts the bolus of food from the pharynx to the stomach. Peristalsis begins in the esophagus and occurs along the entire length of the digestive tract.

The Wall of the Digestive Tract

The wall of the digestive tract typically contains a number of layers. As an example, we will consider the various layers of the esophagus (Fig. 7.4). Still, it should be mentioned that the esophagus lacks an outer serous membrane typical of the other digestive organs. The typical tissue layers of the wall of the digestive tract are:

Mucosa (mucous membrane layer) A layer of epithelium supported by connective tissue and smooth muscle lines the **lumen** (central cavity) and contains glandular epithelial cells that secrete digestive enzymes and goblet cells that secrete mucus.

Submucosa (submucosal layer) A broad band of loose connective tissue that contains blood vessels lies beneath the mucosa and binds the mucosa to the muscularis. Lymph nodules, called Peyer's patches, are in the submucosa. Like the tonsils, they help protect us from disease.

Muscularis (smooth muscle layer) Two layers of smooth muscle make up this section. The inner, circular layer encircles the gut; the outer, longitudinal layer lies in the same direction as the gut. (The stomach also has oblique muscles.)

Serosa (serous membrane layer) Most of the digestive tract has a serosa, a very thin, outermost layer of squamous epithelium supported by connective tissue. The serosa secretes a serous fluid that keeps the outer surface of the intestines moist so that the organs of the abdominal cavity slide against one another. The esophagus has an outer layer composed only of loose connective tissue called the adventitia.

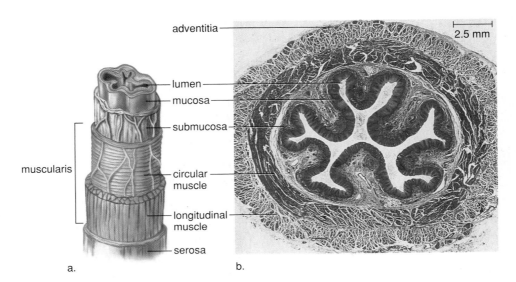

Figure 7.4 Wall of the digestive tract.
a. Several different types of tissues are found in the wall of the digestive tract. Note the placement of circular muscle inside longitudinal muscle.
b. Micrograph of the wall of the esophagus. Note the absence of serosa in the esophagus.

The Stomach

The **stomach** (Fig. 7.5) is a thick-walled, J-shaped organ that lies on the left side of the body beneath the diaphragm. The stomach is continuous with the esophagus above and the duodenum of the small intestine below. The stomach stores food and aids in digestion. The wall of the stomach has deep folds, which disappear as the stomach fills to an approximate capacity of one liter. Its muscular wall churns, mixing the food with gastric juice. The term *gastric* always refers to the stomach.

The columnar epithelial lining of the stomach has millions of gastric pits, which lead into **gastric glands.** The gastric glands produce gastric juice. Gastric juice contains an enzyme called **pepsin,** which digests protein, plus hydrochloric acid (HCl) and mucus. HCl causes the stomach to have a high acidity with a pH of about 2, and this is beneficial because it kills most bacteria present in food. Although HCl does not digest food, it does break down the connective tissue of meat and activate pepsin. The wall of the stomach is protected from the contents of the stomach, which include pepsin and HCL, by a thick layer of mucus secreted by goblet cells in its lining. If, by chance, HCl penetrates this mucus, the wall can begin to break down, and an ulcer results. An **ulcer** is an open sore in the wall caused by the gradual disintegration of tissue. It now appears that most ulcers are due to a bacterial infection *(Helicobacter pylori)* that impairs the ability of epithelial cells to produce protective mucus.

Alcohol is absorbed in the stomach, but food substances are not. Normally, the stomach empties in about 2–6 hours. When food leaves the stomach, it is a thick, soupy liquid called **chyme.** Chyme enters the small intestine in squirts by way of a sphincter that repeatedly opens and closes.

The stomach can expand to accommodate large amounts of food. When food is present, the stomach churns, mixing food with acidic gastric juice.

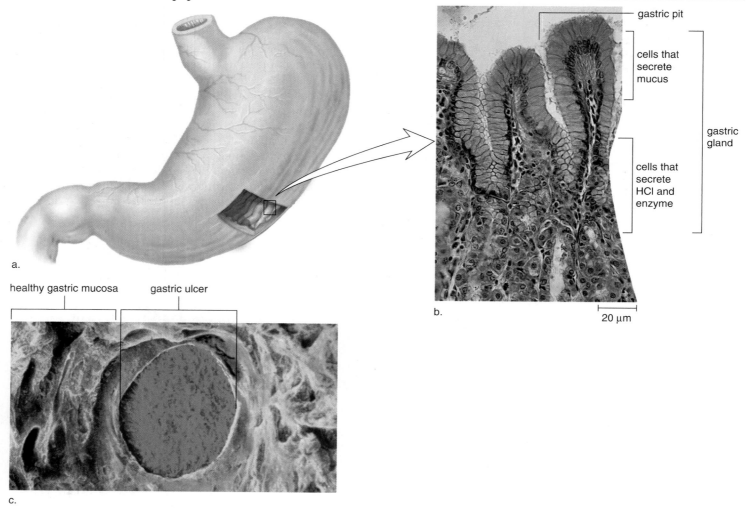

a.

healthy gastric mucosa   gastric ulcer

c.

gastric pit

cells that secrete mucus

gastric gland

cells that secrete HCl and enzyme

b.   20 μm

Figure 7.5   **Anatomy and histology of the stomach.**
a. The stomach has a thick wall with folds that allow it to expand and fill with food. **b.** The lining contains gastric glands, which secrete mucus and a gastric juice active in protein digestion. **c.** A bleeding ulcer viewed through an endoscope (a tubular instrument bearing a tiny lens and a light source) inserted into the abdominal cavity.

The Small Intestine

The **small intestine** is named for its small diameter (compared with that of the large intestine), but perhaps it should be called the long intestine. The small intestine averages about 6 meters (18 ft) in length, compared with the large intestine, which is about 1.5 meters (4½ ft) in length.

The first 25 cm of the small intestine is called the **duodenum.** A duct brings bile from the liver and gallbladder, and pancreatic juice from the pancreas, into the small intestine (see Fig. 7.1). **Bile** emulsifies fat—emulsification causes fat droplets to disperse in water. The intestine has a slightly basic pH because pancreatic juice contains sodium bicarbonate ($NaHCO_3$), which neutralizes chyme. The enzymes in pancreatic juice and the enzymes produced by the intestinal wall complete the process of food digestion.

It has been suggested that the surface area of the small intestine is approximately that of a tennis court. What factors contribute to increasing its surface area? The wall of the small intestine contains finger-like projections called villi (sing., **villus**), which give the intestinal wall a soft, velvety appearance (Fig. 7.6). A villus has an outer layer of columnar epithelial cells, and each of these cells has thousands of microscopic extensions called microvilli. Collectively, in electron micrographs, microvilli give the villi a fuzzy border known as a "brush border." Since the microvilli bear the intestinal enzymes, these enzymes are called brush-border enzymes. The microvilli greatly increase the surface area of the villus for the absorption of nutrients.

Nutrients are absorbed into the vessels of a villus (see Fig. 7.12). A villus contains blood capillaries and a small lymphatic capillary, called a **lacteal.** The lymphatic system is an adjunct to the cardiovascular system; its vessels carry a fluid called lymph to the cardiovascular veins. Sugars (digested from carbohydrates) and amino acids (digested from proteins) enter the blood capillaries of a villus. Glycerol and fatty acids (digested from fats) enter the epithelial cells of the villi, and within these cells are joined and packaged as lipoprotein droplets, called chylomicrons, which enter a lacteal. After nutrients are absorbed, they are eventually carried to all the cells of the body by the bloodstream.

The large surface area of the small intestine facilitates absorption of nutrients into the cardiovascular system (sugars and amino acids) and the lymphatic system (fats).

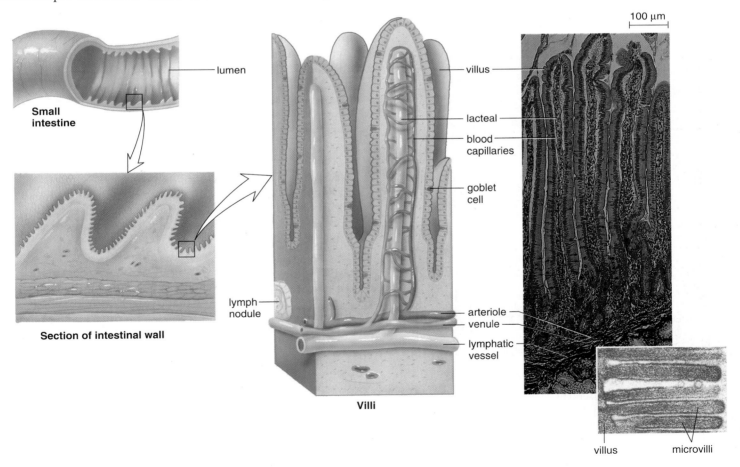

Figure 7.6 **Anatomy of the small intestine.**
The wall of the small intestine has folds that bear finger-like projections called villi. The products of digestion are absorbed into the blood capillaries and the lacteals of the villi by microvilli, which project from the villi.

Regulation of Digestive Secretions

The secretion of digestive juices is promoted by the nervous system and by hormones. A **hormone** is a substance produced by one set of cells that affects a different set of cells, the so-called target cells. Hormones are usually transported by the bloodstream. For example, when a person has eaten a meal particularly rich in protein, the stomach produces the hormone gastrin. Gastrin enters the bloodstream, and soon the stomach is churning, and the secretory activity of gastric glands is increasing. A hormone produced by the duodenal wall, GIP (gastric inhibitory peptide), works opposite to gastrin: It inhibits gastric gland secretion.

Cells of the duodenal wall produce two other hormones that are of particular interest—secretin and CCK (cholecystokinin). Acid, especially hydrochloric acid (HCl) present in chyme, stimulates the release of secretin, while partially digested protein and fat stimulate the release of CCK. Soon after these hormones enter the bloodstream, the pancreas increases its output of pancreatic juice, which helps digest food, and the gallbladder increases its output of bile. The gallbladder contracts to release stored bile. Figure 7.7 summarizes the actions of gastrin, secretin, and CCK.

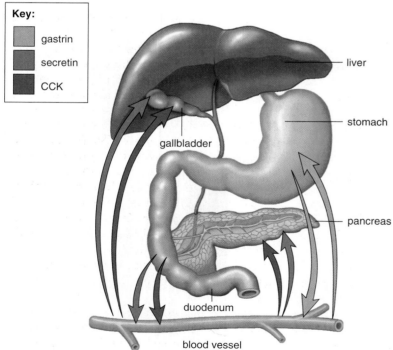

Key:

- gastrin
- secretin
- CCK

liver

stomach

gallbladder

pancreas

duodenum

blood vessel

Figure 7.7 **Hormonal control of digestive gland secretions.** Gastrin (blue), produced by the lower part of the stomach, enters the bloodstream and thereafter stimulates the upper part of the stomach to produce more gastric juice. Secretin (green) and CCK (purple), produced by the duodenal wall, stimulate the pancreas to secrete its juice and the gallbladder to release bile.

The Large Intestine

The **large intestine,** which includes the cecum, the colon, the rectum, and the anal canal, is larger in diameter than the small intestine (6.5 cm compared with 2.5 cm), but it is shorter in length (see Fig. 7.1). The large intestine absorbs water, salts, and some vitamins. It also stores indigestible material until it is eliminated at the anus.

The **cecum,** which lies below the junction with the small intestine, is the blind end of the large intestine. The cecum usually has a small projection called the **vermiform appendix** (*vermiform* means worm-like) (Fig. 7.8). In humans, the appendix also may play a role in fighting infections. This organ is subject to inflammation, a condition called appendicitis. If inflamed, the appendix should be removed before the fluid content rises to the point that the appendix bursts, a situation that may cause **peritonitis,** a generalized infection of the lining of the abdominal cavity. Peritonitis can lead to death.

The **colon** includes the ascending colon, which goes up the right side of the body to the level of the liver; the transverse colon, which crosses the abdominal cavity just below the liver and the stomach; the descending colon, which passes down the left side of the body; and the sigmoid colon, which enters the **rectum,** the last 20 cm of the large intestine. The rectum opens at the **anus,** where **defecation,** the expulsion of feces, occurs. When feces are forced into the rectum by peristalsis, a defecation reflex occurs. The stretching of the rectal wall initiates nerve impulses to the spinal cord, and shortly thereafter the rectal muscles contract and the anal sphincters relax (Fig. 7.9). Ridding the body of indigestible remains is another way the digestive system helps maintain homeostasis.

Feces are three-quarters water and one-quarter solids. Bacteria, dietary **fiber** (indigestible remains), and other indigestible materials are in the solid portion. Bacterial action on indigestible materials causes the odor of feces and also accounts for the presence of gas. A breakdown product of bilirubin (see page 125) and the presence of oxidized iron cause the brown color of feces.

For many years, it was believed that facultative bacteria (bacteria that can live with or without oxygen), such as *Escherichia coli,* were the major inhabitants of the colon, but new culture methods show that over 99% of the colon bacteria are obligate anaerobes (bacteria that die in the presence of oxygen). Not only do the bacteria break down indigestible material, but they also produce B complex vitamins and most of the vitamin K needed by our bodies. In this way, they perform a service for us.

Water is considered unsafe for swimming when the coliform (nonpathogenic intestinal) bacterial count reaches a certain number. A high count indicates that a significant amount of feces has entered the water. The more feces present, the greater the possibility that disease-causing bacteria are also present.

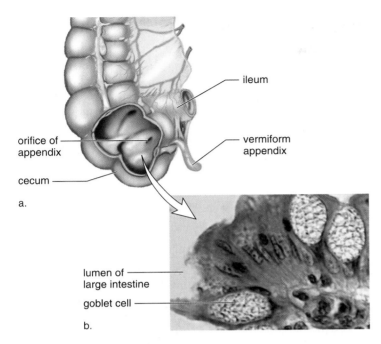

a.

b.

Figure 7.8   Large intestine.
a. The small intestine enters the cecum, which is the blind end of the ascending colon. The vermiform appendix is attached to the cecum.
b. The intestinal mucosa has many goblet cells.

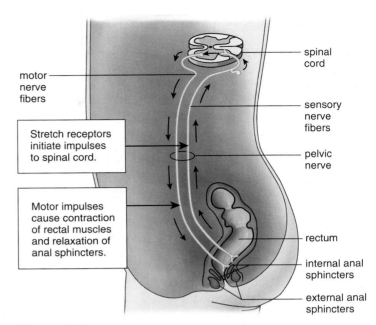

Figure 7.9   Defecation reflex.
The accumulation of feces in the rectum causes it to stretch, which initiates a reflex action resulting in rectal contraction and expulsion of the fecal material from the anus.

Polyps

The colon is subject to the development of **polyps,** small growths arising from the epithelial lining. Polyps, whether benign or cancerous, can be removed surgically. If colon cancer is detected while still confined to a polyp, the expected outcome is a complete cure. Some investigators believe that dietary fat increases the likelihood of colon cancer because dietary fat causes an increase in bile secretion. It could be that intestinal bacteria convert bile salts to substances that promote the development of cancer. On the other hand, fiber in the diet seems to inhibit the development of colon cancer. Dietary fiber absorbs water and adds bulk, thereby diluting the concentration of bile salts and facilitating the movement of substances through the intestine. Regular elimination reduces the time that the colon wall is exposed to any cancer-promoting agents in feces.

Diarrhea and Constipation

Two common complaints associated with the large intestine are **diarrhea** and **constipation.** The major causes of diarrhea are infection of the lower intestinal tract and nervous stimulation. In the case of infection, such as food poisoning caused by eating contaminated food, the intestinal wall becomes irritated, and peristalsis increases. Water is not absorbed, and the diarrhea that results rids the body of the infectious organisms. In nervous diarrhea, the nervous system stimulates the intestinal wall, and diarrhea results. Prolonged diarrhea can lead to dehydration because of water loss and to disturbances in the heart's contraction due to an imbalance of salts in the blood.

When a person is constipated, the feces are dry and hard. One reason for this condition is that socialized persons have learned to inhibit defecation to the point that the urge to defecate is ignored. Two components of the diet that can help prevent constipation are water and fiber. Water intake prevents drying out of the feces, and fiber provides the bulk needed for elimination. The frequent use of laxatives is discouraged. If, however, it is necessary to take a laxative, a bulk laxative is the most natural because, like fiber, it produces a soft mass of cellulose in the colon. Lubricants, such as mineral oil, make the colon slippery; saline laxatives, such as milk of magnesia, act osmotically—they prevent water from being absorbed and, depending on the dosage, may even cause water to enter the colon. Some laxatives are irritants, meaning that they increase peristalsis to the degree that the contents of the colon are expelled.

Chronic constipation is associated with the development of hemorrhoids, enlarged and inflamed blood vessels at the anus. Other contributing factors include pregnancy, aging, and anal intercourse.

The large intestine does not produce digestive enzymes; it does absorb water, salts, and some vitamins.

7.2 Three Accessory Organs

The pancreas, liver, and gallbladder are accessory digestive organs. Figure 7.10a shows how the pancreatic duct from the pancreas and the common bile duct from the liver and gallbladder enter the duodenum.

The Pancreas

The **pancreas** lies deep in the abdominal cavity, resting on the posterior abdominal wall. It is an elongated and somewhat flattened organ that has both an endocrine and an exocrine function. As an endocrine gland, it secretes insulin and glucagon, hormones that help keep the blood glucose level within normal limits. In this chapter, however, we are interested in its exocrine function. Most pancreatic cells produce pancreatic juice, which contains sodium bicarbonate ($NaHCO_3$) and digestive enzymes for all types of food. Sodium bicarbonate neutralizes acid chyme from the stomach. **Pancreatic amylase** digests starch, **trypsin** digests protein, and **lipase** digests fat.

The Liver

The **liver,** which is the largest gland in the body, lies mainly in the upper right section of the abdominal cavity, under the diaphragm (see Fig. 7.1). The liver contains approximately 100,000 lobules that serve as its structural and functional units (Fig. 7.10b). Triads consisting of these three structures are located between the lobules: a bile duct that takes bile away from the liver; a branch of the hepatic artery that brings O_2-rich blood to the liver; and a branch of the hepatic portal vein that transports nutrients from the intestines. The central veins of lobules enter a hepatic vein. In Figure 7.11, trace the path of blood from the intestines to the liver via the hepatic portal vein and from the liver to the inferior vena cava via the hepatic veins.

In some ways, the liver acts as the gatekeeper to the blood (Table 7.2). As blood from the hepatic portal vein passes through the liver, it removes poisonous substances and detoxifies them. The liver also removes and stores iron and the fat-soluble vitamins A, D, E, K, and B_{12}. The liver makes the plasma proteins and helps regulate the quantity of cholesterol in the blood.

The liver maintains the blood glucose level at about 100 mg/100 ml (0.1%), even though a person eats intermittently. When insulin is present, any excess glucose present in blood is removed and stored by the liver as glycogen. Between meals, glycogen is broken down to glucose, which enters the hepatic veins, and in this way, the blood glucose level remains constant.

If the supply of glycogen is depleted, the liver converts glycerol (from fats) and amino acids to glucose molecules. The conversion of amino acids to glucose necessitates deamination, the removal of amino groups. By a complex metabolic pathway, the liver then combines ammonia with carbon dioxide to form urea. Urea is the usual nitrogenous waste product from amino acid breakdown in humans.

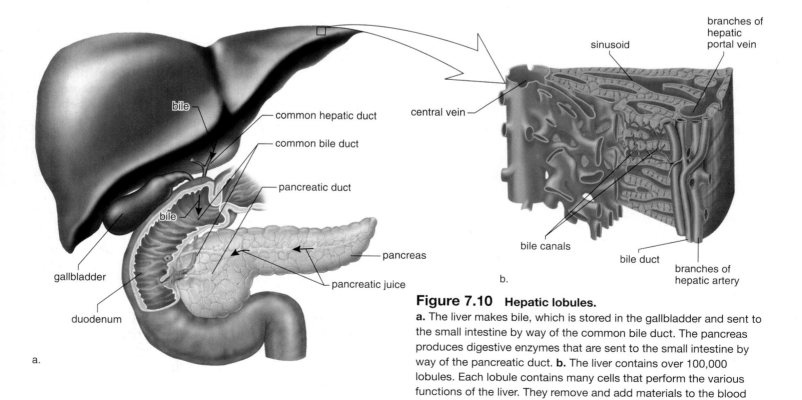

Figure 7.10 **Hepatic lobules.**

a. The liver makes bile, which is stored in the gallbladder and sent to the small intestine by way of the common bile duct. The pancreas produces digestive enzymes that are sent to the small intestine by way of the pancreatic duct. **b.** The liver contains over 100,000 lobules. Each lobule contains many cells that perform the various functions of the liver. They remove and add materials to the blood and deposit bile in a duct.

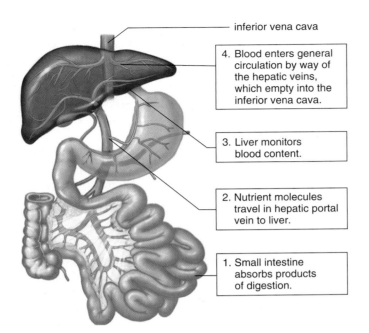

inferior vena cava

4. Blood enters general circulation by way of the hepatic veins, which empty into the inferior vena cava.

3. Liver monitors blood content.

2. Nutrient molecules travel in hepatic portal vein to liver.

1. Small intestine absorbs products of digestion.

Figure 7.11   Hepatic portal system.
The hepatic portal vein takes the products of digestion from the digestive system to the liver, where they are processed before entering a hepatic vein.

The liver produces bile, which is stored in the gallbladder. Bile has a yellowish green color because it contains the bile pigment bilirubin, derived from the breakdown of hemoglobin, the red pigment of red blood cells. Bile also contains bile salts. Bile salts are derived from cholesterol, and they emulsify fat in the small intestine. When fat is emulsified, it breaks up into droplets, providing a much larger surface area, which can be acted upon by a digestive enzyme from the pancreas.

Liver Disorders

Hepatitis and cirrhosis are two serious diseases that affect the entire liver and hinder its ability to repair itself. Therefore, they are life-threatening diseases. When a person has a liver ailment, jaundice may occur. **Jaundice** is a yellowish tint to the whites of the eyes and also to the skin of light-pigmented persons. Bilirubin is deposited in the skin, due to an abnormally large amount in the blood. Jaundice can result from **hepatitis,** inflammation of the liver. Viral hepatitis occurs in several forms. Hepatitis A is usually acquired from sewage-contaminated drinking water. Hepatitis B, which is usually spread by sexual contact, can also be spread by blood transfusions or contaminated needles. The hepatitis B virus is more contagious than the AIDS virus, which is spread in the same way. Thankfully, however, a vaccine is now available for hepatitis B. Hepatitis C, for which there is no vaccine, is usually acquired by contact with infected blood and can lead to chronic hepatitis, liver cancer, and death.

Table 7.2	Functions of the Liver

1. Destroys old red blood cells, excretes bilirubin, a breakdown product of hemoglobin in bile, a liver product

2. Detoxifies blood by removing and metabolizing poisonous substances

3. Stores iron (Fe^{2+}) and the fat-soluble vitamins A, D, E, and K

4. Makes plasma proteins, such as albumins and fibrinogen, from amino acids

5. Stores glucose as glycogen after a meal, and breaks down glycogen to glucose to maintain the glucose concentration of blood between eating periods

6. Produces urea after breaking down amino acids

7. Helps regulate blood cholesterol level, converting some to bile salts

Cirrhosis is another chronic disease of the liver. First, the organ becomes fatty, and then liver tissue is replaced by inactive fibrous scar tissue. Cirrhosis of the liver is often seen in alcoholics, due to malnutrition and to the excessive amounts of alcohol (a toxin) the liver is forced to break down.

The liver has amazing regenerative powers and can recover if the rate of regeneration exceeds the rate of damage. During liver failure, however, there may not be enough time to let the liver heal itself. Liver transplantation is usually the preferred treatment for liver failure, but artificial livers have been developed and tried in a few cases. One type is a cartridge that contains liver cells. The patient's blood passes through the cellulose acetate tubing of the cartridge and is serviced in the same manner as with a normal liver.

The Gallbladder

The **gallbladder** is a pear-shaped, muscular sac attached to the surface of the liver (see Fig. 7.1). About 1,000 mL of bile is produced by the liver each day, and any excess is stored in the gallbladder. Water is reabsorbed by the gallbladder so that bile becomes a thick, mucus-like material. When needed, bile leaves the gallbladder and proceeds to the duodenum via the common bile duct.

The cholesterol content of bile can come out of solution and form crystals. If the crystals grow in size, they form gallstones. The passage of the stones from the gallbladder may block the common bile duct and cause obstructive jaundice and pain. Then, the gallbladder must be removed.

The pancreas produces pancreatic juice, which contains enzymes for the digestion of food. Among the liver's many functions is the production of bile, which is stored in the gallbladder.

7.3 Digestive Enzymes

The digestive enzymes are **hydrolytic enzymes,** which break down substances by the introduction of water at specific bonds. Digestive enzymes, like other enzymes, are proteins with a particular shape that fits their substrate. They also have an optimum pH, which maintains their shape, thereby enabling them to speed up their specific reaction.

The various digestive enzymes present in the gastric, pancreatic, and intestinal juices, mentioned previously, help break down carbohydrates, proteins, nucleic acids, and fats, the major components of food. Starch is a carbohydrate, and its digestion begins in the mouth. Saliva from the salivary glands has a neutral pH and contains **salivary amylase,** the first enzyme to act on starch:

$$\text{starch} + H_2O \xrightarrow{\text{salivary amylase}} \text{maltose}$$

In this equation, salivary amylase is written above the arrow to indicate that it is neither a reactant nor a product in the reaction. It merely speeds the reaction in which its substrate, starch, is digested to many molecules of maltose, a disaccharide. Maltose molecules cannot be absorbed by the intestine; additional digestive action in the small intestine converts maltose to glucose, which can be absorbed.

Protein digestion begins in the stomach. Gastric juice secreted by gastric glands has a very low pH—about 2—because it contains hydrochloric acid (HCl). Pepsinogen, a precursor that is converted to the enzyme **pepsin** when exposed to HCl, is also present in gastric juice. Pepsin acts on protein to produce peptides:

$$\text{protein} + H_2O \xrightarrow{\text{pepsin}} \text{peptides}$$

Peptides vary in length, but they always consist of a number of linked amino acids. Peptides are usually too large to be absorbed by the intestinal lining, but later they are broken down to amino acids in the small intestine.

Starch, proteins, nucleic acids, and fats are all enzymatically broken down in the small intestine. Pancreatic juice, which enters the duodenum, has a basic pH because it contains sodium bicarbonate (NaHCO$_3$). Sodium bicarbonate neutralizes chyme, producing the slightly basic pH that is optimum for pancreatic enzymes. One pancreatic enzyme, **pancreatic amylase,** digests starch:

$$\text{starch} + H_2O \xrightarrow{\text{pancreatic amylase}} \text{maltose}$$

Another pancreatic enzyme, **trypsin,** digests protein:

$$\text{protein} + H_2O \xrightarrow{\text{trypsin}} \text{peptides}$$

Trypsin is secreted as trypsinogen, which is converted to trypsin in the duodenum.

Peptidases and **maltase,** enzymes produced by the small intestine, complete the digestion of protein to amino acids and starch to glucose, respectively. Amino acids and glucose are small molecules that cross the cells of the villi and enter the blood (Figs. 7.12a,b). Peptides, which result from the first step in protein digestion, are digested to amino acids by peptidases:

$$\text{protein} + H_2O \xrightarrow{\text{peptidases}} \text{amino acids}$$

Maltose, a disaccharide that results from the first step in starch digestion, is digested to glucose by maltase:

$$\text{maltose} + H_2O \xrightarrow{\text{maltase}} \text{glucose} + \text{glucose}$$

Other disaccharides, each of which has its own enzyme, are digested in the small intestine. The absence of any one of these enzymes can cause illness. For example, many people, including as many as 75% of African Americans, cannot digest lactose, the sugar found in milk, because they do not produce lactase, the enzyme that converts lactose to its components, glucose and galactose. Drinking untreated milk often gives these individuals the symptoms of **lactose intolerance** (diarrhea, gas, cramps), caused by a large quantity of nondigested lactose in the intestine. In most areas, it is possible to purchase milk made lactose-free by the addition of synthetic lactase or *Lactobacillus acidophilus* bacteria, which break down lactose.

Lipase, a third pancreatic enzyme, digests fat molecules in the fat droplets after they have been emulsified by bile salts:

$$\text{fat} \xrightarrow{\text{bile salts}} \text{fat droplets}$$

$$\text{fat droplets} + H_2O \xrightarrow{\text{lipase}} \text{monoglycerides} + \text{fatty acids}$$

The end products of lipase digestion are monoglycerides (glycerol + one fatty acid) and fatty acids. As mentioned previously, these enter the cells of the villi, and within these cells, they are rejoined and packaged as lipoprotein droplets, called chylomicrons. Chylomicrons enter the lacteals (Fig. 7.12c).

Each type of food is broken down by specific enzymes. Table 7.3 lists some of the major digestive enzymes produced by the digestive tract, salivary glands, or the pancreas.

Digestive enzymes present in digestive juices help break down food to the nutrient molecules: glucose, amino acids, fatty acids, and glycerol. The first two are absorbed into the blood capillaries of the villi, and the last two re-form within epithelial cells before entering the lacteals as lipoprotein droplets.

Table 7.3	Major Digestive Enzymes			
Enzyme	**Produced By**	**Site of Action**	**Optimum pH**	**Digestion**
CARBOHYDRATE DIGESTION:				
Salivary amylase	Salivary glands	Mouth	Neutral	Starch + H_2O → maltose
Pancreatic amylase	Pancreas	Small intestine	Basic	Starch + H_2O → maltose
Maltase	Small intestine	Small intestine	Basic	Maltose + H_2O → glucose + glucose
PROTEIN DIGESTION:				
Pepsin	Gastric glands	Stomach	Acidic	Protein + H_2O → peptides
Trypsin	Pancreas	Small intestine	Basic	Protein + H_2O → peptides
Peptidases	Small intestine	Small intestine	Basic	Peptide + H_2O → amino acids
NUCLEIC ACID DIGESTION:				
Nuclease	Pancreas	Small intestine	Basic	RNA and DNA + H_2O → nucleotides
Nucleosidases	Small intestine	Small intestine	Basic	Nucleotide + H_2O → base + sugar + phosphate
FAT DIGESTION:				
Lipase	Pancreas	Small intestine	Basic	Fat droplet + H_2O → monoglycerides + fatty acids

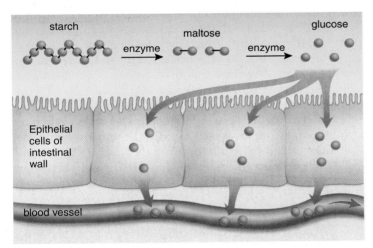

a.

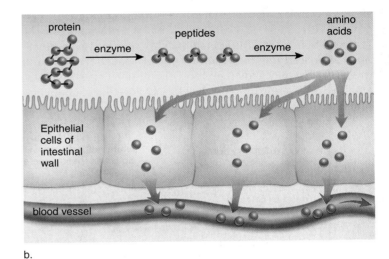

b.

Figure 7.12 Digestion and absorption of nutrients.
a. Starch is digested to glucose, which is actively transported into the epithelial cells of intestinal villi. From there, glucose moves into the bloodstream. **b.** Proteins are digested to amino acids, which are actively transported into the epithelial cells of intestinal villi. From there, amino acids move into the bloodstream. **c.** Fats are emulsified by bile and digested to monoglycerides and fatty acids. These diffuse into epithelial cells, where they recombine and join with proteins to form lipoproteins, called chylomicrons. Chylomicrons enter a lacteal.

c.

7.4 Nutrition

A **nutrient** is a component of food that performs a physiological function in the body. The six major classes of nutrients are: carbohydrates, fats, proteins, vitamins, minerals, and water. The nutrients in our diet provide us with energy, promote growth and development, and regulate cellular metabolism. Carbohydrates and fats are the major sources of energy for the body. Proteins can be used for energy but their primary function is to promote growth and development. Along with vitamins and minerals, proteins also help regulate metabolism, because nearly all enzymes are proteins. Water is necessary to metabolism because the content of a cell is about 70–80% water.

This chapter discusses five of the six major classes of nutrients; it does not discuss the contribution made by water. Food choices to fulfill your nutrient needs constitute the diet. It is important to understand the contribution of each class of nutrients so that you can understand the need for a balanced diet. Nutritionists often present dietary recommendations in a pyramid form. The broad base of the pyramid tells the viewer the foods to emphasize and the tip shows foods to minimize. The food pyramid in Figure 7.13 is a relatively new one designed by nutritionists at the Harvard School of Public Health. This pyramid was developed after studying the relationship between diet and health in various surveys, such as the 121,700-participant Nurses' Health Study sponsored by the Harvard Medical School and other similar studies.

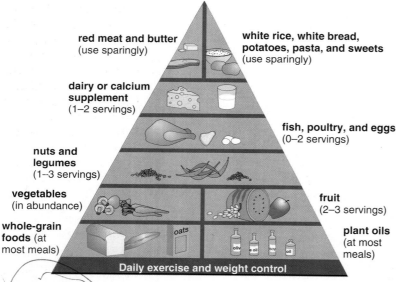

Figure 7.13   Food guide pyramid.
Nutritionists at Harvard Medical School support this food pyramid as a guide to better health. Notice that the pyramid suggests that plant oils are preferable to saturated fats, such as butter; that whole grains, such as those in cereals, are preferable to refined carbohydrates, such as those in white bread and pasta; and that fish and poultry are healthier sources of protein than is red meat.
Source: Data from the U.S. Department of Agriculture.

Carbohydrates

Carbohydrates are digested to simple sugars, which are or can be converted to glucose, the sugar that cells prefer as an energy source. As mentioned earlier in this chapter, glucose is stored by the liver in the form of glycogen. Between eating periods, the blood glucose level is maintained at about 100 mg/dL by the breakdown of glycogen or by the conversion of fat or amino acids to glucose. While body cells can utilize fatty acids as an energy source, brain cells require glucose. For this reason alone, it is necessary to include carbohydrates in the diet.

Complex sources of carbohydrates, such as whole-grain foods featured in Figure 7.14, are recommended because they are digested to sugars gradually and contain fiber. Insoluble fiber, such as that found in wheat bran, has a laxative effect and may possibly guard against colon cancer by limiting the amount of time cancer-causing substances are in contact with the intestinal wall. Soluble fiber, such as that found in oat bran, combines with bile acids and cholesterol in the intestine and prevents them from being absorbed. The liver then removes cholesterol from the blood and changes it to bile acids, replacing the bile acids that were lost. A diet too high in fiber can be detrimental, possibly impairing the body's ability to absorb iron, zinc, and calcium.

Simple sugars in foods, such as candy and ice cream, immediately enter the bloodstream as do those from the digestion of starch within white bread and potatoes. These foods are said to have a high **glycemic index (GI),** because the blood glucose response to these foods is high. When the blood glucose level rises rapidly, the pancreas produces an overload of insulin to bring the level under control. (Cells take up glucose in response to insulin.) Investigators tell us that a chronically high insulin level may lead

Figure 7.14   Complex carbohydrates.
Energy needs should be met by consuming complex carbohydrates, such as those shown here, rather than foods consisting of simple carbohydrates, such as candy and ice cream, or refined carbohydrates, such as white bread.

Table 7.4	Reducing High-Glycemic Index Carbohydrates

To reduce dietary sugar:

1. Eat fewer sweets, such as candy, soft drinks, ice cream, and pastry.
2. Eat fresh fruits or fruits canned without heavy syrup.
3. Use less sugar—white, brown, or raw—and less honey and syrups.
4. Avoid sweetened breakfast cereals.
5. Eat less jelly, jam, and preserves.
6. Eat fresh fruit; especially avoid artificial fruit juices.
7. When cooking, use spices, such as cinnamon, instead of sugar to flavor foods.
8. Do not put sugar in tea or coffee.
9. Avoid potatoes and processed foods made from refined carbohydrates, such as white bread, rice, and pasta.

Table 7.5	Complementary Proteins		
Legumes	**Seeds and Nuts**	**Grains**	**Vegetables**
Green peas	Sunflower seeds	Wheat	Leafy green (e.g., spinach)
Navy beans	Sesame seeds	Rice	
Soybeans	Macadamia nuts	Corn	Broccoli
Black-eyed peas	Brazil nuts	Barley	Cauliflower
Pinto beans	Peanuts	Oats	Cabbage
Lima beans	Cashews	Rye	Artichoke hearts
Kidney beans	Hazelnuts		
Chickpeas	Almonds		
Black beans	Nut butter		

to insulin resistance and diabetes type 2 and increased fat metabolism. Researchers warn that increased deposition of fat and fatty acid metabolism can lead to an increased risk of coronary heart disease, liver ailments, and several types of cancer.

Table 7.4 gives suggestions on how to reduce your intake of high-GI carbohydrates.

Proteins

Foods rich in protein include: red meat, fish, poultry, dairy products, legumes (i.e., peas and beans), nuts, and cereals. Following digestion of protein, amino acids enter the bloodstream and are transported to the tissues. Ordinarily, amino acids are not used as an energy source. Most are incorporated into structural proteins found in muscles, skin, hair, and nails. Others are used to synthesize such proteins as hemoglobin, plasma proteins, enzymes, and hormones.

Adequate protein formation requires 20 different types of amino acids. Of these, eight are required from the diet in adults (nine in children) because the body is unable to produce them. These are termed the **essential amino acids.** The body produces the other amino acids by simply transforming one type into another. Some protein sources, such as meat, milk, and eggs, are complete; they provide all 20 types of amino acids. Legumes (beans and peas), other types of vegetables, seeds and nuts, and also grains supply us with amino acids, but each of these alone is an incomplete protein source, because of a deficiency in at least one of the essential amino acids. Absence of one essential amino acid prevents utilization of the other 19 amino acids. Therefore, vegetarians are counseled to combine two or more incomplete types of plant products to acquire all the essential amino acids. Table 7.5 lists complementary proteins—

sources of protein whose amino acid contents complement each other so that all the essential amino acids are present in the diet. Soybeans and tofu, which is made from soybeans, are rich in amino acids, but even so, you have to combine tofu with a complementary protein to acquire all the essential amino acids. Table 7.5 will allow you to select various combinations of plant products, in order to make sure the diet contains the essential amino acids, when it does not contain meat.

Amino acids are not stored in the body, and a daily supply is needed. However, it does not take very much protein to meet the daily requirement. Two servings of meat a day (one serving is equal in size to a deck of cards) is usually plenty. While the body is harmed if the amount of protein in the diet is severely limited, it is also likely harmed if the diet contains an overabundance of protein. Deamination of excess amino acids in the liver results in urea, our main nitrogen excretion product. The water needed for excretion of urea can cause dehydration when a person is exercising and losing water by sweating. High-protein diets, especially those rich in animal proteins, can also increase calcium loss in urine. Excretion of calcium can lead to kidney stones. The same comments apply to protein and amino acid supplements, which are generally not recommended by nutritionists.

Certain types of meat, especially red meat, are known to be high in saturated fats, while other sources, such as chicken, fish, and eggs, are more likely to be low in saturated fats. As discussed in the next section, an intake of saturated fats leads to cardiovascular disease. In one study, it was found that Hawaiians who have switched back to a diet that is rich in protein from plants have a reduced incidence of cardiovascular disease and cancer, compared with those who follow a modern diet, which is rich in animal protein and fat.

Table 7.6	Reducing Certain Lipids

To reduce saturated fats and trans-fats in the diet:

1. Choose poultry, fish, or dry beans and peas as a protein source.
2. Remove skin from poultry, and trim fat from red meats before cooking; place on a rack so that fat drains off.
3. Broil, boil, or bake rather than fry.
4. Limit your intake of butter, cream, trans-fats, shortenings, and tropical oils (coconut and palm oils).*
5. Use herbs and spices to season vegetables instead of butter, margarine, or sauces. Use lemon juice instead of salad dressing.
6. Drink skim milk instead of whole milk, and use skim milk in cooking and baking.

To reduce dietary cholesterol:

1. Avoid cheese, egg yolks, liver, and certain shellfish (shrimp and lobster). Preferably, eat white fish and poultry.
2. Substitute egg whites for egg yolks in both cooking and eating.
3. Include soluble fiber in the diet. Oat bran, oatmeal, beans, corn, and fruits, such as apples, citrus fruits, and cranberries are high in soluble fiber.

*Although coconut and palm oils are from plant sources, they are mostly saturated fats.

Lipids

Fats, oils, and cholesterol are lipids. Saturated fats, which are solids at room temperature, usually have an animal origin. Two well-known exceptions are palm oil and coconut oil, which contain mostly saturated fats and come from the plants mentioned. Butter and meats, such as marbled red meats and bacon, contain saturated fats. As discussed below, saturated fats are particularly associated with cardiovascular disease. The worst offenders are those that contain trans- (for transformed) fatty acids. These arise when unsaturated fatty acids are hydrogenated to produce a solid fat. Found largely in commercially produced products, trans-fatty acids may reduce the function of the cell-membrane receptors that clear cholesterol from the bloodstream.

Oils contain unsaturated fatty acids, which do not promote cardiovascular disease. Not only that, unsaturated oils, like whole grains and vegetables, have a low glycemic index and are more filling. Each type of oil has a percentage of monounsaturated and polyunsaturated fatty acids. Corn oil and safflower oil are high in polyunsaturated fatty acids. Polyunsaturated oils are nutritionally essential because they are the only type of fat that contains linoleic acid and linolenic acid, two fatty acids the body cannot make. The body needs these two polyunsaturated fatty acids to produce various hormones and the plasma membrane of cells. Since these fatty acids must be supplied by diet, they are called **essential fatty acids.**

Olive and canola oil are well known to contain a larger percentage of monounsaturated fatty acids than other types of cooking oils. Omega-3 fatty acids—with a double bond in the third position—are believed to be especially protective against heart disease. Some cold-water fishes, such as salmon, sardines, and trout, are rich sources of omega-3, but they contain only about half that of flaxseed oil, the best source from plants.

Fats That Cause Disease

Cardiovascular disease is often due to arteries blocked by **plaque,** which contains saturated fats and cholesterol. Cholesterol is carried in the blood by two types of lipoproteins: low-density lipoprotein (LDL) and high-density lipoprotein (HDL). LDL is thought of as "bad" because it carries cholesterol from the liver to the cells, while HDL is thought of as "good" because it carries cholesterol to the liver, which takes it up and converts it to bile salts. Saturated fats tend to raise LDL cholesterol levels, while unsaturated fats lower LDL cholesterol levels.

Controlled-feeding studies of laboratory animals and statistical studies that have examined trans-fat intake in relation to the risk of heart disease and diabetes indicate that trans-fats are more prone to cause these diseases than saturated fats. Trans-fatty acids are found in commercially packaged goods, such as cookies and crackers, commercially fried foods, such as french fries from some fast-food chains, packaged snacks, such as microwaved popcorn, as well as in vegetable shortening and some margarines. Any packaged goods that contain partially hydrogenated vegetable oils or "shortening" most likely contain trans-fat.

In addition to avoiding trans-fatty acids and saturated fats, everyone should use diet and exercise to keep their cholesterol level within normal limits, so that medications will not be needed for this purpose. Table 7.6 gives suggestions on how to reduce dietary saturated fat and cholesterol. It is not a good idea to rely on commercially produced low-fat foods or those that contain fake fat (e.g., olestra) to reduce total fat intake. In some products, such as carbohydrates, namely sugars, have replaced the fat; and in others, protein is used. We have already discussed the dangers of simple sugars in the diet, and while replacement of fat with protein is nutritionally more sound, protein still contributes calories to the diet. Nutritionists also express concern about the consumption of fake fat, because high levels of intake can lead to limited absorption of fat-soluble vitamins, diarrhea, and rectal leakage. However, products containing olestra often have extra fat-soluble vitamins added.

Proper nutrition includes avoiding carbohydrates with a high glycemic index, consuming protein in moderation but taking in all the essential amino acids, and limiting saturated fats, especially trans-fats.

Health Focus

Very Low Carbohydrate Diets

People following a low-carbohydrate diet seem to think that weight gain is caused by carbohydrates, an idea that cannot be supported scientifically. Weight gain is caused by consuming too many calories, whether they are from carbohydrate, protein, or fat. Logically, you are more likely to gain weight from protein and fats than from carbohydrates because dietary fat has more than double the amount of calories per gram than carbohydrate. Protein has slightly higher amounts of energy per gram, making protein and fat more energy-dense than carbohydrate.

Many health professionals do not approve of a very low carbohydrate diet, especially when it also restricts fruits and vegetables and allows unlimited access to protein and fats, as in the Atkins diet. Recent studies have compared two groups: one group followed the Atkins diet and another used a traditional low-fat, high-carbohydrate diet. The Atkins group showed the most weight loss without adverse effect on the cardiovascular and diabetic risk factors in the short term. After 12 months, those on both diets had regained about half the lost weight and there was no longer any statistical difference in weight loss between the two groups. Because of the large dropout rate, it has not been possible to determine if the Atkins diet is safe for the long-term.

Knowledge of how the human body works suggests that the initial weight loss experienced by people on a very low carbohydrate diet is due to a loss of water. As you know, glucose is stored as glycogen in the liver and muscles. When carbohydrates are restricted in the diet, the body first breaks down its glycogen before it turns to burning fat. For every gram of glycogen released from the tissues, three grams of water is lost. Once the person starts eating carbohydrates again, the glycogen and water content of the tissues is restored.

Because a person on a very low carbohydrate diet has limited glucose and glycogen to metabolize, the body must break down protein and fat as a source of energy. When protein and fat are metabolized, the body produces molecules called ketones—the same as diabetics do because glucose is not available to cells. This state, known as "ketosis," is often an indication that body protein from muscles in being broken down, in addition to stored fat. In other words, the body's muscles are wasting away. Ketones make the blood acidic and the kidneys, in particular, are called upon to adjust the pH of the blood. Should the kidneys be unable to do so, the results can be fatal. In other words, a very low carbohydrate diet challenges the body to maintain homeostasis. In any case, a low blood pH increases the likelihood of osteoporosis and kidney stones due to increased excretion of calcium.

Some organs of the body, such as the brain, can only use glucose as an energy source; therefore, the liver usually converts protein to glucose, in order to keep the glucose content of the blood constant. When protein is broken down, the amino groups are converted to urea, the main nitrogenous end product of human metabolism. Again, the kidneys are called upon to do extra work by ridding the body of urea. It is better to be protective of one's kidneys rather than to stress them.

Usually, a very low carbohydrate diet includes a higher amount of saturated fat than usual, if only because meat is usually high in saturated fats. As you know, a diet high in saturated fat leads to the development of plaque in the coronary arteries, and therefore coronary heart disease. Consequently, a person on a low-carbohydrate diet should be sure to consume a variety of fats from plant sources (e.g., olives, olive oil, canola oil, peanuts, peanut oil, soy, and soy oil) rather than from animal sources (e.g., butter, and meat fat).

Vegetarians who consume predominantly plant-based foods are generally slimmer and have much lower rates of obesity, heart disease, and cancer than people who eat meat-based diets. Some plant-based foods, such as whole-grain cereals, grainy bread, natural muesli, brown rice, and certain fruits, have a low glycemic index (GI) and need not be avoided. It is far better to use low-GI carbohydrates to stave off hunger than saturated fat because of the health consequences of eating saturated fats. A very low carbohydrate diet that is low in fiber, vitamins, and minerals increases the risk of cancer, in addition to heart disease and osteoporosis (Fig. 7A).

Ultimately, to avoid weight gain, energy intake should not exceed energy output over a period of time. It is possible to achieve weight loss with a balanced diet that restricts portion sizes and avoids processed foods rich in refined carbohydrates and fat. Also, we should not fail to recognize the benefits of regular physical activity for long-term weight management and good health.

Figure 7A   Fruit is a healthy and low-calorie snack.

Vitamins

Vitamins are organic compounds (other than carbohydrate, fat, and protein) that the body uses for metabolic purposes but is unable to produce in adequate quantity. Many vitamins are portions of coenzymes, which are enzyme helpers. For example, niacin is part of the coenzyme NAD, and riboflavin is part of another dehydrogenase, FAD, discussed in Chapter 3. Coenzymes are needed in only small amounts because each can be used over and over again. Not all vitamins are coenzymes; vitamin A, for example, is a precursor for the visual pigment that prevents night blindness. If vitamins are lacking in the diet, various symptoms develop (Fig. 7.15). Altogether, there are 13 vitamins, which are divided into those that are fat-soluble (Table 7.7) and those that are water-soluble (Table 7.8).

Antioxidants

Over the past 20 years, numerous statistical studies have been done to determine whether a diet rich in fruits and vegetables can protect against cancer. Cellular metabolism generates free radicals, unstable molecules that carry an extra electron. The most common free radicals in cells are superoxide (O_2^-) and hydroxide (OH^-). In order to stabilize themselves, free radicals donate an electron to DNA, to proteins (including enzymes), or to lipids, which are found in plasma membranes. Such donations most likely damage these cellular molecules and thereby may lead to disorders, perhaps even cancer.

Vitamins C, E, and A are believed to defend the body against free radicals, and therefore they are termed antioxidants. These vitamins are especially abundant in fruits and vegetables. The dietary guidelines shown in Figure 7.13 suggest that we eat a minimum of five servings of fruits and vegetables a day. To achieve this goal, we should include salad greens, raw or cooked vegetables, dried fruit, and fruit juice, in addition to apples and oranges and other fresh fruits.

Dietary supplements may provide a potential safeguard against cancer and cardiovascular disease, but nutritionists do not think people should take supplements instead of improving their intake of fruits and vegetables. There are many beneficial compounds in fruits that cannot be obtained from a vitamin pill. These compounds enhance one another's absorption or action and also perform independent biological functions.

Vitamin D

Skin cells contain a precursor cholesterol molecule that is converted to vitamin D after UV exposure. Vitamin D leaves the skin and is modified first in the kidneys and then in the liver until finally it becomes calcitriol. Calcitriol promotes the absorption of calcium by the intestines. The lack of vitamin D leads to rickets in children (Fig. 7.15*a*). Rickets, characterized by bowing of the legs, is caused by defective mineralization of the skeleton. Most milk today is fortified with vitamin D, which helps prevent the occurrence of rickets.

> Vitamins are essential to cellular metabolism; many protect against identifiable illnesses and conditions.

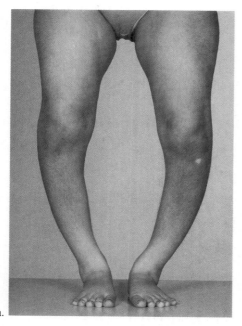
a.

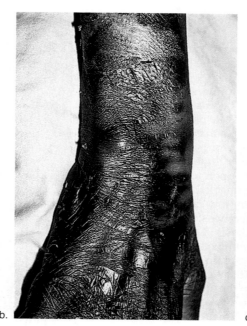
b.

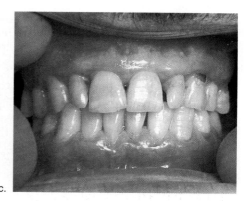
c.

Figure 7.15   Illnesses due to vitamin deficiency.
a. Bowing of bones (rickets) due to vitamin D deficiency. **b.** Dermatitis (pellagra) of areas exposed to light due to niacin (vitamin B$_3$) deficiency. **c.** Bleeding of gums (scurvy) due to vitamin C deficiency.

| Table 7.7 | Fat-Soluble Vitamins | | | |

Vitamin	Functions	Food Sources	Conditions with	
			Too Little	Too Much
Vitamin A	Antioxidant synthesized from beta-carotene; needed for healthy eyes, skin, hair, and mucous membranes, and for proper bone growth	Deep yellow/orange and leafy, dark green vegetables, fruits, cheese, whole milk, butter, eggs	Night blindness, impaired growth of bones and teeth	Headache, dizziness, nausea, hair loss, abnormal development of fetus
Vitamin D	A group of steroids needed for development and maintenance of bones and teeth	Milk fortified with vitamin D, fish liver oil; also made in the skin when exposed to sunlight	Rickets, decalcification and weakening of bones	Calcification of soft tissues, diarrhea, possible renal damage
Vitamin E	Antioxidant that prevents oxidation of vitamin A and polyunsaturated fatty acids	Leafy green vegetables, fruits, vegetable oils, nuts, whole-grain breads and cereals	Unknown	Diarrhea, nausea, headaches, fatigue, muscle weakness
Vitamin K	Needed for synthesis of substances active in clotting of blood	Leafy green vegetables, cabbage, cauliflower	Easy bruising and bleeding	Can interfere with anticoagulant medication

| Table 7.8 | Water-Soluble Vitamins | | | |

Vitamin	Functions	Food Sources	Conditions with	
			Too Little	Too Much
Vitamin C	Antioxidant; needed for forming collagen; helps maintain capillaries, bones, and teeth	Citrus fruits, leafy green vegetables, tomatoes, potatoes, cabbage	Scurvy, delayed wound healing, infections	Gout, kidney stones, diarrhea, decreased copper
Thiamine (vitamin B_1)	Part of coenzyme needed for cellular respiration; also promotes activity of the nervous system	Whole-grain cereals, dried beans and peas, sunflower seeds, nuts	Beriberi, muscular weakness, enlarged heart	Can interfere with absorption of other vitamins
Riboflavin (vitamin B_2)	Part of coenzymes, such as FAD[1]; aids cellular respiration, including oxidation of protein and fat	Nuts, dairy products, whole-grain cereals, poultry, leafy green vegetables	Dermatitis, blurred vision, growth failure	Unknown
Niacin (nicotinic acid)	Part of coenzymes NAD[2]; needed for cellular respiration, including oxidation of protein and fat	Peanuts, poultry, whole-grain cereals, leafy green vegetables, beans	Pellagra, diarrhea, mental disorders	High blood sugar and uric acid, vasodilation, etc.
Folacin (folic acid)	Coenzyme needed for production of hemoglobin and formation of DNA	Dark leafy green vegetables, nuts, beans, whole-grain cereals	Megaloblastic anemia, spina bifida	May mask B_{12} deficiency
Vitamin B_6	Coenzyme needed for synthesis of hormones and hemoglobin; CNS control	Whole-grain cereals, bananas, beans, poultry, nuts, leafy green vegetables	Rarely, convulsions, vomiting, seborrhea, muscular weakness	Insomnia, neuropathy
Pantothenic acid	Part of coenzyme A needed for oxidation of carbohydrates and fats; aids in the formation of hormones and certain neurotransmitters	Nuts, beans, dark green vegetables, poultry, fruits, milk	Rarely, loss of appetite, mental depression, numbness	Unknown
Vitamin B_{12}	Complex, cobalt-containing compound; part of the coenzyme needed for synthesis of nucleic acids and myelin	Dairy products, fish, poultry, eggs, fortified cereals	Pernicious anemia	Unknown
Biotin	Coenzyme needed for metabolism of amino acids and fatty acids	Generally in foods, especially eggs	Skin rash, nausea, fatigue	Unknown

[1]FAD = flavin adenine dinucleotide
[2]NAD = nicotinamide adenine dinucleotide

Minerals

In addition to vitamins, various **minerals** are required by the body. Minerals are divided into major minerals and trace minerals. The body contains more than 5 grams of each major mineral and less than 5 grams of each trace mineral (Fig. 7.16). The major minerals are constituents of cells and body fluids and are structural components of tissues. For example, calcium (present as Ca^{2+}) is needed for the construction of bones and teeth and for nerve conduction and muscle contraction. Phosphorus (present as PO_4^{3-}) is stored in the bones and teeth and is a part of phospholipids, ATP, and the nucleic acids. Potassium (K^+) is the major positive ion inside cells and is important in nerve conduction and muscle contraction, as is sodium (Na^+). Sodium also plays a major role in regulating the body's water balance, as does chloride (Cl^-). Magnesium (Mg^{2+}) is critical to the functioning of hundreds of enzymes. Sulfur (S^{2-}) helps proteins maintain their normal shape.

The trace minerals are parts of larger molecules. For example, iron (Fe^{2+}) is present in hemoglobin, and iodine (I^-) is a part of thyroxine and triiodothyronine, hormones produced by the thyroid gland. Zinc (Zn^{2+}), copper (Cu^{2+}), and manganese (Mn^{2+}) are present in enzymes that catalyze a variety of reactions. Proteins, called zinc-finger proteins because of their characteristic shapes, bind to DNA when a particular gene is to be activated. As research continues, more and more elements are added to the list of trace minerals considered essential. During the past three decades, for example, very small amounts of selenium, molybdenum, chromium, nickel, vanadium, silicon, and even arsenic have been found to be essential to good health. Table 7.9 lists the functions of various minerals and gives their food sources and signs of deficiency and toxicity.

Occasionally, individuals do not receive enough iron (especially women), calcium, magnesium, or zinc in their diets. Adult females need more iron in the diet than males (18 mg compared with 10 mg) because they lose hemoglobin each month during menstruation. Stress can bring on a magnesium deficiency, and due to its high-fiber content, a vegetarian diet may make zinc less available to the body. However, a varied and complete diet usually supplies enough of each type of mineral.

Calcium

Many people take calcium supplements to counteract **osteoporosis,** a degenerative bone disease that afflicts an estimated one fourth of older men and one half of older women in the United States. Osteoporosis develops because bone-eating cells called osteoclasts are more active than bone-forming cells called osteoblasts. Therefore, the bones are porous, and they break easily because they lack sufficient calcium. Due to recent studies that show consuming more calcium does slow bone loss in elderly people, the guidelines have been revised. A calcium intake of 1,000 mg a day is recommended for men and for women who are premenopausal, and 1,300 mg a day is recommended for postmenopausal women. To achieve this amount, supplemental calcium is most likely necessary.

Vitamin D is an essential companion to calcium in preventing osteoporosis. Other vitamins may also be helpful; for example, magnesium has been found to suppress the cycle that leads to bone loss. In addition to adequate calcium and vitamin intake, exercise helps prevent osteoporosis. Risk factors for osteoporosis include drinking more than nine cups of caffeinated coffee per day and smoking. Medications are also available that slow bone loss while increasing skeletal mass. These are still being studied for their effectiveness and possible side effects.

Sodium

The recommended amount of sodium intake per day is 500 mg, although the average American takes in 4,000–4,700 mg every day. In recent years, this imbalance has caused concern because sodium in the form of salt intensifies hypertension (high blood pressure) if you already have it. About one

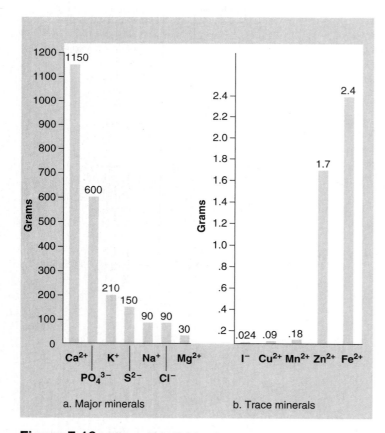

Figure 7.16   Minerals in the body.
a. The major minerals are present in amounts larger than 5 g (about a teaspoon). **b.** Trace minerals are present in lesser amounts.

Table 7.9	Minerals				
Mineral	**Functions**	**Food Sources**	**Conditions with**		
			Too Little	*Too Much*	
MAJOR (MORE THAN 100 MG/DAY NEEDED)					
Calcium (Ca^{2+})	Strong bones and teeth, nerve conduction, muscle contraction	Dairy products, leafy green vegetables	Stunted growth in children, low bone density in adults	Kidney stones; interferes with iron and zinc absorption	
Phosphorus (PO_4^{3-})	Bone and soft tissue growth; part of phospholipids, ATP, and nucleic acids	Meat, dairy products, sunflower seeds, food additives	Weakness, confusion, pain in bones and joints	Low blood and bone calcium levels	
Potassium (K^+)	Nerve conduction, muscle contraction	Many fruits and vegetables, bran	Paralysis, irregular heartbeat, eventual death	Vomiting, heart attack, death	
Sulfur (S^{2-})	Stabilizes protein shape, neutralizes toxic substances	Meat, dairy products, legumes	Not likely	In animals, depresses growth	
Sodium (Na^+)	Nerve conduction, pH and water balance	Table salt	Lethargy, muscle cramps, loss of appetite	Edema, high blood pressure	
Chloride (Cl^-)	Water balance	Table salt	Not likely	Vomiting, dehydration	
Magnesium (Mg^{2+})	Part of various enzymes for nerve and muscle contraction, protein synthesis	Whole grains, leafy green vegetables	Muscle spasm, irregular heartbeat, convulsions, confusion, personality changes	Diarrhea	
TRACE (LESS THAN 20 MG/DAY NEEDED)					
Zinc (Zn^{2+})	Protein synthesis, wound healing, fetal development and growth, immune function	Meats, legumes, whole grains	Delayed wound healing, night blindness, diarrhea, mental lethargy	Anemia, diarrhea, vomiting, renal failure, abnormal cholesterol levels	
Iron (Fe^{2+})	Hemoglobin synthesis	Whole grains, meats, prune juice	Anemia, physical and mental sluggishness	Iron toxicity disease, organ failure, eventual death	
Copper (Cu^{2+})	Hemoglobin synthesis	Meat, nuts, legumes	Anemia, stunted growth in children	Damage to internal organs if not excreted	
Iodine (I^-)	Thyroid hormone synthesis	Iodized table salt, seafood	Thyroid deficiency	Depressed thyroid function, anxiety	
Selenium (SeO_4^{2-})	Part of antioxidant enzyme	Seafood, meats, eggs	Vascular collapse, possible cancer development	Hair and fingernail loss, discolored skin	
Manganese (Mn^{2+})	Part of enzymes	Nuts, legumes, green vegetables	Weakness and confusion	Confusion, coma, death	

third of the sodium we consume occurs naturally in foods; another third is added during commercial processing; and we add the last third either during home cooking or at the table in the form of table salt.

Clearly, it is possible to cut down on the amount of sodium in the diet. Table 7.10 gives recommendations for doing so.

Both major and trace minerals play specific roles in the body. Calcium is needed for strong bones, for example. Excess sodium in the diet can contribute to hypertension; therefore, excess sodium intake should be avoided.

Table 7.10	Reducing Dietary Sodium

To reduce dietary sodium:

1. Use spices instead of salt to flavor foods.
2. Add little or no salt to foods at the table, and add only small amounts of salt when you cook.
3. Eat unsalted crackers, pretzels, potato chips, nuts, and popcorn.
4. Avoid hot dogs, ham, bacon, luncheon meats, smoked salmon, sardines, and anchovies.
5. Avoid processed cheese and canned or dehydrated soups.
6. Avoid brine-soaked foods, such as pickles or olives.
7. Read nutrition labels to avoid high-salt products.

Persons with obesity have

- weight 20% or more above appropriate weight for height.
- body fat content in excess of that consistent with optimal health.
- low levels of exercise.

Figure 7.17 **Recognizing obesity.**

Eating Disorders

Authorities recognize three primary eating disorders: obesity, bulimia nervosa, and anorexia nervosa. Although they exist in a continuum as far as body weight is concerned, they all represent an inability to maintain normal body weight because of eating habits.

Obesity

As indicated in Figure 7.17, **obesity** is most often defined as a body weight 20% or more above the ideal weight for a person's height. By this standard, 28% of women and 10% of men in the United States are obese. Moderate obesity is 41–100% above ideal weight, and severe obesity is 100% or more above ideal weight.

Obesity is most likely caused by a combination of hormonal, metabolic, and social factors. It is known that obese individuals have more fat cells than normal, and when they lose weight, the fat cells simply get smaller; they don't disappear. The social factors that cause obesity include the eating habits of other family members. Consistently eating fatty foods, for example, will make you gain weight. Sedentary activities, such as watching television instead of exercising, also determine how much body fat you have. The risk of heart disease is higher in obese individuals, and this alone tells us that excess body fat is not consistent with optimal health.

The treatment depends on the degree of obesity. Surgery to remove body fat may be required for those who are greatly overweight. But for most people, a knowledge of good eating habits along with behavior modification may suffice, particularly if a balanced diet is accompanied by a sensible exercise program. A lifelong commitment to a properly planned program is the best way to prevent a cycle of weight gain followed by weight loss. Such a cycle is not conducive to good health.

Bulimia Nervosa

Bulimia nervosa can coexist with either obesity or anorexia nervosa, which is discussed next. People with this condition have the habit of eating to excess (called binge eating) and then purging themselves by some artificial means, such as self-induced vomiting or use of a laxative. Bulimic individuals are overconcerned about their body shape and weight, and therefore they may be on a very restrictive diet. A restrictive diet may bring on the desire to binge, and typically the person chooses to consume sweets, such as cakes, cookies, and ice cream (Fig. 7.18). The amount of food consumed is far beyond the normal number of calories for one meal, and the person keeps on eating until every bit is gone. Then, a feeling of guilt most likely brings on the next phase, which is a purging of all the calories that have been taken in.

Bulimia can be dangerous to your health. Blood composition is altered, leading to an abnormal heart rhythm, and damage to the kidneys can even result in death. At the very least, vomiting can lead to inflammation of the pharynx and esophagus, and stomach acids can cause the teeth to erode. The esophagus and stomach may even rupture and tear due to strong contractions during vomiting.

The most important aspect of treatment is to get the patient on a sensible and consistent diet. Again, behavioral modification is helpful, and so perhaps is psychotherapy to help the patient understand the emotional causes of the behavior. Medications, including antidepressants, have sometimes helped to reduce the bulimic cycle and restore normal appetite.

Obesity and bulimia nervosa have complex causes and may be damaging to health. Therefore, they require competent medical attention.

Anorexia Nervosa

In **anorexia nervosa,** a morbid fear of gaining weight causes the person to be on a very restrictive diet. Athletes such as distance runners, wrestlers, and dancers are at risk of anorexia nervosa because they believe that being thin gives them a competitive edge. In addition to eating only low-calorie foods, the person may induce vomiting and use laxatives to bring about further weight loss. No matter how thin they have become, people with anorexia nervosa think they are overweight (Fig. 7.19). Such a distorted self-image may prevent recognition of the need for medical help.

Actually, the person is starving and has all the symptoms of starvation, including low blood pressure, irregular heartbeat, constipation, and constant chilliness. Bone density decreases and stress fractures occur. The body begins to shut down; menstruation ceases in females; the internal organs, including the brain, don't function well; and the skin dries up. Impairment of the pancreas and digestive tract means that any food consumed does not provide nourishment. Death may be imminent. If so, the only recourse may be hospitalization and force-feeding. Eventually, it is necessary to use behavior therapy and psychotherapy to enlist the cooperation of the person to eat properly. Family therapy may be necessary, because anorexia nervosa in children and teens is believed to be a way for them to gain some control over their lives.

In anorexia nervosa, the individual has a distorted body image and always feels fat. Because anorexia has complex causes, competent medical help is often necessary.

Persons with bulimia nervosa have

- recurrent episodes of binge eating characterized by consuming an amount of food much higher than normal for one sitting and a sense of lack of control over eating during the episode.
- an obsession about their body shape and weight.
- increase in fine body hair, halitosis, and gingivitis.

Body weight is regulated by

- a restrictive diet, excessive exercise.
- purging (self-induced vomiting or misuse of laxatives).

Figure 7.18   **Bulimia nervosa.**
Bulimia nervosa can be recognized by its significant characteristics, listed in the box above.

Persons with anorexia nervosa have

- a morbid fear of gaining weight; body weight no more than 85% normal.
- a distorted body image so that person feels fat even when emaciated.
- in females, an absence of a menstrual cycle for at least three months.

Body weight is kept too low by either/or

- a restrictive diet, often with excessive exercise.
- binge eating/purging (person engages in binge eating and then self-induces vomiting or misuses laxatives).

Figure 7.19   **Anorexia nervosa.**
Anorexia nervosa can be recognized by its significant characteristics, listed in the box above.

Summarizing the Concepts

7.1 The Digestive Tract

The digestive tract consists of the mouth, pharynx, esophagus, stomach, small intestine, and large intestine. Only these structures actually contain food, while the salivary glands, liver, and pancreas supply substances that aid in the digestion of food.

The salivary glands send saliva into the mouth, where the teeth chew the food and the tongue forms a bolus for swallowing. Saliva contains salivary amylase, an enzyme that begins the digestion of starch.

The air passage and food passage cross in the pharynx. When a person swallows, the air passage is usually blocked off, and food must enter the esophagus, where peristalsis begins.

The stomach expands and stores food. While food is in the stomach, the stomach churns, mixing food with the acidic gastric juices. Gastric juices contain pepsin, an enzyme that digests protein.

The duodenum of the small intestine receives bile from the liver and pancreatic juice from the pancreas. Bile, which is produced in the liver and stored in the gallbladder, emulsifies fat and readies it for digestion by lipase, an enzyme produced by the pancreas. The pancreas also produces enzymes that digest starch (pancreatic amylase) and protein (trypsin). The intestinal enzymes finish the process of chemical digestion.

The walls of the small intestine have finger-like projections called villi where small nutrient molecules are absorbed. Amino acids and glucose enter the blood vessels of a villus. Glycerol and fatty acids are joined and packaged as lipoproteins before entering lymphatic vessels called lacteals in a villus.

The large intestine consists of the cecum, the colon (including the ascending, transverse, descending, and sigmoid colon), and the rectum, which ends at the anus. The large intestine does not produce digestive enzymes; it does absorb water, salts, and some vitamins. Reduced water absorption results in diarrhea. The intake of water and fiber help prevent constipation.

7.2 Three Accessory Organs

Three accessory organs of digestion—the pancreas, liver, and gallbladder—send secretions to the duodenum via ducts. The pancreas produces pancreatic juice, which contains digestive enzymes for carbohydrate, protein, and fat.

The liver produces bile, which is stored in the gallbladder. The liver receives blood from the small intestine by way of the hepatic portal vein. It has numerous important functions, and any malfunction of the liver is a matter of considerable concern.

7.3 Digestive Enzymes

Digestive enzymes are present in digestive juices and break down food into the nutrient molecules glucose, amino acids, fatty acids, and glycerol (see Table 7.3). Salivary amylase and pancreatic amylase begin the digestion of starch. Pepsin and trypsin digest protein to peptides. Lipase digests fat to glycerol and fatty acids, and then these are packaged as lipoproteins. Intestinal enzymes finish the digestion of starch and protein.

Digestive enzymes have the usual enzymatic properties. They are specific to their substrate and speed up specific reactions at optimum body temperature and pH.

7.4 Nutrition

The nutrients released by the digestive process should provide us with an adequate amount of energy, essential amino acids and fatty acids, and all necessary vitamins and minerals.

Carbohydrates are necessary in the diet, but high-glycemic index carbohydrates (simple sugars and refined starches) are not helpful because they cause a rapid release of insulin that can lead to health problems. Proteins supply us with essential amino acids, but it is wise to avoid meats that are fatty because fats from animal sources are saturated. While unsaturated fatty acids, particularly the omega-3 fatty acids, are protective against cardiovascular disease, the saturated fatty acids lead to plaque, which occludes blood vessels. Aside from carbohydrates, proteins, and fats, the body requires vitamins and minerals. The vitamins A, E, and C are antioxidants that protect cell contents from damage due to free radicals. The mineral calcium is needed for strong bones.

Studying the Concepts

1. List the organs of the digestive tract, and state the contribution of each to the digestive process. 116–23
2. Discuss the absorption of the products of digestion into the lymphatic and cardiovascular systems. 121, 126–27
3. Name and state the functions of the hormones that assist the nervous system in regulating digestive secretions. 122
4. Name the accessory organs, and describe the part they play in the digestion of food. 124–25
5. Choose and discuss any three functions of the liver. 124–25
6. Name and discuss two serious illnesses of the liver. 125
7. Discuss the digestion of starch, protein, and fat, listing all the steps that occur with each of these. 126–27
8. What is the chief contribution of each of these constituents of the diet: a. carbohydrates; b. proteins; c. fats; d. fruits and vegetables; e. calcium and other minerals? 128–30, 132–35
9. Why should the amount of saturated fat be curtailed in the diet? 129–30
10. Name and discuss three eating disorders. 136–37

Thinking Critically About the Concepts

Refer to the opening vignette on page 115, and then answer these questions.

1. Knowing what you do about the digestive system and nutrition, how do you think a radical procedure like this will affect the physiology of Monica's digestive system and other organs of her body?
2. How will rerouting her small intestine affect her ability to properly digest food and absorb nutrients, and what kind of nutritional changes will she have to make?
3. How do you think these severe dietary restrictions will affect her, especially at a point in her life when she is still growing and maturing?

Testing Your Knowledge of the Concepts

Choose the best answer for each question.

1. Tracing the path of food in the following list (a–f), which step is out of order first?
   a. mouth
   b. pharynx
   c. esophagus
   d. small intestine
   e. stomach
   f. large intestine

2. The appendix connects to the
   a. cecum.
   b. small intestine.
   c. esophagus.
   d. liver.
   e. All of these are correct.

3. Which association is incorrect?
   a. mouth—starch digestion
   b. esophagus—protein digestion
   c. small intestine—starch, lipid, protein digestion
   d. stomach—food storage
   e. liver—production of bile

4. Why can a person not swallow food and talk at the same time?
   a. In order to swallow, the epiglottis must close off the trachea.
   b. The brain cannot control two activities at once.
   c. In order to speak, air must come through the larynx to form sounds.
   d. A swallowing reflex is only initiated when the mouth is closed.
   e. Both a and c are correct.

5. Which association is incorrect?
   a. pancreas—produces alkaline secretions and enzymes
   b. salivary glands—produce saliva and amylase
   c. gallbladder—produces digestive enzymes
   d. liver—produces bile

6. Which of the following could be absorbed directly without need of digestion?
   a. glucose
   b. fat
   c. polysaccharides
   d. protein
   e. nucleic acid

7. Peristalsis occurs
   a. from the mouth to the small intestine.
   b. from the beginning of the esophagus to the anus.
   c. only in the stomach.
   d. only in the small and large intestine.
   e. only in the esophagus and stomach.

8. An organ is a structure made of two or more tissues performing a common function. Which of the four tissue types are present in the wall of the digestive tract?
   a. epithelium
   b. connective tissue
   c. nervous tissue
   d. muscle tissue
   e. All of these are correct.

9. Which association is incorrect?
   a. protein—trypsin
   b. fat—bile
   c. fat—lipase
   d. maltose—pepsin
   e. starch—amylase

10. Most of the products of digestion are absorbed across the
    a. squamous epithelium of the esophagus.
    b. striated walls of the trachea.
    c. convoluted walls of the stomach.
    d. finger-like villi of the small intestine.
    e. smooth wall of the large intestine.

11. Bile
    a. is an important enzyme for the digestion of fats.
    b. cannot be stored.
    c. is made by the gallbladder.
    d. emulsifies fat.
    e. All of these are correct.

12. Which of the following is not a function of the liver in adults?
    a. Produces bile.
    b. Detoxifies alcohol.
    c. Stores glucose.
    d. Produces urea.
    e. Makes red blood cells.

13. The large intestine
    a. digests all types of food.
    b. is the longest part of the intestinal tract.
    c. absorbs water.
    d. is connected to the stomach.
    e. is subject to hepatitis.

In questions 14–18, match each function to an organ in the key.

Key:
   a. mouth
   b. esophagus
   c. stomach
   d. small intestine
   e. large intestine

14. Stores nondigestible remains

15. Serves as a passageway

16. Stores food

17. Absorbs nutrients

18. Receives food

19. How many small servings of meat are sufficient in the daily diet?
    a. 6–11
    b. 2–4
    c. 2–3
    d. 3–4

20. The amino acids that must be consumed in the diet are called essential. Nonessential amino acids
    a. can be produced by the body.
    b. are only needed occasionally.
    c. are stored in the body until needed.
    d. can be taken in by supplements.

21. Which of the following are often organic portions of important coenzymes?
    a. minerals
    b. vitamins
    c. protein
    d. carbohydrates

22. Bulimia nervosa is not characterized by
    a. a restrictive diet often with excessive exercise.
    b. binge eating followed by purging.
    c. an obsession about body shape and weight.
    d. a distorted body image so a person feels fat even when emaciated.

23. Predict and explain the expected digestive results per test tube for this experiment.

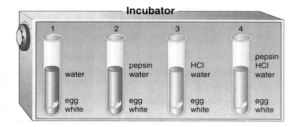

Incubator

24. The products of digestion are
    a. large macromolecules needed by the body.
    b. enzymes needed to digest food.
    c. small nutrient molecules that can be absorbed.
    d. regulatory hormones of various kinds.
    e. the food we eat.

In questions 25–29, match each statement to a layer of the wall of the esophagus in the key. Answers are used more than once.

Key:
   a. mucosa   c. muscularis
   b. submucosa   d. serosa

25. Loose connective tissue that contains lymph nodules.

26. Contains a layer of epithelium that lines the lumen.

27. Very thin layer of squamous epithelium that secretes a fluid, keeping the organ moist.

28. Contains digestive glands and mucus-secreting goblet cells.

29. Two layers of smooth muscle.

In questions 30–36, match each statement to an answer in the key. Answers are used more than once. Some may have more than one answer.

Key:
   a. gastrin
   b. secretin
   c. CCK
   d. All of these are correct.
   e. None of these is correct.

30. Stimulates gallbladder to release bile

31. Hormone carried in bloodstream

32. Stimulates the stomach to digest protein

33. Enzyme that digests food

34. Secreted by duodenum

35. Stimulates the salivary glands to release saliva

36. Secreted by the stomach

Understanding Key Terms

anorexia nervosa 137	liver 124
anus 122	lumen 119
bile 121	maltase 126
bulimia nervosa 136	mineral 134
cecum 122	nasopharynx 118
chyme 120	nutrient 128
cirrhosis 125	obesity 136
colon 122	osteoporosis 134
constipation 123	pancreas 124
defecation 122	pancreatic amylase 124, 126
dental caries 117	pepsin 120, 126
diarrhea 123	peptidase 126
duodenum 121	peristalsis 118
epiglottis 118	peritonitis 122
esophagus 118	pharynx 117
essential amino acids 129	plaque 130
essential fatty acids 130	polyp 123
fiber 122	rectum 122
gallbladder 125	reflex action 118
gastric gland 120	salivary amylase 116, 126
glottis 118	salivary gland 116
glycemic index (GI) 128	small intestine 121
hard palate 116	soft palate 116
heartburn 119	sphincter 118
hepatitis 125	stomach 120
hormone 122	tonsillitis 116
hydrolytic enzyme 126	trypsin 124, 126
jaundice 125	ulcer 120
lacteal 121	vermiform appendix 122
lactose intolerance 126	villus 121
large intestine 122	vitamin 132
lipase 124, 126	

Match the key terms to these definitions.

a. _____ Essential requirement in the diet, needed in small amounts. Often a part of a coenzyme.

b. _____ Fat-digesting enzyme secreted by the pancreas.

c. _____ Lymphatic vessel in an intestinal villus; it aids in the absorption of fats.

d. _____ Muscular tube for moving swallowed food from the pharynx to the stomach.

e. _____ Organ attached to the liver that serves to store and concentrate bile.

Online Learning Center

www.mhhe.com/maderhuman9

The Online Learning Center provides a wealth of information fully organized and integrated by chapter. You will find practice quizzes, interactive activities, labeling exercises, flashcards, and much more that will complement your learning and understanding of human biology.

CHAPTER 8

Respiratory System

CHAPTER CONCEPTS

8.1 The Respiratory System
- What events are required in order to supply cells with oxygen and rid them of carbon dioxide?   142
- How is air that is inhaled or exhaled modified by respiratory surfaces?   142
- What is the path of air, and what are the functions of the organs along that path?   143–45

8.2 Mechanism of Breathing
- Why do physicians measure our ability to move air into and out of the lungs? What measurements do they take?   146
- How is breathing achieved? Is pressure within the lungs greatest during inspiration or expiration?   148–49
- What controls the breathing rate?   149

8.3 Gas Exchanges in the Body
- What are the differences between external respiration and internal respiration?   150–51
- What respiratory pigment is found in human red blood cells? How does it function in the transport of oxygen; carbon dioxide?   150–51

8.4 Respiration and Health
- What are some common respiratory infections and disorders of the upper respiratory tract? Of the lower respiratory tract?   152–54
- What are three respiratory disorders commonly associated with smoking tobacco?   153–54

Just before winning a gold metal for the 400-m race at the 2004 Olympic games, Jeremy Wariner (*center*) of the United States warmed up by stretching, sprinting, and jogging. Onlookers may have thought he was trying to prevent an injury when he ran the race. Maybe, but this type of warmup can also help a runner win the race, primarily because it causes an increase in blood flow to the leg muscles. A good warmup can increase the number of open capillary beds in the region as much as 1,000%. More blood flow brings the fuel and oxygen a runner's working muscles will need, and it also removes the waste products they generate during the race. When muscles contract, lots of CO_2, H^+, and lactic acid enter the bloodstream, and so does heat.

Hemoglobin, the respiratory pigment that carries oxygen, is well adapted to these conditions. As acidity and temperature rise, hemoglobin tends to release more oxygen than otherwise. In distance runners, the body temperature can rise from 98.6°F to 102°F, and pH can be reduced from 7.4 to 6.9, greatly facilitating the release of extra O_2 (20% or more) into the runner's exercising leg muscles.

World-class athletes, such as Jeremy Wariner, need every advantage in order to win a race. Therefore, a prerace warmup is critical, so that the cardiovascular and respiratory systems are ready to perform, even from the moment the race begins. Only if these systems are ready can an athlete hope to win a gold medal at the Olympic games. Even though you may not be a world-class athlete, your cardiovascular and respiratory systems still need to perform optimally when you exercise. Therefore, a warmup is essential for you also, regardless of your chosen sport.

8.1 The Respiratory System

The organs of the respiratory system ensure that oxygen enters the body and carbon dioxide leaves the body. During **inspiration,** or inhalation (breathing in), and **expiration,** or exhalation (breathing out), air is conducted toward or away from the lungs by a series of cavities, tubes, and openings, illustrated in Figure 8.1. **Ventilation** is another term for breathing that encompasses both inspiration and expiration.

The respiratory system also works with the cardiovascular system to accomplish these events:

1. external respiration: exchange of gases (oxygen and carbon dioxide) between air and blood.
2. internal respiration: exchange of gases between blood and tissue fluid.
3. transport of gases to and from the lungs and the tissues.

Cellular respiration uses the oxygen and produces the carbon dioxide that makes gas exchange with the environment necessary. Ventilation and the three events listed here allow cellular respiration to continue.

The Respiratory Tract

Table 8.1 traces the path of air from the nose to the lungs. As air moves along the airways, it is cleansed, warmed, and moistened. Cleansing is accomplished by coarse hairs, cilia, and mucus in the region of the nostrils and by cilia and mucus in the rest of the nasal cavity and the other airways of the respiratory tract. In the nose, the hairs and the cilia act as a screening device. In the trachea and other airways, the cilia beat upward, carrying mucus, dust, and occasional bits of food that "went down the wrong way" into the pharynx, where the accumulation can be swallowed or expectorated. The air is warmed by heat given off by the blood vessels lying close to the lining of the airways, and it is moistened by the wet surface of these passages.

Conversely, as air moves out during expiration, it cools and loses its moisture. As the air cools, it deposits its moisture on the lining of the trachea and the nose, and the nose may even drip as a result of this condensation. The air still retains so much moisture, however, that upon expiration on a cold day, it condenses and forms a small cloud.

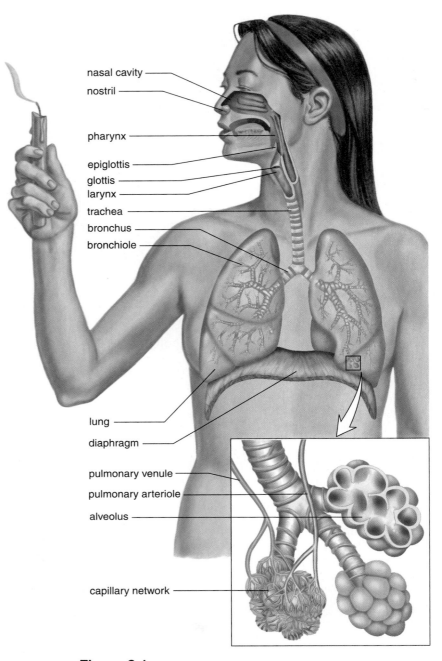

Figure 8.1   The respiratory tract.
The respiratory tract extends from the nose to the lungs. The lungs are composed of air sacs called alveoli. Gas exchange occurs between the air in the alveoli and the blood within a capillary network that surrounds the alveoli. Notice in the blowup that the pulmonary arteriole is colored blue—it carries O_2-poor blood away from the heart to the alveoli. Then, carbon dioxide leaves the blood, and oxygen enters the blood. The pulmonary venule is colored red—it carries O_2-rich blood from the alveoli toward the heart.

Table 8.1	Path of Air	
Structure	**Description**	**Function**
The Upper Respiratory Tract		
Nares	Openings into the nasal cavities	Passage of air into nasal cavities
Nasal cavities	Hollow spaces in nose	Filter, warm, and moisten air
Pharynx	Chamber posterior to oral cavity; lies between nasal cavity and larynx	Connection to surrounding regions
Glottis	Opening into larynx	Passage of air into larynx
Larynx	Cartilaginous organ that houses vocal cords (voice box); composed of the nasopharynx, oropharynx, and the laryngopharynx	Sound production
The Lower Respiratory Tract		
Trachea	Flexible tube that connects larynx with bronchi	Passage of air to bronchi
Bronchi	Paired tubes inferior to the trachea that enter the lungs	Passage of air to lungs
Bronchioles	Branched tubes that lead from bronchi to alveoli (air sacs)	Passage of air to each alveolus
Lungs	Soft, cone-shaped organs that occupy lateral portions of thoracic cavity	Contain alveoli and blood vessels

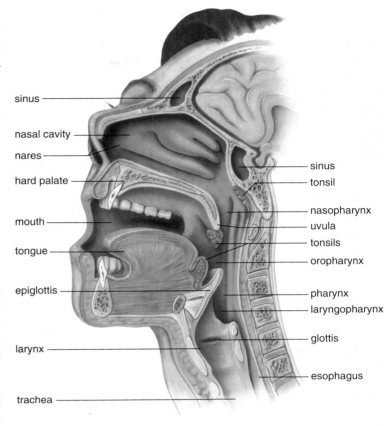

Figure 8.2   The path of air.
This drawing shows the path of air from the nasal cavities to the trachea, which is a part of the lower respiratory tract. The other organs are in the upper respiratory tract.

The Nose

The nose opens at the nares (nostrils) that lead to the **nasal cavities.** The nasal cavities are narrow canals separated from one another by a septum composed of bone and cartilage (Fig. 8.2). Special ciliated cells in the narrow upper recesses of the nasal cavities act as odor receptors. Nerves lead from these cells to the brain, where the impulses generated by the odor receptors are interpreted as smell.

The tear (lacrimal) glands drain into the nasal cavities by way of tear ducts. For this reason, crying produces a runny nose. The nasal cavities also communicate with the cranial sinuses, air-filled mucosa-lined spaces in the skull. If inflammation due to a cold or an allergic reaction blocks the ducts leading from the sinuses, fluid may accumulate, causing a sinus headache.

The nasal cavities empty into the nasopharynx, the upper portion of the pharynx. The auditory tubes lead from the nasopharynx to the middle ears.

The Pharynx

The **pharynx** is a funnel-shaped passageway that connects the nasal and oral cavities to the larynx. Therefore, the pharynx,

which is commonly referred to as the "throat," has three parts: the nasopharynx, where the nasal cavities open above the soft palate; the oropharynx, where the oral cavity opens; and the laryngopharynx, which opens into the larynx.

The tonsils form a protective ring at the junction of the oral cavity and the pharynx. Being lymphatic tissue, the tonsils contain lymphocytes that protect against invasion of foreign antigens that are inhaled. In the tonsils, B cells and T cells are prepared to respond to antigens that may subsequently invade internal tissues and fluids. Therefore, the respiratory tract assists the immune system in maintaining homeostasis.

In the pharynx, the air passage and the food passage cross because the larynx, which receives air, is ventral to the esophagus, which receives food. The larynx lies at the top of the trachea. The larynx and trachea are normally open, allowing air to pass, but the esophagus is normally closed and opens only when a person swallows.

Air from either the nose or the mouth enters the pharynx and then continues to the lungs.

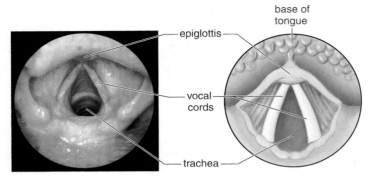

Figure 8.3   **Placement of the vocal cords.**
Viewed from above, the vocal cords can be seen to stretch across the glottis, the opening to the trachea. When air is expelled through the glottis, the vocal cords vibrate, producing sound. The glottis is narrow when we produce a high-pitched sound, and it widens as the pitch deepens.

The Larynx

The **larynx** is a cartilaginous structure that serves as a passageway for air between the pharynx and the trachea. The larynx can be pictured as a triangular box whose apex, the Adam's apple, is located at the front of the neck. At the

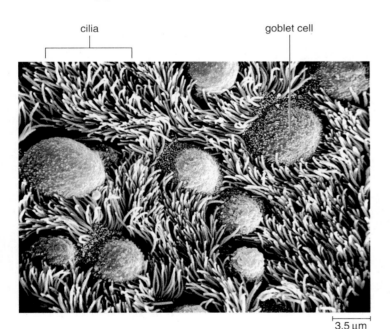

Figure 8.4   **Trachea.**
Scanning electron micrograph of the surface of the mucous membrane lining the trachea consisting of goblet cells and ciliated cells. The cilia sweep mucus and debris embedded in it toward the pharynx, where it is swallowed or expectorated. Smoking causes the cilia to disappear; consequently, debris now enters the bronchi and lungs.
© Dr. Kessel & Dr. Kardon/Tissues & Organs/Visuals Unlimited

top of the larynx is a variable-sized opening called the **glottis.** When food is swallowed, the larynx moves upward against the **epiglottis,** a flap of tissue that prevents food from passing into the larynx. You can detect this movement by placing your hand gently on your larynx and swallowing.

The larynx is called the voice box because it houses the vocal cords. The **vocal cords** are mucosal folds supported by elastic ligaments, which are stretched across the glottis (Fig. 8.3). When air passes through the glottis, the vocal cords vibrate, producing sound. At the time of puberty, the growth of the larynx and the vocal cords is much more rapid and accentuated in the male than in the female, causing the male to have a more prominent Adam's apple and a deeper voice. The voice "breaks" in the young male due to his inability to control the longer vocal cords. These changes cause the lower pitch of the voice in males.

The high or low pitch of the voice is regulated when speaking and singing by changing the tension on the vocal cords. The greater the tension, as when the glottis becomes narrower, the higher the pitch. When the glottis is wider, the pitch is lower (Fig. 8.3, *right*). The loudness, or intensity, of the voice depends upon the amplitude of the vibrations—that is, the degree to which the vocal cords vibrate.

The Trachea

Whereas the nasal cavities, pharynx, and larynx are a part of the upper respiratory tract, the trachea and the rest of the respiratory system are in the lower respiratory tract. The **trachea,** commonly called the windpipe, is a tube connecting the larynx to the primary bronchi. Its walls consist of connective tissue and smooth muscle reinforced by C-shaped cartilaginous rings.

The trachea lies ventral to the esophagus. The open part of the C-shaped rings faces the esophagus, and this allows the esophagus to expand when swallowing. The mucous membrane that lines the trachea has an outer layer of pseudostratified ciliated columnar epithelium. (*Pseudostratified* means that while the epithelium appears to be layered, actually each cell touches the basement membrane.) The cilia that project from the epithelium keep the lungs clean by sweeping mucus, produced by goblet cells, and debris toward the pharynx (Fig. 8.4). When one coughs, the tracheal wall contracts, narrowing its diameter. Therefore, coughing causes air to move more rapidly through the trachea, helping to expel mucus and foreign objects. Smoking is known to destroy the cilia, and consequently the soot in cigarette smoke collects in the lungs. Smoking is discussed more fully in the Health Focus on page 155.

If the trachea is blocked because of illness or the accidental swallowing of a foreign object, it is possible to insert a breathing tube by way of an incision made in the trachea. This tube acts as an artificial air intake and exhaust duct. The operation is called a **tracheostomy.**

The Bronchial Tree

The trachea divides into right and left primary bronchi (sing., **bronchus**), which lead into the right and left lungs (see Fig. 8.1). The bronchi branch into a great number of secondary bronchi that eventually lead to **bronchioles.** The bronchi resemble the trachea in structure, but as the bronchial tubes divide and subdivide, their walls become thinner, and the small rings of cartilage are no longer present. During an asthma attack, the smooth muscle of the bronchioles contracts, causing bronchiolar constriction and characteristic wheezing. Each bronchiole leads to an elongated space enclosed by a multitude of air pockets, or sacs, called alveoli (sing., **alveolus**). The components of the bronchiole tree beyond the primary bronchi compose the lungs.

The Lungs

The **lungs** are paired, cone-shaped organs that occupy the thoracic cavity, except for the central area that contains the trachea, the heart, and esophagus. The right lung has three lobes, and the left lung has two lobes, allowing room for the heart, which points left. A lobe is further divided into lobules, and each lobule has a bronchiole serving many alveoli.

The lungs follow the contours of the thoracic cavity including the diaphragm, the muscle that separates the thoracic cavity from the abdominal cavity. Each lung is enclosed by pleura, a double layer of serous membrane that produces serous fluid. The parietal pleura adheres to the thoracic cavity and the visceral pleura adheres to the surface of the lung. Surface tension is the tendency for water molecules to cling to one another due to hydrogen bonding between molecules. Surface tension holds the two pleural layers together, and therefore the lungs must follow the movement of the thorax when breathing occurs.

The Alveoli

The lungs have about 300 million alveoli, with a total cross-sectional area of 50–70 m². Each alveolar sac is surrounded by blood capillaries. The wall of the sac and the wall of the capillary are largely simple squamous epithelium—thin flattened cells—and this facilitates gas exchange. Gas exchange occurs between air in the alveoli and blood in the capillaries (Fig. 8.5). Oxygen diffuses across the alveolar wall and enters the bloodstream, while carbon dioxide diffuses from the blood across the alveolar wall to enter the alveoli.

The alveoli of human lungs are lined with a **surfactant,** a film of lipoprotein that lowers the surface tension and prevents them from closing. The lungs collapse in some newborn babies, especially premature infants, who lack this film. The condition, called **infant respiratory distress syndrome,** is now treatable by surfactant replacement therapy.

Air passes through the nose, pharynx, larynx, trachea, and bronchial tree before reaching the lungs.

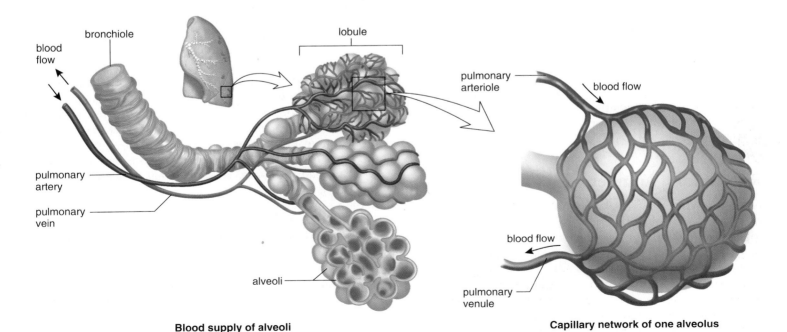

Blood supply of alveoli

Capillary network of one alveolus

Figure 8.5 **Gas exchange in the lungs.**
The lungs consist of alveoli surrounded by an extensive capillary network. Notice that the pulmonary artery and arteriole carry O_2-poor blood (colored blue), and the pulmonary vein and venule carry O_2-rich blood (colored red).

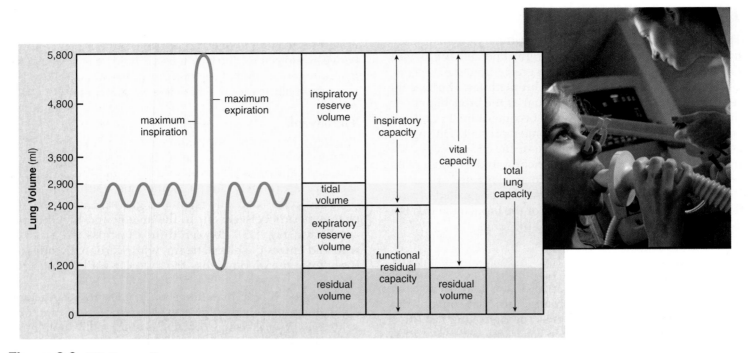

Figure 8.6 **Vital capacity.**
A spirometer measures the amount of air inhaled and exhaled with each breath. During inspiration, the pen moves up, and during expiration, the pen moves down. Vital capacity (red) is the maximum amount of air a person can exhale after taking the deepest inhalation possible.

8.2 Mechanism of Breathing

As ventilation occurs, air moves into the lungs from the nose or mouth during inspiration and then moves out of the lungs during expiration. A free flow of air from the nose or mouth to the lungs and from the lungs to the nose or mouth is vitally important. Therefore, a technique has been developed that allows physicians to determine if there is a medical problem that prevents the lungs from filling with air upon inspiration and releasing it from the body upon expiration. This technique is illustrated in Figure 8.6, which shows the measurements recorded by a spirometer when a person breathes as directed by a technician.

Respiratory Volumes

Normally when we are relaxed, only a small amount of air moves in and out with each breath. This amount of air, called the **tidal volume,** is only about 500 mL.

It is possible to increase the amount of air inhaled, and therefore the amount exhaled, by deep breathing. The maximum volume of air that can be moved in plus the maximum amount that can be moved out during a single breath is called the **vital capacity.** It's called vital capacity because your life depends on breathing, and the more air you can move, the better off you are. A number of different illnesses, discussed at the end of this chapter, can decrease vital capacity.

Vital capacity varies by how much we can increase inspiration and expiration over the tidal volume amount. We can increase inspiration by expanding the chest and therefore, the lungs. Forced inspiration **(inspiratory reserve volume)** usually increases by 2,900 mL, and that's quite a bit more than a tidal volume of only 500 mL! We can increase expiration by contracting the abdominal and thoracic muscles. This so-called **expiratory reserve volume** is usually about 1,400 mL of air. You can see from Figure 8.6 that vital capacity is the sum of tidal, inspiratory reserve, and expiratory reserve volumes.

It's a curious fact that some of the inhaled air never reaches the lungs; instead, it fills the nasal cavities, trachea, bronchi, and bronchioles (see Fig. 8.1). These passages are not used for gas exchange, and therefore they are said to contain **dead air space.** To ensure that inhaled air reaches the lungs, it is better to breathe slowly and deeply. Also, note in Figure 8.6 that even after a very deep exhalation, some air (about 1,000 mL) remains in the lungs; this is called the **residual volume.** This air is no longer useful for gas exchange. In some lung diseases to be discussed later, the residual volume builds up because the individual has difficulty emptying the lungs. This means that the vital capacity is reduced because the lungs are filled with useless air.

The air used for gas exchange excludes both the air in the dead space of the respiratory tract and the residual volume in the lungs.

Ecology Focus

Photochemical Smog Can Kill

Most industrialized cities have photochemical smog, at least occasionally. Photochemical smog arises when primary pollutants react with one another under the influence of sunlight to form a more deadly combination of chemicals. For example, two primary pollutants, nitrogen oxides (NO_x) and volatile organic compounds (VOCs) including hydrocarbons, as well as alcohols, aldehydes, and ethers, react with one another in the presence of sunlight to produce nitrogen dioxide (NO_2), ozone (O_3), and PAN (peroxyacetylnitrate). Ozone and PAN are commonly referred to as oxidants. Breathing oxidants affects the respiratory and nervous systems, resulting in respiratory distress, headache, and exhaustion.

Cities with warm, sunny climates that are large and industrialized, such as Los Angeles, Denver, and Salt Lake City in the United States, Sydney in Australia, Mexico City in Mexico, and Buenos Aires in Argentina, are particularly susceptible to photochemical smog. If the city is surrounded by hills, a thermal inversion may aggravate the situation. Normally, warm air near the ground rises, so that pollutants are dispersed and carried away by air currents. But sometimes during a thermal inversion, smog gets trapped near the Earth by a blanket of warm air (Fig. 8A). This may occur when a cold front brings in cold air, which settles beneath a warm layer. The trapped pollutants cannot disperse, and

the results are dangerous to one's respiratory health. Even healthy adults experience a reduction in lung capacity when exposed to photochemical smog for long periods or during vigorous outdoor activities. Repeated exposures to high concentrations of ozone are associated with respiratory problems, such as an increased rate of lung infections and permanent lung damage. Children, the elderly, asthmatics, and individuals with emphysema or other similar disorders are particularly at risk.

Even though we have federal legislation to bring air pollution under control, more than half the people in the United States live in cities polluted by too much smog. In the long run, pollution prevention is usually easier and cheaper than pollution cleanup. Some prevention suggestions are as follows:

- Encourage use of public transportation and burn fuels that do not produce pollutants.
- Increase recycling in order to reduce the amount of waste that is incinerated.
- Reduce energy use so that power plants need to provide less.
- Use renewable energy sources, such as solar, wind, or water power.
- Require industries to meet clean-air standards.

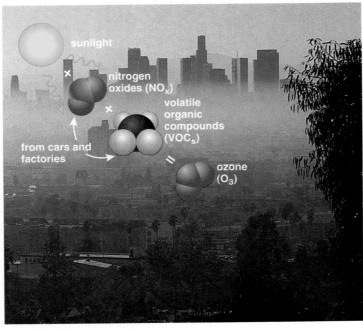

a. Ground-level ozone formation

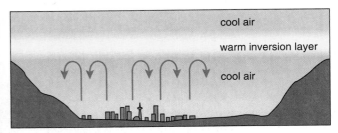

b. Normal pattern

c. Thermal inversion

Figure 8A Thermal inversion.
a. Los Angeles is the "air pollution capital" of the world. Its millions of cars and thousands of factories make it particularly susceptible to photochemical smog, which contains ozone due to the chemical reaction shown. **b.** Normally, pollutants escape into the atmosphere when warm air rises. **c.** During a thermal inversion, a layer of warm air (warm inversion layer) overlies and traps pollutants in cool air below.

Inspiration and Expiration

To understand ventilation, the manner in which air enters and exits the lungs, it is necessary to remember the following facts:

1. Normally, there is a continuous column of air from the pharynx to the alveoli of the lungs.
2. The lungs lie within the sealed-off thoracic cavity. The rib cage, consisting of the ribs joined to the vertebral column posteriorly and to the sternum anteriorly, forms the top and sides of the thoracic cavity. The intercostal muscles lie between the ribs. The diaphragm and connective tissue form the floor of the thoracic cavity.
3. The lungs adhere to the thoracic wall by way of the pleura. Any space between the two pleurae is minimal due to the surface tension of the fluid between them.

Inspiration

Inspiration is the active phase of ventilation because this is the phase in which the diaphragm and the external intercostal muscles contract (Fig. 8.7*a*). In its relaxed state, the diaphragm is dome-shaped; during deep inspiration, it contracts and lowers. Also, the external intercostal muscles contract, and the rib cage moves upward and outward.

Following contraction of the diaphragm and the external intercostal muscles, the volume of the thoracic cavity will be larger than it was before. As the thoracic volume increases, the lungs expand. Now the air pressure within the alveoli decreases, creating a partial vacuum. Because alveolar pressure is now less than atmospheric pressure (air pressure outside the lungs), air naturally flows from outside the body into the respiratory passages and into the alveoli.

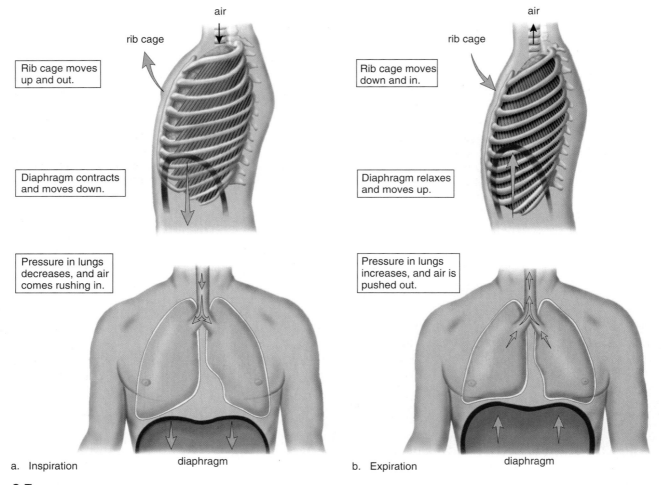

air

rib cage

Rib cage moves up and out.

Diaphragm contracts and moves down.

Pressure in lungs decreases, and air comes rushing in.

a. Inspiration

diaphragm

air

rib cage

Rib cage moves down and in.

Diaphragm relaxes and moves up.

Pressure in lungs increases, and air is pushed out.

b. Expiration

diaphragm

Figure 8.7 **Inspiration versus expiration.**
To understand ventilation, it is necessary to realize that the lungs adhere to the thoracic cavity by way of the pleura. **a.** During inspiration, the thoracic cavity and, therefore, the lungs expand so that air is drawn in. **b.** During expiration, the thoracic cavity and, therefore, the lungs resume their original positions and pressures. Now air is forced out.

It is important to realize that air comes into the lungs because they have already opened up; air does not force the lungs open. This is why it is sometimes said that *humans inhale by negative pressure.* The creation of a partial vacuum in the alveoli causes air to enter the lungs. While inspiration is the active phase of breathing, the actual flow of air into the alveoli is passive.

Expiration

Usually, expiration is the passive phase of breathing, and no effort is required to bring it about. During expiration, the elastic properties of the thoracic wall and lungs cause them to recoil. In addition, the lungs recoil because the surface tension of the fluid lining the alveoli tends to draw them closed. During expiration, the abdominal organs press up against the diaphragm, and the rib cage moves down and inward (Fig. 8.7b). What keeps the alveoli from collapsing as a part of expiration? Recall that the presence of surfactant lowers the surface tension within the alveoli. Also, as the lungs recoil, the pressure between the pleura decreases, and this tends to make the alveoli stay open. The importance of the reduced intrapleural pressure is demonstrated when, by design or accident, air enters the intrapleural space. Now the lung collapses.

The diaphragm and external intercostal muscles are usually relaxed when expiration occurs. However, when breathing is deeper and/or more rapid, expiration can be active. Contraction of the internal intercostal muscles can force the rib cage to move downward and inward. Also, when the abdominal wall muscles contract, they push on the viscera, which push against the diaphragm, and the increased pressure in the thoracic cavity helps expel air.

Control of Ventilation

Normally, adults have a breathing rate of 12 to 20 ventilations per minute. The rhythm of ventilation is controlled by a **respiratory center** located in the medulla oblongata of the brain.

The respiratory center automatically sends out impulses by way of nerves to the diaphragm and the external intercostal muscles of the rib cage, causing inspiration to occur (Fig. 8.8). When the respiratory center stops sending neuronal signals to the diaphragm and the rib cage, the diaphragm relaxes and resumes its dome shape. Now expiration occurs.

Although the respiratory center automatically controls the rate and depth of breathing, its activity can also be influenced by nervous input and chemical input. Following forced inspiration, stretch receptors in the alveolar walls initiate inhibitory nerve impulses that travel from the inflated lungs to the respiratory center. This stops the respiratory center from sending out nerve impulses.

Chemical Input   The respiratory center is directly sensitive to the levels of hydrogen ions (H^+). However, when

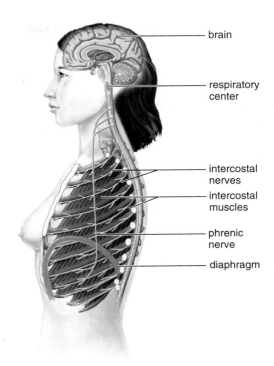

Figure 8.8   Nervous control of breathing.
During inspiration, the respiratory center, located in the medulla oblongata, stimulates the external intercostal (rib) muscles to contract via the intercostal nerves and stimulates the diaphragm to contract via the phrenic nerve. The thoracic cavity, and then the lungs, expand and air comes rushing in. Expiration occurs due to a lack of stimulation from the respiratory center to the diaphragm and intercostal muscles. Now, as the thoracic cavity, and then the lungs, resume their original size, air is pushed out.

carbon dioxide (CO_2) enters the blood, it reacts with water and releases hydrogen ions. In this way, carbon dioxide participates in regulating the breathing rate. When hydrogen ions rise in the blood, the respiratory center increases the rate and depth of breathing. The center is not affected directly by low oxygen (O_2) levels. However, chemoreceptors in the **carotid bodies,** located in the carotid arteries, and in the **aortic bodies,** located in the aorta, are sensitive to the level of oxygen in the blood. When the concentration of oxygen decreases, these bodies communicate with the respiratory center, and the rate and depth of breathing increase.

During inspiration, due to nervous stimulation, the diaphragm lowers, and the rib cage lifts up and out. During expiration, due to a lack of nervous stimulation, the diaphragm rises, and the rib cage lowers.

8.3 Gas Exchanges in the Body

Gas exchange is critical to homeostasis. The act of breathing brings oxygen in air to the lungs and carbon dioxide from the lungs to outside the body. As mentioned previously, respiration includes not only the exchange of gases in the lungs, but also the exchange of gases in the tissues (Fig. 8.9).

The principles of diffusion, alone, govern whether O_2 or CO_2 enters or leaves the blood in the lungs and in the tissues. Gases exert pressure, and the amount of pressure each gas exerts is called its partial pressure, symbolized as P_{O_2} and P_{CO_2}. If the partial pressure of oxygen differs across a membrane, oxygen will diffuse from the higher to lower partial pressure.

External Respiration

External respiration refers to the exchange of gases between air in the alveoli and blood in the pulmonary capillaries (see Fig. 8.5). Blood in the pulmonary capillaries has a higher P_{CO_2} than atmospheric air. Therefore, *CO_2 diffuses out of the plasma into the lungs.* Most of the CO_2 is carried as **bicarbonate ions** (HCO_3^-). As the little remaining free CO_2 begins to diffuse out, the following reaction is driven to the right:

$$H^+ + HCO_3^- \xrightarrow{\text{carbonic anhydrase}} H_2CO_3 \longrightarrow H_2O + CO_2$$

hydrogen ion   bicarbonate ion   carbonic acid   water   carbon dioxide

The enzyme **carbonic anhydrase,** present in red blood cells, speeds the breakdown of carbonic acid (H_2CO_3).

What happens if you hyperventilate (breathe at a high rate), and therefore push this reaction far to the right? The blood will have fewer hydrogen ions, and alkalosis, a high blood pH, results. In that case, breathing will be inhibited, but in the meantime, you may suffer various symptoms from dizziness to tetanic contractions of the muscles. What happens if you hypoventilate (breathe at a low rate) and this reaction does not occur? Hydrogen ions build up in the blood, and acidosis will occur. Buffers may compensate for the low pH, and breathing will most likely increase. Otherwise, you may become comatose and die.

The pressure pattern for O_2 during external respiration is the reverse of that for CO_2. Blood in the pulmonary capillaries is low in oxygen, and alveolar air contains a higher partial pressure of oxygen. Therefore, *O_2 diffuses into plasma and then into red blood cells in the lungs.* Hemoglobin takes up this oxygen and becomes **oxyhemoglobin** (HbO_2):

$$Hb + O_2 \longrightarrow HbO_2$$

deoxyhemoglobin   oxygen   oxyhemoglobin

Internal Respiration

Internal respiration refers to the exchange of gases between the blood in systemic capillaries and the tissue fluid. In Figure 8.9, internal respiration is shown in the upper body and the lower body; however, the same events occur in both regions. Blood in the systemic capillaries is a bright red color because red blood cells contain oxyhemoglobin. Because the temperature in the tissues is higher and the pH is lower, oxyhemoglobin naturally gives up oxygen. After oxyhemoglobin gives up O_2, it diffuses out of the blood into the tissues:

$$HbO_2 \longrightarrow Hb + O_2$$

oxyhemoglobin   deoxyhemoglobin   oxygen

Oxygen diffuses out of the blood into the tissues because the P_{O_2} of tissue fluid is lower than that of blood. The lower P_{O_2} is due to cells continuously using up oxygen in cellular respiration. *Carbon dioxide diffuses into the blood from the tissues* because the P_{CO_2} of tissue fluid is higher than that of blood. Carbon dioxide, produced continuously by cells, collects in tissue fluid.

After CO_2 diffuses into the blood, it enters the red blood cells, where a small amount is taken up by hemoglobin, forming **carbaminohemoglobin** ($HbCO_2$). Most of the CO_2 combines with water, forming carbonic acid (H_2CO_3), which dissociates to hydrogen ions (H^+) and bicarbonate ions (HCO_3^-). The increased concentration of CO_2 in the blood drives the reaction to the right:

$$CO_2 + H_2O \xrightarrow{\text{carbonic anhydrase}} H_2CO_3 \longrightarrow H^+ + HCO_3^-$$

carbon dioxide   water   carbonic acid   hydrogen ion   bicarbonate ion

The enzyme carbonic anhydrase, mentioned previously, speeds the reaction. Bicarbonate ions diffuse out of red blood cells and are carried in the plasma. The globin portion of hemoglobin combines with excess hydrogen ions produced by the overall reaction, and Hb becomes HHb, called **reduced hemoglobin.** In this way, the pH of blood remains fairly constant. Blood that leaves the systemic capillaries is a dark maroon color because red blood cells contain reduced hemoglobin.

Hemoglobin activity is essential to the transport of gases, and therefore to external and internal respiration. External and internal respiration are the movement of gases between pulmonary capillaries and alveoli and between the systemic capillaries and body tissue fluid, respectively. Both processes depend on the process of diffusion.

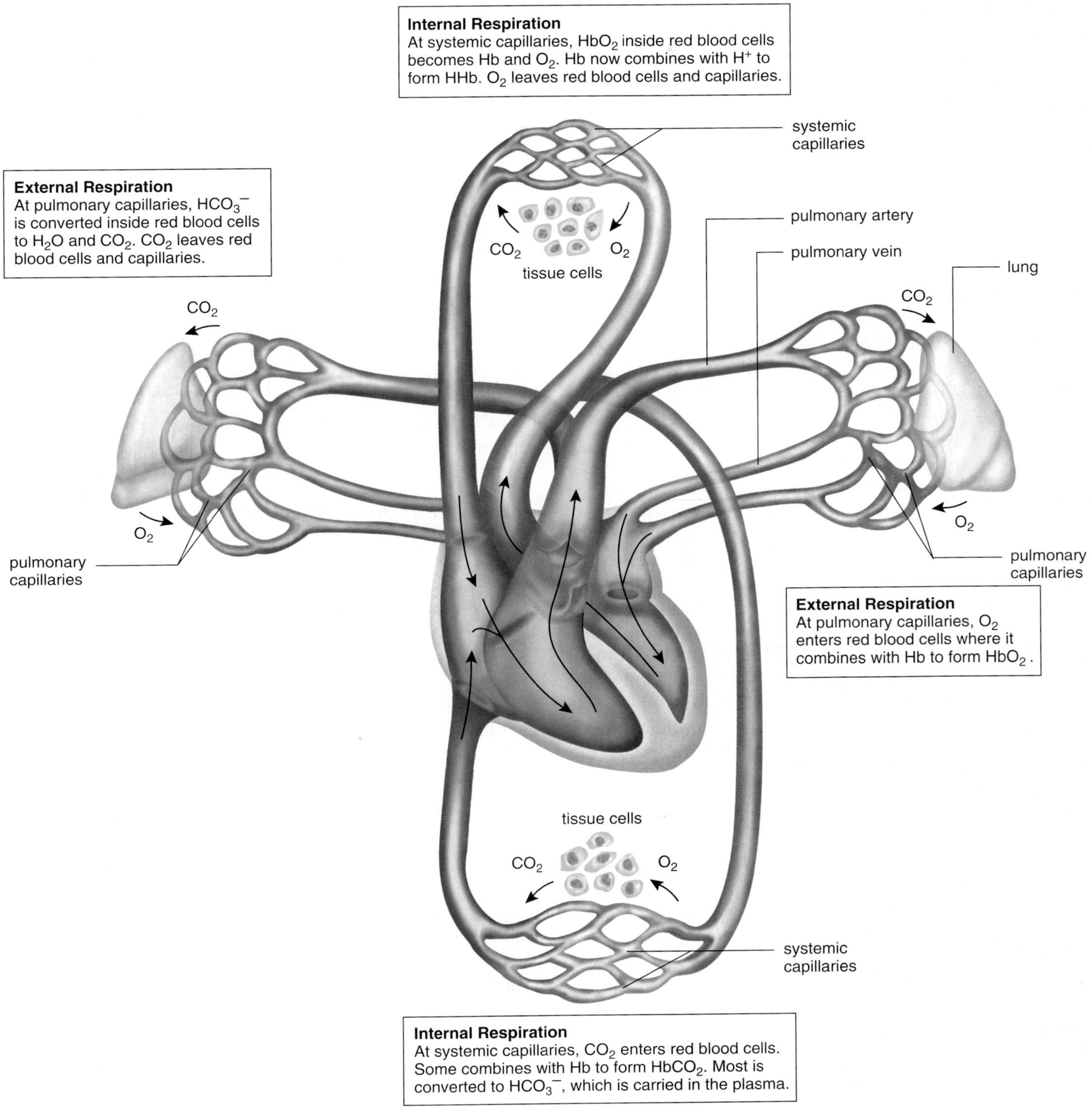

Visual Focus

Internal Respiration
At systemic capillaries, HbO$_2$ inside red blood cells becomes Hb and O$_2$. Hb now combines with H$^+$ to form HHb. O$_2$ leaves red blood cells and capillaries.

External Respiration
At pulmonary capillaries, HCO$_3^-$ is converted inside red blood cells to H$_2$O and CO$_2$. CO$_2$ leaves red blood cells and capillaries.

External Respiration
At pulmonary capillaries, O$_2$ enters red blood cells where it combines with Hb to form HbO$_2$.

Internal Respiration
At systemic capillaries, CO$_2$ enters red blood cells. Some combines with Hb to form HbCO$_2$. Most is converted to HCO$_3^-$, which is carried in the plasma.

systemic capillaries · pulmonary artery · pulmonary vein · lung · tissue cells · CO$_2$ · O$_2$ · pulmonary capillaries

Figure 8.9   External and internal respiration.
During external respiration in the lungs, CO$_2$ leaves the blood and O$_2$ enters the blood. During internal respiration in the tissues, O$_2$ leaves the blood and CO$_2$ enters the blood.

8.4 Respiration and Health

The respiratory tract is constantly exposed to environmental air. The quality of this air and whether it contains infectious pathogens, such as bacteria and viruses, can affect our health.

Upper Respiratory Tract Infections

The upper respiratory tract consists of the nasal cavities, the pharynx, and the larynx. Upper respiratory infections (URI) can spread from the nasal cavities to the sinuses, middle ears, and larynx. Viral infections sometimes lead to secondary bacterial infections. What we call "strep throat" is a primary bacterial infection caused by *Streptococcus pyogenes* that can lead to a generalized upper respiratory infection and even a systemic (affecting the body as a whole) infection. Although antibiotics have no effect on viral infections, they are successfully used to treat most bacterial infections, including strep throat. The symptoms of strep throat are severe sore throat, high fever, and white patches on a dark red throat.

Sinusitis

Sinusitis is an infection of the cranial sinuses, the cavities within the facial skeleton that drain into the nasal cavities. Only about 1–3% of URIs are accompanied by sinusitis. Sinusitis develops when nasal congestion blocks the tiny openings leading to the sinuses. Symptoms include postnasal discharge, as well as facial pain that worsens when the patient bends forward. Pain and tenderness usually occur over the lower forehead or over the cheeks. If the latter, toothache is also a complaint. Successful treatment depends on restoring proper drainage of the sinuses. Even a hot shower and sleeping upright can be helpful. Otherwise, spray decongestants are preferred over oral antihistamines, which thicken rather than liquefy the material trapped in the sinuses.

Otitis Media

Otitis media is an infection of the middle ear. The middle ear is not a part of the respiratory tract, but this infection is considered here because it is a complication often seen in children who have a nasal infection. Infection can spread by way of the **auditory (Eustachian) tube** that leads from the nasopharynx to the middle ear. Pain is the primary symptom of a middle ear infection. A sense of fullness, hearing loss, vertigo (dizziness), and fever may also be present. Antibiotics are prescribed if necessary, but physicians are aware today that overuse of antibiotics can lead to resistance of bacteria to antibiotics. Tubes (called tympanostomy tubes) are sometimes placed in the eardrums of children with multiple recurrences to help prevent the buildup of pressure in the middle ear and the possibility of hearing loss. Normally, the tubes fall out with time.

Tonsillitis

Tonsillitis occurs when the **tonsils,** masses of lymphatic tissue in the pharynx, become inflamed and enlarged. The tonsils in the posterior wall of the nasopharynx are often called adenoids. If tonsillitis occurs frequently and enlargement makes breathing difficult, the tonsils can be removed surgically in a **tonsillectomy.** Fewer tonsillectomies are performed today than in the past because we now know that the tonsils remove many of the pathogens that enter the pharynx; therefore, they are a first line of defense against invasion of the body.

Laryngitis

Laryngitis is an infection of the larynx with accompanying hoarseness leading to the inability to talk in an audible voice. Usually, laryngitis disappears with treatment of the URI. Persistent hoarseness without the presence of a URI is one of the warning signs of cancer, and therefore should be looked into by a physician.

Lower Respiratory Tract Disorders

Lower respiratory tract disorders include infections, restrictive pulmonary disorders, obstructive pulmonary disorders, and lung cancer.

Lower Respiratory Infections

Acute bronchitis, pneumonia, and tuberculosis are infections of the lower respiratory tract. **Acute bronchitis** is an infection of the primary and secondary bronchi. Usually, it is preceded by a viral URI that has led to a secondary bacterial infection. Most likely, a nonproductive cough has become a deep cough that expectorates mucus and perhaps pus.

Pneumonia is a viral or bacterial infection of the lungs in which the bronchi and alveoli fill with thick fluid (Fig. 8.10). Most often, it is preceded by influenza. High fever and chills, with headache and chest pain, are symptoms of pneumonia. Rather than being a generalized lung infection, pneumonia may be localized in specific lobules of the lungs; obviously, the more lobules involved, the more serious is the infection. Pneumonia can be caused by a bacterium that is usually held in check but has gained the upper hand due to stress and/or reduced immunity. AIDS patients are subject to a particularly rare form of pneumonia caused by the protozoan *Pneumocystis jiroveci* (formerly *Pneumocystis carinii*). Pneumonia of this type is almost never seen in individuals with a healthy immune system.

Pulmonary tuberculosis is caused by the tubercle bacillus, a type of bacterium. When tubercle bacilli invade the lung tissue, the cells build a protective capsule around the foreigners, isolating them from the rest of the body. This tiny capsule is called a tubercle. If the resistance of the body is high, the imprisoned organisms die, but if the resistance is low, the organisms eventually can be liberated. If a chest X ray detects active tubercles, the individual is put on appropriate drug therapy to ensure the localization of the disease and the eventual destruction of any live bacteria. It is possible to tell if a person has ever been exposed to tuberculosis with a test in which a highly diluted extract of the bacillus is injected into the skin of the patient. A person who has never been in contact with the tubercle bacillus shows no reaction, but one who has had or is fighting an infection shows an area of inflammation that peaks in about 48 hours.

Restrictive Pulmonary Disorders

In restrictive pulmonary disorders, vital capacity is reduced because the lungs have lost their elasticity. Inhaling particles such as silica (sand), coal dust, asbestos, and, now it seems, fiberglass can lead to **pulmonary fibrosis,** a condition in which fibrous connective tissue builds up in the lungs. The lungs cannot inflate properly and are always tending toward deflation. Breathing asbestos is also associated with the development of cancer. Because asbestos was formerly used widely as a fireproofing and insulating agent, unwarranted exposure has occurred. It has been projected that 2 million deaths caused by asbestos exposure—mostly in the workplace—will occur in the United States between 1990 and 2020.

Obstructive Pulmonary Disorders

In obstructive pulmonary disorders, air does not flow freely in the airways, and the time it takes to inhale or exhale maximally is greatly increased. Several disorders, including chronic bronchitis, emphysema, and asthma, are collectively referred to as chronic obstructive pulmonary disease (COPD) because they tend to recur.

In **chronic bronchitis,** the airways are inflamed and filled with mucus. A cough that brings up mucus is common. The bronchi have undergone degenerative changes, including

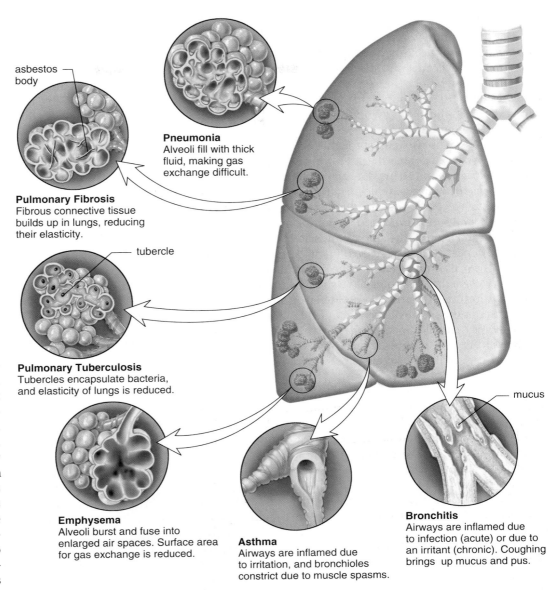

Figure 8.10   Common bronchial and pulmonary diseases.
Exposure to infectious pathogens and/or polluted air, including tobacco smoke, causes the diseases and disorders shown here.

the loss of cilia and their normal cleansing action. Under these conditions, an infection is more likely to occur. Smoking is the most frequent cause of chronic bronchitis. Exposure to other pollutants can also cause chronic bronchitis.

Emphysema is a chronic and incurable disorder in which the alveoli are distended and their walls damaged so that the surface area available for gas exchange is reduced. Emphysema is often preceded by chronic bronchitis. Air trapped in the lungs leads to alveolar damage and a noticeable ballooning of the chest. The elastic recoil of the lungs is reduced, so not only are the airways narrowed, but the driving force behind expiration is also reduced. The victim is breathless and may have a cough. Because the surface area for gas exchange is reduced, less oxygen reaches the heart and the brain. Even so, the heart works furiously to force more blood through the lungs, and an increased workload on the heart can result. Lack of oxygen to the brain can make the person feel depressed, sluggish, and irritable. Exercise, drug therapy, supplemental oxygen, and giving up smoking may relieve the symptoms and possibly slow the progression of emphysema.

Asthma is a disease of the bronchi and bronchioles that is marked by wheezing, breathlessness, and sometimes a cough and expectoration of mucus. The airways are unusually sensitive to specific irritants, which can include a wide range of allergens such as pollen, animal dander, dust, tobacco smoke, and industrial fumes. Even cold air can be an irritant. When exposed to the irritant, the smooth muscle in the bronchioles undergoes spasms. It now appears that chemical mediators given off by immune cells in the bronchioles cause the spasms. Most asthma patients have some degree of bronchial inflammation that reduces the diameter of the airways and contributes to the seriousness of an attack. Asthma is not curable, but it is treatable. Special inhalers can control the inflammation and hopefully prevent an attack, while other types of inhalers can stop the muscle spasms should an attack occur.

Lung Cancer

Lung cancer is more prevalent in men than in women, but recently lung cancer has surpassed breast cancer as a cause of death in women. The recent increase in the incidence of lung cancer in women is directly correlated to increased numbers of women who smoke. Autopsies on smokers have revealed the progressive steps by which the most common form of lung cancer develops. The first event appears to be thickening and callusing of the cells lining the bronchi. (Callusing occurs whenever cells are exposed to irritants.) Then cilia are lost, making it impossible to prevent dust and dirt from settling in the lungs. Following this, cells with atypical nuclei appear in the callused lining. A tumor consisting of disordered cells with atypical nuclei is considered cancer in situ (at one location). A normal lung versus a lung with cancerous tumors is shown in Figure 8.11. A final step occurs when some of these cells break loose and penetrate other tissues, a process called metastasis. Now the cancer has spread. The original tumor may grow until a bronchus is blocked, cutting off the supply of air to that lung. The entire lung then collapses, the secretions trapped in the lung spaces become infected, and pneumonia or a lung abscess (localized area of pus) results. The only treatment that offers a possibility of cure is to remove a lobe or the whole lung before metastasis has had time to occur. This operation is called **pneumonectomy.** If the cancer has spread, chemotherapy and radiation are also required.

The Health Focus on page 155 lists the various illnesses, including cancer, that are apt to occur when a person smokes. Current research indicates that passive smoking (second-hand smoke)—exposure to smoke related by others who are smoking—can also cause lung cancer and other illnesses associated with smoking. If a person stops voluntary smoking and avoids passive smoking and if the body tissues are not already cancerous, the lungs may return to normal over time.

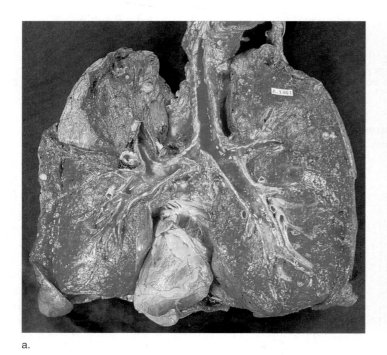

a.

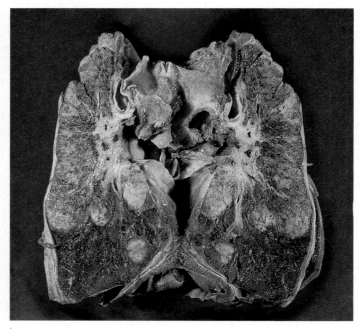

b.

Figure 8.11   **Normal lung versus cancerous lung.**
a. Normal lung with heart in place. Note the healthy red color. **b.** Lungs of a heavy smoker. Notice how black the lungs are except where cancerous tumors have formed.

Health Focus

The Most Often Asked Questions About Tobacco and Health

Is there a safe way to smoke?

No. All forms of tobacco can cause damage, and smoking even a small amount is dangerous. Tobacco is perhaps the only legal product whose advertised and intended use—that is, smoking it—will hurt the body.

Does smoking cause cancer?

Yes, and not only lung cancer. Besides lung cancer, smoking a pipe, cigarettes, or cigars is also a major cause of cancers of the mouth, larynx (voice box), and esophagus. In addition, smoking increases the risk of cancer of the bladder, kidney, pancreas, stomach, and uterine cervix.

What are the chances of being cured of lung cancer?

Very low; the five-year survival rate is only 13%. Fortunately, lung cancer is a largely preventable disease. In other words, by not smoking, you can probably prevent it.

Does smoking cause other lung diseases?

Yes. It leads to chronic bronchitis, a disease in which the airways produce excess mucus, forcing the smoker to cough frequently. Smoking is also the major cause of emphysema, a disease that slowly destroys a person's ability to breathe. Chances of chronic bronchitis and pulmonary emphysema are higher in smokers than in nonsmokers.

Why do smokers have "smoker's cough"?

Normally, cilia (tiny hair-like formations that line the airways) beat outwards and "sweep" harmful material out of the lungs. Smoke, however, decreases this sweeping action, so some of the poisons in the smoke remain in the lungs.

If you smoke but don't inhale, is there any danger?

Yes. Wherever smoke touches living cells, it does harm. So, even if smokers of pipes, cigarettes, and cigars don't inhale, they are at an increased risk for lip, mouth, and tongue cancer.

Does smoking affect the heart?

Yes. Smoking increases the risk of heart disease, which is the United States' number-one killer. Smoking, high blood pressure, high cholesterol, and lack of exercise are all risk factors for heart disease. Smoking alone doubles the risk of heart disease.

Is there any risk for pregnant women and their babies?

Pregnant women who smoke endanger the health and lives of their unborn babies. When a pregnant woman smokes, she really is smoking for two because the nicotine, carbon monoxide, and other dangerous chemicals in smoke enter her bloodstream and then pass into the baby's body. Smoking mothers have more stillbirths and babies of low birth weight than nonsmoking mothers.

Does smoking cause any special health problems for women?

Yes. Women who smoke and use the birth control pill have an increased risk of stroke and blood clots in the legs. In addition, women who smoke increase their chances of getting cancer of the uterine cervix.

What are some of the short-term effects of smoking cigarettes?

Almost immediately, smoking can make it hard to breathe. Within a short time, it can also worsen asthma and allergies. Only seven seconds after a smoker takes a puff, nicotine reaches the brain, where it produces a morphine-like effect.

Are there any other risks to the smoker?

Yes, there are many more risks. Smoking contributes to the likelihood of stroke, which is the third leading cause of death in the United States. Smokers are more likely to have and die from stomach ulcers than nonsmokers. Smokers have a higher incidence of cancer in general. If a person smokes and is exposed to radon or asbestos, the risk for lung cancer increases dramatically.

What are the dangers of passive smoking?

Passive smoking causes lung cancer in healthy nonsmokers. Children whose parents smoke are more likely to suffer from pneumonia or bronchitis in the first two years of life than children who come from smoke-free households. Passive smokers have a 30% greater risk of developing lung cancer than do nonsmokers who live in a smoke-free house.

Are chewing tobacco and snuff safe alternatives to cigarette smoking?

No, they are not. Many people who use chewing tobacco or snuff believe it can't harm them because there is no smoke. Wrong. Smokeless tobacco contains nicotine, the same addicting drug found in cigarettes and cigars. While not inhaled through the lungs, the juice from smokeless tobacco is absorbed through the lining of the mouth. There it can cause sores and white patches, which often lead to cancer of the mouth. Snuff dippers actually take in an average of over ten times more cancer-causing substances than cigarette smokers.

Bioethical Focus

Bans on Smoking

In 1964, the surgeon general of the United States made it known to the general public that smoking was hazardous to our health and thereafter, a health warning was placed on packs of cigarettes. At that time, 40.4% of adults smoked, but by 1990, only about 26% of adults smoked. In the meantime, however, the public became aware that passive smoking—that is, just being in the vicinity of someone who is smoking—can also lead to cancer and other health problems. By now, many state and local governments have passed legislation that bans smoking in public places such as restaurants, elevators, public meeting rooms, and in the workplace.

Is legislation that restricts the freedom to smoke ethical? Or is such legislation akin to racism and creating a population of second-class citizens who are segregated from the majority on the basis of a habit? Are the desires of nonsmokers being allowed to infringe on the rights of smokers? Or is this legislation one way to help smokers become nonsmokers? One study showed that workplace bans on smoking reduce the daily consumption of cigarettes among smokers by 10%.

Is legislation that disallows smoking in family-style restaurants fair, especially if bars and restaurants associated with casinos are not included in the ban on smoking? The selling of tobacco and even the increased need for health care it generates helps the economy. One smoker writes, "Smoking causes people to drink more, eat more, and leave larger tips. Smoking also powers the economy of Wall Street." Is this a reason to allow smoking to continue? Or should we simply require all places of business to put in improved air filtration systems? Would that do away with the dangers of passive smoking?

Does legislation that bans smoking in certain areas represent government invasion of our privacy? If yes, is reducing the chance of cancer a good enough reason to allow the government to invade our privacy? Some people are prone to cancer more than others. Should we all be regulated by the same legislation? Are we our brother's keeper, meaning that we have to look out for one another?

Decide Your Opinion

1. Is legislation that bans smoking in public places creating a group of second-class citizens whose rights are being denied?
2. Should we be concerned about passing and following legislation that possibly puts a damper on the economy, even if it does improve the health of people?
3. Are bans on smoking an invasion of our privacy? If so, is prevention of cancer in certain persons a good enough reason to risk a possible invasion of our privacy?

Summarizing the Concepts

8.1 The Respiratory System
The respiratory tract consists of the nose (nasal cavities), the nasopharynx, the pharynx, the larynx (which contains the vocal cords), the trachea, the bronchi, the bronchioles, and the lungs. The bronchi, along with the pulmonary arteries and veins, enter the lungs, which consist of the alveoli, air sacs surrounded by a capillary network.

8.2 Mechanism of Breathing
Inspiration begins when the respiratory center in the medulla oblongata sends excitatory nerve impulses to the diaphragm and the muscles of the rib cage. As they contract, the diaphragm lowers, and the rib cage moves upward and outward; the lungs expand, creating a partial vacuum, which causes air to rush in (inspiration). The respiratory center now stops sending impulses to the diaphragm and muscles of the rib cage. As the diaphragm relaxes, it resumes its dome shape, and as the rib cage retracts, air is pushed out of the lungs (expiration).

8.3 Gas Exchanges in the Body
External respiration occurs in the lungs when CO_2 leaves blood via the alveoli and O_2 enters blood from the alveoli. Diffusion accounts for the passage of molecules in different directions: There is more carbon dioxide in pulmonary blood when it enters the lungs than in alveoli, and there is more oxygen in alveoli than in pulmonary blood when it enters the lungs. Because carbon dioxide is present in blood as the bicarbonate ion (HCO_3^-), carbonic acid first forms and is broken down to carbon dioxide and water. Then, carbon dioxide diffuses out of the blood. Oxygen is transported to the tissues in combination with hemoglobin as oxyhemoglobin (HbO_2).

Internal respiration occurs in the tissues when O_2 leaves blood and CO_2 enters blood. When carbon dioxide enters blood, carbonic acid forms and is broken down to the bicarbonate ion (HCO_3^-) and hydrogen ions. Carbon dioxide is mainly carried to the lungs within the plasma as the bicarbonate ion. Hemoglobin combines with hydrogen ions and becomes reduced (HHb).

8.4 Respiration and Health
A number of illnesses are associated with the respiratory tract. These disorders can be divided into those that affect the upper respiratory tract and those that affect the lower respiratory tract. Infections of the nasal cavities, sinuses, throat, tonsils, and larynx are all well known. In addition, infections can spread from the nasopharynx to the ears.

The lower respiratory tract is subject to infections such as acute bronchitis, pneumonia, and pulmonary tuberculosis. In restrictive pulmonary disorders, exemplified by pulmonary fibrosis, the lungs lose their elasticity. In obstructive pulmonary disorders, exemplified by chronic bronchitis, emphysema, and asthma, the bronchi (and bronchioles) do not effectively conduct air to and from the lungs. Smoking, which is associated with chronic bronchitis and emphysema, can eventually lead to lung cancer.

Studying the Concepts

1. Name and explain the four phases of respiration. 142
2. What is the path of air from the nose to the lungs? What are the special functions of the nasal cavity, the larynx, and the alveoli? 143–45
3. What is the difference between tidal volume and vital capacity? Of the air we inhale, some is not used for gas exchange. Why not? 146
4. What are the steps in inspiration and expiration? How is breathing controlled? 148–49
5. Discuss the events of external respiration, and include two pertinent equations in your discussion. 150
6. What two equations pertain to the exchange of gases during internal respiration? 150
7. Name and describe several upper and several lower respiratory tract disorders (other than cancer). If appropriate, explain why breathing is difficult with these conditions. 152–54
8. List the steps by which lung cancer develops. 154

Thinking Critically About the Concepts

Refer to the opening vignette on page 141, and then answer these questions.

1. Why are distance-running performances not as good when the weather is cold?
2. Why are distance-running performances not as good when it is hot?

Testing Your Knowledge of the Concepts

Choose the best answer for each question.

1. Which of these is anatomically incorrect?
   a. The nose has two nasal cavities.
   b. The pharynx connects the nasal and oral cavities to the larynx.
   c. The larynx contains the vocal cords.
   d. The trachea enters the lungs.
   e. The lungs contain many alveoli.

2. How is inhaled air modified before it reaches the lungs?
   a. It must be humidified.   c. It must be filtered.
   b. It must be warmed.   d. All of these are correct.

3. What is the name of the structure that prevents food from entering the trachea?
   a. glottis   c. epiglottis
   b. septum   d. Adam's apple

4. The maximum volume of air that can be moved in and out during a single breath is called the
   a. expiratory and inspiratory reserve volume.
   b. residual volume.
   c. tidal volume.
   d. vital capacity.
   e. functional residual capacity.

5. Internal respiration refers to
   a. the exchange of gases between alveolar air and the blood in the lungs.
   b. the movement of air into the lungs.
   c. the exchange of gases between the blood and tissue fluid.
   d. cellular respiration, resulting in the production of ATP.

6. The chemical reaction that converts carbon dioxide to a bicarbonate ion takes place in
   a. the blood plasma.   c. the alveolus.
   b. red blood cells.   d. the hemoglobin molecule.

7. If air enters the intrapleural space (the space between the pleura),
   a. a lobe of the lung can collapse.
   b. the lungs could swell and burst.
   c. the diaphragm will contract.
   d. nothing will happen because air is needed in the intrapleural space.

8. The enzyme carbonic anhydrase
   a. causes the blood to be more basic in the tissues.
   b. speeds up the conversion of carbonic acid to carbon dioxide and water and the reverse.
   c. actively transports carbon dioxide out of capillaries.
   d. is active only at high altitudes.
   e. All of these are correct.

9. Which of these statements is true?
   a. The P_{O_2}, temperature, and pH are higher in the lungs.
   b. The P_{O_2}, temperature, and pH are lower in the lungs.
   c. The P_{O_2} and temperature are higher and the pH is lower in the lungs.
   d. The P_{O_2} and temperature are lower and the pH is higher in the lungs.
   e. The P_{O_2} and pH are higher, but the temperature is lower in the lungs.

10. Air enters the human lungs because
    a. atmospheric pressure is lower than the pressure inside the lungs.
    b. atmospheric pressure is greater than the pressure inside the lungs.
    c. although the pressures are the same inside and outside, the partial pressure of oxygen is lower within the lungs.
    d. the residual air in the lungs causes the partial pressure of oxygen to be lower than it is outside.

11. In humans, the respiratory center
    a. is stimulated by carbon dioxide.
    b. is located in the medulla oblongata.
    c. controls the rate of breathing.
    d. All of these are correct.

In questions 12–16, match each description with a structure in the key.

Key:

   a. pharynx   d. trachea
   b. glottis   e. bronchi
   c. larynx   f. bronchioles

12. Branched tubes that lead from bronchi to the alveoli

13. Reinforced tube that connects larynx with bronchi

14. Chamber behind oral cavity and between nasal cavity and larynx

15. Opening into larynx

16. Divisions of the trachea that enter lungs

17. Which of these is incorrect concerning inspiration?
    a. Rib cage moves up and out.
    b. Diaphragm contracts and moves down.
    c. Pressure in lungs decreases, and air comes rushing in.
    d. The lungs expand because air comes rushing in.

18. Label this diagram of the human respiratory tract.

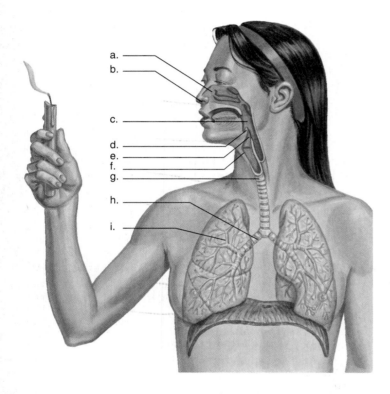

a. _____
b. _____
c. _____
d. _____
e. _____
f. _____
g. _____
h. _____
i. _____

Understanding Key Terms

acute bronchitis 152
alveolus 145
aortic body 149
asthma 154
auditory (Eustachian) tube 152
bicarbonate ion 150
bronchiole 145
bronchus 145
carbaminohemoglobin 150
carbonic anhydrase 150
carotid body 149

chronic bronchitis 153
dead air space 146
emphysema 153
epiglottis 144
expiration 142
expiratory reserve
    volume 146
external respiration 150
glottis 144
infant respiratory distress
    syndrome 145

inspiration 142
inspiratory reserve
    volume 146
internal respiration 150
laryngitis 152
larynx 144
lung cancer 154
lungs 145
nasal cavity 143
otitis media 152
oxyhemoglobin 150
pharynx 143
pneumonectomy 154
pneumonia 152
pulmonary fibrosis 153

pulmonary tuberculosis 152
reduced hemoglobin 150
residual volume 146
respiratory center 149
sinusitis 152
surfactant 145
tidal volume 146
tonsillectomy 152
tonsillitis 152
tonsils 152
trachea 144
tracheostomy 144
ventilation 142
vital capacity 146
vocal cord 144

Match the key terms to these definitions.

a. _____ Common passageway for both food intake and air movement, located between the mouth and the esophagus.

b. _____ Sensory receptor in the aortic arch sensitive to the O_2 content of the blood.

c. _____ Fold of tissue across the glottis within the larynx; creates vocal sounds when it vibrates.

d. _____ Form in which most of the carbon dioxide is transported in the bloodstream.

e. _____ Stage during breathing when air is pushed out of the lungs.

Online Learning Center

www.mhhe.com/maderhuman9

The Online Learning Center provides a wealth of information fully organized and integrated by chapter. You will find practice quizzes, interactive activities, labeling exercises, flashcards, and much more that will complement your learning and understanding of human biology.

Looking at Both Sides

Each day, the Internet, media, and other people present you with opposing viewpoints on a wide range of subjects. Your ability to develop an informed opinion on an issue, and talk to others about it, is extremely important.

To expand and enhance your knowledge of a highly relevant bioethical issue, visit the "Student Edition" of the Online Learning Center. Under "Course-Wide Content," select "Looking at Both Sides." Once there, you will be asked to complete activities that will increase your understanding of a current bioethical issue related to this chapter and allow you to defend your opinion.

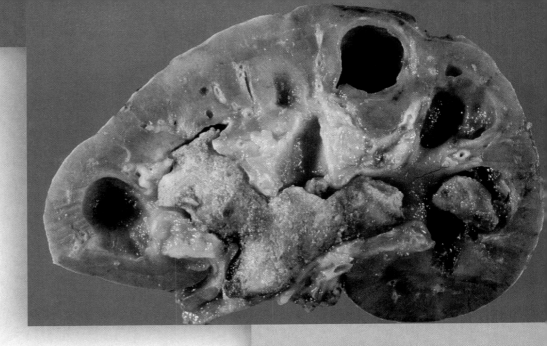

CHAPTER 9

Urinary System and Excretion

CHAPTER CONCEPTS

9.1 Urinary System
- What are the functions and what are the organs of the urinary system? 160
- In what four ways do the kidneys help maintain homeostasis? 160

9.2 Kidney Structure
- What are the three major areas of a kidney? 163
- What microscopic structure is responsible for the production of urine? 163
- How do the parts of a nephron differ? 165

9.3 Urine Formation
- What are the major processes in urine formation? 166–67
- How does the nephron carry out these processes? 167

9.4 Regulatory Functions of the Kidneys
- Where and how is water reabsorbed so that urine is concentrated? 168–69
- What three hormones influence urine production and kidney function? How do these hormones work together? 168–69
- How do the kidneys regulate the pH of body fluids? 170

9.5 Problems with Kidney Function
- What are the most common causes of renal disease, and how can it be treated? 171

9.6 Homeostasis
- How does the urinary system work with the other systems of the body to maintain homeostasis? 172–73
- How do the kidneys regulate the pH of body fluids? 172

One day, Bill experienced a terrible pain in his back that spread across his abdomen. When he started to feel nauseated and noticed blood in his urine, Bill went to a urologist, a physician specializing in the urinary system. An abdominal X ray showed that Bill had a kidney stone.

Kidney stones can be made of substances crystallized from urine, such as calcium oxalate or uric acid. Some factors that may increase the risk of kidney stones include diet, urinary tract infection, and certain metabolic disorders. Some stones are tiny, like grains of sand—these usually pass through the urinary tract with no treatment, other than plenty of fluids and perhaps pain medication. Sometimes, a larger stone blocks the drainage of urine from the kidney.

Bill's stone was too large to be passed, but not so large that he needed surgery. Instead, he underwent extracorporeal shock wave lithotripsy (ESWL), where sound waves are directed at the kidney stone, breaking it into small pieces that are later passed.

Bill wanted to reduce his chances of developing another kidney stone. His urologist advised him to drink plenty of water. Since his stone contained calcium oxalate, Bill learned to avoid overeating foods high in oxalate, such as rhubarb, spinach, chocolate, and tea. To prevent elevated levels of calcium in his urine, he would need to limit his intake of animal protein and salt. However, Bill was surprised that he didn't need to eliminate dietary calcium, as it may help prevent the formation of calcium oxalate stones.

9.1 Urinary System

The kidneys are the primary organs of excretion (Fig. 9.1). **Excretion** is the removal of metabolic wastes from the body. People sometimes confuse the terms excretion and defecation, but they do not refer to the same process. Defecation, the elimination of feces from the body, is a function of the digestive system. Excretion, on the other hand, is the elimination of metabolic wastes, which are the products of metabolism. For example, the undigested food and bacteria that make up feces have never been a part of the functioning of the body, while the substances excreted in urine were once metabolites in the body.

Functions of the Urinary System

The urinary system produces urine and conducts it to outside the body (Fig. 9.1). As the kidneys produce urine, they carry out the following four functions that contribute to homeostasis:

1. *Excretion of Metabolic Wastes*   The kidneys excrete metabolic wastes, notably nitrogenous wastes. Urea is the primary nitrogenous end product of metabolism in human beings, but humans also excrete some ammonium, creatinine, and uric acid.

    Urea is a byproduct of amino acid metabolism. The breakdown of amino acids in the liver releases ammonia, which the liver rapidly combines with carbon dioxide to produce urea. Ammonia is very toxic to cells, but urea is much less toxic.

    Creatine phosphate is a high-energy phosphate reserve molecule in muscles. The metabolic breakdown of creatine phosphate results in **creatinine.**

    The breakdown of nucleotides, such as those containing adenine and thymine, produces **uric acid.** Uric acid is rather insoluble. If too much uric acid is present in blood, crystals form and precipitate out. Crystals of uric acid sometimes collect in the joints, producing a painful ailment called **gout.**
2. *Maintenance of Water-Salt Balance*   A principal function of the kidneys is to maintain the appropriate water-salt balance of the blood. As we shall see, blood volume is intimately associated with the salt balance of the body. As you know, salts, such as NaCl, have the ability to cause osmosis, the diffusion of water—in this case, into the blood. The more salts there are in the blood, the greater the blood volume and the greater the blood pressure. In this way, the kidneys are involved in regulating blood pressure.

    The kidneys also maintain the appropriate level of other ions, such as potassium ions (K^+), bicarbonate ions (HCO_3^-), and calcium ions (Ca^{2+}), in the blood.
3. *Maintenance of Acid-Base Balance*   The kidneys regulate the acid-base balance of the blood. In order for a person

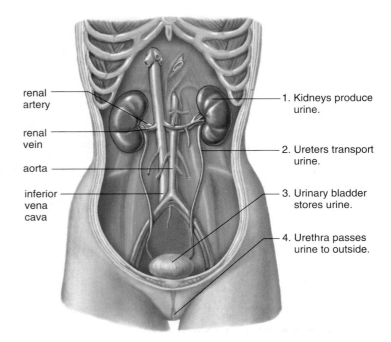

Figure 9.1   The urinary system.
Urine is found only within the kidneys, the ureters, the urinary bladder, and the urethra.

renal artery

renal vein

aorta

inferior vena cava

1. Kidneys produce urine.

2. Ureters transport urine.

3. Urinary bladder stores urine.

4. Urethra passes urine to outside.

to remain healthy, the blood pH should be just about 7.4. The kidneys monitor and help control blood pH, mainly by excreting hydrogen ions (H^+) and reabsorbing the bicarbonate ions (HCO_3^-) as needed to keep blood pH at 7.4. Urine usually has a pH of 6 or lower because our diet often contains acidic foods.
4. *Secretion of Hormones*   The kidneys assist the endocrine system in hormone secretion. The kidneys release renin, a substance that leads to the secretion of the hormone aldosterone from the adrenal cortex, the outer portion of the adrenal glands, which lie atop the kidneys. As described in Section 9.4, aldosterone promotes the reabsorption of sodium ions (Na^+) by the kidneys.

    Whenever the oxygen-carrying capacity of the blood is reduced, the kidneys secrete the hormone **erythropoietin,** which stimulates red blood cell production.

    The kidneys also help activate vitamin D from the skin. Vitamin D is a molecule that promotes calcium (Ca^{2+}) absorption from the digestive tract.

The kidneys are the primary organs of excretion, particularly of nitrogenous wastes. The kidneys are also major organs of homeostasis because they regulate the water-salt balance and the acid-base balance of the blood, as well as the secretion of certain hormones.

Organs of the Urinary System

The urinary system consists of the kidneys, ureters, urinary bladder, and urethra (see Fig. 9.1).

Kidneys

The **kidneys** are paired organs located near the small of the back, on either side of the vertebral column. They lie in depressions beneath the peritoneum, where they receive some protection from the lower rib cage. A sharp blow to the back can dislodge a kidney, which is then called a **floating kidney.**

The kidneys are bean-shaped and reddish brown in color. The fist-sized organs are covered by a tough capsule of fibrous connective tissue, called a renal capsule. Masses of adipose tissue adhere to each kidney. The concave side of a kidney has a depression, where a **renal artery** enters and a **renal vein** and a ureter exit the kidney.

Ureters

The **ureters** conduct urine from the kidneys to the bladder. They are small, muscular tubes about 25 cm long and 5 mm in diameter. Each descends beneath the peritoneum to enter the bladder at its dorsal surface. The wall of a ureter has three layers: an inner mucosa (mucous membrane), a smooth muscle layer, and an outer fibrous coat of connective tissue. Peristaltic contractions cause urine to enter the bladder even if a person is lying down. Urine enters the bladder in spurts that occur at the rate of one to five per minute.

Urinary Bladder

The **urinary bladder** stores urine until it is expelled from the body. The bladder has three openings: two for the ureters and one for the urethra, which drains the bladder (Fig. 9.2).

The bladder wall is expandable because it contains a middle layer of circular fibers and two layers of longitudinal muscle. The epithelium of the mucosa becomes thinner, and folds in the mucosa called *rugae* disappear as the bladder enlarges.

The bladder has other features that allow it to retain urine. After urine enters the bladder from a ureter, small folds of bladder mucosa act like a valve to prevent backward flow. Two sphincters in close proximity are found where the urethra exits the bladder. The internal sphincter occurs around the opening to the urethra. An external sphincter is composed of skeletal muscle that can be voluntarily controlled.

Urethra

The **urethra** is a small tube that extends from the urinary bladder to an external opening. Therefore, its function is to remove urine from the body. The urethra has a different length in females than in males. In females, the urethra is only about 4 cm long. The short length of the female urethra makes bacterial invasion easier, as discussed in the Health

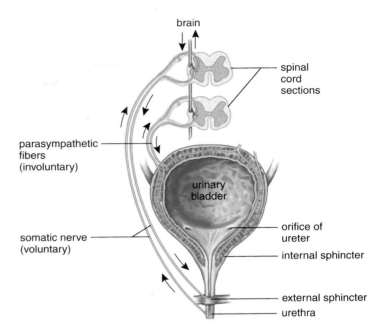

Figure 9.2 Urination.
As the bladder fills with urine, sensory impulses go to the spinal cord and then to the brain. The brain can override the urge to urinate. When urination occurs, motor nerve impulses cause the bladder to contract and the sphincters to relax.

Focus on page 162. In males, the urethra averages 20 cm when the penis is flaccid (limp, nonerect). As the urethra leaves the male urinary bladder, it is encircled by the prostate gland. The prostate is subject to enlargement and cancer. When it enlarges, the prostate gland can restrict urination. Medical and surgical procedures can usually correct the condition and restore a normal flow of urine.

In females, the reproductive and urinary systems are not connected. In males, the urethra carries urine during urination and sperm during ejaculation. This double function of the urethra in males does not alter the path of urine.

Urination

When the urinary bladder fills to about 250 mL with urine, stretch receptors send sensory nerve impulses to the spinal cord. Subsequently, motor nerve impulses from the spinal cord cause the urinary bladder to contract and the sphincters to relax so that urination, also called **micturition,** is possible (Fig. 9.2). In older children and adults, the brain controls this reflex, delaying urination until a suitable time.

Only the urinary system, consisting of the kidneys, ureters, urinary bladder, and urethra, contains urine.

Urinary Tract Infections Require Attention

Although males can get a urinary tract infection, the condition is 50 times more common in women. The explanation lies in a comparison of male and female anatomy (Fig. 9A). The female urethral and anal openings are closer together, and the shorter urethra makes it easier for bacteria from the bowels to enter and start an infection. Although it is possible to have no outward signs of an infection, urination is usually painful, and patients often describe a burning sensation. The urge to pass urine is frequent, but it may be difficult to start the stream. Chills with fever, nausea, and vomiting may be present.

Urinary tract infections confined to the urethra are called urethritis. If the bladder is involved, it is called cystitis. Should the infection reach the kidneys, the person has pyelonephritis. *Escherichia coli (E. coli)*, a normal bacterial resident of the large intestine, is usually the cause of infection. Since the infection is caused by a bacterium, it is curable by antibiotic therapy. However, reinfection is possible as soon as antibiotic therapy is finished.

It makes sense to try to prevent infection in the first place. The following tips might help.

Men and women should drink from 2 to 2.5 liters of liquid a day, preferably water. Try to avoid caffeinated drinks, which may be irritating. Cranberry juice is recommended because it contains a substance that stops bacteria from sticking to the bladder wall once an infection has set in.

Since sexually transmitted diseases such as gonorrhea, chlamydia, or herpes can cause symptoms of a urinary tract infection, all personal behaviors should be examined carefully, and suitable adjustments made to avoid urinary tract infections.

Women may have a urinary tract infection for the first time shortly after they become sexually active. The term "honeymoon cystitis" was coined because of the common association of urinary tract infections with sexual intercourse. Washing the genitals before having sex so as not to introduce bacteria from the anus into the urethra is recommended. Also, urinating immediately before and after sex helps flush out any bacteria that are present. A diaphragm being used for contraception may press on the urethra and prevent adequate emptying of the bladder, increasing the risk of cystitis. A sex partner may have an asymptomatic (no symptoms) urinary infection that causes a woman to become infected repeatedly.

Women should wipe from the front to the back after using the toilet. Perfumed toilet paper and any other perfumed products that come in contact with the genitals may be irritating. Wearing loose clothing and cotton underwear discourages the growth of bacteria, while tight clothing, such as jeans or panty hose, provides an environment for the growth of bacteria.

Personal hygiene is especially important at the time of menstruation. Hands should be washed before and after changing napkins and/or tampons. Superabsorbent tampons that are changed infrequently may encourage the growth of bacteria. Also, sexual intercourse may cause menstrual flow to enter the urethra.

In males, the prostate is a gland that surrounds the urethra just below the bladder (Fig. 9A). The prostate contributes secretions to semen whenever semen enters the urethra prior to ejaculation. An infection of the prostate, called prostatitis, is often accompanied by a urinary tract infection. Fever is present, and the prostate is tender and inflamed. The patient may have to be hospitalized and treated with a broad-spectrum antibiotic. Prostatitis, which in a young male is often preceded by a sexually transmitted disease, can lead to a chronic condition. Chronic prostatitis may be asymptomatic or, as is more typical, the man may experience irritation upon urinating and/or difficulty in urinating. The latter can lead to the need for surgery to remove the obstruction to urine flow.

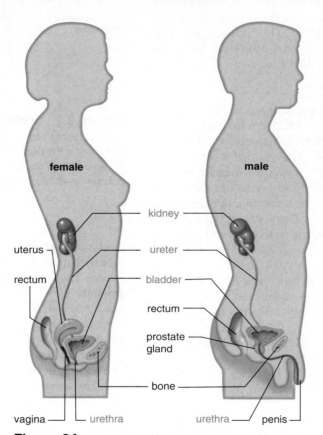

Figure 9A   Female versus male urinary tract.
Females have a short urinary tract compared with males. This means that it is easier for bacteria to invade the urethra and helps explain why females are 50 times more likely than males to get a urinary tract infection.

9.2 Kidney Structure

When a kidney is sliced lengthwise, it is possible to see that many branches of the renal artery and vein reach inside the kidney (Fig. 9.3a). If the blood vessels are removed, it is easier to identify the three regions of a kidney. The **renal cortex** is an outer, granulated layer that dips down in between a radially striated inner layer called the renal medulla. The **renal medulla** consists of cone-shaped tissue masses called renal pyramids. The **renal pelvis** is a central space, or cavity, that is continuous with the ureter (Fig. 9.3b).

Microscopically, the kidney is composed of over one million **nephrons,** sometimes called renal, or kidney, tubules (Fig. 9.3c). The nephrons produce urine and are positioned so that the urine flows into a collecting duct. Several nephrons enter the same collecting duct; the collecting ducts eventually enter the renal pelvis.

Macroscopically, a kidney has three regions: the renal cortex, the renal medulla, and the renal pelvis, which is continuous with the ureter. Microscopically, a kidney contains over one million nephrons.

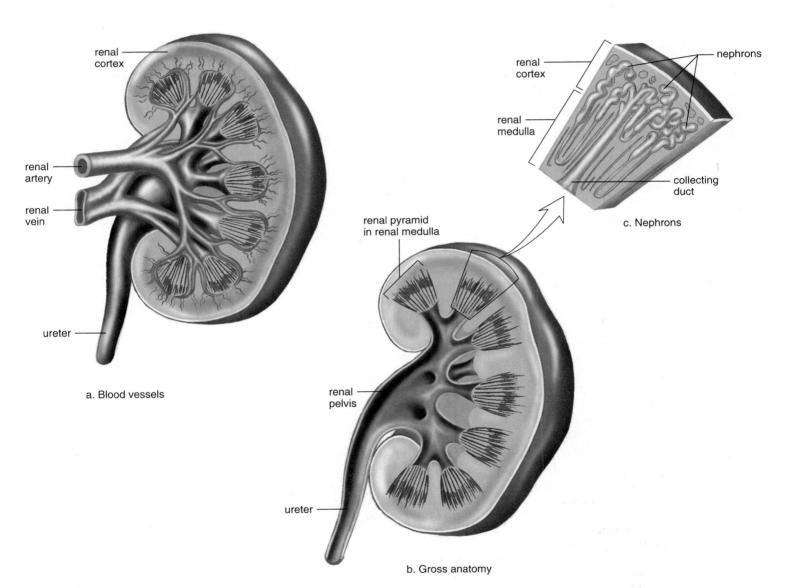

a. Blood vessels

b. Gross anatomy

c. Nephrons

Figure 9.3   Gross anatomy of the kidney.
a. A longitudinal section of the kidney showing the blood supply. Note that the renal artery divides into smaller arteries, and these divide into arterioles. Venules join to form small veins, which join to form the renal vein. **b.** The same section without the blood supply. Now it is easier to distinguish the renal cortex, the renal medulla, and the renal pelvis, which connects with the ureter. The renal medulla consists of the renal pyramids. **c.** An enlargement showing the placement of nephrons.

Anatomy of a Nephron

Each nephron has its own blood supply, including two capillary regions (Fig. 9.4). From the renal artery, an afferent arteriole leads to the **glomerulus,** a knot of capillaries inside the glomerular capsule. Blood leaving the glomerulus enters the efferent arteriole. Blood pressure is higher in the glomerulus because the efferent arteriole is narrower than the afferent arteriole. The efferent arteriole takes blood to the **peritubular capillary network,** which surrounds the rest of the nephron. From there, the blood goes into a venule that carries blood into the renal vein.

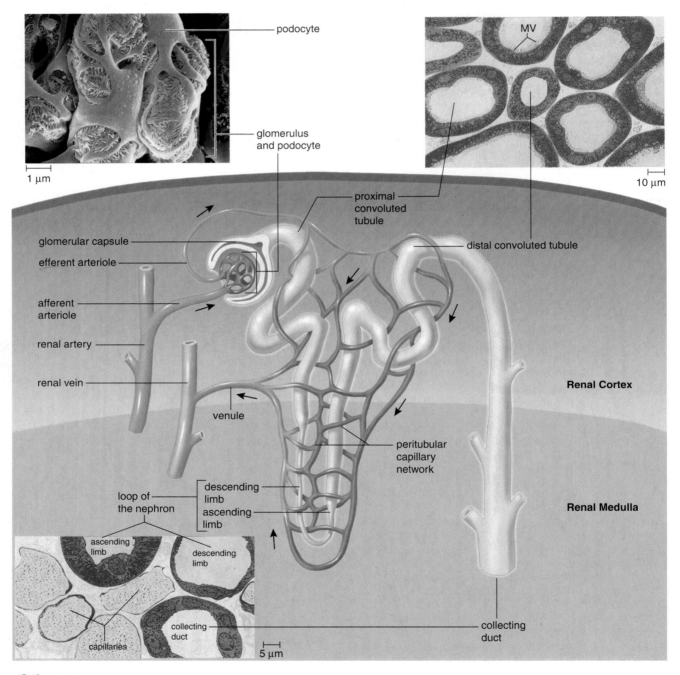

Figure 9.4   Nephron anatomy.
A nephron is made up of a glomerular capsule, the proximal convoluted tubule, the loop of the nephron, the distal convoluted tubule, and the collecting duct. The photomicrographs show the microscopic anatomy of these structures. You can trace the path of blood about the nephron by following the arrows. (MV = microvilli)

Parts of a Nephron

Each nephron is made up of several parts (Fig. 9.4). Some functions are shared by all parts of the neprhon; however, the specific structure of each part is especially suited to a particular function.

First, the closed end of the nephron is pushed in on itself to form a cup-like structure called the **glomerular capsule** (Bowman's capsule). The outer layer of the glomerular capsule is composed of squamous epithelial cells; the inner layer is made up of podocytes that have long cytoplasmic extensions. The podocytes cling to the capillary walls of the glomerulus and leave pores that allow easy passage of small molecules from the glomerulus to the inside of the glomerular capsule. This process, called glomerular filtration, produces a filtrate of the blood.

Next, there is a **proximal convoluted tubule.** The cuboidal epithelial cells lining this part of the nephron have numerous microvilli, about 1 µm in length, that are tightly packed and form a brush border (Fig. 9.5). A brush border greatly increases the surface area for the tubular reabsorption of filtrate components. Each cell also has many mitochondria, which can supply energy for active transport of molecules from the lumen to the peritubular capillary network.

Simple squamous epithelium appears as the tube narrows and makes a U-turn called the **loop of the nephron** (loop of Henle). Each loop consists of a descending limb that allows water to leave and an ascending limb that extrudes salt (NaCl). Indeed, as we shall see, this activity facilitates the reabsorption of water by the nephron and collecting duct.

The cuboidal epithelial cells of the **distal convoluted tubule** have numerous mitochondria, but they lack microvilli. This means that the distal convoluted tubule is not specialized for reabsorption but can participate in moving molecules from the blood into the tubule, a process called tubular secretion. The distal convoluted tubules of several nephrons enter one collecting duct. Many **collecting ducts** carry urine to the renal pelvis.

As shown in Figure 9.4, the glomerular capsule and the convoluted tubules always lie within the renal cortex. The loop of the nephron dips down into the renal medulla; a few nephrons have a very long loop of the nephron, which penetrates deep into the renal medulla. Collecting ducts are also located in the renal medulla, and together they give the renal pyramids their appearance.

Each part of a nephron is anatomically suited to its specific function in urine formation.

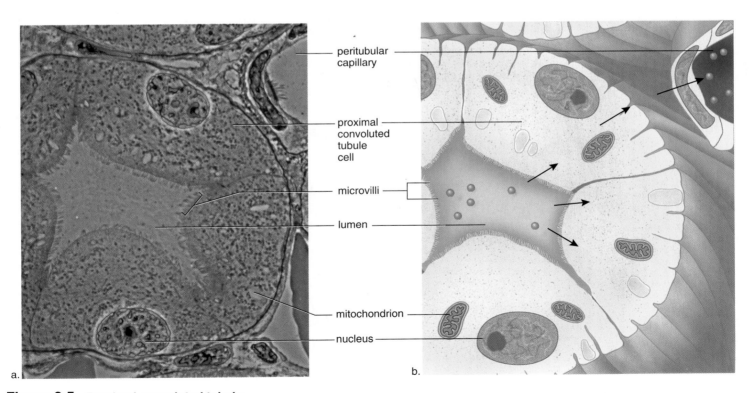

Figure 9.5   Proximal convoluted tubule.
a. This photomicrograph shows that the cells lining the proximal convoluted tubule have a brush-like border composed of microvilli, which greatly increase the surface area exposed to the lumen. The peritubular capillary network surrounds the cells. **b.** Diagrammatic representation of (a) shows that each cell has many mitochondria, which supply the energy needed for active transport, the process that moves molecules (green) from the lumen of the tubule to the capillary, as indicated by the arrows.

Visual Focus

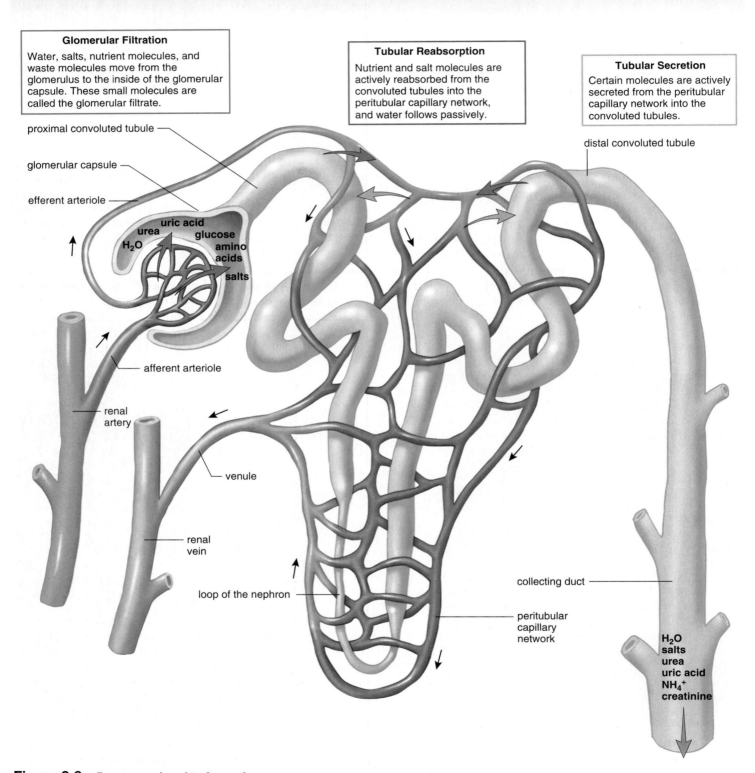

Glomerular Filtration

Water, salts, nutrient molecules, and waste molecules move from the glomerulus to the inside of the glomerular capsule. These small molecules are called the glomerular filtrate.

Tubular Reabsorption

Nutrient and salt molecules are actively reabsorbed from the convoluted tubules into the peritubular capillary network, and water follows passively.

Tubular Secretion

Certain molecules are actively secreted from the peritubular capillary network into the convoluted tubules.

proximal convoluted tubule

glomerular capsule

efferent arteriole

uric acid
urea
H_2O
glucose
amino acids
salts

distal convoluted tubule

afferent arteriole

renal artery

venule

renal vein

loop of the nephron

collecting duct

peritubular capillary network

H_2O
salts
urea
uric acid
NH_4^+
creatinine

Figure 9.6 **Processes in urine formation.**

Top: The three main steps in urine formation are described in boxes that are color-coded to arrows showing the movement of molecules into or out of the nephron at specific locations. In the end, urine is composed of the substances within the collecting duct (see gray arrow, *lower right*).

9.3 Urine Formation

Figure 9.6 gives an overview of urine formation, which is divided into three processes:

Glomerular Filtration

Glomerular filtration occurs when whole blood enters the glomerulus by way of the afferent arteriole. Due to glomerular blood pressure, water and small molecules move from the glomerulus to the inside of the glomerular capsule. This is a filtration process because large molecules and formed elements are unable to pass through the capillary wall. In effect, then, blood in the glomerulus has two portions, the filterable components and the nonfilterable components:

Filterable Blood Components	Nonfilterable Blood Components
Water	Formed elements (blood cells and platelets)
Nitrogenous wastes	Plasma proteins
Nutrients	
Salts (ions)	

The nonfilterable components leave the glomerulus by way of the efferent arteriole. The **glomerular filtrate** inside the glomerular capsule now contains the filterable blood components in approximately the same concentration as plasma.

As indicated in Table 9.1, nephrons in the kidneys filter 180 liters of water per day, along with a considerable amount of small molecules (such as glucose) and ions (such as sodium). If the composition of urine were the same as that of the glomerular filtrate, the body would continually lose water, salts, and nutrients. Therefore, we can conclude that the composition of the filtrate must be altered as this fluid passes through the remainder of the tubule.

Tubular Reabsorption

Tubular reabsorption occurs as molecules and ions are both passively and actively reabsorbed from the nephron into the blood of the peritubular capillary network. The osmolarity of the blood is maintained by the presence of both plasma proteins and salt. When sodium ions (Na^+) are actively reabsorbed, chloride ions (Cl^-) follow passively. The reabsorption of salt (Na^+Cl^-) increases the osmolarity of the blood compared with the filtrate, and therefore water moves passively from the tubule into the blood. About 65% of Na^+ is reabsorbed at the proximal convoluted tubule.

Nutrients such as glucose and amino acids return to the peritubular capillaries almost exclusively at the proximal convoluted tubule. This is a selective process because only molecules recognized by carrier proteins are actively reabsorbed. Glucose is an example of a molecule that ordinarily is completely reabsorbed because there is a plentiful supply

Table 9.1	Reabsorption from Nephrons		
Substance	Amount Filtered (per day)	Amount Excreted (per day)	Reabsorption (%)
Water, L	180	1.8	99.0
Sodium, g	630	3.2	99.5
Glucose, g	180	0.0	100.0
Urea, g	54	30.0	44.0

L = liters, g = grams

of carrier proteins for it. However, every substance has a maximum rate of transport, and after all its carriers are in use, any excess in the filtrate will appear in the urine. In diabetes mellitus, because the liver and muscles fail to store glucose as glycogen, the blood glucose level is above normal and glucose appears in the urine. The presence of excess glucose in the filtrate raises its osmolarity, and therefore less water is reabsorbed into the peritubular capillary network. The frequent urination and increased thirst experienced by untreated diabetics are due to the fact that less water is being reabsorbed from the filtrate into the blood.

We have seen that the filtrate that enters the proximal convoluted tubule is divided into two portions, components that are reabsorbed from the tubule into blood, and components that are not reabsorbed and continue to pass through the nephron to be further processed into urine:

Reabsorbed Filtrate Components	Nonreabsorbed Filtrate Components
Most water	Some water
Nutrients	Much nitrogenous waste
Required salts (ions)	Excess salts (ions)

The substances that are not reabsorbed become the tubular fluid, which enters the loop of the nephron.

Tubular Secretion

Tubular secretion is a second way by which substances are removed from blood and added to the tubular fluid. Hydrogen ions, creatinine, and drugs such as penicillin are some of the substances that are moved by active transport from blood into the kidney tubule. In the end, urine contains substances that have undergone glomerular filtration but have not been reabsorbed, and substances that have undergone tubular secretion. Tubular secretion is now known to occur along the length of the kidney tubule.

Glomerular filtration and tubular secretion add molecules to urine; tubular reabsorption removes them.

9.4 Regulatory Functions of the Kidneys

The kidneys maintain the water-salt balance of the blood within normal limits. In this way, they also maintain the blood volume and blood pressure. Most of the water and salt (NaCl) present in the filtrate is reabsorbed across the wall of the proximal convoluted tubule.

Reabsorption of Water

The excretion of a hypertonic urine (one that is more concentrated than blood) is dependent upon the reabsorption of water from the loop of the nephron and the collecting duct. We can think of reabsorption of water as requiring (1) reabsorption of salt and (2) establishment of a solute gradient dependent on salt and urea before (3) water is reabsorbed.

1. *Reabsorption of Salt* The kidneys regulate the salt balance in blood by controlling the excretion and the reabsorption of various ions. Sodium (Na^+) is an important ion in plasma that must be regulated, but the kidneys also excrete or reabsorb other ions, such as potassium ions (K^+), bicarbonate ions (HCO_3^-), and magnesium ions (Mg^{2+}), as needed.

Usually, more than 99% of sodium (Na^+) filtered at the glomerulus is returned to the blood. Most sodium (67%) is reabsorbed at the proximal convoluted tubule, and a sizable amount (25%) is extruded by the ascending limb of the loop of the nephron. The rest is reabsorbed from the distal convoluted tubule and collecting duct.

Hormones regulate the reabsorption of sodium at the distal convoluted tubule. **Aldosterone** is a hormone secreted by the adrenal cortex. Aldosterone promotes the excretion of potassium ions (K^+) and the reabsorption of sodium ions (Na^+). The release of aldosterone is set in motion by the kidneys themselves. The **juxtaglomerular apparatus** is a region of contact between the afferent arteriole and the distal convoluted tubule (Fig. 9.7). When blood volume, and therefore blood pressure, is not sufficient to promote glomerular filtration, the juxtaglomerular apparatus secretes renin. **Renin** is an enzyme that changes angiotensinogen (a large plasma protein produced by the liver) into angiotensin I. Later, angiotensin I is converted to angiotensin II, a powerful vasoconstrictor that also stimulates the adrenal cortex to release aldosterone. The reabsorption of sodium ions is followed by the reabsorption of water. Therefore, blood volume and blood pressure increase.

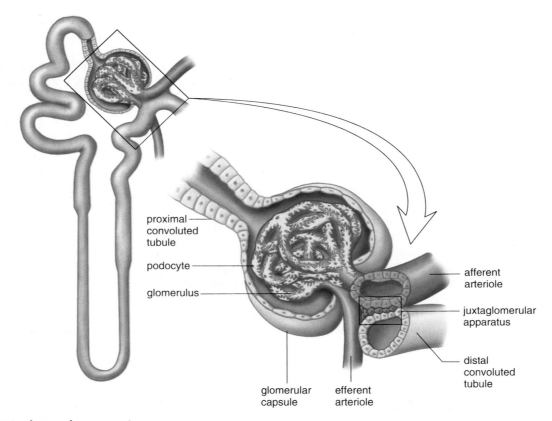

Figure 9.7 **Juxtaglomerular apparatus.**
This drawing shows that the afferent arteriole and the distal convoluted tubule usually lie next to each other. The juxtaglomerular apparatus occurs where they touch. The juxtaglomerular apparatus secretes renin, a substance that leads to the release of aldosterone by the adrenal cortex. Reabsorption of sodium ions and then water now occurs. Thereafter, blood volume and blood pressure increase.

Atrial natriuretic hormone (ANH) is a hormone secreted by the atria of the heart when cardiac cells are stretched due to increased blood volume. ANH inhibits the secretion of renin by the juxtaglomerular apparatus and the secretion of aldosterone by the adrenal cortex. Its effect, therefore, is to promote the excretion of Na^+, called natriuresis.

2. *Establishment of a Solute Gradient*   A long loop of the nephron, which typically penetrates deep into the renal medulla, is made up of a descending limb and an ascending limb. Salt (Na^+Cl^-) passively diffuses out of the lower portion of the ascending limb but the upper, thick portion of the limb actively extrudes salt out into the tissue of the outer renal medulla (Fig. 9.8). (In both instances, the movement of Na^+ precedes the movement of Cl^-.) Less and less salt is available for transport as fluid moves up the thick portion of the

ascending limb. Because of these circumstances, there is an osmotic gradient within the tissues of the renal medulla—the concentration of salt is greater in the direction of the inner medulla. (Note that water cannot leave the ascending limb because the limb is impermeable to water.)

The large arrow in Figure 9.8 indicates that the innermost portion of the inner medulla has the highest concentration of solutes. This cannot be due to salt because active transport of salt does not start until fluid reaches the thick portion of the ascending limb. Urea is believed to leak from the lower portion of the collecting duct, and it is this molecule that contributes to the high solute concentration of the inner medulla.

3. *Reabsorption of Water*   Because of the osmotic gradient within the renal medulla, water leaves the descending limb along its entire length. This is a countercurrent mechanism: as water diffuses out of the descending limb, the remaining fluid within the limb encounters an even greater osmotic concentration of solute; therefore, water continues to leave the descending limb from the top to the bottom.

Fluid enters the collecting duct from the distal convoluted tubule. This fluid is isotonic to the cells of the renal cortex. This means that to this point, the net effect of reabsorption of water and salt is the production of a fluid that has the same tonicity as blood plasma. However, the filtrate within the collecting duct also encounters the same osmotic gradient mentioned earlier (Fig. 9.8). Therefore, water diffuses out of the collecting duct into the renal medulla, and the urine within the collecting duct becomes hypertonic to blood plasma.

Antidiuretic hormone (ADH) released by the posterior lobe of the pituitary plays a role in water reabsorption at the collecting duct. In order to understand the action of this hormone, consider its name. Diuresis means increased amount of urine, and antidiuresis means decreased amount of urine. When ADH is present, more water is reabsorbed (blood volume and pressure rise), and a decreased amount of urine results. Usually, ADH is secreted at night to compensate for water loss through sweating. This explains why the first urine of the day is more concentrated.

Diuretics

Diuretics are chemicals that increase the flow of urine. Drinking alcohol causes diuresis because it inhibits the secretion of ADH. The dehydration that follows is believed to contribute to the symptoms of a hangover. Caffeine is a diuretic because it increases the glomerular filtration rate and decreases the tubular reabsorption of Na^+. Diuretic drugs developed to counteract high blood pressure inhibit active transport of Na^+ at the loop of the nephron or at the distal convoluted tubule. A decrease in water reabsorption and a decrease in blood volume follow.

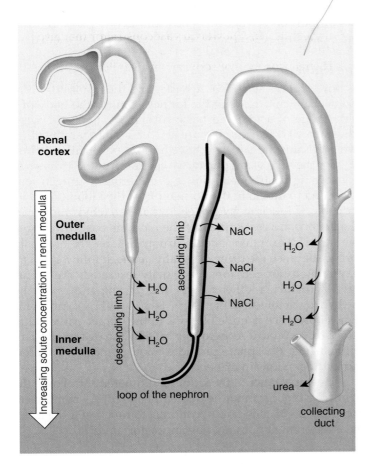

Figure 9.8   Reabsorption of water at the loop of the nephron and the collecting duct.
Salt (NaCl) diffuses and is actively transported out of the ascending limb of the loop of the nephron into the renal medulla. (The thick black line means the ascending limb is impermeable to water.) Also, urea is believed to leak from the collecting duct and to enter the tissues of the renal medulla. This creates a hypertonic environment, which draws water out of the descending limb and the collecting duct. This water is returned to the cardiovascular system.

Acid-Base Balance

The pH scale, as discussed in Chapter 2, page 20, can be used to indicate the basicity (alkalinity) or the acidity of body fluids. A basic solution has a lesser hydrogen ion concentration [H^+] than the neutral pH of 7.0, and an acidic solution has a greater [H^+] than neutral pH. The normal pH for body fluids is about 7.4. This is the pH at which our proteins, such as cellular enzymes, function properly. If the blood pH rises above 7.4, a person is said to have **alkalosis,** and if the blood pH decreases below 7.4, a person is said to have **acidosis.** Alkalosis and acidosis are abnormal conditions that may need medical attention.

The foods we eat add basic or acidic substances to the blood, and so does metabolism. For example, cellular respiration adds carbon dioxide that combines with water to form carbonic acid, and fermentation adds lactic acid. The pH of body fluids stays at just about 7.4 via several mechanisms, primarily acid-base buffer systems, the respiratory center, and the kidneys.

Acid-Base Buffer Systems

The pH of the blood stays near 7.4 because the blood is buffered. A **buffer** is a chemical or a combination of chemicals that can take up excess hydrogen ions (H^+) or excess hydroxide ions (OH^-). One of the most important buffers in the blood is a combination of carbonic acid (H_2CO_3) and bicarbonate ions (HCO_3^-). When hydrogen ions (H^+) are added to blood, the following reaction occurs:

$$H^+ + HCO_3^- \rightarrow H_2CO_3$$

When hydroxide ions (OH^-) are added to blood, this reaction occurs:

$$OH^- + H_2CO_3 \rightarrow HCO_3^- + H_2O$$

These reactions temporarily prevent any significant change in blood pH. A blood buffer, however, can be overwhelmed unless some more permanent adjustment is made. The next adjustment to keep the pH of the blood constant occurs at pulmonary capillaries.

Respiratory Center

As discussed in Chapter 8, the respiratory center in the medulla oblongata increases the breathing rate if the hydrogen ion concentration of the blood rises. Increasing the breathing rate rids the body of hydrogen ions because the following reaction takes place in pulmonary capillaries:

$$H^+ + HCO_3^- \rightleftharpoons H_2CO_3 \rightleftharpoons H_2O + CO_2$$

In other words, when carbon dioxide is exhaled, this reaction shifts to the right, and the amount of hydrogen ions is reduced.

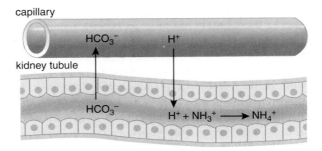

Figure 9.9   Acid-base balance.
In the kidneys, bicarbonate ions (HCO_3^-) are reabsorbed and hydrogen ions (H^+) are excreted as needed to maintain the pH of the blood. Excess hydrogen ions are buffered, for example, by ammonia (NH_3), which becomes ammonium (NH_4^+). Ammonia is produced in tubule cells by the deamination of amino acids.

It is important to have the correct proportion of carbonic acid and bicarbonate ions in the blood. Breathing readjusts this proportion so that this particular acid-base buffer system can continue to absorb both H^+ and OH^- as needed.

The Kidneys

As powerful as the acid-base buffer and the respiratory center mechanisms are, only the kidneys can rid the body of a wide range of acidic and basic substances, and otherwise, adjust the pH. The kidneys are slower acting than the other two mechanisms, but they have a more powerful effect on pH. For the sake of simplicity, we can think of the kidneys as reabsorbing bicarbonate ions and excreting hydrogen ions as needed to maintain the normal pH of the blood (Fig. 9.9). If the blood is acidic, hydrogen ions are excreted, and bicarbonate ions are reabsorbed. If the blood is basic, hydrogen ions are not excreted, and bicarbonate ions are not reabsorbed. Because the urine is usually acidic, it follows that an excess of hydrogen ions is usually excreted. Ammonia (NH_3) provides another means of buffering and removing the hydrogen ions in urine: ($NH_3 + H^+ \rightarrow NH_4^+$). Ammonia (whose presence is quite obvious in the diaper pail or kitty litter box) is produced in tubule cells by the deamination of amino acids. Phosphate provides another means of buffering hydrogen ions in urine.

The importance of the kidneys' ultimate control over the pH of the blood cannot be overemphasized. As mentioned, the enzymes of cells cannot continue to function if the internal environment does not have near-normal pH.

The kidneys, under the influence of the hormones aldosterone and ANH, regulate the reabsorption of salt. The reabsorption of salt and then water affects blood volume and pressure. The kidneys are more powerful regulators of acid-base (pH) balance than are blood buffers and the respiratory center.

9.5 Problems with Kidney Function

Many types of illnesses, especially diabetes, hypertension, and inherited conditions, cause progressive renal disease and renal failure. Infections are also contributory. If the infection is localized in the urethra, it is called **urethritis.** If the infection invades the urinary bladder, it is called **cystitis.** Finally, if the kidneys are affected, the infection is called **pyelonephritis.**

Urinary tract infections, an enlarged prostate gland, pH imbalances, or simply an intake of too much calcium, can lead to kidney stones. Kidney stones are hard granules made of calcium, phosphate, uric acid, and protein. Kidney stones form in the renal pelvis and usually pass unnoticed in the urine flow. If they grow to several centimeters and block the renal pelvis or ureter, a reverse pressure builds up and destroys nephrons. When a large kidney stone passes, strong contractions within a ureter can be excruciatingly painful.

One of the first signs of nephron damage is albumin, white blood cells, or even red blood cells in the urine and can be detected when a urinalysis is done. If damage is so extensive that more than two thirds of the nephrons are inoperative, urea and other waste substances accumulate in the blood. This condition is called **uremia.** Although nitrogenous wastes can cause serious damage, the retention of water and salts is of even greater concern. The latter causes edema, fluid accumulation in the body tissues. Imbalance in the ionic composition of body fluids can lead to loss of consciousness and to heart failure.

Hemodialysis

Patients with renal failure can undergo **hemodialysis,** utilizing either an artificial kidney machine or continuous ambulatory peritoneal dialysis (CAPD). *Dialysis* is defined as the diffusion of dissolved molecules through a semipermeable natural or synthetic membrane that has pore sizes that allow only small molecules to pass through. In an artificial kidney machine (Fig. 9.10), the patient's blood is passed through a membranous tube, which is in contact with a dialysis solution, or **dialysate.** Substances more concentrated in the blood diffuse into the dialysate, and substances more concentrated in the dialysate diffuse into the blood. The dialysate is continuously replaced to maintain favorable concentration gradients. In this way, the artificial kidney can be utilized either to extract substances from blood, including waste products or toxic chemicals and drugs, or to add substances to blood—for example, bicarbonate ions (HCO_3^-) if the blood is acidic. In the course of a 3–6 hour

hemodialysis, from 50 to 250 grams of urea can be removed from a patient, which greatly exceeds the amount excreted by normal kidneys. Therefore, a patient needs to undergo treatment only about twice a week.

CAPD is so named because the peritoneum is the dialysis membrane. A fresh amount of dialysate is introduced directly into the abdominal cavity from a bag that is temporarily attached to a permanently implanted plastic tube. The dialysate flows into the peritoneal cavity by gravity. Waste and salt molecules pass from the blood vessels in the abdominal wall into the dialysate before the fluid is collected 4–8 hours later. The solution is drained into a bag from the abdominal cavity by gravity, and then it is discarded. One advantage of CAPD over an artificial kidney machine is that the individual can go about his or her normal activities during CAPD.

Replacing a Kidney

Patients with renal failure sometimes undergo a kidney transplant operation, during which a functioning kidney from a donor is received. As with all organ transplants, there is the possibility of organ rejection. Receiving a kidney from a close relative has the highest chance of success. The current one-year survival rate is 97% if the kidney is received from a relative and 90% if it is received from a nonrelative. In the future, it may be possible to use kidneys from pigs, especially bred so that they are not antigenic to humans, or kidneys created in the laboratory.

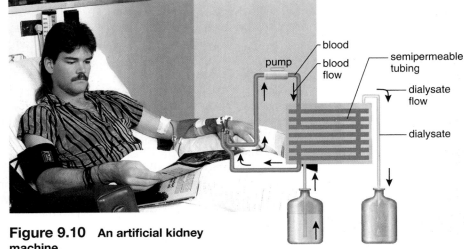

Figure 9.10   An artificial kidney machine.
As the patient's blood is pumped through dialysis tubing, it is exposed to a dialysate (dialysis solution). Wastes exit from blood into the solution because of a pre-established concentration gradient. In this way, blood is not only cleansed, but its water-salt and acid-base balances can also be adjusted.

9.6 Homeostasis

Just as the environment around us is degraded by pollution, the body suffers if wastes are not dealt with effectively. Metabolic waste removal is absolutely necessary for maintaining homeostasis. The blood must constantly be cleansed of the nitrogenous wastes, which are end products of metabolism. The liver produces urea and muscles make creatinine. These wastes, and also uric acid from the cells, are carried by the cardiovascular system to the kidneys. The urine-producing kidneys are responsible for the excretion of nitrogenous wastes. They are assisted to a limited degree by the sweat glands in the skin, which excrete perspiration, a mixture of water, salt, and some urea. In times of kidney failure, urea is excreted by the sweat glands and forms a so-called urea frost on the skin.

Aside from the excretion of nitrogenous wastes, the kidneys are primary organs of homeostasis because they maintain the water-salt (electrolyte) and the acid-base balance of the blood. If blood does not have the usual water-salt balance, blood volume and blood pressure are affected. Without adequate blood pressure, exchange across capillary walls cannot take place, nor is glomerular filtration possible in the kidneys themselves.

What happens if you have insufficient Na^+ in your blood and tissue fluid? This can occur due to prolonged heavy sweating, as in athletes running a marathon. And the problem can be worsened by consuming too much water, which dilutes the remaining Na^+ in the body. This is why sports beverages contain sodium. Too low a concentration of Na^+ in the blood activates the renin-angiotensin-aldosterone sequence, and then the kidneys increase Na^+ reabsorption in order to conserve as much as possible. Subsequently, the osmolarity of the blood and the blood pressure return to normal.

On the other hand, think of what would happen if you ate a big tub of salty popcorn at the movies. When salt (NaCl) is absorbed from the digestive tract, the Na^+ content of the blood increases above normal and the body retains water. Tissue fluid volume increases, which is why you may notice swelling (edema) in your legs and feet after consuming salty food. Likewise, blood volume and blood pressure rise. Elevated blood pressure is detected by specialized cells in the aortic and carotid sinuses, and the kidneys respond by reducing Na^+ and water reabsorption. Excess Na^+ and water leave the body in the urine, and the result is that blood volume, pressure, and tissue fluid volume return to normal.

How is the acid-base balance of the blood maintained? Two closely associated mechanisms work to offset short-term challenges to the acid-base balance. These are the blood bicarbonate (HCO_3-) buffering system and the process of breathing. Usually, the excretion of carbon dioxide (CO_2) by the lungs helps to keep blood pH within normal limits. What happens when you hold your breath? Since you aren't expelling CO_2 from your lungs, blood pH decreases; the

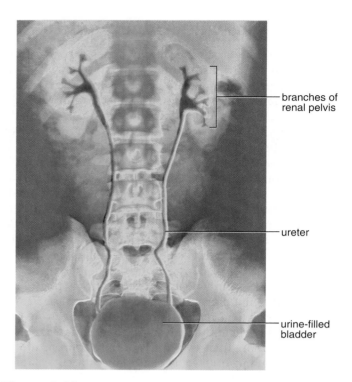

branches of renal pelvis

ureter

urine-filled bladder

Figure 9.11   X-ray enhanced picture of the urinary system.

blood becomes more acidic. Indeed, when this happens, chemoreceptors in the carotid bodies (located in the carotid arteries) and in the aortic bodies (located in the aorta) stimulate the respiratory center, and you experience the overwhelming urge to take a breath.

As powerful as the combined bicarbonate buffer and breathing systems are, only the kidneys can rid the body of a wide range of acidic and basic substances—thus, the importance of the kidneys' ultimate control over blood pH cannot be overemphasized. The kidneys are slower acting than the buffer/breathing mechanism, but their effect on blood pH is stronger. They do this by adjusting the secretion of hydrogen ions and bicarbonate ions as needed.

Aside from producing renin, the kidneys assist the endocrine system and also the cardiovascular system by producing erythropoietin. Erythropoietin stimulates red bone marrow to produce red blood cells. The kidneys assist the skeletal, nervous, and muscular systems by helping to regulate the amount of calcium ions (Ca^{2+}) in the blood. The kidneys convert vitamin D to its active form needed for Ca^{2+} absorption by the digestive tract, and they regulate the excretion of electrolytes, including Ca^{2+}. The kidneys also regulate the sodium (Na^+) and potassium (K^+) content of the blood. These ions are necessary to the contraction of the heart and other muscles in the body, and are also needed for nerve conduction. So, while we tend to remember that the kidneys excrete urea, we must also keep in mind all the other functions of the kidneys that are absolutely essential to homeostasis (Fig. 9.11).

Human Systems Work Together

All systems of the body work with the urinary system to maintain homeostasis. These systems are especially noteworthy.

Urinary System

As an aid to all the systems, the kidneys excrete nitrogenous wastes, maintain the water-salt balance and the acid-base balance of the blood. The urinary system also specifically helps the other systems, as mentioned below.

Cardiovascular System

Production of renin by the kidneys helps maintain blood pressure. Blood vessels transport nitrogenous wastes to the kidneys and carbon dioxide to the lungs. The buffering system of the blood helps the kidneys maintain the acid-base balance.

Digestive System

The liver produces urea excreted by the kidneys. The yellow pigment found in urine, called urochrome (breakdown product of hemoglobin), is produced by the liver. The digestive system absorbs nutrients, ions, and water. These help the kidneys maintain the proper level of ions and water in the blood.

Muscular System

The kidneys regulate the amount of ions in the blood. These ions are necessary to the contraction of muscles, including those that propel fluids in the ureters and urethra.

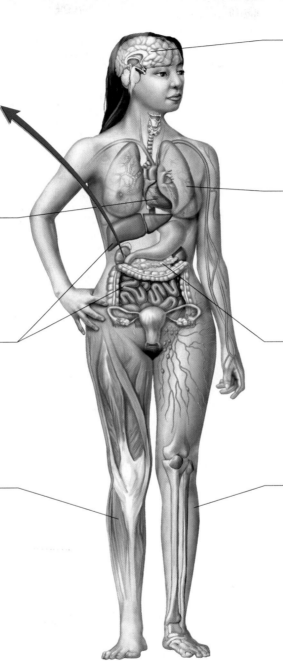

Nervous System

The kidneys regulate the amount of ions (e.g., K^+, Na^+, Ca^{2+}) in the blood. These ions are necessary for nerve impulse conduction. The nervous system controls urination.

Respiratory System

The kidneys help the lungs by excreting carbon dioxide as bicarbonate ions, while the lungs help the kidneys maintain the acid-base balance of the blood by excreting carbon dioxide.

Endocrine System

The kidneys produce renin, leading to the production of aldosterone, a hormone that helps the kidneys maintain the water-salt balance. The kidneys produce the hormone erythropoietin, and they change vitamin D to a hormone. The posterior pituitary produces ADH, which regulates water retention by the kidneys.

Integumentary System

Sweat glands excrete perspiration, which is a solution of water, salt, and some urea.

Summarizing the Concepts

9.1 Urinary System
As the kidneys produce urine, they excrete nitrogenous wastes, including urea, uric acid, and creatinine. They maintain the normal water-salt balance and the acid-base balance of the blood, as well as assisting the endocrine system. The kidneys secrete erythropoietin, which stimulates red blood cell production. They also release renin, which leads to the secretion of aldosterone by the adrenal cortex.

After leaving the kidneys, urine is conducted by the ureters to the bladder, where it is stored before being released by way of the urethra.

9.2 Kidney Structure
Macroscopically, the kidneys are divided into the renal cortex, renal medulla, and renal pelvis. Microscopically, they contain the nephrons. Each nephron has its own blood supply; the afferent arteriole approaches the glomerular capsule and divides to become the glomerulus, a knot of capillaries. The efferent arteriole leaves the glomerulus and immediately branches into the peritubular capillary network.

Each region of the nephron is anatomically suited to its task in urine formation. Spaces between podocytes of the glomerular capsule allow small molecules to enter the tubule from the glomerulus. The cuboidal epithelial cells of the proximal convoluted tubule have many mitochondria and microvilli to carry out reabsorption from the tubule to the blood. In contrast, the cuboidal epithelial cells of the distal convoluted tubule have numerous mitochondria that provide energy for active transport of molecules from the blood to the tubule.

9.3 Urine Formation
Urine is composed primarily of nitrogenous waste products and salts in water. The steps in urine formation are glomerular filtration, tubular reabsorption, and tubular secretion (see Fig. 9.6).

9.4 Regulatory Functions of the Kidneys
Reabsorption of water and the production of a hypertonic urine involves the following: (1) reabsorption of salts. Two hormones, aldosterone and ANH, control the kidneys' reabsorption of sodium (Na^+). The reabsorption of salt increases blood volume and pressure because more water is also reabsorbed. (2) Establishment of a solute gradient that increases toward the inner medulla. The ascending limb of the loop of the nephron establishes this gradient. (3) This gradient draws water from the descending limb of the loop of the nephron and also from the collecting duct. The permeability of the collecting duct is under the control of the hormone ADH.

The kidneys keep blood pH within normal limits. They reabsorb HCO_3^- and excrete H^+ as needed to maintain the pH at about 7.4. Ammonia buffers H^+ in the urine.

9.5 Problems with Kidney Function
Various types of problems, including diabetes, kidney stones, and infections, can lead to renal failure, which necessitates undergoing hemodialysis by utilizing a kidney machine or CAPD, or by receiving a kidney transplant.

9.6 Homeostasis
The kidneys keep blood pH within normal limits. They reabsorb HCO_3^- and excrete H^+ as needed to maintain the pH at about 7.4.

The kidneys also maintain the water-salt balance of blood. The urinary system works with the other systems of the body to maintain homeostasis in the ways described in Human Systems Work Together on page 173.

Studying the Concepts

1. List and explain four functions of the urinary system. 160
2. Describe the path of urine and the function of each organ mentioned. 160–61
3. Explain how urination is controlled. 161
4. Describe the macroscopic anatomy of a kidney. 163
5. Trace the path of blood about a nephron. 164
6. Name the parts of a nephron, and describe the structure of each part. 165
7. State and describe the three processes involved in urine formation. 166–67
8. Where in particular are water and salt reabsorbed along the length of the nephron? Describe the contribution of the loop of the nephron. 168–69
9. Name and describe the action of antidiuretic hormone (ADH), the renin-aldosterone connection, and atrial natriuretic hormone (ANH). 168–69
10. How do the kidneys maintain the pH of the blood within normal limits? 170
11. Explain how the artificial kidney machine works. 171
12. How does the urinary system contribute to homeostasis? What other systems of the body, in particular, assist the urinary system? 172–73

Thinking Critically About the Concepts

Refer to the opening vignette on page 159, and then answer these questions.

1. What effect would a kidney stone, which blocks the flow of urine, have on urine formation?
2. Do you think this might damage the kidney itself, and if so, why?
3. Since kidney function is vital to homeostasis, what "backup" does the body have in case a large stone blocks the drainage of urine from a kidney?

Testing Your Knowledge of the Concepts

Choose the best answer for each question.

1. Which of these functions of the kidneys are mismatched?
   a. excretes metabolic wastes—rids the body of urea
   b. maintains the water-salt balance—helps regulate blood pressure
   c. maintains the acid-base balance—rids the body of uric acid
   d. secretes hormones—secretes erythropoietin
   e. All of these are correct.

2. Which part of a nephron is out of sequence first?
   a. glomerular capsule
   b. proximal convoluted tubule

c. distal convoluted tubule
d. loop of the nephron
e. collecting duct

3. Which of these hormones is most likely to directly cause a drop in blood pressure?
    a. aldosterone
    b. antidiuretic hormone (ADH)
    c. erythropoietin
    d. atrial natriuretic hormone (ANH)

4. To lower blood acidity,
    a. hydrogen ions are excreted, and bicarbonate ions are reabsorbed.
    b. hydrogen ions are reabsorbed, and bicarbonate ions are excreted.
    c. hydrogen ions and bicarbonate ions are reabsorbed.
    d. hydrogen ions and bicarbonate ions are excreted.
    e. urea, uric acid, and ammonia are excreted.

5. Excretion of a hypertonic urine in humans is best associated with the
    a. glomerular capsule and the tubules.
    b. proximal convoluted tubule only.
    c. loop of the nephron and collecting duct.
    d. distal convoluted tubule and peritubular capillary.

6. The presence of ADH (antidiuretic hormone) causes an individual to excrete
    a. sugars.
    b. less water.
    c. more water.
    d. Both a and c are correct.

7. In humans, water is
    a. found in the glomerular filtrate.
    b. reabsorbed from the nephron.
    c. in the urine.
    d. All of these are correct.

8. Glomerular filtration is associated with the
    a. glomerular capsule.
    b. distal convoluted tubule.
    c. collecting duct.
    d. All of these are correct.

9. Which of the following is a structural difference between the urinary systems of males and females?
    a. Males have a longer urethra than females.
    b. In males, the urethra passes through the prostate.
    c. In males, the urethra serves both the urinary and reproductive systems.
    d. All of these are correct.

10. The function of erythropoietin is
    a. reabsorption of sodium ions.
    b. excretion of potassium ions.
    c. reabsorption of water.
    d. to stimulate red blood cell production.
    e. to increase blood pressure.

11. The function of the loop of the nephron in the process of urine formation is
    a. reabsorption of water.
    b. production of filtrate.
    c. reabsorption of solutes.
    d. secretion of solutes.

12. Which of the following materials would not normally be filtered from the blood at the glomerulus?
    a. water
    b. urea
    c. protein
    d. glucose
    e. sodium ions

13. Which of the following materials would not be maximally reabsorbed from the filtrate?
    a. water
    b. glucose
    c. sodium ions
    d. urea
    e. amino acids

14. The renal medulla has a striped appearance due to the presence of which structure(s)?
    a. loops of the nephron
    b. collecting ducts
    c. peritubular capillaries
    d. Both a and b are correct.

15. By what process are most molecules secreted from the blood into the tubule?
    a. osmosis
    b. diffusion
    c. active transport
    d. facilitated diffusion

16. Which of the following is not correct?
    a. Uric acid is produced from the breakdown of amino acids.
    b. Creatinine is produced from breakdown reactions in the muscles.
    c. Urea is the primary nitrogenous waste of humans.
    d. Ammonia results from the deamination of amino acids.

17. When tracing the path of blood, the blood vessel that follows the renal artery is the
    a. peritubular capillary.
    b. efferent arteriole.
    c. afferent arteriole.
    d. renal vein.
    e. glomerulus.

18. When tracing the path of filtrate, the loop of the nephron follows which structure?
    a. collecting duct
    b. distal convoluted tubule
    c. proximal convoluted tubule
    d. glomerulus
    e. renal pelvis

In questions 19–25, match the function of the urinary system to the human organ system in the key.

Key:

a. muscular system
b. nervous system
c. endocrine system
d. cardiovascular system
e. respiratory system
f. digestive system
g. reproductive system

19. Liver synthesizes urea.

20. Smooth muscular contraction assists voiding of urine.

21. ADH, aldosterone, and atrial natriuretic hormone regulate reabsorption of Na^+ by kidneys.

22. Lungs excrete carbon dioxide and also convert angiotensin I to angiotensin II, leading to kidney regulation.

23. Brain controls nerves, which innervate muscles that permit urination.

24. Blood vessels deliver waste to be excreted.

25. Penis in males contains the urethra and performs urination.

26. Sodium is actively extruded from which part of the nephron?
    a. descending portion of the proximal convoluted tubule
    b. ascending portion of the loop of the nephron
    c. ascending portion of the distal convoluted tubule
    d. descending portion of the collecting duct

In questions 27–30, match these substances to the processes of urine formation in the key. Answers can be used more than once, and each question can have more than one answer.

Key:

    a. glomerular filtration
    b. tubular reabsorption
    c. tubular secretion

27. Glucose

28. Amino acids

29. Urea

30. H$^+$

31. Which portion of the nephron has cells with a brush border and many mitochondria?
    a. glomerular capsule   d. distal convoluted tubule
    b. proximal convoluted tubule e. collecting duct
    c. loop of the nephron

32. Label this diagram of a nephron.

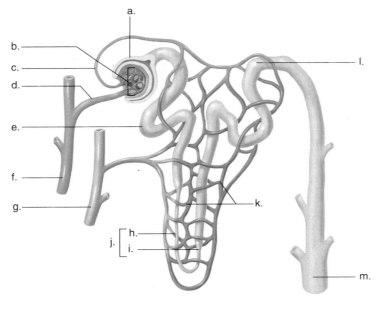

33. Absorption of the glomerular filtrate occurs primarily at the
    a. proximal convoluted tubule.
    b. distal convoluted tubule.
    c. loop of the nephron.
    d. collecting duct.

34. A countercurrent mechanism draws water from the
    a. proximal convoluted tubule.
    b. descending limb of the loop of the nephron.

    c. distal convoluted tubule.
    d. collecting duct.
    e. Both b and d are correct.

acidosis 170
aldosterone 168
alkalosis 170
antidiuretic hormone
    (ADH) 169
atrial natriuretic
    hormone (ANH) 169
buffer 170
collecting duct 165
creatinine 160
cystitis 171
dialysate 171
distal convoluted tubule 165
diuretic 169
erythropoietin 160
excretion 160
floating kidney 161
glomerular capsule
    (Bowman's capsule) 165
glomerular filtrate 167
glomerular filtration 167
glomerulus 164
gout 160
hemodialysis 171
juxtaglomerular apparatus 168

kidney 161
loop of the nephron (loop
    of Henle) 165
micturition 161
nephron 163
peritubular capillary
    network 164
proximal convoluted
    tubule 165
pyelonephritis 171
renal artery 161
renal cortex 163
renal medulla 163
renal pelvis 163
renal vein 161
renin 168
tubular reabsorption 167
tubular secretion 167
urea 160
uremia 171
ureter 161
urethra 161
urethritis 171
uric acid 160
urinary bladder 161

Match the key terms to these definitions.

    a. _____ Drug used to counteract hypertension by causing the excretion of water.

    b. _____ Removal of metabolic wastes from the body.

    c. _____ Tubular structure that receives urine from the bladder and carries it to the outside of the body.

    d. _____ Hollow chamber in the kidney that lies inside the renal medulla and receives freshly prepared urine from the collecting ducts.

    e. _____ Filtered portion of blood contained within the glomerular capsule.

www.mhhe.com/maderhuman9

The Online Learning Center provides a wealth of information fully organized and integrated by chapter. You will find practice quizzes, interactive activities, labeling exercises, flashcards, and much more that will complement your learning and understanding of human biology.

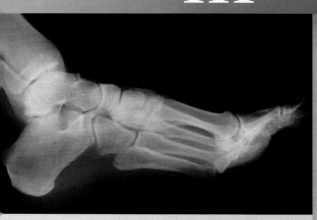

CHAPTER *10*

Skeletal System

10 Skeletal System 177

11 Muscular System 197

The skeletal and muscular systems give the body its shape and allow it to move. The skeletal system protects and supports other organs: The skull protects the brain, and the rib cage protects the lungs and heart; the pelvis supports the organs of the abdominal cavity. The skeletal system also contributes to homeostasis because it stores minerals and produces the formed elements of the blood.

Contraction of the skeletal muscles permits us to move from place to place but also accounts for our facial expressions and our ability to speak. Homeostasis would be impossible without movements of the rib cage and diaphragm for breathing, and contraction of the heart to keep the blood moving. Smooth muscle contraction allows the other internal organs to function; it helps move food along the digestive tract and urine along the urinary tract. Indeed, our lives depend on the functioning of the skeletal and muscular systems.

C H A P T E R   C O N C E P T S

10.1 Tissues of the Skeletal System
- What is the anatomy of compact bone? Of spongy bone?   178
- What are the three types of cartilage, and where are they found in the body?   178
- What type of connective tissue makes up ligaments and tendons?   178
- What is the structure of a typical bone, such as a long bone?   178–79

10.2 Bone Growth, Remodeling, and Repair
- What are the types of cells involved in bone growth, remodeling, and repair?   180
- How does bone growth occur during development?   180–81
- What hormones are involved in bone growth?   182
- How does remodeling affect the blood calcium concentration?   182–83
- How does bone repair itself?   183

10.3 Bones of the Skeleton
- What are the functions of the skeletal system?   185
- What are the bones of the axial and the appendicular skeletons?   185–91
- What are the bones of the cranium, and how are they situated?   186
- What are the bones of the face, and how do they contribute to facial features?   187
- What are the structure and function of the various types of vertebrae and the rib cage?   188–89
- What are the bones of a pectoral girdle and upper limb? Of the pelvic girdle and lower limb? How do these bones function?   190–91

10.4 Articulations
- What are the different types of articulations, and what types of movements are permitted by synovial joints?   192–93
- What are the symptoms of arthritic joints, and what treatments are available?   193

Jared sat up as the library loudspeaker announced the closing of the library in 10 minutes. He had been studying in the same position, hunched over a pile of books for several hours. As he stretched, he felt an aching pain in his lower back. He didn't think it was much of a problem, but when he awoke the next morning, in even greater pain, he began to wonder if he hadn't done some damage to his back.

Eighty percent of adults will experience some significant lower back pain during their lifetime. The lower back is a complex feat of engineering. Five lumbar vertebrae connect the upper spine to the pelvis. Between the vertebral bones are disks that act as stabilizers and shock absorbers. These are all interconnected with ligaments that help support the position of the vertebral column. Finally, muscles connect to the bones to provide the strength necessary for standing, sitting, and lifting. The muscles, ligaments, and bones all work together to provide the necessary support for these movements.

The most common causes of lower back injury are sprains and strains. A sprain occurs when the ligaments are torn from their attachments on the vertebrae. A strain occurs when the muscles are stretched or torn. These are often caused by lack of conditioning (exercise and stretching), improper use (standing, sitting, or lifting incorrectly), and obesity.

10.1   Tissues of the Skeletal System

The bones are largely composed of connective tissue—bone, cartilage, and fibrous connective tissues. Connective tissue contains cells separated by a matrix that contains fibers.

Bone

Bones are strong because their matrix contains mineral salts, notably calcium phosphate, in addition to protein fibers. **Compact bone** is highly organized and composed of tubular units called osteons. In a cross section of an osteon, bone cells called **osteocytes** lie in lacunae, which are tiny chambers arranged in concentric circles around a central canal (Fig. 10.1). Matrix fills the space between the rows of lacunae. Tiny canals called canaliculi (sing., canaliculus) run through the matrix, connecting the lacunae with one another and with the central canal. The cells stay in contact by strands of cytoplasm that extend into the canaliculi. Osteocytes nearest the center of an osteon exchange nutrients and wastes with the blood vessels in the central canal. These cells then pass on nutrients and collect wastes from the other cells via the gap junctions.

Compared with compact bone, **spongy bone** has an unorganized appearance (Fig. 10.1). It contains numerous thin plates (called trabeculae) separated by unequal spaces. Although this makes spongy bone lighter than compact bone, spongy bone is still designed for strength. Just as braces are used for support in buildings, the trabeculae follow lines of stress. The spaces of spongy bone are often filled with **red bone marrow,** a specialized tissue that produces all types of blood cells. The osteocytes of spongy bone are irregularly placed within the trabeculae, and canaliculi bring them nutrients from the red bone marrow.

Cartilage

Cartilage is not as strong as bone, but it is more flexible because the matrix is gel-like and contains many collagenous and elastic fibers. The cells, called **chondrocytes,** lie within lacunae that are irregularly grouped. Cartilage has no nerves, making it well suited for padding joints where the stresses of movement are intense. Cartilage also has no blood vessels, making it slow to heal.

The three types of cartilage differ according to the type and arrangement of fibers in the matrix. *Hyaline cartilage* is firm and somewhat flexible. The matrix appears uniform and glassy, but actually it contains a generous supply of collagen fibers. Hyaline cartilage is found at the ends of long bones, in the nose, at the ends of the ribs, and in the larynx and trachea.

Fibrocartilage is stronger than hyaline cartilage because the matrix contains wide rows of thick, collagen fibers. Fibrocartilage is able to withstand both tension and pressure, and is found where support is of prime importance—in the disks located between the vertebrae and also in the cartilage of the knee.

Elastic cartilage is more flexible than hyaline cartilage because the matrix contains mostly elastin fibers. This type of cartilage is found in the ear flaps and the epiglottis.

Fibrous Connective Tissue

Fibrous connective tissue contains rows of cells called fibroblasts separated by bundles of collagenous fibers. This tissue makes up the **ligaments** that connect bone to bone and the **tendons** that connect muscles to a bone at **joints,** which are also called articulations.

Structure of a Typical Bone

Figure 10.1 shows how the tissues we have been discussing are arranged in a long bone. The expanded region at the end of a long bone is called an epiphysis (pl., epiphyses). The epiphyses are composed largely of spongy bone that contains red bone marrow, where blood cells are made. The epiphyses are coated with a thin layer of hyaline cartilage, which is called **articular cartilage** because it occurs at a joint.

The shaft, or main portion of the bone, is called the diaphysis. The diaphysis has a large **medullary cavity** whose walls are composed of compact bone. The medullary cavity is lined with a thin, vascular membrane (the endosteum) and is filled with yellow bone marrow that stores fat.

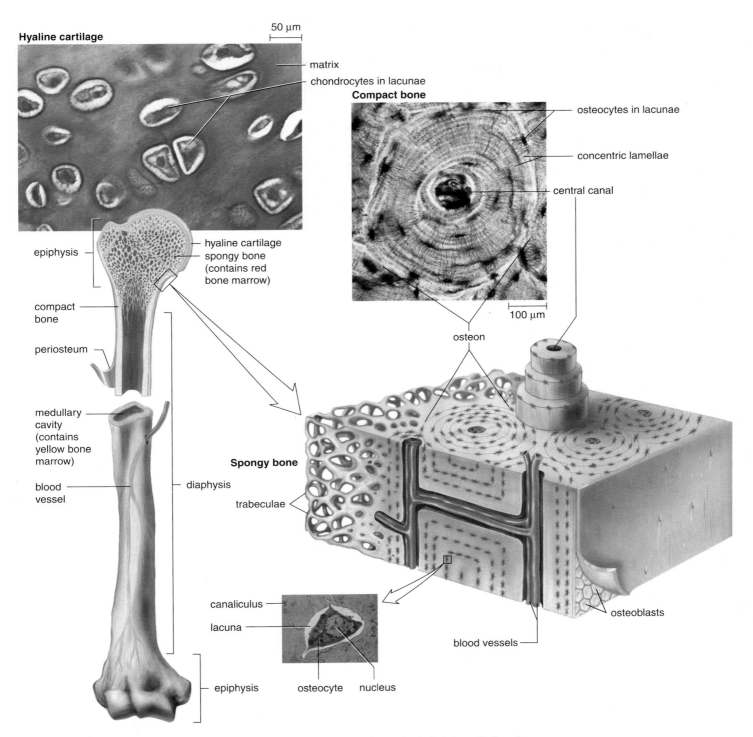

Figure 10.1   Anatomy of a long bone, from the macroscopic to the microscopic level.

A long bone is encased by the periosteum except at the epiphyses, where it is covered by hyaline (articular) cartilage (see micrograph, *top left*). Spongy bone located in each epiphysis may contain red bone marrow. The diaphysis contains yellow bone marrow and is bordered by compact bone, which is shown in the enlargement and micrograph *(top right)*.

Except for the articular cartilage on its ends, a long bone is completely covered by a layer of fibrous connective tissue called the **periosteum.** This covering contains blood vessels, lymphatic vessels, and nerves. Note in Figure 10.1 how a blood vessel penetrates the periosteum and enters the bone where it gives off branches within the central canals. The periosteum is continuous with ligaments and tendons that are connected to a bone.

10.2 Bone Growth, Remodeling, and Repair

The importance of the skeleton to the human form is evident by its early appearance during development. The skeleton starts forming at about 6 weeks, when the embryo is only about 12 mm (0.5 inches) long. Most bones grow in length and width through adolescence but some continue enlarging until about age 25. In a sense, bones can grow throughout a lifetime, because they are able to respond to stress by changing size, shape, and strength. This process is called remodeling. If a bone fractures, it can heal by what is called bone repair.

Bones are composed of living tissues, as exemplified by their ability to grow, remodel, and undergo repair. Several different types of cells are involved in bone growth, remodeling, and repair:

Osteoblasts are bone-forming cells. They secrete the organic matrix of bone and promote the deposition of calcium salts into the matrix.

Osteocytes are mature bone cells derived from osteoblasts. They maintain the structure of bone.

Osteoclasts are bone-absorbing cells. They break down bone and assist in depositing calcium and phosphate in the blood.

Throughout life, osteoclasts are removing the matrix of bone and osteoblasts are building it up. When osteoblasts are surrounded by calcified matrix, they become the osteocytes within lacunae.

Bone Development and Growth

The term **ossification** refers to the formation of bone. The bones of the skeleton form during embryonic development in two distinctive ways: intramembranous ossification and endochondral ossification (Fig. 10.2).

Intramembranous Ossification

In **intramembranous ossification,** bones develop between sheets of fibrous connective tissue. Flat bones, such as the bones of the skull, are examples of intramembranous bones.

Ossification occurs in two locations: inside and outside. Inside, cells derived from connective tissue cells become osteoblasts located in ossification centers. The osteoblasts secrete the organic matrix of bone consisting of mucopolysaccharides and collagen fibrils. Calcification occurs when calcium salts are added to the organic matrix. The osteoblasts promote calcification. Ossification results in the trabeculae of spongy bone, and spongy bone remains on the inside. Recall that red bone marrow is associated with spongy bone and flat bones, such as those of the skull and clavicles (collarbones).

A periosteum forms on the the outside of flat bones and the osteoblasts that carry out ossification are derived from the periosteum. Outside, ossification proceeds the same way as inside, only the trabeculae of spongy bone continue to grow thicker. Finally, the trabeculae fuse and become compact bone. The compact bone forms a bone collar that surrounds the spongy bone on the inside.

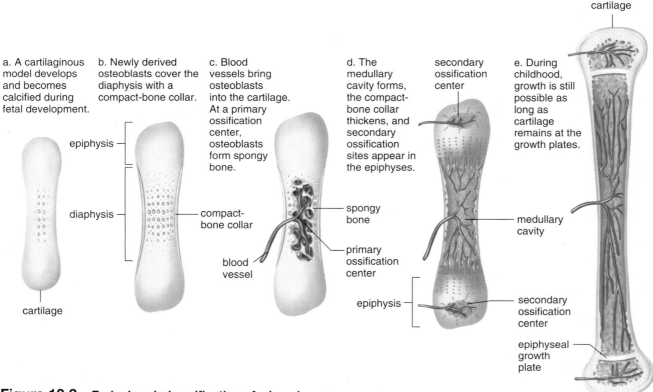

a. A cartilaginous model develops and becomes calcified during fetal development.

b. Newly derived osteoblasts cover the diaphysis with a compact-bone collar.

c. Blood vessels bring osteoblasts into the cartilage. At a primary ossification center, osteoblasts form spongy bone.

d. The medullary cavity forms, the compact-bone collar thickens, and secondary ossification sites appear in the epiphyses.

e. During childhood, growth is still possible as long as cartilage remains at the growth plates.

epiphysis

diaphysis

cartilage

compact-bone collar

blood vessel

spongy bone

primary ossification center

secondary ossification center

epiphysis

medullary cavity

secondary ossification center

joint cartilage

epiphyseal growth plate

Figure 10.2   **Endochondral ossification of a long bone.**

Endochondral Ossification

Most of the bones of the human skeleton are formed by **endochondral ossification.** During endochondral ossification, bone replaces the cartilaginous models of the bones. Gradually, the cartilage is replaced by the calcified bone matrix that makes these bones capable of bearing weight.

Inside, bone formation spreads from the center to the ends and this accounts for the term used for this type of ossification. The long bones, such as the tibia, provide examples of endochondral ossification (Fig. 10.2).

1. *The cartilage model.* Chondrocytes lay down hyaline cartilage, which is shaped like the future bones. Therefore, they are called cartilage models of the future bones. As the cartilage models calcify, the chondrocytes die off.
2. *The bone collar.* Osteoblasts, derived from the newly formed periosteum, secrete the organic bone matrix and the matrix undergoes calcification. The result is a bone collar, which covers the diaphysis (Fig. 10.2). The bone collar is composed of compact bone. In time, the bone collar thickens.
3. *The primary ossification center.* Blood vessels bring osteoblasts to the interior and they begin to lay down spongy bone. This region is called a primary ossification center because it is the first center for bone formation.
4. *The medullary cavity and secondary ossification sites.* The spongy bone of the diaphysis is absorbed by osteoclasts, and the cavity created becomes the medullary cavity. Shortly after birth, secondary ossification centers form in the epiphyses. Spongy bone persists in the epiphyses, and they contain red bone

marrow for quite some time. Cartilage is present at two locations: the epiphyseal (growth) plate and articular cartilage.

5. *The epiphyseal (growth) plate.* A band of cartilage called a **growth plate** remains between the primary ossification center and each secondary center. The limbs keep increasing in length as long as growth plates are still present.

Figure 10.3 shows that the epiphyseal plate contains four layers. The layer nearest the epiphysis rests and serves to attach the epiphysis to the diaphysis. The next layer is undergoing mitosis and producing new cells. In the third layer, the cartilage cells are dying off, and in the fourth layer, bone is forming. Osteoblasts invade this layer, and bone formation occurs as the bone increases in length. The epiphyses of bones can enlarge because the inside layer of articular cartilage also undergoes ossification in the manner described.

The diameter of a bone enlarges as a bone lengthens. Osteoblasts derived from the periosteum are active in new bone deposition as osteoclasts enlarge the medullary cavity from inside.

Final Size of the Bones   When the epiphyseal plates close, bone length can no longer occur. The epiphyseal plates in the arms and legs of women close at about age 18, while they do not close in men until about age 20. Portions of other types of bones may continue to grow until age 25. Hormones are chemical messengers secreted by the endocrine glands and distributed about the body by the bloodstream. Hormones control the activity of the epiphyseal plate, as is discussed next.

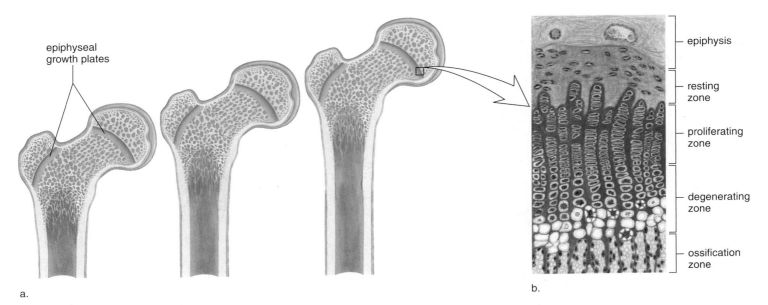

a.

b.

Figure 10.3   Bone growth in length.
a. Length of a bone increases when cartilage is replaced by bone at the growth plate. **b.** Chondrocytes produce new cartilage at the upper layer (resting zone) nearest the epiphysis, and cartilage becomes bone at the lower layer (ossification zone) closest to diaphysis.

Hormones Affect Bone Growth

The importance of bone growth is signified by the involvement of several hormones in bone growth. A hormone is a chemical messenger, produced by one part of the body, which acts on a different part of the body.

Vitamin D is formed in the skin, when it is exposed to sunlight, but it can also be consumed in the diet. Milk, in particular, is often fortified with vitamin D today. In the kidneys, vitamin D is converted to a hormone that acts on the intestinal tract. The chief function of vitamin D is intestinal absorption of calcium. In the absence of vitamin D, children can develop rickets, a condition marked by bone deformities including bowed long bones (Fig. 10.4).

Growth hormone (GH) directly stimulates growth of the epiphyseal plate, as well as bone growth in general. However, growth hormone will be somewhat ineffective if the metabolic activity of cells is not promoted. Thyroid hormone, in particular, promotes the metabolic activity of cells. Too much growth hormone during childhood can produce excessive growth and even gigantism, while too little can cause dwarfism. Too much GH produces gigantism in youths prior to epiphyseal fusion, and acromegaly in adults following epiphyseal fusion (see Fig. 14.6 and Fig. 14.7).

Adolescents usually experience a dramatic increase in height called the growth spurt due to an increased level of sex hormones, which apparently stimulate osteoblast activity to the point that the epiphyseal plates become "paved over" by the faster growing bone tissue, within one or two years of the onset of puberty.

Bone Remodeling and Its Role in Homeostasis

Bone is constantly being broken down by osteoclasts and re-formed by osteoblasts in the adult. As much as 18% of bone is recycled each year. This process of bone renewal, often called **bone remodeling,** normally keeps bones strong (Fig. 10.5). In Paget's disease, new bone is generated at a faster-than-normal rate. This rapid remodeling produces bone that's softer and weaker than normal bone and can cause bone pain, deformities, and fractures.

Bone recycling allows the body to regulate the amount of calcium in the blood. To illustrate that the blood calcium level is critical, recall that calcium is required for blood to clot. Also, if the blood calcium concentration is too high, neurons and muscle cells no longer function, and if it falls too low, they become so excited, convulsions occur. The bones are the storage sites for calcium—if the blood calcium rises above normal, at least some of the excess is deposited in the bones and if the blood calcium dips too low, calcium is removed from the bones to bring it back up to the normal level.

Two hormones, in particular, are involved in regulating the blood calcium level. Parathyroid hormone (PTH) accelerates bone recycling, and in that way, increases the blood calcium level. Calcitonin is a hormone that acts opposite to PTH. The female sex hormone estrogen can actually increase the number of osteoblasts, and the reduction of estrogen in older women is often given as reason for the development of weak bones, called osteoporosis. Osteoporosis is discussed

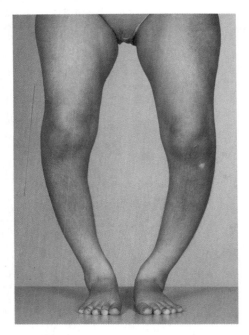

Figure 10.4   Rickets.
Rickets occurs when children have a deficiency of vitamin D. Production of vitamin D in skin exposed to sunlight was the chief source of vitamin D until early in the twentieth century when a form of vitamin D was discovered in fish liver oil. Now, vitamin D is available in tablet form.

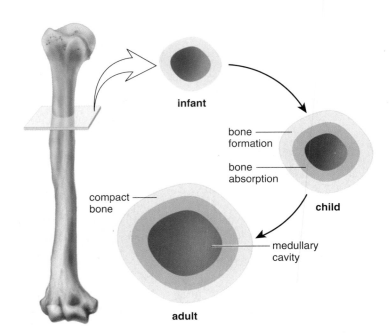

Figure 10.5   Bone growth and remodeling.
Diameter of a bone increases as bone absorption occurs inside the shaft and is matched by bone formation outside the shaft.

in the Health Focus on page 184. In the young adult the activity of osteoclasts is matched by the activity of osteoblasts, and bone mass remains stable until about age 45 years in women. After that age, bone mass starts to decrease. Men also experience osteoporosis later in life.

Bone remodeling also accounts for why bones can respond to stress (Fig. 10.5). If you engage in an activity that calls upon the use of a particular bone, it will enlarge in diameter at the region most affected by the activity. During this process, osteoblasts in the periosteum form compact bone around the external bone surface and osteoclasts break down bone on the internal bone surface, around the medullary cavity. This prevents the bones from getting too heavy and thick. Today, exercises, such as walking, jogging, and weight lifting, are recommended ways of keeping the bones strong because they stimulate the work of osteoblasts instead of osteoclasts.

Bone Repair

Repair of a bone is required after it breaks or fractures. Fracture repair takes place over a span of several months in a series of four steps, shown in Figure 10.6 and listed here:

1. *Hematoma.* After a fracture, blood escapes from ruptured blood vessels and forms a hematoma (mass of clotted blood) in the space between the broken bones within 6–8 hours.

2. *Fibrocartilaginous callus.* Tissue repair begins, and a fibrocartilaginous callus fills the space between the ends of the broken bone for about three weeks.

3. *Bony callus.* Osteoblasts produce trabeculae of spongy bone and convert the fibrocartilage callus to a bony callus that joins the broken bones together and lasts about three to four months.

4. *Remodeling.* Osteoblasts build new compact bone at the periphery, and osteoclasts absorb the spongy bone, creating a new medullary cavity.

In some ways, bone repair parallels the development of a bone except that the first step, hematoma, indicates that injury has occurred, and then a fibrocartilaginous callus precedes the production of compact bone.

The naming of fractures tells you what kind of break occurred. A fracture is complete if the bone is broken clear through and incomplete if the bone is not separated into two parts. A fracture is simple if it does not pierce the skin and compound if it does pierce the skin. Impacted means that the broken ends are wedged into each other, and a spiral fracture occurs when the break is ragged due to twisting of a bone.

Bone is living tissue. It develops, grows, remodels, and repairs itself. In all these processes, osteoclasts break down bone, and osteoblasts build bone.

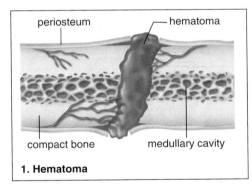
1. Hematoma
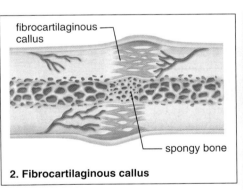
2. Fibrocartilaginous callus
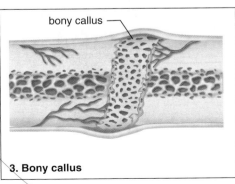
3. Bony callus
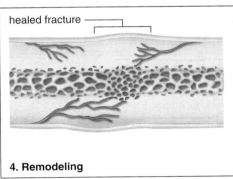
4. Remodeling

a.   b.

Figure 10.6   Bone fracture and repair.
a. Steps in the repair of a fracture. **b.** A cast helps stabilize the bones while repair takes place. Fiberglass casts are now replacing plaster of Paris as the usual material for a cast.

Health Focus

You Can Avoid Osteoporosis

Osteoporosis is a condition in which the bones are weakened due to a decrease in the bone mass that makes up the skeleton. Throughout life, bones are continuously remodeled. While a child is growing, the rate of bone formation is greater than the rate of bone breakdown. The skeletal mass continues to increase until ages 20–30. After that, the rates of formation and breakdown of bone mass are equal until ages 40–50. Then, reabsorption begins to exceed formation, and the total bone mass slowly decreases.

Young people should be aware of the following risk factors for osteoporosis:

- white or Asian race
- thin body type
- family history of osteoporosis
- early menopause (before age 45)
- smoking
- a diet low in calcium, or excessive alcohol consumption and caffeine intake
- sedentary lifestyle

The stronger your bones are when young, the less likely you are to get osteoporosis when older. Adequate dietary calcium throughout life is an important protection against osteoporosis. The U.S. National Institutes of Health recommend a calcium intake of 1,200–1,500 mg per day during puberty. Males and females require 1,000 mg per day until age 65 and 1,500 mg per day after age 65. In postmenopausal women not receiving estrogen replacement therapy, 1,500 mg per day is desirable.

Over time, men are apt to lose 25% and women 35% of their bone mass. But we have to consider that men tend to have denser bones than women anyway, and their testosterone (male sex hormone) level generally does not begin to decline significantly until after age 65. In contrast, the estrogen (female sex hormone) level in women begins to decline at about age 45. Since sex hormones play an important role in maintaining bone strength, this difference means that women are more likely than men to suffer fractures, involving especially the hip, vertebrae, long bones, and pelvis. Although osteoporosis may at times be the result of various disease processes, it is essentially a disease of aging.

A small daily amount of vitamin D is also necessary to absorb calcium from the digestive tract. Exposure to sunlight is required to allow skin to synthesize vitamin D. If you reside on or north of a "line" drawn from Boston to Milwaukee, to Minneapolis, to Boise, chances are, you're not getting enough vitamin D during the winter months. Therefore, you should avail yourself of vitamin D present in fortified foods such as low-fat milk and cereal or by taking a vitamin supplement.

Presently, bone density is measured by a method called dual-energy X-ray absorptiometry (DEXA). This test measures bone density based on the absorption of photons generated by an X-ray tube. Soon there may be a blood and urine test to detect the biochemical markers of bone loss, making it possible for all older women and at-risk men to be screened in their doctor's office for osteoporosis.

If the bones are already thin, it is worthwhile to take other measures to gain bone density because even a slight increase can significantly reduce fracture risk. A combination of exercise and drug treatment, as recommended by a physician, may yield the best results. Very inactive people, such as those confined to bed, lose bone mass 25 times faster than people who are moderately active. Thus, regular, moderate, weight-bearing exercise like walking or jogging is another good way to maintain bone strength (Fig. 10A).

A wide variety of prescribed drugs that have different modes of action are available. Hormone therapy includes black cohosh, which is a phytoestrogen (estrogen made by a plant as opposed to an animal). Calcitonin is a naturally occurring hormone whose main site of action is the skeleton, where it inhibits the action of osteoclasts, the cells that break down bone. Also, alendronate is a drug that acts similarly to calcitonin. After three years of alendronate therapy, an increase in spinal density by about 8% and hip density by about 7% is obtained. Promising new drugs include slow-release fluoride therapy and certain growth hormones. These medications stimulate the formation of new bone.

Figure 10A **Preventing osteoporosis.**

a. Exercise can help prevent osteoporosis. **b.** Normal bone growth compared with bone from a person with osteoporosis illustrating why osteoporosis is described as "weak bones."

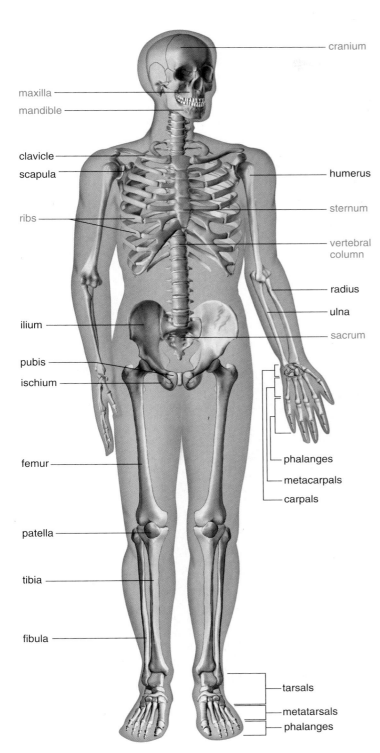

- cranium
- maxilla
- mandible
- clavicle
- scapula
- humerus
- sternum
- ribs
- vertebral column
- radius
- ulna
- ilium
- sacrum
- pubis
- ischium
- phalanges
- metacarpals
- carpals
- femur
- patella
- tibia
- fibula
- tarsals
- metatarsals
- phalanges

Figure 10.7 **The skeleton.**
The skeleton of a human adult contains bones that belong to the axial skeleton (red labels) and those that belong to the appendicular skeleton (black labels). The bones of the axial skeleton are located along the body's axis and the bones of the appendicular skeleton are located in the girdles and appendages.

10.3 Bones of the Skeleton

We will discuss the functions of the skeleton in relation to particular bones:

The skeleton supports the body. The bones of the legs (the femur in particular and also the tibia) support the entire body when we are standing, and the coxal bones of the pelvic girdle support the abdominal cavity.

The skeleton protects soft body parts. The bones of the skull protect the brain; the rib cage, composed of the ribs, thoracic vertebrae, and sternum, protects the heart and lungs.

The skeleton produces blood cells. All bones in the fetus have spongy bone containing red bone marrow that produces blood cells. In the adult, the flat bones of the skull, ribs, sternum, clavicles, epiphyses of larger long bones, such as the femur, and also the vertebrae and pelvis produce blood cells.

The skeleton stores minerals and fat. All bones have a matrix that contains calcium phosphate. When bones are remodeled, osteoclasts break down bone and assist in returning calcium ions and phosphate ions to the bloodstream. Fat is stored in yellow bone marrow.

The skeleton, along with the muscles, permits flexible body movement. While articulations (joints) occur between all the bones, we associate body movement in particular with the bones of the legs (especially the femur and tibia) and the feet (tarsals, metatarsals, and phalanges) because we use them when walking.

Classification of the Bones

The bones are classified according to their shape. For example, long bones, exemplified by the humerus and femur, are longer than they are wide. Short bones, such as the carpals and tarsals, are cube-shaped—that is, their lengths and widths are about equal. Flat bones, such as those of the skull, are plate-like with broad surfaces. Round bones, exemplified by the patella, are circular in shape. Irregular bones, such as the vertebrae and facial bones, have varied shapes that permit connections with other bones.

The 206 bones of the skeleton are also classified according to whether they occur in the axial skeleton or the appendicular skeleton. The axial skeleton is in the midline of the body, and the appendicular skeleton consists of the limbs along with their girdles (Fig. 10.7).

The bones of the skeleton are not smooth; they have articulating depressions and protuberances at various joints. They also have projections where the muscles attach and openings for nerves and/or blood vessels to pass through.

The skeleton is divided into the axial and appendicular skeletons. Each has different types of bones with protuberances at joints and processes where the muscles attach.

The Axial Skeleton

The **axial skeleton** lies in the mid-line of the body and consists of the skull, hyoid bone, vertebral column, the rib cage, and the ear ossicles.

The Skull

The **skull** is formed by the cranium (braincase) and the facial bones. It should be noted, however, that some cranial bones contribute to the face.

The Cranium   The cranium protects the brain. In adults, it is composed of eight bones fitted tightly together. In newborns, certain cranial bones are not completely formed and instead are joined by membranous regions called **fontanels.** The fontanels usually close by the age of 16 months by the process of intramembranous ossification.

Some of the bones of the cranium contain the **sinuses,** air spaces lined by mucous membrane. The sinuses reduce the weight of the skull and give a resonant sound to the voice. Two sinuses called the mastoid sinuses drain into the middle ear. **Mastoiditis,** a condition that can lead to deafness, is an inflammation of these sinuses.

The major bones of the cranium have the same names as the lobes of the brain: frontal, parietal, occipital, and temporal. On the top of the cranium (Fig. 10.8*a*), the **frontal bone** forms the forehead, the **parietal bones** extend to the sides, and the **occipital bone** curves to form the base of the skull. Here there is a large opening, the **foramen magnum** (Fig. 10.8*b*), through which the spinal cord passes and becomes the brainstem. Below the much larger parietal bones, each temporal bone has an opening (external auditory canal) that leads to the middle ear.

The **sphenoid bone,** which is shaped like a bat with outstretched wings, extends across the floor of the cranium from one side to the other. The sphenoid is the keystone of the cranial bones because all the other bones articulate with it. The sphenoid completes the sides of the skull and also contributes to forming the orbits (eye sockets). The **ethmoid bone,** which lies in front of the sphenoid, also helps form the orbits and the nasal septum. The orbits are completed by various facial bones. The eye sockets are called orbits because we can rotate our eyes.

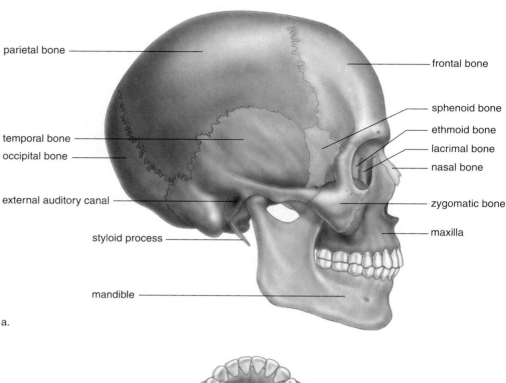

a.

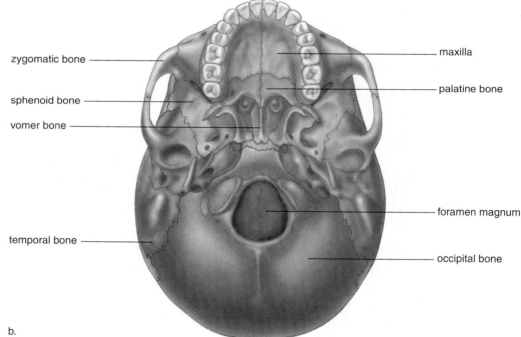

b.

Figure 10.8   Bones of the skull.
a. Lateral view. **b.** Inferior view.

The cranium contains eight bones: the frontal, two parietal, the occipital, two temporal, the sphenoid, and the ethmoid.

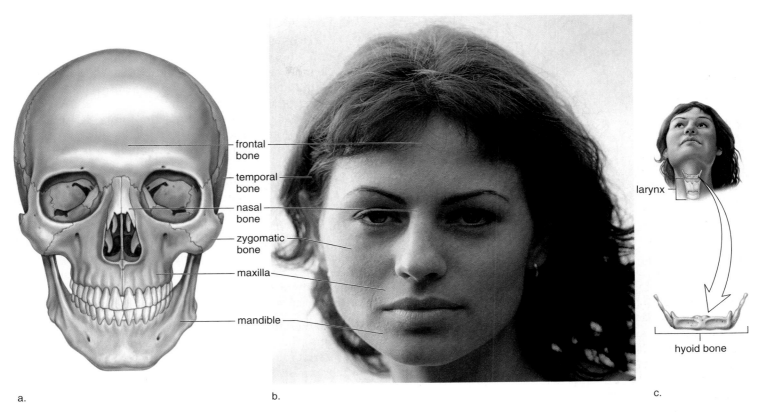

frontal
bone

temporal
bone

nasal
bone

zygomatic
bone

maxilla

mandible

larynx

hyoid bone

a.   b.   c.

Figure 10.9   **Bones of the face and the hyoid.**
a. The frontal bone forms the forehead and eyebrow ridges; the zygomatic bones form the cheekbones; and the maxillae have numerous functions.
They assist in the formation of the eye sockets, and the nasal cavity. They form the upper jaw and contain sockets for the upper teeth. The
mandible is the lower jaw with sockets for the lower teeth. The mandible has a projection we call the chin. **b.** The maxillae, frontal, and nasal
bones help form the external nose. **c.** The hyoid bone is located as shown.

The Facial Bones   The most prominent of the facial bones
are the mandible, the maxillae (sing., maxilla), the zygomatic
bones, and the nasal bones.

The **mandible,** or lower jaw, is the only movable portion
of the skull (Fig. 10.9*a,b*), and its action permits us to chew
our food. It also forms the chin. Tooth sockets are located on
the mandible and on the **maxillae,** the bones that form the
upper jaw and also the anterior portion of the hard palate.
The palatine bones make up the posterior portion of the
hard palate and the floor of the nose (see Fig. 10.8*b*).

The lips and cheeks have a core of skeletal muscle. The
zygomatic bones are the cheekbone prominences, and the
nasal bones form the bridge of the nose. Other bones (e.g.,
ethmoid and vomer) are a part of the nasal septum, which
divides the interior of the nose into two nasal cavities. The
lacrimal bone (see Fig. 10.8*a*) contains the opening for the
nasolacrimal canal, which brings tears from the eyes to
the nose.

Certain cranial bones contribute to the face. The sphenoid
bones account for the flattened areas we call the temples. The
frontal bone forms the forehead and has supraorbital ridges
where the eyebrows are located. Glasses sit where the frontal
bone joins the nasal bones.

Although the ears are formed only by cartilage and not by
bone, the nose is a mixture of bones, cartilages, and connective
tissues. The cartilages complete the tip of the nose, and fibrous
connective tissue forms the flared sides of the nose.

Among the facial bones, the mandible is the lower
jaw where the chin is located, the two maxillae
form the upper jaw, the two zygomatic bones are
the cheekbones, and the two nasal bones form
the bridge of the nose.

The Hyoid Bone

Although the **hyoid bone** is not part of the skull, it will be
mentioned here because it is a part of the axial skeleton. It is
the only bone in the body that does not articulate with another
bone (Fig. 10.9*c*). It is attached to the temporal bones by muscles and ligaments and to the larynx by a membrane. The larynx is the voice box at the top of the trachea in the neck region.
The hyoid bone anchors the tongue and serves as the site for
the attachment of muscles associated with swallowing.

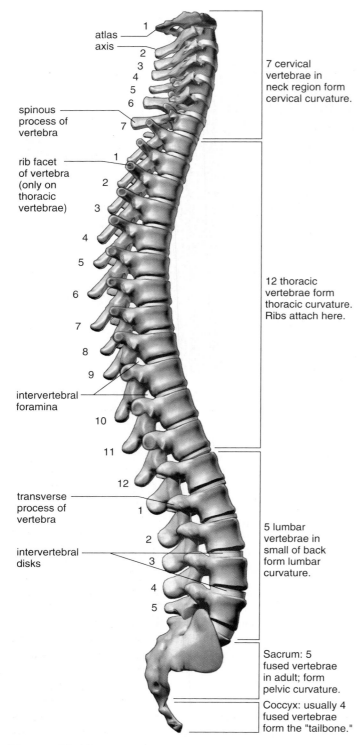

atlas
axis

7 cervical vertebrae in neck region form cervical curvature.

spinous process of vertebra

rib facet of vertebra (only on thoracic vertebrae)

12 thoracic vertebrae form thoracic curvature. Ribs attach here.

intervertebral foramina

transverse process of vertebra

intervertebral disks

5 lumbar vertebrae in small of back form lumbar curvature.

Sacrum: 5 fused vertebrae in adult; form pelvic curvature.

Coccyx: usually 4 fused vertebrae form the "tailbone."

Figure 10.10   The vertebral column.
The vertebral column is made up of 33 vertebrae separated by intervertebral disks. The intervertebral disks make the column flexible. The vertebrae are named for their location in the vertebral column. For example, the thoracic vertebrate are located in the thorax. Note that humans have a coccyx, which is also called a tailbone.

The Vertebral Column

The **vertebral column** consists of 33 vertebrae (Fig. 10.10). Normally, the vertebral column has four curvatures that provide more resilience and strength for an upright posture than a straight column could provide. **Scoliosis** is an abnormal lateral (sideways) curvature of the spine. Two other well-known abnormal curvatures are kyphosis, an abnormal posterior curvature that often results in a hunchback, and lordosis, an abnormal anterior curvature resulting in a swayback.

The vertebral column forms when the vertebrae join. The spinal cord, which passes through the vertebral canal, gives off the spinal nerves at the intervertebral foramina. Spinal nerves function to control skeletal muscle contraction among other functions. The spinous processes of the vertebrae can be felt as bony projections along the midline of the back. The spinous processes and also the transverse processes, which extend laterally, serve as attachment sites for the muscles that move the vertebral column.

Types of Vertebrae   The various vertebrae are named according to their location in the vertebral column. The cervical vertebrae are located in the neck. The first cervical vertebra, called the **atlas,** holds up the head. It is so named because Atlas, of Greek mythology, held up the world. Movement of the atlas permits the "yes" motion of the head. It also allows the head to tilt from side to side. The second cervical vertebra is called the **axis** because it allows a degree of rotation, as when we shake the head "no." The thoracic vertebrae have long, thin, spinous processes and articular facets for the attachment of the ribs (Fig. 10.11*a*). Lumbar vertebrae have a large body and thick processes. The five sacral vertebrae are fused together in the sacrum. The coccyx, or tailbone, is usually composed of four fused vertebrae.

Intervertebral Disks   Between the vertebrae are **intervertebral disks** composed of fibrocartilage that acts as a kind of padding. They prevent the vertebrae from grinding against one another and absorb shock caused by movements such as running, jumping, and even walking. The presence of the disks allows the vertebrae to move as we bend forward, backward, and from side to side. Unfortunately, these disks become weakened with age and can herniate and rupture. Pain results if a disk presses against the spinal cord and/or spinal nerves. If that occurs, surgical removal of the disk may relieve the pain.

The vertebral column forms when the vertebrae join. The vertebral column supports the head and trunk, protects the spinal cord, and serves as a site for muscle attachment. The intervertebral disks provide padding and account for the flexibility of the column.

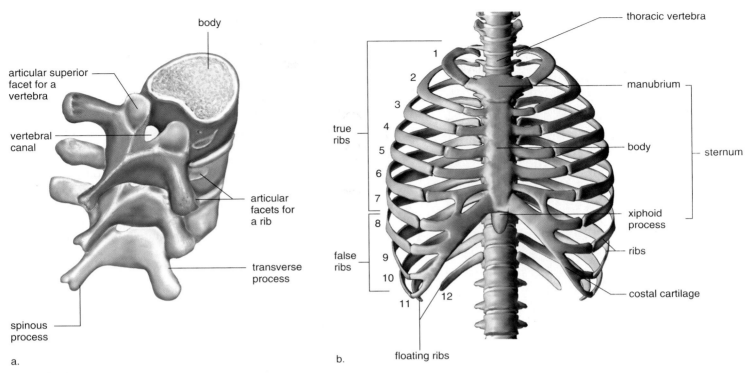

a.

b.

Figure 10.11 **Thoracic vertebrae and the rib cage.**
a. The thoracic vertebrae articulate with one another and also with the ribs at articular facets. A thoracic vertebra has two facets for articulation with a rib; one is on the body, and the other is on the transverse process. **b.** The rib cage consists of the 12 thoracic vertebrae, the 12 pairs of ribs, the costal cartilages, and the sternum. The rib cage protects the lungs and the heart.

The Rib Cage

The rib cage, also called the thoracic cage, is composed of the thoracic vertebrae, the ribs and their associated cartilages, and the sternum (Fig. 10.11b). The rib cage is part of the axial skeleton.

The rib cage demonstrates how the skeleton is protective but also flexible. The rib cage protects the heart and lungs; yet it swings outward and upward upon inspiration and then downward and inward upon expiration.

The Ribs

A rib is flattened bone that originates at the thoracic vertebrae and proceeds toward the anterior thoracic wall. There are 12 pairs of ribs. All 12 pairs connect directly to the thoracic vertebrae in the back. A rib articulates with the body and transverse process of its corresponding thoracic vertebra. Each rib curves outward and then forward and downward.

The upper seven pairs of ribs connect directly to the sternum by means of costal cartilages. These are called the "true ribs." The next three pairs of ribs do not connect directly to the sternum, and they are called the "false ribs." They attach to the sternum by means of a common cartilage. The last two pairs are called "floating ribs" because they do not attach to the sternum at all.

The Sternum

The **sternum** lies in the midline of the body. It, along with the ribs, helps protect the heart and lungs. The sternum, or breastbone, is a flat bone that has the shape of a knife.

The sternum is composed of three bones that fuse during fetal development. These bones are the manubrium (the handle), the body (the blade), and the xiphoid process (the point of blade). The manubrium articulates with the clavicles of the appendicular skeleton and the first pair of ribs. The manubrium joins with the body of the sternum at an angle. This is an important anatomical landmark because it occurs at the level of the second rib and therefore allows the ribs to be counted. Counting the ribs is sometimes done to determine where the apex of the heart is located—usually between the fifth and sixth ribs.

The xiphoid process is the third part of the sternum. Composed of hyaline cartilage in the child, it becomes ossified in the adult. The variably shaped xiphoid process serves as an attachment site for the diaphragm, which divides the thoracic cavity from the abdominal cavity.

The rib (thoracic) cage, consisting of the thoracic vertebrae, the ribs, costal cartilages, and the sternum, protects the heart and lungs in the thoracic cavity.

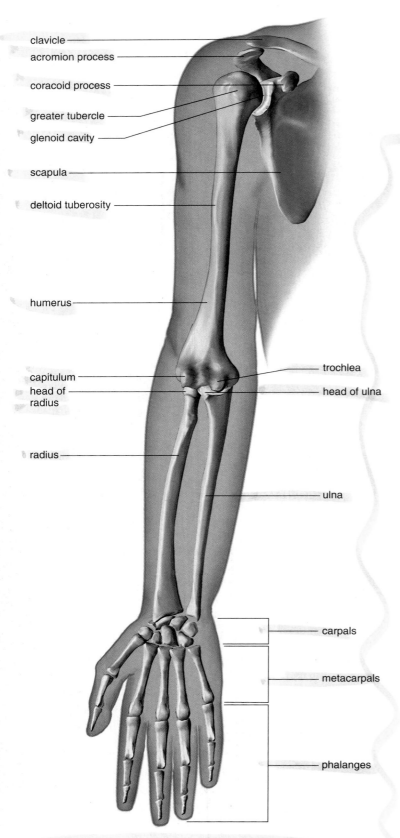

clavicle
acromion process
coracoid process
greater tubercle
glenoid cavity
scapula
deltoid tuberosity
humerus
capitulum
head of radius
radius
trochlea
head of ulna
ulna
carpals
metacarpals
phalanges

Figure 10.12   Bones of a pectoral (shoulder) girdle and upper limb.

The Appendicular Skeleton

The **appendicular skeleton** consists of the bones within the pectoral and pelvic girdles and their attached limbs. A pectoral (shoulder) girdle and upper limb are specialized for flexibility; the pelvic (hip) girdle and lower limbs are specialized for strength.

The Pectoral Girdle and Upper Limb

The body has left and right **pectoral girdles;** each consists of a scapula (shoulder blade) and a clavicle (collarbone) (Fig. 10.12). The **clavicle** extends across the top of the thorax; it articulates with (joins with) the sternum and the acromion process of the **scapula,** a visible bone in the back. The muscles of the arm and chest attach to the coracoid process of the scapula. The **glenoid cavity** of the scapula articulates with and is much smaller than the head of the humerus. This allows the arm to move in almost any direction, but reduces stability. This is the joint that is most apt to dislocate. Ligaments, and also tendons, stabilize this joint. Tendons that extend to the humerus from four small muscles originating on the scapula form the **rotator cuff.** Vigorous circular movements of the arm can lead to rotator cuff injuries.

The components of a pectoral girdle follow freely the movements of the upper limb, which consists of the humerus within the arm and the radius and ulna within the forearm. The **humerus,** the single long bone in the arm, has a smoothly rounded head that fits into the glenoid cavity of the scapula as mentioned. The shaft of the humerus has a tuberosity (protuberance) where the deltoid, a shoulder muscle, attaches. After death, enlargement of this tuberosity can be used as evidence that the person did a lot of heavy lifting.

The far end of the humerus has two protuberances, called the capitulum and the trochlea, which articulate respectively with the **radius** and the **ulna** at the elbow. The bump at the back of the elbow is the olecranon process of the ulna.

When the upper limb is held so that the palm is turned forward, the radius and ulna are about parallel to each other. When the upper limb is turned so that the palm is turned backward, the radius crosses in front of the ulna, a feature that contributes to the easy twisting motion of the forearm.

The hand has many bones, and this increases its flexibility. The wrist has eight **carpal** bones, which look like small pebbles. From these, five **metacarpal** bones fan out to form a framework for the palm. The metacarpal bone that leads to the thumb is opposable to the other digits. (**Digits** is a term that refers to either fingers or toes.) The knuckles are the enlarged distal ends of the metacarpals. Beyond the metacarpals are the **phalanges,** the bones of the fingers and the thumb. The phalanges of the hand are long, slender, and lightweight.

The pectoral girdle and upper limb are specialized for flexibility of movement.

The Pelvic Girdle and Lower Limb

Figure 10.13 shows how the lower limb is attached to the pelvic girdle. The **pelvic girdle** (hip girdle) consists of two heavy, large coxal bones (hipbones). The **pelvis** is a basin composed of the pelvic girdle, sacrum, and coccyx. The pelvis bears the weight of the body, protects the organs within the pelvic cavity, and serves as the place of attachment for the legs.

Each **coxal bone** has three parts: the ilium, the ischium, and the pubis, which are fused in the adult (Fig. 10.13). The hip socket, called the acetabulum, occurs where these three bones meet. The ilium is the largest part of the coxal bones, and our hips occur where it flares out. We sit on the ischium, which has a posterior spine called the ischial spine. The pubis, from which the term pubic hair is derived, is the anterior part of a coxal bone. The two pubic bones are joined together by a fibrocartilaginous joint, the **pubic symphysis.**

The male and female pelves differ from each other. In the female, the iliac bones are more flared; the pelvic cavity is more shallow, but the outlet is wider. These adaptations facilitate giving birth.

The **femur** (thighbone) is the longest and strongest bone in the body. The head of the femur articulates with the coxal bones at the acetabulum, and the short neck better positions the legs for walking. The femur has two large processes, the greater and lesser trochanters, which are places of attachment for thigh muscles, buttock muscles, and hip flexors. At its distal end, the femur has medial and lateral condyles that articulate with the tibia of the leg. This is the region of the knee and the **patella,** or kneecap. The patella is held in place by the quadriceps tendon, which continues as a ligament that attaches to the tibial tuberosity. At the distal end, the medial malleolus of the tibia causes the inner bulge of the ankle. The **fibula** is the more slender bone in the leg. The fibula has a head that articulates with the tibia and a distal lateral malleolus that forms the outer bulge of the ankle.

Each foot has an ankle, an instep, and five toes. The many bones of the foot give it considerable flexibility, especially on rough surfaces. The ankle contains seven **tarsal** bones, one of which (the talus) can move freely where it joins the tibia and fibula. Strange to say, the calcaneus, or heel bone, is also considered part of the ankle. The talus and calcaneus support the weight of the body.

The instep has five elongated **metatarsal** bones. The distal end of the metatarsals forms the ball of the foot. If the ligaments that bind the metatarsals together become weakened, flat feet are apt to result. The bones of the toes are called **phalanges,** just like those of the fingers, but in the foot, the phalanges are stout and extremely sturdy.

The pelvic girdle and lower limb are adapted to supporting the weight of the body. The femur is the longest and strongest bone in the body.

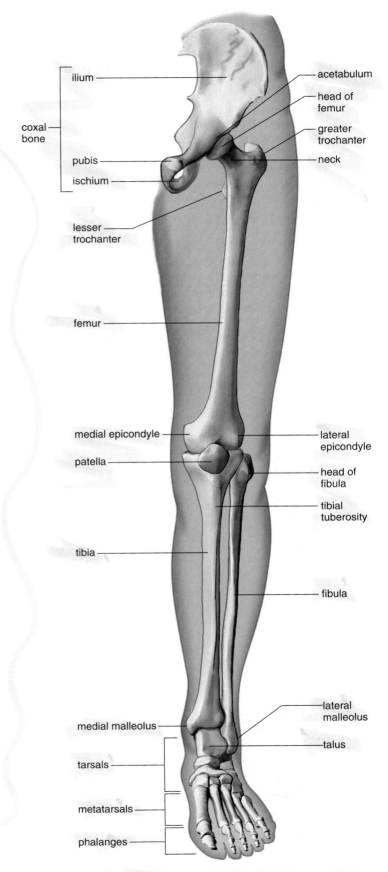

Figure 10.13   **Bones of the pelvic girdle and lower limb.**

10.4 Articulations

Bones are joined at the joints, which are classified as fibrous, cartilaginous, or synovial. Many fibrous joints, such as the **sutures** between the cranial bones, are immovable. Cartilaginous joints are connected by hyaline cartilage, as in the costal cartilages that join the ribs to the sternum, or by fibrocartilage, as in the intervertebral disks. Cartilaginous joints tend to be slightly movable. Synovial joints are freely movable.

In **synovial joints,** the two bones are separated by a cavity. Ligaments hold the two bones in place as they form a capsule. Tendons also help stabilize the joint. The joint capsule is lined by a **synovial membrane,** which produces synovial fluid, a lubricant for the joint. The knee is an example of a synovial joint (Fig. 10.14). Aside from articular cartilage, the knee contains menisci (sing., **meniscus**), crescent-shaped pieces of hyaline cartilage between the bones. These give added stability and act as shock absorbers. Unfortunately, athletes often suffer injury to the menisci, known as torn cartilage. The knee joint also contains 13 fluid-filled sacs called bursae (sing., **bursa**), which ease friction between the tendons and ligaments. Inflammation of the bursae is called **bursitis;** tennis elbow is a form of bursitis.

There are different types of synovial joints. The knee and elbow joints are **hinge joints** because, like a hinged door, they largely permit movement in one direction only.

The joint between the radius and ulna is a pivot joint in which only rotation is possible. More movable are the **ball-and-socket joints;** for example, the ball of the femur fits into a socket on the hipbone. Ball-and-socket joints allow movement in all planes, even rotational movement.

Movements Permitted by Synovial Joints

Intact skeletal muscles are attached to bones by tendons that span joints. When a muscle contracts, one bone moves in relation to another bone. The more common types of movements are described here.

Angular Movements (Fig. 10.15a,b)

Flexion decreases the joint angle. Flexion of the elbow moves the forearm toward the upper arm; flexion of the knee moves the lower leg toward the upper leg. *Dorsiflexion* is flexion of the foot upward, as when you stand on your heels; *plantar flexion* is flexion of the foot downward, as when you stand on your toes.

Extension increases the joint angle. Extension of the flexed elbow straightens the arm so that there is a 180° angle at the elbow. Hyperextension occurs when a portion of the body part is extended beyond 180°. It is possible to hyperextend the head and the trunk of the body.

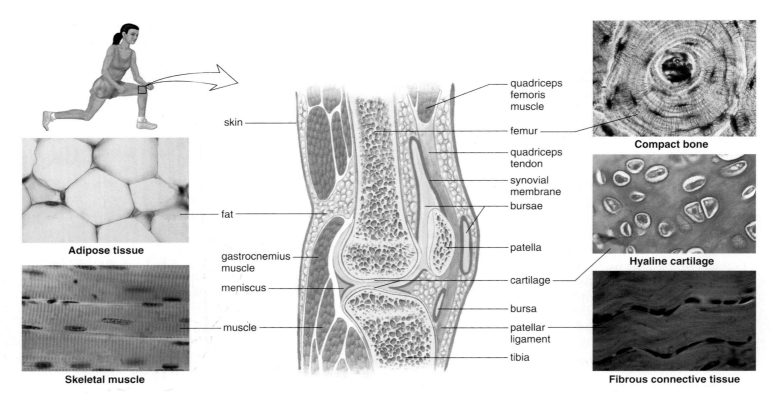

Figure 10.14   Knee joint.
The knee joint is a synovial joint. Notice the cavity between the bones, which is encased by ligaments and lined by synovial membrane. The patella (kneecap) serves to guide the quadriceps tendon over the joint when flexion or extension occurs.

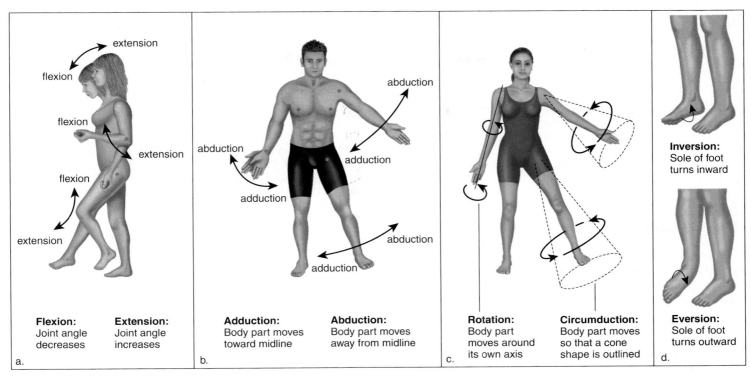

Figure 10.15 **Joint movements.**
a. Flexion and extension. **b.** Adduction and abduction. **c.** Rotation and circumduction. **d.** Inversion and eversion. Circles indicate pivot points.

Adduction is the movement of a body part toward the midline. For example, adduction of the arms or legs moves them back to the sides, toward the body.

Abduction is the movement of a body part laterally, away from the midline. Abduction of the arms or legs moves them laterally, away from the body.

Circular Movements (Fig. 10.15c)

Rotation is the movement of a body part around its own axis, as when the head is turned to answer "no" or when the arm is twisted one way and then the other.

Circumduction is the movement of a body part in a wide circle, as when a person makes arm circles. If the motion is observed carefully, one can see that, because the proximal end of the arm is stationary, the shape outlined by the arm is actually a cone.

Supination is the rotation of the lower arm so that the palm is upward; **pronation** is the opposite—the movement of the lower arm so that the palm is downward.

Special Movements (Fig. 10.15d)

Inversion and **eversion** are terms that apply only to the feet. Inversion is turning the foot so that the sole is inward, and eversion is turning the foot so that the sole is outward.

Elevation and **depression** are the lifting up and down, respectively, of a body part, such as when you shrug your shoulders.

Osteoarthritis

Rheumatoid arthritis (inflamed joint) is not as common as **osteoarthritis** (deterioration of an overworked joint). Constant compression and abrasion continually damage articular cartilage, and eventually it softens, cracks, and wears away entirely in some areas. As the osteoarthritis progresses, the exposed bone thickens and forms spurs that cause the bone ends to enlarge and joint movement to be restricted.

Today, replacement of damaged joints with a prosthesis (artificial substitute) is often possible. Before taking that route, some people have said that they find glucosamine chondroitin supplements beneficial. Glucosamine, an amino sugar, is thought to promote the formation and repair of cartilage. Chondroitin, a carbohydrate, is a cartilage component that is thought to promote water retention, elasticity, and to inhibit enzymes that break down cartilage. Both compounds are naturally produced by the body.

Movements at joints are classified as angular, circular, and special.

Summarizing the Concepts

10.1 Tissues of the Skeletal System
A system is made up of organs, and each organ is made up of tissues. The organs known as bones are largely composed of connective tissue, particularly bone, cartilage, and fibrous connective tissue. In a long bone, hyaline (articular) cartilage covers the ends, while periosteum (fibrous connective tissue) covers the rest of the bone. Spongy bone, which may contain red bone marrow, is in the epiphyses, while yellow bone marrow is in the medullary cavity of the diaphysis. The wall of the diaphysis is compact bone.

10.2 Bone Growth, Remodeling, and Repair
The prenatal human skeleton is, at first, cartilaginous, but is later replaced by a bony skeleton. During adult life, bone is constantly being broken down by osteoclasts and then rebuilt by osteoblasts that become osteocytes in lacunae. Ossification (development of bone) can be intramembranous ossification, or endochondral ossification. The latter process replaces a cartilaginous model of the bone. Certain hormones, namely vitamin D, growth hormone, and sex hormones, affect bone growth. During bone remodeling, a lifelong process, bone is constantly renewed providing an opportunity for blood calcium regulation. Repair of a fracture requires four steps: (1) hematoma, (2) fibrocartilaginous callus, (3) bony callus, and (4) remodeling.

10.3 Bones of the Skeleton
The skeleton supports and protects the body, permits flexible movement, produces blood cells, and serves as a storehouse for mineral salts, particularly calcium phosphate.

The axial skeleton lies in the midline of the body and consists of the skull, the hyoid bone, the vertebral column, and the rib cage. The skull contains the cranium, which protects the brain and the facial bones. On the face, the frontal bone forms the forehead; the maxillae extend from the frontal bone to the upper row of teeth; the zygomatic bones are the cheekbones; and the nasal bones form the bridge of the nose. The rest of the nose is a mixture of cartilages and connective tissues. The ears are cartilaginous. The mandible is the lower jaw and accounts for the chin.

The appendicular skeleton consists of the bones of the pectoral girdles, upper limbs, pelvic girdle, and lower limbs. The pectoral girdles and upper limbs are adapted for flexibility. The glenoid cavity of the scapula is barely large enough to receive the head of the humerus, and this means that dislocated shoulders are more likely to happen than dislocated hips. The pelvic girdle and the lower limbs are adapted for strength; the femur is the strongest bone in the body. However, the foot, like the hand, is flexible because it contains so many bones. Both the fingers and the toes are called digits, and the term phalanges refers to the bones of each.

10.4 Articulations
There are three types of joints: Fibrous joints, such as the sutures of the cranium, are immovable; cartilaginous joints, such as those between the ribs and sternum and the pubic symphysis, are slightly movable; and synovial joints, having a membrane-lined (synovial membrane) cavity, are freely movable. The kinds of synovial joints, and the movements they permit, are varied.

Studying the Concepts

1. A bone is an organ composed of what types of tissues? What are some differences between compact bone tissue and spongy bone tissue? 178–79
2. Describe the makeup of a long bone. 178–79
3. What types of cells are involved in bone growth, remodeling, and repair? 180
4. What are the two types of ossification? Describe endochondral ossification and growth in length of a long bone. 180–81
5. What hormones affect bone growth? 182
6. How does bone remodeling and growth in bone diameter occur? 182–83
7. What are the four steps required for fracture repair? 183
8. What are the functions of the skeleton? 185
9. What are the bones of the cranium and the face? Associate the parts of the face with particular bones or cartilages. 186–87
10. What are the parts of the vertebral column, and what are its curvatures? Distinguish between the atlas, axis, sacrum, and coccyx. 188
11. What are the bones of the rib cage, and what are several functions of the rib cage? 189
12. What are the bones of a pectoral girdle? Give examples to demonstrate the flexibility of the pectoral girdle. Where does the scapula articulate with the clavicle? 190
13. What are the bones of the upper limb? Name several projections of the humerus. Of the elbow. 190
14. What are the bones of the pelvic girdle, and what are their functions? Give examples to demonstrate the strength and stability of the pelvic girdle. 191
15. What are the bones of the lower limb? Name several projections of the femur. Of the ankle. 191
16. How are joints classified? Give examples of the different types of synovial joints and the movements they permit. 192–93

Thinking Critically About the Concepts

Refer to the opening vignette on page 178, and then answer these questions.

1. What advantage is there to having a curved vertebral column rather than a straight one?
2. Why should you lift heavy objects with your leg muscles, instead of your back muscles?
3. What types of back injuries would show up on an X ray? What types would not?
4. How do you maintain healthy bones?

Testing Your Knowledge of the Concepts

Choose the best answer for each question.

1. A bone is considered
   a. a tissue.
   b. an organ.
   c. a cell.
   d. a system.
   e. a part of the integumentary system.

In questions 2–7, match each bone to a location in the key.

Key:

a. forehead   e. shoulder blade
b. chin   f. hip
c. cheekbone   g. arm
d. collarbone

2. Zygomatic bone

3. Clavicle

4. Frontal bone

5. Humerus

6. Coxal bone

7. Scapula

In questions 8–13, match each bone to a feature in the key.

Key:

a. glenoid cavity
b. olecranon process
c. acetabulum
d. spinous process
e. greater and lesser trochanters
f. xiphoid process

8. Femur

9. Scapula

10. Ulna

11. Coxal bone

12. Sternum

13. Vertebra

14. Spongy bone
a. contains osteons.
b. contains red bone marrow, where blood cells are formed.
c. lends no strength to bones.
d. takes up most of a leg bone.
e. All of these are correct.

15. Which of these associations is mismatched?
a. slightly movable joint—vertebrae
b. hinge joint—hip
c. synovial joint—elbow
d. immovable joint—sutures in cranium

16. The bone cell that is responsible for breaking down bone tissue is the _____, while the bone cell that produces new bone tissue is the _____.
a. osteoclast, osteoblast
b. osteocyte, osteoclast
c. osteoblast, osteocyte
d. osteocyte, osteoblast
e. osteoclast, osteocyte

17. All blood cells—red, white, and platelets—are produced by which of the following?
a. yellow bone marrow
b. red bone marrow
c. periosteum
d. medullary cavity

18. Which of the following is not a group into which bones are classified?
a. long bones   d. flat bones
b. short bones   e. irregular bones
c. compact bones

19. This bone is the only movable bone of the skull.
a. sphenoid   d. maxilla
b. frontal   e. temporal
c. mandible

20. Which of the following is not a function of the skeletal system?
a. production of blood cells
b. storage of minerals
c. involved in movement
d. storage of fat
e. production of body heat

21. When you bend your arm, the bump seen as your elbow is part of the
a. humerus.
b. radius.
c. ulna.
d. carpal.

22. The bump seen on the outside of the ankle is part of the
a. femur.   c. fibula.
b. tibia.   d. tarsal bones.

In questions 23–27, indicate whether the statement is true (T) or false (F).

23. The pectoral girdle is specialized for weight-bearing, while the pelvic girdle is specialized for flexibility of movement. _____

24. The term phalanges refers to the bones in both the fingers and the toes. _____

25. Bones synthesize vitamin D for the body. _____

26. Bones store minerals and fat. _____

27. Most bones develop through endochondral ossification. ___True___

28. Which of the following is not a bone of the appendicular skeleton?
a. the scapula   c. a metatarsal bone
b. a rib   d. the patella

29. Which of the following statements is incorrect?
a. A growth plate occurs between the primary ossification center and a secondary center.
b. Each temporal bone has an opening that leads to the middle ear.
c. Intervertebral disks are composed of fibrocartilage.
d. Bone cells are rigid and hard because they are dead.
e. The sternum is composed of three bones that fuse during fetal development.

30. A fontanel is
a. a site for blood cell formation.
b. found only in a fetus before birth.
c. a cavity in the skull.
d. a membranous area on a forming skull.
e. the articulation between a rib and a vertebra.

31. Which of the following is not a long bone?
    a. hyoid bone   d. fibula
    b. humerus   e. ulna
    c. metatarsal bone

32. The clavicle articulates with
    a. the scapula and humerus.
    b. the humerus and manubrium.
    c. the sternum and scapula.
    d. the manubrium, scapula, and humerus.
    e. the femur and the tibia.

33. Label this diagram of the pelvis and lower limb.

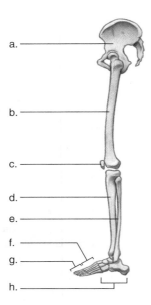

a. _____
b. _____
c. _____
d. _____
e. _____
f. _____
g. _____
h. _____

34. The vertebrae that articulate with the ribs are the
    a. lumbar vertebrae.
    b. sacral vertebrae.
    c. thoracic vertebrae.
    d. cervical vertebrae.
    e. coccyx.

In questions 35–39, match each term with the correct characteristic given in the key.

Key:
    a. closing the angle at a joint
    b. movement in all planes
    c. made of cartilage
    d. movement toward the body
    e. fluid-filled sac

35. Ball-and-socket joints

36. Flexion

37. Bursa

38. Meniscus

39. Adduction

Understanding Key Terms

appendicular skeleton 190
articular cartilage 178
axial skeleton 186
ball-and-socket joint 192
bone remodeling 182
bursa 192
bursitis 192
cartilage 178
chondrocyte 178
compact bone 178
endochondral ossification 181
fibrous connective tissue 178
fontanel 186
foramen magnum 186
growth plate 181
hinge joint 192
intervertebral disk 188
intramembranous
    ossification 180
joint 178
ligament 178
mastoiditis 186
medullary cavity 178

meniscus 192
ossification 180
osteoarthritis 193
osteoblast 180
osteoclast 180
osteocyte 178, 180
pectoral girdle 190
pelvic girdle 191
pelvis 191
periosteum 179
pubic symphysis 191
red bone marrow 178
rotator cuff 190
scoliosis 188
sinus 186
skull 186
spongy bone 178
suture 192
synovial joint 192
synovial membrane 192
tendon 178
vertebral column 188

Match the key terms to these definitions.

a. _____ Cartilaginous wedge that separates the surfaces of bones in a synovial joint.

b. _____ Type of bone that contains osteons consisting of concentric layers of matrix and osteocytes in lacunae.

c. _____ Cavity or hollow space in the cranium.

d. _____ Membranous region located between certain cranial bones in the skull of a fetus or infant.

e. _____ Mature bone cell located within the lacunae of bone.

Online Learning Center

www.mhhe.com/maderhuman9

The Online Learning Center provides a wealth of information fully organized and integrated by chapter. You will find practice quizzes, interactive activities, labeling exercises, flashcards, and much more that will complement your learning and understanding of human biology.

CHAPTER 11

Muscular System

CHAPTER CONCEPTS

11.1 Types and Functions of Muscles
- What are the three types of muscles in the human body? 198
- What are the functions of skeletal muscles? 198
- How do skeletal muscles work together to cause bones to move? 199
- What are the major skeletal muscles in the body? 200–201

11.2 Mechanism of Skeletal Muscle Fiber Contraction
- What are the microscopic levels of structure of a skeletal muscle? 202–3
- How does contraction of a skeletal muscle come about? 204–5
- What is the role of ATP in muscle contraction? 205

11.3 Whole Muscle Contraction
- How is the contraction of whole muscles studied in the laboratory? 206
- How is moderate tension, or tone, maintained by skeletal muscles? 206

11.4 Energy for Muscle Contraction
- What are the sources of ATP for muscle contraction? 208–9

11.5 Muscular Disorders
- What are tendinitis and bursitis? 210
- What are two more serious muscular conditions? 210

11.6 Homeostasis
- How does the muscular system work with the other systems of the body to maintain homeostasis? 212–13

L isa's hero is Florence Griffith Joyner, known as Flo Jo, who won gold medals and set world records in both the 100- and 200-meter races at the 1988 Olympic Games in Seoul, South Korea. Sprinters are built for explosive, quick speed over short distances and times. On the other hand, long-distance runners are able to run at a steady pace for hours on end. Does genetics or training account for this difference in ability?

Genetics might determine what type of muscles we have. Slow-twitch muscle fibers are needed for distance running, while fast-twitch muscle fibers are needed by sprinters. Both fast- and slow-twitch fibers generate the same force per contraction, but fast-twitch fibers contract more rapidly. Usually, the muscles of our legs contain 50% of each type. Olympic sprinters have been shown to possess approximately 80% fast-twitch fibers in their major leg muscles. Were they born that way, or did the type of fibers in their leg muscles change due to training?

Animal studies suggest that muscle fibers can change from fast to slow with endurance training. This would mean that you can increase your ability to perform as a long-distance runner. Some think, also, that you can maximize the size of fast-twitch fibers with weight training and plyometric exercise (training for power and explosiveness), but this idea is very controversial. Fiber type counts but we know for sure that other systems also improve with training. Cardiovascular and respiratory efficiency improve with training. Any way you look at it, training is very important to the athlete.

11.1 Types and Functions of Muscles

All muscles, regardless of their particular type, can contract—that is, shorten—and when muscles contract, some part of the body or the entire body moves.

Types of Muscles

Humans have three types of muscle tissue: smooth, cardiac, and skeletal (Fig. 11.1). The cells of these tissues are called **muscle fibers.**

Smooth muscle fibers are spindle-shaped cells, each with a single nucleus (uninucleated). The cells are usually arranged in parallel lines, forming sheets. Striations (bands of light and dark) are seen in cardiac and skeletal muscle but not in tissue of this type. Smooth muscle is located in the walls of hollow internal organs, and it causes these walls to contract. Contraction of smooth muscle is involuntary, occurring without conscious control. Although smooth muscle is slower to contract than skeletal muscle, it can sustain prolonged contractions and does not fatigue easily.

Cardiac muscle forms the heart wall. Its fibers are generally uninucleated, striated, tubular, and branched, which allows the fibers to interlock at intercalated disks. Intercalated disks permit contractions to spread quickly throughout the heart. Cardiac fibers relax completely between contractions, which prevents fatigue. Contraction of cardiac muscle is rhythmical; it occurs without outside nervous stimulation and without conscious control. Thus, cardiac muscle contraction is involuntary.

Skeletal muscle fibers are tubular, multinucleated, and striated. They make up the skeletal muscles attached to the skeleton. They run the length of the muscle and can be quite long. Skeletal muscle is voluntary because its contraction can be consciously stimulated and controlled by the nervous system. Skeletal muscles have numerous functions.

Functions of Skeletal Muscles

Skeletal muscles support the body. Skeletal muscle contraction opposes the force of gravity and allows us to remain upright.

Skeletal muscles make bones move. Muscle contraction accounts not only for the movement of arms and legs but also for movements of the eyes, facial expressions, and breathing.

Skeletal muscles help maintain a constant body temperature. Skeletal muscle contraction causes ATP to break down, releasing heat that is distributed about the body.

Skeletal muscle contraction assists movement in cardiovascular and lymphatic vessels. The pressure of skeletal muscle contraction keeps blood moving in cardiovascular veins and lymph moving in lymphatic vessels.

Skeletal muscles help protect internal organs and stabilize joints. Muscles pad the bones that protect organs, and they have tendons that help hold bones together at joints.

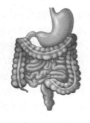
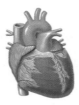

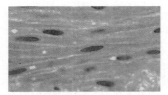

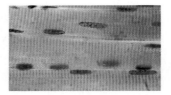

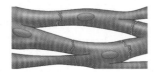

Smooth muscle
- has spindle-shaped, nonstriated uninucleated fibers.
- occurs in walls of internal organs.
- is involuntary.

Cardiac muscle
- has striated, branched, generally uninucleated fibers.
- occurs in walls of heart.
- is involuntary.

Skeletal muscle
- has striated, tubular, multinucleated fibers.
- is usually attached to skeleton.
- is voluntary.

Figure 11.1 **Types of muscles.**
Human muscles are of three types: smooth, cardiac, and skeletal. These muscles have different characteristics, as noted.

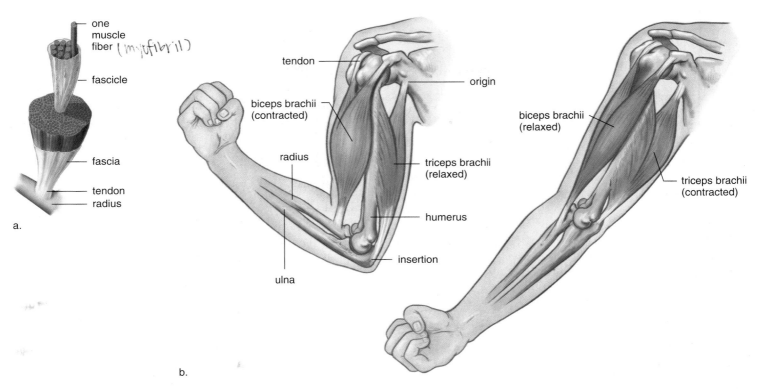

Figure 11.2   **Skeletal muscles as exemplified by the biceps brachii and the triceps brachii.**
a. A fascia covers the surface of a muscle and contributes to the tendon, which attaches the muscle to a bone. Connective tissue also separates bundles of muscle fibers that make up a skeletal muscle. **b.** The origin of a skeletal muscle is on a bone that remains stationary, and the insertion of a muscle is on a bone that moves when the muscle contracts. The muscles in this drawing are antagonistic. When the biceps brachii contracts, the forearm flexes, and when the triceps brachii contracts, the forearm extends.

Skeletal Muscles of the Body

In the animal kingdom, humans are vertebrates, animals whose skeletal muscles lie outside an internal skeleton that has jointed appendages. Our skeletal muscles are attached to the skeleton, and their contraction causes the movement of bones at a joint.

Basic Structure of Skeletal Muscles

Skeletal muscles are well organized. A whole muscle contains bundles of skeletal muscle fibers called fascicles (Fig. 11.2a). Within a fascicle, each fiber is surrounded by connective tissue, and the fascicle itself is also surrounded by connective tissue. Muscles are covered with fascia, a type of connective tissue that extends beyond the muscle and becomes its **tendon.** Tendons quite often extend past a joint before anchoring a muscle to a bone.

Skeletal Muscles Work in Pairs

In general, each muscle is concerned with the movement of only one bone. For the sake of discussion, we can imagine the movement of that bone and no others. The **origin** of a muscle is on a stationary bone, and the **insertion** of a muscle is on a bone that moves.

Skeletal muscles usually function in groups. Consequently, to make a particular movement, your nervous system does not stimulate a single muscle, it stimulates an appropriate group of muscles. Even so, for any particular movement, one muscle does most of the work and is called the prime mover. While a prime mover is working, however, certain muscles, called the synergists, are assisting the prime mover and making its action more effective.

When muscles contract, they shorten. Therefore, muscles can only pull; they cannot push. This means that muscles work in opposite pairs. The muscle that acts opposite to a prime mover is called an antagonist. For example, the biceps brachii and the triceps brachii are antagonists; one flexes the forearm, and the other extends the forearm (Fig. 11.2b). If both of these muscles contracted at once, the forearm would remain rigid. Smooth body movements depend on an antagonist relaxing when a prime mover is acting.

For help in learning the functions of muscles, you may want to concentrate on which ones work with or opposite a particular muscle.

When muscles cooperate to achieve movement, some act as prime movers, others are synergists, and still others are antagonists.

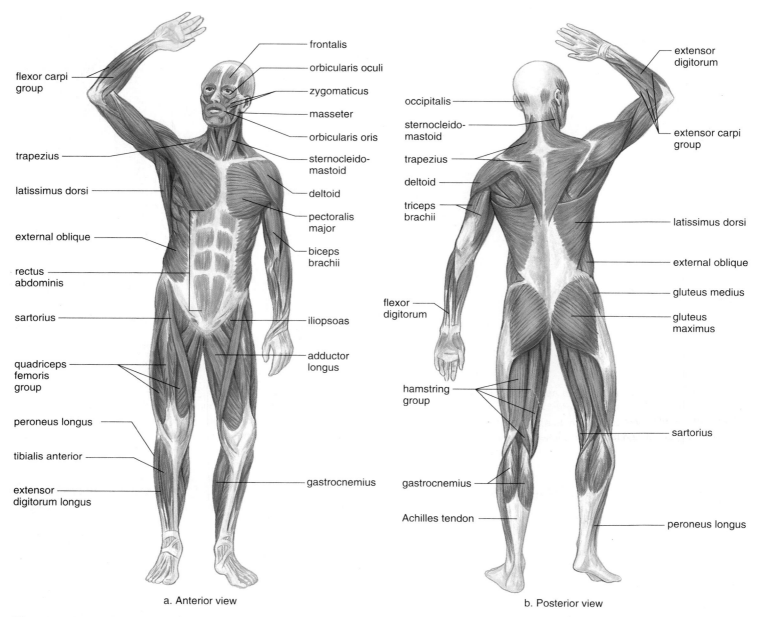

Figure 11.3   Human musculature.
Superficial skeletal muscles in (**a**) anterior and (**b**) posterior view.

Names and Actions of Skeletal Muscles

Figure 11.3 illustrates the location of major skeletal muscles, and Tables 11.1 and 11.2 list their actions. Recall that extension increases the joint angle, and flexion decreases the joint angle; abduction is the movement of a body part sideways away from the midline, and adduction is the movement of a body part toward the midline.

The names of muscles are based on various characteristics, as shown in the following examples:

1. Size. The gluteus maximus that makes up the buttocks is the largest muscle.

2. Shape. The deltoid is shaped like a triangle. (The Greek letter delta has this appearance: Δ.)
3. Location. The frontalis overlies the frontal bone.
4. Direction of muscle fibers. The rectus abdominis is a longitudinal muscle of the abdomen (rectus means straight).
5. Attachment. For example, the sternocleidomastoid is attached to the sternum, clavicle, and mastoid process.
6. Number of attachments. The biceps brachii has two attachments, or origins.
7. Action. The extensor digitorum extends the fingers, or digits.

Table 11.1	Muscles (anterior view)

Name	Action
HEAD AND NECK	
Frontalis	Wrinkles forehead and lifts eyebrows
Orbicularis oculi	Closes eye (winking)
Zygomaticus	Raises corner of mouth (smiling)
Masseter	Closes jaw
Orbicularis oris	Closes and protrudes lips (kissing)
UPPER LIMB AND TRUNK	
External oblique	Compresses abdomen; rotates trunk
Rectus abdominis	Flexes spine; compresses abdomen
Pectoralis major	Flexes and adducts shoulder and arm ventrally (pulls arm across chest)
Deltoid	Abducts and raises arm at shoulder joint
Biceps brachii	Flexes forearm and supinates hand
LOWER LIMB	
Adductor longus	Adducts and flexes thigh
Iliopsoas	Flexes thigh at hip joint
Sartorius	Rotates thigh (sitting cross-legged)
Quadriceps femoris group	Extends leg
Peroneus longus	Everts foot
Tibialis anterior	Dorsiflexes and inverts foot
Flexor digitorum longus	Flexes toes
Extensor digitorum longus	Extends toes

Table 11.2	Muscles (posterior view)

Name	Action
HEAD AND NECK	
Occipitalis	Moves scalp backward
Sternocleidomastoid	Turns head to side; flexes neck and head
Trapezius	Extends head; raises and adducts shoulders dorsally (shrugging shoulders)
UPPER LIMB AND TRUNK	
Latissimus dorsi	Extends and adducts shoulder and arm dorsally (pulls arm across back)
Deltoid	Abducts and raises arm at shoulder joint
External oblique	Rotates trunk
Triceps brachii	Extends forearm
Flexor carpi group	Flexes hand
Extensor carpi group	Extends hand
Flexor digitorum	Flexes fingers
Extensor digitorum	Extends fingers
BUTTOCKS AND LOWER LIMB	
Gluteus medius	Abducts thigh
Gluteus maximus	Extends thigh (forms buttocks)
Hamstring group	Flexes leg and extends thigh at hip joint
Gastrocnemius	Flexes leg and foot (tiptoeing)

11.2 Mechanism of Skeletal Muscle Fiber Contraction

We have already examined the structure of skeletal muscle, as seen with the light microscope. As you know, skeletal muscle tissue has alternating light and dark bands, giving it a striated appearance. Now we will see that these bands are due to the arrangement of myofilaments in a muscle fiber.

Muscle Fiber

A muscle fiber is a cell containing the usual cellular components, but special names have been assigned to some of these components (Table 11.3 and Fig. 11.4). The plasma membrane is called the **sarcolemma;** the cytoplasm is the sarcoplasm; and the endoplasmic reticulum is the **sarcoplasmic reticulum.** A muscle fiber also has some unique anatomical characteristics. One feature is its T (for transverse) system; the sarcolemma forms **T (transverse) tubules** that penetrate, or dip down, into the cell so that they come into contact—but do not fuse—with expanded portions of the sarcoplasmic reticulum. The expanded portions of the sarcoplasmic reticulum are calcium storage sites. Calcium ions (Ca^{2+}), as we shall see, are essential for muscle contraction.

The sarcoplasmic reticulum encases hundreds and sometimes even thousands of **myofibrils,** each about 1 μm in diameter, which are the contractile portions of the muscle fibers. Any other organelles, such as mitochondria, are located in the sarcoplasm between the myofibrils. The sarcoplasm also contains glycogen, which provides stored

energy for muscle contraction, and the red pigment myoglobin, which binds oxygen until it is needed for muscle contraction.

Myofibrils and Sarcomeres

Myofibrils are cylindrical in shape and run the length of the muscle fiber. The light microscope shows that skeletal muscle fibers have light and dark bands called striations. The electron microscope shows that the striations of skeletal muscle fibers are formed by the placement of myofilaments within units of myofibrils called **sarcomeres.** A sarcomere extends between two dark lines called the Z lines. A sarcomere contains two types of protein myofilaments. The thick filaments are made up of a protein called **myosin,** and the thin filaments are made up of a protein called **actin.** Other proteins are also present. The I band is light colored because it contains only actin filaments attached to a Z line. The dark regions of the A band contain overlapping actin and myosin filaments, and its H zone has only myosin filaments.

Myofilaments

The thick and thin filaments differ in the following ways:

Thick Filaments   A thick filament is composed of several hundred molecules of the protein myosin. Each myosin molecule is shaped like a golf club, with the straight portion of the molecule ending in a double globular head, or *crossbridge*. The cross-bridges occur on each side of a sarcomere but not in the middle.

Thin Filaments   Primarily, a thin filament consists of two intertwining strands of the protein actin. Two other proteins, called tropomyosin and troponin, also play a role, as we will discuss later in this section.

Sliding Filaments   We will also see that when muscles are stimulated, impulses travel down a T tubule, and calcium is released from the sarcoplasmic reticulum. Now the muscle fiber contracts as the sarcomeres, within the myofibrils, shorten. When a sarcomere shortens, the actin (thin) filaments slide past the myosin (thick) filaments and approach one another. This causes the I band to shorten and the H zone to almost or completely disappear. The movement of actin filaments in relation to myosin filaments is called the **sliding filament model** of muscle contraction. During the sliding process, the sarcomere shortens, even though the filaments themselves remain the same length. ATP supplies the energy for muscle contraction. Although the actin filaments slide past the myosin filaments, it is the myosin filaments that do the work. Myosin filaments break down ATP and have cross-bridges that pull the actin filaments toward the center of the sarcomere.

When muscle fibers are stimulated to contract, myofilaments slide past one another, causing sarcomeres to shorten.

Table 11.3	Microscopic Anatomy of a Muscle
Name	**Function**
Sarcolemma	Plasma membrane of a muscle fiber that forms T tubules
Sarcoplasm	Cytoplasm of a muscle fiber that contains the organelles, including myofibrils
Glycogen	A polysaccharide that stores energy for muscle contraction
Myoglobin	A red pigment that stores oxygen for muscle contraction
T tubule	Extension of the sarcolemma that extends into the muscle fiber and conveys impulses that cause Ca^{2+} to be released from the sarcoplasmic reticulum
Sarcoplasmic reticulum	The smooth ER of a muscle fiber that stores Ca^{2+}
Myofibril	A bundle of myofilaments that contracts
Myofilament	Actin filaments and myosin filaments, whose structure and functions account for muscle striations and contractions

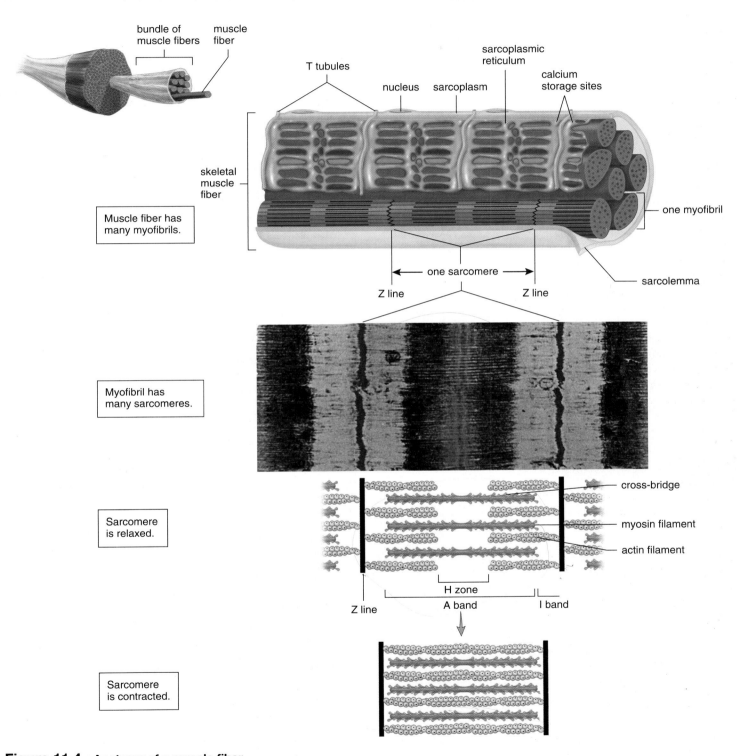

bundle of muscle fibers
muscle fiber

T tubules
nucleus
sarcoplasm
sarcoplasmic reticulum
calcium storage sites

skeletal muscle fiber

Muscle fiber has many myofibrils.

one myofibril

one sarcomere

Z line   Z line

sarcolemma

Myofibril has many sarcomeres.

Sarcomere is relaxed.

cross-bridge
myosin filament
actin filament

H zone

Z line   A band   I band

Sarcomere is contracted.

Figure 11.4 Anatomy of a muscle fiber.
A muscle fiber has many myofibrils. The sarcomeres of a myofibril contain myosin and actin filaments, whose arrangement gives rise to the striations characteristic of skeletal muscle tissue. Muscle contraction occurs when sarcomeres shorten and actin filaments slide past myosin filaments.

Skeletal Muscle Contraction

Muscle fibers are stimulated to contract by motor neurons whose axons are in nerves. The axon of one motor neuron can stimulate from a few to several muscle fibers of a muscle because each axon has several branches. A branch of an axon ends in an axon terminal that lies in close proximity to the sarcolemma of a muscle fiber. A small gap, called a synaptic cleft, separates the axon terminal from the sarcolemma. This entire region is called a **neuromuscular junction** (Fig. 11.5).

Axon terminals contain synaptic vesicles that are filled with the neurotransmitter acetylcholine (ACh). When nerve impulses, traveling down a motor neuron, arrive at an axon terminal, the synaptic vesicles release ACh into the synaptic cleft. It quickly diffuses across the cleft and binds to receptors in the sarcolemma. Now, the sarcolemma generates impulses that spread over the sarcolemma and down T tubules to the sarcoplasmic reticulum. The release of Ca^{2+} from the sarcoplasmic reticulum causes the filaments within the sarcomeres to slide past one another. Sarcomere contraction results in myofibril contraction, which, in turn, results in muscle fiber, and finally, muscle contraction.

Botox is a trade name for botulinum toxin A, a neurotoxin produced by a bacterium. Botox, which can be injected by a physician to prevent wrinkling of the brow and skin about the eyes, prevents the release of ACh, and therefore, the contraction of muscles in these areas.

At a neuromuscular junction, nerve impulses bring about the release of neurotransmitter molecules that signal a muscle fiber to contract.

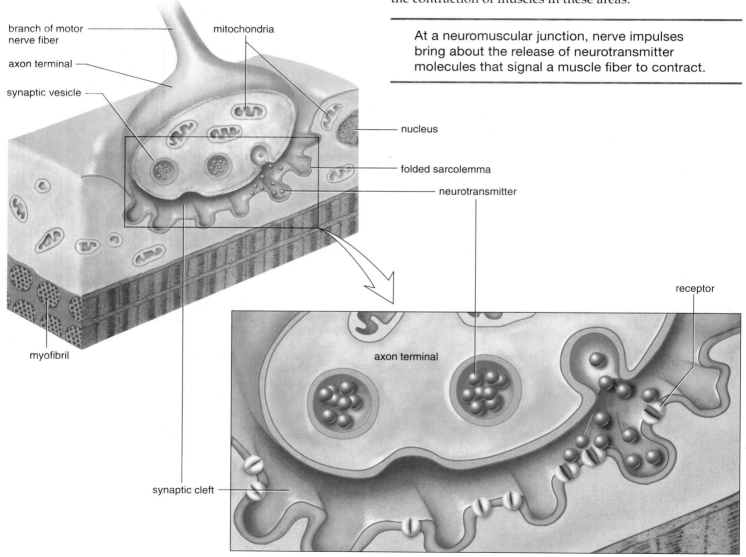

Figure 11.5 Neuromuscular junction.
The branch of a motor nerve fiber terminates in an axon terminal that meets, but does not touch, a muscle fiber. A synaptic cleft separates the axon terminal from the sarcolemma of the muscle fiber. Nerve impulses traveling down a motor fiber cause synaptic vesicles to discharge acetylcholine, which diffuses across the synaptic cleft. When the neurotransmitter is received by the sarcolemma of a muscle fiber, impulses begin and lead to muscle fiber contractions.

The Role of Actin and Myosin

Figure 11.6 shows the placement of two other proteins associated with an actin filament. Threads of **tropomyosin** wind about an actin filament, and **troponin** occurs at intervals along the threads. When Ca^{2+} ions are released from the sarcoplasmic reticulum, they combine with troponin, and this causes the tropomyosin threads to shift their position. Now, binding sites for myosin are exposed.

The double globular heads of a myosin filament have ATP binding sites, where an ATPase splits ATP into ADP and ℗. The ADP and ℗ remain on the myosin heads until the heads attach to an actin filament, forming cross-bridges. Now, ADP and ℗ are released, and the cross-bridges change their positions. This is the power stroke that pulls the actin filament toward the center of the sarcomere. When ATP molecules again bind to the myosin heads, the cross-bridges are broken, and heads detach from actin filament. Actin filaments move nearer the center of the sarcomere each time the cycle is repeated. When nerve impulses cease, the sarcoplasmic reticulum actively transports Ca^{2+} back into the sarcoplasmic reticulum, and the muscle relaxes.

After Ca^{2+} binds to troponin, myosin filaments break down ATP and attach to actin filaments, forming cross-bridges that pull actin filaments to the center of a sarcomere.

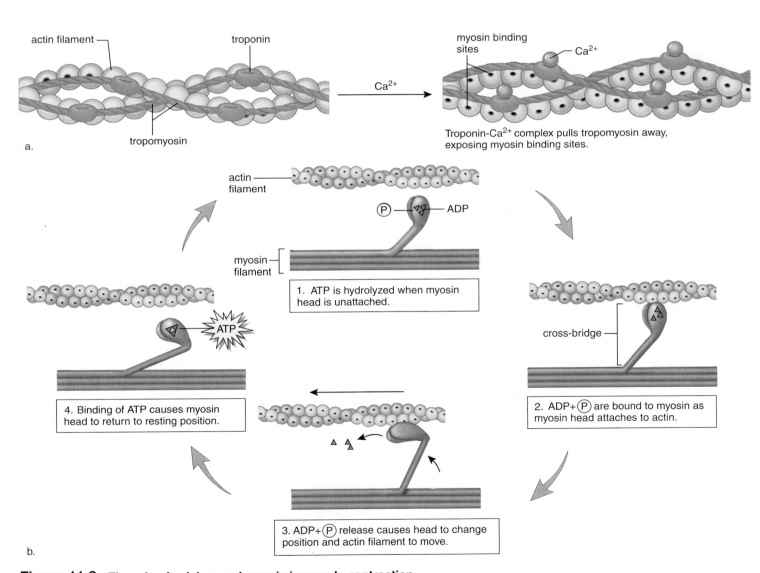

Figure 11.6 **The role of calcium and myosin in muscle contraction.**
a. Upon release, calcium (Ca^{2+}) binds to troponin, exposing myosin-binding sites. **b.** After breaking down ATP, myosin heads bind to an actin filament, and later, a power stroke causes the actin filament to move.

11.3 Whole Muscle Contraction

Muscles can be studied in the laboratory in an effort to understand whole muscle contraction in the body.

In the Laboratory

When a muscle fiber is isolated, placed on a microscope slide, and provided with ATP plus various salts, it contracts completely along its entire length. This observation has resulted in the **all-or-none law:** A muscle fiber contracts completely or not at all. In contrast, a whole muscle shows degrees of contraction. To study whole muscle contraction in the laboratory, an isolated muscle is stimulated electrically, and the mechanical force of contraction is recorded as a visual pattern called a **myogram.** When the strength of the stimulus is above a threshold level, the muscle contracts and then relaxes. This action—a single contraction that lasts only a fraction of a second—is called a **muscle twitch.** Figure 11.7a is a myogram of a muscle twitch, which is customarily divided into three stages: the latent period, or the period of time between stimulation and initiation of contraction; the contraction period, when the muscle shortens; and the relaxation period, when the muscle returns to its former length. It's interesting to use our knowledge of muscle fiber contraction to understand these events. From our study thus far, we know that a muscle fiber in an intact muscle contracts when calcium leaves storage sacs and relaxes when calcium returns to storage sacs.

But unlike the contraction of a muscle fiber, a muscle has degrees of contraction, and a twitch can vary in height (strength) depending on the degree of stimulation. Why should that be? Obviously, a stronger stimulation causes more individual fibers to contract than before.

If a whole muscle is given a rapid series of stimuli, it can respond to the next stimulus without relaxing completely. Summation is increased muscle contraction until maximal sustained contraction, called **tetanus,** is achieved (Fig. 11.7b). The myogram no longer shows individual twitches; rather, the twitches are fused and blended completely into a straight line. Tetanus continues until the muscle fatigues due to depletion of energy reserves. Fatigue is apparent when a muscle relaxes, even though stimulation continues.

In the Body

In the body, muscles are stimulated to contract by nerves. As mentioned, each axon within a nerve stimulates a number of muscle fibers. A nerve fiber, together with all of the muscle fibers it innervates, is called a **motor unit.** A motor unit obeys the all-or-none law. Why? Because all the muscle fibers in a motor unit are stimulated at once, and they all either contract or do not contract. A variable of interest is the number of muscle fibers within a motor unit. For example, in the ocular muscles that move the eyes, the innervation ratio is one motor axon per 23 muscle fibers, while in the

gastrocnemius muscle of the leg, the ratio is about one motor axon per 1,000 muscle fibers. Thus, moving the eyes requires finer control than moving the legs.

Tetanic contractions ordinarily occur in the body because, as the intensity of nervous stimulation increases, more and more motor units are activated. This phenomenon, known as recruitment, results in stronger and stronger muscle contractions. But, while some muscle fibers are contracting, others are relaxing. Because of this, intact muscles rarely fatigue completely. Even when muscles appear to be at rest, they exhibit tone, in which some of their fibers are always contracting. **Muscle tone** is particularly important in maintaining posture. If all the fibers within the muscles of the neck, trunk, and legs were to suddenly relax, the body would collapse.

Observation of muscle contraction in the laboratory helps explain how muscles contract in the body. A muscle at rest exhibits tone, and a contracting muscle exhibits degrees of contraction dependent on recruitment.

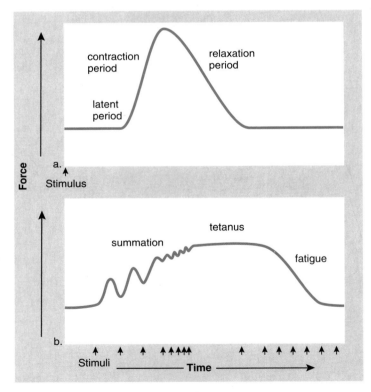

Figure 11.7 Physiology of skeletal muscle contraction.
Stimulation of a muscle dissected from a frog resulted in these myograms. **a.** A simple muscle twitch has three periods: latent, contraction, and relaxation. **b.** Summation and tetanus. When the muscle is not permitted to relax completely between stimuli, the contraction gradually increases in intensity. The muscle becomes maximally contracted until it fatigues.

Health Focus

Exercise, Exercise, Exercise

Exercise programs improve muscular strength, muscular endurance, and flexibility. Muscular strength is the force a muscle group (or muscle) can exert against a resistance in one maximal effort. Muscular endurance is judged by the ability of a muscle to contract repeatedly or to sustain a contraction for an extended period. Flexibility is tested by observing the range of motion about a joint.

Exercise also improves cardiorespiratory endurance. The heart rate and capacity increase, and the air passages dilate so that the heart and lungs are able to support prolonged muscular activity. The blood level of high-density lipoprotein (HDL), the molecule that prevents the development of plaque in blood vessels, increases. Also, body composition—that is, the proportion of protein to fat—changes favorably when you exercise.

Exercise also seems to help prevent certain kinds of cancer. Cancer prevention involves eating properly, not smoking, avoiding cancer-causing chemicals and radiation, undergoing appropriate medical screening tests, and knowing the early warning signs of cancer. However, studies show that people who exercise are less likely to develop colon, breast, cervical, uterine, and ovarian cancers.

Physical training with weights can improve the density and strength of bones and the strength and endurance of muscles in all adults, regardless of age. Even men and women in their eighties and nineties can make substantial gains in bone and muscle strength that help them lead more independent lives. Exercise helps prevent osteoporosis, a condition in which the bones are weak and tend to break. Exercise promotes the activity of osteoblasts in young as well as older people. The stronger the bones when a person is young, the less chance of osteoporosis as that person ages. Exercise helps prevent weight gain, not only because the level of activity increases but also because muscles metabolize faster than other tissues. As a person becomes more muscular, the body is less likely to accumulate fat.

Exercise relieves depression and enhances the mood. Some people report that exercise actually makes them feel more energetic, and that after exercising, particularly in the late afternoon, they sleep better that night. Self-esteem rises because of improved appearance, as well as other factors that are not well understood. For example, vigorous exercise releases endorphins, hormone-like chemicals that are known to alleviate pain and provide a feeling of tranquility.

A sensible exercise program is one that provides all of these benefits without the detriments of a too-strenuous program. Overexertion can actually be harmful to the body and might result in sports injuries, such as lower back strains or torn ligaments of the knees. The beneficial programs suggested in Table 11A are tailored according to age.

Dr. Arthur Leon at the University of Minnesota performed a study involving 12,000 men, and the results showed that only moderate exercise is needed to lower the risk of a heart attack by one third. In another study conducted by the Institute for Aerobics Research in Dallas, Texas, which included 10,000 men and more than 3,000 women, even a little exercise was found to lower the risk of death from cardiovascular diseases and cancer. Increasing daily activity by walking to the corner store instead of driving and by taking the stairs instead of the elevator can improve your health.

Table 11A	A Checklist for Staying Fit		
Children, 7–12	**Teenagers, 13–18**	**Adults, 19–55**	**Seniors, 56 and Up**
Vigorous activity 1–2 hrs daily	Vigorous activity 1 hr 3–5 days a week, otherwise 1/2 hr daily moderate activity	Vigorous activity 1 hr 3 days a week, otherwise 1/2 hr daily moderate activity	Moderate exercise 1 hr daily 3 days a week, otherwise 1/2 hr daily moderate activity
Free play	Build muscle with calisthenics	Exercise to prevent lower back pain: aerobics, stretching, yoga	Take a daily walk
Build motor skills through team sports, dance, swimming	Do aerobic exercise to control buildup of fat cells	Take active vacations: hike, bicycle, cross-country ski	Do daily stretching exercises
Encourage more exercise outside of physical education classes	Pursue tennis, swimming, horseback riding—sports that can be enjoyed for a lifetime	Find exercise partners: join a running club, bicycle club, outing group	Learn a new sport or activity: golf, fishing, ballroom dancing
Initiate family outings: bowling, boating, camping, hiking	Continue team sports, dancing, hiking, swimming	Initiate family outings: bowling, boating, camping, hiking	Try low-impact aerobics. Before undertaking new exercises, consult your doctor

11.4 Energy for Muscle Contraction

ATP, produced previous to strenuous exercise, lasts a few seconds, and then muscles acquire new ATP in three different ways: creatine phosphate breakdown, cellular respiration, and fermentation (Fig. 11.8). Creatine phosphate breakdown and fermentation are anaerobic, meaning that they do not require oxygen. Creatine phosphate breakdown is used first. It is a way to acquire ATP before oxygen starts entering mitochondria. Cellular respiration is aerobic and only takes place when oxygen is available. If exercise is vigorous to the point that oxygen cannot be delivered fast enough to working muscles, then fermentation occurs. Fermentation brings on oxygen deficit.

Creatine Phosphate Breakdown

<u>Creatine phosphate</u> is a high-energy compound built up when a muscle is resting. Creatine phosphate cannot participate directly in muscle contraction. Instead, it can regenerate ATP by the following reaction:

creatine phosphate ⟶ creatine

This reaction occurs in the midst of sliding filaments, and therefore is the speediest way to make ATP available to muscles. Creatine phosphate provides enough energy for only about eight seconds of intense activity, and then it is spent. Creatine phosphate is rebuilt when a muscle is resting by transferring a phosphate group from ATP to creatine.

Cellular Respiration

Cellular respiration, completed in mitochondria, usually provides most of a muscle's ATP. Glycogen and fat are stored in muscle cells. Therefore, a muscle cell can use glucose, from glycogen, and fatty acids, from fat, as fuel to produce ATP if oxygen is available:

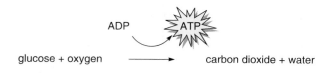

glucose + oxygen ⟶ carbon dioxide + water

Myoglobin, an oxygen carrier similar to hemoglobin, is synthesized in muscle cells, and its presence accounts for the reddish brown color of skeletal muscle fibers. Myoglobin has a higher affinity for oxygen than does hemoglobin. Therefore, it can temporarily store oxygen and make it available to mitochondria when cellular respiration begins. The resulting carbon dioxide leaves the body at the lungs and water simply enters the extracellular space. The by-product, heat, keeps the entire body warm.

Fermentation

Fermentation, such as creatine phosphate breakdown, supplies ATP without consuming oxygen. During fermentation, glucose is broken down to lactate (lactic acid):

glucose ⟶ lactate

The accumulation of lactate in a muscle fiber makes the cytoplasm more acidic, and eventually, enzymes cease to function well. If fermentation continues longer than 2 or 3 minutes, cramping and fatigue set in. Cramping seems to be due to lack of the ATP needed to pump calcium ions back into the sarcoplasmic reticulum and to break the linkages between the actin and myosin filaments so that muscle fibers can relax.

Oxygen Deficit

When a muscle uses fermentation to supply its energy needs, it incurs an **oxygen deficit.** Oxygen deficit is obvious when a person continues to breathe heavily after exercising. The ability to run up an oxygen deficit is one of muscle tissue's greatest assets. Brain tissue cannot last nearly as long without oxygen as muscles can.

In people who train, the number of muscle mitochondria increases, and so fermentation is not needed to produce ATP. Their mitochondria can start consuming oxygen as soon as the ADP concentration starts rising during muscle contraction. Because mitochondria can break down fatty acid instead of glucose, blood glucose is spared for the activity of the brain. (The brain, unlike other organs, can only utilize glucose to produce ATP.) Because less lactate is produced in people who train, the pH of the blood remains steady, and there is less of an oxygen deficit.

Repaying an oxygen deficit requires replenishing creatine phosphate supplies and disposing of lactate. Lactate can be changed back to pyruvate and metabolized completely in mitochondria, or it can be sent to the liver to reconstruct glycogen. A marathon runner who has just crossed the finish line is not usually exhausted due to oxygen deficit. Instead, the runner has used up all the muscles', and probably the liver's, glycogen supply. It takes about two days to replace glycogen stores on a high-carbohydrate diet.

Working muscles require a supply of ATP. Anaerobic creatine phosphate breakdown and fermentation can quickly generate ATP. Cellular respiration in mitochondria is best for sustained exercise.

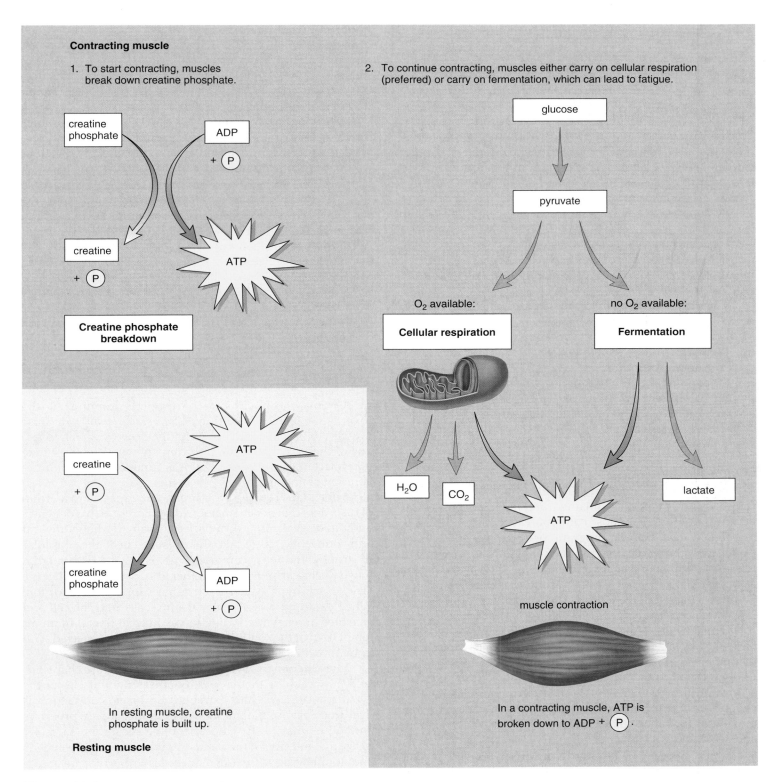

Contracting muscle

1. To start contracting, muscles break down creatine phosphate.

creatine phosphate

ADP + (P)

creatine + (P)

ATP

Creatine phosphate breakdown

2. To continue contracting, muscles either carry on cellular respiration (preferred) or carry on fermentation, which can lead to fatigue.

glucose

pyruvate

O_2 available:

Cellular respiration

no O_2 available:

Fermentation

H_2O CO_2

ATP

lactate

muscle contraction

creatine + (P)

ATP

creatine phosphate

ADP + (P)

In resting muscle, creatine phosphate is built up.

Resting muscle

In a contracting muscle, ATP is broken down to ADP + (P).

Figure 11.8 **Energy sources for muscle contraction.**
In a resting muscle (lighter screen), creatine phosphate builds up and is stored in the muscle. When a muscle starts contracting (darker screen) the muscle has several ways to acquire ATP. (1) When the muscle starts contracting, a muscle breaks down stored creatine phosphate and this generates some ATP that is used immediately. (2) To continue contracting, a muscle carries on cellular respiration as long as oxygen (O_2) is available. When O_2 is not available, a muscle carries on fermentation for a limited period of time. Unfortunately, fermentation results in only a small amount of ATP (compared to cellular respiration) and lactate builds up. Once the muscle resumes resting (lighter screen), creatine phosphate builds up again.

11.5 Muscular Disorders

Muscular disorders are divided into those that are spasms and injuries and those that are diseases.

Spasms and Injuries

Spasms are sudden and involuntary muscular contractions most often accompanied by pain. Spasms can occur in smooth and skeletal muscles. A spasm of the intestinal tract is a type of colic sometimes called a bellyache. Multiple spasms of skeletal muscles are called a seizure or convulsion. Cramps are strong, painful spasms, especially of the leg and foot, usually due to strenuous activity. Cramps can even occur when sleeping after a strenuous workout. Facial tics, such as periodic eye blinking, head turning, or grimacing, are spasms that can be controlled voluntarily, but only with great effort.

A **strain** is due to an injury that causes overstretching of a muscle near a joint, but a **sprain** is a twisting of a joint leading to swelling and injury not only of muscles but also of ligaments, tendons, blood vessels, and nerves. The ankle is often subject to sprains.

Myalgia refers to achy muscles. It is often an accompaniment of influenza or other viral illnesses. Myalgia may accompany myositis, which is inflammation of the muscles, either in response to viral infection or as an immune system disorder.

Tendinitis and Bursitis

In **tendinitis,** the normal smooth gliding motion of a tendon is impaired, the tendon is inflamed, and movement of a joint becomes painful. The most common cause of tendinitis is overuse. A new exercise program, or an increased level of exercise, can bring on the symptoms of tendinitis. As we age, tendons lose their elasticity and ability to glide as smoothly as they once did; therefore, tendinitis is more common. Some speculate that the tendons are not being supplied with adequate nutrients because of a change in the blood vessels.

Tennis elbow, a form of tendinitis, is suspected when a patient complains of elbow pain. The condition is thought to be due to small tears of the tendons that attach the muscles of the forearm to the humerus at the elbow joint. The wrist extensors, in particular, have been implicated in causing the symptoms of tennis elbow. Patients complain of pain on the outside of the elbow that is worsened by grasping objects and cocking the wrist back.

Every person has hundreds of bursae located in the joints throughout the body. A bursa, which provides a smooth, slippery surface where muscles and tendons glide over bones, has been likened to a plastic bag filled with a small amount of oil. Bursitis is an inflammation of a bursa. Bursitis usually results from a repetitive movement or from prolonged and excessive pressure. Patients who rest on their elbows for long periods or those who bend their elbows frequently and repetitively (for example, using a vacuum for hours at a time) can develop elbow bursitis, also called olecranon bursitis. Similarly, in other parts of the body, repetitive use or frequent pressure can irritate a bursa and lead to inflammation. Systemic inflammatory conditions, such as rheumatoid arthritis, contribute to a person developing inflammation of a bursa.

Over-the-counter and prescribed nonsteroidal anti-inflammatory drugs, commonly referred to as NSAIDs (pronounced en-sayds) are the most commonly used medications for treating arthritis, bursitis, and tendinitis. Medicines such as ibuprofen (Motrin) and naproxen (Aleve) are available over the counter, whereas other medications must be prescribed. Cortisone injections are also a common, nonsurgical way to treat tendinitis and bursitis. Cortisone is a steroid hormone produced naturally by the adrenal gland. The adrenal glands release cortisone into the bloodstream when the body is under stress but its action is relatively short-lived. Injectable cortisone, a close derivative of the body's own product, is synthetically produced today. Synthetic cortisone is injected into the specific area of inflammation and not into the bloodstream.

Diseases

In persons who have not been properly immunized, the toxin of the tetanus bacterium (*Clostridium tetani*) can cause muscles to lock in paralysis. A rigidly locked jaw, **lockjaw,** is one of the first signs of an infection known as tetanus. Like other bacterial infections, tetanus is curable with the administration of an antibiotic.

Muscular dystrophy is a broad term applied to a group of disorders that are characterized by a progressive degeneration and weakening of muscles. As muscle fibers die, fat and connective tissue take their place. Duchenne muscular dystrophy, the most common type, is inherited through a flawed gene carried by the mother. It is now known that the lack of a protein called dystrophin causes the condition. When dystrophin is absent, calcium leaks into the cell and activates an enzyme that dissolves muscle fibers. In an attempt to treat the condition, muscles have been injected with immature muscle cells that do produce dystrophin.

Myasthenia gravis is an autoimmune disease characterized by weakness that especially affects the muscles of the eyelids, face, neck, and extremities. Muscle contraction is impaired because the immune system mistakenly produces antibodies that destroy acetylcholine receptors. In many cases, the first sign of the disease is a drooping of the eyelids and double vision. Treatment includes drugs that are antagonistic to the enzyme acetylcholinesterase (see page 222).

At one time or another, many people suffer from a muscular disorder, such as a sprain or tendinitis. Muscular dystrophy and myasthenia gravis are less common.

Bioethical Focus

Performance-Enhancing Drugs

As we learned in the opening vignette on page 197, some athletes may be better at one sport than another, depending on whether their muscles contain fast- or slow-twitch fibers. A natural advantage of this sort does not bar an athlete from participating in and winning a medal in a particular sport at the Olympic Games. Also, some athletes have an advantage over others due to improved equipment and special shoes, advances in sports nutrition, new weight- and endurance-training regimens, specialized techniques based on their particular anatomy and physiology, and almost miraculous medical treatments for injuries. Such advantages are not considered reason enough to bar an athlete from receiving a medal. However, if athletes take any number of performance-enhancing drugs, they are barred from getting a medal (Fig. 11A).

In the past, athletes have turned to other dangerous and potentially life-threatening techniques to improve their edge. It was fairly common for wrestlers to use severe dehydration, diuretics, and laxatives to lose weight in order to participate in a lower weight class. In blood doping, blood is removed from an athlete's body several weeks before a competition and then reinjected into the body right before the event. A heart attack or stroke can occur due to increased blood viscosity resulting from the increased amount of red blood cells.

Anabolic steroids are one class of drugs commonly abused by athletes today. Although illegal, many of these drugs are available for sale on the Internet. Anabolic steroids are synthetic substances related to male sex hormones that bulk up muscle mass and increase strength. When abused at high doses, they also increase hostility and aggression, and cause heart disease, liver cancer, acne, eating disorders, sterility, and stunted height. Withdrawal leads to mood swings, fatigue, depression, and often suicide attempts. Despite these drawbacks, some athletes still want to use these drugs. Should they be allowed to?

On the horizon are other ways that might give some athletes an advantage over their competitors. Gene therapy may soon be available to help the aging and diseased repair and strengthen their skeletal muscles. The gene for insulin-like growth factor may help increase the growth of skeletal muscles in these patients. The gene for erythropoietin can cause those with anemia to increase the number of red blood cells. Gene therapy utilizing these genes is still in the experimental, animal-testing stage. When ready for use in humans, such gene therapy will be well within the guidelines for medical treatment of human disorders. But should

Figure 11A   Anabolic steroid use.
In 1988, Ben Johnson won an Olympic gold medal for the 100-meter sprint, but had to return it a few days later because he tested positive for anabolic steroids.

they be used by athletes to enhance their performance? Why or why not?

Should the International Olympic Committee outlaw the taking of any medication or the use of any procedure to enhance an athlete's performance. On what basis? "Unfair advantage" cannot be cited because some athletes naturally have an unfair advantage over other athletes to begin with. Should performance-enhancing drugs or procedures be outlawed on the basis of health reasons? Excessive practice alone and a purposeful decrease or increase in weight to better perform in a sport can also injure a person's health. In other words, how can you justify allowing some behaviors that enhance performance and not others?

Decide Your Opinion

1. Do you believe that the techniques athletes use to train and enhance their performance should be regulated in any way? Why or why not? Does this apply to high school athletes as well?
2. Is it acceptable for athletes to endanger their health by practicing excessively? By gaining or losing weight? By taking drugs? Why or why not?
3. Who, if anyone, should be in charge of regulating the behavior of athletes so that they do not harm themselves?

11.6 Homeostasis

Movement is essential to maintaining homeostasis. The skeletal and muscular systems work together to enable body movement (Fig. 11.9). This is most evidently illustrated by what happens when skeletal muscles contract and pull on the bones to which they are attached, causing movement at joints. Body movement of this sort allows us to respond to certain types of changes in the environment. For instance, if you are sitting in the sun and start to feel hot, you can get up and move to a shady spot.

The muscular and skeletal systems work for other types of movements that are just as important for maintaining homeostasis. Contraction of skeletal muscles associated with the jaw and tongue allow you to grind food with the teeth. The rhythmic smooth-muscle contractions of peristalsis move ingested materials through the digestive tract. These processes are necessary for supplying the body's cells with nutrients. The ceaseless beating of your heart, which propels blood into the arterial system, is the contraction of cardiac muscle. Contractions of skeletal muscles in the body, especially those associated with breathing and leg movements, aid in the process of venous return by pushing blood back toward the heart. This is why soldiers and marching bands are cautioned not to lock their knees when standing at attention—the reduction in venous return causes a drop in blood pressure that can result in fainting. The pressure exerted by skeletal muscle contraction also helps to squeeze tissue fluid into the lymphatic capillaries, where it is referred to as lymph.

Protection

Do the skeletal and muscular systems contribute to homeostasis in other ways? Indeed they do. The skeletal system plays a simple yet important role just by protecting the soft internal organs of your body, such as the brain, spinal cord, kidneys, liver, and most of the endocrine glands. All of these, particularly the nervous and endocrine organs, must be protected so that they can carry out activities necessary for homeostasis.

Calcium Metabolism

Under the direction of the endocrine system, the skeletal system performs tasks that are vital for calcium homeostasis. Calcium ions (Ca^{2+}) are needed for a variety of processes in your body, such as muscle contraction and nerve conduction. They are also necessary for the regulation of cellular metabolism by acting in cellular messenger systems. Thus, it is important to always maintain an adequate level of Ca^{2+} in the blood. When you have plenty of Ca^{2+} in your blood, the hormone calcitonin from the thyroid gland ensures that calcium salts are deposited in bone tissue. Thus, the skeleton acts as a reservoir for storage of this important mineral. If your blood Ca^{2+} level starts to fall, parathyroid hormone

Figure 11.9   Muscles and bones.
Muscles and bones work closely together to create movements.

secretion stimulates osteoclasts to break down bone tissue and thereby make Ca^{2+} available to the blood. Vitamin D is needed for the absorption of Ca^{2+} from the digestive tract, which is why vitamin D deficiency can result in weak bones. It is easy to get enough of this vitamin, since your skin produces it when exposed to sunlight and the milk you buy at the grocery store is fortified with vitamin D.

The bones of your skeleton contain two types of marrow: yellow and red. Fat is stored in yellow bone marrow, thus making it part of the body's energy reserves. Red bone marrow is the site of red blood cell production. The red blood cells are the carriers of oxygen in the blood. Oxygen is necessary for the production of ATP by aerobic cellular respiration. White blood cells also originate in the red bone marrow. The white cells are involved in defending your body against pathogens and cancerous cells; without them, you would soon succumb to disease and die.

Maintaining Body Temperature

The muscular system contributes to body temperature. When you are very cold, smooth muscle in the blood vessels that supply your skin constrict, reducing the amount of blood that is close to the surface of the body. This helps to conserve heat in the body's core, where vital organs lie. If you are cold enough, you may start to experience involuntary skeletal muscle contractions, known as shivering. This is initiated by temperature-sensitive neurons in the hypothalamus of the brain. Skeletal muscle contraction requires ATP, and using ATP generates heat. You may also notice that you get goose bumps when you are cold. This is because arrector pili muscles, tiny bundles of smooth muscle attached to the hair follicles, contract and cause the hairs to stand up. This is not very helpful in keeping humans warm, but it is quite effective in our furrier fellow mammals. Think of a cat or dog outside on a cold winter day. Its fur is a better insulator when standing up than lying flat. Goose bumps can also be a sign of fear. Although a human with goose bumps may not look very impressive, a frightened or aggressive animal whose fur is standing on end looks bigger and (hopefully) more intimidating to a predator or rival.

Human Systems Work Together

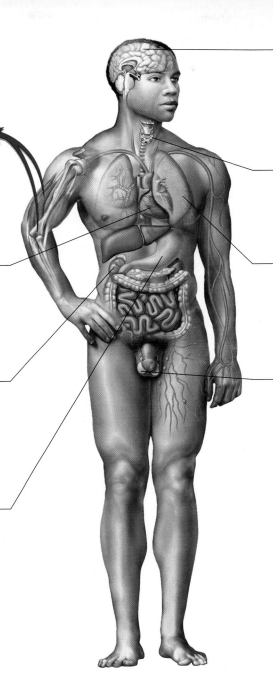

The muscular and skeletal systems work together to maintain homeostasis. The systems listed here in particular also work with these two systems.

Muscular and Skeletal Systems

These systems allow the body to move, and they provide support and protection for internal organs. Muscle contraction provides heat to warm the body; bones play a role in Ca^{2+} balance. These systems specifically help the other systems as mentioned below.

Cardiovascular System

Red bone marrow produces the blood cells. The rib cage protects the heart; red bone marrow stores Ca^{2+} for blood clotting. Muscle contraction keeps blood moving in the heart and blood vessels, particularly the veins.

Urinary System

Muscle contraction moves the fluid within ureters, bladder, and urethra. Kidneys activate vitamin D needed for Ca^{2+} absorption and help maintain the blood level of Ca^{2+} for bone growth and repair, and for muscle contraction.

Digestive System

Jaws contain teeth that chew food; the hyoid bone assists swallowing. Muscle contraction accounts for chewing of food and peristalsis to move food along digestive tract. The digestive tract absorbs ions needed for strong bones and muscle contraction.

Nervous System

Bones store Ca^{2+} needed for muscle contraction and nerve impulse conduction. The nervous system stimulates muscles and sends sensory input from joints to the brain. Muscle contraction moves eyes, permits speech, and creates facial expressions.

Endocrine System

Growth hormone and sex hormones regulate bone and muscle development; parathyroid hormone and calcitonin regulate Ca^{2+} content of bones.

Respiratory System

The rib cage protects lungs, and rib cage movement assists breathing, as does muscle contraction. Breathing provides the oxygen needed for ATP production so muscles can move.

Reproductive System

Muscle contraction moves gametes in oviducts, and uterine contraction occurs during childbirth. Sex hormones influence bone growth and density; androgens promote muscle growth.

Summarizing the Concepts

11.1 Types and Functions of Muscles
Humans have three types of muscle tissue (smooth, cardiac, and skeletal) that differ in anatomy. Skeletal muscle is voluntary, while smooth and cardiac are involuntary. Muscles have various functions; they provide movement and heat, help maintain posture, and protect underlying organs.

A whole skeletal muscle contains bundles of muscle fibers called fascicles. Skeletal muscles are usually attached to the skeleton by tendons. Some muscles are prime movers, some are synergists, and others are antagonists.

Muscles are named for their size, shape, location, direction of fibers, number of attachments, and action.

11.2 Mechanism of Skeletal Muscle Fiber Contraction
Muscle fibers contain myofibrils, and myofibrils contain actin and myosin filaments. Nerve impulses travel down motor neurons and stimulate muscle fibers at neuromuscular junctions. The sarcolemma of a muscle fiber forms T tubules that extend into the fiber and almost touch the sarcoplasmic reticulum, which stores calcium ions. When calcium ions are released into muscle fibers, actin filaments slide past myosin filaments within the sarcomeres of a myofibril.

At a neuromuscular junction, synaptic vesicles release acetylcholine (ACh), which binds to protein receptors on the sarcolemma, causing impulses to travel down the T tubules and calcium to leave the sarcoplasmic reticulum. Myofibril contraction follows.

Calcium ions bind to troponin and cause the tropomyosin threads that wind around actin filaments to shift their position, revealing myosin-binding sites. The myosin filament is composed of many myosin molecules, each containing a head with an ATP-binding site. Myosin is an ATPase, and once it breaks down ATP, the myosin head is ready to attach to actin. The release of ADP and ℗ causes the head to change its position. This is the power stroke that causes the actin filament to slide toward the center of a sarcomere. When myosin breaks down another ATP, the head detaches from actin, and the cycle begins again.

11.3 Whole Muscle Contraction
In the laboratory, muscle contraction is described in terms of a muscle twitch, summation, and tetanus. In the body, muscles exhibit tone, in which a continuous slight tension is maintained by muscle fibers that take turns contracting. The strength of muscle contraction varies according to recruitment of motor units.

11.4 Energy for Muscle Contraction
A muscle fiber has three ways to acquire ATP for muscle contraction. (1) Creatine phosphate, built up when a muscle is resting, can donate a high-energy phosphate to ADP, forming ATP. (2) Fermentation results in oxygen deficit because oxygen is needed to complete the metabolism of the lactic acid that accumulates. Both of these processes quickly produce ATP for muscle contraction. (3) Cellular respiration takes longer because oxygen must be transported to mitochondria before the process can be completed.

11.5 Muscular Disorders
Muscular disorders include spasms and injuries as well as such diseases as lockjaw, muscular dystrophy, and myasthenia gravis.

11.6 Homeostasis
The muscular system works with the other systems of the body in the ways described in Human Systems Work Together on page 213.

Studying the Concepts

1. What are the three types of muscles in the human body? 198
2. List and discuss the functions of muscles. 198
3. Give an example that illustrates how muscles work in antagonistic pairs. 199
4. What criteria are used to name muscles? Give an example for each one. 200–201
5. Describe the microscopic anatomy of a muscle fiber and explain the sliding filament model of muscle contraction. 202–3
6. Describe the structure and function of a neuromuscular junction. 204
7. Describe the cyclical events as myosin pulls actin toward the center of a sarcomere. 205
8. Contrast a muscle twitch with summation and tetanus. 206
9. What is muscle tone, and how is it maintained? 206
10. What are the three ways a muscle fiber can acquire ATP for muscle contraction? How are the three ways interrelated? 208–9
11. What are some common muscular disorders? What types of diseases are more serious? 210
12. How does the muscular system help maintain homeostasis? 212–13

Thinking Critically About the Concepts

Refer to the opening vignette on page 197, and then answer these questions.

1. What differences exist at the cellular level between fast-twitch and slow-twitch muscle fibers?
2. Why are fast-twitch muscle fibers better suited for quick, short bursts of speed?
3. What other things besides muscle fibers could affect an athlete's performance on a particular race day?
4. Why is the breast meat of a bird made up of fast-twitch fibers?

Testing Your Knowledge of the Concepts

Choose the best answer for each question.

1. Which of the following characteristics is not used to name muscles?
   a. strength of contraction
   b. size
   c. shape
   d. location
   e. number of attachments

2. Impulses that move down the T system of a muscle fiber most directly cause
   a. movement of tropomyosin.
   b. attachment of the cross-bridges to myosin.
   c. release of Ca^{2+} from the sarcoplasmic reticulum.
   d. splitting of ATP.

3. Which of the following statements about cross-bridges is false?
   a. They are composed of myosin.
   b. They bind to ATP after they detach from actin.
   c. They contain an ATPase.
   d. They split ATP before they attach to actin.

4. Which statement about sarcomere contraction is incorrect?
   a. The A bands shorten.
   b. The H zones shorten.
   c. The I bands shorten.
   d. The sarcomeres shorten.

5. Which of the following muscles would have motor units with the lowest innervation ratio?
   a. leg muscles
   b. arm muscles
   c. muscles that move the fingers
   d. muscles of the trunk

6. Muscles are covered by fibrous connective tissue called the
   a. fascicle.   c. fascia.
   b. tendon.   d. retinaculum.

7. Label this diagram of a muscle fiber, using these terms: myofibril, T tubule, sarcomere, sarcolemma, sarcoplasmic reticulum, Z line.

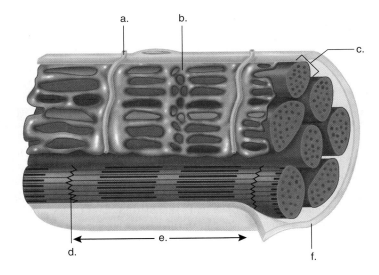

8. As ADP and Ⓟ are released from a myosin head,
   a. actin filaments move toward the H zone.
   b. myosin cross-bridges pull the thin filaments.
   c. a sarcomere shortens.
   d. Only a and c are correct.
   e. All of these are correct.

9. Which of these is a direct source of energy for muscle contraction?
   a. ATP   d. glycogen
   b. creatine phosphate   e. Both a and b are correct.
   c. lactic acid

10. When muscles contract,
    a. sarcomeres increase in length.
    b. actin breaks down ATP.
    c. myosin slides past actin.
    d. the H zone disappears.
    e. calcium is taken up by the sarcoplasmic reticulum.

11. Nervous stimulation of muscles
    a. occurs at a neuromuscular junction.
    b. results in an impulse that travels down the T system.
    c. causes calcium to be released from expanded regions of the sarcoplasmic reticulum.
    d. All of these are correct.

12. In a muscle fiber,
    a. the sarcolemma is connective tissue holding the myofibrils together.
    b. the T system consists of tubules.
    c. both actin and myosin filaments have cross-bridges.
    d. there is no endoplasmic reticulum.
    e. All of these are correct.

13. To increase the force of muscle contraction,
    a. individual muscle cells have to contract with greater force.
    b. motor units have to contract with greater force.
    c. motor units need to be recruited.
    d. All of the above are correct.
    e. None of the above is correct.

14. Lack of calcium in muscles will
    a. result in no contraction.
    b. cause weak contraction.
    c. cause strong contraction.
    d. will have no effect.
    e. None of the above is correct.

15. Which of these energy relationships are mismatched?
    a. creatine phosphate—anaerobic
    b. cellular respiration—aerobic
    c. fermentation—anaerobic
    d. oxygen deficit—anaerobic
    e. All of these are properly matched.

16. During muscle contraction,
    a. ATP is hydrolyzed when the myosin head is unattached.
    b. ADP and Ⓟ are released as the myosin head attaches to actin.
    c. ADP and Ⓟ release causes the head to change position and actin filaments to move.
    d. release of ATP causes the myosin head to return to resting position.
    e. Both b and d are correct.

17. Proper functioning of a neuromuscular junction requires the
    a. presence of acetylcholine.
    b. presence of a synaptic cleft.
    c. presence of a motor terminal.
    d. sarcolemma of a muscle cell.
    e. All of these are correct.

18. Which of these join a larger structure to a smaller structure?
    a. muscle fiber—myofibril
    b. myofibril—sarcomere
    c. sarcomere—actin filament
    d. actin filament—myosin filament
    e. All but d are correct.

In questions 19–22, match each muscle to a region of the body in the key.

Key:
- a. head and neck
- b. trunk
- c. arm
- d. thigh

19. Hamstring group

20. Trapezius

21. Rectus abdominis

22. Triceps brachii

In questions 23–26, match each function to a muscle of the buttocks and legs in the key.

Key:
- a. gluteus medius
- b. gluteus maximus
- c. hamstring group
- d. gastrocnemius

23. Flexes leg and extends thigh

24. Abducts thigh

25. Flexes leg and foot

26. Extends thigh

In questions 27–29, match each function to a muscle of the face in the key.

Key:
- a. frontalis
- b. orbicularis oculi
- c. zygomaticus

27. Raises corner of mouth

28. Wrinkles forehead and lifts eyebrows

29. Closes eye

In questions 30–32, match the functions to a muscle of the upper limb and trunk in the key.

Key:
- a. external oblique
- b. rectus abdominis
- c. pectoralis major

30. Compresses abdomen; rotates trunk

31. Flexes and abducts shoulder

32. Flexes spine; compresses abdomen

In questions 33–35, match each function to a muscle of the lower limb in the key.

Key:
- a. adductor longus
- b. iliopsoas
- c. sartorius

33. Flexes thigh at hip joint

34. Adducts and flexes thigh

35. Rotates thigh

Understanding Key Terms

actin 202	origin 199
all-or-none law 206	oxygen deficit 208
cardiac muscle 198	sarcolemma 202
creatine phosphate 208	sarcomere 202
insertion 199	sarcoplasmic reticulum 202
lockjaw 210	skeletal muscle 198
motor unit 206	sliding filament model 202
muscle fiber 198	smooth muscle 198
muscle tone 206	spasm 210
muscle twitch 206	sprain 210
muscular dystrophy 210	strain 210
myalgia 210	T (transverse) tubule 202
myasthenia gravis 210	tendinitis 210
myofibril 202	tendon 199
myogram 206	tetanus 206
myosin 202	tropomyosin 205
neuromuscular junction 204	troponin 205

Match the key terms to these definitions.

a. _____ Structural and functional unit of a myofibril; contains actin and myosin filaments.

b. _____ End of a muscle that is attached to a movable bone.

c. _____ A condition of the body that occurs as a result of fermentation, an anaerobic process.

d. _____ Sustained maximal muscle contraction.

Online Learning Center

www.mhhe.com/maderhuman9

The Online Learning Center provides a wealth of information fully organized and integrated by chapter. You will find practice quizzes, interactive activities, labeling exercises, flashcards, and much more that will complement your learning and understanding of human biology.

Looking at Both Sides

Each day, the Internet, media, and other people present you with opposing viewpoints on a wide range of subjects. Your ability to develop an informed opinion on an issue, and talk to others about it, is extremely important.

To expand and enhance your knowledge of a highly relevant bioethical issue, visit the "Student Edition" of the Online Learning Center. Under "Course-Wide Content," select "Looking at Both Sides." Once there, you will be asked to complete activities that will increase your understanding of a current bioethical issue related to this chapter and allow you to defend your opinion.

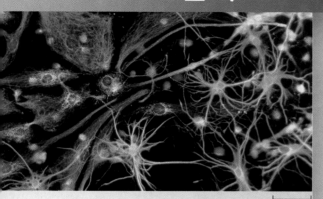

0.2 μm

12 Nervous System 217

13 Senses 243

14 Endocrine System 265

The nervous system is the ultimate coordinator of homeostasis. Nerves bring information to the brain and spinal cord from sensory receptors that detect changes both inside and outside the body. Then nerves take the commands sent by the brain and spinal cord to effectors, allowing the body to respond to these changes. For example, after low blood pressure stimulates internal receptors, the cardiovascular center in the brain sends out nerve impulses that constrict blood vessels, causing blood pressure to rise.

The endocrine system, like the nervous system, regulates other organs, but it acts more slowly and brings about a response that lasts longer. The endocrine organs secrete chemical signals called hormones into the bloodstream. After arriving at their target organs, hormones alter cellular metabolism.

Despite their very different modes of operation, we now know that the nervous system and the endocrine system are joined in numerous ways.

C H A P T E R   **12**

Nervous System

C H A P T E R   C O N C E P T S

12.1 Nervous Tissue
- What are the two major divisions of the nervous system? 218
- What are the three types of neurons and what are the three parts of a neuron? 218
- What is a nerve impulse and how is it propagated? 220
- Since neurons don't physically touch, how is an impulse transmitted from one neuron to the next? 222

12.2 The Central Nervous System
- What structures compose the central nervous system? 224
- What are the two functions of the spinal cord? 225
- What are the four major parts of the brain and the general function of each? 226–29
- What brain structure is responsible for a person being awake and alert, asleep, or comatose? 229

12.3 The Limbic System and Higher Mental Functions
- What is the function of the limbic system? 230
- What limbic system structures are involved in learning and long-term memory? 230–31
- What areas of the cerebrum are involved in language and speech? Where are they located? 231

12.4 The Peripheral Nervous System
- How many cranial nerves are there? How many spinal nerves are there? 232
- What is the fastest way for you to react to a stimulus? 233
- What is the autonomic system, and how does it function? 234–35

12.5 Drug Abuse
- How can the abuse of drugs, including alcohol and nicotine, affect the nervous system? 237–39

Lou Gehrig, a member of the National Baseball Hall of Fame, first played for the New York Yankees in 1923 and ultimately became team captain. He was an exceptional batter, with a lifetime average of .340. Up until 1939, Gehrig had been a strong, healthy individual, even earning the nickname "Iron Horse." But he retired from baseball because he had begun experiencing weakness and lack of coordination. He had been diagnosed as having amyotrophic lateral sclerosis (ALS), now widely known as Lou Gehrig's disease.

ALS is a disease of nerve cells known as motor neurons. Motor neurons are responsible for relaying signals from the brain and spinal cord to the skeletal muscles for voluntary movement. In ALS, motor neurons gradually die, causing the muscles they normally communicate with to become weak and then atrophy (waste away). Even the muscles needed for swallowing and respiration are eventually affected. Other types of neurons survive, so a person with ALS can still sense and think normally.

Although a small proportion of ALS cases are due to an inherited genetic defect, the cause of most cases is unknown. Interestingly, the prevalence of ALS appears to be greater in people who are slim and athletic, for reasons that are still not clear. ALS is a fatal disease. Many people die within just three to five years of receiving a diagnosis of ALS, as did Lou Gehrig. He died in 1941, shortly before his 38th birthday. At this time, there is still no cure.

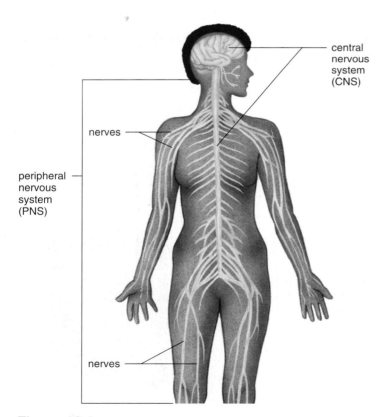

Figure 12.1   **Organization of the nervous system.**
The central nervous system (CNS) consists of the brain and spinal cord. The peripheral nervous system (PNS) consists of the nerves, which lie outside the CNS.

12.1 Nervous Tissue

In the nervous system, the brain carries out all sorts of higher mental functions that help account for our individual personalities. The nervous system also allows us to respond to external stimuli and, along with the endocrine system, is involved in coordination of internal systems. Therefore, the nervous system is critical to homeostasis.

The nervous system has two major divisions (Fig. 12.1). The **central nervous system (CNS)** consists of the brain and spinal cord, which are located in the midline of the body. The **peripheral nervous system (PNS)** consists of nerves. Nerves lie outside the CNS. The division between the CNS and the PNS is arbitrary; the two systems work together and are connected to each other.

Nervous tissue contains two types of cells: neurons and neuroglia (neuroglial cells). **Neurons** are the cells that transmit nerve impulses between parts of the nervous system; **neuroglia** support and nourish neurons. Neuroglia were discussed in Chapter 4, and this section discusses the structure and function of neurons.

Neuron Structure

Although the nervous system is extremely complex, the principles of its operation are simple. Classified according to function, the three types of neurons are: sensory neurons, interneurons, and motor neurons (Fig. 12.2). Their functions are best described in relation to the CNS. A **sensory neuron** takes nerve impulses (messages) from a sensory receptor to the CNS. **Sensory receptors** are special structures that detect changes in the environment. An **interneuron** lies entirely within the CNS. Interneurons can receive input from sensory neurons and also from other interneurons in the CNS. Thereafter, they sum up all the nerve impulses received from these neurons before they communicate with motor neurons. A **motor neuron** takes nerve impulses away from the CNS to an effector (muscle fiber or gland). **Effectors** carry out our responses to environmental changes, whether they are external or internal.

Neurons vary in appearance, but all of them have just three parts: a cell body, dendrites, and an axon. The **cell body** contains the nucleus, as well as other organelles. **Dendrites** are the many short extensions that receive signals from sensory receptors or other neurons. These signals can result in nerve impulses that are then conducted by an axon. The **axon** is the portion of a neuron that conducts nerve impulses. An axon can be quite long, and when present in nerves, an axon is called a nerve fiber.

Notice that in sensory neurons, a very long axon carries nerve impulses from the dendrites associated with a sensory receptor to the CNS and that this axon bypasses the cell body. In interneurons and motor neurons, on the other hand, multiple dendrites take signals to the cell body and then an axon conducts nerve impulses away from the cell body.

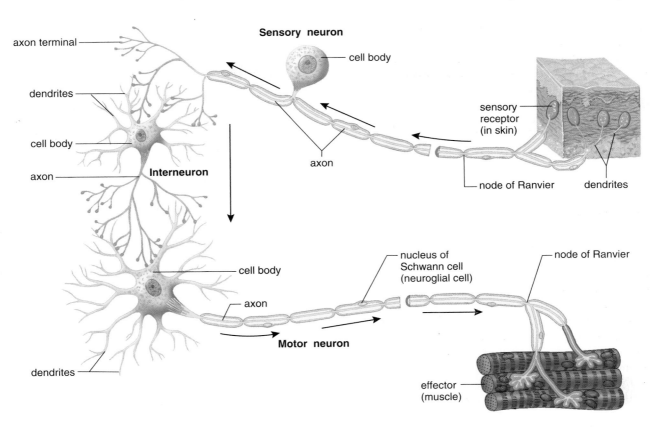

Figure 12.2   Types of neurons.
A sensory neuron, an interneuron, and a motor neuron are drawn here to show their arrangement in the body. (The breaks indicate that the fibers are much longer than shown.) How does this arrangement correlate with the function of each neuron?

Myelin Sheath

Some axons are covered by a protective **myelin sheath.** In the PNS, this covering is formed by a type of neuroglia called **Schwann cells,** which contain myelin, a lipid substance, in their plasma membranes. The myelin sheath develops when Schwann cells wrap themselves around an axon many times. Because each Schwann cell only covers a portion of an axon, the myelin sheath is interrupted. The gaps where there is no myelin sheath are called **nodes of Ranvier** (Fig. 12.3).

Long axons tend to have a myelin sheath, but short axons do not. The gray matter of the CNS is gray because it contains no myelinated axons; the white matter of the CNS is white because it does. Multiple sclerosis (MS) is a disease of the myelin sheath in the CNS. Lesions develop that interfere with normal conduction of nerve impulses, and various neuromuscular symptoms are the result.

In the PNS, myelin gives nerve fibers their white, glistening appearance and serves as an excellent insulator. The myelin sheath also plays an important role in nerve regeneration within the PNS. If an axon is accidentally severed, the myelin sheath remains and serves as a passageway for new fiber growth.

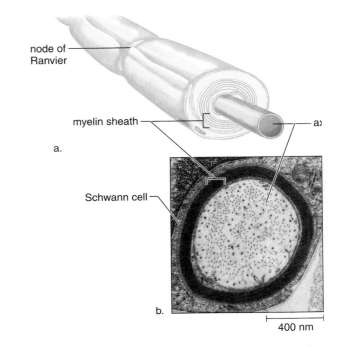

Figure 12.3   Myelin sheath.
a. In the PNS, a myelin sheath forms when Schwann cells wrap themselves around an axon. **b.** Electron micrograph of a cross section of an axon surrounded by a myelin sheath.

The Nerve Impulse

Nerve impulses convey information in the nervous system. The nerve impulse is studied by using excised axons and a voltmeter called an **oscilloscope.** Voltage, often measured in millivolts (mV), is a measure of the electrical potential difference between two points, which in this case are the inside and the outside of the axon. Voltage is displayed on the oscilloscope screen as a trace, or pattern, over time.

Resting Potential

In the experimental setup shown in Figure 12.4a and b an oscilloscope is wired to two electrodes: One electrode is placed inside an axon, and the other electrode is placed outside. The axon is essentially a membranous tube filled with axoplasm (cytoplasm of the axon). When the axon is not conducting an impulse, the internal electrode detects a potential difference across a membrane equal to about -65 mV; the inside of the axon is negative compared with the outside. This is the **resting potential** because the axon is not conducting an impulse.

The resting potential correlates with a difference in ion distribution on either side of the axomembrane (plasma membrane of the axon). As Figure 12.4a shows, the concentration of sodium ions (Na^+) is greater outside the axon than inside, and the concentration of potassium ions (K^+) is greater inside the axon than outside. The unequal distribution of these ions is due to the action of the **sodium-potassium pump,** a membrane protein that actively transports Na^+ out of and K^+ into the axon (see Fig. 3.8b). The work of the pump maintains the unequal distribution of Na^+ and K^+ across the membrane.

The pump is always working because the membrane is somewhat permeable to these ions, and they tend to diffuse toward their lesser concentration. Since the membrane is more permeable to K^+ than to Na^+, there are always more positive ions outside the membrane than inside. Large, negatively charged organic ions in the axoplasm also contribute to the polarity across a resting axomembrane.

An unequal distribution of ions (Na^+ on the outside; K^+ and organic ions on the inside) causes the inside of an axon to be negative compared with the outside.

Action Potential

An **action potential** is a rapid change in polarity across an axomembrane as the nerve impulse occurs. An action potential is an all-or-none phenomenon. If a stimulus causes the axomembrane to depolarize to a certain level, called **threshold,** an action potential occurs. The strength of an action potential does not change, but an intense stimulus can cause an axon to fire (start an axon potential) more often in a given time interval than a weak stimulus.

The action potential requires two types of gated channel proteins in the membrane. One gated channel protein opens to allow Na^+ to pass through the membrane, and another opens to allow K^+ to pass through the membrane (Fig. 12.4c,d).

Sodium Gates Open   When an action potential occurs, the gates of sodium channels open first, and Na^+ flows into the axon. As Na^+ moves to inside the axon, the membrane potential changes from -65 mV to $+40$ mV. This is a *depolarization* because the charge inside the axon changes from negative to positive.

Potassium Gates Open   Second, the gates of potassium channels open, and K^+ flows to outside the axon. As K^+ moves to outside the axon, the action potential changes from $+40$ mV back to -65 mV. This is a *repolarization* because the inside of the axon resumes a negative charge as K^+ exits the axon.

Following an Action Potential

After an action potential has passed by, the sodium-potassium pump restores the resting potential by moving the potassium back to the inside and sodium back to the outside.

During the depolarization phase of a nerve impulse, Na^+ moves to inside the axon, and during repolarization K^+ moves to outside the axon.

Propagation of an Action Potential

An action potential travels down an axon. In nonmyelinated axons, each successive portion of the axon undergoes a depolarization and then a repolarization. As soon as an action potential has moved on, the previous portion of an axon undergoes a **refractory period,** during which the sodium gates are unable to open. This ensures that the action potential cannot move backward and instead always moves down an axon toward its branches.

In myelinated axons, the gated ion channels that produce an action potential are concentrated at the nodes of Ranvier. Since ion exchange occurs only at the nodes, the action potential travels faster than in nonmyelinated axons. This is called saltatory conduction, meaning that the action potential "jumps" from node to node. Speeds of 200 m per second (450 miles per hour) have been recorded.

An action potential travels along the length of an axon.

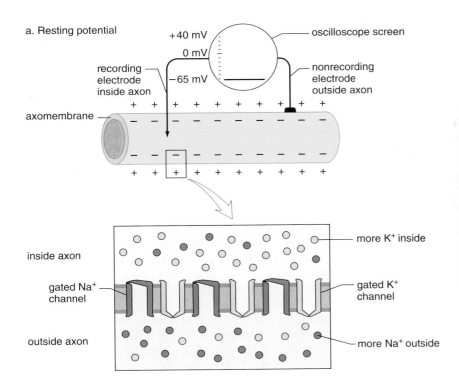

a. Resting potential

+40 mV

0 mV

oscilloscope screen

−65 mV

recording electrode inside axon

nonrecording electrode outside axon

axomembrane

inside axon

gated Na⁺ channel

more K⁺ inside

gated K⁺ channel

outside axon

more Na⁺ outside

b. Experimenter using oscilloscope

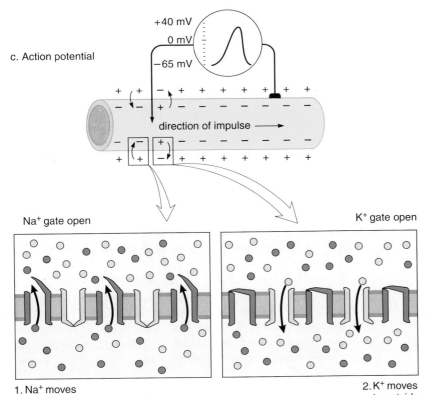

c. Action potential

+40 mV

0 mV

−65 mV

direction of impulse →

Na⁺ gate open

K⁺ gate open

1. Na⁺ moves to inside

2. K⁺ moves to outside

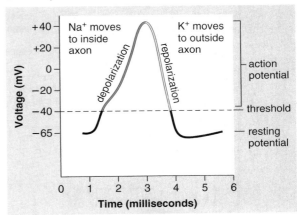

d. Action potential trace

Na⁺ moves to inside axon

K⁺ moves to outside axon

depolarization

repolarization

action potential

threshold

resting potential

Voltage (mV)

+40, +20, 0, −20, −40, −65

Time (milliseconds)

0 1 2 3 4 5 6

Figure 12.4   Resting and action potential.
a. Resting potential. There are more Na⁺ ions outside the axon and more K⁺ ions inside the axon. **b.** An oscilloscope, an instrument that measures voltage, records a resting potential of −65 mV. **c.** Action potential. A depolarization occurs when Na⁺ gates open and Na⁺ moves to inside the axon; a repolarization occurs when K⁺ gates open and K⁺ moves to outside the axon. **d.** Enlargement of the action potential in (**c**), as seen on the oscilloscope screen.

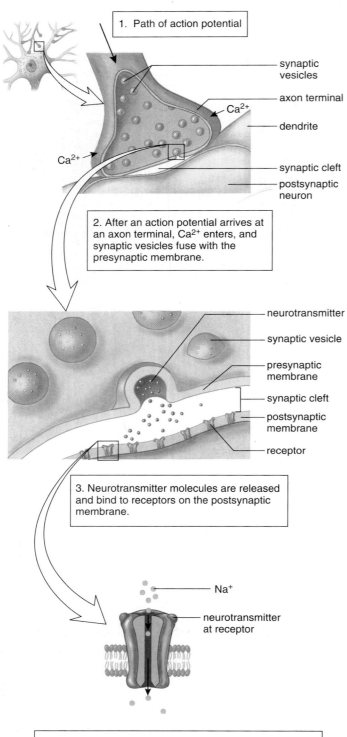

1. Path of action potential

— synaptic vesicles
— axon terminal
Ca²⁺
— dendrite
Ca²⁺
— synaptic cleft
— postsynaptic neuron

2. After an action potential arrives at an axon terminal, Ca²⁺ enters, and synaptic vesicles fuse with the presynaptic membrane.

— neurotransmitter
— synaptic vesicle
— presynaptic membrane
— synaptic cleft
— postsynaptic membrane
— receptor

3. Neurotransmitter molecules are released and bind to receptors on the postsynaptic membrane.

— Na⁺
— neurotransmitter at receptor

4. When an excitatory neurotransmitter binds to a receptor, Na⁺ diffuses into the postsynaptic neuron, and an action potential begins.

Figure 12.5   Synapse structure and function.
Transmission across a synapse from one neuron to another occurs when a neurotransmitter, released at the presynaptic membrane, diffuses across a synaptic cleft and binds to a receptor in the postsynaptic membrane.

The Synapse

Every axon branches into many fine endings, each tipped by a small swelling called an **axon terminal.** Each terminal lies very close to either the dendrite or the cell body of another neuron. This region of close proximity is called a **synapse** (Fig. 12.5). At a synapse, the membrane of the first neuron is called the *pre*synaptic membrane, and the membrane of the next neuron is called the *post*synaptic membrane. The small gap between is the **synaptic cleft.**

Transmission across a synapse is carried out by molecules called **neurotransmitters,** which are stored in synaptic vesicles in the axon terminals. These events occur: (1) nerve impulses traveling along an axon reach an axon terminal. (2) Calcium ions enter the terminal and they stimulate synaptic vesicles to merge with the presynaptic membrane. (3) Neurotransmitter molecules are released into the synaptic cleft and they diffuse across the cleft to the postsynaptic membrane, where they bind with specific receptor proteins. (4) Depending on the type of neurotransmitter, the response of the postsynaptic neuron can be toward excitation or toward inhibition. In Figure 12.5, excitation occurs because this neurotransmitter has caused Na⁺ to diffuse into the postsynaptic neuron. Inhibition would occur if a neurotransmitter caused K⁺ to enter the postsynaptic neuron.

Neurotransmitter Molecules

At least 25 different neurotransmitters have been identified, and a few of these are listed in Table 12.1. Two very well-known neurotransmitters are **acetylcholine (ACh)** and **norepinephrine (NE).** Both of these neurotransmitters are active in both the CNS and PNS. In the PNS, these neurotransmitters act at regions similar to synapses called neuromuscular junctions as discussed in Chapter 11.

Once a neurotransmitter has been released into a synaptic cleft and has initiated a response, it is removed from the cleft. In some synapses, the postsynaptic membrane contains enzymes that rapidly inactivate the neurotransmitter. For example, the enzyme **acetylcholinesterase (AChE)** breaks down acetylcholine. In other synapses, the presynaptic membrane rapidly reabsorbs the neurotransmitter, possibly for repackaging in synaptic vesicles or for molecular breakdown.

The short existence of neurotransmitters at a synapse prevents continuous stimulation (or inhibition) of postsynaptic membranes. The postsynaptic cell needs to be able to respond quickly to changing conditions; if the neurotransmitter were to linger in the cleft, the postsynaptic cell would be unable to respond to a new signal from a presynaptic cell.

Transmission across a synapse depends on the release of neurotransmitters, which diffuse across the synaptic cleft from one neuron to the next.

Synaptic Integration

A single neuron has many dendrites plus the cell body, and all of these can have synapses with many other neurons. Therefore, a neuron is on the receiving end of many signals (potential change), which can be either excitatory or inhibitory. An excitatory neurotransmitter produces a signal that drives the neuron closer to an action potential; an inhibitory neurotransmitter produces a signal that drives the neuron farther from an action potential.

Neurons integrate these incoming signals. **Integration** is the summing up of excitatory and inhibitory signals (Fig. 12.6). If a neuron receives enough excitatory signals (either from different synapses or at a rapid rate from one synapse) to outweigh the inhibitory ones, chances are, the axon will transmit a nerve impulse. On the other hand, if a neuron receives more inhibitory than excitatory signals, the summing up of these signals may prohibit the axon from firing.

It is of interest to note here that many drugs affect the nervous system by interfering with the actions of neurotransmitters. As described in Figure 12.18, a drug, for example a local anesthetic, might block the release of an excitatory neurotransmitter, while an antidepressant might alter the reuptake or prevent the breakdown of a excitatory transmitter.

Integration is the summing up of inhibitory and excitatory signals received by a postsynaptic neuron.

Table 12.1	Commonly Known Neurotransmitters

Neurotransmitter	Comments
Acetylcholine	Active in CNS and PNS; if present in excess, it overcomes acetylcholinesterase and becomes a poison.
Norepinephrine	Active in CNS and PNS; chemically related to epinephrine (adrenaline), a heart stimulator.
Dopamine	Active in CNS; loss of dopamine neurons causes Parkinson disease.
Serotonin	Active inhibitory neurotransmitter in the CNS; some drugs elevate mood and counter anxiety by increasing serotonin levels.
Glutamate	Most common excitatory neurotransmitter in the CNS; the food additive, monosodium glutamate, affects the nervous system in some people.
Gamma–amino-butyric acid (GABA)	Inhibitory neurotransmitter, whose action is mimicked by the drug benzodiazepine, which reduces anxiety and produces sedation.
Endorphins	Active in CNS, especially in pain pathways; its receptors are activated by narcotic drugs: opium, morphine, heroin, and codeine.

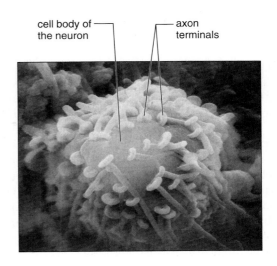

cell body of the neuron — axon terminals

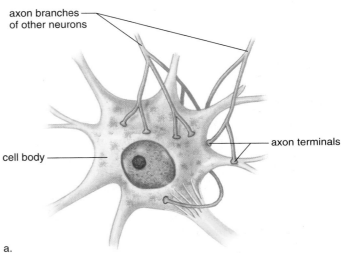

axon branches of other neurons

cell body — axon terminals

a.

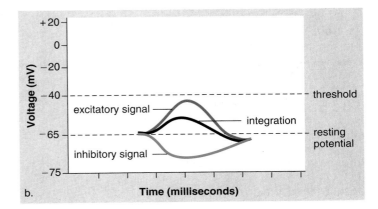

b.

Figure 12.6 Integration.

a. Many axons synapse with each neuron. **b.** Inhibitory signals and excitatory signals are summed up in the dendrite and cell body of the postsynaptic neuron. Only if the combined signals cause the membrane potential to rise above threshold does an action potential occur. In this example, threshold was not reached.

12.2 The Central Nervous System

The spinal cord and the brain make up the CNS, where sensory information is received and motor control is initiated. Figure 12.7 illustrates how the CNS relates to the PNS. Both the spinal cord and the brain are protected by bone; the spinal cord is surrounded by vertebrae, and the brain is enclosed by the skull. Also, both the spinal cord and the brain are wrapped in protective membranes known as **meninges** (sing., meninx). The spaces between the meninges are filled with **cerebrospinal fluid,** which cushions and protects the CNS. A small amount of this fluid is sometimes withdrawn from around the cord for laboratory testing when a spinal tap (lumbar puncture) is performed. Meningitis is an infection of the meninges.

Cerebrospinal fluid is also contained within the ventricles of the brain and in the central canal of the spinal cord. The brain has four **ventricles,** interconnecting chambers that produce and serve as a reservoir for cerebrospinal fluid. Normally, any excess cerebrospinal fluid drains away into the cardiovascular system. However, blockages can occur. In an infant, the brain can enlarge due to cerebrospinal fluid accumulation, resulting in a condition called hydrocephalus ("water on the brain"). If cerebrospinal fluid collects in an adult, the brain cannot enlarge, and instead is pushed against the skull, possibly becoming injured.

The CNS is composed of two types of nervous tissue—gray matter and white matter. **Gray matter** is gray because it contains cell bodies and short, nonmyelinated fibers. **White matter** is white because it contains myelinated axons that run together in bundles called **tracts.**

The CNS, which lies in the midline of the body and consists of the brain and the spinal cord, receives sensory information and initiates motor control.

The Spinal Cord

The **spinal cord** extends from the base of the brain through a large opening in the skull called the foramen magnum and into the vertebral canal formed by openings in the vertebrae.

Structure of the Spinal Cord

Figure 12.8*a* shows how an individual vertebra protects the spinal cord. The spinal nerves project from the cord between the vertebrae that make up the vertebral column. Intervertebral disks separate the vertebrae, and if a disk slips a bit and presses on the spinal cord, pain results.

A cross section of the spinal cord shows a central canal, gray matter, and white matter (Fig. 12.8*b,c*). The central canal contains cerebrospinal fluid, as do the meninges that protect the spinal cord. The gray matter is

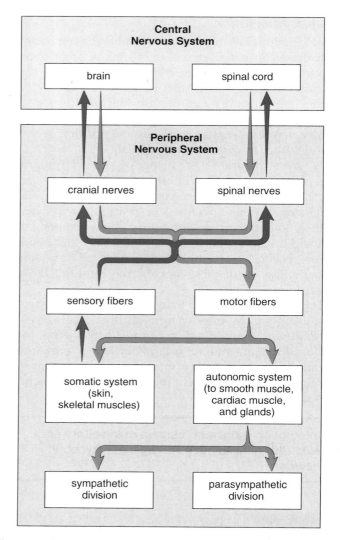

Figure 12.7   Organization of the nervous system.
The CNS is composed of the spinal cord and brain; the PNS contains cranial and spinal nerves. Nerves may contain both sensory and motor fibers. In the somatic system, nerves conduct impulses from sensory receptors to the CNS and motor impulses from the CNS to the skeletal muscles. In the autonomic system, consisting of the sympathetic and parasympathetic divisions, motor impulses travel to smooth muscle, cardiac muscle, and the glands.

centrally located and shaped like the letter H. Portions of sensory neurons and motor neurons are found there, as are interneurons that communicate with these two types of neurons. The dorsal root of a spinal nerve contains sensory fibers entering the gray matter, and the ventral root of a spinal nerve contains motor fibers exiting the gray matter. The dorsal and ventral roots join before the spinal nerve leaves the vertebral canal. Spinal nerves are a part of the PNS.

The white matter of the spinal cord occurs in areas around the gray matter. The white matter contains ascending tracts taking information to the brain (primarily located dorsally) and descending tracts taking information from the brain (primarily located ventrally). Because many tracts cross just after they enter and exit the brain, the left side of the brain controls the right side of the body, and the right side of the brain controls the left side of the body.

The spinal cord extends from the base of the brain into the vertebral canal formed by the vertebrae. A cross section shows that the spinal cord has a central canal, gray matter, and white matter.

Functions of the Spinal Cord

The spinal cord provides a means of communication between the brain and the peripheral nerves that leave the cord. When someone touches your hand, sensory receptors generate nerve impulses that pass through sensory fibers to the spinal cord and up ascending tracts to the brain. When we voluntarily move our limbs, motor impulses originating in the brain pass down descending tracts to the spinal cord and out to our muscles by way of motor fibers. Therefore, if the spinal cord is severed, we suffer a loss of sensation and a loss of voluntary control—that is, paralysis. If the cut occurs in the thoracic region, the lower body and legs are paralyzed, a condition known as paraplegia. If the injury is in the neck region, all four limbs are usually affected, a condition called quadriplegia.

We will see that the spinal cord is also the center for thousands of reflex arcs. A stimulus causes sensory receptors to generate nerve impulses that travel in sensory axons to the spinal cord. Interneurons integrate the incoming data and relay signals to motor neurons. A response to the stimulus occurs when motor axons cause skeletal muscles to contract. Each interneuron in the spinal cord has synapses with many other neurons, and therefore they send signals to several other interneurons and motor neurons.

The spinal cord plays a similar role for the internal organs. For example, when blood pressure falls, internal receptors in the carotid arteries and aorta generate nerve impulses that pass through sensory fibers to the cord and then up an ascending tract to a cardiovascular center in the brain. Thereafter, nerve impulses pass down a descending tract to the spinal cord. Motor impulses then cause blood vessels to constrict so that the blood pressure rises.

The spinal cord serves as a means of communication between the brain and much of the body. The spinal cord is also a center for reflex actions.

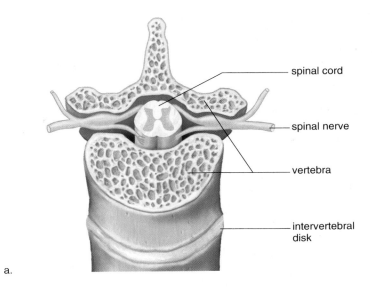

a.

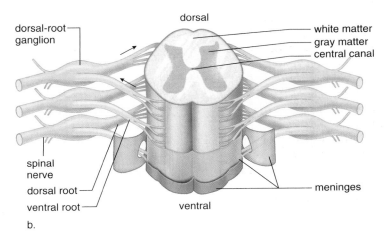

b.

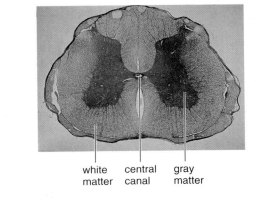

c.

Figure 12.8 **Spinal cord.**
a. The spinal cord passes through the vertebral canal formed by the vertebrae. **b.** The spinal cord has a central canal filled with cerebrospinal fluid, gray matter in an H-shaped configuration, and white matter as shown. The white matter contains tracts that take nerve impulses to and from the brain. **c.** Photomicrograph of a cross section of the spinal cord.

The Brain

The human **brain** has been called the last great frontier of biology. The goal of modern neuroscience is to understand the structure and function of the brain's various parts so well that it will be possible to prevent or correct the thousands of mental disorders that rob human beings of a normal life. This section gives only a glimpse of what is known about the brain and the modern avenues of research.

We will discuss the parts of the brain with reference to the cerebrum, the diencephalon, the cerebellum, and the brainstem. The brain's four ventricles (described on page 224) are called, in turn, the two lateral ventricles, the third ventricle, and the fourth ventricle. It may be helpful for you to associate the cerebrum with the two lateral ventricles, the diencephalon with the third ventricle, and the brainstem and the cerebellum with the fourth ventricle (Fig. 12.9a).

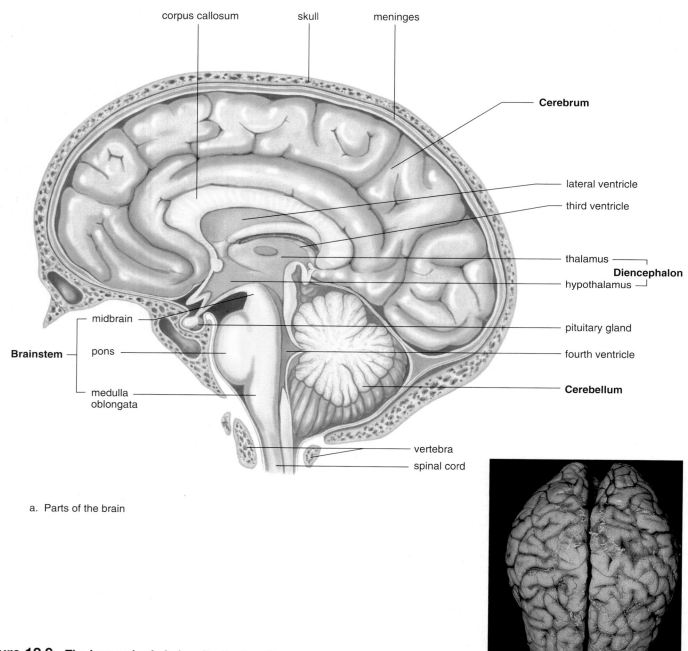

a. Parts of the brain

b. Cerebral hemispheres

Figure 12.9 **The human brain in longitudinal section.**
a. The cerebrum is the largest part of the brain in humans. **b.** Viewed from above, the cerebrum has a left and right cerebral hemisphere. The hemispheres are connected by the corpus callosum.

The Cerebrum

The **cerebrum,** also called the telencephalon, is the largest portion of the brain in humans. The cerebrum is the last center to receive sensory input and carry out integration before commanding voluntary motor responses. It communicates with and coordinates the activities of the other parts of the brain. As we shall see, the cerebrum carries out higher thought processes required for learning and memory and for language and speech.

Cerebral Hemispheres   Just as the human body has two halves, so does the cerebrum. These halves are called the left and right **cerebral hemispheres** (Fig. 12.9b). A deep groove called the longitudinal fissure divides the left and right cerebral hemispheres. Still, the two cerebral hemispheres are connected by a bridge of tracts within the corpus callosum.

Shallow grooves called sulci (sing., sulcus) divide each hemisphere into lobes (Fig. 12.10). The *frontal lobe* is the most ventral of the lobes (directly behind the forehead). The *parietal lobe* is dorsal to the frontal lobe. The *occipital lobe* is dorsal to the parietal lobe (at the rear of the head). The *temporal lobe* lies inferior to the frontal and parietal lobes (at the temple and the ear).

Each lobe is associated with particular functions as indicated in Figure 12.10.

The Cerebral Cortex   The **cerebral cortex** is a thin but highly convoluted outer layer of gray matter that covers the cerebral hemispheres. The cerebral cortex contains over one billion cell bodies and is the region of the brain that accounts for sensation, voluntary movement, and all the thought processes we associate with consciousness.

Primary Motor and Sensory Areas of the Cortex   The cerebral cortex contains motor areas and sensory areas, as well as association areas. The **primary motor area** is in the frontal lobe just ventral to (before) the central sulcus. Voluntary commands to skeletal muscles begin in the primary motor area, and each part of the body is controlled by a certain section. For example, the versatile human hand takes up an especially large portion of the primary motor area (Fig 12.11).

The **primary somatosensory area** is just dorsal to the central sulcus in the parietal lobe. Sensory information from the skin and skeletal muscles arrives here, where each part of the body is sequentially represented. A *primary visual area* in the occipital lobe receives information from our eyes, and a *primary auditory area* in the temporal lobe receives information from our ears. A *primary taste area* also in the parietal lobe accounts for taste sensations, and a primary olfactory area for smell is located in the temporal lobe.

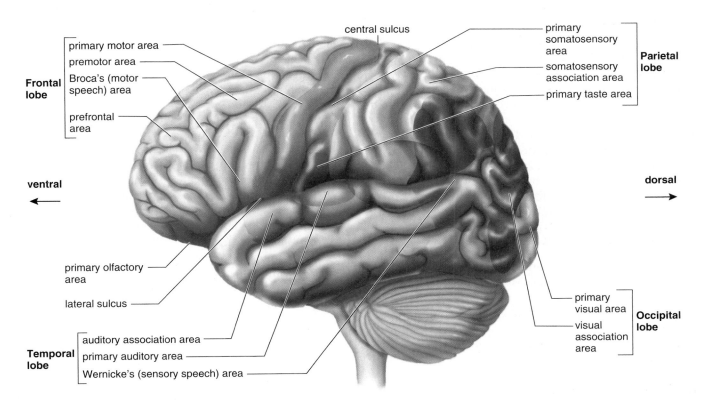

Figure 12.10   **The lobes of a cerebral hemisphere.**
Each cerebral hemisphere is divided into four lobes: frontal, parietal, temporal, and occipital. The frontal lobe contains centers for reasoning and movement, the parietal lobe for somatic sensing and taste, the temporal lobe for hearing, and the occipital for vision.

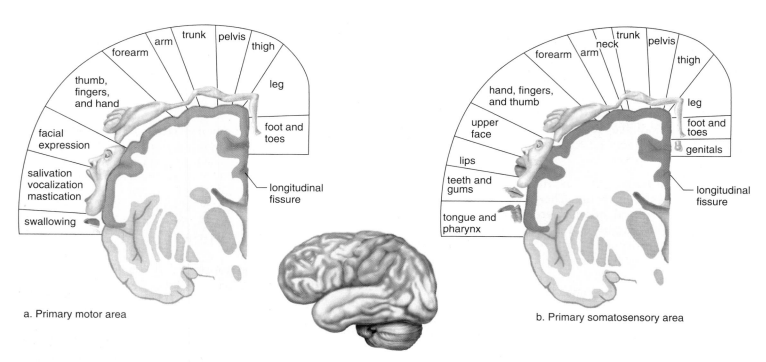

Figure 12.11   The primary motor area and the primary somatosensory area.
The primary motor area (**a**) and the somatosensory area (**b**). The size of each body region shown indicates the relative amount of cortex devoted to that body region.

Association Areas   **Association areas** are places where integration occurs. Ventral to the primary motor area is a premotor area. The premotor area organizes motor functions for skilled motor activities, such as walking and talking at the same time, and then the primary motor area sends signals to the cerebellum, which integrates them. A momentary lack of oxygen during birth can damage the motor areas of the cerebral cortex so that cerebral palsy, a condition characterized by a spastic weakness of the arms and legs, develops. The *somatosensory association area*, located just dorsal to the primary somatosensory area, processes and analyzes sensory information from the skin and muscles. The *visual association area* in the occipital lobe associates new visual information with previously received visual information. It might "decide," for example, if we have seen this face, scene, or symbol before. The *auditory association area* in the temporal lobe performs the same functions with regard to sounds.

Processing Centers   Processing centers of the cortex receive information from the other association areas and perform higher level analytical functions. The **prefrontal area,** an association area in the frontal lobe, receives information from the other association areas and uses this information to reason and plan our actions. Integration in this area accounts for our most cherished human abilities; to think critically and to formulate appropriate behaviors.

The unique ability of humans to speak is partially dependent upon two processing centers found only in the left cerebral cortex. **Wernicke's area** is located in the dorsal part of the left temporal lobe, and **Broca's area** is located in the left frontal lobe. Broca's area is located just ventral to the portion of the primary motor area for speech musculature (lips, tongue, larynx, and so forth) (Fig. 12.11). Wernicke's area helps us understand both the written and spoken word and sends the information to Broca's area. Broca's area adds grammatical refinements and directs the primary motor area to stimulate the appropriate muscles for speaking and writing.

Central White Matter   Much of the rest of the cerebrum is composed of white matter. As you know, white matter in the CNS consists of long myelinated axons organized into tracts. Descending tracts from the primary motor area communicate with lower brain centers, and ascending tracts from lower brain centers send sensory information up to the primary somatosensory area. Because the tracts cross over in the medulla, the left side of the cerebrum controls the right side of the body, and vice versa. Tracts within the cerebrum also take information between the different sensory, motor, and association areas pictured in Figure 12.10. As previously mentioned, the corpus callosum contains tracts that join the two cerebral hemispheres.

Basal Nuclei   While the bulk of the cerebrum is composed of tracts, there are masses of gray matter located deep within the white matter. These so-called **basal nuclei** (formerly termed basal ganglia) integrate motor commands, ensuring that proper muscle groups are activated or inhibited. Huntington disease and Parkinson disease, which are both characterized by uncontrollable movements, are believed to be due to malfunctioning of the basal nuclei.

The Diencephalon

The hypothalamus and the thalamus are in the **diencephalon,** a region that encircles the third ventricle. The **hypothalamus** forms the floor of the third ventricle. The hypothalamus is an integrating center that helps maintain homeostasis by regulating hunger, sleep, thirst, body temperature, and water balance. The hypothalamus controls the pituitary gland and thereby serves as a link between the nervous and endocrine systems.

The **thalamus** consists of two masses of gray matter located in the sides and roof of the third ventricle. The thalamus is on the receiving end for all sensory input except smell. Visual, auditory, and somatosensory information arrives at the thalamus via the cranial nerves and tracts from the spinal cord. The thalamus integrates this information and sends it on to the appropriate portions of the cerebrum. The thalamus is involved in arousal of the cerebrum, and it also participates in higher mental functions such as memory and emotions.

The pineal gland, which secretes the hormone melatonin, is located in the diencephalon. Presently there is much popular interest in the role of melatonin in our daily rhythms; some researchers believe it can help ameliorate jet lag or insomnia. Scientists are also interested in the possibility that the hormone may regulate the onset of puberty.

The Cerebellum

The **cerebellum** is separated from the brainstem by the fourth ventricle. The cerebellum has two portions that are joined by a narrow median portion. Each portion is primarily composed of white matter, which in longitudinal section has a tree-like pattern called arbor vitae. Overlying the white matter is a thin layer of gray matter that forms a series of complex folds.

The cerebellum receives sensory input from the eyes, ears, joints, and muscles about the present position of body parts, and it also receives motor output from the cerebral cortex about where these parts should be located. After integrating this information, the cerebellum sends motor impulses by way of the brainstem to the skeletal muscles. In this way, the cerebellum maintains posture and balance. It also ensures that all of the muscles work together to produce smooth, coordinated voluntary movements. The cerebellum assists the learning of new motor skills such as playing the piano or hitting a baseball.

The Brainstem

The **brainstem** contains the midbrain, the pons, and the medulla oblongata (see Fig. 12.9*a*). The **midbrain** acts as a relay station for tracts passing between the cerebrum and the spinal cord or cerebellum. It also has reflex centers for visual, auditory, and tactile responses. The word **pons** means "bridge" in Latin, and true to its name, the pons contains bundles of axons traveling between the cerebellum and the rest of the CNS. In addition, the pons functions with the medulla oblongata to regulate breathing rate and has reflex centers concerned with head movements in response to visual and auditory stimuli.

The **medulla oblongata** contains a number of reflex centers for regulating heartbeat, breathing, and vasoconstriction (blood pressure). It also contains the reflex centers for vomiting, coughing, sneezing, hiccuping, and swallowing. The medulla oblongata lies just superior to the spinal cord, and it contains tracts that ascend or descend between the spinal cord and higher brain centers.

The Reticular Formation The **reticular formation** is a complex network of **nuclei** (masses of gray matter) and fibers that extend the length of the brainstem (Fig. 12.12). The reticular formation is a major component of the reticular activating system (RAS), which receives sensory signals and sends them up to higher centers, and motor signals, which it sends to the spinal cord.

The RAS arouses the cerebrum via the thalamus and causes a person to be alert. If you want to awaken the RAS, surprise it with sudden stimuli, such as an alarm clock ringing, bright lights, smelling salts, or splashing cold water on your face. Apparently, the RAS can filter out unnecessary sensory stimuli, explaining why you can study with the TV on. To inactivate the RAS, remove visual or auditory stimuli, allowing yourself to become drowsy and drop off to sleep. General anesthetics function by artificially suppressing the RAS. A severe injury to the RAS can cause a person to be comatose, from which recovery may be impossible.

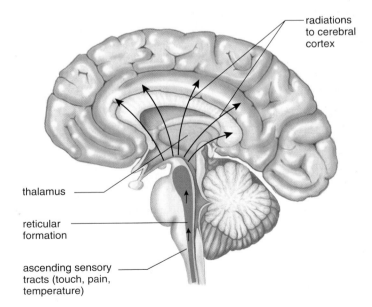

radiations to cerebral cortex

thalamus

reticular formation

ascending sensory tracts (touch, pain, temperature)

Figure 12.12 The reticular activating system.
The reticular formation receives and sends on motor and sensory information to various parts of the CNS. One portion, the reticular activating system (RAS; see arrows), arouses the cerebrum and, in this way, controls alertness versus sleep.

12.3 The Limbic System and Higher Mental Functions

The limbic system is intimately involved in our emotions and higher mental functions. After a short description, we will discuss the functions of the limbic system.

Limbic System

The **limbic system** is a complex network of tracts and nuclei that incorporates medial portions of the cerebral lobes, the basal nuclei, and the diencephalon (Fig. 12.13). The limbic system blends primitive emotions and higher mental functions into a united whole. It accounts for why activities such as sexual behavior and eating seem pleasurable and also why, say, mental stress can cause high blood pressure.

Two significant structures within the limbic system are the hippocampus and the amygdala, which are essential for learning and memory. The **hippocampus**, a structure deep in the temporal lobe, is well situated in the brain to make the prefrontal area aware of past experiences stored in association areas. The **amygdala**, in particular, can cause these experiences to have emotional overtones.

The prefrontal area consults the hippocampus and in this way memories can be used to modify our behavior. However, the inclusion of the frontal lobe in the limbic system means that reason can keep us from acting out strong feelings.

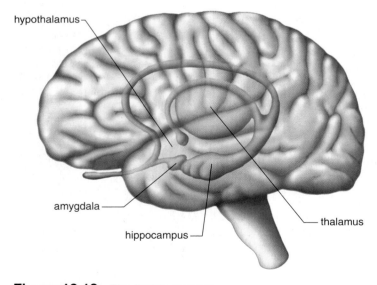

Figure 12.13   The limbic system.
In the limbic system (in blue), structures deep within each cerebral hemisphere and surrounding the diencephalon join higher mental functions, such as reasoning, with more primitive feelings, such as fear and pleasure. Therefore, primitive feelings can influence our behavior, but reason can also keep them in check.

Higher Mental Functions

As in other areas of biological research, brain research has progressed due to technological breakthroughs. Neuroscientists now have a wide range of techniques at their disposal for studying the human brain, including modern technologies that allow us to record its functioning.

Memory and Learning

Just as the connecting tracts of the corpus callosum are evidence that the two cerebral hemispheres work together, so the limbic system indicates that cortical areas may work with lower centers to produce learning and memory. **Memory** is the ability to hold a thought in mind or to recall events from the past, ranging from a word we learned only yesterday to an early emotional experience that has shaped our lives. **Learning** takes place when we retain and utilize past memories.

Types of Memory   We have all tried to remember a seven-digit telephone number for a short period of time. If we say we are trying to keep it in the forefront of our brain, we are exactly correct. The prefrontal area, which is active during **short-term memory,** lies just dorsal to our forehead! There are some telephone numbers that we have memorized; in other words, they have gone into **long-term memory.** Think of a telephone number you know by heart, and try to bring it to mind without also thinking about the place or person associated with that number. Most likely you cannot, because typically long-term memory is a mixture of what is called **semantic memory** (numbers, words, etc.) and **episodic memory** (persons, events, etc.). Due to brain damage, some people lose one type of memory but not the other. For example, without a working episodic memory, they can carry on a conversation but have no recollection of recent events. If you are talking to them and then leave the room, they don't remember you when you come back!

Skill memory is another type of memory that can exist independent of episodic memory. Skill memory is involved in performing motor activities such as riding a bike or playing ice hockey. When a person first learns a skill, more areas of the cerebral cortex are involved than after the skill is perfected. In other words, you have to think about what you are doing when you learn a skill, but later the actions become automatic. Skill memory involves all the motor areas of the cerebrum below the level of consciousness.

Long-Term Memory Storage and Retrieval   Our long-term memories are apparently stored in bits and pieces throughout the sensory association areas of the cerebral cortex. Visions are stored in the vision association area, sounds are stored in the auditory association area, and so forth. As previously mentioned, the hippocampus serves as a bridge between the sensory association areas, where memories are stored, and the prefrontal area, where memories are utilized. The prefrontal area communicates with the hippocampus, when memories are stored and when these memories are

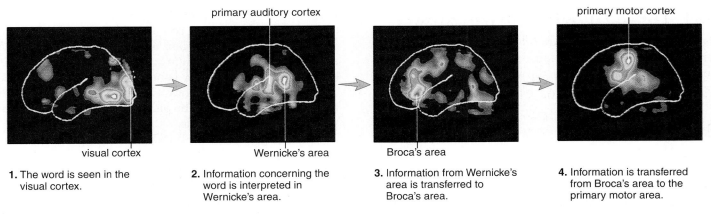

primary auditory cortex

primary motor cortex

visual cortex

Wernicke's area

Broca's area

1. The word is seen in the visual cortex.

2. Information concerning the word is interpreted in Wernicke's area.

3. Information from Wernicke's area is transferred to Broca's area.

4. Information is transferred from Broca's area to the primary motor area.

Figure 12.14 **Language and speech.**
These functional images were captured by a high-speed computer during PET (positron emission tomography) scanning of the brain. A radioactively labeled solution is injected into the subject, and then the subject is asked to perform certain activities. Cross-sectional images of the the brain generated by the computer reveal where activity is occurring because the solution is preferentially taken up by active brain tissue and not by inactive brain tissue. These PET images show the cortical pathway for reading words and then speaking them. Red indicates the most active areas of the brain, and blue indicates the least active areas.

brought to mind. Why are some memories so emotionally charged? The amygdala seems to be responsible for fear conditioning and associating danger with sensory stimuli received from both the diencephalon and the cortical sensory areas.

Long-Term Potentiation While it is helpful to know the memory functions of various portions of the brain, an important step toward curing mental disorders is understanding memory on the cellular level. **Long-term potentiation (LTP)** is an enhanced response at synapses within the hippocampus. LTP is probably essential to memory storage, but unfortunately, it sometimes causes a postsynaptic neuron to become so excited that it undergoes apoptosis, a form of cell death. This phenomenon, called excitotoxicity, may develop due to a mutation. (The longer we live, the more likely it is that any particular mutation will occur.) Excitotoxicity is due to the action of the neurotransmitter glutamate, which is active in the hippocampus. When glutamate binds with a specific type of receptor in the postsynaptic membrane, calcium (Ca^{2+}) may enter and remain, leading to the death of a cell. A gradual extinction of brain cells in the hippocampus and other parts of the brain occurs in persons with Alzheimer disease (AD).

Language and Speech

Language depends on semantic memory. Therefore, we would expect some of the same areas in the brain to be involved in both memory and language. Any disruption of these pathways could very well contribute to an inability to comprehend our environment and use speech correctly.

Seeing and hearing words depends on sensory centers in the occipital and temporal lobes, respectively. Damage to Wernicke's area, discussed earlier, results in the inability to

comprehend speech. Damage to Broca's area, on the other hand, results in the inability to speak and write. The functions of the visual cortex, Wernicke's area, and Broca's area are shown in Figure 12.14.

One interesting aside pertaining to language and speech is the recognition that the left brain and the right brain may have different functions. Consistent with the recognition that the left hemisphere, not the right, contains Broca's area and Wernicke's area, it appears that the left hemisphere plays a role of great importance in language functions. In an attempt to cure epilepsy in the early 1940s, the corpus callosum was surgically severed in some patients. If viewed only by the right hemisphere, these so-called split-brain patients could choose the proper object for a particular use but were unable to name it. Later, the left brain was contrasted with the right brain along these lines:

Left Hemisphere	Right Hemisphere
Verbal	Nonverbal, visuospatial
Logical, analytical	Intuitive
Rational	Creative

Researchers now believe that the hemispheres process the same information differently. The left hemisphere is more global, whereas the right hemisphere is more specific in its approach.

Memory has been studied at various levels—behavioral, structural, and cellular. Special areas in the left hemisphere help account for our ability to comprehend and use speech.

12.4 The Peripheral Nervous System

The peripheral nervous system (PNS) lies outside the central nervous system and is composed of nerves and ganglia. **Nerves** are bundles of axons; the axons that occur in nerves are called nerve fibers:

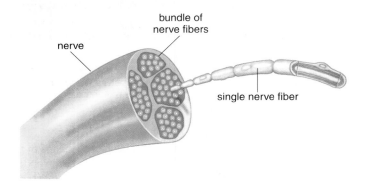

Sensory fibers carry information to the CNS, and motor fibers carry information away from the CNS. Ganglia (sing., **ganglion**) are swellings associated with nerves that contain collections of cell bodies.

Humans have 12 pairs of **cranial nerves** attached to the brain. By convention, the pairs of cranial nerves are referred to by roman numerals (Fig. 12.15*a*). Some of these are sensory nerves—that is, they contain only sensory fibers; some are motor nerves that contain only motor fibers; and others are mixed nerves that contain both sensory and motor fibers. Cranial nerves are largely concerned with the head, neck, and facial regions of the body. However, the vagus nerve (**X**) has branches not only to the pharynx and larynx, but also to most of the internal organs.

The **spinal nerves** of humans emerge in 31 pairs from either side of the spinal cord. Each spinal nerve originates when two short branches, or roots, join together (Fig. 12.15*b*). The dorsal root (at the back) contains sensory fibers that conduct impulses inward (toward the spinal cord) from sensory receptors. The cell body of a sensory neuron is in a **dorsal-root ganglion.** The ventral root (at the front) contains motor fibers that conduct impulses outward (away from the cord) to effectors. Notice, then, that all spinal nerves are mixed nerves that contain many sensory and motor fibers. Each spinal nerve serves the particular region of the body in which it is located. For example, the intercostal muscles of the rib cage are innervated by thoracic nerves.

In the PNS, cranial nerves take impulses to and from the brain, and spinal nerves take impulses to and from the spinal cord.

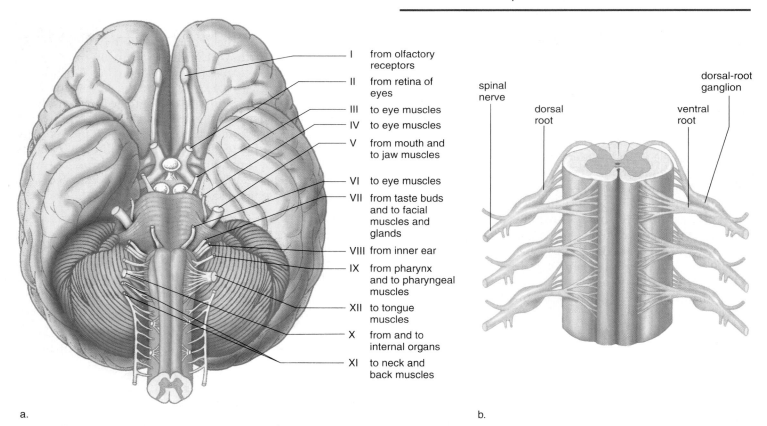

I   from olfactory receptors

II   from retina of eyes

III   to eye muscles

IV   to eye muscles

V   from mouth and to jaw muscles

VI   to eye muscles

VII   from taste buds and to facial muscles and glands

VIII   from inner ear

IX   from pharynx and to pharyngeal muscles

XII   to tongue muscles

X   from and to internal organs

XI   to neck and back muscles

a.

b.

Figure 12.15   Cranial and spinal nerves.
a. Ventral surface of the brain showing the attachment of the 12 pairs of cranial nerves. **b.** Cross section of the spinal cord, showing three pairs of spinal nerves. The human body has 31 pairs of spinal nerves altogether, and each spinal nerve has a dorsal root and a ventral root attached to the spinal cord.

Somatic System

The PNS is subdivided into the somatic system and the autonomic system. The **somatic system** serves the skin, skeletal muscles, and tendons. It includes nerves that take sensory information from external sensory receptors to the CNS and motor commands away from the CNS to the skeletal muscles. Some actions in the somatic system are due to **reflexes,** automatic responses to a stimulus. A reflex occurs quickly, without our even having to think about it. Other actions are voluntary, and these always originate in the cerebral cortex, as when we decide to move a limb.

The Reflex Arc

Figure 12.16 illustrates the path of a reflex that involves only the spinal cord. If your hand touches a sharp pin, sensory receptors in the skin generate nerve impulses that move along sensory fibers through the dorsal-root ganglia toward the spinal cord. Sensory neurons that enter the cord dorsally pass signals on to many interneurons. Some of these interneurons synapse with motor neurons whose short dendrites and cell bodies are in the spinal cord. Nerve impulses travel along these motor fibers to an effector, which brings about a response to the stimulus. In this case, the effector is a muscle, which contracts so that you withdraw your hand from the pin. Various other reactions are also possible—you will most likely look at the pin, wince, and cry out in pain. This whole series of responses occurs because some of the interneurons involved carry nerve impulses to the brain. The brain makes you aware of the stimulus and directs these other reactions to it. You don't feel pain until the brain receives the information and interprets it.

> In the somatic system, nerves take messages from external sensory receptors to the CNS and take motor commands to the skeletal muscles. Involuntary reflexes allow us to respond rapidly to external stimuli.

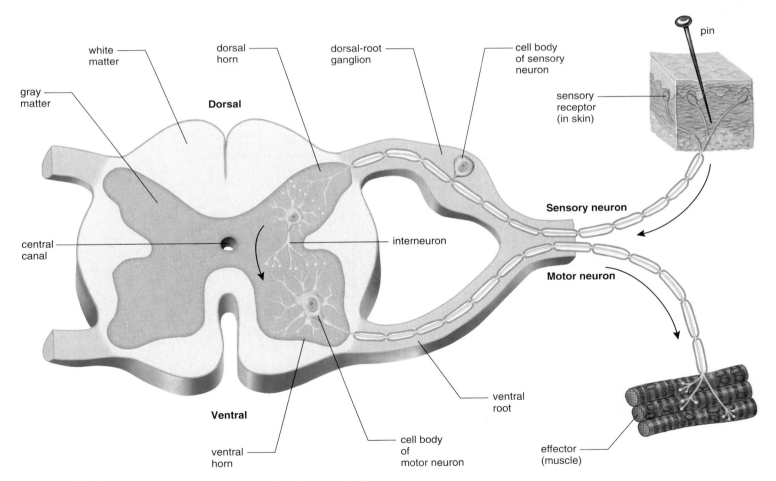

Figure 12.16 **A reflex arc showing the path of a spinal reflex.**
A stimulus (e.g., a pinprick) causes sensory receptors in the skin to generate nerve impulses that travel in sensory axons to the spinal cord. Interneurons integrate data from sensory neurons and then relay signals to motor neurons. Motor axons convey nerve impulses from the spinal cord to a skeletal muscle, which contracts. Removal of the pin could be the response to the stimulus in this example.

Visual Focus

Sympathetic division

Parasympathetic division

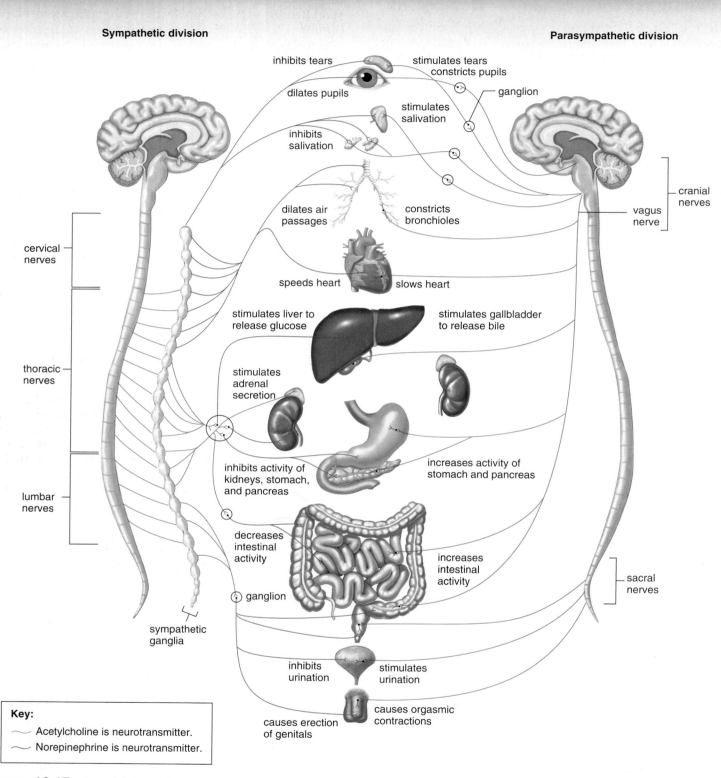

inhibits tears

stimulates tears
constricts pupils

dilates pupils

ganglion

stimulates
salivation

inhibits
salivation

cranial
nerves

dilates air
passages

constricts
bronchioles

vagus
nerve

cervical
nerves

speeds heart

slows heart

stimulates liver to
release glucose

stimulates gallbladder
to release bile

thoracic
nerves

stimulates
adrenal
secretion

lumbar
nerves

inhibits activity of
kidneys, stomach,
and pancreas

increases activity of
stomach and pancreas

decreases
intestinal
activity

increases
intestinal
activity

sacral
nerves

ganglion

sympathetic
ganglia

inhibits
urination

stimulates
urination

causes erection
of genitals

causes orgasmic
contractions

Key:

〜 Acetylcholine is neurotransmitter.

〜 Norepinephrine is neurotransmitter.

Figure 12.17 **Autonomic system structure and function.**
Sympathetic preganglionic fibers *(left)* arise from the thoracic and lumbar portions of the spinal cord; parasympathetic preganglionic fibers *(right)* arise from the cranial and sacral portions of the spinal cord. The two divisions innervate the same organs but have antagonistic effects.

Autonomic System

The **autonomic system** of the PNS regulates the activity of cardiac and smooth muscles and glands. The system is divided into the sympathetic and parasympathetic divisions (Fig. 12.17). These two divisions have several features in common: (1) They function automatically and usually in an involuntary manner; (2) they innervate all internal organs; and (3) they utilize two neurons and one ganglion for each impulse. The first neuron has a cell body within the CNS and a preganglionic fiber. The second neuron has a cell body within the ganglion and a postganglionic fiber.

Reflex actions, such as those that regulate the blood pressure and breathing rate, are especially important to the maintenance of homeostasis. These reflexes begin when the sensory neurons in contact with internal organs send messages to the CNS. They are completed by motor neurons within the autonomic system.

Sympathetic Division

Most preganglionic fibers of the **sympathetic division** arise from the middle, or thoracolumbar, portion of the spinal cord and almost immediately terminate in ganglia that lie near the cord. Therefore, in this division, the preganglionic fiber is short, but the postganglionic fiber that makes contact with an organ is long:

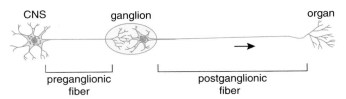

The sympathetic division is especially important during emergency situations when you might be required to fight or take flight. It accelerates the heartbeat and dilates the bronchi; active muscles, after all, require a ready supply of glucose and oxygen. On the other hand, the sympathetic division inhibits the digestive tract—digestion is not an immediate necessity if you are under attack. The neurotransmitter released by the postganglionic axon is primarily norepinephrine (NE). The structure of NE is like that of epinephrine (adrenaline), an adrenal medulla hormone that usually increases heart rate and contractility.

The sympathetic division brings about those responses we associate with "fight or flight."

Parasympathetic Division

The **parasympathetic division** includes a few cranial nerves (e.g., the vagus nerve) as well as fibers that arise from the sacral (bottom) portion of the spinal cord. Therefore, this division is often referred to as the craniosacral portion of the autonomic system. In the parasympathetic division, the preganglionic fiber is long, and the postganglionic fiber is short because the ganglia lie near or within the organ:

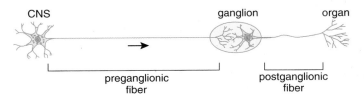

The parasympathetic division, sometimes called the housekeeper division, promotes all the internal responses we associate with a relaxed state; for example, it causes the pupil of the eye to contract, promotes digestion of food, and retards the heartbeat. The neurotransmitter utilized by the parasympathetic division is acetylcholine (ACh).

Table 12.2 summarizes the features and functions of the motor divisions of the somatic and autonomic systems.

The parasympathetic division brings about the responses we associate with a relaxed state.

Table 12.2	Comparison of Somatic Motor and Autonomic Motor Pathways		
	Somatic Motor Pathway	**Autonomic Motor Pathways**	
		Sympathetic	**Parasympathetic**
Type of control	Voluntary/involuntary	Involuntary	Involuntary
Number of neurons per message	One	Two (preganglionic shorter than postganglionic)	Two (preganglionic longer than postganglionic)
Location of motor fiber	Most cranial nerves and all spinal nerves	Thoracolumbar spinal nerves	Cranial (e.g., vagus) and sacral spinal nerves
Neurotransmitter	Acetylcholine	Norepinephrine	Acetylcholine
Effectors	Skeletal muscles	Smooth and cardiac muscle, glands	Smooth and cardiac muscle, glands

Health Focus

Degenerative Brain Disorders

Many researchers are now engaged in studying Alzheimer and Parkinson diseases, which are degenerative brain disorders.

Alzheimer Disease

Signs of **Alzheimer disease (AD)** may appear before the age of 50, but it is usually seen in individuals past the age of 65. One of the early symptoms is loss of memory, particularly for recent events. Characteristically, the person asks the same question repeatedly and becomes disoriented even in familiar places. Signs of mental disturbance are frequently seen. Gradually, the person loses the ability to perform any type of daily activity and becomes bedridden. Death is usually due to pneumonia or some other such illness.

In AD patients, abnormal neurons are present throughout the brain but especially in the hippocampus and amygdala. These neurons have two abnormalities: (1) plaques, containing a protein called beta amyloid, envelop the axon, and (2) neurofibrillary tangles are in the axons and extend upward to surround the nucleus (Fig. 12A). The neurofibrillary tangles arise because a protein called tau no longer has the correct shape. Tau holds microtubules in place so that they support the structure of neurons. When tau changes shape, it grabs onto other tau molecules, and the tangles result. Researchers are working furiously to discover the cause of beta amyloid plaques and neurofibrillary tangles. Several genes that predispose a person to AD have been identified. One of them, called $APOE_4$, is found in 65% of persons with AD. But it is unknown why inheritance of this gene leads to AD neurons.

Researchers do know that plasma membrane enzymes, called secretases, snip beta amyloid from a larger molecule, even in healthy cells. People with AD produce too much beta amyloid, particularly one very sticky type. The beta amyloid plaques grow so dense that they trigger an inflammatory reaction that ends in neuron death. Some researchers are trying to block a type of secretase enzyme, thinking that this will stop the formation of beta amyloid plaques.

Now, new evidence has been gathered that the presence of plaques does precede the formation of tangles. Researchers injected mutant mice that developed both plaques and misshapen tau with antibodies against beta amyloid. In some mice, this treatment removed, first, the plaques and, then, the tau. This bolsters the hypothesis that beta amyloid blocks the work of proteosomes, complexes that ordinarily clear the cell of any excess protein, including tau.

Frank M. LaFerla, of the University of California, Irvine, who led a team doing this work, suggests that amyloid works with tau to kill neurons and trigger the confusion and memory loss so characteristic of AD. Based on this research, it should appear that treatment for AD in humans should begin as early as possible, and that it should be continued indefinitely. If the tau had already formed tangles, it was too late, and only the plaques disappeared. Also, the treatment didn't last long and the plaques reappeared within two weeks.

Parkinson Disease

Parkinson disease is characterized by a gradual loss of motor control beginning between the ages of 50 and 60. Eventually, the person has a wide-eyed, unblinking expression, involuntary tremors of the fingers and thumbs, muscular rigidity, and a shuffling gait. Speaking and performing ordinary daily tasks become laborious.

In Parkinson patients, the basal nuclei (see page 228) function improperly because of a degeneration of the dopamine-releasing neurons in the brain. Without dopamine, which is an inhibitory neurotransmitter, the excessive excitatory signals from the motor cortex and other brain areas result in the symptoms of Parkinson disease.

Unfortunately, it is not possible to give Parkinson patients dopamine directly because of the impermeability of the capillaries serving the brain. However, symptoms can be alleviated by giving patients L-dopa, a chemical that can be changed to dopamine in the body, until too few cells are left to do the job. Then, patients must turn to a number of controversial surgical procedures. Implantation of dopamine-secreting tissue from various sources has been tried with mixed results.

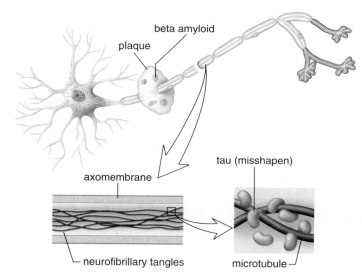

Figure 12A Alzheimer disease.
Some of the neurons of Alzheimer disease (AD) patients have beta amyloid plaques and neurofibrillary tangles. AD neurons are present throughout the brain but concentrated in the hippocampus and amygdala.

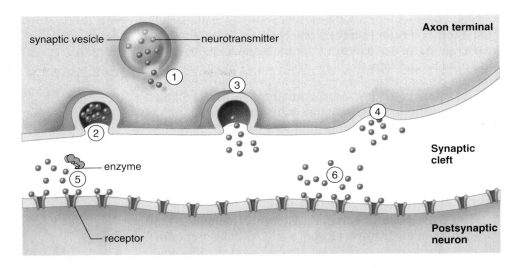

Figure 12.18 Drug actions at a synapse.
A drug can ① cause the neurotransmitter (NT) to leak out of a synaptic vesicle into the axon terminal; ② prevent release of NT into the synaptic cleft; ③ promote release of NT into the synaptic cleft; ④ prevent reuptake of NT by the presynaptic membrane; ⑤ block the enzyme that causes breakdown of the NT; or ⑥ bind to a receptor, mimicking the action of an NT.

12.5 Drug Abuse

A wide variety of drugs affect the nervous system and can alter the mood and/or emotional state. Such drugs have two general effects: (1) They affect the limbic system, and (2) they either promote or decrease the action of a particular neurotransmitter (Fig. 12.18). Stimulants are drugs that increase the likelihood of neuron excitation, and depressants decrease the likelihood of excitation. Increasingly, researchers believe that dopamine, among other neurotransmitters in the brain, is responsible for mood. Cocaine is known to potentiate the effects of dopamine by interfering with its uptake from synaptic clefts. Many of the new medications developed to counter drug dependence and mental illness affect the release, reception, or breakdown of dopamine.

Dopamine is a neurotransmitter that is important in the workings of the brain's built-in *reward circuit.* The reward circuit is a collection of neurons that, under normal circumstances, promotes healthy activities, such as consuming food. We continually engage in beneficial behavior because the reward circuit makes us feel good. However, certain drugs may artificially stimulate the reward circuit. Drug abusers may neglect their basic physical needs in favor of continued use of drugs.

Drug abuse is apparent when a person takes a drug at a dose level and under circumstances that increase the potential for a harmful effect. Drug abusers are apt to display a psychological and/or physical dependence on the drug. Psychological dependence is apparent when a person craves the drug, spends time seeking the drug, and takes it regularly. With physical dependence, formerly called "addiction," the person has become tolerant to the drug—that is, more of the drug is needed to get the same effect, and withdrawal symptoms, including diarrhea, occur when he or she stops taking the drug. Diarrhea occurs because heroin decreases intestinal motility and the body compensates for this effect by producing substances that increase peristalsis. Without the presence of heroin, the substances that lead to increased peristalsis have free reign and diarrhea results.

Alcohol

It is possible that alcohol influences the action of GABA, an inhibiting neurotransmitter, or glutamate, an excitatory neurotransmitter. Once imbibed, alcohol is primarily metabolized in the liver, where it disrupts the normal workings of this organ so that fats cannot be broken down. Fat accumulation, the first stage of liver deterioration, begins after only a single night of heavy drinking. If heavy drinking continues, fibrous scar tissue appears during a second stage of deterioration. If heavy drinking stops, the liver can still recover and become normal once again. If not, the final and irrevocable stage, cirrhosis of the liver, occurs: Liver cells die, harden, and turn orange (cirrhosis means orange).

Alcohol requires no digestion and it can be absorbed unchanged from the stomach and small intestine. Table 12.3 lists the behavioral effects of alcohol, according to the blood level.

Table 12.3	Blood Alcohol Level and Behavioral Effects
Percent blood alcohol level	**Behavioral effects**
0.05	Lowered alertness, usually good feeling, release of inhibitions, impaired judgment
0.10	Slowed reaction times and impaired motor function, less caution
0.15	Large, consistent increases in reaction time
0.20	Marked depression in sensory and motor capability, decidedly intoxicated
0.25	Severe motor disturbance, staggering, sensory perceptions greatly impaired, smashed!
0.30	Stuporous but conscious—no comprehension of what's going on
0.35	Surgical anesthesia; minimal level causing death

Ray, O. and Ksir, C., *Drugs, Society, and Human Behaviors*, 7th edition, 1999, McGraw-Hill Publishing, Inc.

Alcohol taken with or after a meal is absorbed more slowly than if imbibed before a meal. Alcohol is used by the body as an energy source, but it lacks the vitamins, minerals, essential amino acids, and fatty acids the body needs to stay healthy. For this reason, many alcoholics are undernourished and prone to illness. Alcohol causes weight gain because other calories that might be burned are not. In other words, alcohol will decrease the rate at which humans burn fat for energy. More important, withdrawal symptoms are severe following prolonged heavy use of alcohol. Death is more likely to occur than with withdrawal from other addictive drugs. That's why its recommended that detoxification (allowing the body to rid itself of alcohol) occur in a medical setting.

The United States surgeon general recommends that pregnant women drink no alcohol at all. Alcohol crosses the placenta freely and causes fetal alcohol syndrome in newborns, which is characterized by mental retardation and various physical defects.

Nicotine

Nicotine, an alkaloid derived from tobacco, is also a widely used neurological agent (Fig. 12.19). Cigarette smoking produces a rapid distribution of nicotine to the brain, with drug levels peaking within 10 seconds of inhalation. The acute effects of nicotine dissipate in a few minutes, causing the smoker to repeatedly smoke during the day to maintain the drug's pleasurable effects.

In the central nervous system, nicotine causes neurons to release the neurotransmitter dopamine. The excess dopamine has a reinforcing effect that leads to dependence on the drug. In the peripheral nervous system, nicotine stimulates the same postsynaptic receptors as acetylcholine and leads to increased activity of the skeletal muscles. It also increases the heart rate and blood pressure, as well as digestive tract mobility.

Many smokers find it difficult to give up the habit because nicotine induces both physiological and psychological dependence. Smokers report that smoking helps alleviate their mood but this has been difficult to substantiate. In contrast, the experience of being addicted to tobacco appears to add to, rather than relieve, stress in the everyday lives of smokers. Withdrawal symptoms include headache, stomach pain, irritability, insomnia, worsened cognitive performance, and the urge to smoke.

Cigarette smoking in young women who are sexually active is most unfortunate because if they become pregnant, nicotine, like other psychoactive drugs, adversely affects a developing embryo and fetus.

Cocaine

Cocaine is an alkaloid derived from the shrub *Erythroxylon coca*. The major routes of administration of cocaine are sniffing or snorting, injecting, and smoking. Snorting is the process of inhaling cocaine powder through the nose, where

Figure 12.19   Why do people use drugs?
Social motivations may be at play if a person smokes and drinks only in the presence of others. Other factors may be at work if the activity occurs to excess when the person is alone.

it is absorbed into the bloodstream through the nasal tissues. Injecting requires the use of a needle to release the drug directly into the bloodstream. "Crack" is the street name given to cocaine that has been processed to a free base for smoking. Ammonia or baking soda, water, and heat are used to change cocaine hydrochloride to a form that can be smoked. The term *crack* refers to the crackling sound heard when the mixture is smoked. Smoking allows extremely high doses of cocaine to reach the brain very quickly and, in the nonaddicted, brings an intense and immediate high.

Cocaine is a strong central nervous system stimulant that interferes with the synaptic uptake of dopamine, and this causes the user to experience a rush sensation. The epinephrine-like effects of dopamine account for the state of arousal that lasts for only minutes after the rush experience. A cocaine binge can go on for days, after which the individual suffers a crash. During the binge period, the user is hyperactive and has little desire for food or sleep but has an increased sex drive. During the crash period, the user is fatigued, depressed, and irritable; has memory and concentration problems; and displays no interest in sex. Indeed, men are often impotent.

Cocaine causes extreme physical dependence. A tolerance may develop and many addicts report that they seek but fail to achieve as much pleasure as they did from their first exposure. With continued cocaine use, the body begins to make less dopamine to compensate for a seemingly excess supply. The user, therefore, experiences tolerance, withdrawal symptoms, and an intense craving for cocaine. These are indications that the person is highly dependent upon the drug. Overdosing on cocaine can cause seizures and cardiac and respiratory arrest. It is possible that long-term cocaine abuse causes brain damage. Babies born to addicts suffer

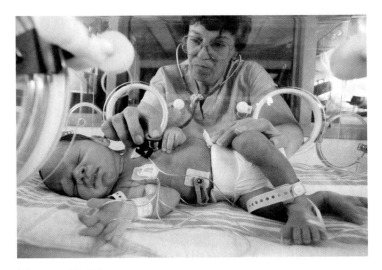

Figure 12.20 Drug abuse affects babies.
Infants whose mothers abused cocaine or heroin may go through
withdrawal at birth. Symptoms include hyperactivity, sleep and
feeding problems, a high-pitched cry, fussiness, breathing problems,
diarrhea, vomiting, and convulsions.

withdrawal symptoms and may have neurological and developmental problems. (Fig. 12.20).

Methamphetamine

Methamphetamine is available as a powder (speed) or as
crystals (crystal meth or ice). The production of methamphetamine is a fairly simple process, which makes it easy to
produce in makeshift home laboratories. The crystals are
smoked and the effects are almost instantaneous, and nearly
as quick when snorted. The effects last four to eight hours
when smoked.

Methamphetamine is close in structure to amphetamine—it has a methyl group that does not appear in amphetamine. This methyl group increases the CNS potency of
the drug. Methamphetamine attaches to the same receptors
as dopamine and norepinephrine and it hinders the reuptake of these substances. Methamphetamine reverses the effects of fatigue, maintains wakefulness, and temporarily ele-
vates the mood of the user. After the initial rush, there is
typically a state of high agitation that, in some individuals,
leads to violent behavior. Chronic use can lead to what is
called amphetamine psychosis resulting in paranoia, auditory and visual hallucinations, self-absorption, irritability,
and aggressive, erratic behavior.

Methamphetamine causes significant tolerance as well
as psychological dependence. The user is likely to have
strong cravings for more meth, while at the same time being
unable to reach a satisfactory high.

Ecstasy is the street name for MDMA (methylenedioxymethamphetamine), a drug that has the same effects as
methamphetamine but without hallucinations. Ecstasy
comes in a pill form and it often contains other drugs

besides MDMA, some of which are more dangerous. Deaths
are usually linked to the club scene.

Heroin

Heroin is derived from morphine, an alkaloid of opium.
Once heroin is injected into a vein, a feeling of euphoria,
along with relief of any pain, occurs within 3 to 6 minutes.
Side effects can include nausea, vomiting, dysphoria, and
respiratory and circulatory depression.

Heroin binds to receptors meant for the endorphins, the
special neurotransmitters that kill pain and produce a feeling of tranquility. With time, the body's production of
endorphins decreases. Tolerance develops so that the user
needs to take more of the drug just to prevent withdrawal
symptoms. The euphoria originally experienced upon injection is no longer felt.

Heroin withdrawal symptoms include perspiration,
dilation of pupils, tremors, restlessness, abdominal cramps,
gooseflesh, vomiting, and an increase in systolic blood pressure and respiratory rate. People who are excessively
dependent may experience convulsions, respiratory failure,
and death. Infants born to women who are physically
dependent also experience these withdrawal symptoms
(Fig. 12.20).

Marijuana

The dried flowering tops, leaves, and stems of the Indian
hemp plant *Cannabis sativa* contain and are covered by a resin
that is rich in THC (tetrahydrocannabinol). The names
cannabis and *marijuana* apply to either the plant or THC. Usually, marijuana is smoked in a cigarette form called a "joint."

The occasional user of marijuana experiences a mild
euphoria along with alterations in vision and judgment, which
result in distortions of space and time. Motor incoordination,
including the inability to speak coherently, takes place. Heavy
use can result in hallucinations, anxiety, depression, rapid flow
of ideas, body image distortions, paranoid reactions, and similar psychotic symptoms. The terms *cannabis psychosis* and
cannabis delirium refer to such reactions. Craving and difficulty
in stopping usage can occur as a result of regular use.

Recently, researchers have found that marijuana binds
to a receptor for anandamide, a normal molecule in the
body. Some researchers believe that long-term marijuana
use leads to brain impairment. Fetal cannabis syndrome,
which resembles fetal alcohol syndrome, has been reported.
Some psychologists believe that marijuana use among adolescents is a way to avoid dealing with the personal problems that often develop during that stage of life.

Neurological drugs either potentiate or dampen
the effect of the body's neurotransmitters. The
body compensates for their presence, leading to
dependency.

Summarizing the Concepts

12.1 Nervous Tissue
There are three types of neurons. Sensory neurons take nerve impulses from sensory receptors to the CNS; interneurons occur within the CNS; and motor neurons take nerve impulses from the CNS to effectors (muscles or glands). A neuron is composed of dendrites, a cell body, and an axon. Long axons are covered by a myelin sheath.

When an axon is not conducting a nerve impulse, the inside of the axon is negative (-65 mV) compared with the outside. The sodium-potassium pump actively transports Na^+ out of an axon and K^+ to the inside of an axon. The resting potential is due to the leakage of K^+ to the outside of the neuron. When an axon is conducting a nerve impulse (action potential), Na^+ first moves into the axoplasm, and then K^+ moves out of the axoplasm.

Transmission of a nerve impulse from one neuron to another takes place when a neurotransmitter molecule is released into a synaptic cleft. The binding of the neurotransmitter to receptors in the postsynaptic membrane causes excitation or inhibition. Integration is the summing of excitatory and inhibitory signals.

12.2 The Central Nervous System
The CNS consists of the spinal cord and brain, which are both protected by bone. The CNS receives and integrates sensory input and formulates motor output. The gray matter of the spinal cord contains neuron cell bodies; the white matter consists of myelinated axons that occur in bundles called tracts. The spinal cord sends sensory information to the brain, receives motor output from the brain, and carries out reflex actions.

In the brain, the cerebrum has two cerebral hemispheres connected by the corpus callosum. Sensation, reasoning, learning and memory, and language and speech take place in the cerebrum. The cerebral cortex is a thin layer of gray matter covering the cerebrum. The cerebral cortex of each cerebral hemisphere has four lobes: a frontal, parietal, occipital, and temporal lobe. The primary motor area in the frontal lobe sends out motor commands to lower brain centers, which pass them on to motor neurons. The primary somatosensory area in the parietal lobe receives sensory information from lower brain centers in communication with sensory neurons. Association areas are located in all the lobes.

The brain has a number of other regions. The hypothalamus controls homeostasis, and the thalamus specializes in sending sensory input on to the cerebrum. The cerebellum primarily coordinates skeletal muscle contractions. The medulla oblongata and the pons have centers for vital functions such as breathing and the heartbeat.

12.3 The Limbic System and Higher Mental Functions
The limbic system connects portions of the cerebral cortex with the hypothalamus, thalamus, and basal nuclei. In the limbic system, the hippocampus acts as a conduit for sending messages to long-term memory and retrieving them once again. The amygdala adds emotional overtones to memories.

12.4 The Peripheral Nervous System
The PNS contains only nerves and ganglia. Voluntary actions always involve the cerebrum, but reflexes are automatic, and some do not require involvement of the brain. In the somatic system, for example, a stimulus causes sensory receptors to generate nerve impulses that are then conducted by sensory fibers to interneurons in the spinal cord. Interneurons signal motor neurons, which conduct nerve impulses to a skeletal muscle that contracts, producing the response to the stimulus.

The autonomic (involuntary) system controls the smooth muscle of the internal organs and glands. The sympathetic division is associated with responses that occur during times of stress, and the parasympathetic system is associated with responses that occur during times of relaxation.

12.5 Drug Abuse
Although neurological drugs are quite varied, each type has been found to either promote or prevent the action of a particular neurotransmitter.

Studying the Concepts

1. What are the three types of neurons, and what is their relationship to the CNS? Describe the structure and function of the three parts of a neuron. 218
2. What is the resting potential, and how is it brought about? 220
3. Describe the two parts of an action potential and the changes that can be associated with each part. 220
4. What is a neurotransmitter, where is it stored, how does it function, and how is it destroyed? Name two well-known neurotransmitters. 222–23
5. The CNS contains two portions. Describe the structure and function of the spinal cord. 224–25
6. Name the major parts of the brain, and give a function for each. 226–29
7. Name the lobes of the cerebral hemispheres, and describe the function of primary motor, primary somatosensory, and association areas. 227–28
8. What is the reticular formation? 229
9. What is the limbic system, and how is it involved in higher mental functions? 230–31
10. Language and speech require what portions of the brain? What is the left brain/right brain hypothesis? 231
11. The PNS contains what two types of nerves? Why is a spinal nerve called a mixed nerve? 232
12. What is the somatic system? Trace the path of a reflex arc. 233
13. What is the autonomic system, and what are its two major divisions? Give several similarities and differences between these divisions. 234–35
14. Describe the physiological effects and mode of action of alcohol, nicotine, cocaine, methamphetamine, heroin, and marijuana. 237–39

Thinking Critically About the Concepts

Refer to the opening vignette on page 218, and then answer these questions.

1. If a person became paralyzed due to a spinal cord injury, how would his or her symptoms differ from those of ALS?
2. How might sensory reception differ between a person with a spinal cord injury and one with ALS?

Testing Your Knowledge of the Concepts

Choose the best answer for each question.

1. The neuroglial cells that form myelin sheaths in the PNS are
   a. oligodendrocytes.
   b. ganglionic cells.
   c. Schwann cells.
   d. astrocytes.
   e. microglia.

2. Repolarization of an axon during an action potential is produced by
   a. inward diffusion of Na^+.
   b. outward diffusion of K^+.
   c. inward active transport of Na^+.
   d. active extrusion of K^+.

3. The hypothalamus does not
   a. control skeletal muscles.
   b. regulate thirst.
   c. control the pituitary gland.
   d. regulate body temperature.

4. The spinal cord does not contain
   a. the central canal.
   b. white matter area.
   c. association areas.
   d. the dorsal root.
   e. tracts.

5. A reflex arc
   a. always involves the spinal cord.
   b. occurs only in the arms and legs.
   c. usually involves only one sensory and one motor neuron.
   d. allows a quicker response than voluntary movement.

6. A drug that inactivates acetylcholinesterase
   a. stops the release of ACh from presynaptic endings.
   b. prevents the attachment of ACh to its receptor.
   c. increases the ability of ACh to stimulate muscle contraction.
   d. All of these are correct.

7. Which of the following statements about autonomic neurons is correct?
   a. They are motor neurons.
   b. The preganglionic neurons have cell bodies in the CNS.
   c. The postganglionic neurons innervate smooth muscles, cardiac muscle, and glands.
   d. All of these are correct.

8. Which of the following fibers release norepinephrine?
   a. preganglionic sympathetic axons
   b. postganglionic sympathetic axons
   c. preganglionic parasympathetic axons
   d. postganglionic parasympathetic axons

9. The sympathetic division of the autonomic system stimulation does not cause
   a. the liver to release glycogen.
   b. dilation of bronchioles.
   c. the gastrointestinal tract to digest food.
   d. an increase in the heart rate.

10. Integration
    a. is the summing up of excitatory and inhibitory signals.
    b. precedes neuron firing.
    c. involves synapses.
    d. is dependent on neurotransmitters.
    e. All of these are correct.

11. Which of these are the first and last elements in a spinal reflex?
    a. axon and dendrite
    b. sensory receptor and muscle effector
    c. ventral horn and dorsal horn
    d. brain and skeletal muscle
    e. motor neuron and sensory neuron

12. A spinal nerve takes nerve impulses
    a. to the CNS.
    b. away from the CNS.
    c. both to and away from the CNS.
    d. from the CNS to the spinal cord.

13. Which of these correctly describes the distribution of ions on either side of an axon when it is not conducting a nerve impulse?
    a. more sodium ions (Na^+) outside and more potassium ions (K^+) inside
    b. more K^+ outside and less Na^+ inside
    c. charged protein outside; Na^+ and K^+ inside
    d. Na^+ and K^+ outside and water only inside
    e. chlorine ions (Cl^-) on outside and K^+ and Na^+ on inside

14. When the action potential begins, sodium gates open, allowing Na^+ to cross the membrane. Now the polarity changes to
    a. negative outside and positive inside.
    b. positive outside and negative inside.
    c. There is no difference in charge between outside and inside.
    d. neutral outside and positive inside.
    e. All of these are correct.

15. Transmission of the nerve impulse across a synapse is accomplished by the
    a. movement of Na^+ and K^+.
    b. release of a neurotransmitter by a dendrite.
    c. release of a neurotransmitter by an axon.
    d. release of a neurotransmitter by a cell body.
    e. All of these are correct.

16. The autonomic system has two divisions, called the
    a. CNS and PNS.
    b. somatic and skeletal divisions.
    c. efferent and afferent divisions.
    d. sympathetic and parasympathetic divisions.

17. Synaptic vesicles are
    a. at the ends of dendrites and axons.
    b. at the ends of axons only.
    c. along the length of all long fibers.
    d. All of these are correct.

18. Which of these would be covered by a myelin sheath?
    a. short dendrites
    b. globular cell bodies
    c. long axons
    d. interneurons
    e. All of these are correct.

19. When you remove your hand from a hot stove, which system is least likely to be involved?
    a. somatic system
    b. autonomic system
    c. central nervous system
    d. peripheral nervous system

20. The spinal cord communicates with the brain via
    a. the gray matter of the cord and brain.
    b. sensory nerve fibers in a spinal nerve.
    c. the sympathetic system.
    d. tracts in the white matter.
    e. ventricles in the brain and the spinal cord.

21. Which two parts of the brain are least likely to work together?
    a. thalamus and cerebrum
    b. cerebrum and cerebellum
    c. hypothalamus and medulla oblongata
    d. cerebellum and medulla oblongata
    e. reticular formation and thalamus

22. Which of these is an incorrect contrast between these two areas of the brain?

	Primary Motor	**Primary Somatosensory**

    a. ventral to the central sulcus—dorsal to the central sulcus
    b. controls skeletal muscles—receives sensory information
    c. communicates directly with association areas in the parietal lobe—communicates directly with association areas in the frontal lobe
    d. has connections with the cerebellum—has connections with the thalamus
    e. All of these are contrasts between the two areas.

23. Label this diagram.

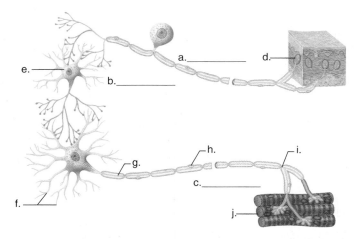

e. _____
b. _____
a. _____
d. _____
h. _____
i. _____
g. _____
c. _____
f. _____
j. _____

Understanding Key Terms

acetylcholine (ACh) 222
acetylcholinesterase (AChE) 222
action potential 220
Alzheimer disease (AD) 236
amygdala 230
association area 228
autonomic system 235
axon 218
axon terminal 222
basal nuclei 228
brain 226
brainstem 229
Broca's area 228
cell body 218
central nervous system (CNS) 218
cerebellum 229
cerebral cortex 227
cerebral hemisphere 227
cerebrospinal fluid 224
cerebrum 227
cranial nerve 232
dendrite 218
diencephalon 229
dorsal-root ganglion 232
drug abuse 237
effector 218
episodic memory 230
ganglion 232
gray matter 224
hippocampus 230
hypothalamus 229
integration 223
interneuron 218
learning 230
limbic system 230
long-term memory 230
long-term potentiation (LTP) 231
medulla oblongata 229
memory 230
meninges (sing., meninx) 224
midbrain 229
motor neuron 218
myelin sheath 219
nerve 232
nerve impulse 220
neuroglia 218
neuron 218
neurotransmitter 222
node of Ranvier 219
norepinephrine (NE) 222
nuclei 229
oscilloscope 220
parasympathetic division 235
Parkinson disease 236
peripheral nervous system (PNS) 218
pons 229
prefrontal area 228
primary motor area 227
primary somatosensory area 227
reflex 233
refractory period 220
resting potential 220
reticular formation 229
Schwann cell 219
semantic memory 230
sensory neuron 218
sensory receptor 218
short-term memory 230
skill memory 230
sodium-potassium pump 220
somatic system 233
spinal cord 224
spinal nerve 232
sympathetic division 235
synapse 222
synaptic cleft 222
thalamus 229
threshold 220
tract 224
ventricle 224
Wernicke's area 228
white matter 224

Match the key terms to these definitions.

a. _____ Automatic, involuntary response of an organism to a stimulus.

b. _____ Chemical stored at the ends of axons that is responsible for transmission across a synapse.

c. _____ Part of the peripheral nervous system that regulates internal organs.

d. _____ Collection of neuron cell bodies, usually outside the central nervous system.

e. _____ Neurotransmitter active in the somatic system of the peripheral nervous system.

Online Learning Center

www.mhhe.com/maderhuman9

The Online Learning Center provides a wealth of information fully organized and integrated by chapter. You will find practice quizzes, interactive activities, labeling exercises, flashcards, and much more that will complement your learning and understanding of human biology.

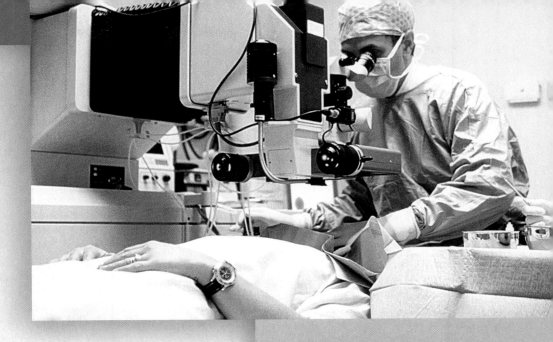

Senses

C H A P T E R   C O N C E P T S

13.1 Sensory Receptors and Sensations
- What is the function of a sensory receptor? 244
- What is the difference between sensation and perception? 244–45

13.2 Proprioceptors and Cutaneous Receptors
- What is the function of proprioceptors? 246
- What are the functions of cutaneous receptors in the skin? 246–47

13.3 Senses of Taste and Smell
- Taste cells are what type of sensory receptor? What are the four types of taste that result from stimulating these receptors? 248
- What are the receptors responsible for smell called, and where are they located? 249

13.4 Sense of Vision
- What parts of the eye assist in focusing an image on the retina? 251
- What are the two types of photoreceptors? 252
- Once photoreceptors initiate a visual signal, what other cells in the eye integrate the signal and pass it on to the cerebrum? 253–54

13.5 Sense of Hearing
- What parts in the ear assist in amplifying sound waves? 256–57
- What receptors allow us to hear? Where are these receptors located? How do they function? 257

13.6 Sense of Equilibrium
- Where are the receptors that detect rotation located? How do they function? 260–61
- Where are the receptors that detect gravity located? How do they function? 260–61

Carrie has an important decision to make. She has worn glasses and contacts since she was a little girl. Recently, she learned about LASIK eye surgery. LASIK is an acronym that stands for laser-assisted in situ keratomileusis. During this procedure, a laser is used to change the shape of the cornea, the transparent layer that covers the front of the eye. It will permanently cause light rays to be focused on the retina, the sensory part of the eye. Both eyes can be done at the same time, or they can be done in separate sessions. Carrie will be able to stay awake throughout the entire procedure. She will not even need to stay in the hospital.

Carrie is excited about the possibility of having normal vision, but the procedure is not risk-free. Although the majority of people who have LASIK eye surgery are satisfied with the outcome, there are exceptions. Some people have visual problems, such as "halos" or "starbursts" around bright lights, and blurred or double vision. A few experience permanent vision loss. Others see some improvement after the surgery, but must still wear glasses or contact lenses. Additional surgeries may be necessary. And the procedure, which can be expensive, is not usually covered by insurance. After the surgery, Carrie will have to use eyedrops to fight possible infection and inflammation while her corneas heal. Over the next few months, she will need to visit the ophthalmologist for additional checkups as her vision stabilizes.

13.1 Sensory Receptors and Sensations

Sensory receptors are dendrites specialized to detect certain types of stimuli (sing., **stimulus**). **Exteroceptors** are sensory receptors that detect stimuli from outside the body, such as those that result in taste, smell, vision, hearing, and equilibrium (Table 13.1). **Interoceptors** receive stimuli from inside the body. For example, among interoceptors, pressoreceptors respond to changes in blood pressure, osmoreceptors detect changes in blood volume, and chemoreceptors monitor the pH of the blood.

Interoceptors are directly involved in homeostasis and are regulated by a negative feedback mechanism. For example, when blood pressure rises, pressoreceptors signal a regulatory center in the brain, which sends out nerve impulses to the arterial walls, causing them to relax; the blood pressure then falls. Therefore, the pressoreceptors are no longer stimulated, and the system shuts down.

Exteroceptors such as those in the eyes and ears are not directly involved in homeostasis and continually send messages to the central nervous system regarding environmental conditions.

Types of Sensory Receptors

Sensory receptors in humans can be classified into just four categories: chemoreceptors, photoreceptors, mechanoreceptors, and thermoreceptors.

Chemoreceptors respond to chemical substances in the immediate vicinity. As Table 13.1 indicates, taste and smell depend on this type of sensory receptor, but certain chemoreceptors in various other organs are sensitive to internal conditions. Chemoreceptors that monitor blood pH are located in the carotid arteries and aorta. If the pH lowers, the breathing rate increases. As more carbon dioxide is expired, the blood pH rises.

Pain receptors (nociceptors) are a type of chemoreceptor. They are naked dendrites that respond to chemicals released by damaged tissues. Pain receptors are protective because they alert us to possible danger. For example, without the pain of appendicitis, we might never seek the medical help needed to avoid a ruptured appendix.

Photoreceptors respond to light energy. Our eyes contain photoreceptors that are sensitive to light rays and thereby provide us with a sense of vision. Stimulation of the photoreceptors known as rod cells results in black-and-white vision, while stimulation of the photoreceptors known as cone cells results in color vision.

Mechanoreceptors are stimulated by mechanical forces, which most often result in pressure of some sort. When we hear, airborne sound waves are converted to fluid-borne pressure waves that can be detected by mechanoreceptors in the inner ear. Similarly, mechanoreceptors are responding to fluid-borne pressure waves when we detect changes in gravity and motion, helping us keep our balance. These receptors are in the vestibule and semicircular canals of the inner ear, respectively. The sense of touch depends on pressure receptors that are sensitive to either strong or slight pressures. Pressoreceptors located in certain arteries detect changes in blood pressure, and stretch receptors in the lungs detect the degree of lung inflation. Proprioceptors, which respond to the stretching of muscle fibers, tendons, joints, and ligaments, make us aware of the position of our limbs.

Thermoreceptors located in the hypothalamus and skin are stimulated by changes in temperature. Those that respond when temperatures rise are called warmth receptors, and those that respond when temperatures lower are called cold receptors.

The sensory receptors are categorized as chemoreceptors, photoreceptors, mechanoreceptors, and thermoreceptors.

How Sensation Occurs

Sensory receptors respond to environmental stimuli by generating nerve impulses. **Sensation** occurs when nerve

Table 13.1	Exteroceptors				
Sensory Receptor	**Stimulus**	**Category**	**Sense**	**Sensory Organ**	
Taste cells	Chemicals	Chemoreceptor	Taste	Taste buds	
Olfactory cells	Chemicals	Chemoreceptor	Smell	Olfactory epithelium	
Rod cells and cone cells in retina	Light rays	Photoreceptor	Vision	Eye	
Hair cells in spiral organ	Sound waves	Mechanoreceptor	Hearing	Ear	
Hair cells in semicircular canals	Motion	Mechanoreceptor	Rotational equilibrium	Ear	
Hair cells in vestibule	Gravity	Mechanoreceptor	Gravitational equilibrium	Ear	

impulses arrive at the cerebral cortex of the brain. **Perception** occurs when the cerebral cortex interprets the meaning of sensations.

As we discussed in Chapter 12, sensory receptors are the first element in a reflex arc. We are only aware of a reflex action when sensory information reaches the brain. At that time, the brain integrates this information with other information received from other sensory receptors. After all, if you burn yourself and quickly remove your hand from a hot stove, the brain receives information not only from your skin, but also from your eyes, nose, and all sorts of sensory receptors.

Some sensory receptors are free nerve endings or encapsulated nerve endings, while others are specialized cells closely associated with neurons. The plasma membrane of a sensory receptor contains receptor proteins that react to the stimulus. For example, the receptor proteins in the plasma membrane of chemoreceptors bind to certain molecules. When this happens, ion channels open, and ions flow across the plasma membrane. If the stimulus is sufficient, nerve impulses begin and are carried by a sensory nerve fiber within the PNS to the CNS (Fig. 13.1). The stronger the stimulus, the greater the frequency of nerve impulses. Nerve impulses that reach the spinal cord first are conveyed to the brain by ascending tracts. If nerve impulses finally reach the cerebral cortex, sensation and perception occur.

All sensory receptors initiate nerve impulses; the sensation that results depends on the part of the brain receiving the nerve impulses. Nerve impulses that begin in the optic nerve eventually reach the visual areas of the cerebral cortex and, thereafter, we see objects. Nerve impulses that begin in the auditory nerve eventually reach the auditory areas of the cerebral cortex and, thereafter, we hear sounds. If it were possible to switch these nerves, stimulation of the eyes would result in hearing! On the other hand, when a blow to the eye stimulates photoreceptors, we "see stars" because nerve impulses from the eyes can only result in sight.

Before sensory receptors initiate nerve impulses, they carry out **integration,** the summing up of signals. One type of integration is called **sensory adaptation,** a decrease in response to a stimulus. We have all had the experience of smelling an odor when we first enter a room and then later not being aware of it at all. Some authorities believe that when sensory adaptation occurs, sensory receptors have stopped sending impulses to the brain. Others believe that the reticular activating system (RAS) has filtered out the ongoing stimuli. You will recall that sensory information is conveyed from the brainstem through the thalamus to the cerebral cortex by the RAS. The thalamus acts as a gatekeeper and only passes on information of immediate importance. Just as we gradually become unaware of particular environmental stimuli, we can suddenly become aware of stimuli that may have been present

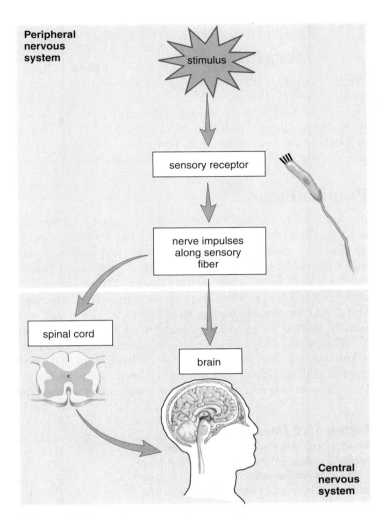

Figure 13.1 Sensation and perception.
The stimulus is received by a sensory receptor, which generates nerve impulses (action potentials). Nerve impulses are conducted to the CNS by sensory fibers within the PNS, and only those impulses that reach the cerebral cortex result in sensation and perception.

for some time. This can be attributed to the workings of the RAS, which has synapses with all the great ascending sensory tracts.

The functioning of our sensory receptors makes a significant contribution to homeostasis. Without sensory input, we would not receive information about our internal and external environment. This information leads to appropriate reflex and voluntary actions to keep the internal environment constant.

Sensation occurs when nerve impulses reach the cerebral cortex of the brain. Perception, which also occurs in the cerebral cortex, is an interpretation of the meaning of sensations.

13.2 Proprioceptors and Cutaneous Receptors

Sensory receptors in the muscles, joints and tendons, other internal organs, and skin send nerve impulses to the spinal cord. From there, they travel up the spinal cord in tracts to the somatosensory areas of the cerebral cortex (see Fig. 12.10). These general sensory receptors can be categorized into three types: proprioceptors, cutaneous receptors, and pain receptors.

Proprioceptors

Proprioceptors are mechanoreceptors involved in reflex actions that maintain muscle tone, and thereby the body's equilibrium and posture. They help us know the position of our limbs in space by detecting the degree of muscle relaxation, the stretch of tendons, and the movement of ligaments. Muscle spindles act to increase the degree of muscle contraction, and Golgi tendon organs act to decrease it. The result is a muscle that has the proper length and tension, or muscle tone.

Figure 13.2 illustrates the activity of a muscle spindle. In a muscle spindle, sensory nerve endings are wrapped around thin muscle cells within a connective tissue sheath. When the muscle relaxes and undue stretching of the muscle

spindle occurs, nerve impulses are generated. The rapidity of the nerve impulses generated by the muscle spindle is proportional to the stretching of a muscle. A reflex action then occurs, which results in contraction of muscle fibers adjoining the muscle spindle. The knee-jerk reflex, which involves muscle spindles, offers an opportunity for physicians to test a reflex action. The information sent by muscle spindles to the CNS is used to maintain the body's equilibrium and posture, despite the force of gravity always acting upon the skeleton and muscles.

Cutaneous Receptors

The skin is composed of two layers: the epidermis and the dermis. In Figure 13.3, the artist has dramatically indicated these two layers by separating the epidermis from the dermis in one location. The epidermis is stratified squamous epithelium in which cells become keratinized as they rise to the surface, where they are sloughed off. The dermis is a thick connective tissue layer. The dermis contains **cutaneous receptors,** which make the skin sensitive to touch, pressure, pain, and temperature (warmth and cold). The dermis is a mosaic of these tiny receptors, as you can determine by slowly passing a metal probe

Figure 13.2   Muscle spindle.
When a muscle is stretched, a muscle spindle sends ① sensory nerve impulses to the spinal cord. ② Motor nerve impulses from the spinal cord result in muscle fiber contraction so that muscle tone is maintained.

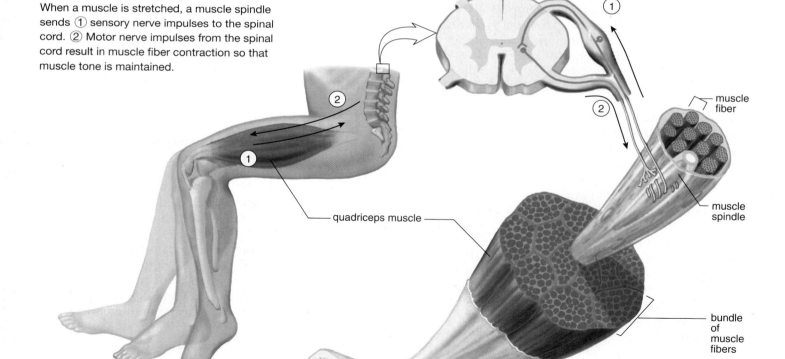

muscle fiber

muscle spindle

bundle of muscle fibers

quadriceps muscle

tendon

over your skin. At certain points, you will feel touch or pressure, and at others, you will feel heat or cold (depending on the probe's temperature).

Three types of cutaneous receptors are sensitive to fine touch. *Meissner corpuscles* are concentrated in the fingertips, the palms, the lips, the tongue, the nipples, the penis, and the clitoris. *Merkel disks* are found where the epidermis meets the dermis. A free nerve ending called a *root hair plexus* winds around the base of a hair follicle and fires if the hair is touched.

The three different types of cutaneous receptors that are sensitive to pressure are Pacinian corpuscles, Ruffini endings, and Krause end bulbs. *Pacinian corpuscles* are onion-shaped sensory receptors that lie deep inside the dermis. *Ruffini endings* and *Krause end bulbs* are encapsulated by sheaths of connective tissue and contain lacy networks of nerve fibers.

Temperature receptors are simply free nerve endings in the epidermis. Some free nerve endings are responsive to cold; others are responsive to warmth. Cold receptors are far more numerous than warmth receptors, but the two types have no known structural differences.

Pain Receptors

Like the skin, many internal organs have pain receptors, also called *nociceptors*, which are sensitive to chemicals released by damaged tissues. When inflammation occurs, due to mechanical, thermal, or electrical stimuli or toxic substances, cells release chemicals that stimulate pain receptors. Aspirin and ibuprofen reduce pain by inhibiting the synthesis of one class of these chemicals.

Sometimes, stimulation of internal pain receptors is felt as pain from the skin, as well as the internal organs. This is called **referred pain.** Some internal organs have a referred pain relationship with areas located in the skin of the back, groin, and abdomen; for example, pain from the heart is felt in the left shoulder and arm. This most likely happens when nerve impulses from the pain receptors of internal organs travel to the spinal cord and synapse with neurons also receiving impulses from the skin.

Proprioceptors help maintain our posture; sensory receptors in the skin are sensitive to touch, pressure, pain, and temperature.

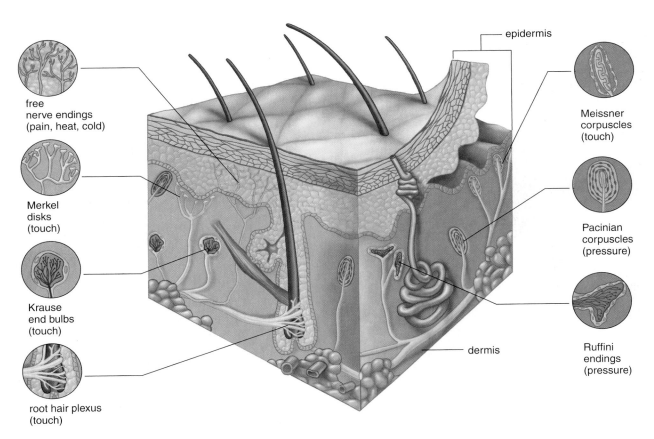

Figure 13.3 Sensory receptors in human skin.
The classical view is that each sensory receptor has the main function shown here. However, investigators report that matters are not so clear-cut. For example, microscopic examination of the skin of the ear shows only free nerve endings (pain receptors), and yet the skin of the ear is sensitive to all sensations. Therefore, it appears that the receptors of the skin are somewhat, but not completely, specialized.

13.3   Senses of Taste and Smell

Taste and smell are called chemical senses because their receptors are sensitive to molecules in the food we eat and the air we breathe. Taste cells and olfactory cells bear chemoreceptors.

Chemoreceptors are also in the carotid arteries and in the aorta, where they are primarily sensitive to the pH of the blood. These bodies communicate via sensory nerve fibers with the respiratory center in the medulla oblongata. When the pH drops, they signal this center, and immediately thereafter, the breathing rate increases. The expiration of CO_2 raises the pH of the blood.

Sense of Taste

The sensory receptors for the sense of taste, the taste cells, are located in **taste buds.** Taste buds are embedded in epithelium primarily on the tongue (Fig. 13.4). Many lie along the walls of the papillae, the small elevations on the tongue that are visible to the naked eye. Isolated taste buds are also present on the hard palate, the pharynx, and the epiglottis. We have at least four primary types of taste, but the taste buds for each are located throughout the tongue (Fig. 13.4a).

Even so, certain regions of the tongue are most sensitive to particular tastes: The tip of the tongue is most sensitive to sweet tastes; the margins to salty and sour tastes; and the rear of the tongue to bitter tastes.

How the Brain Receives Taste Information

Taste buds open at a taste pore. They have supporting cells and a number of elongated taste cells that end in microvilli. When molecules bind to receptor proteins of the microvilli, nerve impulses are generated in sensory nerve fibers that go to the brain. When they reach the gustatory (taste) cortex, they are interpreted as particular tastes.

Since we can respond to a range of sweet, sour, salty, and bitter tastes, the brain appears to survey the overall pattern of incoming sensory impulses and to take a "weighted average" of their taste messages as the perceived taste. Again, we can note that even though our senses depend on sensory receptors, the cortex integrates the incoming information and gives us our sense perceptions.

The microvilli of taste cells have receptor proteins for molecules that cause the brain to distinguish among sweet, sour, salty, and bitter tastes.

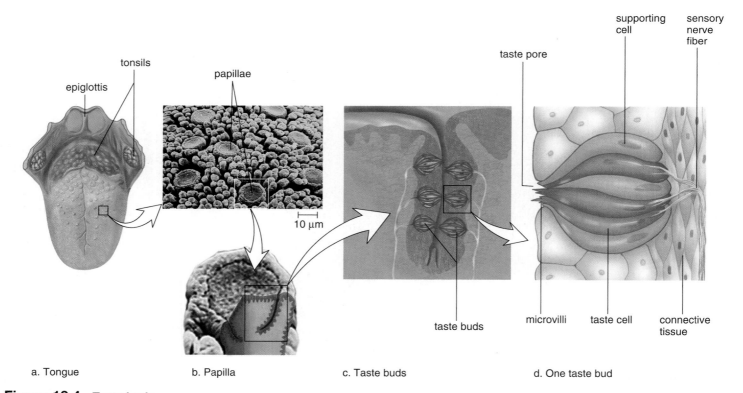

a. Tongue   b. Papilla   c. Taste buds   d. One taste bud

Figure 13.4   Taste buds.
a. Papillae on the tongue contain taste buds that are sensitive to sweet, sour, salty, and bitter tastes. **b.** Enlargement of papilla. **c.** Taste buds occur along the walls of the papillae. **d.** Taste cells end in microvilli that bear receptor proteins for certain molecules. When molecules bind to the receptor proteins, nerve impulses are generated that go to the brain, where the sensation of taste occurs.

Sense of Smell

Approximately 80–90% of what we perceive as "taste" actually is due to the sense of smell, which accounts for how dull food tastes when we have a head cold or a stuffed-up nose. Our sense of smell depends on **olfactory cells** located within olfactory epithelium high in the roof of the nasal cavity (Fig. 13.5). Olfactory cells are modified neurons. Each cell ends in a tuft of about five olfactory cilia, which bear receptor proteins for odor molecules.

How the Brain Receives Odor Information

Each olfactory cell has only one out of 1,000 different types of receptor proteins. Nerve fibers from like olfactory cells lead to the same neuron in the olfactory bulb, an extension of the brain. An odor contains many odor molecules, which activate a characteristic combination of receptor proteins. For example, a rose might stimulate olfactory cells, designated by purple and green in Figure 13.5, while a hyacinth might stimulate a different combination. An odor's signature in the olfactory bulb is determined by which neurons are stimulated. The neurons communicate this information via the olfactory tract to the brain; when it reaches the olfactory cortex, we know we have smelled a rose or a hyacinth.

Have you ever noticed that a certain aroma vividly brings to mind a certain person or place? A person's perfume may remind you of someone else, or the smell of boxwood may remind you of your grandfather's farm. The olfactory bulbs have direct connections with the limbic system and its centers for emotions and memory. One investigator showed that when subjects smelled an orange while viewing a painting, they not only remembered the painting when asked about it later, but they also had many deep feelings about it.

> Olfactory epithelium contains olfactory cells. The cilia of olfactory cells have receptor proteins for odor molecules that cause the brain to distinguish odors.

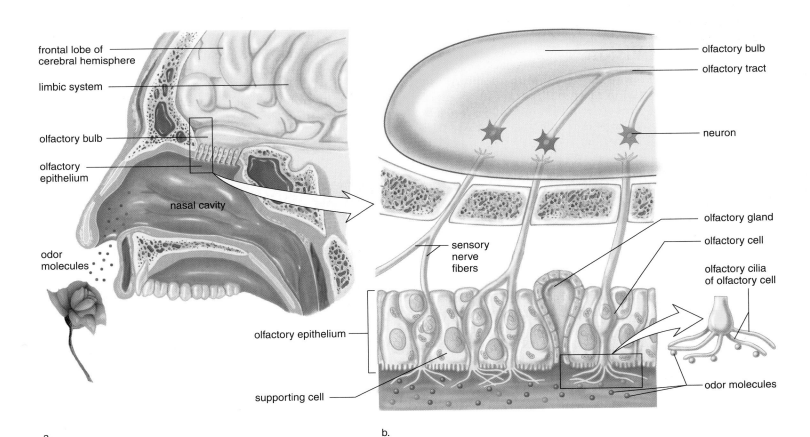

a.   b.

Figure 13.5 Olfactory cell location and anatomy.

a. The olfactory epithelium in humans is located high in the nasal cavity. **b.** Olfactory cells end in cilia that bear receptor proteins for specific odor molecules. The cilia of each olfactory cell can bind to only one type of odor molecule (signified here by color). If a rose causes olfactory cells sensitive to "purple" and "green" odor molecules to be stimulated, then neurons designated by purple and green in the olfactory bulb are activated. The primary olfactory area of the cerebral cortex interprets the pattern of stimulation as the scent of a rose.

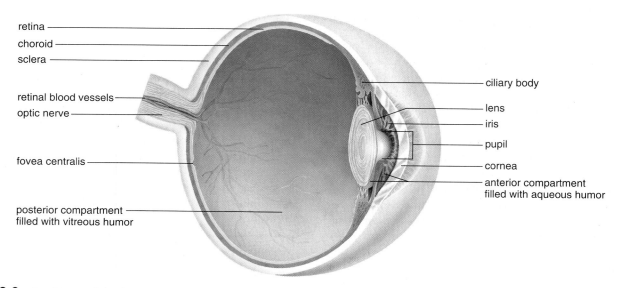

Figure 13.6   **Anatomy of the human eye.**
The sclera, the outer layer of the eye, becomes the cornea. The choroid, the middle layer, is continuous with the ciliary body and the iris. The retina, the inner layer, contains the photoreceptors for vision; the fovea centralis is the region where vision is most acute.

13.4 Sense of Vision

Vision requires the work of the eyes and the brain. As we shall see, much processing of stimuli occurs in the eyes before nerve impulses are sent to the brain. Still, researchers estimate that at least a third of the cerebral cortex takes part in processing visual information.

Anatomy and Physiology of the Eye

The eyeball, which is an elongated sphere about 2.5 cm in diameter, has three layers, or coats: the sclera, the choroid, and the retina (Fig. 13.6 and Table 13.2). The outer layer, the **sclera,** is white and fibrous except for the **cornea,** which is made of transparent collagen fibers. The cornea is the window of the eye.

The middle, thin, darkly pigmented layer, the **choroid,** is vascular and absorbs stray light rays that photoreceptors have not absorbed. Toward the front, the choroid becomes the donut-shaped **iris.** The iris regulates the size of the **pupil,** a hole in the center of the iris through which light enters the eyeball. The color of the iris (and therefore the color of your eyes) correlates with its pigmentation. Heavily pigmented eyes are brown, while lightly pigmented eyes are green or blue. Behind the iris, the choroid thickens and forms the circular ciliary body. The **ciliary body** contains the ciliary muscle, which controls the shape of the lens for near and far vision.

The **lens,** attached to the ciliary body by ligaments, divides the eye into two compartments; the one in front of

the lens is the anterior compartment, and the one behind the lens is the posterior compartment. The anterior compartment is filled with a clear, watery fluid called the **aqueous humor.** A small amount of aqueous humor is continually produced each day. Normally, it leaves the anterior compartment by way of tiny ducts. When a per-

Table 13.2	Functions of the Parts of the Eye
Part	**Function**
Sclera	Protects and supports eyeball
Cornea	Refracts light rays
Pupil	Admits light
Choroid	Absorbs stray light
Ciliary body	Holds lens in place, accommodation
Iris	Regulates light entrance
Retina	Contains sensory receptors for sight
Rod cells	Make black-and-white vision possible
Cone cells	Make color vision possible
Fovea centralis	Makes acute vision possible
Other	
Lens	Refracts and focuses light rays
Humors	Transmit light rays and support eyeball
Optic nerve	Transmits impulse to brain

son has **glaucoma,** these drainage ducts are blocked, and aqueous humor builds up. If glaucoma is not treated, the resulting pressure compresses the arteries that serve the nerve fibers of the retina, where photoreceptors are located. The nerve fibers begin to die due to lack of nutrients, and the person becomes partially blind. Eventually, total blindness can result.

The third layer of the eye, the **retina,** is located in the posterior compartment, which is filled with a clear, gelatinous material called the **vitreous humor.** The retina contains photoreceptors called rod cells and cone cells. The rods are very sensitive to light, but they do not see color; therefore, at night or in a darkened room we see only shades of gray. The cones, which require bright light, are sensitive to different wavelengths of light, and therefore we have the ability to distinguish colors. The retina has a very special region called the **fovea centralis** where cone cells are densely packed. Light is normally focused on the fovea when we look directly at an object. This is helpful because vision is most acute in the fovea centralis. Sensory fibers from the retina form the **optic nerve,** which takes nerve impulses to the visual cortex.

The eye has three layers: the outer sclera, the middle choroid, and the inner retina. Only the retina contains photoreceptors for light energy.

Function of the Lens

The lens, assisted by the cornea and the humors, focuses images on the retina (Fig. 13.7a). Focusing starts with the cornea and continues as the rays pass through the lens and the humors. The image produced is much smaller than the object because light rays are bent (refracted) when they are brought into **focus.** If the eyeball is too long or too short, the person may need corrective lenses to bring the image into focus. Notice that the image on the retina is inverted (upside down) and reversed from left to right.

Visual accommodation occurs for close vision. During visual accommodation, the lens rounds up, in order to bring the image to focus on the retina. The shape of the lens is controlled by the ciliary muscle, within the ciliary body. When we view a distant object, the ciliary muscle is relaxed, causing the suspensory ligaments attached to the ciliary body to be taut; therefore, the lens remains relatively flat (Fig. 13.7b). When we view a near object, the ciliary muscle contracts, releasing the tension on the suspensory ligaments, and the lens rounds up due to its natural elasticity (Fig. 13.7c). Now the image is focused on the retina. Because close work requires contraction of the ciliary muscle, it very often causes muscle fatigue, known as eyestrain. Usually after the age of 40, the lens loses some of its

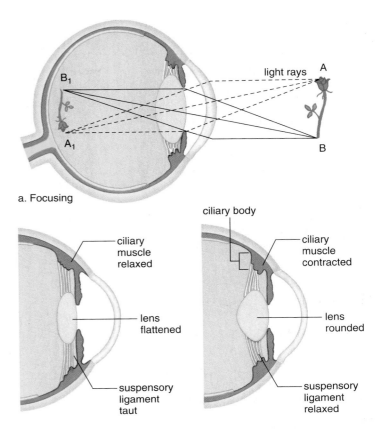

a. Focusing

b. Focusing on distant object   c. Focusing on near object

Figure 13.7 Focusing.
a. Light rays from each point on an object are bent by the cornea and the lens in such a way that an inverted and reversed image of the object forms on the retina. **b.** When focusing on a distant object, the lens is flat because the ciliary muscle is relaxed and the suspensory ligament is taut. **c.** When focusing on a near object, the lens accommodates; it becomes rounded because the ciliary muscle contracts, causing the suspensory ligament to relax.

elasticity and is unable to accommodate. Bifocal lenses may then be necessary for those who already have corrective lenses.

With aging, or possibly exposure to the sun, the lens is subject to cataracts. The lens becomes opaque and, therefore, incapable of transmitting rays of light. Today, the lens is usually surgically replaced with an artificial lens. In the future, it may be possible to restore the original configuration of the proteins making up the lens.

The lens, assisted by the cornea and the humors, focuses images on the retina. When viewing a close object, the lens rounds up, in order to bring the image to focus on the retina.

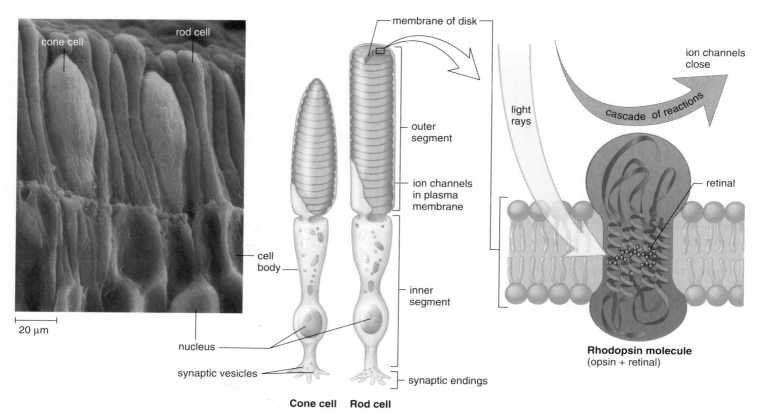

Figure 13.8 Photoreceptors in the eye.
The outer segment of rods and cones contains stacks of membranous disks, which contain visual pigments. In rods, the membrane of each disk contains rhodopsin, a complex molecule containing the protein opsin and the pigment retinal. When rhodopsin absorbs light energy, it splits, releasing opsin, which sets in motion a cascade of reactions that cause ion channels in the plasma membrane to close. Thereafter, signals pass to other neurons in the retina.

Visual Pathway to the Brain

The pathway for vision begins once light has been focused on the photoreceptors in the retina. Some integration occurs in the retina, where nerve impulses begin before the optic nerve transmits them to the brain.

Function of Photoreceptors Figure 13.8 illustrates the structure of the photoreceptors called **rod cells** and **cone cells.** Both rods and cones have an outer segment joined to an inner segment by a stalk. Pigment molecules are embedded in the membrane of the many disks present in the outer segment. Synaptic vesicles are located at the synaptic endings of the inner segment.

The visual pigment in rods is a deep purple pigment called rhodopsin. **Rhodopsin** is a complex molecule made up of the protein opsin and a light-absorbing molecule called **retinal,** which is a derivative of vitamin A. When a rod absorbs light, rhodopsin splits into opsin and retinal, leading to a cascade of reactions and the closure of ion channels in the rod cell's plasma membrane. The release of inhibitory transmitter molecules from the rod's synaptic vesicles ceases. Thereafter, signals go to other neurons in the retina. Rods are very sensitive to light, and therefore, are suited to night vision. (Because carrots are rich in vitamin A, it is true that eating carrots can improve your night vision.) Rod cells are plentiful throughout the entire retina; therefore, they also provide us with peripheral vision and perception of motion.

The cones, on the other hand, are located primarily in the fovea and are activated by bright light. They allow us to detect the fine detail and the color of an object. **Color vision** depends on three different kinds of cones, which contain pigments called the B (blue), G (green), and R (red) pigments. Each pigment is made up of retinal and opsin, but there is a slight difference in the opsin structure of each, which accounts for their individual absorption patterns. Various combinations of cones are believed to be stimulated by in-between shades of color.

The receptors for sight are the rods and the cones. The rods permit vision in dim light at night, and the cones permit vision in the bright light needed for color vision.

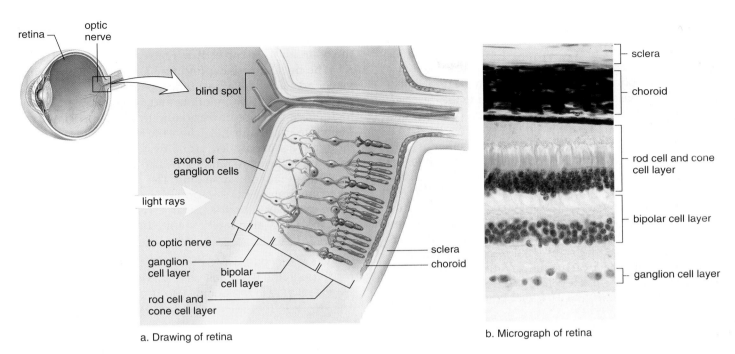

a. Drawing of retina

b. Micrograph of retina

Figure 13.9   **Structure and function of the retina.**
a. The retina is the inner coat of the eyeball. The rod and cone cell layer of the retina is located nearest the choroid. The rod cells and cone cells synapse with bipolar cells, which synapse with ganglion cells. Integration of signals occurs at these synapses; therefore, much processing occurs in bipolar and ganglion cells. Further, notice that many rod cells share one bipolar cell, but cone cells do not. Certain cone cells synapse with only one bipolar cell. Cone cells, in general, distinguish more detail than do rod cells. **b.** This micrograph shows that the sclera and choroid are relatively thin compared with the retina, which has several layers of cells. The choroid absorbs stray light rays and the sclera is the protective outer coat of the eye.

Function of the Retina   The retina has three layers of neurons (Fig. 13.9). The layer closest to the choroid contains the rod cells and cone cells; the middle layer contains bipolar cells; and the innermost layer contains ganglion cells, whose sensory fibers become the optic nerve. Only the rod cells and the cone cells are sensitive to light, and therefore, light must penetrate to the back of the retina before they are stimulated.

The rod cells and the cone cells synapse with the bipolar cells, which, in turn, synapse with ganglion cells whose axons become the optic nerve. Notice in Figure 13.9 that there are many more rod cells and cone cells than ganglion cells. In fact, the retina has as many as 150 million rod cells and 6 million cone cells but only 1 million ganglion cells. The sensitivity of cones versus rods is mirrored by how directly they connect to ganglion cells. As many as 150 rods may activate the same ganglion cell. No wonder stimulation of rods results in vision that is blurred and indistinct. In contrast, some cone cells in the fovea centralis activate only one ganglion cell. This explains why cones, especially in the fovea, provide us with a sharper, more detailed image of an object.

As signals pass to bipolar cells and ganglion cells, integration occurs. Each ganglion cell receives signals from rod cells covering about 1 mm^2 of retina (about the size of a thumbtack hole). This region is the ganglion cell's receptive field. Some time ago, scientists discovered that a ganglion cell is stimulated only by signals received from the center of its receptive field; otherwise, it is inhibited. If all the rod cells in the receptive field receive light, the ganglion cell responds in a neutral way—that is, it reacts only weakly or perhaps not at all. This supports the hypothesis that considerable processing occurs in the retina before ganglion cells generate nerve impulses, which are carried in the optic nerve to the visual cortex. Additional integration occurs in the visual cortex.

Synaptic integration and processing begin in the retina before nerve impulses are sent to the brain.

Blind Spot   Figure 13.9 provides an opportunity to point out that there are no rods and cones where the optic nerve exits the retina. Therefore, no vision is possible in this area. You can prove this to yourself by putting a dot to the right of center on a piece of paper. Use your right hand to move the paper slowly toward your right eye, while you look straight ahead. The dot will disappear at one point—this is your **blind spot.**

From the Retina to the Visual Cortex As stated, the axons of ganglion cells in the retina assemble to form the optic nerves. The optic nerves carry nerve impulses from the eyes to the optic chiasma. The **optic chiasma** has an **X** shape, formed by a crossing-over of optic nerve fibers. Fibers from the right half of each retina converge and continue on together in the *right optic tract*, and fibers from the left half of each retina converge and continue on together in the *left optic tract*.

The optic tracts sweep around the hypothalamus, and most fibers synapse with neurons in nuclei (masses of neuron cell bodies) within the thalamus. Axons from the thalamic nuclei form optic radiations that take nerve impulses to the *visual cortex* within the occipital lobe. Notice that the image arriving at the thalamus, and therefore, the visual cortex, has been split because the left optic tract carries information about the right portion of the visual field and the right optic tract carries information about the left portion of the visual field. Therefore, the right and left visual cortices must communicate with each other for us to see the entire visual field. Also, because the image is inverted and reversed (see Fig. 13.7 and Fig. 13.10), it must be righted in the brain for us to correctly perceive the visual field.

The most surprising finding has been that the primary visual area acts like a post office, parceling out information regarding color, form, motion, and possibly other attributes to different portions of the adjoining visual association area. Therefore, the brain has taken the visual field apart, even though we see a unified visual field. The visual association areas are believed to rebuild the field and give us an understanding of it at the same time. The ability of the visual cortex to integrate various information might help explain why nerve impulses from tongue touch receptors arriving at the somatosensory area can be shunted to the visual cortex.

The visual pathway begins in the retina and passes through the thalamus before reaching the primary visual area in the occipital lobe of the brain.

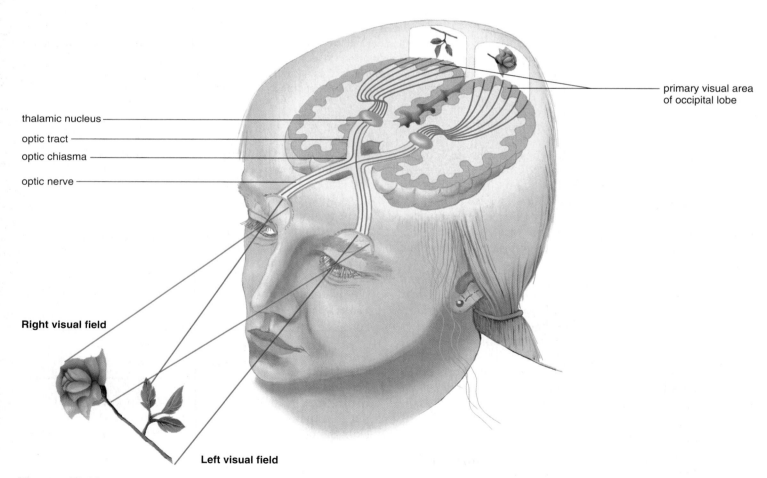

Figure 13.10 Optic chiasma.
Both eyes "see" the entire visual field. Because of the optic chiasma, data from the right half of each retina go to the right visual cortex, and data from the left half of the retina go to the left visual cortex. These data are then combined to allow us to see the entire visual field. Note that the visual pathway to the brain includes the thalamus, which has the ability to filter sensory stimuli.

Abnormalities of the Eye

Color blindness and misshapen eyeballs are two common abnormalities of the eye.

Color Blindness

Complete color blindness is extremely rare. In most instances, only one type of cone is defective or deficient in number. The most common mutation is the inability to see the colors red and green. This abnormality affects 5–8% of the male population. If the eye lacks cones that respond to red wavelengths, green colors are accentuated, and vice versa.

Distance Vision

If you can see from 20 feet what a person with normal vision can see from 20 feet, you are said to have 20/20 vision. Persons who can see close objects but cannot see the letters from this distance are said to be nearsighted. **Nearsighted** people can see close objects better than they can see objects at a distance. These individuals have an elongated eyeball, and when they attempt to look at a distant object, the image is brought to focus in front of the retina (Fig. 13.11*a*). They can see close objects because the lens can compensate for the long eyeball. To see distant objects, these people can wear concave lenses, which diverge the light rays so that the image focuses on the retina.

Rather than wear glasses or contact lenses, many nearsighted people are now choosing to undergo LASIK surgery. First, specialists determine how much the cornea needs to be flattened to achieve visual acuity. Controlled by a computer, the laser then removes this amount of the cornea. Most patients achieve at least 20/40 vision, but a few complain of glare and varying visual acuity.

Persons who can easily see the optometrist's chart but cannot see close objects well are **farsighted;** these individuals can see distant objects better than they can see close objects. They have a shortened eyeball, and when they try to see close objects, the image is focused behind the retina (Fig. 13.11*b*). When the object is distant, the lens can compensate for the short eyeball. When the object is close, these persons must wear convex lenses to increase the

bending of light rays so that the image can be focused on the retina.

When the cornea or lens is uneven, the image is fuzzy. The light rays cannot be evenly focused on the retina. This condition, called **astigmatism,** can be corrected by an unevenly ground lens to compensate for the uneven cornea (Fig. 13.11*c*).

The shape of the eyeball determines the need for corrective lenses. If the shape is too long, a person is nearsighted. If the shape is too short, a person is farsighted.

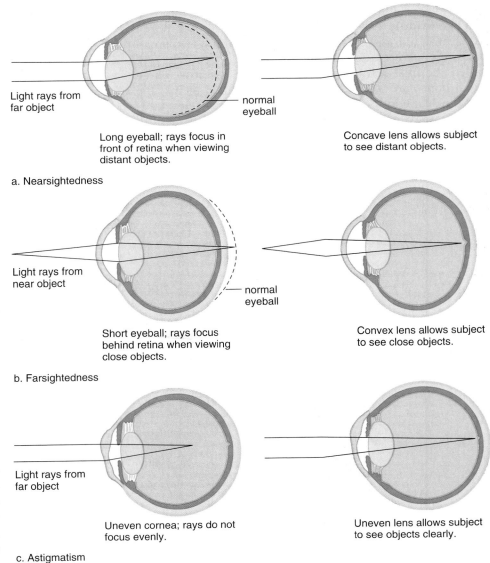

Light rays from far object

normal eyeball

Long eyeball; rays focus in front of retina when viewing distant objects.

a. Nearsightedness

Concave lens allows subject to see distant objects.

Light rays from near object

normal eyeball

Short eyeball; rays focus behind retina when viewing close objects.

b. Farsightedness

Convex lens allows subject to see close objects.

Light rays from far object

Uneven cornea; rays do not focus evenly.

c. Astigmatism

Uneven lens allows subject to see objects clearly.

Figure 13.11   **Common abnormalities of the eye, with possible corrective lenses.**
a. A concave lens in nearsighted persons focuses light rays on the retina. **b.** A convex lens in farsighted persons focuses light rays on the retina. **c.** An uneven lens in persons with astigmatism focuses light rays on the retina.

13.5 Sense of Hearing

The ear has two sensory functions: hearing and balance (equilibrium). The sensory receptors for both of these are located in the inner ear, and each consists of **hair cells** with stereocilia (actually long microvilli) that are sensitive to mechanical stimulation. They are mechanoreceptors.

Anatomy and Physiology of the Ear

Figure 13.12 shows that the ear has three divisions: outer, middle, and inner. The **outer ear** consists of the **pinna** (external flap) and the **auditory canal.** The opening of the auditory canal is lined with fine hairs and sweat glands. Modified sweat glands are located in the upper wall of the canal; they secrete earwax, a substance that helps guard the ear against the entrance of foreign materials, such as air pollutants.

The **middle ear** begins at the **tympanic membrane** (eardrum) and ends at a bony wall containing two small openings covered by membranes. These openings are called the **oval window** and the **round window.** Three small bones are found between the tympanic membrane and the oval window. Collectively called the **ossicles,** individually they are the **malleus** (hammer), the **incus** (anvil), and the **stapes** (stirrup) because their shapes resemble these objects. The malleus adheres to the tympanic membrane, and the stapes touches the oval window. An

auditory tube (eustachian tube), which extends from the middle ear to the nasopharynx, permits equalization of air pressure. Chewing gum, yawning, and swallowing in elevators and airplanes help move air through the auditory tubes upon ascent and descent. As this occurs, we often hear the ears "pop."

Whereas the outer ear and the middle ear contain air, the inner ear is filled with fluid. Anatomically speaking, the **inner ear** has three areas: The **semicircular canals** and the **vestibule** are both concerned with equilibrium; the **cochlea** is concerned with hearing. The cochlea resembles the shell of a snail because it spirals.

Auditory Pathway to the Brain

The sound pathway begins with the auditory canal. Thereafter, hearing requires the other parts of the ear, the cochlear nerve, and the brain. Hearing loss is discussed in the Health Focus on pages 258–59.

Through the Auditory Canal and Middle Ear   The process of hearing begins when sound waves enter the auditory canal. Just as ripples travel across the surface of a pond, sound waves travel by the successive vibrations of molecules. Ordinarily, sound waves do not carry much energy, but when a large number of waves strike the tympanic membrane, it moves back and forth (vibrates) ever so slightly. The malleus then takes the pressure from the inner

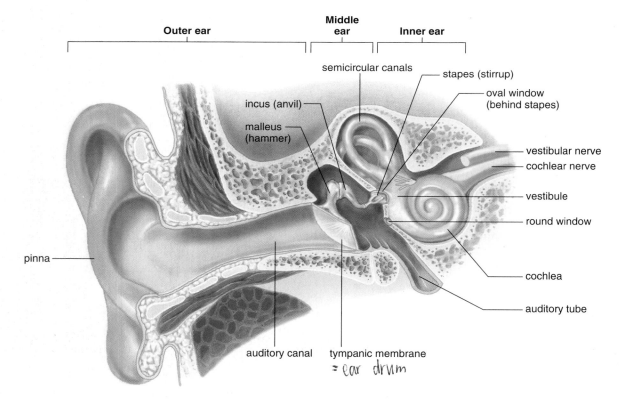

Figure 13.12   Anatomy of the human ear.
In the middle ear, the malleus (hammer), the incus (anvil), and the stapes (stirrup) amplify sound waves. In the inner ear, the mechanoreceptors for equilibrium are in the semicircular canals and the vestibule, and the mechanoreceptors for hearing are in the cochlea.

surface of the tympanic membrane and passes it, by means of the incus, to the stapes in such a way that the pressure is multiplied about 20 times as it moves. The stapes strikes the membrane of the oval window, causing it to vibrate, and in this way, the pressure is passed to the fluid within the cochlea.

From the Cochlea to the Auditory Cortex   If the cochlea is unwound and examined in cross section (Fig. 13.13), you can see that it has three canals: the vestibular canal, the **cochlear canal,** and the tympanic canal. The sense organ for hearing, called the **spiral organ** (organ of Corti), is located in the cochlear canal. The spiral organ consists of little hair cells and a gelatinous material called the **tectorial membrane.** The hair cells sit on the basilar membrane and their stereocilia are embedded in the tectorial membrane.

When the stapes strikes the membrane of the oval window, pressure waves move from the vestibular canal to the tympanic canal across the basilar membrane. The basilar membrane moves up and down, and the stereocilia of the hair cells embedded in the tectorial membrane bend. Then, nerve impulses begin in the **cochlear nerve** and travel to the brain. When they reach the auditory cortex in the temporal lobe, they are interpreted as a sound.

Each part of the spiral organ is sensitive to different wave frequencies, or pitch. Near the tip, the spiral organ responds to low pitches, such as a tuba, and near the base, it responds to higher pitches, such as a bell or a whistle. The nerve fibers from each region along the length of the spiral organ lead to slightly different areas in the auditory cortex. The pitch sensation we experience depends upon which region of the basilar membrane vibrates and which area of the auditory cortex is stimulated.

Volume is a function of the amplitude of sound waves. Loud noises cause the fluid within the vestibular canal to exert more pressure and the basilar membrane to vibrate to a greater extent. The resulting increased stimulation is interpreted by the brain as volume. It is believed that the brain interprets the tone of a sound based on the distribution of the hair cells stimulated.

The mechanoreceptors for hearing are hair cells on the basilar membrane of the spiral organ.

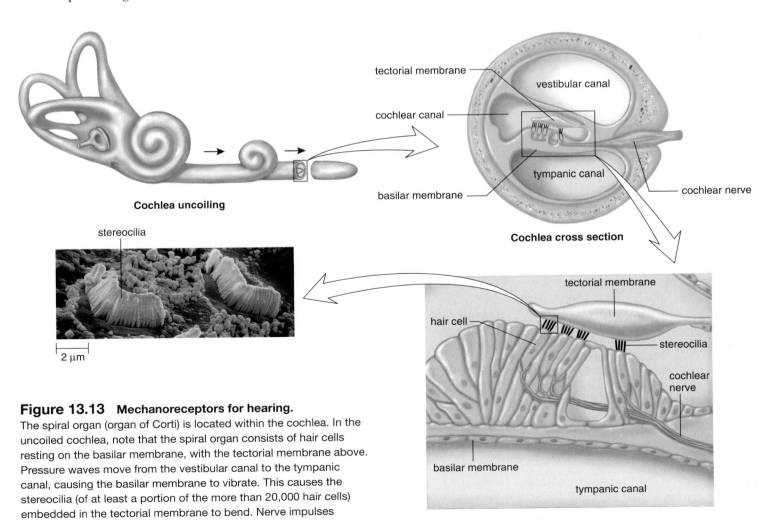

Figure 13.13   Mechanoreceptors for hearing.
The spiral organ (organ of Corti) is located within the cochlea. In the uncoiled cochlea, note that the spiral organ consists of hair cells resting on the basilar membrane, with the tectorial membrane above. Pressure waves move from the vestibular canal to the tympanic canal, causing the basilar membrane to vibrate. This causes the stereocilia (of at least a portion of the more than 20,000 hair cells) embedded in the tectorial membrane to bend. Nerve impulses traveling in the cochlear nerve result in hearing.

Health Focus

Hearing Loss

It is easy to take the sense of hearing for granted. But in fact many people eventually lose some or all of their ability to hear. There are two broad categories of hearing loss: conduction deafness and nerve deafness. In conduction deafness, sound waves are not conducted to the cochlea by the usual pathway: through the auditory canal to the tympanic membrane, then via the ossicles and oval window to the fluid-filled cochlea. Instead, sound waves must travel through the bones of the skull. In nerve deafness, sound waves are transmitted normally to the cochlea, but there is a problem with the nervous structures associated with hearing, such as the hair cells of the spiral organ, the cochlear nerve, or even the auditory portions of the cerebral cortex.

There are numerous causes of conduction deafness. Anything that affects the ability of the tympanic membrane to vibrate may result in hearing loss. For example, earwax can build up in the auditory canal, and press on the membrane. Inserting objects into the ear can damage the tympanic membrane (hence the warning, "the only thing you should stick in your ear is your elbow").

Otitis media is an infection of the middle ear that can lead to conduction deafness. It typically occurs when an upper respiratory infection, such as a cold, leads to swelling of the auditory tube, creating a vacuum that pulls fluid into the middle ear. The fluid provides an ideal environment for bacteria or viruses, and the pressure it exerts causes symptoms such as pain, tinnitus (ringing in the ears), and hearing loss. The loss is usually incomplete, and rarely permanent. However, when such hearing loss occurs in very young children, it can delay their speech development. If the tympanic membrane ruptures under pressure, it usually heals on its own in a matter of weeks. If it does not rupture, fluid may linger in the middle ear, and in some cases a tube must be surgically inserted for drainage.

Some people develop conduction deafness as they get older. This may result from otosclerosis, a condition in which bony growth gradually fuses the ossicles of the middle ear. The good news is that otosclerosis is often correctable with surgery.

Noise exposure is a common and usually preventable cause of nerve deafness. Noise volume is measured in units called decibels (dB). Table 13A provides a list of some common sources of noise with their levels in dB and predicted effects on hearing. Any noise above a level of 80 dB could result in damage to the hair cells of the organ of Corti. Eventually, the stereocilia and then the hair cells disappear completely (Fig. 13A). If listening to city traffic for extended periods can damage hearing, it stands to reason that frequent attendance at rock concerts, constantly playing a stereo loudly, or using earphones at high volume is also damaging to hearing. The first hint of danger could be temporary hearing loss, a "full" feeling in the ears, muffled hearing, or tinnitus (e.g., ringing in the ears). If you have any of these symptoms, modify your listening habits immediately to prevent further damage. If exposure to noise is unavoidable, specially designed noise-reduction earmuffs are available, and it is also possible to purchase earplugs made from a compressible, sponge-like material at the drugstore or sporting-goods store. These earplugs are not the same as those worn for swimming, and they should not be used interchangeably.

Aside from loud music, noisy indoor or outdoor equipment, such as a rug-cleaning machine or a chain saw, is also troublesome. Even motorcycles and recreational vehicles such as snowmobiles and motocross bikes can contribute to a gradual loss of hearing. Exposure to intense sounds of short duration, such as a burst of gunfire, can result in an immediate hearing loss. Hunters may have a significant hearing reduction in the ear opposite the shoulder where the gun is carried. The butt of the rifle offers some protection to the ear nearest the gun when it is shot.

Certain over-the-counter and prescription drugs have the potential to cause nerve deafness when taken in combination or excessive amounts. Such medications include: anti-inflammatory drugs such as aspirin, ibuprofen, and naproxen; antibiotics such as neomycin; anticancer drugs such as cisplatin; the antimalarial drug quinine; and certain blood pressure medications such as furosemide. Sometimes hearing is restored when a person stops taking the medication, but in other cases the damage is permanent.

One uncommon cause of deafness is autoimmune inner ear disease (AIED). Like any autoimmune disease, AIED occurs when a person's immune system turns against normal, healthy tissue, like the spiral organ. A person who develops AIED typically experiences symptoms such as dizziness and tinnitus in addition to hearing loss. Although AIED can be treated with drugs that suppress the immune system, the drugs themselves can have serious side effects, and may only slow the disease.

Hearing aids can help with partial hearing loss such as that caused by chronic noise exposure, but they do so by amplifying sound waves rather than restoring lost hearing. Most amplify all sound waves equally, which is why it may be difficult for someone wearing a hearing aid to carry on a conversation in a noisy restaurant. Some of the newer and more expensive hearing aids are programmable, so the level of amplification can be adjusted depending on the noise level of one's surroundings.

Through the use of cochlear implants, there is hope today for people who have little or no hearing due to cochlear damage. A person with a cochlear implant wears a microphone that picks up sounds and sends them to a processor, which relays signals to a small receiver implanted beneath the scalp. The receiver transmits signals through a number of electrodes to the origins of the cochlear nerve. Cochlear implants are not yet capable of producing all the nuances of normal hearing, but they do allow people who have them to understand speech and perceive sounds such as alarms and telephones.

Table 13A Noises That Affect Hearing

Type of Noise	Sound Level (decibels)	Effect
"Boom car," jet engine, shotgun, rock concert	Over 125	Beyond threshold of pain; potential for hearing loss high
Nightclub, "boom box," thunderclap	Over 120	Hearing loss likely
Chain saw, pneumatic drill, jackhammer, symphony orchestra, snowmobile, garbage truck, cement mixer	100–200	Regular exposure of more than 1 min risks permanent hearing loss
Farm tractor, newspaper press, subway, motorcycle	90–100	Fifteen minutes of unprotected exposure potentially harmful
Lawn mower, food blender	85–90	Continuous daily exposure for more than 8 hrs can cause hearing damage
Diesel truck, average city traffic noise	80–85	Annoying; constant exposure may cause hearing damage

Source: National Institute on Deafness and Other Communication Disorders, January 1990, National Institutes of Health.

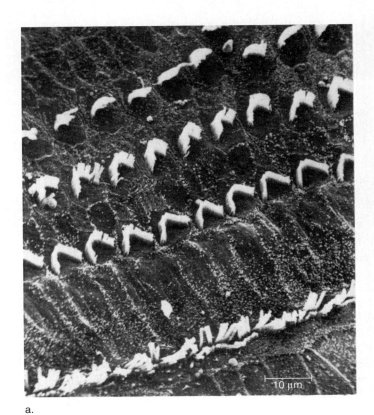
a.

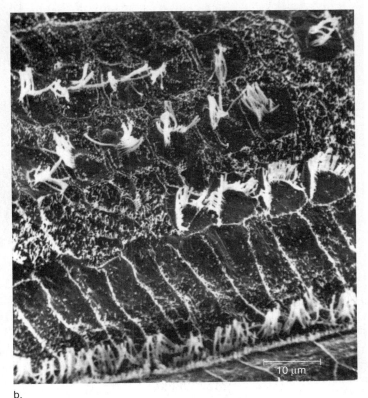
b.

Figure 13A Hair cell damage.

a. Normal hair cells in the spiral organ of a guinea pig. **b.** Damaged cells. This damage occurred after 24-hour exposure to a noise level equivalent to that at a heavy-metal rock concert (see Table 13A). Hearing is permanently impaired because lost cells will not be replaced, and damaged cells may also die.

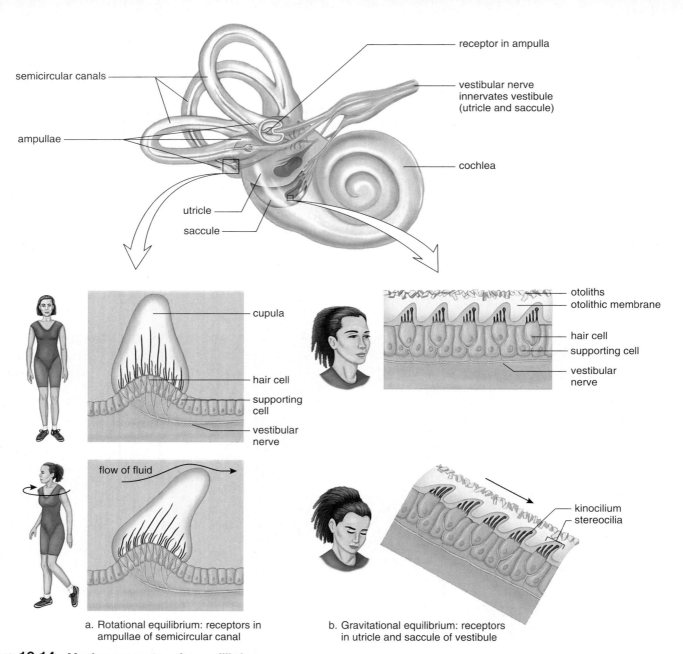

a. Rotational equilibrium: receptors in ampullae of semicircular canal

b. Gravitational equilibrium: receptors in utricle and saccule of vestibule

Figure 13.14 **Mechanoreceptors for equilibrium.**

a. Rotational equilibrium. The ampullae of the semicircular canals contain hair cells with stereocilia embedded in a cupula. When the head rotates, the cupula is displaced, bending the stereocilia. Thereafter, nerve impulses travel in the vestibular nerve to the brain. **b.** Gravitational equilibrium. The utricle and the saccule contain hair cells with stereocilia embedded in an otolithic membrane. When the head bends, otoliths are displaced, causing the membrane to sag and the stereocilia to bend. If the stereocilia bend toward the kinocilium, the longest of the stereocilia, nerve impulses increase in the vestibular nerve. If the stereocilia bend away from the kinocilium, nerve impulses decrease in the vestibular nerve. This difference tells the brain in which direction the head moved.

13.6 Sense of Equilibrium

Mechanoreceptors in the semicircular canals detect rotational and/or angular movement of the head **(rotational equilibrium)**, while mechanoreceptors in the utricle and saccule detect movement of the head in the vertical or horizontal planes **(gravitational equilibrium)** (Fig. 13.14 and Table 13.3).

Through their communication with the brain, these mechanoreceptors help us achieve equilibrium, but other structures in the body are also involved. For example, we already mentioned that proprioceptors are necessary for maintaining our equilibrium. Vision, if available, provides extremely helpful input the brain can act upon.

Rotational Equilibrium Pathway

Rotational equilibrium involves the three semicircular canals, which are arranged so that there is one in each dimension of space. The base of each of the three canals, called the **ampulla,** is slightly enlarged. Little hair cells, whose stereocilia are embedded within a gelatinous material called a cupula, are found within the ampullae. Because of the way the semicircular canals are arranged, each ampulla responds to head rotation in a different plane of space. As fluid within a semicircular canal flows over and displaces a cupula, the stereocilia of the hair cells bend, and the pattern of impulses carried by the vestibular nerve to the brainstem and cerebellum changes. The brain uses information from the hair cells within ampulla of the semicircular canals to maintain rotational equilibrium through appropriate motor output to various skeletal muscles that can right our present position in space as need be.

Sometimes, data regarding rotational equilibrium bring about unfortunate circumstances. For example, continuous movement of fluid in the semicircular canals causes one form of motion sickness. **Vertigo** is dizziness and a sensation of rotation. It is possible to simulate a feeling of vertigo by spinning rapidly and stopping suddenly. When the eyes are rapidly jerked back to a midline position, the person feels like the room is spinning. This shows that the eyes are also involved in our sense of equilibrium.

Gravitational Equilibrium Pathway

Gravitational equilibrium depends on the **utricle** and **saccule,** two membranous sacs located in the vestibule. Both of these sacs contain little hair cells, whose stereocilia are embedded within a gelatinous material called an otolithic membrane. Calcium carbonate ($CaCO_3$) granules, or **otoliths,** rest on this membrane. The utricle is especially sensitive to horizontal (back-forth) movements and the bending of the head, while the saccule responds best to vertical (up-down) movements.

When the body is still, the otoliths in the utricle and the saccule rest on the otolithic membrane above the hair cells. When the head bends or the body moves in the horizontal and vertical planes, the otoliths are displaced and the otolithic membrane sags, bending the stereocilia of the hair cells beneath. If the stereocilia move toward the largest stereocilium, called the kinocilium, nerve impulses increase in the vestibular nerve. If the stereocilia move away from the kinocilium, nerve impulses decrease in the vestibular nerve. If you are upside down, nerve impulses in the vestibular nerve cease. These data reach the vestibular cortex, which uses them to determine the direction of the movement of the head at the moment. The brain uses this information to maintain gravitational equilibrium through appropriate motor output to various skeletal muscles that can right our present position in space as need be.

The semicircular canals contribute to the sense of rotational equilibrium, and the utricle and the saccule function in gravitational equilibrium.

Table 13.3	Functions of the Parts of the Ear		
Part	**Medium**	**Function**	**Mechanoreceptor**
Outer Ear	Air		
Pinna		Collects sound waves	—
Auditory canal		Filters air	—
Middle Ear	Air		
Tympanic membrane and ossicles		Amplify sound waves	—
Auditory tube		Equalizes air pressure	—
Inner Ear	Fluid		
Semicircular canals		Rotational equilibrium	Stereocilia embedded in cupula
Vestibule (contains utricle and saccule)		Gravitational equilibrium	Stereocilia embedded in otolithic membrane
Cochlea (spiral organ)		Hearing	Stereocilia embedded in tectorial membrane

Summarizing the Concepts

13.1 Sensory Receptors and Sensations

Each type of sensory receptor detects a particular kind of stimulus. When stimulation occurs, sensory receptors initiate nerve impulses that are transmitted to the spinal cord and/or brain. Sensation occurs when nerve impulses reach the cerebral cortex. Perception is an interpretation of the meaning of sensations.

13.2 Proprioceptors and Cutaneous Receptors

Proprioception is illustrated by the action of muscle spindles that are stimulated when muscle fibers stretch. A reflex action, which is illustrated by the knee reflex, causes the muscle fibers to contract. Proprioception helps maintain equilibrium and posture.

The skin contains sensory receptors, called cutaneous receptors, for touch, pressure, temperature (warmth and cold), and pain. The pain of internal organs is sometimes felt in the skin and is called referred pain.

13.3 Sense of Taste and Smell

Taste and smell are due to chemoreceptors that are stimulated by molecules in the environment. After molecules bind to plasma membrane receptor proteins on the microvilli of taste cells and the cilia of olfactory cells, nerve impulses eventually reach the cerebral cortex, which determines the taste and odor according to the pattern of stimulation. The gustatory (taste) cortex responds to a range of salty, sour, sweet, and bitter tastes.

13.4 Sense of Vision

Vision depends on the eye, the optic nerves, and the visual areas of the cerebral cortex. The eye has three layers. The outer layer, the sclera, can be seen as the white of the eye; it also becomes the transparent bulge in the front of the eye called the cornea. The middle pigmented layer, called the choroid, absorbs stray light rays. The rod cells (sensory receptors for dim light) and the cone cells (sensory receptors for bright light and color) are located in the retina, the inner layer of the eyeball. The cornea, the humors, and especially the lens bring the light rays to focus on the retina. To see a close object, accommodation occurs as the lens rounds up.

The visual pathway begins when light strikes rhodopsin within the membranous disks of rod cells; rhodopsin splits into opsin and retinal. A cascade of reactions leads to the closing of ion channels in a rod cell's plasma membrane. Inhibitory transmitter molecules are no longer released, and signals are passed to other neurons in the retina.

Integration occurs in the retina, which is composed of three layers of cells: the rod and cone layer, the bipolar cell layer, and the ganglion cell layer. Integration also occurs in the brain. The visual field is taken apart by the optic chiasma and by the primary visual area in the cerebral cortex, which parcels out signals for color, form, and motion to the visual association area. Then the cortex rebuilds the field.

13.5 Sense of Hearing

Hearing depends on the ear, the cochlear nerve, and the auditory areas of the cerebral cortex.

The ear is divided into three parts: outer, middle, and inner. The outer ear consists of the pinna and the auditory canal, which direct sound waves to the middle ear. The middle ear begins with the tympanic membrane and contains the ossicles (malleus, incus, and stapes). The malleus is attached to the tympanic membrane, and the stapes is attached to the oval window, which is covered by a membrane. The inner ear contains the cochlea and the semicircular canals, plus the utricle and the saccule.

The auditory pathway begins when the outer ear receives and the middle ear amplifies the sound waves that then strike the oval window membrane. Its vibrations set up pressure waves across the cochlear canal, which contains the spiral organ, consisting of hair cells whose stereocilia are embedded within the tectorial membrane. When the basilar membrane vibrates, the stereocilia of the hair cells bend. Nerve impulses begin in the cochlear nerve and are carried to the primary auditory area in the temporal lobe of the cerebral cortex.

13.6 Sense of Equilibrium

The ear also contains mechanoreceptors for our sense of equilibrium. Rotational equilibrium depends on the stimulation of hair cells within the ampullae of the semicircular canals. Gravitational equilibrium relies on the stimulation of hair cells within the utricle and the saccule.

Studying the Concepts

1. What are the four types of sensory receptors in the human body? 244
2. Explain sensation, from the reception of stimuli to the passage of nerve impulses to the brain. 244–45
3. Explain how muscle spindles are involved in proprioception. What do the cutaneous receptors sense? 246–47
4. What causes pain, and what is referred pain? 247
5. Describe the structure of a taste bud, and tell how a taste cell functions. 248
6. Describe the structure and function of the olfactory epithelium. How does the sense of smell come about? 249
7. Describe the anatomy of the eye, and explain focusing and visual accommodation. 250–51
8. Describe the structure and function of rod cells and cone cells. 252
9. Explain the process of integration in the retina and the brain. 253–54
10. Relate the need for corrective lenses to three possible eyeball shapes. 255
11. Describe the anatomy of the ear and how we hear. 256–57
12. Describe the roles of the semicircular canals, the utricle, and the saccule in maintaining equilibrium. 260–61

Thinking Critically About the Concepts

Refer to the opening vignette on page 243, and then answer these questions.

1. Now that you have learned what causes nearsightedness, can you explain how changing the shape of the cornea could help to correct it?
2. What types of visual problems could not be treated with LASIK surgery?
3. What do you think happens when a young person who has had LASIK becomes older and the lens becomes stiff?

Testing Your Knowledge of the Concepts

Choose the best answer for each question.

1. A sensory receptor
   a. is the first portion of a reflex arc.
   b. initiates nerve impulses.
   c. can be internal or external.
   d. All of these are correct.

2. Which of these is an incorrect difference between olfactory receptors and equilibrium receptors?

   Olfactory Receptors

   a. Located in nasal cavities.
   b. Chemoreceptors.
   c. Respond to molecules in the air.
   d. Communicate with brain via a tract.
   e. All of these contrasts are correct.

   Equilibrium Receptors

   Located in the inner ear.
   Mechanoreceptors.
   Respond to movements of the body.
   Communicate with brain via vestibular nerve.

3. Which of these is an incorrect difference between proprioceptors and cutaneous receptors?

   Proprioceptors

   a. Located in muscles and tendons.
   b. Chemoreceptors.
   c. Respond to tension.
   d. Interoceptors.
   e. All of these contrasts are correct.

   Cutaneous Receptors

   Located in the skin.
   Mechanoreceptors.
   Respond to pain, hot, cold, touch, pressure.
   Exteroceptors.

4. Which of the following gives the correct path for light rays entering the human eye?
   a. sclera, retina, choroid, lens, cornea
   b. fovea centralis, pupil, aqueous humor, lens
   c. cornea, pupil, lens, vitreous humor, retina
   d. cornea, fovea centralis, lens, choroid, rods
   e. optic nerve, sclera, choroid, retina, humors

5. Which structure of the eye is incorrectly matched with its function?
   a. lens—focusing
   b. cones—color vision
   c. iris—regulation of amount of light
   d. choroid—location of cones
   e. sclera—protection

6. Which of the following wouldn't you mention if you were tracing the path of sound vibrations?
   a. auditory canal
   b. tympanic membrane
   c. ossicles
   d. semicircular canals
   e. cochlea

7. Which one of these correctly describes the location of the spiral organ?
   a. between the tympanic membrane and the oval window in the inner ear
   b. in the utricle and saccule within the vestibule
   c. between the tectorial membrane and the basilar membrane in the cochlear canal
   d. between the nasal cavities and the throat
   e. between the outer and inner ear within the semicircular canals

8. Which of these associations is incorrectly matched?
   a. semicircular canals—inner ear
   b. utricle and saccule—outer ear
   c. auditory canal—outer ear
   d. cochlea—inner ear
   e. ossicles—middle ear

9. Retinal is
   a. a derivative of vitamin A.
   b. sensitive to light energy.
   c. a part of rhodopsin.
   d. found in both rods and cones.
   e. All of these are correct.

10. Both olfactory receptors and sound receptors
    a. are chemoreceptors.
    b. are a part of the brain.
    c. are mechanoreceptors.
    d. initiate nerve impulses.
    e. All of these are correct.

11. In order to focus on objects that are close to the viewer,
    a. the suspensory ligaments must be pulled tight.
    b. the lens needs to become more rounded.
    c. the ciliary muscle will be relaxed.
    d. the image must focus on the area of the optic nerve.

12. Which abnormality of the eye is incorrectly matched with its cause?
    a. astigmatism—either the lens or cornea is not even
    b. farsightedness—eyeball is shorter than usual
    c. nearsightedness—image focuses behind the retina
    d. color blindness—genetic disorder in which certain types of cones may be missing

13. Which of the following structures would allow you to know that you were upside down, even if you were in total darkness?
    a. utricle and saccule
    b. cochlea
    c. semicircular canals
    d. tectorial membrane

14. Which of the following could result in hearing loss?
    a. certain antibiotics
    b. earphone use
    c. consistent use of loud equipment such as a jackhammer
    d. use of firearms
    e. All of these are correct.

15. Conscious interpretation of changes in the internal and external environment is called
    a. responsiveness.
    b. perception.
    c. sensation.
    d. accommodation.

16. Label this diagram of an eye. State a function for each structure labeled.

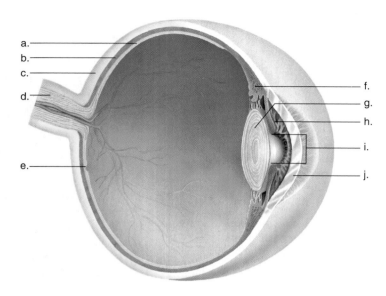

a.

b.

c.

d.

e.

f.

g.

h.

i.

j.

17. Receptors that are sensitive to changes in blood pressure are
    a. interoceptors.
    b. exteroceptors.
    c. proprioceptors.
    d. nociceptors.

18. Pain perceived as coming from another location is known as
    a. intercepted pain.
    b. phantom pain.
    c. referred pain.
    d. parietal pain.

19. The thin, darkly pigmented layer that underlies most of the sclera is
    a. the conjunctiva.
    b. the cornea.
    c. the retina.
    d. the choroid.

20. Adjustment of lens to focus on objects close to the viewer is called
    a. convergence.
    b. visual accommodation.
    c. focusing.
    d. constriction.

21. The middle ear is separated from the inner ear by
    a. the oval window.
    b. the tympanic membrane.
    c. the round window.
    d. Both a and c are correct.

22. Tasting something "sweet" versus "salty" is a result of
    a. activating different sensory receptors.
    b. activating many versus few sensory receptors.
    c. activating no sensory receptors.
    d. None of the above is correct.

Understanding Key Terms

ampulla 261
aqueous humor 250
astigmatism 255
auditory canal 256
auditory tube 256
blind spot 253
chemoreceptor 244
choroid 250
ciliary body 250
cochlea 256
cochlear canal 257
cochlear nerve 257
color vision 252
cone cell 252
cornea 250
cutaneous receptor 246
exteroceptor 244
farsighted 255
focus 251
fovea centralis 251
glaucoma 251
gravitational equilibrium 261
hair cell 256
incus 256
inner ear 256
integration 245
interoceptor 244
iris 250
lens 250
malleus 256
mechanoreceptor 244
middle ear 256
nearsighted 255
olfactory cell 249
optic chiasma 254
optic nerve 251

ossicle 256
otolith 261
outer ear 256
oval window 256
pain receptor 244
perception 245
photoreceptor 244
pinna 256
proprioceptor 246
pupil 250
referred pain 247
retina 251
retinal 252
rhodopsin 252
rod cell 252
rotational equilibrium 261
round window 256
saccule 261
sclera 250
semicircular canal 256
sensation 244
sensory adaptation 245
sensory receptor 244
spiral organ 257
stapes 256
stimulus 244
taste bud 248
tectorial membrane 257
thermoreceptor 244
tympanic membrane 256
utricle 261
vertigo 261
vestibule 256
visual accommodation 251
vitreous humor 251

Match the key terms to these definitions.

a. _____ Structure that receives sensory stimuli and is a part of a sensory neuron or transmits signals to a sensory neuron.

b. _____ Inner layer of the eyeball containing the photoreceptors—rod cells and cone cells.

c. _____ Outer, white, fibrous layer of the eye that surrounds the eye except for transparent cornea.

d. _____ Receptor that is sensitive to chemical stimulation—for example, receptors for taste and smell.

e. _____ Specialized region of the cochlea containing the hair cells for sound detection and discrimination.

Online Learning Center

www.mhhe.com/maderhuman9

The Online Learning Center provides a wealth of information fully organized and integrated by chapter. You will find practice quizzes, interactive activities, labeling exercises, flashcards, and much more that will complement your learning and understanding of human biology.

C H A P T E R   C O N C E P T S

14.1 Endocrine Glands
- How can the nervous system be contrasted with the endocrine system? 266
- What is a chemical signal, and what type of chemical signal are hormones? 268–69
- How do hormones affect the metabolism of cells? 268–69

14.2 Hypothalamus and Pituitary Gland
- What role does the hypothalamus play in the endocrine system? 270–71
- What hormones are produced by the anterior pituitary? 270–71

14.3 Thyroid and Parathyroid Glands
- What hormones are produced by the thyroid gland? What is the function of each? 273–74
- What hormone is produced by the parathyroid gland? What is the function of this hormone? It acts antagonistically to what hormone produced by the thyroid? 274

14.4 Adrenal Glands
- What hormones are produced by the adrenal glands? 275–77

14.5 Pancreas
- What hormones are produced by the pancreas? How does each affect blood glucose? 278
- What causes the condition known as diabetes mellitus? 279

14.6 Other Endocrine Glands
- What other body organs and tissues may function as endocrine glands? 280–82

14.7 Homeostasis
- How does the endocrine system work with the other systems in the body to achieve homeostasis? 284–85

Harry stood before the mirror, making sure his appearance would be just right. Tonight was the big junior high dance, and he was taking Mary on his first date. He noticed that he was getting a slight growth of hair on his upper lip and chin, and he couldn't decide whether to shave or let it grow. But the facial hair didn't concern him nearly as much as his voice—the change of pitch, which he could not control, was quite embarrassing. Although some of the kids laughed when this happened, he hoped Mary would not be one of them. Harry wondered why he cared what Mary thought; just last year he wouldn't even have wanted to go to the dance, let alone go on a date with a girl.

Harry was experiencing normal signs of puberty brought on by an increase in sex hormones. During puberty, sexual organs mature, and the secondary sex characteristics appear. As the larynx grows larger, the voice changes more dramatically in boys than in girls. Girls usually undergo a growth spurt before boys, and therefore girls are often taller than boys during early adolescence. Underarm hair appears in both sexes, usually before pubic hair does, but only boys are expected to get facial hair. Increased activity of oil glands in the skin can cause facial blemishes, or acne. In girls, breasts begin to develop and menstruation begins. Boys have their first ejaculation.

14.1 Endocrine Glands

The nervous system and the endocrine system both regulate the other organ systems. Control of the other systems permits coordination of their functions and brings about homeostasis. As we saw in the previous two chapters, the nervous system is composed of neurons. In this system, sensory receptors (specialized dendrites) detect changes in the internal and external environment. The CNS integrates the information and can respond by stimulating muscles and glands. Communication in this system depends on nerve impulses, conducted in axons, and neurotransmitters, which cross synapses. Axon conduction occurs rapidly and so does diffusion of a neurotransmitter across the short distance of a synapse. In other words, the nervous system is organized to respond rapidly to stimuli. This is particularly useful if the stimulus is an external event that endangers our safety—we can move quickly to avoid being hurt.

The endocrine system functions differently (Table 14.1). The endocrine system is notably composed of glands. These glands secrete **hormones,** which are carried by the bloodstream to target cells throughout the body (Fig. 14.1 and Table 14.2). The blood concentration of a substance often prompts an endocrine gland to secrete its hormone. For example, as discussed previously in Chapter 11, the parathyroid glands secrete a hormone when the blood Ca^{2+} level falls below normal. Hormones influence the metabolism of cells; the growth and development of body parts. In our example, parathyroid hormone (PTH) causes bone to break down and release Ca^{2+}. It takes time to deliver hormones and it takes time for cells to respond, but the effect is longer lasting. In other words, the endocrine system is organized for a slow but prolonged response.

Endocrine glands can be contrasted with exocrine glands. Exocrine glands have ducts and secrete their products into these ducts, which take them to the lumens of other organs or outside the body. For example, the salivary glands send saliva into the mouth by way of the salivary ducts. **Endocrine glands,** as stated, secrete their products into the bloodstream, which delivers them throughout the body. It must be stressed that only certain cells, called target cells, can respond to certain hormones. If a cell can respond to a hormone, the hormone and receptor proteins in the plasma membrane bind together as a key fits a lock.

It is of interest to note that both the nervous system and the endocrine system make use of negative feedback mechanisms. As mentioned previously, if the blood pressure falls, sensory receptors signal a control center in the brain. This center sends out nerve impulses to the arterial walls, so that they constrict and blood pressure rises. Now, the sensory receptors are no longer stimulated and the system is inactivated. Similarly, to continue our example, when the blood Ca^{2+} level rises, the parathyroid gland no longer secretes PTH.

Table 14.1	Comparison of Nervous and Endocrine Systems	
	Nervous System	**Endocrine System**
Composed of	Neurons	Usually glands
Delivery	Nerve impulse and neurotransmitter	Hormone
How delivered	Axon and synapse	Usually bloodstream
Target	Muscle and glands	Cells throughout body
Response	Rapid, short-lived	Slow, long-lasting
Controlled by	Negative feedback	Negative feedback

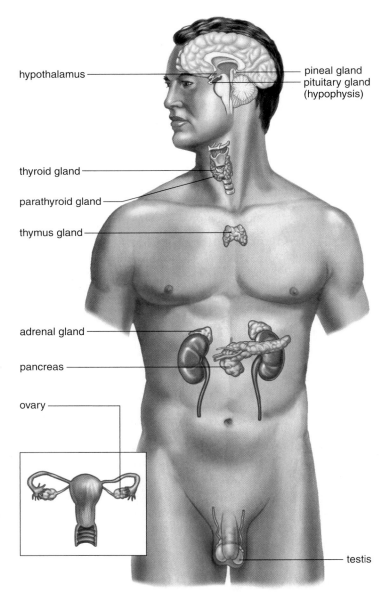

hypothalamus

pineal gland
pituitary gland (hypophysis)

thyroid gland

parathyroid gland

thymus gland

adrenal gland

pancreas

ovary

testis

Figure 14.1   The endocrine system.

Table 14.2 Principal Endocrine Glands and Hormones

Endocrine Gland	Hormone Released	Chemical Class	Target Tissues/Organs	Chief ... of H...
Hypothalamus	Hypothalamic-releasing and -inhibiting hormones	Peptide	Anterior pituitary	Regu...
Pituitary gland				
Posterior pituitary	Antidiuretic (ADH)	Peptide	Kidneys	Stimulates water re... kidne...
	Oxytocin	Peptide	Uterus, mammary glands	Stimulates urine muscle cont... release of mil by mammary glands
Anterior pituitary	Thyroid-stimulating (TSH)	Glycoprotein	Thyroid	Stimulates thy...
	Adrenocorticotropic (ACTH)	Peptide	Adrenal cortex	Stimulates adren... cortex
	Gonadotropic (FSH, LH)	Glycoprotein	Gonads	Egg and sperm pr... sex hormone produ ction;
	Prolactin (PRL)	Protein	Mammary glands	Milk production
	Growth (GH)	Protein	Soft tissues, bones	Cell division, protein sy...is, and bone growth
	Melanocyte-stimulating (MSH)	Peptide	Melanocytes in skin	Unknown function in hum... regulates skin color in lowe...
Thyroid	Thyroxine (T_4) and triiodothyronine (T_3)	Iodinated amino acid	All tissues	Increases metabolic rate; regrates growth and development
	Calcitonin	Peptide	Bones, kidneys, intestine	Lowers blood calcium level
Parathyroids	Parathyroid (PTH)	Peptide	Bones, kidneys, intestine	Raises blood calcium level
Adrenal gland				
Adrenal cortex	Glucocorticoids (cortisol)	Steroid	All tissues	Raise blood glucose level; stimulate breakdown of protein
	Mineralocorticoids (aldosterone)	Steroid	Kidneys	Reabsorb sodium and excrete potassium
	Sex hormones	Steroid	Gonads, skin, muscles, bones	Stimulate reproductive organs and bring about sex characteristics
Adrenal medulla	Epinephrine and norepinephrine	Modified amino acid	Cardiac and other muscles	Released in emergency situations; raise blood glucose level
...ncreas	Insulin	Protein	Liver, muscles, adipose tissue	Lowers blood glucose level; promotes formation of glycogen
	Glucagon	Protein	Liver, muscles, adipose tissue	Raises blood glucose level
	Androgens (testosterone)	Steroid	Gonads, skin, muscles, bones	Stimulate male sex characteristics
	Estrogens and progesterone	Steroid	Gonads, skin, muscles, bones	Stimulate female sex characteristics
	Thymosins	Peptide	T lymphocytes	Stimulate production and maturation of T lymphocytes
	Melatonin	Modified amino acid	Brain	Controls circadian and circannual rhythms; possibly involved in maturation of sexual organs

...s Are
...al Signals

...es are a type of chemical signal.
...cal signals are a means of com-
...cation between cells, between body
...s, and even between individuals.
...ey typically affect the metabolism of
...ells that have receptors to reeive them
(Fig. 14.2). In a condition caled androgen insensitivity, an ndivdual has X
and Y sex chromoses aid the testes,
which remain in e abdominal cavity,
produce the sex ly cells lack receptors
However, the ...mbine with testosterone
that are able ...ual appears to be a nor-
and the inc...
mal fema ...osterone, most hormones
    Lik...stance between body parts.
act a...l in the bloodstream from the
The...at produced them to their target
gl...lso counted as hormones are the
...ons produced by neurosecretory
...in the hypothalamus, a part of the
...n. They travel in the capillary net-
...ork that runs between the hypothala-
...nus and the pituitary gland. Some of
these secretions stimulate the pituitary
to secrete its hormones, and others prevent it from doing so.

    Not all hormones act between body parts. As we shall
see, prostaglandins are a good example of a *local hormone*.

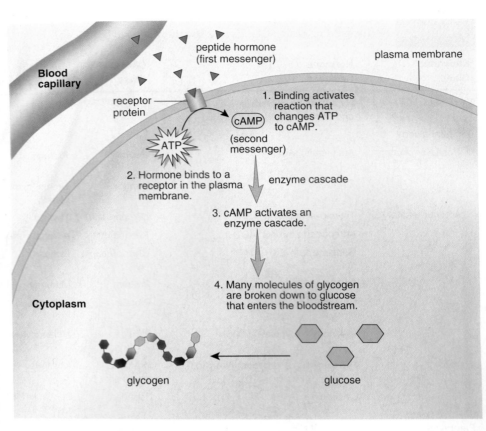

Figure 14.3   Peptide hormone.
A peptide hormone (first messenger) binds to a receptor in the plasma membrane. Thereaft...
cyclic AMP (second messenger) forms and activates an enzyme cascade.

1. Binding activates reaction that changes ATP to cAMP.
2. Hormone binds to a receptor in the plasma membrane.
3. cAMP activates an enzyme cascade.
4. Many molecules of glycogen are broken down to glucose that enters the bloodstream.

peptide hormone (first messenger)

plasma membrane

Blood capillary

receptor protein

cAMP (second messenger)

ATP

enzyme cascade

Cytoplasm

glycogen   glucose

After prostaglandins are produced, they are not carr...
bloodstream; instead, they affect neighboring c...
times promoting pain and inflammation. Also, g...
are local hormones that promote cell division ...
    Chemical signals that affect the metaboli...
the behavior of other individuals are c...
Pheromones are exemplified in other...
humans. Still, studies suggest that w...
odors of men who are immunologi...
selves. Choosing a mate of a diff...
ceivably improve the immune r...
studies indicate that axillary...
strual cycle. Women who l...
have menstrual cycles in ...
that a woman's axillar...
cycle by a few days.

The Action of ...

Hormones h...
these effect...
ticular su...
Some bring a...
in some way. ...
hormones can influe...

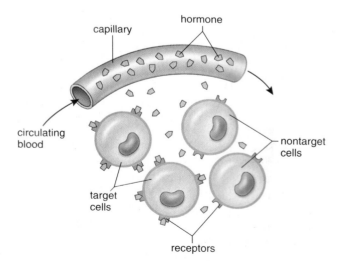

Figure 14.2   Target cell concept.
Most hormones are distributed by the bloodstream to target cells.
Target cells have receptors for the hormone, and the hormone
combines with the receptor as a key fits a lock.

hormone

capillary

circulating blood

nontarget cells

target cells

receptors

Pa...
Gonad...
Teste...
Ovaries
Thymus
Pineal gland

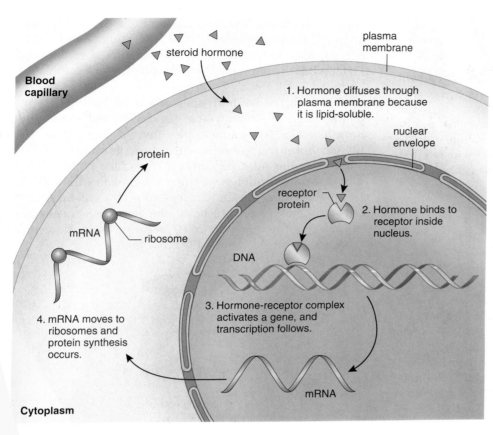

Blood capillary

steroid hormone

plasma membrane

1. Hormone diffuses through plasma membrane because it is lipid-soluble.

nuclear envelope

protein

receptor protein

mRNA — ribosome

2. Hormone binds to receptor inside nucleus.

DNA

3. Hormone-receptor complex activates a gene, and transcription follows.

4. mRNA moves to ribosomes and protein synthesis occurs.

mRNA

Cytoplasm

Figure 14.4 Steroid hormone.

A steroid hormone passes directly through the target cell's plasma membrane before binding to a receptor in the nucleus or cytoplasm. The hormone-receptor complex binds to DNA, and gene expression follows.

of a peptide hormone and the other typifies the action of a steroid hormone. The term **peptide hormone** is used to refer to hormones that are peptides, proteins, glycoproteins, or modified amino acids. **Steroid hormones** have the same type of four carbon rings because they are all derived from cholesterol (see Fig. 2.23).

Action of Peptide Hormones Most hormonal glands produce peptide hormones (see Table 14.2). The actions of these hormones can vary, and we will concentrate on their actions in muscle cells after the hormone epinephrine binds a receptor in the plasma membrane (Fig. 14.3). In muscle cells, the reception of epinephrine leads to the breakdown of glycogen to glucose, which ends up in the blood. The immediate result of binding is the formation of cyclic adenosine monophosphate (cAMP). Cyclic AMP has an extra phosphate group attached to adenosine at two locations. Therefore, the molecule is cyclic. Cyclic AMP activates a protein kinase enzyme in the cell, and this one, in turn, activates another enzyme, and so forth. The enzymatic reactions that follows cAMP is called an enzyme cascade. Because each enzyme acts over and over again at every step of the way, more enzymes are involved. Finally, many mol-

ecules of glucose glucose, which

Typical of hormone never en fore, the hormone is senger, while cAMP, metabolic machinery in the **second messenger.** To terminology, let's imagine that the nal medulla, which produces ep rine, is like the office that ser out a courier (i.e., the hormone epineph rine is the first messenger) to a factory (the cell). The courier doesn't have a pass to enter the factory when he arrives at the factory, he through the screen door the foreman office wants the factory to produce home ticular product. The foreman (in par the second messenger) walks oMP, flips a switch that starts the mac (the enzymatic pathway), and a pro is made.

The Action of Steroid Hormones The number of glands that produce steroid hormones is limited to the adrenal cortex, the ovaries, and the testes (see Table 14.2). Thyroid hormones act similarly to steroid hormones, even though they have a different structure.

Steroid hormones do not bind to plasma membrane receptors, and instead they are able to enter the cell because they are lipids (Fig. 14.4). Once inside, steroid hormones bind to receptors, usually in the nucleus but sometimes in the cytoplasm. Inside the nucleus, the hormone-receptor complex binds with DNA and activates transcription of certain genes. Translation of messenger RNA (mRNA) transcripts results in enzymes and other proteins that can carry out a response to the hormonal signal.

Steroids act more slowly than peptides because it takes more time to synthesize new proteins than to activate enzymes already present in cells. Their action lasts longer, however.

Hormones bind to receptor proteins in target cells. Peptide hormones (e.g., epinephrine) bind to a receptor in the plasma membrane and cause the formation of cAMP, which activates an enzyme cascade. Steroid hormones diffuse through the plasma membrane and enter the nucleus to bind with a receptor. The complex affects gene activity and protein synthesis.

Hypothalamus and Pituitary Gland

The **hypothalamus** regulates the internal environment through the autonomic system. For example, it helps control the heartbeat, body temperature, and water balance. The hypothalamus also controls the glandular secretions of the **pituitary gland.** The pituitary, a small gland about 1 cm in diameter, is connected to the hypothalamus by a stalk-like structure. The pituitary has two portions: the posterior and the anterior pituitary.

Posterior Pituitary

Neurons in the hypothalamus called neurosecretory cells produce hormones **antidiuretic hormone (ADH)** and oxytocin (Fig. 14.5, *left*). These hormones pass through axons into the **posterior pituitary** where they are stored in axon endings. Certain neurons in the hypothalamus are sensitive to the water-salt balance of the blood. When these cells determine that the blood is too concentrated, ADH is released from the posterior pituitary. Upon reaching the kidneys, ADH causes more water to be reabsorbed into kidney capillaries. As the blood becomes dilute, ADH is no longer released. This is an example of control by negative feedback because the effect of the hormone (to dilute blood) acts to shut down the release of the hormone. Negative feedback maintains stable conditions and homeostasis.

Inability to produce ADH causes diabetes insipidus (watery urine), in which a person produces copious amounts of urine with a resultant loss of ions from the blood. The condition can be corrected by the administration of ADH.

Oxytocin, the other hormone made in the hypothalamus, causes uterine contraction during childbirth and milk letdown when a baby is nursing. The more the uterus contracts during labor, the more nerve impulses reach the hypothalamus, causing oxytocin to be released. The sound of a baby crying may also stimulate the release of oxytocin. Similarly, the more a baby suckles, the more oxytocin is released. In both instances, the release of oxytocin from the posterior pituitary is controlled by **positive feedback**—that is, the stimulus continues to bring about an effect that ever increases in intensity. Positive feedback terminates due to some external event as when a baby is full and stops suckling. Positive feedback is not a way to maintain stable conditions and homeostasis.

Anterior Pituitary

A portal system, consisting of two capillary systems connected by a vein, lies between the hypothalamus and the **anterior pituitary** (Fig. 14.5, *right*). The hypothalamus controls the anterior pituitary by producing **hypothalamic-releasing** and **hypothalamic-inhibiting hormones.** For example, there is a thyroid-releasing hormone (TRH) and a thyroid-inhibiting hormone (TIH). TRH stimulates the anterior pituitary to secrete thyroid-stimulating hormone, and TIH inhibits the pituitary from secreting thyroid-stimulating hormone.

Three of the six hormones produced by the anterior pituitary have an effect on other glands: **Thyroid-stimulating hormone (TSH)** stimulates the thyroid to produce the thyroid hormones; **adrenocorticotropic hormone (ACTH)** stimulates the adrenal cortex to produce cortisol; and **gonadotropic hormones** stimulate the gonads—the testes in males and the ovaries in females—to produce gametes and sex hormones. In each instance, the blood level of the last hormone in the sequence exerts negative feedback control over the secretion of the first two hormones:

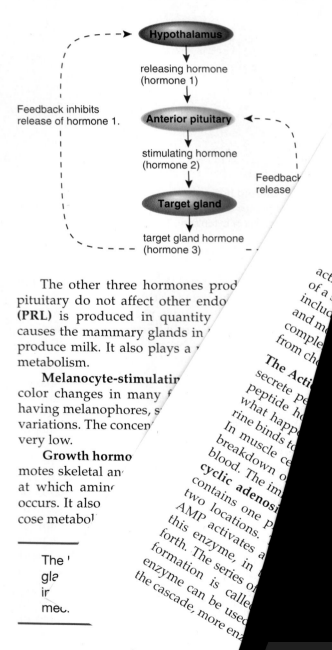

The other three hormones produced by the anterior pituitary do not affect other endocrine glands. Prolactin **(PRL)** is produced in quantity only after childbirth. It causes the mammary glands in the breasts to develop and produce milk. It also plays a role in carbohydrate and fat metabolism.

Melanocyte-stimulating hormone (MSH) causes color changes in many fishes, amphibians, and reptiles having melanophores, special skin cells that produce color variations. The concentration of this hormone in humans is very low.

Growth hormone (GH), or somatotropin, promotes skeletal and muscular growth. It increases the rate at which amino acids enter cells and protein synthesis occurs. It also promotes fat metabolism as opposed to glucose metabolism.

Visual Focus

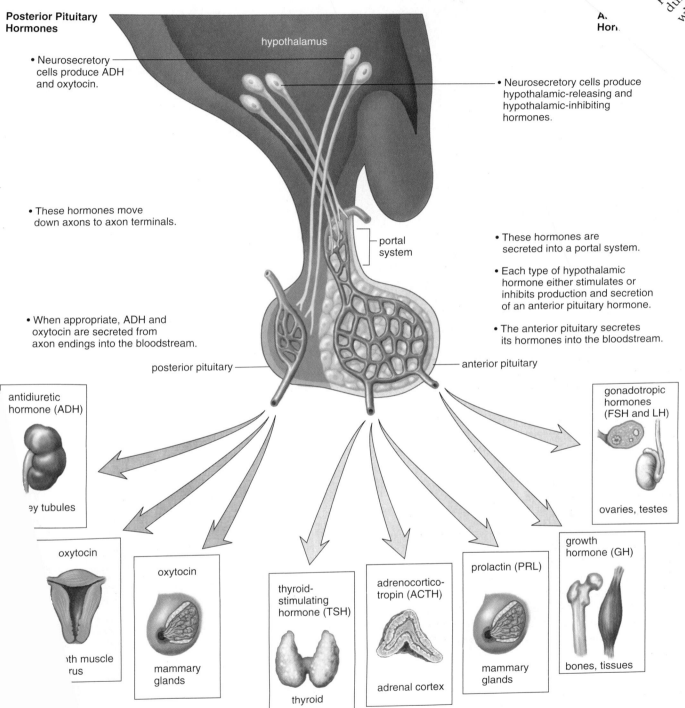

Posterior Pituitary Hormones

- Neurosecretory cells produce ADH and oxytocin.

- These hormones move down axons to axon terminals.

- When appropriate, ADH and oxytocin are secreted from axon endings into the bloodstream.

hypothalamus

- Neurosecretory cells produce hypothalamic-releasing and hypothalamic-inhibiting hormones.

portal system

- These hormones are secreted into a portal system.

- Each type of hypothalamic hormone either stimulates or inhibits production and secretion of an anterior pituitary hormone.

- The anterior pituitary secretes its hormones into the bloodstream.

posterior pituitary

anterior pituitary

antidiuretic hormone (ADH)

ey tubules

oxytocin

th muscle rus

oxytocin

mammary glands

thyroid-stimulating hormone (TSH)

thyroid

adrenocortico-tropin (ACTH)

adrenal cortex

prolactin (PRL)

mammary glands

gonadotropic hormones (FSH and LH)

ovaries, testes

growth hormone (GH)

bones, tissues

othalamus and the pituitary.

s produces two hormones, ADH and oxytocin, which are stored and secreted by the posterior pituitary. *Right:* The
the secretions of the anterior pituitary, and the anterior pituitary controls the secretions of the thyroid, adrenal cortex, and
ndocrine glands.

of Growth Hormone

produced by the anterior
ary. The quantity is greatest
g childhood and adolescence,
en most body growth is occur-
g (Fig. 14.6a). If too little GH is
produced during childhood, the
individual has **pituitary dwarfism,**
characterized by perfect proportions but small stature. If too much
GH is secreted, a person can become a giant (Fig. 14.6b). Giants
usually have poor health, primarily
because GH has a secondary effect
on the blood sugar level, promoting
an illness called diabetes mellitus
(see page 279).

On occasion, GH is overproduced in the adult, and a condition
called **acromegaly** results. Since
long bone growth is no longer possible in adults, only the feet, hands,
and face (particularly the chin, nose,
and eyebrow ridges) can respond,
and these portions of the body
become overly large (Fig. 14.7).

The amount of growth
hormone produced during
childhood affects the
height of an individual.

a.

b.

Figure 14.6   **Effect of growth hormone.**
a. The amount of growth hormone produced by the anterior pituitary during childh
height of an individual. Plentiful growth hormone produces very tall basketball pl
growth hormone can lead to gigantism, while an insufficient amount results in li
even pituitary dwarfism.

Age 9

Age 16

Age 33

Figure 14.7   **Acromegaly.**
Acromegaly is caused by overproduction of GH in the adult. It is characterized by enlarge
as a person ages.

ki

sm
in u

Figure 14.5   Hy
Left: The hypothalamu
hypothalamus controls
gonads, which are also

14.3 Thyroid and Parathyroid Glands

The **thyroid gland** is a large gland located in the neck, where it is attached to the trachea just below the larynx (see Fig. 14.1). The parathyroid glands are embedded in the posterior surface of the thyroid gland.

Thyroid Gland

The thyroid gland is composed of a large number of follicles, each a small spherical structure made of thyroid cells filled with triiodothyronine (T_3), which contains three iodine atoms, and **thyroxine (T_4),** which contains four.

Effects of Thyroid Hormones

To produce triiodothyronine and thyroxine, the thyroid gland actively acquires iodine. The concentration of iodine in the thyroid gland can increase to as much as 25 times that of the blood. If iodine is lacking in the diet, the thyroid gland is unable to produce the thyroid hormones. In response to constant stimulation by the anterior pituitary, the thyroid enlarges, resulting in a **simple goiter** (Fig. 14.8*a*). Some years ago, it was discovered that the use of iodized salt allows the thyroid to produce the thyroid hormones and, therefore, helps prevent simple goiter.

Thyroid hormones increase the metabolic rate. They do not have a target organ; instead, they stimulate all cells of

the body to metabolize at a fast[...] ken down, and more energy is ut[...]

If the thyroid fails to develop pro[...] **congenital hypothyroidism** results (F[...] with this condition are short and stock[...] treme hypothyroidism (undersecretion of [...] since infancy or childhood. Thyroid hormon[...] initiate growth, but unless treatment is begun wit[...] two months of life, mental retardation results. Th[...] rence of hypothyroidism in adult produces the con[...] known as **myxedema** (Fig. 14.8*c*), which is characterized [...] lethargy, weight gain, loss of hair, slow pulse rate, lowered body temperature, and thickness and finess of the skin. The administration of adequate doses of thyroid hormones restores normal function and appearance.

In the case of hyperthyroidism (oversec[...] hormone), or Graves disease, the thyroid gland of thyroid and a goiter forms. This type of goiter is called overactive, **goiter.** The eyes protrude because of edema in **thalmic** tissues and swelling of the muscles that move the socket patient usually becomes hyperactive, nervous and [...] The and suffers from insomnia. Removal or destructio[...] portion of the thyroid by means of radioactive iodi[...] sometimes effective in curing the condition. Hypert[...] roidism can also be caused by a thyroid tumor, which is usu[...] ally detected as a lump during physical examination. Again, the treatment is surgery in combination with administration of radioactive iodine. The prognosis for most patients is excellent.

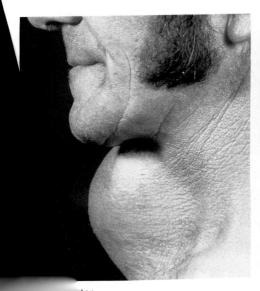

b. Congenital hypothyroidism

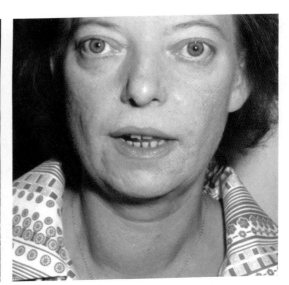

c. Exophthalmic goiter

3   Abnormalities of the thyroid.
[...]hyroid gland is often caused by a lack of iodine in the diet. Without iodine, the thyroid is unable to produce its hormones, and [...]r pituitary stimulation causes the gland to enlarge. **b.** Children with congenital hypothyroidism have hypothyroidism—that is, [...]rly childhood they do not grow or develop as others do. **c.** Adults with myxedema have muscle weakness, low body [...]ss, dry skin, and puffiness of the skin.

...nin

...m (Ca^{2+}) plays a significant role in both nervous con-
...on and muscle contraction. It is also necessary for
...d clotting. The blood Ca^{2+} level is regulated in part by
...citonin, a hormone secreted by the thyroid gland when
...e blood Ca^{2+} level rises (Fig. 14.9). The primary effect of
...alcitonin is to bring about the deposit of Ca^{2+} in the bones.
It does this by temporarily reducing the activity and number
of osteoclasts. When the blood Ca^{2+} level lowers to normal,
the release of calcitonin by the thyroid is inhibited, but a low
level stimulates the release of **parathyroid hormone (PTH)**
by the parathyroid glands.

Parathyroid Glands

Many years ago, the four parathyroid glands were sometimes mistakenly removed during thyroid surgery because
of their size and location. PTH, the hormone produced by
the **parathyroid glands,** causes the blood Ca^{2+} level to
increase.

A low blood Ca^{2+} level stimulates the release of PTH.
PTH promotes the activity of osteoclasts and the release of
calcium from the bones. PTH also promotes the reabsorption of calcium by the kidneys, where it activates vitamin D.
Activated vitamin D is a hormone sometimes called calcitriol, which stimulates the absorption of Ca^{2+} from the
intestine. These effects bring the blood
Ca^{2+} level back to the normal range so
that the parathyroid glands no longer
secrete PTH.

When insufficient PTH production
leads to a dramatic drop in the blood
calcium level, tetany results. In **tetany,**
the body shakes from continuous muscle contraction. This effect is brought
about by increased excitability of the
nerves, which initiate nerve impulses
spontaneously and without rest.

The antagonistic actions of
calcitonin from the thyroid
gland and PTH from the
parathyroid glands maintain
the blood calcium level within
normal limits.

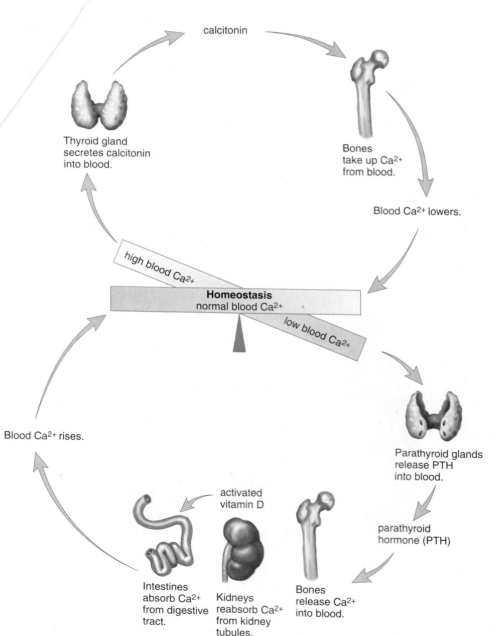

calcitonin

Thyroid gland
secretes calcitonin
into blood.

Bones
take up Ca^{2+}
from blood.

Blood Ca^{2+} lowers.

high blood Ca^{2+}

Homeostasis
normal blood Ca^{2+}

low blood Ca^{2+}

Blood Ca^{2+} rises.

activated
vitamin D

Intestines
absorb Ca^{2+}
from digestive
tract.

Kidneys
reabsorb Ca^{2+}
from kidney
tubules.

Bones
release Ca^{2+}
into blood.

Parathyroid glands
release PTH
into blood.

parathyroid
hormone (PTH)

Figure 14.9 P
calcium level.
Top: When the
high, the thyr
Calcitonin p
the bones
returns t
Ca^{2+} le
relea
cau
c

ret

a. Simple g

Figure 1
a. An enlarg
continued a
since infancy
temperature,

14.4 Adrenal Glands

The **adrenal glands** sit atop the kidneys (see Fig. 14.1). Each adrenal gland consists of an inner portion called the **adrenal medulla** and an outer portion called the **adrenal cortex.** These portions, like the anterior and the posterior pituitary, are two functionally distinct endocrine glands. The adrenal medulla is under nervous control, and portions of the adrenal cortex are under the control of ACTH, an anterior pituitary hormone. Stress of all types, including emotional and physical trauma, prompts the hypothalamus to stimulate a portion of the adrenal glands (Fig. 14.10).

Adrenal Medulla

The hypothalamus initiates nerve impulses that travel by way of the brainstem, spinal cord, and sympathetic nerve fibers to the adrenal medulla, which then secretes its hormones.

Epinephrine (adrenaline) and **norepinephrine** (noradrenaline) produced by the adrenal medulla rapidly bring about all the body changes that occur when an individual reacts to an emergency situation. The effect of these hormones prov... to stress.

Adrenal Cortex

In contrast, the hormones produced by the a... provide a long-term response... stress (Fig. 14.1... major types of hormones produced by the adrenal c... the mineralocorticoids and the glucocorticoids. The m... **alocorticoids** regulate salt and water balance, leading ... increases in blood volume and blood pressure. The **gluco-corticoids,** under the control of ACTH, ...ulate carbohydrate, protein, and fat metabolism, leading to ...increase in blood glucose level. Glucocorticoids also su...ss the body's inflammatory response. Cortisone, the ...ication often administered for inflammation of joints, is a ...ocorticoid.

The adrenal cortex also secretes a small a...st of male sex hormones and a small amount of female s...mones in both sexes. That is, in both males and females ...male and female sex hormones are produced by the ...nal cortex.

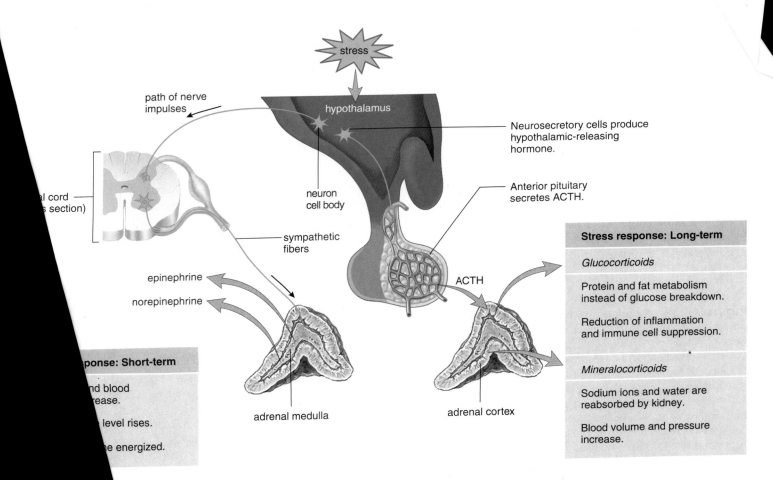

The adrenal glands and stress.
...dulla and the adrenal cortex are under the control of the hypothalamus when they help us respond to stress. *Left:* The
...des a rapid, but short-term, stress response. *Right:* The adrenal cortex provides a slower, but long-term, stress response.

corticoids

stimulates a portion of the adrenal cortex to secrete the
corticoids. **Cortisol** and also cortisone are biologically
ificant glucocorticoids. Glucocorticoids raise the blood
ucose level in at least two ways: (1) They promote the
breakdown of muscle proteins to amino acids, which are
taken up by the liver from the bloodstream. The liver then
breaks down these excess amino acids to glucose, which enters the blood. (2) They promote the metabolism of fatty
acids rather than carbohydrates, and this spares glucose.

The glucocorticoids also counteract the inflammatory response that leads to the pain and swelling of joints in arthritis
and bursitis. The administration of cortisone aids these conditions because it reduces inflammation. Very high levels of
glucocorticoids in the blood can suppress the body's defense system, including the inflamma-
tory response that occurs at infection
sites. Cortisone and other glucocorticoids
relieve swelling and pain from inflammation, but by suppressing pain and
immunity, they can also make a person
highly susceptible to injury and infection.

Mineralocorticoids

Aldosterone is the most important of the
mineralocorticoids. The aldosterone primarily targets the kidney, where it promotes renal absorption of sodium (Na^+)
and renal excretion of potassium (K^+).

The secretion of mineralocorticoids
is not controlled by the anterior pituitary. When the blood Na^+ level and
therefore the blood pressure are low, the
kidneys secrete **renin** (Fig. 14.11). Renin
is an enzyme that converts the plasma
protein angiotensinogen to angiotensin
I, which is changed to angiotensin II by
a converting enzyme found in lung

capillaries. Angiotensin II stimulates the adrenal cortex to
release aldosterone. The effect of this system, called the
renin-angiotensin-aldosterone system, is to raise blood pressure in two ways: Angiotensin II constricts the arterioles,
and aldosterone causes the kidneys to reabsorb Na^+. When
the blood Na^+ level rises, water is reabsorbed, in part, because the hypothalamus secretes ADH (see page 270). Reabsorption means that water enters kidney capillaries and thus
the blood. Then blood pressure increases to normal.

When the atria of the heart are stretched due to a great
increase in blood volume, cardiac cells release a hormone
called **atrial natriuretic hormone (ANH),** which inhibits the
secretion of aldosterone from the adrenal cortex. The effect
of this hormone is to cause the excretion of Na^+—that is,
natriuresis. When Na^+ is excreted, so is water, and therefore
blood pressure lowers to normal.

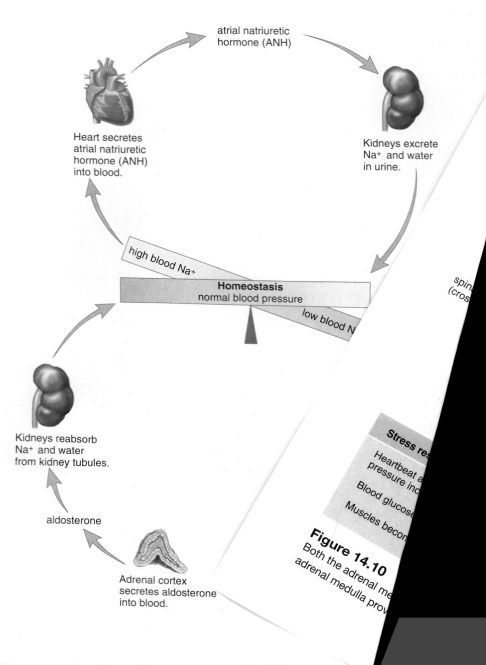

**Figure 14.11   Regulation of blood
pressure and volume.**

Bottom: When the blood sodium (Na^+) level is
low, a low blood pressure causes the kidneys
to secrete renin. Renin leads to the secretion
of aldosterone from the adrenal cortex.
Aldosterone causes the kidneys to reabsorb
Na^+, and water follows, so that blood volume
and pressure return to normal. *Top:* When a
high blood Na^+ level accompanies a high
blood volume, the heart secretes atrial
natriuretic hormone (ANH). ANH causes the
kidneys to excrete Na^+, and water follows. The
blood volume and pressure return to normal.

Table 14.2	Principal Endocrine Glands and Hormones			
Endocrine Gland	Hormone Released	Chemical Class	Target Tissues/Organs	Chief Function(s) of Hormone
Hypothalamus	Hypothalamic-releasing and -inhibiting hormones	Peptide	Anterior pituitary	Regulate anterior pituitary hormones
Pituitary gland				
Posterior pituitary	Antidiuretic (ADH)	Peptide	Kidneys	Stimulates water reabsorption by kidneys
	Oxytocin	Peptide	Uterus, mammary glands	Stimulates uterine muscle contraction; release of milk by mammary glands
Anterior pituitary	Thyroid-stimulating (TSH)	Glycoprotein	Thyroid	Stimulates thyroid
	Adrenocorticotropic (ACTH)	Peptide	Adrenal cortex	Stimulates adrenal cortex
	Gonadotropic (FSH, LH)	Glycoprotein	Gonads	Egg and sperm production; sex hormone production
	Prolactin (PRL)	Protein	Mammary glands	Milk production
	Growth (GH)	Protein	Soft tissues, bones	Cell division, protein synthesis, and bone growth
	Melanocyte-stimulating (MSH)	Peptide	Melanocytes in skin	Unknown function in humans; regulates skin color in lower vertebrates
Thyroid	Thyroxine (T_4) and triiodothyronine (T_3)	Iodinated amino acid	All tissues	Increases metabolic rate; regulates growth and development
	Calcitonin	Peptide	Bones, kidneys, intestine	Lowers blood calcium level
Parathyroids	Parathyroid (PTH)	Peptide	Bones, kidneys, intestine	Raises blood calcium level
Adrenal gland				
Adrenal cortex	Glucocorticoids (cortisol)	Steroid	All tissues	Raise blood glucose level; stimulate breakdown of protein
	Mineralocorticoids (aldosterone)	Steroid	Kidneys	Reabsorb sodium and excrete potassium
	Sex hormones	Steroid	Gonads, skin, muscles, bones	Stimulate reproductive organs and bring about sex characteristics
Adrenal medulla	Epinephrine and norepinephrine	Modified amino acid	Cardiac and other muscles	Released in emergency situations; raise blood glucose level
Pancreas	Insulin	Protein	Liver, muscles, adipose tissue	Lowers blood glucose level; promotes formation of glycogen
	Glucagon	Protein	Liver, muscles, adipose tissue	Raises blood glucose level
Gonads				
Testes	Androgens (testosterone)	Steroid	Gonads, skin, muscles, bones	Stimulate male sex characteristics
Ovaries	Estrogens and progesterone	Steroid	Gonads, skin, muscles, bones	Stimulate female sex characteristics
Thymus	Thymosins	Peptide	T lymphocytes	Stimulate production and maturation of T lymphocytes
Pineal gland	Melatonin	Modified amino acid	Brain	Controls circadian and circannual rhythms; possibly involved in maturation of sexual organs

Hormones Are Chemical Signals

Hormones are a type of chemical signal. **Chemical signals** are a means of communication between cells, between body parts, and even between individuals. They typically affect the metabolism of cells that have receptors to receive them (Fig. 14.2). In a condition called androgen insensitivity, an individual has X and Y sex chromosomes and the testes, which remain in the abdominal cavity, produce the sex hormone testosterone. However, the body cells lack receptors that are able to combine with testosterone and the individual appears to be a normal female.

Like testosterone, most hormones act at a distance between body parts. They travel in the bloodstream from the gland that produced them to their target cells. Also counted as hormones are the secretions produced by neurosecretory cells in the hypothalamus, a part of the brain. They travel in the capillary network that runs between the hypothalamus and the pituitary gland. Some of these secretions stimulate the pituitary to secrete its hormones, and others prevent it from doing so.

Not all hormones act between body parts. As we shall see, prostaglandins are a good example of a *local hormone*.

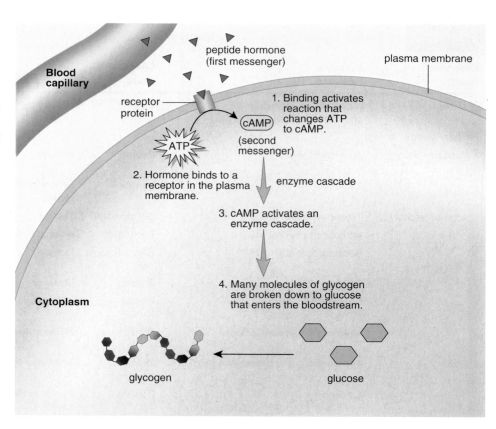

Figure 14.3   Peptide hormone.
A peptide hormone (first messenger) binds to a receptor in the plasma membrane. Thereafter, cyclic AMP (second messenger) forms and activates an enzyme cascade.

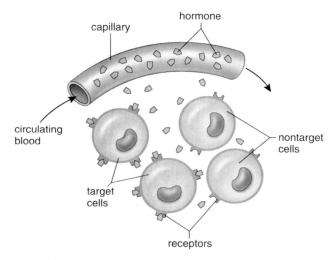

Figure 14.2   Target cell concept.
Most hormones are distributed by the bloodstream to target cells. Target cells have receptors for the hormone, and the hormone combines with the receptor as a key fits a lock.

After prostaglandins are produced, they are not carried in the bloodstream; instead, they affect neighboring cells, sometimes promoting pain and inflammation. Also, growth factors are local hormones that promote cell division and mitosis.

Chemical signals that affect the metabolism and influence the behavior of other individuals are called **pheromones.** Pheromones are exemplified in other animals but not in humans. Still, studies suggest that women prefer the armpit odors of men who are immunologically different from themselves. Choosing a mate of a different HLA type could conceivably improve the immune response of offspring. Several studies indicate that axillary secretions can affect the menstrual cycle. Women who live in the same household often have menstrual cycles in synchrony. Researchers have found that a woman's axillary extract can alter another woman's cycle by a few days.

The Action of Hormones

Hormones have a wide range of effects on cells. Some of these effects induce a target cell to increase its uptake of particular substances, such as glucose, or ions, such as calcium. Some bring about an alteration of the target cell's structure in some way. Here, we will concentrate on two ways hormones can influence cell metabolism. One typifies the ecules of glycogen are broken down to glucose, which enters the bloodstream.

Typical of epinephrine, a peptide hormone never enters the cell. Therefore, the hormone is called the **first messenger,** while cAMP, which sets the metabolic machinery in motion, is called the **second messenger.** To explain this terminology, let's imagine that the adrenal medulla, which produces epinephrine, is like the home office that sends out a courier (i.e., the hormone epinephrine is the first messenger) to a factory (the cell). The courier doesn't have a pass to enter the factory, so when he arrives at the factory, he tells a foreman through the screen door that the home office wants the factory to produce a particular product. The foreman (i.e., cAMP, the second messenger) walks over and flips a switch that starts the machinery (the enzymatic pathway), and a product is made.

The Action of Steroid Hormones   The number of glands that produce steroid hormones is limited to the adrenal cortex, the ovaries, and the testes (see Table 14.2). Thyroid hormones act similarly to steroid hormones, even though they have a different structure.

Steroid hormones do not bind to plasma membrane receptors, and instead they are able to enter the cell because they are lipids (Fig. 14.4). Once inside, steroid hormones bind to receptors, usually in the nucleus but sometimes in the cytoplasm. Inside the nucleus, the hormone-receptor complex binds with DNA and activates transcription of certain genes. Translation of messenger RNA (mRNA) transcripts results in enzymes and other proteins that can carry out a response to the hormonal signal.

Steroids act more slowly than peptides because it takes more time to synthesize new proteins than to activate enzymes already present in cells. Their action lasts longer, however.

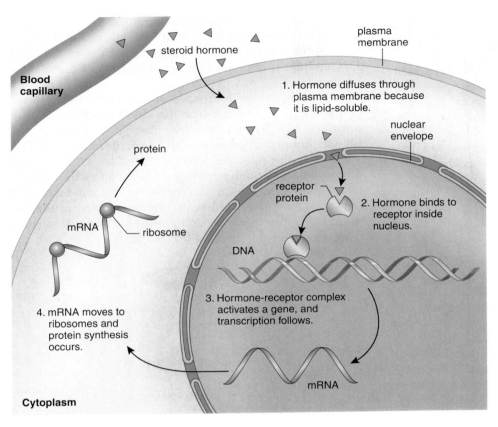

Figure 14.4   Steroid hormone.
A steroid hormone passes directly through the target cell's plasma membrane before binding to a receptor in the nucleus or cytoplasm. The hormone-receptor complex binds to DNA, and gene expression follows.

action of a peptide hormone and the other typifies the action of a steroid hormone. The term **peptide hormone** is used to include hormones that are peptides, proteins, glycoproteins, and modified amino acids. **Steroid hormones** have the same complex of four carbon rings because they are all derived from cholesterol (see Fig. 2.23).

The Action of Peptide Hormones   Most hormonal glands secrete peptide hormones (see Table 14.2). The actions of peptide hormones can vary, and we will concentrate on what happens in muscle cells after the hormone epinephrine binds to a receptor in the plasma membrane (Fig. 14.3). In muscle cells, the reception of epinephrine leads to the breakdown of glycogen to glucose, which ends up in the blood. The immediate result of binding is the formation of **cyclic adenosine monophosphate (cAMP).** Cyclic AMP contains one phosphate group attached to adenosine at two locations. Therefore, the molecule is cyclic. Cyclic AMP activates a protein kinase enzyme in the cell, and this enzyme, in turn, activates another enzyme, and so forth. The series of enzymatic reactions that follows cAMP formation is called an enzyme cascade. Because each enzyme can be used over and over again at every step of the cascade, more enzymes are involved. Finally, many mol-

---

Hormones bind to receptor proteins in target cells. Peptide hormones (e.g., epinephrine) bind to a receptor in the plasma membrane and cause the formation of cAMP, which activates an enzyme cascade. Steroid hormones diffuse through the plasma membrane and enter the nucleus to bind with a receptor. The complex affects gene activity and protein synthesis.

14.2 Hypothalamus and Pituitary Gland

The **hypothalamus** regulates the internal environment through the autonomic system. For example, it helps control heartbeat, body temperature, and water balance. The hypothalamus also controls the glandular secretions of the **pituitary gland.** The pituitary, a small gland about 1 cm in diameter, is connected to the hypothalamus by a stalk-like structure. The pituitary has two portions: the posterior and the anterior pituitary.

Posterior Pituitary

Neurons in the hypothalamus called neurosecretory cells produce the hormones **antidiuretic hormone (ADH)** and oxytocin (Fig. 14.5, *left*). These hormones pass through axons into the **posterior pituitary** where they are stored in axon endings. Certain neurons in the hypothalamus are sensitive to the water-salt balance of the blood. When these cells determine that the blood is too concentrated, ADH is released from the posterior pituitary. Upon reaching the kidneys, ADH causes more water to be reabsorbed into kidney capillaries. As the blood becomes dilute, ADH is no longer released. This is an example of control by negative feedback because the effect of the hormone (to dilute blood) acts to shut down the release of the hormone. Negative feedback maintains stable conditions and homeostasis.

Inability to produce ADH causes diabetes insipidus (watery urine), in which a person produces copious amounts of urine with a resultant loss of ions from the blood. The condition can be corrected by the administration of ADH.

Oxytocin, the other hormone made in the hypothalamus, causes uterine contraction during childbirth and milk letdown when a baby is nursing. The more the uterus contracts during labor, the more nerve impulses reach the hypothalamus, causing oxytocin to be released. The sound of a baby crying may also stimulate the release of oxytocin. Similarly, the more a baby suckles, the more oxytocin is released. In both instances, the release of oxytocin from the posterior pituitary is controlled by **positive feedback**—that is, the stimulus continues to bring about an effect that ever increases in intensity. Positive feedback terminates due to some external event as when a baby is full and stops suckling. Positive feedback is not a way to maintain stable conditions and homeostasis.

Anterior Pituitary

A portal system, consisting of two capillary systems connected by a vein, lies between the hypothalamus and the **anterior pituitary** (Fig. 14.5, *right*). The hypothalamus controls the anterior pituitary by producing **hypothalamic-releasing** and **hypothalamic-inhibiting hormones.** For example, there is a thyroid-releasing hormone (TRH) and a thyroid-inhibiting hormone (TIH). TRH stimulates the anterior pituitary to secrete thyroid-stimulating hormone, and TIH inhibits the pituitary from secreting thyroid-stimulating hormone.

Three of the six hormones produced by the anterior pituitary have an effect on other glands: **Thyroid-stimulating hormone (TSH)** stimulates the thyroid to produce the thyroid hormones; **adrenocorticotropic hormone (ACTH)** stimulates the adrenal cortex to produce cortisol; and **gonadotropic hormones** stimulate the gonads—the testes in males and the ovaries in females—to produce gametes and sex hormones. In each instance, the blood level of the last hormone in the sequence exerts negative feedback control over the secretion of the first two hormones:

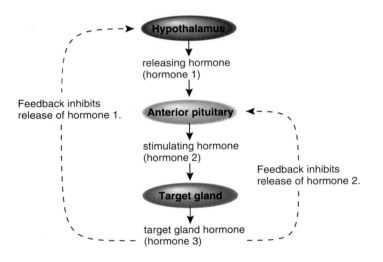

The other three hormones produced by the anterior pituitary do not affect other endocrine glands. **Prolactin (PRL)** is produced in quantity only after childbirth. It causes the mammary glands in the breasts to develop and produce milk. It also plays a role in carbohydrate and fat metabolism.

Melanocyte-stimulating hormone (MSH) causes skin-color changes in many fishes, amphibians, and reptiles having melanophores, special skin cells that produce color variations. The concentration of this hormone in humans is very low.

Growth hormone (GH), or somatotropic hormone, promotes skeletal and muscular growth. It stimulates the rate at which amino acids enter cells and protein synthesis occurs. It also promotes fat metabolism as opposed to glucose metabolism.

The hypothalamus, the anterior pituitary, and other glands controlled by the anterior pituitary are all involved in self-regulating negative feedback mechanisms that maintain stable conditions.

Visual Focus

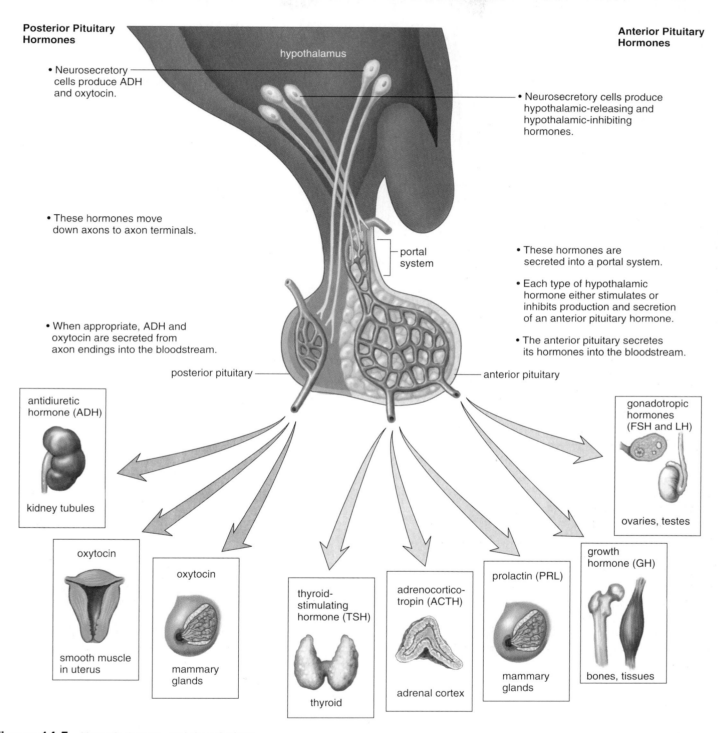

Posterior Pituitary Hormones

- Neurosecretory cells produce ADH and oxytocin.

- These hormones move down axons to axon terminals.

- When appropriate, ADH and oxytocin are secreted from axon endings into the bloodstream.

hypothalamus

portal system

posterior pituitary

anterior pituitary

Anterior Pituitary Hormones

- Neurosecretory cells produce hypothalamic-releasing and hypothalamic-inhibiting hormones.

- These hormones are secreted into a portal system.

- Each type of hypothalamic hormone either stimulates or inhibits production and secretion of an anterior pituitary hormone.

- The anterior pituitary secretes its hormones into the bloodstream.

antidiuretic hormone (ADH)

kidney tubules

oxytocin

smooth muscle in uterus

oxytocin

mammary glands

thyroid-stimulating hormone (TSH)

thyroid

adrenocortico-tropin (ACTH)

adrenal cortex

prolactin (PRL)

mammary glands

gonadotropic hormones (FSH and LH)

ovaries, testes

growth hormone (GH)

bones, tissues

Figure 14.5 Hypothalamus and the pituitary.
Left: The hypothalamus produces two hormones, ADH and oxytocin, which are stored and secreted by the posterior pituitary. *Right:* The hypothalamus controls the secretions of the anterior pituitary, and the anterior pituitary controls the secretions of the thyroid, adrenal cortex, and gonads, which are also endocrine glands.

271

Effects of Growth Hormone

GH is produced by the anterior pituitary. The quantity is greatest during childhood and adolescence, when most body growth is occurring (Fig. 14.6*a*). If too little GH is produced during childhood, the individual has **pituitary dwarfism,** characterized by perfect proportions but small stature. If too much GH is secreted, a person can become a giant (Fig. 14.6*b*). Giants usually have poor health, primarily because GH has a secondary effect on the blood sugar level, promoting an illness called diabetes mellitus (see page 279).

On occasion, GH is overproduced in the adult, and a condition called **acromegaly** results. Since long bone growth is no longer possible in adults, only the feet, hands, and face (particularly the chin, nose, and eyebrow ridges) can respond, and these portions of the body become overly large (Fig. 14.7).

The amount of growth hormone produced during childhood affects the height of an individual.

a.   b.

Figure 14.6   Effect of growth hormone.
a. The amount of growth hormone produced by the anterior pituitary during childhood affects the height of an individual. Plentiful growth hormone produces very tall basketball players. **b.** Too much growth hormone can lead to gigantism, while an insufficient amount results in limited stature and even pituitary dwarfism.

Age 9   Age 16   Age 33   Age 52

Figure 14.7   Acromegaly.
Acromegaly is caused by overproduction of GH in the adult. It is characterized by enlargement of the bones in the face, the fingers, and the toes as a person ages.

14.3 Thyroid and Parathyroid Glands

The **thyroid gland** is a large gland located in the neck, where it is attached to the trachea just below the larynx (see Fig. 14.1). The parathyroid glands are embedded in the posterior surface of the thyroid gland.

Thyroid Gland

The thyroid gland is composed of a large number of follicles, each a small spherical structure made of thyroid cells filled with triiodothyronine (T_3), which contains three iodine atoms, and **thyroxine (T_4),** which contains four.

Effects of Thyroid Hormones

To produce triiodothyronine and thyroxine, the thyroid gland actively acquires iodine. The concentration of iodine in the thyroid gland can increase to as much as 25 times that of the blood. If iodine is lacking in the diet, the thyroid gland is unable to produce the thyroid hormones. In response to constant stimulation by the anterior pituitary, the thyroid enlarges, resulting in a **simple goiter** (Fig. 14.8a). Some years ago, it was discovered that the use of iodized salt allows the thyroid to produce the thyroid hormones and, therefore, helps prevent simple goiter.

Thyroid hormones increase the metabolic rate. They do not have a target organ; instead, they stimulate all cells of the body to metabolize at a faster rate. More glucose is broken down, and more energy is utilized.

If the thyroid fails to develop properly, a condition called **congenital hypothyroidism** results (Fig. 14.8b). Individuals with this condition are short and stocky and have had extreme hypothyroidism (undersecretion of thyroid hormone) since infancy or childhood. Thyroid hormone therapy can initiate growth, but unless treatment is begun within the first two months of life, mental retardation results. The occurrence of hypothyroidism in adults produces the condition known as **myxedema** (Fig. 14.8c), which is characterized by lethargy, weight gain, loss of hair, slower pulse rate, lowered body temperature, and thickness and puffiness of the skin. The administration of adequate doses of thyroid hormones restores normal function and appearance.

In the case of hyperthyroidism (oversecretion of thyroid hormone), or Graves disease, the thyroid gland is overactive, and a goiter forms. This type of goiter is called **exophthalmic goiter.** The eyes protrude because of edema in eye socket tissues and swelling of the muscles that move the eyes. The patient usually becomes hyperactive, nervous and irritable, and suffers from insomnia. Removal or destruction of a portion of the thyroid by means of radioactive iodine is sometimes effective in curing the condition. Hyperthyroidism can also be caused by a thyroid tumor, which is usually detected as a lump during physical examination. Again, the treatment is surgery in combination with administration of radioactive iodine. The prognosis for most patients is excellent.

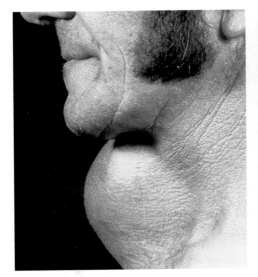

a. Simple goiter

b. Congenital hypothyroidism

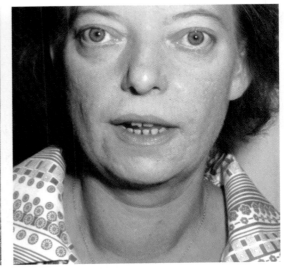

c. Exophthalmic goiter

Figure 14.8   Abnormalities of the thyroid.
a. An enlarged thyroid gland is often caused by a lack of iodine in the diet. Without iodine, the thyroid is unable to produce its hormones, and continued anterior pituitary stimulation causes the gland to enlarge. **b.** Children with congenital hypothyroidism have hypothyroidism—that is, since infancy or early childhood they do not grow or develop as others do. **c.** Adults with myxedema have muscle weakness, low body temperature, hair loss, dry skin, and puffiness of the skin.

Calcitonin

Calcium (Ca^{2+}) plays a significant role in both nervous conduction and muscle contraction. It is also necessary for blood clotting. The blood Ca^{2+} level is regulated in part by **calcitonin,** a hormone secreted by the thyroid gland when the blood Ca^{2+} level rises (Fig. 14.9). The primary effect of calcitonin is to bring about the deposit of Ca^{2+} in the bones. It does this by temporarily reducing the activity and number of osteoclasts. When the blood Ca^{2+} level lowers to normal, the release of calcitonin by the thyroid is inhibited, but a low level stimulates the release of **parathyroid hormone (PTH)** by the parathyroid glands.

Parathyroid Glands

Many years ago, the four parathyroid glands were sometimes mistakenly removed during thyroid surgery because of their size and location. PTH, the hormone produced by the **parathyroid glands,** causes the blood Ca^{2+} level to increase.

A low blood Ca^{2+} level stimulates the release of PTH. PTH promotes the activity of osteoclasts and the release of calcium from the bones. PTH also promotes the reabsorption of calcium by the kidneys, where it activates vitamin D. Activated vitamin D is a hormone sometimes called calcitriol, which stimulates the absorption of Ca^{2+} from the intestine. These effects bring the blood Ca^{2+} level back to the normal range so that the parathyroid glands no longer secrete PTH.

When insufficient PTH production leads to a dramatic drop in the blood calcium level, tetany results. In **tetany,** the body shakes from continuous muscle contraction. This effect is brought about by increased excitability of the nerves, which initiate nerve impulses spontaneously and without rest.

> The antagonistic actions of calcitonin from the thyroid gland and PTH from the parathyroid glands maintain the blood calcium level within normal limits.

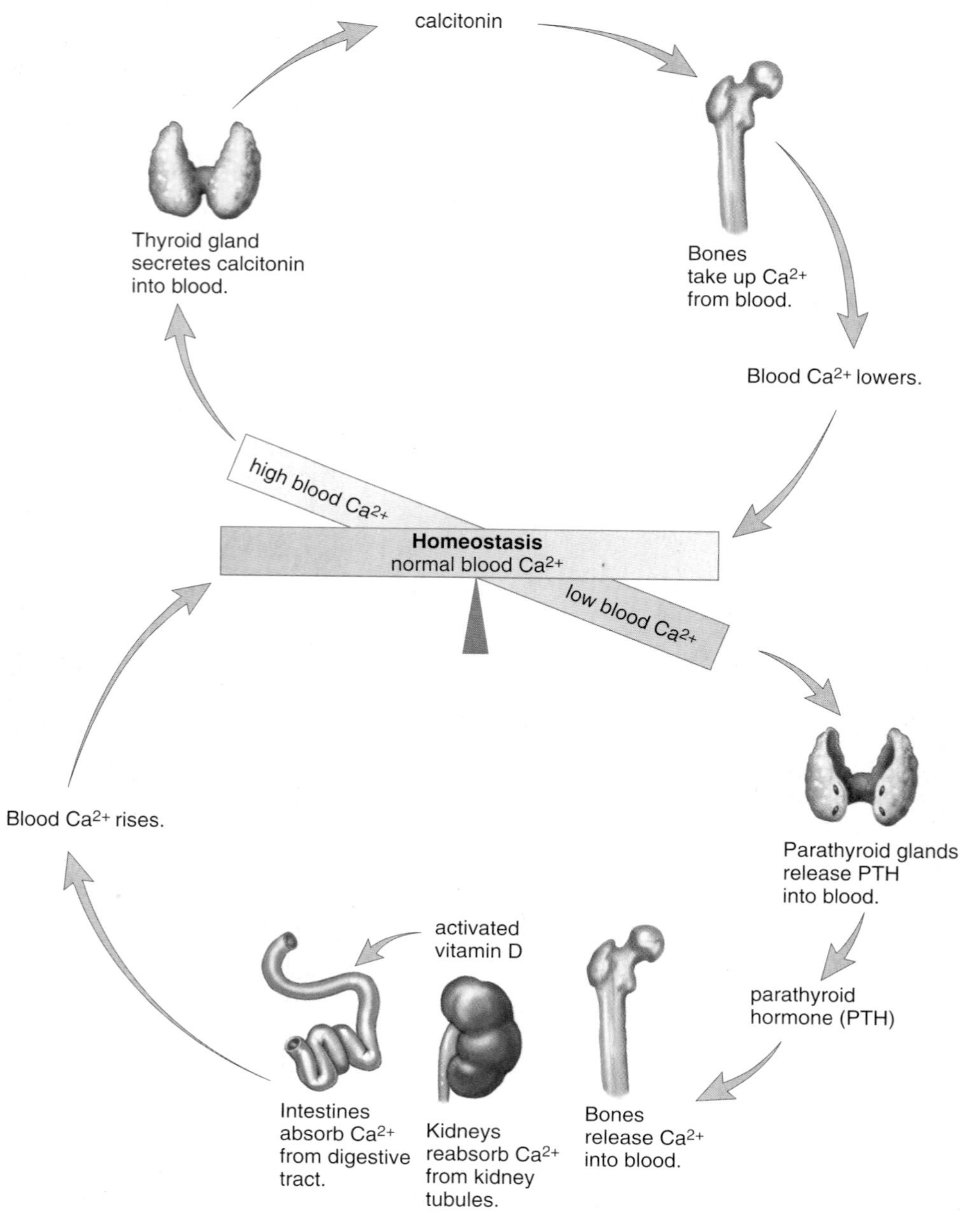

calcitonin

Thyroid gland secretes calcitonin into blood.

Bones take up Ca^{2+} from blood.

Blood Ca^{2+} lowers.

high blood Ca^{2+}

Homeostasis normal blood Ca^{2+}

low blood Ca^{2+}

Blood Ca^{2+} rises.

activated vitamin D

Intestines absorb Ca^{2+} from digestive tract.

Kidneys reabsorb Ca^{2+} from kidney tubules.

Bones release Ca^{2+} into blood.

Parathyroid glands release PTH into blood.

parathyroid hormone (PTH)

Figure 14.9 **Regulation of blood calcium level.**
Top: When the blood calcium (Ca^{2+}) level is high, the thyroid gland secretes calcitonin. Calcitonin promotes the uptake of Ca^{2+} by the bones, and therefore the blood Ca^{2+} level returns to normal. *Bottom:* When the blood Ca^{2+} level is low, the parathyroid glands release parathyroid hormone (PTH). PTH causes the bones to release Ca^{2+}. It also causes the kidneys to reabsorb Ca^{2+} and activate vitamin D; thereafter, the intestines absorb Ca^{2+}. Therefore, the blood Ca^{2+} level returns to normal.

14.4 Adrenal Glands

The **adrenal glands** sit atop the kidneys (see Fig. 14.1). Each adrenal gland consists of an inner portion called the **adrenal medulla** and an outer portion called the **adrenal cortex.** These portions, like the anterior and the posterior pituitary, are two functionally distinct endocrine glands. The adrenal medulla is under nervous control, and portions of the adrenal cortex are under the control of ACTH, an anterior pituitary hormone. Stress of all types, including emotional and physical trauma, prompts the hypothalamus to stimulate a portion of the adrenal glands (Fig. 14.10).

Adrenal Medulla

The hypothalamus initiates nerve impulses that travel by way of the brainstem, spinal cord, and sympathetic nerve fibers to the adrenal medulla, which then secretes its hormones.

Epinephrine (adrenaline) and **norepinephrine** (noradrenaline) produced by the adrenal medulla rapidly bring about all the body changes that occur when an individual reacts to an emergency situation in a fight-or-flight manner. The effect of these hormones provide a short-term response to stress.

Adrenal Cortex

In contrast, the hormones produced by the adrenal cortex provide a long-term response to stress (Fig. 14.10). The two major types of hormones produced by the adrenal cortex are the mineralocorticoids and the glucocorticoids. The **mineralocorticoids** regulate salt and water balance, leading to increases in blood volume and blood pressure. The **glucocorticoids,** under the control of ACTH, regulate carbohydrate, protein, and fat metabolism, leading to an increase in blood glucose level. Glucocorticoids also suppress the body's inflammatory response. Cortisone, the medication often administered for inflammation of joints, is a glucocorticoid.

The adrenal cortex also secretes a small amount of male sex hormones and a small amount of female sex hormones in both sexes. That is, in both males and females, both male and female sex hormones are produced by the adrenal cortex.

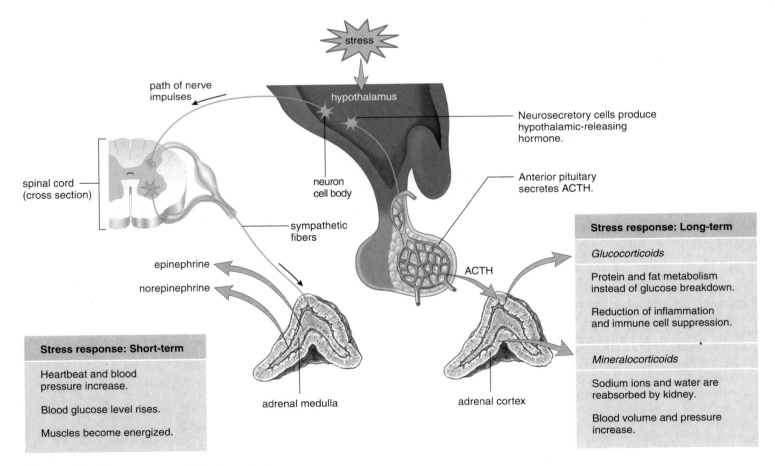

Figure 14.10   The adrenal glands and stress.
Both the adrenal medulla and the adrenal cortex are under the control of the hypothalamus when they help us respond to stress. *Left:* The adrenal medulla provides a rapid, but short-term, stress response. *Right:* The adrenal cortex provides a slower, but long-term, stress response.

Glucocorticoids

ACTH stimulates a portion of the adrenal cortex to secrete the glucocorticoids. **Cortisol** and also cortisone are biologically significant glucocorticoids. Glucocorticoids raise the blood glucose level in at least two ways: (1) They promote the breakdown of muscle proteins to amino acids, which are taken up by the liver from the bloodstream. The liver then breaks down these excess amino acids to glucose, which enters the blood. (2) They promote the metabolism of fatty acids rather than carbohydrates, and this spares glucose.

The glucorticoids also counteract the inflammatory response that leads to the pain and swelling of joints in arthritis and bursitis. The administration of cortisone aids these conditions because it reduces inflammation. Very high levels of glucocorticoids in the blood can suppress the body's defense system, including the inflammatory response that occurs at infection sites. Cortisone and other glucocorticoids can relieve swelling and pain from inflammation, but by suppressing pain and immunity, they can also make a person highly susceptible to injury and infection.

Mineralocorticoids

Aldosterone is the most important of the mineralocorticoids. The aldosterone primarily targets the kidney, where it promotes renal absorption of sodium (Na^+) and renal excretion of potassium (K^+).

The secretion of mineralocorticoids is not controlled by the anterior pituitary. When the blood Na^+ level and therefore the blood pressure are low, the kidneys secrete **renin** (Fig. 14.11). Renin is an enzyme that converts the plasma protein angiotensinogen to angiotensin I, which is changed to angiotensin II by a converting enzyme found in lung capillaries. Angiotensin II stimulates the adrenal cortex to release aldosterone. The effect of this system, called the renin-angiotensin-aldosterone system, is to raise blood pressure in two ways: Angiotensin II constricts the arterioles, and aldosterone causes the kidneys to reabsorb Na^+. When the blood Na^+ level rises, water is reabsorbed, in part, because the hypothalamus secretes ADH (see page 270). Reabsorption means that water enters kidney capillaries and thus the blood. Then blood pressure increases to normal.

When the atria of the heart are stretched due to a great increase in blood volume, cardiac cells release a hormone called **atrial natriuretic hormone (ANH),** which inhibits the secretion of aldosterone from the adrenal cortex. The effect of this hormone is to cause the excretion of Na^+—that is, *natriuresis*. When Na^+ is excreted, so is water, and therefore blood pressure lowers to normal.

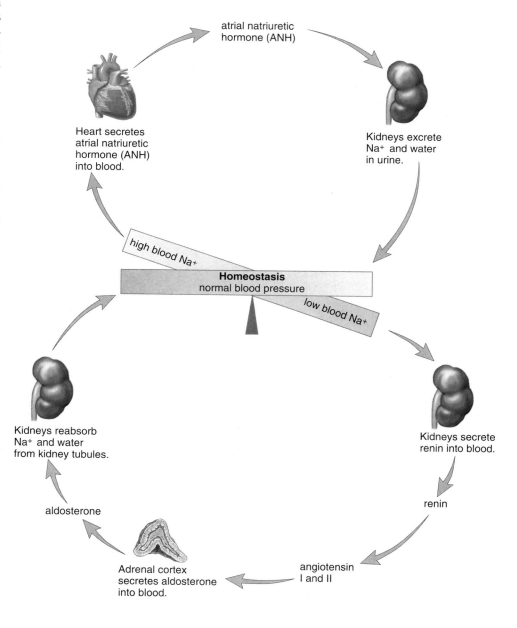

Figure 14.11   Regulation of blood pressure and volume.

Bottom: When the blood sodium (Na^+) level is low, a low blood pressure causes the kidneys to secrete renin. Renin leads to the secretion of aldosterone from the adrenal cortex. Aldosterone causes the kidneys to reabsorb Na^+, and water follows, so that blood volume and pressure return to normal. *Top:* When a high blood Na^+ level accompanies a high blood volume, the heart secretes atrial natriuretic hormone (ANH). ANH causes the kidneys to excrete Na^+, and water follows. The blood volume and pressure return to normal.

Malfunction of the Adrenal Cortex

When the level of glucocorticoids is low due to hyposecretion, a person develops **Addison disease.** The presence of excessive but ineffective ACTH causes a bronzing of the skin because ACTH, like MSH, can lead to a buildup of melanin (Fig. 14.12). Without the glucocorticoids, glucose cannot be replenished when a stressful situation arises. Even a mild infection can lead to death. In some cases, hyposecretion of aldosterone results in a loss of sodium and water, the development of low blood pressure, and possibly severe dehydration. Left untreated, Addison disease can be fatal.

When the level of glucorticoids is high due to hypersecretion, a person develops **Cushing syndrome.** The excess glucocorticoids result in a tendency toward diabetes mellitus, as muscle protein is metabolized and subcutaneous fat is deposited in the midsection. The trunk is obese, while the arms and legs remain a normal size. Children will show obesity and poor growth in height (Fig. 14.13). Depending on the cause and duration of the Cushing syndrome, some people may have more dramatic changes, including masculinization with increased blood pressure and weight gain.

The adrenal cortex hormones are essential to homeostasis. Addison disease is due to adrenal cortex hyposecretion, and Cushing syndrome is due to adrenal cortex hypersecretion.

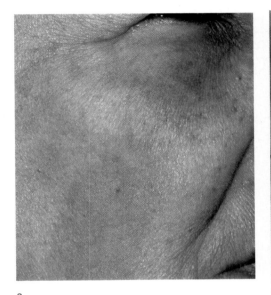
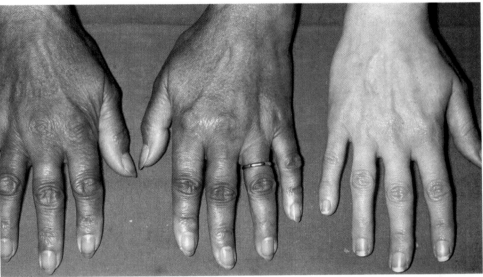

a.   b.

Figure 14.12 **Addison disease.**
Addison disease is characterized by a peculiar bronzing of the skin, particularly noticeable in these light-skinned individuals. Note the color of (**a**) the face and (**b**) the hands compared with the hand of an individual without the disease.

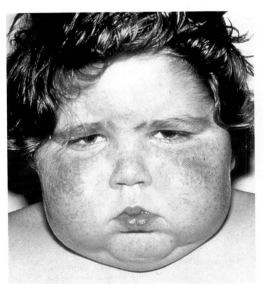
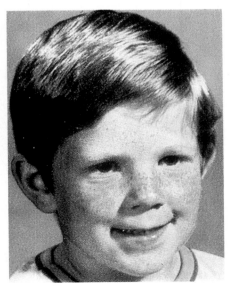

Figure 14.13 **Cushing syndrome.**
Cushing syndrome results from hypersecretion of adrenal cortex hormones. *Left:* Patient first diagnosed with Cushing syndrome. *Right:* Four months later, after therapy.

14.5 Pancreas

The **pancreas** is a long organ that lies transversely in the abdomen between the kidneys and near the duodenum of the small intestine. It is composed of two types of tissue. Exocrine tissue produces and secretes digestive juices that go by way of ducts to the small intestine. Endocrine tissue, called the **pancreatic islets** (islets of Langerhans), produces and secretes the hormones **insulin** and **glucagon** directly into the blood (Fig. 14.14).

Insulin is secreted when the blood glucose level is high, which usually occurs just after eating. Insulin stimulates the uptake of glucose by cells, especially liver cells, muscle cells, and adipose tissue cells. In liver and muscle cells, glucose is then stored as glycogen. In muscle cells, the glucose supplies energy for muscle contraction, and in fat cells, glucose enters the metabolic pool and thereby supplies

glycerol for the formation of fat. In these various ways, insulin lowers the blood glucose level.

Glucagon is secreted from the pancreas, usually before eating, when the blood glucose level is low. The major target tissues of glucagon are the liver and adipose tissue. Glucagon stimulates the liver to break down glycogen to glucose and to use fat and protein in preference to glucose as energy sources. Adipose tissue cells break down fat to glycerol and fatty acids. The liver takes these up and uses them as substrates for glucose formation. In these ways, glucagon raises the blood glucose level.

The two antagonistic hormones insulin and glucagon, both produced by the pancreas, maintain the normal level of glucose in the blood.

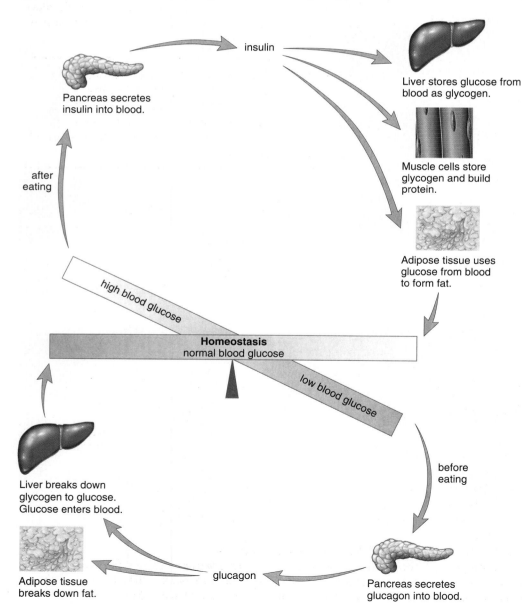

Pancreas secretes insulin into blood.

insulin

Liver stores glucose from blood as glycogen.

Muscle cells store glycogen and build protein.

Adipose tissue uses glucose from blood to form fat.

after eating

high blood glucose

Homeostasis
normal blood glucose

low blood glucose

Liver breaks down glycogen to glucose. Glucose enters blood.

Adipose tissue breaks down fat.

glucagon

before eating

Pancreas secretes glucagon into blood.

Figure 14.14   Regulation of blood glucose level.

Top: When the blood glucose level is high, the pancreas secretes insulin. Insulin promotes the storage of glucose as glycogen and the synthesis of proteins and fats (as opposed to their use as energy sources). Therefore, insulin lowers the blood glucose level. *Bottom:* When the blood glucose level is low, the pancreas secretes glucagon. Glucagon acts opposite to insulin; therefore, glucagon raises the blood glucose level to normal.

Diabetes Mellitus

Diabetes mellitus is a fairly common hormonal disease in which liver cells, and indeed most body cells, are unable to take up glucose as they should. Therefore, cellular famine exists in the midst of plenty, and the person becomes extremely hungry. As the blood glucose level rises, glucose, along with water, is excreted in the urine. Urination is frequent, and the loss of water causes the diabetic to be extremely thirsty.

The glucose tolerance test assists in the diagnosis of diabetes mellitus. After the patient is given 100 grams of glucose, the blood glucose concentration is measured at intervals. In a diabetic, the blood glucose level rises greatly and remains elevated for several hours (Fig. 14.15). In the meantime, glucose appears in the urine. In a nondiabetic, the blood glucose level rises somewhat and then returns to normal after about 2 hours.

Types of Diabetes

There are two types of diabetes mellitus. In *diabetes type 1*, the pancreas is not producing insulin. This condition is believed to be brought on by exposure to an environmental agent, most likely a virus, whose presence causes cytotoxic T cells to destroy the pancreatic islets. The body turns to the metabolism of fat, which leads to the buildup of ketones in the blood, called ketonuria, and, in turn, to acidosis (acid blood), which can lead to coma and death. As a result, the individual must have daily insulin injections. These injections control the diabetic symptoms but can still cause inconveniences, since either an overdose of insulin or missing a meal can bring on the symptoms of hypoglycemia (low blood sugar). These symptoms include perspiration, pale skin, shallow breathing, and anxiety. Because the brain requires a constant supply of sugar, unconsciousness can result. The cure is quite simple: Immediate ingestion of a sugar cube or fruit juice can very quickly counteract hypoglycemia.

It is possible to transplant a working pancreas into patients with diabetes type 1. To do away with the necessity of taking immunosuppressive drugs after the transplant, fetal pancreatic islet cells have been injected into patients. Another experimental procedure is to place pancreatic islet cells in a capsule that allows insulin to get out but prevents antibodies and T-lymphocytes from getting in. This artificial organ is implanted in the abdominal cavity.

Of the 16 million people who now have diabetes in the United States, most have *diabetes type 2*. Often, the patient is obese—adipose tissue produces a substance that impairs insulin receptor function. Normally, but not in diabetes type 2, the binding of insulin to a receptor causes the number of glucose transporters to increase in the plasma membrane.

Also, the blood insulin level is low and cells do not have enough insulin receptors.

It is possible to prevent or at least control diabetes type 2 by adhering to a low-fat, low-sugar diet and exercising regularly. If this fails, oral drugs that stimulate the pancreas to secrete more insulin and enhance the metabolism of glucose in the liver and muscle cells are available. It's projected as many as 7 million Americans may have diabetes type 2 without being aware of it. Yet, the effects of untreated diabetes type 2 are as serious as those of diabetes type 1.

Long-term complications of both types of diabetes are blindness, kidney disease, and cardiovascular disorders, including atherosclerosis, heart disease, stroke, and reduced circulation. The latter can lead to gangrene in the arms and legs. Pregnancy carries an increased risk of diabetic coma, and the child of a diabetic is somewhat more likely to be stillborn or to die shortly after birth. These complications of diabetes are not expected to appear if the mother's blood glucose level is carefully regulated and kept within normal limits.

Diabetes mellitus is caused by the lack of insulin or by the inability of cells to respond to the presence of insulin, a hormone that lowers the blood glucose level by causing cells to take it up. Following uptake, the liver and muscle cells store glucose as glycogen.

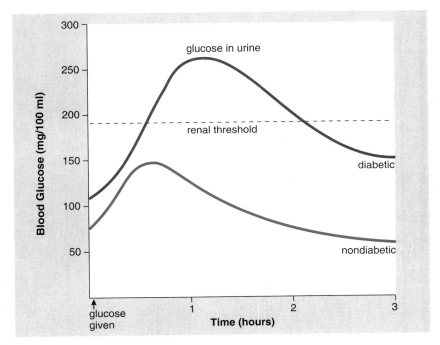

Figure 14.15   Glucose tolerance test.
Following the administration of 100 grams of glucose, the blood glucose level rises dramatically in the diabetic and glucose appears in the urine. Also, the blood glucose level at 2 hours is equal to more than 200 mg/100 mL.

14.6 Other Endocrine Glands

The **gonads** are the testes in males and the ovaries in females. The gonads are endocrine glands. Other lesser known glands and some tissues also produce hormones.

Testes and Ovaries

The **testes** are located in the scrotum, and the **ovaries** are located in the pelvic cavity. The testes produce **androgens** (e.g., **testosterone**), which are the male sex hormones, and the ovaries produce estrogen and progesterone, the female sex hormones. The hypothalamus and the pituitary gland control the hormonal secretions of these organs in the same manner previously described for the thyroid gland.

Greatly increased testosterone secretion at the time of puberty stimulates the growth of the penis and the testes. Testosterone also brings about and maintains the male secondary sex characteristics that develop during puberty, including the growth of a beard, axillary (underarm) hair, and pubic hair. It prompts the larynx and the vocal cords to enlarge, causing the voice to lower. It is partially responsible for the muscular strength of males, and this is why some athletes take supplemental amounts of **anabolic steroids,** which are either testosterone or related chemicals. The contraindications of taking anabolic steroids are listed in Figure 14.16. Testosterone also stimulates oil and sweat glands in the skin; therefore, it is largely responsible for acne and body odor. Another side effect of testosterone is baldness. Genes for baldness are probably inherited by both sexes, but baldness is seen more often in males because of the presence of testosterone.

The female sex hormones, **estrogens** (often referred to in the singular) and **progesterone,** have many effects on the body. In particular, estrogen secreted at the time of puberty stimulates the growth of the uterus and the vagina. Estrogen is necessary for egg maturation and largely responsible for the secondary sex characteristics in females, including female body hair and fat distribution. In general, females have a more rounded appearance than males because of a greater accumulation of fat beneath the skin. Also, the pelvic girdle is wider in females than in males, resulting in a larger pelvic cavity. Both estrogen and progesterone are required for breast development and for regulation of the uterine cycle, which includes monthly menstruation (discharge of blood and mucosal tissues from the uterus).

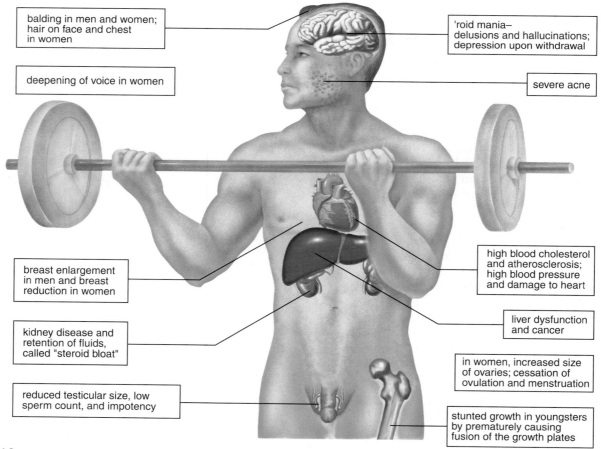

balding in men and women; hair on face and chest in women

deepening of voice in women

'roid mania–delusions and hallucinations; depression upon withdrawal

severe acne

breast enlargement in men and breast reduction in women

kidney disease and retention of fluids, called "steroid bloat"

reduced testicular size, low sperm count, and impotency

high blood cholesterol and atherosclerosis; high blood pressure and damage to heart

liver dysfunction and cancer

in women, increased size of ovaries; cessation of ovulation and menstruation

stunted growth in youngsters by prematurely causing fusion of the growth plates

Figure 14.16 **The effects of anabolic steroid use.**

Health Focus

Melatonin

Melatonin has one of the most striking patterns of secretion of any hormone, yet is one of the least understood. A major impediment to understanding melatonin has been that its administration does not cause dramatic changes in the body like many of the hormones you are studying in this chapter. It is produced by the pineal gland of the brain and is often referred to as the "hormone of darkness" because, as shown in Figure 14A, it is secreted only at night and is inhibited by light (which has caused some to refer to it as the werewolf hormone!). It was this unique pattern of secretion that provided clues to one of its major functions: as a hormone that supplies time-of-day information to the body. Most of our cells are unable to assess the time of day and depend on a special center in the brain called the suprachiasmatic nucleus (SCN), to keep time. The SCN informs the cells of the body when it is night and time to rest by directing the pineal gland to secrete melatonin.

One of the clearest effects of melatonin is its ability to reset the body's internal clock, for example, in blind people, in those suffering from jet lag, and in night-shift workers. Melatonin administered in the afternoon shifts the sleep cycle so that people wake up and go to sleep earlier; melatonin given in the morning causes people to wake up and go to sleep later. This capability of melatonin to shift the body's internal clock will likely find increasing use in the future as travel for business and pleasure become more international. It also should be especially useful in sports where teams playing in international competitions now have to arrive a week before an event in order for their internal rhythms to shift naturally so they can play at their physiological best.

Another timekeeping function of melatonin is its role in orchestrating seasonal changes. For example, it plays a major part in signaling the body of hibernators that it is time to hibernate. In this capacity, it is believed that melatonin is instrumental in causing tissues to shift into a state of metabolic inactivity during hibernation. This capability has led some researchers to propose that melatonin might be able to induce a hibernation-like state in donor organs prior to transplantation in order to prolong their "shelf life." In seasonally reproducing animals, melatonin plays a part in directing the reproductive system to become inactive. Because of this ability to regulate seasonal activities, there has been interest in the role that melatonin might play in seasonal affective disorder (SAD), which makes some people depressed in the winter. The present evidence indicates that the short days of winter cause excess melatonin to be produced in individuals susceptible to SAD, but not in unaffected people. It appears that in people with SAD, the melatonin system does not respond to artificial lighting, while in unaffected people the system ceases production of melatonin in response to artificial lighting. Interestingly, in many people with SAD, special bright lights that mimic sunlight are effective in shutting down melatonin and alleviating depression.

Although melatonin is widely advertised as a sleep aid, there is controversy among scientists about what role it plays in sleep. It does not appear to work like a sleeping pill and simply induce sleep, rather it seems to produce a physiological bias toward sleep. As people get older, the amount of melatonin they produce at night decreases, while insomnia and other sleep problems increase (about 25% of people over 65 have insomnia). Alzheimer's patients have sleep problems because this normal age-dependent decrease in melatonin is highly exaggerated in them. Melatonin levels in late-stage Alzheimer's victims have been reported to be only one-fifth those of age-matched controls. Fortunately, a few studies have already shown that melatonin treatment can cause significant improvements in the sleep quality of both elderly insomniacs and Alzheimer's patients. If melatonin can be used to reestablish more normal sleep patterns in Alzheimer's patients, it should help delay their institutionalization and reduce the psychological, physical, and monetary burden of this devastating disease.

Figure 14A Melatonin production.
Melatonin production is greatest at night when we are sleeping. Light suppresses melatonin production (**a**), so its secreted for a longer time in the winter (**b**) than in the summer (**c**).

Thymus Gland

The lobular **thymus gland** lies just beneath the sternum (see Fig. 14.1). This organ reaches its largest size and is most active during childhood. With aging, the organ gets smaller and becomes fatty. Lymphocytes that originate in the bone marrow and then pass through the thymus are transformed into T-lymphocytes. The lobules of the thymus are lined by epithelial cells that secrete hormones called **thymosins.** These hormones aid in the differentiation of lymphocytes packed inside the lobules. Although the hormones secreted by the thymus ordinarily work in the thymus, there is hope that these hormones could be injected into AIDS or cancer patients, where they would enhance T-lymphocyte function.

Pineal Gland

The **pineal gland,** which is located in the brain (see Fig. 14.1), produces the hormone **melatonin,** primarily at night. Melatonin is involved in our daily sleep-wake cycle; normally we grow sleepy at night when melatonin levels increase and awaken once daylight returns and melatonin levels are low. Daily 24-hour cycles such as this are called **circadian rhythms** and, as discussed in the Health Focus on page 281, circadian rhythms are controlled by a biological clock located in the hypothalamus.

Animal research suggests that melatonin also regulates sexual development. In keeping with these findings, it has been noted that children whose pineal gland has been destroyed due to a brain tumor experience early puberty.

The gonads, thymus, and pineal gland are also endocrine organs. The gonads secrete the sex hormones, the thymus secretes thymosins, and the pineal gland secretes melatonin.

Hormones from Other Tissues

Some organs that are not considered endocrine glands do indeed secrete hormones. We have already mentioned that the heart produces atrial natriuretic hormone (see page 276). And you will recall that the stomach and the small intestine produce peptide hormones that regulate digestive secretions. A number of other types of tissues produce hormones.

Leptin

Leptin is a protein hormone produced by adipose tissue. Leptin acts on the hypothalamus, where it signals satiety—that is, the individual has had enough to eat. Strange to say, the blood of obese individuals may be rich in leptin. It is possible that the leptin they produce is ineffective because of

a genetic mutation, or else their hypothalamic cells lack a suitable number of receptors for leptin.

Growth Factors

A number of different types of organs and cells produce peptide **growth factors,** which stimulate cell division and mitosis. They are like hormones in that they act on cell types with specific receptors to receive them. Some are released into the blood; others diffuse to nearby cells. Growth factors of particular interest are the following:

Granulocyte and macrophage colony-stimulating factor (GM-CSF) is secreted by many different tissues. GM-CSF causes bone marrow stem cells to form either granulocyte or macrophage cells, depending on whether the concentration is low or high.

Platelet-derived growth factor is released from platelets and from many other cell types. It helps in wound healing and causes an increase in the number of fibroblasts, smooth muscle cells, and certain cells of the nervous system.

Epidermal growth factor and *nerve growth factor* stimulate the cells indicated by their names, as well as many others. These growth factors are also important in wound healing.

Tumor angiogenesis factor stimulates the formation of capillary networks and is released by tumor cells. One treatment for cancer is to prevent the activity of this growth factor.

Prostaglandins

Prostaglandins are potent chemical signals produced within cells from arachidonate, a fatty acid. Prostaglandins are not distributed in the blood; instead, they act locally, quite close to where they were produced. In the uterus, prostaglandins cause muscles to contract; therefore, they are implicated in the pain and discomfort of menstruation in some women. Also, prostaglandins mediate the effects of pyrogens, chemicals that are believed to reset the temperature regulatory center in the brain. Aspirin reduces body temperature and controls pain because of its effect on prostaglandins.

Certain prostaglandins reduce gastric secretion and have been used to treat gastric reflux; others lower blood pressure and have been used to treat hypertension; and yet others inhibit platelet aggregation and have been used to prevent thrombosis. However, different prostaglandins have contrary effects, and it has been very difficult to successfully standardize their use. Therefore, prostaglandin therapy is still considered experimental.

Many tissues, aside from the traditional endocrine glands, produce hormones. Some of these enter the bloodstream, and some act only locally.

Bioethical Focus

Hormone Replacement Therapy

Menopause is the time in a woman's life when menstruation comes to an end. During menopause, which may begin as early as 35 years of age, the ovaries gradually produce lower levels of the sex hormones. Doctors may recommend using hormone replacement therapy (HRT) to counter some of the problems often associated with menopause (hot flashes, night sweats, sleeplessness, mood swings, and vaginal dryness) or to prevent some long-term conditions that are more common in postmenopausal women, such as osteoporosis. HRT used to be quite common. Data from a 1997 national survey showed that 45% of U.S. women born between 1897 and 1950 used menopausal hormones for at least one month, and 20% continued use for five or more years.

In recent years, a number of long-term studies have attempted to assess the risks and benefits of HRT. The best data comes from the Women's Health Initiative (WHI), a large, randomized clinical trial of over 16,000 healthy women, ages 50 through 79, in which half of the participants took hormones and the other half took a placebo pill (which does not contain any drug). The trial, sponsored by the National Institutes of Health (NIH), was halted early when, in July 2002, investigators reported that the overall risks of HRT outweighed the benefits. What were the results of this study with regard to quality of life, cancer and cardiovascular disease risk, and osteoporosis?

Quality of Life On the basis of the WHI study and others, HRT has no significant effects on the general health, vitality, mental health, depressive symptoms, or sexual satisfaction of women. Although hormone use was associated with a small benefit in terms of sleep disturbance, physical functioning, and bodily pain after one year of use, the effect was too small to be considered clinically significant. However, the risk of developing dementia (including Alzheimer disease) was double in women age 65 and older.

Cancer HRT significantly increased the risk of developing breast cancer in women ages 50 to 64. Current hormone users were also more likely to die from breast cancer than women who did not use them. Within about five years of stopping use, the increased risk largely disappeared. Although not as definite as breast cancer, the possibility exists that HRT also increases a woman's risk of endometrial cancer (cancer of the lining of the uterus) and ovarian cancer.

As a benefit, women on HRT have fewer cases of colorectal cancer compared with women taking a placebo.

Cardiovascular Disease HRT may increase the risk of heart disease among generally healthy postmenopausal women. The greatest increased risk occurred in the first year. Women on HRT have double the combined rate of blood clots in the lungs and legs. Studies have consistently reported increased risks of blood clots in the lungs (pulmonary embolisms) and deep veins in the legs with hormone use. The WHI study also indicated that the risk of a stroke increases when women use HRT.

Figure 14B   Thinking it through.
Menopausal women are now advised to consult their physicians and then to decide for themselves if they wish to be on hormone replacement therapy.

Osteoporosis Osteoporosis is the loss of bone mass and density, which causes bones to become fragile and increases the chance of bone fractures. As a benefit, estrogen alone and estrogen combined with progestin have been shown to protect against osteoporosis. Results from the WHI showed that estrogen plus progestin can prevent fractures of the hip, vertebrae, and other bones.

Conclusion The WHI found that use of this estrogen plus progestin pill increases the risk of breast cancer, heart disease, stroke, and blood clots. The study also found that there were fewer cases of hip fractures and colon cancer among women using estrogen plus progestin than in those taking a placebo. Therefore, women are now advised to discuss the pros and cons of HRT with their physician and decide for themselves if they wish to use it (Fig. 14B). In other words, the patient has to be aware of the risks and accept the responsibility for taking replacement hormones.

Decide Your Opinion

1. Should physicians wait to recommend medications until they are certain about their benefits? Or, are they duty-bound to make recommendations based on incomplete information if there is a possibility of improving the health of millions of people?
2. Should patients accept the responsibility of deciding for themselves if they should take a medicine, or should physicians assume this responsibility?
3. HRT must be prescribed by a physician. Should women who suffered health consequences after undergoing HRT be encouraged to sue the physicians who wrote prescriptions that allowed them to use the therapy?

14.7 Homeostasis

The nervous and endocrine systems exert control over the other systems and thereby maintain homeostasis.

Responding to External Changes

The nervous system is particularly able to respond to changes in the external environment. Some responses are automatic as you can testify by trying this: Take a piece of clear plastic and hold it just in front of your face. Get someone to gently toss a soft object, such as a wadded-up piece of paper, at the plastic. Can you prevent yourself from blinking? This reflex protects your eyes.

The eyes and other organs that have sensory receptors provide us with valuable information about the external environment. The central nervous system, which is on the receiving end of millions of bits of information, integrates information, compares it with previously stored memories, and "decides" on the proper course of action. Suppose you have spent the morning skiing; your muscles ache, your stomach churns, and your toes are cold. The brain will send out the motor impulses that will soon have you recovering from your exertions. The nervous system often responds to changes in the external environment through body movement. It gives us the ability to stay in as moderate an environment as possible—one that is not too hot or cold, for example. Otherwise, we test the ability of the nervous system to maintain homeostasis despite extreme conditions.

Responding to Internal Changes

The governance of internal organs usually requires that the nervous and endocrine systems work together, usually below the level of consciousness. Subconscious control often depends on reflex actions that involve the hypothalamus and the medulla oblongata. Let's take blood pressure as an example. You've just run three miles to raise money for hunger relief and decide to sit down under a tree to rest a bit. When you stand up to push off again, you feel faint, but it quickly passes because the medulla oblongata responds to input from the baroreceptors in the aortic arch and carotid arteries and immediately acts through the sympathetic system to increase heart rate and constrict the blood vessels so that your blood pressure rises. Sweating may have upset the water-salt balance of your blood. If so, the hormone aldosterone from the adrenal cortex will act on the kidney tubules to conserve Na^+ and water reabsorption will follow. The hypothalamus can also help by sending antidiruetic hormone (ADH), to the posterior pituitary gland, which releases it into the blood. ADH actively promotes water reabsorption by the kidney tubules.

Recall from Chapter 9 that certain drugs, such as alcohol, can affect ADH secretion. When you consume alcohol, it is quickly absorbed across the stomach lining into the

Figure 14.17 **Control of reproduction.**
Successful reproduction requires the participation of both the nervous and endocrine systems.

bloodstream, where it travels to the hypothalamus and inhibits ADH secretion. When ADH levels fall, the kidney tubules absorb less water. The result is increased production of dilute urine. Excessive water loss, or dehydration, is a disturbance of homeostasis. This is why drinking alcohol when you are exercising, or simply perspiring heavily on a hot day, is not a good idea. Instead of keeping you hydrated, an alcoholic beverage, such as beer, will have just the opposite effect.

Controlling the Reproductive System

Few systems intrigue us more than the reproductive system, which couldn't function without nervous and endocrine control (Fig. 14.17). The hypothalamus controls the anterior pituitary, which in turn controls the release of hormones from the testes and the ovaries and the production of their gametes. The nervous system directly controls the muscular contractions of the ducts, which propel the sperm, and the oviducts, which move a developing embryo to the uterus, where development continues. Without the positive feedback cycle involving oxytocin, produced by the hypothalamus and released by posterior pituitary, birth might not occur.

The Neuroendocrine System

The nervous and endocrine systems work so closely together, they form what is sometimes called the neuroendocrine system. As we have seen, the hypothalamus certainly bridges the regulatory activities of both the nervous and endocrine systems. In addition to producing the hormones released by the posterior pituitary, the hypothalamus produces hormones that control the anterior pituitary. And the hypothalamus acts directly through the nerves of the autonomic system to control other organs. The hypothalamus truly belongs to both the nervous and endocrine systems. Indeed, it is often and appropriately referred to as a neuroendocrine organ.

Human Systems Work Together

The nervous and endocrine systems work together to maintain homeostasis. The systems listed here in particular also work with these two systems.

Nervous and Endocrine Systems

The nervous and endocrine systems coordinate the activities of the other systems. The brain receives sensory input and controls the activity of muscles and various glands. The endocrine system secretes hormones that influence the metabolism of cells, the growth and development of body parts, and homeostasis.

Cardiovascular System

Nerves and epinephrine regulate contraction of the heart and constriction/dilation of blood vessels. Hormones regulate blood glucose and ion levels. Growth factors promote blood cell formation. Blood vessels transport hormones to target cells.

Respiratory System

The respiratory center in the brain regulates the breathing rate. The lungs carry on gas exchange for the benefit of all systems, including the nervous and endocrine systems.

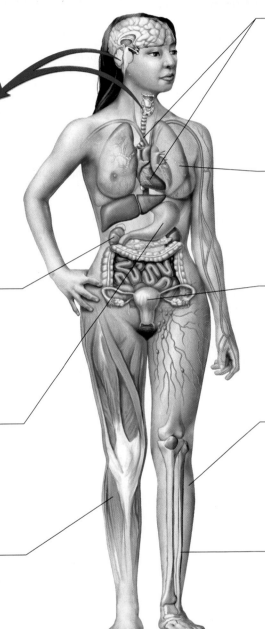

Urinary System

Nerves stimulate muscles that permit urination. Hormones (ADH and aldosterone) help kidneys regulate the water-salt balance and the acid-base balance of the blood.

Reproductive System

Nerves stimulate contractions that move gametes in ducts, and uterine contraction that occurs during childbirth. Sex hormones influence the development of the secondary sex characteristics.

Digestive System

Nerves stimulate smooth muscle and permit digestive tract movements. Hormones help regulate digestive juices that break down food to nutrients for neurons and glands.

Integumentary System

Nerves activate sweat glands and arrector pili muscles. Sensory receptors in skin send information to the brain about the external environment. Skin protects neurons and glands.

Muscular System

Nerves stimulate muscles, whose contractions allow us to move out of danger. Androgens promote growth of skeletal muscles. Sensory receptors in muscles and joints send information to the brain. Muscles protect neurons and glands.

Skeletal System

Growth hormone and sex hormones regulate the size of the bones; parathyroid hormone and calcitonin regulate their Ca^{2+} content and therefore bone strength. Bones protect nerves and glands.

Summarizing the Concepts

14.1 Endocrine Glands

The nervous and endocrine systems can be contrasted as in Table 14.1. Endocrine glands secrete hormones into the bloodstream, and from there they are distributed to target organs or tissues.

Hormones are a type of chemical signal that usually act at a distance between body parts. Hormones are either peptides or steroids. Reception of a peptide hormone at the plasma membrane activates an enzyme cascade inside the cell. Steroid hormones combine with a receptor in the cell, and the complex attaches to and activates DNA. Protein synthesis follows.

14.2 Hypothalamus and Pituitary Gland

Neurosecretory cells in the hypothalamus produce antidiuretic hormone (ADH) and oxytocin, which are stored in axon endings in the posterior pituitary until they are released.

The hypothalamus produces hypothalamic-releasing and hypothalamic-inhibiting hormones, which pass to the anterior pituitary by way of a portal system. The anterior pituitary produces at least six types of hormones, and some of these stimulate other hormonal glands to secrete hormones.

14.3 Thyroid and Parathyroid Glands

The thyroid gland requires iodine to produce triiodothyronine and thyroxine, which increase the metabolic rate. If iodine is available in limited quantities, a simple goiter develops; if the thyroid is overactive, an exophthalmic goiter develops. The thyroid gland also produces calcitonin, which helps lower the blood calcium level. The parathyroid glands secrete parathyroid hormone, which raises the blood calcium and decreases the blood phosphate levels.

14.4 Adrenal Glands

The adrenal glands respond to stress: Immediately, the adrenal medulla secretes epinephrine and norepinephrine, which bring about responses we associate with emergency situations. On a long-term basis, the adrenal cortex produces the glucocorticoids (e.g., cortisol), under the control ACTH, and the mineralocorticoids (e.g., aldosterone). Cortisol stimulates hydrolysis of proteins to amino acids that are converted to glucose; in this way, it raises the blood glucose level. Aldosterone causes the kidneys to reabsorb sodium ions (Na^+) and to excrete potassium ions (K^+). Addison disease develops when the adrenal cortex is underactive, and Cushing syndrome develops when the adrenal cortex is overactive.

14.5 Pancreas

The pancreatic islets secrete insulin, which lowers the blood glucose level, and glucagon, which has the opposite effect. The most common illness caused by hormonal imbalance is diabetes mellitus, which is due to the failure of the pancreas to produce insulin or the failure of the cells to take it up.

14.6 Other Endocrine Glands

The gonads produce the sex hormones. The thymus secretes thymosins, which stimulate T-lymphocyte production and maturation. The pineal gland produces melatonin, which may be involved in circadian rhythms and the development of the reproductive organs.

Tissues also produce hormones. Adipose tissue produces leptin, which acts on the hypothalamus, and various tissues produce growth factors. Prostaglandins are produced and act locally.

14.7 Homeostasis

The nervous and endocrine systems exert control over the other systems, and thereby, maintain homeostasis. The nervous system is particularly able to respond to the external environment, after receiving data from the sensory receptors. Sensory receptors are present in such organs as the eyes and ears. The governance of internal organs requires the nervous and endocrine systems to work together, usually below the level of consciousness. Subconscious control often depends on reflex actions that involve the hypothalamus and medulla oblongata. The nervous and endocrine systems work so closely together that they form what is sometimes called the neuroendocrine system.

Studying the Concepts

1. Compare the endocrine system to the nervous system. 266
2. Compare the effects of peptide and steroid hormones on the cell. 268–69
3. Explain the relationship of the hypothalamus to the posterior pituitary gland and to the anterior pituitary gland. List the hormones secreted by the posterior and anterior pituitary glands. 270–72
4. Give an example of the negative feedback relationship among the hypothalamus, the anterior pituitary, and other endocrine glands. 270
5. Discuss the effect of growth hormone on the body and the result of having too much or too little growth hormone when a young person is growing. What is the result if the anterior pituitary produces growth hormone in an adult? 272
6. What types of goiters and other conditions are associated with a malfunctioning thyroid? Explain each type. 273
7. How do the thyroid and the parathyroid work together to control the blood calcium level? 274
8. How do the adrenal glands respond to stress? What hormones are secreted by the adrenal medulla and the adrenal cortex? What effects do these hormones have? 275–276
9. What are the symptoms of Addison disease and Cushing syndrome? 277
10. Draw a diagram to explain how insulin and glucagon maintain the blood glucose level. Use your diagram to explain the major symptoms of diabetes type 1. 278–79
11. Name the other endocrine glands discussed in this chapter, and discuss the functions of the hormones they secrete. 280–82
12. What are leptin, growth factors, and prostaglandins? How do these substances act? 282
13. How do the nervous and the endocrine systems work together with other systems to maintain homeostasis? 284–85

Thinking Critically About the Concepts

Refer to the opening vignette on page 265, and then answer these questions.

1. Increased secretion by the hypothalamus is credited with jump-starting puberty. Why would that be a reasonable hypothesis?
2. A person with a Y chromosome develops into a male because of the presence of a gene on the Y chromosome called the *SRY* (sex-determining region of the Y) gene. What would happen if an X chromosome, by chance, has this gene in an XX individual? Is it a true statement, then, that only XY individuals can be males?

3. Androgens (e.g., testosterone) have numerous effects on the body. Which one is of interest to most athletes abusing anabolic steroids? Females who take steroids should expect what other less desirable changes?

4. Harry was becoming interested in girls. Can sex hormones affect the brain? What is the most obvious example that they can? (Hint, consider the diagram on page 270.)

Testing Your Knowledge of the Concepts

Choose the best answer for each question.

1. Hormones are never
   a. steroids.
   b. amino acids.
   c. glycoproteins.
   d. fats (triglycerides).

2. _____ glands are ductless.
   a. Exocrine
   b. Endocrine
   c. Both a and b are correct.
   d. Neither a nor b is correct.

3. _____ is released through positive feedback and causes _____.
   a. Insulin, stomach contractions
   b. Oxytocin, stomach contractions
   c. Oxytocin, uterine contractions
   d. None of these is correct.

4. Growth hormone is produced by the
   a. posterior adrenal gland.
   b. posterior pituitary.
   c. anterior pituitary.
   d. kidneys.
   e. None of these is correct.

5. Bodily response to stress includes
   a. water reabsorption by the kidneys.
   b. blood pressure increase.
   c. increase in blood glucose levels.
   d. heart rate increase.
   e. All of these are correct.

6. Glucagon causes
   a. use of fat for energy.
   b. glycogen to be converted to glucose.
   c. use of amino acids to form fats.
   d. Both a and b are correct.
   e. None of these is correct.

7. Long-term complications of diabetes include
   a. blindness.
   b. kidney disease.
   c. circulatory disorders.
   d. All of these are correct.
   e. None of these is correct.

In questions 8–12, match the hormones to the correct gland in the key.

Key:

   a. glucagon
   b. prostaglandin
   c. melatonin
   d. insulin
   e. leptin

8. Raises blood glucose levels

9. Conversion of glucose to glycogen

10. Hunger control

11. Controls circadian rhythms

12. Causes uterine contractions

13. Which hormones can cross cell membranes?
    a. peptide hormones
    b. steroid hormones
    c. Both a and b are correct.
    d. Neither a nor b is correct.

14. Anabolic steroid use can cause
    a. liver damage.
    b. severe acne.
    c. balding.
    d. reduced testicular size.
    e. All of these are correct.

15. PTH causes the blood levels of calcium to _____ and calcitonin causes it to _____.
    a. increase, increase
    b. increase, decrease
    c. decrease, increase
    d. decrease, decrease

16. Lack of aldosterone will cause a blood imbalance of
    a. sodium.
    b. potassium.
    c. water.
    d. All of the above are correct.
    e. None of these is correct.

17. Complete the diagram below.

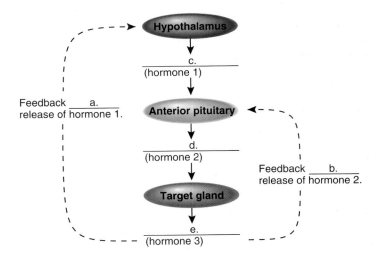

18. The anterior pituitary controls the secretion(s) of
    a. both the adrenal medulla and the adrenal cortex.
    b. both thyroid and adrenal cortex.
    c. both ovaries and testes.
    d. Both b and c are correct.

19. Diabetes mellitus is associated with
    a. too much insulin in the blood.
    b. too high a blood glucose level.
    c. blood that is too dilute.
    d. All of these are correct.

In questions 20–24, match the hormones to the correct gland in the key.

Key:

    a. pancreas
    b. anterior pituitary
    c. posterior pituitary
    d. thyroid
    e. adrenal medulla
    f. adrenal cortex

20. Cortisol

21. Growth hormone (GH)

22. Oxytocin storage

23. Insulin

24. Epinephrine

25. Which of these is not a pair of antagonistic hormones?
    a. insulin—glucagon
    b. calcitonin—parathyroid hormone
    c. cortisol—epinephrine
    d. aldosterone—atrial natriuretic hormone (ANH)
    e. thyroxine—growth hormone

26. Which hormone and condition is mismatched?
    a. growth hormone—acromegaly
    b. thyroxine—goiter
    c. parathyroid hormone—tetany
    d. cortisol—myxedema
    e. insulin—diabetes

Understanding Key Terms

acromegaly 272
Addison disease 277
adrenal cortex 275
adrenal gland 275
adrenal medulla 275
adrenocorticotropic
    hormone (ACTH) 270
aldosterone 276
anabolic steroid 280
androgen 280
anterior pituitary 270
antidiuretic hormone
    (ADH) 270
atrial natriuretic
    hormone (ANH) 276
calcitonin 274
chemical signal 268
circadian rhythm 282
congenital hypothyroidism 273
cortisol 276
Cushing syndrome 277

cyclic adenosine monophos-
    phate (cAMP) 269
diabetes mellitus 279
endocrine gland 266
epinephrine 275
estrogen 280
exophthalmic goiter 273
first messenger 269
glucagon 278
glucocorticoid 275
gonad 280
gonadotropic hormone 270
growth factor 282
growth hormone (GH) 270
hormone 266
hypothalamic-inhibiting
    hormone 270
hypothalamic-releasing
    hormone 270
hypothalamus 270
insulin 278

leptin 282
melanocyte-stimulating
    hormone (MSH) 270
melatonin 282
mineralocorticoid 275
myxedema 273
norepinephrine 275
ovary 280
oxytocin 270
pancreas 278
pancreatic islets 278
parathyroid gland 274
parathyroid hormone
    (PTH) 274
peptide hormone 269
pheromone 268
pineal gland 282
pituitary dwarfism 272
pituitary gland 270

positive feedback 270
posterior pituitary 270
progesterone 280
prolactin (PRL) 270
prostaglandin 282
renin 276
second messenger 269
simple goiter 273
steroid hormone 269
testes 280
testosterone 280
tetany 274
thymosin 282
thymus gland 282
thyroid gland 273
thyroid-stimulating
    hormone (TSH) 270
thyroxine (T$_4$) 273

Match the key terms to these definitions.

a. _____ Organ that is in the neck and secretes several important hormones, including thyroxine and calcitonin.

b. _____ Condition characterized by high blood glucose level and the appearance of glucose in the urine.

c. _____ Hormone secreted by the anterior pituitary that stimulates portions of the adrenal cortex.

d. _____ Type of hormone that causes the activation of an enzyme cascade in cells.

e. _____ Hormone released by the posterior pituitary that causes contraction of the uterus and milk letdown.

Online Learning Center

www.mhhe.com/maderhuman9

The Online Learning Center provides a wealth of information fully organized and integrated by chapter. You will find practice quizzes, interactive activities, labeling exercises, flashcards, and much more that will complement your learning and understanding of human biology.

Looking at Both Sides

Each day, the Internet, media, and other people present you with opposing viewpoints on a wide range of subjects. Your ability to develop an informed opinion on an issue, and talk to others about it, is extremely important.

To expand and enhance your knowledge of a highly relevant bioethical issue, visit the "Student Edition" of the Online Learning Center. Under "Course-Wide Content," select "Looking at Both Sides." Once there, you will be asked to complete activities that will increase your understanding of a current bioethical issue related to this chapter and allow you to defend your opinion.

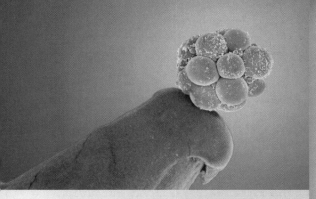

C H A P T E R 15

15 Reproductive System 289

16 Development and Aging 309

Human beings are either male or female. The reproductive organs of each sex produce the sex cells that join prior to the development of a new individual. The embryo develops into a fetus within the body of the female, and birth usually occurs when there is a reasonable chance for independent existence.

We are in the midst of a sexual revolution. We have the freedom to engage in varied sexual practices and to reproduce by assisted reproductive technologies, such as in vitro fertilization. With freedom comes a responsibility to be familiar with the biology of reproduction and health-related issues, not only for ourselves, but for our potential offspring.

Reproductive System

C H A P T E R   C O N C E P T S

15.1 Male Reproductive System

- What male structures function to produce sperm and seminal fluid? Which of these structures are involved in transport of semen out of the body? 290–91
- What endocrine glands and hormones are involved in promoting and maintaining the sex characteristics of males? 293

15.2 Female Reproductive System

- Among the female structures, which produce the egg, transport the egg, house a developing embryo, and serve as the birth canal? 294–95

15.3 Female Hormone Levels

- Which endocrine glands and hormones control the menstrual cycle and maintain pregnancy? 296–99
- What additional effects do these hormones have on the female body? 300

15.4 Control of Reproduction

- What are some common birth control methods available to men and women today? 301–2
- If a couple has trouble conceiving a child, what options can they explore? 304

Prior to 1978, infertile couples had two options: adopt or be childless. Today, infertile couples have many options; some estimate that, thanks to modern science, there are as many as 50 ways to make a baby! Fertility drugs, in vitro fertilization (test tube babies), artificial insemination, and surrogate motherhood are just a few variations on the traditional method of sperm meeting egg. If several of these are used at once, it is even possible for a child to have several parents.

For others, modern science has also developed many novel ways to prevent sperm from meeting egg. Besides traditional barrier methods of birth control such as condoms or diaphragms, many females use what are called "hormonal" methods of birth control. These are based on our knowledge of how hormones regulate the female reproductive cycle. A woman can take in the hormones orally (the pill), through a periodic injection, through implants placed in her arm, through a ring placed near her cervix, and even through a patch simply placed on the skin! This knowledge has also led to the development of a morning-after pill that ensures pregnancy will not occur after unprotected intercourse.

Intervention to promote human reproduction and also to prevent it give rise to many ethical questions that our society continues to debate with much emotion.

15.1 Male Reproductive System

The male reproductive system includes the organs depicted in Figure 15.1. The male gonads, or primary sex organs, are paired **testes** (sing., testis), which are suspended within the sacs of the **scrotum.**

Sperm produced by the testes mature within the **epididymis** (pl., epididymides), which is a tightly coiled duct lying just outside each testis. Maturation seems to be required in order for sperm to swim to the egg. When sperm leave an epididymis, they enter a **vas deferens** (pl., vasa deferentia), also called the ductus deferens, where they may also be stored for a time. Each vas deferens passes into the abdominal cavity, where it curves around the bladder and empties into an ejaculatory duct. The ejaculatory ducts enter the **urethra.**

At the time of ejaculation, sperm leave the penis in a fluid called **semen.** The seminal vesicles, the prostate gland, and the bulbourethral glands (Cowper glands) add secretions to seminal fluid. The pair of **seminal vesicles** lie at the base of the bladder, and each has a duct that joins with a vas deferens. The **prostate gland** is a single, donut-shaped gland that surrounds

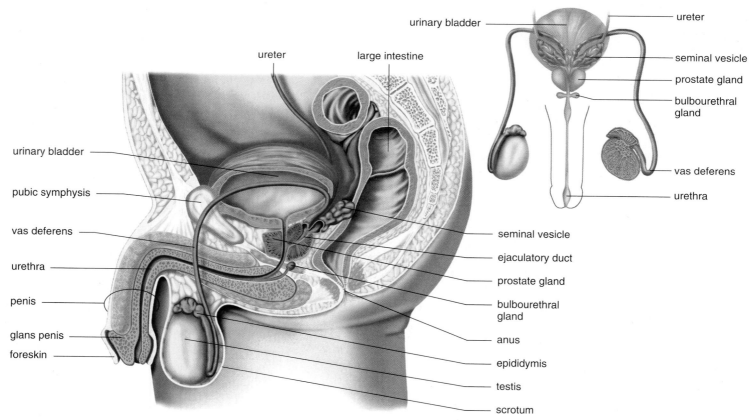

Figure 15.1   The male reproductive system.
The testes produce sperm. The seminal vesicles, the prostate gland, and the bulbourethral glands provide a fluid medium for the sperm, which move from the vas deferens through the ejaculatory duct to the urethra in the penis. The foreskin (prepuce) is removed when a penis is circumcised.

the upper portion of the urethra just below the bladder. In older men, the prostate can enlarge and squeeze off the urethra, making urination painful and difficult. The condition can be treated medically. **Bulbourethral glands** are pea-sized organs that lie posterior to the prostate on either side of the urethra. Their secretion makes the seminal fluid gelatinous.

Each component of seminal fluid seems to have a particular function. Sperm are more viable in a basic solution, and seminal fluid, which is milky in appearance, has a slightly basic pH (about 7.5). Swimming sperm require energy, and seminal fluid contains the sugar fructose, which presumably serves as an energy source. Semen also contains prostaglandins, chemicals that cause the uterus to contract. Some investigators believe that uterine contractions help propel the sperm toward the egg.

Orgasm in Males

The **penis** (Fig. 15.2) is the male organ of sexual intercourse. The penis has a long shaft and an enlarged tip called the glans penis. The glans penis is normally covered by a layer of skin called the foreskin. Circumcision, the surgical removal of the foreskin, is usually done soon after birth.

Spongy, erectile tissue containing distensible blood spaces extends through the shaft of the penis. During sexual arousal, autonomic nerve impulses lead to the production of cyclic guanosine monophosphate (cGMP) in smooth muscle cells, and the erectile tissue fills with blood. The veins that take blood away from the penis are compressed, and the penis becomes erect. **Erectile dysfunction** (formerly called impotency) exists when the erectile tissue doesn't expand enough to compress the veins. During an erection, a sphincter closes off the bladder so that no urine enters the urethra.

(The urethra carries either urine or semen at different times.) The drug sildenafil (Viagra) alters male chemistry in a way that ensures a full erection. However, the same chemical effects cause vision problems in some males taking Viagra.

As sexual stimulation intensifies, sperm enter the urethra from each vas deferens, and the glands contribute secretions to the seminal fluid. Once seminal fluid is in the urethra, rhythmic muscle contractions cause it to be expelled from the penis in spurts (ejaculation).

The contractions that expel seminal fluid from the penis are a part of male orgasm, the physiological and psychological sensations that occur at the climax of sexual stimulation. The psychological sensation of pleasure is centered in the brain, but the physiological reactions involve the genital (reproductive) organs and associated muscles, as well as the entire body. Marked muscular tension is followed by contraction and relaxation.

Following ejaculation and/or loss of sexual arousal, the penis returns to its normal flaccid state. After ejaculation, a male typically experiences a period of time, called the refractory period, during which stimulation does not bring about an erection. The length of the refractory period increases with age.

There may be in excess of 400 million sperm in the 3.5 mL of semen expelled during ejaculation. The sperm count can be much lower than this, however, and fertilization of the egg by a sperm can still take place.

Sperm are produced in the testes, mature in the epididymis, and pass from the vas deferens to the urethra. After glands add fluid to sperm, semen is ejaculated from the penis at the time of male orgasm.

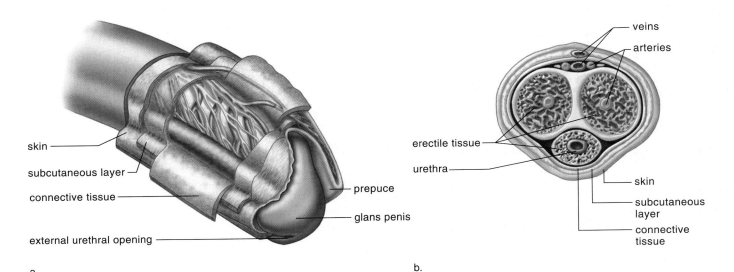

a.

b.

Figure 15.2   Penis anatomy.
a. Beneath the skin and the connective tissue lies the urethra, surrounded by erectile tissue, so called because it expands during an erection. This tissue expands to form the glans penis, which in uncircumcised males is partially covered by the foreskin (prepuce). **b.** Two other columns of erectile tissue in the penis are located dorsally.

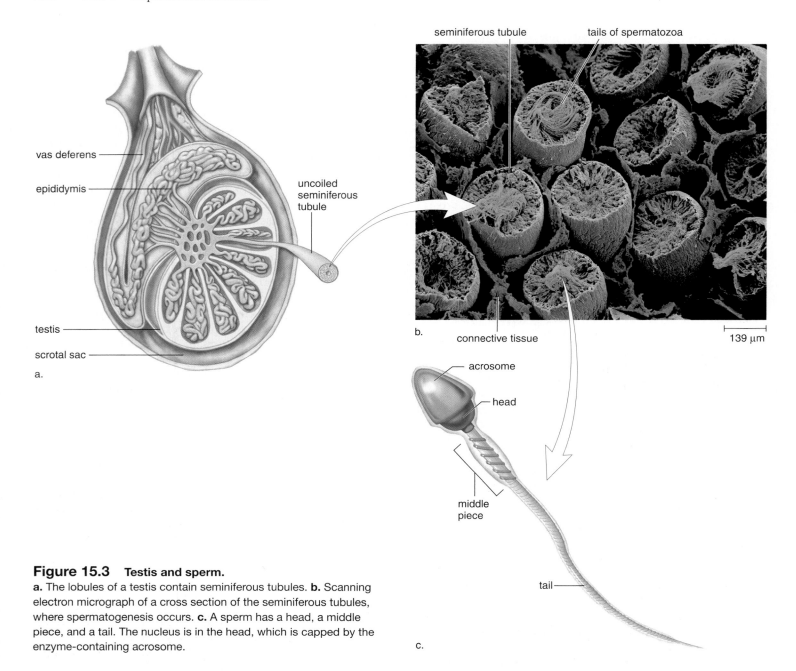

Figure 15.3   Testis and sperm.
a. The lobules of a testis contain seminiferous tubules. **b.** Scanning electron micrograph of a cross section of the seminiferous tubules, where spermatogenesis occurs. **c.** A sperm has a head, a middle piece, and a tail. The nucleus is in the head, which is capped by the enzyme-containing acrosome.

Male Gonads, the Testes

The testes, which produce sperm and also the male sex hormones, lie outside the abdominal cavity of the male, within the scrotum. The testes begin their development inside the abdominal cavity but descend into the scrotal sacs during the last two months of fetal development. If, by chance, the testes do not descend and the male is not treated or operated on to place the testes in the scrotum, sterility—the inability to produce offspring—usually follows. This is because the internal temperature of the body is too high to produce viable sperm. The scrotum helps regulate the temperature of the testes by holding them closer or farther away from the body.

Seminiferous Tubules

A longitudinal section of a testis shows that it is composed of compartments called lobules, each of which contains one to three tightly coiled **seminiferous tubules** (Fig. 15.3*a*). Altogether, these tubules have a combined length of approximately 250 meters. A microscopic cross section of a seminiferous tubule reveals that it is packed with cells undergoing **spermatogenesis** (Fig. 15.3*b,c*), the production of sperm. Newly formed cells move away from the outer wall, increase in size, and undergo cell division to become spermatids. Spermatids then differentiate into sperm. Also present are large cells that support, nourish, and regulate the spermatogenic cells.

Table 15.1	Male Reproductive Organs
Organ	**Function**
Testes	Produce sperm and sex hormones
Epididymides	Ducts where sperm mature and some sperm are stored
Vasa deferentia	Conduct and store sperm
Seminal vesicles	Contribute nutrients and fluid to semen
Prostate gland	Contributes fluid to semen
Urethra	Conducts sperm
Bulbourethral glands	Contribute mucoid fluid to semen
Penis	Organ of sexual intercourse

Mature **sperm,** or spermatozoa, have three distinct parts: a head, a middle piece, and a tail (Fig. 15.3*c*). Mitochondria in the middle piece provide energy for the movement of the tail, which is a flagellum. The head contains a nucleus covered by a cap called the **acrosome,** which stores enzymes needed to penetrate the egg. The ejaculated semen of a normal human male contains several hundred million sperm, but only one sperm normally enters an egg. Sperm usually do not live more than 48 hours in the female genital tract.

Interstitial Cells

The male sex hormones, the androgens, are secreted by cells that lie between the seminiferous tubules. Therefore, they are called **interstitial cells.** The most important of the androgens is testosterone, whose functions are discussed next.

Hormonal Regulation in Males

The hypothalamus has ultimate control of the testes' sexual function because it secretes a hormone called **gonadotropin-releasing hormone,** or **GnRH,** that stimulates the anterior pituitary to secrete the gonadotropic hormones. There are two gonadotropic hormones, **follicle-stimulating hormone (FSH)** and **luteinizing hormone (LH),** which are present in both males and females. In males, FSH promotes the production of sperm in the seminiferous tubules.

LH in males controls the production of testosterone by the interstitial cells. All these hormones are involved in a negative feedback relationship that maintains the fairly constant production of sperm and testosterone (Fig. 15.4).

Testosterone, the main sex hormone in males, is essential for the normal development and functioning of the organs listed in Table 15.1. Testosterone also brings about and maintains the male secondary sex characteristics that develop at the time of puberty. Males are generally taller than females and have broader shoulders and longer legs relative to trunk length. The deeper voices of males compared with those of females are due to a larger larynx with longer vocal cords. Since the so-called Adam's apple is a part of the larynx,

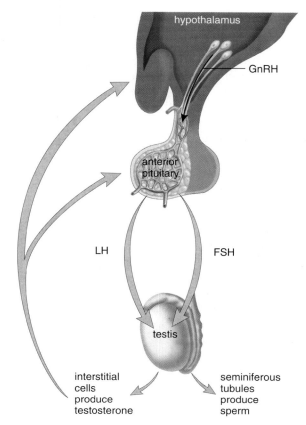

Figure 15.4 Hormonal control of testes.
GnRH (gonadotropin-releasing hormone) stimulates the anterior pituitary to secrete the gonadotropic hormones: Follicle-stimulating hormone (FSH) stimulates the production of sperm, and luteinizing hormone (LH) stimulates the production of testosterone. Testosterone and inhibin exert negative feedback control over the hypothalamus and the anterior pituitary, and this regulates the level of testosterone in the blood.

it is usually more prominent in males than in females. Testosterone causes males to develop noticeable hair on the face, chest, and occasionally other regions of the body, such as the back. A related chemical also leads to the receding hairline and pattern baldness that occur in males.

Testosterone is responsible for the greater muscular development in males. Knowing this, both males and females sometimes take anabolic steroids, which are either testosterone or related steroid hormones resembling testosterone. Health problems involving the kidneys, the cardiovascular system, and hormonal imbalances can arise from such use. The testes shrink in size, and feminization of other male traits occurs (see Fig. 14.16).

The gonads in males are the testes, which produce sperm as well as testosterone, the most significant male sex hormone.

15.2 Female Reproductive System

The female reproductive system includes the organs depicted in Figure 15.5 and listed in Table 15.2. The female gonads are paired **ovaries** that lie in shallow depressions, one on each side of the upper pelvic cavity. **Oogenesis** is the production of an **egg,** the female gamete. The ovaries alternate in producing one egg a month. **Ovulation** is the process by which an egg bursts from an ovary and usually enters an oviduct.

The Genital Tract

The **oviducts,** also called the uterine or fallopian tubes, extend from the uterus to the ovaries; however, the oviducts are not attached to the ovaries. Instead, they have finger-like projections called fimbriae (sing., **fimbria**) that sweep over the ovaries. When an egg bursts from an ovary during ovulation, it usually is swept into an oviduct by the combined action of the fimbriae and the beating of cilia that line the oviducts.

Once in the oviduct, the egg is propelled slowly by ciliary movement and tubular muscle contraction toward the uterus. An egg only lives approximately 6–24 hours, unless fertilization occurs. Fertilization, and therefore **zygote** formation, usually takes place in the oviduct. The developing embryo normally arrives at the uterus after several days and then **implantation** occurs—the embryo embeds in the uterine lining, which has been prepared to receive it.

The **uterus** is a thick-walled, muscular organ about the size and shape of an inverted pear. Normally, it lies above and is tipped over the urinary bladder. The oviducts join the uterus at its upper end, while at its lower end, the **cervix** enters the vagina nearly at a right angle.

Cancer of the cervix is a common form of cancer in women. Early detection is possible by means of a **Pap test,** which requires the removal of a few cells from the region of the cervix for microscopic examination. If the cells are cancerous, a physician may recommend a hysterectomy. A

Table 15.2	Female Reproductive Organs
Organ	**Function**
Ovaries	Produce egg and sex hormones
Oviducts (uterine or fallopian tubes)	Conduct egg; location of fertilization
Uterus (womb)	Houses developing fetus
Cervix	Contains opening to uterus
Vagina	Receives penis during sexual intercourse; serves as birth canal and as an exit for menstrual flow

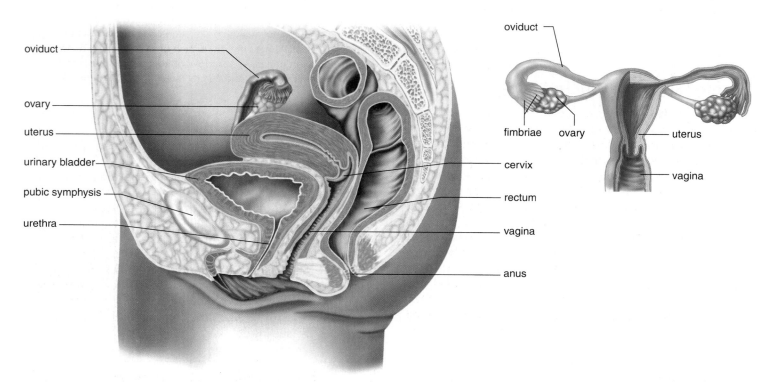

Figure 15.5   **The female reproductive system.**
The ovaries usually release one egg a month; fertilization occurs in the oviduct, and development occurs in the uterus. The vagina is the birth canal, as well as the organ of sexual intercourse and outlet for menstrual flow.

hysterectomy is the removal of the uterus, including the cervix. Removal of the ovaries in addition to the uterus is technically termed an ovariohysterectomy (radical hysterectomy). Because the vagina remains, the woman can still engage in sexual intercourse.

Development of the embryo and fetus normally takes place in the uterus. This organ, sometimes called the womb, is approximately 5 cm wide in its usual state but is capable of stretching to over 30 cm wide to accommodate a growing fetus. The lining of the uterus, called the **endometrium,** participates in the formation of the placenta (see page 300), which supplies nutrients needed for embryonic and fetal development. The endometrium has two layers: a basal layer and an inner, functional layer. In the nonpregnant female, the functional layer of the endometrium varies in thickness according to a monthly reproductive cycle called the uterine cycle.

A small opening in the cervix leads to the vaginal canal. The **vagina** is a tube that lies at a 45° angle to the small of the back. The mucosal lining of the vagina lies in folds and can extend. This is especially important when the vagina serves as the birth canal, and it facilitates sexual intercourse, when the vagina receives the penis. The vagina also acts as an exit for menstrual flow.

> Once each month, an egg produced by an ovary enters an oviduct. If fertilization occurs, the developing embryo is propelled by cilia to the uterus, where it implants in the endometrium.

External Genitals

The external genital organs of the female are known collectively as the **vulva** (Fig. 15.6). The vulva includes two large, hair-covered folds of skin called the labia majora. The labia majora extend backward from the mons pubis, a fatty prominence underlying the pubic hair. The labia minora are two small folds lying just inside the labia majora. They extend forward from the vaginal opening to encircle and form a foreskin for the glans clitoris. The glans clitoris is the organ of sexual arousal in females and, like the penis, contains a shaft of erectile tissue that becomes engorged with blood during sexual stimulation.

The cleft between the labia minora contains the openings of the urethra and the vagina. The vagina may be partially closed by a ring of tissue called the hymen. The hymen is ordinarily ruptured by sexual intercourse or by other types of physical activities. If remnants of the hymen persist after sexual intercourse, they can be surgically removed.

Notice that the urinary and reproductive systems in the female are entirely separate. For example, the urethra carries only urine, and the vagina serves only as the birth canal and the organ for sexual intercourse.

Orgasm in Females

Upon sexual stimulation, the labia minora, the vaginal wall, and the clitoris become engorged with blood. The breasts also swell, and the nipples become erect. The labia majora enlarge, redden, and spread away from the vaginal opening.

The vagina expands and elongates. Blood vessels in the vaginal wall release small droplets of fluid that seep into the vagina and lubricate it. Mucus-secreting glands beneath the labia minora on either side of the vagina also provide lubrication for entry of the penis into the vagina. Although the vagina is the organ of sexual intercourse in females, the clitoris plays a significant role in the female sexual response. The extremely sensitive clitoris can swell to two or three times its usual size. The thrusting of the penis and the pressure of the pubic symphyses of the partners act to stimulate the clitoris.

Orgasm occurs at the height of the sexual response. Blood pressure and pulse rate rise, breathing quickens, and the walls of the uterus and oviducts contract rhythmically. A sensation of intense pleasure is followed by relaxation when organs return to their normal size. Females have no refractory period, and multiple orgasms can occur during a single sexual experience.

> The vagina and the external genitals, especially the clitoris, play an active role in the sexual response of females, which culminates in uterine and oviduct contractions.

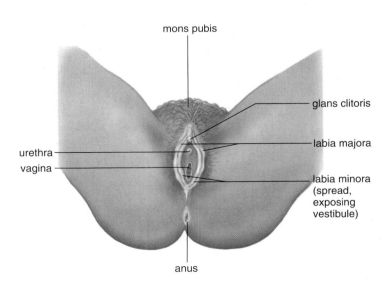

Figure 15.6   External genitals of the female.
At birth, the opening of the vagina is partially blocked by a membrane called the hymen. Physical activities and sexual intercourse rupture the hymen.

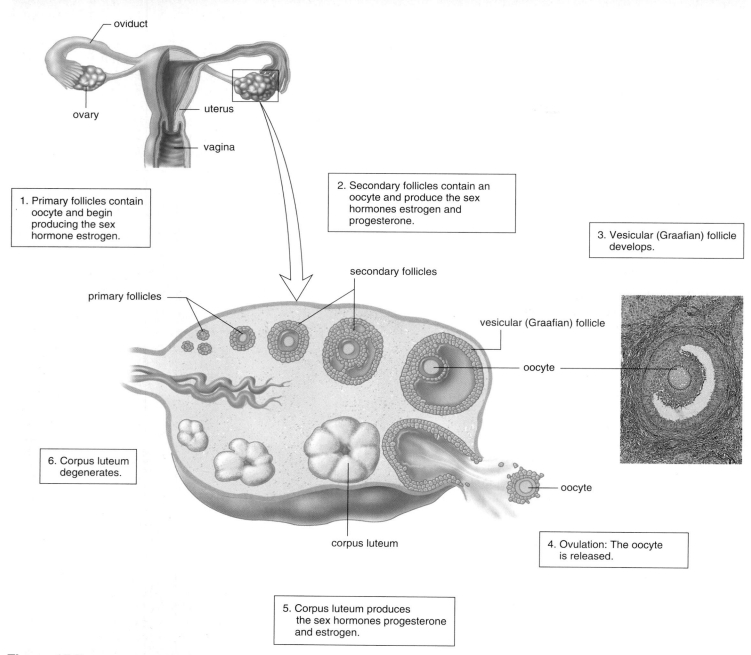

oviduct

ovary

uterus

vagina

1. Primary follicles contain oocyte and begin producing the sex hormone estrogen.

2. Secondary follicles contain an oocyte and produce the sex hormones estrogen and progesterone.

3. Vesicular (Graafian) follicle develops.

secondary follicles

primary follicles

vesicular (Graafian) follicle

oocyte

oocyte

6. Corpus luteum degenerates.

corpus luteum

oocyte

4. Ovulation: The oocyte is released.

5. Corpus luteum produces the sex hormones progesterone and estrogen.

Figure 15.7   Ovarian cycle.
As a follicle matures, the oocyte enlarges and is surrounded by layers of follicle cells and fluid. Eventually, ovulation occurs, the mature follicle ruptures, and the oocyte is released. A single follicle actually goes through all stages in one place within the ovary.

15.3 Female Hormone Levels

Hormone levels cycle in the female on a monthly basis, and the ovarian cycle drives the uterine cycle, as discussed in this section.

Ovarian Cycle: Nonpregnant

A longitudinal section through an ovary shows that it is made up of an outer region and an inner region (Fig. 15.7). In the outer region are many **follicles,** and each one contains an immature egg, called an oocyte. A female is born with as many as 2 million follicles, but the number is reduced to 300,000–400,000 by the time of puberty. Only a small number of follicles (about 400) ever mature because a female usually produces only one egg per month during her reproductive years. Oocytes, present at birth, age as the woman ages. This may be one reason older women are more likely to have difficulty becoming pregnant and are more likely to produce children with genetic defects.

The **ovarian cycle** occurs as a follicle changes from a primary to a secondary to a vesicular (Graafian) follicle (Fig. 15.7). Epithelial cells of a primary follicle surround a primary oocyte. Pools of follicular fluid surround the oocyte in a secondary follicle. In a vesicular follicle, a fluid-filled cavity increases to the point that the follicle wall balloons out on the surface of the ovary.

As the vesicular follicle develops, an oocyte becomes visible. The vesicular follicle bursts, releasing the oocyte (often called an egg) surrounded by a clear membrane. This process is referred to as ovulation. Once a vesicular follicle has lost the oocyte, it develops into a **corpus luteum,** a gland-like structure.

The oocyte enters an oviduct. Fertilization does not occur; the oocyte disintegrates and the corpus luteum begins to degenerate after about ten days.

Phases of the Ovarian Cycle

The ovarian cycle is commonly divided into two phases. The first half of the cycle is called the follicular phase and the second half is the luteal phase. During the *follicular phase,* follicle-stimulating hormone (FSH), produced by the anterior pituitary, promotes the development of a follicle in the ovary, which secretes estrogen and progesterone (Fig. 15.8). As the estrogen level in the blood rises, it exerts feedback control over the anterior pituitary secretion of FSH so that the follicular phase comes to an end.

Presumably, an estrogen spike causes a sudden secretion of a large amount of GnRH from the hypothalamus. This leads to a surge of LH production by the anterior pituitary and to ovulation at about the 14th day of a 28-day cycle.

Now, the *luteal phase* begins. During the luteal phase of the ovarian cycle, LH promotes the development of the corpus luteum, which secretes estrogen and progesterone. When pregnancy does not occur, a uterine hormone causes the corpus luteum to regress and a new cycle begins with menstruation.

One ovarian follicle per month produces an oocyte (egg). Following ovulation, the follicle develops into corpus luteum. When fertilization does not occur, the oocyte disintegrates and the corpus luteum degenerates.

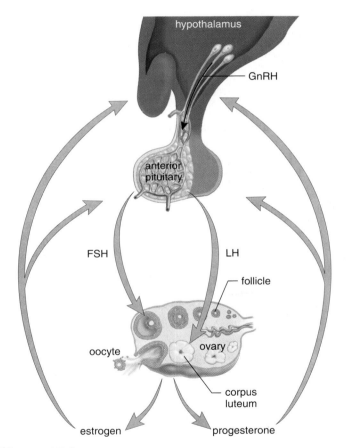

Figure 15.8   Hormonal control of ovaries.
The hypothalamus produces GnRH (gonadotropin-releasing hormone). GnRH stimulates the anterior pituitary to produce follicle-stimulating hormone (FSH) and luteinizing hormone (LH). FSH stimulates the follicle to produce estrogen, and LH stimulates the corpus luteum to produce progesterone. Estrogen and progesterone maintain the sexual organs (e.g., uterus) and the secondary sex characteristics, and exert feedback control over the hypothalamus and the anterior pituitary.

The Uterine Cycle: Nonpregnant

The female sex hormones, **estrogen** and **progesterone,** have numerous functions. One function of these hormones affects the endometrium, causing the uterus to undergo a cyclical series of events known as the **uterine cycle** (Fig. 15.9). Twenty-eight-day cycles are divided as follows:

During *days 1–5,* a low level of estrogen and progesterone in the body causes the endometrium to disintegrate and its blood vessels to rupture. On day one of the cycle, a flow of blood and tissues, known as the menses, passes out of the vagina during **menstruation,** also called the menstrual period.

During *days 6–13,* increased production of estrogen by a new ovarian follicle in the ovary causes the endometrium to thicken and become vascular and glandular. This is called the proliferative phase of the uterine cycle.

On *day 14* of a 28-day cycle, ovulation usually occurs.

During *days 15–28,* increased production of progesterone by the corpus luteum in the ovary causes the endometrium of the uterus to double or triple in thickness (from 1 mm to 2–3 mm) and the uterine glands to mature, producing a thick mucoid secretion. This is called the secretory phase of the uterine cycle. The endometrium is now prepared to receive the developing embryo. If this does not occur, the corpus luteum in the ovary regresses, and the low level of sex hormones in the female body results in the endometrium breaking down during menstruation.

Table 15.3 compares the stages of the uterine cycle with those of the ovarian cycle when pregnancy does not occur.

Menstruation

During menstruation, arteries that supply the lining of the uterus constrict and the capillaries weaken. Blood spilling from the damaged vessels detaches layers of the lining, not all at once, but in random patches. Endometrium, mucus, and blood descend from the uterus, through the vagina, creating menstrual flow. Fibrinolysin, an enzyme released by dying cells, prevents the blood from clotting. Menstruating lasts from three to five days, as the uterus sloughs off the thick lining that was three weeks in the making.

Painful Menstruation and Premenstrual Syndrome

About half of all women complain of painful menstruation, characterized by agonizing cramps, headaches, backaches, and nausea. Painful menstruation is the leading cause of lost time from school and work among young women.

Researchers have shown that prostaglandin levels are four or five times higher in women who experience painful menstruation than in those whose menstrual periods are

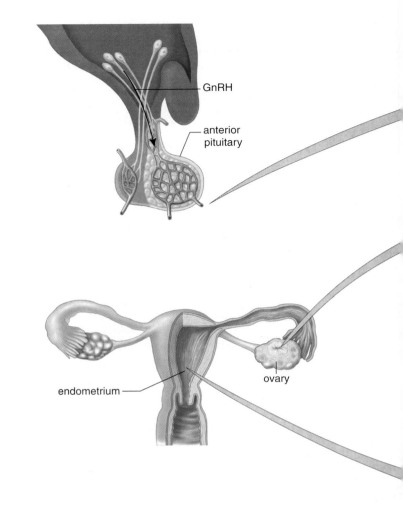

relatively painless. Protaglandins are known to cause muscle contractions, particularly uterine contraction during childbirth.

Self-help measures for painful menstruation include application of a heating pad to the lower abdomen, the intake of warm beverages, and taking warm showers or baths. Over-the-counter anti-inflammatory medicines may be helpful; if not, a physician can prescribe other medications.

Premenstrual syndrome (PMS) is a group of symptoms related to the menstrual cycle. Anywhere from two weeks to a few days before menstruation, a significant number of women experience such symptoms as irrational mood swings, headaches, joint pain, digestive upsets, and sore breasts. The mood swings can be particularly troublesome if they lead to behaviors uncharacteristic of the individual.

Self-help measures include adopting a healthy lifestyle, such as that recommended for cardiovascular health on page 90. Avoiding salt, sugar, caffeine, and alcohol, especially when symptoms are present, can possibly help. Severe symptoms may require the intervention of a physician.

During the uterine cycle, the endometrium builds up and then is broken down during menstruation.

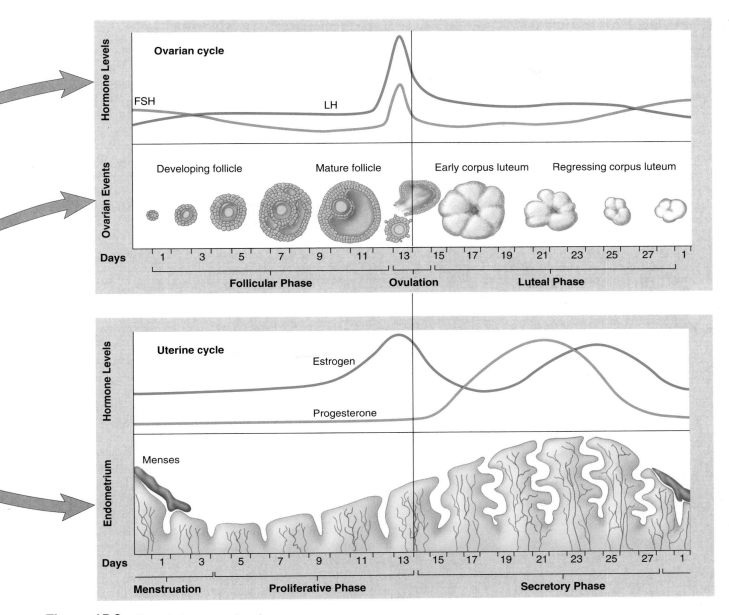

Figure 15.9   Female hormone levels.
During the follicular phase, FSH released by the anterior pituitary promotes the maturation of a follicle in the ovary. The ovarian follicle produces increasing levels of estrogen, which causes the endometrium to thicken during the proliferative phase of the uterine cycle. After ovulation and during the luteal phase of the ovarian cycle, LH promotes the development of the corpus luteum. Progesterone in particular causes the endometrial lining to become secretory. Menses, due to the breakdown of the endometrium, begins when progesterone production declines to a low level.

Table 15.3	Ovarian and Uterine Cycles: Nonpregnant		
Ovarian Cycle	**Events**	**Uterine Cycle**	**Events**
Follicular phase—Days 1–13	FSH secretion begins.	Menstruation—Days 1–5	Endometrium breaks down.
	Follicle maturation occurs.	Proliferative phase—Days 6–13	Endometrium rebuilds.
	Estrogen secretion is prominent.		
Ovulation—Day 14*	LH spike occurs.		
Luteal phase—Days 15–28	LH secretion continues. Corpus luteum forms.	Secretory phase—Days 15–28	Endometrium thickens, and glands are secretory.
	Progesterone secretion is prominent.		

*Assuming a 28-day cycle.

Fertilization and Pregnancy

Following unprotected sexual intercourse, many sperm will most likely make their way into the oviduct, where the egg is located following ovulation. Only one sperm fertilizes the egg and it becomes a zygote, which begins development even as it travels down the oviduct to the uterus. The endometrium is now prepared to receive the developing embryo, which becomes implanted in the lining several days following fertilization (Fig. 15.10). Pregnancy has now begun; an abortion is the removal of an implanted embryo.

The **placenta,** which sustains the developing embryo and later fetus, originates from both maternal and fetal tissues. It is the region of exchange of molecules between fetal and maternal blood, although the two rarely mix. At first, the placenta produces **human chorionic gonadotropin (HCG),** which maintains the corpus luteum in the ovary until the placenta begins its own production of estrogen and progesterone. A pregnancy test detects the presence of HCG in the blood or urine. If this molecule is present, a woman is pregnant.

Estrogen and progesterone produced by the placenta have two effects: They shut down the anterior pituitary so that no new follicle in the ovaries matures, and they maintain the endometrium so that the corpus luteum in the ovary is no longer needed. Usually, there is no menstruation during pregnancy.

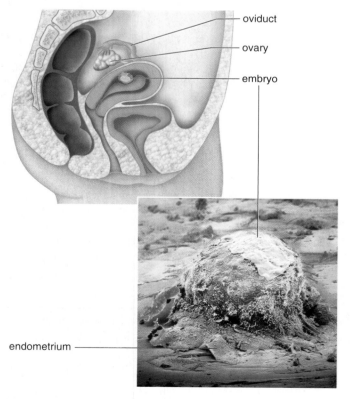

oviduct

ovary

embryo

endometrium

Figure 15.10 **Implantation.**
A scanning electron micrograph showing an embryo implanted in the endometrium on day 12 following fertilization.

Estrogen and Progesterone

Estrogen and progesterone affect not only the uterus but other parts of the body as well. Estrogen is largely responsible for the secondary sex characteristics in females, including body hair and fat distribution. In general, females have a more rounded appearance than males because of a greater accumulation of fat beneath the skin. Like males, females develop axillary and pubic hair during puberty. In females, the upper border of pubic hair is horizontal, but in males, it tapers toward the navel. Both estrogen and progesterone are also required for breast development. Other hormones are involved in milk production following pregnancy and milk letdown when a baby begins to nurse.

The pelvic girdle is wider and deeper in females, so the pelvic cavity usually has a larger relative size compared with that of males. This means that females have wider hips than males and that their thighs converge at a greater angle toward the knees. Because the female pelvis tilts forward, females tend to have more of a lower back curve than males, an abdominal bulge, and protruding buttocks.

Menopause

Menopause, the period in a woman's life during which the ovarian and uterine cycles cease, is likely to occur between ages 45 and 55. The ovaries are no longer responsive to the gonadotropic hormones produced by the anterior pituitary, and the ovaries no longer secrete estrogen or progesterone. At the onset of menopause, the uterine cycle becomes irregular, but as long as menstruation occurs, it is still possible for a woman to conceive. Therefore, a woman is usually not considered to have completed menopause until menstruation is absent for a year.

The hormonal changes during menopause often produce physical symptoms, such as "hot flashes" (caused by circulatory irregularities), dizziness, headaches, insomnia, sleepiness, and depression. These symptoms may be mild or even absent. Women sometimes report an increased sex drive following menopause. It has been suggested that this may be due to androgen production by the adrenal cortex.

Until recently, many women took combined estrogen-progestin drugs to ease menopausal symptoms. However, a new study conducted by the Women's Health Initiative (WHI), found that the long-term use of the combined drugs by most menopausal women caused increases in breast cancer, heart attacks, strokes, and blood clots. Those risks outweigh the drugs' actual benefits—a small decrease in hip fractures and a decrease in cases of colorectal cancer.

Estrogen and progesterone produced by the ovaries are the female sex hormones. They foster the development of the reproductive organs, maintain the uterine cycle, and bring about the secondary sex characteristics in females.

15.4 Control of Reproduction

Several means are available to dampen or enhance our reproductive potential. **Birth control methods** are used to regulate the number of children an individual or couple will have.

Birth Control Methods

The most reliable method of birth control is abstinence—that is, not engaging in sexual intercourse. This form of birth control has the added advantage of preventing transmission of a sexually transmitted disease. Table 15.4 lists other means of birth control used in the United States, and rates their effectiveness. For example, with the birth control pill, we expect 100% effectiveness and no sexually active women will get pregnant within the year. On the other hand, with natural family planning, one of the least effective methods given in the table, we expect that 70% will not get pregnant and 30% will get pregnant within the year.

Figure 15.11 features some of the most effective and commonly used means of birth control. **Contraceptives** are medications and devices that reduce the chance of pregnancy. Oral contraception **(birth control pills)** often involves taking a combination of estrogen and progesterone on a daily basis (Fig. 15.11a). The estrogen and progesterone in the birth control pill or a patch applied to the skin effectively shut down the pituitary production of both FSH and LH so that no follicle in the ovary begins to develop in the ovary; since ovulation does not occur, pregnancy cannot take place. Because of possible side effects, women taking birth control pills should see a physician regularly.

An **intrauterine device (IUD)** is a small piece of molded plastic that is inserted into the uterus by a physician. IUDs are believed to alter the environment of the uterus and oviducts so that fertilization probably will not occur—but if fertilization should occur, implantation cannot take place. The type of IUD featured in Figure 15.11b has copper wire wrapped around the plastic.

The **diaphragm** is a soft latex cup with a flexible rim that lodges behind the pubic bone and fits over the cervix (Fig. 15.11c). Each woman must be properly fitted by a physician, and the diaphragm can be inserted into the vagina no more than 2 hours before sexual relations. Also, it must be used with spermicidal jelly or cream and should be left in place at least 6 hours after sexual relations. The cervical cap is a minidiaphragm.

There has been a renewal of interest in barrier methods of birth control, because these methods offer some protection against sexually transmitted diseases. A **female condom,** now available, consists of a large polyurethane tube with a flexible ring that fits onto the cervix (Fig. 15.11d). The open end of the tube has a ring that covers the external genitals. A **male condom** is most often a latex sheath that fits over the erect penis. The ejaculate is trapped inside the sheath, and thus does not enter the vagina. When used in conjunction with a spermicide, the protection is better than with the condom alone.

Contraceptive implants utilize a synthetic progesterone to prevent ovulation by disrupting the ovarian cycle. The older version of the implant consists of six match-sized, time-release capsules that are surgically implanted under the skin of a woman's upper arm. The newest version consists of a single capsule that remains effective for about three years (Fig. 15.11e).

Contraceptive injections are available as progesterone only (Fig. 15.11f) or a combination of estrogen and progesterone. The length of time between injections can vary from three months to a few weeks.

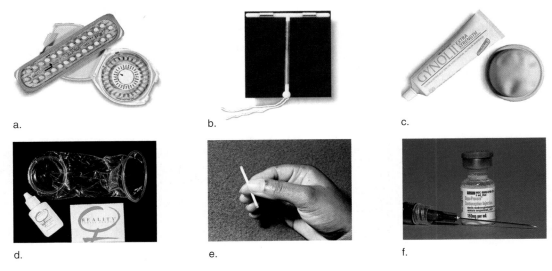

a.   b.   c.

d.   e.   f.

Figure 15.11   Various birth control devices.
a. Oral contraception (birth control pills). **b.** Intrauterine device. **c.** Spermicidal jelly and diaphragm. **d.** Female condom. **e.** Contraceptive implant. **f.** Contraceptive injections.

Contraceptive vaccines are now being developed. For example, a vaccine intended to immunize women against HCG, the hormone so necessary to maintaining the implantation of the embryo, was successful in a limited clinical trial. Since HCG is not normally present in the body, no autoimmune reaction is expected, but the immunization does wear off with time. Others believe that it would also be possible to develop a safe antisperm vaccine that could be used in women.

Morning-After Pills

A morning-after pill, or emergency contraception, refers to a medication that will prevent pregnancy after unprotected intercourse. The expression "morning-after pill" is a misnomer in that the medication can begin one to several days after unprotected intercourse.

One type, a kit called Preven, contains four synthetic progesterone pills; two are taken up to 72 hours after unprotected intercourse, and two more are taken 12 hours later.

The medication upsets the normal uterine cycle, making it difficult for an embryo to implant itself in the endometrium. In a recent study, it was estimated that the medication was 85% effective in preventing unintended pregnancies.

Mifepristone, better known as RU-486, is a pill that is presently used to cause the loss of an implanted embryo by blocking the progesterone receptor proteins of endometrial cells. Without functioning receptors for progesterone, the endometrium sloughs off, carrying the embryo with it. When taken in conjunction with a prostaglandin to induce uterine contractions, RU-486 is 95% effective. It is possible that some day this medication will also be a "morning-after pill," taken when menstruation is late without evidence that pregnancy has occurred.

The birth control methods and devices now available vary in effectiveness. New methods of birth control are expected to be developed.

Table 15.4   Common Birth Control Methods

Name	Procedure	Methodology	Effectiveness	Risk
Abstinence	Refrain from sexual intercourse	No sperm in vagina	100%	None
Vasectomy	Vasa deferentia are cut and tied	No sperm in seminal fluid	Almost 100%	Irreversible sterility
Tubal ligation	Oviducts cut and tied	No eggs in oviduct	Almost 100%	Irreversible sterility
Oral contraception (or a patch applied to skin)	Hormone medication taken daily	Anterior pituitary does not release FSH and LH	Almost 100%	Thromboembolism, especially in smokers
Contraceptive implants	Tubes of progestin (form of progesterone) implanted under skin	Anterior pituitary does not release FSH and LH	More than 90%	Presently none known
Contraceptive injections	Injections of hormones	Anterior pituitary does not release FSH and LH	About 99%	Osteoporosis?
Intrauterine device (IUD)	Plastic coil inserted into uterus by physician	Prevents implantation	More than 90%	Infection (pelvic inflammatory disease)
Diaphragm	Latex cup inserted into vagina to cover cervix before intercourse	Blocks entrance of sperm to uterus	With jelly, about 90%	Latex, spermicide allergy
Cervical cap	Latex cap held by suction over cervix	Delivers spermicide near cervix	Almost 85%	UTI,[1] latex or spermicide allergy
Male condom	Latex sheath fitted over erect penis	Traps sperm and prevents STDs	About 85%	Latex allergy
Female condom	Polyurethane liner fitted inside vagina	Blocks entrance of sperm to uterus and prevents STDs	About 85%	—
Coitus interruptus	Penis withdrawn before ejaculation	Prevents ejaculate from entering	About 75%	Presently none known
Jellies, creams, foams	These spermicidal products inserted before intercourse	Kill a large number of sperm	About 75%	UTI,[2] vaginitis, allergy
Natural family planning	Day of ovulation determined by record keeping, various methods of testing	Intercourse avoided on certain days of the month	About 70%	Presently none known
Douche	Vagina cleansed after intercourse	Washes out sperm	Less than 70%	Presently none known

[1]Effectiveness cited here is dependent on using the method properly.
[2]UTI = urinary tract infection.

Ecology Focus

Endocrine-Disrupting Contaminants

Rachel Carson's book *Silent Spring*, published in 1962, predicted that pesticides would have a deleterious effect on animal life. Soon thereafter, it was found that pesticides caused the thinning of eggshells in bald eagles to the point that their eggs broke and the chicks died. Additionally, populations of terns, gulls, cormorants, and lake trout declined after they ate fish contaminated by high levels of environmental toxins. The concern was so great that the United States Environmental Protection Agency (EPA) came into existence. The efforts of this agency and civilian environmental groups have brought about a reduction in pollution release and a cleaning up of emissions. Even so, we are now aware of more subtle effects that pollutants can have.

Hormones influence nearly all aspects of physiology and behavior in animals. Therefore, when wildlife in contaminated areas began to exhibit certain types of abnormalities, researchers began to think that certain pollutants can affect the endocrine system. In England, male fish exposed to sewage developed ovarian tissue and produced a metabolite normally found only in females during egg formation. In California, western gulls displayed abnormalities in gonad structure and nesting behaviors. Hatchling alligators in Florida possessed abnormal gonads and hormone concentrations linked to nesting.

At first, such effects seemed to indicate only the involvement of the female hormone estrogen, and researchers therefore called the contaminants ecoestrogens. However, further study brought more information to light. Many of the contaminants interact with hormone receptors, and in that way cause developmental effects. Others bind directly with sex hormones, such as testosterone and estrogen. Still others alter the physiology of the growth hormones and neurotransmitters responsible for brain development and behavior. Therefore, the preferred term today for these pollutants is endocrine-disrupting contaminants (EDCs).

Many EDCs are chemicals used as pesticides and herbicides in agriculture, and some are associated with the manufacture of various other synthetic organic compounds such as PCBs (polychlorinated biphenyls). Some chemicals shown to influence hormones are found in plastics, food additives, and personal hygiene products. In mice, phthalate esters, which are plastic components, affect neonatal development when present in the part-per-trillion range. It is of great concern that EDCs have been found at levels comparable to functional hormone levels in the human body. Furthermore, it is not surprising that EDCs are affecting the endocrine systems of a wide range of organisms (Fig. 15A).

Scientists and those representing industrial manufacturers continue to debate whether EDCs pose a health risk to humans. Some suspect that EDCs lower sperm counts, reduce male and female fertility, and increase rates of certain cancers (breast, ovarian, testicular, and prostate). Additionally, some studies suggest that EDCs contribute to learning deficits and behavioral problems in children. Laboratory and field research continues to identify chemicals that have the ability to influence the endocrine system. Millions of tons of potential EDCs are produced annually in the United States, and the EPA is under pressure to certify these compounds as safe. The European Economic Community has already restricted the use of certain EDCs and has banned the production of specific plastic components intended for use by children. Only through continued scientific research and the cooperation of industry can we identify the risks that EDCs pose to the environment, wildlife, and humans.

Figure 15A Exposure to endocrine-disrupting contaminants.
Various types of wildlife, as well as humans, are exposed to endocrine-disrupting contaminants that can seriously affect their health and reproductive abilities.

Infertility

Infertility is the failure of a couple to achieve pregnancy after one year of regular, unprotected intercourse. The American Medical Association (AMA) estimates that 15% of all couples are infertile. The cause of infertility can be attributed to the male (40%), the female (40%), or both (20%).

Causes of Infertility

The most frequent cause of infertility in males is low sperm count and/or a large proportion of abnormal sperm, which can be due to environmental influences. The public is particularly concerned about endocrine-disrupting contaminants (EDCs), which are discussed in the Ecology Focus on page 303. But thus far, it appears that a sedentary lifestyle coupled with smoking and alcohol consumption most often leads to male infertility. When males spend most of the day sitting in front of a computer or the TV or driving, the testes temperature remains too high for adequate sperm production.

Body weight appears to be the most significant factor in causing female infertility. In women of normal weight, fat cells produce a hormone called leptin that stimulates the hypothalamus to release GnRH. In overweight women, the ovaries often contain many small follicles, and the woman fails to ovulate. Other causes of infertility in females are blocked oviducts due to pelvic inflammatory disease (see page 454) and endometriosis. Endometriosis is the presence of uterine tissue outside the uterus, particularly in the oviducts and on the abdominal organs. Backward flow of menstrual fluid allows living uterine cells to establish themselves in the abdominal cavity, where they go through the usual uterine cycle, causing pain and structural abnormalities that make it more difficult for a woman to conceive.

Sometimes the causes of infertility can be corrected by medical intervention so that couples can have children. If no obstruction is apparent and body weight is normal, it is possible to give females fertility drugs, which are gonadotropic hormones that stimulate the ovaries and bring about ovulation. Such hormone treatments may cause multiple ovulations and multiple births.

When reproduction does not occur in the usual manner, many couples adopt a child. Others sometimes try one of the assisted reproductive technologies discussed in the following paragraphs.

Assisted Reproductive Technologies

Assisted reproductive technologies (ART) consist of techniques used to increase the chances of pregnancy. Often, sperm and/or eggs are retrieved from the testes and ovaries, and fertilization takes place in a clinical or laboratory setting.

Artificial Insemination by Donor (AID)   During artificial insemination, sperm are placed in the vagina by a physician. Sometimes a woman is artificially inseminated by her part-

ner's sperm. This is especially helpful if the partner has a low sperm count, because the sperm can be collected over a period of time and concentrated so that the sperm count is sufficient to result in fertilization. Often, however, a woman is inseminated by sperm acquired from a donor who is a complete stranger to her. At times, a combination of partner and donor sperm is used.

A variation of AID is *intrauterine insemination (IUI)*. In IUI, fertility drugs are given to stimulate the ovaries, and then the donor's sperm is placed in the uterus, rather than in the vagina.

If the prospective parents wish, sperm can be sorted into those that are believed to be X-bearing or Y-bearing to increase the chances of having a child of the desired sex.

In Vitro Fertilization (IVF)   During IVF, conception occurs in laboratory glassware. Ultrasound machines can now spot follicles in the ovaries that hold immature eggs; therefore, the latest method is to forgo the administration of fertility drugs and retrieve immature eggs by using a needle. The immature eggs are then brought to maturity in glassware before concentrated sperm are added. After about two to four days, the embryos are ready to be transferred to the uterus of the woman, who is now in the secretory phase of her uterine cycle. If desired, the embryos can be tested for a genetic disease, and only those found to be free of disease will be used. If implantation is successful, development is normal and continues to term.

Gamete Intrafallopian Transfer (GIFT)   The term **gamete** refers to a sex cell, either a sperm or an egg. GIFT was devised to overcome the low success rate (15–20%) of in vitro fertilization. The method is exactly the same as in vitro fertilization, except the eggs and the sperm are placed in the oviducts immediately after they have been brought together. GIFT has the advantage of being a one-step procedure for the woman—the eggs are removed and reintroduced all in the same time period. A variation on this procedure is to fertilize the eggs in the laboratory and then place the zygotes in the oviducts.

Surrogate Mothers   In some instances, women are contracted and paid to have babies. These women are called surrogate mothers. The sperm and even the egg can be contributed by the contracting parents.

Intracytoplasmic Sperm Injection (ICSI)   In this highly sophisticated procedure, a single sperm is injected into an egg. It is used effectively when a man has severe infertility problems.

When corrective procedures fail to reverse infertility, assisted reproductive technologies may be considered.

Bioethical Focus

Designer Children

Human beings have always attempted to influence the characteristics of their children. For example, couples have attempted to determine the sex of their children for centuries through a variety of methods. Amniocentesis has allowed us to test fetuses for chromosomal abnormalities and debilitating developmental defects before birth. Modern genetic testing technology enables parents to directly select children bearing desired traits, even at the very earliest stages of development.

Recently, a couple selected an embryo because, as a newborn, the individual could save the life of his sister (Fig. 15B). The couple, Jack and Lisa Nash, had a daughter with Fanconi's anemia, a rare inherited disorder in which affected persons cannot properly repair DNA damage that results from certain toxins. The disease primarily afflicts the bone marrow, and therefore results in a reduction of all types of blood cells. Anemia occurs, due to a deficiency of red blood cells. Patients are also at high risk of infection, because of low white blood cell numbers, and of leukemia, because white blood cells cannot properly repair any damage to their DNA.

Fanconi's anemia may be treated by a traditional bone marrow transplant, or by an adult stem cell transplant, preferably from a parent or sibling, because the risk of rejection is lower. Adult stem cells are almost always the preferred treatment option, because stem cells are hardier and much less likely to be rejected than a bone marrow transplant. Recall that the umbilical cord of a newborn is a rich source of adult stem cells for all types of blood cells. (Called adult because they are not embryonic stem cells.)

The selection of an embryo on the basis of genes is accomplished by extracting a sample of the DNA, determining its sequence, and comparing it with known sequences for diseases. In this case, doctors examined the DNA of embryos to see if they had the gene in question, that the newborn would be healthy, and also would be able to benefit his sister. The parents underwent in vitro fertilization, and the 15 resulting embryos were screened to see if they were both free of the inherited disease and a match for their daughter. Two embryos met these requirements, but only one implanted in the uterus and it developed into a healthy baby boy. Adult stem cells were harvested from the umbilical cord of the newborn and were successfully used to treat his sister's anemia. The physician who performed the genetic screening stated that he has received numerous inquiries about performing the procedure for other couples with diseased children.

This case, and other related cases, has raised a number of ethical issues surrounding prenatal selection of children based on genetic traits. While the AMA insists that selection based on traits not related to disease is unethical, the AMA's chair of the Council on Ethical and Judicial Affairs made an exception for this case, because the child was selected for

Figure 15B   The Nash family.
Jack, Molly holding baby Adam, and Lisa Nash. Adam was genetically selected as an embryo because the stem cells of his umbilical cord would save the life of his sister, Molly.

medical reasons. Dr. Jacques Montagut, who helped develop in vitro fertilization, believes that it is dangerous to bear children for the purpose of curing others, and compared it with "a new form of biological slavery." Still others think that, soon, children will be selected for less altruistic reasons, such as for their height, physical prowess, or intellectual abilities.

Decide Your Opinion

1. In general, do you think it is ethical to have children to cure medically related conditions, regardless of how fertilization occurred? If not, do you agree with the AMA that this case is an acceptable exception?
2. Because the brother was created ostensibly as a treatment for his sister's disease, do you believe that there is a moral obligation to provide him with compensation?
3. Would embryonic stem cells, derived from an aborted fetus and cultured in the laboratory, be an acceptable substitute?
4. Would you willingly donate sperm or eggs for in vitro fertilization to produce a healthy child for a couple who could not have one because of the risk of an inherited disease, such as Fanconi's anemia?

Summarizing the Concepts

15.1 Male Reproductive System

In males, spermatogenesis, occurring in seminiferous tubules of the testes, produces sperm that mature and are stored in the epididymides. Sperm may also be stored in the vasa deferentia before entering the urethra, along with secretions produced by the seminal vesicles, prostate gland, and bulbourethral glands. Sperm and these secretions are called semen, or seminal fluid.

The external genitals of males are the penis, the organ of sexual intercourse, and the scrotum, which contains the testes. Orgasm in males is a physical and emotional climax during sexual intercourse that results in ejaculation of semen from the penis.

Hormonal regulation, involving secretions from the hypothalamus, the anterior pituitary, and the testes, maintains testosterone, produced by the interstitial cells of the testes, at a fairly constant level. FSH from the anterior pituitary promotes spermatogenesis in the seminiferous tubules, and LH promotes testosterone production by the interstitial cells.

15.2 Female Reproductive System

In females, oogenesis occurring within the ovaries typically produces one mature follicle each month. This follicle balloons out of the ovary and bursts, releasing an egg, which enters an oviduct. The oviducts lead to the uterus, where implantation and development occur. The external genital area includes the vaginal opening, the clitoris, the labia minora, and the labia majora.

The vagina is the organ of sexual intercourse and the birth canal in females. The vagina and the external genitals, especially the clitoris, play an active role in orgasm, which culminates in uterine and oviduct contractions.

15.3 Female Hormone Levels

In the nonpregnant female, the ovarian cycle is under the hormonal control of the hypothalamus and the anterior pituitary. During the first half of the cycle, FSH from the anterior pituitary causes maturation of a follicle that secretes estrogen and some progesterone. After ovulation and during the second half of the cycle, LH from the anterior pituitary converts the follicle into the corpus luteum, which secretes progesterone and some estrogen.

Estrogen and progesterone regulate the uterine cycle. Estrogen causes the endometrium to rebuild. Ovulation usually occurs on day 14 of a 28-day cycle. Progesterone produced by the corpus luteum causes the endometrium to thicken and become secretory. Then a low level of hormones causes the endometrium to break down, as menstruation occurs.

If fertilization takes place, the embryo implants itself in the thickened endometrium. If fertilization and implantation occur, the corpus luteum in the ovary is maintained because of HCG production by the placenta, and therefore progesterone production does not cease. Menstruation usually does not occur during pregnancy.

15.4 Control of Reproduction

Numerous birth control methods and devices, such as the birth control pill, diaphragm, and condom, are available for those who wish to prevent pregnancy. Effectiveness varies, and research is being conducted to find new and possibly better methods. A morning-after pill for unprotected intercourse is now on the market.

Some couples are infertile, and if so, they may use assisted reproductive technologies in order to have a child. Artificial insemination and in vitro fertilization have been followed by more sophisticated techniques such as intracytoplasmic sperm injection.

Studying the Concepts

1. Outline the path of sperm. What glands contribute fluids to semen? 290–91
2. Discuss the anatomy and physiology of the testes. Describe the structure of sperm. 292–93
3. Name the endocrine glands involved in maintaining the sex characteristics of males and the hormones produced by each. 293
4. Describe the organs of the female genital tract. Where do fertilization and implantation occur? Name two functions of the vagina. 294–95
5. Name and describe the external genitals in females. 295
6. Discuss the anatomy and the physiology of the ovaries. Describe the ovarian cycle in the nonpregnant female. 296–97
7. Describe the uterine cycle, and relate it to the ovarian cycle. 298–99
8. In what way is menstruation prevented if pregnancy occurs? 300
9. Describe other functions of the female sex hormones aside from control of the ovarian and uterine cycles. 300
10. Discuss the various means of birth control and their relative effectiveness in preventing pregnancy. 301–2
11. Describe how in vitro fertilization is carried out. 304

Thinking Critically About the Concepts

Refer to the opening vignette on page 290, and then answer these questions.

1. Should there be government regulations on treatments for infertility?
2. If infertility is caused by genetic factors, are we increasing the possibility of bringing children into the world with abnormalities by developing techniques that allow infertile couples to have children?
3. What problems do you see in developing a male birth control pill?

Testing Your Knowledge of the Concepts

Choose the best answer for each question.

1. Label this diagram of the male reproductive system, and trace the path of sperm.

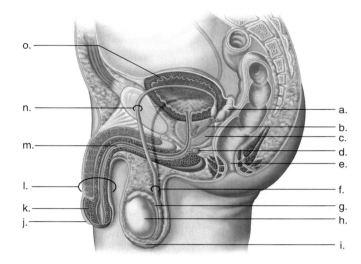

2. Which of these associations is mismatched?
   a. interstitial cells—testosterone
   b. seminiferous tubules—sperm production
   c. vasa deferentia—seminal fluid production
   d. urethra—conducts sperm

3. Follicle-stimulating hormone (FSH)
   a. is secreted by females but not by males.
   b. stimulates the seminiferous tubules to produce sperm.
   c. secretion is controlled by gonadotropin-releasing hormone (GnRH).
   d. Both b and c are correct.

4. In tracing the path of sperm, you would mention the vasa deferentia before the
   a. testes.   c. urethra.
   b. epididymides.   d. uterus.

5. An oocyte is fertilized in the
   a. vagina.   c. oviduct.
   b. uterus.   d. ovary.

6. Semen does not contain
   a. prostate fluid.   d. prostaglandins.
   b. urine.   e. Both b and d are correct.
   c. fructose.

7. Luteinizing hormone in males
   a. stimulates sperm development.
   b. triggers ovulation.
   c. is responsible for secondary sex characteristics.
   d. controls testosterone production by interstitial cells.

8. The release of the oocyte from the follicle is caused by
   a. a decreasing level of estrogen.
   b. a surge in the level of follicle-stimulating hormone.
   c. a surge in the level of luteinizing hormone.
   d. progesterone released from the corpus luteum.

9. For nine months, pregnancy is maintained by the
   a. anterior pituitary.   c. corpus luteum.
   b. ovaries.   d. placenta.

In questions 10–12, match each method of protection with a means of birth control in the key.

Key:

   a. vasectomy
   b. oral contraception
   c. intrauterine device (IUD)
   d. diaphragm
   e. male condom
   f. coitus interruptus

10. Blocks entrance of sperm to uterus

11. Traps sperm and also prevents STDs

12. Prevents implantation of an embryo

13. Following implantation, the corpus luteum is maintained by
    a. estrogen.
    b. progesterone.
    c. follicle-stimulating hormone.
    d. human chorionic gonadotropin.

14. During pregnancy,
    a. the ovarian and uterine cycles occur more quickly than before.
    b. GnRH is produced at a higher level than before.
    c. the ovarian and uterine cycles do not occur.
    d. the female secondary sex characteristics are not maintained.

15. Female oral contraceptives prevent pregnancy because
    a. the pill inhibits the release of luteinizing hormone.
    b. oral contraceptives prevent the release of an egg.
    c. follicle-stimulating hormone is not released.
    d. All of these are correct.

16. Which contraceptive method is most effective?
    a. abstinence
    b. diaphragm
    c. IUD
    d. Depo-Provera injection

17. Infertility is most often due to
    a. the male.
    b. the female.
    c. both.
    d. males and females are equally likely to be the cause of infertility.

18. Possible causes of male sterility include
    a. high testes temperature.
    b. exposure to endocrine-disrupting contaminants.
    c. production of abnormal sperm.
    d. All of these are correct.

19. Endometriosis, a common cause of infertility, involves
    a. inflammation of the ovaries.
    b. removal of the uterus.
    c. presence of uterine tissue in an oviduct or in the abdomen.
    d. inflammation of the uterus.

20. On about which days of the uterine cycle does menstruation usually occur?
    a. 1–5
    b. 5–10
    c. 14–20
    d. 15–28
    e. 28–35

21. Which of the following statements is incorrect?
    a. Fertilization usually occurs in the oviduct.
    b. Development begins before implantation.
    c. The placenta produces a hormone.
    d. There is usually no menstruation during pregnancy.
    e. All of these are correct.

22. Which of the following is the primary sex organ of the male?
    a. penis
    b. scrotum
    c. testis
    d. prostate

23. The scrotum is
    a. part of the primary sex organ.
    b. important in regulating the temperature of the testes.
    c. poorly innervated.
    d. an extension of the spermatic cord.

24. Testosterone is produced and secreted by
    a. spermatogonia.
    b. sustentacular cells.
    c. seminiferous tubules.
    d. interstitial cells.

25. Which of the following is incorrect?
    a. The lifetime of a sperm in the female tract is usually not longer than 48 hours.
    b. Testosterone is required for sperm production.
    c. The head of a sperm cell contains a nucleus.
    d. Spermatogenesis eventually exhausts the number of spermatogonia.

26. Which of the following is not in the path of sperm?
    a. epididymis
    b. seminal vesicle
    c. ejaculatory duct
    d. vas deferens

27. In an uncircumcised male, the prepuce covers
    a. the glans penis.
    b. the erectile tissue of the penis.
    c. the urethra of the penis.
    d. the shaft of the penis.

28. Secondary sex characteristics are
    a. the only body features that regress as we age.
    b. the same in males and females.
    c. those characteristics that develop only after puberty.
    d. the only reproductive structures that are affected by hormones.

Understanding Key Terms

acrosome 293
birth control method 301
birth control pill 301
bulbourethral gland 291
cervix 294
contraceptive 301
contraceptive implant 301
contraceptive injection 301
contraceptive vaccine 302
corpus luteum 297
diaphragm 301
egg 294
endometrium 295
epididymis 290
erectile dysfunction 291
estrogen 298
female condom 301
fimbria 294

follicle 297
follicle-stimulating hormone (FSH) 293
gamete 304
gonadotropin-releasing hormone (GnRH) 293
human chorionic gonadotropin (HCG) 300
implantation 294
infertility 304
interstitial cell 293
intrauterine device (IUD) 301
luteinizing hormone (LH) 293
male condom 301
menopause 300
menstruation 298
oogenesis 294
ovarian cycle 297
ovary 294
oviduct 294
ovulation 294

Pap test 294
penis 291
placenta 300
progesterone 298
prostate gland 290
scrotum 290
semen 290
seminal vesicle 290
seminiferous tubule 292
sperm 293
spermatogenesis 292
testes 290
testosterone 293
urethra 290
uterine cycle 298
uterus 294
vagina 295
vas deferens 290
vulva 295
zygote 294

Match the key terms to these definitions.

a. _____ Release of an oocyte from the ovary.

b. _____ Female sex hormone that causes the endometrium of the uterus to become secretory during the uterine cycle; along with estrogen, it maintains secondary sex characteristics in females.

c. _____ Thick, whitish fluid consisting of sperm and secretions from several glands of the male reproductive tract.

d. _____ Narrow end of the uterus, which projects into the vagina.

e. _____ Cap at the anterior end of a sperm that partially covers the nucleus and contains enzymes that help the sperm penetrate the egg.

Online Learning Center

www.mhhe.com/maderhuman9

The Online Learning Center provides a wealth of information fully organized and integrated by chapter. You will find practice quizzes, interactive activities, labeling exercises, flashcards, and much more that will complement your learning and understanding of human biology.

Looking at Both Sides

Each day, the Internet, media, and other people present you with opposing viewpoints on a wide range of subjects. Your ability to develop an informed opinion on an issue, and talk to others about it, is extremely important.

To expand and enhance your knowledge of a highly relevant bioethical issue, visit the "Student Edition" of the Online Learning Center. Under "Course-Wide Content," select "Looking at Both Sides." Once there, you will be asked to complete activities that will increase your understanding of a current bioethical issue related to this chapter and allow you to defend your opinion.

CHAPTER 16

Development and Aging

C H A P T E R   C O N C E P T S

16.1 Fertilization
- How does fertilization occur? 310

16.2 Development Before Birth
- Development involves what processes? 311
- What are the extraembryonic membranes? What is their function? 311
- What happens during pre-embryonic development? 313 During embryonic development? 315–17
- What is the path of blood through the heart and the rest of the fetus's body? Where does exchange of gases, nutrients, and wastes take place? 318
- What happens during fetal development? 319
- How do male and female sex organs develop? What causes ambiguous sex determination? 320–21

16.3 Pregnancy and Birth
- What physical and physiological changes can a pregnant woman expect? 324
- What are the stages of birth, and what happens during each stage? 324–25

16.4 Development After Birth
- What are the different hypotheses of aging? 326–27
- What is the effect of aging on the various body systems? 327–28
- What is the best way to keep healthy, even though aging occurs? 328

The tiny infant drifts into sleep, tired from the exertion of being born. It took nine months to reach this point. However, the newborn's journey of development is far from over.

Her existence commenced with one cell, formed when a single sperm fertilized an egg. As the developmental program unfolded, a series of cell divisions produced a hollow ball of cells. From this simple beginning, the tissues and then the organs gradually formed.

Even before this child's conception, her mother took good care of her own body to ensure that it could support a pregnancy. She watched her diet, didn't smoke, and during pregnancy, she abstained from alcohol. For quite a while, the baby will be completely dependent on her parents' devoted care. And during the years ahead, she will learn from them the essentials of good health.

A healthy lifestyle is important, because the baby has many changes to go through as she develops from a child to an adolescent and eventually to an adult. In order to reach her potential, she will need to have good nutrition and get plenty of exercise. During her lifetime, she will inevitably experience injuries. The body's efforts to heal itself are also considered part of development and are affected by overall wellness.

Even after the infant has grown up, her body will undergo changes due to aging. But maintaining good health habits can help her to avoid some age-related illnesses and lessen the effects of others.

Years of development await this infant. She is a complete, new individual, ready to meet the world. Well, maybe after a little nap. . . .

16.1 Fertilization

Fertilization results in a **zygote,** the first cell of the new individual. Figure 16.1 shows the manner in which an egg is fertilized by a sperm in humans.

Sperm and Egg Anatomy

A sperm has three distinct parts: a head, a middle piece, and a tail. The tail is a flagellum, which allows the sperm to swim toward the egg, and the middle piece contains energy-producing mitochondria. The head contains a nucleus and is capped by a membrane-bound acrosome. Notice that only the nucleus from the sperm head fuses with the egg nucleus. Therefore, the zygote receives cytoplasm and organelles only from the mother.

The plasma membrane of the egg is surrounded by an extracellular matrix termed the zona pellucida. In turn, the zona pellucida is surrounded by a few layers of adhering follicular cells, collectively called the corona radiata. These cells nourished the egg when it was in a follicle of the ovary.

Steps of Fertilization

During fertilization, (1) several sperm penetrate the corona radiata, (2) several sperm attempt to penetrate the zona pellucida, and (3) one sperm enters the egg. The acrosome plays a role in allowing sperm to penetrate the zona pellucida. After a sperm head binds tightly to the zona pellucida, the acrosome releases digestive enzymes that forge a pathway for the sperm through the zona pellucida. When a sperm binds to the egg, their plasma membranes fuse, and this sperm (the head, the middle piece, and usually the tail) enters the egg. Fusion of the sperm nucleus and the egg nucleus follows.

To ensure proper development, only one sperm should enter an egg. Prevention of polyspermy (entrance of more than one sperm) depends on changes in the egg's plasma membrane and in the zona pellucida. As soon as a sperm touches an egg, the egg's plasma membrane depolarizes (from 265 mV to 10 mV), and this prevents the binding of any other sperm. Then the egg releases substances that lead to a lifting of the zona pellucida away from the surface of the egg. Now sperm cannot bind to the zona pellucida either.

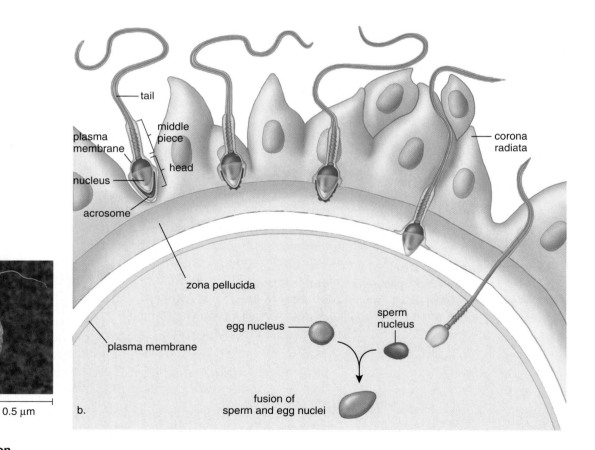

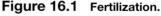

a. |——————| 0.5 µm   b.

Figure 16.1   Fertilization.
a. During fertilization, a single sperm enters the egg. **b.** A sperm makes its way through the corona radiata. The head of a sperm has a membrane-bound acrosome filled with enzymes. When released, these enzymes digest a pathway for the sperm through the zona pellucida. After it binds to the plasma membrane of the egg, a sperm enters the egg. When the sperm nucleus fuses with the egg nucleus, fertilization is complete.

16.2 Development Before Birth

Before we discuss the stages of development, you will want to become familiar with the processes of development and the names and functions of the extraembryonic membranes.

Processes of Development

As a human being develops, these processes occur:

Cleavage   Immediately after fertilization, the zygote begins to divide so that there are first 2, then 4, 8, 16, and 32 cells, and so forth. Increase in size does not accompany these divisions (see Fig. 16.3). Cell division during cleavage is mitotic, and each cell receives a full complement of chromosomes and genes.

Growth   During embryonic development, cell division is accompanied by an increase in size of the daughter cells.

Morphogenesis   Morphogenesis refers to the shaping of the embryo and is first evident when certain cells are seen to move, or migrate, in relation to other cells. By these movements, the embryo begins to assume various shapes.

Differentiation   When cells take on a specific structure and function, differentiation occurs. The first system to become visibly differentiated is the nervous system.

Extraembryonic Membranes

The **extraembryonic membranes** are not part of the embryo and fetus; instead, as implied by their name, they are outside the embryo (Fig. 16.2). The names of the extraembryonic membranes in humans are strange to us because they are named for their function in shelled animals! In shelled animals, the chorion lies next to the shell and carries on gas exchange. The amnion contains the protective amniotic fluid, which bathes the developing embryo. The allantois collects nitrogenous wastes, and the yolk sac surrounds the yolk, which provides nourishment.

The functions of the extraembryonic membranes are different in humans because humans develop inside the uterus. The extraembryonic membranes have these functions in humans:

1. **Chorion.** The chorion develops into the fetal half of the **placenta,** the organ that provides the embryo/fetus with nourishment and oxygen and takes away its waste.
2. **Yolk sac.** The yolk sac has little yolk and is the first site of blood cell formation.
3. **Allantois.** The allantois blood vessels become the umbilical blood vessels.
4. **Amnion.** The amnion contains fluid to cushion and protect the embryo, which develops into a fetus.

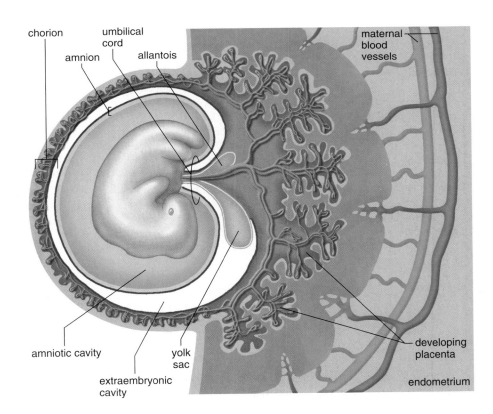

Figure 16.2   The extraembryonic membranes.
The extraembryonic membranes. The chorion and amnion surround the embryo. The two other extraembryonic membranes, the yolk sac and allantois, contribute to the umbilical cord.

Table 16.1	Human Development	

Time	Events for Mother	Events for Baby
Pre-Embryonic Development		
First week	Ovulation occurs.	Fertilization occurs. Cell division begins and continues. Chorion appears.
Embryonic Development		
Second week	Symptoms of early pregnancy (nausea, breast swelling and tenderness, fatigue) are present. Blood pregnancy test is positive.	Implantation occurs. Amnion and yolk sac appear. Embryo has tissues. Placenta begins to form.
Third week	First menstruation is missed. Urine pregnancy test is positive. Symptoms of early pregnancy continue.	Nervous system begins to develop. Allantois and blood vessels are present. Placenta is well formed.
Fourth week		Limb buds form. Heart is noticeable and beating. Nervous system is prominent. Embryo has tail. Other systems form.
Fifth week	Uterus is the size of a hen's egg. Mother feels frequent need to urinate due to pressure of growing uterus on bladder.	Embryo is curved. Head is large. Limb buds show divisions. Nose, eyes, and ears are noticeable.
Sixth week	Uterus is the size of an orange.	Fingers and toes are present. Skeleton is cartilaginous.
Two months	Uterus can be felt above the pubic bone.	All systems are developing. Bone is replacing cartilage. Facial features are becoming refined. Embryo is about 38 mm ($1\frac{1}{2}$ in.) long.
Fetal Development		
Third month	Uterus is the size of a grapefruit.	Gender can be distinguished by ultrasound. Fingernails appear.
Fourth month	Fetal movement is felt by a mother who has previously been pregnant.	Skeleton is visible. Hair begins to appear. Fetus is about 150 mm (6 in.) long and weighs about 170 grams (6 oz).
Fifth month	Fetal movement is felt by a mother who has not previously been pregnant. Uterus reaches up to level of umbilicus, and pregnancy is obvious.	Protective cheesy coating, called vernix caseosa, begins to be deposited. Heartbeat can be heard.
Sixth month	Doctor can tell where baby's head, back, and limbs are. Breasts have enlarged, nipples and areolae are darkly pigmented, and colostrum is produced.	Body is covered with fine hair called lanugo. Skin is wrinkled and reddish.
Seventh month	Uterus reaches halfway between umbilicus and rib cage.	Testes descend into scrotum. Eyes are open. Fetus is about 300 mm (12 in.) long and weighs about 1,350 grams (3 lb).
Eighth month	Weight gain is averaging about a pound a week. Standing and walking are difficult for the mother because her center of gravity is thrown forward.	Body hair begins to disappear. Subcutaneous fat begins to be deposited.
Ninth month	Uterus is up to rib cage, causing shortness of breath and heartburn. Sleeping becomes difficult.	Fetus is ready for birth. It is about 530 mm ($20\frac{1}{2}$ in.) long and weighs about 3,400 grams ($7\frac{1}{2}$ lb).

Stages of Development

Development encompasses the events that occur from fertilization to birth. In humans, this **gestation** period is usually calculated by adding 280 days to the start of the last menstruation, a date that is usually known. However, only about 5% of babies actually arrive on the predicted date.

Pre-Embryonic Development

Table 16.1 shows that we can subdivide development into pre-embryonic, embryonic, and fetal development. **Pre-embryonic development** encompasses the events of the first week, as shown in Figure 16.3.

Immediately after fertilization, the zygote divides repeatedly as it passes down the oviduct to the uterus. A **morula** is a compact ball of embryonic cells that becomes a **blastocyst.** The many cells of the blastocyst arrange themselves so that there is an **inner cell mass** surrounded by a layer of cells, the **trophoblast.** The inner cell mass will become the embryo and the trophoblast will become the chorion. The early appearance of the chorion emphasizes the complete dependence of the developing embryo on this extraembryonic membrane.

Each cell within the inner cell mass has the genetic capability of becoming any type of tissue. This recognition has recently led to a proposed new procedure called therapeutic cloning, as discussed in the Health Focus on page 314. Sometimes during development, the cells of the morula separate, or the inner cell mass splits, and two pre-embryos are present rather than one. If all goes well, these two pre-embryos will be identical twins because they have inherited exactly the same chromosomes. Fraternal twins, who arise when two different eggs are fertilized by two different sperm, do not have identical chromosomes.

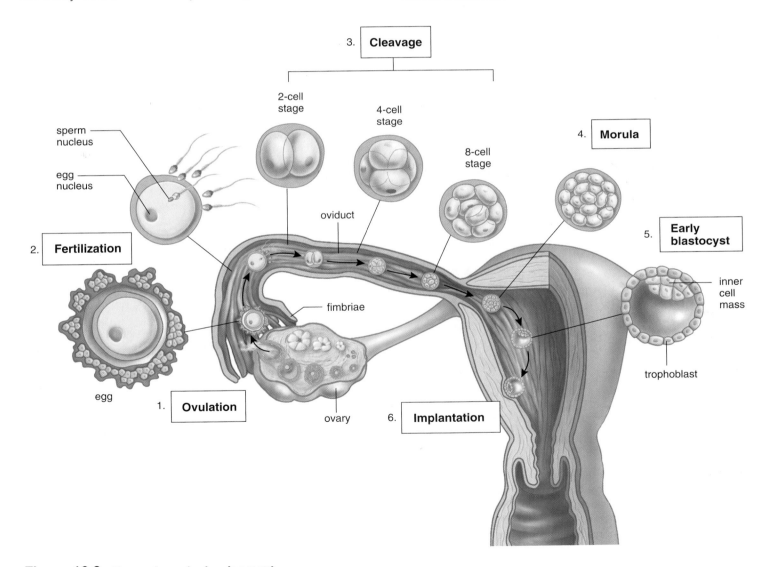

Figure 16.3 **Pre-embryonic development.**
(1) At ovulation the egg leaves the ovary. (2) Fertilization occurs in the upper third of the oviduct. (3) The zygote is termed a pre-embryo when cell division (cleavage) begins. (4) Cleavage produces a morula. (5) When implantation occurs the blastocyst becomes an embryo.

Reproductive and Therapeutic Cloning

Reproductive cloning and therapeutic cloning are done for different purposes. In reproductive cloning, the desired end is an individual that is genetically identical to the original individual. At one time, it was thought that the cloning of adult animals would be impossible because investigators found it difficult to have the nucleus of an adult cell "start over," even when it was placed in an enucleated egg cell. (An enucleated egg cell has had its own nucleus removed.)

In March 1997, Scottish investigators announced they had cloned a sheep called Dolly. How was their procedure different from all the others that had been attempted? Unlike other attempts, the donor cells were starved before the cell's nucleus was placed in an enucleated egg. Starving the donor cells caused them to stop dividing and go into a resting stage, and this made the nuclei amenable to cytoplasmic signals for initiation of development (Fig. 16Aa). By now, it is common practice to clone all sorts of farm animals that have desirable traits and even to clone rare animals that might otherwise become extinct.

In the United States, no federal funds can be used on experiments to clone human beings. Cloning is wasteful—even in the case of Dolly, out of 29 clones, only one was successful. Also, there is concern that cloned animals may not be healthy. Dolly was euthanized in 2003 because she was suffering from lung cancer and crippling arthritis. She had lived only half the normal life span for a Dorset sheep.

In therapeutic cloning, the desired end is not an individual; rather, it is mature cells of various cell types. The purpose of therapeutic cloning is (1) to learn more about how specialization of cells occurs and (2) to provide cells and tissues that could be used to treat human illnesses, such as diabetes, spinal cord injuries, Parkinson disease, and so forth.

There are two possible ways to carry out therapeutic cloning. The first way is to use the exact same procedure as reproductive cloning, except embryonic cells, called *embryonic stem cells*, are separated and each is subjected to a treatment that causes it to develop into a particular type of cell, such as red blood cells, muscle cells, or nerve cells (Fig. 16Ab). Some have ethical concerns about this type of therapeutic cloning, which is still very experimental, because if the embryo were allowed to continue development, it would become an individual.

The second way to carry out therapeutic cloning is to use *adult stem cells*. Stem cells are found in many organs of the adult's body; for example, the skin has stem cells that constantly divide and produce new skin cells. The bone marrow has stem cells that produce new blood cells as does the umbilical cord of newborns. It has already been possible to use stem cells from the brain to regenerate nerve tissue for the treatment of Parkinson disease. However, the goal is to develop techniques that would allow scientists to turn any adult stem cell into any type of specialized cell. Many investigators are engaged in this endeavor. In order to do this, scientists need to know how to control gene expression.

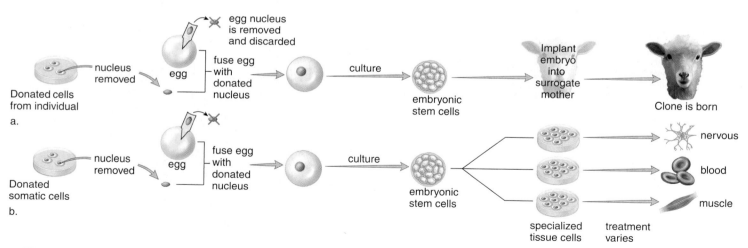

Figure 16A Two types of cloning.

a. The purpose of reproductive cloning is to produce an individual that is genetically identical to the one that donated a nucleus. The nucleus is placed in an enucleated egg, and, after several divisions, the embryo comes to term in a surrogate mother. **b.** The purpose of therapeutic cloning is to produce specialized tissue cells. A nucleus is placed in an enucleated egg, and, after several divisions, the embryonic cells (called embryonic stem cells) are separated and treated to become specialized cells.

Embryonic Development

Embryonic development begins with the second week and lasts until the end of the second month of development.

Second Week   At the end of the first week, the **embryo** usually begins the process of implanting itself in the wall of the uterus. If **implantation** is successful, the woman is clinically pregnant. On occasion, it happens that the embryo implants itself in a location other than the uterus—most likely, the oviduct. Such a so-called **ectopic pregnancy** cannot succeed because an oviduct is unable to support it.

During implantation, the trophoblast secretes enzymes to digest away some of the tissue and blood vessels of the endometrium of the uterus. The trophoblast also begins to secrete **human chorionic gonadotropin (HCG),** the hormone that is the basis for the pregnancy test. HCG acts like luteinizing hormone (LH) in that it serves to maintain the corpus luteum past the time it normally disintegrates. Because it is being stimulated, the corpus luteum secretes progesterone, the endometrium is maintained, and the expected menstruation does not occur.

The embryo is now about the size of the period at the end of this sentence. As the week progresses, the inner cell mass detaches itself from the trophoblast and becomes the **embryonic disk,** and two more extraembryonic membranes form (Fig. 16.4*a*). The yolk sac is the first site of blood cell formation. The amniotic cavity surrounds the embryo (and then the fetus) as it develops. In humans, amniotic fluid acts as an insulator against cold and heat and also absorbs shock, such as that caused by the mother exercising.

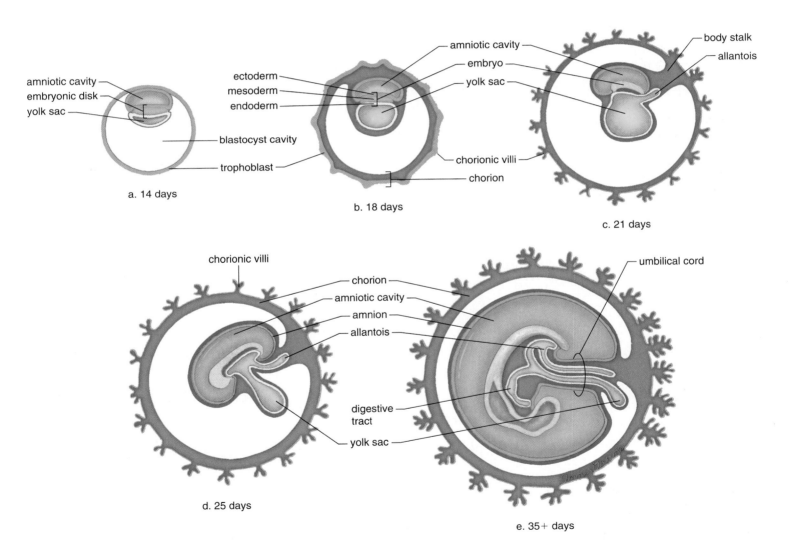

Figure 16.4   Embryonic development.
a. At first, no organs are present in the embryo, only tissues. The amniotic cavity is above the embryonic disk, and the yolk sac is below.
b. The chorion develops villi, the structures so important to exchange between mother and child. **c, d.** The allantois and yolk sac, two more extraembryonic membranes, are positioned inside the body stalk as it becomes the umbilical cord. **e.** At 35+ days, the embryo has a head region and a tail region. The umbilical cord takes blood vessels between the embryo and the chorion (placenta).

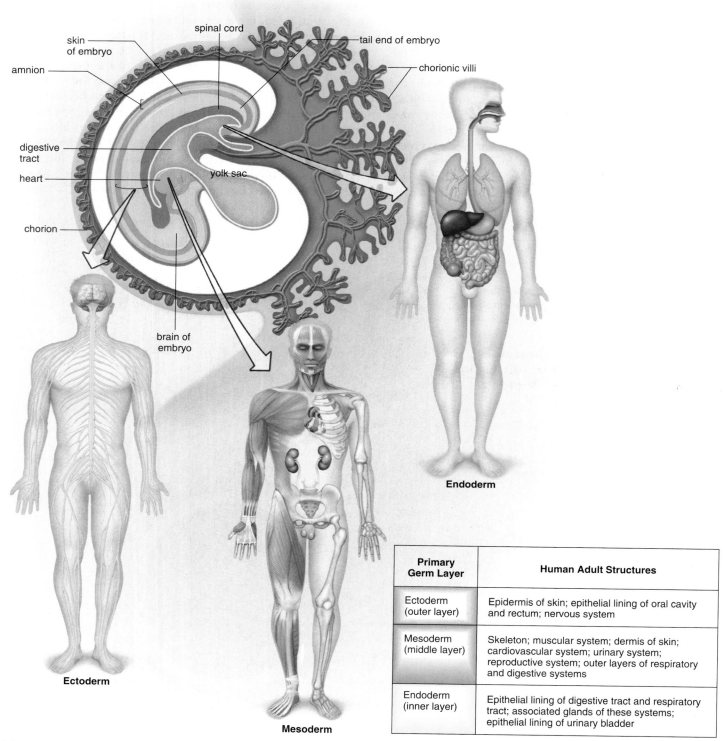

skin of embryo

amnion

spinal cord

tail end of embryo

chorionic villi

digestive tract

yolk sac

heart

chorion

brain of embryo

Ectoderm

Mesoderm

Endoderm

Primary Germ Layer	Human Adult Structures
Ectoderm (outer layer)	Epidermis of skin; epithelial lining of oral cavity and rectum; nervous system
Mesoderm (middle layer)	Skeleton; muscular system; dermis of skin; cardiovascular system; urinary system; reproductive system; outer layers of respiratory and digestive systems
Endoderm (inner layer)	Epithelial lining of digestive tract and respiratory tract; associated glands of these systems; epithelial lining of urinary bladder

Figure 16.5   An embryo has three primary germ layers.
The three germ layers are ectoderm, mesoderm, and endoderm. Organs and tissues can be traced back to a particular germ layer as indicated in this illustration.

With the start of the major event called **gastrulation,** the inner cell mass becomes the embryonic disk. Gastrulation is an example of morphogenesis (see page 311) during which cells move or migrate, in this case to become tissue layers called the **primary germ layers.** By the time gastrulation is complete, the embryonic disk has become an embryo with three primary germ layers: ectoderm, mesoderm, and endoderm. Figure 16.5 shows the significance of the primary germ layers—all the organs of an individual can be traced back to one of the primary germ layers. When the trophoblast is reinforced by mesoderm, it becomes the chorion.

Third Week   Two important organ systems make their appearance during the third week. The nervous system is the first organ system to be visually evident. At first, a thickening appears along the entire posterior length of the embryo, and then invagination occurs as neural folds appear. When the neural folds meet at the midline, the neural tube, which later develops into the brain and the spinal cord, is formed.

Development of the heart begins in the third week and continues into the fourth week. At first, there are right and left heart tubes; when these fuse, the heart begins pumping blood, even though the chambers of the heart are not fully formed. The veins enter posteriorly, and the arteries exit anteriorly from this largely tubular heart, but later the heart twists so that all major blood vessels are located anteriorly.

Fourth and Fifth Weeks   At four weeks, the embryo is barely larger than the height of this print. A body stalk connects the caudal (tail) end of the embryo with the chorion, which has tree-like projections called **chorionic villi** (see Fig. 16.4c, d). The fourth extraembryonic membrane, the allantois, lies within the body stalk, and its blood vessels become the umbilical blood vessels. The head and the tail then lift up, and the body stalk moves anteriorly by constriction. Once this process is complete, the **umbilical cord,** which connects the developing embryo to the placenta, is fully formed (see Fig. 16.4e).

Little flippers called limb buds appear (Fig. 16.6); later, the arms and the legs develop from the limb buds, and even the hands and the feet become apparent. At the same time—during the fifth week—the head enlarges and the sense organs become more prominent. It is possible to make out the developing eyes and ears, and even the nose.

Sixth Through Eighth Weeks   During the sixth through eighth weeks of development, the embryo changes to a form that is easily recognized as a human being. Concurrent with brain development, the head achieves its normal relationship with the body as a neck region develops. The nervous system is developed well enough to permit reflex actions, such as a startle response to touch. At the end of this period, the embryo is about 38 mm (1.5 in.) long and weighs no more than an aspirin tablet, even though all organ systems have been established.

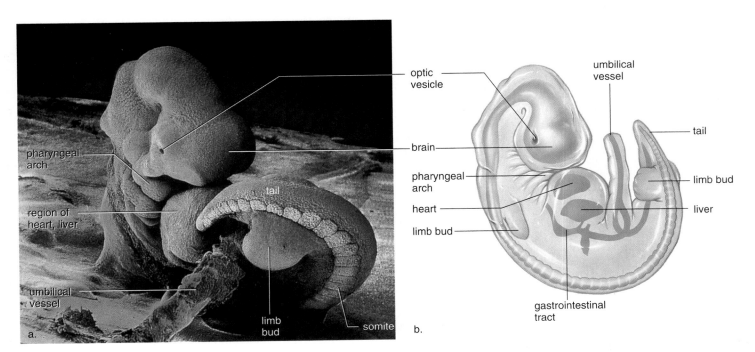

Figure 16.6   **Human embryo at beginning of fifth week.**
a. Scanning electron micrograph. **b.** The embryo is curled so that the head touches the region of the heart and liver. The organs of the gastrointestinal tract are forming, and the arms and the legs develop from the bulges called limb buds. The tail is an evolutionary remnant; its bones regress and become those of the coccyx (tailbone). In humans the pharyngeal arches support pouches that become the auditory tubes, the tonsils, the thymus gland, and the parathyroid glands.

Fetal Circulation and the Placenta

By the tenth week, the placenta is formed fully and begins to produce progesterone and estrogen. These hormones have two functions (1) because of negative feedback on the hypothalamus and anterior pituitary, they prevent any new follicles from maturing, and (2) they maintain the endometrium—menstruation does not usually occur during pregnancy.

The placenta has a fetal side contributed by the chorion and a maternal side consisting of uterine tissues (Fig. 16.7). The blood of the mother and the fetus never mix since exchange always takes place across the villi. Carbon dioxide and other wastes move from the fetal side to the maternal side, and nutrients and oxygen move from the maternal side to the fetal side of the placenta by diffusion. Harmful chemicals can also cross the placenta, and this is of particular concern during the embryonic period, when various structures are first forming. Each organ or part seems to have a sensitive period during which a substance can alter its normal function. The Bioethical Focus on page 329 concerns maternal behaviors that can prevent certain birth defects.

Path of Fetal Blood

The umbilical cord, which stretches between the placenta and the fetus, is the lifeline of the fetus because it contains the umbilical arteries and veins. Blood within the fetal aorta travels to its various branches, including the iliac arteries, which connect to the *umbilical arteries* going to the placenta. The *umbilical vein* carries blood rich in nutrients and oxygen away from the placenta to the fetus. The umbilical vein enters the liver and then joins the *venous duct*, which merges with the inferior vena cava, a vessel that returns blood to the heart. In the fetus, blood entering the right side of the heart is O_2-rich (not O_2-poor as in the adult). This blood bypasses the lungs by two routes: (1) some is shunted into the left atrium through the *oval opening* and (2) some enters the aorta by way of the *arterial duct*, a connection between the pulmonary artery and the aorta.

Various circulatory changes occur at birth due to the tying of the cord and the expansion of the lungs. The lack of any one of these changes might cause the "blue baby" syndrome in which the skin is blue due to O_2-poor blood. (1) Return of this blood to the left side of the heart usually causes a flap to cover the oval opening. Although incomplete closure occurs in nearly one out of four individuals, passage of the blood from the right atrium to the left atrium rarely occurs because either the opening is small or it closes when the atria contract. (2) The arterial duct closes at birth because endothelial cells divide and block off the duct. (3) Remains of the arterial duct and parts of the umbilical arteries and vein later are transformed into connective tissue.

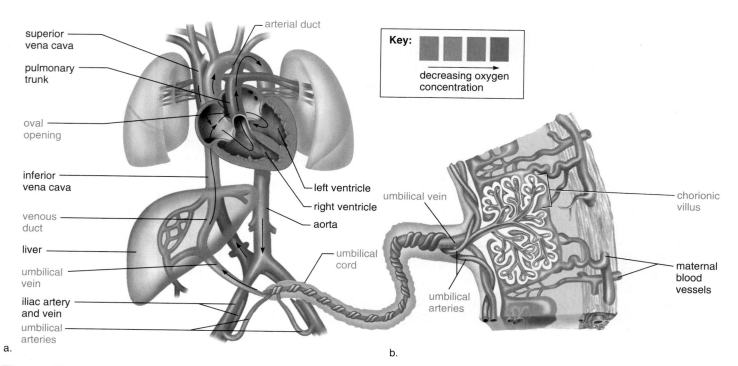

Key: decreasing oxygen concentration

superior vena cava
pulmonary trunk
oval opening
inferior vena cava
venous duct
liver
umbilical vein
iliac artery and vein
umbilical arteries

arterial duct
left ventricle
right ventricle
aorta
umbilical cord
umbilical arteries

umbilical vein
chorionic villus
maternal blood vessels

a.

b.

Figure 16.7 Fetal circulation and the placenta.

a. Trace the path of blood by following the arrows. The structures in red are unique to the fetus. **b.** At the placenta, an exchange of molecules between fetal and maternal blood takes place across the walls of the chorionic villi.

Fetal Development and Birth

Fetal development includes the third through the ninth months of development. At this time, the fetus is recognizably human (Fig. 16.8) but many refinements still need to be added. The fetus usually increases in size and gains the weight that will be needed to allow it to live as an independent individual.

Third and Fourth Months

At the beginning of the third month, the fetal head is still very large relative to the rest of the body, the nose is flat, the eyes are far apart, and the ears are well formed. Head growth now begins to slow down as the rest of the body increases in length. Epidermal refinements, such as fingernails, nipples, eyelashes, eyebrows, and hair on the head, appear.

Cartilage begins to be replaced by bone as ossification centers appear in most of the bones. Cartilage remains at the ends of the long bones, and ossification is not complete until age 18 or 20 years. The skull has six large membranous areas called **fontanels,** which permit a certain amount of flexibility as the head passes through the birth canal and allow rapid growth of the brain during infancy. Progressive fusion of the skull bones causes the fontanels to close, usually by 2 years of age.

Sometime during the third month, it is possible to distinguish males from females. As discussed on page 320, the presence of an SRY gene, usually on the Y chromosome, leads to the development of testes and male genitals. Otherwise ovaries and females genitals develop. At this time, either testes or ovaries are located within the abdominal cavity, but later, in the last trimester of fetal development, the testes descend into the scrotal sacs (scrotum). Sometimes the testes fail to descend, and in that case, an operation may be done later to place them in their proper location.

During the fourth month, the fetal heartbeat is loud enough to be heard when a physician applies a stethoscope to the mother's abdomen. By the end of this month, the fetus is about 152 mm (6 in.) in length and weighs about 171 g (6 oz).

Fifth Through Seventh Months

During the fifth through seventh months (Fig. 16.8), the mother begins to feel movement. At first, there is only a fluttering sensation, but as the fetal legs grow and develop, kicks and jabs are felt. The fetus, though, is in the fetal position, with the head bent down and in contact with the flexed knees.

The wrinkled, translucent skin is covered by a fine down called **lanugo.** This in turn is coated with a white, greasy, cheese-like substance called **vernix caseosa,** which probably protects the delicate skin from the amniotic fluid. The eyelids are now fully open.

At the end of this period, the fetus's length has increased to about 300 mm (12 in.), and it weighs about 1,380 g (3 lb). It is possible that, if born now, the baby will survive.

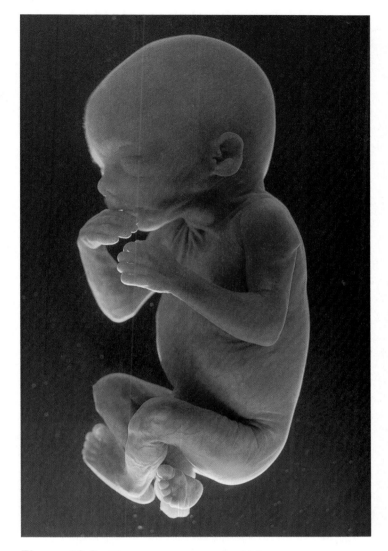

Figure 16.8   **Five- to seven-month-old fetus.**

Eighth Through Ninth Months

At the end of nine months, the fetus is about 530 mm (20½ in.) long and weighs about 3,400 g (7½ lb). Weight gain is due largely to an accumulation of fat beneath the skin. Full-term babies have the best chance of survival, while premature babies are subject to various challenges, such as respiratory distress syndrome because their lungs are underdeveloped (see page 145), jaundice (see page 125), and infections.

As the end of development approaches, the fetus usually rotates so that the head is pointed toward the cervix. However, if the fetus does not turn, a **breech birth** (rump first) is likely. It is very difficult for the cervix to expand enough to accommodate this form of birth, and asphyxiation of the baby is more likely to occur. Thus, a **cesarean section** may be prescribed for delivery of the fetus (incision through the abdominal and uterine walls). Birth is discussed on page 325.

Development of Male and Female Sex Organs

The sex of an individual is determined at the moment of fertilization. All individuals have 23 pairs of chromosomes but typically in males, one of these pairs is an X and Y, while females have two X chromosomes. During the first several weeks of development, it is impossible to tell by external inspection whether the unborn child is a boy or a girl. Gonads don't start developing until the seventh week of development. The tissue that gives rise to the gonads is called indifferent because it can become testes or ovaries depending on the action of hormones.

In Figure 16.9a, notice that at six weeks both males and females have the same types of ducts. During this indifferent stage, an embryo has the potential to develop into a male or a female. If a gene called SRY is present, testes develop and testosterone produced by the testes stimulate the Wolffian ducts to become male genital ducts. The Wolffian ducts enter the urethra, which belongs to both the urinary and reproductive systems in males. An anti-Müllerian hormone causes the Müllerian ducts to regress. In the absence of an SRY gene, ovaries develop instead of testes from the same indifferent tissue. Now the Wolffian ducts regress, and under the influence of estrogen from the ovaries the Müllerian ducts develop into the uterus and oviducts. Estrogen has no effect on the Wolffian duct, which degenerates in females. A developing vagina also extends from the uterus. There is no connection between the urinary and genital systems in females.

At 14 weeks, both the primitive testes and ovaries are located deep inside the abdominal cavity. An inspection of the interior of the testes would show that sperm are even now starting to develop, and similarly, the ovaries already contain large numbers of tiny follicles, each having an ovum. Toward the end of development, the testes descend into the scrotal sac; the ovaries remain in the abdominal cavity.

Figure 16.9b shows the development of the external genitals. These tissues are also indifferent at first—they can develop into either male or female genitals. At six weeks, a small bud appears between the legs; this can develop into the male penis or the female clitoris. At nine weeks, a urogenital groove bordered by two swellings appears. By 14 weeks, this groove has disappeared in males, and the scrotum has formed from the original swellings. In females, the groove persists and becomes the vaginal opening. Labia majora and labia minora are present instead of a scrotum. These changes are due to the presence or absence of another hormone produced by the testes. It is called dihydrotestosterone (DHT), which is derived from testosterone.

The SRY Gene

It's not correct to say that all XY individuals develop into males. Some XY individuals, who are said to have the XY female syndrome, become females instead of males. Similarly, some XX individuals, who are said to have XX male syndrome, develop into males. In individuals with the XY female syndrome, a piece of the Y chromosome is missing. In individuals with the XX male syndrome, this same small piece is present on an X chromosome. The piece of a Y chromosome that causes male genitals to develop is called the SRY (sex determining region of the Y) gene. The SRY gene is one that is able to turn on other genes. It causes testes to form and then the testes secrete three different types of hormones.

The Hormones of Male Development

These testes' hormones are required for male development:

1. Testosterone stimulates development of the epididymides, vas deferentia, seminal vesicles, and ejaculatory duct.
2. Anti-Müllerian hormone prevents further development of female structures and instead causes them to degenerate.
3. Dihydrotestosterone, which is derived from testosterone, directs the development of the urethra, prostate gland, penis, and scrotum.

The absence of any one or more of these hormones results in ambiguous sex determination in which the individual has the external appearance of a female, although the gonads of a female are absent.

Ambiguous Sex Determination

In *androgen insensitivity syndrome,* these three types of hormones are produced by testes during development, but the individual develops as a female because the plasma membrane receptors for testosterone are absent in other bodily tissues. The external genitalia develop as female and the Wolffian duct degenerates internally. Because the individual does not develop a scrotum, the testes fail to descend and instead remain deep within the body. The individual develops the secondary sex characteristics of a female and no abnormality is suspected until the individual fails to menstruate.

True gonadal hermaphroditism in which a person has both ovarian and testicular tissue is rare. However, it is estimated that about 1% of the population may have *male pseudohermaphroditism.* The individual appears to be a normal female until puberty because anti-Müllerian hormone is produced and the female set of tubes degenerated. However, the testes never produce testosterone or dihydrotestosterone. At puberty, the clitoris begins to enlarge as a response to testosterone produced by the adrenal cortex. The clitoris even looks like a penis; the voice deepens, and muscles enlarge. There is no breast development and the individual does not menstruate. In the Dominican Republic, this syndrome is called guevedoces, which means "penis at age 12."

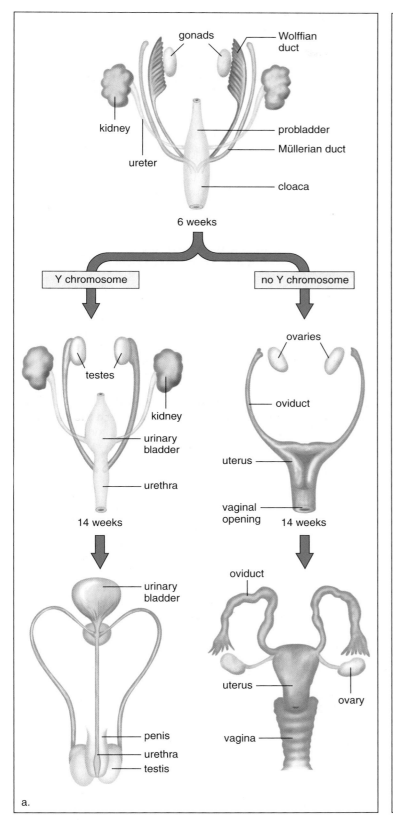

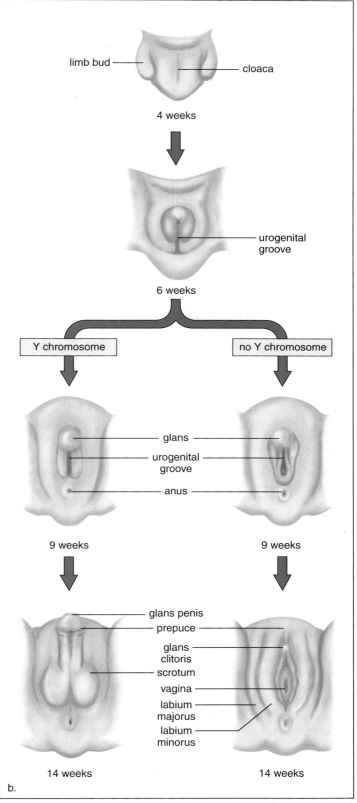

Figure 16.9 **Male and female organs.**

a. Development of gonads and ducts. **b.** Development of external genitals.

Health Focus

Preventing Birth Defects

Although some congenital (birth) defects are not preventable, certain ones are, and therefore all females of childbearing age are advised to take everyday precautions to protect any future and/or presently developing embryos and fetuses from these defects. For example, it is best if a woman has a physical exam even before she becomes pregnant. At that time, it can be determined if she has been immunized against rubella (German measles). Depending on exactly when a pregnant woman has the disease, rubella can cause blindness, deafness, mental retardation, heart malformations, and other serious problems in an unborn child. A vaccine to prevent the disease can be given to a woman before she gets pregnant, but cannot be given to a woman who is already pregnant because it contains live viruses. Also, the presence of human immunodeficiency virus (HIV) (the causative agent for acquired immunodeficiency syndrome, AIDS) should be tested for because preventative therapies are available to improve maternal and infant health.

Good health habits are a must during pregnancy, including proper nutrition, adequate rest, and exercise. Moderate exercise can usually continue throughout pregnancy and hopefully will contribute to ease of delivery. Basic nutrients are required in adequate amounts to meet the demands of both fetus and mother. A growing number of studies confirm that small, thin newborns are more likely to develop certain chronic diseases, such as diabetes and high blood pressure, when they become adults than are babies who are born heavier.

An increased amount of minerals, such as calcium for bone growth and iron for red blood cell formation, and certain vitamins, such as vitamin B_6 for proper metabolism and folate (folic acid), are required. Pregnant women need more folate a day to meet an increased rate of cell division and DNA synthesis in their own bodies and that of the developing child. A maternal deficiency of folate has been linked to development of neural tube defects in the fetus. These defects include spina bifida (spinal cord or spinal fluid bulge through the back) and anencephaly (absence of a brain). Perhaps as many as 75% of these defects could be prevented by adequate folate intake even before pregnancy occurs. Consuming fortified breakfast cereals is a good way to meet folate needs, because they contain a more absorbable form of folate.

Good health habits include avoiding substances that can cross the placenta and harm the fetus (Table 16A). Cigarette smoke poses a serious threat to the health of a fetus because it contains not only carbon monoxide but also other fetotoxic chemicals. Children born to smoking mothers have a greater chance of a cleft lip or palate, increased incidence of respiratory diseases, and later on, more reading disorders than those born to mothers who did not smoke during their pregnancy.

Alcohol easily crosses the placenta, and even one drink a day appears to increase the chance of a miscarriage. The more alcohol consumed, the greater the chances of physical abnormalities if the pregnancy continues. Heavy consumption of alcohol puts a fetus at risk for a mental defect because alcohol enters the brain of the fetus. Babies born to heavy drinkers are apt to undergo delirium tremens after birth—shaking, vomiting, and extreme irritability—and to have fetal alcohol syndrome (FAS). Babies with FAS have decreased weight, height, and head size, with malformation of the head and face (Fig. 16B). Later, mental retardation is common, as are numerous other physical malformations.

Certainly, illegal drugs, such as marijuana, cocaine, and heroin, should be completely avoided during pregnancy. *Crack babies* now make up 60% of drug-affected babies. Cocaine use causes severe fluctuations in a mother's blood pressure that temporarily deprive the developing fetus's brain of oxygen. Cocaine babies have visual problems, lack coordination, and are mentally retarded.

Children born to women who received X-ray treatment during pregnancy for, say, cancer are apt to have birth defects and/or to develop leukemia later. It takes a lower amount of X rays to cause mutations in a developing embryo or fetus than in an adult. Dental and other diagnostic X rays that result in only a small amount of radiation are probably safe. Still, a woman should be sure a physician knows that she is or may be pregnant. Similarly, toxic chemicals, such as pesticides, and many organic industrial chemicals, such as vinyl chloride, formaldehyde, asbestos, and benzenes, are mutagenic and can cross the placenta, resulting in abnormalities. Lead circulating in a pregnant woman's blood can cause a child to be mentally retarded. Agents that produce abnormalities during development are called teratogens.

A woman has to be very careful about taking medications and supplements while pregnant. Excessive vitamin A, sometimes used to treat acne, may damage an embryo. In the 1950s and 1960s, DES (diethylstilbestrol), a synthetic hormone related to the natural female hormone estrogen, was given to pregnant women to prevent cramps, bleeding, and threatened miscarriage. But in the 1970s and 1980s, some adolescent girls and young women whose mothers had been treated with DES showed various abnormalities of the reproductive organs and an increased tendency toward cervical cancer. Other sex hormones, including birth control pills, can possibly cause abnormal fetal development, including abnormalities of the sex organs.

Table 16A	Behaviors Harmful to the Unborn
Drinking alcohol	
Smoking cigarettes	
Taking illegal drugs	
Taking any medication not approved by a physician	

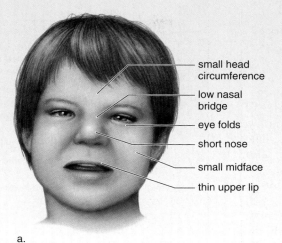

small head circumference

low nasal bridge

eye folds

short nose

small midface

thin upper lip

a.

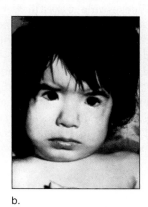

b.

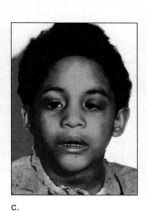

c.

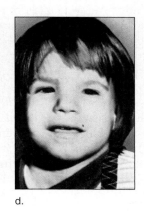

d.

Figure 16B Fetal alcohol syndrome.
Fetal alcohol syndrome is characterized by certain features. **a.** These features include malformations of the head and face. **b-d.** Photos of children who have fetal alcohol syndrome.

An Rh-negative woman who has given birth to an Rh-positive child should receive an Rh immunoglobulin injection within 72 hours to prevent her body from producing Rh antibodies. She will start producing these antibodies when some of the child's Rh-positive red blood cells enter her bloodstream, possibly before but particularly at birth. Rh antibodies can cause nervous system and heart defects in a fetus. The first Rh-positive baby is not usually affected. But in subsequent pregnancies, antibodies created at the time of the first birth cross the placenta and begin to destroy the blood cells of the fetus, thereby causing anemia and other complications.

The birth defects we have been discussing are particularly preventable because they are not due to inheritance of an abnormal number of chromosomes or any other genetic abnormality. More women are having babies after the age of 35, and first births among women older than 40 have increased by 50% since 1980. The chance of an older woman bearing a child with a birth defect unrelated to genetic inheritance is no greater than that of a younger woman. However, as discussed in Chapter 19, there is a greater risk of an older woman having a child with a chromosomal abnormality leading to premature delivery, cesarean section, a low birth weight, or certain syndromes. Some chromosomal and other genetic defects can be detected in utero so that therapy for these disorders can begin as soon as possible.

Now that physicians and laypeople are aware of the various ways birth defects can be prevented, it is hoped that the incidence of birth defects will decrease in the future.

The drug thalidomide was a popular tranquilizer during the 1950s and 1960s in many European countries and to a degree in the United States. The drug, which was taken to prevent nausea in pregnant women, arrested the development of arms and legs in some children and also damaged heart and blood vessels, ears, and the digestive tract. Some mothers of affected children report that they took the drug for only a few days. Because of such experiences, physicians are generally very cautious about prescribing drugs during pregnancy, and no pregnant woman should take any drug—even ordinary cold remedies or aspirin—without checking first with her physician.

Unfortunately, immunization for sexually transmitted diseases is not possible. The HIV virus can cross the placenta and cause mental retardation. As mentioned, proper medication can greatly reduce the chance of this happening. When a mother has herpes, gonorrhea, or chlamydia, newborns can become infected as they pass through the birth canal. Blindness and other physical and mental defects may develop. Birth by cesarean section could prevent these occurrences.

323

16.3 Pregnancy and Birth

Major changes take place in the mother's body during pregnancy. When first pregnant, the mother may experience nausea and vomiting, loss of appetite, and fatigue. These symptoms subside, and some mothers report increased energy levels and a general sense of well-being despite an increase in weight. During pregnancy, the mother gains weight due to breast and uterine enlargement, weight of the fetus, amount of amniotic fluid, size of the placenta, her own increase in total body fluid; and an increase in storage of proteins, fats, and minerals. The increased weight can lead to lordosis (swayback) and lower back pain.

Aside from an increase in weight, many of the physiological changes in the mother are due to the presence of the placental hormones that support fetal development (Table 16.2). Progesterone decreases uterine motility by relaxing smooth muscle, including the smooth muscle in the walls of arteries. The arteries expand, and this leads to a low blood pressure that sets in motion the renin-angiotensin-aldosterone mechanism, which is promoted by estrogen. Aldosterone activity promotes sodium and water retention, and blood volume increases until it reaches its peak sometime during weeks 28–32 of pregnancy. Altogether, blood volume increases from 5 L to 7 L—a 40% rise. An increase in the number of red blood cells follows. With the rise in blood volume, cardiac output increases by 20–30%. Blood flow to the kidneys, placenta, skin, and breasts rises significantly. Smooth muscle relaxation also explains the common gastrointestinal effects of pregnancy. The heartburn experienced by many is due to relaxation of the esophageal sphincter and reflux of stomach contents into the esophagus. Constipation is caused by a decrease in intestinal tract motility.

Of interest is the increase in pulmonary values in a pregnant woman. The bronchial tubes relax, but this alone cannot explain the typical 40% increase in vital capacity and tidal volume. The increasing size of the uterus from a nonpregnant weight of 60–80 g to 900–1,200 g contributes to an improvement in respiratory functions. The uterus comes to occupy most of the abdominal cavity, reaching nearly to the xiphoid process of the sternum. This increase in size not only pushes the intestines, liver, stomach, and diaphragm superiorly, but it also widens the thoracic cavity. Compared with nonpregnant values, the maternal oxygen level changes little, but blood carbon dioxide levels fall by 20%, creating a concentration gradient favorable to the flow of carbon dioxide from fetal blood to maternal blood at the placenta.

The enlargement of the uterus does result in some problems. In the pelvic cavity, compression of the ureters and urinary bladder can result in stress incontinence. Compression of the inferior vena cava, especially when lying down, decreases venous return, and the result is edema and varicose veins.

Table 16.2	Effects of Placental Hormones on Mother
Hormone	**Chief Effects**
Progesterone	Relaxation of smooth muscle; reduced uterine motility; reduced maternal immune response to fetus
Estrogen	Increased uterine blood flow; increased renin-angiotensin-aldosterone activity; increased protein biosynthesis by the liver
Peptide hormones	Increased insulin resistance

Source: Moore, Thomas R., *Gestation Encyclopedia of Human Biology*, Vol. 7, 7th edition. Copyright © 1997 Academic Press.

Aside from the steroid hormones progesterone and estrogen, the placenta also produces some peptide hormones. One of these makes cells resistant to insulin, and the result can be pregnancy-induced diabetes. Some of the integumentary changes observed during pregnancy are also due to placental hormones. **Striae gravidarum,** commonly called "stretch marks," typically form over the abdomen and lower breasts in response to increased steroid hormone levels rather than stretching of the skin. Melanocyte activity also increases during pregnancy. Darkening of the areolae, skin in the line from the navel to the pubis, areas of the face and neck, and vulva is common.

Birth

The uterus has contractions throughout pregnancy. At first, these are light, lasting about 20–30 seconds and occurring every 15–20 minutes. Near the end of pregnancy, the contractions may become stronger and more frequent so that a woman thinks she is in labor. "False-labor" contractions are called **Braxton Hicks contractions.** However, the onset of true labor is marked by uterine contractions that occur regularly every 15–20 minutes and last for 40 seconds or longer.

A positive feedback mechanism can explain the onset and continuation of labor. Uterine contractions are induced by a stretching of the cervix, which also brings about the release of oxytocin from the posterior pituitary gland. Oxytocin stimulates the uterine muscles, both directly and through the action of prostaglandins. Uterine contractions push the fetus downward, and the cervix stretches even more. This cycle keeps repeating itself until birth occurs.

Prior to or at the first stage of **parturition,** which is the process of giving birth to an offspring, there can be a "bloody show" caused by expulsion of a mucous plug from the cervical canal. This plug prevents bacteria and sperm from entering the uterus during pregnancy.

Stage 1

During the first stage of labor, the uterine contractions of labor occur in such a way that the cervical canal slowly disappears as the lower part of the uterus is pulled upward toward the baby's head. This process is called effacement, or "taking up the cervix." With further contractions, the baby's head acts as a wedge to assist cervical dilation (Fig. 16.10*b*). If the amniotic membrane has not already ruptured, it is apt to do so during this stage, releasing the amniotic fluid, which leaks out of the vagina (an event sometimes referred to as "breaking water"). The first stage of parturition ends once the cervix is dilated completely.

Stage 2

During the second stage of parturition, the uterine contractions occur every 1–2 minutes and last about 1 minute each. They are accompanied by a desire to push, or bear down. As the baby's head gradually descends into the vagina, the desire to push becomes greater. When the baby's head

reaches the exterior, it turns so that the back of the head is uppermost (Fig. 16.10*c*). To enlarge the vaginal orifice an **episiotomy** is often performed. This incision, which enlarges the opening, is sewn together later. As soon as the head is delivered, the physician may hold the head and guide it downward, while one shoulder and then the other emerges. The rest of the baby follows easily.

Once the baby is breathing normally, the umbilical cord is cut and tied, severing the child from the placenta. The stump of the cord shrivels and leaves a scar, which is the umbilicus.

Stage 3

The placenta, or **afterbirth,** is delivered during the third stage of parturition (Fig. 16.10*d*). About 15 minutes after delivery of the baby, uterine muscular contractions shrink the uterus and dislodge the placenta. The placenta then is expelled into the vagina. As soon as the placenta and its membranes are delivered, the third stage of parturition is complete.

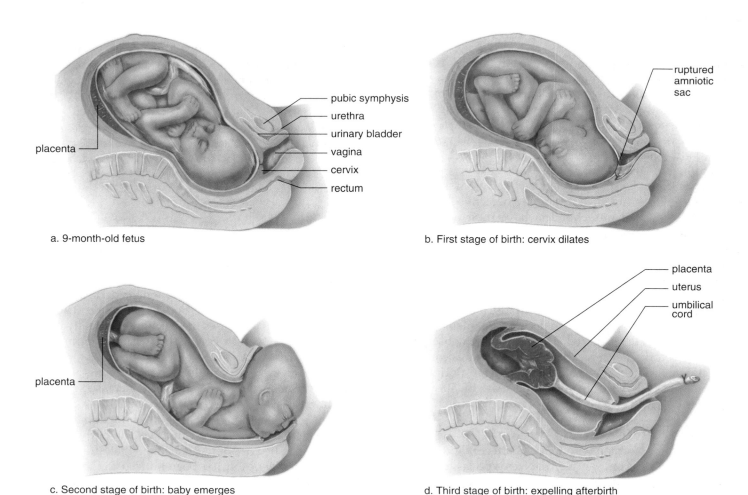

a. 9-month-old fetus

b. First stage of birth: cervix dilates

c. Second stage of birth: baby emerges

d. Third stage of birth: expelling afterbirth

Figure 16.10   Three stages of parturition (birth).
a. Position of fetus just before birth begins. **b.** Dilation of cervix. **c.** Birth of baby. **d.** Expulsion of afterbirth.

16.4 Development After Birth

Development does not cease once birth has occurred but continues throughout the stages of life: infancy, childhood, adolescence, and adulthood. **Aging** encompasses these progressive changes that contribute to an increased risk of infirmity, disease, and death (Fig. 16.11).

Today, **gerontology,** the study of aging, is of great interest because there are now more older individuals in our society than ever before, and the number is expected to rise dramatically. In the next half-century, the number of people over age 75 will rise from the present 8 million to 14.5 million, and the number over age 80 will rise from 5 million to 12 million. The human life span is judged to be a maximum of 120–125 years. The present goal of gerontology is not necessarily to increase the life span, but to increase the health span, the number of years that an individual enjoys the full functions of all body parts and processes.

Hypotheses of Aging

Of the many hypotheses about the cause of aging, three are considered here.

Genetic in Origin

Several lines of research indicate that aging has a genetic basis. Researchers working with simple organisms, such as yeast and roundworms, have identified a host of genes, whose expression decreases the life span. If these genes are silenced through mutations or restricted food intake the organism lives longer. What do these genes have in common? Apparently, when these genes are inactive, mitochondria do not produce energy—the cell uses alternative pathways. The current *mitochondrial hypothesis of aging* has been supported by engineering mice that have a defective DNA polymerase. (Recall that mitochondria have their own DNA.) These mice aged much faster than their peers. Why? Possibly because their defective mitochondria produced more free radicals than usual. Free radicals (see page 132) are unstable molecules that carry an extra electron. To become stable, free radicals donate an electron to another molecule, such as DNA or proteins (e.g., enzymes) or lipids, found in plasma membranes. Eventually, these molecules are unable to function, and the cell is destroyed. The well known observation that a low-calorie diet can expand the life span is consistent with the mitochondrial hypothesis of aging. Caloric restriction also shuts down the genes that decrease the life span— the genes that turn on the activity of mitochondria!

Whole-Body Process

A decline in the hormonal system can affect many different organs of the body. For example, diabetes type 2 is common in older individuals. The pancreas makes insulin, but the cells lack the receptors that enable them to respond. Menopause in women occurs for a similar reason. The bloodstream contains adequate amounts of follicle-stimulating hormone, but the

Figure 16.11   Aging.
Aging is a slow process during which the body undergoes changes that eventually bring about death, even if no marked disease or disorder is present. Medical science is trying to extend the human life span and the health span, the length of time the body functions normally.

ovaries do not respond. Perhaps aging results from the loss of hormonal activities and a decline in the functions they control.

The immune system, too, no longer performs as it once did, and this can affect the body as a whole. The thymus gland gradually decreases in size, and eventually most of it is replaced by fat and connective tissue. The incidence of cancer increases among the elderly, which may signify that the immune system is no longer functioning as it should. This idea is also substantiated by the increased incidence of autoimmune diseases in older individuals.

It is possible, though, that aging is not due to the failure of a particular system that can affect the body as a whole, but to a specific type of tissue change that affects all organs and even the genes. It has been noticed for some time that proteins—such as the collagen fibers present in many support tissues—become increasingly cross-linked as people age. Undoubtedly, this cross-linking contributes to the stiffening and loss of elasticity characteristic of aging tendons and ligaments. It may also account for the inability of such organs as the blood vessels, the heart, and the lungs to function as they once did. Some researchers have now found that glucose has the tendency to attach to any type of protein, which is the first step in a cross-linking process. They are presently experimenting with drugs that can prevent cross-linking.

Extrinsic Factors

The current data about the effects of aging are often based on comparisons of the elderly to younger age groups. But perhaps today's elderly were not as aware when they were younger of the importance of, for example, diet and exercise to general health. It is possible, then, that much of what we attribute to aging is instead due to years of poor health habits.

Consider, for example, osteoporosis. This condition is associated with a progressive decline in bone density in both males and females so that fractures are more likely to occur after only minimal trauma. Osteoporosis is common in the elderly—by age 65, one-third of women will have vertebral fractures, and by age 81, one-third of women and one-sixth of men will have suffered a hip fracture. While there is no denying that a decline in bone mass occurs as a result of aging, certain extrinsic factors are also important. The occurrence of osteoporosis itself is associated with cigarette smoking, heavy alcohol intake, and inadequate calcium intake. Not only is it possible to eliminate these negative factors by personal choice, but it is also possible to add a positive factor. A moderate exercise program has been found to slow down the progressive loss of bone mass.

Even more important, a sensible exercise program and a proper diet that includes at least five servings of fruits and vegetables a day will most likely help eliminate cardiovascular disease. Experts no longer believe that the cardiovascular system necessarily suffers a large decrease in functioning ability with age. Persons 65 years of age and older can have well-functioning hearts and open coronary arteries if their health habits are good and they continue to exercise regularly.

Effect of Age on Body Systems

Data about how aging affects body systems are necessarily based on past events. It is possible that, in the future, age will not have these effects or at least not to the same degree as those described here.

Skin

As aging occurs, skin becomes thinner and less elastic because the number of elastic fibers decreases and the collagen fibers undergo cross-linking, as discussed previously. Also, there is less adipose tissue in the subcutaneous layer; therefore, older people are more likely to feel cold. The loss of thickness partially accounts for sagging and wrinkling of the skin.

Homeostatic adjustment to heat is also limited because there are fewer sweat glands for sweating to occur. Because of fewer hair follicles, the hair on the scalp and the extremities thins out. The number of oil (sebaceous) glands is reduced, and the skin tends to crack. Older people also experience a decrease in the number of melanocytes, making their hair gray and their skin pale. In contrast, some of the remaining pigment cells are larger, and pigmented blotches appear on the skin.

Processing and Transporting

Cardiovascular disorders are the leading cause of death today. The heart shrinks because of a reduction in cardiac muscle cell size. This leads to loss of cardiac muscle strength and reduced cardiac output. Still, the heart, in the absence of disease, is able to meet the demands of increased activity because it can double its rate or triple the amount of blood pumped each minute even though the maximum possible output declines.

Because the middle layer of arteries contains elastic fibers, which are most likely subject to cross-linking, the arteries become more rigid with time, and their size is further reduced by plaque, a buildup of fatty material. Therefore, blood pressure readings gradually rise. Such changes are common in individuals living in Western industrialized countries but not in agricultural societies. A diet low in cholesterol and saturated fatty acids has been suggested as a way to control degenerative changes in the cardiovascular system.

Blood flow to the liver is reduced, and this organ does not metabolize drugs as efficiently as before. This means that, as a person gets older, less medication is needed to maintain the same level of a drug in the bloodstream.

Cardiovascular problems are often accompanied by respiratory disorders, and vice versa. Growing inelasticity of lung tissue means that ventilation is reduced. Because we rarely use the entire vital capacity, these effects are not noticed unless the demand for oxygen increases.

Blood supply to the kidneys is also reduced. The kidneys become smaller and less efficient at filtering wastes. Salt and water balance is difficult to maintain, and the elderly dehydrate faster than young people do. Difficulties involving urination include incontinence (lack of bladder control) and the inability to urinate. In men, the prostate gland may enlarge and reduce the diameter of the urethra, making urination so difficult that surgery is often needed.

The loss of teeth, which is frequently seen in elderly people, is more apt to be the result of long-term neglect than aging. The digestive tract loses tone, and secretion of saliva and gastric juice is reduced, but there is no indication of reduced absorption. Therefore, an adequate diet, rather than vitamin and mineral supplements, is recommended. Elderly people commonly complain of constipation, increased gas, and heartburn; gastritis, ulcers, and cancer can also occur.

Integration and Coordination

While most tissues of the body regularly replace their cells, some at a faster rate than others, the brain and the muscles ordinarily do not. However, contrary to previous opinion, recent studies show that few neural cells of the cerebral cortex are lost during the normal aging process. This means that cognitive skills remain unchanged even though a loss in short-term memory characteristically occurs. Although the elderly learn more slowly than the young, they can acquire and remember new material. The results of tests indicate that, when more time is given for the subject to respond, age differences in learning decrease.

Neurons are extremely sensitive to oxygen deficiency, and if neuron death does occur, it may be due not to aging itself but to reduced blood flow in narrowed blood vessels. Specific disorders, such as depression, Parkinson disease, and Alzheimer disease, are sometimes seen in the elderly, but they are not common. Reaction time, however, does slow, and more stimulation is needed for hearing, taste, and smell receptors to function as before. After age 50, the ability to hear tones at higher frequencies decreases gradually, and this can make it difficult to identify individual voices and to understand conversation in a group. The lens of the eye does not accommodate as well and also may develop a cataract. Glaucoma, the buildup of pressure due to increased fluid, is more likely to develop because of a reduction in the size of the anterior cavity of the eye.

Loss of skeletal muscle mass is not uncommon, but it can be controlled by following a regular exercise program. The capacity to do heavy labor decreases, but routine physical work should be no problem. A decrease in the strength of the respiratory muscles and inflexibility of the rib cage contribute to the inability of the lungs to expand as before, and reduced muscularity of the urinary bladder contributes to an inability to empty the bladder completely, and therefore to the occurrence of urinary infections.

As noted before, aging is accompanied by a decline in bone density. Osteoporosis, characterized by a loss of calcium and other minerals from bone, is not uncommon, but evidence indicates that proper health habits can prevent its occurrence. Arthritis, which causes pain upon movement of a joint, is also seen.

Weight gain occurs because the basal metabolism decreases and inactivity increases. Muscle mass is replaced by stored fat and retained water.

The Reproductive System

Females undergo menopause, and thereafter the level of female sex hormones in the blood falls markedly. The uterus and the cervix decrease in size, and the walls of the oviducts and the vagina become thinner. The external genitals become less pronounced. In males, the level of androgens falls gradually over the age span of 50–90, but sperm production continues until death.

Figure 16.12   Remaining active.
The aim of gerontology is to allow the elderly to enjoy living.

It is of interest that, as a group, females live longer than males. Males suffer a marked increase in heart disease in their forties, but an increase is not noted in females until after menopause, when women lead men in the incidence of stroke. Men are still more likely than women to have a heart attack, however. At one time it was thought that estrogen offers women some protection against cardiovascular disorders but this hypothesis is called into question because postmenopausal administration of estrogen has been shown to increase the risk of cardiovascular disorders in women.

Conclusion

We have listed many adverse effects of aging, but it is important to emphasize that although such effects are seen, they are not inevitable (Fig. 16.12). We must discover any extrinsic factors that precipitate these adverse effects and guard against them. Just as it is wise to make the proper preparations to remain financially independent when older, it is also wise to realize that biologically successful old age begins with the health habits developed when we are younger.

The deterioration of organ systems associated with aging can possibly be prevented in part by utilizing good health habits.

Bioethical Focus

Maternal Health Habits

The fetus is subject to harm if the mother uses medicines and drugs of abuse, including nicotine and alcohol. Also, various sexually transmitted diseases, notably HIV infection, can be passed on to the fetus by way of the placenta. Women need to know how to protect their unborn children from harm. Indeed, if they are sexually active, their behavior should be protective, even if they are using a recognized form of birth control. Harm can occur before a woman realizes she is pregnant!

Because maternal health habits can affect a child before it is born, there has been a growing acceptance of prosecuting women when a newborn has a condition, such as fetal alcohol syndrome, that could only have been caused by the drinking habits of the mother. Employers have also become aware that they might be subject to prosecution if the workplace exposes pregnant employees to toxins. To protect themselves, Johnson Controls, a U.S. battery manufacturer, developed a fetal protection policy. No woman who could bear a child was offered a job that might expose her to toxins that could negatively affect the development of her baby. To get such a job, a woman had to show that she had been sterilized or was otherwise incapable of having children. In 1991, the U.S. Supreme Court declared this policy unconstitutional on the basis of sexual discrimination. The decision was hailed as a victory for women, but was it? The decision was written in such a way that women alone, and not an employer, are responsible for any harm done to the fetus by workplace toxins.

Some have noted that prosecuting women for causing prenatal harm can itself have a detrimental effect. The women may tend to avoid prenatal treatment, thereby increasing the risk to their children. Or they may opt for an abortion in order to avoid the possibility of prosecution. Women feel they are in a no-win situation. If they have a child that has been harmed due to their behavior, they are bad mothers; if they abort, they are also bad.

Figure 16C **Health habits.**
Should a pregnant woman be liable for poor health habits that could harm her child?

Decide Your Opinion

1. Do you believe a woman should be prosecuted if her child is born with a preventable condition? Why or why not?
2. Is the woman or the physician responsible when a woman of childbearing age takes a prescribed medication that harms an unborn child? Is the employer or the woman responsible when a workplace toxin harms an unborn child?
3. Should sexually active women who can bear a child be expected to avoid substances or situations that could possibly harm an unborn child, even if they are using birth control? Why or why not?

Summarizing the Concepts

16.1 Fertilization
During fertilization, a sperm nucleus fuses with the egg nucleus. The resulting zygote begins to develop into a mass of cells, which travels down the uterine tube and embeds itself in the endometrium. Cells surrounding the embryo produce HCG, the hormone whose presence indicates that the female is pregnant.

16.2 Development Before Birth
Cleavage, growth, morphogenesis, and differentiation are the processes of development. The extraembryonic membranes—the chorion, yolk sac, allantois, and amnion—have functions that allow internal development.

At the end of the embryonic period, all organ systems are established, and there is a mature and functioning placenta. The embryo is only about 38 mm (1½ in.) long.

To support development, the umbilical arteries and vein take blood to and from the placenta, where exchanges take place that supply the fetus with oxygen and nutrients and rid the fetus of carbon dioxide and wastes. The venous duct joins the umbilical vein to the inferior vena cava. The oval duct and arterial duct allow the blood to pass through the heart without going to the lungs.

Fetal development extends from the third through the ninth months. During the third and fourth months, the skeleton is becoming ossified. The sex of the fetus becomes distinguishable. The presence of an *SRY* gene, usually on the Y chromosome, sets in motion a series of events that leads to the development of testes and the male genitals. Otherwise, ovaries and female genitals develop.

During the fifth through the ninth months, the fetus continues to grow and to gain weight. Babies born after six or seven months may survive, but full-term babies have a better chance of survival.

16.3 Pregnancy and Birth

During pregnancy, the mother gains weight as the uterus comes to occupy most of the abdominal cavity with resultant annoyances, such as incontinence. Many of the complaints of pregnancy, such as constipation, heartburn, darkening of certain skin areas, and diabetes of pregnancy, are due to the presence of the placental hormones.

A positive feedback mechanism that involves uterine contractions and oxytocin explains the onset and continuation of labor. During stage 1 of parturition, the cervix dilates. During stage 2, the child is born. During stage 3, the afterbirth is expelled.

16.4 Development After Birth

Development after birth consists of infancy, childhood, adolescence, and adulthood. Young adults are at their prime, and then the aging process begins. Aging encompasses progressive changes from about age 20 on that contribute to an increased risk of infirmity, disease, and death. Perhaps aging is genetic in origin, perhaps it is due to a change that affects the whole body, or perhaps it is due to extrinsic factors.

Studying the Concepts

1. Describe the process of fertilization and the processes of development. 310–11
2. Name the four extraembryonic membranes, and give a function for each. 311
3. What events occur during pre-embryonic development? 313
4. What is the basis of the pregnancy test? 315
5. Specifically, what events normally occur during embryonic development? 315–17 What events normally occur during fetal development? 319
6. Describe fetal circulation and the structure and function of the placenta. 318
7. Describe the development of the male and female sex organs. Describe two ambiguous sex determination syndromes. 320–21
8. In general, describe the physical changes in the mother during pregnancy. 324
9. What are the three stages of birth? Describe the events of each stage. 325
10. Discuss three hypotheses concerning aging. What major changes in body systems have been observed as adults age? 326–28

Thinking Critically About the Concepts

Refer to the opening vignette on page 309, and then answer these questions.

1. Support the contention that it is appropriate to look at development in this way.

2. Do genes determine destiny, considering that they control development?
3. Aside from genes, what else affects development?

Testing Your Knowledge of the Concepts

Choose the best answer for each question.

1. When all three germ layers are present (ectoderm, endoderm, and mesoderm), what event has occurred?
   a. blastulation
   b. limb formation
   c. gastrulation
   d. morulation
   e. blastopore formation

2. Which of these is not a process of development?
   a. cleavage
   b. parturition
   c. growth
   d. morphogenesis
   e. differentiation

3. Which of these is mismatched?
   a. chorion—sense perception
   b. yolk sac—first site of blood cell formation
   c. allantois—umbilical blood vessels
   d. amnion—contains fluid that protects embryo

4. In human development, which part of the blastocyst will develop into a fetus?
   a. morula
   b. trophoblast
   c. inner cell mass
   d. chorion
   e. yolk sac

5. In humans, the fetus eventually
   a. has four extraembryonic membranes.
   b. has developed organs and is recognizably human.
   c. depends upon the placenta for excretion of wastes and acquisition of nutrients.
   d. All of these are correct.

6. The placenta does not
   a. produce estrogen and progesterone.
   b. exchange dissolved gases.
   c. supply nutrients.
   d. cause the embryo to implant itself.

7. Human chorionic gonadotropin is a
   a. hormone.
   b. basis of pregnancy test.
   c. cause of ectopic pregnancy.
   d. Both a and b are correct.

8. Which hormone can be administered to begin the process of childbirth?
   a. estrogen
   b. oxytocin
   c. prolactin
   d. testosterone
   e. Both b and d are correct.

9. Only one sperm enters an egg because
   a. sperm have an acrosome.
   b. the corona radiata gets larger.
   c. the zona pellucida lifts up.
   d. the plasma membrane hardens.
   e. All of these are correct.

10. Which is a correct sequence that ends with the stage that implants?
    a. morula, blastocyst, embryonic disk, gastrula
    b. ovulation, fertilization, cleavage, morula, early blastocyst
    c. embryonic disk, gastrula, primitive streak, neurula
    d. primitive streak, neurula, extraembryonic membranes, chorion
    e. cleavage, neurula, early blastocyst, morula

11. Differentiation is equivalent to which term?
    a. morphogenesis
    b. growth
    c. specialization
    d. gastrulation
    e. induction

12. Which association is not correct?
    a. third week—development of heart
    b. fourth and fifth weeks—limb buds appear
    c. sixth through eighth weeks—germ layers appear for the first time
    d. All of these are correct.

13. Which association is not correct?
    a. third and fourth months—fetal heart has formed but it does not beat
    b. fifth through seventh months—mother feels movement
    c. eighth through ninth months—usually head is now pointed toward the cervix
    d. All of these are correct.

14. Which process refers to the shaping of the embryo and involves cell migration?
    a. cleavage
    b. differentiation
    c. growth
    d. induction
    e. morphogenesis

15. Structures that develop and become part of the placenta are the
    a. amniotic villi.
    b. yolk sac villi.
    c. allantois villi.
    d. chorionic villi.
    e. Both a and c are correct.

16. Which of these sequences correctly traces the path of blood in the fetus?
    a. umbilical arteries, umbilical vein, venous duct, iliac artery, heart
    b. oval opening, superior vena cava, pulmonary trunk, heart, aorta
    c. pulmonary trunk, superior vena cava, oval opening, heart
    d. umbilical arteries, placenta, umbilical vein, venous duct, heart
    e. Both a and d are correct.

17. Which of these is a hormone involved in development of male and female sex organs?
    a. estrogen
    b. anti-Müllerian hormone
    c. dihydrotestosterone
    d. testosterone
    e. All of these hormones are involved.

18. Which of these structures is not a circulatory feature unique to the fetus?
    a. arterial duct
    b. oval opening
    c. umbilical vein
    d. venous duct
    e. All of these are unique to the fetus.

19. Label this diagram illustrating the placement of the extraembryonic membranes, and give a function for each membrane in humans.

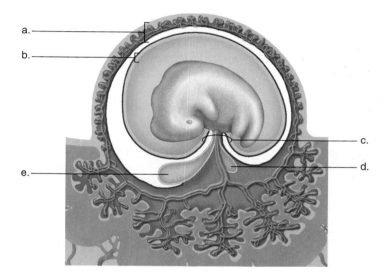

20. Which of these statements is correct?
    a. Fetal circulation, like adult circulation, takes blood equally to a pulmonary circuit and a systemic circuit.
    b. Fetal circulation shunts blood away from the lungs but makes full use of the systemic circuit.
    c. Fetal circulation includes exchange of substances between fetal blood and maternal blood at the placenta.
    d. Unlike adult circulation, fetal blood always carries O_2-rich blood and therefore has no need for the pulmonary circuit.
    e. Both b and c are correct.

21. At 25 days, the embryo has
    a. become a fetus.
    b. all the extraembryonic membranes.
    c. a nervous system and a digestive system.
    d. already undergone gastrulation.
    e. Both b and d are correct.

22. At two months, the embryo has
    a. become a fetus.
    b. body systems, but they don't function yet.
    c. a head, arms, and legs.
    d. a nose and eyes.
    e. All but b are correct.

23. Which of these statements is correct?
    a. The head starts out big but then gets smaller.
    b. The hands and feet begin as paddle-like structures.
    c. The heart is at first tubular.
    d. The placenta functions until birth occurs.
    e. All of these are correct statements.

24. Which length can be best associated with the embryo at the end of two months when it becomes a fetus?
    a. less than 1 mm, which is microscopic
    b. 38 mm, which is about 1½ in.
    c. 1 ft, which is about ⅓ m
    d. same length as a fetus at birth, which is about 20 in.
    e. Length varies too much to say.

25. Male/female gender of the fetus can be accurately determined as soon as the
    a. embryo is a zygote.
    b. germ layers have appeared.
    c. vertebrae have appeared.
    d. embryo is a fetus.
    e. embryo is about three months.

26. Label this diagram illustrating the fetal circulatory system.

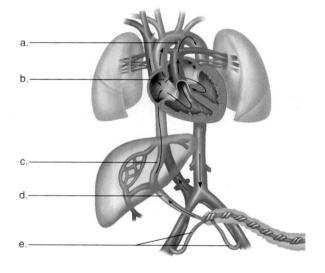

Understanding Key Terms

afterbirth 325
aging 326
allantois 311
amnion 311
blastocyst 313
Braxton Hicks contraction 324
breech birth 319
cesarean section 319
chorion 311
chorionic villi 317
cleavage 311
differentiation 311
ectopic pregnancy 315
embryo 315
embryonic development 315
embryonic disk 315

episiotomy 325
extraembryonic
    membrane 311
fertilization 310
fetal development 319
fontanel 319
gastrulation 317
gerontology 326
gestation 313
growth 311
human chorionic gonadotropin
    (HCG) 315
implantation 315
inner cell mass 313
lanugo 319
morphogenesis 311
morula 313
parturition 324
placenta 311
pre-embryonic
    development 313
primary germ layer 317
striae gravidarum 324
trophoblast 313
umbilical cord 317
vernix caseosa 319
yolk sac 311
zygote 310

Match the key terms to these definitions.

a. _____ Short, fine hair that is present during the later portion of fetal development.

b. _____ Developmental process by which a cell becomes specialized for a particular function.

c. _____ Extraembryonic membrane that forms a fluid-filled sac around the embryo.

d. _____ Union of a sperm nucleus and an egg nucleus, which creates a zygote with the diploid number of chromosomes.

e. _____ One of three layers of cells in the early embryo; each layer gives rise to specific organs as development proceeds.

Online Learning Center

www.mhhe.com/maderhuman9

The Online Learning Center provides a wealth of information fully organized and integrated by chapter. You will find practice quizzes, interactive activities, labeling exercises, flashcards, and much more that will complement your learning and understanding of human biology.

Looking at Both Sides

Each day, the Internet, media, and other people present you with opposing viewpoints on a wide range of subjects. Your ability to develop an informed opinion on an issue, and talk to others about it, is extremely important.

To expand and enhance your knowledge of a highly relevant bioethical issue, visit the "Student Edition" of the Online Learning Center. Under, "Course-Wide Content," select "Looking at Both Sides." Once there, you will be asked to complete activities that will increase your understanding of a current bioethical issue related to this chapter and allow you to defend your opinion.

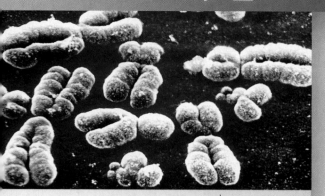

1 µm

17 Cell Division and the Human Life Cycle 333

18 Patterns of Inheritance 351

19 DNA Biology and Technology 367

20 Genetic Counseling 389

The human life cycle involves two types of nuclear divisions called mitosis and meiosis. Mitosis maintains the chromosome number during growth and repair, and meiosis reduces the chromosome number during gamete production. Gametes carry half the total number of chromosomes, as well as variable combinations of chromosomes and genes. It is sometimes possible to determine the chances of an offspring receiving a particular parental gene, and therefore having a particular appearance.

Genes, constructed of DNA, control not only the metabolism of the cell but also the characteristics of the individual. The base sequence of DNA within the human chromosomes is now known. This knowledge is expected to assist researchers in developing drugs to combat human ills. Biotechnology is a new and burgeoning field that permits DNA to be extracted from one organism and inserted into a different organism, also for a purpose useful to human beings.

Today, genetic counseling involves advising parents about the chances of their passing on a chromosome or genetic disorder based on family history. In the future, it should be possible to determine the mutations an individual carries, how these can be treated, and how to prevent them from being passed on.

CHAPTER **17**

Cell Division and the Human Life Cycle

C H A P T E R   C O N C E P T S

17.1 Cell Increase and Decrease
- What are somatic cells, and what process increases the number of somatic cells? What process decreases the number of somatic cells?   334
- What are the four stages of the cell cycle?   334–35
- How do the stages of the cell cycle prepare a cell for mitosis?   334–35

17.2 Mitosis
- Following mitosis, how does the chromosome number of the daughter cells compare with the chromosome number of the parent cell?   337
- What are the phases of mitosis and what happens during each phase?   338–39
- How is the cytoplasm divided between the daughter cells, following mitosis?   339

17.3 Meiosis
- Following meiosis, how does the chromosome number of the daughter cells compare to the chromosome number of the parent cell?   340
- How does meiosis reduce the likelihood that gametes will have the same combination of chromosomes and genes?   341
- What are the phases of meiosis and what happens during each phase?   341–43

17.4 Comparison of Meiosis with Mitosis
- What are the major differences between meiosis and mitosis?   344–45

17.5 The Human Life Cycle
- The human life cycle involves what two types of nuclear divisions?   346
- What is the function of mitosis and meiosis in humans?   346
- How does the process of spermatogenesis differ from oogenesis?   346–47

Apoptosis. What does it have to do with you? Well, just ask Joe about his toes. On both feet, the second and third toes are incompletely separated. Why? Because when he was a fetus, apoptosis (programmed cell death) failed to occur to a sufficient degree. During development, hands and feet look like paddles at first, and then later, apoptosis fashions fingers and toes.

Joe is actually fortunate that the lack of apoptosis during one stage of development left him with only a small anomaly. Just as cells must divide in order for a child to grow or a cut to heal, so apoptosis must occur for parts to take shape and for cancer cells to die. From the fertilization of the egg to the death of the individual, cell division and apoptosis are in balance for the person to remain healthy.

Signals received at the plasma membrane tell the cell whether cell division or apoptosis is required. During both processes, specific enzymes are activated—one set makes more cells, and the second set destroys cells. The genes too are involved. They respond to the signals and direct which enzymes will be present—those that build or those that tear down.

17.1 Cell Increase and Decrease

As we have often seen, opposing events often keep the body in balance and maintain homeostasis. For example, consider that some carrier proteins transport molecules into the cell and others transport molecules out of the cell. Some hormones increase the level of blood glucose, and others decrease the level. Similarly, two opposing processes keep the number of cells in the body at an appropriate level. Cell division increases the number of **somatic** (body) **cells.** Cell division consists of **mitosis,** which is division of the nucleus, and **cytokinesis,** which is division of the cytoplasm. **Apoptosis,** programmed cell death, decreases the number of cells.

Both mitosis and apoptosis are normal parts of growth and development. An organism begins as a single cell that repeatedly divides to produce many cells, but eventually some cells must die for the organism to take shape. For example, when a tadpole becomes a frog, the tail disappears as apoptosis occurs. As mentioned above, the fingers and toes of a human embryo are at first webbed, but then they are usually freed from one another as a result of apoptosis.

Cell division occurs during your entire life. Even now, your body is producing thousands of new red blood cells, skin cells, and cells that line your respiratory and digestive tracts. Also, if you suffer a cut, cell division will repair the injury. Apoptosis occurs all the time too, particularly if an abnormal cell that could become cancerous appears. Death of a cell through apoptosis prevents a tumor from developing.

The Cell Cycle

Cell division is a part of the cell cycle. The **cell cycle** is an orderly set of stages that take place between the time a cell divides and the time the resulting cells also divide.

Some cells become specialized and no longer enter the cell cycle.

In order to understand the cell cycle it is necessary to recall the structure of a cell (see Fig. 3.3). A human cell has a plasma membrane, which encloses the cytoplasm, the content of the cell outside the nucleus. In the cytoplasm are various organelles, which carry on various functions necessary to the life of the cell. When a cell is not undergoing division, the DNA (and associated proteins) within a nucleus is a tangled mass of thin threads called chromatin.

The Stages of Interphase

As Figure 17.1 shows, most of the cell cycle is spent in **interphase.** This is the time when the organelles carry on their usual functions. Also, the cell gets ready to divide: It grows larger, the number of organelles doubles, and the amount of chromatin doubles as DNA replicates. For mammalian cells, interphase lasts for about 20 hours, which is 90% of the cell cycle.

The event of DNA synthesis permits interphase to be divided into three stages: the G_1 stage occurs before DNA synthesis, the S stage includes DNA synthesis, and the G_2 stage occurs after DNA synthesis. Originally, G stood for the "gaps" that occur in DNA synthesis, during interphase. But now that we know growth occurs during these stages, the G can be thought of as standing for growth. Let us see what specifically happens during each of these stages.

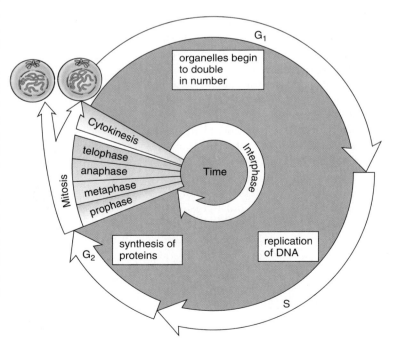

Figure 17.1   The cell cycle.
The cell cycle has four stages. During interphase, which consists of G_1, S, and G_2, the cell gets ready to divide, and during the mitotic stage, nuclear division and cytokinesis (cytoplasmic division) occur.

G_1 *stage.* A cell doubles its organelles (e.g., mitochondria and ribosomes), and it accumulates the materials needed for DNA synthesis.

S stage. DNA replication occurs; a copy is made of all the DNA in the cell.

G_2 *stage.* The cell synthesizes the proteins needed for cell division, such as the protein found in microtubules. The role of microtubules in cell division is described in a later section.

The amount of time the cell takes for interphase varies widely. Some cells, such as nerve and muscle cells, typically do not complete the cell cycle and are permanently arrested in G_1. These cells are said to have entered a G_0 stage. Embryonic cells spend very little time in G_1 and complete the cell cycle in a few hours.

The Mitotic Stage

Following interphase, the cell enters the M (for mitotic) stage. This stage not only includes mitosis, it also includes cytokinesis.

As described in the Health Focus on page 336, by now chromatin has become the chromosomes. Each species has a characteristic number of chromosomes; humans have 46. Various proteins assist in changing chromatin into chromosomes that are visible under the microscope when stained (see Fig. 17A). Because DNA replication occurred during the S stage, each chromosome consists of two identical DNA strands, called the sister chromatids. Another way of expressing these events is to say that DNA replication has resulted in duplicated chromosomes. During mitosis, which consists of the phases noted in Figure 17.1, the sister chromatids of each chromosome separate, becoming chromosomes that are distributed to two daughter nuclei. When cytokinesis is complete, two daughter cells are now present. Mammalian cells usually require only about 4 hours to complete the mitotic stage.

Control of the Cell Cycle

The cell cycle is controlled by internal and external chemical signals. The growth factors discussed on page 282 are external signals received at the plasma membrane, which can cause cells to undergo the cell cycle repeatedly. Researchers have identified an internal signal called cyclin that increases and decreases as the cell cycle continues. Cyclin has to be present for the cell to proceed from the G_2 stage to the M stage, and for the cell to proceed from the G_1 stage to the S stage.

DNA damage can stop the cell cycle in the G_1 stage. The protein p53 attempts to bring about DNA repair, but if DNA repair is not possible, p53 brings about apoptosis. We now know that many forms of tumors contain cells that lack an active p53 protein. Without an active p53 protein, cancer develops.

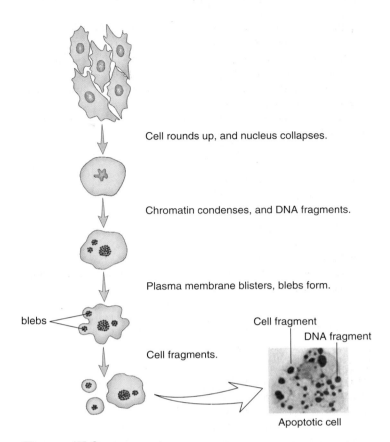

Cell rounds up, and nucleus collapses.

Chromatin condenses, and DNA fragments.

Plasma membrane blisters, blebs form.

blebs

Cell fragments.

Cell fragment
DNA fragment

Apoptotic cell

Figure 17.2   Apoptosis.
Apoptosis is a sequence of events that results in a fragmented cell. The fragments are phagocytized by white blood cells and neighboring tissue cells.

Apoptosis

Apoptosis is often defined as programmed cell death because the cell progresses through a usual series of events that bring about its destruction (Fig. 17.2). The cell rounds up and loses contact with its neighbors. The nucleus fragments, and the plasma membrane develops blisters, or blebs. Finally, the cell fragments, and its bits and pieces are engulfed by white blood cells and/or neighboring cells. A remarkable finding of the past few years is that cells routinely harbor the enzymes, now called caspases, that bring about apoptosis. The enzymes are ordinarily held in check by inhibitors, but they can be unleashed either by internal or external signals. There are two sets of caspases. The first set are the "initiators" that receive the signal to activate the "executioners," which then activate the enzymes that dismantle the cell. For example, executioners turn on enzymes that tear apart the cytoskeleton and enzymes that chop up DNA.

Cell division and apoptosis are two opposing processes that keep the number of healthy cells in balance.

Health Focus

Chromosome Organization

Health depends on the proper distribution of DNA from the parent cell to the daughter cells. (These terms have nothing to do with gender; they are simply a way to designate the beginning cell and the resulting cell.) Unless the daughter cells get a complete copy of DNA, any number of illnesses could possibly develop, because the daughter cells require a copy of all the genes.

Especially in eukaryotic cells, such as human cells, passage of DNA to the daughter cells presents a problem because of the large quantity of DNA found in the nucleus. For example, a human cell contains about 2 m of DNA within a nucleus that is only 5 to 8 μm in diameter. But our DNA is packaged into chromosomes, which do fit inside the nucleus and allow DNA to be distributed to the daughter cells. Because the nucleus houses DNA, it is the command center for the cell.

When a human cell is not undergoing cell division, the DNA and associated proteins have the appearance of thin threads called chromatin. Closer examination reveals that DNA is periodically wound around a core of eight protein molecules, and as a result, the entire molecule looks like beads on a string. The protein molecules are histones and each bead is called a nucleosome (Fig. 17A).

Just before nuclear division occurs, chromatin coils tightly into a fiber that has six nucleosomes to a turn. Then, the fiber loops back and forth and condenses to produce highly condensed chromosomes. We can see chromosomes microscopically because just before division occurs a chromosome is 10,000 times more compact than is chromatin.

Another important event, which has occurred in preparation for distribution of chromosomes, is DNA replication. During replication, DNA is copied. By the time we can clearly see the chromosomes, they are duplicated. A duplicated chromosome is composed of two identical halves called chromatids. The chromatids are held together at a constricted region called a centromere.

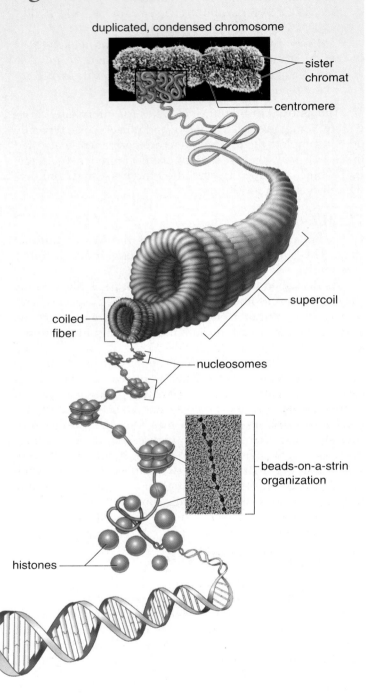

Figure 17A Levels of chromosome organization.
Histones are responsible for packaging chromatin so that it fits into the nucleus and so that it becomes highly condensed when nuclear division occurs.

17.2 Mitosis

Mitosis *is nuclear division that produces two new cells, each with the same number and kinds of chromosomes as the cell that divides.* The cell that divides is called the **parent cell** and the new cells are called the **daughter cells.** Because the parent cell and daughter cell have the same number and kinds of chromosomes, they are genetically identical.

Overview of Mitosis

As mentioned, when mitosis is going to occur, chromatin in the nucleus becomes highly condensed, and the chromosomes become visible. Because replication of DNA occurred, each chromosome is now duplicated and is composed of two identical parts, called sister chromatids, held together at a **centromere.** They are called sister chromatids because they contain the same genes.

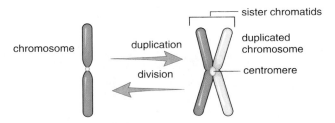

Figure 17.3 gives an overview of mitosis; for simplicity, only four chromosomes are depicted. (In determining the number of chromosomes, it is necessary to count only the number of independent centromeres.) The complete number of chromosomes is called the **diploid (2n)** number for reasons that will be explained later.

During mitosis, the centromeres divide and the sister chromatids separate. (Following separation, each chromatid is called a chromosome.) Each daughter cell gets a complete set of chromosomes and is 2n. Therefore, each daughter cell receives the same number and kinds of chromosomes as the parent cell, and each daughter cell is genetically identical to the other and to the parent cell.

The Spindle

Another event of importance during meiosis is the duplication of the **centrosome,** the microtubule organizing center of the cell. After centrosomes duplicate, they separate and form the poles of the **mitotic spindle,** where they assemble the microtubules that make up the spindle fibers. The chromosomes are attached to the spindle fibers (Fig. 17.4). An array of microtubules, called an **aster,** is also at the poles.

The **centrioles** are short cylinders of microtubules that are present in centrosomes. The centrioles lie at right angles to one another. What role the centrioles play in the centrosome is not presently known. They could possibly assist in the formation of the spindle that separates the chromatids during mitosis.

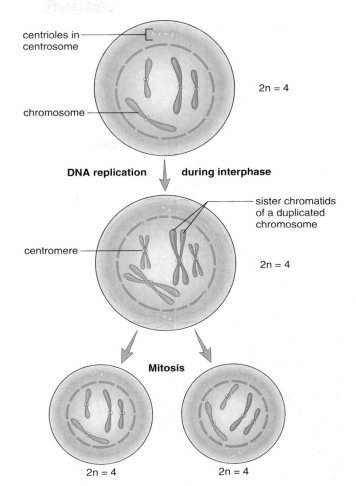

Figure 17.3   **Mitosis overview.**
Following DNA replication, each chromosome is duplicated. When the centromeres split, the sister chromatids, now called chromosomes, move into daughter nuclei. (The blue and red chromosomes were inherited from different parents.)

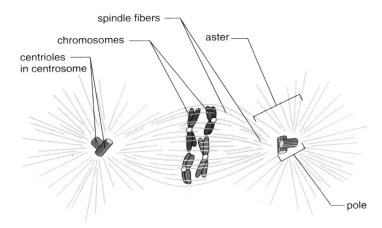

Figure 17.4   **The mitotic spindle.**
Before mitosis begins, the centrosome and the centrioles duplicate; during mitosis, they separate and the mitotic spindle, composed of microtubules, forms between them.

Phases of Mitosis

Mitosis follows interphase (Fig. 17.5). As an aid in describing the events of mitosis, the process is divided into four phases: prophase, metaphase, anaphase, and telophase (Fig. 17.6). Although the stages of mitosis are depicted as if they were separate, they are actually continuous, and one stage flows from the other with no noticeable interruption.

Prophase

Several events occur during **prophase** that visibly indicate the cell is preparing to divide. The centrosomes outside the nucleus have duplicated, and they begin moving away from one another toward opposite ends of the nucleus. Spindle fibers appear between the separating centrosomes, the nuclear envelope begins to fragment, and the nucleolus, a special region of DNA, disappears as the chromosomes coil and become condensed.

The chromosomes are now visible. Each is composed of two sister chromatids held together at a centromere. Spindle fibers attach to the centromeres as the chromosomes continue to shorten and to thicken. During prophase, chromosomes are randomly placed in the nucleus (Fig. 17.6).

Metaphase

During **metaphase,** the nuclear envelope is fragmented, and the spindle occupies the region formerly occupied by the nucleus. The chromosomes are now at the equator (center) of the spindle. Metaphase is characterized by a fully formed spindle, and the chromosomes, each with two sister chromatids, are aligned at the equator (Fig. 17.6).

Anaphase

At the start of **anaphase,** the centromeres uniting the sister chromatids divide. Then the sister chromatids separate, becoming chromosomes that move toward opposite poles of the spindle. Separation of the sister chromatids ensures that each cell receives a copy of each type of chromosome, and thereby has a full complement of genes. Anaphase is

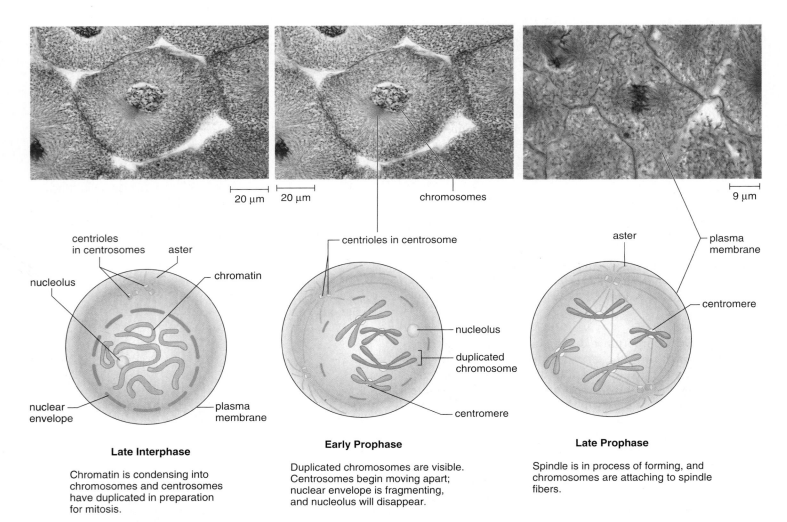

Late Interphase

Chromatin is condensing into chromosomes and centrosomes have duplicated in preparation for mitosis.

Figure 17.5   Late interphase.

Early Prophase

Duplicated chromosomes are visible. Centrosomes begin moving apart; nuclear envelope is fragmenting, and nucleolus will disappear.

Figure 17.6   Phases of mitosis.

Late Prophase

Spindle is in process of forming, and chromosomes are attaching to spindle fibers.

characterized by the 2n (diploid) number of chromosomes moving toward each pole.

Remember that counting the number of centromeres indicates the number of chromosomes. Therefore, in Figure 17.6, each pole receives four chromosomes: two are red and two are blue.

Function of the Spindle   The spindle brings about chromosomal movement. Two types of spindle fibers are involved in the movement of chromosomes during anaphase. One type extends from the poles to the equator of the spindle; there, they overlap. As mitosis proceeds, these fibers increase in length, and this helps push the chromosomes apart. The chromosomes themselves are attached to other spindle fibers that simply extend from their centromeres to the poles. These fibers (composed of microtubules that can disassemble) get shorter and shorter as the chromosomes move toward the poles. Therefore, they pull the chromosomes apart.

Spindle fibers, as stated earlier, are composed of microtubules. Microtubules can assemble and disassemble by the addition or subtraction of tubulin (protein) subunits. This is what enables spindle fibers to lengthen and shorten, and what ultimately causes the movement of the chromosomes.

Telophase

Telophase begins when the chromosomes arrive at the poles. During telophase, the chromosomes become indistinct chromatin again. The spindle disappears as the nuclear envelope components reassemble in each cell. Each nucleus has a nucleolus because each has a region of the DNA, where ribosomal subunits are produced. Telophase is characterized by the presence of two daughter nuclei.

Cytokinesis

Cytokinesis, which generally follows mitosis, is the division of the cytoplasm and organelles. In human cells, a slight indentation, called a **cleavage furrow,** passes around the circumference of the cell. Actin filaments form a contractile ring, and as the ring gets smaller and smaller, the cleavage furrow pinches the cell in half. As a result, each cell becomes enclosed by its own plasma membrane.

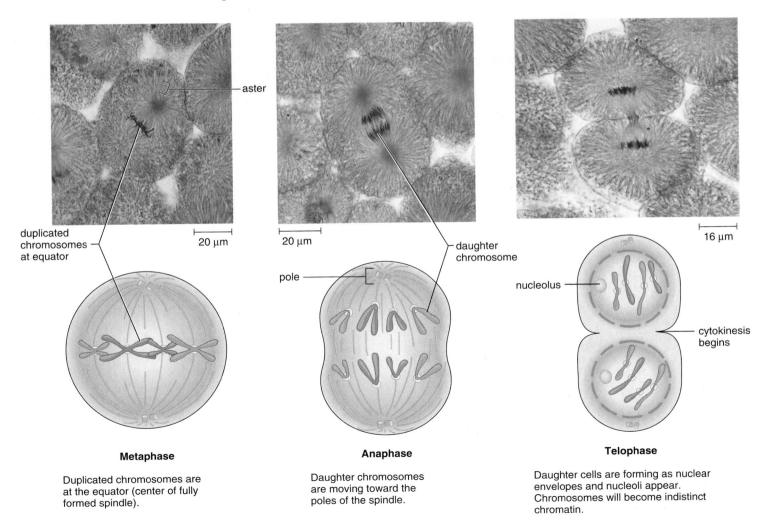

Metaphase

Duplicated chromosomes are at the equator (center of fully formed spindle).

Anaphase

Daughter chromosomes are moving toward the poles of the spindle.

Telophase

Daughter cells are forming as nuclear envelopes and nucleoli appear. Chromosomes will become indistinct chromatin.

17.3 Meiosis

Meiosis, which requires two nuclear divisions, results in *four daughter cells, each having one of each kind of chromosome, and therefore half as many chromosomes as the parent cell.* The parent cell has the diploid (2n) number of chromosomes, while the daughter cells have half this number, which is called the **haploid (n)** number of chromosomes. Therefore, meiosis is often called reduction division. The daughter cells that result from meiosis go on to become the gametes.

In Figure 17.7, the diploid (2n) number of chromosomes is four chromosomes. The parent cell has the 2n number of chromosomes while the daughter cells have the haploid (n) number of chromosomes, which is equal to two chromosomes.

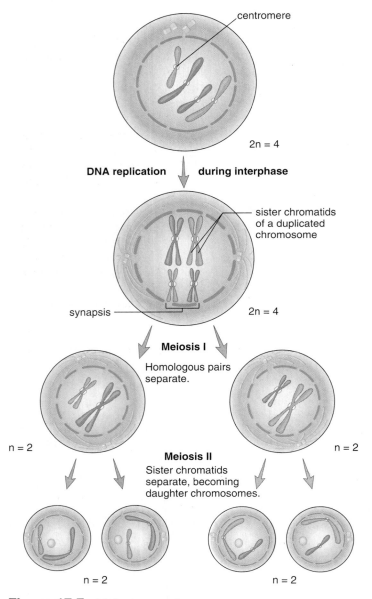

Figure 17.7   Meiosis overview.
DNA replication is followed by meiosis I when homologous chromosomes pair and then separate. During meiosis II, the sister chromatids become chromosomes that move into daughter nuclei.

Overview of Meiosis

At the start of meiosis, the parent cell has the diploid number of chromosomes. When a cell is 2n, or diploid, the chromosomes occur in pairs. For example, the 46 chromosomes of humans occur in 23 pairs of chromosomes. In Figure 17.7, there are two pairs of chromosomes. The short chromosomes are one pair and the long chromosomes are another. The members of a pair are called **homologous chromosomes,** or **homologues,** because they look alike and carry genes for the same traits, such as type of hair or color of eyes.

Meiosis I

The two cell divisions of meiosis are called meiosis I and meiosis II. Prior to meiosis I, DNA replication has occurred, and the chromosomes are duplicated. Each chromosome consists of two chromatids held together at a centromere. During meiosis I, the homologous chromosomes come together and line up side by side. This so-called **synapsis** results in an association of four chromatids that stay in close proximity during the first two phases of meiosis I. Synapsis is quite significant because its occurrence leads to a reduction of the chromosome number.

Because of synapsis, there are pairs of homologous chromosomes at the equator during meiosis I. Notice that only during meiosis I is it possible to observe paired chromosomes at the equator. When the members of these pairs separate, each daughter nucleus receives one member of each pair. Therefore, each daughter cell now has the haploid (n) number of chromosomes, as you can verify by counting its centromeres. Each chromosome, however, is still duplicated, and no replication of DNA occurs between meiosis I and meiosis II.

Meiosis II and Fertilization

During meiosis II, the centromeres divide and the sister chromatids separate, becoming chromosomes that are distributed to daughter nuclei. In the end, each of four daughter cells has the n, or haploid, number of chromosomes, and each chromosome consists of one chromatid.

In humans, the daughter cells mature into **gametes** (sex cells—sperm and egg) that fuse during fertilization. **Fertilization** restores the diploid number of chromosomes in the **zygote,** the first cell of the new individual. If the gametes carried the diploid, instead of the haploid number of chromosomes, the chromosome number would double with each fertilization. After several generations, the zygote would be nothing but chromosomes.

During meiosis I, homologous chromosomes pair up and then separate. Each daughter nucleus receives one copy of each kind of chromosome. Following meiosis II, there are four haploid daughter cells, and each chromosome consists of one chromatid.

Stages of Meiosis

Meiosis is a part of sexual reproduction. The process of meiosis ensures that the next generation of individuals will have the diploid number of chromosomes and a combination of characteristics different from that of either parent. Both meiosis I and meiosis II have the same four stages of nuclear division as did mitosis—prophase, metaphase, anaphase, and telophase.

Prophase I

In prophase I, synapsis occurs, and then the spindle appears, while the nuclear envelope fragments and the nucleolus disappears. During synapsis, the homologous chromosomes come together and line up side by side. Now, an exchange of genetic material may occur between the nonsister chromatids of the homologous pair (Fig. 17.8). This exchange is called **crossing-over.** Crossing-over means that the chromatids held together by a centromere are no longer identical. When the chromatids separate during meiosis II, the daughter cells will receive chromosomes with recombined genetic material.

In order to appreciate the significance of crossing-over, it is necessary to realize that the members of a homologous pair can carry slightly different instructions for the same genetic trait. For example, one homologue may carry instructions for brown eyes, while the corresponding homologue may carry instructions for blue eyes. Therefore, crossing causes the offspring to receive a different combination of instructions from the mother and father of the offspring.

Metaphase I

During metaphase I, the homologous pairs align independently at the equator. This means that the maternal or paternal member may be oriented toward either pole. Figure 17.9 shows four possible orientations for a cell that contains only three pairs of chromosomes. Each orientation will result in gametes that have a different combination

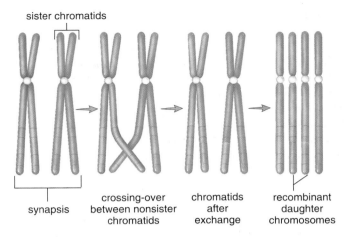

Figure 17.8   Synapsis and crossing-over.
During meiosis I, *from left to right*, duplicated homologous chromosomes undergo synapsis and line up with each other. During crossing-over, nonsister chromatids break and then rejoin. Two of the resulting chromosomes will have a different combination of genes than they had before.

of maternal and paternal chromosomes. For example, only the first alignment will result in gametes with either three paternal or three maternal chromosomes. Gametes from the other cells will have a different combination of chromosomes.

Once all possible orientations are considered, the result will be 2^3, or 8, possible combinations of maternal and paternal chromosomes in the resulting gametes from this cell. In humans, where there are 23 pairs of chromosomes, the number of possible chromosomal combinations in the gametes is a staggering 2^{23}, or 8,388,608. And this does not even consider the genetic variations that are introduced due to crossing-over.

The events of prophase I and metaphase I help ensure that gametes will not have the same combination of chromosomes and genes.

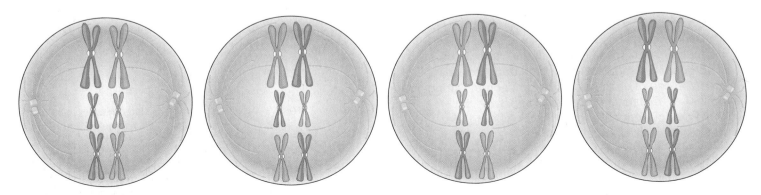

Figure 17.9   Independent alignment.
Four possible orientations of homologous pairs at the equator are shown for metaphase I of a cell that has three pairs of homologous chromosomes. Each of these orientations will result in daughter nuclei with a different combination of parent chromosomes. When a cell has three pairs of homologous chromosomes, there will be 2^3 possible combinations of parent chromosomes in the daughter nuclei.

First Division: All Phases

The phases of meiosis I for an animal cell are diagrammed in Figure 17.10a. Synapsis and crossing-over, which occur during prophase I, were discussed earlier. Crossing-over is represented by an exchange of "color." During metaphase I, as discussed, homologous pairs align independently at the equator. The maternal homologue (e.g., red) may be orientated toward either pole, and the paternal (e.g., blue) homologue may be aligned toward either pole. This means that all possible combinations of chromosomes can occur in the daughter nuclei. During anaphase I, homologous chromosomes separate and, then, move to opposite poles of the spindle. Each chromosome still consists of two chromatids.

In some species, a telophase I phase occurs at the end of meiosis I. If so, the nuclear envelopes re-form, and nucleoli appear. This phase may or may not be accompanied by cytokinesis, which is separation of the cytoplasm.

Interkinesis

The period between meiosis I and meiosis II is called **interkinesis.** No replication of DNA occurs during interkinesis. Why is this appropriate? Because the chromosomes are already duplicated.

The Second Division and Cytokinesis

The phases of meiosis II are diagrammed in Figure 17.10b. At the beginning of prophase II, a spindle appears while the nuclear envelope disassembles and the nucleolus disappears. Each duplicated chromosome attaches to the spindle independently. During metaphase II, the chromosomes are lined up at the equator. At the start of anaphase II, the centromeres split. The sister chromatids of each chromosome separate and move toward the poles. Each pole receives the same number of chromosomes. In telophase II, the spindle disappears as nuclear envelopes form.

During cytokinesis, the plasma membrane furrows to give two complete cells, each of which has the haploid, or n, number of chromosomes. Since each cell from meiosis I undergoes meiosis II, there are four daughter cells altogether.

Meiosis involves two cell divisions. During meiosis I, synapsis and crossing-over occur. Homologous chromosomes separate, and each daughter cell receives one of each kind of chromosome. During meiosis II, the sister chromatids separate, and there are four daughter cells, each with the haploid number of chromosomes.

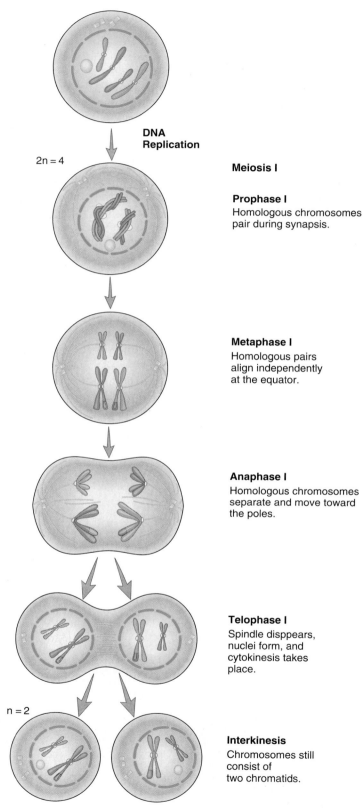

DNA Replication

2n = 4

Meiosis I

Prophase I
Homologous chromosomes pair during synapsis.

Metaphase I
Homologous pairs align independently at the equator.

Anaphase I
Homologous chromosomes separate and move toward the poles.

Telophase I
Spindle disppears, nuclei form, and cytokinesis takes place.

n = 2

Interkinesis
Chromosomes still consist of two chromatids.

a.

Meiosis II

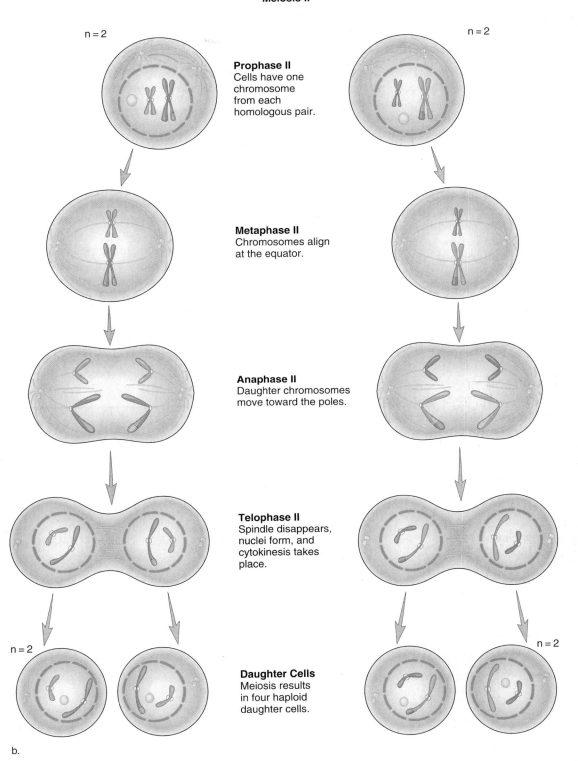

n = 2

Prophase II
Cells have one chromosome from each homologous pair.

n = 2

Metaphase II
Chromosomes align at the equator.

Anaphase II
Daughter chromosomes move toward the poles.

Telophase II
Spindle disappears, nuclei form, and cytokinesis takes place.

n = 2

n = 2

Daughter Cells
Meiosis results in four haploid daughter cells.

b.

Figure 17.10   Meiosis I and meiosis II.
a. During meiosis I, homologous pairs of chromosomes undergo synapsis and then separate so that each daughter cell has only one chromosome from each original homologous pair. Notice that each daughter cell is haploid and each chromosome still has two chromatids.
b. During meiosis II, sister chromatids separate and the resulting chromosomes go into the daughter nuclei. (The blue chromosomes were inherited from one parent, and the red from the other.)

17.4 Comparison of Meiosis with Mitosis

Figure 17.11 compares meiosis to mitosis. You will want to notice that:

- DNA replication takes place only once prior to both meiosis and mitosis. However, meiosis requires two nuclear divisions, but mitosis requires only one.
- Four daughter nuclei are produced by meiosis, and following cytokinesis, there are four daughter cells. Mitosis followed by cytokinesis results in two daughter cells.
- The four daughter cells following meiosis are haploid and have half the chromosome number of the parent cell. The daughter cells following mitosis have the same chromosome number as the parent cell.
- The daughter cells from meiosis are not genetically identical to each other or to the parent cell. The daughter cells from mitosis are genetically identical to each other and to the parent cell.

The specific differences between these nuclear divisions can be categorized according to occurrence and process.

Occurrence

Meiosis occurs only at certain times in the life cycle of sexually reproducing organisms. In humans, meiosis occurs only in the reproductive organs and produces the gametes. Mitosis is more common because it occurs in all tissues during growth and repair.

Process

To summarize the process, Tables 17.1 and 17.2 separately compare meiosis I and meiosis II with mitosis.

Comparison of Meiosis I with Mitosis

Notice that these events distinguish meiosis I from mitosis:

- Homologous chromosomes pair and undergo crossing-over during prophase I of meiosis, but not during mitosis.
- Paired homologous chromosomes align at the equator during metaphase I in meiosis. These paired chromosomes have four chromatids altogether. Individual chromosomes align at the equator during metaphase in mitosis. They each have two chromatids.
- Homologous chromosomes (with centromeres intact) separate and move to opposite poles during anaphase I in meiosis. Centromeres split, and sister chromatids, now called chromosomes, move to opposite poles during anaphase in mitosis.

Comparison of Meiosis II with Mitosis

The events of meiosis II are just like those of mitosis except in meiosis II, the nuclei contain the haploid number of chromosomes.

Meiosis is a specialized process that reduces the chromosome number and occurs only during the production of gametes. Mitosis is a process that occurs during growth and repair of all tissues.

Table 17.1	Comparison of Meiosis I with Mitosis

Meiosis I	Mitosis
Prophase I	*Prophase*
Pairing of homologous chromosomes	No pairing of chromosomes
Metaphase I	*Metaphase*
Homologous duplicated chromosomes at equator	Duplicated chromosomes at equator
Anaphase I	*Anaphase*
Homologous chromosomes separate.	Sister chromatids separate, becoming daughter chromosomes that move to the poles.
Telophase I	*Telophase*
Two haploid daughter cells	Two daughter cells, identical to the parent cell

Table 17.2	Comparison of Meiosis II with Mitosis

Meiosis II	Mitosis
Prophase II	*Prophase*
No pairing of chromosomes	No pairing of chromosomes
Metaphase II	*Metaphase*
Haploid number of duplicated chromosomes at equator	Duplicated chromosomes at equator
Anaphase I	*Anaphase*
Sister chromatids separate, becoming daughter chromosomes that move to the poles.	Sister chromatids separate, becoming daughter chromosomes that move to the poles.
Telophase II	*Telophase*
Four haploid daughter cells	Two daughter cells, identical to the parent cell

Meiosis

Mitosis

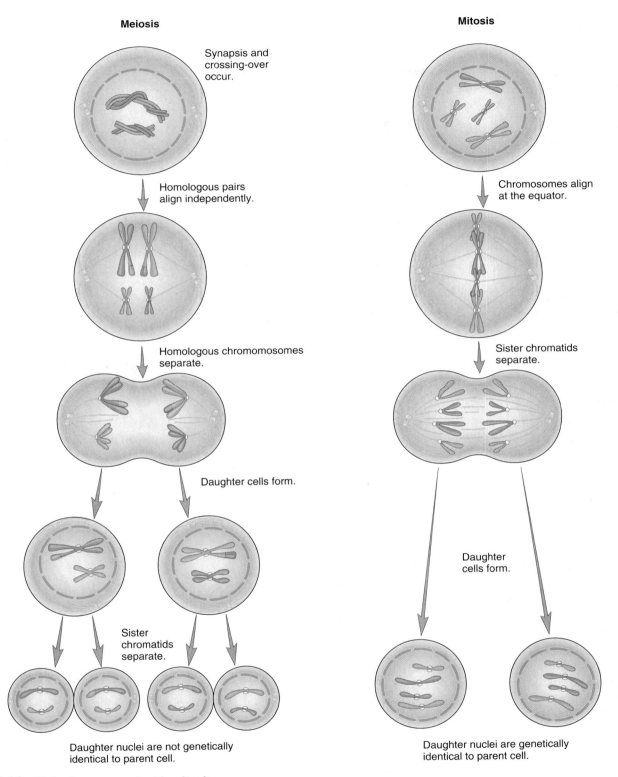

Synapsis and crossing-over occur.

Homologous pairs align independently.

Homologous chromomosomes separate.

Daughter cells form.

Sister chromatids separate.

Daughter nuclei are not genetically identical to parent cell.

Chromosomes align at the equator.

Sister chromatids separate.

Daughter cells form.

Daughter nuclei are genetically identical to parent cell.

Figure 17.11   Meiosis compared with mitosis.

Why does meiosis produce daughter cells with half the number and mitosis produces daughter cells with the same number of chromosomes as the parent cell? Compare metaphase I of meiosis with metaphase of mitosis. Only in metaphase I are the homologous chromosomes paired at the equator. Members of the homologous chromosomes separate during anaphase I, and therefore, the daughter cells are haploid. The blue chromosomes were inherited from one parent, and the red from the other. The exchange of color between nonsister chromatids represents crossing-over during meiosis I.

17.5 The Human Life Cycle

The human life cycle requires both meiosis and mitosis (Fig. 17.12). In both sexes, meiosis is a part of gametogenesis, production of the gametes, which are the sperm and egg. A haploid sperm and a haploid egg join at fertilization, and the resulting zygote has the full, or diploid, number of chromosomes. As a result of meiosis, the chromosome number stays constant generation after generation. During development of the fetus and growth after birth, mitosis keeps the chromosome number constant in all the cells of the body. As a result of mitosis, each somatic cell in the body has the diploid number of chromosomes.

The Functions of Mitosis and Meiosis

Mitosis and meiosis have different roles to play in the life cycle of human beings.

Mitosis occurs in humans when tissues grow or when repair occurs. Growth occurs during development before birth, and it occurs as a child becomes an adult. Also, when a cut heals or a broken bone mends, mitosis has occurred.

In many organs, the cell cycle, which includes mitosis, continually produces new cells throughout the life span. These organs contain stem cells (often called adult stem cells), which can continually divide. Stem cells in the red bone marrow repeatedly divide to produce millions of cells that go on to become the various types of blood cells. The possibility exists that researchers will be able to manipulate red bone marrow stem cells to become various types of tissues that can be used to cure illnesses. Some researchers prefer to use embryonic stem cells for this purpose as discussed on page 305.

The functions of meiosis are to keep the chromosome number constant from generation to generation and to provide genetic recombination. Because the gametes are haploid, the zygote has only the diploid number of chromosomes. Genetic recombination is ensured in three ways: crossing-over and independent alignment were discussed on page 341. Also, because the zygote receives chromosomes from both parents during fertilization, recombination occurs.

Spermatogenesis and Oogenesis

Meiosis is a part of **spermatogenesis,** the production of sperm in males, and **oogenesis,** the production of eggs in females (Fig. 17.13). Following meiosis, the daughter cells mature to become the gametes.

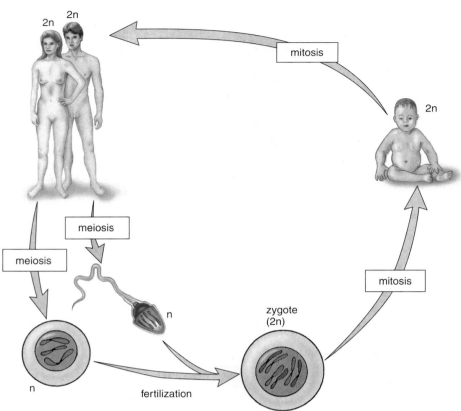

Figure 17.12   Life cycle of humans.
Meiosis in human males is a part of sperm production, and meiosis in human females is a part of egg production. When a haploid sperm fertilizes a haploid egg, the zygote is diploid. The zygote undergoes mitosis as it develops into a newborn child. Mitosis continues after birth, until the individual reaches maturity; then the life cycle begins again.

Spermatogenesis

After puberty, the time of life when the sex organs mature, spermatogenesis is continual in the testes of human males. As many as 300,000 sperm are produced per minute, or 400 million per day.

Spermatogenesis is shown in Figure 17.13*a*. The so-called *primary spermatocytes*, which are diploid (2n), divide during meiosis I to form two *secondary spermatocytes*, which are haploid (n). Secondary spermatocytes divide during meiosis II to produce four *spermatids*, which are also haploid (n). What's the difference between the chromosomes in haploid secondary spermatocytes and those in haploid spermatids? The chromosomes in secondary spermatocytes are duplicated and consist of two chromatids, while those in spermatids consist of only one. Spermatids mature into sperm (spermatozoa). In human males, sperm have 23 chromosomes, which is the haploid number. The process of meiosis in males always results in four cells that become sperm. In other words, all four daughter cells—the spermatids—become sperm.

Oogenesis

As you know, the ovary of a female contains many immature follicles (see Fig 15.7). Each of these follicles contains a primary oocyte arrested in prophase I. As shown in Figure 17.13*b*, a primary oocyte, which is diploid (2n), divides during meiosis I into two cells, each of which is haploid. Note that the chromosomes are duplicated. One of these cells, termed the **secondary oocyte,** receives almost all the cytoplasm. The other is the first polar body. A **polar body** is a nonfunctioning cell that occurs during oogenesis. The first polar body contains duplicated chromosomes and completes meiosis II occasionally. The secondary oocyte begins meiosis II but stops at metaphase II until circumstances are suitable.

The secondary oocyte (for convenience, called the egg) leaves the ovary during ovulation and enters an oviduct, where it may be fertilized by a sperm. If so, the oocyte is activated to complete the second meiotic division. Following meiosis II, there is one egg and two or possibly three polar bodies. The mature egg has 23 chromosomes. The polar bodies disintegrate. They are a way to discard unnecessary chromosomes, while retaining much of the cytoplasm in the egg.

The human life cycle contains both mitosis and meiosis. Meiosis occurs in the testes of males during spermatogenesis and in the ovaries of females during oogenesis.

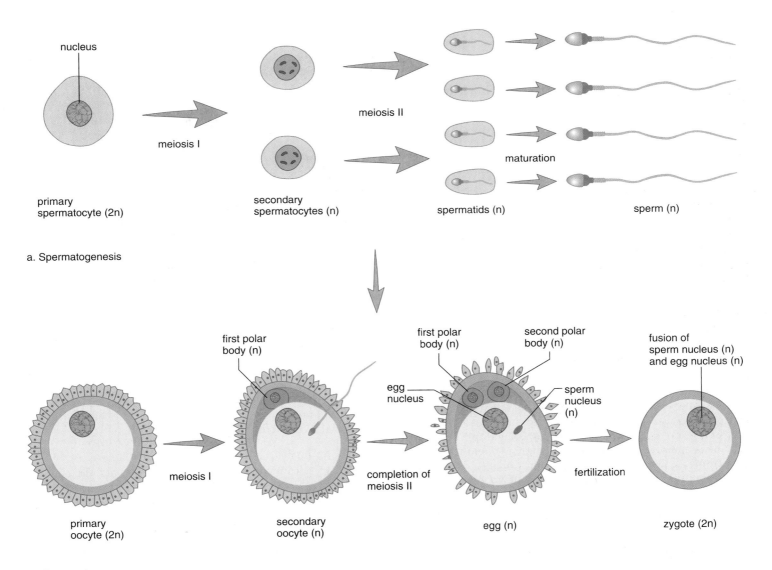

Figure 17.13   Spermatogenesis and oogenesis.
Spermatogenesis (**a**) produces four viable sperm, whereas oogenesis (**b**) produces one egg and two polar bodies. In humans, both sperm and egg have 23 chromosomes each; therefore, following fertilization, the zygote has 46 chromosomes.

Bioethical Focus

Genetic Testing for Cancer Genes

Several genetic tests are now available to detect certain cancer genes. If women test positive for defective *BRACA1* and *BRCA2* genes, they have an increased risk for early-onset breast and ovarian cancer. If individuals test positive for the *APC* gene, they are at greater risk for the development of colon cancer. Other genetic tests exist for rare cancers, including retinoblastoma and Wilms tumor.

Advocates for genetic testing say that it can alert those who test positive for these mutated genes to undergo more frequent mammograms or colonoscopies. Early detection of cancer clearly offers the best chance for successful treatment. Others feel that genetic testing is unnecessary because nothing can presently be done to prevent the disease. Perhaps it is enough for those who have a family history of cancer to schedule more frequent checkups, beginning at a younger age.

People opposed to genetic testing worry that a woman with defective *BRACA1* and *BRCA2* genes might make the unnecessary decision to have a radical mastectomy. In a study of 177 patients who underwent *APC* gene testing for susceptibility to colon cancer, less than 20% received any counseling before the test. Moreover, physicians misinterpreted the test results in nearly one third of the cases. It's possible, too, that people who test negative for a particular genetic mutation may believe that they are not at risk for cancer. This might encourage them not to have routine cancer screening. Regular testing and avoiding known causes of cancer—such as smoking, a high-fat diet, or too much sunlight—are important for everyone.

Decide Your Opinion

1. Should everyone be aware that genetic testing for certain cancers is a possibility, or should such testing be confined to a research setting? Explain.
2. If genetic testing for cancer were offered to you, would you take advantage of it? Why or why not?
3. Are protective measures to avoid cancer more important than testing? Explain.

Summarizing the Concepts

17.1 Cell Increase and Decrease

Cell division increases the number of cells in the body, and apoptosis reduces this number when appropriate. Cells go through a cell cycle that includes (1) interphase and (2) cell division, consisting of mitosis and cytokinesis. Interphase, in turn, includes G_1 (growth as certain organelles double), S (DNA synthesis), and G_2 (growth as the cell prepares to divide). Cell division occurs during the mitotic stage (M) when daughter cells receive a full complement of chromosomes.

The cell cycle is controlled by chemical signals. DNA damage is a reason the cell cycle stops, and the p53 protein initiates apoptosis. During apoptosis, the enzymes called caspases bring about destruction of the nucleus and the rest of the cell.

17.2 Mitosis

The total number of chromosomes is the diploid number, and half this number is the haploid number.

Replication of DNA nuclear division. The duplicated chromosome is composed of two sister chromatids held together at a centromere. During mitosis, the centromeres divide, and the chromatids become chromosomes that go into each new nucleus.

Mitosis has the following phases: (1) prophase—in early prophase, chromosomes have no particular arrangement, and in late prophase the chromosomes are attached to spindle fibers; (2) metaphase, when the chromosomes are aligned at the equator; (3) anaphase, when the chromatids separate, becoming chromosomes that move toward the poles; and (4) telophase, when new nuclear envelopes form around the chromosomes and cytokinesis begins. Cytokinesis occurs by furrowing at a cleavage furrow in animal cells.

17.3 Meiosis

Meiosis is a part of sexual reproduction. During meiosis I, homologues separate, and this leads to daughter cells with half, or the haploid number of homologous chromosomes. During meiosis II, chromatids separate, becoming chromosomes that are distributed to daughter nuclei. In humans, the daughter cells become gametes, and upon fertilization, the zygote has the diploid number of chromosomes, the same as its parents had.

Meiosis utilizes two nuclear divisions. Crossing-over during prophase I and independent alignment of chromosomes during metaphase I ensure genetic recombination in daughter cells. When the homologous chromosomes separate during anaphase I, each daughter nucleus receives one member from each pair of chromosomes. Therefore, the daughter cells are haploid. Distribution of chromosomes derived from sister chromatids during meiosis II then leads to a total of four new cells, each with the haploid number of chromosomes.

Meiosis results in genetic recombination due to independent alignment of homologous chromosomes and crossing-over. Fertilization also contributes to genetic recombination.

17.4 Comparison of Meiosis with Mitosis

Figure 17.11 contrasts the phases of mitosis with the phases of meiosis.

17.5 The Human Life Cycle

The human life cycle involves both mitosis and meiosis. Mitosis ensures that each somatic cell has the diploid number of chromosomes. Mitosis is necessary to growth and repair of tissues. Meiosis is a part of spermatogenesis and oogenesis. It keeps the chromosome number constant between generations and ensures genetic recombination. Spermatogenesis in males produces four viable sperm, while oogenesis in females produces one egg and two or three polar bodies. Oogenesis goes to completion if a sperm fertilizes the developing egg.

Studying the Concepts

1. Describe the role of cell division and apoptosis in humans. 334
2. What are the stages of the cell cycle? 334–35
3. Describe the phases of mitosis; include in your description the terms centrioles, nucleolus, spindle, and furrowing. 337–39
4. How do the terms diploid (2n) and haploid (n) pertain to meiosis? 340
5. Describe crossing-over during prophase I and independent alignment during metaphase I. 341
6. Describe the other phases of meiosis I and the phases of meiosis II. 342–43
7. Contrast meiosis and mitosis. 344–45
8. Draw a diagram describing the human life cycle. 346
9. What are the functions of mitosis and meiosis in the life cycle of humans? 346
10. How does spermatogenesis in males compare with oogenesis in females? 346–47

Thinking Critically About the Concepts

Refer to the opening vignette on page 334, and then answer these questions.

1. When is apoptosis appropriate during development? During adulthood?
2. The immune system and apoptosis work together to kill cancer cells. What must the immune system utilize to turn on the genes for apoptosis?
3. What gene, in particular, must be turned on when apoptosis occurs?
4. Cancer is characterized by uncontrolled cell growth. What activity becomes uncontrollable in cells when cancer results?

Testing Your Knowledge of the Concepts

Choose the best answer for each question.

1. Spindle fibers begin to appear during
   a. prophase.
   b. metaphase.
   c. anaphase.
   d. interphase.

2. DNA synthesis occurs during
   a. interphase.
   b. prophase.
   c. metaphase.
   d. telophase.

In questions 3–6, match the part of the diagram of the cell cycle to the statements provided.

3. DNA replication

4. Organelles double

5. Cell prepares to divide

6. Cytokinesis occurs

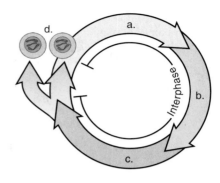

7. Which is not a part of the mitosis stage?
   a. anaphase   c. interphase
   b. telophase   d. metaphase

In questions 8–12, match the part of the diagram to the appropriate statement.

8. Meiosis II

9. Primary spermatocyte

10. Sperm

11. Secondary spermatocyte

12. Spermatids

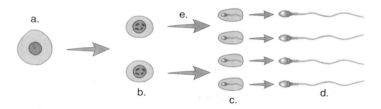

13. The end products of _____ are _____ cells.
   a. mitosis, diploid
   b. meiosis, haploid
   c. meiosis, diploid
   d. Both a and b are correct.

14. Programmed cell death is called
   a. mitosis.   c. cytokinesis.
   b. meiosis.   d. apoptosis.

15. Which helps to ensure that genetic diversity will be maintained?
   a. independent alignment during metaphase I
   b. crossing-over during prophase I
   c. recombination at fertilization
   d. All of these are correct.

16. Which will contribute genetically to the zygote?
   a. secondary oocyte
   b. first polar body
   c. second polar body
   d. None of the above is correct.

17. _____ ensures the same number of chromosomes from one _____ to the next.
   a. Meiosis, somatic cell
   b. Meiosis, generation
   c. Mitosis, generation
   d. None of the above is correct.

18. In human beings, mitosis is necessary to
    a. growth and repair of tissues.
    b. formation of the gametes.
    c. maintaining the chromosome number in all body cells.
    d. the death of unnecessary cells.
    e. Both a and c are correct.

For questions 19–22, match the descriptions that follow to the terms in the key. Answers may be used more than once.

Key:

    a. centriole   c. chromosome
    b. cell body   d. centromere

19. Point of attachment for sister chromatids

20. Found at a pole in the center of an aster

21. Coiled and condensed chromatin

22. Can have two chromatids

23. If a parent cell has 14 chromosomes prior to mitosis, how many chromosomes will the daughter cells have?
    a. 28
    b. 14
    c. seven
    d. any number between 7 and 28

24. In which phase of mitosis are chromosomes moving toward the poles?
    a. prophase   d. telophase
    b. metaphase   e. Both b and c are correct.
    c. anaphase

25. If a parent cell has 12 chromosomes, the daughter cells following meiosis II will have
    a. 12 chromosomes.
    b. 24 chromosomes.
    c. six chromosomes.
    d. Any of these could be correct.

26. At the equator during metaphase I of meiosis, there are
    a. single chromosomes.
    b. unpaired duplicated chromosomes.
    c. homologous pairs.
    d. always 23 chromosomes.

27. Crossing-over occurs between
    a. sister chromatids of the same chromosomes.
    b. chromatids of nonhomologous chromosomes.
    c. nonsister chromatids of a homologous pair.
    d. two daughter nuclei.
    e. Both b and c are correct.

28. Which of these drawings represents metaphase I of meiosis?

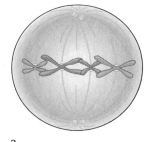
a.

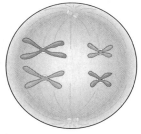
b.

Understanding Key Terms

anaphase 338
apoptosis 334
aster 337
cell cycle 334
centriole 337
centromere 337
centrosome 337
cleavage furrow 339
crossing-over 341
cytokinesis 334
daughter cell 337
diploid (2n) 337
fertilization 340
gamete 340
haploid (n) 340
homologous chromosome 340
homologue 340

interkinesis 342
interphase 334
meiosis 340
metaphase 338
mitosis 334, 337
mitotic spindle 337
oogenesis 346
parent cell 337
polar body 347
prophase 338
secondary oocyte 347
somatic cell 334
spermatogenesis 346
synapsis 340
telophase 339
zygote 340

Match the key terms to these definitions.

a. _____ Members of a pair that synapse during prophase I and are aligned together at the equator during metaphase I.

b. _____ Repeating sequence of events in human cells consisting of interphase, when growth and DNA synthesis occur, and a mitotic stage, when cell division occurs.

c. _____ Structure consisting of fibers, poles, and asters in animal cells that brings about the movement of chromosomes during cell division.

d. _____ Nonfunctioning daughter cell that has little cytoplasm and is formed during oogenesis.

e. _____ Half the diploid number; the number of chromosomes in the gametes.

Online Learning Center

www.mhhe.com/maderhuman9

The Online Learning Center provides a wealth of information fully organized and integrated by chapter. You will find practice quizzes, interactive activities, labeling exercises, flashcards, and much more that will complement your learning and understanding of human biology.

Looking at Both Sides

Each day, the Internet, media, and other people present you with opposing viewpoints on a wide range of subjects. Your ability to develop an informed opinion on an issue, and talk to others about it, is extremely important.

To expand and enhance your knowledge of a highly relevant bioethical issue, visit the "Student Edition" of the Online Learning Center. Under "Course-Wide Content," select "Looking at Both Sides." Once there, you will be asked to complete activities that will increase your understanding of a current bioethical issue related to this chapter and allow you to defend your opinion.

CHAPTER 18

Patterns of Inheritance

C H A P T E R   C O N C E P T S

18.1 Genotype and Phenotype
- What is the difference between genotype and phenotype? 352
- What are the three possible genotypes and the two possible phenotypes for a characteristic that is controlled by two alleles, one being dominant and the other recessive?   352

18.2 One- and Two-Trait Inheritance
- Why do gametes have only one allele for each pair of alleles being considered?   353
- What phenotypic ratios are expected for all possible crosses involving only one trait?   354–55
- What is the relationship between the events of meiosis and genetic diversity among the gametes?   356
- What phenotypic ratios are expected for all possible crosses involving two traits?   357–58

18.3 Beyond Simple Inheritance Patterns
- What are some examples of human multifactorial traits?   359
- What type of studies show that human inheritance is influenced by the environment?   360
- What is an example of incomplete dominance in humans?   360
- How is ABO blood type an example of codominance and multiple allele inheritance?   361

18.4 Sex-Linked Inheritance
- Why are more males than females color blind?   362
- What phenotypic ratios are expected for all possible crosses involving an X-linked recessive allele; involving one X-linked dominant allele?   362–63
- What is a mixed genetics problem and how would you construct the gametes for the individuals in such a problem?   363

Michael Douglas strikingly resembles his father, Kirk Douglas. A look-alike relationship between one generation and the next has been noted for some time, but now we know the reason for it. Genes!

Through the process of sexual reproduction, Kirk Douglas passed on a copy of half of his genes to his son. Why doesn't Michael Douglas look exactly like this father? For precisely the same reason: Kirk Douglas gave Michael only half his genes; his mother gave him the other half.

We know today that many hundreds of genes are located on each of the chromosomes that come together when the sperm fertilizes the egg. Each gene controls some particular characteristic of the cell or individual. Why do the Douglases have a cleft chin? The genes involved specified the proteins that brought about cleft chin.

We now recognize the power of genes and have learned how to manipulate some genes for our own purposes. What would Michael Douglas do if he wanted a son who looked exactly like him? He would think about having just his genes used to start a new life. That's called reproductive cloning, a process that has not yet been accomplished in humans and is not legal in the United States.

18.1 Genotype and Phenotype

Genotype refers to the genes of the individual. Alternative forms of a gene having the same position (locus) on a pair of chromosomes and affecting the same trait are called **alleles.** It is customary to designate an allele by a letter, which represents the specific trait (characteristic) it controls; a **dominant allele** is assigned an uppercase (capital) letter, while a **recessive allele** is given the same letter but in lowercase. In humans, for example, unattached (free) earlobes are dominant over attached earlobes, so a suitable key would be *E* for unattached earlobes and *e* for attached earlobes.

Alleles occur in pairs; therefore, the individual normally has two alleles for a trait. Just as one of each pair of chromosomes is inherited from each parent, so too is one of each pair of alleles inherited from each parent. Indeed, the alleles occur in the same location, called their **loci,** on a pair of homologous chromosomes.

Figure 18.1 shows three possible fertilizations, the resulting genetic makeup of the zygote and, therefore, the individual. In the first instance, the chromosomes of both the sperm and the egg carry an *E*. Consequently, the zygote and subsequent individual have the alleles *EE*, which may be called a **homozygous dominant** genotype. A person with genotype *EE* obviously has unattached earlobes. The physical appearance of the individual—in this case, unattached earlobes—is called the **phenotype.** Notice in Figure 18.1 that the genotype (letters) and then the phenotype (description) are given after the drawing.

In the second fertilization, the zygote has received two recessive alleles *(ee)*, and the genotype is called **homozygous recessive.** An individual with this genotype has the recessive phenotype, which is attached earlobes. In the third fertilization, the resulting individual has the alleles *Ee*, which is called a **heterozygous** genotype. A heterozygote shows the dominant phenotype; therefore, this individual has unattached earlobes.

How many dominant alleles must an individual inherit in order to have the dominant phenotype? These examples show that a dominant allele contributed from only one parent can bring about a particular dominant phenotype. How many recessive alleles must an individual inherit in order to have the recessive phenotype? A recessive allele must be received from both parents to bring about the recessive phenotype.

The genotype, whether homozygous dominant *(EE)*, homozygous recessive *(ee)*, or heterozygous *(Ee)*, tells what alleles a person carries. The phenotype—for example, attached or unattached earlobes—tells what the person looks like. A person can have the dominant phenotype or the recessive phenotype.

Key:
E = Unattached earlobes (dominant allele)
e = Attached earlobes (recessive allele)

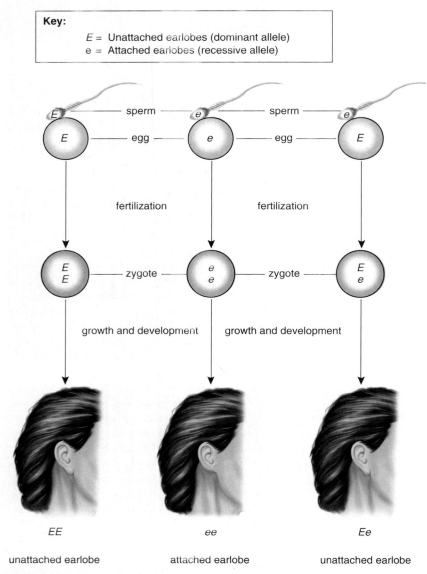

EE — unattached earlobe
ee — attached earlobe
Ee — unattached earlobe

Figure 18.1   Genetic inheritance.
Individuals inherit a minimum of two alleles for every characteristic of their anatomy and physiology. The inheritance of a single dominant allele *(E)* causes an individual to have unattached earlobes; two recessive alleles *(ee)* cause an individual to have attached earlobes. Notice that each individual receives one allele from the father (by way of a sperm) and one allele from the mother (by way of an egg).

18.2 One- and Two-Trait Inheritance

In one-trait crosses, the inheritance of only one set of alleles is being considered, and in two-trait crosses, the inheritance of two sets of alleles is being considered. For both types of crosses, it will be necessary to determine the gametes of both individuals who are reproducing.

Forming the Gametes

During gametogenesis, the chromosome number is reduced. Whereas the individual has 46 chromosomes, a gamete has only 23 chromosomes. (If this did not happen, each new generation of individuals would have twice as many chromosomes as their parents.) Reduction of the chromosome number occurs when the homologous chromosomes separate as meiosis occurs. Since the alleles are on the chromosomes, they also separate during meiosis, and therefore, the gametes carry only one allele for each trait. *In the simplest of terms, no two letters in a gamete can be the same letter of the alphabet.*

If an individual carried the alleles *EE,* all the gametes would carry an *E* since that is the only choice. Similarly, if an individual carried the alleles *ee,* all the gametes would carry an *e.*

What if an individual were *Ee?* Half of the gametes would carry an *E* and half would carry an *e.* Figure 18.2 shows the genotypes and phenotypes for certain other traits in humans, and you can practice deciding what alleles the gametes would carry in order to produce these genotypes. If the genotype is *EeSs,* all combinations of any two different letters can be present. Therefore, *ES, eS, Es,* and *es* are all possible.

Practice Problems 1*

1. For each of the following genotypes, give all possible gametes.
   a. *WW*
   b. *WWSs*
   c. *Tt*
   d. *Ttgg*
   e. *AaBb*
2. For each of the following, state whether a genotype or a gamete is represented.
   a. *D*
   b. *Ll*
   c. *Pw*
   d. *LlGg*
3. What is the genotype of the individual from the following crosses?
   a. *ES* × *es*
   b. *eS* × *eS*

*Answers to Practice Problems appear in Appendix A.

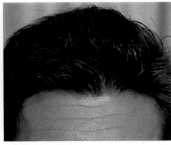

a. Widow's peak: *WW* or *Ww*   b. Straight hairline: *ww*

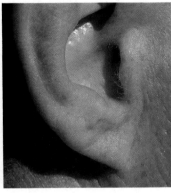
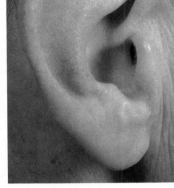

c. Unattached earlobes: *EE* or *Ee*   d. Attached earlobes: *ee*

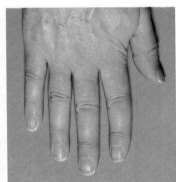
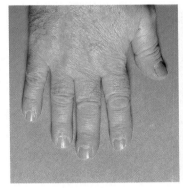

e. Short fingers: *SS* or *Ss*   f. Long fingers: *ss*

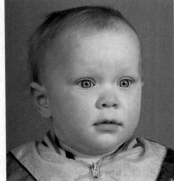

g. Freckles: *FF* or *Ff*   h. No freckles: *ff*

Figure 18.2   Common inherited traits in human beings.
The alleles indicate which traits are dominant and which are recessive.

One-Trait Crosses

Many times, parents would like to know the chances of having a child with a certain genotype and, therefore, a certain phenotype. To illustrate, let us consider a particular cross. If a homozygous dominant man with unattached earlobes reproduces with a woman with attached earlobes, what kind of earlobes will their children have?

In solving the problem, we (1) use the key already given on page 352 to indicate the genotype of each parent; (2) determine what the possible gametes are for each parent; (3) combine all possible gametes; and (4), finally, determine the genotypes and the phenotypes of all the offspring.

In the following diagram, the letters in the first row give the genotypes of the parents. Each parent has only one type of gamete with regard to earlobes, and therefore all the children have a similar genotype and phenotype. The children are heterozygous *(Ee)* and have unattached earlobes. When writing a heterozygous genotype, always put the capital letter first to avoid confusion.

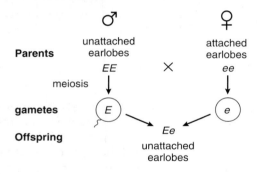

These children are **monohybrids**; that is, they are heterozygous for only one pair of alleles. If they reproduce with someone else of the same genotype, what type of earlobes will their children have? In this problem (*Ee* × *Ee*), each parent has two possible types of gametes (*E* or *e*), and we must ensure that all types of sperm have an equal chance to fertilize all possible types of eggs. One way to do this is to use a **Punnett square** (Fig. 18.3), in which all possible types of sperm are lined up vertically and all possible types of eggs are lined up horizontally (or vice versa), and every possible combination of gametes occurs within the squares.

After we determine the genotypes and the phenotypes of the offspring, we can first determine the genotypic and then the phenotypic ratio. The genotypic ratio is 1 *EE*:2, *Ee*: 1:*ee* or simply 1:2:1, but the phenotypic ratio is 3:1. Why? Because three individuals will have unattached earlobes and one will have attached earlobes.

This 3:1 phenotypic ratio is always expected for a monohybrid cross when one allele is completely dominant over the other. The exact ratio is more likely to be observed if a large number of matings take place and if a large number of offspring result. Only then do all possible kinds of

sperm have an equal chance of fertilizing all possible kinds of eggs. Naturally, we do not routinely observe hundreds of offspring from a single type of cross in humans. The best interpretation of Figure 18.3, in humans, is to say that each child has three chances out of four to have unattached earlobes, or one chance out of four to have attached earlobes.

It is important to realize that *chance has no memory*; for example, if two heterozygous parents already have three children with unattached earlobes and are expecting a fourth child, this child still has a 75% chance of having unattached earlobes and a 25% chance of having attached earlobes.

When solving a genetics problem, it is assumed that all possible types of sperm fertilize all possible types of eggs. The results can be expressed as an expected phenotypic ratio; it is also possible to state the chance of an offspring showing a particular phenotype.

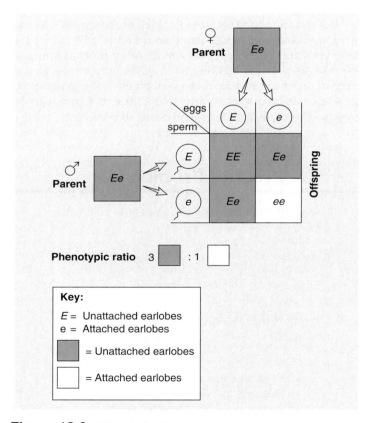

Figure 18.3 **Monohybrid cross.**
A Punnett square diagrams the results of a cross. When the parents are heterozygous, each child has a 75% chance of having the dominant phenotype and a 25% chance of having the recessive phenotype.

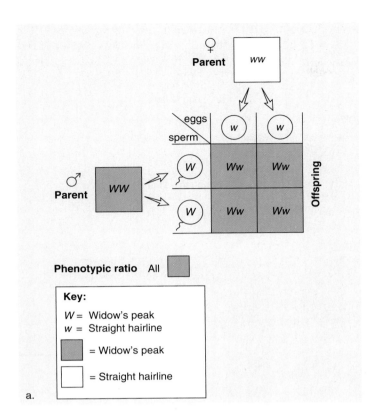

Phenotypic ratio   All

Key:

W = Widow's peak
w = Straight hairline

= Widow's peak

= Straight hairline

a.

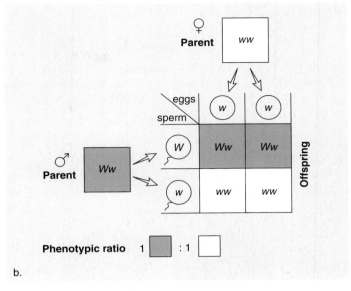

Phenotypic ratio   1   : 1

b.

Figure 18.4   One-trait crosses.
This cross will determine if an individual with the dominant phenotype is homozygous or heterozygous. **a.** Because all offspring show the dominant characteristic, the individual is most likely homozygous, as shown. **b.** Because the offspring show a 1:1 phenotypic ratio, the individual is heterozygous, as shown.

Other One-Trait Crosses

It is not possible to tell by inspection if a person expressing a dominant allele is homozygous dominant or heterozygous. However, it is sometimes possible to tell by the results of a cross. For example, Figure 18.4 shows two possible results when a man with a widow's peak reproduces with a woman who has a straight hairline. If the man is homozygous dominant, all his children will have a widow's peak. If the man is heterozygous, each child has a 50% chance of having a straight hairline. The birth of just one child with a straight hairline indicates that the man is heterozygous.

Consider, also, that a person's parentage sometimes tells you that he is heterozygous. In Figure 18.4, each of the offspring with a widow's peak has to be heterozygous. Why? Because one of the parents was homozygous recessive, and therefore had to give each offspring a *w*.

The Punnett Square and Probability

The Punnett square allows you to figure the chances or the probability that an offspring will have a particular genotype/phenotype. The two laws of probability are the product rule and the sum rule. The product rule says that the chance of two different events occurring together is the product (multiplication) of their chance occurring separately. The sum rule says the chance of any event that can occur in more than one way is the sum (addition) of the individual chances.

Notice that when you bring the allele(s) donated by the sperm and egg together into the same square, in all combinations, you are using the product rule because the father gives an offspring a certain chance of getting a particular allele and the mother gives a certain chance of getting an allele for the same trait. When you add up the results of bringing the various alleles together, you are using the sum rule.

Practice Problems 2*

1. A man with a widow's peak has a mother with a straight hairline. Widow's peak (*W*) is dominant over straight hairline (*w*). What is the genotype of the man?
2. Both a man and a woman are heterozygous for freckles. Freckles (*F*) are dominant over no freckles (*f*). What is the chance that their child will have freckles?
3. Both you and your sister or brother have attached earlobes, yet your parents have unattached earlobes. Unattached earlobes (*E*) are dominant over attached earlobes (*e*). What are the genotypes of your parents?
4. A father has dimples, the mother does not have dimples, and all five of their children have dimples. Dimples (*D*) are dominant over no dimples (*d*). Give the probable genotypes of all persons concerned.

*Answers to Practice Problems appear in Appendix A.

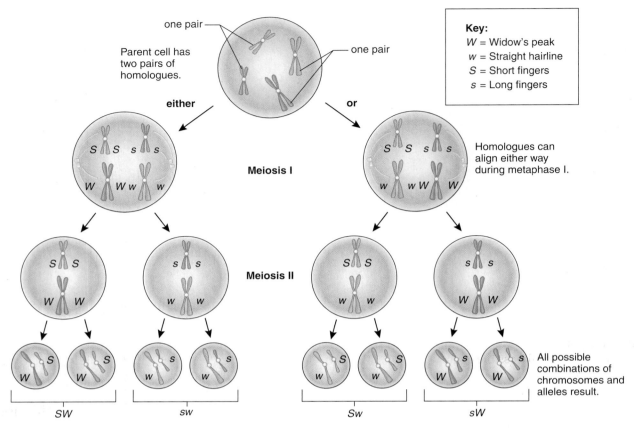

Figure 18.5 Meiosis and genetic diversity among gametes.
A cell has two pairs of homologous chromosomes (homologues) recognized by length, not color. The homologues, and the alleles they carry, align independently during meiosis. Therefore, all possible combinations of chromosomes and alleles occur in the gametes.

Two-Trait Crosses

Figure 18.5 allows you to relate the events of meiosis to the formation of gametes, when a cross involves two traits. In the example given, a cell has two pairs of homologues, recognized by length—one pair of homologues is short and the other is long. (The color signifies that we inherit chromosomes from our parents; one homologue of each pair is the "paternal" chromosome, and the other is the "maternal" chromosome.)

Because the homologues separate during meiosis I, each gamete receives one member from each pair of homologues. Because the homologues separate independently—it matters not which member of a pair goes into which gamete—all possible combinations of alleles occur in the gametes. In the simplest of terms, a gamete in Figure 18.5 will *receive one short and one long chromosome of either color.* Therefore, all possible combinations of chromosomes and alleles are in the gametes.

Specifically, assume that the alleles for two genes are on these homologues. The alleles *S* and *s* are on one pair of

homologues, and the alleles *W* and *w* are on the other pair of homologues. First notice that because the homologues separate, a gamete will have either an *S* or an *s* and either a *W* or a *w* and never two of the same letter of the alphabet. Also, because the homologues align independently at the equator, either the paternal or maternal chromosome of each pair can face either pole.

Therefore, there are no restrictions as to which homologue goes into which gamete; a gamete can receive either an *S* or an *s* and either a *W* or a *w* in any combination. In the end, the gametes will collectively have all possible combinations of alleles.

Figure 18.5 illustrates that the alleles separate, and they separate independently because of the manner in which meiosis occurs. Because it does not matter which homologue of a pair faces which spindle pole, all possible combinations of alleles occur in the gametes.

The Dihybrid Cross

In the two-trait cross depicted in Figure 18.6, a person homozygous for widow's peak and short fingers (*WWSS*) reproduces with one who has a straight hairline and long fingers (*wwss*). The gametes for the *WWSS* parent must be *WS* and the gametes for the *wwss* parent must be *ws*. Therefore, the offspring will all have the genotype *WwSs* and the same phenotype (widow's peak with short fingers). This genotype is called a **dihybrid** because the individual is heterozygous in two regards: hairline and fingers.

When a dihybrid *WwSs* reproduces with another dihybrid that is *WwSs*, what gametes are possible? Each gamete can have only one letter of each kind in all possible combinations. Therefore, these are the gametes for both dihybrids: *WS*, *Ws*, *wS*, and *ws*.

A Punnett square makes sure that all possible sperm fertilize all possible eggs. If so, these are the expected phenotypic results:

9 widow's peak and short fingers:

3 widow's peak and long fingers:

3 straight hairline and short fingers:

1 straight hairline and long fingers.

This 9:3:3:1 phenotypic ratio is always expected for a dihybrid cross when simple dominance is present. We can use this expected ratio to predict the chances of each child receiving a certain phenotype. For example, the chance of getting the two dominant phenotypes together is 9 out of 16, and the chance of getting the two recessive phenotypes together is 1 out of 16.

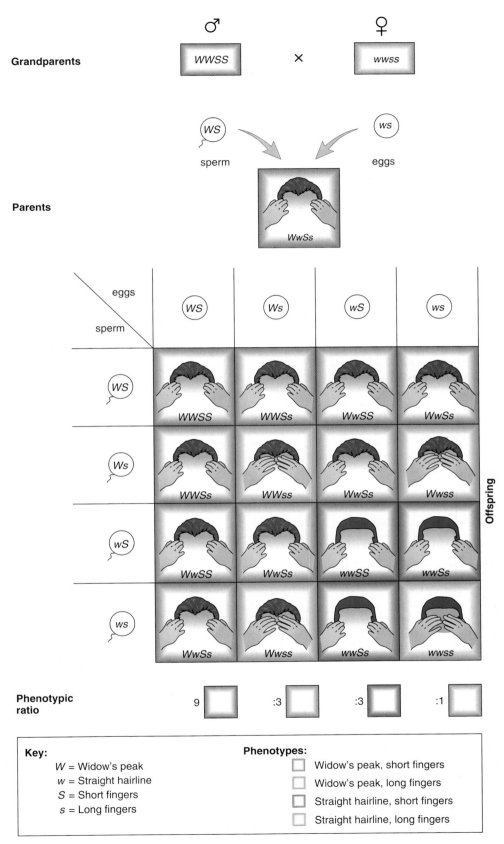

Figure 18.6   Dihybrid cross.
Since each dihybrid can form four possible types of gametes, four different phenotypes occur among the offspring in the proportions shown.

Other Two-Trait Crosses

It is not possible to tell by inspection whether an individual expressing the dominant alleles for two traits is homozygous dominant or heterozygous. But, if the individual reproduces with the homozygous recessive, it may be possible to tell. For example, if a man homozygous dominant for widow's peak and short fingers reproduces with a female who is homozygous recessive for both traits, then all his children will have the dominant phenotypes. However, if a man is heterozygous for both traits, then each child has a 25% chance of showing either one or both recessive traits. A Punnett square (Fig. 18.7) shows that the expected ratio is 1 widow's peak with short fingers: 1 widow's peak with long fingers: 1 straight hairline with short fingers: 1 straight hairline with long fingers, or 1:1:1:1.

For practical purposes, if an individual with the dominant phenotype, in either trait, has an offspring with the recessive phenotype, that individual has to be heterozygous for that trait. Also, it is possible to tell if a person is heterozygous by knowing the parentage. In Figure 18.7, no offspring showing a dominant phenotype is homozygous dominant for either trait. Why? Because the mother is homozygous recessive for that trait.

Table 18.1 gives the phenotypic results for the certain crosses we have studied. These crosses always give these phenotypic results, and therefore, it is not necessary to do a Punnett square to arrive at the results.

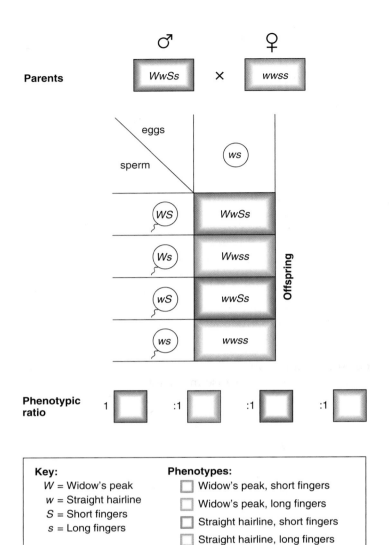

Figure 18.7   Two-traits cross.
The results of this cross indicate that the individual with the dominant phenotypes is heterozygous for both traits because some of the children are homozygous recessive for one or both traits. The chance of receiving any possible phenotype is 25%.

Practice Problems 3*

1. Attached earlobes and straight hairline are recessive. What genotype does a man with unattached earlobes and a widow's peak have if his mother has attached earlobes and a straight hairline?
2. What genotype do children have if one parent is homozygous recessive for earlobes and homozygous dominant for hairline, and the other is homozygous dominant for unattached earlobes and homozygous recessive for hairline?
3. If an individual from this cross reproduces with another of the same genotype, what are the chances that they will have a child with a straight hairline and attached earlobes?
4. A child who does not have dimples or freckles is born to a man who has dimples and freckles (both dominant) and a woman who does not. What are the genotypes of all persons concerned?

*Answers to Practice Problems appear in Appendix A.

Table 18.1	Phenotypic Ratios of Common Crosses
Genotypes	**Phenotypes**
Monohybrid X monohybrid	3:1 (dominant to recessive)
Monohybrid X recessive	1:1 (dominant to recessive)
Dihybrid X dihybrid	9:3:3:1 (9 both dominant, 3 one dominant, 3 other dominant, 1 both recessive)
Dihybrid X recessive	1:1:1:1 (all possible combinations in equal number)

18.3 Beyond Simple Inheritance Patterns

Certain traits, such as those studied in Section 18.1, are controlled by one set of alleles that follows a simple dominant or recessive inheritance. We now know of many other types of inheritance patterns.

Multifactorial Inheritance

Many traits, such as size or height, shape, weight, skin color, metabolic rate, and behavior are governed by several sets of alleles. **Multifactorial inheritance** occurs when a trait is governed by two or more sets of alleles. The individual has a copy of all allelic pairs, possibly located on many different pairs of chromosomes. Each dominant allele codes for a product, and therefore, the dominant alleles have a quantitative effect on the phenotype, and these effects are additive. The result is a *continuous variation* of phenotypes, resulting in a distribution of these phenotypes that resembles a bell-shaped curve. The more genes involved, the more continuous the variations and distribution of the phenotypes. Also, environmental effects cause many intervening phenotypes; in the case of height, differences in nutrition bring about a bell-shaped curve (Fig. 18.8).

Skin Color

Skin color is an example of a multifactorial trait that is likely controlled by many pairs of alleles. Even so, we will use the simplest model and assume that skin has only two pairs of alleles (*Aa* and *Bb*) and that each capital letter contributes pigment to the skin. When a very dark person reproduces with a very light person, the children have medium-brown skin. When two people with the genotype *AaBb* reproduce with one another, the children may range in skin color from very dark to very light:

Genotypes	Phenotypes
AABB	Very dark
AABb or *AaBB*	Dark
AaBb or *AAbb* or *aaBB*	Medium brown
Aabb or *aaBb*	Light
aabb	Very light

Notice, again, that a range of phenotypes exists and several possible phenotypes fall between the two extremes. Therefore, the distribution of these phenotypes is expected to follow a bell-shaped curve, meaning that few people have the extreme phenotypes and most people have the phenotype that lies in the middle.

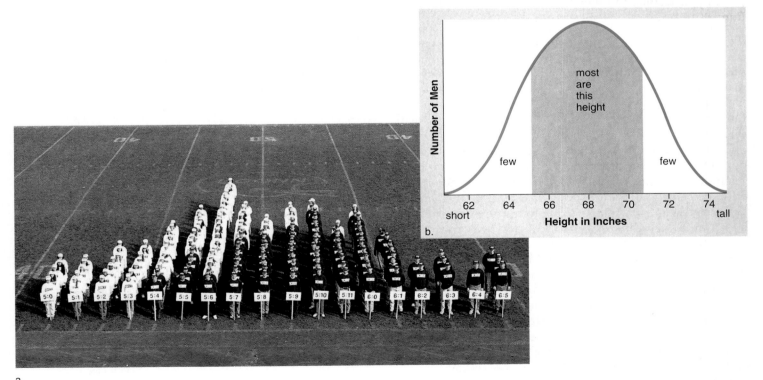

a.

b.

Figure 18.8 Multifactorial inheritance.
When you record the heights of a large group of people chosen at random, the values follow a bell-shaped curve. Such a continuous distribution is due to control of a trait by several sets of alleles. Environmental effects are also involved.

Figure 18.9 **Coat color in Himalayan rabbits.**
Hair growing under an ice pack in these rabbits is black. The dark ears, nose, and feet of these rabbits are believed to be due to a lower body temperature in these areas.

Environmental Influences

The environment can influence the phenotype. The coats of Siamese cats and Himalayan rabbits are darker in color at the ears, nose, paws, and tail. Himalayan rabbits are known to be homozygous for the allele *ch*, which is involved in the production of melanin. Experimental evidence suggests that the enzyme coded for by this gene is active only at a low temperature and that, therefore, black fur occurs only at the extremities where body heat is lost to the environment (Fig. 18.9).

Multifactorial traits seem to be particularly influenced by the environment. Because many human traits are most likely multifactorial ones, investigators try to determine what percentage of various traits is due to nature (inheritance) and what percentage is due to nurture (the environment). Some studies use identical and fraternal twins separated from birth because, then, it's known that the twins have a different environment. The supposition is that, if identical twins in different environments share the same trait, that trait is most likely inherited. Identical twins are more similar in their intellectual talents, personality traits, and levels of lifelong happiness than are fraternal twins separated from birth. Biologists conclude that all behavioral traits are partly heritable and that genes exert their effects by acting together in complex combinations susceptible to environmental influences.

Incomplete Dominance and Codominance

Incomplete dominance occurs when the heterozygote is intermediate between the two homozygotes. For example,

when a curly-haired individual reproduces with a straight-haired individual, their children have wavy hair. When two wavy-haired persons reproduce, the expected phenotypic ratio among the offspring is 1:2:1—that is, one curly-haired child to two with wavy hair to one with straight hair (Fig. 18.10). We can explain incomplete dominance by assuming that only one allele codes for a product and the single dose of the product gives the intermediate result.

Codominance occurs when alleles are equally expressed in a heterozygote. A familiar example is the human blood type AB, in which the red blood cells have the characteristics of both type A and type B blood. We can explain codominance by assuming that both genes code for a product, and we observe the results of both products being present. Blood type inheritance is said to be an example of multiple alleles.

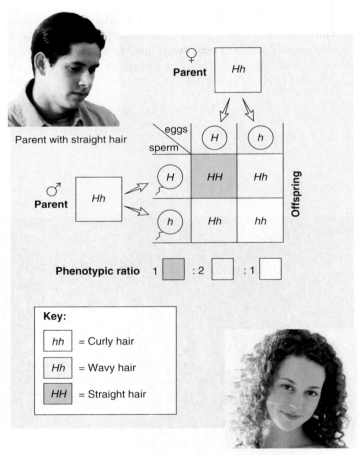

Figure 18.10 **Incomplete dominance.**
Neither straight nor curly hair is dominant. When two wavy-haired individuals reproduce, each offspring has a 25% chance of having either straight or curly hair and a 50% chance of having wavy hair, the intermediate phenotype.

Multiple Allele Inheritance

When a trait is controlled by **multiple alleles,** the gene exists in several allelic forms. But each person usually has only two of the possible alleles.

ABO Blood Types

Three alleles for the same gene control the inheritance of ABO blood types. These alleles determine the presence or absence of antigens on red blood cells:

I^A = A antigen on red blood cells

I^B = B antigen on red blood cells

i = Neither A nor B antigen on red blood cells

Each person has only two of the three possible alleles, and both I^A and I^B are dominant over i. Therefore, there are two possible genotypes for type A blood and two possible genotypes for type B blood. On the other hand, I^A and I^B are fully expressed in the presence of the other. Therefore, if a person inherits one of each of these alleles, that person will have type AB blood. Type O blood can result only from the inheritance of two i alleles.

The possible genotypes and phenotypes for blood type are as follows:

Phenotype	Genotype
A	$I^A I^A$, $I^A i$
B	$I^B I^B$, $I^B i$
AB	$I^A I^B$
O	ii

Figure 18.11 shows that matings between certain genotypes can have surprising results in terms of blood type.

Blood typing can sometimes aid in paternity suits. However, a blood test of a supposed father can only suggest that he *might* be the father, not that he definitely *is* the father. For example, it is possible, but not definite, that a man with type A blood (genotype $I^A i$) is the father of a child with type O blood. On the other hand, a blood test sometimes can definitely prove that a man is not the father. For example, a man with type AB blood cannot possibly be the father of a child with type O blood. Therefore, blood tests can be used in legal cases only to try to exclude a man from possible paternity.

As a point of interest, the Rh factor is inherited separately from A, B, AB, or O blood types. When you are Rh positive, your red blood cells have a particular antigen, and when you are Rh negative, that antigen is absent. There are multiple alleles for Rh$^-$, but they are all recessive to Rh$^+$.

Inheritance by multiple alleles occurs when a gene exists in more than two allelic forms. However, each individual usually inherits only two alleles for these genes.

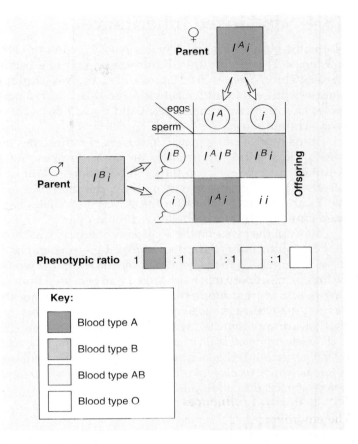

Figure 18.11 **Inheritance of blood type.**
As shown here, a cross between individuals with type A blood and type B blood can result in any one of the four blood types. Why? Because these parents are $I^A i$ and $I^B i$. If both parents were type AB blood, no child would have what blood type?

Practice Problems 4*

1. A multifactorial trait is controlled by three pairs of alleles. What are the two extreme genotypes for this trait?
2. What is the genotype of the lightest child that could result from a mating between two medium-brown individuals?
3. A child with type O blood is born to a mother with type A blood. What is the genotype of the child? The mother? What are the possible genotypes of the father?
4. From the following blood types, determine which baby belongs to which parents:

   Baby 1, type O   Mrs. Doe, type A
   Baby 2, type B   Mr. Doe, type A
                           Mrs. Jones, type A
                           Mr. Jones, type AB

*Answers to Practice Problems appear in Appendix A.

18.4 Sex-Linked Inheritance

Normally, both males and females have 23 pairs of chromosomes; 22 pairs are called **autosomes,** and one pair is the sex chromosomes. These are called the **sex chromosomes** because they differ between the sexes. In humans, males have the sex chromosomes X and Y, and females have two X chromosomes.

Traits controlled by genes on the sex chromosomes are said to be **sex-linked;** an allele on an X chromosome is **X-linked,** and an allele on the Y chromosome is Y-linked. Most sex-linked genes are only on the X chromosomes, and the Y chromosome is blank for these. Very few alleles have been found on the much smaller Y chromosome.

Many of the genes on the X chromosomes, such as those that determine normal as opposed to red-green color blindness, are unrelated to the gender of the individual. It would be logical to suppose that a sex-linked trait is passed from father to son or from mother to daughter, but this is not the case. A male always receives an X-linked allele from his mother, from whom he inherited an X chromosome. *The Y chromosome from the father does not carry an allele for the trait.* Usually, a sex-linked genetic disorder is recessive; therefore, a female must receive two alleles, one from each parent, before she has the condition.

X-Linked Alleles

When considering X-linked traits, the allele on the X chromosome is shown as a letter attached to the X chromosome. For example, this is the key for red-green color blindness, a well-known X-linked recessive disorder:

X^B = normal vision

X^b = color blindness

The possible genotypes and phenotypes in both males and females are:

Genotypes	Phenotypes
$X^B X^B$	Female who has normal color vision
$X^B X^b$	Carrier female who has normal color vision
$X^b X^b$	Female who is color-blind
$X^B Y$	Male who has normal vision
$X^b Y$	Male who is color-blind

The second genotype is a carrier female because, although a female with this genotype appears normal, she is capable of passing on an allele for color blindness. Color-blind females are rare because they must receive the allele from both parents; color-blind males are more common because they need only one recessive allele to be color-blind. The allele for color blindness must be inherited from their mother because it is on the X chromosome; males only inherit the Y chromosome from their father.

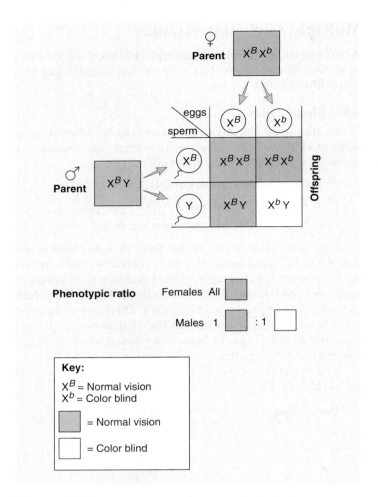

Figure 18.12   Cross involving an X-linked allele.
The male parent is normal, but the female parent is a carrier—an allele for color blindness is located on one of her X chromosomes. Therefore, each son has a 50% chance of being color-blind. The daughters will appear normal, but each one has a 50% chance of being a carrier.

X-Linked Problems

Now, let us consider a mating between a man with normal vision and a heterozygous woman (Fig. 18.12). What is the chance that this couple will have a color-blind daughter? A color-blind son? All daughters will have normal color vision because they all receive an X^B from their father. The sons, however, have a 50% chance of being color-blind, depending on whether they receive an X^B or an X^b from their mother. The inheritance of a Y chromosome from their father cannot offset the inheritance of an X^b from their mother. Because the Y chromosome doesn't have an allele for the trait, it can't possibly prevent color blindness in a son. Notice in Figure 18.12 that the phenotypic results for sex-linked traits are given separately for males and females.

How is it possible to determine that a female is a carrier for an X-linked trait? As shown in Figure 18.12, if a woman has a son with an X-linked recessive trait, she has to be a carrier. Also, the parentage of the woman can determine that she is a carrier. If the father of a woman has an X-linked recessive trait, the woman must be a carrier.

Mixed Problems

How do you write the genotype of a person in a two-trait cross if only one trait is X-linked and the other is autosomal? For example, what is the genotype of a man who has a straight hairline and is color-blind? Only the color-blind allele is attached to the X chromosome, and the genotype is wwX^bY.

How about a woman who is heterozygous for both traits? The genotype is WwX^BX^b. What are the gametes for this woman? Each gamete must have only one allele for each trait, and all combinations are possible. Therefore, her gametes are: WX^B, WX^b, wX^B, and wX^b.

The X chromosome carries alleles that are not on the Y chromosome. Therefore, a recessive allele on the X chromosome, which was inherited from his mother, is expressed in males.

Practice Problems 5*

1. Both the mother and the father of a color-blind male appear to be normal. From whom did the son inherit the allele for color blindness? What are the genotypes of the mother, the father, and the son?
2. A woman is color-blind. What are the chances that her sons will be color-blind? If she is married to a man with normal vision, what are the chances that her daughters will be color-blind? Will be carriers?
3. Both the husband and wife have normal vision. The wife gives birth to a color-blind daughter. Is it more likely the father had normal vision or was color-blind? What does this lead you to deduce about the girl's parentage?
4. What is the genotype of a color-blind male with long fingers if s = long fingers? If all his children have normal vision and short fingers, what is the likely genotype of the mother?

*Answers to Practice Problems appear in Appendix A.

Bioethical Focus

Choosing Gender

You may feel it is ethically wrong to choose which particular embryo can continue development following in vitro fertilization (see Bioethical Focus on page 305). But, what about choosing whether an X-bearing or Y-bearing sperm should fertilize the egg? As you know, the sex of a child depends upon whether an X-bearing sperm or a Y-bearing sperm enters the egg. A new technique has been developed that can separate X-bearing sperm from Y-bearing sperm. First, the sperm are dosed with a DNA-staining chemical. Because the X chromosome has slightly more DNA than the Y chromosome, it takes up more dye. When a laser beam shines on the sperm, the X-bearing sperm shine a little more brightly than the Y-bearing sperm. A machine sorts the sperm into two groups on this basis. The results are not perfect. Following artificial insemination, there's about an 85% success rate for a girl and about a 65% success rate for a boy.

Some might believe that this is the simplest way to make sure they have a healthy child if the mother is a carrier of an X-linked genetic disorder, such as hemophilia or Duchenne muscular dystrophy. Previously, a pregnant woman with these concerns had to wait for the results of an amniocentesis test and then decide whether to abort the pregnancy if it were a boy. Is it better to increase the chances of a girl to begin with?

Or, do you believe that gender selection is not acceptable for any reason? Even if it doesn't lead to a society with far more members of one sex than another, there could be a problem. Once you separate reproduction from the sex act, it might open the door to genetically designing children in the future. On the other hand, is it acceptable to bring a child into the world with a genetic disorder that may cause an early death or a lifelong disability? Would it be better to select sperm for a girl, who at worst would be a carrier like her mother?

Decide Your Opinion

1. Do you think it is acceptable to choose the gender of a baby? Even if it requires artificial insemination at a clinic? Why or why not?
2. Do you see any difference between choosing gender or choosing embryos free of a genetic disease for reproduction purposes? Explain.
3. If selecting sperm is less expensive than selecting embryos, should women who are carriers of X-linked genetic disorders be encouraged to use this method of producing children who are free of the disease?

Summarizing the Concepts

18.1 Genotype and Phenotype
It is customary to use letters to represent the genotypes of individuals. Homozygous dominant (two capital letters) and heterozygous (a capital letter and a lowercase letter) exhibit the dominant phenotype. Homozygous recessive (two lowercase letters) exhibits the recessive phenotype.

18.2 One- and Two-Trait Inheritance
Whereas the individual has two alleles (copies of a gene) for each trait, the gametes have only one allele for each trait. A Punnett square can help determine the phenotypic ratio among offspring because it gives the results when all possible sperm types are given an equal chance to fertilize all possible egg types, for a particular cross. When a heterozygous individual reproduces with another heterozygote, there is a 75% chance the child will have the dominant phenotype and a 25% chance the child will have the recessive phenotype. When a heterozygous individual reproduces with a pure recessive, the offspring has a 50% chance of having either phenotype.

It is impossible to determine, by inspection, if a person with the dominant phenotype is homozygous or heterozygous. But when a cross with a pure recessive results in a phenotypic ratio of 1:1, the person has to be heterozygous. Each child from such a cross has a 50% chance of having the recessive phenotype and a 50% chance of having the dominant phenotype.

Because of meiosis, the gametes have only one of each pair of homologous chromosomes/alleles and in all possible combinations. Therefore, individuals heterozygous for two traits can form four types of gametes, and the phenotypic ratio for a dihybrid cross is 9:3:3:1; $9/16$ of the offspring have the two dominant traits, $3/16$ have one of the dominant traits with one of the recessive traits, $3/16$ have the other dominant trait with the other recessive trait, and $1/16$ have both recessive traits. It is impossible to determine, by inspection, if a person with the dominant phenotype for two traits is homozygous or heterozygous for each trait. But when a cross with a pure recessive results in a phenotypic ratio of 1:1:1:1, the person has to be heterozygous in both traits. Each child from such a cross has a 25% chance for each possible phenotype.

18.3 Beyond Simple Inheritance Patterns
There are many other types of inheritance beyond simple dominant/recessive patterns. They are multifactorial inheritance (skin color), degrees of dominance (curly hair), and multiple alleles (ABO blood type).

For multifactorial traits, each of several genes contributes to the overall phenotype in equal, small degrees. The environment plays a role in the continuously varying expression that follows a bell-shaped curve. Twin studies have allowed investigators to determine that behavioral traits are most likely multifactorial ones.

18.4 Sex-Linked Inheritance
Some traits are sex-linked, meaning that although they do not determine gender, they are carried on the sex chromosomes. Most of the alleles for these traits are carried on the X chromosome, and the Y is blank. It is customary to show an X-linked allele as a superscript on the X chromosome (for example, X^b). The phenotypic results of crosses are given for females and males separately.

An X-linked recessive allele is always expressed in males because it is the only allele a son receives for an X-linked trait. Also, notice that the recessive allele has to have come from his mother because a father does not pass on an allele for an X-linked trait to a son.

Studying the Concepts

1. What is the difference between the genotype and the phenotype of an individual? For which phenotype—dominant or recessive—are there two possible genotypes? 352
2. Why do the gametes have only one allele for each trait? Explain why Aa is a genotype for an individual and not a gamete. 353
3. What is the chance of producing a child with the dominant phenotype from each of the following crosses? 354–55
   $AA \times AA$
   $Aa \times AA$
   $Aa \times Aa$
   $aa \times aa$
4. Which of the crosses in question 3 can result in an offspring with the recessive phenotype? Explain. 354–55
5. What does the phrase "chance has no memory" mean? 354
6. What are the expected results of the following crosses? 354–58
   monohybrid × monohybrid
   monohybrid × recessive
   dihybrid × dihybrid
   dihybrid × recessive in both traits
7. Which of these crosses would best allow you to determine that an individual with the dominant phenotype is homozygous or heterozygous? 354–58
8. Show the events of meiosis, also explain why all possible combinations of alleles occur in the gametes. 356
9. What is the genotype of a heterozygote with a widow's peak and short fingers? Give all possible gametes for this individual. 357
10. Give examples of these patterns of inheritance: multifactorial inheritance, incomplete dominance/codominance, and multiple alleles. 359–61
11. If a trait is on an autosome, how do you give the genotype for a homozygous dominant female? If a trait is on an X chromosome, how do you give the genotype for a homozygous dominant female? 362
12. What phenotypic ratio is expected when a woman who is a carrier for color blindness reproduces with a man who has normal vision? 362
13. How do you give the genotype for a woman who is homozygous dominant for widow's peak and is color-blind? 363

Thinking Critically About the Concepts

Refer to the opening vignette on page 351, and then answer these questions.

1. Of all the patterns of inheritance discussed in this chapter, which most likely governs cleft chin?
2. What would be the genotype and phenotype of their children if Michael Douglas is homozygous dominant for cleft chin and homozygous recessive for type of hairline, and his wife, Catherine Zeta-Jones, is homozygous recessive for type of chin and homozygous recessive for type of hairline?
3. Suppose crossing-over occurred between the nonsister chromatids in Michael Douglas, with regard to cleft chin. What would be the genotypes and phenotypes of their children?

Testing Your Knowledge of the Concepts

Choose the best answer for each question. Assume simple dominance unless told otherwise.

1. Which of these is a correct statement?
   a. Each gamete contains two alleles for each trait.
   b. Each individual has one allele for each trait.
   c. Fertilization gives each new individual one allele for each trait.
   d. All of these are correct.
   e. None of these is correct.

2. Which of the following indicates a heterozygous individual?
   a. *AB*
   b. *AA*
   c. *Aa*
   d. *aa*

3. Which of these could be a normal gamete?
   a. *A*
   b. *Aa*
   c. *AA*
   d. None of these is correct.

4. List the gametes produced by *AaBb*.
   a. *Aa, Bb*
   b. *A, a, B, b*
   c. *AB, ab*
   d. *AB, Ab, aB, ab*

5. Homologous chromosomes have
   a. genes for the same traits.
   b. the same shape and size.
   c. the same DNA base sequences.
   d. All of these are correct.

6. In humans, pointed eyebrows (*P*) are dominant over smooth eyebrows (*p*). Mary's father has pointed eyebrows, but she and her mother have smooth. What is the genotype of the father?
   a. *pp*
   b. *Pp*
   c. *PPpp*
   d. *pp*
   e. Any one of these are correct.

7. The genotypic ratio from a monohybrid cross is
   a. 1:1.
   b. 3:1.
   c. 1:2:1.
   d. 9:3:3:1.
   e. 1:1:1:1.

8. A straight hairline is recessive. If two parents with a widow's peak have a child with a straight hairline, then what is the chance that their next child will have a straight hairline?
   a. no chance
   b. 1/4
   c. 3/16
   d. 1/2
   e. 1/16

9. What is the chance that an *Aa* individual will be produced from an *Aa* × *Aa* cross?
   a. 50%
   b. 75%
   c. 0%
   d. 25%
   e. 100%

10. The genotype of an individual, with the dominant phenotype, can be determined best by reproduction with
   a. the recessive genotype or phenotype.
   b. a heterozygote.
   c. the dominant phenotype.
   d. the homozygous dominant.
   e. Both a and b are correct.

11. Using the diagram below, show how four types of gametes (*SW, sw, Sw, sW*) are produced from the dihybrid individual represented in the top circle.

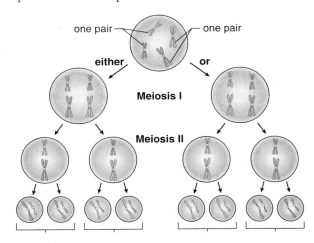

12. Because the homologous chromosomes align independently at the equator during meiosis
   a. all possible combinations of alleles can occur in the gametes.
   b. only the parental combinations of gametes can occur in the gametes.
   c. only the nonparental combinations of gametes can occur in the gametes.

13. What is the chance that a dihybrid cross will produce a homozygous recessive in both traits?
   a. 9/16
   b. 1/4
   c. 1/16
   d. 3/16
   e. 1/8

14. Which of the following is not a feature of multifactorial inheritance?
   a. Effects of dominant alleles are additive.
   b. Genes affecting the trait may be on multiple chromosomes.
   c. Environment influences phenotype.
   d. Recessive alleles are harmful.

15. The ABO blood system exhibits
   a. codominance.
   b. dominance.
   c. multiple alleles.
   d. All of these are correct.
   e. None of these is correct.

For questions 16–19, match the cross type with the expected ratios in the key. Each answer can be used more than once.

Key:

   a. 3:1
   b. 1:1
   c. 9:3:3:1
   d. 1:1:1:1

16. Phenotypic ratio, when a dihybrid reproduces with a dihybrid

17. Phenotypic ratio, when a monohybrid reproduces with a monohybrid

18. Phenotypic ratio, when a dihybrid reproduces with the homozygous recessive in both traits

19. Phenotypic ratio, when a monohybrid reproduces with a homozygous recessive for the trait

20. The occurrence of the type AB blood shows that two alleles involved in determining blood type are
    a. completely dominant.
    b. incompletely dominant.
    c. codominant.

21. Assume two normal parents have a color-blind son. Which parent is responsible for color blindness in the son?
    a. the mother
    b. the father
    c. either parent
    d. None of these is correct—two normal parents cannot have a color-blind son.

22. If a child has type O blood and the mother has type A, then which of the following could be the blood type of the child's father?
    a. A only
    b. B only
    c. O only
    d. A or O
    e. A, B, or O

23. Cleft chin is a dominant trait. A man without a cleft chin marries a woman with a cleft whose mother lacked the cleft. What proportion of their children would lack the cleft chin?
    a. 1/4
    b. 1/2
    c. 3/4
    d. All of these are correct.
    e. None of these is correct.

24. A researcher does a statistical study of a population and finds that the phenotypes for a particular trait follow a bell-shaped curve. He concludes rightly that the trait is governed by
    a. codominant genes.
    b. simple dominance.
    c. an X-linked gene.
    d. multifactorial genes, plus the environment.

25. Alice and Henry are at the opposite extremes for a multifactorial trait. Their children will
    a. be bell-shaped.
    b. be a phenotype typical of a 3:1 ratio.
    c. have the middle phenotype between their two parents.
    d. look like one parent or the other.

26. A woman with very light skin has medium-brown parents. If this woman reproduces with a light-skinned man, what is the darkest skin color possible for their children?
    a. dark skin
    b. light skin
    c. medium-brown skin
    d. Any one of these may occur.

27. A woman is color-blind, and her spouse has normal vision. What are the chances of a color-blind son, daughter?
    a. 0% for son, 100% for daughter
    b. 100% for son, 0% for daughter
    c. 50% for son, 50% for daughter
    d. 75% for son, 25% for daughter

28. Two wavy-haired individuals (neither curly hair nor straight hair are completely dominant) reproduce. What are the chances that their children will have wavy hair?
    a. 0%
    b. 25%
    c. 50%
    d. 100%

Understanding Key Terms

allele 352	locus (pl., loci) 352
autosome 362	monohybrid 354
codominance 360	multifactorial inheritance 359
dihybrid 357	multiple allele 361
dominant allele 352	phenotype 352
genotype 352	Punnett square 354
heterozygous 352	recessive allele 352
homozygous dominant 352	sex chromosome 362
homozygous recessive 352	sex-linked 362
incomplete dominance 360	X-linked 362

Match the terms to these definitions:

a. _____ Grid-like device used to calculate the expected results of simple genetic crosses.

b. _____ Alternative forms of a gene that occur at the same locus on homologous chromosomes.

c. _____ Allele that exerts its phenotypic effect in the heterozygote; it masks the expression of the recessive allele.

d. _____ Particular site where a gene is found on a chromosome.

e. _____ Alleles of an individual for a particular trait or traits such as *BB* or *Aa* or *BBAa*

Online Learning Center

www.mhhe.com/maderhuman9

The Online Learning Center provides a wealth of information fully organized and integrated by chapter. You will find practice quizzes, interactive activities, labeling exercises, flashcards, and much more that will complement your learning and understanding of human biology.

Looking at Both Sides

Each day, the Internet, media, and other people present you with opposing viewpoints on a wide range of subjects. Your ability to develop an informed opinion on an issue, and talk to others about it, is extremely important.

To expand and enhance your knowledge of a highly relevant bioethical issue, visit the "Student Edition" of the Online Learning Center. Under "Course-Wide Content," select "Looking at Both Sides." Once there, you will be asked to complete activities that will increase your understanding of a current bioethical issue related to this chapter and allow you to defend your opinion.

C H A P T E R   C O N C E P T S

19.1 DNA and RNA Structure and Function
- How does the structure of DNA allow it to be replicated?   368–69
- How is RNA structure similar to, but also different from, that of DNA? What are the different forms of RNA?   370

19.2 Gene Expression
- What is the structure of a protein, and what function do proteins perform in a metabolic pathway?   371
- What are the two steps of gene expression, and how are they carried out?   372–76
- What are various levels of genetic control in human cells? How is transcriptional control achieved?   377

19.3 Genomics
- What are genomics and proteomics?   378–79
- Why is the genome now said to be three-dimensional?   379

19.4 DNA Technology
- What two genetic engineering techniques allow scientists to clone a gene?   380–81
- How and why is DNA fingerprinting done?   382
- What is biotechnology, and what are some kinds of biotechnology products?   383–84
- In what ways does genetic engineering improve agricultural plants and farm animals?   384

Arthur Lee Whitfield was released from prison, August 23, 2004, after DNA fingerprinting proved he had not raped two women in 1981. He had served 22 years of a 63-year sentence. DNA fingerprinting, which is based on the sequence of one's bases in DNA, is so called because it is a pattern unique to the individual as is a traditional fingerprint.

Whitfield had always said he was innocent, but a jury sentenced him to 45 years in prison based, in part, on a victim's identification of him. Whitfield pled guilty to the second rape charge, in exchange for an 18-year sentence and the hope he would live to see his family again.

The Virginia state legislature decided that inmates could now use DNA evidence to prove their innocence, and this prompted Whitfield to ask for DNA testing of the biological evidence saved from his jury trial. DNA fingerprinting of the semen sample, taken from the vagina of the rape victim, did not match that of Whitfield's DNA, and, instead, matched that of another man, who was convicted for an unrelated rape.

Whitfield couldn't believe it when he was told he was free. He was 27 when he went to jail; now he is 49. Despite the intervening years, his niece, grand-niece, mother, and sister were all there to welcome him home. The night of the rapes he was with his family at a next-door neighbor's birthday party, but the jury had not believed him.

Attorneys are hopeful that other inmates will also be set free in Virginia on the basis of DNA fingerprinting, which is now allowable evidence.

19.1 DNA and RNA Structure and Function

You know that **DNA (deoxyribonucleic acid)** is the genetic material, and that DNA is largely found in the chromosomes, located in the nucleus of a cell. Any genetic material has to be able to do three things: (1) replicate so that it can be transmitted to the next generation, (2) store information, and (3) undergo mutations that provide genetic variability. We want to explore how DNA is able to accomplish these tasks, but first we have to review the structure of DNA.

Structure of DNA

DNA is a **double helix;** it is composed of two strands that spiral about each other (Fig. 19.1a). Each strand is a polynucleotide because it is composed of a series of nucleotides. A nucleotide is a molecule composed of three subunits—phosphoric acid (phosphate), a pentose sugar (deoxyribose), and a nitrogen-containing base. Looking at just one strand of DNA, notice that the phosphate and sugar molecules make up a backbone and the bases project

to one side. Put the two strands together and DNA resembles a ladder (Fig. 19.1b). The phosphate-sugar backbones make up the supports of the ladder, and the rungs of the ladder are the paired bases. The bases are held together by hydrogen bonding: A pairs with T, by forming two hydrogen bonds, and G pairs with C, by forming three hydrogen bonds, or vice versa. This is called **complementary base pairing.**

The bases are important to the functioning of DNA, so it will be helpful to remember that a purine (has two rings) is always paired with a pyrimidine (has one ring) like this:

Purines	Pyrimidines
Adenine (A)	Thymine (T)
Guanine (G)	Cytosine (C)

You might also want to note that two strands of DNA are antiparallel—that is, they run in opposite directions, which you can verify by noticing that in one strand the sugar molecules appear right-side up and in the other they appear upside down. This technicality, while important, need not concern us.

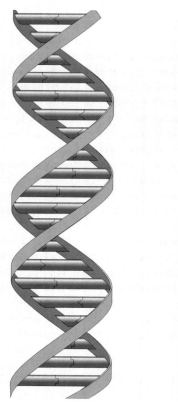

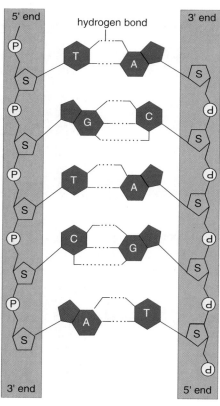

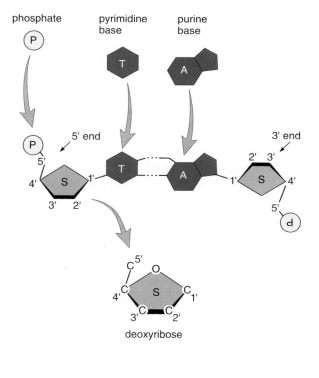

a. Double helix   b. Ladder structure   c. One pair of bases

Figure 19.1   Overview of DNA structure.
a. DNA double helix. **b.** When the helix is unwound, a ladder configuration shows that the supports are composed of sugar (S) and phosphate (P) molecules and the rungs are complementary bases. Notice that the bases in DNA pair in such a way that the phosphate-sugar backbones are oriented in different directions. **c.** The DNA strands are antiparallel, which is apparent by numbering the carbon atoms in deoxyribose.

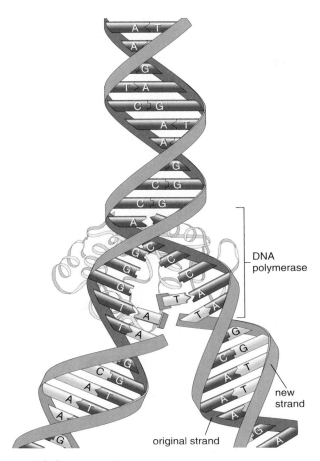

DNA
polymerase

new
strand

original strand

Figure 19.2   **Overview of DNA replication.**
Replication is called semiconservative because each new double
helix is composed of an original strand and a new strand.

Parental DNA molecule
contains so-called original
strands hydrogen-bonded
by complementary base
pairing.

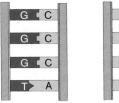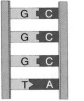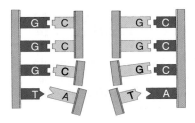

Region of replication.
Parental DNA is unwound
and unzipped. New
nucleotides are pairing
with those in original strands.

Replication is complete.
Each double helix is
composed of an original
(parental) strand and a
new (daughter) strand.

Figure 19.3   **Ladder configuration and DNA replication.**
Use of the ladder configuration better illustrates how complementary
nucleotides, available in the cell, pair with those of each old strand
before they are joined together to form a daughter strand.

Replication of DNA

When cells divide, each new cell gets an exact copy of DNA.
The process of copying a DNA helix is called **DNA replication.** The double-stranded structure of DNA allows each original strand to serve as a **template** (mold) for the formation of
a complementary new strand. DNA replication is termed
semiconservative because each new double helix has one original strand and one new strand. In other words, one of the
original strands is conserved, or present, in each new double
helix. Because each original strand has produced a new
strand through complementary base pairing, there are now
two DNA helices identical to each other and to the original
molecule (Fig. 19.2).

Figure 19.3 shows how complementary nucleotides pair
in the daughter strand.

1. Before replication begins, the two strands that make up
   parental DNA are hydrogen-bonded to each other.
2. An enzyme unwinds and "unzips" double-stranded
   DNA (i.e., the weak hydrogen bonds between the
   paired bases break).
3. New complementary DNA nucleotides, always present
   in the nucleus, fit into place by the process of

complementary base pairing. These are positioned and
joined by the enzyme *DNA polymerase*.
4. To complete replication, an enzyme seals any breaks in
   the sugar-phosphate backbone.
5. The two double helix molecules are identical to each
   other and to the original DNA molecule.

Rarely, a replication error occurs— the sequence of the
bases in the new strand is not correct. But, if an error does
occur, the cell has repair enzymes that usually fix it. A replication error that persists is a **mutation,** a permanent change
in the sequence of bases that can possibly cause a change in
the phenotype and introduce variability. Such variabilities
make you different from your neighbor and humans different from other animals.

DNA is a double helix with phosphate-sugar
backbones on the outside and complementary
paired bases on the inside. During DNA
replication, DNA unwinds and unzips, and new
strands form that are complementary to the
original strands.

The Structure and Function of RNA

RNA (ribonucleic acid) is made up of nucleotides containing the sugar ribose. This sugar accounts for the scientific name of this polynucleotide. The four nucleotides that make up the RNA molecule have the following bases: adenine (A), **uracil (U)**, cytosine (C), and guanine (G) (Fig. 19.4). Notice that in RNA, the base uracil replaces the base thymine.

RNA, unlike DNA, is single-stranded (Fig. 19.4), but the single RNA strand sometimes doubles back on itself, and complementary base pairing still occurs. Similarities and differences between these two nucleic acid molecules are listed in Table 19.1.

In general, RNA is a helper to DNA, allowing protein synthesis to occur according to the stored genetic information that DNA provides. There are three types of RNA, each with a specific function in protein synthesis.

Ribosomal RNA

Ribosomal RNA (rRNA) is produced in the nucleolus of a nucleus where a portion of DNA serves as a template for its formation. Ribosomal RNA joins with proteins made in the cytoplasm to form the subunits of ribosomes. The subunits leave the nucleus and come together in the cytoplasm when protein synthesis is about to begin. Proteins are synthesized at the ribosomes, which in low-power electron micrographs look like granules arranged along the endoplasmic reticulum, a system of tubules and saccules within the cytoplasm. Some ribosomes appear free in the cytoplasm or in clusters called polyribosomes.

Messenger RNA

Messenger RNA (mRNA) is produced in the nucleus where DNA serves as a template for its formation. This type of RNA carries genetic information from DNA to the ribosomes in the cytoplasm where protein synthesis occurs. Messenger RNA is a linear molecule.

Transfer RNA

Transfer RNA (tRNA) is produced in the nucleus, and a portion of DNA also serves as a template for its production. Appropriate to its name, tRNA transfers amino acids to the ribosomes, where the amino acids are joined, forming a protein. There are 20 different types of amino acids in proteins; therefore, at least 20 tRNAs must be functioning in the cell. Each type of tRNA carries only one type of amino acid.

RNA is a polynucleotide that functions during protein synthesis in various ways. There are three types of RNA, each with a specific role.

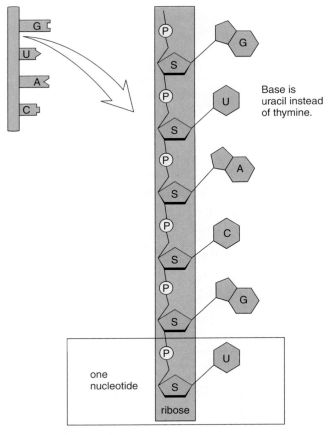

Figure 19.4   Structure of RNA.

Like DNA, RNA is a polymer of nucleotides. In an RNA nucleotide, the sugar ribose is attached to a phosphate molecule and to a base: G, U, A, or C. Notice that in RNA, the base uracil replaces thymine as one of the pyrimidine bases. RNA is single-stranded, whereas DNA is double-stranded.

Table 19.1	DNA-RNA Similarities and Differences

DNA-RNA SIMILARITIES

Both are nucleic acids

Both are composed of nucleotides

Both have a sugar-phosphate backbone

Both have four different types of bases

DNA-RNA DIFFERENCES

DNA	RNA
Found in nucleus	Found in nucleus and cytoplasm
The genetic material	Helper to DNA
Sugar is deoxyribose	Sugar is ribose
Bases are A, T, C, G	Bases are A, U, C, G
Double-stranded	Single-stranded
Is transcribed (to give mRNA)	Is translated (to give proteins)

19.2 Gene Expression

As we shall see, DNA provides the cell with a blueprint for synthesizing proteins. DNA resides in the nucleus, and protein synthesis occurs in the cytoplasm. First, mRNA carries a copy of DNA's blueprint into the cytoplasm, and second, the other RNA molecules we just discussed are involved in bringing about protein synthesis.

Before discussing the mechanics of gene expression, let's review the structure of proteins.

Structure and Function of Proteins

Proteins are composed of subunits called amino acids (Table 19.2). Twenty different amino acids are commonly found in proteins, which are synthesized at the ribosomes in the cytoplasm of cells. Proteins differ because the number and order of their amino acids differ. Figure 19.5 shows that the sequence of amino acids in a protein leads to its particular shape. The shape of a protein is extremely important because it helps determine a protein's function.

Proteins are found in all parts of the body; some are structural proteins, and some are enzymes. The protein hemoglobin is responsible for the red color of red blood cells. Albumins and globulins (antibodies) are well-known plasma proteins. Muscle cells contain the proteins actin and myosin, which give muscles substance and the ability to contract.

Enzymes are organic catalysts that speed reactions in cells. The reactions in cells form metabolic or chemical pathways. A pathway can be represented as follows:

$$\begin{array}{cccc} E_A & E_B & E_C & E_D \\ A \rightarrow B & \rightarrow C & \rightarrow D & \rightarrow E \end{array}$$

In this pathway, the letters are molecules, and the notations over the arrows are enzymes: Molecule A becomes molecule B, and enzyme E_A speeds the reaction; molecule B becomes molecule C, and enzyme E_B speeds the reaction; and so forth. Enzymes are *specific*: Enzyme E_A can only convert A to B, enzyme E_B can only convert B to C, and so forth.

Proteins determine the structure and function of the various cells in the body.

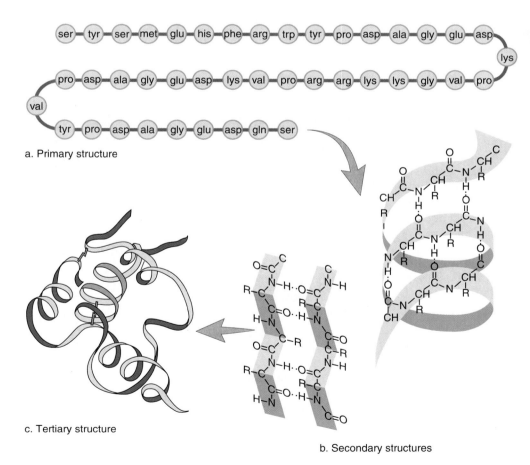

a. Primary structure

c. Tertiary structure

b. Secondary structures

Table 19.2	Amino Acids
Amino Acid	**Abbreviation**
alanine	ala
arginine	arg
asparagine	asn
aspartic acid	asp
cysteine	cys
glutamine	gln
glutamic acid	glu
glycine	gly
histidine	his
isoleucine	ile
leucine	leu
lysine	lys
methionine	met
phenylalanine	phe
proline	pro
serine	ser
threonine	thr
tryptophan	trp
tyrosine	tyr
valine	val

Figure 19.5 Protein structure.
ACTH (adrenocorticotropic hormone) is a hormone produced by the anterior pituitary, which stimulates the adrenal cortex to produce cortisol. **a.** The primary structure of a protein is the sequence of its amino acids. **b.** The secondary structure can be either a helix or pleated sheet. **c.** The tertiary structure is the final three-dimensional shape.

Gene Expression: An Overview

The first step in gene expression is called transcription, and the second step is called translation (Fig. 19.6). During **transcription,** a strand of mRNA forms that is complementary to a portion of DNA. The mRNA molecule that forms is a *transcript* of a gene. Transcription means to make a faithful copy, and in this case, a sequence of nucleotides in DNA is copied to a sequence of nucleotides in mRNA.

Protein synthesis occurs during **translation** according to the information provided by mRNA. Translation means to put information into a different language. In this case, a sequence of *nucleotides* is translated into the sequence of *amino acids.* This is only possible if the bases in DNA and mRNA code for amino acids. This code is called the genetic code.

The Genetic Code

Recognizing that there must be a genetic code, investigators wanted to know how four bases (A, C, G, U) could provide enough combinations to code for 20 amino acids? If the code were a singlet code (only one base stands for an amino acid), only four amino acids could be encoded. If the code were a doublet (any two bases stand for one amino acid), it would still not be possible to code for 20 amino acids, but if the code were a triplet, then the four bases could supply 64 different triplets, far more than needed to code for 20 different amino acids. It should come as no surprise, then, to learn that the code is a **triplet code.**

Each three-letter (base) unit of an mRNA molecule is called a **codon.** The translation of all 64 mRNA codons has been determined (Fig. 19.7). Sixty-one triplets correspond to a particular amino acid; the remaining three are stop codons, which signal polypeptide termination. The one codon that stands for the amino acid methionine is also a start codon signaling polypeptide initiation. Notice, too, that most amino acids have more than one codon; leucine, serine, and arginine have six different codons, for example. This offers some protection against possibly harmful mutations that change the sequence of the bases.

To crack the code, a cell-free experiment was done: Artificial RNA was added to a medium containing bacterial ribosomes and a mixture of amino acids. Comparison of the bases in the RNA, with the resulting polypeptide, allowed investigators to decipher the code. For example, an mRNA with a sequence of repeating guanines (GGG'GGG'...) would encode a string of glycine amino acids.

The genetic code is just about universal in living things. This suggests that the code dates back to the very first organisms on Earth and that all living things are related.

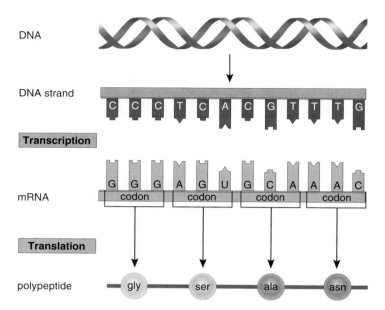

Figure 19.6   **Overview of gene expression.**
Transcription occurs when DNA acts as a template for RNA (e.g., mRNA) synthesis. (Notice that uracil (U), in RNA, takes the place of thymine (T), in DNA.) Translation occurs when the sequence of codons of mRNA specify the sequence of amino acids in a polypeptide.

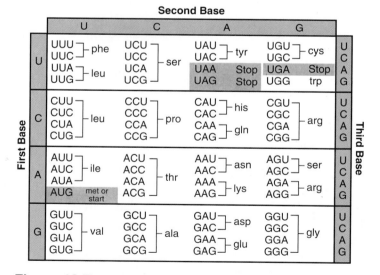

Figure 19.7   **Messenger RNA codons.**
Notice that in this chart, each of the codons (white rectangles) are composed of three letters representing the first base, second base, and third base. For example, find the rectangle where C for the first base and A for the second base intersect. You will see that U, C, A, or G can be the third base. CAU and CAC are codons for his (histidine); CAA and CAG are codons for glu (glutamine) (as per Table 19.2).

Transcription

During transcription, a segment of the DNA serves as a template for the production of an RNA molecule. Although all three classes of RNA are formed by transcription, we will focus on transcription to form mRNA.

Messenger RNA

Transcription begins when the enzyme **RNA polymerase** opens up the DNA helix just in front of it so that complementary base pairing can occur. Then, RNA polymerase joins the RNA nucleotides, and an mRNA molecule results. When mRNA forms, it has a sequence of bases complementary to DNA; wherever A, T, G, or C is present in the DNA template, U, A, C, or G is incorporated into the mRNA molecule (Fig. 19.8). Now, mRNA is a faithful copy of the sequence of bases in DNA.

Processing of mRNA   After the mRNA is transcribed in human cells, it must be *processed* before entering the cytoplasm.

The newly synthesized *primary mRNA* molecule becomes a *mature mRNA* molecule after processing (Fig. 19.9). Most genes in humans are interrupted by segments of DNA that are not part of the gene. These portions are called *introns* because they are intragene segments. The other portions of the gene are called *exons* because they are ultimately expressed. Only exons result in a protein product.

Primary mRNA contains bases that are complementary to both exons and introns, but during processing, (1) one end of the mRNA is capped, by the addition of an altered guanine nucleotide, and the other end is given a tail, by the addition of adenosine nucleotides. (2) The introns are removed, and the exons are joined to form a mature mRNA molecule consisting of continuous exons. This *splicing* of mRNA is done by a complex composed of both RNA and protein. Surprisingly, RNA, not the protein, is the enzyme, and so it is called a *ribozyme*.

Ordinarily, processing brings together all the exons of a gene. In some instances, cells use only certain exons rather than all of them to form a mature RNA transcript. The result can be a different protein product in each cell. Alternate mRNA splicing is believed to account for the ability of a single gene to result in two different proteins in a cell.

The enzyme RNA polymerase copies a strand of the DNA into a complementary RNA molecule. In eukaryotic cells, the primary mRNA molecule is processed by modification of the 5′ and 3′ ends and removal of the introns. The mature mRNA leaves the nucleus.

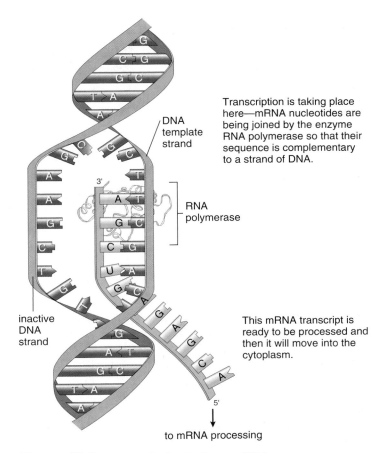

Transcription is taking place here—mRNA nucleotides are being joined by the enzyme RNA polymerase so that their sequence is complementary to a strand of DNA.

DNA template strand

RNA polymerase

inactive DNA strand

This mRNA transcript is ready to be processed and then it will move into the cytoplasm.

to mRNA processing

Figure 19.8   Transcription to form mRNA.
During transcription, complementary RNA is made from a DNA template. A portion of DNA unwinds and unzips at the point of attachment of RNA polymerase. A strand of mRNA is produced when complementary bases join in the order dictated by the sequence of bases in template DNA.

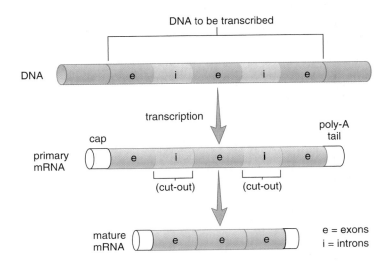

DNA to be transcribed

DNA

transcription

cap

poly-A tail

primary mRNA

(cut-out)   (cut-out)

mature mRNA

e = exons
i = introns

Figure 19.9   mRNA processing.
During processing, a cap and tail are added to mRNA, and the introns are removed so that only exons remain.

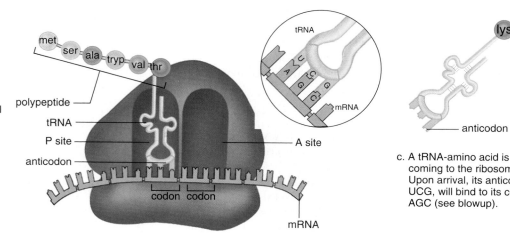

a. An mRNA is threaded between ribosomal subunits and a polypeptide extends to the side.

b. A ribosome has two binding sites where codons bind to anticodons. A tRNA bearing a polypeptide is at the P site and a tRNA-amino acid is approaching the A site.

c. A tRNA-amino acid is coming to the ribosome. Upon arrival, its anticodon, UCG, will bind to its codon, AGC (see blowup).

Figure 19.10   Ribosome structure and function.
Protein synthesis occurs at a ribosome. **a.** Side view of a ribosome showing mRNA and growing polypeptide. **b.** Structure and function of a large ribosomal subunit. **c.** tRNA structure and function.

Translation

During translation, transfer RNA (tRNA) molecules bring amino acids to the ribosomes (Fig. 19.10), where polypeptide synthesis occurs. A ribosome consists of a large and a small subunit that join together in the cytoplasm just as protein synthesis begins. Each ribosome has a binding site for mRNA, as well as binding sites for two tRNA molecules at a time. Usually, there is more than one tRNA molecule for each of the 20 amino acids found in proteins. The amino acid binds to one end of the molecule. Therefore, the entire complex is designated as tRNA–amino acid. At the other end of each tRNA is a specific **anticodon,** a group of three bases complementary to an mRNA codon. The tRNA molecules come to the ribosome at the A (for amino acid) site where each anticodon pairs by hydrogen bonding with a codon.

The order in which tRNA-amino acids come to the ribosome is directed by the sequence of the mRNA codons. In this way, the order of codons in mRNA brings about a particular order of amino acids in a protein. The tRNA that is attached to the growing polypeptide is at the P site of a ribosome, as shown in Figure 19.10.

If the codon sequence is ACC, GUA, and AAA, what will be the sequence of amino acids in a portion of the polypeptide? Inspection of Table 19.2 (see page 371) allows us to determine this:

Codon	Anticodon	Amino Acid
ACC	UGG	Threonine
GUA	CAU	Valine
AAA	UUU	Lysine

Polypeptide synthesis requires three steps: initiation, elongation, and termination (Fig. 19.11).

1. During *initiation,* mRNA binds to the smaller of the two ribosomal subunits; then the larger subunit associates with the smaller one.
2. During *elongation,* the polypeptide lengthens one amino acid at a time. An incoming tRNA–amino acid complex arrives at the A site and then receives the peptide from the outgoing tRNA. The ribosome moves laterally so that again the P site is filled by a tRNA-peptide complex. The A site is now available to receive another incoming tRNA–amino acid complex. In this manner, the peptide grows, and the linear structure of a polypeptide comes about. (The particular shape of a polypeptide is formed later.)
3. Then *termination* of synthesis occurs at a codon that means stop and does not code for an amino acid. The ribosome dissociates into its two subunits and falls off the mRNA molecule.

During elongation, about five amino acids are added to a polypeptide every second. However, many ribosomes are at work forming the same polypeptide. As soon as the initial portion of mRNA has been translated by one ribosome, and the ribosome has begun to move down the mRNA, another ribosome attaches to the mRNA. Therefore, several ribosomes, collectively called a **polyribosome,** can move along one mRNA at a time. And several polypeptides of the same type can be synthesized using one mRNA molecule (Fig. 19.12).

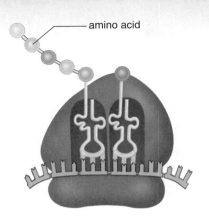

amino acid

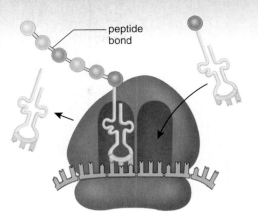

peptide bond

(2) Elongation occurs in two stages.
a. tRNA-polypeptide is at the P site and a tRNA-amino acid is at the A site. The polypeptide will be transferred to the tRNA-amino acid.

b. The ribosome has moved to the right and the tRNA-polypeptide at the P site is now longer by one amino acid. One tRNA is outgoing and another tRNA is incoming.

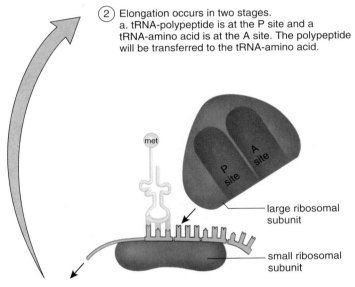

met

A site

P site

large ribosomal subunit

small ribosomal subunit

free polypeptide

(1) Initiation. The small ribosomal subunit, the mRNA, the first tRNA-amino acid, and the large ribosomal subunit come together.

(3) Termination. When the ribosome reaches a stop codon, all participants separate and the polypeptide is released.

Figure 19.11 **Polypeptide synthesis.**
Polypeptide synthesis takes place at a ribosome and has three steps: (1) initiation, (2) elongation, and (3) termination.

Figure 19.12 **Polyribosome structure.**
Several ribosomes, collectively called a polyribosome, move along an mRNA molecule at one time. They function independently of one another; therefore, several polypeptides can be made simultaneously.

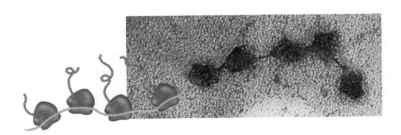

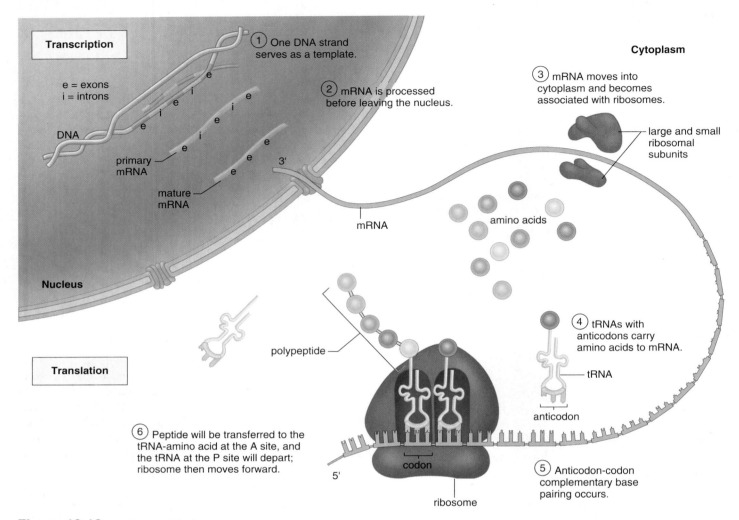

Figure 19.13   Gene expression.
Gene expression leads to the formation of a product, most often a protein. The two steps required for gene expression are transcription, which occurs in the nucleus, and translation, which occurs in the cytoplasm at the ribosomes.

Review of Gene Expression

DNA in the nucleus contains a *triplet code*. Each group of three bases stands for a specific amino acid (Fig. 19.13 and Table 19.3). During transcription, a segment of a DNA strand serves as a template for the formation of mRNA. The bases in mRNA are complementary to those in DNA; every three bases is a *codon* for a certain amino acid. Messenger RNA is processed before it leaves the nucleus, during which time the introns are removed and the ends are modified. Messenger RNA carries a sequence of codons to the *ribosomes*, which are composed of rRNA and proteins. A tRNA bonded to a particular amino acid has an *anticodon* that pairs with a codon in mRNA. During translation, tRNAs and their attached amino acids arrive at the ribosomes, where the linear sequence of codons of mRNA determines the order in which amino acids become incorporated into a protein.

Table 19.3	Participants in Gene Expression	
Name of Molecule	**Special Significance**	**Definition**
DNA	Genetic information	Sequence of DNA bases
mRNA	Codons	Sequence of three RNA bases complementary to DNA
tRNA	Anticodon	Sequence of three RNA bases complementary to codon
rRNA	Ribosome	Site of protein synthesis
Amino acid	Building block for protein	Transported to ribosome by tRNA
Protein	Enzyme, structural protein, or secretory product	Amino acids joined in a predetermined order

The Regulation of Gene Expression

All cells receive a copy of all genes; however, cells differ as to which genes are actively expressed. Muscle cells, for example, have a different set of genes that are turned on in the nucleus and different proteins that are active in the cytoplasm than do nerve cells. A variety of mechanisms regulate gene expression, from transcription to protein activity in our cells. These mechanisms can be grouped under four primary levels of control, two that pertain to the nucleus and two that pertain to the cytoplasm:

1. *Transcriptional control* In the nucleus, a number of mechanisms regulate which genes are transcribed and/or the rate at which transcription of the genes occurs. These include the organization of chromatin and the use of transcription factors that initiate transcription, the first step in gene expression.

2. *Posttranscriptional control* Posttranscriptional control occurs in the nucleus after DNA is transcribed and mRNA is formed. How mRNA is processed before it leaves the nucleus and also how fast mature mRNA leaves the nucleus can affect the amount of gene expression.

3. *Translational control* Translational control occurs in the cytoplasm after mRNA leaves the nucleus and before there is a protein product. The life expectancy of mRNA molecules (how long they exist in the cytoplasm) can vary, as can their ability to bind ribosomes. It is also possible that some mRNAs may need additional changes before they are translated at all.

4. *Posttranslational control* Posttranslational control, which also occurs in the cytoplasm, occurs after protein synthesis. The polypeptide product may have to undergo additional changes before it is biologically functional. Also, a functional enzyme is subject to feedback control—the binding of an enzyme's product can change its shape so that it is no longer able to carry out its reaction.

Activated Chromatin

For a gene to be transcribed in human cells, the chromosome in that region must first decondense. The chromosomes within the developing egg cells of many vertebrates are called lampbrush chromosomes because they have many loops that appear to be bristles (Fig. 19.14). Here mRNA is being synthesized in great quantity; then protein synthesis can be carried out, despite rapid cell division during development.

Transcription Activators

In human cells, **transcription activators** are DNA-binding proteins. Every cell contains many different types of transcription activators, and a specific combination is believed to regulate the activity of any particular gene. After the right combination of transcription activators binds to DNA, an RNA polymerase attaches to DNA and begins the process of transcription.

As cells mature, they differentiate and become specialized. Specialization is determined by which genes are active, and therefore, perhaps, by which transcription activators are present in that cell. Signals received from inside and outside the cell could turn on or off genes that code for certain transcription factors. For example, the gene for fetal hemoglobin ordinarily gets turned off as a newborn matures; therefore, one possible treatment for sickle-cell disease is to turn this gene on again.

Regulation of gene expression occurs at four levels. The first level, transcriptional control, involves organization of chromatin and the use of transcription activators that bind to DNA.

Figure 19.14 · **Lampbrush chromosomes.**
These chromosomes, seen in amphibian egg cells, give evidence that when mRNA is being synthesized, chromosomes decondense. Each chromosome has many loops extending from its axis (white on the micrograph). Many mRNA transcripts are being made off these DNA loops (red).

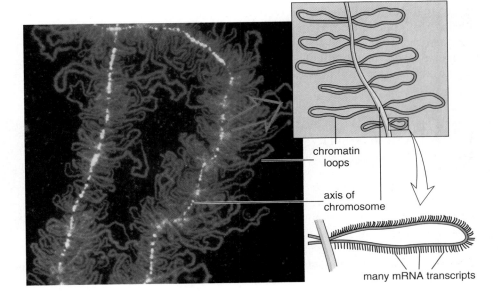

chromatin loops

axis of chromosome

many mRNA transcripts

19.3 Genomics

In the previous century, researchers discovered the structure of DNA, how DNA replicates, and how protein synthesis occurs. Genetics in the 21st century concerns **genomics,** the study of genomes—our genes, and the genes of other organisms. The enormity of the task can be appreciated by knowing that, at the very least, we have 30,000 genes that code for proteins, and many organisms have more encoding genes than we do.

Sequencing the Bases

We now have a working draft of the sequence of all the base pairs in all the DNA in all our chromosomes. This feat was accomplished by the U.S. Human Genome Project, a 13-year effort that involved both university and private laboratories around the world. How did they do it? First, investigators developed a laboratory procedure that would allow them to decipher a short sequence of base pairs, and then an instrument was devised that would carry out this procedure automatically. Over a 13-year span, DNA sequencers were constantly improved, until today, we have instruments that can automatically analyze up to 2 million base pairs of DNA in a 24-hour period.

Genome Comparisons

The genomes of many other organisms, such as a common bacterium, yeast, and mouse, are also in the final-draft stage (Table 19.4). There are many similarities between the sequence of our bases and those of other organisms whose DNA sequences are also known. From this, we can conclude that we share a large number of genes with much simpler organisms, such as bacteria! With a genome size of 3 billion base pairs, there are also many differences.

In one study, researchers compared our genome with that of chromosome 22 in chimpanzees. Among the many genes that differed in sequence were three types of particular interest: a gene for proper speech development, several for hearing, and several for smell. The gene necessary for proper speech development is thought to have played an important role in human evolution. You can suppose that

changes in hearing may have facilitated using language for communication between people. Changes in smell genes are a little more problematic. The investigators speculated that the olfaction genes may have affected dietary changes or sexual selection. Or, they may have been involved in other traits, rather than just smell (Fig. 19.15).

The researchers were surprised to find that many of the other genes they located and studied are known to cause human diseases, if abnormal. They wondered if comparing genomes would be a way of finding genes that are associated with human diseases. Investigators are taking all sorts of avenues to link human base sequence differences to illnesses.

The HapMap Project

The HapMap project is a new undertaking, whose goal is to catalog common sequence differences that occur in human beings. People have been found to inherit patterns of sequence differences, now called haplotypes. For example, if one haplotype of a person has an A rather than a G at a particular location in a chromosome, there are probably other particular base differences near the A. To discover the most common haplotypes, genetic data from African, Asian, and European populations will be analyzed (Fig. 19.16). The goal of the project is to link haplotypes to the risk for specific illnesses, hoping that it will lead to new methods of preventing, diagnosing, and treating disease.

Table 19.4	Sequenced Genomes
Year Sequenced	**Organisms**
2004	*Rattus norvegicus*, the brown Norway rat
2002	*Mus musculus*, the mouse; *Fugu rubripes*, the Japanese puffer fish
2000	*Drosophila melanogaster*, the fruit fly
1998	*Caenorhabditis elegans*, a form of roundworm
1997	*Escherichia coli*, a bacterium
1996	*Methanococcus jannaschii*, an archaea
1995	*Saccaromyces cerevisiae*, a form of yeast; *Haemophilus influenzae*, a bacterium that causes bacterial meningitis

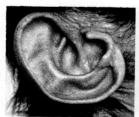
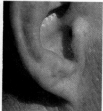
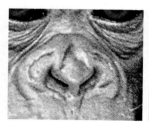

a.   b.   c.

Figure 19.15   **Studying genomic differences between chimpanzees and humans.**
Did changes in the genes for **(a)** speech, **(b)** hearing, and **(c)** smell influence the evolution of humans?

Figure 19.16 Studying genomic differences among people. The HapMap project will compare sequences among African, Asian, and European populations.

Proteomics and Bioinformatics

Proteomics is the study of the structure, function, and interaction of cellular proteins. The known sequence of bases in the human genome predicts that at least 30,000 genes are translated into proteins. The translation of all of these genes results in a collection of proteins, called the human proteome.

Computer modeling of the three-dimensional shape of these proteins is an important part of proteomics. If the primary structure of these proteins is now known, it should be possible to predict their final three-dimensional shape. The study of protein function is also essential to the discovery of better drugs. One day, it may be possible to correlate drug treatment to the particular genome of the individual to increase efficiency and decrease side effects.

Bioinformatics is the application of computer technologies to the study of the genome. Genomics and proteomics produce raw data, and these fields depend upon computer analysis to find significant patterns in the data. As a result of bioinformatics, scientists are hopeful of finding cause-and-effect relationships between various genetic profiles and genetic disorders caused by multifactor genes.

Also, the current genome sequence contains 82 gene "deserts," with no known function. Bioinformatics might find these regions have functions by correlating any sequence changes with resulting phenotypes. New computational tools will, most likely, be needed in order to accomplish these goals.

Expanding Present-Day Genomics

Investigators now believe that our genome is three-dimensional. The sections of DNA that encode proteins are but one dimension—what are the other two? The second layer are DNA sequences that interrupt and separate the genes. These sections have been preserved and this suggests that they may have important functions. Could it be that these sequences do contribute to what makes one person different from another? Doesn't it seem strange that fruit flies have fewer coding genes than roundworms, and rice plants have more than humans? Our protein-coding sequences account for less than 2% of the DNA in the human chromosomes. The rest has been dismissed as evolutionary junk. But is it? Some investigators have found so far that much of the "junk" codes for RNA and they are trying to discover what this RNA does.

The third layer to our genome lies outside DNA! It's called the epigenic layer because it consists of the proteins, such as histones and other chemicals, that surround and adhere to DNA. The epigenic layer seems to play an important role in growth, aging, and cancer and might explain the unusual patterns of inheritance of certain diseases. It's possible the epigenic layer will be easier for us to modify than the other layers of the genome.

Sequencing the base pairs of the human genome has led to several in-depth studies of the genome and a desire to find new medicines.

19.4 DNA Technology

Knowledge of DNA biology has led to our ability to manipulate the genes of organisms. We can clone genes and then use them to alter the genomes of viruses and cells, whether bacterial, plant, or animal cells. This is called **genetic engineering.** Genetic engineering can be used to produce a product or to cure various human ills.

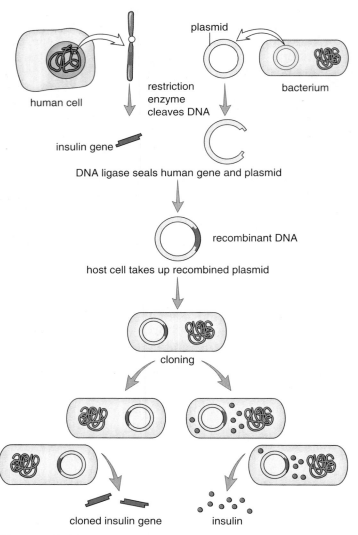

Figure 19.17   **Cloning of a human gene.**
Human DNA and plasmid DNA are cleaved by the same type of restriction enzyme and spliced together by the enzyme DNA ligase. Gene cloning is achieved when a host cell takes up the recombinant plasmid, and as the cell reproduces, the plasmid is replicated. Multiple copies of the gene are now available to an investigator. If the insulin gene functions normally as expected, insulin may also be retrieved.

The Cloning of a Gene

In biology, **cloning** is the production of identical copies through some asexual means. The members of a bacterial colony on a petri dish are clones because they all came from the division of the same original cell. And human identical twins are clones. The first two cells of the embryo separated and each became a complete individual.

Gene cloning is the production of many identical copies of the same gene. Biologists clone genes for a number of reasons. They might want to determine the difference in base sequence between a normal gene and a mutated gene, for example. Or they might use the genes to alter the phenotype of other organisms in a beneficial way. When the organism is a human, we call it gene therapy. If the organism is not human, we call it a transgenic organism.

Scientists might instead be interested in the protein coded for by the cloned gene. In any case, they begin by using one of two ways to clone the gene.

Using Recombinant DNA Technology

Recombinant DNA (rDNA) contains DNA from two or more different sources (Fig. 19.17). To make rDNA, a researcher needs a **vector,** a piece of DNA that can be manipulated in order to add foreign DNA to it. One common vector is a plasmid. **Plasmids** are small accessory rings of DNA from bacteria that are not part of the bacterial chromosome and are capable of replicating on their own. Plasmids were discovered by investigators studying the bacterium *Escherichia coli (E. coli)*.

Two enzymes are needed to introduce foreign DNA into vector DNA: (1) a **restriction enzyme** to cleave DNA, and (2) **DNA ligase** to seal DNA into an opening created by the restriction enzyme. Hundreds of restriction enzymes occur naturally in bacteria, where they cut up any viral DNA that enters the cell. They are called restriction enzymes because they *restrict* the growth of viruses, but they also can be used as molecular scissors to cut double-stranded DNA at a specific site. For example, the restriction enzyme called *Eco*RI always recognizes and cuts double-stranded DNA in this manner when DNA has the sequence of bases GAATTC:

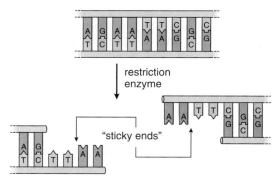

Notice that a gap now exists into which a piece of foreign DNA can be placed if it ends in bases complementary to those exposed by the restriction enzyme. To ensure this, it is only necessary to cleave the foreign DNA with the same type of restriction enzyme. The single-stranded, but complementary, ends of the two DNA molecules are called "sticky ends" because they can bind a piece of foreign DNA by complementary base pairing. Sticky ends facilitate the insertion of foreign DNA into vector DNA.

DNA ligase, an enzyme that functions in DNA replication to seal any breaks in the double-stranded helix, is then used to seal the foreign piece of DNA into the vector. Bacterial cells take up recombinant plasmids from the medium, especially if the cells are treated to make them more permeable. Thereafter, as the plasmid replicates, the gene is cloned.

Using the Polymerase Chain Reaction

The **polymerase chain reaction (PCR)** can create millions of copies of a segment of DNA very quickly in a test tube without the use of a vector or a host cell. The original sample of PCR is usually just a portion of the entire genome. PCR is very specific—it *amplifies* (makes copies of) a targeted DNA sequence that can be less than one part in a million of the total DNA sample!

PCR requires the use of DNA polymerase, the enzyme that carries out DNA replication; a set of primers; and a sup-
ply of nucleotides for the new DNA strands. Primers are single-stranded DNA sequences that start the replication process on each strand. PCR is a chain reaction because the targeted DNA is repeatedly replicated as long as the process continues. The process is shown in Figure 19.18. The amount of DNA doubles with each replication cycle; after one cycle, there are two copies of the targeted DNA sequence, after two cycles, there are four copies, and so forth.

PCR has been in use for several years, and now almost every laboratory has automated PCR machines to carry out the procedure. Automation became possible after a temperature-insensitive (thermostable) DNA polymerase was extracted from the bacterium *Thermus aquaticus,* which lives in hot springs. During the PCR cycle, the mixture of DNA and primers is heated to 95°C to separate the two strands of the double helix so that the primers can bind to single-stranded DNA. The enzyme can withstand the high temperature used to separate double-stranded DNA; therefore, replication does not have to be interrupted by the need to add more enzyme.

DNA amplified by PCR is often analyzed for various purposes. Mitochondrial DNA base sequences in modern living populations were used to decipher the evolutionary history of human populations. Since so little DNA is required for PCR to be effective, it has even been possible to sequence DNA taken from a 76,000-year-old mummified human brain.

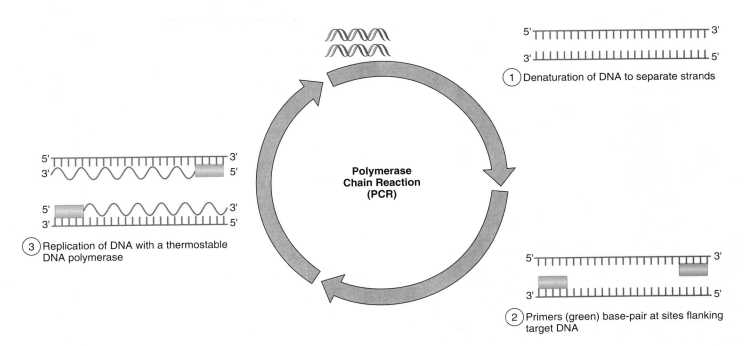

Figure 19.18   Polymerase chain reaction.

At the start of PCR, double-stranded DNA, DNA polymerase, two primers for flanking a targeted sequence, and a supply of the four DNA are placed in a test tube. First cycle: 1. High heat for 5 minutes separates the two strands of the DNA. 2. Cooling for 2 minutes allows the primers (green) to pair with the DNA strands, as shown. 3. Moderate heat for 2–5 minutes allows DNA polymerase (wavy lines) to copy the DNA between the primers. Future cycles (not shown): At the end of the second cycle, four identical copies of targeted DNA are present. After 25–30 cycles, over 30,000,000 copies of the targeted DNA are present.

Applications

A relevant application of PCR is to help identify an individual through DNA fingerprinting. As described in the introduction to the chapter, Arthur Lee Whitfield was set free after it was determined that his DNA fingerprint did not match that of sperm taken from the vagina of a rape victim. DNA fingerprinting can identify the parents of a child or someone who died, such as the victims of the attacks of September 11, 2001. All that is needed is a match between the DNA of the deceased and skin cells left on a personal item, such as a toothbrush or cigarette butt.

Today, DNA fingerprinting makes use of sections of DNA that do not code for protein. Some of the noncoding DNA has functions such as regulation of the coding genes, keeping the chromosomes intact, or serving as introns. The other noncoding regions—the regions that seem to have no

function—consist of nothing but two to five bases repeated over and over again as in ATCATCATCATC. People differ by how many times such a sequence is repeated because the number of repeats is inherited!

How can this difference between people be detected? Recall that PCR amplifies only particular portions of the DNA. Therefore, the greater the number of repeats, the greater the relative amount of DNA that will result after PCR amplification is done. It is possible to measure this amount of DNA by using a technique called gel electrophoresis. During gel electrophoresis, samples of DNA migrate through a jelly-like material (the gel) according to size. The smaller the amount of DNA, the farther it migrates (Fig. 19.19). It is customary to test for the number of repeats at several locations in order to further define the individual, comparing the individuals' profile with known frequency distributions for each portion.

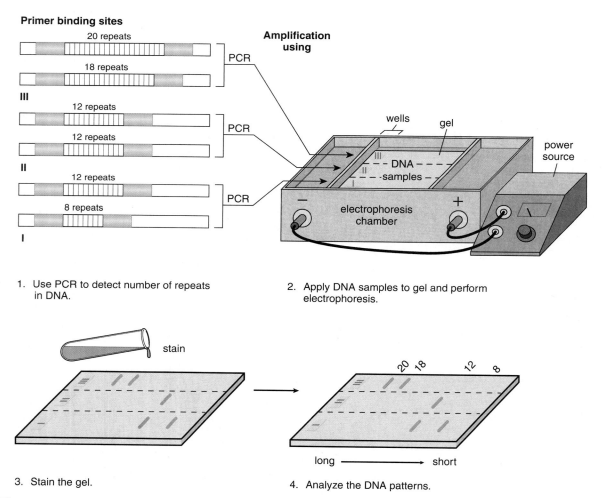

Figure 19.19   **Use of PCR to perform DNA fingerprinting.**

People differ by the number of base repeats in particular regions of DNA. Therefore, it is possible to use these regions to do DNA fingerprinting as in this example. Primers bind on either side of the repeat segment before amplification begins. Both strands of the DNA double helix are amplified because a person can be heterozygous for the number of repeats as in individual I and III. The amount of amplified DNA is detected by separating the samples of DNA by gel electrophoresis. The lower the number of repeats, the farther the DNA sample migrates along the gel.

Biotechnology

Biotechnology uses natural biological systems to create a product or to achieve an end desired by human beings. A relevant application of recombination DNA technology is to genetically engineer organisms to make biotechnology products (Fig. 19.20). Organisms that have had a foreign gene inserted into them are called **transgenic organisms.**

Transgenic Bacteria

Transgenic bacteria are grown in huge vats called bioreactors. The bacteria express the cloned gene, and the gene product is often collected from the medium the bacteria are grown in. Biotechnology products produced by bacteria, that are now on the market, include insulin, human growth hormone, t-PA (tissue plasminogen activator), and hepatitis B vaccine.

Transgenic bacteria have many other uses as well. Some have been produced to promote the health of plants. For example, bacteria that normally live on plants and encourage the formation of ice crystals have been changed from frost-plus to frost-minus bacteria. Also, a bacterium that normally colonizes the roots of corn plants has now been endowed with genes (from another bacterium) that code for an insect toxin. The toxin protects the roots from insects.

Bacteria can be selected for their ability to degrade a particular substance, and this ability can then be enhanced by genetic engineering. For instance, naturally occurring bacteria that eat oil can be genetically engineered to do an even better job of cleaning up beaches after oil spills (Fig. 19.21). Bacteria can also remove sulfur from coal before it is burned and help clean up toxic waste dumps. One such strain was given genes that allowed it to clean up levels of toxins that would have killed other strains. Further, these bacteria were given "suicide" genes that caused them to self-destruct when the job had been accomplished.

Organic chemicals are often synthesized by having catalysts act on precursor molecules or by using bacteria to carry out the synthesis. Today, it is possible to go one step further and manipulate the genes that code for these enzymes. For instance, biochemists discovered a strain of bacteria that is especially good at producing phenylalanine, an organic chemical needed to make aspartame, the dipeptide sweetener better known as NutraSweet. They isolated, altered, and cloned the appropriate genes so that various bacteria could be genetically engineered to produce phenylalanine.

Many major mining companies already use bacteria to obtain various metals. Genetic engineering can enhance the ability of bacteria to extract copper, uranium, and gold from low-grade sources. Some mining companies are testing genetically engineered organisms that have improved bioleaching capabilities.

Bacteria are being genetically altered to perform all sorts of tasks, not only in the factory, but also in the environment.

Figure 19.20   Biotechnology products.
Products such as clotting factor VIII, which is administered to hemophiliacs, can be made by transgenic bacteria, plants, or animals. After being processed and packaged, they are sold as commercial products.

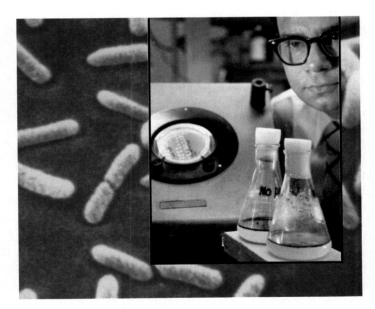

Figure 19.21   Bioremediation.
Bacteria capable of decomposing oil have been engineered and patented by the investigator Dr. Chakrabarty. In the inset, the flask toward the rear contains oil and no bacteria; the flask toward the front contains the bacteria and is almost clear of oil.

Transgenic Plants

Techniques have been developed to introduce foreign genes into immature plant embryos or into plant cells called protoplasts that have had the cell wall removed. It is possible to treat protoplasts with an electric current while they are suspended in a liquid containing foreign DNA. The electric current makes tiny, self-sealing holes in the plasma membrane through which genetic material can enter. Protoplasts go on to develop into mature plants containing and expressing the foreign DNA.

Foreign genes transferred to cotton, corn, and potato strains have made these plants resistant to pests because their cells now produce an insect toxin. Similarly, soybeans have been made resistant to a common herbicide. Some corn and cotton plants are both pest- and herbicide-resistant. These and other genetically engineered crops that are expected to have increased yields are now sold commercially. As discussed in the Health Focus on page 385, the public is concerned about the possible effect of genetically modified crops on their health and the environment.

The hope is that plants can one day be engineered to have leaves boost their intake of carbon dioxide or cut down on water loss or to increase the yield of grain crops. Already, it is possible to water tomato plants with salt water instead of fresh water, because they have been genetically modified to sequester the salt in their leaves.

Plants are also being engineered to produce human proteins, such as hormones, clotting factors, and antibodies, in their seeds. One type of antibody made by corn can deliver radioisotopes to tumor cells, and another made by soybeans can be used to treat genital herpes.

Transgenic Animals

Techniques have been developed to insert genes into the eggs of animals. It is possible to microinject foreign genes into eggs by hand, but another method uses vortex mixing. The eggs are placed in an agitator with DNA and silicon carbide needles. The needles make tiny holes in the eggs through which the DNA can enter. When these eggs are fertilized, the resulting offspring are transgenic animals. Using this technique, many types of animal eggs have acquired the gene for bovine growth hormone (bGH). The procedure has been used to produce larger fishes, cows, pigs, rabbits, and sheep.

Gene pharming, the use of transgenic farm animals to produce pharmaceuticals, is being pursued by a number of firms. Figure 19.22 outlines the procedure for producing transgenic mammals. DNA containing the gene of interest is injected into donor eggs. Following in vitro fertilization, the zygotes are placed in host females, where they develop. After female offspring mature, the product is secreted in their milk. Plans are under way to produce drugs for the treatment of cystic fibrosis, cancer, blood diseases, and other disorders by this method.

a.

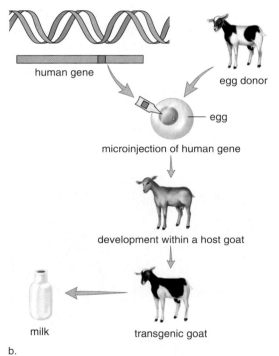
b.

Figure 19.22 **Transgenic animals.**
a. This goat is genetically engineered to produce antithrombin III, an anticoagulant, which is secreted in her milk. **b.** To produce this goat, a donor egg was microinjected with a human gene, and development occurred within a host goat. The host gave birth to the transgenic goat that produces the biotechnology product in her milk.

Plants are genetically engineered to improve yield, and animals are engineered to increase their size. Gene pharming, the use of transgenic animals to produce pharmaceuticals in milk, is now a reality.

Health Focus

Are Genetically Engineered Foods Safe?

A series of focus groups conducted by the Food and Drug Administration (FDA) in 2000 showed that although most participants believed that genetically engineered foods might offer benefits, they also feared unknown long-term health consequences that might be associated with the technology. In Canada, Conrad G. Brunk, a bioethicist at the University of Waterloo in Ontario, has said, "When it comes to human and environmental safety, there should be clear evidence of the absence of risks. The mere absence of evidence is not enough."

The discovery by activists that a genetically engineered corn called StarLink had inadvertently made it into the food supply triggered the recall of taco shells, tortillas, and many other corn-based foodstuffs from supermarkets. Further, the makers of StarLink were forced to buy back StarLink from farmers and to compensate food producers at an estimated cost of several hundred million dollars. StarLink is a type of "BT" corn. It contains a foreign gene taken from a common soil organism, *Bacillus thuringiensis*, whose insecticidal properties have been long known. About a dozen BT varieties, including corn, potato, and even a tomato, have now been approved for human consumption. These strains contain a gene for an insecticidal protein called CrylA. The makers of StarLink decided to use a gene for a related protein called Cry9C. They thought that using this molecule might slow down the chances of pest resistance to BT corn. In order to get FDA approval for use in foods, the makers of StarLink performed the required tests. Like the other now-approved strains, StarLink wasn't poisonous to rodents, and its biochemical structure is not similar to those of most food allergens. But the Cry9C protein resisted digestion longer than the other BT proteins when it was put in simulated stomach acid and subjected to heat. Because most food allergens are stable like this, StarLink was not approved for human consumption.

The scientific community is now trying to devise more tests for allergens because it has not been possible to determine conclusively whether Cry9C is or is not an allergen. Also, at this point, it is unclear how resistant to digestion a protein must be in order to be an allergen, and it is also unclear what degree of sequence similarity a potential allergen must have to a known allergen to raise concern. Dean D. Metcalfe, chief of the Laboratory of Allergic Diseases at the National Institute of Allergy and Infectious Diseases, said, "We need to understand thresholds for sensitization to food allergens and thresholds for elicitation of a reaction with food allergens."

Other scientists are concerned about the following potential drawbacks to the planting of BT corn: (1) resistance among populations of the target pest, (2) exchange of genetic material between the transgenic crop and related plant species, and (3) BT crops' impact on nontarget species. They feel that many more studies are needed before it can be said for certain that BT corn has no ecological drawbacks.

Despite controversies, the planting of genetically engineered corn increased in 2001. The USDA reports that U.S. farmers planted genetically engineered corn on 26% of all corn acres, 1% more than in 2000. In all, U.S. farmers planted at least 72 million acres with mostly genetically engineered corn, soybeans, and cotton (Fig. 19A). The public wants all genetically engineered foods to be labeled as such, but this may not be easy to accomplish because, for example, most cornmeal is derived from both conventional and genetically engineered corn. So far, there has been no attempt to sort out one type of food product from the other.

a.

c.

b.

Figure 19A Genetically engineered crops.
Genetically engineered (**a**) corn, (**b**) soybeans, and (**c**) cotton crops are increasingly being planted by today's farmers.

Bioethical Focus

DNA Fingerprinting and the Criminal Justice System

Traditional fingerprinting has been used for years to identify criminals and to exonerate those wrongly accused of crimes. The opportunity now arises to use DNA fingerprinting in the same way. DNA fingerprinting requires only a small DNA sample. This sample can come from blood left at the scene of the crime, semen from a rape case, even a single hair root!

The DNA is amplified, cut with restriction enzymes, and separated by gel electrophoresis to produce a unique DNA fragment pattern. The same procedure is done several times with different restriction enzymes, making it nearly impossible that anyone else in the world would have the same set of patterns. Advocates of DNA fingerprinting claim that identification is "beyond a reasonable doubt."

Opponents of this technology, however, point out that it is not without its problems. Police or laboratory negligence can invalidate the evidence. For example, during the O. J. Simpson trial, the defense claimed that the DNA evidence was inadmissible because it could not be proven that the police had not "planted" O. J.'s blood at the crime scene. There have also been reported problems with sloppy laboratory procedures and the credibility of forensic experts.

In addition to identifying criminals, DNA fingerprinting can be used to establish paternity and maternity, determine nationality for immigration purposes, and identify victims of a national disaster, such as the terrorist attacks of September 11, 2001.

Considering the usefulness of DNA fingerprints, perhaps everyone should be required to contribute blood to create a national DNA fingerprint databank. Some say, however, this would constitute an unreasonable search, which is unconstitutional.

Decide Your Opinion

1. Would you be willing to provide your DNA for a national DNA databank? Why or why not? What types of privacy restrictions would you want on your DNA?
2. If not everyone, do you think that convicted felons, at least, should be required to provide DNA for a databank?
3. Should all defendants have access to DNA fingerprinting (at government expense) to prove they didn't do a crime? Should this include those already convicted of crimes who want to reopen their cases using new DNA evidence?

Summarizing the Concepts

19.1 DNA and RNA Structure and Function

DNA is a double helix composed of two nucleic acid strands that are held together by weak hydrogen bonds between the bases: A is bonded to T, and C is bonded to G. During replication, the DNA strands unzip, and then a new complementary strand forms opposite each old strand. This results in two identical DNA molecules.

RNA is a single-stranded nucleic acid in which U (uracil) occurs instead of T (thymine). The three forms of RNA—rRNA, mRNA, and tRNA—are active during protein synthesis.

19.2 Gene Expression

Proteins differ from one another by the sequence of their amino acids. DNA has a code that specifies this sequence. Gene expression requires transcription and translation. During transcription, the DNA code (triplet of three bases) is passed to an mRNA that then contains codons. Introns are removed from mRNA during mRNA processing. During translation, tRNA molecules bind to their amino acids, and then their anticodons pair with mRNA codons. In the end, each protein has a sequence of amino acids according to the blueprint provided by the sequence of nucleotides in DNA.

Control of gene expression can occur at four levels in a human cell: at the time of transcription; after transcription and during mRNA processing; during translation; and after translation—before, at, or after protein synthesis. It is known that chromatin has to be decondensed for transcription to occur and that transcription activators control the activity of genes in human cells.

19.3 Genomics

Now that we know the sequence of all our DNA, progress is proceeding on other fronts. In particular, investigators want to discover the abnormal sequences that lead to human illnesses and develop drugs to combat these illnesses. The latter requires proteomics—knowledge of the structure and function of proteins in the cell. Also important is bioinformatics, the computerized assemblage of new-found genetic information.

19.4 DNA Technology

It is possible to clone a gene by utilizing recombinant DNA technology or the polymerase chain reaction (PCR). Recombinant DNA contains DNA from two different sources. The foreign gene and vector DNA are cut by the same restriction enzyme and, then, the foreign gene is sealed into vector DNA. Bacteria will take up recombinant plasmids.

PCR uses the enzyme DNA polymerase to quickly make multiple copies of a specific piece (target) of DNA. Following PCR, it is possible to carry out DNA fingerprinting.

Biotechnology uses natural biological systems to create a product or to achieve an end desired by human beings. Transgenic organisms have had a foreign gene inserted into them. Genetically engineered bacteria, agricultural plants, and farm animals now produce commercial products of interest to humans, such as hormones and vaccines. Bacteria secrete the product. The seeds of plants and the milk of animals contain the product.

Transgenic bacteria have been produced to promote the health of plants, perform bioremediation, extract minerals, and produce chemicals. Transgenic crops that have been engineered to resist herbicides and pests are commercially available. Transgenic animals have been given various genes, in particular the one for bovine growth hormone (bGH). Cloning of transgenic animals is now being done.

Studying the Concepts

1. Describe the structure of DNA and how this structure contributes to the ease of DNA replication. 368–69
2. Describe the structure of RNA, and compare it with the structure of DNA. 370
3. Name and discuss the roles of three different types of RNA. 370
4. Describe the structure and function of a protein and the manner in which DNA codes for a particular protein. 371–72
5. Describe the process of transcription and the three steps of translation. If the code is TTT, CAT, TGG, CCG, what are the codons, and what is the sequence of amino acids? 372–75
6. What are the four levels of genetic control in human cells? Describe two means by which transcription is regulated. 377
7. What developments have occurred since the human genome was sequenced? 378–79
8. What is the methodology for producing recombinant DNA to be used in gene cloning? 380–81
9. What is the polymerase chain reaction (PCR), and how is it carried out to produce multiple copies of a DNA segment? 381
10. What is the purpose of and how is DNA fingerprinting carried out? 382
11. For what purposes have bacteria, plants, and animals been genetically altered? 383–84

Thinking Critically About the Concepts

Refer to the opening vignette on page 367, and then answer the following.

1. Why can DNA fingerprints be used to tell who is related to whom?
2. What causes one person's DNA fingerprint to be different from another's?
3. Assuming a reputable laboratory is doing the testing, why would DNA fingerprinting be better evidence of guilt than eyewitness identification?

Testing Your Knowledge of the Concepts

Choose the best answer for each question.

1. The double-helix model of DNA resembles a twisted ladder in which the rungs of the ladder are
   a. complementary base pairs.
   b. A paired with G and C paired with T.
   c. A paired with T and G paired with C.
   d. a sugar-phosphate paired with a sugar-phosphate.
   e. Both a and c are correct.
2. In a DNA molecule, the
   a. backbone is sugar and phosphate molecules.
   b. bases are bonded to the sugars.
   c. sugars are bonded to the phosphates.
   d. bases are hydrogen-bonded to one another.
   e. All of these are correct.

3. The enzyme responsible for adding new nucleotides to a growing DNA chain during DNA replication is
   a. helicase.
   b. RNA polymerase.
   c. DNA polymerase.
   d. ribozymes.
4. RNA processing
   a. takes place in the cytoplasm.
   b. is the same as transcription.
   c. is an event that occurs after RNA is transcribed.
   d. is the rejection of old, worn-out RNA.
   e. Both a and c are correct.
5. During protein synthesis, an anticodon of a tRNA pairs with
   a. amino acids in the polypeptide.
   b. DNA nucleotide bases.
   c. rRNA nucleotide bases.
   d. mRNA nucleotide bases.
   e. other tRNA nucleotide bases.
6. Which of these associations does not correctly compare DNA and RNA?

DNA	RNA
a. Contains the base thymine.	Contains the base uracil.
b. Is double-stranded.	Is also double-stranded.
c. Is a helix.	Is not a helix.
d. The sugar is deoxyribose.	The sugar is ribose.

7. The process of converting the information contained in the nucleotide sequence of RNA into a sequence of amino acids is called
   a. transcription.
   b. translation.
   c. translocation.
   d. replication.
8. Which of the following is involved in controlling gene expression?
   a. the occurrence of transcription
   b. activity of the polypeptide product
   c. life expectancy of the mRNA molecule in the cell
   d. All of these are involved.
9. Complementary base pairing
   a. involves T, A, G, C.
   b. is necessary to replication.
   c. utilizes hydrogen bonds.
   d. occurs when ribose binds with deoxyribose.
   e. All but d are correct.
10. Which one or more of the following does not characterize the process of transcription?
    a. RNA is made off of one strand of the DNA.
    b. In making RNA, the base uracil of RNA pairs with the base adenine of DNA.
    c. The enzyme RNA polymerase synthesizes RNA.
    d. RNA is made in the cytoplasm.
11. Translation can be defined as
    a. the making of protein using mRNA and tRNA.
    b. the making of RNA from a DNA template.
    c. the gathering of amino acids by tRNA molecules in the cytoplasm.
    d. the removal of introns from mRNA.

12. Using the following key, put the phrases in the correct order to form a plasmid-carrying recombinant DNA.

Key:

(1) Use restriction enzymes.
(2) Use DNA ligase.
(3) Remove plasmid from parent bacterium.
(4) Introduce plasmid into new host bacterium.
    a. 1, 2, 3, 4
    b. 4, 3, 2, 1
    c. 3, 1, 2, 4
    d. 2, 3, 1, 4

13. Which of the following is not a clone?
    a. colony of identical bacterial cells
    b. identical quintuplets
    c. a forest of identical trees
    d. eggs produced by oogenesis
    e. copies of a gene through PCR

14. PCR
    a. utilizes RNA polymerase.
    b. takes place in huge bioreactors.
    c. utilizes a temperature-insensitive enzyme.
    d. makes lots of nonidentical copies of DNA.
    e. All of these are correct.

15. DNA fingerprinting can be used for which of the following?
    a. identifying human remains
    b. identifying infectious diseases
    c. finding evolutionary links between organisms
    d. solving crimes
    e. All of these are correct.

16. Following is a segment of a DNA molecule. (Remember that only one strand is transcribed.) What are (a) the RNA codons and (b) the tRNA anticodons?

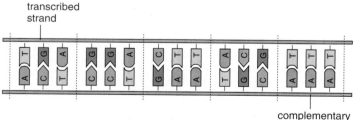

transcribed strand

complementary strand

17. Restriction enzymes found in bacterial cells are ordinarily used
    a. during DNA replication.
    b. to degrade the bacterial cell's DNA.
    c. to degrade viral DNA that enters the cell.
    d. to attach pieces of DNA together.

18. Which of the following is a benefit to having insulin produced by biotechnology?
    a. It is just as effective.
    b. It can be mass-produced.
    c. It is nonallergenic.
    d. It is less expensive.
    e. All of these are correct.

Understanding Key Terms

anticodon 374
bioinformatics 379
biotechnology 383
cloning 380
codon 372
complementary base
    pairing 368
DNA (deoxyribonucleic
    acid) 368
DNA ligase 380
DNA replication 369
double helix 368
gene cloning 380
genetic engineering 380
genomics 378
messenger RNA (mRNA) 370
mutation 369
plasmid 380

polymerase chain reaction
    (PCR) 381
polyribosome 374
proteomics 379
recombinant DNA (rDNA) 380
restriction enzyme 380
ribosomal RNA (rRNA) 370
RNA (ribonucleic acid) 370
RNA polymerase 373
template 369
transcription 372
transcription activator 377
transfer RNA (tRNA) 370
transgenic organism 383
translation 372
triplet code 372
uracil (U) 370
vector 380

Match the key terms to these definitions.

a. _____ Cluster of ribosomes attached to the same mRNA molecule; each ribosome is producing a copy of the same polypeptide.

b. _____ Free-living organism in the environment that has had a foreign gene inserted into it.

c. _____ Pattern or guide used to make copies.

d. _____ Process resulting in the production of a strand of RNA that is complementary to a segment of DNA.

e. _____ A means to transfer foreign genetic material into a cell.

Online Learning Center

www.mhhe.com/maderhuman9

The Online Learning Center provides a wealth of information fully organized and integrated by chapter. You will find practice quizzes, interactive activities, labeling exercises, flashcards, and much more that will complement your learning and understanding of human biology.

Looking at Both Sides

Each day, the Internet, media, and other people present you with opposing viewpoints on a wide range of subjects. Your ability to develop an informed opinion on an issue, and talk to others about it, is extremely important.

To expand and enhance your knowledge of a highly relevant bioethical issue, visit the "Student Edition" of the Online Learning Center. Under "Course-Wide Content," select "Looking at Both Sides." Once there, you will be asked to complete activities that will increase your understanding of a current bioethical issue related to this chapter and allow you to defend your opinion.

CHAPTER 20

Genetic Counseling

C H A P T E R   C O N C E P T S

20.1 Counseling for Chromosomal Disorders
- What do you call a visual display of an individual's chromosomes arranged by pairs? 390–91
- How is it possible to acquire chromosomes from an adult for study? To acquire fetal chromosomes? 390–91
- What process usually causes an individual to have an abnormal number of chromosomes? 392
- What is the specific chromosome abnormality of a person with Down syndrome? 393
- What are some syndromes that result from inheritance of an abnormal sex chromosome number? 394–95
- What are other types of chromosome mutations, aside from abnormal chromosome number? 396–97

20.2 Counseling for Genetic Disorders: The Present
- What is a pedigree, and how do you use it to recognize an autosomal recessive/dominant disorder and an X-linked recessive disorder? 398–99
- What are the symptoms of the genetic disorders discussed in this chapter? 400–402
- Presently, how is it possible to test for genetic disorders? How is it possible to test the fetus, the embryo, or the egg? 403–5

20.3 Counseling for Genetic Disorders: The Future
- How will a genetic profile be acquired, and how will genetic profiles be used? 406
- What is gene therapy, and how is it carried out? 408

Chris Burke was born with three copies of chromosome 21. He has Down syndrome. His parents were advised to put him in an institution.

The abnormalities associated with Down syndrome are numerous and diverse: All body parts tend to be short, the face is usually broad and flat, the nose is typically small, the eyes slant, and the eyelids have a fold. The tongue is large and furrowed. Malformations of the heart, digestive tract, kidneys, thyroid gland, and adrenal glands commonly occur. And intelligence is usually below normal. But Chris's parents persevered, and they gave Chris the same loving care and attention they gave their other children, and it paid off. Chris is remarkably talented. He is a playwright, actor, and musician. He starred in *Life Goes On*, a TV series written just for him, and he is frequently asked to be a guest star in a number of TV shows. His love of music and collaboration with other musicians has led to the release of several albums—like Chris, the songs are uplifting and inspirational. Chris is pictured above. You can read more about this remarkable young man in his autobiography, *A Special Kind of Hero*.

20.1 Counseling for Chromosomal Disorders

Now that potential parents are becoming aware that many illnesses are caused by abnormal chromosomal inheritance or by faulty genes, more couples are seeking **genetic counseling** as a means to determine the risk of a chromosomal mutation or genetic mutation in the family. For example, they might be prompted to seek counseling after several miscarriages, if several relatives have a particular medical condition, or if they already have a child with a genetic defect. The counselor will help the couple understand the mode of inheritance and the medical consequences of a particular genetic disorder, as well as making them aware of the possible decisions they might wish to make.

Various human disorders result from abnormal chromosome number or structure. Such disorders often result in a **syndrome,** which is a group of symptoms that always occur together. Table 20.1 lists several syndromes that are due to an abnormal chromosome number. If the woman is pregnant and there is concern that the unborn child might have a chromosomal defect, the counselor might recommend karyotyping the fetus's chromosomes.

Karyotyping

A **karyotype** is a visual display of the chromosomes arranged by size, shape, and banding pattern. Any cell in the body, except red blood cells, which lack a nucleus, can be a source of chromosomes for karyotyping. In adults, it is easiest to use white blood cells separated from a blood sample for this purpose. In fetuses, whose chromosomes are often examined in order to be forewarned of a syndrome, cells can be obtained by either amniocentesis or chorionic villi sampling.

Amniocentesis is a procedure for obtaining a sample of amniotic fluid from the uterus of a pregnant woman. Blood tests and age of the mother are used to determine when the procedure should be done. The risk of spontaneous abortion increases by about 0.3% due to amniocen-

tesis, and doctors use the procedure only if it is medically warranted.

Amniocentesis is not usually performed until about the 14th–17th week of pregnancy. A long needle is passed through the abdominal and uterine walls to withdraw a small amount of amniotic fluid, which also contains fetal cells (Fig. 20.1a). Tests are done on the amniotic fluid. Karyotyping the chromosomes may be delayed as long as four weeks so that the cells can be cultured to increase their number.

Chorionic villi sampling (CVS) is a procedure for obtaining chorionic cells in the region where the placenta has developed. This procedure can be done as early as the fifth week of pregnancy. A long, thin suction tube is inserted through the vagina into the uterus (Fig. 20.1b). Ultrasound, which gives a picture of the uterine contents, is used to place the tube between the uterine lining and the chorionic villi. Then a sampling of chorionic cells is obtained by suction. The cells do not have to be cultured, and karyotyping can be done immediately. But testing amniotic fluid is not possible because no amniotic fluid is collected. Also, CVS carries a greater risk of spontaneous abortion than amniocentesis—0.8% compared with 0.3%. The advantage of CVS is getting the results of karyotyping at an earlier date.

The Karyotype

After a cell sample has been obtained, the cells are stimulated to divide in a culture medium. A chemical is used to stop mitosis during metaphase when chromosomes are the most highly compacted and condensed. The cells are then killed, spread on a microscope slide, and dried. Stains are applied to the slides, and the cells are photographed. Staining causes the chromosomes to have dark and light cross-bands of varying widths, and these can be used, in addition to size and shape, to help pair up the chromosomes. Today, a computer is used to arrange the chromosomes in pairs (Fig. 20.1c). The karyotype of a person who has Down syndrome usually has three number 21 chromosomes, instead of the usual two number 21 chromosomes (Fig. 20.1d,e).

Table 20.1	Syndromes from Abnormal Chromosome Numbers				
Syndrome	**Sex**	**Disorder**	**Chromosome Number**	**Frequency**	
				Spontaneous Abortions	*Live Births*
Down	M or F	Trisomy 21	47	1/40	1/800
Poly-X	F	XXX (or XXXX)	47 or 48	0	1/1,500
Klinefelter	M	XXY (or XXXY)	47 or 48	1/300	1/800
Jacobs	M	XYY	47	?	1/1,000
Turner	F	X	45	1/18	1/2,500

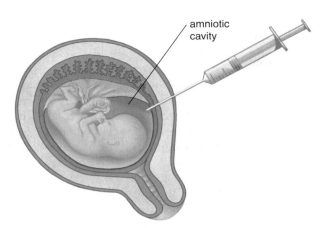

amniotic
cavity

a. During amniocentesis, a long needle
   is used to withdraw amniotic fluid
   containing fetal cells.

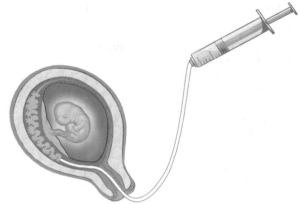

b. During chorionic villi sampling, a suction tube
   is used to remove cells from the chorion,
   where the placenta developed.

c. Cells are microscopically examined
   and photographed. Computer arranges
   the chromosomes into pairs.

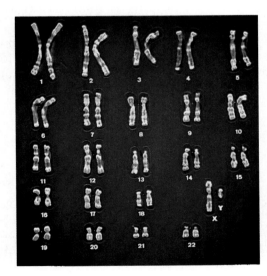

d. Normal male karyotype
   with 46 chromosomes

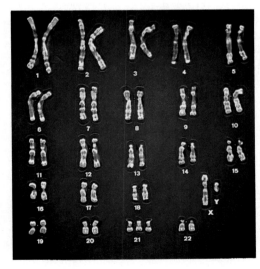

e. Down syndrome karyotype
   with an extra chromosome 21

Figure 20.1   **Human karyotype preparation.**
A karyotype is an arrangement of an individual's chromosomes into numbered pairs according to their size, shape, and banding pattern.
a. Amniocentesis and (**b**) chorionic villi sampling provide cells for karyotyping to determine if the unborn child has a chromosomal abnormality.
c. After cells are treated as described in the text, a computer constructs the karyotype. **d.** Karyotype of a normal male. **e.** Karyotype of a male with Down syndrome. A Down syndrome karyotype has three number 21 chromosomes.

Changes in Chromosome Number

Normally, an individual receives 22 pairs of autosomes and two sex chromosomes. Sometimes individuals are born with either too many or too few autosomes or sex chromosomes, most likely due to nondisjunction during meiosis. **Nondisjunction** occurs during meiosis I, when both members of a homologous pair go into the same daughter cell, or during meiosis II, when the sister chromatids fail to separate and both daughter chromosomes go into the same gamete. Figure 20.2 assumes that nondisjunction has occurred during oogenesis; some abnormal eggs have 24 chromosomes, while others have only 22 chromosomes. If an egg with 24 chromosomes is fertilized with a normal sperm, the result is a **trisomy,** so called because one type of chromosome is present in three copies. If an egg with 22 chromosomes is fertilized with a normal sperm, the result is a **monosomy,** so called because one type of chromosome is present in a single copy.

Normal development depends on the presence of exactly two of each kind of chromosome. Too many chromosomes is tolerated better than a deficiency of chromosomes, and several trisomies are known to occur in humans. Among autosomal trisomies, only trisomy 21 (Down syndrome) has a reasonable chance of survival after birth. This

is probably due to the fact that chromosome 21 is the smallest of the chromosomes.

The chances of survival are greater when trisomy or monosomy involves the sex chromosomes. In normal XX females, one of the X chromosomes becomes a darkly staining mass of chromatin called a **Barr body** (after the person who discovered it). A Barr body is an inactive X chromosome; therefore, we now know that the cells of females function with a single X chromosome just as those of males do. This is most likely the reason why a zygote with one X chromosome (Turner syndrome) can survive. Then too, all extra X chromosomes beyond a single one become Barr bodies, and this explains why poly-X females and XXY males are seen fairly frequently. An extra Y chromosome, called Jacobs syndrome, is tolerated in humans, most likely because the Y chromosome carries few genes. Jacobs syndrome (XYY) is due to nondisjunction during meiosis II of spermatogenesis. We know this because two Ys are present only during meiosis II in males.

Nondisjunction changes the chromosome number in gametes. Offspring sometimes inherit an extra chromosome (trisomy) or are missing a chromosome (monosomy).

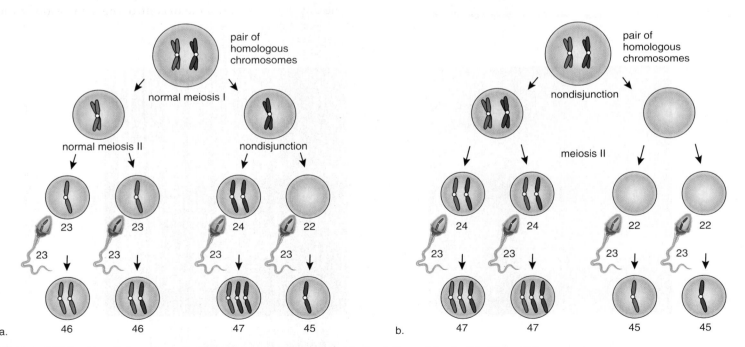

Figure 20.2   Nondisjunction of chromosomes during oogenesis, followed by fertilization with normal sperm.
a. Nondisjunction can occur during meiosis II if the sister chromatids separate, but the resulting chromosomes go into the same daughter cell. Then the egg will have one more (24) or one less (22) than the usual number of chromosomes. Fertilization of these abnormal eggs with normal sperm produces an abnormal zygote with 47 or 45 chromosomes. **b.** Nondisjunction can also occur during meiosis I and result in abnormal eggs that also have one more or one less than the normal number of chromosomes. Fertilization of these abnormal eggs with normal sperm results in a zygote with an abnormal chromosome number and the syndromes listed in Table 20.1.

Down Syndrome

The most common autosomal trisomy seen among humans is Down syndrome, also called trisomy 21 (Fig. 20.3). This syndrome is easily recognized by these characteristics: short stature; an eyelid fold; a flat face; stubby fingers; a wide gap between the first and second toes; a large, fissured tongue; a round head; a palm crease, the so-called simian line; and, unfortunately, mental retardation, which can sometimes be severe.

Persons with Down syndrome usually have three copies of chromosome 21 because the egg had two copies instead of one. (In 23% of the cases studied, however, the sperm had the extra chromosome 21.) The chances of a woman having a Down syndrome child increase rapidly with age, starting at about age 40, and the reasons for this are still being determined.

Although an older woman is more likely to have a Down syndrome child, most babies with Down syndrome are born to women younger than age 40 because this is the age group having the most babies. Karyotyping can detect a Down syndrome child. However, young women are not routinely encouraged to undergo the procedures necessary to get a sample of fetal cells (i.e., amniocentesis or chorionic villi sampling) because the risk of complications is greater than the risk of having a Down syndrome child. Fortunately, a test based on substances in maternal blood can help identify fetuses who may need to be karyotyped.

The genes that cause Down syndrome are located on the bottom third of chromosome 21 (Fig. 20.3b), and extensive investigative work has been directed toward discovering the specific genes responsible for the characteristics of the syndrome. Thus far, investigators have discovered several genes that may account for various conditions seen in persons with Down syndrome. For example, they have located genes most likely responsible for the increased tendency toward leukemia, cataracts, accelerated rate of aging, and mental retardation. The gene for mental retardation, dubbed the *Gart* gene, causes an increased level of purines in the blood, a finding associated with mental retardation. One day, it may be possible to control the expression of the *Gart* gene even before birth so that at least this symptom of Down syndrome does not appear.

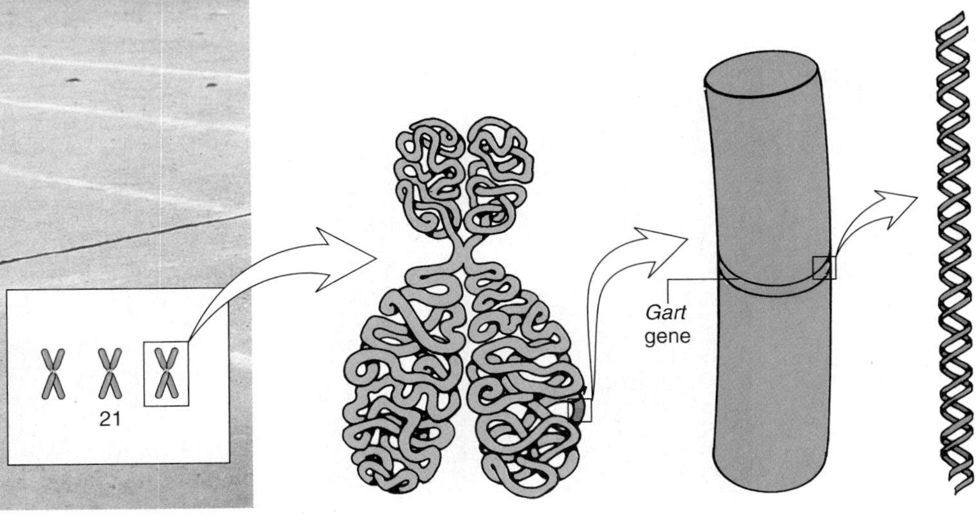

Figure 20.3 **Abnormal autosomal chromosome number.**
Persons with Down syndrome have an extra chromosome 21. **a.** Common characteristics of the syndrome include a wide, rounded face and a fold on the upper eyelids. Mental retardation, along with an enlarged tongue, makes it difficult for a person with Down syndrome to speak distinctly. **b.** Karyotype of an individual with Down syndrome shows an extra chromosome 21. More sophisticated technologies allow investigators to pinpoint the location of specific genes associated with the syndrome. An extra copy of the *Gart* gene, which leads to a high level of purines in the blood, may account for the mental retardation seen in persons with Down syndrome.

Changes in Sex Chromosome Number

An abnormal sex chromosome number is the result of inheriting too many or too few X or Y chromosomes. Figure 20.2 can be used to illustrate nondisjunction of the sex chromosomes during oogenesis, if you assume that the chromosomes shown represent X chromosomes. Nondisjunction during oogenesis or spermatogenesis can result in gametes that have too few or too many X or Y chromosomes. After fertilization, the syndromes listed in Table 20.1 (other than Down syndrome, which is autosomal) are possibilities.

A person with Turner syndrome (XO) is a female, and a person with Klinefelter syndrome (XXY) is a male. This shows that in humans, the presence of a Y chromosome, not the number of X chromosomes, determines maleness. The *SRY* (*sex-determining region of Y*) gene, on the short arm of the Y chromosome, produces a hormone called testis-determining factor, which plays a critical role in the development of male genitals.

Turner Syndrome   From birth, an individual with Turner syndrome has only one sex chromosome, an X (Fig. 20.4*a*). As adults, Turner females are short, with a broad chest and folds of skin on the back of the neck. The ovaries, oviducts, and uterus are very small and underdeveloped. Turner females do not undergo puberty or menstruate, and their breasts do not develop. However, some have given birth following in vitro fertilization using donor eggs. They usually are of normal intelligence and can lead fairly normal lives if they receive hormone supplements.

Klinefelter Syndrome   A male with Klinefelter syndrome has two or more X chromosomes, in addition to a Y chromosome (Fig. 20.4*b*). Counting the number of Barr bodies can tell the number of extra X chromosomes. As adults, the person has underdeveloped testes and prostate gland and no facial hair. But there may be some breast development. Affected individuals have large hands and feet and very long arms and legs. They are usually slow to learn but not mentally retarded unless they inherit more than two X chromosomes. No matter how many X chromosomes there are, an individual with a Y chromosome is usually a male (see pages 320–321).

The Health Focus on the next page tells of the experiences of a person with Klinefelter syndrome who suggests that it is best for parents to know right away that they have a child with this disorder because much can be done to help the child lead a normal life.

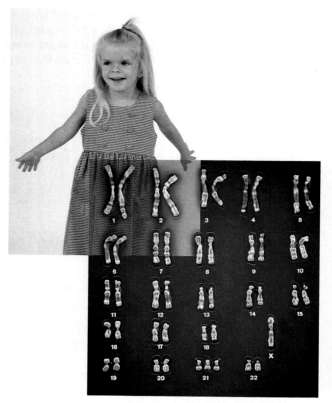

a. Turner syndrome

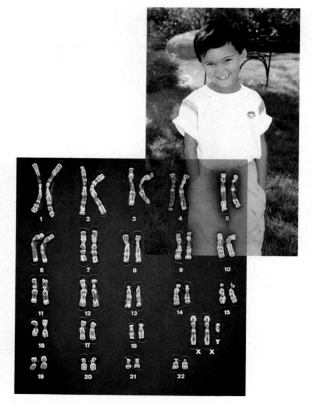

b. Klinefelter syndrome

Figure 20.4   **Abnormal sex chromosome number.**
People with (**a**) Turner syndrome, who have only one sex chromosome, an X, as shown, and (**b**) Klinefelter syndrome, who have more than one X chromosome plus a Y chromosome, as shown, can look relatively normal (especially as children) and can lead relatively normal lives.

Poly-X Females A poly-X female has more than two X chromosomes and extra Barr bodies in the nucleus. Females with three X chromosomes have no distinctive phenotype, aside from a tendency to be tall and thin. Although some have delayed motor and language development, most poly-X females are not mentally retarded. Some may have menstrual difficulties, but many menstruate regularly and are fertile. Their children usually have a normal karyotype.

Females with more than three X chromosomes occur rarely. Unlike XXX females, XXXX females are usually severely retarded. Various physical abnormalities are seen but they may menstruate normally.

Jacobs Syndrome XYY males with Jacobs syndrome can only result from nondisjunction during spermatogenesis. Affected males are usually taller than average, suffer from persistent acne, and tend to have speech and reading problems. At one time, it was suggested that these men were likely to be criminally aggressive, but it has since been shown that the incidence of such behavior among them may be no greater than among XY males.

Several syndromes are due to an abnormal number of sex chromosomes (see also Table 20.1).

Health Focus

Living with Klinefelter Syndrome

In 1996, at the age of 25, I was diagnosed with Klinefelter syndrome (KS). Being diagnosed has changed my life for the better.

I was a happy baby, but when I was still very young, my parents began to believe that there was something wrong with me. I knew something was different about me, too, as early on as five years old. I was very shy and had trouble making friends. One minute I'd be well behaved, and the next I'd be picking fights and flying into a rage. Many psychologists, therapists, and doctors tested me because of school and social problems and severe mood changes. Their only diagnosis was "learning disabilities" in such areas as reading comprehension, abstract thinking, word retrieval, and auditory processing. No one could figure out what the real problem was, and I hated the tutoring sessions I had. In the seventh grade, a psychologist told me that I was stupid and lazy, I would probably live at home for the rest of my life, and I would never amount to anything. For the next five years, he was basically right, and I barely graduated from high school.

I believe, though, that I have succeeded because I was told that I would fail. I quit the tutoring sessions when I enrolled at a community college; I decided I could figure things out on my own. I received an associate degree there, then transferred to a small liberal arts college. I never told anyone about my learning disabilities and never sought special help. However, I never had a semester below a 3.0, and I graduated with two B.S. degrees. I was accepted into a graduate program but decided instead to accept a job as a software engineer even though I did not have an educational background in this field. As I later learned, many KS'ers excel in computer skills. I had been using a computer for many years and had learned everything I needed to know on my own, through trial and error.

Around the time I started the computer job, I went to my physician for a physical. He sent me for blood tests because he noticed that my testes were smaller than usual. The results were conclusive: Klinefelter syndrome with sex chromosomes XXY. I initially felt denial, depression, and anger, even though I now had an explanation for many of the problems I had experienced all my life. But then I decided to learn as much as I could about the condition and treatments available. I now give myself a testosterone injection once every two weeks, and it has made me a different person, with improved learning abilities and stronger thought processes in addition to a more outgoing personality.

I found, though, that the best possible path I could take was to help others live with the condition. I attended my first support group meeting four months after I was diagnosed. By spring 1997, I had developed an interest in KS that was more than just a part-time hobby. I wanted to be able to work with this condition and help people forever. I have been very involved in KS conferences and have helped to start support groups in the U.S., Spain, and Australia.

Since my diagnosis, it has been my dream to have a son with KS, although when I was diagnosed, I found out it was unlikely that I could have biological children. Through my work with KS, I had the opportunity to meet my fiancee Chris. She has two wonderful children: a daughter, and a son who has the same condition that I do. There are a lot of similarities between my stepson and me, and I am happy I will be able to help him get the head start in coping with KS that I never had. I also look forward to many more years of helping other people seek diagnosis and live a good life with Klinefelter syndrome.

Stefan Schwarz
stefan13@mail.ptd.net

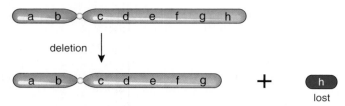

deletion

a.

b.

Figure 20.5   Deletion.

a. When chromosome 7 loses an end piece, the result is Williams syndrome. **b.** These children, although unrelated, have the same appearance, health, and behavioral problems.

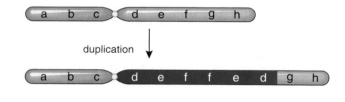

duplication

a.

b.

Figure 20.6   Duplication.

a. When a piece of chromosome 15 is duplicated and inverted, (**b**) a syndrome results in which the child has poor muscle tone and autistic characteristics.

Changes in Chromosomal Structure

A mutation is a permanent genetic change. A change in chromosomal structure that can be detected microscopically is a **chromosomal mutation.** A skilled technician is able to detect differences in chromosomal structure based on a change in the normal banding patterns (see Fig. 20.1*d,e*).

Chromosomal mutations occur when chromosomes suffer breaks. Various environmental agents—radiation, certain organic chemicals, or even viruses—can cause chromosomes to break apart. Ordinarily, when breaks occur in chromosomes, the segments reunite to give the same sequence of genes. But their failure to reunite correctly can result in one of several types of mutations: deletion, duplication, translocation, or inversion. Chromosomal mutations can occur during meiosis, and if the offspring inherits the abnormal chromosome, a syndrome may very well develop.

Deletions and Duplications

A **deletion** occurs when a single break causes a chromosome to lose an end piece or when two simultaneous breaks lead to the loss of an internal chromosomal segment. An individual who inherits a normal chromosome from one parent and a chromosome with a deletion from the other parent no longer has a pair of alleles for each trait, and a syndrome can result.

Williams syndrome occurs when chromosome 7 loses a tiny end piece (Fig. 20.5). Children who have this syndrome look like pixies because they have turned-up noses, wide mouths, a small chin, and large ears. Although their academic skills are poor, they exhibit excellent verbal and musical abilities. The gene that governs the production of the protein elastin is missing, and this affects the health of the cardiovascular system and causes their skin to age prematurely. Such individuals are very friendly but need an ordered life, perhaps because of the loss of a gene for a protein that is normally active in the brain.

Cri du chat (cat's cry) syndrome is seen when chromosome 5 is missing an end piece. The affected individual has a small head, is mentally retarded, and has facial abnormalities. Abnormal development of the glottis and larynx results in the most characteristic symptom—the infant's cry resembles that of a cat.

In a **duplication,** a chromosomal segment is repeated in the same chromosome or in a nonhomologous chromosome. In any case, the individual has more than two alleles for certain traits. An inverted duplication is known to occur in chromosome 15. **Inversion** means that a segment joins in the direction opposite from normal. Children with this syndrome, called inv dup 15 syndrome, have poor muscle tone, mental retardation, seizures, a curved spine, and autistic characteristics, including poor speech, hand flapping, and lack of eye contact (Fig. 20.6).

Translocation A **translocation** is the exchange of chromosomal segments between two nonhomologous chromosomes. A person who has both of the involved chromosomes has the normal amount of genetic material and is healthy, unless the chromosome exchange breaks an allele into two pieces. The person who inherits only one of the translocated chromosomes will no doubt have only one copy of certain alleles and three copies of certain other alleles. A genetic counselor begins to suspect a translocation has occurred when spontaneous abortions are commonplace and family members suffer from various syndromes. A special microscopic technique allows a technician to determine that a translocation has occurred.

In 5% of cases, a translocation that occurred in a previous generation between chromosomes 21 and 14 is the cause of Down syndrome. The affected person inherits two normal chromosomes 21 and an abnormal chromosome 14 that contains a segment of chromosome 21. In these cases, Down syndrome is not related to the age of the mother, but instead tends to run in the family of either the father or the mother.

Figure 20.7 shows a father and son who have a translocation between chromosomes 2 and 20. Although they have the normal amount of genetic material, they have the distinctive face, abnormalities of the eyes and internal organs, and severe itching characteristic of Alagille syndrome. People with this syndrome ordinarily have a deletion on chromosome 20; therefore, it can be deduced that the translocation disrupted an allele on chromosome 20 in the father. The symptoms of Alagille syndrome range from mild to severe, so some people may not be aware they have the syndrome. This father did not realize it until he had a child with the syndrome.

Inversion

An inversion occurs when a segment of a chromosome is turned 180 degrees so the alleles are in the opposite order. In other words, as is the case in Figure 20.8, ABCDEFG could become ABEDCDFG. You might think this is not a problem because the same genes are present, but the reverse sequence of alleles can lead to altered gene activity.

Crossing-over between an inverted chromosome and the noninverted homologue can lead to recombinant chromosomes that have both duplicated and deleted segments. This happens because alignment between the two homologues is only possible when the inverted chromosome forms a loop (Fig. 20.8).

Chromosomal mutations can lead to various syndromes among offspring when the mutation produces chromosomes that have deleted, duplicated, translocated, and inverted segments.

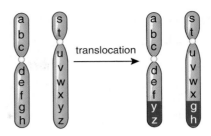

a.

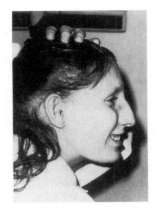

b.

Figure 20.7 **Translocation.**
a. When chromosomes 2 and 20 exchange segments, (**b**) Alagille syndrome, with distinctive facial features, sometimes results because the translocation disrupts an allele on chromosome 20.

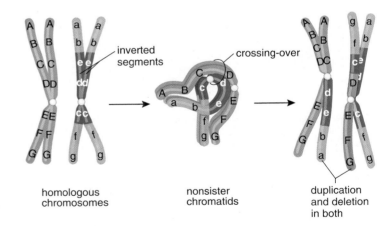

homologous chromosomes · nonsister chromatids · duplication and deletion in both

Figure 20.8 **Inversion.**
(Left) A segment is inverted in the sister chromatids of one homologue. Notice that in the shaded segment, *edc* occurs instead of *cde*. *(Middle)* The nonsister chromatids can pair only when the inverted sequence forms an internal loop. After crossing over, a duplication and a deletion can occur. *(Right)* The nonsister chromatid on the left has *AB* and *ab* sequences and neither *fg* nor *FG* genes. The nonsister chromatid on the right has *gf* and *FG* sequences and neither *AB* nor *ab* genes.

20.2 Counseling for Genetic Disorders: The Present

Even if no chromosomal abnormality is likely, amniocentesis still might be done because it is now possible to perform biochemical tests to detect over 400 different genetic disorders in the fetus. The genetic counselor determines ahead of time what tests might be warranted. To do this, the counselor needs to know the medical history of the family in order to construct a pedigree.

Family Pedigrees

A **pedigree** is a chart of a family's history with regard to a particular genetic trait. In the chart, males are designated by squares and females by circles. Shaded circles and squares are affected individuals; they have a genetic disorder. A line between a square and a circle represents a union. A vertical line going downward leads directly to a single child; if there are more children, they are placed off a horizontal line.

From the counselor's knowledge of genetic disorders, he or she might already know if an inherited trait is autosomal dominant, autosomal recessive, or X-linked recessive. If not, the pedigree might help the counselor decide the pattern of inheritance. The counselor can then determine the chances that any child born to the couple will have the abnormal phenotype.

Pedigrees for Autosomal Disorders

Could the following pattern of inheritance be that of an autosomal dominant or an autosomal recessive characteristic?

pattern I

In this pattern, the child is affected, but neither parent is; this can only happen if the disorder is recessive and the parents are heterozygotes. Notice that the parents are **carriers** because they are unaffected but are capable of having a child with the genetic disorder. If the family pedigree suggests that the parents are carriers for an autosomal recessive disorder, the counselor might suggest confirming this by doing the appropriate genetic test. Then, if the parents so desire, it would be possible to do prenatal testing for the genetic disorder (see pages 404–5).

Notice that in the pedigree shown in Figure 20.9, cousins are the parents of three children, two of whom have the disorder. Aside from illustrating that reproduction between cousins is more likely to bring out recessive traits, this pedigree also illustrates that "chance has no memory;" therefore, each child born to heterozygous parents has a 25% chance of having the disorder. In other words, it is

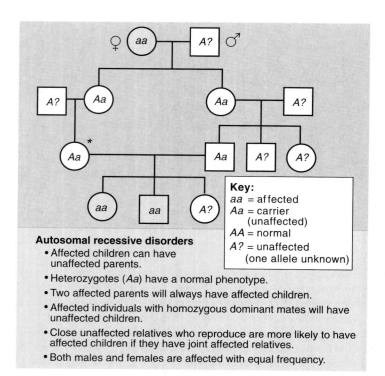

Figure 20.9 **Pedigree for an autosomal recessive.**
The list gives ways to recognize an autosomal recessive disorder. How would you know that the individual at the * is heterozygous?

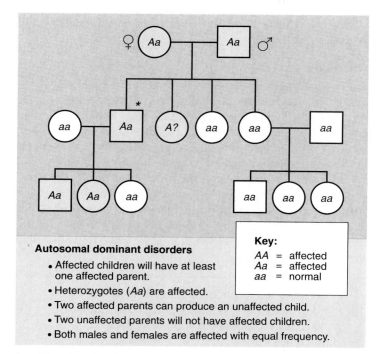

Figure 20.10 **Pedigree for an autosomal dominant.**
The list gives ways to recognize an autosomal dominant disorder. How would you know that the individual at the * is heterozygous?

possible that if a heterozygous couple has four children, each child might have the condition.

Now consider this pattern of inheritance:

pattern II

In this pattern, the child is unaffected, but the parents are both affected. This can happen if the condition is autosomal dominant and the parents are *Aa*. Figure 20.10 lists other ways to recognize an autosomal dominant pattern of inheritance. This pedigree illustrates that when both parents are unaffected, all their children are unaffected. Why? Because neither parent has a dominant gene that causes the condition to pass on.

Pedigrees for Sex-Linked Disorders

Sex-linked disorders can be carried on the X or Y chromosome.

X-Linked Disorders   Figure 20.11 gives a pedigree chart for an *X-linked recessive disorder*. Recall that sons inherit an X-linked recessive allele from their mothers because their fathers gave them a Y chromosome. More males than females have the disorder because recessive alleles on the X chromosome are always expressed in males—the Y chromosome lacks an allele for the disorder. Females who have the condition inherited the allele from both their mother and their father, and all the sons of this female will have the condition. If a male has an X-linked recessive condition, his

daughters are carriers, even if his partner is normal. Therefore, X-linked recessive conditions often pass from grandfather to grandson. Figure 20.11 lists other ways to recognize a recessive X-linked disorder.

Only a few known traits are *X-linked dominant*. If a disorder is X-linked dominant, affected males pass the trait *only* to daughters, who have a 100% chance of having the condition. Females can pass an X-linked dominant allele to both sons and daughters. If a female is heterozygous and her partner is normal, each child has a 50% chance of escaping an X-linked dominant disorder, depending on which maternal X chromosome is inherited.

Y-Linked Disorders   A few genetic disorders are carried on the Y chromosome; one that is well known is involved in determining gender during development. Others code for membrane proteins, including an enzyme that regulates the movement of ADP into and ATP out of mitochondria! How would a counselor recognize a Y-linked pattern of inheritance? Y-linked disorders are present only in males and are passed directly from father to *all* sons because males must inherit a Y chromosome from their fathers.

Unusual Inheritance Patterns

No doubt a genetic counselor will occasionally come across some rather unusual inheritance patterns. For example, a mother (and not a father) passes mutated mitochondrial genes to her offspring through the cytoplasm of the egg. (The sperm contains little or no cytoplasm.) Genetic disorders due to mutated mitochondrial DNA usually manifest themselves in defective energy metabolism.

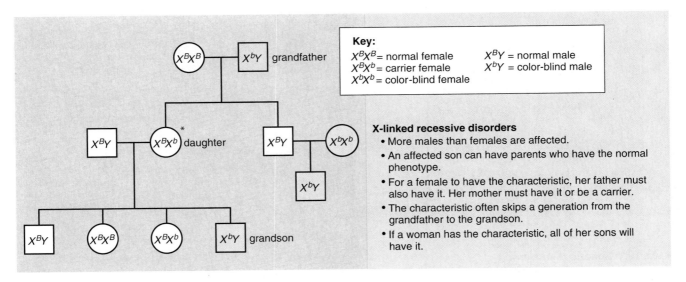

Figure 20.11   Pedigree for an X-linked recessive.
The list gives ways of recognizing an X-linked recessive disorder—in this case, color blindness. How would you know the individual at the * is a carrier?

Genetic Disorders of Interest

Medical genetics has traditionally focused on disorders caused by single gene mutations, and we will discuss a few of the better-known disorders.

Autosomal Recessive Disorders

Inheritance of two recessive alleles is required before an autosomal recessive disorder will appear.

Tay-Sachs   Tay-Sachs disease is a well-known autosomal recessive disorder that occurs usually among Jewish people in the United States, most of whom are of central and eastern European descent. Tay-Sachs disease results from a lack of the enzyme hexosaminidase A (Hex A) and the subsequent storage of its substrate, a glycosphingolipid, in lysosomes. Lysosomes build up in many body cells, but the primary sites of storage are the cells of the brain, which accounts for the onset of symptoms and the progressive deterioration of psychomotor functions (Fig. 20.12a).

At first, it is not apparent that a baby has Tay-Sachs disease. However, development begins to slow down between four and eight months of age, and neurological impairment and psychomotor difficulties then become apparent. The child gradually becomes blind and helpless, develops uncontrollable seizures, and eventually becomes paralyzed.

Cystic Fibrosis   Cystic fibrosis is an autosomal recessive disorder that occurs among all ethnic groups, but it is the most common lethal genetic disorder among Caucasians in the United States. Research has demonstrated that chloride ions (Cl^-) fail to pass through a plasma membrane channel protein in the cells of these patients (Fig. 20.12b). Ordinarily, after chloride ions have passed through the membrane, sodium ions (Na^+) and water follow. It is believed that lack of water is the cause of abnormally thick mucus in bronchial tubes and pancreatic ducts. In these children, the mucus in the bronchial tubes and pancreatic ducts is particularly thick and viscous, interfering with the function of the lungs and pancreas. To ease breathing, the thick mucus in the lungs has to be manually loosened periodically, but still the lungs become infected frequently. Clogged pancreatic ducts prevent digestive enzymes from reaching the small intestine, and to improve digestion, patients take digestive enzymes mixed with applesauce before every meal.

Phenylketonuria   Phenylketonuria (PKU) is an autosomal recessive metabolic disorder that affects nervous system development. Affected individuals lack an enzyme that is needed for the normal metabolism of the amino acid phenylalanine, and therefore, it appears in the urine and the blood. Newborns are routinely tested in the hospital for elevated levels of phenylalanine in the blood. If elevated levels are detected, newborns will develop normally if they are placed on a diet low in phenylalanine, which must be continued until the brain is fully developed, around the age of seven, or else severe mental retardation develops. Some doctors recommend that the diet continue for life, but in any case, a pregnant woman with phenylketonuria must be on the diet, in order to protect her unborn child from harm.

Sickle-Cell Disease   Sickle-cell disease (Fig. 20.13a) is an autosomal recessive disorder in which the red blood cells are not biconcave disks like normal red blood cells; they are irregular. In fact, many are sickle-shaped. The defect is caused by an abnormal hemoglobin that differs from normal hemoglobin by one amino acid in the protein globin. The single amino acid change causes hemoglobin molecules to stack up and form insoluble rods, and the red blood cells become sickle-shaped.

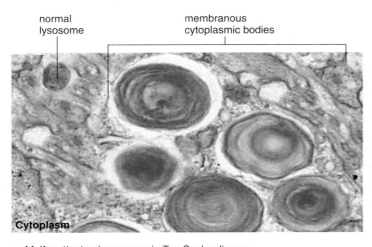

a. Malfunctioning lysosomes in Tay-Sachs disease.

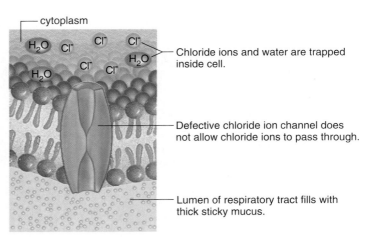

b. Malfunctioning channel protein in cystic fibrosis.

Figure 20.12   Genetic disorders.
a. A cortical neuron in Tay-Sachs disease contains many membranous cytoplasmic bodies (MCB) stored in the cell because of a deficient lysosomal enzyme. The MCBs are made up of various types of lipids in specific proportions. **b.** Cystic fibrosis is due to a faulty protein that is supposed to regulate the flow of chloride ions into and out of cells through a channel protein.

Because sickle-shaped cells can't pass along narrow capillary passageways as disk-shaped cells can, they clog the vessels and break down. This is why persons with sickle-cell disease suffer from poor circulation, anemia, and low resistance to infection. Internal hemorrhaging leads to further complications, such as jaundice, episodic pain in the abdomen and joints, and damage to internal organs.

Sickle-cell heterozygotes have sickle-cell traits in which the blood cells are normal unless they experience dehydration or mild oxygen deprivation. Still, at present, most experts believe that persons with the sickle-cell trait do not need to restrict their physical activity.

Autosomal Dominant Disorders

Inheritance of only one dominant allele is necessary for an autosomal dominant genetic disorder to appear. We discuss only two of the many autosomal dominant disorders here.

Marfan Syndrome   Marfan syndrome, an autosomal dominant disorder, is caused by a defect in an elastic connective tissue protein, called fibrillin. This protein is normally abundant in the lens of the eye, the bones of limbs, fingers, and ribs, and also in the wall of the aorta. This explains why the affected person often has a dislocated lens, long limbs and fingers, and a caved-in chest. The aorta wall is weak and can possibly burst without warning. A tissue graft can strengthen the aorta, but Marfan patients with aortic symptoms still should not overexert themselves.

Huntington Disease   Huntington disease is a neurological disorder that leads to progressive degeneration of brain cells (Fig. 20.13b). The disease is caused by a mutated copy of the gene for a protein, called huntingtin. Most patients appear normal until they are of middle age and have already had children, who may later also be stricken. Occasionally, the first sign of the disease will appear during the teen years or even earlier. There is no effective treatment, and death comes 10 to 15 years after the onset of symptoms.

Several years ago, researchers found that the gene for Huntington disease was located on chromosome 4. A test was developed for the presence of the gene, but few people want to know if they have inherited the gene because there is no cure. At least now we know that the disease stems from a mutation that causes the huntingtin protein to have too many copies of the amino acid glutamine. The normal version of huntingtin has stretches of between 10 and 25 glutamines. If huntingtin has more than 36 glutamines, it changes shape and forms large clumps inside neurons. Even worse, it attracts and causes other proteins to clump with it. One of these proteins, called CBP, helps nerve cells survive. Researchers hope they may be able to combat the disease by boosting CBP levels.

Incompletely Dominant Disorders

The prognosis in **familial hypercholesterolemia (FH)** parallels the number of LDL-cholesterol receptor proteins in the plasma membrane. A person with two mutated alleles lacks LDL-cholesterol receptors; a person with only one mutated allele has half the normal number of receptors, and a person with two normal alleles has the usual number of receptors.

The presence of excessive cholesterol in the blood causes cardiovascular disease. Therefore, those with no receptors die of cardiovascular disease as children. Individuals with half the number of receptors may die when young or after they have reached middle age. People with the full number of receptors do not have familial hypercholesterolemia (Fig. 20.14a).

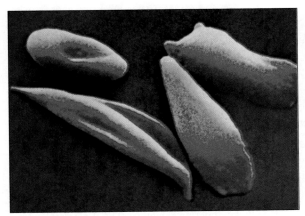

a. Abnormally shaped red blood cells in sickle-cell disease.

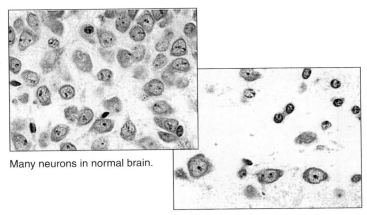

Many neurons in normal brain.

b.   Loss of neurons in Huntington brain.

Figure 20.13   Genetic disorders.
a. Persons with sickle-cell disease have sickle-shaped red blood cells because of an abnormal hemoglobin A molecule. **b.** Huntington disease is characterized by increasingly serious psychomotor and mental disturbances because of a loss of nerve cells.

X-Linked Recessive Disorders

Most X-linked disorders are recessive; therefore, more males than females are affected. **Color blindness,** an X-linked recessive disorder, does not prevent males from leading a normal life. About 8% of Caucasian men have red-green color blindness. Most of these see brighter greens as tans, olive greens as browns, and reds as reddish browns. A few cannot tell reds from greens at all. They see only yellows, blues, blacks, whites, and grays.

Muscular Dystrophy   Duchenne **muscular dystrophy** is an X-linked recessive disorder characterized by a wasting away of the muscles. Symptoms, such as waddling gait, toe walking, frequent falls, and difficulty in rising, may appear as soon as the child starts to walk. Muscle weakness intensifies until the individual is confined to a wheelchair. Death usually occurs by age 20; therefore, affected males are rarely fathers. The recessive allele remains in the population by passage from carrier mother to carrier daughter.

The absence of a protein, now called dystrophin, is the cause of Duchenne muscular dystrophy. Much investigative work determined that dystrophin is involved in the release of calcium from the sarcoplasmic reticulum in muscle fibers. The lack of dystrophin causes calcium to leak into the cell, which promotes the action of an enzyme that dissolves muscle fibers. When the body attempts to repair the tissue, fibrous tissue forms (Fig. 20.14*b*), and this cuts off the blood supply so that more and more cells die. Immature muscle cells can be injected into muscles, but it takes 100,000 cells for dystrophin production to increase by 30–40%.

Hemophilia   There are two common types of hemophilia, an X-linked recessive disorder. Hemophilia A is due to the absence or minimal presence of a clotting factor known as factor VIII, and hemophilia B is due to the absence of clotting factor IX. Hemophilia is called the bleeder's disease because the affected person's blood either does not clot or clots very slowly. Although hemophiliacs bleed externally after an injury, they also bleed internally, particularly around joints. Hemorrhages can be stopped with transfusions of fresh blood (or plasma) or concentrates of the clotting protein. Also, factors VIII and IX are now available as a biotechnology product.

At the turn of the century, hemophilia was prevalent among the royal families of Europe, and all of the affected males could trace their ancestry to Queen Victoria of England. Of Queen Victoria's 20 grandchildren, four grandsons had hemophilia, and four granddaughters were carriers. Because none of Queen Victoria's relatives were affected, it seems that the faulty allele she carried arose by mutation, either in Victoria or in one of her parents. Her carrier daughters, Alice and Beatrice, introduced the allele into the ruling houses of Russia and Spain, respectively. Alexis, the last heir to the Russian throne before the Russian Revolution, was a hemophiliac. There are no hemophiliacs in the present British royal family because Victoria's eldest son, King Edward VII, did not receive the allele.

Inherited disorders are autosomal recessive, autosomal dominant, incompletely dominant, or X-linked recessive.

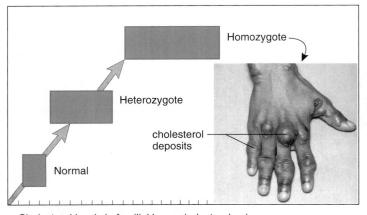

a. Cholesterol levels in familial hypercholesterolemia

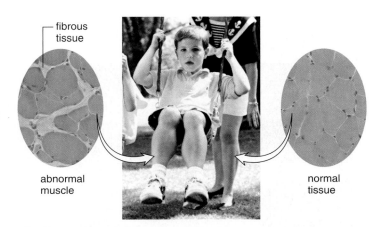

b. Abnormal muscle in muscular dystrophy

Figure 20.14   Genetic disorders.
a. Familial hypercholesterolemia is incompletely dominant. Persons with one mutated allele have an abnormally high level of cholesterol in the blood, and those with two mutated alleles have a higher level still. **b.** In muscular dystrophy, an X-linked recessive disorder, calves enlarge because fibrous tissue develops as muscles waste away, due to lack of the protein dystrophin.

Testing for Genetic Disorders

Prospective parents will know if either has an autosomal dominant disorder because the person will show it. However, genetic testing is required to detect if either is a carrier for an autosomal recessive disorder that runs in their family. In any case, a genetic counselor will explain to a couple the chances a child will have the disorder. If a woman is already pregnant, the parents may want to know if the unborn child has the disorder. If the woman is not pregnant, the parents may opt for testing of the embryo or egg before she does become pregnant.

Testing depends on the genetic disorder of interest. In some instances, it is appropriate to test for a particular protein, and in others to test for the mutated gene.

Testing for a Protein

Some genetic mutations lead to disorders caused by a missing enzyme. For example, babies with Tay-Sachs disease lack an enzyme called hexosaminidase A (hex A). It is possible to test for the quantity of hex A in a sample of cells and from that, determine whether the individual is likely homozygous normal, a carrier, or has Tay-Sachs disease. If the parents are carriers, each child has a 25% chance of having Tay-Sachs disease. This knowledge may lead prospective parents to opt for testing of the embryo or egg, as discussed on the next page.

In the case of PKU, an enzyme is missing, but the test is for an excess amount of the enzyme's substrate, namely phenylalanine. Paper disks containing the newborn's blood are placed on a bacterial culture, and if the bacteria grow around them, the newborn has PKU.

Testing the DNA

Two types of DNA testing are possible: testing for a genetic marker and using a DNA probe.

Genetic Markers Testing for a genetic marker is possible when the DNA base sequence abnormality is known. It is possible to test people for Huntington disease because the abnormality is known. This abnormality in sequence is a **genetic marker.** As you know, restriction enzymes (see page 498) cleave DNA at particular base sequences. Therefore, fragments that result from the use of a restriction enzyme will be differently sized according to whether the individual has or does not have Huntington disease. Figure 20.15 gives an example for possible results.

DNA Probes A **DNA probe** is a single-stranded piece of DNA that will bind to complementary DNA. For the purpose of genetic testing, the DNA probe bears a genetic mutation of interest. A DNA chip is a new technology that can test for many genetic disorders at a time. A DNA chip is a very small glass square that contains several rows of DNA probes. DNA from an individual is cut into fragments using restriction enzymes, and the fragments are tagged with a fluorescent dye and converted to single DNA strands before being applied to the chip (Fig. 20.16). Fragments that contain a mutated gene bind to one of the probes, and binding is detected by a laser scanner. Therefore, the results tell if an individual has particular mutated genes.

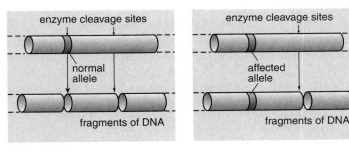

a. Normal fragmentation pattern   b. Genetic disorder fragmentation pattern

Figure 20.15 **Use of a genetic marker to test for a genetic mutation.**
a. In this example, DNA from a normal individual has certain restriction enzyme cleavage sites. **b.** DNA from another individual lacks one of the cleavage sites, and this loss indicates that the person has a mutated gene. In heterozygotes, half of their DNA would have the cleavage site, and half would not have it. (In other instances, the gain in a cleavage site could be an indication of a mutation.)

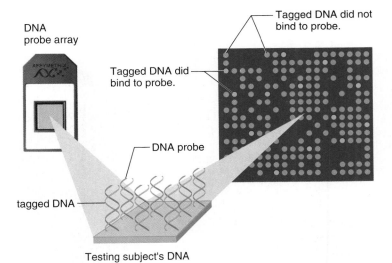

Testing subject's DNA

Figure 20.16 **Use of a DNA chip to test for mutated genes.**
This DNA chip contains rows of DNA probes for mutations that indicate the presence of particular genetic disorders. If single-stranded DNA fragments derived from an individual's DNA bind (hybridize) to a probe, the individual has the mutation. Heterozygotes would not have as much binding as homozygotes.

Testing the Fetus

Various types of procedures are available to test for a genetic defect (see page 403). To prevent having a child with a genetic defect, some prospective parents may wish to test the fetus or the embryo before birth; or even the egg before in vitro fertilization. Ultrasound is a way to view the fetus before birth and there are ways to obtain and test fetal cells before birth.

Ultrasound   Ultrasounds are images that help doctors evaluate fetal anatomy. An ultrasound probe scans over the mother's abdomen and a transducer transmits high-frequency sound waves that are transformed into a picture on a video screen. This picture shows the fetus inside the uterus (Fig. 20.17).

Ultrasound, done after 16 weeks' gestation, can be used to tell the baby's age and size, and whether there is more than one baby. It's also possible to tell if a baby has a serious condition, such as spina bifida, the most common neural tube defect. Spina bifida results when the spine fails to close properly during the first month of pregnancy. In severe cases, the spinal cord protrudes through the back and may be covered by skin or a thin membrane. Surgery to close a newborn's back is generally performed within 24 hours after birth. Closure minimizes the risk of infection and helps preserve spinal cord functions.

Testing Fetal Cells   Fetal cells can be tested for various genetic disorders. If the fetus has an incurable disorder, such as Tay-Sachs disease or will have Huntington disease, the parents may wish to consider an abortion. For testing purposes, fetal cells may be acquired through the following means.

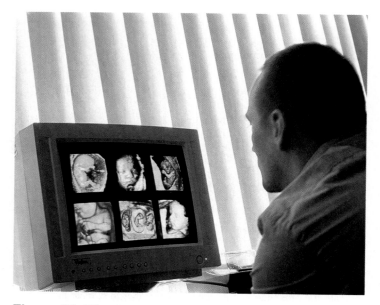

Figure 20.17   Ultrasound.
An ultrasound exam produces images of the fetus that can allow physicians to detect serious defects, such as a neural tube defect. Today, ultrasound can produce images that look three-dimensional.

Amniocentesis.   As mentioned on page 390, amniocentesis is not performed until a woman is at least 12 weeks (three months) pregnant. Possible loss of the fetus is slightly less than for chorionic villi sampling (CVS). The wait for genetic testing of cells (about 20 days), however, is longer than for CVS. Because amniotic fluid is collected, it can be tested for alpha fetoprotein (AFP), a chemical that is present when a fetus has a neural tube defect.

Chorionic villi sampling (CVS).   As mentioned on page 390, this procedure is done earlier than amniocentesis—as early as seven weeks. There is a slightly higher risk of miscarriage, and the occurrence of induced fetal facial and limb abnormalities has been reported but not confirmed. Because no amniotic fluid is collected, the AFP test cannot be done. The wait for genetic test results (about 10 days) is less than that for amniocentesis.

Fetal cells in mother's blood.   As early as nine weeks into the pregnancy, a small number of fetal cells can be isolated from the mother's blood using a cell sorter. It is best to gather nucleated fetal red blood cells from the mother's blood, because like any red blood cell, they are short-lived, and therefore must be due to the present pregnancy.

Only about 1/70,000 blood cells in a mother's blood are fetal cells, and therefore, a PCR (see page 381) has to be used to amplify the DNA from the few cells collected. Only the types of DNA tests mentioned on page 403 can be done, but the procedure poses no risk whatsoever to the fetus.

Testing the Embryo and Egg

As discussed in Chapter 15, in vitro fertilization (IVF) is carried out in laboratory glassware. The physician obtains eggs from the prospective mother and sperm from the prospective father, and places them in the same receptacle, where fertilization occurs. Following IVF, by now a routine procedure, it is possible to test the embryo. Prior to IVF, it is possible to test the egg for any genetic defect. In any case, only normal embryos are transferred to the uterus for further development.

Testing the Embryo   If prospective parents are carriers for one of the genetic disorders discussed on pages 400–402, they may want the assurance that their offspring will be free of the disorder. Testing the embryo will provide this assurance.

Following IVF, the zygote (fertilized egg) divides. When the embryo has six to eight cells (Fig. 20.18), removal of one of these cells for testing purposes has no effect on normal development. Only embryos that test negative for the genetic disorders of interest are placed in the uterus to continue developing.

So far, about 1,000 children, free of alleles for genetic disorders that run in their families, have been born worldwide following embryo testing. In the future, it's possible that embryos who test positive for a disorder could be treated by gene therapy, so that they, too, would be allowed to continue to term.

Testing the Egg   Recall that meiosis in females results in a single egg and at least two polar bodies (see page 347). Polar bodies, which later disintegrate, receive very little cytoplasm, but they do receive a haploid number of chromosomes. When a woman is heterozygous for a recessive genetic disorder, about half the polar bodies will have received the mutated allele, and in these instances the egg received the normal allele. Therefore, if a polar body tests positive for a mutated allele, the egg received the normal allele. Only normal eggs are then used for IVF. Even if the sperm should happen to carry the mutation, the zygote will, at worst, be heterozygous. But the phenotype will appear normal.

If, in the future, gene therapy becomes routine, it's possible that an egg could be given genes that control traits desired by the parents, such as musical or athletic ability, prior to IVF.

Today, genetic counseling is most appropriate for determining the presence of genetic disorders caused by single gene defects, whose pattern of inheritance is shown by a family pedigree. Genetic testing involves protein and DNA testing and testing of the fetus, embryo, or egg.

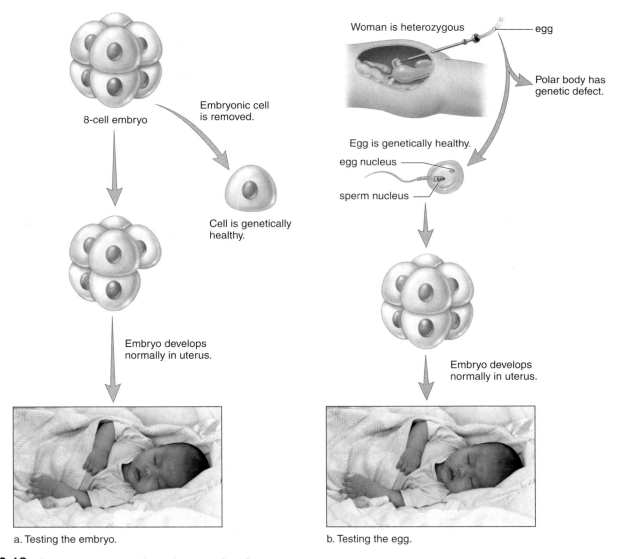

a. Testing the embryo.

b. Testing the egg.

Figure 20.18   Prepregnancy testing of egg and embryo.
a. Following IVF and cleavage, genetic analysis is performed on one cell removed from an eight-celled embryo. If it is found to be free of the genetic defect of concern, the seven-celled embryo is implanted in the uterus and develops into a newborn with a normal phenotype.
b. Chromosomal and genetic analysis is performed on a polar body attached to an egg. If the egg is free of a genetic defect, it is used for IVF and the embryo is implanted in the uterus for further development.

20.3 Counseling for Genetic Disorders: The Future

We learned in the previous chapter that *genomics* includes the study of the Human Genome Project (see page 378). Scientists have a working draft that tells them the order of the base pairs in all the chromosomes. The Health Focus on the next page speculates on the possible future practical benefits of having sequenced our genome. Indeed, investigators have now turned their attention in particular to linking abnormalities in base sequences to diseases. For example, which changes in the normal sequence can be associated with heart disease, or cancer, or diabetes type 2? Such multifactorial traits may be due to several changes within various sections of a person's DNA. Once we have such information, routine genetic profiling might be a part of providing good medical care.

The Genetic Profile

The complete **genetic profile** would tell how a person's genome differs from the norm. Perhaps one day, it will be possible to quickly sequence anyone's DNA. Comparing the sequence to a standard sequence would indicate any abnormalities. Such differences might indicate a propensity toward particular disorders.

Then, too, DNA chips (or DNA microarrays) will soon be available, which could rapidly identify the complete genotype, including all the various mutations in the genome of an individual. Already, chips are available that hold tens of thousands of genes. Therefore, acquiring a genetic profile would be easy. The patient need only provide a few cells, even by simply swabbing the inside of a cheek. Then, DNA is removed from the cells, amplified by PCR, if need be, and cut into fragments, which are tagged by a fluorescent dye. The fragments are applied to a DNA chip, and the results are read.

Benefits of Genetic Profiling

With the help of a genetic counselor, individuals would be educated about their genetic profile. It's possible that a person has or will have a genetic disorder caused by a single pair of alleles (see pages 400–402). Multifactorial traits are more common, however, and in these instances, the genetic profile will indicate an increased or decreased risk for a disorder. Risk information can be used to design a program of medical surveillance and to foster a lifestyle that would reduce the risk. For example, suppose an individual has mutations common to people with colon cancer. If so, an annual colonoscopy would be helpful so that any abnormal growths could be detected and removed before they become invasive.

The genetic profile may indicate what particular drug therapy or what gene therapy might be most appropriate

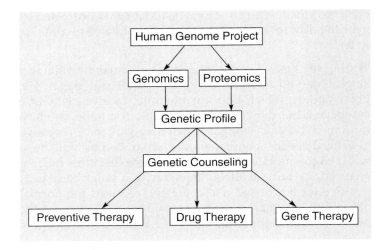

a.

b.

Figure 20.19   Genetic counseling in the future.
a. It's hoped that sequencing the human genome will lead to better health care for the individual. Knowing an individual's genetic profile is expected to make it possible to suggest preventive therapy, design the right drug therapy, and make gene therapy for any present or predicted conditions more likely. **b.** A genetic counselor discusses his genetic profile with a patient.

for the individual (Fig. 20.19). Drugs tend to be proteins or small molecules that affect the behavior of proteins. Recall that *proteomics* is the study of cellular proteins; often discovering their tertiary structure is the first step to understanding what they do in a cell. The field of proteomics is especially pertinent to human disease, because it deals with the development of new drugs for the treatment of genetic disorders.

Investigators are hopeful that sequencing the human genome will lead to providing patients with better preventive care, more effective drugs, and, if necessary, successful gene therapy.

New Cures on the Horizon

Now that we know the sequence of the bases in the DNA of all the human chromosomes, biologists all over the world believe this knowledge will result in rapid medical advances for ourselves and our children.

First prediction: Many new medicines tailored to the individual will be available.

Most drugs are proteins or small chemicals that are able to interact with proteins. Today's drugs were usually discovered in a hit-or-miss fashion, but now researchers will be able to take a more systematic approach to finding effective medicines. In a recent search for a medicine that makes wounds heal, researchers cultured skin cells with 14 proteins (found by chance) that can cause skin cells to grow. Only one of these proteins made skin cells

First prediction
Many new medicines will be coming.

grow and did nothing else. They expect this protein to become an effective drug for conditions such as venous ulcers, which are skin lesions that affect many thousands of people in the United States. Tests leading to effective medicines can be carried out with many more proteins that scientists will discover by examining the human genome.

As you know, many drugs potentially have unwanted side effects. Why do some people and not others have one or more of the side effects? Most likely, this is because people have different genetic profiles. It is expected that a physician will be able to match patients to drugs that are safe for them on the basis of their genetic profiles.

One study found that various combinations of mutations can lead to the development of asthma. A particular drug, called albuterol, is effective and safe for patients with certain combinations of mutations and not others. This example and others show that many diseases are multifactorial and that only a genetic profile is able to detect which mutations are causing an individual to have a disease and how it should be properly treated.

Second prediction: A longer and healthier life will be yours.

Pre-embryonic gene therapy may become routine once we discover the genes that contribute to a longer and healthier life. We know that the presence of free radicals causes cellular molecules to become unstable and cells to die. Certain genes are believed to code for antioxidant enzymes that detoxify free radicals. It could be that human beings

with particular forms of these genes have more efficient antioxidant enzymes, and therefore live longer. If so, researchers will no doubt be able to locate these genes and also others that promote a longer, healthier life.

Perhaps certain genetic profiles allow some people to live far beyond the normal life span. Researchers may be able to find which genes allow individuals to live a long time and make them available to the general public. Then, many more people would live longer and healthier lives.

Second prediction
A longer and healthier life will be yours.

Third prediction: You will be able to design your children.

Genome sequence data will be used to identify many more mutant genes that cause genetic disorders than are presently known. In the future, it may be possible to cure genetic disorders before the child is born by adding a normal gene to any egg that carries a mutant gene. Or an artificial chromosome, constructed to carry a large number of corrective genes, could automatically be placed in eggs. In vitro fertilization would have to be utilized in order to take advantage of such measures for cur-

Third prediction
You will be able to design your children.

ing genetic disorders before conception.

Genome sequence data can also be used to identify polygenic genes for traits such as height, intelligence, or behavioral characteristics. A couple could decide on their own which genes they wish to use to enhance a child's phenotype. In other words, the sequencing of the human genome may bring about a genetically just society, in which all types of genes would be accessible to all parents.

Gene Therapy

Gene therapy is the insertion of genetic material into human cells for the treatment of a disorder. Gene therapy is also appropriate for the treatment of genetic disorders and various other human illnesses, such as cardiovascular disease and cancer. Gene therapy includes both ex vivo (outside the body) and in vivo (inside the body) therapy.

Ex Vivo Gene Therapy

Figure 20.20 describes a methodology for treating children who have SCID (severe combined immunodeficiency). These children lack the enzyme ADA (adenosine deaminase), which is involved in the maturation of T and B cells. In order to carry out gene therapy, bone marrow stem cells are removed from the blood and infected with an RNA retrovirus that carries a normal gene for the enzyme. Then, the cells are returned to the patient. Bone marrow stem cells are preferred for this procedure because they divide to produce more cells with the same genes. Patients who have undergone this procedure show significantly improved immune function associated with a sustained rise in the level of ADA enzyme activity in the blood.

As discussed on page 401, in one form of familial hypercholesterolemia, the liver cells lack receptor proteins for removing cholesterol from the blood. The high levels of blood cholesterol make the patient subject to fatal heart attacks at a young age. A small portion of the liver is surgically excised and then infected with a retrovirus containing a normal gene for the receptor before being returned to the patient. Several patients have experienced lowered serum cholesterol levels following this procedure.

In Vivo Gene Therapy

Cystic fibrosis patients (see page 400) lack a gene that codes for the transmembrane carrier of the chloride ion. They often die due to numerous infections of the respiratory tract. In gene therapy trials, the gene needed to cure cystic fibrosis is sprayed into the nose or delivered to the lower respiratory tract by an adenovirus vector or by the use of liposomes, microscopic vesicles made of lipoproteins. Investigators are trying to improve uptake and are also hypothesizing that a combination of different vectors might be more successful.

Genes are being used to treat medical conditions, such as poor coronary circulation. It has been known for some time that VEGF (vascular endothelial growth factor) can cause the growth of new blood vessels. The gene that codes for this growth factor can be injected alone or within a virus into the heart to stimulate branching of coronary blood vessels. Patients report that they have less chest pain and can run longer on a treadmill.

Gene therapy is increasingly used as a part of cancer therapy. Genes are being used to make healthy cells more tolerant of chemotherapy, while making tumor cells more sensitive. The tumor suppressor gene *p53* brings about apoptosis (cell death). There is much interest in finding a way to selectively introduce *p53* into cancer cells and to, thereby, kill them.

The new fields of genomics and proteomics may lead to renewed interest in gene therapy.

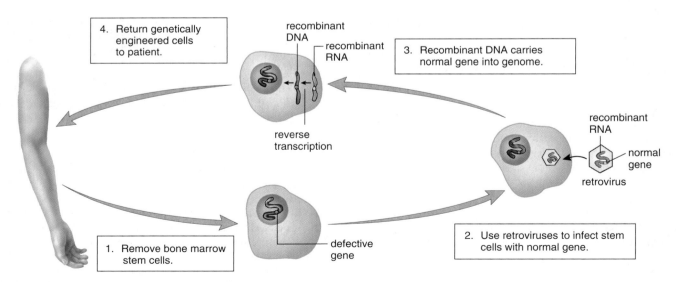

Figure 20.20   Ex vivo gene therapy in humans.
Bone marrow stem cells are withdrawn from the body, an RNA retrovirus is used to insert a normal gene into them, and they are returned to the body.

Bioethical Focus

Genetic Profiling

Now that the human genome has been sequenced, researchers are using various means to discover which sequencing differences among people might forecast the possibility of a future disease. No doubt, there are benefits to genetic profiling. For example, knowledge of your genes might indicate your susceptibility to various types of cancer. This information could be used to develop a prevention program, including the avoidance of environmental influences associated with the disease. Also, you would be less inclined to smoke if you knew your genes make it almost inevitable that smoking will give you lung cancer. Are there any reasons not to be in favor of genetic profiling?

People, however, worry that insurance companies and employers could use a genetic profile against them. Perhaps employers will not hire, or insurance companies will not insure, those who have a propensity for particular diseases. The federal government, and about 25 states, have passed laws prohibiting genetic discrimination by health insurers, and 11 have passed laws prohibiting genetic discrimination by employers. The legislation states that genetic information cannot be released to anyone without the subject's permission. Is such legislation enough to allay our fears of discrimination? Might an employer not hire you or an insurance company not insure you simply because you will not grant permission to access your genetic profile (Fig. 20A)? Say two women are being considered for the same position, and each meets all the basic requirements for the job. The first denies access to her genetic profile, while the second one grants permission to look at her genetic profile. Thinking that the first woman might have something to hide, the employer hires the second one. The possibility that sick days may be needed by the first woman makes the second woman the more cost-effective choice. People who have genetic profiles proving they are likely to be healthy in the future might even use them in order to have an advantage over those who have profiles showing that they are likely to develop serious illnesses in the future. In this way, we might create a genetic underclass.

Genetic information is sometimes misunderstood, particularly by laypeople. In the past, for example, as an effort to combat sickle-cell disease, many people were screened for it. Unfortunately, those who were found to have the sickle-cell trait, and not the actual disease, experienced discrimination at school, or from employers and insurance carriers. Is possible misunderstanding of the results enough not to do genetic profiling, or do the potential benefits outweigh the risks?

On the other hand, employers may fear that the government might use genetic information one day to require them to provide an environment specific to every employee's need, in order to prevent future illness. Would you approve of this, or should individuals be required to leave an area or job that

Figure 20A **Interviewing for a position.**
If a prospective employer asked for your genetic profile, would you be inclined to give him permission to view it?

exposes them to an environmental influence that could be detrimental to their health?

Some people believe that free access to genetic profiling data is absolutely essential to developing better preventive care for all. If researchers can match genetic profiles to environmental conditions that bring on illnesses, they could come up with better prevention guidelines for the next generation. Should genetic profiles and health records become public information under these circumstances? It would particularly help in the study of complex diseases, such as cardiovascular disorders, noninsulin-dependent diabetes, and juvenile rheumatoid arthritis. Perhaps there would be some way to protect privacy and still make the information known?

If present legislation to protect privacy is inadequate, what could be done to truly keep such information private? Should the information be coded in some way, so that only the medical profession can read it? Should people be responsible for keeping the only copy of their profiles, which would be coded so that even they cannot read it? Or, do you believe that anyone should have access to anyone's profile, for whatever reason?

Decide Your Opinion

1. Should people be encouraged or even required to have their DNA analyzed so that they can develop programs to possibly prevent future illness?
2. Should employers be encouraged or required to provide an environment suitable to a person's genetic profile? Or, should the individual avoid a work environment that could bring on an illness?
3. How can we balance individual rights with the public health benefit of matching genetic profiles to detrimental environments?

Summarizing the Concepts

20.1 Counseling for Chromosomal Disorders
It is possible to karyotype the chromosomes of a cell arrested in metaphase of mitosis. Amniocentesis and chorionic villi sampling can provide fetal cells for the karyotyping of chromosomes when a chromosomal abnormality may have been inherited.

Nondisjunction during meiosis can result in an abnormal number of autosomes or sex chromosomes in the gametes. Down syndrome results when an individual inherits three copies of chromosome 21. Females who are XO have Turner syndrome, and those who are XXX are poly-X females. Males with Klinefelter syndrome are XXY. Males who are XYY have Jacobs syndrome.

Changes in chromosomal structure also affect the phenotype. Chromosomal mutations include deletions, duplications, translocations, and inversions. In Williams syndrome, one copy of chromosome 7 has a deletion. In cri du chat syndrome, one copy of chromosome 5 has a deletion. In inv dup 15 syndrome, chromosome 15 has an inverted duplication. Translocations do not necessarily cause any difficulties if the person has inherited both translocated chromosomes. However, the translocation can disrupt a particular allele, and then a syndrome will follow. An inversion can lead to chromosomes that have a deletion and a duplication when the inverted piece loops back to align with the noninverted homologue, and crossing-over follows between the nonsister chromatids.

20.2 Counseling for Genetic Disorders: The Present
A family pedigree is a visual representation of the history of a genetic disorder in a family. Constructing pedigrees helps a genetic counselor decide whether a genetic disorder that runs in a family is autosomal recessive (see Fig. 20.9) or dominant (see Fig 20.10); X-linked (see Fig. 20.11); or some other pattern of inheritance. After deciding the pattern of inheritance, a counselor will be able to tell prospective parents the chances that any child born to them will have the genetic disorder.

Today, we have been most successful in identifying genetic disorders caused by single gene mutations. Tay-Sachs disease (a lysosomal storage disease), cystic fibrosis (faulty regulator of chloride channel), phenylketonuria (inability to metabolize phenylalanine), and sickle-cell disease (sickle-shaped red blood cells) are all autosomal recessive disorders. Marfan syndrome (defective elastic connective tissue), and Huntington disease (abnormal huntingtin protein) are both autosomal dominant disorders. Familial hypercholesterolemia (liver cells lack cholesterol receptors) is an incompletely dominant autosomal disorder. Among X-linked disorders are muscular dystrophy (absence of dystrophin leads to muscle weakness) and hemophilia (inability of blood to clot).

Testing for genetic disorders includes testing for a protein and testing the DNA. For example, persons with Tay-Sachs disease lack the enzyme hex A, and those with PKU have much phenylalamine in their blood. To test the DNA for mutations, it is possible to compare fragment sizes, following the use of restriction enzymes to the normal pattern, or to see if the fragments bind to DNA probes that contain the mutation.

The fetus, embryo, or egg can be tested for a genetic defect that indicates the newborn will not be normal. An ultrasound allows for the detection of severe abnormalities, such as spina bifida. Fetal cells can be obtained by amniocentesis, chorionic villi sampling, and by sorting fetal cells from the mother's blood. Following in vitro fertilization, it is possible to test the embryo. A cell is removed from an eight-celled embryo, and if it is found to be genetically healthy, the embryo is implanted in the uterus, where it develops to term. Before IVF, a polar body can be tested. If the woman is heterozygous and the polar body has the genetic defect, the egg does not have it. Following IVF, the embryo is implanted in the uterus.

20.3 Counseling for Genetic Disorders: The Future
Researchers now know the sequence of the base pairs along the length of the human chromosomes.

One day, genetic counselors may order a genetic profile that can be easily obtained by the use of a DNA chip that contains all our genes. The genetic profile will have three benefits: preventive therapy, appropriate drug therapy, and better gene therapy.

During gene therapy, a genetic defect is treated by giving the patient a foreign gene. During ex vivo therapy, cells are removed from the patient, treated, and returned to the patient. In vivo therapy consists of directly giving the patient a foreign gene that will improve his/her health.

Studying the Concepts

1. What is genetic counseling? 390
2. What is a karyotype, and when and how is karyotyping of fetal cells done? 390–91
3. What is nondisjuction, and how does it occur? 392
4. Describe Down syndrome, the most common autosomal chromosome abnormality in humans. 393
5. List four sex chromosomal abnormalities that have to do with an abnormal number of sex chromosomes. 394–95
6. List other types of chromosomal mutations that can affect the phenotype. 396–97
7. How is a pedigree constructed? List the ways to recognize an autosomal genetic disorder and an X-linked recessive genetic disorder when examining a pedigree chart. 398–99
8. Describe the autosomal recessive/dominant disorders and the X-linked recessive disorders discussed in the text. 400–402
9. Why can certain genetic disorders be detected by testing for a protein? 403
10. What are the two types of DNA testing for a genetic disorder? In general, describe each method. 403
11. How is it possible to obtain fetal cells for DNA testing? To test an egg before in vitro fertilization and an embryo after in vitro fertilization? 404–5
12. What is genetic profiling? Explain and give examples of ex vivo and in vivo gene therapies in humans. 406–9

Thinking Critically About the Concepts

Refer to the opening vignette on page 389, and then answer these questions.

1. Normally, how many chromosomes of each type do individuals have? Why?
2. Some individuals with Down syndrome are severely affected and some are mildly affected. What explanation might a researcher studying epigenomics (see page 393) offer?
3. Consider that a female can be a heterozygote for an X-linked disorder, such as absence of sweat glands. Why would you expect some portions of a heterozygote's skin to lack sweat glands and some portions to have sweat glands?
4. In what way will genomics be helpful to those with chromosomal disorders?

Testing Your Knowledge of the Concepts

Choose the best answer for each question.

1. A karyotype is prepared
    a. for an unborn child through amniocentesis or chorionic villi sampling.
    b. by arranging chromosomes into pairs by size, shape, and banding patterns.
    c. as a means of diagnosing an abnormal chromosome disorder.
    d. using a photograph of a cell sample arrested during metaphase.
    e. All of the above are correct.

2. Chromosomes from an adult are most easily acquired for study using
    a. amniotic fluid.
    b. placental cells.
    c. a saliva sample.
    d. a blood sample.
    e. a hair sample.

3. An individual can have too many or too few chromosomes due to which of these?
    a. nondisjunction
    b. a Barr body
    c. a trisomy
    d. amniocentesis
    e. a monosomy

For questions 4–8, match the chromosome disorder to its description in the key.

Key:

    a. female with undeveloped ovaries and uterus, unable to undergo puberty, normal intelligence, lives normally with hormone replacement
    b. XXY male, can inherit more than two X chromosomes
    c. male or female, mentally retarded, short stature, flat face, stubby fingers, large tongue, simian palm crease
    d. XXX or XXXX female
    e. caused by nondisjunction during spermatogenesis

4. Klinefelter syndrome

5. Poly-X female

6. Down syndrome

7. Turner syndrome

8. Jacobs syndrome

For questions 9–12, match the chromosome mutation to its description in the key.

Key:

    a. turned-up nose, wide mouth, small chin, large ears, academic skills poor, excellent verbal and musical abilities, prematurely aging cardiovascular system
    b. deletion in chromosome 5
    c. poor muscle tone, mental retardation, seizures, curved spine, autistic characteristics, poor speech, hand flapping, lack of eye contact
    d. translocation between chromosomes 2 and 20

9. Alagille syndrome

10. inv dup 15 syndrome

11. Williams syndrome

12. Cri du chat syndrome

13. The pedigree chart below pertains to color blindness. The genotype of the individual at the * is _____.

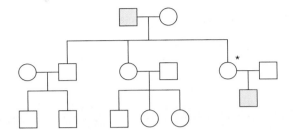

14. Which of the following is incorrect regarding genetic testing? Genetic testing
    a. is beneficial in determining if parents are carriers for autosomal recessive disorders.
    b. can determine if the enzyme hexosaminidase A is present in an unborn fetus.
    c. can be carried out on an embryo prior to implantation.
    d. using polar bodies can provide information about eggs.
    e. is routinely used to determine genetic defects caused by multiple genes.

15. Parents who do not have Tay-Sachs disease (recessive) produce a child who has Tay-Sachs disease. What are the chances that each child born to this couple will have Tay-Sachs disease?
    a. 100%
    b. 75%
    c. 25%
    d. 0%
    e. All of these are correct.

16. Which is a late-onset neuromuscular genetic disorder?
    a. cystic fibrosis
    b. Huntington disease
    c. phenylketonuria
    d. Tay-Sachs disease

17. Two affected parents have an unaffected child. The trait involved is
    a. autosomal recessive.
    b. incompletely dominant.
    c. controlled by multiple alleles.
    d. autosomal dominant.

18. Gene therapy has been used to treat which of the following disorders?
    a. cystic fibrosis
    b. hypercholesterolemia
    c. severe combined immunodeficiency
    d. All of these are correct.

19. A boy is color-blind, which is correct?
    a. His father must be color blind.
    b. His mother must be color blind or a carrier.
    c. His father must be normal or a carrier.
    d. His siblings are also color blind.
    e. Both b and d are correct.

20. Does the following pedigree represent an autosomal dominant trait, an autosomal recessive trait, or an X-linked recessive trait?

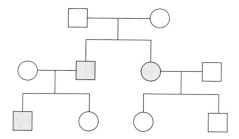

Additional Genetics Problems

1. A color-blind female and normal male have children.
   a. What are the chances their son will be color blind?
   b. What are the chances their daughter will be color blind?

2. A man has Duchenne muscular dystrophy.
   a. What are the possible genotypes of his mother?
   b. If he lived to produce a child with a normal female, what are the chances a daughter would have the disease?

3. A girl is a hemophiliac. What are the possible genotypes of her parents?

4. A woman has Marfan syndrome, inherited from her father. She has a young son who also shows signs of the syndrome.
   a. What are the possible genotypes of the child?
   b. What are the possible genotypes of his father?

5. A 25-year-old man believes he has Huntington disease and does not want to pass this trait down to his children.
   a. If he does have the disease, is it possible for him to father a normal son? Explain.
   b. If he does have the disease, is it possible for him to father a normal daughter? Explain.

6. A child has familial hypercholesterolemia and has half the normal number of receptors for cholesterol.
   a. What are the possible genotypes of his parents? Keep in mind, they lived long enough to have children.
   b. Could he live long enough to have children? Explain, using his genotype.

7. A woman has cystic fibrosis in her family and does not want to have a child that suffers from the disease. She and her spouse go in for genetic testing and counseling. What are the chances they could have a child with the disease?

8. Parents who do not have Tay-Sachs disease produce a child who has Tay-Sachs disease. What is the genotype of each parent? What are the chances that each child will have Tay-Sachs disease?

9. A baby tests positive for phenylketonuria. Could either parent have a homozygous genotype? If so, what would be the genotype?

Understanding Key Terms

amniocentesis 390
Barr body 392
carrier 398
chorionic villi
    sampling (CVS) 390
chromosomal mutation 396
color blindness 402
cystic fibrosis 400
deletion 396
DNA probe 403
Duchenne muscular
    dystrophy 402
duplication 396
familial hypercholesterolemia
    (FH) 401
gene therapy 408

genetic counseling 390
genetic marker 403
genetic profile 406
Huntington disease 401
inversion 396
karyotype 390
Marfan syndrome 401
monosomy 392
nondisjunction 392
pedigree 398
phenylketonuria (PKU) 400
sickle-cell disease 400
syndrome 390
Tay-Sachs disease 400
translocation 397
trisomy 392

Match the key terms to these definitions.

a. _____ Duplicated chromosome arranged by pairs according to their size, shape, and general appearance.

b. _____ Removal of cells from a portion of the placenta for karyotyping of the fetus.

c. _____ Dark-staining body in the nuclei of female mammals that contains a condensed, inactive X chromosome.

d. _____ Change in chromosome structure in which a segment of a chromosome is turned around 180°.

e. _____ Autosomal recessive disorder in which thick mucus fills the bronchial tubes and pancreatic ducts leading to respiratory and disgestive difficulties.

Online Learning Center

www.mhhe.com/maderhuman9

The Online Learning Center provides a wealth of information fully organized and integrated by chapter. You will find practice quizzes, interactive activities, labeling exercises, flashcards, and much more that will complement your learning and understanding of human biology.

Looking at Both Sides

Each day, the Internet, media, and other people present you with opposing viewpoints on a wide range of subjects. Your ability to develop an informed opinion on an issue, and talk to others about it, is extremely important.

To expand and enhance your knowledge of a highly relevant bioethical issue, visit the "Student Edition" of the Online Learning Center. Under "Course-Wide Content," select "Looking at Both Sides." Once there, you will be asked to complete activities that will increase your understanding of a current bioethical issue related to this chapter and allow you to defend your opinion.

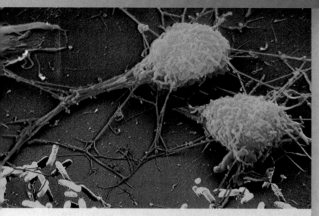

21 Defenses Against Disease 413

22 Parasites and Pathogens 431

23 Sexually Transmitted Diseases 453

24 Cancer 471

CHAPTER **21**

Defenses Against Disease

Disease can be defined as any abnormal condition of the body. In that case, you would expect this part of the book to discuss infectious diseases and all the other organic or genetic disorders common to humans. You will be relieved to know that this part instead will limit the term *disease* to mean infectious diseases and cancer. The rationale becomes clear when we consider that the immune system ordinarily protects us from infectious diseases and cancer. The immune system is able to recognize, and ordinarily to act against, any cell that displays proteins (called antigens) that are not found in the body. It is said that the immune system can tell "self" from "nonself."

Most likely, you can accept the concept that parasites (e.g., viruses, bacteria, and larger forms of life) display antigens that tip off the immune system to their presence. But cancer cells aren't invaders as parasites are. They are the body's own cells that have undergone genetic mutations. Mutations allow cancer cells to grow uncontrollably, resulting in a tumor. They also allow cancer cells to become malignant so that they travel in blood vessels or lymphatic vessels to other parts of the body, forming other tumors. These same mutations also cause cancer cells to carry antigens that the immune system ordinarily recognizes. Malignancy develops only when the immune system, for some unknown reason, fails to do its job.

CHAPTER CONCEPTS

21.1 Organs, Tissues, and Cells of the Immune System
- Which organs are primary lymphatic organs? Secondary lymphatic organs? 414
- How do the primary and secondary lymphatic organs function in immunity? 414–15

21.2 Nonspecific and Specific Defenses
- How does nonspecific defense differ from specific defense? 417
- What are some examples of the body's nonspecific defenses? 417–18
- Which blood cells are mainly responsible for specific defense, and how do they function? 418–23

21.3 Acquired Immunity
- What is acquired immunity? What are the different types of acquired immunity, and what are some examples of each? 424–26

21.4 Immunity Side Effects
- What types of complications and disorders are associated with the functioning of the immune system? 426–28

Weight loss, hand tremors, and insomnia sent Barbara to a doctor. The doctor said she had hyperthyroidism, also called Graves disease. A patient with Graves disease produces autoantibodies to the thyroid-stimulating hormone (TSH) receptor in the plasma membrane. The result is an overactive thyroid that produces too much of the thyroid's hormones.

Ordinarily, antibodies only attack foreign invaders, such as bacteria and viruses, and are part of the protective activity of the immune system. When the system runs amok and produces autoantibodies to self-components, the result is an autoimmune disease, such as Graves disease.

In this chapter, you will learn about some of the myriad defense mechanisms that protect you against infectious disease. These natural processes can also be activated through vaccination. But sometimes the immune system responds when it shouldn't. Then, allergies and autoimmune diseases result.

21.1   Organs, Tissues, and Cells of the Immune System

The **immune system,** which plays an important role in keeping us healthy, consists of a network of lymphatic organs, tissues, and cells as well as products of these cells, including antibodies and regulatory agents. **Antibodies** are proteins produced by the body in response to the presence of a foreign substance called an antigen. An **antigen** is a part of a molecule that can be recognized by lymphocytes because it binds to an antigen receptor. **Immunity** is the ability to react to antigens so that the body remains free of disease. **Disease,** a state of homeostatic imbalance, can be due to infection by foreign agents or to failure of the immune system to function properly.

Primary Lymphatic Organs

Lymphatic organs contain large numbers of lymphocytes, the type of white blood cell that plays a pivotal role in immunity (Fig. 21.1). The *primary lymphatic organs* are the red bone marrow and the thymus gland. Lymphocytes originate and/or mature in these organs.

Red Bone Marrow

Red bone marrow is the site of stem cells that are ever capable of dividing and producing blood cells. Some of these cells become the various types of white blood cells: neutrophils, eosinophils, basophils, monocytes, and lymphocytes.

In a child, most bones have red bone marrow, but in an adult it is present only at the ends of certain bones, the skull, the sternum, the ribs, the clavicle, the pelvic bones, and the vertebral column.

The red bone marrow consists of a network of connective tissue fibers, which support the stem cells and their progeny. They are packed around thin-walled sinuses filled with venous blood. Differentiated blood cells enter the bloodstream at these sinuses.

Lymphocytes differentiate into the B lymphocytes and the T lymphocytes. Bone marrow is not only the source of B lymphocytes, but also the place where B lymphocytes mature. T lymphocytes mature in the thymus gland.

Thymus Gland

The soft, bilobed **thymus gland** is located anterior to the ascending aorta and posterior to the sternum in the upper thoracic cavity. The thymus varies in size, but it is larger in children and shrinks as we get older. Connective tissue divides the thymus into lobules, which are filled with lymphocytes. The thymus gland produces thymic hormones, such as thymosin, that are thought to aid in maturation of T lymphocytes. Thymosin may also have other functions in immunity.

Immature T lymphocytes migrate from the bone marrow through the bloodstream to the thymus, where they mature. Only about 5% of these cells ever leave the thymus. These T lymphocytes have survived a critical test: If any show the ability to react with "self" cells, they die. If they have the potential to attack a foreign cell, they leave the thymus.

The thymus is absolutely critical to immunity; without a thymus, a person does not reject foreign tissues, blood lymphocyte levels are drastically reduced, and the body's response to most antigens is poor or absent.

Secondary Lymphatic Organs

The secondary lymphatic organs are the spleen, lymph nodes, and other organs, such as the tonsils, Peyer's patches, and the appendix. All the secondary organs are places where lymphocytes encounter and bind with antigens, after which they proliferate and become actively engaged cells.

Spleen

The **spleen** is located in the upper left region of the abdominal cavity posterior to the stomach. Connective tissue divides the spleen into partial compartments, each of which contains tissue known as white pulp and red pulp. The white pulp contains a concentration of lymphocytes; the red pulp, which surrounds venous sinuses, is involved in filtering the blood. Blood entering the spleen must pass through the sinuses before exiting. Lymphocytes and macrophages react to pathogens, and macrophages engulf debris and also remove any old, worn-out red blood cells.

The spleen's outer capsule is relatively thin, and an infection or a blow can cause the spleen to burst. Although its functions are replaced by other organs, a person without a spleen is often slightly more susceptible to infections and may have to receive antibiotic therapy indefinitely.

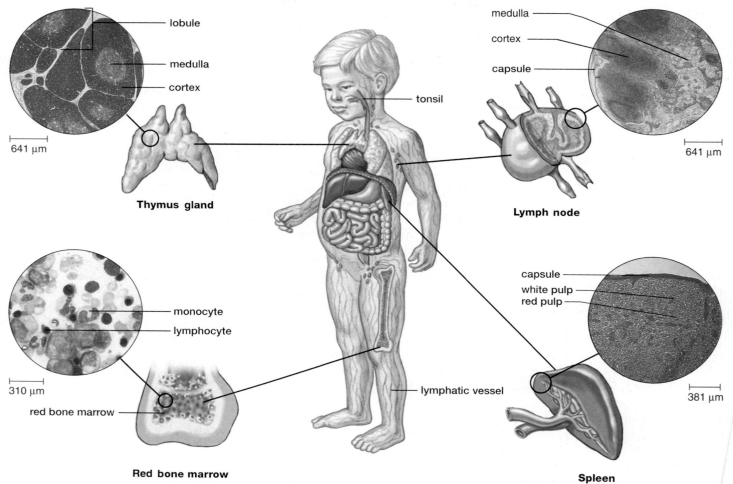

Figure 21.1   The lymphatic organs.
Left: The thymus gland and the red bone marrow are primary lymphatic organs. *Right:* Lymph nodes and the spleen, as well as other lymphatic organs such as the tonsils, are secondary lymphatic organs. In the spleen, the white pulp stains purple on a typical slide.

Lymph Nodes

Lymph nodes, which are small (about 1–25 mm in diameter), ovoid structures, occur along lymphatic vessels. Connective tissue forms the capsule of a lymph node and also divides the organ into compartments. Each compartment contains a nodule packed with B lymphocytes and a sinus that increases in size toward the center of the node. As lymph courses through the sinuses, it is filtered by macrophages, which engulf pathogens and debris. T lymphocytes, also present in sinuses, fight infections and attack cancer cells.

Lymph nodes are named for their location. Each cavity of the body contains lymph nodes except the dorsal cavity. Some nodes are superficial. For example, inguinal nodes are in the groin, and axillary nodes are in the armpits. Physicians often feel for the presence of swollen, tender lymph nodes in the neck as evidence that the body is fighting an infection. This is a noninvasive, preliminary way to help make such a diagnosis.

Other Lymphatic Organs

The **tonsils** are patches of lymphatic tissue located in a ring about the pharynx (see Fig. 8.2). The tonsils perform the same functions as lymph nodes, but because of their location, they are the first to encounter pathogens and antigens that enter the body by way of the nose and mouth.

Peyer's patches located in the intestinal wall and the **vermiform appendix** attached to the cecum, a blind pouch of the large intestine, encounter pathogens that enter the body by way of the intestinal tract.

Lymphocytes and other white blood cells are produced by the red bone marrow, which is a primary lymphatic organ along with the thymus, where T lymphocytes mature. Lymphocytes congregate in the secondary lymphatic organs: the spleen, the lymph nodes, and other organs, such as the tonsils.

Visual Focus

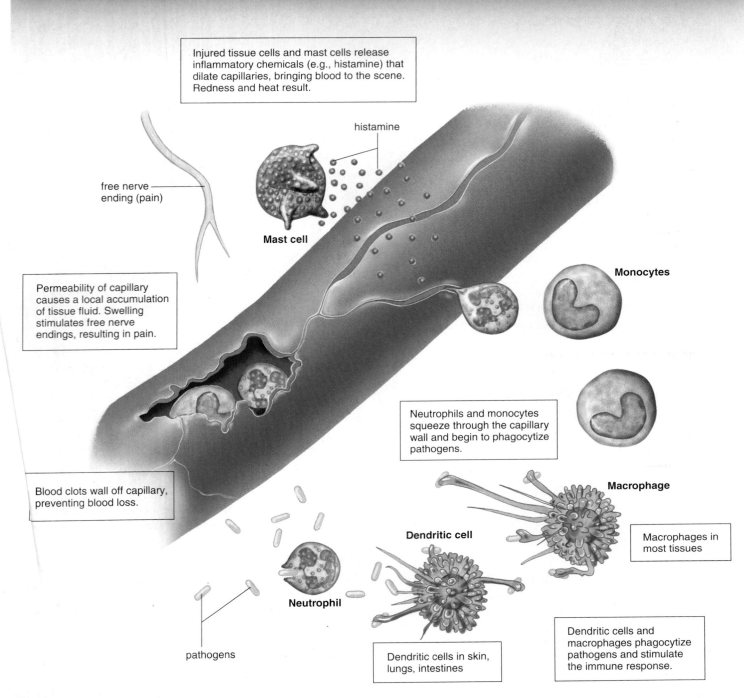

Injured tissue cells and mast cells release inflammatory chemicals (e.g., histamine) that dilate capillaries, bringing blood to the scene. Redness and heat result.

histamine

free nerve ending (pain)

Mast cell

Monocytes

Permeability of capillary causes a local accumulation of tissue fluid. Swelling stimulates free nerve endings, resulting in pain.

Neutrophils and monocytes squeeze through the capillary wall and begin to phagocytize pathogens.

Blood clots wall off capillary, preventing blood loss.

Macrophage

Dendritic cell

Macrophages in most tissues

Neutrophil

pathogens

Dendritic cells in skin, lungs, intestines

Dendritic cells and macrophages phagocytize pathogens and stimulate the immune response.

Figure 21.2 Inflammatory reaction.
When a blood vessel is injured, mast cells, a type of white blood cell found in tissue around blood vessels, release substances, such as histamine. Histamine dilates blood vessels and increases permeability so that tissue fluid leaks from the vessel. Swelling in the area stimulates pain receptors (free nerve endings). Neutrophils and monocytes squeeze through the capillary wall. These white blood cells begin to phagocytize pathogens (e.g., disease-causing viruses and bacteria). Dendritic cells and macrophages are even better at phagocytizing pathogens, and these cells go on to stimulate other immune cells. Blood clotting seals off the capillary, preventing blood loss and pathogen spread.

21.2 Nonspecific and Specific Defenses

Immunity includes nonspecific defenses and specific defenses. The four types of nonspecific defenses—barriers to entry, the inflammatory reaction, natural killer cells, and protective proteins—are effective against many types of infectious agents. Specific defenses are effective against a particular infectious agent.

Barriers to Entry

Skin and the mucous membranes lining the respiratory, digestive, and urinary tracts serve as mechanical barriers to entry by pathogens. Oil gland secretions contain chemicals that weaken or kill certain bacteria on the skin. The upper respiratory tract is lined by ciliated cells that sweep mucus and trapped particles up into the throat, where they can be swallowed or expectorated (coughed out). The stomach has an acidic pH, which inhibits the growth of or kills many types of bacteria. The various bacteria that normally reside in the intestine and other areas, such as the vagina, prevent pathogens from taking up residence.

Inflammatory Reaction

Whenever tissue is damaged by physical or chemical agents or by pathogens, a series of events occur that is known as the **inflammatory reaction.** Figure 21.2 illustrates the participants in the inflammatory reaction.

An inflamed area has four outward signs: redness, heat, swelling, and pain. All of these signs are due to capillary changes in the damaged area. Chemical mediators, such as **histamine** released by damaged tissue cells, and **mast cells,** widely distributed in connective tissues, cause the capillaries to dilate and become more permeable. Excess blood flow, due to enlarged capillaries, causes the skin to redden and become warm. Increased permeability of capillaries allows proteins and fluids to escape into the tissues, resulting in swelling. The swollen area stimulates free nerve endings, causing the sensation of pain.

Migration of phagocytes, namely neutrophils and monocytes, also occurs during the inflammatory reaction. Neutrophils and monocytes are amoeboid and can change shape to squeeze through capillary walls and

enter tissue fluid. Also present are **dendritic cells,** notably in the skin and mucous membranes, and **macrophages** in other tissues that are able to devour many pathogens and still survive (Fig. 21.3). Macrophages also release colony-stimulating factors, which pass by way of blood to the red bone marrow, where the factors stimulate the production and the release of white blood cells, primarily neutrophils. Neutrophils, dendritic cells, and macrophages engulf pathogens, which are destroyed by enzymes when endocytic vesicles combine with lysosome. As the infection is being overcome, some phagocytes die. These—along with dead tissue cells, dead bacteria, and living white blood cells—form pus, a whitish material. The presence of pus indicates that the body is trying to overcome an infection.

The inflammatory reaction can be accompanied by other responses to the injury. A blood clot can form to seal a break in a blood vessel. Antigens, chemical mediators, dendritic cells, and macrophages move through the tissue fluid and lymph to the lymph nodes. There, B lymphocytes and T lymphocytes are activated to mount a specific defense to the infection.

Sometimes an inflammation persists, and the result is chronic inflammation that is often treated by administering anti-inflammatory agents, such as aspirin, ibuprofen, or cortisone. These medications act against the chemical mediators released by the white blood cells in the damaged area.

The inflammatory reaction is a "call to arms"—it marshals phagocytic white blood cells to the site of bacterial invasion and stimulates the immune system to react against a possible infection.

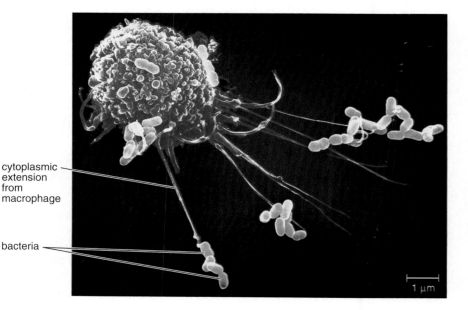

cytoplasmic extension from macrophage

bacteria

1 μm

Figure 21.3 Macrophage engulfing bacteria.

Natural Killer Cells

Natural killer (NK) cells are large, granular lymphocytes that kill virus-infected cells and tumor cells by cell-to-cell contact. What makes an NK cell attack and kill a cell? The cells of your body ordinarily have "self" proteins on their surface, which bind to receptors on NK cells. Sometimes, virus-infected cells and tumor cells undergo alterations and lose their self proteins. When NK cells can find no self proteins to bind to, they kill the cell by the same method as cytotoxic T cells (see page 423). NK cells are not specific; they have no memory; and their numbers do not increase when exposed to a particular antigen.

Protective Proteins

The **complement system,** often simply called complement, is composed of a number of blood plasma proteins designated by the letter C and a subscript. The complement proteins "complement" certain immune responses, which accounts for their name. For example, they are involved in and amplify the inflammatory response because certain complement proteins can bind to mast cells and trigger histamine release, and others can attract phagocytes to the scene. Some complement proteins bind to the surface of pathogens already coated with antibodies (see page 420), which ensures that the pathogens will be phagocytized by a neutrophil, dendritic cell, or macrophage.

Certain other complement proteins join to form a **membrane attack complex** that produces holes in the surface of bacteria and some viruses. Fluids and salts then enter the bacterial cell or virus to the point that they burst (Fig. 21.4).

Interferons are proteins produced by virus-infected cells as a warning to noninfected cells in the area. Interferon binds to receptors of noninfected cells, causing them to prepare for possible attack by producing substances that interfere with viral replication. Interferons are used as treatment in certain viral infections, such as hepatitis C.

Specific Defenses

When nonspecific defenses have failed to prevent an infection, specific defenses come into play. Because specific defenses do not ordinarily react to our own normal cells, it is said that the immune system is able to distinguish "self" from "nonself." Specific defenses take five to seven days to become fully activated, and they usually last for some time; for example, once we recover from measles, we usually do not get measles a second time.

Specific defenses primarily depend on the action of lymphocytes, which differentiate as either B lymphocytes (B cells) or T lymphocytes (T cells). B cells and T cells are capable of recognizing antigens because they have specific antigen receptors—plasma membrane receptor proteins, whose shape allows them to combine with particular antigens. Each lymphocyte has only one type receptor. It is often said that the receptor and the antigen fit together like a lock and a key. Because we encounter a million different antigens during our lifetime, we need a diversity of B cells and T cells to protect us against them. Remarkably, diversification occurs to such an extent, during the maturation process, that there are specific B cells and/or T cells for any possible antigen.

B cells give rise to plasma cells, which produce antibodies, which are capable of combining with and neutralizing a particular antigen. In contrast, **T cells** do not produce antibodies. Instead, they differentiate into either helper T cells, which release chemicals to regulate the immune response, or cytotoxic T cells, which attack and kill virus-infected cells and tumor cells.

B Cells and Antibody-Mediated Immunity

The receptor on a B cell is called a *B-cell receptor (BCR).* A B cell is activated in a lymph node or spleen when its BCRs bind to a specific antigen. Thereafter, the B cell divides by mitosis many times. In other words, it makes many clones of

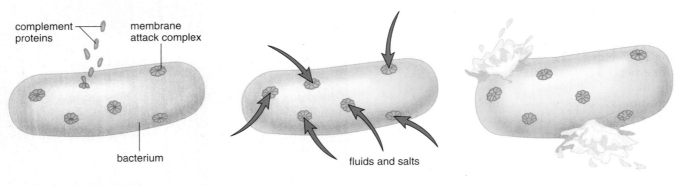

complement proteins   membrane attack complex

bacterium

fluids and salts

Complement proteins form a membrane attack complex in the bacterial cell wall and membrane.

Holes in the middle of the complexes allow fluids and salts to enter the bacterium.

Bacterium expands until it bursts.

Figure 21.4   Action of the complement system against a bacterium.
When complement proteins in the blood plasma are activated by an immune response, they form a membrane attack complex that makes holes in bacterial cell walls and plasma membranes, allowing fluids and salts to enter until the cell eventually bursts.

itself. Most of the resulting cells (clones) become **plasma cells,** which circulate in the blood and lymph. Plasma cells are larger than regular B cells because they have extensive rough endoplasmic reticulum for the mass production and secretion of antibodies to a specific antigen. Antibodies are identical to the BCR of the B cell that was activated.

The **clonal selection theory** states that an antigen selects, then binds to the BCR of only one type B cell or T cell, and then this B cell or T cell clones. Note in Figure 21.5 that each B cell has a specific BCR represented by shape. Only the B cell with a BCR that has a shape that fits the antigen (red circle) undergoes clonal expansion. During clonal expansion, cytokines secreted by helper T cells (see page 423) stimulate B cells to clone. Some cloned B cells become memory cells, which are the means by which long-term immunity is possible. If the same antigen enters the system again, memory B cells quickly divide and give rise to more plasma cells capable of quickly producing the correct type antibody.

Once the threat of an infection has passed, the development of new plasma cells ceases, and those present undergo apoptosis. **Apoptosis** is the process of programmed cell death (PCD) involving a cascade of specific cellular events leading to the death and destruction of the cell (see page 335).

Defense by B cells is called **antibody-mediated immunity** because the various types of activated B cells become plasma cells that produce antibodies. It is also called humoral immunity because these antibodies are present in blood and lymph. A humor is any fluid normally occurring in the body.

Characteristics of B Cells

- Antibody-mediated immunity against pathogens
- Produced and mature in bone marrow
- Reside in lymph nodes and spleen, circulate in blood and lymph
- Directly recognize antigen and then undergo clonal selection
- Clonal expansion produces antibody-secreting plasma cells as well as memory B cells

---

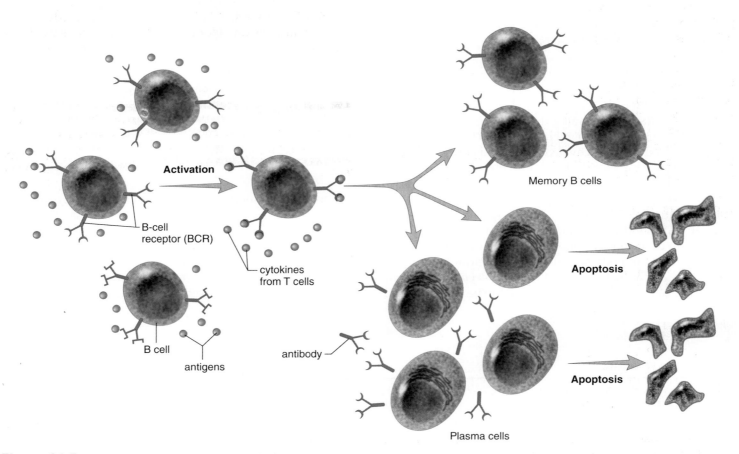

Figure 21.5   Clonal selection theory as it applies to B cells.
Each B cell has a B-cell receptor (BCR) designated by shape that will combine with a specific antigen. Activation of a B cell occurs when its BCR can combine with an antigen (red circle). In the presence of cytokines, the B cell undergoes clonal expansion, producing many plasma cells that secrete antibodies specific to the antigen and memory B cells that immediately recognize the antigen in the future. After the infection passes, plasma cells undergo apoptosis.

Structure of an Antibody   Antibodies are also called **immunoglobulins (Igs).** They are typically Y-shaped molecules with two arms. Each arm has a "heavy" (long) polypeptide chain and a "light" (short) polypeptide chain. These chains have constant regions, where the sequence of amino acids is set, and variable regions, where the sequence of amino acids varies between antibodies (Fig. 21.6). The constant regions are not identical among all the antibodies. Instead, they are almost the same within a particular antibody class. The variable regions become hypervariable at their tips and form antigen-binding sites, and their shape is specific for a particular antigen. It is the variable and hypervariable regions that change to be specific for a particular antigen. The antigen combines with the antibody at the antigen-binding site in a lock-and-key manner.

The antigen-antibody reaction can take several forms, but quite often the reaction produces complexes of antigens combined with antibodies. Such antigen-antibody complexes, sometimes called immune complexes, mark the antigens for destruction. For example, an antigen-antibody complex may be engulfed by neutrophils or macrophages, or it may activate complement. Complement makes pathogens more susceptible to phagocytosis, as discussed previously.

Types of Antibodies   There are five different classes of circulating antibodies (Table 21.1). IgG antibodies are the major type in blood, lymph, and tissue fluid. IgG antibodies bind to pathogens and their toxins. They can activate the complement system. IgGs are the only antibodies that can cross the placenta, and along with IgAs, are in breast milk. IgM antibodies are pentamers, meaning that they contain five of the Y-shaped structures shown in Figure 21.6a. These antibodies are the first produced by activated B cells, and are the first seen in the blood after a vaccination or infection. They disappear before the infection ends. They are good activators of the complement system. IgMs are the antibodies in plasma that can cause red blood cells to clump. IgA antibodies are monomers in blood and lymph or dimers in tears, saliva, gastric juice, and mucous secretions. They are the main type of antibody found in body secretions. IgAs bind to pathogens before they reach the bloodstream. IgD molecules appear in the surface of B cells when they are ready to be activated. IgE

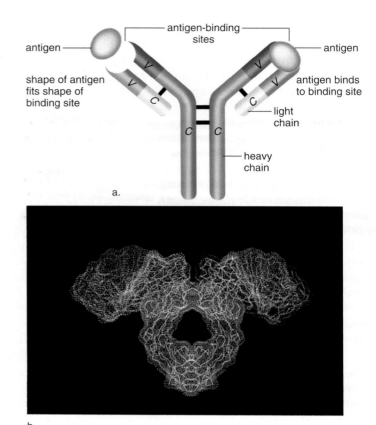

Figure 21.6   **Structure of an antibody.**
a. An antibody contains two heavy (long) polypeptide chains and two light (short) chains arranged so there are two variable regions, where a particular antigen is capable of binding with an antibody (*V* = variable region, *C* = constant region). **b.** Computer model of an antibody molecule. The antigen combines with the two side branches.

antibodies are important in the immune system's response to parasites (e.g., parasitic worms). They are best known, however, for immediate allergic responses, including anaphylactic shock (see page 426) and asthma (see page 427). IgE antibodies bind to receptors on basophils and mast cells. Once bound, these antibodies allow mast cells and basophils to react to the antigen in an antigen-specific manner.

Table 21.1	Antibodies	
Class	**Presence**	**Function**
IgG	Main antibody type in circulation	Binds to pathogens, activates complement, and enhances phagocytosis
IgM	Antibody type found in circulation; largest antibody	Activates complement; clumps cells
IgA	Main antibody type in secretions such as saliva and milk	Prevents pathogens from attaching to epithelial cells in digestive and respiratory tract
IgD	Antibody type found on surface of immature B cells	Presence signifies readiness of B cell
IgE	Antibody type found as antigen receptors on basophils in blood and on mast cells in tissues	Responsible for immediate allergic response and protection against certain parasitic worms

Pesticide: An Asset and a Liability

A pesticide is any one of 55,000 chemical products used to kill insects, plants, fungi, or rodents that interfere with human activities. Increasingly, we have discovered that pesticides are harmful to both the environment and to humans (Fig. 21A). The effect of pesticides on the immune system is a new area of concern; no testing except for skin sensitization has thus far been required before pesticide products are put on the market. Contact or respiratory allergic responses are among the most immediately obvious toxic effects of pesticides. But pesticides can also cause suppression of the immune system, leading to increased susceptibility to infection or tumor development. Lymphocyte impairment was found following the worst industrial accident in the world,

Figure 21A Pesticide warning signs indicate that pesticides are harmful to our health.

which took place in India in 1984. Nerve gas used to produce an insecticide was released into the air; 3,700 people were killed, and 30,000 were injured. Vietnam veterans claim a variety of health effects due to contact with a herbicide called Agent Orange that was used as a defoliant during the Vietnam War. The Environmental Protection Agency (EPA) says that pesticide residues on food possibly cause suppression of the immune system, disorders of the nervous system, birth defects, and cancer. The immune, nervous, and endocrine systems communicate with one another by way of hormones, and what affects one system can affect the other. In men, testicular atrophy, low sperm counts, and abnormal sperm may be due to the ability of pesticides to mimic the effects of estrogen, a female sex hormone.

The argument for using pesticides at first seems attractive. Pesticides are meant to kill off disease-causing agents, increase crop yield, and work quickly with minimal risk. But over time, it has been found that pesticides do not meet these claims. Instead, pests become resistant to pesticides, which kill off their natural enemies in addition to the pest. Then the pest population explodes. For example, at first DDT did a marvelous job of killing off the mosquitoes that carry malaria; now malaria is as big a problem as ever. In the meantime, DDT has accumulated in the tissues of wildlife and humans, causing harmful effects. The problem was made obvious when birds of prey became unable to reproduce due to weak eggshells. The use of DDT is now banned in the United States.

There are alternatives to the use of pesticides. Integrated pest management uses a diversified environment, mechanical and physical means, natural enemies, disruption of reproduction, and resistant plants to control rather than eradicate pest populations. Chemicals are used only as a last resort. Maintaining hedgerows, weedy patches, and certain trees can provide diverse habitats and food for predators and parasites that help control pests. The use of strip farming and crop rotation by farmers denies pests a continuous food source.

Natural enemies abound in the environment. When lacewings were released in cotton fields, they reduced the boll weevil population by 96% and increased cotton yield threefold. A predatory moth was used to reclaim 60 million acres in Australia overrun by the prickly pear cactus, and another type of moth is now used to control alligator weed in the southern United States. Also in the United States, the *Chrysolina* beetle controls Klamath weed, except in shady places where a root-boring beetle is more effective.

Sex attractants and sterile insects are used in other types of biological control. In Sweden and Norway, scientists synthesized the sex pheromone of the *Ips* bark beetle, which attacks spruce trees. Almost 100,000 baited traps collected females normally attracted to males emitting this pheromone. Sterile males have also been used to reduce pest populations. The screwworm fly parasitizes cattle in the United States. Flies raised in a laboratory were made sterile by exposure to radiation. The entire Southeast was freed from this parasite when female flies mated with sterile males and then laid eggs that did not hatch.

In general, biological control is a more sophisticated method of controlling pests than the use of pesticides. It requires an in-depth knowledge of pests and/or their life cycles. Because it does not have an immediate effect on the pest population, the effects of biological control may not be apparent to the farmer or gardener who eventually benefits from it.

Citizens can promote biological control of pests by:

- Urging elected officials to support legislation to protect humans and the environment against the use of pesticides.
- Allowing native plants to grow on all or most of the land to give natural predators a place to live.
- Cutting down on the use of pesticides, herbicides, and fertilizers for the lawn, garden, and house.
- Using alternative methods such as cleanliness and good sanitation to keep household pests under control.
- Disposing of pesticides in a safe manner.

T Cells and Cell-Mediated Immunity

When a T cell leaves the thymus, it has a unique *T-cell receptor (TCR)* just as B cells have. Unlike B cells, however, T cells are unable to recognize an antigen without help. The antigen must be displayed to them by an **antigen-presenting cell (APC),** such as a dendritic cell or a macrophage. After phagocytizing a pathogen, APCs travel to a lymph node or spleen, where T cells also congregate. In the meantime, the APC has broken the pathogen apart in a lysosome. A piece of the pathogen is then displayed in the groove of an MHC (major histocompatibility complex) protein on the cell's surface. MHC proteins are called "self" proteins because they mark cells as belonging to a particular individual and make transplantation of organs difficult.

In Figure 21.7, the different types of T cells have specific TCRs represented by their different shapes. A macrophage is presenting an antigen to a T cell. This T cell has the specific TCR that will combine with this particular antigen, represented by a red circle. Now, the T cell is activated and undergoes clonal expansion. Many copies of the activated T cell are produced during clonal expansion. There are two classes of MHC proteins (called MHC I and MHC II). If an APC displays an antigen within the groove of an MHC I protein, the activated T cell will form cytotoxic T cells. If an APC displays an antigen within the groove of an MHC II protein, the activated T cell will form helper T cells.

As the illness disappears, the immune reaction wanes, and activated T cells become susceptible to apoptosis. As mentioned previously, apoptosis contributes to homeostasis by regulating the number of cells present in an organ, or in this case, in the immune system. When apoptosis does not occur as it should, T-cell cancers (i.e., lymphomas and leukemias) can result. Also, in the thymus, any T cell that has the potential to destroy the body's own cells undergoes apoptosis.

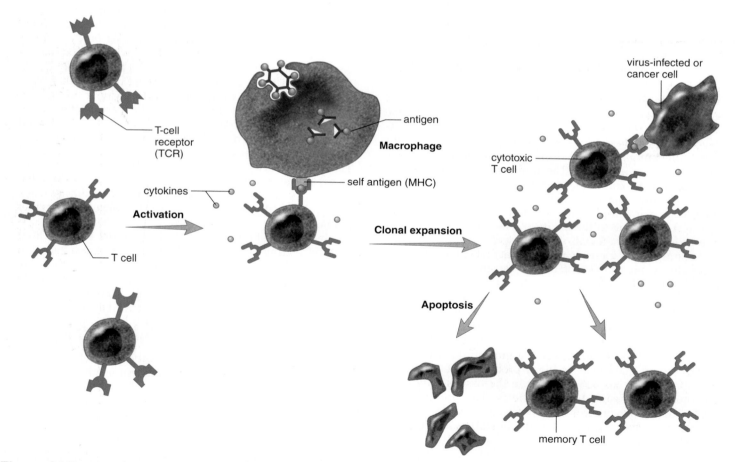

Figure 21.7   Clonal selection theory as it applies to T cells.
Each T cell has a T-cell receptor (TCR) designated by shape that will combine only with a specific antigen. Activation of a T cell occurs when its TCR can combine with an antigen. A macrophage presents the antigen (red circle) in the groove of an MHC protein. Thereafter, the T cell undergoes clonal expansion, and many copies of the same type T cell are produced. After the immune response has been successful, the majority of T cells undergo apoptosis, but a small number are memory T cells. Memory T cells provide protection should the same antigen enter the body again at a future time.

Types of T Cells The two main types of T cells are cytotoxic T cells and helper T cells. **Cytotoxic T cells** have storage vacuoles containing perforins and storage vacuoles containing enzymes called granzymes. After a cytotoxic T cell binds to a virus-infected cell or tumor cell, it releases perforin molecules, which perforate the plasma membrane, forming a pore. Cytotoxic T cells then deliver granzymes into the pore, and these cause the cell to undergo apoptosis and die. Once cytotoxic T cells have released the perforins and granzymes, they move on to the next target cell. Cytotoxic T cells are responsible for so-called **cell-mediated immunity** (Fig. 21.8).

Helper T cells regulate immunity by secreting **cytokines,** the chemicals that enhance the response of all types of immune cells. B cells cannot be activated without T-cell help. Because the human immunodeficiency virus (HIV), the virus that causes AIDS, infects helper T cells and other cells of the immune system, it inactivates the immune response and makes HIV-infected individuals susceptible to opportunistic infections. Infected macrophages and dendritic cells serve as reservoirs for the HIV virus.

Notice in Figure 21.7 that a few of the clonally expanded T cells are memory T cells. They remain in the body and can jump-start an immune reaction to an antigen previously present in the body.

Characteristics of T Cells

- Cell-mediated immunity against virus-infected cells and cancer cells
- Produced in bone marrow, mature in thymus
- Antigen must be presented in groove of an MHC molecule
- Cytotoxic T cells destroy nonself antigen-bearing cells
- Helper T cells secrete cytokines that control the immune response

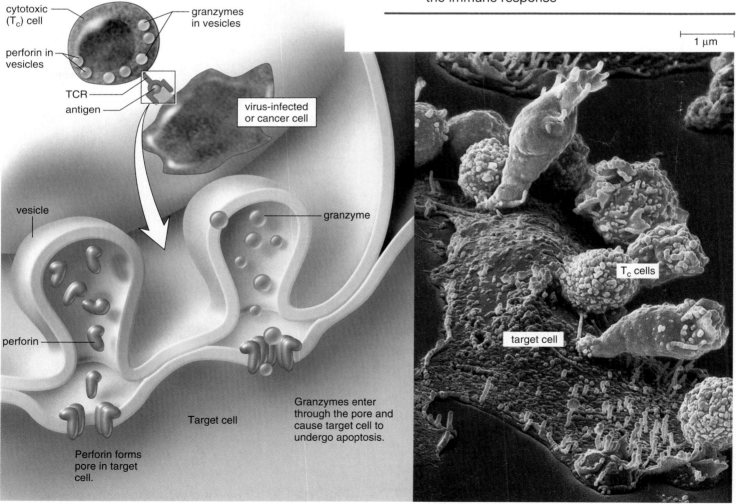

Figure 21.8 **Cell-mediated immunity.**
a. How a T cell destroys a virus-infected cell or cancer cell. **b.** The scanning electron micrograph shows cytotoxic T cells attacking and destroying a cancer cell (target cell).

21.3 Acquired Immunity

Immunity occurs naturally through infection or is brought about artificially (induced) by medical intervention. The two types of acquired immunity are active and passive. In **active immunity,** the individual alone produces antibodies against an antigen; in **passive immunity,** the individual is given prepared antibodies via an injection.

Active Immunity

Active immunity sometimes develops naturally after a person is infected with a pathogen. However, active immunity is often induced when a person is well so that future infection will not take place. To prevent infections, people can be artificially immunized against them. The United States is committed to immunizing all children against the common types of childhood disease.

Immunization involves the use of **vaccines,** substances that contain an antigen to which the immune system responds. Traditionally, vaccines are the pathogens themselves, or their products, that have been treated so they are no longer virulent (able to cause disease). Today, it is possible to genetically engineer bacteria to mass-produce a protein from pathogens, and this protein can be used as a vaccine. This method has now produced a vaccine against hepatitis B, a viral-induced disease, and is being used to prepare a vaccine against malaria, a protozoan-induced disease.

After a vaccine is given, it is possible to follow an immune response by determining the amount of antibody present in a sample of plasma—this is called the **antibody titer.** After the first exposure to a vaccine, a primary response occurs. For a period of several days, no antibodies are present; then the titer rises slowly, levels off, and gradually declines as the antibodies bind to the antigen or simply break down (Fig. 21.9). After a second exposure to the vaccine, a secondary response is expected. The titer rises rapidly to a level much greater than before; then it slowly declines. The second exposure is called a "booster" because it boosts the antibody titer to a high level. The high antibody titer now is expected to help prevent disease symptoms even if the individual is exposed to the disease-causing antigen.

Active immunity depends upon the presence of memory B cells and memory T cells that are capable of responding to lower doses of antigen. Active immunity is usually long-lasting, although a booster may be required every so many years.

Active (long-lasting) immunity can be induced by the use of vaccines. Active immunity depends upon the presence of memory B cells and memory T cells in the body.

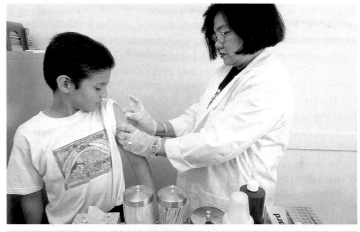

Suggested Immunization Schedule

Vaccine	Age (months)	Age (years)
Hepatitis B	Birth–18	11–12
Diphtheria, tetanus, pertussis (DTP)	2, 4, 6, 15–18	4–6
Tetanus only		11–12, 14–16
Haemophilus influenzae, type b	2, 4, 6, 12–15	
Polio	2, 4, 6–18	4–6
Pneumococcal	2, 4, 6, 12–15	
Measles, mumps, rubella (MMR)	12–15	4–6, 11–12
Varicella (chickenpox)	12–18	11–12
Hepatitis A (in selected areas)	24	4–12
Human papilloma-virus, type 16	–	12–14

a.

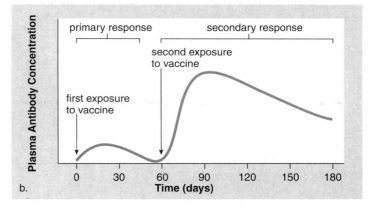

b.

Figure 21.9   **Active immunity due to immunizations.**
a. Suggested immunization schedule for infants and children.
b. During immunization, the primary response, after the first exposure to a vaccine, is minimal, but the secondary response, which may occur after the second exposure, shows a dramatic rise in the amount of antibody present in plasma.

Passive Immunity

Passive immunity occurs when an individual is given prepared antibodies (immunoglobulins) to combat a disease. Since these antibodies are not produced by the individual's plasma cells, passive immunity is temporary. For example, newborn infants are passively immune to some diseases because IgG antibodies have crossed the placenta from the mother's blood (Fig. 21.10*a*). These antibodies soon disappear, however, so within a few months, infants become more susceptible to infections. Breast-feeding prolongs the natural passive immunity an infant receives from the mother because IgG and IgA antibodies are present in the mother's milk (Fig. 21.10*b*).

Even though passive immunity does not last, it is sometimes used to prevent illness in a patient who has been unexpectedly exposed to an infectious disease. Usually, the patient receives a gamma globulin injection (serum that contains antibodies), perhaps taken from individuals who have recovered from the illness (Fig 21.10*c*). In the past, horses were immunized, and serum was taken from them to provide the needed antibodies against such diseases as diphtheria, botulism, and tetanus. Unfortunately, a patient who received these antibodies became ill about 50% of the time, because the serum contained proteins that the individual's immune system recognized as foreign. This was called serum sickness. Passive immunity using horse antibodies against poisonous snake and spider venom is still used today. Antivenom antibodies are immunoglobulins produced in horses. Problems can also occur with products made in other ways. An immunoglobulin intravenous product called Gammagard was withdrawn from the market because of its possible implication in the transmission of hepatitis.

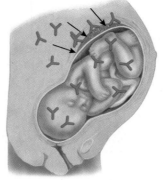

a. Antibodies (IgG) cross the placenta.

b. Antibodies (IgG, IgA) are secreted into breast milk.

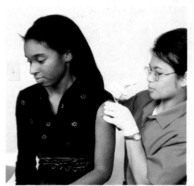

c. Antibodies can be injected by a physician.

Figure 21.10   Passive immunity.
During passive immunity, antibodies are received (**a**) by crossing the placenta, (**b**) in breast milk, or (**c**) by injection. Because the body is not producing the antibodies, passive immunity is short-lived.

> Passive immunity provides protection when an individual is in immediate danger of succumbing to an infectious disease. Passive immunity is temporary because there are no memory cells.

Cytokines and Immunity

Cytokines are signaling molecules produced by T lymphocytes, macrophages, and other cells. Because cytokines regulate white blood cell formation and/or function, they are being investigated as a possible adjunct therapy for cancer and AIDS. Both interferon and **interleukins,** which are cytokines produced by various white blood cells, have been used as immunotherapeutic drugs, particularly to enhance the ability of the individual's own T cells to fight cancer.

Because most cancer cells carry an altered protein on their cell surface, they should be attacked and destroyed by cytotoxic T cells. Whenever cancer develops, it is possible that cytotoxic T cells have not been activated. In that case, cytokines might awaken the immune system and lead to the destruction of the cancer. In one technique being investigated, researchers first withdraw T cells from the patient, present cancer cell antigens to them, and then activate the cells by culturing them in the presence of an interleukin. The T cells are reinjected into the patient, who is given doses of interleukin to maintain the killer activity of the T cells.

Scientists who are actively engaged in interleukin research believe that interleukins soon will be used as adjuncts for vaccines, for the treatment of chronic infectious disease, and perhaps for the treatment of cancer. Interleukin antagonists also may prove helpful in preventing skin and organ rejection, autoimmune diseases, and allergies.

Monoclonal Antibodies

Every plasma cell derived from the same B cell secretes antibodies against a specific antigen. These are **monoclonal antibodies** because all of them are the same type and because they are produced by plasma cells derived from the same B cell. One method of producing monoclonal antibodies in vitro (outside the body in glassware) is

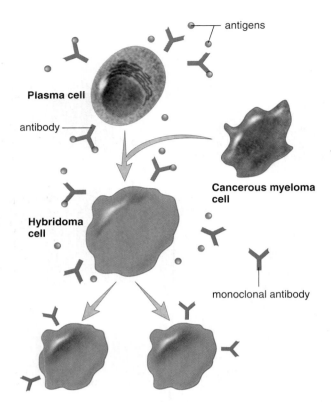

Figure 21.11   Production of monoclonal antibodies.
Plasma cells of the same type (derived from immunized mice) are fused with myeloma (cancerous) cells, producing hybridoma cells that are "immortal." Hybridoma cells divide and continue to produce the same type of antibody, called monoclonal antibodies.

depicted in Figure 21.11. B lymphocytes are removed from an animal (today, usually mice are used) and are exposed to a particular antigen. The resulting plasma cells are fused with myeloma cells (malignant plasma cells that live and divide indefinitely; they are immortal cells). The fused cells are called hybridomas—*hybrid-* because they result from the fusion of two different cells, and *-oma* because one of the cells is a cancer cell.

At present, monoclonal antibodies are being used for quick and certain diagnosis of various conditions. For example, a particular hormone is present in the urine of a pregnant woman. A monoclonal antibody can be used to detect this hormone; if it is present, the woman knows she is pregnant. Monoclonal antibodies are also used to identify infections. And because they can distinguish between cancerous and normal tissue cells, they are used to carry radioactive isotopes or toxic drugs to tumors, which can then be selectively destroyed. Herceptin is a monoclonal antibody used in the treatment of breast cancer. It binds to a protein receptor on breast cancer cells and prevents the cancer cells from dividing so fast. Antibodies that bind to cancer cells also can activate complement, can increase phagocytosis by macrophages and neutrophils, and can attract NK cells.

21.4 Immunity Side Effects

Sometimes the immune system responds in a manner that harms the body, as when individuals develop allergies, receive an incompatible blood type, suffer tissue rejection, or have an autoimmune disease.

Allergies

Allergies are hypersensitivities to substances, such as pollen, food, or animal hair, that ordinarily would do no harm to the body. The response to these antigens, called **allergens,** usually includes some degree of tissue damage.

An **immediate allergic response** can occur within seconds of contact with the antigen. The response is caused by antibodies known as IgE (see Table 21.1). IgE antibodies are attached to the plasma membrane of mast cells in the tissues and also to basophils in the blood. When an allergen attaches to the IgE antibodies on these cells, mast cells release histamine and other substances that bring about the allergic symptoms. When pollen is an allergen, histamine stimulates the mucous membranes of the nose and eyes to release fluid, causing the runny nose and watery eyes typical of **hay fever.** If a person has **asthma,** as discussed in the Health Focus on page 427, the airways leading to the lungs constrict, resulting in difficult breathing accompanied by wheezing. When food contains an allergen, nausea, vomiting, and diarrhea result.

Anaphylactic shock is an immediate allergic response that occurs because the allergen has entered the bloodstream. Bee stings and penicillin shots are known to cause this reaction because both inject the allergen into the blood. Anaphylactic shock is characterized by a sudden and life-threatening drop in blood pressure due to increased permeability of the capillaries by histamine. Taking epinephrine can delay this reaction until medical help is available.

People with allergies produce ten times more IgE than those people without allergies. A new treatment using injections of monoclonal IgG antibodies for IgEs is currently being tested in individuals with severe food allergies. More routinely, injections of the allergen are given so that the body will build up high quantities of IgG antibodies. The hope is that these will combine with allergens received from the environment before they have a chance to reach the IgE antibodies located in the membrane of mast cells and basophils.

A **delayed allergic response** is initiated by memory T cells at the site of allergen contact in the body. The allergic response is regulated by the cytokines secreted by both T cells and macrophages. A classic example of a delayed allergic response is the skin test for tuberculosis (TB). When the test result is positive, the tissue where the antigen was injected becomes red and hardened. This shows that there was prior exposure to tubercle bacilli, the cause of TB. Contact dermatitis, which occurs when a person is allergic to poison ivy, jewelry, cosmetics, and many other substances that touch the skin, is also an example of a delayed allergic response.

Health Focus

Preventing Asthma

During an asthma attack, the muscles around the airways tighten, and the lining inside the airways swells or thickens and gets clogged with lots of thick mucus. This makes it hard to breathe. A significant number of asthma attacks are cause by allergens that attach to IgE antibodies located in the plasma membrane of mast cells (see Figure 21B). The release of histamine and other chemicals bring on the symptoms of asthma.

The number of children who suffer from asthma attacks is on the increase, and researchers want to know why. The results of a survey carried out in Salzburg, Austria, in 1999 showed that children who lived in rural areas and had regular contact with farm animals were considerably less likely to have asthma. The following year, a study carried out in Arizona indicated that young children who attended daycare or who had older siblings suffered from more infections, but were less likely to develop asthma. A recent study, conducted by the National Institute of Allergy and Infectious Diseases, found that children raised in a house with two or more dogs or cats during the first year of life may be less likely to develop allergic diseases. These children were 66–77% less likely to have IgE-class antibodies to common allergens as children exposed to only one or no pets during the first year.

Consider also, that numerous circumstances, such as safety considerations, indoor entertainment systems, and lack of outdoor play areas, are causing children in our modern world to spend more time indoors. A mania for household cleanliness might insulate some of them from sustained contact with ordinary dirt. Could it be that exposure to the antigens of the natural world from an early age could help prevent inappropriate immune responses, such as allergies and asthma? Some researchers think this is a logical hypothesis.

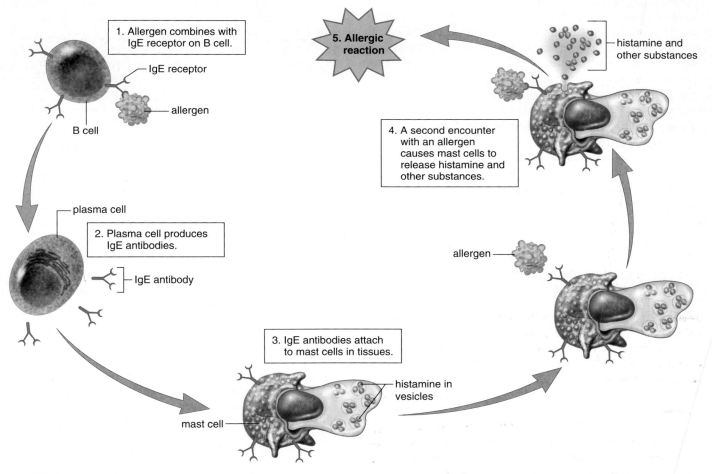

Figure 21B   **Allergic reaction.**

When an allergen combines with IgE antibodies attached to mast cells, the release of histamine, in particular, leads to an allergic rea

Tissue Rejection

Certain organs, such as skin, the heart, and the kidneys, could be transplanted easily from one person to another if the body did not attempt to reject them. Rejection of transplanted tissue results because the recipient's immune system recognizes that the transplanted tissue is not "self." Cytotoxic T cells respond by causing disintegration of the transplanted tissue.

Organ rejection can be controlled by carefully selecting the organ to be transplanted and administering **immunosuppressive** drugs. It is best if the transplanted organ has the same type of MHC antigens as those of the recipient, because cytotoxic T cells recognize foreign MHC antigens. Two well-known immunosuppressive drugs, cyclosporine and tacrolimus, both act by inhibiting the response of T cells to cytokines.

Researchers hope that tissue engineering, including the production of organs that lack antigens, will one day do away with the problem of rejection.

Xenotransplantation is the use of animal organs instead of human organs in transplant patients. Scientists have chosen to use the pig because animal husbandry has long included the raising of pigs as a meat source, and pigs are prolific. Genetic engineering can make pig organs less antigenic. The ultimate goal is to make pig organs as widely accepted as type O blood. An alternative to xenotransplantation exists because bioengineering is making organs in the laboratory. Scientists are ready to test a lab-grown urinary bladder in human patients.

When tissue rejection occurs, the immune system has recognized and destroyed cells that bear foreign MHC antigens.

Diseases of the Immune System

When a person has an **autoimmune disease,** cytotoxic T cells or antibodies mistakenly attack the body's own cells as if they bear foreign antigens. Exactly what causes autoimmune diseases is not known. However, sometimes they occur after an individual has recovered from an infection.

In the autoimmune disease **myasthenia gravis,** neuromuscular junctions do not work properly, and muscular weakness results. In **multiple sclerosis (MS),** the myelin sheath of nerve fibers breaks down, and this causes various neuromuscular symptoms. A person with **systemic lupus erythematosus (SLE)** has various symptoms prior to death due to kidney damage. In **rheumatoid arthritis,** the joints are affected. Researchers suggest that heart damage following rheumatic fever and diabetes type 1 are also autoimmune illnesses. As yet, there are no cures for autoimmune diseases, but they can be controlled with drugs.

When a person has an immune deficiency, the immune system is unable to protect the body against disease. Acquired immunodeficiency syndrome (AIDS) is an example of an acquired immune deficiency. As a result of a weakened immune system, AIDS patients show a greater susceptibility to a variety of diseases and also have a higher risk of cancer. Immune deficiency may also be congenital (i.e., inherited). Infrequently, a child may be born with an impaired B- or T-cell system caused by a defect in lymphocyte development. In **severe combined immunodeficiency disease (SCID),** both antibody- and cell-mediated immunity are lacking or inadequate. Without treatment, even common infections can be fatal. Gene therapy has been successful in SCID patients.

Diseases of the immune system are autoimmune or immune deficiency disorders.

Summarizing the Concepts

21.1 Organs, Tissues, and Cells of the Immune System

The immune system consists of lymphatic organs, tissues, and cells as well as the products of these cells. The primary lymphatic organs are (1) the red bone marrow, where all blood cells are made and the B lymphocytes mature, and (2) the thymus gland, where T lymphocytes mature.

The secondary lymphatic organs are the spleen, lymph nodes, and other organs such as the tonsils, Peyer's patches, and the appendix. Blood is cleansed of pathogens and debris in the spleen, and lymph is cleansed of pathogens and debris in the nodes. The other organs mentioned are the first line of defense against pathogens that enter the body.

21.2 Nonspecific and Specific Defenses

Immunity involves nonspecific and specific defenses. Nonspecific defenses include barriers to entry, the inflammatory reaction, natural killer cells, and protective proteins.

Specific defenses require B lymphocytes and T lymphocytes, also called B cells and T cells. B cells undergo clonal selection with production of plasma cells and memory B cells after their B-cell receptor combines with a specific antigen. Plasma cells secrete antibodies and eventually undergo apoptosis. Plasma cells are responsible for antibody-mediated immunity. An antibody is usually a Y-shaped molecule that has two binding sites for a specific antigen. Memory B cells remain in the body and produce antibodies if the same antigen enters the body at a later date.

T cells have T-cell receptors and are responsible for cell-mediated immunity. For a T cell to recognize an antigen, the antigen must be presented by an antigen-presenting cell (APC), a dendritic cell, or a macrophage, along with an MHC (major histocompatibility complex). Thereafter, the activated T cell undergoes clonal expansion until the illness has been stemmed. Then, most of the activated T cells undergo apoptosis. A few cells remain, however, as memory T cells.

The two main types of T cells are cytotoxic T cells and helper T cells. Cytotoxic T cells kill virus-infected or cancer cells on contact because they bear a nonself protein. Helper T cells produce cytokines and stimulate other immune cells.

21.3 Acquired Immunity

Active (long-lived) immunity can be induced by vaccines when a person is well and in no immediate danger of contracting an infectious disease. Active immunity depends upon the presence of memory cells in the body.

Passive immunity is needed when an individual is in immediate danger of succumbing to an infectious disease. Passive immunity is short-lived because the antibodies are administered to and not made by the individual. Cytokines, including interferon, are a form of passive immunity used to treat AIDS and to promote the body's ability to recover from cancer. Monoclonal antibodies, which are produced by the same plasma cell, have various functions, from detecting infections to treating cancer.

21.4 Immunity Side Effects

Allergic responses occur when the immune system reacts vigorously to substances not normally recognized as foreign. Immediate allergic responses, usually consisting of cold-like symptoms, are due to the activity of antibodies. Delayed allergic responses, such as contact dermatitis, are due to the activity of T cells. Immunity side effects also include blood-type reactions, tissue rejection, and autoimmune diseases.

Studying the Concepts

1. Describe the structure and function of the primary lymphatic organs. 414
2. What are the secondary lymphatic organs, and what role do they play in immunity? 414–15
3. What are the body's nonspecific defense mechanisms? 416–18
4. Describe the inflammatory reaction, and give a role for each type of cell and molecule that participates in the reaction. 416–17
5. What is the clonal selection theory as it applies to B cells? B cells are responsible for which type of immunity? 418–19
6. Describe the structure of an antibody, and define the terms *variable regions* and *constant regions*. 420
7. Describe the clonal selection theory as it applies to T cells. 422
8. Name the two main types of T cells, and state their functions. 423
9. How is active immunity artificially achieved? How is passive immunity achieved? 424–25
10. What are cytokines, and how are they used in immunotherapy? 425
11. How are monoclonal antibodies produced, and what are their applications? 425–26
12. Discuss allergies, tissue rejection, and autoimmune diseases as they relate to the immune system. 426–28

Thinking Critically About the Concepts

Refer to the opening vignette on page 414, and then answer these questions.

1. What are some of the other conditions that are the result of autoantibodies attacking the body's own cells?
2. Are antibodies part of the specific (acquired) defense system, or the nonspecific (innate) system?
3. Which cell type is responsible for antibody production?

Testing Your Knowledge of the Concepts

Choose the best answer for each question.

1. Which of the following is a function of the spleen?
   a. Produces T cells.
   b. Removes worn-out red blood cells.
   c. Produces immunoglobulins.
   d. Produces macrophages.
   e. Regulates the immune system.

2. Which of the following is a function of the thymus gland?
   a. Production of red blood cells.
   b. Secretion of antibodies.
   c. Production and maintenance of stem cells.
   d. Site for the maturation of T lymphocytes.

3. Which of these pertain(s) to T cells?
   a. Have specific receptors.
   b. Are of more than one type.
   c. Are responsible for cell-mediated immunity.
   d. Stimulate antibody production by B cells.
   e. All of these are correct.

4. Which one of these does not pertain to B cells?
   a. Have passed through the thymus.
   b. Have specific receptors.
   c. Are responsible for antibody-mediated immunity.
   d. Synthesize and liberate antibodies.

For questions 5–10, match the lymphatic organs in the key to the description of its location.

Key:

   a. vermiform appendix
   b. lymph nodes
   c. Peyer's patches
   d. spleen
   e. thymus gland
   f. tonsils

5. Arranged in a ring around the pharynx
6. In the intestinal wall
7. Occur along lymphatic vessels
8. Upper left abdominal cavity, posterior to the stomach
9. Attached to the cecum
10. Anterior to the ascending aorta, posterior to the sternum

11. During a secondary immune response,
    a. antibodies are made quickly and in great amounts.
    b. antibody production lasts longer than in a primary response.
    c. antibodies of the IgG class are produced.
    d. lymphocyte cloning occurs.
    e. All of these are correct.

12. Acquired immunity may be produced by
    a. having a disease.
    b. receiving a vaccine.
    c. receiving gamma globulin injections.
    d. Both a and b are correct.
    e. Both b and c are correct.

13. Which of the following is a function of the secondary lymphatic organs?
    a. transportation of lymph
    b. production of lymphocytes
    c. location where lymphocytes encounter antigens
    d. All of the above are correct.

14. Which organ or structure contains white and red pulp?
    a. lymph node
    b. red bone marrow
    c. spleen
    d. thymus
    e. tonsil

15. Defense mechanisms that function to protect the body against many infectious agents are called
    a. specific.
    b. nonspecific.
    c. barriers to entry.
    d. immunity.

16. Label a–c on the following IgG molecule using these terms: antigen-binding sites, light chain, heavy chain.

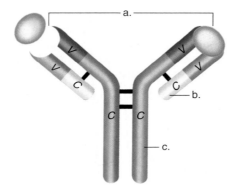

    d. What do *V* and *C* stand for in the diagram?

17. Which of the following is most directly responsible for the increase in capillary permeability during the inflammatory reaction?
    a. pain
    b. white blood cells
    c. histamine
    d. tissue damage

18. A main goal of the inflammatory reaction is to
    a. bring more oxygen to damaged tissues.
    b. decrease blood loss from a wound.
    c. increase the number of white blood cells in the damaged tissues.
    d. prevent entry of pathogens into damaged tissues.

19. Which of the following is not correct concerning interferon?
    a. Interferon is a protective protein.
    b. Virus-infected cells produce interferon.
    c. Interferon binds to and disables viruses.
    d. Interferon is specific to each species.

Understanding Key Terms

active immunity 424
allergen 426
allergy 426
anaphylactic shock 426
antibody 414
antibody-mediated
    immunity 419
antibody titer 424
antigen 414
antigen-presenting cell
    (APC) 422
apoptosis 419
asthma 426
autoimmune disease 428
B cell 418
cell-mediated immunity 423
clonal selection theory 419
complement system 418
cytokine 423, 425
cytotoxic T cell 423
delayed allergic response 426
dendritic cell 417
disease 414
hay fever 426
helper T cell 423
histamine 417
immediate allergic
    response 426
immune system 414
immunity 414
immunization 424

immunoglobulin (Ig) 420
immunosuppressive 428
inflammatory reaction 417
interferon 418
interleukin 425
lymphatic organ 414
lymph node 415
macrophage 417
mast cell 417
membrane attack complex 418
monoclonal antibody 425
multiple sclerosis (MS) 428
myasthenia gravis 428
natural killer (NK) cell 418
passive immunity 424
Peyer's patches 415
plasma cell 419
red bone marrow 414
rheumatoid arthritis 428
severe combined
    immunodeficiency disease
    (SCID) 428
spleen 414
systemic lupus erythematosus
    (SLE) 428
T cell 418
thymus gland 414
tonsils 415
vaccine 424
vermiform appendix 415
xenotransplantation 428

Match the key terms to these definitions.

a. _____ Antigens prepared in such a way that they can promote active immunity without causing disease.

b. _____ Series of proteins in plasma that form a nonspecific defense mechanism against pathogen invasion.

c. _____ Foreign substance, usually a protein, that stimulates the immune system to react, such as by producing antibodies.

d. _____ Process of programmed cell death involving a cascade of specific cellular events leading to the death and destruction of the cell.

e. _____ Type of lymphocyte that matures in the thymus gland and exists in three varieties, one of which kills antigen-bearing cells outright.

Online Learning Center

www.mhhe.com/maderhuman9

The Online Learning Center provides a wealth of information fully organized and integrated by chapter. You will find practice quizzes, interactive activities, labeling exercises, flashcards, and much more that will complement your learning and understanding of human biology.

CHAPTER *22*

Parasites and Pathogens

CHAPTER CONCEPTS

22.1 Microbes and You
- How do microbes directly benefit you?   432
- What makes some microbes virulent?   434
- What are the different ways you can catch an infectious disease?   434–35

22.2 Viruses as Infectious Agents
- Are viruses alive? How can they replicate?   436
- Why aren't you immune to influenza once you've had it before?   437
- What diseases are caused by herpes viruses?   438
- What does chickenpox have to do with shingles?   438

22.3 Bacteria as Infectious Agents
- What is the structure of a bacterium, and how do the cell walls of Gram-positive and Gram-negative bacteria differ?   441
- What complications are possible after a strep infection?   442
- Why is tuberculosis on the rise today?   443
- What are the two major types of food poisoning?   444

22.4 Other Infectious Agents
- What types of diseases are caused by fungi?   446
- What is the most widespread and dangerous protozoan disease?   447
- Why isn't schistosomiasis prevalent in this country?   449

Modern air travel presents a swift means of transporting a newly emerged pathogen halfway around the world. In March 2003 after visiting Hong Kong, a passenger returning to Toronto inadvertently carried a virus that started a mini-epidemic there. The unwelcome disease was the newly diagnosed syndrome called severe acute respiratory syndrome (SARS).

SARS apparently originated in southern China in late 2002 and was first recognized as a serious global health threat in February 2003. Before the 2003 outbreak was over, SARS had spread to over 25 countries in Asia, Europe, North America, and South America. During this time, over 8,000 people were infected and 774 died. The cause of this highly contagious respiratory syndrome was identified as a coronavirus, which was named SARS-associated coronavirus (SARS-CoV).

Although SARS is a "new" infectious disease caused by a virus that is newly described by science, it carries with it the legacy of centuries of invasions of the human body by a legion of microbial agents.

Any infectious agent requires a method of getting into the body. Can this agent be identified by laboratory tests? How does the body respond to the infection? There is often an incubation period between infection and the onset of symptoms. Certain signs and symptoms of the infection are generally recognizable. What kind of treatment is available? These and other questions must be answered if medical practitioners are to identify the agent, treat victims, and control or prevent an epidemic.

22.1 Microbes and You

The diversity of life on Earth is enormous, especially when you consider that most living things are too small to be seen with the naked eye. Scientists use microscopes to visualize *microbes* and a battery of biochemical and genetic tests to study them. Microorganisms are widely distributed in the environment. They cover inanimate objects and the surfaces of plants and animals; they even reside within the bodies of macroscopic organisms, including ourselves. Local environments determine where microscopic organisms can live and what they do there. Knowing the characteristics of microbes allows us to take advantage of their many activities.

Activities of Microbes

We will discuss three activities of microbes that are of particular use to humans.

Ecological Contributions: Nutrient Cycling

When a tree falls to the forest floor, it eventually rots because decomposers, including bacteria and fungi, break down the remains of dead organisms to inorganic nutrients, which plants then take from the soil. Without the microorganisms of decay, the work of photosynthesizing food for all living things would stop.

Further, inorganic nutrients such as nitrogen, sulfur, and phosphorus, along with other minerals, move through biogeochemical cycles that make them available to living things. Not only plants but also animals depend on these cycles in order to have food to eat and oxygen to breathe. Without the activity of decomposing microbes, the biosphere, including ourselves, would cease to exist (Fig. 22.1*a*).

Economic and Aesthetic Contributions

Many of us do not realize that we eat microbial products every day (Fig. 22.1*b*). Bread, beer, and wine are the products of microbial action, mainly alcohol fermentation by yeasts. Sour milk products, such as yogurt, butter, and cheese, are created by lactic acid bacteria. The end product of fermentation for them is lactic acid among other molecules. Pickled foods, such as sauerkraut and olives, are made by a similar process in which bacteria produce acids and other compounds that flavor food. Low-fat salad dressings and desserts contain gels and gums derived from algae, which are aquatic photosynthesizers.

Many products of microbial metabolism are useful to us and are produced on a large scale in bioreactor vats. These products include vitamins, antibiotics, insulin, and enzymes used in detergents.

Contributions to Our Health

The bacteria and other organisms that routinely live on or in organs are called their normal *microflora* (Fig. 22.1*c*). The large intestine is packed full of bacteria, termed coliforms because they live in the colon. These bacteria digest compounds that would otherwise be indigestible, and thereby provide us with additional nutrients, vitamins, and fatty acids that the body cannot synthesize. The normal microflora, the "good" bacteria, help protect us from the "bad" bacteria. For example, the normal microflora of the vagina maintain a pH that discourages the proliferation of infectious organisms.

The activities of microbes contribute to the Earth's ecology, our economy, and our health.

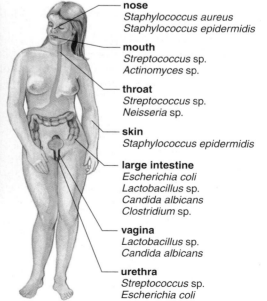

a.   b.

nose
Staphylococcus aureus
Staphylococcus epidermidis

mouth
Streptococcus sp.
Actinomyces sp.

throat
Streptococcus sp.
Neisseria sp.

skin
Staphylococcus epidermidis

large intestine
Escherichia coli
Lactobacillus sp.
Candida albicans
Clostridium sp.

vagina
Lactobacillus sp.
Candida albicans

urethra
Streptococcus sp.
Escherichia coli

Figure 22.1   Services of bacteria.
a. Bacteria and fungi of decay contribute to biogeochemical cycles, which are necessary to the continuance of ecosystems and ourselves. **b.** The growth and activity of microorganisms are used to produce foods such as those pictured here. **c.** The normal microflora (a few examples are given) in these organs help prevent disease-causing agents from taking hold.

c.

Health Focus

BioDefense

Bioterrorism is the intentional use of microorganisms or their toxins to cause death or disease in humans, animals, or plants on which humans depend. The public was alarmed when an act of bioterrorism closely followed an attack on the World Trade Center in New York on September 11, 2001. Highly infectious endospores of *Bacillus anthracis* were disseminated through the United States postal system, leading to the deaths of several innocent individuals who came in contact with the contaminated envelopes. Anthrax, caused by this bacterium, is generally a disease of hoofed animals. Anthrax endospores remain viable for decades.

Numerous potential bioterrorism agents have been identified. Plague is a disease of rodents that is transmitted to humans by the bite of fleas. Serious cases of plague, like that of anthrax, can be acquired through inhalation of the organism. Tularemia, often called rabbit fever, is caused by an extremely virulent bacterium that infects many wild animal species, especially rodents. Several viral agents that cause equine encephalitis are known for their bioterrorism capabilities, as are the viruses that cause Ebola and other hemorrhagic fevers. Another area of concern is botulism, caused by toxins of *Clostridium botulinum*. These neurotoxins are produced during germination of endospores that occur naturally in soil and marine mud. When they find their way into food and water supplies, serious illness can occur. What all of these agents have in common is that they can kill humans in large numbers.

The possibility of a biological attack in the United States has been recognized for many years. During World War I, in Europe, farm animals were deliberately infected with anthrax and other agents. During World War II, there were allegations, but only a few documented attempts, of bioterrorism. One attempt involved a scheme to spread plague by dropping fleas into an area.

Following World War II, the Centers for Disease Control and Prevention (CDC) established the Epidemic Intelligence Service (EIS) to monitor and help protect the United States against bioterrorism. Since 1998, the CDC, in conjunction with other government agencies, has been actively preparing for the possibility of domestic bioterrorism. To guard against a successful biological attack, these areas of concern have been identified.

Rapid identification of the agent involved. Once the agent is identified, steps can be taken to limit exposure to the agent and to ensure the proper treatment of those already exposed. Toward this end, communication systems have been put in place to alert the proper agencies and personnel of an attack. Training programs have been implemented so that public health practitioners, medical personal, public safety officers, and emergency room staff can respond quickly.

Adequate stockpiles of pharmaceuticals. The CDC is currently working with industries to ensure the availability of drugs, vaccines, and other medical

Figure 22A   Prevention of bioterrorism attacks.
Adequate planning by the Epidemic Intelligence Service and other governmental agencies will be needed to prevent bioterrorism attacks.

equipment required to treat victims of intentional outbreaks. The possibility of a biological attack has lead to efforts to develop improved vaccines for known biological agents, such as smallpox and tularemia.

Improved surveillance. New and improved surveillance methods are being investigated. These include recognizing early signs of a disease statistically, before actual clinical reports are evaluated. Other events that must be investigated immediately include unusual purchases of equipment or medications that might predict an attack.

Research reviews. A review system to guard against bioterrorism-related misuse of legitimate research has been recommended. Areas that invite scrutiny involve efforts to increase the virulence, host range, or transmissibility of pathogens. Also, research to decrease the effectiveness of antimicrobial drugs is of concern.

Government defense and scientific institutes are struggling with other questions, such as:

1. Should the government establish a new agency, under a single umbrella, to deal with the challenges involved in developing drugs, vaccines, and other medical interventions against biowarfare agents?
2. How much oversight should there be over ongoing research areas?
3. Should there be any publication of research in sensitive bioterrorism areas?
4. How much funding should there be for the prevention of bioterrorism?

Pathogenicity

Microbes that can cause disease are called **pathogens.** Pathogens can cause disease because they have various **virulence factors** that give them an ability to overcome the defenses of a potential host.

Virulence Factors

These are some of the more common virulence factors associated with microorganisms:

Flagella Some bacteria, such as the one that causes cholera, and *Salmonella,* which causes food poisoning, have flagella, organs of locomotion, that allow these bacteria to migrate through the mucous layer of the small intestine to reach the underlying epithelium.

Adhesion Factors The bacteria that cause gonorrhea, namely *Neisseria gonorrhoeae,* have adhesion factors, which allow them to adhere to cells and subsequently colonize tissues.

Invasive Factors Among other bacteria, certain strains of *Staphylococcus* have enzymes that break down the ground substance of connective tissue, allowing them to invade underlying tissue. If a disease becomes system-wide, or **systemic,** it is likely to be more serious than if it were localized. For example, *Salmonella enteritidis* causes food poisoning, but in most cases the host recovers without treatment or serious illness. *Salmonella typhi,* however, has virulence factors that allow the bacterium to penetrate beyond the digestive tract and cause typhoid fever.

Toxins Small organic molecules, small pieces of protein (peptides), or parts of bacterial cell wall that are released when a bacterium dies are termed toxins because they are poisonous to us. Notice that toxins are specific to the particular bacterium.

   E. coli O157:H7, a strain that causes a serious intestinal disease, has acquired the ability to make verotoxin, commonly produced by *Shigella dysentariae.* This toxin causes epidemic dysentery. Also, this strain is able to stick to the lining of the intestine more efficiently than *E. coli* so that it remains there instead of being expelled with the feces. *Clostridium tetani,* the cause of tetanus, proliferates under anaerobic conditions. The bacteria never leave the site of a wound, but the tetanus toxin does move throughout the body. This toxin prevents the relaxation of muscles. In time, the body contorts because all its muscles have contracted. Eventually, suffocation occurs.

Capsules *Streptococcus pneumoniae* is known in medical microbiology as the pneumococcus because of its consistent involvement in pneumonia. This bacterium has a polysaccharide capsule that protects the bacteria from phagocytosis.

Survival Mechanisms Some bacteria, such as *Mycobacterium tuberculosis,* are able to multiply in the very phagocytic cells that are supposed to destroy them.

Epidemiology

Epidemiology is the study of the occurrence, distribution, and control of disease in a population. Epidemiology helps determine how best to protect the public from coming down with a disease. **Infectious diseases** are illnesses caused by the presence of a pathogen or its product. (Pathogens that are highly transmissible by a direct means are termed **contagious.**) Infections can be separated into those that are acute and those that are chronic. **Acute infections** occur quickly and have severe symptoms, but last for only a short time. The common cold is an acute infection that persists for little more than a week. **Chronic infections** have less severe symptoms over a longer time than acute infections. In sleeping sickness, periods of symptoms are interspersed with periods of relative health. Eventually, chronic infections damage vital organs, leading to death.

Modes of Transmission

Pathogens have four modes of transmission: direct contact, airborne, vehicle, and vector-borne (Fig. 22.2).

Direct Contact Transmission Many pathogens can only be transmitted by direct contact—that is, you must come into contact with the body fluids or lesions of the infected person. Pathogens, such as the tuberculosis bacterium, are transmitted by *droplets* in the breath. Health professionals and visitors must wear surgical masks when near these patients, who must be kept in isolation. Many other pathogens are transmitted through droplets released when a person coughs or sneezes. The most deadly form of the plague can

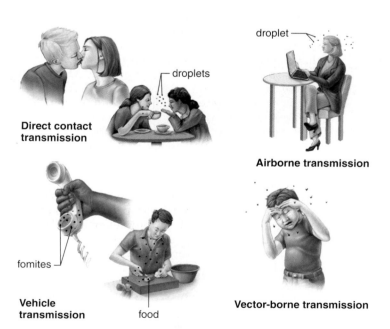

Figure 22.2 Transmission of diseases.
Examples of four modes of disease transmission are shown. During transmission an infectious agent passes between people.

be transmitted in this way. Contact with the blood or semen of infected individuals is crucial to the transmission of the AIDS virus and hepatitis, while contact with skin lesions leads to the transmission of herpes.

Airborne Transmission   When airborne, the pathogen is suspended in the air and travels a meter or more from the source to the host. Sometimes, the pathogens travel in *droplet nuclei*, which are small particles that result from the evaporation of droplets. Or they can survive for a relatively long time in dust, creating an epidemiological problem, particularly in hospitals.

Vehicle Transmission   A **vehicle,** which is an inanimate substance or medium, can transmit disease to a large group of individuals. Food and water are common vehicles for spreading disease. Many individuals may contract food poisoning caused by *Salmonella* from a salad bar, for example. Inanimate objects that transmit disease are called **fomites.** Cold viruses can survive for some time on surfaces, such as desks or doorknobs. Some fomites cause disease through puncture wounds. When needles and nails puncture the skin, they can introduce a pathogen into the tissues of the body.

Vector-Borne Transmission   A **vector** is an animal that carries a disease-causing agent from one host to another. The classic vectors are insects, such as the mosquito. Vectors are important for the transmission of many pathogens, including bacteria, viruses, and protists. When an individual infected with malaria is bitten by a mosquito, the parasite passes into the body of the mosquito with its blood meal.

When the mosquito bites an uninfected individual, the parasite passes into the blood, and the person becomes infected. Ticks, lice, fleas, and certain flies are also common disease vectors. The bites of dogs, raccoons, and bats are known to transmit rabies. Often, our best defense against the spread of a vector-borne disease is control of vector populations; for example, eliminating sources of standing water and spraying for mosquitoes can control the outbreak of malaria.

Disease Categories

Four categories describe the extent of infectious diseases such as those listed in Table 22.1:

1. **Sporadic occurrences** are limited in scope, affecting a few individuals in a small area. For example, a single ventilation system can infect a few people with Legionnaires' disease.
2. An **endemic** disease is caused by an infectious agent that is always present in a population. Hantavirus is endemic in the rodent population in certain portions of the western United States. As discussed in the Health Focus on page 433, bioterrorism is the use of an infectious agent to start an epidemic.
3. **Epidemics** are more widespread. For example, a high number of cases of the flu in the state of Michigan would exemplify an epidemic outbreak.
4. A **pandemic** is a disease that occurs worldwide. The massive influenza outbreak of 1918 was a pandemic, killing millions around the world.

Table 22.1	Common Viral Diseases in Humans		
Disease	**Virus**	**Transmission**	**Comments**
Acquired immunodeficiency syndrome (AIDS)	Human immunodeficiency virus (HIV)	Direct contact	Sexually transmitted disease; latent infection
Chickenpox, shingles	Varicella-zoster	Airborne, direct contact	Latent infection; not a pox virus
Cold sores, genital herpes	Herpes virus	Direct contact	Latent infections; genital herpes, sexually transmitted.
Common cold	Rhinovirus	Airborne, vehicles, direct contact	Hundreds of variants
German measles	Rubella	Airborne	Not related to measles; mild in adults, serious congenital; part of MMR vaccine
Hepatitis A	Hepatovirus	Fecal-oral route	Foodborne disease; acute liver infection
Hepatitis B	Orthohepadnavirus	Blood/bodily fluid	Chronic liver infection
Measles	Rubeola	Airborne, direct contact	Very contagious; part of MMR vaccine
Mumps	Rubulavirus	Airborne	Swollen salivary glands; part of MMR vaccine
Polio	Poliovirus	Fecal-oral route	Salk/Sabin vaccines; paralysis is rare
Rabies	Lyssa-virus	Animal vector	Hydrophobia; foaming mouth; dementia
Smallpox	Variola	Airborne, direct contact	Eradicated; high mortality rate
Genital warts	Papillomavirus	Direct contact	Sexually transmitted disease
Yellow fever	Flavivirus	Mosquito vector	First viral disease described

22.2 Viruses as Infectious Agents

Viruses bridge the gap between the living and the nonliving. Outside a host, viruses are essentially chemicals that can be stored on a shelf. But when the opportunity arises, viruses replicate inside cells, and during this period of time, they clearly appear to be alive.

Structure and Replication of Viruses

Viruses are acellular—not composed of cells. They are obligate parasites, meaning that they must replicate inside a living cell. Therefore, viruses cause disease (see Table 22.1)

Virus particles are generally very small, ranging from 0.2 to 2 μm. A virus is about ten times smaller than a bacterium. A virus always has two parts: an outer **capsid** composed of protein units, and an inner core of nucleic acid. In contrast to cellular organisms, the viral genome need not be double-stranded DNA, nor even DNA. Indeed, some viruses have an RNA genome. The genome of a virus carries the genetic information needed to produce more viruses. A virus may also contain various enzymes that help the replication process.

In addition to a capsid, some viruses have an envelope, which is derived from the host plasma membrane. The envelope contains host proteins and also viral glycoproteins, called spikes, that react with specific receptors on the surface of the target cell. This bonding allows the virus to enter the host cell. Inside the host, viruses with an envelope have a distinct advantage because with a membranous envelope, a virus looks more like a host cell.

As illustrated in Figure 22.3, replication of an animal virus with a DNA genome involves these steps:

1. *Attachment.* Spikes projecting through the envelope allow the virus to bind only to specific host cells. These cells have receptor proteins to which a virus can bind.
2. *Penetration.* After the viral particle is brought into the cell, uncoating—the removal of the capsid—follows, and DNA is released.
3. *Replication.* During viral replication, the host cell's enzymes make many copies of viral DNA.
4. *Biosynthesis.* Capsid proteins are synthesized by host cell ribosomes according to viral DNA and RNA instructions.
5. *Maturation.* Viral proteins and DNA replicates are assembled to form new viral particles.
6. *Release.* During budding, the virus gets its envelope, which consists of host plasma membrane components and envelope spikes that were coded for by viral DNA.

Some viruses that enter human cells—for example, the papillomaviruses, the herpesviruses, the hepatitis viruses, and the adenoviruses—can undergo a period of **latency,** during which they are hidden in the cell and do not reproduce. Certain environmental factors, such as ultraviolet radiation, can induce the virus to reproduce and bud from the cell.

Outside a living cell, viruses are nonliving particles composed of protein and nucleic acid. Inside the host cell, viruses replicate by a series of steps.

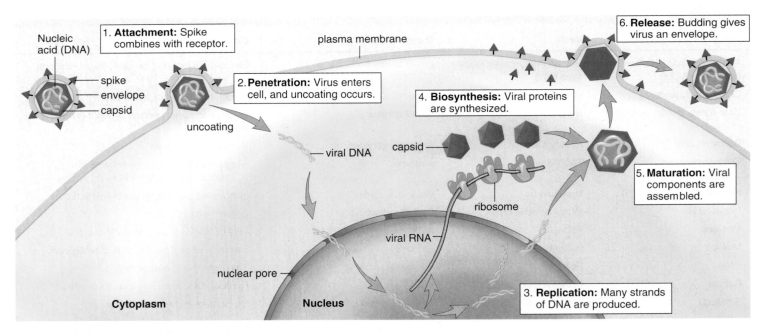

Figure 22.3   Replication of an animal virus.
Notice that the mode of entry requires uncoating and the virus acquires an envelope when it buds from the host cell.

Viral Diseases

Among the viral diseases listed in Table 22.1 (page 435), we will discuss influenza, herpes infections, measles, and the common cold. Emerging viral pathogens are discussed on page 440.

Influenza

Flu is characterized by many of the same symptoms as the common cold, but a flu infection also includes fever, chills, nausea, and vomiting. Flu outbreaks tend to be epidemic, affecting many people in a large geographical area.

Structure   The **influenza virus** has spikes projecting from its envelope (Fig. 22.4). The genome of the influenza virus is composed of eight separate pieces of RNA.

The surface of the influenza virus contains two antigens on its spikes, neuraminidase (N antigen) and hemagglutinin (H antigen). These two antigens are virulence factors that help the virus attach to the host cells. After recovering from the flu, your body has antibodies and immune cells able to recognize particular N and H antigens displayed by the virus that infected you. Should the same strain attack again, your body can respond and prevent illness.

Epidemiology   You might ask why you can get the flu again. The answer is that you are only immune to strains that have infected you previously. *Antigenic drift* occurs when mutations bring about small changes in the N and H antigens (Fig. 22.4*a*). If the drift is sufficiently large, an epidemic spread of the disease can occur and account for the yearly outbreaks of influenza.

Antigenic shift occurs when two different influenza viruses, by chance, attack the same cell (Fig. 22.4*b*). The two genomes can reassort during viral replication. The reassortment event generates virus particles that contain RNA genome segments from each of the original viruses that infected the cell. Such large changes can occur in N and H antigens that no one will be immune. The result is a worldwide pandemic. Pandemics occur about every seven years.

Reassortment events are most serious when genome segments from animal influenza viruses mix with those of human influenza viruses. When a swine flu virus attacks the same cell as a human flu virus, the progeny may display an N or H antigen from the swine virus. Such an occurrence led to the devastating flu of 1918 that killed tens of millions worldwide. The World Health Organization believes a similar event may occur due to a "bird flu" virus, which infects people in Southeast Asia. New influenza virus types are often seen first in Southeast Asia, where much of the society is agrarian and has closer contact with livestock. The flu strains that proliferate in that region during winter in the Southern Hemisphere move to the United States during the winter months of the Northern Hemisphere. The types of influenza viruses prevalent in Southeast Asia are closely monitored and form the basis for developing the specific flu vaccine given in the United States that year.

The influenza virus is an example of a virus that frequently mutates, making long-lasting immunity difficult to achieve.

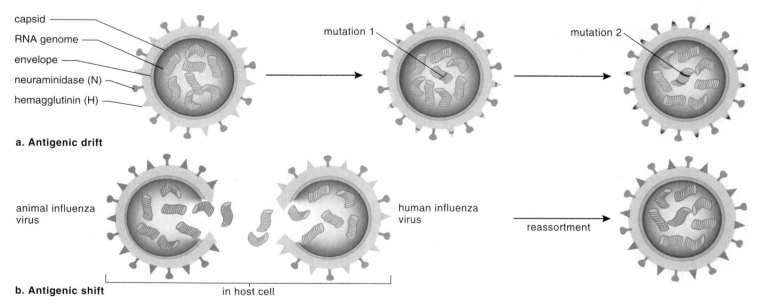

a. Antigenic drift

b. Antigenic shift

Figure 22.4   Influenza virus.

a. Antigenic drift. Mutations can cause a gradual change in the antigens in the capsid spikes so that antibody against the original virus becomes less effective. **b.** Antigenic shift. With shift, an abrupt, major change occurs in antigens of capsid spikes because the virus acquires one or more new genome segments. Now, human antibodies are sure to be ineffective, and most people will become ill when they are exposed to the virus.

Herpes

A number of viruses can become latent. The herpesviruses cause chronic infections because they are latent for much of the time.

Herpes Simplex Virus Type 1 (HSV-1)   HSV-1 is generally associated with the occurrence of cold sores and fever blisters around the mouth. It is estimated that 70–90% of the adult population is infected with HSV-1, usually as infants. After the initial infection, the virus particles migrate to spinal ganglia. There the virus enters a latent state by integrating its DNA genome into the genome of the host cell. In about half of infected individuals, symptoms eventually recur. The viral genome is induced to replicate by various stresses, including excessive sunlight, fever, trauma, and emotional disturbance. The newly formed viruses migrate back to the original site of infection where they cause a recurrence of lesions.

Herpes Simplex Virus Type 2 (HSV-2)   A herpes infection of the genitals is generally caused by HSV-2, which is transmitted through sexual contact. Crossover infections with HSV-1, which causes cold sores, and HSV-2, which causes genital herpes, occur due to the practice of oral sex. HSV-2 is remarkable in its rate of replication; it rapidly produces progeny virus in large numbers. The site of infection generally displays blisters filled with a clear fluid that is very infectious. The blisters are usually painful in men but not as painful in women. Condoms do not usually prevent the transmission of herpes because the lesions are most often found on the labia majora in women and at the base of the penis in men.

Genital herpes infections are widespread in the United States, affecting as many as 40% of the adult population. HSV-2 travels to spinal ganglia, where it remains in a latent state by integrating its genome into the host cell genome. But about 88% of individuals infected with genital herpes will have recurrences of symptoms due to stress. The disease is transmissible to someone else even when obvious signs of infection are absent.

Pregnant women who have a genital herpes infection should plan for a cesarean delivery. Infection can occur in the birth canal, and herpes is one of the greatest life-threatening diseases of newborns.

Varicella-Zoster Virus   This herpesvirus causes chickenpox, a childhood disease (Fig. 22.5). After the initial infection, which includes fever and a characteristic rash, the virus remains latent in spinal ganglia. Later in life, usually after age 60, the virus can reemerge as a related disease called **shingles,** or herpes zoster. Painful cutaneous blisters form along the path of a single sensory neuron within the upper chest or face (Fig. 22.6). The symptoms may last for several weeks or, in some cases, months.

Viruses in the herpes family exemplify viruses that cause chronic infections because latency is interrupted by periods of activity.

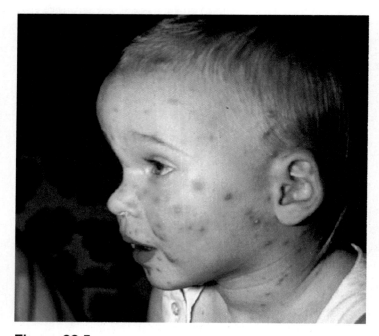

Figure 22.5   Chickenpox (varicella).
A child with chickenpox showing characteristic lesions, pus-filled blisters that break and crust.

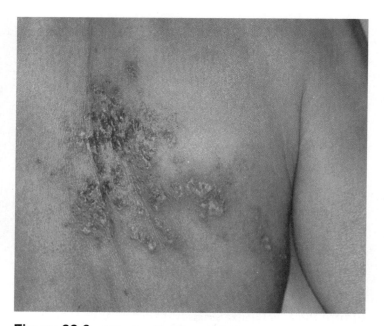

Figure 22.6   Shingles (herpes zoster).
The rash is like that of chickenpox, except that it is present along a sensory nerve on one side of the body.

Measles

Measles

Measles (or rubeola, after the name of the virus) is perhaps the most contagious of all human diseases. In unvaccinated populations, all children will contract the disease. Measles is a major killer worldwide, affecting as many as 50 million people each year and killing four million, mainly children, each year. In the United States, the number of cases has dropped from 5 million each year to a few thousand since the measles vaccine was introduced in 1963. The vaccine against measles is usually given to infants in combination with vaccines against mumps and rubella, called the MMR vaccine (see page 424). Outbreaks sometimes occur in colleges because the vaccine may have been given too early or did not take, and the close contacts of the college environment expose susceptible individuals.

Transmission and Symptoms The measles virus is spread through the respiratory route as airborne particles. An incubation period of 7–12 days precedes the onset of flu-like symptoms, including a fever. An early telltale sign of measles is the presence of Koplik spots, red patches with white specks in the mouth near the molars. A red rash develops on the face and moves to the trunk and extremities (Fig. 22.7). The rash lasts for several days and may become confluent. Encephalitis (brain swelling), often leading to permanent neurological damage, develops in about 1 in 1,000 cases. In the more-developed countries, the fatality rate for measles is about 1 in 3,000; however, in less-developed countries, the fatality rate is 10–15%. The measles virus passes through the placenta and can be very harmful to the fetus.

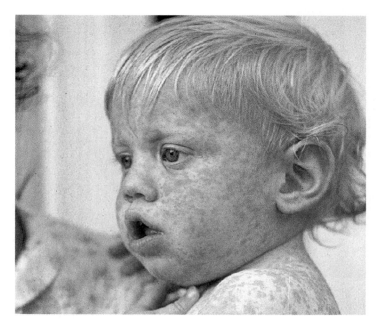

Figure 22.7 Measles (rubeola).
Besides a rash, measles symptoms usually include a fever, a runny nose, and a bad cough.

Common Cold

Common Cold

Perhaps we are most familiar with the viral disease known as a cold. Although half of all colds are caused by rhinoviruses, a variety of other viral pathogens leads to the symptoms associated with the common cold. There are likely more than 200 different cold viruses. Vaccines against each are not a viable option, and individuals become immune only to the cold viruses they have encountered.

Transmission and Symptoms Cold viruses are transmitted through airborne droplets, by direct contact, and by vehicles. Many believe that hand-to-hand contact is the most effective route of transmission. Antibacterial hand creams that are essentially alcohol gels do not usually protect against these nonenveloped viruses. Within three to seven days after exposure, the common symptoms of nasal discharge, sore throat, cough, and malaise begin. The disease is self-limiting, and spontaneous recovery occurs in seven to ten days. The cold viruses tend to prefer growth temperatures that are slightly lower than normal body temperature—hence, their preference for colonization of the nasopharynx. Viral replication leads to cell damage and an immune response that includes edema. The influx of fluids to the tissues leads to the characteristic symptoms.

The incidence of colds increases during the cold winter months, although the reason for this is unclear. It may be the result of spending more time indoors with infected individuals.

Prions

Prions, proteinaceous infectious particles, cause a group of degenerative diseases of the nervous system and also wasting diseases. Originally thought to be viral diseases, prions cause *Creutzfeldt-Jakob disease* in humans, scrapie in sheep, and bovine spongiform encephalopathy, commonly called *mad cow disease*. These infections are apparently transmitted by ingestion of brain and nerve tissues from infected individuals. A type of prion disease called kuru was first noted in a cannibalistic tribe in the Kuru region of Papua New Guinea. Transmission from animals to humans is disputed.

Prions are proteins of unknown function in the brains of healthy individuals. Disease occurs when certain prion proteins change their shape into a "rogue" form that can convert normal prion proteins into the rogue configuration. Loss of nervous tissue and the presence of calcified plaques occur in the brain. The incidence of prion diseases in humans is extraordinarily low. A person is far more likely to die in a soccer accident than of a prion disease.

Measles is the most contagious of all viral diseases, while the common cold may be the most familiar. Some infectious diseases once thought to be viral diseases are caused by prions.

Health Focus

Emerging Viral Pathogens

You hear about it on the evening news—a new viral pathogen has emerged (Fig. 22B). West Nile virus. SARS. Hantavirus. HIV. Where do these apparently new pathogens come from? How do they cause such widespread diseases? A best-selling novel from a decade ago, *The Hot Zone*, told the story of the Drs. Jaax when they were working on viruses for the military in the Washington, DC area. An outbreak of Ebola virus in a colony of monkeys had to be confirmed and contained. Ebola is one of a group of viruses that cause hemorrhagic fevers. These terrible pathogens quickly cause extensive tissue damage, leading to internal bleeding, multiple organ failure, and death. The Ebola that the Jaax encountered was called the Reston strain, for Reston, Virginia, where the animals were housed. There are also Sudan and Zaire strains of Ebola, named for outbreaks in those places. Lassa virus, which can cause a hemorrhagic fever, was named after Lassa, Nigeria.

Infectious diseases in humans seem to "emerge" in several different ways. In some cases, the virus is simply transported from one location to another. Flu strains move from Southeast Asia to the United States each year. The West Nile virus is making headlines because it has changed its range, being transported into the United States and taking hold in bird and mosquito populations. Severe Acute Respiratory Syndrome (SARS) was clearly transported from Southeast Asia to Toronto, Canada. A world where you can wake up in Bangkok and sleep in Los Angeles is a world where disease can spread at unprecedented rates.

Some viruses that infect both may cause a more serious disease in humans than animals. Animal populations can maintain the disease, acting as a reservoir. Diseases with animal reservoirs are hard to control. Smallpox could be eradicated because it infects only humans.

Many viral diseases are transmitted by vectors, usually insects, that carry disease from an infected individual to a healthy individual. Diseases spread by insects may require massive efforts to control the vector population. A disease can emerge when a mutation allows a virus to use a different insect vector. If a virus transmitted by a rare species of mosquito can now be transmitted by a more common species, a disease can spread more easily. This illustrates that the mode of transmission can be very important. What if the HIV virus was transmitted like the common cold?

Viruses can emerge through the acquisition of new surface antigens. The immune system, unable to recognize the new "face" of the virus, allows it to cause disease. Viruses that continually change their "faces," such as HIV, are far more difficult to eradicate. Presently, there is concern about the "bird flu." It arose in Southeast Asia, in a region where markets are overcrowded with humans and animals. The infecting virus carries surface antigens from a human flu virus and from a bird flu virus. The bird flu has a relatively high mortality rate, has been seen infrequently by a human immune system, and may cause a pandemic, if there is no time to prepare sufficient vaccine. Luckily, the disease doesn't transmit among humans very well.

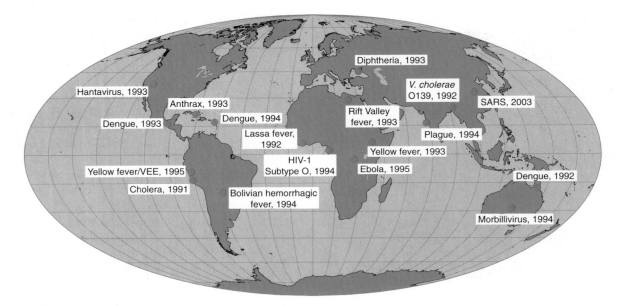

Figure 22B Emerging diseases.
Emerging diseases, such as those noted here according to their country of origin, are new or demonstrate increased prevalence. These disease-causing agents may have acquired a new ability to infect humans or spread to locations that allowed them to infect an increased number of humans.

22.3 Bacteria as Infectious Agents

Dozens of bacteria cause a wide range of diseases, from mild to fatal. They are the major cause of preventable infections and death. However, as illustrated in Figure 22.1, bacteria also perform many services for human beings.

Structure

Bacteria are at least ten times larger than a virus but at least ten times smaller than a human cell. Although bacteria are cellular, they lack the membrane-bound nucleus found in human cells (Fig. 22.8). Human cells and all others that have a membrane-bound nucleus are called **eukaryotic** (true nucleus) **cells.** The DNA of **prokaryotic** (before nucleus) **cells,** such as bacteria, have their single circular strand of DNA in a special region of the cell called a **nucleoid.** Many bacteria are unattached, single cells, while others form

chains or clusters. Most bacteria are either rods, called **bacilli** (sing., bacillus), or spheres, called **cocci** (sing., coccus). Bacteria growing under appropriate conditions divide by **binary fission** in which one parent cell splits into two daughter cells. Although bacteria do not sexually reproduce, they have other means of sharing genes.

The cell walls of bacteria have distinguishing features that aid in their identification. The **Gram stain** is used as a preliminary way to identify a bacterial pathogen. The cell wall of *Gram-positive* bacteria has a thick layer of a complex protein-carbohydrate molecule called **peptidoglycan** (Fig. 22.9a). *Gram-negative* bacteria do not bind the Gram stain, and they have a much thinner layer of peptidoglycan (Fig. 22.9b).

Gram-negative bacteria have a so-called outer membrane beyond the peptidoglycan layer. The outer membrane is made up of complex protein-lipid molecules called lipopolysaccharides. When the immune system attacks Gram-negative bacteria, they release lipopolysaccharides that initiate a cascade of events leading to inflammation reactions and fever.

Bacteria are prokaryotic cells that occur usually as bacilli or cocci. Some are Gram-positive, and some are Gram-negative.

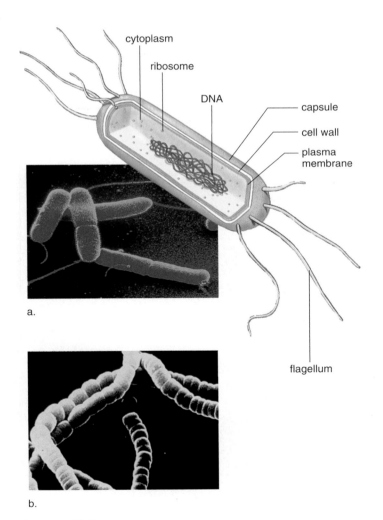

Figure 22.8 **Bacterial structure.**
a. A bacterium has a nucleoid region instead of the membrane-bounded nucleus found in human cells. Most bacteria are bacilli (rod-shaped) or (**b**) cocci (spheres).

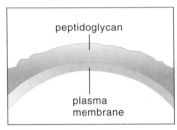

a. Gram-positive cell   b. Gram-negative cell

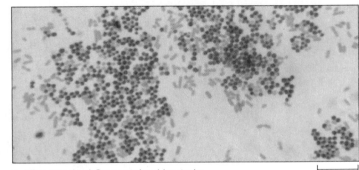

c. Micrograph of Gram stained bacteria   10 µm

Figure 22.9 **Gram stain.**
a. Gram-positive cells have a thick layer of peptidoglycan, and (**b**) Gram-negative cells have a very thin layer of peptidoglycan. (Also note the outer membrane of Gram-negative bacteria.) **c.** This difference causes Gram-positive cells to stain purple and Gram-negative cells to stain reddish pink when a counterstain is applied.

Bacterial Diseases

Among the bacterial diseases listed in Table 22.2 (see page 444), we will discuss strep infections, staph infections, tuberculosis, and food poisoning.

Strep Infections

Gram-positive bacteria in the genus *Streptococcus* occur as chains of cells (Fig. 22.10*a*). Bacteria belonging to this genus cause a greater variety of human diseases than any other group of bacteria.

The most common and the mildest illness caused by streptococci is pharyngitis, a severe sore throat colloquially called **strep throat.** Strep throat is contracted by inhaling small droplets in the air or by consuming contaminated raw milk. The disease is generally limited to the throat and does not affect other parts of the body. However, when the *Streptococcus* strain causing the strep throat has the ability to produce an erythrogenic toxin, **scarlet fever** can result. The patient's immune response to this toxin leads to an extensive rash that looks like scalded skin. A membrane peels off the tongue, making the tongue appear bright red. This toxin can lead to fatal septic shock.

An extremely strong immune response to a strep throat can lead to **rheumatic fever,** characterized by a high fever, swollen joints, and possible heart damage. Although rarely seen in the United States today, in the early 20th century, rheumatic fever killed more school-age children than all other diseases combined. Rheumatic fever is a leading cause of heart disease worldwide.

Streptococci are also important agents in pneumonias. *Streptococcus pneumoniae* is endemic in the human population; the health of an individual determines his or her susceptibility to this disease. *Streptococcus pyogenes* causes relatively mild skin diseases such as **impetigo** (Fig. 22.10*b*). But if this bacterium has certain virulence factors it causes **necrotizing fasciitis,** also termed galloping gangrene, in which rapid tissue damage can lead to amputation of infected limbs or, in 40% of cases, rapid death (Fig. 22.10*c*).

Staph Infections

Staphylococcus aureus is a Gram-positive bacterium that occurs singly or in irregular clusters. This bacterium often lives in the nose or on the skin of healthy people. When it penetrates the skin or invades other parts of the body, a staph infection may result. Staph bacteria that are resistant to the action of methicillin and related antibiotics are referred to as "methicillin-resistant staph aureus" or MRSA. MRSA are not only resistant to all penicillin-like antibiotics, but they are often resistant to many other types of antibiotics, as well. In the past, MRSA has been a problem mainly in health-care settings, such as hospitals and nursing homes. Recently however, there have been many reports of MRSA infections occurring among persons in the general community.

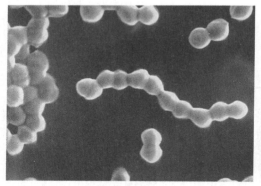

a. Scanning electron micrograph   0.5 μm

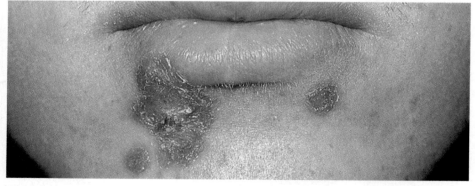

b. Impetigo

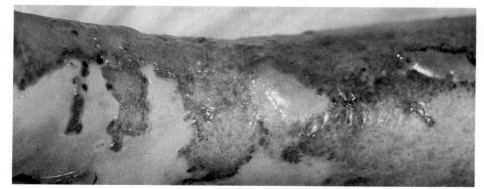

c. Flesh-eating disease

Figure 22.10 *Streptococcus pyogenes.*
a. This species causes more types of human disease than any other. **b.** Impetigo is a common mild skin infection. **c.** Flesh-eating disease is rare and life-threatening.

Tuberculosis

When first described by Robert Koch, in 1882, **tuberculosis (TB)** caused one of every seven deaths in Europe. Today, it is estimated that one third of the world's population is infected with TB, causing over 3 million deaths each year. A vaccine for TB is not widely used in the United States because it is inconsistent in its protection against pulmonary TB and its use leads to false positives for an infection. The common *tuberculin skin test* injects a tuberculin protein derivative that elicits an immune response in individuals who have active TB, or have been exposed to TB in their lifetimes.

Tuberculosis is a chronic disease caused by *Mycobacterium tuberculosis*, a bacterium that usually infects the lungs. The bacterium is very slow-growing, has a cell wall and a habit of growing inside phagocytes that makes it extremely resistant to the immune defense mechanisms. It is most serious for the elderly, the infirm, immunocompromised individuals (e.g., AIDS patients), and indigent populations because of poor nutrition.

Due to a TB infection, lesions in the alveoli can produce dense structures in the lungs called **tubercles** (Fig. 22.11). These can persist for years, causing symptoms that include coughing, which spreads the bacteria to other areas of the lungs and to other individuals. Eventually, the tubercles are destroyed, and the dead tissue calcifies, leaving characteristic spots observed with chest X-rays (Fig. 22.12).

TB can be treated with antibiotics, but these must be consistently taken for months or years to be effective. As discussed in the Health Focus on page 445, resistance to antibiotics, in general, is a growing problem. Unfortunately, populations most susceptible to TB are least likely to successfully complete the antibiotic regime. Of much concern is the fact that inadequate antibiotic therapy has now led to resistant strains of tuberculosis.

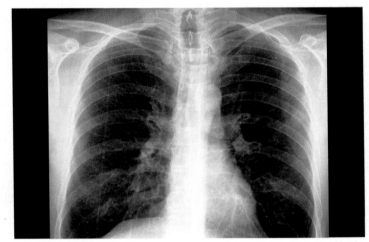

a. Normal individual

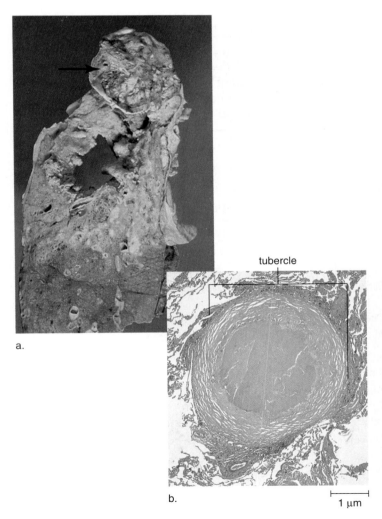

tubercle

a.

b.

1 µm

Figure 22.11 Tuberculosis.
a. Lung tissue with a large cavity surrounded by tubercles, a hard calcified nodule, where the bacterium is trapped. **b.** Photomicrograph shows one tubercle, with a diseased center, in cross section.

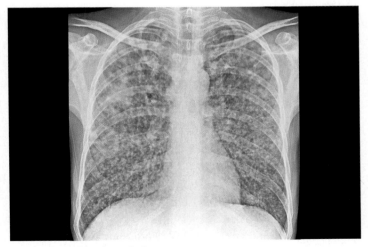

b. Individual with tuberculosis

Figure 22.12 Comparative chest X-rays.
a. Chest X-ray of an individual without tuberculosis. **b.** Chest X-ray of a person with tuberculosis.

Food Poisoning

Food poisoning refers to an illness that is caused by eating contaminated food. Guidelines and regulations for the safe cooking and handling of food in the United States are meant to guard against food poisoning, but it still occurs. *Salmonella* is found in poultry, eggs, unprocessed milk, meat, and water. It may also be carried by pets, such as turtles and birds. When *Salmonella* causes food poisoning, the bacterium must grow in the intestine for several days or weeks before the toxin produced by the bacterium leads to a diarrhea that lasts for a couple of days. *Staphylococcus* produces a toxin that contaminates foods, such as salad dressings, cream-filled pastries, and milk products, if they are kept warm for an hour or two. Boiling will kill bacteria, but will not affect any toxin in food.

Clostridium botulinum, a common soil bacterium related to the tetanus bacterium, also produces toxins in food (Fig. 22.13). This bacterium causes **botulism,** an infection that poisons the respiratory muscles. When canning, people often fail to heat food above the boiling point of water. Under these conditions, *Clostridium* can produce **endospores,** a resistant resting stage that survives unfavorable conditions, and therefore can survive the canning process. These spores then germinate and grow in the airless environment of the can. They produce a neurotoxin that is perhaps the most toxic substance on Earth. They also produce gas that may make the can bulge, an indication of contamination.

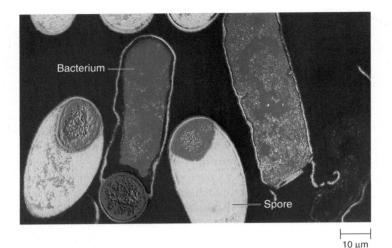

Figure 22.13 *Clostridium botulinum.*
This bacterium produces endospores, structures that can only be destroyed by exposing them to a temperature of 122° C for at least 15 minutes. If not destroyed, endospores can germinate to release active bacteria that produce a deadly toxin.

The streptococci are a group of bacteria that cause the greatest variety of human diseases. The causative agent of TB kills more people worldwide than any other disease. Food poisoning is caused by a variety of bacteria.

Table 22.2	Common Bacterial Diseases		
Disease	**Bacterium**	**Transmission**	**Comments**
Cholera	*Vibrio cholerae*	Vehicle by water/food	Periodic epidemics
Diphtheria	*Corynebacterium diphtheriae*	Airborne	Part of DTP vaccine
Epidemic typhus	*Rickettsia prowazekii*	Louse vector	High mortality (50%) without treatment
Food poisoning, pimples, wound infections	*Staphylococcus aureus*	Vehicles, direct contact	Many diseases/virulence factors
Gonorrhea	*Neisseria gonorrhoeae*	Direct contact	Sexually transmitted disease
Legionnaires' disease	*Legionella pneumophila*	Airborne	Sporadic incidence
Leprosy	*Mycobacterium leprae*	Direct contact	Chronic and disfiguring
Pertussis (whooping cough)	*Bordetella pertussis*	Airborne	Very contagious, part of DTP vaccine
Plague	*Yersinia pestis*	Flea and animal vectors	Black death; pneumonic form 100% fatal, bubonic form 50–70% fatal
Shigellosis	*Shigella dysentariae*	Vehicle by water/food	Epidemic dysentery
Strep throat, scarlet fever, rheumatic fever, impetigo	*Streptococcus pyogenes*	Airborne	Causes more types of disease than any other bacterium
Syphilis	*Treponema pallidum*	Direct contact	Sexually transmitted disease, three chronic stages
Tetanus	*Clostridium tetani*	Vehicle by fomites	Lockjaw, part of DTP vaccine
Trachoma	*Chlamydia trachomatis*	Direct contact, vehicles	Top cause of preventable blindness
Tuberculosis	*Mycobacterium tuberculosis*	Airborne	Chronic, most infectious disease deaths
"Walking" pneumonia	*Mycoplasma pneumoniae*	Airborne, direct contact	No cell walls

Health Focus

Antibiotics

Originally termed "magic bullets," antibiotics are supposed to kill the invader, while leaving the host unharmed. Antibiotics are antimicrobial agents produced naturally by a bacterium or fungus to fend off competing organisms in the environment. Now, humans use bacterial or fungal fermentation to produce antibiotics in large commercial bioreactors.

Because bacterial cells differ in structure and function from human cells, it is possible to find compounds that selectively kill them, while leaving the human patient unharmed. Protozoans, fungi, and helminths are far more closely related to humans, and therefore it is more difficult to find antibiotics that will kill these organisms without harming the human host. Viruses take over the machinery of host cells for viral reproduction; therefore, selective antiviral compounds are difficult to discover, and few are known.

Figure 22C **Antibiotic therapy.**

Types of Antibiotics

Antibacterial agents tend to either inhibit cell wall biosynthesis or protein synthesis by bacteria. Penicillin, a naturally occurring compound produced by the common bread mold *Penicillium,* acts by inhibiting the synthesis of the peptidoglycan found in bacterial cell walls. Naturally occurring penicillins can be chemically modified into a wide variety of "cillin" antibiotics, such as ampicillin, carbenicillin, and amoxicillin, that exhibit different qualities and spectrums of activity. The spectrum of an antibiotic is the range of organisms for which it is effective. The cephalosporins, such as Ciprofloxacin, inhibit peptidoglycan synthesis in the same way as the cillins. But Vancomycin inhibits bacterial cell wall synthesis by a different mechanism.

Some antibiotics target the activity of bacterial ribosomes, whose composition differs somewhat from that of human ribosomes. Erythromycin, a broad-spectrum antibiotic, is often used as a substitute for penicillin. Aminoglycosides are another class of antibacterial compounds that block the action of ribosomes. Tetracyclines are a group of related agents that inhibit bacterial protein synthesis. These compounds have the broadest spectrum of any of the antibiotics. They move easily throughout the body and into the cells. Tetracyclines are often used against intracellular parasites, such as chlamydias and rickettsias.

Few antiviral agents are available; the most widely prescribed are derivatives of acyclovir. These compounds mimic nucleic acid bases and disrupt viral genome reproduction. Acyclovir is commonly used to treat recurrences of herpes. As discussed in Chapter 23, a variety of antiviral agents have been developed to limit the growth of HIV and retard the onset of AIDS.

It is difficult to kill eukaryotic pathogens, but researchers have been able to exploit a few biochemical differences. For example, the synthesis of sterols in fungi differs somewhat from the same pathways in humans. A variety of fungicides are directed against sterol synthesis, such as topical agents for treating yeast and tinea infections. The medicine usually used to treat systemic fungal infections (griseofulvin) has a mechanism that is poorly understood. Malaria is treated with quinine derivatives, such as chloroquine. These agents have significant side effects in humans, leaving the patient semiconscious with hallucinations for several days in many cases. There are few effective treatments for helminths (see page 449), but a medicine has been developed for an *Ascaris* infection.

Problems Associated with Antibiotic Therapy

Some patients are allergic to antibiotics, and the reaction can be fatal. Antibiotics not only kill off disease-causing bacteria, but they also reduce the number of beneficial bacteria in the intestinal tract and other locations. Therefore, the growth of pathogenic microbes begins to flourish. Diarrhea can result, as can a vaginal yeast infection. The use of antibiotics probably prevents natural immunity from occurring and most likely leads to the need for recurring antibiotic therapy. Most important, perhaps, is the growing resistance of certain strains of bacteria to antibiotics. Whereas penicillin was once 100% effective against hospital strains of *Staphylococcus aureus,* today it is far less effective. Penicillin and tetracycline, long used to cure gonorrhea, now have a failure rate of more than 20% against certain strains of gonococci. Pulmonary tuberculosis is on the rise, particularly among AIDS patients, the homeless, and the rural poor, and the strains are resistant to the usual combined antibiotic therapy.

To keep antibiotics effective, the following steps are recommended:

Steps to Prevent Resistant Diseases

1. Never take an antibiotic for a viral infection, such as a cold or flu.

2. Take antibiotics exactly and only as a doctor prescribes.

3. Wash your hands frequently and thoroughly.

4. Always handle food safely:
   Keep your hands, utensils, and countertops clean.
   Keep raw meat, poultry, and fish—or their juices—from contacting other foods.
   Cook foods thoroughly and refrigerate foods promptly.

5. Get vaccinated when vaccines are available.

6. Exercise, eat right, drink lots of water, and get plenty of sleep.

Some believe that if antibiotic use is not strictly limited, resistant strains of bacteria will completely replace present strains, and antibiotic therapy will no longer be effective.

22.4 Other Infectious Agents

Fungi, protozoans, and a variety of worms also cause diseases in humans.

Fungi

Fungi are more closely related to animals than are bacteria because their cells are eukaryotic as are those of animals, including humans. Molds and yeasts constitute the microscopic fungi even though they produce large, visible colonies on old bread. Yeasts are usually unicellular and reproduce by budding. Molds are filamentous and exist as chains of cells, called hyphae.

Mycoses are diseases caused by fungi. The strong similarities between fungal cells and human cells make it difficult to design antibiotics that act against fungi and do not harm humans. Among the diseases listed in Table 22.3 (see page 448), we will discuss tineas, which are skin infections; candidiasis, a common vaginal infection; and histoplasmosis.

Tineas

The pathogenic fungi causing the cutaneous diseases called tineas are commonly found in the environment, in soils, on surfaces, and on pets. The fungi release enzymes that degrade the keratin and collagen in skin. The area of infection becomes red and inflamed. In **ringworm,** the fungal colony grows outward, forming a ring of inflammation. The center of the lesion begins to heal so that the lesion gets the characteristic red ring surrounding an area of healed skin. Tinea of the scalp is rampant among school-age children, affecting as much as 30% of that population.

Tinea can occur almost anywhere, including the groin (jock itch), the beard, and the hands. In infants, a scalp infection can lead to permanent hair loss. Athlete's foot is a form of tinea that causes itching and peeling of the skin between the toes (Fig. 22.14). It is transmitted by way of locker-room floors and showers and can lead to chronic nail infections. Most infections are treated topically, but chronic infections require oral antibiotics.

Candidiasis

The yeast *Candida albicans,* which causes the widest variety of fungal infections, is part of most people's normal microflora on the skin, and in the mouth, intestine, and vagina. **Candidiasis** is observed when the balance of the normal microflora is disrupted by taking antibiotics or immunosuppressive drugs or by having an immunodeficiency disease.

In the vagina, bacteria called *Lactobacillus* normally produce organic acids that lower the pH of the vagina. When these bacteria are inhibited, *Candida* can proliferate, leading to inflammation, itching, and a cheesy, yellow-white discharge. Males who contract the disease through sexual contact develop pustules.

Oral thrush is a *Candida* infection of the mouth that is common in newborns and AIDS patients. Bleeding gums and white patches on the tongue are common symptoms. *Candida* can also cause chronic infections of the skin in AIDS patients. In some cases, *Candida* invades the body, causing a systemic infection that can damage the heart, brain, and other organs. A systemic infection often results from intravenous drug use.

Histoplasmosis

Histoplasma capsulatum, a soil organism found in bird droppings, causes systemic mycosis (Fig. 22.15). Over 40 million people in the United States are infected, and 500,000 new cases occur annually. The vast majority of cases are in the Midwest. Less than half of those infected notice any symptoms. About 3,000 have a severe disease, and about 50 die each year from **histoplasmosis.** In this disease, the fungal pathogen lives and grows within cells of the immune system. Lesions in the lungs leave calcifications that resemble those of TB. In chronic cases, histoplasmosis is not easily distinguished from TB. The fungus can also cause oral lesions and inflammations of the lymph nodes and organs.

Fungi cause several diseases, including those of the skin, vagina, and blood.

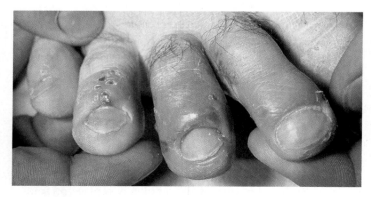

Figure 22.14 **Athlete's foot.**
Tinea pedis is usually caused by species of *Trichophyton*.

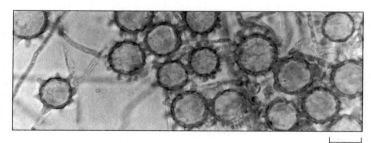

10 µm

Figure 22.15 *Histoplasma capsulatum.*
The mold phase of this organism produces large spores, called conidia, with projecting knobs.

Protozoans

The protozoans are generally eukaryotic unicellular organisms with a nucleus and organelles. Among the protozoan diseases listed in Table 22.4 (see page 448), we will discuss malaria and giardiasis in detail.

Malaria

Malaria is the most widespread and dangerous of the diseases caused by protozoans. It is endemic in approximately 50% of the habitable surface of the Earth. Some 300 million people are infected worldwide, and 2–4 million die each year, a million of these under age five. Although presently rare in the United States, malaria was widespread there until the mosquitoes that transmit the disease were brought under control. One quarter of all Civil War hospitalizations were due to malaria. The disease can be caused by one of several *Plasmodium* species, each of which has a complex life cycle (Fig. 22.16). Sexual reproduction requiring the joining of

gametes occurs in the mosquito, and then many parasites migrate to the salivary glands. After the parasite passes to a human through the bite of a mosquito, a series of developmental stages occurs in liver cells and then in blood cells. In some cases, as many as 40% of the patient's blood cells are infected. The infected blood cells burst in virtual synchrony, releasing huge numbers of parasites. This causes anemia and "sludge blood," which can damage organs. The cycle repeats every two or three days, with chills, high fever, and vomiting. Some forms of malaria have a 50% mortality rate if left untreated. Survivors gain limited immunity to reinfection. No vaccine is available for malaria in part due to its complex life cycle. Efforts to control malaria worldwide by attacking mosquito populations have been unsuccessful. A related protozoan, *Toxoplasma*, is commonly transmitted by cats. **Toxoplasmosis** generally causes no appreciable symptoms, but infection is harmful to the developing fetus. This is why it is recommended that pregnant women take steps to prevent fecal-oral transmission if their cat is a potential carrier.

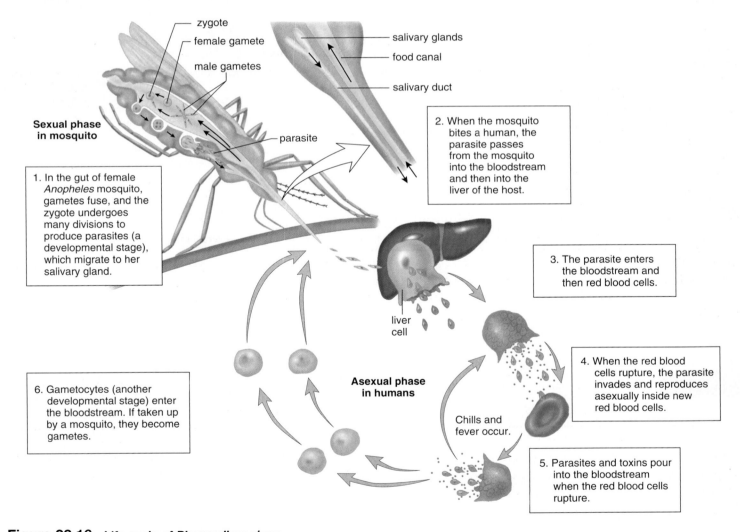

Figure 22.16   Life cycle of *Plasmodium vivax.*
The *Anopheles* mosquito is a vector that carries the infection from human to human. Asexual reproduction occurs in humans, while sexual reproduction takes place within the *Anopheles* mosquito.

Giardiasis and Related Diseases

Giardiasis, the most common water-borne diarrheal disease in the United States, is caused by *Giardia,* a flagellated protozoan (Fig. 22.17*a*). Often mild or asymptomatic, the watery diarrhea it causes is particularly dangerous for young children. Chronic infections can result in a malabsorption syndrome and wasting. *Giardia* is common in surface waters used as sources for drinking water. The microbe produces cysts that are very resistant to chemical and physical damage. The cysts often pass through the sand filters in water treatment plants and are not killed by chlorine disinfection. *Giardia* infections are rampant in day-care centers because the cysts are found in feces. In less-developed countries, 30% of children under age two are infected. It is estimated that 200 million people worldwide are infected with *Giardia.* In the United States, about 7% of the population are healthy carriers of the disease.

A related protozoan disease, cryptosporidiosis, is caused by *Cryptosporidium.* The organism and its cysts are common in surface waters and in the feces of animals and birds. In the United States, 90% of sewage samples and 75% of rivers are contaminated with *Cryptosporidium.* Infection usually leads to a self-limiting gastroenteritis, but can result in a fatal, watery diarrhea in some cases. *Giardia* and *Cryptosporidium* are two of the most important reasons that natural surface waters must be boiled before being ingested.

Another flagellate, *Trypanosoma brucei,* is the cause of African sleeping sickness, which is transmitted by the tsetse fly. It lives in the patient's blood, causing an inflammation that decreases oxygen flow to the brain (Fig. 22.17*b*). The possibility of an infection is confined to tropical Africa where tsetse flies live in woodlands and thickets of the savannah and the dense vegetation along streams. Although rare, the number of cases in travelers, primarily to East African game parks, has increased in recent years. Travelers who sustain tsetse fly bites and become ill with high fever are advised to seek early medical attention.

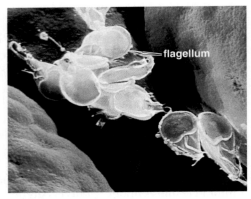

a.

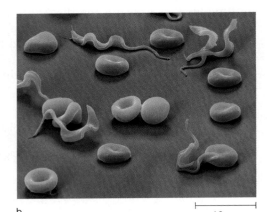

b.   10 μm

Figure 22.17   Flagellates.
a. *Giardia lamblia* in the intestine.
b. *Trypanosoma brucei* in the blood.

Table 22.3	Common Fungal Diseases		
Disease	**Fungus**	**Transmission**	**Comments**
Athlete's foot	*Trichophyton rubrum*	Vehicle, direct contact	Also ringworm of scalp, groin, and elsewhere
Blastomycosis	*Blastomyces dermatitidis*	Airborne	Systemic biowarfare agent
Histoplasmosis	*Histoplasma capsulatum*	Vehicle by soil, airborne	Ohio Valley fever
Pneumocystis pneumonia	*Pneumocystis jiroveci*	Airborne	Common in AIDS patients
Thrush, vaginal yeast infections	*Candida albicans*	Airborne, direct contact	Opportunistic infection

Table 22.4	Common Protozoan Diseases		
Disease	**Protozoan**	**Transmission**	**Comments**
Amebic dysentery	*Entamoeba histolytica*	Vehicle by water/food	500 million annual cases
Chagas disease	*Trypanosoma cruzi*	Kissing bug vector	Chronic infection
Cryptosporidiosis	*Cryptosporidium parvum*	Vehicle by water	Epidemic dysentery from drinking waters
Giardiasis	*Giardia lamblia*	Vehicle by water	Epidemic dysentery from drinking waters
Leishmaniasis	*Leishmania braziliensis*	Sand fly vector	Disfiguring and chronic
Malaria	*Plasmodium falciparum*	Mosquito vector	Other species: *P. vivax, P. ovale, P. malariae*
Toxoplasmosis	*Toxoplasma gondii*	Direct contact with animals	Congenital infections

Helminths

The **helminths** include blood flukes and roundworms that cause human infections. *Schistosoma* are blood flukes that have a complex life cycle. Eggs are released in feces or urine and enter surface waters. The larvae enter and develop in a snail host. A swimming form emerges from the snail and penetrates human skin in seconds. The fluke then moves from the lungs to the veins of the intestine. The flukes can persist for 25 years or more. They produce large masses of eggs that become lodged in blood vessels and tissues. Eventually, fluids accumulate in the abdomen. The liver and spleen become enlarged. **Schistosomiasis** is one of the causes of the swollen belly seen in children in less-developed nations. Infection elicits an immune response and formation of lesions, like those of tuberculosis and histoplasmosis, that destroy tissues. It is estimated that worldwide 250 million people are infected, and over 500,000 die each year. More than 400,000 cases occur in the United States, mainly in the immigrant population. The disease does not spread in the United States due to good sanitation practices. But a related condition, called swimmer's itch, does occur.

Ascaris lumbricoides is a roundworm about the size and general shape of the common earthworm, reaching 8 inches or more in length. The eggs, transmitted in fecal matter, release larvae in the human intestine. The larvae penetrate the intestinal wall, enter the bloodstream, and move to the lungs. After going through several developmental stages, they are coughed up into the esophagus and swallowed. Upon maturity, the adult worms remain in the intestines where they feed on digesting foodstuffs. Although the host may have no symptoms, this is a vitality-sapping infection that can lead to physical and mental retardation. When a bolus of worms appears in the feces, it is possible to diagnose an *Ascaris* infection. The disease is endemic worldwide; over a billion people are infected with roundworms. A related nematode leads to **trichinosis,** in which a parasitic roundworm resides in muscle tissue.

Bioethical Focus

Growth Promoters

Antimicrobials have been used as growth promoters in the livestock industry since the early 1950s. The belief is that low levels of antimicrobials added to animal feed stimulate animal growth and shorten the time from birth to market.

The increased use of these antimicrobials as growth promoters has paralleled a rising influx of increasingly antimicrobial-resistant bacteria. The list of resistant bacteria is increasing and includes the bacterial pathogens *Salmonella, Campylobacter,* and *Enterococcus.* In 1994, vancomycin-resistant enterococci (VRE) were isolated from chickens in the United Kingdom. There was also an increase in the number of VRE infections in hospitals and there was evidence that farm animals were serving as a reservoir for the bacteria. This caused particular concern because VRE are resistant to all commonly used antimicrobial drugs. Vancomycin had previously been the drug of last resort when treating *Enterococcus* infections.

In 1995, the Danish minister of agriculture banned the use of avoparcin in animals grown in Denmark. In 1997, the European Union (EU) Commission agreed to ban the use of avoparcin as a growth promoter in all EU member states. Since that time, both Denmark and the EU have banned other antimicrobial growth promoters that belong to those classes of antimicrobials used to treat humans. Studies show that productivity remained the same and animal mortality rates remained even or appeared to decline slightly. Feed requirements increased somewhat; however, the increase in cost was offset by not having to purchase antimicrobials.

The major result of the ban has been a dramatic decline in antimicrobial resistance to several of the infectious agents in Denmark and other affected countries. Apparently, the use of growth promotion helped to maintain high levels of antibiotic resistance, particularly in *Enterococcus.* There has also been a decline in resistance among *Campylobacter* and *Salmonella* in areas where the ban is in effect.

The United States and Canada permits the use of many antimicrobial growth promoters. At least 17 classes of antimicrobial growth promoters are approved for use in the United States, including several that belong to the same antibiotic classes as those used to treat humans.

The World Health Organization (WHO) has declared the use of these agents a major public health concern. Several groups in the United States, including the Institute of Medicine, recommend that the FDA ban antimicrobial growth promoters that are the same-type antibiotic prescribed to treat infections in humans.

Decide Your Opinion

1. In light of the evidence of a serious public health threat, should the United States and Canada follow the lead of the EU and impose bans of these products? Why or why not?

Summarizing the Concepts

22.1 Microbes and You

Microbes perform valuable services, which can be divided into ecological contributions, economic and aesthetic contributions, and health contributions.

Microbes that possess virulence factors are pathogens. Possession of flagella, adhesion factors, invasive factors, toxins, capsules and survival mechanisms can all be virulence factors

Epidemiology involves knowledge of modes of transmission whether by direct contact, airborne, vehicle, or vector-borne.

22.2 Viruses as Infectious Agents

Viruses are not cellular—they are always composed of an outer capsid made of protein units and a nucleic acid core. The nucleic acid can be DNA (either double- or single-stranded) or RNA. All viruses can only replicate inside a living cell. Viruses that infect humans replicate by this series of phases: attachment, penetration, replication, biosynthesis, maturation, and release.

Among the many viral diseases (see Table 22.1), the influenza virus typifies one that mutates frequently, and this makes long-lasting immunity difficult to achieve. The herpesviruses typify those that lead to chronic infections because they have latent states. Measles is the most contagious of all human diseases. The sheer number of viruses that can cause a cold allows us to come down with one more often than we like.

22.3 Bacteria as Infectious Agents

Bacteria are single cells that usually have a rod shape (bacillus) or a spherical shape (coccus), sometimes occurring as a cluster or in chains. A bacterium doesn't have a nucleus or any of the other organelles typical of a human cell. Its DNA is in a region of the cell known as a nucleoid. Bacteria reproduce by binary fission. The Gram stain aids in the identification of a bacterium.

Among the many disease-causing bacteria (see Table 22.2), the streptococci cause many more different types of infections than any other genus. A strep throat can lead to scarlet fever and/or rheumatic fever, depending on the virulence of the streptococcal strain causing the infection. *Streptococcus pyogenes* causes impetigo, a skin infection, and streptococci are also sometimes "flesh-eating" bacteria.

Tuberculosis is a chronic infection caused by *Mycobacterium tuberculosis*. Active lesions in the alveoli lead to dense structures called tubercles that eventually calcify. Chest X-rays help diagnose a tuberculosis infection.

Food poisoning is caused by toxins released by a bacterium such as *Salmonella,* which can also reproduce in the body, or by staphylococci that reproduce in food, releasing a toxin that remains even after the food is heated to a high temperature. Botulism is caused by *Clostridium botulinum,* which can endure boiling temperatures because it produces endospores. The endospores germinate, and the resulting bacteria release a toxin inside canned foods.

22.4 Other Infectious Agents

Among the many infections caused by fungi (see Table 22.3), tineas take the form of ringworm and athlete's foot. Candidiasis, a type of vaginitis, is caused by *Candida albicans. Histoplasma capsulatum* causes histoplasmosis, a serious infection because it can become systemic.

Among the many infections caused by protozoans (see Table 22.4), malaria is the most widespread and dangerous. The *Anopheles* mosquito is the vector for malaria, which reproduces inside red blood cells. *Giardia,* which causes giardiasis, a gastrointestinal infection, lives in surface waters.

A variety of worms also cause human illnesses. Schistosomiasis is caused by a blood fluke that also has a snail host. The fluke enters the body and destroys tissues.

Studying the Concepts

1. Describe the ways that humans use microbes to their benefit. 432
2. Name several virulence factors, and tell how they affect the activity of bacteria. 434
3. Describe the four major routes of disease transmission. 434–35
4. Describe the structure and life cycle of an animal virus. 436
5. Explain why flu shots are recommended every year. 437
6. Describe the relationship between chickenpox and shingles. 438
7. Why do outbreaks of measles sometimes occur in college dorms? 439
8. How do prions differ from viruses? What diseases are caused by prions? 439
9. Describe the structure and means of cell division of a bacterium. 441
10. What is the structural difference between Gram-positive and Gram-negative bacteria? 441
11. Why are strep throat infections treated aggressively by physicians? 442
12. What is the relationship between impetigo and flesh-eating disease? 442
13. Why is tuberculosis a serious threat today? 443
14. What two types of fungi cause diseases in humans? Describe their structure. 446
15. Describe the tinea infections, candidiasis, and histoplasmosis. 446
16. What type of organism causes malaria? How is malaria transmitted? How is giardiasis transmitted? 447–48
17. What are the helminths? What two diseases do helminths commonly cause in less-developed countries? 449

Thinking Critically About the Concepts

Refer to the opening vignette on page 431, and then answer these questions.

1. One laboratory test for SARS-CoV is the polymerase chain reaction, or PCR. What does this test detect?
2. What steps might public health practitioners take to prevent further SARS epidemics?
3. What steps can you take to protect yourself from SARS and other related infections?

Testing Your Knowledge of the Concepts

Choose the best answer for each question.

1. Normal microflora
   a. are "good" bacteria.
   b. routinely live on or in our organs.
   c. include coliform bacteria in the large intestine.
   d. All of these are correct.

2. Virulence factors can enable a microbe to
   a. produce a toxin.
   b. invade cells.
   c. adhere to surfaces.
   d. All of these are correct.

3. The study of the occurrence, distribution, and control of disease in a population is
   a. bacteriology.
   b. microbiology.
   c. mycology.
   d. epidemiology.
   e. pathogenicity.

4. The mode of transmission that includes transmission via droplets released when a person sneezes is
   a. airborne transmission.
   b. direct contact transmission.
   c. vector-borne transmission.
   d. vehicle transmission.

5. Which of the following is an inanimate object that serves to transmit a pathogen to a individual?
   a. fomite
   b. vehicle
   c. vector
   d. Both a and b are correct.
   e. a, b, and c are all correct.

6. Small changes in the antigens of viruses due to mutation lead to
   a. antigenic shift.
   b. antigenic drift.
   c. antigenic schism.
   d. antigenic transduction.
   e. antigenic reduction.

7. New influenza viruses often appear in Southeast Asia because
   a. adequate health care is less available in that region.
   b. that society has closer contact with livestock.
   c. the climate in that region supports pathogen reproduction.
   d. All of these are correct.

8. Which of the following causes an infection of the genitals?
   a. herpes simplex virus type 1
   b. herpes simplex virus type 2
   c. varicella-zoster virus
   d. rubeola

9. People do not become immune to the common cold because
   a. memory lymphocytes are not produced during the infection.
   b. memory lymphocytes only last a few months.
   c. infections become latent and viruses remain in the body.
   d. many different viruses cause the common cold.

10. Eggs responsible for *Ascaris* infection are transmitted via
    a. mosquito.
    b. snail.
    c. undercooked pork.
    d. fecal material.

11. Selective antiviral compounds are uncommon because viruses
    a. are resistant to most chemicals.
    b. use structures in host cells for viral reproduction.
    c. are structurally complex.
    d. have life cycles that require many host organisms.

12. Viruses differ from bacteria in that viruses
    a. contain DNA.
    b. are not cellular.
    c. cause disease.
    d. can be transmitted by a vector.
    e. are microbes.

13. Viral capsids are composed of
    a. protein.
    b. lipid.
    c. carbohydrate.
    d. DNA.
    e. RNA.

14. Viruses that hide in host cells in an inactive form are called
    a. latent viruses.
    b. hiding viruses.
    c. acute viruses.
    d. lytic viruses.
    e. stasis viruses.

15. A re-emergence of the chickenpox virus in older adults is called
    a. malaria.
    b. chickenpox.
    c. smallpox.
    d. shingles.
    e. polio.

16. A prion is made of
    a. protein.
    b. nucleic acid.
    c. lipid.
    d. carbohydrate.
    e. Both a and c are correct.

17. Lesions in the lung caused by TB are called
    a. tubercles.
    b. histomas.
    c. plaques.
    d. somatosomes.
    e. pulmonary ablations.

18. Which of the following is often associated with improper canning practices?
    a. *Staphylococcus*
    b. *Clostridium botulinum*
    c. *Salmonella*
    d. *Giardia*
    e. *Streptomyces*

19. Which of the following is a protozoan often found in drinking waters?
    a. *Staphylococcus*
    b. *Clostridium botulinum*
    c. *Salmonella*
    d. *Giardia*
    e. *Streptomyces*

20. Diseases caused by fungi are called
    a. fungicides.
    b. septations.
    c. mycoses.
    d. septicemias.
    e. hyphoids.

21. Which of the following is not a place where tinea infections can occur?
    a. feet
    b. groin
    c. scalp
    d. hands
    e. All of these places can be infected.

22. Which of the following is the causative agent of vaginal yeast infections?
    a. bacteria
    b. fungi
    c. protozoans
    d. helminths
    e. None of these are correct.

23. Which of the following is the vector that transmits the *Plasmodium* parasite of malaria?
    a. sand fly
    b. kissing bug
    c. flea
    d. tick
    e. mosquito

24. Penicillin blocks the synthesis of which of the following?
    a. proteins
    b. nucleic acids
    c. peptidoglycan
    d. cellulose
    e. sterols

Understanding Key Terms

acute infection 434
bacillus (pl., bacilli) 441
binary fission 441
botulism 444
candidiasis 446

capsid 436
chronic infection 434
coccus (pl., cocci) 441
contagious 434
endemic 435

endospore 444
epidemic 435
epidemiology 434
eukaryotic cell 441
fomite 435
food poisoning 444
giardiasis 448
Gram stain 441
helminth 449
histoplasmosis 446
impetigo 442
infectious disease 434
influenza virus 437
latency 436
malaria 447
mycosis (pl., mycoses) 446
necrotizing fasciitis 442
nucleoid 441
pandemic 435

pathogen 434
peptidoglycan 441
prion 439
prokaryotic cell 441
rheumatic fever 442
ringworm 446
scarlet fever 442
schistosomiasis 449
shingles 438
sporadic occurrence 435
strep throat 442
systemic 434
toxoplasmosis 447
trichinosis 449
tubercle 443
tuberculosis (TB) 443
vector 435
vehicle 435
virulence factor 434

Match the key terms to these definitions.

a. _____ Rod-shaped bacterial cells.

b. _____ Worldwide epidemic.

c. _____ The science dealing with the incidence, distribution, and control of disease in a population.

d. _____ Cell type having a membrane-bounded nucleus.

e. _____ Resistant form that is able to harbor and transmit a pathogenic organism.

Online Learning Center

www.mhhe.com/maderhuman9

The Online Learning Center provides a wealth of information fully organized and integrated by chapter. You will find practice quizzes, interactive activities, labeling exercises, flashcards, and much more that will complement your learning and understanding of human biology.

Looking at Both Sides

Each day, the Internet, media, and other people present you with opposing viewpoints on a wide range of subjects. Your ability to develop an informed opinion on an issue, and talk to others about it, is extremely important.

To expand and enhance your knowledge of a highly relevant bioethical issue, visit the "Student Edition" of the Online Learning Center. Under "Course-Wide Content," select "Looking at Both Sides." Once there, you will be asked to complete activities that will increase your understanding of a current bioethical issue related to this chapter and allow you to defend your opinion.

CHAPTER

23

Sexually Transmitted Diseases

C H A P T E R C O N C E P T S

23.1 Bacterial Infections
- Why are chlamydia infections particularly troublesome?   454
- What kinds of complications can accompany gonorrhea?   454–55
- What are the three stages of syphilis?   456

23.2 Viral Infections
- Can the herpes virus be transmitted even if a partner has no symptoms at the time?   457
- Genital warts are associated with what other medical condition in women?   458
- What organ in the body is most affected by a hepatitis infection?   458

23.3 Other Infections
- Can pubic lice be transmitted other than by sexual interactions?   459
- How common is bacterial vaginosis, and what are the possible consequences of an infection?   459
- What are the symptoms of trichomoniasis, and why should it be treated?   459

23.4 AIDS (Acquired Immunodeficiency Syndrome)
- How many people in the world currently have an HIV infection? What continent is particularly affected?   460–61
- What are the three categories of an HIV infection?   462–64
- What treatments are currently available for an HIV infection?   466

Jennifer W. is sitting in a doctor's office, quietly explaining that every time she goes to the bathroom, she has this terrible burning pain. She goes on and confesses to blisters on the genitals and a vaginal discharge. She doesn't want to tell her friends. She can't tell her parents.

At least she is telling the doctor.

The source of Jennifer's agony is genital herpes, a very common—and very embarrassing—condition. **Sexually transmitted diseases (STDs)** are contagious diseases caused by pathogens that are passed from one human to another by sexual contact. Genital herpes is an STD caused by a virus. As in Jennifer's case, most people catch the disease by having sex with someone who's infected but may have no symptoms at the moment. That's because herpesviruses—as well as AIDS and a host of other STDs—can lie latent in the body. Even if you can't see the disease, you should try to prevent passing it by (1) practicing abstinence; (2) having a monogamous (always the same partner) sexual relationship with someone who does not have an STD and is not an intravenous drug user; or (3) always using a female or male latex condom in the proper manner. You should also avoid oral/genital contact—just touching the genitals can transfer an STD in some cases.

After taking a prescription drug, Jennifer recovered from her present symptoms of a herpes infection. But she'll never be free of the virus, a possible recurrence of symptoms, or the knowledge that her pain could have been avoided.

23.1 Bacterial Infections

More than 25 diseases are spread primarily through sexual activity. Among the most common bacterial infections are chlamydia, gonorrhea, and syphilis.

Chlamydia

Chlamydia is named for the tiny bacterium that causes it, *Chlamydia trachomatis*. For years, chlamydiae were considered more closely related to viruses than to bacteria, but today it is known that these organisms are cellular. Even so, like a virus, chlamydia grows within body cells. After the bacterium enters a cell by endocytosis, its life cycle occurs inside the endocytic vacuole, which eventually bursts and liberates many new infective chlamydiae.

Chlamydia is the leading STD in the United States. As many as 18% of American women have vaginal chlamydial infections, and most of those cases are asymptomatic. It is estimated that the infection rate could be as high as 50% on college and university campuses. For every reported case in men, more than five cases are detected in women. This is mainly due to increased detection of asymptomatic infections through screening. The low rates in men suggest that many of the sex partners of women with chlamydia are not diagnosed or reported.

Symptoms

Chlamydial infections of the lower reproductive tract usually are mild or asymptomatic, especially in women. About 8–21 days after infection, men may experience a mild burning sensation on urination and a mucoid discharge. Women may have a vaginal discharge along with the symptoms of a urinary tract infection. If untreated or treated inappropriately, there is a particular risk of the infection spreading from the cervix to the oviducts so that **pelvic inflammatory disease (PID)** results. This very painful condition can lead to a blockage of the oviducts, with the possibility of sterility or ectopic pregnancy.

Some health authorities believe that chlamydial infections increase the possibility of premature and stillborn births. If a newborn comes in contact with chlamydia during delivery, pneumonia or inflammation of the eyes can result (Fig. 23.1). Erythromycin eyedrops at birth prevent this occurrence. If a chlamydial infection is detected in a pregnant woman, erythromycin should be administered during pregnancy.

Diagnosis and Treatment

New and faster laboratory tests are now available for detecting a chlamydial infection. However, their expense sometimes prevents public clinics from using them. Criteria that could help physicians decide which women should be tested include: being no more than 24 years old; having had a new sex partner within the preceding two months;

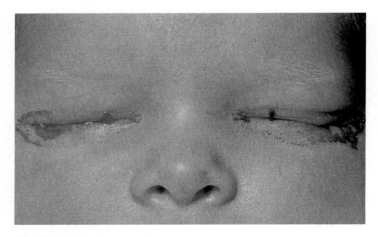

Figure 23.1 **Chlamydia eye infection.**
This newborn's eyes were infected after passing through the birth canal of an infected mother.

experiencing a cervical discharge; bleeding during parts of the vaginal exam; and using a nonbarrier method of contraception. Antibiotic treatment is possible and an antibiotic is used that can also cure gonorrhea, as discussed next.

PID and sterility are possible effects of a chlamydial infection in women. This condition may accompany a gonorrheal infection, discussed next.

Gonorrhea

Gonorrhea is caused by the bacterium *Neisseria gonorrhoeae*, which is a diplococcus, meaning that generally there are two spherical cells in close proximity. Reported gonorrhea rates declined steadily until the late 1990s, and then they increased by about 9% (Fig. 23.2). Rates of infection remain high among adolescents, young adults, and African Americans. Also, women using the birth control pill have a greater risk of contracting gonorrhea because hormonal contraceptives cause the genital tract to be more receptive to pathogens.

Persons with gonorrhea often have chlamydia, a secondary infection. Infection with either gonorrhea or chlamydia increases the risk of an infection with HIV.

Symptoms

The diagnosis of gonorrhea in men is not difficult as long as they display typical symptoms (as many as 20% of men may be asymptomatic). The patient complains of pain during urination and has a milky urethral discharge three to five days after contact with the pathogen. In women, the bacteria may first settle within the vagina or near the cervix, from which they may spread to the oviducts. Unfortunately, the majority of women are asymptomatic until they develop severe pain

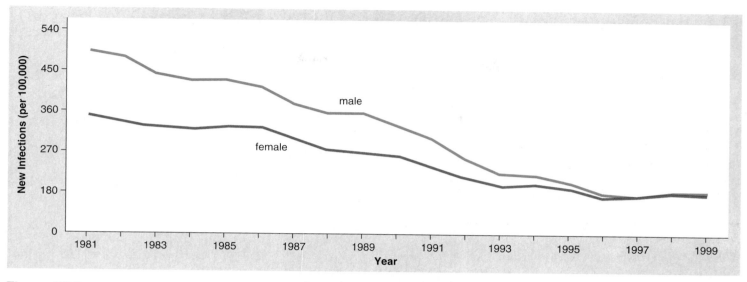

Figure 23.2 **Gonorrhea rates by gender, United States, 1981–1999.**
During the period from 1997 to 1999, epidemiologists reported an increase of 8.8% among men and 9% among women. Before then, the disease was on the decline.

in the abdominal region due to PID. PID from gonorrhea is especially apt to occur in women using an IUD (intrauterine device) as a birth control measure.

PID due to a chlamydial or gonorrheal infection affects many thousands of women each year in the United States. PID-induced scarring of oviducts will cause infertility in about 20%, ectopic pregnancy in 9%, and chronic pelvic pain in 18%.

Gonorrhea proctitis is an infection of the anus, with symptoms that include anal pain and blood or pus in the feces. Oral/genital contact can cause infection of the mouth, the throat, and the tonsils. Gonorrhea can spread to internal parts of the body, causing heart damage or arthritis. If, by chance, the person touches infected genitals and then his or her eyes, a severe eye infection can result (Fig. 23.3).

Eye infection leading to blindness can occur as a baby passes through the birth canal. Because of this, all newborns receive erythromycin eyedrops as a protective measure.

Transmission and Treatment

The chances of getting a gonorrheal infection from an infected partner are good. Women have a 50–60% risk, while men have a 20% risk of contracting the disease after even a single exposure to an infected partner. Therefore, the preventive measures listed in the introduction to this chapter on page 453 should be followed.

Blood tests for gonorrhea are being developed, but in the meantime, it is necessary to diagnose the condition by microscopically examining the discharge of men or by growing a culture of the bacterium from either the male or the female to positively identify the organism. Because no blood test is available, it is very difficult to recognize asymptomatic carriers, who are capable of passing on the condition without realizing it.

It is standard medical practice to treat anyone who is known or suspected to have either gonorrhea or chlamydia as if they have both diseases and treat with antibiotics appropriate for both diseases. Penicillin and tetracycline are no longer suitable treatment choices due to resistance. The antibiotic cephalosporin is now recommended.

Gonorrheal infections presently show a slight increase in prevalence at a time when resistance to antibiotic therapy is occurring.

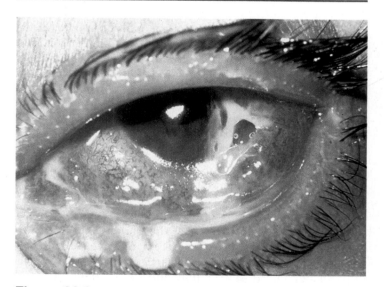

Figure 23.3 **Secondary sites for a gonorrheal infection.**
Gonorrheal infection of the eyes can happen when a newborn passes through the birth canal. Manual transfer from the genitals to the eyes is also possible.

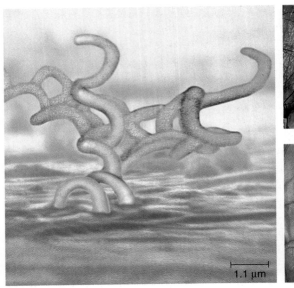

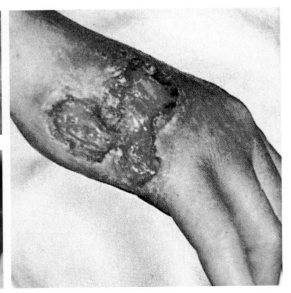

1.1 µm

a.   b.

Figure 23.4   Syphilis.

a. Scanning electron micrograph of *Treponema pallidum*, the cause of syphilis. **b.** The three stages of syphilis. The primary stage of syphilis is a chancre at the site where the bacterium enters the body. The secondary stage is a body rash that occurs even on the palms of the hands and soles of the feet. In the tertiary stage, gummas may appear on the skin or internal organs.

Syphilis

Syphilis is caused by a bacterium called *Treponema pallidum*, an actively motile, corkscrew-like organism that is classified as a spirochete (Fig. 23.4*a*). The number of new cases of syphilis in 2001 were the fewest in the United States since 1945. However, outbreaks of syphilis have recently been reported among gay and bisexual men.

Syphilis has three stages, which can be separated by latent periods, during which the bacteria are not multiplying (Fig. 23.4*b*). During the primary stage, a hard chancre (ulcerated sore with hard edges) indicates the site of infection. The chancre can go unnoticed, especially since it usually heals spontaneously, leaving little scarring. During the secondary stage, the bacterium has spread throughout the body, and the individual breaks out in a rash. Curiously, the rash does not itch and is seen even on the palms of the hands and the soles of the feet. Hair loss can occur, and infectious gray patches may appear on the mucous membranes, including the mouth. These symptoms disappear of their own accord.

Not all cases of secondary syphilis go on to the tertiary stage. Some spontaneously resolve the infection, and some do not progress beyond the secondary stage. During a tertiary stage, which lasts until the patient dies, syphilis may affect the cardiovascular system, and weakened arterial walls (aneurysms) are seen, particularly in the aorta. In other instances, the disease may affect the nervous system. The patient may become mentally impaired, blind, walk with a shuffle, or show signs of insanity. Gummas, large destructive ulcers, may develop on the skin or within the internal organs. Congenital syphilis is caused by syphilitic

bacteria crossing the placenta. The possibility exists that a child can be stillborn, born blind, or with other anatomical malformations.

Diagnosis and Treatment

Syphilis can be diagnosed through blood tests or by microscopic examination of fluids from lesions. One blood test is based on the presence of reagin, an antibody that appears during the course of the disease. Currently, the most common test is rapid plasma reagin (RPR), which is used for screening large numbers of test serums. Because the blood tests can give a false positive, they are followed up by microscopic detection. Dark-field microscopic examination of fluids from lesions can detect the living organism. Alternatively, test serum is added to a freeze-dried *T. pallidum* on a slide. Any antibodies present that react to *T. pallidum* are detected by fluorescent-labeled antibodies to human gamma globulin. The organism will then fluoresce when examined under a fluorescence microscope.

Syphilis is a devastating disease. Control of syphilis depends on prompt and adequate treatment of all new cases; therefore, it is crucial for all sexual contacts to be traced so that they can be treated. The cure for all stages of syphilis is some form of penicillin. To prevent transmission, the general instructions given in the introduction to this chapter (see page 453) should be faithfully followed.

Syphilis is a devastating sexually transmitted disease. Although it is curable by antibiotic therapy, the chance of resistance is always a threat.

23.2 Viral Infections

Among the many sexually transmitted diseases, the most common ones caused by a virus are genital herpes, human papillomavirus, and hepatitis B. AIDS, which is also caused by a virus, is discussed in detail in Section 23.4.

Herpes Infections

There are several types of herpesviruses, and only the ones called herpes simplex viruses (HSV) cause sexually transmitted diseases. The two types of HSVs are: HSV-1, which usually causes cold sores and fever blisters, and HSV-2, which more often causes **genital herpes.** Crossover infections do occur, however. That is, type 1 has been known to cause a genital infection, while type 2 has been known to cause cold sores and fever blisters.

It is estimated that 45 million persons are now infected with herpes and that a million more become infected each year, most of them teens and young adults.

Genital Herpes

Some people have no symptoms of a genital herpes infection. Others may experience a tingling or itching sensation before blisters appear on the genitals (within 2–20 days) (Fig. 23.5). Once the blisters rupture, they leave painful ulcers that may take as long as three weeks or as little as five days to heal. The blisters may be accompanied by fever, pain during urination, swollen lymph nodes in the groin, and in women, a copious vaginal discharge.

After the ulcers heal, the disease is only latent. Blisters can recur, although usually at less frequent intervals and with milder symptoms. Again, fever, stress, sunlight, and menstruation are associated with a recurrence of symptoms. When no symptoms are present, the virus primarily resides in the ganglia of sensory nerves associated with the affected skin. Although HSV-2 was formerly thought to cause cervical cancer, this is no longer believed to be the case.

The herpesvirus can cross the placenta and infect an infant before birth. An infant can also be born with a herpes infection if it comes in contact with a lesion in the birth canal. Either way, the newborn will have a herpes infection. At worst, the infant can be gravely ill, become blind, have neurological disorders, including brain damage, or die. Birth by cesarean section can prevent infection during birth, and therefore all pregnant women infected with the virus should be sure to tell their health-care provider.

Transmission Outside a monogamous relationship, people are at risk for a herpes infection no matter how young they are. Viruses capable of reproduction have occasionally been cultured from the skin of infected persons with no lesions; therefore, the virus can be spread even when no lesions are visible. Persons who are infected should take extreme care to prevent the possibility of spreading the infection to other parts of their own body, such as the eyes. Certainly, sexual contact should be avoided until all lesions are completely healed, and then the general directions given on page 453 for avoiding STD transfer should be followed.

Treatment Presently, there is no cure for genital herpes. The drugs acyclovir and vidarabine disrupt viral reproduction. The ointment form of acyclovir (Zovirax) relieves initial symptoms, and the oral form, valacyclovir (Valtrex), is the drug of choice to prevent the recurrence of symptoms. Other drugs, which are similar in chemical composition and effect, are also available; research is being conducted in an attempt to develop a vaccine.

Herpes simplex viruses cause genital herpes, an extremely infectious disease whose symptoms recur and for which there is no cure.

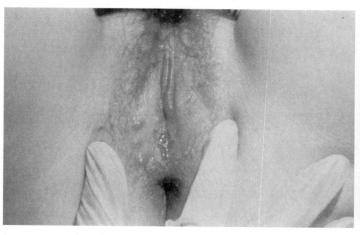

a.

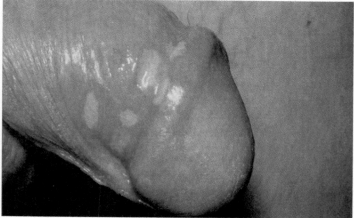

b.

Figure 23.5 **Genital herpes.**
Symptoms of genital herpes are due to an outbreak of blisters, which can be present on the labia of females (**a**) or on the penis of males (**b**).

Genital Warts

Human papillomaviruses (HPVs) cause warts, including common warts, plantar warts, and also genital warts, which are sexually transmitted. Over 6.2 million persons become infected each year with a form of HPV that causes **genital warts** (Fig. 23.6), but only a portion seek medical help. An estimated 20 million people in the United States have an infection that can be transmitted to others.

Transmission and Symptoms

Quite often, carriers of genital warts do not detect any sign of warts, although flat lesions may be present. When present, the warts commonly are seen on the penis and foreskin of men and near the vaginal opening in women. A newborn can become infected while passing through the birth canal.

Genital warts are associated with cancer of the cervix, as well as tumors of the vulva, the vagina, the anus, the penis, and the mouth. Some researchers believe that HPVs are involved in 90–95% of all cases of cancer of the cervix. Teenagers with multiple sex partners seem particularly susceptible to HPV infections. More cases of cancer of the cervix are being seen among this age group.

Treatment

Presently, there is no cure for an HPV infection, but it can be treated effectively by surgery, freezing, application of an acid, or laser burning, depending on severity. Also, even after treatment, the virus can be transmitted. There is no effective manner to prevent transmission of HPV except abstinence or a monogamous relationship with someone known to be free of the virus. Scientists have developed a vaccine against the most common HPV and are working on developing others. Children, especially girls, should be vaccinated before they become sexually active.

Genital warts is a prevalent STD associated with cervical cancer in women.

Hepatitis

There are several types of **hepatitis.** The most common type of hepatitis, hepatitis A, is caused by the HAV (hepatitis A virus). It is usually acquired from sewage-contaminated drinking water and food. It can also be sexually transmitted through oral/anal contact. A hepatitis A vaccine is available and recommended to most individuals.

Hepatitis C, caused by HCV, is most frequently caused by illegal injection of drugs. This type of hepatitis is also of great concern. Infection can lead to chronic hepatitis, liver cancer, and death.

Hepatitis E, caused by HEV, is usually seen in developing countries. Only imported cases—that is, occurring in travelers to the country or in visitors to endemic regions—have been reported in the United States.

Hepatitis B

HBV is a DNA virus that is spread in the same way as HIV, the cause of AIDS—through sharing needles by drug abusers and through sexual contact between heterosexuals or between homosexual men. Therefore, it is common for an AIDS patient to also have an HBV infection. Also, like HIV, HBV can be passed from mother to child by way of the placenta.

About 70% of infected persons have flu-like symptoms, including fatigue, fever, headache, nausea, vomiting, muscle aches, and dull pain in the upper right of the abdomen. Jaundice, a yellowish cast to the skin, can also be present. Some persons have an acute infection that lasts only three to four weeks. Others have a chronic form of the disease that leads to liver failure and the need for a liver transplant. Death from chronic liver disease occurs in 15–25% of infected persons.

Although there are drugs in use for treatment of chronic hepatitis B, prevention is imperative. The general directions given on page 453 should be followed, but inoculation with the HBV vaccine is the best protection. The vaccine, which is safe and does not cause any major side effects, is now on the list of recommended immunizations for children (see Fig. 21.9).

Hepatitis B is an infection that can lead to liver failure. Because it is spread in the same way as AIDS, many persons are infected with both viruses at the same time.

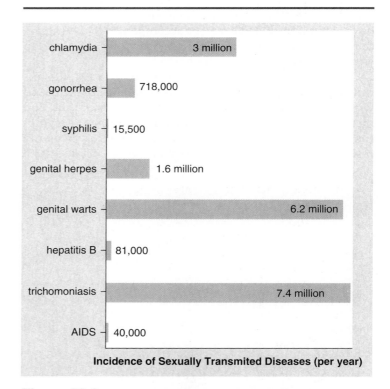

Incidence of Sexually Transmitted Diseases (per year)

Figure 23.6   Incidence of new cases of common STDs.
In the United States, more than 65 million people are living with an incurable STD. An additional 16.5 million people become infected with one or more STDs each year. Approximately one-fourth of these new infections occur in teenagers. Despite STDs being quite widespread, many people remain unaware of the risks and the consequences, sometimes deadly, of becoming infected.

23.3 Other Infections

Here, we consider infections with pubic lice and various vaginal infections.

Pubic Lice (Crabs)

The parasitic crab louse *Phthirus pubis* (an insect) takes its name from its resemblance to a small crab (Fig. 23.7). The louse infests the pubic hair, causing an STD, commonly known as pubic lice, or crabs. The condition can be contracted by direct contact with an infested person or by contact with his or her clothing or bedding. Female lice lay their eggs around the base of the hair, and these eggs hatch within a few days to produce a larger number of animals that suck blood from their host and cause severe itching, particularly at night.

In contrast to most types of STDs, self-diagnosis and self-treatment that does not require shaving are possible. Usually, a person finds and identifies adult lice or their numerous eggs on or near the pubic hairs. Medications such as lindane are applied to the infested area; all sexual partners need to be treated also. Undergarments, sheets, and night clothing should be washed by machine in hot water.

Vaginal Infections

Among the microflora of the vagina, lactobacilli help maintain a healthy environment. An increase in the growth of *Gardnerella vaginalis* with a decrease in lactobacilli results in the development of **bacterial vaginosis (BV).** BV is believed to account for 50% of vaginitis cases in American women. The overgrowth of the bacterium and consequent symptoms can also be due to nonsexual reasons, but males who are symptomless may pass on the bacteria to women, who then exhibit symptoms.

A woman with BV usually has a thin, gray discharge that resembles flour paste and has a foul smell. The smell is particularly noticeable after sexual intercourse because the alkaline seminal fluid causes the bacteria to release the chemicals that cause the smell. Untreated BV may increase the risk of PID and an HIV infection. Both intravaginal creams and oral medications are available.

Trichomoniasis is a sexually transmitted disease caused by the protozoan *Trichomonas vaginalis* (Fig. 23.8a). The organism accounts for about one-fourth of all cases of vaginitis. Trichomoniasis is characterized by the presence of an abundant, frothy, white or yellow, foul-smelling vaginal discharge accompanied by itching that can be severe. Trichomoniasis is most often acquired through sexual intercourse, and an asymptomatic partner is usually the reservoir of infection. To avoid passing the condition back and forth, both partners should be treated simultaneously. If this is done, a cure rate of approximately 95% is expected.

Figure 23.7
Sexually transmitted animal. This parasitic crab louse, *Phthirus pubis*, infests the pubic hair of humans.

250 μm

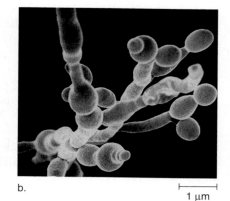

a.   8 μm   b.   1 μm

Figure 23.8   Organisms that cause vaginitis.
a. *Trichomonas vaginalis*, a protozoan. **b.** *Candida albicans*, a yeast.

If untreated, the *Trichomonas* invades the urinary tract, and some health authorities believe it can affect the cells of the cervix, eventually causing cervical cancer. Although the cause is not known, both BV and trichomoniasis in a pregnant woman can result in premature birth and/or an infant with low birth weight.

Candida albicans (Fig. 23.8b) is usually found in the vagina, but the growth of this yeast sometimes increases beyond normal in women who are taking an antibiotic or the birth control pill. An estimated 13 million cases of **candidal vaginitis** occur annually. A woman usually notices a white, clumpy discharge that looks something like cottage cheese. Associated symptoms include intense itching and soreness of the vaginal and vulval tissues, which typically become red and dry. Over-the-counter intravaginal preparations are available, but self-treatment may not be wise because a mistake in diagnosis can have serious consequences. Treatment should continue well beyond the two days it takes for symptoms to disappear.

Various organisms cause vaginal infections. It is important to be diagnosed and treated to avoid possible complications. A parasitic louse causes the condition known as crabs.

23.4 AIDS (Acquired Immunodeficiency Syndrome)

The organism that causes **acquired immunodeficiency syndrome (AIDS)** is a virus called **human immunodeficiency virus (HIV).** HIV attacks the type of lymphocyte known as helper T cells. As helper T cells decline in number, the immune system becomes compromised.

Origin of HIV

It is generally accepted that HIV originated in Africa and then spread to the United States and Europe by way of the Caribbean. HIV has been found in a preserved 1959 blood sample taken from a man who lived in an African country, now called the Democratic Republic of the Congo. Even before this discovery, scientists speculated that an immunodeficiency virus may have evolved into HIV during the late 1950s.

Of the two types of HIV, HIV-2 corresponds to a type of immunodeficiency virus found in the green monkey, which lives in western Africa. Recently, it was announced that researchers have found a virus identical to HIV-1 in a subgroup of chimpanzees once common in west-central Africa. Perhaps, HIV viruses were originally found only in nonhuman primates. They could have mutated to HIV after humans ate nonhuman primates for meat.

British scientists have been able to show that AIDS came to their country perhaps as early as 1959. They examined the preserved tissues of a Manchester seaman who died that year and concluded that he most likely died of AIDS. Similarly, it is thought that HIV entered the United States on numerous occasions as early as the 1950s. But the first documented case is a 15-year-old male who died in Missouri in 1969 with skin lesions now known to be characteristic of an AIDS-related cancer. Doctors froze some of his tissues because they could not identify the cause of death. Researchers also want to test the preserved tissue samples of a 49-year-old Haitian who died in New York in 1959 of the type of pneumonia now known to be AIDS-related.

Throughout the 1960s, it was customary in the United States to list leukemia as the cause of death in immunodeficient patients. Most likely, some of these people actually died of AIDS. Since HIV is not extremely infectious, it took several decades for the number of AIDS cases to increase to the point that AIDS became recognizable as a specific and separate disease. The name AIDS was coined in 1982, and HIV was found to be the cause of AIDS in 1983–84.

AIDS most likely originated in the 1950s, but it wasn't until 1983 that HIV was recognized as its cause.

Transmission and Prevalence of AIDS

HIV is transmitted by sexual contact with an infected person, including vaginal or rectal intercourse and oral/genital contact. Also, needle-sharing among intravenous drug users is high-risk behavior. A less common mode of transmission (and now rare in countries where blood is screened for HIV) is through transfusions of infected blood or blood-clotting factors. Babies born to HIV-infected women may become infected before or during birth, or through breast-feeding after birth. Table 23.1 summarizes the most frequent ways by which HIV is transmitted.

Prevalence of AIDS

AIDS is pandemic because the disease is prevalent in the entire human population around the globe (Fig. 23.9). Today, 34.7 million adults and 1.4 million children are estimated to be living with an HIV infection, and 21.8 million persons have died of AIDS worldwide.

More-Developed Countries   The incidence of HIV infection in the more-developed countries of North America and western Europe and elsewhere is modest. The incidence ranges from 0.02% in Japan to 0.6% in the United States and 0.7% in Portugal. Further, the introduction of combination drug therapy has resulted in a drastic decrease in overall AIDS deaths since 1995. In the United States, HIV first spread through the homosexual community, and male-to-male sexual contact still accounts for the largest percentage of new AIDS cases. But the rate of new HIV infections is now rising faster among heterosexuals than homosexuals. Even now, 26% of all people with AIDS in the United States are women, and they account for 33% of all newly diagnosed cases of HIV infection. In 1986, the majority of AIDS cases occurred among Caucasians; today, this proportion has shifted to minorities. There is one more statistic to call to your attention. Most new HIV infections are occurring among teenagers and young adults; even with drug therapy, these young people will probably not escape eventually coming down with AIDS.

Table 23.1	Transmission of HIV

POSSIBLE ROUTES

Homosexual and heterosexual contact

Intravenous drug use

Transfusion (unlikely in U.S.)

Crossing placenta during pregnancy; breast-feeding

RISK FACTORS

Promiscuous behavior (large number of partners, sex with a prostitute)

Drug abuse with needle-sharing

Presence of another sexually transmitted disease

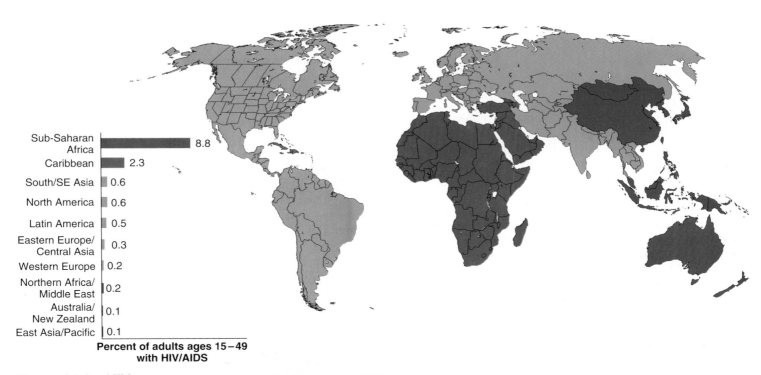

Figure 23.9   HIV prevalence rates in adults at the end of 2000.

HIV/AIDS occurs in all continents and countries of the globe, and presently 34.7 million adults and 1.4 million children younger than 15 are infected worldwide. Clearly, sub-Saharan Africa is the hardest hit, probably because HIV is an emerging disease that began in Africa, possibly by jumping from a non-human primate to a human.

Less-Developed Countries   In the largest countries of Latin America and the Caribbean, with an incidence of 2.3% and 0.5%, respectively, the AIDS epidemic has charted a course similar to that in North America. HIV/AIDS was first seen among homosexuals and intravenous drug users. Now it is increasingly being spread by heterosexual contact.

Haiti, with an overall HIV prevalence in adults of about 5%, is the worst-affected country outside of Africa. In sub-Saharan Africa, 26 million people are infected with HIV. This is almost 9% of the total adult population between 15 and 49 years of age. The increasing number of deaths among young adults means that there will be more people in their 60s and 70s than in their 40s and 50s. Many are concerned about how families in Africa will cope when the old have to care for their grandchildren and when these grandchildren have to assume adult responsibilities much sooner than they ordinarily would.

Some countries in Africa are affected more than others. HIV prevalence in South Africa grew from 1% of the adult population in 1990 to about 20% today. Similarly, Botswana was essentially free of the disease in 1990; now 45–50% of young adults age 20–30 years are infected with HIV. A certain subtype of HIV-1, namely HIV-1C, has brought about this great devastation. HIV-1C has a greater ease of transmission, and also multiplies and mutates faster than all the other subtypes. Most likely, HIV-1C has already spread from Africa to western India, and a

hybrid virus containing some HIV-1C genetic material has reached mainland China.

The Future   It's quite possible that in 5–20 years the more-developed countries, including the United States, will experience a new epidemic of AIDS caused by HIV-1C. Therefore, it behooves the more-developed countries to do all they can to help African countries aggressively seek a solution to this new HIV epidemic.

AIDS in the United States is presently caused by HIV-1B, and drug therapy has brought the condition under control. But the drug therapy has two dangers. People may become lax in their efforts to avoid infection because they know that drug therapy is available. Also, the use of drugs leads to drug-resistant viruses. Even now, some HIV-1B viruses have become drug-resistant when patients have failed to adhere to their drug regimens. We cannot escape the conclusion that all persons should do everything they can to avoid becoming infected. Behaviors that help prevent transmission are discussed in the Health Focus on page 463.

New HIV infections are increasing faster among heterosexuals than homosexuals; women in the United States now account for nearly 26% of AIDS cases.

Phases of an HIV Infection

The following description of the phases of an HIV infection pertains to an HIV-1B infection, the type now prevalent in the United States. The HIV viruses primarily infect helper T lymphocytes that are also called CD4 T lymphocytes, or simply CD4 T cells. These cells display a molecule called CD4 on their surface. Helper T cells, you will recall, ordinarily stimulate B lymphocytes to produce antibodies and cytotoxic T cells to destroy cells that are infected with a virus.

The Centers for Disease Control and Prevention now recognize three phases of an HIV-1B infection. During the acute phase, no symptoms are apparent, yet the person is highly infectious. During the chronic phase, the individual loses weight, suffers from diarrhea, and most likely develops infections such as thrush or genital herpes. The final phase of an HIV infection is AIDS, when the person comes down with pneumonia, cancer, and other serious conditions.

Category A: Acute Phase

A normal CD4 T-cell count is at least 800 cells per cubic millimeter of blood ($800/mm^3$). This first phase of an HIV infection is characterized by a CD4 T-cell count of $500/mm^3$ or greater (Fig. 23.10). This count is sufficient for the immune system to function normally.

Today, investigators are able to track not only the blood level of CD4 T cells, but also the viral load. The viral load is the number of HIV particles in the blood. At the start of an HIV-1B infection, the virus is replicating ferociously, and the killing of CD4 T cells is evident because the blood level of these cells drops dramatically. For a few weeks, however, people don't usually have any symptoms at all. Then, a few (1–2%) do have mononucleosis-like symptoms that may include fever, chills, aches, swollen lymph nodes, and an itchy rash. These symptoms disappear, and no other symptoms appear for quite some time. The HIV blood test commonly used at clinics is not yet positive because it tests for the presence of antibodies, not for the presence of HIV itself. This means that the person is highly infectious, even though the HIV blood test is negative. For this reason, all persons need to follow the guidelines for preventing the transmission of HIV as outlined in the Health Focus on page 463.

After a period of time, the body responds to the infection by increased activity of immune cells, and the HIV blood test becomes positive. During this phase, the number of CD4 T cells is greater than the viral load (Fig. 23.10). But some investigators believe that a great unseen battle is going on. The body is staying ahead of the hordes of viruses entering the blood by producing as many as 1–2 billion new helper T lymphocytes each day. This is called the "kitchen sink model" for CD4 loss. The sink's faucet (production of new CD4 T cells) and the sink's drain (destruction of CD4 T cells) are wide open. As long as the body can produce enough new CD4 T cells to keep pace with the destruction of these cells by HIV and by cytotoxic T cells, the person has a healthy immune system that can deal with the infection.

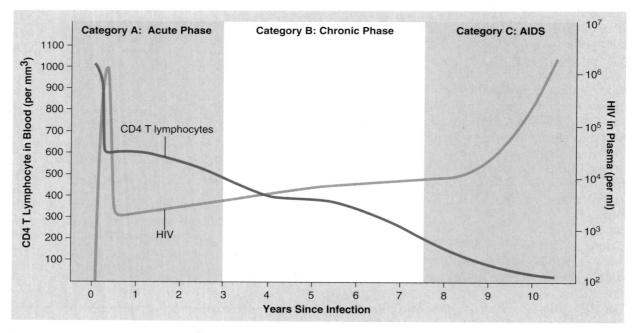

Figure 23.10 **Stages of an HIV infection.**

In category A individuals, the number of HIV particles in plasma rises upon infection and then falls. The number of CD4 T lymphocytes falls, but stays above 400/mm³. In category B individuals, the number of HIV particles in plasma is slowly rising, and the number of T lymphocytes is decreasing. In category C individuals, the number of HIV particles in plasma rises dramatically as the number of T lymphocytes falls below 200/mm³.

Health Focus

Preventing Transmission of STDs

Sexual Activities Transmit STDs

Because sexual activities transmit STDs, individuals should either abstain from sexual intercourse or develop a long-term monogamous (always the same partner) sexual relationship with a partner who is free of STDs (Fig. 23A).

Refrain from multiple sex partners or having relations with someone who has multiple sex partners. If you have sex with two other people and each of these has sex with two people and so forth, the number of people who are relating is quite large.

Remember that the prevalence of AIDS is presently higher among homosexuals and bisexuals than among those who are heterosexual.

Be aware that having relations with an intravenous drug user is risky because the behavior of this group risks AIDS and hepatitis B. Be aware that anyone who already has another STD is more susceptible to an HIV infection.

Avoid anal-rectal intercourse (in which the penis is inserted into the rectum) because this behavior increases the risk of an HIV infection. The lining of the rectum is thin, and infected CD4 T cells can easily enter the body there. Also, the rectum is supplied with many blood vessels, and insertion of the penis into the rectum is likely to cause tearing and bleeding that facilitate the entrance of HIV. The vaginal lining is thick and difficult to penetrate, but the lining of the uterus is only one cell thick and does allow CD4 T cells to enter.

Practice Safer Sex

Always use a latex condom during sexual intercourse if you are not in a monogamous relationship. Be sure to follow the directions supplied by the manufacturer for the use of a condom. At one time, condom users were advised to use nonoxynol-9 in conjunction with a condom, but recent testing shows that this spermicide has no effect on microbes, including HIV.

Avoid fellatio (kissing and insertion of the penis into a partner's mouth) *and cunnilingus* (kissing and insertion of the tongue into the vagina) because they may be a means of transmission. The mouth and gums often have cuts and sores that facilitate catching an STD.

Practice penile, vaginal, oral, and hand cleanliness. Be aware that hormonal contraceptives make the female genital tract receptive to the transmission of STDs, including HIV.

Be cautious about using alcohol or any drug that may prevent you from being able to control your behavior.

Drug Use Transmits HIV

Stop, if necessary, or do not start the habit of injecting drugs into your veins. Be aware that HIV and hepatitis B can be spread by blood-to-blood contact.

Always use a new sterile needle for injection or one that has been cleaned in bleach if you are a drug user and cannot stop your behavior.

Figure 23A Sexual activities transmit STDs.

Figure 23B Sharing needles transmits STDs.

Category B: Chronic Phase

Several months to several years after infection, an untreated individual will probably progress to category B. During this phase, the CD4 T-cell count is 200–499/mm³ of blood, and the number of HIV particles is on the rise (Fig. 23.10). Most likely, symptoms will begin to appear, including swollen lymph nodes in the neck, armpits, or groin that persist for three months or more; severe fatigue not related to exercise or drug use; unexplained persistent or recurrent fevers, often with night sweats; persistent cough not associated with smoking, a cold, or the flu; and persistent diarrhea. Also possible are signs of nervous system impairment, including loss of memory, inability to think clearly, loss of judgment, and/or depression.

The development of non-life-threatening but recurrent infections is a signal that full-blown AIDS will occur shortly. One possible infection is thrush, a *Candida albicans* infection that is identified by the presence of white spots and ulcers on the tongue and inside the mouth. The fungus may also spread to the vagina, resulting in a chronic infection there. Another frequent infection is herpes simplex, with painful and persistent sores on the skin surrounding the anus, the genital area, and/or the mouth.

Category C: AIDS

When a person has AIDS, the CD4 T-cell count has fallen below 200/mm³, and the lymph nodes have degenerated. The patient is extremely thin and weak due to persistent diarrhea and coughing, and will most likely develop one of the opportunistic infections. An **opportunistic infection** is one that has the *opportunity* to occur only because the immune system is severely weakened. Persons with AIDS die

from one or more of the following diseases rather than from the HIV infection itself:

- *Pneumocystis jiroveci* pneumonia. The lungs become useless as they fill with fluid and debris due to an infection with an organism now considered a fungus.
- *Mycobacterium tuberculosis*. This bacterial infection, usually of the lungs, is seen more often as an infection of lymph nodes and other organs in patients with AIDS.
- Toxoplasmic encephalitis is caused by a protozoan parasite. The infection is acquired by eating flesh of infected herbivorous animals or food items contaminated with fecal material from cats. Many people harbor a latent infection in the brain or muscle, but in AIDS patients, the infection leads to loss of brain cells, seizures, and weakness.
- Kaposi's sarcoma is an unusual cancer of the blood vessels, which gives rise to reddish purple, coin-sized spots and lesions on the skin.
- Invasive cervical cancer. This cancer of the cervix spreads to nearby tissues.

Although newly developed drugs can deal with opportunistic diseases, most AIDS patients are repeatedly hospitalized due to weight loss, constant fatigue, and multiple infections (Fig. 23.11). Death usually follows in two to four years.

During the acute phase of an HIV infection, the person is highly infectious; during the chronic phase, swollen lymph nodes and various infections may occur; during the last phase, which is called AIDS, the patient usually succumbs to an opportunistic infection.

a. AIDS patient Tom Moran, July 1987

b. AIDS patient Tom Moran, early January 1988

c. AIDS patient Tom Moran, late January 1988

Figure 23.11 A patient with AIDS.
These photos show how the health of a patient with AIDS deteriorates.

HIV Structure and Life Cycle

Like many other animal viruses, HIV has an envelope with spikes, a capsid, and a nucleic acid genome. The genome for an HIV virus consists of RNA instead of DNA. In addition, HIV is a retrovirus. A **retrovirus** uses reverse transcription of its genome from RNA into DNA for insertion of a complementary copy of its genome into the host's genome.

Inside the HIV capsid are RNA and three viral enzymes of interest:

Reverse transcriptase: carries out reverse transcription when a DNA copy is made of the viral genome.

Integrase: carries out integration of the DNA copy of the viral genome into the host genome.

Protease: cleaves long polypeptides to make them suitable for viral use.

Life Cycle

The events that occur in the reproductive cycle of an HIV virus (Fig. 23.12) are essentially the same as those for the DNA virus, but extra steps are needed because HIV is a retrovirus.

1. *Attachment*. During attachment, the HIV virus binds to the plasma membrane. HIV has an envelope marker, and this marker allows the virus to bind to a CD4 receptor in the host-cell plasma membrane.
2. *Fusion*. After attachment occurs, the HIV virus fuses with the plasma membrane, and the virus enters the cell.
3. *Entry*. A process called uncoating removes the capsid, and RNA is released.
4. *Reverse transcription*. This event in the reproductive cycle is unique to retroviruses. The enzyme called reverse transcriptase makes a DNA copy of retroviruses' RNA genetic material. Usually in cells, DNA is transcribed into RNA. Retroviruses can do the opposite only because they have a unique enzyme from which they take their name. (*Retro* in Latin means reverse.)
5. *Integration*. The viral enzyme integrase now splices viral DNA into a host chromosome. The term **HIV provirus** refers to viral DNA integrated into host DNA. HIV is usually transmitted to another person by means of cells that contain proviruses. Also, proviruses serve as a latent reservoir for HIV during drug treatment. Even if drug therapy results in an

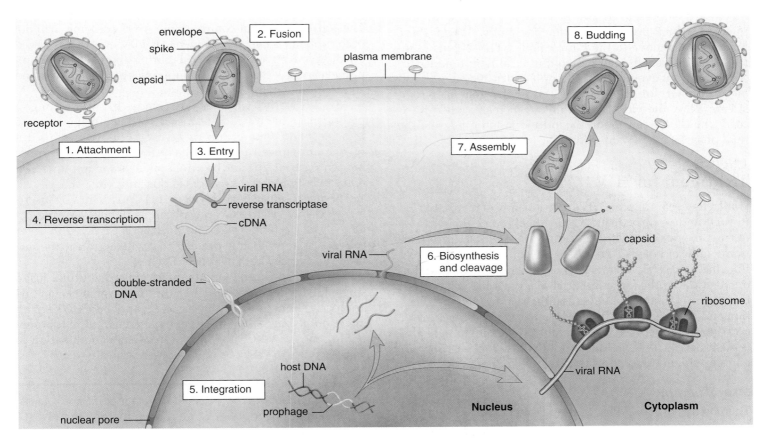

Figure 23.12 Reproduction of HIV.
HIV is a retrovirus that utilizes reverse transcription to produce viral DNA. Viral DNA integrates into the cell's chromosomes before it reproduces and buds from the cell.

undetectable viral load, investigators know that there are still proviruses inside infected lymphocytes.

6. *Biosynthesis and cleavage.* When the provirus is activated, perhaps by a new and different infection, the normal cell machinery directs the production of more viral RNA. Some of this RNA becomes the genetic material for new virus particles. The rest of viral RNA brings about the synthesis of very long polypeptides. These polypeptides have to be cut up into smaller pieces. This cutting process, called cleavage, depends on a third HIV enzyme called protease.

7. *Assembly.* Capsid proteins, viral enzymes, and RNA can now be assembled to form new viral particles.

8. *Budding.* During budding, the virus gets its envelope and envelope marker coded for by the viral genetic material.

The life cycle of an HIV virus includes transmission to a new host. Body secretions, such as semen from an infected male, contain proviruses inside CD4 T lymphocytes. When this semen is discharged into the vagina, rectum, or mouth, infected CD4 T cells migrate through the organ's lining and enter the body. The receptive partner in anal-rectal intercourse appears to be most at risk because the lining of the rectum is apparently prone to penetration. CD4 macrophages present in tissues are believed to be the first infected when proviruses enter the body. When these macrophages move to the lymph nodes, HIV begins to infect CD4 T cells. HIV can hide out in local lymph nodes for some time, but eventually the lymph nodes degenerate, and large numbers of HIV particles enter the general bloodstream. Now the viral load begins to increase; when it exceeds the CD4 T-cell count, the individual progresses to the final phase of an HIV infection.

Treatment for HIV

Until a few years ago, an HIV infection almost invariably led to AIDS and an early death. The medical profession was able to treat the opportunistic infections that stemmed from immune failure, but had no drugs for controlling HIV itself. But since late 1995, scientists have gained a much better understanding of the structure of HIV and its life cycle. Now, therapy is available that successfully controls HIV replication and keeps patients in the chronic phase of infection for a variable number of years so that the development of AIDS is postponed. However, this is not the case for those in poor nations with limited funds for drug treatment of the disease.

Drug Therapy

There is no cure for AIDS, but a treatment called highly active antiretroviral therapy (HAART) is usually able to stop HIV replication to such an extent that the viral load becomes undetectable. HAART utilizes a combination of drugs that interfere with the life cycle of HIV. Entry inhibitors stop HIV from entering a cell by, for example, preventing the virus from binding to a receptor in the plasma membrane. Reverse transcriptase inhibitors, such as zidovudine (AZT), interfere with the operation of the reverse transcriptase enzyme. Integrase inhibitors prevent HIV from inserting its own genetic material into that of the host cells. Protease inhibitors prevent protease from cutting up newly created polypeptides. Assembly and budding inhibitors are in the experimental stage, and none are available as yet. The hope is that by giving a patient a combination of these drugs, the virus is less likely to replicate, successfully mutate in a particular way making drug therapy ineffective, or become resistant to drug therapy.

Investigators have found that when HAART is discontinued, the virus rebounds; therefore, therapy must be continued indefinitely. An HIV-positive pregnant woman who takes reverse transcriptase inhibitors during her pregnancy reduces the chances of HIV transmission to her newborn. If possible, drug therapy should be delayed until the 10th to 12th week of pregnancy to minimize any adverse effects of AZT on fetal development. But, if treatment begins at this time, the chance of transmission is reduced by 66%. If treatment is delayed until the last few weeks of a pregnancy, transmission of HIV to an offspring is still cut by 50%.

Vaccines

The consensus is that control of the AIDS epidemic will not occur until a vaccine that prevents an HIV infection is developed. An effective vaccine should bring about a twofold immune response: production of antibodies by plasma cells and stimulation of cytotoxic T cells.

Traditionally, vaccines are made by weakening a pathogen so that it will not cause disease when it is injected into the body. One group of investigators using this approach announced that they have found a way to expose hidden parts of gp120 (the viral spike) so the immune system can better learn to recognize this antigen.

Some scientists have developed DNA vaccines by inserting pieces of viral DNA into plasmids, which are rings of DNA from bacterial cells. This vaccine is expected to enter cells and start producing proteins that will migrate to the surface, and thereby alert cytotoxic T cells.

Others have been working on vaccines that utilize just a single HIV protein, such as gp120, as the vaccine. So far, this approach has not resulted in sufficient antibodies to keep an infection at bay. After many clinical trials, none too successful, most investigators now agree that a combination of various types of vaccines may be the best strategy.

HIV is a retrovirus, and its life cycle includes reverse transcription. Current drug therapy is aimed against its three enzymes: reverse transcriptase, integrase, and protease. Research into a possible vaccine continues.

Bioethical Focus

Providing Access to HIV/AIDS Medications

In sub-Saharan Africa, over 26 million people are living with AIDS. In the United States, the average AIDS patient has access to medications to treat AIDS-related infections and to the antiretroviral drugs (ARVs) that reverse the effects of HIV in infected individuals. In sub-Saharan Africa, these drugs are either not available, or the cost is way beyond the means of the average citizen.

The epidemic is exacting an enormous toll on the social and economic fabric of many countries in the subcontinent. Those primarily affected are in their prime productive years. The people that work in industry, the agriculture workers that provide food for the population, truck drivers, all the folks that sustain the economy. And most are parents. At this time, it is estimated that 11 million children in sub-Saharan Africa are orphaned.

International aid agencies, such as Medecins sans Frontieres (MSF), are actively working to provide affordable treatment to patients in these countries. The obstacles are overwhelming. Inadequate infrastructure and poor techniques impede basic medical services. Civil strife can interrupt access to clinics. One of the biggest problems, however, is cost. The cost of the drugs is way beyond the ability of countries and people in Africa to pay for them.

The countries of the world belong to an organization called the World Trade Organization (WTO) and this organization has modified the TRIPS (trade-related aspects of intellectual property rights) agreement. It says despite pharmaceutical companies having patents that forbid anyone else from making the same drug for less cost, these patents should not prevent member countries from taking measures to protect public health. Therefore, WTO countries agree to extend exemptions on pharmaceutical patent protection for less-developed countries, until 2016. It allows member governments to grant others the right to make or use a patented product without consent of the original patent holder. A subsequent ruling in 2003 allows for the import of these products by poorer countries.

The end result has been two polarized camps: the pharmaceutical industry and the international aid organizations. The pharmaceutical industry argues in favor of stringent patent protection. In the United States, this industry spends $30 billion a year to develop new products. Only one of the 5,000–10,000 drugs developed and reviewed makes it to the market; only one-third of these make any money. This fraction must support all of the research, overhead, production, and marketing costs. Without adequate patent protection, the companies would not be able to make this investment.

Although a patent is issued for a 20-year period, the reality is about 12 years of actual profit. After the patent expiration, the drugs can be produced and sold by generic manufacturers. Without significant drug development by

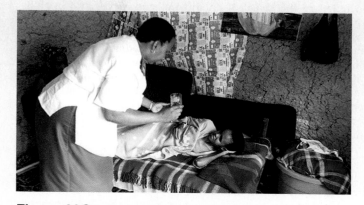

Figure 23C   **AIDS in Africa.**
Making anti-retroviral drugs available to Africans at a reduced price raises many ethical questions.

the established industry, there would be fewer drugs for the generic drug industry to copy and market.

The arguments for not recognizing the patents of drug companies is put forth by MSF and other international aid organizations. These organizations point to the millions of sufferers that could be helped by importing drugs at below market rates. They state that allowing these poorest countries to import generic medicines would involve about 1% of the market and would not have an effect on the pharmaceutical industry profits. They further claim that the prices set for patented medicines usually are far in excess of production costs.

In contrast to the manner in which the TRIPS agreement deals with the drug companies, the agreement says that performers have the right to prevent unauthorized recording, reproduction, and broadcast of live performances (bootlegging) for no less than 50 years. Should those who create drugs be afforded less protection than those who create new musical pieces? How can we be sure that an exception for poor countries would not lead to many other exceptions, to the point that drug companies would have to go out of business?

Or, do you feel that drug companies make far too much money and their profits should be curtailed, by whatever means possible?

Decide Your Opinion

1. What do you see as the main concerns surrounding the cost of drugs to poor countries, to poor individuals?
2. Should the pharmaceutical industry be made to bear the cost of ARVs (anti-retroviral drugs) for the entire world? Why or why not? If no, who should pay for these drugs?
3. What would be a fair way to set the cost of these drugs?

Summarizing the Concepts

23.1 Bacterial Infections

Bacteria are the cause of chlamydia, gonorrhea, and syphilis. Chlamydia is caused by a tiny bacterium of the same name. These bacteria develop inside endocytic vacuoles that eventually burst and liberate infective chlamydiae. Chlamydia can be asymptomatic, or it can produce symptoms of a urinary tract infection. Both chlamydia and gonorrhea can result in PID, leading to sterility and ectopic pregnancy. Gonorrhea is caused by the bacterium *Neisseria gonorrhoeae*, a diplococcus. Gonorrhea may not cause symptoms, particularly in women, but men may experience painful urination and a thick, milky discharge. Syphilis is caused by a bacterium called *Treponema pallidum*, an actively motile, corkscrew-like organism. Syphilis is a systemic disease that should be cured in its early stages before possible deterioration of the nervous system and cardiovascular system takes place.

Abstinence, a monogamous relationship, or use of a condom can help prevent the transmission of viral and bacterial STDs.

23.2 Viral Infections

Viruses are the cause of genital herpes, genital warts, hepatitis B, and AIDS. Genital herpes is caused by herpes simplex virus (HSV): Type 1 usually causes cold sores and fever blisters, while type 2 often causes genital herpes. Genital herpes is a disease that causes painful blisters on the genitals. Genital warts are caused by human papillomavirus (HPV), which is a cuboidal DNA virus that reproduces in the nuclei of skin cells. Genital warts is a disease characterized by warts on the penis and foreskin in men and near the vaginal opening in women. Hepatitis B, which is spread in the same manner as AIDS, can lead to liver failure.

Medications have been developed to control AIDS and genital herpes, but there is no cure for these conditions, and no vaccines are available. Of all the viral STDs, only a vaccine for hepatitis B exists at the present time.

23.3 Other Infections

Pubic lice is an STD caused by an insect. Significant types of vaginal infections are bacterial vaginosis, caused by a bacterium; trichomoniasis, caused by a protozoan; and candidiasis, caused by a yeast.

23.4 AIDS (Acquired Immunodeficiency Syndrome)

HIV is the cause of AIDS, a disease that is now pandemic. HIV-1C is rampaging through Africa and may eventually cause a new epidemic in the United States, where HIV-1B currently causes most infections. An HIV infection has three phases; the last phase is called AIDS. By this time, the immune system is devastated, and the individual dies of an opportunistic disease. Today, anti-retroviral therapy is expanding the lifespan of people infected with HIV.

Studying the Concepts

1. Describe the symptoms and results of a chlamydial infection and gonorrhea in men and in women. What is PID, and how does it affect reproduction? 454–55
2. Describe the three stages of syphilis. 456
3. Give the cause and symptoms of genital herpes, genital warts, and a hepatitis B infection. 457–58
4. How does the newborn acquire an infection of chlamydia, gonorrhea, syphilis, herpes, or genital warts? What effects do these infections have on infants? 454–58
5. Describe the symptoms of three types of pubic lice and of vaginitis. 459
6. How did AIDS arise, and how prevalent is it today? 460–61
7. List and describe the phases of an HIV infection. 462–64
8. Describe the life cycle of HIV, and tell how the life cycle relates to drug therapy for an HIV infection. 465–66
9. What types of vaccines are being prepared to prevent an HIV infection? 466

Thinking Critically About the Concepts

Refer to the opening vignette on page 453, and then answer these questions.

1. Explain why Jennifer will never be free of genital herpes, even if it disappears at times.
2. Explain why an antibiotic will not cure Jennifer of genital herpes.
3. What is the surest way of protecting yourself from any sexually transmitted disease?

Testing Your Knowledge of the Concepts

Choose the best answer for each question.

1. Which of the following may lead to pelvic inflammatory disease if untreated?
   a. chlamydia
   b. gonorrhea
   c. AIDS
   d. Both a and b are correct.

2. Which of the following may cause an eye infection in newborns delivered to infected mothers?
   a. chlamydia
   b. gonorrhea
   c. AIDS
   d. Both a and b are correct.

3. Which of the following infections can result from the transmission of bacteria across the placenta?
   a. chlamydia
   b. gonorrhea
   c. syphilis
   d. herpes

4. For which of the following infections is there, at present, no cure?
   a. chlamydia
   b. gonorrhea
   c. syphilis
   d. herpes

5. Which of the following is indicative of the third stage of a syphilis infection?
   a. chancre
   b. rash
   c. gumma
   d. erythema
   e. generalized edema

6. Which of the following are routinely diagnosed by using a blood test?
   a. chlamydia
   b. gonorrhea
   c. syphilis
   d. HIV infection
   e. Both c and d are correct.

7. Which of the following is associated with cancer of the cervix?
   a. herpes
   b. genital warts
   c. hepatitis
   d. syphilis

For questions 8–11, match the statement with the disease. A question can have more than one answer.

Key:

   a. chlamydia
   b. gonorrhea
   c. syphilis
   d. genital herpes
   e. genital warts
   f. hepatitis B
   g. trichomoniasis

8. Antibiotic therapy is usually effective.

9. Not caused by a bacterium nor a virus.

10. Pelvic inflammatory disease can lead to sterility.

11. Associated with cancer.

12. Which of these infections is transmitted in the same manner as AIDS?
    a. herpes
    b. hepatitis B
    c. syphilis
    d. genital warts

13. Which sexually transmitted disease has the greatest number of new cases each year?
    a. chlamydia
    b. genital warts
    c. genital herpes
    d. gonorrhea

14. Which sexually transmitted disease is not caused by a virus?
    a. genital warts
    b. genital herpes
    c. hepatitis
    d. All of these are caused by a virus.

15. Which of the following does not cause a type of vaginal infection?
    a. bacteria
    b. protozoa
    c. fungi
    d. insects

16. A partner can pass on an infection, even though she/he has no obvious signs of
    a. chlamydia and gonorrhea.
    b. genital herpes and genital warts.
    c. hepatitis B.
    d. All of these are correct.

17. HIV can be passed from mother to child
    a. across the placenta.
    b. during delivery.
    c. in breast milk.
    d. All of these are correct.

18. In which of these groups is the incidence of HIV infection increasing?
    a. heterosexuals
    b. minorities
    c. teenagers and young adults
    d. All of these are correct.

19. The HIV virus primarily infects
    a. B lymphocytes.
    b. helper T lymphocytes.
    c. cytotoxic T lymphocytes.
    d. All of these are correct.

20. The HIV blood test commonly used at clinics test for the presence of
    a. HIV viruses.
    b. helper T cells.
    c. cytotoxic T cells.
    d. antibodies.

21. The HIV provirus is inserted into a host chromosome during which stage of the HIV life cycle?
    a. attachment
    b. fusion
    c. integration
    d. biosynthesis

22. Which of these is true about genital herpes?
    a. undergoes latency
    b. occurs in both males and females
    c. can be passed on by natural childbirth
    d. All of these are true.

23. Which stage of the HIV life cycle is unique to retroviruses?
    a. uncoating
    b. reverse transcription
    c. integration
    d. biosynthesis

24. During which stage of the HIV life cycle is viral RNA and protein produced?
    a. fusion
    b. replication
    c. biosynthesis
    d. maturation

25. During which stage of the HIV life cycle is a DNA copy of the viral genome created?
    a. uncoating
    b. reverse transcription
    c. integration
    d. biosynthesis

26. Which of the following is the least likely route for transmission of HIV?
    a. homosexual contact
    b. heterosexual contact
    c. blood transfusions
    d. breast-feeding
    e. sharing utensils

27. Which continent has the greatest prevalence rate of HIV infection?
    a. Asia
    b. Africa
    c. North America
    d. Europe
    e. South America

28. Which of the following strains of HIV is the most easily transmitted and the fastest growing?
    a. HIV-1A
    b. HIV-1B
    c. HIV-1C
    d. HIV-1D
    e. HIV-1E

For questions 29–32, match the description to the category of an HIV infection.

Key:

    a. Category A
    b. Category B
    c. Category C
    d. All categories
    e. No category

29. The number of CD4 T lymphocytes declines.

30. Nonspecific symptoms occur, such as night sweats, cough, or diarrhea.

31. Person has few, if any, symptoms.

32. Infected person dies from an opportunistic infection.

33. Which of the following is not an opportunistic infection observed in AIDS patients?
    a. pneumocystis pneumonia
    b. tuberculosis
    c. toxoplasmic encephalitis
    d. choriogenic aphasia
    e. All of these are correct.

34. Which of these is true about sexually active individuals?
    a. Young people cannot get an HIV infection.
    b. White people cannot get an HIV infection.
    c. Heterosexuals cannot get an HIV infection.
    d. Women cannot pass on an HIV infection, only men.
    e. All of these are false.

Understanding Key Terms

acquired immunodeficiency syndrome (AIDS) 460
bacterial vaginosis (BV) 459
candidal vaginitis 459
chlamydia 454
genital herpes 457
genital warts 458
gonorrhea 454
hepatitis 458
HIV provirus 465
human immunodeficiency virus (HIV) 460
opportunistic infection 464
pelvic inflammatory disease (PID) 454
retrovirus 465
sexually transmitted disease (STD) 453
syphilis 456
trichomoniasis 459

Match the key terms to these definitions.

    a. _____ Inflammation of the liver.

    b. _____ Disease state of the reproductive organs, usually caused by a chlamydial infection or gonorrhea.

    c. _____ RNA virus containing the enzyme reverse transcriptase that carries out RNA/DNA transcription.

    d. _____ A disease that only occurs in a host with impaired defense mechanisms.

    e. _____ Type of vaginitis caused by a yeast.

Online Learning Center

www.mhhe.com/maderhuman9

The Online Learning Center provides a wealth of information fully organized and integrated by chapter. You will find practice quizzes, interactive activities, labeling exercises, flashcards, and much more that will complement your learning and understanding of human biology.

Looking at Both Sides

Each day, the Internet, media, and other people present you with opposing viewpoints on a wide range of subjects. Your ability to develop an informed opinion on an issue, and talk to others about it, is extremely important.

To expand and enhance your knowledge of a highly relevant bioethical issue, visit the "Student Edition" of the Online Learning Center. Under "Course-Wide Content," select "Looking at Both Sides." Once there, you will be asked to complete activities that will increase your understanding of a current bioethical issue related to this chapter and allow you to defend your opinion.

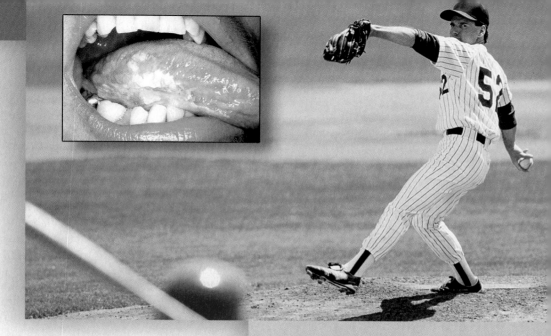

CHAPTER *24*

Cancer

CHAPTER CONCEPTS

24.1 Cancer Cells
- What characteristics of cancer cells allow them to grow uncontrollably?   472–73
- Mutations in what two types of genes lead to uncontrollable growth?   474
- What three types of cancer are responsible for the most cancer deaths?   475

24.2 Causes of Cancer
- What evidence is there that you can inherit genes that lead to cancer?   476
- What environmental carcinogens, in particular, are known to play a role in the development of cancer?   476–77
- What protective steps can you take to reduce your risk of cancer?   478

24.3 Diagnosis and Treatment
- What routine screening tests are available to detect and diagnose cancer?   479–80
- What three types of therapy are presently the standard ways to treat cancer?   481–82
- What is an active form of immunotherapy and a passive form of immunotherapy for cancer?   483
- What type of p53 therapy is available?   483
- What is the rational for antiangiogenesis therapy?   483

If there's one thing Tom loves, it's baseball. He played every afternoon and weekends, while growing up. Now, he is the pitcher on his high school team. One of his teammates was given a free sample of chewing tobacco and Tom tried it. It felt good having that smooth mound in his mouth and it made spitting all the easier.

Tom eventually found that he was using tobacco almost every day, even when it was not his day to pitch. He didn't know it but he had become addicted to nicotine, just as if he smoked tobacco, instead of chewing it. Eventually, he noticed smooth, white patches in his mouth, and the grit and sand in chewing tobacco had eroded the enamel on his teeth. His dentist told him his teeth needed corrective therapy and that the lesions were the first step toward cancer.

Tom decided to read up on what smokeless tobacco contains and found out that it contains over 2,000 chemicals, many of which are known to be carcinogens—cancer-causing chemicals. Smokeless tobacco increases the risk of cancer of the mouth, pharynx, larynx, and esophagus. Pain is rarely an early symptom of oral cancer, and instead the user has white patches in his mouth that won't heal, a prolonged sore throat, difficulty in chewing, and restricted movement of the tongue or jaw.

Tom made the right decision and used a nicotine patch to free himself of his nicotine addiction. He pitches better too—the increased heartbeat he noticed when he chewed tobacco was now gone.

24.1 Cancer Cells

Although **cancer** is actually over a hundred different diseases and each type of cancer can vary from another, these characteristics are common to cancer cells.

Characteristics of Cancer Cells

Cancer cells share characteristics that distinguish them from normal cells (Table 24.1).

Cancer Cells Lack Differentiation

Cancer cells are nonspecialized and do not contribute to the functioning of a body part. A cancer cell does not look like a differentiated epithelial, muscle, nervous, or connective tissue cell; instead, it looks distinctly abnormal.

Cancer Cells Have Abnormal Nuclei

The nuclei of cancer cells are enlarged and may contain an abnormal number of chromosomes. The chromosomes are also abnormal; some parts may be duplicated and some may be deleted. In addition, gene amplification (extra copies of specific genes) is seen much more frequently than in normal cells. Ordinarily, cells with damaged DNA undergo **apoptosis,** or programmed cell death. Cancer cells fail to undergo apoptosis, even though they are abnormal cells.

Cancer cells have also undergone genetic mutations, each one making the cell more abnormal and giving it the ability to produce more of its own kind.

Cancer Cells Have Unlimited Replicative Potential

Ordinarily, cells divide about 60–70 times and then just stop dividing and die. Cancer cells are immortal and keep on dividing for an unlimited number of times.

Just as shoelaces are capped by small pieces of plastic, chromosomes in human cells end with special repetitive DNA sequences called **telomeres.** Specific proteins bind to telomeres and protect the ends of chromosomes from DNA repair enzymes that always tend to bind together naked ends of chromosomes. The telomeres get shorter after each

cell cycle, and eventually the chromosomes do bind together, causing the cell to die. Telomerase is a special enzyme that can rebuild telomere sequences, and in that way prevent these cells from ever losing their potential to divide. The gene that codes for telomerase is turned on in cancer cells. Telomerase continuously rebuilds the telomeres in cancer cells so that the telomeres remain at a constant length and the cell can keep dividing over and over again.

Cancer Cells Form Tumors

Normal cells anchor themselves to a substratum and/or adhere to their neighbors. They exhibit contact inhibition—when they come in contact with a neighbor, they stop dividing. Cancer cells have lost all restraint; they pile on top of one another and grow in multiple layers, forming a **tumor.** As cancer develops, the most aggressive cell becomes the dominant cell of the tumor (Fig. 24.1).

A benign tumor is usually encapsulated and, therefore, will never invade adjacent tissue. Cancer in situ is a tumor of epithelium in its place of origin not always surrounded by a capsule. As yet, the cancer has not penetrated beyond the basement membrane, a layer of nonliving material that anchors epithelial tissue to underlying connective tissue.

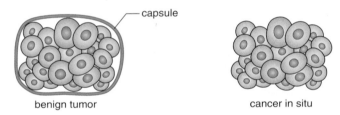

benign tumor   cancer in situ

Cancer Cells Have No Need for Growth Factors

Chemical signals between cells tell them whether they should be dividing or not dividing. These chemical signals, called growth factors, are of two types: stimulatory growth factors and inhibitory growth factors. Cancer cells keep on dividing, even when stimulatory growth factors are absent, and they do not respond to inhibitory growth factors.

Table 24.1	Cancer Cells versus Normal Cells	
Characteristics	**Cancer Cells**	**Normal Cells**
Differentiation	Do not become differentiated	Do become differentiated
Appearance of nucleus	Abnormal nucleus	Normal nucleus
Replicated potential	Unlimited replicated potential	Limited replicated potential
Form tumors	Do form tumors	Do not form tumors
Need for growth factors	Growth factors not needed	Growth factors are needed
Angiogenesis	Induce and sustain angiogenesis	Do not encourage angiogenesis
Metastasis	Metastasize	Do not metastasize

Cancer Cells Gradually Become Abnormal

Figure 24.1 illustrates that **carcinogenesis,** the development of cancer, is a multistage process that can be divided into these three phases:

Initiation: A single cell undergoes a mutation that causes it to begin to divide repeatedly.

Promotion: A tumor develops, and the tumor cells continue to divide. As they divide, they undergo mutations.

Progression: One cell undergoes a mutation that gives it a selective advantage over the other cells. This process is repeated several times, and, eventually, there is a cell that has the ability to invade surrounding tissues.

Cancer Cells Undergo Angiogenesis and Metastasis

To grow larger than about a million cells, about the size of a pea, a tumor must have a well developed capillary network to bring it nutrients and oxygen. **Angiogenesis** is the formation of new blood vessels. The low oxygen content in the middle of a tumor may turn on genes coding for angiogenic growth factors that diffuse into the nearby tissues and cause new vessels to form.

Due to mutations, cancer cells tend to be motile because they have a disorganized internal cytoskeleton and lack intact actin filament bundles. To metastasize, cancer cells must make their way across the basement membrane and into a blood vessel or lymphatic vessel. Cancer cells produce proteinase enzymes that degrade the membrane and allow them to invade underlying tissues. Malignancy is present when cancer cells are found in nearby lymph nodes. When these cells begin new tumors far from the primary tumor, **metastasis** has occurred. Not many cancer cells achieve this feat (maybe 1 in 10,000), but those that successfully metastasize to various parts of the body make the prognosis (the predicted outcome of the disease) for recovery doubtful.

Cancer cells display a number of abnormal characteristics. These characteristics are due to a series of mutations that allow initiation, promotion, and progression to occur, ending with a tumor that can metastasize.

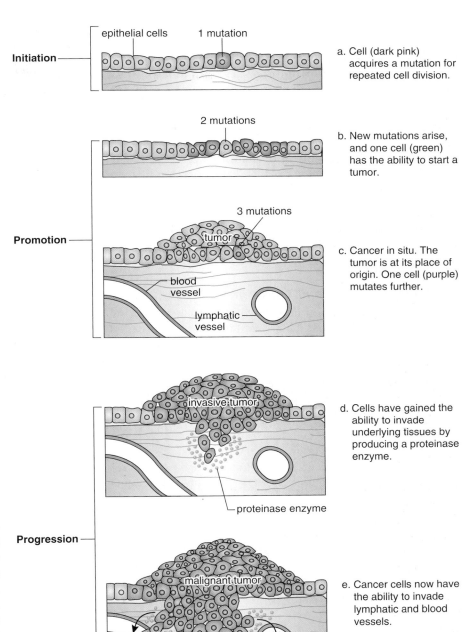

a. Cell (dark pink) acquires a mutation for repeated cell division.

b. New mutations arise, and one cell (green) has the ability to start a tumor.

c. Cancer in situ. The tumor is at its place of origin. One cell (purple) mutates further.

d. Cells have gained the ability to invade underlying tissues by producing a proteinase enzyme.

e. Cancer cells now have the ability to invade lymphatic and blood vessels.

f. New metastatic tumors are found some distance from the tumor.

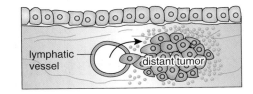

Figure 24.1   Tumor progression.
a. One cell in a tissue mutates. **b.** The mutated cell divides repeatedly (dark pink). **c.** A cell with two mutations (green) forms a tumor. **d.** A cell with three mutations (purple) takes over the tumor, which now can invade underlying tissue. **e.** Tumor cells invade lymphatic and blood vessels. **f.** A new tumor forms at a distant location.

Cancer Is a Genetic Disease

Recall that the cell cycle, as discussed on page 334, consists of interphase, followed by mitosis. *Cyclin* is a molecule that has to be present for a cell to proceed from interphase to mitosis. When cancer develops, the cell cycle occurs repeatedly, in large part, due to mutations in two types of genes. Figure 24.2 shows that:

1. **Proto-oncogenes:** code for proteins that promote the cell cycle and prevent apoptosis. They are often likened to the gas pedal of a car because they cause acceleration of the cell cycle.
2. **Tumor-suppressor genes:** code for proteins that inhibit the cell cycle and promote apoptosis. They are often likened to the brakes of a car because they inhibit acceleration.

Proto-Oncogenes Become Oncogenes

When proto-oncogenes mutate, they become cancer-causing genes called **oncogenes.** These mutations can be called "gain-of-function" mutations because overexpression is the result (Fig. 24.3). Whatever a proto-oncogene does, an oncogene does it better.

A **growth factor** is a signal that activates a cell-signaling pathway, resulting in cell division. Some proto-oncogenes code for a growth factor or for a receptor protein that receives a growth factor. When these proto-oncogenes become oncogenes, receptor proteins are easy to activate and even may be stimulated by a growth factor produced by the receiving cell. Several proto-oncogenes code for Ras proteins that promote mitosis by activating **cyclin.** *Ras* oncogenes are typically found in many different types of cancers. Cyclin D is a proto-oncogene that codes for a cyclin directly. When this gene becomes an oncogene, cyclin is readily available all the time.

p53 is a transcription activator instrumental in stopping the cell cycle and activating repair enzymes. If repair is impossible, the p53 protein promotes *apoptosis*, programmed cell death. Apoptosis is an important way carcinogenesis is prevented. A proto-oncogene codes for a protein that functions to make p53 unavailable. When this proto-oncogene becomes an oncogene, no matter how much p53 is made, none will be available. Many tumors are lacking in p53 activity.

Tumor-Suppressor Genes Become Inactive

When tumor-suppressor genes mutate, their products no longer inhibit the cell cycle nor promote apoptosis. Therefore, these mutations can be called "loss of function" mutations (Fig. 24.3).

The retinoblastoma protein (RB) controls the activity of a transcription activator for cyclin D and other genes whose products promote entry into the S phase of the cell cycle. When the tumor-suppressor gene *p16* mutates, the RB protein is always functional and the result is, again, too much active cyclin D in the cell. The cell experiences repeated rounds of DNA synthesis without the occurrence of mitosis.

The protein Bax promotes apoptosis. When a tumor-suppressor gene *Bax* mutates, the protein Bax is not present, and apoptosis is less likely to occur. The gene contains a run of eight consecutive G bases, making it subject to mutations.

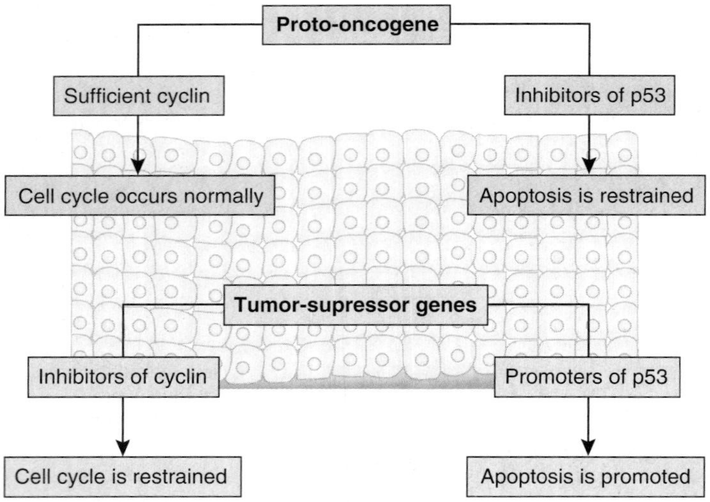

Figure 24.2   Normal cells.
In normal cells, proto-oncogenes code for sufficient cyclin to keep the cell cycle going normally and they code for proteins that inhibit p53 and apoptosis. Tumor-suppressor genes code for proteins that inhibit cyclin, and promote p53 and apoptosis.

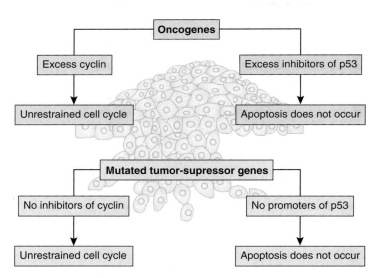

Figure 24.3   Cancer cells.
In cancer cells, oncogenes cause excess cyclin so that the cell cycle is unrestrained, and cause excess inhibitors of p53 so that apoptosis does not occur. Mutated tumor-suppressor genes no longer code for effective inhibitors of cyclin nor for effective promoters of p53 and apoptosis.

Types of Cancer

Statistics indicate that one in three Americans will deal with cancer in their lifetime. Therefore, this is a topic of considerable importance to the health and well being of every individual. **Oncology** is the study of cancer, and a medical specialist in cancer is, therefore, known as an **oncologist.** The patient's prognosis (probable outcome) depends on (1) whether the tumor has invaded surrounding tissues, and (2) whether there are metastatic tumors in distant parts of the body.

Tumors are classified according to their place of origin. **Carcinomas** are cancers of the epithelial tissues and adenocarcinomas are cancers of glandular epithelial cells. Carcinomas include cancer of the skin, breast, liver, pancreas, intestines, lung, prostate, and thyroid. **Sarcomas** are cancers that arise in muscles and connective tissue, such as bone and fibrous connective tissue. **Leukemias** are cancers of the blood, and **lymphomas** are cancers of lymphatic tissue.

Common Cancers

Cancer occurs in all parts of the body, but some organs are more susceptible than others (Fig. 24.4). In the respiratory system, lung cancer is the most common type. Overall, this is one of the most common types of cancer, and smoking is known to increase a person's risk for this disease. In the digestive system, colorectal cancer (colon/rectum) is another common tumor. Other cancers of the digestive system include those of the pancreas, stomach, esophagus, and other organs. In the cardiovascular system, cancers include leukemia and plasma cell tumors. In the lymphatic system, cancers are classified as either Hodgkin's or non-Hodgkin's lymphoma. Thyroid cancer is the most common type of tumor in the endocrine system, whereas brain and spinal tumors are found in the central nervous system.

Breast cancer is one of the most common types of cancer. Although predominantly found in women, occasionally it is also found in men. Cancers of the cervix, ovaries, and other reproductive structures also occur in women. In males, prostate cancer is one of the most common cancers. Other cancers of the male reproductive system include cancer of the testis and the penis. Bladder and kidney cancers are associated with the urinary system. Skin cancers include melanoma and basal cell carcinoma. Oral cavity cancer is more frequent in men than women.

Cancer is a disease in which the cells become increasingly abnormal due to mutations in proto-oncogenes and tumor-suppressor genes. Cancers are classified according to their place of origin and are more common in particular organs of the body.

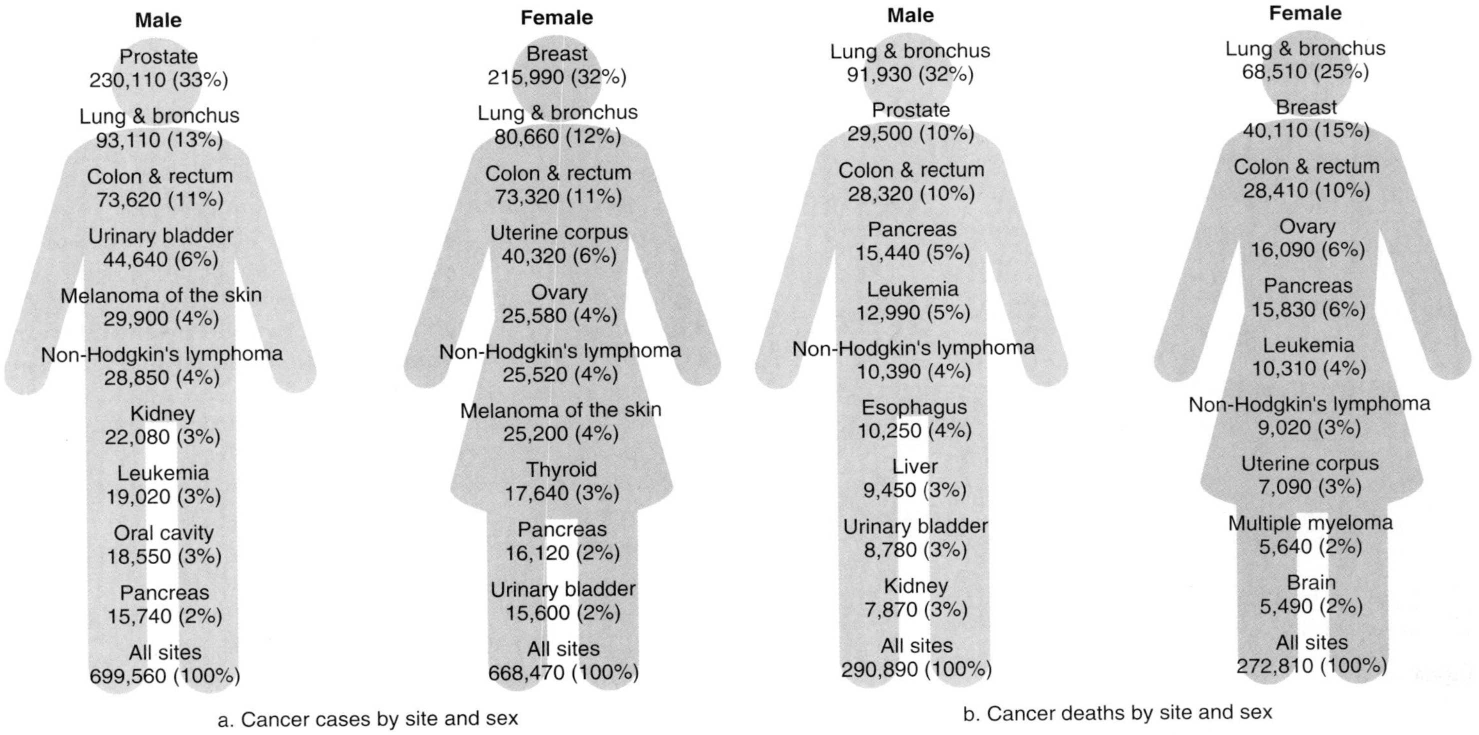

Male
Prostate
230,110 (33%)
Lung & bronchus
93,110 (13%)
Colon & rectum
73,620 (11%)
Urinary bladder
44,640 (6%)
Melanoma of the skin
29,900 (4%)
Non-Hodgkin's lymphoma
28,850 (4%)
Kidney
22,080 (3%)
Leukemia
19,020 (3%)
Oral cavity
18,550 (3%)
Pancreas
15,740 (2%)
All sites
699,560 (100%)

Female
Breast
215,990 (32%)
Lung & bronchus
80,660 (12%)
Colon & rectum
73,320 (11%)
Uterine corpus
40,320 (6%)
Ovary
25,580 (4%)
Non-Hodgkin's lymphoma
25,520 (4%)
Melanoma of the skin
25,200 (4%)
Thyroid
17,640 (3%)
Pancreas
16,120 (2%)
Urinary bladder
15,600 (2%)
All sites
668,470 (100%)

a. Cancer cases by site and sex

Male
Lung & bronchus
91,930 (32%)
Prostate
29,500 (10%)
Colon & rectum
28,320 (10%)
Pancreas
15,440 (5%)
Leukemia
12,990 (5%)
Non-Hodgkin's lymphoma
10,390 (4%)
Esophagus
10,250 (4%)
Liver
9,450 (3%)
Urinary bladder
8,780 (3%)
Kidney
7,870 (3%)
All sites
290,890 (100%)

Female
Lung & bronchus
68,510 (25%)
Breast
40,110 (15%)
Colon & rectum
28,410 (10%)
Ovary
16,090 (6%)
Pancreas
15,830 (6%)
Leukemia
10,310 (4%)
Non-Hodgkin's lymphoma
9,020 (3%)
Uterine corpus
7,090 (3%)
Multiple myeloma
5,640 (2%)
Brain
5,490 (2%)
All sites
272,810 (100%)

b. Cancer deaths by site and sex

Figure 24.4   Types of cancer.
Leading sites of new cancer cases and deaths in the United States, 2004 estimates.

24.2 Causes of Cancer

Our current understanding of the causes of cancer are incomplete; however, by studying patterns of cancer development in populations, scientists have determined that, aside from heredity, there are environmental risk factors for developing cancer. Some people are more sensitive than others to environmental factors that can cause cancer.

Heredity

In 1990, DNA linkage studies on large families identified the first gene associated with breast cancer. Scientists named this gene *breast cancer 1* or *BRCA1* (pronounced brak-uh). Later, they found that breast cancer in other families was due to another breast cancer gene they called *BRCA2*. These genes are tumor-suppressor genes that are known to behave as if they are autosomal recessive alleles. If one mutated allele is inherited from either parent, a mutation in the other allele is required before the predisposition to cancer is increased. Because the first mutated gene is inherited, cancer is more likely wherever the second mutation occurs. If the second mutation occurs in the breast, breast cancer may develop. If the second mutation is in the ovary, ovarian cancer may develop if additional cancer-causing mutations occur.

The *RB* gene is also a tumor-suppressor gene. It takes its name from its association with an eye tumor called a *retino*blastoma tumor, which first appears as a white mass in the retina. When a mutated allele is inherited, it takes another mutated allele to increase the chance of cancer. A tumor in one eye is more usual because it takes mutations in both alleles before cancer can develop (Fig. 24.5).

An abnormal *RET* gene, which predisposes an individual to thyroid cancer, can be passed from parent to child. *RET* is a proto-oncogene known to be inherited in an autosomal dominant manner—only one mutated allele is needed to increase a predisposition to cancer. The remainder of the mutations necessary for a thyroid cancer to develop are acquired (not inherited).

Environmental Carcinogens

A **mutagen** is an agent that causes mutations. A simple laboratory test, called an Ames test, is capable of testing if a substance is mutagenic. A **carcinogen** is a chemical that causes cancer, for example, by being mutagenic. Some carcinogens cause only initiation; others cause initiation and promotion.

Heredity can predispose a person to cancer, but whether it develops or not depends on environmental mutagens, such as the ones we will be discussing.

Radiation

Ionizing radiation, such as in ultraviolet light, radon gas, nuclear fuel, and X-rays, is capable of affecting DNA and causing mutations. Ultraviolet radiation in sunlight and tanning lamps are most likely responsible for the dramatic increases seen in skin cancer in the past several years. Today, at least six cases of skin cancer occur for every one case of lung cancer. Nonmelanoma skin cancers are usually curable through surgery, but melanoma skin cancer tends to metastasize and is responsible for 1–2% of total cancer deaths in the United States.

Another natural source of ionizing radiation is radon gas, which comes from the natural (radioactive) breakdown of uranium in soil, rock, and water. The Environmental Protection Agency recommends that every home be tested for radon because it is the second-leading cause of lung cancer in the United States. The combination of radon gas and smoking cigarettes can be particularly dangerous. A vent pipe system and fan, which pulls radon from beneath the house and vents it to the outside, is the most common way to rid a house of radon after the house is constructed.

Most of us have heard about the damaging effects of the nuclear bomb explosions or accidental emissions from nuclear power plants. For example, more cancer deaths are expected in the vicinity of the Chernobyl Power Station (in Ukraine), which suffered a terrible accident in 1986. Usually, however, diagnostic X-rays account for most of our exposure to artificial sources of radiation. The benefits of these procedures can far outweigh the possible risk, but it is still wise to avoid X-ray procedures that are not medically warranted.

Despite much publicity, scientists have not been able to show a clear relationship between cancer and the nonionizing radiation that comes from electric power lines, household appliances, and cellular telephones.

Organic Chemicals

Certain organic chemicals, particularly synthetic organic chemicals, have been found to be risk factors for cancer. We will take two examples: the organic chemicals that are in tobacco and those that are pollutants in the environment.

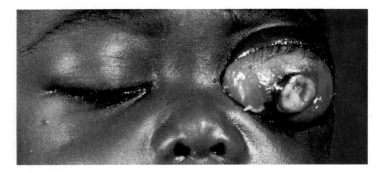

Figure 24.5 Inherited retinoblastoma.
A child is at risk for an eye tumor when a mutated *RB* allele is inherited, even though a second mutation in the normal allele is required before the tumor develops.

Tobacco Smoke Tobacco smoke contains a number of organic chemicals that are known mutagens, including nitroso-nor-nicotine, vinyl chloride, and benzo[a]pyrenes (a known suppressor of p53). Aside from lung cancer, smoking is also implicated in the development of cancers of the mouth, larynx, bladder, kidney, and pancreas. The greater the number of cigarettes smoked per day, the earlier the habit starts, and the higher the tar content, the more likely it is that cancer will develop. On the basis of data, such as shown in Figure 24.6, scientists estimate that about 80% of all cancers, including oral cancer and cancers of the larynx, esophagus, pancreas, bladder, kidney, and cervix, are related to the use of tobacco products. When smoking is combined with drinking alcohol, the risk of these cancers increases even more.

Passive smoking, or inhalation of someone else's tobacco smoke, is also dangerous and probably causes a few thousand deaths each year.

Pollutants Being exposed to substances such as metals, dust, chemicals, or pesticides at work can increase the risk of cancer. Asbestos, nickel, cadmium, uranium, radon, vinyl chloride, benzidine, and benzene are well-known examples of carcinogens in the workplace. For example, inhaling asbestos fibers increases the risk of lung diseases, including cancer, and the cancer risk is especially high for asbestos workers who smoke.

Data show the incidence in soft tissue sarcomas (STS), malignant lymphomas, and non-Hodgkin's lymphomas increases in farmers living in Nebraska and Kansas who used 2,4-D (a commonly used herbicidal agent) on crops and to clear weeds along railroad tracks.

Viruses

Few cancers are caused by viruses. However, at least four types of DNA viruses—hepatitis B and C viruses, Epstein-Barr virus, and human papillomavirus—are directly believed to cause human cancers.

In China, almost all the people have been infected with the hepatitis B virus, and this correlates with the high incidence of liver cancer in that country. For a long time, circumstances suggested that cervical cancer was a sexually transmitted disease, and now human papillomaviruses are routinely isolated from cervical cancers. Burkitt lymphoma occurs frequently in Africa, where virtually all children are infected with the Epstein-Barr virus. In China, the Epstein-Barr virus is isolated in nearly all nasopharyngeal cancer specimens.

RNA-containing retroviruses, in particular, are known to cause cancers in animals. In humans, the retrovirus HTLV-1 (human T-cell lymphotropic virus, type 1) has been shown to cause hairy cell leukemia. This disease occurs frequently in parts of Japan, the Caribbean, and Africa, particularly in regions where people are known to be infected with the virus. HIV, the virus that causes AIDS, and also Kaposi's sarcoma-associated herpesvirus (KSHV) is responsible for the development of Kaposi's sarcoma and certain lymphomas due to the suppression of proper immune system functions.

Dietary Choices

Nutrition is emerging as a way to help prevent cancer. The incidence of breast and prostate cancer parallels a high-fat diet, but so does obesity. The Health Focus on the next page discusses how to protect yourself from cancer. The American Cancer Society recommends consumption of fruits and vegetables, whole grains instead of processed (refined) grains, and limited consumption of red meats (especially high-fat and processed meats). Moderate to vigorous activity for 30–45 minutes a day, five or more days a week, is also recommended.

Development of cancer is determined by a person's genetic profile, plus exposure to environmental carcinogens.

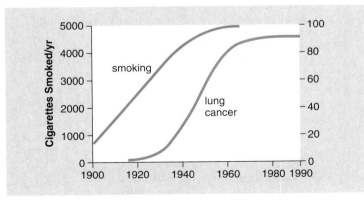
a. Men in the United States

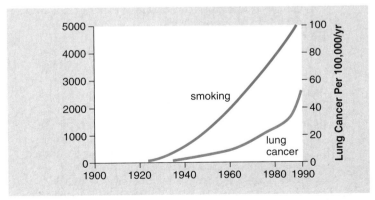
b. Women in the United States

Figure 24.6 **Smoking and cancer.**
a. Note that as the incidence of smoking in men grew, so did the incidence of lung cancer. Lung cancer was rare in 1920, but as more men took up smoking, lung cancer became more common. **b.** As late as 1960, the incidence of lung cancer in women was low and so was the incidence of smoking. As women became smokers, the incidence of lung cancer in women also rose.

Health Focus

Prevention of Cancer

Evidence suggests that the risk of certain types of cancer can be reduced by adopting protective behaviors and the right diet.

Protective Behaviors

These behaviors help prevent cancer:

Don't smoke Cigarette smoking accounts for about 30% of all cancer deaths. Smoking is responsible for 90% of lung cancer cases among men and 79% among women—about 87% altogether. People who smoke two or more packs of cigarettes a day have lung cancer mortality rates 15–25 times greater than those of nonsmokers. Smokeless tobacco (chewing tobacco or snuff) increases the risk of cancers of the mouth, larynx, throat, and esophagus.

Don't sunbathe Almost all cases of basal-cell and squamous-cell skin cancers are considered sun-related. Further, sun exposure is a major factor in the development of melanoma, and the incidence of this cancer increases for people living near the equator.

Avoid alcohol Cancers of the mouth, throat, esophagus, larynx, and liver occur more frequently among heavy drinkers, especially when accompanied by tobacco use (cigarettes or chewing tobacco).

Avoid radiation Excessive exposure to ionizing radiation can increase cancer risk. Even though most medical and dental X-rays are adjusted to deliver the lowest dose possible, unnecessary X-rays should be avoided. Excessive radon exposure in homes increases the risk of lung cancer, especially in cigarette smokers. It is best to test your home and take the proper remedial actions.

Be tested for cancer Do the shower check for breast cancer or testicular cancer. Have other exams done regularly by a physician.

Be aware of occupational hazards Exposure to several different industrial agents (nickel, chromate, asbestos, vinyl chloride, etc.) and/or radiation increases the risk of various cancers. Risk from asbestos is greatly increased when combined with cigarette smoking.

Be aware of postmenopausal hormone therapy A new study conducted by the Women's Health Initiative found that estrogen-progestin combined therapy prescribed to ease the symptoms of menopause increased the incidence of breast cancer. And that the risk outweighed the possible decrease in the number of colorectal cancer cases.

The Right Diet

Statistical studies have suggested that people who follow certain dietary guidelines are less likely to have cancer. The following dietary guidelines greatly reduce your risk of developing cancer:

Avoid obesity The risk of cancer (especially colon, breast, and uterine cancers) is 55% greater among obese women, and the risk of colon cancer is 33% greater among obese men, compared with people of normal weight.

Eat plenty of high-fiber foods Studies have indicated that a high-fiber diet (whole-grain cereals, fruits, and vegetables) protects against colon cancer, a frequent cause of cancer deaths. It is worth noting that foods high in fiber also tend to be low in fat!

Increase consumption of foods that are rich in vitamins A and C Beta-carotene, a precursor of vitamin A, is found in dark green, leafy vegetables; carrots; and various fruits. Vitamin C is present in citrus fruits. These vitamins are called antioxidants because in cells they prevent the formation of free radicals (organic ions having an unpaired electron) that can possibly damage DNA. Vitamin C also prevents the conversion of nitrates and nitrites into carcinogenic nitrosamines in the digestive tract.

Reduce consumption of salt-cured, smoked, or nitrite-cured foods Salt-cured or pickled foods may increase the risk of stomach and esophageal cancers. Smoked foods, such as ham and sausage, contain chemical carcinogens similar to those in tobacco smoke. Nitrites are sometimes added to processed meats (e.g., hot dogs and cold cuts) and other foods to protect them from spoilage; as mentioned previously, nitrites are converted to nitrosamines in the digestive tract.

Include vegetables from the cabbage family in the diet The cabbage family includes cabbage, broccoli, brussels sprouts, kohlrabi, and cauliflower. These vegetables may reduce the risk of gastrointestinal and respiratory tract cancers.

Be moderate in the consumption of alcohol Risks of cancer development rises as the level of alcohol intake increases. The strongest cancer associations are with oral, pharyngeal, esophageal, and laryngeal cancer, but cancer of the breast and liver are also implicated. People who drink and smoke greatly enhance their risk for developing cancer.

24.3 Diagnosis and Treatment

The earlier a cancer is detected, the more likely it can be effectively treated. At present, physicians have ways to detect several types of cancer before they become malignant. But they are always looking for new and better detection methods. A growing number of researchers now believe the future of early detection lies in testing for the molecular fingerprints of a cancer. Several teams of scientists are working on blood, saliva, and urine tests to catch cancerous gene and protein patterns in these bodily fluids before a tumor develops. In the meantime, cancer is usually diagnosed by the methods discussed here.

Diagnosis of Cancer

At present, diagnosis of cancer before metastasis is difficult, although treatment at this stage is usually more successful. The American Cancer Society publicizes seven warning signals, which spell out the word CAUTION and which everyone should be aware of:

C   hange in bowel or bladder habits

A   sore that does not heal

U   nusual bleeding or discharge

T   hickening or lump in breast or elsewhere

I   ndigestion or difficulty in swallowing

O   bvious change in wart or mole

N   agging cough or hoarseness

Keep in mind that these signs do not necessarily mean that you have cancer. However, they are an indication that something is wrong and a medical professional should be consulted. Unfortunately, some of these symptoms are not obvious until cancer has progressed to one of its later stages.

Routine Screening Tests

Self-examination, followed by examination by a physician, can help detect the presence of cancer. For example, the ABCDs of melanoma (The most serious form of skin cancer. Fig. 24.7) is helpful, as is the self-examination for breast and testicular cancer which are discussed in the Health Focus on page 480.

An aim of medicine is to develop tests for cancer that are relatively easy to do, cost little, and are fairly accurate. So far, only the Pap test for cervical cancer fulfills these three requirements. A physician merely takes a sample of cells from the cervix, which are then examined microscopically for signs of abnormality. Regular Pap tests are credited with preventing over 90% of deaths from cervical cancer.

Breast cancer is not as easily detected, but three procedures are recommended. First, every woman should do a monthly breast self-examination. Second, during an annual physical examination, which is recommended especially for women above age 40, a physician does this same procedure. While helpful, this type of examination may not detect lumps before metastasis has already taken place. That is the goal of the third recommended procedure, *mammography,* which is an X-ray study of the breast (Fig. 24.8). However, mammograms do not show all cancers, and new tumors may develop in the interval between mammograms. The objective is that a mammogram will reveal a lump that is too small to be felt and at a time when the cancer is still highly curable.

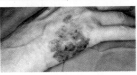
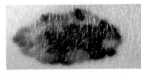

A = Asymmetry, one half the mole does not look like the other half.

B = Border, irregular scalloped or poorly circumscribed border.

C = Color, varied from one area to another; shades of tan, brown, black, or sometimes white, red, or blue.

D = Diameter, larger than 6 mm (the diameter of a pencil eraser).

Figure 24.7   **Detecting melanoma.**
Suspicion of melanoma can begin by discovering a mole that has one or more of these characteristics.

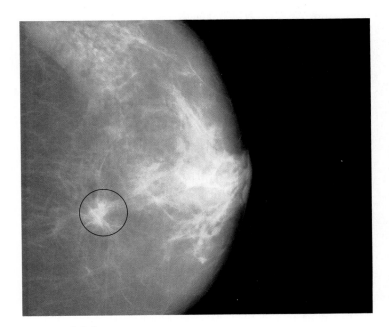

Figure 24.8   **Mammogram.**
An X-ray image of the breast can find tumors too small to be felt.

Health Focus

Shower Check for Cancer

The American Cancer Society urges women to do a breast self-exam and men to do a testicle self-exam every month. Breast cancer and testicular cancer are far more curable if found early, and we must all take on the responsibility of checking for one or the other.

Breast Self-Exam for Women

1. Check your breasts for any lumps, knots, or changes about one week after your period.
2. Place your right hand behind your head. Move your *left* hand over your *right* breast in a circle. Press firmly with the pads of your fingers (Fig. 24A). Also check the armpit.
3. Now place your left hand behind your head and check your *left* breast with your *right* hand in the same manner as before. Also check the armpit.
4. Check your breasts while standing in front of a mirror right after you do your shower check. First, put your hands on your hips and then raise your arms above your head (Fig. 24B). Look for any changes in the way your breasts look: dimpling of the skin, changes in the nipple, or redness or swelling.

5. If you find any changes during your shower or mirror check, see your doctor right away.

You should know that the best check for breast cancer is a mammogram. When your doctor checks your breasts, ask about getting a mammogram.

Testicle Self-Exam for Men

1. Check your testicles once a month.
2. Roll each testicle between your thumb and finger as shown in Figure 24C. Feel for hard lumps or bumps.
3. If you notice a change or have aches or lumps, tell your doctor right away so he or she can recommend proper treatment.

Cancer of the testicles can be cured if you find it early. You should also know that prostate cancer is the most common cancer in men. Men over age 50 should have an annual health checkup that includes a prostate examination.

Information provided by the American Cancer Society. Used by permission.

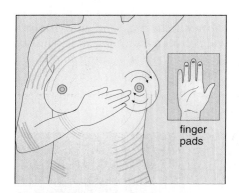

Figure 24A Shower check for breast cancer.

finger pads

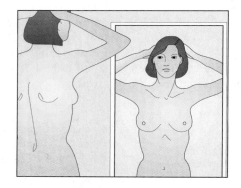

Figure 24B Mirror check for breast cancer.

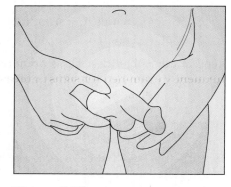

Figure 24C Shower check for testicular cancer.

Screening for colon cancer also depends upon three types of testing. A digital rectal examination performed by a physician is actually of limited value because only a portion of the rectum can be reached by finger. With flexible sigmoidoscopy, the second procedure, a much larger portion of the colon can be examined by using a thin, pliable, lighted tube. Finally, a stool blood test (fecal occult blood test) consists of examining a stool sample to detect any hidden blood. The sample is smeared on a slide, and a chemical is added that changes color in the presence of hemoglobin. This procedure is based on the supposition

that a cancerous polyp bleeds, although some polyps do not bleed, and bleeding is not always due to a polyp. Therefore, the percentage of false negatives and false positives is high. All positive tests are followed up by a colonoscopy, an examination of the entire colon, or by X-ray after a barium enema. If the colonoscope detects polyps, they can be destroyed by laser therapy.

Other tests routinely used are blood tests to detect leukemia and urinalysis for the diagnosis of bladder cancer. Newer tests under consideration are tumor marker tests and tests for oncogenes.

Tumor Marker Tests

Tumor marker tests are blood tests for tumor antigens/antibodies. They are possible because tumors release substances that provoke an antibody response in the body. For example, if an individual has already had colon cancer, it is possible to use the presence of an antigen called *CEA* (for *carcinoembryonic antigen*) to detect any relapses. When the CEA level rises, additional tumor growth has occurred.

There are also tumor marker tests that can be used as an adjunct procedure to detect cancer in the first place. They are not reliable enough to count on solely, but in conjunction with physical examination and ultrasound (see page 479), they are considered useful. For example, there is a *prostate-specific antigen (PSA) test* for prostate cancer, a *CA-125* test for ovarian cancer, and an *alpha-fetoprotein (AFP) test* for liver tumors.

Genetic Tests

Tests for genetic mutations in proto-oncogenes and tumor-suppressor genes are making it possible to detect the likelihood of cancer before the development of a tumor. Tests are available that signal the possibility of colon, bladder, breast, and thyroid cancers, as well as melanoma.

A *ras* oncogene can be detected in stool and urine samples. If the test for *ras* oncogene in the stool is positive, the physician suspects colon cancer, and if the test for *ras* oncogene in urine is positive, the physician suspects bladder cancer.

A genetic test is also available for the presence of *BRCA1* (breast cancer gene 1). A woman who has inherited this gene can choose to either have prophylactic surgery or to be frequently examined for signs of breast cancer.

Physicians now believe that a mutated *RET* gene means that thyroid cancer is present or may occur in the future, and a mutated *p16* gene appears to be associated with melanoma. Genetic testing can also be used to determine if cancer cells still remain after a tumor has been removed. In one study, 50% of the patients still had tumor cells in apparently "clean" margins or in lymph nodes believed to be free of them.

Microsatellites are small regions of DNA that always have di-, tri-, or tetranucleotide repeats. Physicians can use microsatellites to detect chromosomal deletions that accompany bladder cancer. They compare the number of nucleotide DNA repeats in a lymphocyte microsatellite with the number in a microsatellite of a cell found in urine. When the number of repeats is less in the cell from urine, a bladder tumor is suspected. Clinical trials involving this procedure have been so successful that a larger trial involving many institutions is now under way.

Telomerase, you will recall, is the enzyme that keeps telomeres a constant length in cells. The gene that codes for telomerase is turned off in normal cells but is active in cancer cells. Therefore, if the test for the presence of telomerase is positive, the cell is cancerous.

Confirming the Diagnosis

A diagnosis of cancer can be confirmed without major surgery by performing a *biopsy* or using various *imaging procedures*. Needle biopsies allow removal of a few cells for examination, and sophisticated techniques, such as laparoscopy, permit viewing of body parts.

Computerized axial tomography (or CAT scan) uses computer analysis of scanning X-ray images to create cross-sectional pictures that portray a tumor's size and location. Magnetic resonance imaging (MRI) is another type of imaging technique that depends on computer analysis. MRI is particularly useful for analyzing tumors in tissues surrounded by bone, such as tumors of the brain or spinal cord. A radioactive scan obtained after a radioactive isotope is administered can reveal any abnormal isotope accumulation due to a tumor. During ultrasound, echoes of high-frequency sound waves directed at a part of the body are used to reveal the size, shape, and location of tissue masses. Ultrasound can confirm tumors of the stomach, prostate, pancreas, kidney, uterus, and ovary.

Treatment of Cancer

Surgery, radiation, and chemotherapy are the standard methods of cancer therapy. Other methods of therapy are in clinical trials, and if they prove successful, will become more generally available in the future.

Standard Therapies

Surgery Surgery alone is sufficient for cancer in situ. But because there is always the danger that some cancer cells were left behind, surgery is often preceded by and/or followed by radiation therapy.

Radiation Ionizing radiation causes chromosomal breakage and cell cycle disruption. Therefore, dividing cells, such as cancer cells, are more susceptible to its effects than other cells. Powerful X-rays or gamma rays can be administered through an externally applied beam or, in some instances, by implanting tiny radioactive sources into the patient's body. Cancer of the cervix and larynx, early stages of prostate cancer, and Hodgkin disease are often treated with radiation therapy alone.

Although X-rays and gamma rays are the mainstays of radiation therapy, protons and neutrons also work well. Proton beams can be aimed at the tumor like a rifle bullet hitting the bull's-eye of a target.

Side effects of radiation therapy greatly depend upon which part of the body is being irradiated and how much radiation is used. Examples of short-term side effects, which in most cases are temporary, include diarrhea; dry, red or irritated skin, including blistering burns, at the treatment site; dry mouth; fatigue or weakness; hair loss at the treatment site, which in some situations can be permanent; and nausea.

Chemotherapy Radiation is localized therapy, while chemotherapy is a way to catch cancer cells that have spread throughout the body (Fig. 24.9 and Fig. 24.10). One of chemotherapy's main advantages is that—unlike radiation, which treats only the part of the body exposed to the radiation—chemotherapy treats the entire body. As a result, any cells that may have escaped from where the cancer originated are treated. Most chemotherapeutic drugs kill cells by damaging their DNA or interfering with DNA synthesis. The hope is that all cancer cells will be killed, while leaving untouched enough normal cells to allow the body to keep functioning. Combining drugs that have different actions at the cellular level may help destroy a greater number of cancer cells and might reduce the risk of the cancer developing resistance to one particular drug. What chemicals are used is generally based on the type of cancer and the patient's age, general health, and perceived ability to tolerate potential side effects. Some of the types of chemotherapy medications commonly used to treat cancer include:

Alkylating agents. These medications interfere with the growth of cancer cells by blocking the replication of DNA.

Antimetabolites. These drugs block the enzymes needed by cancer cells to live and grow.

Antitumor antibiotics. These antibiotics—different from those used to treat bacterial infections—interfere with DNA, blocking certain enzymes and cell division and changing cell membranes.

Mitotic inhibitors. These drugs inhibit cell division or hinder certain enzymes necessary in the cell reproduction process.

Nitrosoureas. These medications impede the enzymes that help repair DNA.

Whenever possible, chemotherapy is specifically designed for the particular cancer. In Allen's lymphoma/leukemia, for example, it is known that a small portion of chromosome 9 is missing, and therefore DNA metabolism differs in the cancerous cells compared with normal cells. Specific chemotherapy for this cancer is designed to exploit this metabolic difference and destroy the cancerous cells.

One drug, *taxol*, extracted from the bark of the Pacific yew tree, was found to be particularly effective against advanced ovarian cancers, as well as breast, head, and neck tumors. Taxol interferes with microtubules needed for cell division. Now, chemists have synthesized a family of related drugs, called taxoids, which may be more powerful and have fewer side effects than taxol itself.

Certain types of cancer, such as leukemias, lymphomas, and testicular cancer, are now successfully treated by combination chemotherapy alone. The survival rate for children with childhood leukemia is 80%. Hodgkin disease, a lymphoma, once killed two out of three patients. Now, combination therapy, using four different drugs, can wipe out the disease in a matter of months in three out of four patients, even when the cancer is not diagnosed immediately. In other cancers—most notably, breast and colon cancer—chemotherapy can reduce the chance of recurrence after surgery has removed all detectable traces of the disease.

Chemotherapy sometimes fails because cancer cells become resistant to one or several chemotherapeutic drugs, a phenomenon called multidrug resistance. This occurs because all the drugs are capable of interacting with a plasma membrane carrier that pumps them out of the cell. Researchers are testing drugs known to poison the pump in an effort to restore the efficacy of the drugs. Another possibility is to use combinations of drugs with nonoverlapping patterns of toxicity, because cancer cells can't become resistant to many different types at once.

Bone marrow transplants are sometimes done in conjunction with chemotherapy. The red bone marrow contains large populations of dividing cells; therefore, red bone marrow is particularly prone to destruction by chemotherapeutic drugs. In bone marrow autotransplantation, a patient's stem cells are harvested and stored before chemotherapy begins. Quite high doses of radiation or chemotherapeutic drugs are then given within a relatively short time. This prevents multidrug resistance from occurring, and the treatment is more likely to catch each and every cancer cell. Then, the stored stem cells, which are needed to produce blood cells, are returned to the patient by injection. They automatically make their way to bony cavities, where they initiate blood cell formation.

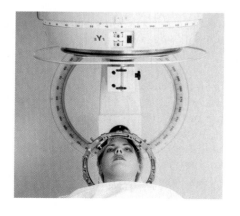

Figure 24.9 X-ray therapy for cancer.
Most people who receive radiation therapy for cancer have external radiation on an outpatient basis. This type of therapy is delivered by a machine to a specific part of the body.

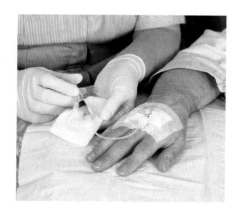

Figure 24.10 Chemotherapy.
The intravenous route is the most common, allowing chemotherapy drugs to spread quickly throughout the entire body by way of the bloodstream.

Newer Therapies

Several therapies are now in clinical trials and are expected to be increasingly used to treat cancer.

Immunotherapy   When cancer develops, the immune system has failed to dispose of cancer cells, even though they bear antigens that make them different from the body's normal cells. The first generation of immunotherapy simply used treated tumor cells mixed with cytokines in an attempt to awaken the body's immune system. A vaccine, called Melacine, which contains broken melanoma cells from two different sources, mobilizes the immune system against melanoma. This vaccine is heading toward possible FDA approval because it has fewer serious side effects than chemotherapy. Another idea is to use immune cells, genetically engineered to bear the tumor's antigens (Fig. 24.11). When these cells are returned to the body, they produce cytokines and present the antigen to cytotoxic T cells, which then go forth and destroy tumor cells in the body.

Passive immunotherapy is also possible. Monoclonal antibodies are antibodies of the same type because they are produced by the same plasma cell (see Fig. 21.11). Some monoclonal antibodies are designed to zero in on the receptor proteins of cancer cells. To increase the killing power of monoclonal antibodies, they are linked to radioactive isotopes or chemotherapeutic drugs. Trastuzumab (Herceptin) is a monoclonal antibody that binds to a growth factor receptor found on the surface of about 30% of breast cancer cells. Because this monoclonal antibody can be combined with a chemotherapy agent, it delivers a double punch. Monoclonal antibodies can help cancer patients after standard treatments have stopped working. It is expected that soon they will be used as initial therapies, in addition to chemotherapy.

***p53* Gene Therapy**   With greater understanding of genes and carcinogenesis, it is not unreasonable to think that gene therapy can help cure human cancers.

Recently, a retrovirus carrying a normal *p53* gene was injected directly into tumor cells of patients with lung cancer. The tumors shrank in three patients and stopped growing in the other three. Researchers believe that *p53* expression is only needed for 24 hours to trigger apoptosis, programmed cell death. And the *p53* gene seems to trigger cell death only in cancer cells—that is, elevating the *p53* level in a normal cell doesn't do any harm, possibly because apoptosis requires extensive DNA damage.

Some investigators prefer working with adenoviruses rather than retroviruses. Ordinarily, when adenoviruses infect a cell, they first produce a protein that inactivates *p53*. In a cleverly designed procedure, investigators genetically engineered an adenovirus that lacks the gene for this protein. Now, the adenovirus can infect and kill only cells that lack a *p53* gene. Which cells are those? Tumor cells, of course. Another plus to this procedure is that the injected adenovirus spreads through the cancer, killing tumor cells as it goes. This genetically engineered virus is now in clinical trials.

Other Therapies   Many other therapies are now being investigated. Among them, drugs that inhibit angiogenesis are a proposed therapy under investigation. Antiangiogenic drugs confine and reduce tumors by breaking up the network of new capillaries in the vicinity of a tumor. A number of antiangiogenic compounds are currently being tested in clinical trials. Two highly effective drugs, called angiostatin and endostatin, have been shown to inhibit angiogenesis in laboratory animals and are expected to do the same in humans.

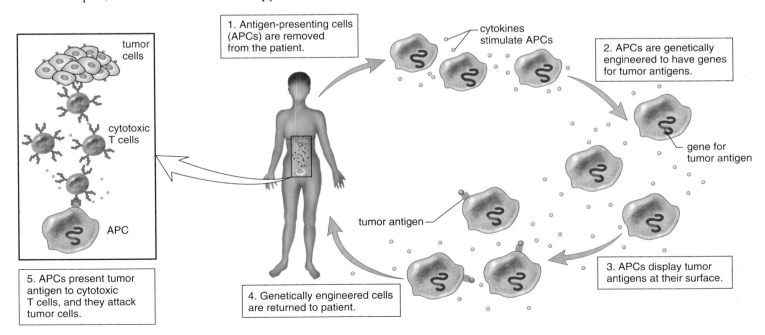

Figure 24.11   Immunotherapy.
Immune system cells are removed and genetically engineered to display tumor antigens. After these cells are returned to the patient, they present the antigen to cytotoxic T cells, which then kill tumor cells.

Bioethical Focus

Tobacco and Alcohol Use

The Health Focus on page 478 promotes a healthy lifestyle as a way to prevent the occurrence of cancer. Tobacco and alcohol use, in particular, increase our chances of developing cancer. Smoking one to two packs of cigarettes a day increases the chances of lung cancer some 20 times, cancer of the larynx 8 times, cancer of the mouth and pharynx 4 times, cancer of the esophagus 3 times, and cancer of the bladder 2 times. Users of smokeless tobacco (chewing tobacco or snuff) are at greater risk for oral cancer. A nonsmoker married to a smoker still has a 25% greater risk of developing lung cancer because of passive smoking. Alcohol plays a role in the development of cancers of the mouth, pharynx, esophagus, larynx, liver, and possibly the breast. The combination of alcohol and tobacco is particularly dangerous (Fig. 24D). Together, they account for 75–85% of all cancers of the mouth, pharynx, and esophagus in the United States.

Do you think society has an obligation to educate young people about the detrimental health effects of using tobacco and alcohol? If yes, do you think public schools should assume this responsibility? Why or why not? What else could be done to educate the public? Should young people be punished if they are caught using tobacco and alcohol? By whom? Or should they be allowed to choose their own lifestyle despite the possibility of future illness?

When people are incapacitated and no longer able to work, they often become a burden on society. The government pays their medical bills and may even be called upon to provide their daily needs. Should the taxes of those of us who have protected our health go to pay these expenses?

Figure 24D   Tobacco smoke and alcohol.
Smoking cigarettes, especially when combined with drinking alcohol, is associated with cancer of the lungs, larynx, mouth, pharynx, bladder, and many other organs.

Decide Your Opinion

1. Should society require that all people be educated about the detrimental effects of tobacco and alcohol use?
2. Even so, should people be allowed to smoke and drink alcohol if it is their choice? Why or why not?
3. Should advertising and/or sales of tobacco and alcohol be restricted? Should society be required to pay the medical bills of those who are ill due to tobacco and alcohol use? Explain your answers.

Summarizing the Concepts

24.1 Cancer Cells

Certain characteristics are common to cancer cells. Cancer cells are not differentiated and do not look like the normal specialized cells. Even though they have abnormal nuclei, cancer cells do not undergo apoptosis, and instead they enter the cell cycle for an unlimited number of times. In normal cells, telomeres get shortened with each cell division, but in cancer cells, the enzyme telomerase rebuilds the telomeres. Cancer cells form tumors and have no need of outside stimulation by growth factors in order to keep dividing. Cancer develops gradually and passes through the phases of initiation, promotion, and progression. Cancer cells are supported by the growth of blood vessels (angiogenesis) and can spread throughout the body (metastasis).

24.2 Causes of Cancer

Cancers that run in families are most likely due to the inheritance of mutated genes that predispose one to carcinogenesis under adverse environmental circumstances. Certain environmental factors are carcinogens. They bring about mutations that lead to cancer. Ultraviolet radiation is a well-known carcinogen for melanoma. Carcinogenic organic chemicals include those in tobacco smoke and pollutants. Tobacco smoke is believed to be involved in the majority of cancer deaths. Industrial chemicals, including pesticides and herbicides, are carcinogenic. Certain viruses, including hepatitis B and C, human papillomavirus, and Epstein-Barr virus, cause specific cancers.

24.3 Diagnosis and Treatment

Procedures to detect specific cancers include the Pap test for cervical cancer and the mammogram for breast cancer. But new techniques, such as tumor marker tests and tests for oncogenes and mutated tumor-suppressor genes, are being developed. Biopsy and imaging are used to confirm the diagnosis of cancer.

Surgery, followed by radiation and/or chemotherapy, is the traditional method of treating cancer. Chemotherapy involving bone marrow transplants has now become fairly routine. Immunotherapy, *p53* gene therapy, and inhibitory drugs for angiogenesis and metastasis are being investigated. One type of *p53* gene therapy ensures that cancer cells undergo apoptosis.

Studying the Concepts

1. List and discuss seven characteristics of cancer cells that cause them to be abnormal. 472–73
2. Why is cancer called a genetic disease? 474
3. What are the three most common types of cancer? 475
4. What role does heredity play in the development of cancer? 476
5. Name three types of carcinogens, and give examples of each type. 476–77
6. What is the standard way to detect cervical cancer, breast cancer, and colon cancer? 479–80
7. Describe and give examples of tumor marker tests and genetic tests for oncogenes and mutated tumor-suppressor genes. 481
8. What are the traditional therapies for cancer? Explain why a bone marrow transplant is sometimes used in conjunction with chemotherapy. 481–82
9. What types of immunotherapy are presently being used in cancer patients? 483
10. Explain the manner in which monoclonal antibodies are used to fight cancer. 483
11. Describe two investigative therapies utilizing the *p53* gene. Why would you expect them to be successful? 483
12. Explain the rationale for drugs that inhibit angiogenesis. 483

Thinking Critically About the Concepts

Refer to the opening vignette on page 471, and then answer these questions.

1. How is it possible that smoking cigarettes and using chewing tobacco can increase the risk of, say, pancreatic cancer?
2. What data would you use to prove to a friend that tobacco use does cause cancer?
3. Would you expect the chemicals in chewing tobacco and cigarette smoke to be mutagenic? Why?
4. What two types of genes would you expect to undergo mutations due to the chemicals in tobacco?

Testing Your Knowledge of the Concepts

Choose the best answer for each question.

1. Whereas, _____ stimulate the cell cycle, _____ inhibit the cell cycle.
   a. tumor-suppressor genes, oncogenes
   b. oncogenes, tumor-suppressor genes
   c. proto-oncogenes, oncogenes
   d. proto-oncogenes, tumor-suppressor genes
2. Growth factors lead to
   a. increased cell division.
   b. the functioning of cyclin proteins.
   c. progression through the cell cycle
   d. All of these are correct.
3. During which stage of the cell cycle does the cell replicate its DNA?
   a. G$_1$ c. M
   b. G$_2$ d. S
4. Which of these is not true of p53?
   a. Mutations of both proto-oncogenes and tumor-suppressor genes lead to inactivity of p53.
   b. Normally, p53 functions to stop the cell cycle and initiate repair enzymes, when necessary.
   c. Normally, p53 restores the length of telomeres.
   d. Cancer cells shut down the activity of p53, even though it may be present.
5. Which association is incorrect?
   a. proto-oncogenes—code for cyclin and proteins that inhibit the activity of p53
   b. oncogenes—"grain of function" genes
   c. mutated tumor-suppressor genes—code for cyclin and proteins that inhibit the activity of p53
   d. mutated tumor-suppressor genes—"loss of function" mutations
   e. Both a and c are incorrect.
6. During which stage of the cell cycle does cell division occur?
   a. G$_1$ d. S
   b. G$_2$ e. All of the above are correct.
   c. M
7. Following each cell cycle, telomeres
   a. get longer.
   b. get shorter.
   c. return to the same length.
   d. bind to cyclin proteins.
8. Concerning the causes of cancer, which one is incorrect?
   a. Genetic mutations cause cancer.
   b. Genetic mutations can be caused by environmental influences, such as radiation, organic chemicals, and viruses.
   c. An active immune system, diet, and exercise can help prevent cancer.
   d. Heredity cannot be a cause of cancer.
9. Why is cancer called a genetic disease?
   a. Cancer is always inherited.
   b. Carcinogenesis is accompanied by mutations.
   c. Cancer causes mutations that are passed on to offspring.
   d. All of these are correct.
10. Leukemia is a form of cancer that affects
   a. lymphatic tissue.
   b. bone tissue.
   c. blood-forming cells.
   d. nervous system structures.
11. Which is the name of the tumor-suppressor gene that causes retinoblastoma?
   a. *p21*   c. *ras*
   b. *RB*   d. *TGF-b*
12. Angiogenic growth factors function to
   a. stimulate the development of new blood vessels.
   b. activate tumor-suppressor genes.
   c. change proto-oncogenes into oncogenes.
   d. promote metastasis.

13. A tumor with cells that spread to secondary locations is referred to as
    a. benign.
    b. cancer in situ.
    c. malignant.
    d. encapsulate.

14. Which of the following is not a type of carcinogen?
    a. tobacco smoke
    b. radiation
    c. pollutants
    d. viruses
    e. All of the above are carcinogens.

15. Human papillomaviruses have been shown to be involved in the formation of _____ cancer.
    a. breast
    b. cervical
    c. kidney
    d. lymphatic

16. Which of the following is not a warning signal for cancer?
    a. sore that does not heal
    b. change in bowel or bladder habits
    c. nagging cough or hoarseness
    d. shortness of breath or fatigue

17. Which of these is mismatched?
    a. breast cancer—mammogram
    b. lung cancer—X-ray
    c. cervical cancer—Pap test
    d. prostate cancer—CA-125 test

18. The most common form of cancer in men is _____ cancer.
    a. colon
    b. lung
    c. prostate
    d. testicular

19. Following a biopsy, what does a doctor look for to diagnose cancer?
    a. He looks for abnormal-appearing cells.
    b. He sees if the cells can divide.
    c. He sees if the cells will respond to growth factors.
    d. He sees if the chromosomes have telomeres.

20. Most chemotherapeutic drugs kill cells by
    a. producing pores in plasma membranes.
    b. interfering with protein synthesis.
    c. interfering with cellular respiration.
    d. interfering with DNA and/or enzymes.

21. Multidrug resistance to chemotherapeutic drugs occurs because
    a. cancer cells can use plasma membrane carriers to pump drugs out of the cell.
    b. one drug may interfere with the activity of another drug.
    c. using several drugs at once will overtax the patient's immune system.
    d. using several drugs at once decreases the effectiveness of radiation therapy.

Understanding Key Terms

angiogenesis 473	metastasis 473
apoptosis 472	mutagen 476
bone marrow transplant 482	oncogene 474
cancer 472	oncologist 475
carcinogen 476	oncology 475
carcinogenesis 473	proto-oncogene 474
carcinoma 475	sarcoma 475
cyclin 474	telomere 472
growth factor 474	tumor 472
leukemia 475	tumor marker test 481
lymphoma 475	tumor-suppressor gene 474

Match the key terms to these definitions.

a. _____ End of chromosome that prevents it from binding to another chromosome; normally get shorter with each cell division.

b. _____ Environmental agent that contributes to the development of cancer.

c. _____ Normal gene involved in cell growth and differentiation that becomes an oncogene through mutation.

d. _____ Formation of new blood vessels, such as a capillary network.

e. _____ Spread of cancer from the place of origin throughout the body; caused by the ability of cancer cells to migrate and invade tissues.

Online Learning Center

www.mhhe.com/maderhuman9

The Online Learning Center provides a wealth of information fully organized and integrated by chapter. You will find practice quizzes, interactive activities, labeling exercises, flashcards, and much more that will complement your learning and understanding of human biology.

Looking at Both Sides

Each day, the Internet, media, and other people present you with opposing viewpoints on a wide range of subjects. Your ability to develop an informed opinion on an issue, and talk to others about it, is extremely important.

To expand and enhance your knowledge of a highly relevant bioethical issue, visit the "Student Edition" of the Online Learning Center. Under "Course-Wide Content," select "Looking at Both Sides." Once there, you will be asked to complete activities that will increase your understanding of a current bioethical issue related to this chapter and allow you to defend your opinion.

25 Human Evolution 487

26 Global Ecology 505

27 Human Population,
Planetary Resources,
and Conservation 521

Like all living things, human beings can trace their ancestry to the first cell(s) to have evolved about 3.5 billion years ago. A chemical evolution produced the first cell(s), and then biological evolution began. The evidence for biological evolution is strong. Living things share biochemical and anatomical characteristics, and the fossil record tells the history of life. Researchers have found that human evolution is complex but still follows the same patterns of evolution as other groups do.

Living things inhabit ecosystems, such as a forest or a pond, where they interact with one another and with the physical environment. Almost all ecosystems today have been affected by human activities. A large city contains little, if any, of the original ecosystem. The use of resources and the resulting pollution is proportionate to the size of the human population. The goal of conservation is to protect biodiversity by preserving ecosystems for the benefit of all living things, including human beings.

CHAPTER **25**

Human Evolution

C H A P T E R   C O N C E P T S

25.1 Origin of Life
- What type of evolution produced the first cells?   488

25.2 Biological Evolution
- What is biological evolution, and what are its two most important aspects?   489
- What type of evidence convinced Charles Darwin that biological evolution does occur?   490
- What process accounts for the great diversity of living things?   492

25.3 Humans Are Primates
- How are humans classified—from domain to species?   493
- What are the characteristics of all primates, and how are primates related to one another?   493–95
- What features are used to distinguish hominid fossils from ape fossils?   494–95

25.4 Evolution of Australopithecines
- Why are australopithecines, living about 4–3 MYA[1], thought to be hominids?   496

25.5 Evolution of Humans
- How might *Homo habilis*, living about 2 MYA, have differed from the australopithecines?   497
- How might *Homo erectus*, living about 1.9–1.6 MYA, have differed from *Homo habilis*?   498
- What is the out-of-Africa hypothesis, and what bearing does it have on the evolution of humans?   499
- How does Cro-Magnon, the first of the modern humans, differ from the other species in the genus *Homo?*   500

[1]MYA = millions of years ago

Marykay sighed as she stared at her dinner plate. This diet was the pits. She was practically living on celery and nonfat cottage cheese, with a handful of lentils, and still was barely losing any weight. The doctor was adamant; she needed to shed some of the excess poundage she was carrying around. Marykay agreed, but it was so incredibly hard.

The 1,600-calorie-a-day diet hadn't produced any change in her weight at all during the three months she tried it. The 1,200-calorie diet had no effect either, except to make her cranky, according to her family. People who knew she was on a serious weight-loss regimen had begun making subtle and not-so-subtle remarks about whether she was "cheating" on her diet. Despite the temptations, she hadn't given in to chocolates and chips, but she hadn't lost any weight, either. She was now down to 800 calories a day and was losing weight, slowly. Maybe the only way to lose weight would be to work out constantly. Her sister, Margaret, managed to stay within a normal weight range, but she went to the gym every day for at least an hour.

Marykay blamed it all on her Irish genes. After all, her ancestors had survived the potato famine in Ireland, while many others had wasted away. Maybe her ancestors were adapted to getting the most out of every mouthful. Now that she thought about it, this might make a good term paper for her evolution course. Metabolic adaptations are just as likely to occur as anatomical adaptations, she thought.

25.1 Origin of Life

Our study of evolution begins with the origin of life. A fundamental principle of biology states that all living things are made of cells and that every cell comes from a preexisting cell (see page 36). But if this is so, how did the first cell come about? Since it was the very first living thing, it had to come from nonliving chemicals. Could there have been a slow increase in the complexity of chemicals—could a **chemical evolution** have produced the first cell(s) on the primitive Earth?

The Primitive Earth

We know that the solar system was in place about 4.6 billion years ago (BYA) and that the gravitational field of the Earth allowed it to have an atmosphere. The Earth's primitive atmosphere was not the same as today's atmosphere. Most likely, the primitive atmosphere was formed by gases escaping from volcanoes. If so, the primitive atmosphere would have consisted mostly of water vapor (H_2O), nitrogen (N_2), and carbon dioxide (CO_2), with only small amounts of hydrogen (H_2) and carbon monoxide (CO). The primitive atmosphere had little, if any, free oxygen.

At first, the Earth and its atmosphere were extremely hot, and water, existing only as a gas, formed dense, thick clouds. Then, as the Earth cooled, water vapor condensed to liquid water, and rain began to fall. It rained in such enormous quantities over hundreds of millions of years that the oceans of the world were produced.

Small Organic Molecules

The rain washed the other gases, such as N_2 and CO_2, into the oceans (Fig. 25.1a). The primitive Earth had many sources of energy, including volcanoes, meteorites, radioactive isotopes, lightning, and ultraviolet radiation. In the presence of so much available energy, the primitive gases may have reacted with one another and produced small organic compounds, such as nucleotides and amino acids (Fig. 25.1b). In 1953, Stanley Miller performed an experiment. He placed a mixture of primitive gases in a closed system, heated the mixture, and circulated it past an electric spark. After cooling, Miller discovered a variety of small organic molecules in the resulting liquid. Other investigators have achieved the same results using various mixtures of gases.

Macromolecules

The newly formed small organic molecules likely joined to produce organic macromolecules (Fig. 25.1c). There are two hypotheses of special interest concerning this stage in the origin of life. One is the **RNA-first hypothesis,** which suggests that only the macromolecule RNA (ribonucleic acid) was needed at this time to progress toward formation of the first cell(s). This hypothesis was formulated after the discovery that RNA can sometimes be both a substrate and an enzyme. Such RNA molecules are called ribozymes. Perhaps RNA could have carried out the processes of life commonly associated today with DNA (deoxyribonucleic acid) and proteins. Scientists who support this hypothesis say that it was an "RNA world" some 3.5 BYA.

Another hypothesis is termed the **protein-first hypothesis.** Sidney Fox has shown that amino acids join together when exposed to dry heat. He suggests that amino acids collected in shallow puddles along the rocky shore, and the heat of the sun caused them to form proteinoids, small polypeptides that have some catalytic properties. When proteinoids are returned to water, they form microspheres, structures composed only of protein that have many of the properties of a cell.

The Protocell

A cell has a lipid-protein membrane. Fox has shown that if lipids are made available to microspheres, the two tend to become associated, producing a lipid-protein membrane. A **protocell,** which could carry on metabolism but could not reproduce, would have come into existence in this manner.

The protocell would have been able to use the still-abundant small organic molecules in the ocean as food. Therefore, the protocell was, most likely, a **heterotroph,** an organism that takes in preformed food. Further, the protocell would have been a fermenter, because there was no free oxygen.

The True Cell

A true cell can reproduce, and in today's cells DNA replicates before cell division occurs. Enzymatic proteins carry out the replication process.

How did the first cell acquire both DNA and enzymatic proteins? Scientists who support the RNA-first hypothesis propose a series of steps. According to this hypothesis, the first cell had RNA genes that, like messenger RNA, could have specified protein synthesis. Some of the proteins formed would have been enzymes. Perhaps one of these enzymes, such as reverse transcriptase found in retroviruses, could use RNA as a template to form DNA. Replication of DNA would then proceed normally.

By contrast, supporters of the protein-first hypothesis suggest that some of the proteins in the protocell would have evolved the enzymatic ability to synthesize DNA from nucleotides in the ocean. Then DNA would have gone on to specify protein synthesis, and in this way the cell could have acquired all its enzymes, even the ones that replicate DNA.

A chemical evolution produced the first cell(s), and then biological evolution began.

25.2 Biological Evolution

The first true cells were the simplest of life-forms; therefore, they must have been **prokaryotic cells,** which lack a nucleus. Later, **eukaryotic cells** (protists), which have nuclei, evolved. Then, multicellularity and the other kingdoms (fungi, plants, and animals) evolved (see Fig. 1.1). Obviously, all these types of organisms—even prokaryotic cells—are alive today. Each type of organism has its own evolutionary history that is traceable back to the first cell(s).

Biological evolution is a change in life-forms that has taken place in the past and will take place in the future. Biological evolution has two important aspects: descent from a common ancestor and adaptation to the environment. Descent from the original cell(s) explains why all living things have a common chemistry and a cellular structure. An **adaptation** is a characteristic that makes an organism able to survive and reproduce in its environment. Adaptations to different environments help explain the diversity of life—why there are so many different types of living things.

Biological evolution explains both the unity (sameness) and diversity of life.

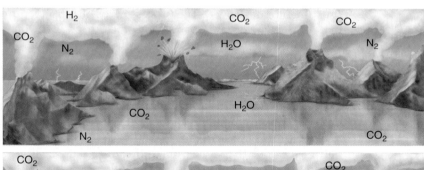

a. The primitive atmosphere contained gases, including H_2O, CO_2, and N_2, that escaped from volcanoes. As the water vapor cooled, some gases were washed into the oceans by rain.

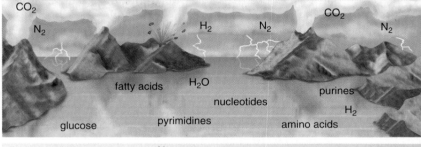

b. The availability of energy from volcanic eruption and lightning allowed gases to form small organic molecules, such as nucleotides and amino acids.

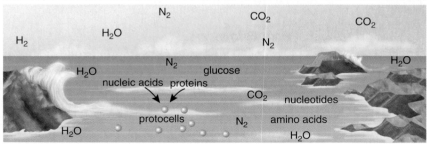

c. Small organic molecules could have joined to form proteins and nucleic acids, which became incorporated into membrane-bound spheres. The spheres became the first cells, called protocells. Later protocells became true cells that could reproduce.

Figure 25.1   Chemical evolution.
A chemical evolution could have produced the protocell, which became a true cell once it had genes composed of DNA and could reproduce.

Common Descent

Charles Darwin was an English naturalist who first formulated the theory of evolution that has since been supported by so much independent data. At the age of 22, Darwin sailed around the world as the naturalist on board the HMS *Beagle*. Between 1831 and 1836, the ship sailed in the tropics of the Southern Hemisphere, where life-forms are more abundant and varied than in Darwin's native England.

Even though it was not his original intent, Darwin began to realize and to gather evidence that life-forms change over time and from place to place. The types of evidence that convinced Darwin that common descent occurs were anatomical, fossil, and biogeographical.

Biogeographical Evidence

Biogeography is the study of the distribution of plants and animals throughout the world. Darwin noted that South America had no rabbits, even though the environment was quite suitable for them. He concluded that there are no rabbits in South America because rabbits originated somewhere else and had no means of reaching South America.

Instead of rabbits, the Patagonian hare exists in the grasslands of South America (Fig. 25.2). This hare has long legs and ears but the face of a guinea pig. Both rabbits and Patagonian hares eat grass, hide in bushes, and move rapidly using long hind legs. Darwin began to think that the Patagonian hare was related to a guinea pig through common descent and that rabbits and Patagonian hares share the same characteristics because they are both adapted to the same type of environment. To take another example of so-called convergent evolution, the marsupials in Australia are adapted for the same lifestyles as are placental mammals on other continents.

Figure 25.2   Patagonian hare.
This animal has the face of a guinea pig and is native to South America, which has no native rabbits. The Patagonian hare has long legs and other adaptations similar to those of rabbits.

Anatomical Evidence

Darwin was able to show that a common descent hypothesis offers a plausible explanation for anatomical similarities among living organisms. Vertebrate forelimbs are used for flight (birds and bats), orientation during swimming (whales and seals), running (horses), climbing (arboreal lizards), or swinging from tree branches (monkeys). Despite dissimilar functions, all vertebrate forelimbs contain the same sets of bones organized in similar ways. The most plausible explanation for this unity is that the basic forelimb plan belonged to a common ancestor and the plan was modified in the various groups as each continued along its own evolutionary pathway. The shared characteristics of vertebrates also explain why their embryological development is so similar.

Vertebrate forelimbs are **homologous structures.** Homologous structures indicate that organisms are related to one another through common descent. **Analogous structures,** such as the wings of birds and insects, have the same function but do not have a common ancestry.

Fossil Evidence

Fossils are the remains and traces of past life. Traces include trails, footprints, burrows, worm casts, or even preserved droppings. Most fossils consist only of hard parts, such as shells, bones, or teeth, because these parts are usually not consumed or destroyed. The process of fossilization requires three steps. The organism must become buried in sediment; the calcium in bone or similar type tissue must mineralize; and then, the surrounding sediment must eventually harden to form rock. Sediment forms a stratum (pl., strata), a recognizable layer in a stratigraphic sequence (Fig. 25.3). Any given stratum is older than the one above it and younger than the one immediately below it. Therefore, the strata allow us to assign a relative date to fossils. An absolute dating method that relies on radioactive data techniques assigns an actual date to a fossil.

The fossils trapped in strata are the **fossil record** that tells us about the history of life. The fossil record supports common descent because similarity of form allows fossils to be linked over time, despite observed changes. In other words, they tell us who is related to whom in the past. Darwin found the fossil remains of a sloth and an armadillo, and the similarity of the fossils to the living animals made him realize that the fossils were related to the modern animals.

Biochemical Evidence

Darwin was not aware, as we are today, that almost all living organisms use the same basic biochemical molecules, including DNA and ATP. Also, organisms use the DNA triplet code and the same 20 amino acids in their proteins. Also of interest, researchers have found that many developmental genes are shared in animals, ranging from worms to humans.

There are no functional reasons why these chemicals need to be so similar. But, their similarity can be explained by hypothesizing descent from a common ancestor.

a.

c.

b.

Figure 25.3 Fossil record.

a. The strata are layers of sediment in which fossils are trapped. The fossils in a given stratum are older than the ones above it and younger than the ones immediately below it. Therefore, the stratigraphic sequence tells us about the history of life. **b.** As paleontologists work, they may disturb and remove layers, carry away excavated soil to a waste or spoil heap, and take away finds. Therefore, they must keep careful records. **c.** In the laboratory, the fossils are carefully cleaned and examined in great detail.

Natural Selection

When Darwin returned home, he spent the next 20 years gathering data to support the principle of biological evolution. His most significant contribution to this principle was a process for **natural selection,** the way a species becomes adapted to its environment. On his trip Darwin visited the Galápagos Islands. He saw a number of finches that resembled one another but had different ways of life. Some were seed-eating ground finches, some cactus-eating ground finches, and some insect-eating tree finches. A warbler-type finch had a beak that could take honey from a flower. A woodpecker-type finch lacked the long tongue of a woodpecker but could use a cactus spine or twig to pull insects from cracks in the bark of a tree. Darwin thought the finches were all descended from a mainland ancestor whose offspring had spread out among the islands and become adapted to different environments.

In order to emphasize the nature of Darwin's natural selection process, it is often contrasted with a process espoused by Jean-Baptiste Lamarck, another 19th-century naturalist. Lamarck's explanation for the long neck of the giraffe was based on the assumption that the ancestors of the modern giraffe were trying to reach into the trees to browse on high-growing vegetation (Fig. 25.4*a*). Continual stretching of the neck caused it to become longer, and this acquired characteristic was passed on to the next generation. Lamarck's process is **teleological** because, according to him, the desired outcome is known ahead of time. This type of explanation has not stood the test of time. Natural selection, on the other hand, is nonteleological and has been fully substantiated by later investigators (Fig. 25.4*b*).

The critical elements of the natural selection process are variation, competition for limited resources, and adaptation as an end result.

- *Variation.* Individual members of a species vary in physical characteristics. Physical variations can be passed from generation to generation. (Darwin was never aware of genes, but we know today that the inheritance of the genotype determines the phenotype.)
- *Competition for limited resources.* Even though each individual could eventually produce many descendants, the number in each generation usually stays about the same. Why? Because resources are limited, and only certain individuals survive and reproduce. These members of a species are able to capture more resources in a particular environment because they have a characteristic that gives them an advantage over other members of their species. The environment "selects" these better-adapted members to have offspring, and therefore to pass on this characteristic.
- *Adaptation.* Each subsequent generation includes more individuals that are adapted in the same way to the environment.

Early giraffes probably had short necks that they stretched to reach food.

Early giraffes probably had necks of various lengths.

Their offspring had longer necks that they stretched to reach food.

Natural selection due to competition led to survival of the longer-necked giraffes and their offspring.

Eventually, the continued stretching of the neck resulted in today's giraffe.

Eventually, only long-necked giraffes survived the competition.

a. Lamarck's proposal   b. Darwin's proposal

Figure 25.4   Mechanism of evolution.
This diagram contrasts Jean-Baptiste Lamarck's process of acquired characteristics with Charles Darwin's process of natural selection. Only natural selection is supported by data.

Natural selection can account for the great diversity of life because environments differ widely.

Living things share characteristics because they are all descended from the first cell(s), and they are diverse because they are adapted to different environments.

25.3 Humans Are Primates

For further study of human evolution, we can turn to the classification system. Biologists classify organisms according to their hypothesized evolutionary relatedness. The organisms in a particular classification category share a set of common anatomical and molecular characteristics. The **binomial name** of an organism gives its genus and species. Organisms in the same domain have only general characteristics in common; those in the same genus have quite specific characteristics in common. Table 25.1 lists some of the characteristics that help classify humans into major categories. The dates in the first column of the table tell us when these groups of animals first appear in the fossil record.

Characteristics of Primates

Primates are members of the order Primates. In contrast to the other orders of placental mammals, primates are adapted to an arboreal life—that is, for living in trees. Primate limbs are mobile, and the hands and feet both have five digits each. Many primates have both an opposable big toe and thumb—that is, the big toe or thumb can touch each of the other toes or fingers. (Humans don't have an opposable big toe, but the thumb is opposable, and this results in a grip that is both powerful and precise.) The opposable thumb allows a primate to easily reach out and bring food, such as fruit, to the mouth. When locomoting, primates grasp and release tree limbs freely because nails have replaced claws.

In primates, the snout is shortened considerably, allowing the eyes to move to the front of the head. The stereoscopic vision (or depth perception) that results permits primates to make accurate judgments about the distance and position of adjoining tree limbs. Some primates, such as humans, who are active during the day, have color vision and greater visual acuity because the retina contains cone cells, in addition to rod cells. Cone cells require bright light, but the image is sharp and in color. The lens of the eye focuses light directly on the fovea, a region of the retina, where cone cells are concentrated.

The evolutionary trend among primates is toward a larger and more complex brain—the brain size is smallest in prosimians and largest in modern humans. The cerebral cortex, with many association areas, expands so much that it becomes extensively folded in humans. The portion of the brain devoted to smell gets smaller, and the portions devoted to sight increase in size and complexity during primate evolution. Also, more and more of the brain is involved in controlling and processing information received from the hands and the thumb. The result is good hand-eye coordination in humans.

It is difficult to care for several offspring while moving from limb to limb, and one birth at a time is the norm in primates. The juvenile period of dependency is extended, and there is an emphasis on learned behavior and complex social interactions.

The order Primates has two suborders. The **prosimians** include the lemurs, tarsiers, and lorises. The **anthropoids** include the monkeys, apes, and humans. This classification tells us that humans are more closely related to the monkeys and apes than they are to the prosimians.

These characteristics especially distinguish primates from other mammals:

- Opposable thumb (and in some cases, big toe)
- Well-developed brain
- Nails (not claws)
- Single birth
- Extended period of parental care
- Emphasis on learned behavior

Table 25.1	Evolution and Classification of Humans	
BYA/MYA*	**Classification Category**	**Characteristics**
2 BYA	Domain Eukarya	Membrane-bound nucleus with several chromosomes; usually sexual reproduction
600 MYA	Kingdom Animalia	Usually motile, multicellular organisms, without cell walls or chlorophyll; usually have an internal cavity for digestion of nutrients
540 MYA	Phylum Chordata	Organisms that at one time in their life history have a dorsal hollow nerve cord, a notochord, and pharyngeal pouches
120 MYA	Class Mammalia	Warm-blooded vertebrates possessing mammary glands; body more or less covered with hair; well-developed brain
60 MYA	Order Primates	Good brain development; opposable thumb and sometimes opposable big toe
7 MYA	Family Hominidae	Limb anatomy suitable for upright stance and bipedal locomotion
3 MYA	Genus *Homo*	Maximum brain development, especially in regard to particular portions; hand anatomy suitable to making and using tools
0.1 MYA	Species *Homo sapiens***	Body proportions of modern humans; speech centers of brain well developed

*BYA = billions of years ago; MYA = millions of years ago.
**To specify an organism, you must use the full binomial name, such as *Homo sapiens*.

The Evolution of Hominids

Once biologists have studied the characteristics of a group of organisms, they can construct an **evolutionary tree** that is a working hypothesis of their past history. The evolutionary tree in Figure 25.5 shows that all primates share one common ancestor and that the other types of primates diverged from the human line of descent over time. For example, prosimians, represented by lemurs, were the first type of primate to diverge, and African apes were the last. Notice that the tree indicates that humans are most closely related to African apes (Fig. 25.6). One of the most unfortunate misconceptions concerning human evolution is the belief that Darwin and others suggested that humans evolved from apes. On the contrary, humans and apes are thought to have shared a common ape-like ancestor. Today's apes are our distant cousins, and we couldn't have evolved from our cousins because we are contemporaries—living on Earth at the same time.

The First Hominids

Biologists have not been able to agree on which extinct form known only by the fossil record is the first hominid.

Hominid is a term that refers to our branch of the evolutionary tree. Any fossil placed in the hominid line of descent is closer to us than to one of the African apes.

When any two lines of descent, called a **lineage,** first diverge from a common ancestor, the genes and proteins of the two lineages are nearly identical. But as time goes by, each lineage accumulates genetic changes, which lead to RNA and protein changes. Many genetic changes are neutral (not tied to adaptation) and accumulate at a fairly constant rate; such changes can be used as a kind of **molecular clock** to indicate the relatedness of two groups and when they diverged from each other. Molecular data suggest that hominids split from the ape line of descent about 6–7 MYA.

Hominid Features

Paleontologists use certain anatomical features when they try to determine if a fossil is a hominid. One of these features is **bipedal posture** (walking on two feet). Until recently, many scientists thought that hominids began to walk upright on two feet because of a dramatic change in climate that caused forests to be replaced by grassland.

Figure 25.5   Primate evolutionary tree.

The ancestor to all primates climbed into one of the first fruit-bearing forests about 66 MYA. The descendants of this ancestor adapted to the new way of life and developed traits, such as a shortened snout and nails instead of claws. The time when the other primates diverged from the human line of descent is largely known from the fossil record. A common ancestor was living at each point of divergence. For example, there was a common ancestor for monkeys, apes, and humans about 33 MYA; one for all apes and humans about 15 MYA; and one for just African apes and humans about 6–7 MYA.

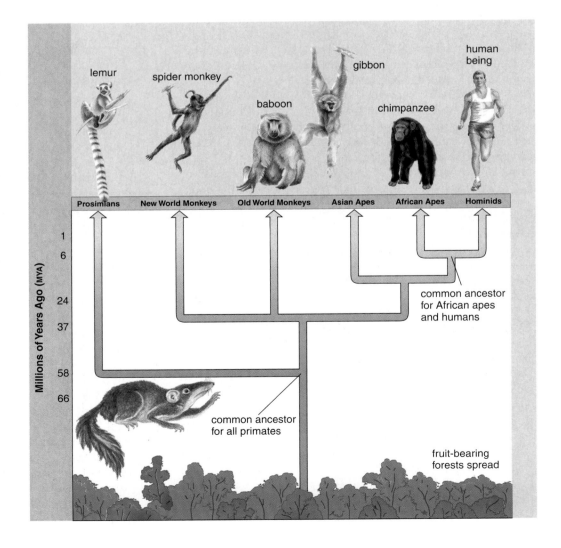

Figure 25.6 Today's apes.
The apes can be divided into the Asian apes (gibbons and orangutans) and the African apes (chimpanzees and gorillas). Molecular data and the location of early hominid fossil remains tell us that we are more closely related to the African than to the Asian apes.

Now, some biologists suggest that the first hominid began to assume a bipedal posture even while it lived in trees. Why? Because they cannot find evidence of a dramatic shift in vegetation about 6–7 MYA. The first hominid's environment is now thought to have included some forest, some woodland, and some grassland. While still living in trees, the first hominids may have walked upright on large branches as they collected fruit from overhead. Then, when they began to forage on the ground among bushes, it would have been easier to shuffle along on their hind limbs. Bipedalism would also have prevented them from getting heatstroke because an upright stance exposes more of the body to breezes. Bipedalism may have been an advantage in still another way. Males may have acquired food far afield, and if they could carry it back to females, they would have been more assured of sex.

Two other hominid features of importance are the shape of the face and brain size. Today's humans have a flatter face and a more pronounced chin than do the apes because the human jaw is shorter than that of the apes. Then, too, our teeth are generally smaller and less specialized; we don't have the sharp canines of an ape, for example. Chimpanzees have a brain size of about 400 cm^3, and modern humans have a brain size of about 1,300 cm^3.

It's hard to decide which fossils are hominids because human features evolved gradually and they didn't evolve at the same rate. Most investigators rely first and foremost on bipedal posture as the hallmark of a hominid, regardless of the size of the brain.

Early Hominids

Fossils, dated at the time the ape and human lineages split, have been found. The oldest of these fossils, called *Sahelanthropus tchaensis*, dated at 7 MYA, was found in Chad, located in central Africa far from eastern and southern Africa, where other hominid fossils were excavated. The only find, a skull, appears to be that of a hominid because it has smaller canines and thicker tooth enamel than an ape. The braincase, however, is very ape-like and it is impossible to tell if this hominid walked upright. Some suggest this fossil is ancestral to the gorilla.

Orrorin tugenensis, dated at 6 MYA and found in eastern Africa, is thought to be another early hominid, especially because the limb anatomy suggests a bipedal posture. However, the canine teeth are large and pointed and the arm and finger bones retain adaptations for climbing. Some suggest this fossil is ancestral to the chimpanzee.

Ardipithecus ramidus kkadabba, found in eastern Africa and dated between 5.8 and 5.2 MYA, is closely related to the later appearing *Ardipithecus ramidus*. This ardipithecine is thought to be closely related to the australopithecines, which are discussed next.

The evolution of bipedalism is used as the distinctive feature that separates hominids from apes. Scientists are still looking for reasons bipedalism evolved.

25.4 Evolution of Australopithecines

The hominid line of descent begins in earnest with the **australopithecines,** a group of individuals that evolved and diversified in Africa. Some australopithecines were slight of frame and termed *gracile* (slender) types. Some were *robust* (powerful) and tended to have strong upper bodies and especially massive jaws. The gracile types most likely fed on soft fruits and leaves, while the robust types had a more fibrous diet that may have included hard nuts.

Southern Africa

The first australopithecine to be discovered was unearthed in southern Africa by Raymond Dart in the 1920s. This hominid, named *Australopithecus africanus,* is a gracile type dated about 2.8 MYA. *A. robustus,* dated from 2 to 1.5 MYA, is a robust type from southern Africa. Both *A. africanus* and *A. robustus* had a brain size of about 500 cm³; their skull differences are essentially due to dental and facial adaptations to different diets.

Limb anatomy suggests these hominids walked upright. Nevertheless, the proportions of the limbs are ape-like: The forelimbs are longer than the hind limbs. Some argue that *A. africanus,* with its relatively large brain, is the best ancestral candidate for early *Homo,* whose limb proportions are similar to those of this fossil.

Eastern Africa

More than 20 years ago, a team led by Donald Johanson unearthed nearly 250 fossils of a hominid called *A. afarensis.* A now-famous female skeleton dated at 3.18 MYA is known worldwide by its field name, Lucy. (The name derives from the Beatles song "Lucy in the Sky with Diamonds.") Although her brain was quite small (400 cm³), the shapes and relative proportions of her limbs indicate that Lucy stood upright and walked bipedally (Fig. 25.7*a*). Even better evidence of bipedal locomotion comes from a trail of footprints in Laetoli dated about 3.7 MYA. The larger prints are double, as though a smaller-sized being was stepping in the footfalls of another—and there are additional small prints off to the side, within hand-holding distance (Fig. 25.7*b*).

Since the australopithecines were ape-like above the waist (small brain) and human-like below the waist (walked erect), it shows that human characteristics did not evolve all at one time. The term **mosaic evolution** is applied when different body parts change at different rates, and therefore at different times.

A. afarensis, a gracile type, is most likely ancestral to the robust types found in eastern Africa: *A. aethiopicus* and *A. boisei.* *A. boisei* had a powerful upper body and the largest molars of any hominid. These robust types died out, and therefore, it is possible that *A. afarensis* is ancestral to both *A. africanus* and early *Homo.*

Australopithecines, which arose in Africa, were hominids. Their remains show that bipedal posture was the first human-like feature to evolve. It is unknown at this time which australopithecine is ancestral to early *Homo*.

a.

b.

Figure 25.7 *Australopithecus afarensis.*
a. A reconstruction of Lucy on display at the St. Louis Zoo. **b.** These fossilized footprints occur in ash from a volcanic eruption some 3.7 MYA. The larger footprints are double (one followed behind the other), and a third, smaller individual was walking to the side. (A female holding the hand of a youngster may have been walking in the footprints of a male.) The footprints suggest that *A. afarensis* walked bipedally.

25.5 Evolution of Humans

Fossils are assigned to the genus *Homo* if (1) the brain size is 600 cm^3 or greater, (2) the jaw and teeth resemble those of humans, and (3) tool use is evident (Fig. 25.8).

Early *Homo*

Homo habilis, dated between 2.0 and 1.9 MYA, may be ancestral to modern humans. Some of these fossils have a brain size as large as 775 cm^3, which is about 45% larger than that of *A. afarensis.* The cheek teeth are smaller than even those of the gracile australopithecines. Therefore, it is likely that these early *Homos* were omnivores who ate meat in addition to plant material. Bones at their campsites bear cut marks, indicating that they used tools to strip them of meat.

The stone tools made by *H. habilis,* whose name means "handy man," are rather crude. It's possible that these are the cores from which they took flakes sharp enough to scrape away hide, cut tendons, and easily remove meat from bones.

Early *Homo* skulls suggest that the portions of the brain associated with speech areas were enlarged. We can speculate that the ability to speak may have led to hunting cooperatively. Other members of the group may have remained plant gatherers, and if so, both hunters and gatherers most likely ate together and shared their food. In this way, society and culture could have begun. **Culture,** which encompasses human behavior and products (e.g., technology and the arts), depends upon the capacity to speak and transmit knowledge. We can further speculate that the advantages of a culture to *H. habilis* may have hastened the extinction of the australopithecines.

H. habilis warrants classification as *Homo* because of brain size, dentition, and tool use. These early *Homos* may have had the rudiments of a culture.

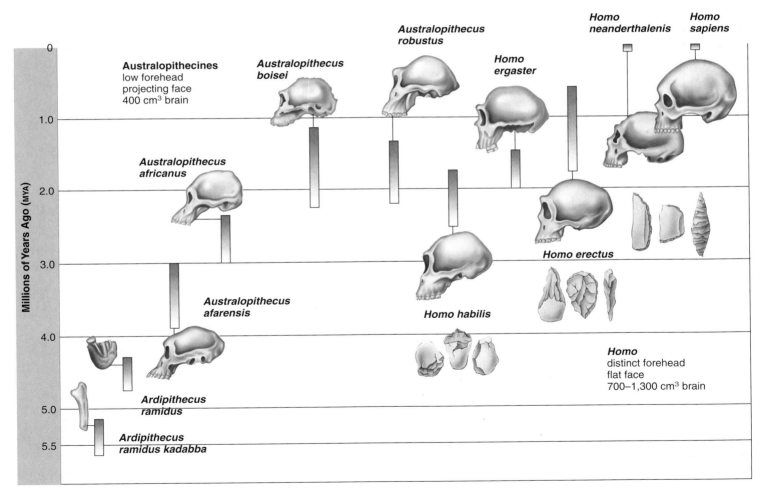

Figure 25.8 Human evolution.
The length of time each species existed is indicated by the vertical gray lines. Notice that there have been times when two or more hominids existed at the same time. Therefore, human evolution resembles a "bush" rather than a single branch. (*Left*) Australopithecines have a low forehead, projecting face, and a brain size of about 400 cm^3. (*Right*) *Homos* have an increasingly high forehead, a flat face, and a brain size of 700 to 1,300 cm^3.

Homo erectus

Homo erectus and like fossils are found in Africa, Asia, and Europe and dated between 1.9 and 0.3 MYA. A Dutch anatomist named Eugene Dubois was the first to unearth *H. erectus* bones in Java in 1891, and since that time many other fossils have been found in the same area. Although all fossils assigned the name *H. erectus* are similar in appearance, enough discrepancy exists to suggest that several different species have been included in this group. In particular, some experts suggest that the African and Asian forms are two different species (Fig. 25.9).

Compared with *H. habilis*, *H. erectus* had a larger brain (about 1,000 cm^3) and a flatter face. The nose projected, however. This type of nose is adaptive for a hot, dry climate because it permits water to be removed before air leaves the body. The recovery of an almost complete skeleton of a 10-year-old boy indicates that *H. erectus* was much taller than the hominids discussed thus far. Males were 1.8 meters tall (about 6 feet), and females were 1.55 meters (approaching 5 feet). Indeed, these hominids were erect and most likely had a striding gait like ours. The robust and most likely heavily muscled skeleton still retained some australopithecine features. Even so, the size of the birth canal indicates that infants were born in an immature state that required an extended period of care.

H. erectus may have first appeared in Africa and then migrated into Asia and Europe. At one time, the migration was thought to have occurred about 1 MYA, but recently *H. erectus* fossil remains in Java and the Republic of Georgia have been dated at 1.9 and 1.6 MYA, respectively. These remains push the evolution of *H. erectus* in Africa to an earlier date than has yet been determined. In any case, such an extensive population movement is a first in the history of humankind and a tribute to the intellectual and physical skills of the species.

H. erectus was the first hominid to use fire, and also fashioned more advanced tools than early *Homos*. These hominids used heavy, teardrop-shaped axes and cleavers as well as flakes, which were probably used for cutting and scraping. It could be that *H. erectus* was a systematic hunter and brought kills to the same site over and over again. In one location, researchers have found over 40,000 bones and 2,647 stones. These sites could have been "home bases" where social interaction occurred and a prolonged childhood allowed time for learning. Perhaps a language evolved and a culture more like our own developed.

H. erectus, which evolved from *H. habilis*, had a striding gait, made well-fashioned tools (perhaps for hunting), and could control fire. This hominid migrated into Europe and Asia from Africa between 2 and 1 MYA.

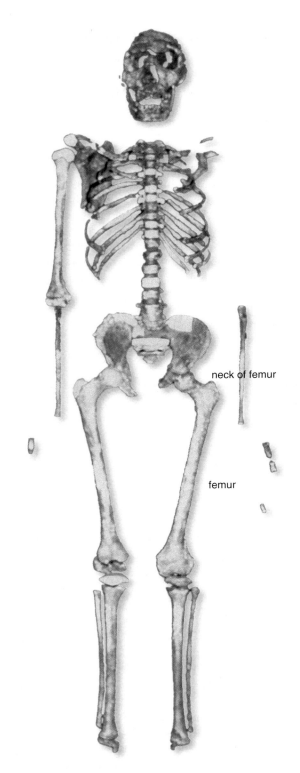

neck of femur

femur

Figure 25.9   *The Turkana boy.*
This skeleton of a 10-year-old boy who lived 1.6 MYA in eastern Africa shows femurs that are angled, with femur necks much longer than in the femurs of modern humans. Some classify this fossil as *H. erectus*, while others assign it to *H. ergaster*, a closely related species.

Evolution of Modern Humans

Most researchers accept the idea that *Homo sapiens* (modern humans) evolved from *H. erectus,* but they differ as to the details. Perhaps *Homo sapiens* evolved from *H. erectus* separately in Asia, Africa, and Europe. The hypothesis that *Homo sapiens* evolved in several different locations is called the **multiregional continuity hypothesis** (Fig. 25.10a). This hypothesis proposes that evolution to modern humans was essentially similar in several different places. If so, each region should show a continuity of its own anatomical characteristics from the time when *H. erectus* first arrived in Europe and Asia.

Opponents argue that it seems highly unlikely that evolution would have produced essentially the same result in these different places. They suggest, instead, the **out-of-Africa hypothesis,** which proposes that *H. sapiens* evolved from *H. erectus* only in Africa, and thereafter *H. sapiens* migrated to Europe and Asia about 100,000 years BP (before present) (Fig. 25.10b). If so, there would be no continuity of characteristics between fossils dated 200,000 years BP and 100,000 years BP in Europe and Asia.

According to which hypothesis would modern humans be most genetically alike? The multiregional continuity hypothesis states that human populations have been evolving separately for a long time, and therefore genetic differences are expected. The out-of-Africa hypothesis states that we are all descended from a few individuals from about 100,000 years BP. Therefore, the out-of-Africa hypothesis suggests that we are more genetically similar.

A few years ago, a study attempted to show that all the people of Europe (and the world, for that matter) have essentially the same mitochondrial DNA. Called the "mitochondrial Eve" hypothesis by the press (note that this is a misnomer because no single ancestor is proposed), the statistics that calculated the date of the African migration were found to be flawed. Still, the raw data—which indicate a close genetic relationship among all Europeans—support the out-of-Africa hypothesis.

These opposing hypotheses have sparked many other innovative studies to test them. The final conclusions are still being determined.

Investigators are currently testing two hypotheses: (1) Modern humans evolved separately in Asia, Africa, and Europe, or (2) modern humans evolved in Africa and then migrated to Asia and Europe.

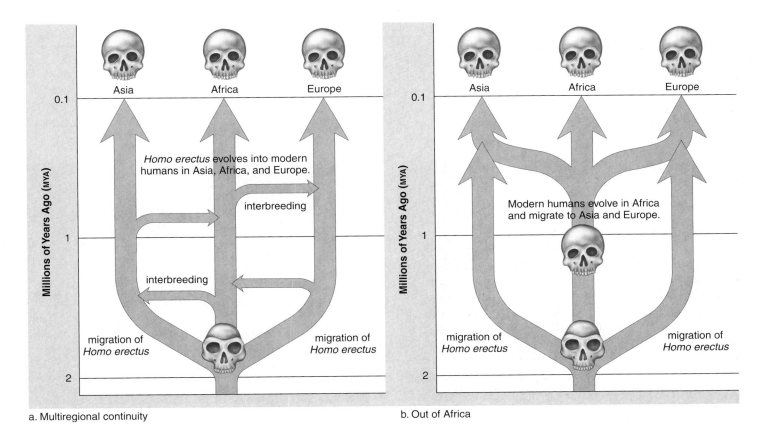

a. Multiregional continuity

b. Out of Africa

Figure 25.10   Evolution of modern humans.
a. The multiregional continuity hypothesis proposes that *Homo sapiens* evolved separately in at least three different places: Asia, Africa, and Europe. Therefore, continuity of genotypes and phenotypes is expected in these regions. **b.** The out-of-Africa hypothesis proposes that *Homo sapiens* evolved only in Africa; then this species migrated and supplanted populations of *Homo* in Asia and Europe about 100,000 years BP.

Neanderthals

Neanderthals (*H. neanderthalensis*) take their name from Germany's Neander Valley, where one of the first Neanderthal skeletons, dated some 200,000 years BP, was discovered. The Neanderthals had massive brow ridges, and their nose, jaws, and teeth protruded far forward. The forehead was low and sloping, and the lower jaw lacked a chin. New fossils show that the pubic bone was long compared with ours.

According to the out-of-Africa hypothesis (see page 499), Neanderthals were eventually supplanted by modern humans. Surprisingly, however, the Neanderthal brain was, on the average, slightly larger than that of *Homo sapiens* (1,400 cm³, compared with 1,360 cm³ in most modern humans). The Neanderthals were heavily muscled, especially in the shoulders and neck (Fig. 25.11). The bones of the limbs were shorter and thicker than those of modern humans. It is hypothesized that a larger brain than that of modern humans was required to control the extra musculature. The Neanderthals lived in Europe and Asia during the last Ice Age, and their sturdy build could have helped conserve heat.

The Neanderthals give evidence of being culturally advanced. Most lived in caves, but those living in the open may have built houses. They manufactured a variety of stone tools, including spear points, which could have been used for hunting, and scrapers and knives, which would have helped in food preparation. They most likely successfully hunted bears, woolly mammoths, rhinoceroses, reindeer, and other contemporary animals. They used and could control fire, which probably helped them cook meat and keep themselves warm. They even buried their dead with flowers and tools and may have had a religion.

Cro-Magnons

Cro-Magnons are the oldest fossils to be designated *Homo sapiens*. In keeping with the out-of-Africa hypothesis, the Cro-Magnons, who are named after a fossil location in France, were the modern humans who entered Asia and Europe from Africa 100,000 years BP or even earlier. Cro-Magnons had a thoroughly modern appearance (Fig. 25.12). They made advanced stone tools, including compound tools, as when stone flakes were fitted to a wooden handle. They may have been the first to throw spears, enabling them to kill animals from a distance, and to make knife-like blades. They were such accomplished hunters that some researchers suggest they were responsible for the extinction of many larger mammals, such as the giant sloth, the mammoth, the saber-toothed tiger, and the giant ox, during the late Pleistocene epoch.

Cro-Magnons hunted cooperatively, and perhaps they were the first to have a language. Most likely, they lived in small groups, with the men hunting by day, while the women remained at home with the children. It's quite possible that this hunting way of life among prehistoric people influences our behavior even today. The Cro-Magnon culture included art. They sculpted small figurines out of reindeer bones and antlers. They also painted beautiful drawings of animals on cave walls in Spain and France (Fig. 25.12).

Most likely, modern humans migrated out of Africa and supplanted other *Homo* species in Asia and Europe. Today, only one *Homo* species exists—namely, *Homo sapiens*.

Figure 25.11 Neanderthals.
This drawing shows that the nose and the mouth of the Neanderthals protruded from their faces, and their muscles were massive. They made stone tools and were most likely excellent hunters.

Figure 25.12 Cro-Magnons.
Cro-Magnon people are one of the earliest groups to be designated *Homo sapiens*. Their tool-making ability and other cultural attributes, including artistic talents, are legendary.

We Are One Species

Human beings are diverse, but even so, we are all classified as *Homo sapiens*. The biological definition of species is a group of organisms able to interbreed and bear fertile offspring. Any two types of humans are able to reproduce with one another, signifying that all humans belong to the same species. While it may appear that various "races" exist, molecular data show that the DNA base sequence varies as much between individuals of the same ethnicity as between individuals of different ethnicities.

It is generally accepted that the human phenotype is adapted to the climate of a region. Although dark skin might seem to protect against the hot rays of the sun, it has been suggested that it is actually a protection against ultraviolet ray absorption. Dark-skinned persons living in southern regions and light-skinned persons living in northern regions absorb the same amount of radiation. (Some absorption is required for vitamin D production.) Other features that correlate with skin color, such as hair type and eye color, may simply be side effects of genes that control skin color.

Differences in body shape represent adaptations to temperature. A squat body with short limbs and a short nose retains more heat than an elongated body with long limbs and a long nose. Also, almond-shaped eyes, a flat nose and forehead, and broad cheeks seem to be adaptations to the last Ice Age.

While some people propose that physical differences warrant assigning humans to different "races," this contention is not borne out by molecular data.

Bioethical Focus

The Theory of Evolution

The term *theory* in science is reserved for those ideas that scientists have found to be all-encompassing because they are based on data collected in a number of different fields. Evolution is a scientific theory. So is the cell theory, which says that all organisms are composed of cells, and so is the atomic theory, which says that all matter is composed of atoms. No one argues that schools should teach alternatives to the cell theory or the atomic theory. Yet controversy reigns over the use of the expression "the theory of evolution."

No wonder most scientists in our country are dismayed when state legislatures or school boards rule that teachers must put forward a variety of "theories" on the origin of life, including one that runs contrary to the mass of data that supports the theory of evolution. An organization in California called the Institute for Creation Research advocates that students be taught an "intelligent-design theory," which says that DNA could never have arisen without the involvement of an "intelligent agent," and that gaps in the fossil record mean that species arose fully developed with no antecedents.

Since our country forbids the mingling of church and state—that is, no purely religious ideas can be taught in the schools—the advocates for an intelligent-design theory are careful not to mention the Bible or any strictly religious ideas (i.e., God created the world in seven days). Still, teachers who have a solid scientific background do not feel comfortable teaching an intelligent-design theory because it does not meet the test of a scientific theory. Science is based on hypotheses that have been tested by observation and/or experimentation. A scientific theory has stood the test of time—that is, no hypotheses that run contrary to the theory have been supported by observation and/or experimentation. On the contrary, the theory of evolution is supported by data collected in such wide-ranging fields as development, anatomy, geology, and biochemistry.

Polls consistently show that nearly half of all Americans prefer to believe the Old Testament account of creation. That, of course, is their right, but should schools be required to teach an intelligent-design theory that traces its roots back to the Old Testament and is not supported by observation and experimentation?

Decide Your Opinion

1. Should teachers be required to teach an intelligent-design theory of the origin of life? Why or why not?
2. Should schools rightly teach that science is based on data collected by testing hypotheses through observation and experimentation? Why or why not?
3. Should schools be required to show that the intelligent-design theory does not meet the test of being scientific? Why or why not?

Summarizing the Concepts

25.1 Origin of Life

Data suggest that a chemical evolution produced the first cell. In the presence of an outside energy source, such as ultraviolet radiation, the primitive atmospheric gases reacted with one another to produce small organic molecules.

Next, macromolecules evolved and interacted. The RNA-first hypothesis is supported by the discovery of RNA enzymes called ribozymes. The protein-first hypothesis is supported by the observation that amino acids polymerize abiotically when exposed to dry heat. The protocell must have been a heterotrophic fermenter living on the preformed organic molecules in the ocean. Eventually, the DNA → RNA → protein self-replicating system evolved, and a true cell that could reproduce came into being.

25.2 Biological Evolution

Descent from a common ancestor explains the unity of living things—for example, why all living things have a cellular structure and a common chemistry. Adaptation to different environments explains the great diversity of living things.

Darwin discovered much evidence for common descent. Biogeography shows that the distribution of organisms on Earth is explainable by assuming that organisms evolved in one locale. The common anatomies and development of a group of organisms are explainable by descent from a common ancestor. The fossil record gives us the history of life in general and allows us to trace the descent of a particular group. Fossils located in later strata are more closely related to modern organisms than fossils located in earlier strata. All organisms have similar biochemical molecules, and this supports the concept of common descent.

Darwin developed a mechanism for adaptation known as natural selection. Members of a population exhibit inherited variations and compete with one another for limited resources. The members with variations that help them survive and reproduce have more offspring, and in this way the adaptive characteristics become widespread in the next generation. The process of natural selection is nonteleological.

25.3 Humans Are Primates

The classification of humans can be used to trace their ancestry. Humans are primates, mammals adapted to living in trees. An evolutionary diagram of primates based on anatomical, molecular, and fossil evidence shows that we share a common ancestor with African apes. The first hominid (humans are in this family) most likely lived about 6–7 MYA. Researchers have singled out certain features—bipedal posture, flat face, and brain size—that identify which fossil finds are hominids. Among the fossils dated 5–7 MYA, ardipithecines were most likely hominids.

25.4 Evolution of Australopithecines

The evolutionary tree of hominids resembles a bush—meaning that there is not a straight line of fossils leading to modern humans. Australopithecines were hominids that lived about 3 MYA. Australopithecines could walk erect, but they had a small brain. This testifies to a mosaic evolution for humans—that is, not all advanced features evolved at the same time. It is uncertain which australopithecine, if any, are ancestral to early *Homo*.

25.5 Evolution of Humans

H. habilis made tools, but fossil evidence shows that *H. erectus* was the first *Homo* to have a brain size of more than 1,000 cm^3. *H. erectus* migrated from Africa into Europe and Asia. They used fire and may have been big-game hunters.

Whereas the multiregional continuity hypothesis suggests that modern humans evolved separately in Europe, Africa, and Asia, the out-of-Africa hypothesis says that *H. sapiens* evolved in Africa but then migrated to Asia and Europe. The Neanderthals were already living in Europe and Asia before modern humans arrived. The Neanderthals did not have the physical traits of modern humans, but they did have culture. Cro-Magnon is a name often given to the first *H. sapiens*. Their tools were sophisticated, and they definitely had a culture, as shown by their paintings on the walls of caves.

Studying the Concepts

1. List and discuss the steps by which a chemical evolution could have produced a protocell. 488–89
2. What is a true cell? How might DNA replication have come about? 489
3. Biological evolution explains what two general observations about living things? 489
4. Show that the fossil record, biogeography, comparative anatomy, and biochemistry all give evidence of evolution. 490
5. Explain Darwin's mechanism of natural selection. How does natural selection result in adaptation to the environment? 492
6. Name the major classification categories. Classify humans, and state some of the characteristics for each category. 493
7. In general, primates are adapted to what type of life? List and discuss several primate characteristics. 493–94
8. Describe an evolutionary tree. What can we learn from the primate evolutionary tree? 494
9. What features do paleontologists use to determine that a fossil is a hominid? 494–95
10. Describe the characteristics of australopithecines, early *Homo*, *Homo erectus*, Neanderthals, and Cro-Magnon. 496–500
11. Which of our ancestors first walked erect? Used tools? Used fire? Drew pictures? 496–500
12. Give evidence that human evolution resembles a bush rather than a single branch. 497
13. Contrast the multiregional continuity hypothesis with the out-of-Africa hypothesis. 499

Thinking Critically About the Concepts

Refer to the opening vignette on page 488, and then answer these questions.

1. How would it be possible for genes to control how efficiently we metabolize?
2. Would more or less ATP be available if a high rate of fat storage occurs in the body?
3. What could be meant by a "thrifty gene" hypothesis to account for the inability of some people to lose weight, despite a restrictive diet? How could such a hypothesis be tested?

Testing Your Knowledge of the Concepts

Choose the best answer for each question.

1. Which of these did Stanley Miller place in his experimental system to show that organic molecules could have arisen from inorganic molecules on the primitive Earth?
   a. microspheres
   b. purines and pyrimidines
   c. primitive gases
   d. only RNA
   e. All of these are correct.

2. Which of these is the chief reason the protocell was probably a fermenter?
   a. The protocell didn't have any enzymes.
   b. The atmosphere didn't have any oxygen.
   c. Fermentation provides the most energy.
   d. There was no ATP yet.
   e. All of these are correct.

3. Evolution of the DNA → RNA → protein system was a milestone because the protocell could now
   a. be a heterotrophic fermenter.
   b. pass on genetic information.
   c. use energy to grow.
   d. take in preformed molecules.
   e. All of these are correct.

4. According to Darwin,
   a. the adapted individual is the one who survives and passes on its genes to offspring.
   b. changes in phenotype are passed on by way of the genotype to the next generation.
   c. organisms are able to bring about a change in their phenotype.
   d. evolution is striving toward particular traits.
   e. All of these are correct.

5. Organisms
   a. compete with other members of their species.
   b. vary in physical characteristics.
   c. are adapted to their environment.
   d. are related by descent from common ancestors.
   e. All of these are correct.

6. If evolution occurs, we would expect different biogeographical regions with similar environments to
   a. all contain the same mix of plants and animals.
   b. each have its own specific mix of plants and animals.
   c. have plants and animals with similar adaptations.
   d. have plants and animals with different adaptations.
   e. Both b and c are correct.

7. The fossil record offers direct evidence for evolution because you can
   a. see that the types of fossils change over time.
   b. sometimes find common ancestors.
   c. trace the ancestry of a particular group.
   d. trace the biological history of living things.
   e. All of these are correct.

8. Organisms such as whales and sea turtles that are adapted to an aquatic way of life
   a. will probably have homologous structures.
   b. will have similar adaptations but not necessarily homologous structures.
   c. may very well have analogous structures.
   d. will have the same degree of fitness.
   e. Both b and c are correct.

9. Which of these gives the correct order of divergence from the main line of descent leading to humans?
   a. prosimians, monkeys, Asian apes, African apes, humans
   b. gibbons, baboons, prosimians, monkeys, African apes, humans
   c. monkeys, gibbons, prosimians, African apes, baboons, humans
   d. African apes, gibbons, monkeys, baboons, prosimians, humans
   e. *H. habilis, H. erectus, H. neanderthalensis,* Cro-Magnon

10. Lucy is a member of what species?
    a. *Homo erectus*
    b. *Australopithecus afarensis*
    c. *H. habilis*
    d. *A. robustus*
    e. *A. anamensis* and *A. afarensis* are alternative forms of Lucy.

11. What possibly may have influenced the evolution of bipedalism?
    a. A larger brain developed.   d. Both b and c are correct.
    b. Gathering of food was easier.   e. Both a and c are correct.
    c. The climate became colder.

12. *H. erectus* could have been the first to
    a. use and control fire.
    b. migrate out of Africa.
    c. make tools.
    d. Both a and b are correct, but c is not.
    e. a, b, and c are correct.

13. Which of these characteristics is not consistent with the others?
    a. opposable thumb   d. well-developed brain
    b. learned behavior   e. stereoscopic vision
    c. multiple births

14. The last common ancestor for African apes and hominids
    a. has been found, and it resembles a gibbon.
    b. has not yet been identified, but it is expected to be dated from about 6–7 MYA.
    c. has been found, and it has been dated at 30 MYA.
    d. is not expected to be found because there was no such common ancestor.
    e. most likely lived in Asia, not Africa.

15. If the multiregional continuity hypothesis is correct, then
    a. hominid fossils in China after 100,000 BP are not expected to resemble earlier fossils.
    b. hominid fossils in China after 100,000 BP are expected to resemble earlier fossils.
    c. the mitochondrial Eve study must be invalid.
    d. Both a and c are correct.
    e. Both b and c are correct.

16. A primate evolutionary tree
    a. exists only for humans.
    b. shows the evolutionary relationship among the different types of primates.
    c. should not include extinct forms.
    d. indicates that the ape lineage and human lineage are still joined.
    e. All of these are correct.

17. In which boxes of the following diagram would you place:
    a. a skull of *Homo sapiens* to describe the out-of-Africa hypothesis _____
    b. a skull of *Homo erectus* _____

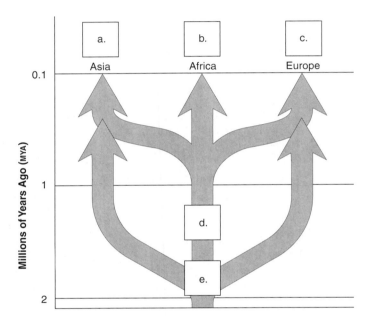

18. Classify humans by filling in the missing lines.
    Domain   Eukarya
    Kingdom   Animalia
    Phylum   a. _____
    b. _____   Mammalia
    c. _____   Primates
    Family   d. _____
    e. _____   *Homo*
    Species   f. _____

In questions 19–22, match each description to a type of evolutionary evidence in the key.

Key:

    a. biogeography
    b. fossil record
    c. comparative biochemistry
    d. comparative anatomy

19. Species change over time.

20. Forms of life are variously distributed.

21. A group of related species have homologous structures.

22. The same types of molecules are found in all living things.

Understanding Key Terms

adaptation 489
analogous structure 490
anthropoid 493
australopithecine 496
binomial name 493
biogeography 490
biological evolution 489
bipedal posture 494
chemical evolution 488
Cro-Magnon 500
culture 497
eukaryotic cell 489
evolutionary tree 494
fossil 490
fossil record 490
heterotroph 488
hominid 494
Homo erectus 498

Homo habilis 497
homologous structure 490
Homo sapiens 499
lineage 494
molecular clock 494
mosaic evolution 496
multiregional continuity hypothesis 499
natural selection 492
Neanderthal 500
out-of-Africa hypothesis 499
primate 493
prokaryotic cell 489
prosimian 493
protein-first hypothesis 488
protocell 488
RNA-first hypothesis 488
teleological 492

Match the key terms to these definitions.

a. _____ Process by which populations become adapted to their environment.

b. _____ Organism's modification in structure, function, or behavior suitable to the environment.

c. _____ Structure that is similar in two or more species because of common ancestry.

d. _____ Increase in the complexity of chemicals over time that could have led to the first cells.

e. _____ Any remains of an organism that have been preserved in the Earth's crust.

Online Learning Center

www.mhhe.com/maderhuman9

The Online Learning Center provides a wealth of information fully organized and integrated by chapter. You will find practice quizzes, interactive activities, labeling exercises, flashcards, and much more that will complement your learning and understanding of human biology.

Looking at Both Sides

Each day, the Internet, media, and other people present you with opposing viewpoints on a wide range of subjects. Your ability to develop an informed opinion on an issue, and talk to others about it, is extremely important.

To expand and enhance your knowledge of a highly relevant bioethical issue, visit the "Student Edition" of the Online Learning Center. Under "Course-Wide Content," select "Looking at Both Sides." Once there, you will be asked to complete activities that will increase your understanding of a current bioethical issue related to this chapter and allow you to defend your opinion.

CHAPTER *26*

Global Ecology

C H A P T E R   C O N C E P T S

26.1 The Scope of Ecology

- What are the levels of organization, from organism to biosphere? What is ecology?   506
- What is the differences between the niche and the habitat of an organism?   506
- Why are autotrophs called producers and heterotrophs called consumers? What are the different types of consumers in an ecosystem?   506
- What two processes characterize an ecosystem? Explain.   507

26.2 Energy Flow

- What type of diagram represents the various paths of energy flow in an ecosystem?   508–9
- What is the difference between a grazing food web and a detrital food web?   508–9
- What type of diagram represents a single path of energy flow in an ecosystem?   509
- What type of diagram illustrates that usable energy is lost in ecosystems?   509

26.3 Global Biogeochemical Cycles

- Chemical cycling in the biosphere may involve what three components?   510
- What are two examples of gaseous biogeochemical cycles? What is an example of a sedimentary biogeochemical cycle?   510
- How do water, phosphorus, nitrogen, and carbon cycle in the biosphere?   510–13
- What ecological problems are associated with each of the cycles? Explain.   510–13

26.4 Global Ecosystems

- Aquatic ecosystems are divided into what two general types? What are some examples of each type?   514
- What is ecological succession?   514
- What are the major terrestrial ecosystems of the world?   514–15
- How does primary productivity differ among aquatic and terrestrial ecosystems?   516

Jessica and Michael have just graduated from college and want to get married and start a family. First, they need jobs. Michael wants to work as a general contractor in housing construction. Jessica wants to work for a conservation organization that protects forests and other natural areas. After all, isn't the environment in danger? In the news, they both hear about extinction of species, contaminated seafood, pesticides and hormones in the food supply, and beaches closed because of sewage contamination, not to mention the hole in the ozone layer. Just as their desired jobs seem contradictory to each other, so are other choices they face that could affect the environment. Should they purchase a small, energy-efficient, economical car, or a large, expensive SUV? A small car makes more sense to them economically, but an SUV is certainly appealing. The extra space would be perfect for all their camping trips and then, of course, there is the "coolness" factor.

Many people struggle with the same issues as Jessica and Michael. How can a society based on resource consumption such as ours still keep the planet healthy? Michael thinks he has found a way. As a general contractor, he could build energy-efficient houses and encourage communities to preserve biodiversity by setting aside land for wildlife. His landscaping could utilize native plants, which would attract birds and butterflies.

What would happen if everyone made choices that helped preserve the environment? We could keep products longer, recycle as much as possible, and practice energy efficiency at home and for transportation. Then the environment would be much better off locally and globally.

26.1 The Scope of Ecology

The **biosphere** is where organisms are found, from the atmosphere above to the depths of the oceans below and everything in between. Organisms are members of **populations** that interact with one another within a **community.** An **ecosystem** is a *biotic* community plus the *abiotic* physical environment. **Ecology** is the study of the interactions of organisms with one another and with the physical environment.

A Biotic Community

The members of one species that live in an area and can potentially interact are a population; all the populations in an area make up a community. Within a community, each population has a habitat and a niche. The **habitat** of an organism is its place of residence—that is, where it can be found, such as under a log or at the bottom of a pond. Its **niche** is its role; how it gets its food and what eats it; how it interacts with other populations in the same community.

Autotrophs require only inorganic nutrients and an outside energy source to produce organic nutrients for their own use and for all the other members of a community. Therefore, they are called **producers**—they produce food (Fig. 26.1). Photosynthetic organisms produce most of the organic nutrients for the biosphere. Algae of all types possess chlorophyll and carry on photosynthesis in freshwater and marine habitats. Algae photosynthesize in aquatic ecosystems, and green plants are the dominant photosynthesizers on land.

Heterotrophs need a source of organic nutrients. They are the **consumers**—they consume food. **Herbivores** are animals that graze directly on plants or algae (Fig 26.1b). In terrestrial habitats, insects are small herbivores, while in aquatic habitats, protists, such as protozoans, play that role. **Carnivores** feed on other animals; birds that feed on insects are carnivores, and so are hawks that feed on birds (Fig. 26.1c). This example allows us to mention that there are primary consumers (e.g., insects), secondary consumers (e.g., insect-eating birds), and tertiary consumers (e.g., hawks). Sometimes tertiary consumers are called top predators. **Omnivores** are animals that feed both on plants and animals. As you most likely know, humans are omnivores.

Another group of organisms in an ecosystem remove and recycle dead bodies and the waste products of others. **Scavengers,** such as vultures and hyenas, clean up dead carcasses of larger animals. **Detritivores,** such as beetles, termites, and worms, consume litter, debris, and dung. **Decomposers,** such as bacteria and fungi (Fig. 26.1d), complete the breakdown of organic matter into organic nutrients that can be used by autotrophs. These organisms ensure the recycling of chemicals within an ecosystem, and therefore, their activities are only second in importance to producers.

 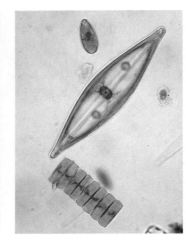

a. Producers

b. Herbivores

c. Carnivores

 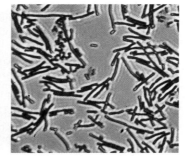

d. Decomposers

Figure 26.1 **Biotic components.**
a. Green plants and diatoms are producers. **b.** Giraffes and caterpillars are herbivores. **c.** An osprey and a praying mantis are carnivores. **d.** Mushrooms and some bacteria are decomposers.

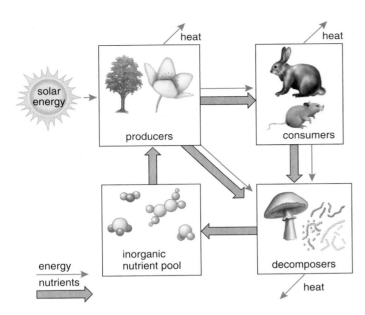

Figure 26.2   **Energy flow and chemical cycling.**
Chemicals cycle, but energy flows through an ecosystem. As energy transformations repeatedly occur, all the energy derived from the sun eventually dissipates as heat.

Energy Flow and Chemical Cycling

When we diagram the interactions of all the populations of an ecosystem, it is possible to illustrate that every ecosystem is characterized by two phenomena: energy flow and chemical cycling. Energy flow begins when producers absorb solar energy, and chemical cycling begins when producers take in inorganic nutrients from the physical environment. Thereafter, producers make organic nutrients (food) directly for themselves and indirectly for the other populations of the ecosystem. Energy flow occurs because as nutrients pass from one population to another, all the energy content is eventually converted to heat, which dissipates in the environment. Therefore, most ecosystems cannot exist without a continual supply of solar energy. Chemicals cycle when inorganic nutrients are returned to the producers from the atmosphere or soil (Fig. 26.2).

Only a portion of the organic nutrients made by autotrophs is passed on to heterotrophs because plants use organic molecules to fuel their own cellular respiration. Similarly, only a small percentage of nutrients taken in by heterotrophs is available to higher-level consumers. Figure 26.3 shows why. Some of the food eaten by a herbivore is never digested and is eliminated as feces. Metabolic wastes are excreted as urine. Of the assimilated energy, a large portion is utilized during cellular respiration and thereafter becomes heat. Only the remaining food, converted into increased body weight (or additional offspring), becomes available to carnivores.

The elimination of feces and urine by a heterotroph, and indeed the death of all organisms, does not mean that

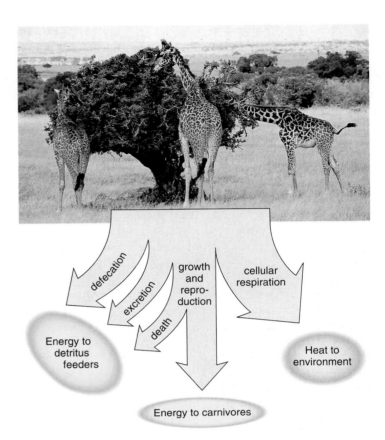

Figure 26.3   **Energy balances.**
Only about 10% of the food energy taken in by a herbivore is passed on to carnivores. A large portion goes to detritus feeders in the ways indicated, and another large portion is used by herbivores for cellular respiration.

substances are lost to an ecosystem. They are nutrients for the scavengers, detritivores, and decomposers. Since these organisms can be food for other heterotrophs of an ecosystem, the situation can get a bit complicated. Still, we can conceive that all the solar energy that enters an ecosystem eventually becomes heat. And this explains why ecosystems depend on a continual supply of solar energy.

The laws of thermodynamics explain why energy flows through an ecosystem. The first law states that energy cannot be created (or destroyed)—it can be changed to different types of energy. The second law states that, with every transformation, some energy is degraded into a less available form, such as heat. Because plants carry on cellular respiration, for example, only about 55% of the original energy absorbed by plants is available to an ecosystem. And, as organisms feed on one another, less and less of this 55% is available in a useable form.

Energy flows through the populations of an ecosystem, while chemicals cycle within and among ecosystems.

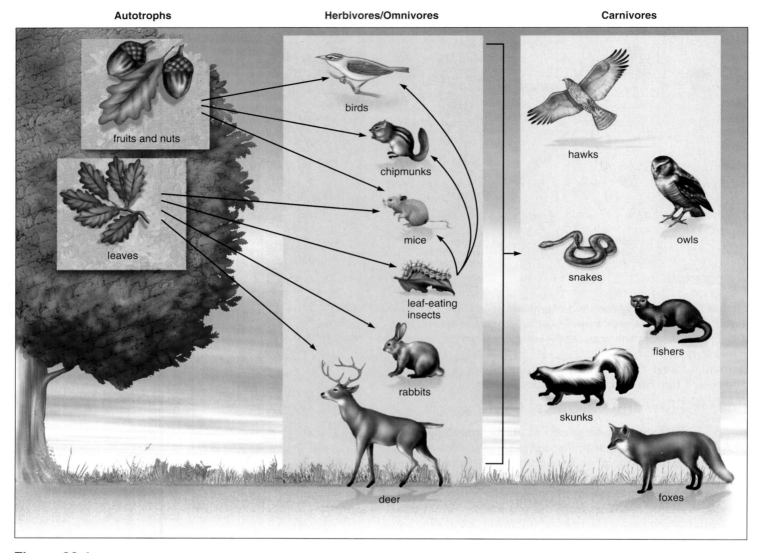

Autotrophs **Herbivores/Omnivores** **Carnivores**

Figure 26.4 **Grazing food webs.**
Food webs are descriptions of who eats whom. For example, birds, which feed on nuts, may be eaten by a hawk. Autotrophs, such as the tree, are producers (first trophic, or feeding, level), the first series of animals are primary consumers (second trophic level), and the next group of animals are secondary consumers (third trophic level).

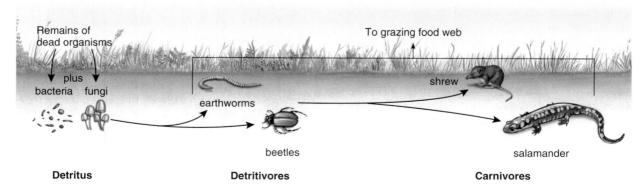

Detritus **Detritivores** **Carnivores**

Figure 26.5 **Detrital food web.**
The arrows illustrate possible detrital food chains, which begin with detritus. A large portion of remains worked on by decomposers are from the grazing food web illustrated in Figure 26.4. The organisms in the detrital food web are sometimes fed on by various animals in the grazing food web, as when robins feed on earthworms. Thus, the grazing food web and the detrital food web are connected to each other.

26.2 Energy Flow

The principles we have been discussing can now be applied to an actual ecosystem—a forest. The various interconnecting paths of energy flow are represented by a **food web,** describing who eats whom. Figure 26.4 is a **grazing food web** because it begins with an oak tree and grass. Caterpillars feed on oak leaves, while mice, rabbits, and deer feed on leaves and grass at or near the ground. Birds, chipmunks, and mice feed on seeds and nuts, but they are considered omnivores because they also feed on caterpillars. These herbivores and omnivores are then food for carnivores.

Figure 26.5 is a **detrital food web,** which begins with detritus. Detritus is food for the decomposers (bacteria and fungi) and for detritivores (i.e., earthworms and beetles) that are, in turn, eaten by shrews and salamanders. Because the members of detrital food webs may become food for aboveground carnivores, the detrital and grazing food webs are joined.

We naturally tend to think that aboveground plants, such as trees, are the largest storage form of organic matter and energy, but this is not necessarily the case. In this particular forest, the organic matter lying on the forest floor and mixed into the soil contains over twice as much energy as the leaves of living trees. Therefore, more energy in a forest may be funneling through the detrital food web than through the grazing food web.

Trophic Levels

You can see that Figure 26.4 would allow us to link organisms one to another in a straight line, according to who eats whom. Such diagrams that show a single path of energy flow are called **food chains.** For example, in the grazing food web, we could find this **grazing food chain:**

Leaves → caterpillars → tree birds → hawks

And in the detrital food web (Fig. 26.5), we could find this **detrital food chain:**

detritus → earthworms → shrews

A **trophic level** is composed of all the organisms that feed at a particular link in a food chain. In the grazing food web in Figure 26.4, going from left to right, the trees are primary producers (first trophic level), the first series of animals are primary consumers (second trophic level), and the next group of animals are secondary consumers (third trophic level).

Ecological Pyramids

The shortness of food chains can be attributed to the loss of energy between trophic levels. In general, only about 10% of the energy of one trophic level is available to the next trophic level. Therefore, if a herbivore population consumes

1,000 kg of plant material, only about 100 kg is converted to herbivore tissue, 10 kg to first-level carnivores, and 1 kg to second-level carnivores. The so-called 10% rule of thumb explains why few carnivores can be supported in a food web. The flow of energy with large losses between successive trophic levels is sometimes depicted as a **ecological pyramid** (Fig. 26.6).

A pyramid based on the number of organisms can be misleading because, for example, one tree can support many herbivores. Pyramids of biomass eliminate size as a factor because **biomass** is the number of organisms multiplied by their weight. You would certainly expect the biomass of the producers to be greater than the biomass of the herbivores and that of the herbivores to be greater than that of the carnivores. In aquatic ecosystems, such as lakes and open seas where algae are the only producers, the herbivores may have a greater biomass than the producers when you take their measurements. Why? The reason is that, over time, the algae reproduce rapidly, but they are also consumed at a high rate.

The flow of energy through the populations explains in large part the organization of an ecosystem depicted in food webs, food chains, and ecological pyramids.

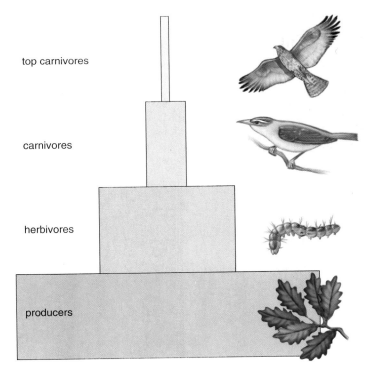

Figure 26.6 Ecological pyramid.
An ecological pyramid reflects the loss of energy from one trophic level to the next. A pyramid of energy, number of organisms, or biomass are all due to this loss of energy.

26.3 Global Biogeochemical Cycles

In this section, we will examine in more detail how chemicals cycle through ecosystems. The pathways by which chemicals circulate through ecosystems involve both living (biotic) and nonliving (geological) components; therefore, they are known as **biogeochemical cycles.** A biogeochemical cycle can be gaseous or sedimentary. In a gaseous cycle, such as the carbon and nitrogen cycles, the element returns to and is withdrawn from the atmosphere as a gas. The phosphorus cycle is a sedimentary cycle: The chemical is absorbed from the soil by plant roots, passed to heterotrophs, and eventually returned to the soil by decomposers.

Chemical cycling may involve these components:

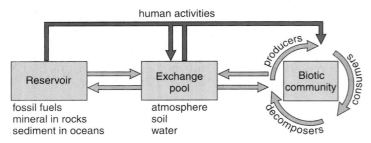

Human activities (purple arrows) remove chemicals from reservoirs and pools and make them available to the biotic community. In this way, human activities result in pollution because it upsets the normal balance of nutrients for producers in the environment.

A *reservoir* is a source normally unavailable to producers, such as carbon in calcium carbonate shells on ocean bottoms. An *exchange pool* is a source from which organisms do generally take chemicals, such as the atmosphere or soil. Chemicals move along food chains in a *biotic community*, perhaps never entering a pool.

The Water Cycle

In the **water (hydrologic) cycle,** fresh water is distilled from salt water (Fig. 26.7). The sun's rays cause fresh water to evaporate from sea water, leaving the salts behind. Water also evaporates from the land. Water vapor rises into the atmosphere, where it forms clouds as it cools and condenses.

When rain or snow falls, some of the water sinks into the ground and depressions become lakes and ponds. Flowing water occurs in rivers and streams. **Aquifers** are rock layers that contain groundwater and release it in wells or springs. Eventually, all water flows into the oceans.

Human Activities

In some arid areas and southern Florida, withdrawals from aquifers exceed any possibility of recharge. This is called "groundwater mining." The groundwater is dropping, and residents may run out of groundwater within a few years. Fresh water makes up only about 3% of the world's water, it is a renewable resource because a new supply is always being produced by rain and snow. However, it is possible to run out of fresh water when the available supply is not adequate and/or is polluted.

In the water cycle, fresh water evaporates from bodies of water. Water that falls on land enters the ground, surface waters, or aquifers. Eventually, all water returns to the oceans.

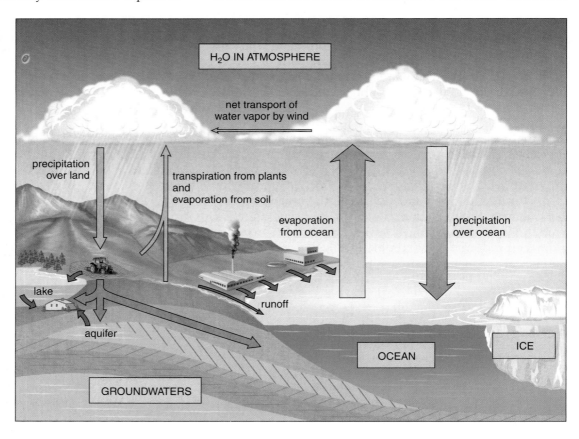

Figure 26.7   The water (hydrologic) cycle.
Purple arrows represent human activities; gray arrows represent natural events.

The Phosphorus Cycle

By following the outer arrows in Figure 26.8, you can verify that phosphate moves from the land to the oceans and then back to the land again. On land, the very slow weathering of rocks makes phosphate ions (PO_4^{3-} and HPO_4^{2-}) available to producers, which take up phosphate from the soil. Producers use phosphate in a variety of molecules, such as phospholipids and nucleotides.

Animals eat producers and incorporate some of the phosphate into teeth, bones, and shells that take many years to decompose. Death and decay of all organisms and also decomposition of animal wastes do, however, make phosphate ions available to producers once again. Because the available amount of phosphate is already being utilized within food chains, phosphate is usually a limiting inorganic nutrient for plants—that is, the lack of it limits their growth.

When phosphate runs off into aquatic ecosystems, algae, the producers in aquatic habitats, acquire phosphate from the water. This phosphate is passed through aquatic food chains but some of it becomes trapped in sediments. Phosphate in marine sediments does not become available to producers on land again until a geological upheaval exposes sedimentary rocks to weathering once more.

Phosphorus does not enter the atmosphere; therefore, the phosphorus cycle is called a sedimentary cycle.

Human Activities

A **transfer rate** is the amount of a nutrient that moves from one component of the environment to another over time. The width of the arrows in Figure 26.8 indicates the transfer rate for phosphate. Human beings boost the transfer rate of phosphate by mining phosphate ores and using them to make fertilizers, animal feed supplements, and detergents. Fertilizers usually contain three basic ingredients: nitrogen, phosphorus, and potassium. Most laundry detergents contain approximately 35% to 75% sodium triphosphate. The amount of phosphate in animal feed varies.

Animal wastes from livestock feedlots, fertilizers from lawns and cropland, and untreated and treated sewage discharged from cities all add excess phosphate to nearby sources of fresh waters. The end result is **cultural eutrophication** (overenrichment), which can lead to an algal bloom, apparent when green scum floats on the water. When the algae die off, the enlarged decomposer population use up all available oxygen during cellular respiration. The result is a massive fish kill.

In the phosphorus cycle, weathering makes phosphate available to the biotic community from a reservoir (rocks) at a very slow rate. Therefore, phosphate is a limiting nutrient in ecosystems.

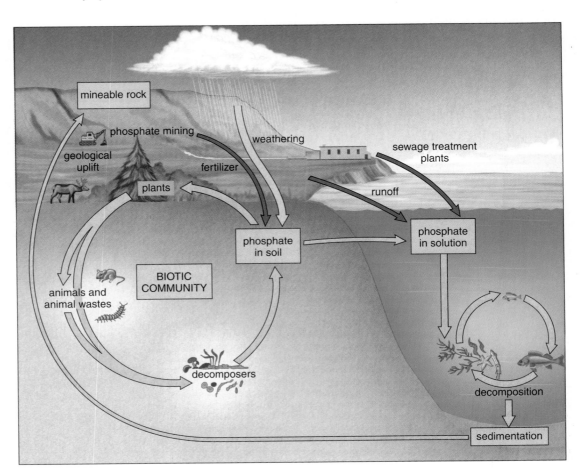

Figure 26.8 **The phosphorus cycle.**
Purple arrows represent human activities; gray arrows represent natural events.

The Nitrogen Cycle

Nitrogen gas (N_2) makes up about 78% of the atmosphere, but plants cannot make use of nitrogen gas. Therefore, nitrogen is also a limiting inorganic nutrient for plants.

Ammonium (NH_4^+) Formation and Use

In the nitrogen cycle, **nitrogen fixation** occurs when nitrogen gas (N_2) is converted to ammonium (NH_4^+), a form plants can use (Fig. 26.9). Some cyanobacteria in aquatic ecosystems and some free-living bacteria in soil are able to fix atmospheric nitrogen in this way. Other nitrogen-fixing bacteria live in nodules on the roots of legumes, such as beans, peas, and clover. They make organic compounds containing nitrogen available to the host plants so that the plant can form proteins and nucleic acids.

Nitrate (NO_3^-) Formation and Use

Plants can also use nitrates (NO_3^-) as a source of nitrogen. The production of nitrates during the nitrogen cycle is called **nitrification.** Nitrification can occur in two ways: (1) Nitrogen gas (N_2) is converted to nitrate (NO_3^-) in the atmosphere when cosmic radiation, meteor trails, and lightning provide the high energy needed for nitrogen to react with oxygen. (2) Ammonium (NH_4^+) in the soil from various sources, including decomposition of organisms and animal wastes, is converted to nitrate by soil bacteria in a two-step process. First, nitrite-producing bacteria convert ammonium to nitrite (NO_2^-), and then nitrate-producing bacteria convert nitrite to nitrate. Notice that the subcycle involving the biotic community does not depend on the presence of nitrogen gas at all.

Formation of Nitrate from Nitrogen Gas

Denitrification is the conversion of nitrate back to nitrogen gas, which enters the atmosphere. Denitrifying bacteria living in the anaerobic mud of lakes, bogs, and estuaries carry out this process as a part of their own metabolism. In the nitrogen cycle, denitrification would counterbalance nitrogen fixation except for human activities.

Human Activities

Human activities significantly alter the transfer rates in the nitrogen cycle by producing fertilizers from N_2—in fact, they nearly double the fixation rate. Fertilizer, which also contains phosphate, runs off into lakes and rivers and results in an overgrowth of algae and rooted aquatic plants. As discussed on page 511, the end result is cultural eutrophication (over-enrichment), which can lead to an algal boom. When the algae die off, enlarged decomposer populations use up all the oxygen in the water, and the result is a massive fish kill.

Fertilizer use also results in the release of nitrous oxide (N_2O), a greenhouse gas that contributes to global warming and depletion of the ozone shield. The ozone shield is a layer of ozone (O_3) that absorbs much of the ultraviolet rays of the sun before they strike the Earth.

In the nitrogen cycle, nitrogen-fixing bacteria (in nodules and in the soil) convert nitrogen gas to ammonium, which plants can use; nitrifying bacteria convert ammonium to nitrate; denitrifying bacteria convert nitrate back to nitrogen gas.

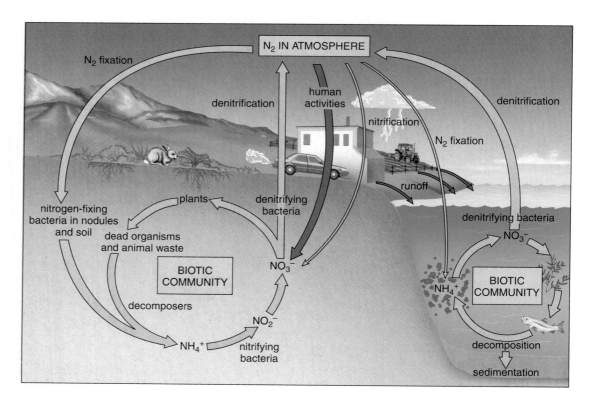

Figure 26.9   The nitrogen cycle.

Purple arrows represent human activities; gray arrows represent natural events.

The Carbon Cycle

The carbon dioxide in the atmosphere is the exchange pool for the carbon cycle. In this cycle, organisms in both terrestrial and aquatic ecosystems exchange carbon dioxide with the atmosphere (Fig. 26.10). On land, plants take up carbon dioxide from the air, and through photosynthesis, they incorporate carbon into nutrients that are used by autotrophs and heterotrophs alike. When organisms, including plants, respire, carbon is returned to the atmosphere as carbon dioxide. Therefore, carbon dioxide recycles to plants by way of the atmosphere.

In aquatic ecosystems, the exchange of carbon dioxide with the atmosphere is indirect. Carbon dioxide from the air combines with water to produce bicarbonate ion (HCO_3^-), a source of carbon for algae that produce food for themselves and for heterotrophs. Similarly, when aquatic organisms respire, the carbon dioxide they give off becomes bicarbonate ion. The amount of bicarbonate in the water is in equilibrium with the amount of carbon dioxide in the air.

Reservoirs Hold Carbon

Living and dead organisms contain organic carbon and serve as one of the reservoirs for the carbon cycle. The world's biotic components, particularly trees, contain 800 billion tons of organic carbon, and an additional 1,000–3,000 billion metric tons are estimated to be held in the remains of plants and animals in the soil. Before decomposition can occur, some of these remains are subjected to physical processes that transform them into coal, oil, and natural gas. We call these materials the **fossil fuels.** Most of the fossil fuels were formed during the Carboniferous period, 286–360 MYA, when an exceptionally large amount of organic matter was buried before decomposing. Another reservoir is the inorganic carbonate that accumulates in limestone and in calcium carbonate shells. Many marine organisms have calcium carbonate shells that remain in bottom sediments long after the organisms have died. Geological forces change these sediments into limestone.

Human Activities

The transfer rates of carbon dioxide due to photosynthesis and cellular respiration, which includes the work of decomposers, are just about even. However, more carbon dioxide is being deposited in the atmosphere than is being removed. This increase is largely due to the burning of fossil fuels and the destruction of forests to make way for farmland and pasture. When we do away with forests, we reduce a reservoir and also the very organisms that take up excess carbon dioxide. Today, the amount of carbon dioxide released into the atmosphere is about twice the amount that remains in the atmosphere. It's believed that most of this dissolves in the ocean.

The increased amount of carbon dioxide (and other gases) in the atmosphere is causing a rise in temperature called **global warming.** These gases allow the sun's rays to pass through, but they absorb and radiate heat back to the Earth, a phenomenon called the **greenhouse effect.** Global warming is expected to cause dire consequences, as discussed in Chapter 27.

The atmosphere is the exchange pool of the carbon cycle. In this cycle, photosynthesis removes, but cellular respiration returns, carbon dioxide to the atmosphere. Forests and dead organisms are carbon reservoirs, as is the ocean.

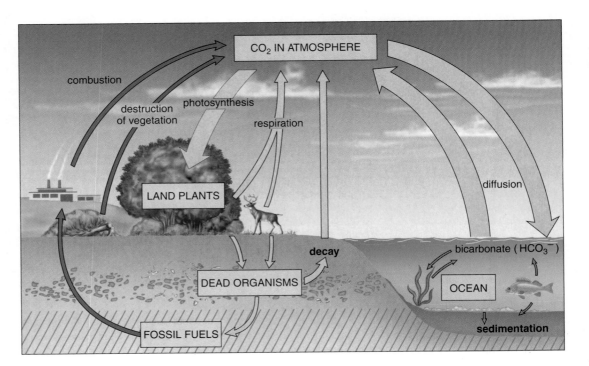

Figure 26.10 **The carbon cycle.**
Purple arrows represent human activities; gray arrows represent natural events.

26.4 Global Ecosystems

The biogeochemical cycles involve all the ecosystems of the world, both aquatic and terrestrial.

Aquatic Ecosystems

Aquatic ecosystems are divided into salt water (marine) and fresh water. Lakes, ponds, rivers, and streams are freshwater ecosystems. Marine ecosystems include the seashores, oceans, coral reefs, and estuaries. The oceans are the most extensive of all ecosystems. They cover nearly three quarters of the Earth. Figure 26.11 features some of the major aquatic ecosystems.

Terrestrial Ecosystems

One of the outstanding characteristics of natural ecosystems is their continuous change. This dynamic nature of a ecosystem is dramatically illustrated by **ecological succession;** a sequential change in the species. A pond can fill in over time and the vegetation changes until trees grow there. An abandoned field changes slowly to become more like the surrounding natural area. The two types of succession are called primary and secondary succession.

Primary succession begins on bare rock. The rock is weathered by abiotic forces, such as wind, rain, and freezing, and then attacked by lichens and mosses. The rock slowly breaks down, becoming soil, permitting grasses, then shrubs and trees, to grow. Secondary succession begins following a disturbance, such as a farm, a fire, or a lumbering operation. There is an herbaceous stage, then shrubs and trees appear. Many factors, including temperature and rainfall, influence which of these ecosystems develop (Fig. 26.12):

Forests—dominated by trees

The three major categories of forests include tropical rain forests, taiga (coniferous forests), and temperate deciduous forests.

Grasslands—dominated by grasses

The two types of grasslands are tropical grasslands (savanna) and temperate grassland (prairie).

Deserts—determined by lack of available moisture

The two desert-like ecosystems are tundra, with little available moisture and very cold temperatures; and deserts, with little moisture and usually, very hot, dry portions of an annual cycle.

Figure 26.11   **A sampling of major aquatic ecosystems.**
Aquatic ecosystems are divided into those that have salt water and those that have fresh water. Among saltwater ecosystems, the open ocean (**a**) does not have nearly the number and variety of species as do coral reefs (**b**) and marshes (**c**). Freshwater ecosystems include streams and rivers (**d**) and also lakes and ponds. We are largely dependent on fresh water for our daily supply of water.

Figure 26.12   The major terrestrial ecosystems.
The tundra is the most northern of the ecosystems and has the lowest average temperature with minimal to moderate rainfall. The taiga, a coniferous forest that encircles the globe, also has a low average temperature, but moderate rainfall. Temperate forests have moderate temperatures and occur where rainfall is moderate, yet sufficient to support trees. A tropical grassland (savanna) has high temperatures and moderate/seasonal rainfall. A temperate grassland (prairie) has low to high temperatures, with low annual rainfall. Deserts have changeable temperatures with minimal rainfall. Tropical rain forests, which generally occur near the equator, have a high average temperature and the greatest amount of rainfall.

Primary Productivity

One way to compare global ecosystems is based on primary productivity. **Primary productivity** is the rate at which the producers in an ecosystem capture and store energy within organic nutrients over a certain period of time. Temperature and rainfall and, secondarily, the nature of the soil, determine the type of vegetation and the primary productivity of an ecosystem. In terrestrial ecosystems, primary productivity is generally lowest at the poles, where the environment for a tundra occurs, and highest at the equator, where tropical rain forests occur (Fig. 26.13). The high productivity of tropical rain forests provides varied niches and much food for consumers. The number and variety of species in tropical rain forests is the highest of all the terrestrial ecosystems. Therefore, conservationists are particularly interested in preserving as much of this ecosystem as possible.

The primary productivity of aquatic ecosystems depends largely on the availability of inorganic nutrients. Estuaries, swamps, and marshes are rich in organic nutrients, and this is where we find a large number of varied species, particularly in the early stages of their development, before they venture forth into the ocean. Therefore, any of these coastal regions are in great need of preservation. The open ocean has a productivity somewhere between that of a desert and the tundra because of the lack of a concentrated supply of inorganic nutrients. Coral reefs exist near the coasts in warm tropical waters, where currents and waves bring nutrients and where sunlight penetrates to the ocean floor. Corals are short, squat, sedentary animals that use their tentacles to remove organic debris from ocean currents. Also, a mutualistic photosynthetic protist lives among their tissues. The protists use the energy of the sun and inorganic nutrients to produce organic food for themselves and the coral. The coral makes its digestive wastes available to the protist. This tight recycling of nutrients contributes to the high primary productivity of coral reefs. Coral reefs are areas of remarkable biological abundance, equivalent to that of tropical rain forests.

Human Impact

Humans have transformed vast areas of many wetlands and ecosystems into farmland, cities, highways, and other developments. Through our resource use and release of pollutants, we have now become an agent of global importance. Yet we still depend on the biodiversity that exists in the Earth's ecosystems and on the interactions of other organisms within the biosphere. These interactions still influence climate, patterns of nutrient cycling and waste processing, and basic biological productivity. The Earth's biotic diversity also provides enjoyment and inspiration to millions of people, who spend billions of dollars to visit coral reefs, deserts, rain forests, and even the Arctic tundra. Unfortunately, as we shall see in Chapter 27, many of the Earth's ecosystems may not survive in their present form for our descendants' benefit. Although most of us value Earth's diversity, we are causing patterns of global change that are adversely affecting every ecosystem on the planet.

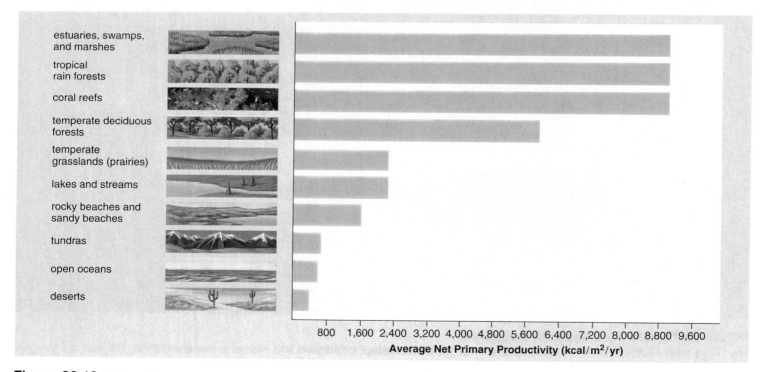

Figure 26.13   Primary productivity.
With few exceptions, the primary productivity of ecosystems is related to the number of different species in the ecosystem. In which terrestrial ecosystems would you expect to find the largest variety of species? In which aquatic ecosystems?

Bioethical Focus

Oil Drilling in the Arctic

The Arctic National Wildlife Refuge (ANWR), established by an act of Congress in 1980, covers a total of 19 million acres of Alaska. ANWR is home to a variety of wildlife, such as caribou, migratory birds, grizzly and polar bears, wolves, and musk oxen (Fig. 26A). In the summer, the adjacent coastal waters host a variety of marine mammals, such as bowhead and gray whales. ANWR also contains substantial oil reserves. These aspects of ANWR have become the focus of much debate, in which the value of a pristine wilderness is weighed against the value of its energy resources.

When ANWR was initially established, its coastal plain area, which covers 1.5 million acres, was designated off-limits to oil drilling without Congressional authorization. No oil production has yet been permitted in the coastal plain. However, it has been proposed that 2,000 acres of the coastal plain be developed for oil drilling. This action could, according to one estimate, yield up to a million barrels of oil per day over the next 20 years. Supporters of this plan note that it would affect only a small proportion of the total area of ANWR. By using the newest drilling methods, removing the oil and disposing of wastes would cause much less disruption to the surface environment compared with techniques used in the past. If drilling in the ANWR coastal plain were permitted, Alaskans would benefit by the creation of new jobs and a boost to the state economy. Advocates also say that this approach would reduce our dependence on foreign oil, and help to buffer us against rising oil prices.

Those who are opposed to drilling in ANWR believe that we should instead focus on reducing our need for energy by making better use of existing resources. For example, it has been suggested that a modest increase in vehicle fuel efficiency would save even more oil than would be gained by drilling in the ANWR coastal plain. Opponents point to the fact that the United States uses approximately 20 million barrels of oil per day, so even if the yield from coastal plain drilling met with advocates' expectations, its contribution to our oil needs would be relatively minor. They suggest that we should put more effort into the development of alternative energy sources, especially those which are renewable. By so doing, we would protect ANWR's wildlife and the rest of our environment at the same time. Furthermore, those who are against ANWR development counter the implication that only a small part of the coastal plain would be affected, because the areas proposed for drilling are fairly scattered. Assembling the infrastructure needed to connect all the potential drilling sites would result in the development of more than 2,000 acres of land.

Decide Your Opinion

1. In the United States, Republicans are generally in favor of oil drilling in ANWR, and Democrats are generally opposed. Should party politics play a role in our decision making?
2. Do you agree or disagree with oil drilling in ANWR? On what basis would you go about making a decision on this issue?
3. According to Figure 26.13, the tundra ecosystem represented in ANWR would have a limited variety of species, compared with, say, a tropical rain forest. Does this influence your decision-making process? Why or why not?

Figure 26A   The terrain and wildlife of the Arctic National Wildlife Refuge.

Summarizing the Concepts

26.1 The Scope of Ecology

Organisms are members of biotic populations that interact in a community. Populations also interact with the abiotic physical environment, and the result is an ecosystem. Ecology is the study of the interactions of organisms with each other and with the physical environment.

In a community, photosynthesizers transform solar energy into food (organic nutrients) for themselves and all heterotrophs. For example, herbivores feed on plants or algae, and carnivores feed on herbivores. Feces, urine, and dead bodies become food for decomposers.

Ecosystems are characterized by energy flow and chemical cycling. Energy flows because as one population feeds on another, energy dissipates as heat. Eventually, all the solar energy that enters an ecosystem is converted to heat, and thus ecosystems require a continual supply of solar energy. Chemicals are not lost from the biosphere as energy is. They recycle within and between ecosystems. Decomposers return inorganic nutrients to autotrophs, and other portions are imported or exported between ecosystems in global cycles.

26.2 Energy Flow

Ecosystems contain food webs, and a diagram of a food web shows how the various organisms are connected by eating relationships. Grazing food chains begin with vegetation that is fed on by a herbivore, which becomes food for a carnivore, and so forth. In detrital food chains, a decomposer acts on organic material in the soil, and when it is fed on by a carnivore, the two food webs are joined. A trophic level is all the organisms that feed at a particular link in a food chain.

Ecological pyramids show trophic levels stacked one on top of the other like building blocks. Generally, they show that biomass and energy content decrease from one trophic level to the next because of a loss of energy. Most pyramids pertain to grazing food webs and largely ignore the detrital food web portion of an ecosystem.

26.3 Global Biogeochemical Cycles

Biogeochemical cycles contain reservoirs, such as fossil fuels, sediments, and rocks, that contain inorganic nutrients available only on a limited basis to living things. Exchange pools are areas such as the atmosphere, soil, and water, which are ready sources of inorganic nutrients for living things. Nutrients cycle among the biotic components of an ecosystem.

In the water cycle, water that evaporates over the ocean is not compensated for by rainfall. Water also evaporates from terrestrial ecosystems. Rainfall over land results in bodies of fresh water plus groundwater, including aquifers. Eventually, all water returns to the oceans.

In the phosphorus cycle, the reservoir is sediments at the bottom of the ocean. Only upheavals make sedimentary rock available on land for slow release of phosphorus to plants by weathering.

In the nitrogen cycle, the reservoir is the atmosphere, and nitrogen gas (N_2) must be converted to a form usable by producers.

Nitrogen-fixing bacteria in root nodules make organic nitrogen available to plants. Nitrogen-fixing bacteria in the soil produce ammonium (NH_4^+), which is taken up by plants along with nitrate. Other bacteria active in the nitrogen cycle are the nitrifying bacteria, which convert ammonium to nitrate (NO_3^-), and the denitrifying bacteria, which reconvert nitrate to N_2.

In the carbon cycle, the reservoir is organic matter, calcium carbonate shells, and limestone. The exchange pool is the atmosphere: Photosynthesis removes carbon dioxide, and respiration and combustion add carbon dioxide to the atmosphere.

26.4 Global Ecosystems

Aquatic ecosystems are either salt water (e.g., oceans, coral reefs) or fresh water (e.g., rivers and streams; lakes and ponds). Oceans cover three quarters of the Earth.

The process of succession from either bare rock or disturbed land results in a climax community, which does not necessarily have to be of the same type at a particular locale. Still, temperature and rainfall influence to a great degree the type of vegetation found in any particular ecosystem. The seven major ecosystems are: tropical rain forest, taiga (coniferous forest), temperate deciduous forest, tropical grassland (savanna), grassland (prairie), tundra, and desert.

The major ecosystems of the world differ in productivity, and therefore, in the variety of species they contain. Marshes, estuaries, and coral reefs have a large number of varied species, and so do tropical rain forests. Therefore, conservationists are particularly interested in conserving them.

Studying the Concepts

1. Distinguish between population, community, ecosystem, biosphere, and ecology. 506
2. What are the habitat and the niche of an organism? 506
3. Name four different types of consumers found in natural ecosystems. 506
4. Tell why energy must flow in an ecosystem, but chemicals cycle. 507
5. Describe two types of food webs and two types of food chains found in terrestrial ecosystems. Which of these typically moves more energy through an ecosystem? 508–9
6. What is a trophic level? An ecological pyramid? 509
7. Give examples of reservoirs and exchange pools in biogeochemical cycles. Which of these is less accessible to biotic communities? 510
8. Draw a diagram to illustrate the water, phosphorus, nitrogen, and carbon biogeochemical cycles, and include in your diagram the manner in which human activities can change a particular transfer rate. 510–13
9. What are the two main types of aquatic ecosystems? Give examples of each type. 514
10. Describe the process of succession. What are the major terrestrial ecosystems? 514–15
11. Which of the aquatic ecosystems and terrestrial ecosystems have the greatest variety of species? 516

Thinking Critically About the Concepts

Refer to the opening vignette on page 505, and then answer these questions.

1. Give some examples to substantiate that our society is based on resource consumption.
2. The evening news frequently tells us whether the GNP (gross national product) has gone up or down. What is the GNP based on?
3. How would it be possible to get young people to think about the environment in addition to the economy?

Testing Your Knowledge of the Concepts

Choose the best answer for each question.

In questions 1–4, match each description to a population in the key.

Key:

   a. producer
   b. consumer
   c. decomposer
   d. herbivore

1. Heterotroph that feeds on plant material.

2. Autotroph that manufactures organic nutrients.

3. Any type of heterotroph that feeds on plant material or on other animals.

4. Heterotroph that breaks down detritus as a source of nutrients.

5. Of the total amount of energy that passes from one trophic level to another, about 10% is
   a. respired and becomes heat.
   b. passed out as feces or urine.
   c. stored as body tissue.
   d. recycled to autotrophs.
   e. All of these are correct.

6. Compare this food chain:
      algae → water fleas → fish → green herons
   with this food chain:
      trees → tent caterpillars → red-eyed vireos → hawks

   Both water fleas and tent caterpillars are
   a. carnivores.
   b. primary consumers.
   c. detritus feeders.
   d. present in grazing and detrital food webs.
   e. Both a and b are correct.

7. Which of the following contribute(s) to the carbon cycle?
   a. respiration
   b. photosynthesis
   c. fossil fuel combustion
   d. decomposition of dead organisms
   e. All of these are correct.

8. How do plants contribute to the carbon cycle?
   a. When plants respire, they release CO_2 into the atmosphere.
   b. When plants photosynthesize, they consume CO_2 from the atmosphere.
   c. When plants photosynthesize, they provide oxygen to heterotrophs.
   d. When plants emigrate, they transport carbon molecules between ecosystems.
   e. Both b and c are correct.

9. How do nitrogen-fixing bacteria in the soil contribute to the nitrogen cycle?
   a. They return nitrogen to the atmosphere.
   b. They change ammonium to nitrate.
   c. They change nitrogen to ammonium.
   d. They withdraw nitrate from the soil.
   e. They decompose and return nitrogen to autotrophs.

10. In what way are decomposers like producers?
   a. Either may be the first member of a grazing or a detrital food chain.
   b. Both produce oxygen for other forms of life.
   c. Both require nutrient molecules and energy.
   d. Both are present only on land.
   e. Both produce organic nutrients for other members of ecosystems.

11. Choose the statement that is true concerning this food chain:
      grass → rabbits → snakes → hawks
   a. Each predator population has a greater biomass than its prey population.
   b. Each prey population has a greater biomass than its predator population.
   c. Each population is omnivorous.
   d. Each population returns inorganic nutrients and energy to the producer.
   e. Both a and c are correct.

12. Label the following diagram of a ecosystem.

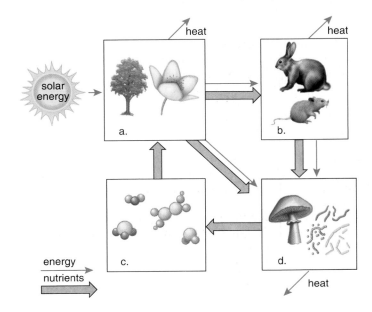

13. On the following diagram, label the trophic levels using two of these terms for each level: producers, top carnivores, secondary consumers, autotrophs, primary consumers, tertiary consumers, carnivores, herbivores.

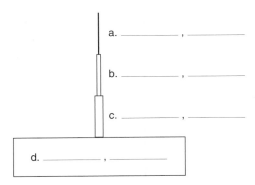

a. _____ , _____

b. _____ , _____

c. _____ , _____

d. _____ , _____

14. Why are ecosystems dependent on a continual supply of solar energy?
    a. Carnivores have a greater biomass than producers.
    b. Decomposers process the greatest amount of energy in an ecosystem.
    c. Energy transformation results in a loss of usable energy to the environment.
    d. Energy cycles within and between ecosystems.

15. Nutrient cycles always involve
    a. rocks as a reservoir.
    b. movement of nutrients through the biotic community.
    c. the atmosphere as an exchange pool.
    d. loss of the nutrients from the biosphere.

For questions 16–19, match each human activity with one or more of the cycles listed in the key. More than one answer can be used, and answers can be used more than once.

Key:

    a. water cycle
    b. carbon cycle
    c. nitrogen cycle
    d. phosphorus cycle
    e. none of these
    f. all of these

16. Drive cars.

17. Use fertilizers.

18. Take showers.

19. Grow crops.

For questions 20–24, match each characteristic to the cycles listed in the key for questions 16–19. More than one answer can be used, and answers can be used more than once.

20. Occurs on land but not in the water.

21. Can occur without the participation of humans.

22. Always involves the participation of decomposers.

23. The atmosphere is involved.

24. Rocks are the reservoir in this cycle.

Understanding Key Terms

aquifer 510
autotroph 506
biogeochemical cycle 510
biomass 509
biosphere 506
carnivore 506
community 506
consumer 506
cultural eutrophication 511
decomposer 506
denitrification 512
detrital food chain 509
detrital food web 509
detrivore 506
ecological pyramid 509
ecological succession 514
ecology 506
ecosystem 506
food chain 509
food web 509

fossil fuel 513
global warming 513
grazing food chain 509
grazing food web 509
greenhouse effect 513
habitat 506
herbivore 506
heterotroph 506
niche 506
nitrification 512
nitrogen fixation 512
omnivore 506
population 506
primary productivity 516
producer 506
scavanger 506
transfer rate 511
trophic level 509
water (hydrologic) cycle 510

Match the key terms to these definitions.

a. _____ Pictorial graph of the trophic levels in a food web—from the producers to the final consumers.

b. _____ Sequential change in the relative dominance of species within an ecosystem; can begin either on bare rock or where soil already exists.

c. _____ Remains of once-living organisms that are burned to release energy, such as coal, oil, and natural gas.

d. _____ Process by which atmospheric nitrogen gas is changed to forms that plants can use.

e. _____ Photosynthetic organism at the start of a grazing food chain that makes its own food.

Online Learning Center

www.mhhe.com/maderhuman9

The Online Learning Center provides a wealth of information fully organized and integrated by chapter. You will find practice quizzes, interactive activities, labeling exercises, flashcards, and much more that will complement your learning and understanding of human biology.

Looking at Both Sides

Each day, the Internet, media, and other people present you with opposing viewpoints on a wide range of subjects. Your ability to develop an informed opinion on an issue, and talk to others about it, is extremely important.

To expand and enhance your knowledge of a highly relevant bioethical issue, visit the "Student Edition" of the Online Learning Center. Under "Course-Wide Content," select "Looking at Both Sides." Once there, you will be asked to complete activities that will increase your understanding of a current bioethical issue related to this chapter and allow you to defend your opinion.

CHAPTER 27

Human Population, Planetary Resources, and Conservation

C H A P T E R   C O N C E P T S

27.1 Human Population Growth
- Are the more-developed countries or the less-developed countries now undergoing exponential population growth?   522–23

27.2 Human Use of Resources and Pollution
- What five resources are maximally utilized by humans?   524
- Which ecosystems suffer the most due to human habitation?   524–25
- How do humans increase the supply of fresh water, and what are the consequences of doing so?   525–26
- What farming methods are in use today, and what are the possible environmental consequences?   526–27
- Why is it better for humans to use renewable rather than nonrenewable sources?   528–29
- The consumption of mineral resources has what environmental consequences?   530
- What hazardous wastes are present in the environment?   530

27.3 Biodiversity
- What are the chief causes of species extinctions?   531–32
- What are the indirect and direct benefits of preserving wildlife?   533–35

27.4 Working Toward a Sustainable Society
- What are the characteristics of today's unsustainable society?   537
- What are the characteristics of a sustainable society?   537–38

James surveyed his ripened fields of corn and was well pleased. As far as the eye could see, the corn was ready for harvesting, and he expected a more bountiful crop and a better profit than he'd had the year before. His heavy farm equipment, needed to quickly bring in the harvest, stood ready for the next day's work. He was grateful that the bank had loaned him the money for additives to apply to his fields.

Even so, James's mind wandered to the fact that his well now contained traces of the pesticides and fertilizers he had so generously used. His wife was expecting, and he sure hoped the baby wouldn't suffer the "blue baby" syndrome he had heard about in other farming families. They said it happens when well water contains nitrates from fertilizers, and the nitrates combine with hemoglobin in the blood. Perhaps he should switch to organic farming like his neighbor Bob. Crop yields were lower, but so were operating costs. Bob said that he required about two-fifths as much fossil fuel to produce one dollar's worth of crop. Using crop rotation instead of fertilizers was cheaper and lessened the need for heavy equipment, which causes soil erosion. Bob was going to use drip irrigation next year and expected even less soil erosion.

Yes, James thought, I'd better get the lowdown from Bob this winter. After all, I want my farm to still be productive for my children one day.

27.1 Human Population Growth

The world's human population has risen steadily (Fig. 27.1). Prior to 1750, the growth of the human population was relatively slow, but as more reproducing individuals were added, growth increased, until the curve began to slope steeply upward, indicating that the population was undergoing **exponential growth.** The number of people added annually to the world population peaked at about 87 million around 1990, and currently it is a little over 79 million per year. That is roughly the population of Germany, the Philippines, or Vietnam.

The **growth rate** of a population is determined by considering the difference between the number of persons born per year (birthrate, or natality) and the number who die per year (death rate, or mortality). It is customary to record these rates per 1,000 persons. For example, the world at the present time has a birthrate of 22 per 1,000 per year, but it has a death rate of 9 per 1,000 per year. This means that the world's population growth, or simply its growth rate, is

$$\frac{22 - 9}{1,000} = \frac{13}{1,000} = 0.013 \times 100 = 1.3\%$$

(Notice that while the birthrate and death rate are expressed in terms of 1,000 persons, the growth rate is expressed per 100 persons, or as a percentage.) After 1750, the world population growth rate steadily increased, until it peaked at 2% in 1965. It has since fallen to its present 1.3%. Yet, the world population is still steadily growing because of its past exponential growth.

In the wild, exponential growth indicates that a population is enjoying its **biotic potential**—that is, the maximum growth rate under ideal conditions. Growth begins to decline because of **environmental resistance,** which includes limiting factors such as food and space. Finally, the population levels off at the carrying capacity. The **carrying capacity** is the maximum population that the environment can support for an indefinite period. The carrying capacity of the Earth for humans has not been determined. Some authorities think the Earth is potentially capable of supporting 50–100 billion people. Others think we already have more humans than the Earth can adequately support.

The MDCs Versus the LDCs

The countries of the world today can be divided into two groups. The *more-developed countries* (MDCs), typified by countries in North America and Europe, are those in which population growth is modest and the people enjoy a good standard of living. The *less-developed countries* (LDCs), typified by some countries in Asia, Africa, and Latin America, are those in which population growth is dramatic and the majority of people live in poverty.

The MDCs

The MDCs did not always have low population increases. Between 1850 and 1950, they doubled their populations, largely because of a decline in the death rate due to development of modern medicine and improvements in public health and socioeconomic conditions. The decline in the death rate was followed shortly thereafter by a decline in the birthrate, so that populations in the MDCs have experienced only modest growth since 1950.

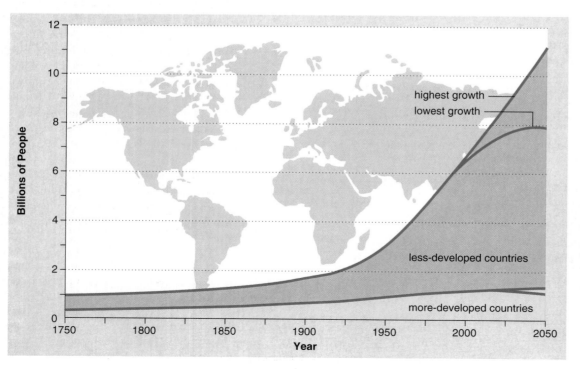

Figure 27.1 **Human population growth.**
It is predicted that the world's population size may level off at 8 billion or increase to more than 11 billion by 2050, depending on the speed with which the growth rate declines.
Source: Population Reference Bureau and United Nations, World Population Projections to 2100 (1998).

The growth rate for the MDCs as a whole is now about 0.1%, but several are not growing at all or are actually decreasing in size. The MDCs are expected to increase by 52 million between 2002 and 2050, but this amount will still keep their total population at just about 1.2 billion. In contrast to other MDCs, there is no leveling off and no end in sight to United States population growth. The United States has a growth rate of 0.6%, and many people immigrate to the United States each year. In addition, a baby boom between 1947 and 1964 means that a large number of U.S. women are still of reproductive age.

The LDCs

The death rate began to decline steeply in the LDCs following World War II with the introduction of modern medicine, but the birthrate remained high. The growth rate of the LDCs peaked at 2.5% between 1960 and 1965. Since that time, the collective growth rate for the LDCs has declined to 1.6%, but some 46 countries have not participated in this decline. Thirty-five of these countries are in sub-Saharan Africa, where women on the average are presently having more than five children each.

Between 2002 and 2050, the population of the LDCs may jump from 5 billion to at least 8 billion. Some of this increase will occur in Africa, but most will occur in Asia because many deaths from AIDS are slowing the growth of the African population. Asia already has 56% of the world's population living on 31% of its arable (farmable) land. Therefore, Asia is expected to experience acute water scarcity, a significant loss of biodiversity, and more urban pollution. Twelve of the world's 15 most polluted cities are in Asia.

Comparing Age Structure

The LDCs are experiencing a population momentum because they have more women entering the reproductive years than older women leaving them. Populations have three age groups: dependent, reproductive, and postreproductive. This is best visualized by plotting the proportion of individuals in each group on a bar graph, thereby producing an age-structure diagram (Fig. 27.2).

Laypeople are sometimes under the impression that if each couple has two children, zero population growth will take place immediately. However, **replacement reproduction,** as this practice is called, will still cause most LDCs today to have a positive growth rate due to the age structure of the population. Because there are more young women entering the reproductive years than older women leaving them, the population continues to increase.

Most MDCs—not including the United States—have a stabilized age-structure diagram. Therefore, their populations are expected to remain just about the same or decline if couples are having fewer than two children each.

Age-structure diagrams can be used to predict future population growth.

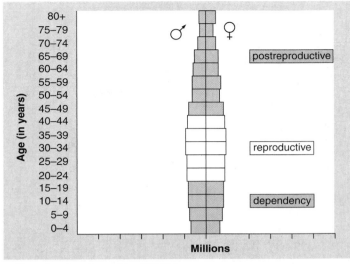

a. More-developed countries (MDCs)

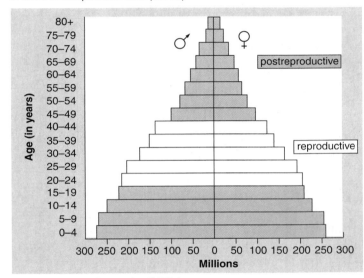

b. Less-developed countries (LDCs)

c.

Figure 27.2   Age-structure diagrams (1998).
The shape of these age-structure diagrams allows us to predict that **(a)** the populations of MDCs are approaching stabilization, and **(b)** the populations of LDCs will continue to increase for some time.
c. Improved women's rights and increasing contraceptive use could change this scenario. Here a community health worker is instructing women in Bangladesh about the use of contraceptives.
Source: United Nations Population Division, 1998.

27.2 Human Use of Resources and Pollution

Human beings have certain basic needs, and a **resource** is anything from the biotic or abiotic environment that helps meet these needs. Land, water, food, energy, and minerals are the maximally used resources that will be discussed in this chapter (Fig. 27.3).

Some resources are nonrenewable, and some are renewable. **Nonrenewable resources** are limited in supply. For example, the amount of land, fossil fuels, and minerals is finite and can be exhausted. Better extraction methods can make more fossil fuels and minerals available. Efficient use, recycling, or substitution can make the supply last longer, but eventually these resources will run out.

Renewable resources are not limited in supply. We can use water and certain forms of energy (e.g., solar energy) or harvest plants and animals for food, and more supply will always be forthcoming. Even with renewable resources, though, we have to be careful not to squander them. Consider, for example, that most species have population thresholds below which they cannot recover, as when the huge herds of buffalo that once roamed the west disappeared after being overexploited.

Unfortunately, a side effect of resource consumption can be pollution. **Pollution** is any alteration of the environment in an undesirable way. Pollution is often caused by human activities. The effect of humans on the environment is proportional to the size of the population. As the population grows, so does the need for resources and the amount of pollution caused by using these resources. Consider that six people adding waste to the ocean may not be alarming, but 6 billion people doing so would certainly affect its cleanliness. Actually, in modern times, the consumption of mineral and energy resources has grown faster than population size, most likely because people in the LDCs have increased their use of them.

Land

People need a place to live. Worldwide, there are currently more than 32 persons for each square kilometer (83 persons per square mile) of all available land, including Antarctica, mountain ranges, jungles, and deserts. Naturally, land is also needed for a variety of uses aside from homes, such as agriculture, electric power plants, manufacturing plants, highways, hospitals, schools, and so on.

Beaches and Human Habitation

At least 40% of the world population lives within 100 km (60 mi) of a coastline, and this number is expected to increase. In the United States today, over half of the population lives within 80 km (50 mi) of the coasts (including the Great Lakes). Living right on the coast is an unfortunate choice because it leads to beach erosion and loss of habitat for marine organisms. The coast is particularly subject to pollution because toxic substances placed in freshwater lakes, rivers, and streams may eventually find their way to the coast. Oil spills at sea cause localized harmful effects also.

Semiarid Lands and Human Habitation

Forty percent of the Earth's lands are already deserts, and land adjacent to a desert is in danger of becoming unable to support human life if it is improperly managed by humans (Fig. 27.4). **Desertification** is the conversion of semiarid land to desertlike conditions.

Quite often, desertification begins when humans allow animals to overgraze the land. The soil can no longer hold rainwater, and it runs off instead of keeping the remaining plants alive or recharging wells. Humans then remove whatever vegetation they can find to use as fuel or fodder for their animals. The end result is a lifeless desert, which is then abandoned as people move on to continue the process

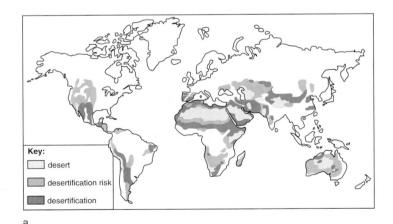
a.

Figure 27.4 **Desertification.**
a. Desertification is a worldwide occurrence that (**b**) reduces the amount of land suitable for human habitation.

b.

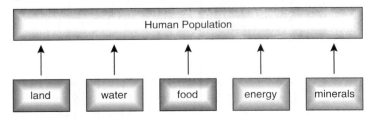

Figure 27.3 **Resources.**
Human beings use land, water, food, energy, and minerals to meet their basic needs, such as a place to live, food to eat, and products that make their lives easier.

someplace else. Some estimate that nearly three quarters of all rangelands worldwide are in danger of desertification. Many famines in Africa are due, at least in part, to degradation of the land to the point that it can no longer support human beings and their livestock.

Tropical Rain Forest and Human Habitation

Deforestation, the removal of trees, has long allowed humans to live in areas where forests once covered the land. The concern of late has been that people are settling in tropical rain forests, such as the Amazon, following the building of roads (Fig. 27.5). This land, too, is subject to desertification. Soil in the tropics is often thin and nutrient-poor because all the nutrients are tied up in the trees and other vegetation. When the trees are felled and the land is used for agriculture or grazing, it quickly loses its fertility and becomes subject to desertification.

Water

In the water-poor areas of the world (Fig. 27.6), people may not have ready access to drinking water, and if they do, the water may be impure. It's considered a human right for people to have clean drinking water, but actually, most fresh water is utilized by industry and agriculture. Worldwide, 70% of all fresh water is used to irrigate crops! Much of a recent surge in demand for water stems from increased industrial activity and irrigation-intensive agriculture, the type of agriculture that now supplies about 40% of the world's food crops. Domestically, in the MDCs, more water is usually used for bathing, flushing toilets, and watering lawns than for drinking and cooking.

Increasing Water Supplies

Although the needs of the human population overall do not exceed the renewable supply, this is not the case in certain regions of the United States and the world. As illustrated in Figure 27.4, about 40% of the world's land is desert, and deserts are bordered by semiarid land. When needed, humans increase the supply of fresh water by damming rivers and withdrawing water from aquifers.

Dams The world's 45,000 large dams catch 14% of all precipitation runoff, provide water for up to 40% of irrigated land, and give some 65 countries more than half their electricity. Damming of certain rivers has been so extensive that they no longer flow as they once did. The Yellow River in China fails to reach the sea most years; the Colorado River barely makes it to the Gulf of California, and even the Rio Grande dries up before it can merge with the Gulf of Mexico. The Nile in Egypt and the Ganges in India are also so overexploited that at some times of the year, they hardly make it to the ocean.

Dams have other drawbacks: (1) They lose water due to evaporation and seepage into underlying rock beds. The amount of water lost sometimes equals the amount they made available! (2) The salt left behind by evaporation and agricultural runoff increases salinity and can make a river's water unusable farther downstream. (3) Dams hold back less water with time because of sediment buildup. Sometimes a reservoir becomes so full of silt that it is no longer useful for storing water.

Aquifers To meet their freshwater needs, people are pumping vast amounts of water from **aquifers,** which are reservoirs found just below or as much as 1 km below the surface. Aquifers hold about 1,000 times the amount of

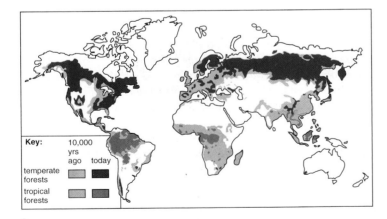

a.

Figure 27.5 Deforestation.
a. Nearly half of the world's forestlands have been cleared for farming, logging, and urbanization. **b.** The soil of tropical rain forests is not suitable for long-term farming.

b.

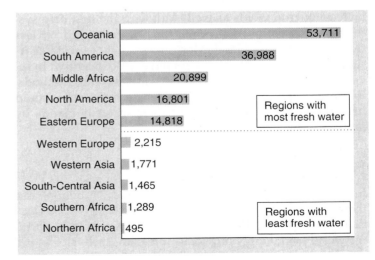

Figure 27.6 Freshwater resources.
Countries and regions within continents differ by the amount of fresh water available. Amounts given are average annual cubic meters per capita.

water that falls on land as precipitation each year. This water accumulates from rain that fell in far-off regions even hundreds of thousands of years ago. In the past 50 years, groundwater depletion has become a problem in many areas of the world. In substantial portions of the High Plains Aquifer, which stretches from South Dakota to the Texas panhandle, more than half of the water has been pumped out. In the 1950s, India had 100,000 motorized pumps in operation; today, India has 20 million pumps, a huge increase in groundwater pumping.

Environmental Consequences   Removal of water is causing land **subsidence,** a settling of the soil as it dries out. In California's San Joaquin valley, an area of more than 13,000 km^2 has subsided at least 30 cm due to groundwater depletion, and in the worst spot, the surface of the ground has dropped more than 9 meters! In some parts of Gujarat, India, the water table has dropped as much as 7 meters. Subsidence damages canals, buildings, and underground pipes. Withdrawal of groundwater can cause **sinkholes,** in which an underground cavern collapses when water no longer holds up its roof.

Saltwater intrusion is another consequence of aquifer depletion. The flow of water from streams and aquifers usually keeps them fairly free of seawater. But as water is withdrawn, the water table can lower to the point that seawater backs up into streams and aquifers. Saltwater intrusion reduces the supply of fresh water along the coast.

Conservation of Water

By 2025, two thirds of the world's population may be living in countries that are facing serious water shortages. Some solutions for expanding water supplies have been suggested. Planting drought- and salt-tolerant crops would help a lot. Using drip irrigation delivers more water to crops and saves about 50% over traditional methods, while increasing crop yields as well. Although the first drip systems were developed in 1960, they're only used on less than 1% of irrigated land. Most governments subsidize irrigation so heavily that farmers have little incentive to invest in drip systems or other water-saving methods. Reusing water and adopting conservation measures could help the world's industries cut their water demands by more than half.

Food

In 1950, the human population numbered 2.5 billion, and there was only enough food to provide less than 2,000 calories per person per day; now, with 6 billion people on Earth, the world food supply provides more than 2,500 calories per person per day. Generally speaking, food comes from three activities: growing crops, raising animals, and fishing the seas. The increase in the food supply has largely been possible because of modern farming methods, which unfortunately include some harmful practices:

1. *Planting of a few genetic varieties.* The majority of farmers practice monoculture. Wheat farmers plant the same type of wheat, and corn farmers plant the same type of corn. Unfortunately, monoculture means that a single type of parasite can cause much devastation.
2. *Heavy use of fertilizers, pesticides, and herbicides.* Fertilizer production is energy intensive, and fertilizer runoff contributes to water pollution. Pesticides reduce soil fertility because they kill off beneficial soil organisms as well as pests, and some pesticides and herbicides are linked to the development of cancer.
3. *Generous irrigation.* As already discussed, water is sometimes taken from aquifers whose water content may in the future become so reduced that it could be too expensive to pump out any more.
4. *Excessive fuel consumption.* Irrigation pumps remove water from aquifers, and large farming machines are used to spread fertilizers, pesticides, and herbicides, as well as to sow and harvest the crops. In effect, modern farming methods transform fossil fuel energy into food energy.

Figure 27.7 shows ways to minimize the harmful effects of modern farming practices.

Soil Loss and Degradation

Land suitable for farming and grazing animals is being degraded worldwide. Topsoil, the topmost portion of the soil, is the richest in organic matter and the most capable of supporting grass and crops. When bare soil is acted on by water and wind, soil erosion occurs and topsoil is lost. As a result, marginal rangeland becomes desertized, and farmland loses its productivity.

The custom of planting the same crop in straight rows that facilitate the use of large farming machines has caused the United States and Canada to have one of the highest rates of soil erosion in the world. Conserving the nutrients now being lost could save farmers $20 billion annually in fertilizer costs. Much of the eroded sediment ends up in lakes and streams, where it reduces the ability of aquatic species to survive.

Between 25% and 35% of the irrigated western croplands are thought to have undergone **salinization,** an accumulation of mineral salts due to the evaporation of excess irrigation water. Salinization makes the land unsuitable for growing crops.

Green Revolutions

About 50 years ago, researchers began to breed tropical wheat and rice varieties specifically for farmers in the LDCs. The dramatic increase in yield due to the introduction of these new varieties around the world was called "the green revolution." These plants helped the world food supply keep pace with the rapid increase in world population. Most green revolution plants are called "high responders" because they need high levels of fertilizer, water, and pesticides in order to produce a high yield. In other words, they require the same subsidies and create the same ecological problems as do modern farming methods.

Genetic Engineering   As we discussed in Chapter 19 (see page 380), genetic engineering can produce transgenic plants with new and different traits, among them, resistance to both insects and herbicides. When herbicide-resistant crops are planted, weeds are easily controlled, less tillage is needed, and soil erosion is minimized. Researchers also want to produce crops that tolerate salt, drought, and cold. Some progress has also been made in increasing the food quality of crops so that they will supply more of the proteins, vitamins, and minerals people need. Genetically engineered crops could result in still another green revolution.

Nevertheless, some citizens are opposed to the use of genetically engineered crops, fearing that they will damage the environment and lead to health problems in humans. The Bioethical Focus on page 385 discusses these problems.

Domestic Livestock

A low-protein, high-carbohydrate diet consisting only of grains such as wheat, rice, or corn can lead to malnutrition. In the LDCs, kwashiorkor, caused by a severe protein deficiency, is seen in infants and children ages 1–3, usually after a new baby arrives in the family and the older children are no longer breastfed. Such children are lethargic, irritable, and have bloated abdomens. Mental retardation is expected.

In the MDCs, many people tend to have more than enough protein in their diet. Almost two thirds of U. S. cropland is devoted to producing livestock feed. This means that a large percentage of the fossil fuel, fertilizer, water, herbicides, and pesticides we use are actually for the purpose of raising livestock. Typically, cattle are range-fed for about four months, and then they are brought to crowded feedlots where they receive growth hormone and antibiotics, while they feed on grain or corn. Most pigs and chickens spend their entire lives cooped up in crowded pens and cages.

If livestock eat a large proportion of the crops in the United States, then raising livestock accounts for much of the pollution associated with farming. Consider, also, that presently, fossil fuel energy is needed not just to produce herbicides and pesticides and to grow food, but also to make the food available to the livestock. Raising livestock is extremely energy-intensive in the MDCs. In addition, water is used to wash livestock wastes into nearby bodies of water, where they add significantly to water pollution. Whereas human wastes are sent to sewage treatment plants, raw animal wastes are not.

For these reasons, it is prudent to recall the ecological energy pyramid (see Fig. 26.6), which shows that as you move up the food chain, energy is lost. As a rule of thumb, for every 10 calories of energy from a plant, only 1 calorie is available for the production of animal tissue in a herbivore. In other words, it is extremely wasteful for the human diet to contain more protein than is needed to maintain good health. It is possible to feed ten times as many people on grain as on meat.

Environmental problems can result from human habitation of the land, increasing freshwater supplies, and the modern-day methods of farming and the raising of domestic livestock.

a. Polyculture

b. Contour farming

c. Biological pest control

Figure 27.7   Conservation methods.
a. Polyculture reduces the ability of one parasite to wipe out an entire crop and reduces the need to use a herbicide to kill weeds. This farmer has planted alfalfa in between strips of corn, which also replenishes the nitrogen content of the soil (instead of adding fertilizers). Alfalfa, a legume, has root nodules that contain nitrogen-fixing bacteria. **b.** Contour farming with no-till conserves topsoil because water has less tendency to run off. **c.** Instead of pesticides, it is sometimes possible to use a natural predator. Here, ladybugs are feeding on cottony-cushion scale insects on citrus trees.

Energy

Modern society runs on various sources of energy. Some of these energy sources are nonrenewable, and others are renewable.

Nonrenewable Sources

Presently, about 6% of the world's energy supply comes from nuclear power, and 75% comes from fossil fuels; both of these are finite, nonrenewable sources. Although it was once predicted that the *nuclear power* industry would fulfill a significant portion of the world's energy needs, this has not happened for two reasons: (1) People are very concerned about nuclear power dangers, such as the meltdown that occurred in 1986 at the Chernobyl nuclear power plant in Russia. (2) Radioactive wastes from nuclear power plants remain a threat to the environment for thousands of years, and we still have not decided how best to safely store them.

Fossil fuels (oil, natural gas, and coal) are so named because they are derived from the compressed remains of plants and animals that died many thousands of years ago. Although the U.S. population makes up about 5% of the world's population, it uses more than half of the fossil fuel energy supply. Comparatively speaking, each person in the MDCs uses approximately as much energy in one day as a person in an LDC does in one year.

Among the fossil fuels, oil burns more cleanly than coal, which may contain a considerable amount of sulfur. So despite the fact that the United States has a goodly supply of coal, imported oil is our preferred fossil fuel today. Even so, the burning of any fossil fuel causes environmental problems because as it burns, pollutants are emitted into the air. Acid rain is discussed on page 21.

Fossil Fuels and Global Climate Change In 1850, the level of carbon dioxide in the atmosphere was about 280 parts per million (ppm), and today it is about 350 ppm. This increase is largely due to the burning of fossil fuels and the burning and clearing of forests to make way for farmland and pasture. Human activities are causing the emission of other gases as well. For example, the amount of methane given off by oil and gas wells, rice paddies, and all sorts of organisms, including domesticated cows, is increasing by about 1% a year. These gases are known as **greenhouse gases** because, just like the panes of a greenhouse, they allow solar radiation to pass through but hinder the escape of infrared heat back into space.

Today, data collected around the world show a steady rise in the concentration of the various greenhouse gases. These data are used to generate computer models that predict the Earth may warm to temperatures never before experienced by living things. The global climate has already warmed about 0.6°C since the industrial revolution. Computer models are unable to consider all possible variables, but the Earth's temperature may rise 1.5°–4.5°C by 2060 if greenhouse emissions continue at the current rates.

Because of global warming, it is predicted that as the oceans warm, temperatures in the polar regions will rise to a greater degree than in other regions. If so, glaciers will melt, and sea levels will rise, not only due to this melting but also because water expands as it warms. Water evaporation will increase, and most likely precipitation will increase along the coasts, while conditions inland become dryer. The occurrence of droughts will reduce agricultural yields, and also cause trees to die off. Coastal agricultural lands, such as the deltas of Bangladesh, India, and China, will be inundated, and billions will have to be spent to keep coastal cities, such as New York, Boston, Miami, and Galveston in the United States, from disappearing into the ocean.

Renewable Energy Sources

Renewable types of energy include hydropower, geothermal, wind, and solar.

Hydropower Hydroelectric plants convert the energy of falling water into electricity (Fig. 27.8*a*). Hydropower accounts for about 10% of the electric power generated in the United States and almost 98% of the total renewable energy used. Brazil, New Zealand, and Switzerland produce at least 75% of their electricity with water power, but Canada is the world's leading hydropower producer. Worldwide, hydropower presently generates 19% of all electricity utilized, but this percentage is expected to rise because of increased use in certain countries. For example, Iceland has an ambitious hydropower project under way because presently it uses only 10% of its potential capacity.

Much of the hydropower development in recent years has been due to the construction of enormous dams, which are known to have detrimental environmental effects (see p. 525). The better choice is believed to be small-scale dams that generate less power per dam but do not have the same environmental impact.

Geothermal Energy Elements such as uranium, thorium, radium, and plutonium undergo radioactive decay below the Earth's surface and then heat the surrounding rocks to hundreds of degrees Celsius. When the rocks are in contact with underground streams or lakes, huge amounts of steam and hot water are produced. This steam can be piped up to the surface to supply hot water for home heating or to run steam-driven turbogenerators. The California's Geysers project is the world's largest geothermal electricity-generating complex.

Wind Power Wind power is expected to account for a significant percentage of our energy needs in the future (Fig. 27.8*b*). Despite the common belief that a huge amount of land is required for the "wind farms" that produce commercial electricity, the actual amount of space for a wind farm compares favorably with the amount of land required by a coal-fired power plant or a solar thermal energy system.

A community that generates its own electricity by using wind power can solve the problem of uneven energy production by selling electricity to a local public utility when an excess is available and buying electricity from the same facility when wind power is in short supply.

Solar Energy and the Solar-Hydrogen Revolution Solar energy is diffuse energy that must be (1) collected, (2) converted to another form, and (3) stored if it is to compete with other available forms of energy. Passive solar heating of a house is successful when the windows of the house face the sun, the building is well insulated, and heat can be stored in water tanks, rocks, bricks, or some other suitable material.

In a **photovoltaic (solar) cell,** a wafer of the electron-emitting metal is in contact with another metal that collects the electrons and passes them along into wires in a steady stream. Spurred by the oil shocks of the 1970s, the U. S. government has been supporting the development of photovoltaics ever since. As a result, the price of buying one has dropped from about $100 per watt to around $4. The photovoltaic cells placed on roofs, for example, generate electricity that can be used inside a building and/or sold back to a power company (Fig. 27.8c).

Several types of solar power plants are now operational in California. In one type, huge reflectors focus sunlight on a pipe containing oil. The heated pipes boil water, generating steam that drives a conventional turbogenerator. In another type, 1,800 sun-tracking mirrors focus sunlight onto a molten salt receiver mounted on a tower (Fig. 27.8d). The hot salt generates steam that drives a turbogenerator.

Scientists are working on the possibility of using solar energy to extract hydrogen from water via electrolysis. The hydrogen can then be used as a clean-burning fuel; when it burns, water is produced. Presently, cars have internal combustion engines that run on gasoline. In the future, vehicles are expected to be powered by fuel cells, which use hydrogen to produce electricity. The electricity runs a motor that propels the vehicle. Fuel cells are now powering buses in Vancouver and Chicago, and more buses are planned.

Hydrogen fuel can be produced locally or in central locations, using energy from photovoltaic cells. If in central locations, hydrogen can be piped to filling stations using the natural gas pipes already plentiful in the United States. The advantages of a solar-hydrogen revolution are at least twofold: (1) The world would no longer be dependent on the Middle East region for oil, and (2) environmental problems, such as global warming, acid rain, and smog, would begin to lessen.

The consumption of nonrenewable energy supplies results in environmental degradation. Renewable energy is expected to be utilized more in the future and a solar-hydrogen revolution is expected.

Figure 27.8 Other renewable energy sources.
a. Hydropower dams provide a clean form of energy but can be ecologically disastrous in other ways. **b.** Wind power requires land on which to place enough windmills to generate energy. **c.** Photovoltaic cells on rooftops and **(d)** sun-tracking mirrors on land can collect diffuse solar energy more cheaply than could be done formerly.

a.

b.

c.

d.

Minerals

Minerals are nonrenewable raw materials in the Earth's crust that can be mined (extracted) and used by humans. Nonrenewable minerals include fossil fuels; nonmetallic raw materials, such as sand, gravel, and phosphate; and metals, such as aluminum, copper, iron, lead, and gold.

The most dangerous metals to human health are the heavy metals: lead, mercury, arsenic, cadmium, tin, chromium, zinc, and copper. They are used to produce batteries, electronics, pesticides, medicines, paints, inks, and dyes. In the ionic form, they enter the body and inhibit vital enzymes. That's why these items should be discarded carefully and taken to hazardous waste sites.

One of the greatest threats to the maintenance of ecosystems and biodiversity is surface mining, called *strip mining*. In the United States, huge machines can go as far as removing mountaintops in order to reach a mineral. The land devoid of vegetation takes on a surreal appearance, and rain washes toxic waste deposits into nearby streams and rivers.

Hazardous Wastes

Every year, countries of the world discard billions of tons of solid waste, some on land and some in fresh and marine waters. An estimated 5 billion metric tons of highly toxic chemicals was improperly discarded in the United States between 1950 and 1975. The public's concern was so great that the Environmental Protection Agency (EPA) came into existence. Using an allocation of monies called the Superfund, the EPA oversees the cleanup of hazardous waste disposal sites in the United States. The ten most commonly found contaminants of the environment are heavy metals (lead, arsenic, cadmium, chromium) and synthetic organic compounds (trichloroethylene, toluene, benzene, polychlorinated biphenyls [PCBs], chloroform, and toluene). Some of these are endocrine-disrupting contaminants (see the Ecology Focus, p. 303).

Synthetic organic chemicals play a role in the production of plastics, pesticides, herbicides, cosmetics, coatings, solvents, wood preservatives, and hundreds of other products. Synthetic organic chemicals include halogenated hydrocarbons, in which halogens (chlorine, bromine, fluorine) have replaced certain hydrogens. One such molecule comprises the **chlorofluorocarbons (CFCs),** a type of halogenated hydrocarbon in which both chlorine and fluorine atoms replace some of the hydrogen atoms. CFCs have brought about a thinning of the Earth's **ozone shield,** which protects terrestrial life from the dangerous effects of ultraviolet radiation. Now that MDCs are no longer using CFCs, the ozone shield is predicted to recover by 2050.

Other synthetic organic chemicals pose a direct and serious threat to the health of living things, including humans. Rachel Carson's book *Silent Spring,* published in 1962, made the public aware of the deleterious effects of pesticides. Sometimes, they accumulate in the mud of deltas and estuaries of highly polluted rivers and cause environmental

problems if disturbed. These wastes enter bodies of water and are subject to **biological magnification** (Fig. 27.9). Decomposers are unable to break down these wastes. They enter and remain in the bodies of organisms because they accumulate in fat and are not excreted. Therefore, they become more concentrated as they pass along a food chain. Biological magnification is most apt to occur in aquatic food chains, which have more links than terrestrial food chains. Humans are the final consumers in both types of food chains, and over the past 25–30 years, a number of toxic chemicals have found their way into breast milk—PCBs, DDT, solvents, and heavy metals.

Raw sewage causes oxygen depletion in lakes and rivers. As the oxygen level decreases, the diversity of life is greatly reduced. Also, human feces can contain pathogenic microorganisms that cause cholera, typhoid fever, and dysentery. In regions of the LDCs where sewage treatment is practically nonexistent, many children die each year from these diseases. Typically, sewage treatment plants use bacteria to break down organic matter to inorganic nutrients, such as nitrates and phosphates, which then enter surface waters. The end result can be cultural eutrophication discussed on page 511.

The consumption of minerals contributes to the buildup of hazardous wastes, including synthetic organic chemicals, in the environment.

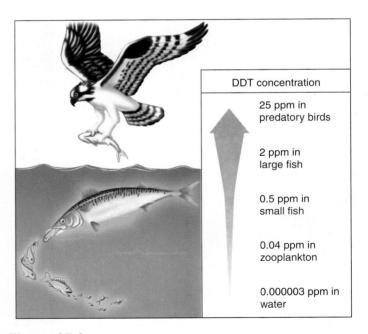

DDT concentration
25 ppm in predatory birds
2 ppm in large fish
0.5 ppm in small fish
0.04 ppm in zooplankton
0.000003 ppm in water

Figure 27.9   Biological magnification.
Various synthetic organic chemicals, such as DDT, accumulate in animal fat. Therefore, the chemical becomes increasingly concentrated at higher trophic levels. By the time DDT was banned in the United States, it had interfered with predatory bird reproduction by causing egg shell thinning.

27.3 Biodiversity

Biodiversity can be defined as the variety of life on Earth, described in terms of the number of different species. We are presently in a biodiversity crisis—the number of extinctions (loss of species) expected to occur in the near future is unparalleled in the history of the Earth.

Loss of Biodiversity

Figure 27.10 identifies the major causes of extinction.

Habitat Loss

Human occupation of the coastline, semiarid lands, tropical rain forests (see pages 524–25), and other areas have contributed to the loss of biodiversity. Scientists are especially concerned about the tropical rain forests and coral reefs because they are particularly rich in species. Already, tropical rain forests have been reduced from their original 14% of landmass to the present 6%. Also, 60% of coral reefs have been destroyed or are on the verge of destruction; its possible that all coral reefs may disappear during the next 40 years.

Alien Species

Alien species, sometimes called exotics, are nonnative members of an ecosystem. Humans have introduced alien species into new ecosystems chiefly due to colonization, horticulture and agriculture, and accidental transport. For example, the pilgrims brought the dandelion to the United States as a familiar salad green. Kudzu is a vine from Japan that the U. S. Department of Agriculture thought would help prevent soil erosion. The plant now covers much landscape in the South, including even walnut, magnolia, and sweet gum trees. The zebra mussel from the Caspian Sea was accidentally introduced into the Great Lakes in 1988. It now forms dense beds that squeeze out native mussels.

Pollution

Pollution brings about environmental change that adversely affects the lives and health of living things. Biodiversity is particularly threatened by the following types of environmental pollution.

Acid rain   The Ecology Focus in Chapter 2, page 21 tells how acid rain decimates forests because it causes trees to weaken and increases their susceptibility to disease and insects.

Global warming   Global warming, an increase in the Earth's temperature due to the presence of greenhouse gases in the atmosphere, is expected to have many detrimental effects, such as destruction of coastal wetlands due to a rise in sea levels; loss of habitat due to temperature shifts; and the death of coral reefs if the temperature increases by 4°C.

Ozone depletion   The release of CFCs into the atmosphere causes the shield to break down, leading to impairment of crop and tree growth and death of plankton that sustains oceanic life.

Synthetic organic chemicals   Many of the organic chemicals released into the environment are endocrine-disrupting contaminants that can possibly affect the endocrine system and reproductive potential of food species and humans.

Overexploitation

Overexploitation occurs when the number of individuals taken from a wild population is so great that the population becomes severely reduced in numbers. A positive feedback cycle explains overexploitation: the smaller the population, the more valuable its members, and the greater the incentive to capture the few remaining organisms.

Markets for decorative plants and exotic pets support both legal and illegal trade in wild species. Rustlers dig up rare cacti, such as the single-crested saguaro, and sell them to gardeners. Parakeets and macaws are among the birds taken from the wild for sale to pet owners. For every bird delivered alive, many more have died in the process. The same holds true for tropical fish, which often come from the coral reefs of Indonesia and the Philippines. Divers dynamite reefs or use plastic squeeze-bottles of cyanide to stun them; in the process, many fish die.

Figure 27.10   Loss of biodiversity.
a. Habitat loss, alien species, pollution, overexploitation, and disease have been identified as causes of extinction of organisms. **b.** Macaws that reside in South American tropical rain forests are endangered for the reasons listed in the graph.

Declining species of mammals are still hunted for their hides, tusks, horns, or bones. Because of its rarity, a single Siberian tiger is now worth more than $500,000—its bones are pulverized and used as a medicinal powder. The horns of rhinoceroses become ornate carved daggers, and their bones are ground up to sell as a medicine. The ivory of an elephant's tusk is used to make art objects, jewelry, or piano keys. The fur of a Bengal tiger sells for as much as $100,000 in Tokyo.

Fish are a renewable resource if harvesting does not exceed the ability of the fish to reproduce. Today, larger and more efficient fishing fleets decimate fishing stocks (Fig. 27.11). Tuna and like fishes are captured by purse-seine fishing, in which a very large net surrounds a school of fish, and then the net is closed in the same manner as a drawstring purse. Dolphins which accompany the tuna are killed by this type of net. Other fishing boats drag huge trawling nets, large enough to accommodate 12 jumbo jets, along the seafloor to capture bottom-dwelling fish. Trawling has been called the marine equivalent of clear-cutting trees because after the net goes by, the sea bottom is devastated. Only large fish are kept; undesirable small fish and sea turtles are discarded, dying, back into the ocean. Cod and haddock, once the most abundant bottom-dwelling fish along the northeast coast, are now often outnumbered by dogfish and skate.

A marine ecosystem can be disrupted by overfishing, as exemplified on the U.S. west coast. When sea otters began to decline in numbers, investigators found that they were being eaten by orcas (killer whales). Usually, orcas prefer seals and sea lions to sea otters, but they began eating sea otters when few seals and sea lions could be found. What caused a decline in seals and sea lions? Their preferred food sources—perch and herring—were no longer plentiful due to overfishing. Ordinarily, sea otters keep the population of sea urchins, which feed on kelp, under control. But with fewer sea otters around, the sea urchin population exploded and decimated the kelp beds. Thus, overfishing set in motion a chain of events that detrimentally altered the food web of an ecosystem.

Disease

Wildlife is subject to emerging diseases just as humans are. Exposure to domestic animals and their pathogens occurs due to the encroachment of humans on wildlife habitats (Fig. 27.12). Wildlife can also be infected by animals not ordinarily encountered. For example, African elephants carry a strain of herpes virus that is fatal to Asian elephants, and deaths can result if the two types of elephants are housed together.

The significant effect of diseases on biodiversity is underscored by a National Wildlife Health Center study that found that almost half of sea otter deaths along the coast of California are due to infectious diseases. Scientists tell us that the number of pathogens that cause disease are on the rise, and just as human health is threatened, so is that of wildlife. Extinctions due simply to disease may occur.

Five causes of extinction have been identified: habitat loss, introduction of alien species, pollution, overexploitation, and disease.

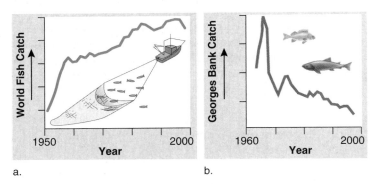

a.   b.

Atlantic Ocean		Pacific Ocean	
Area	Change (%)	Area	Change (%)
Northwest	− 52	Northwest	+ 48
Northeast	+ 1.2	Northeast	no change
Southwest	+ 35	Southwest	+ 22
Southeast	− 52	Southeast	+ 16

c.

Figure 27.11   Fisheries.
a. The world fish catch is now declining because of overexploitation. **b.** Fish catches in the Georges Bank area. **c.** Fish catches in the Atlantic and Pacific oceans, 1970–2000. (Data from U.S. Marine Fisheries Service.)

Figure 27.12   Wildlife is at risk due to disease.
Veterinarians are working on a Florida panther in the wild.

Indirect Value of Biodiversity

To bring about the preservation of wildlife, it is necessary to make all people aware that biodiversity is a resource of immense value. If we want to preserve wildlife, it is more economical to save ecosystems than individual species. Ecosystems perform many services for modern humans, who increasingly live in cities. These services are said to be indirect because they are pervasive and not easily discernible. Even so, our very survival depends on the functions that ecosystems perform for us and they tell us the indirect value of wildlife. Therefore, the indirect value of biodiversity can be associated with the following services.

Biogeochemical Cycles

You'll recall from Chapter 26 that ecosystems are characterized by energy flow and chemical cycling. The biodiversity within ecosystems contributes to the workings of the water, phosphorus, nitrogen, carbon, and other biogeochemical cycles. We depend on these cycles for fresh water, provision of phosphate, uptake of excess soil nitrogen, and removal of carbon dioxide from the atmosphere. When human activities upset the usual workings of biogeochemical cycles, the dire environmental consequences include the release of excess pollutants that are harmful to us. Technology is unable to artificially contribute to or create any of the biogeochemical cycles.

Waste Disposal

Decomposers break down dead organic matter and other types of wastes to inorganic nutrients that are used by the producers within ecosystems. This function aids humans immensely because we dump millions of tons of waste material into natural ecosystems each year. If it were not for decomposition, waste would soon cover the entire surface of our planet. We can build sewage treatment plants, but they are expensive, and few of them break down solid wastes completely to inorganic nutrients. It is less expensive and more efficient to water plants and trees with partially treated wastewater and let soil bacteria cleanse it completely.

Biological communities are also capable of breaking down and immobilizing pollutants, such as heavy metals and pesticides, that humans release into the environment. A review of wetland functions in Canada assigned a value of $50,000 per hectare (2.471 acres, or 10,000 m^2) per year to the ability of natural areas to purify water and take up pollutants.

Provision of Fresh Water

Few terrestrial organisms are adapted to living in a salty environment—they need fresh water. The water cycle continually supplies fresh water to terrestrial ecosystems. Humans use fresh water in innumerable ways, including drinking it and irrigating their crops. Freshwater ecosystems, such as rivers and lakes, also provide us with fish and other types of organisms for food.

Unlike other commodities, there is no substitute for fresh water. We can remove salt from seawater to obtain fresh water, but the cost of desalination is about four to eight times the average cost of fresh water acquired via the water cycle.

Forests and other natural ecosystems exert a "sponge effect." They soak up water and then release it at a regular rate. When rain falls in a natural area, plant foliage and dead leaves lessen its impact, and the soil slowly absorbs it, especially if the soil has been aerated by organisms. The water-holding capacity of forests reduces the possibility of flooding. The value of a marshland outside Boston, Massachusetts, has been estimated at $72,000 per hectare per year solely on its ability to reduce floods. Forests release water slowly for days or weeks after the rains have ceased. Rivers flowing through forests in West Africa release twice as much water halfway through the dry season and between three and five times as much at the end of the dry season, as do rivers from coffee plantations.

Prevention of Soil Erosion

Intact ecosystems naturally retain soil and prevent soil erosion. The importance of this ecosystem attribute is especially observed following deforestation. In Pakistan, the world's largest dam, the Tarbela Dam, is losing its storage capacity of 12 billion cubic meters many years sooner than expected because silt is building up behind the dam, due to deforestation. At one time, the Philippines was exporting $100 million worth of oysters, mussels, clams, and cockles each year. Now, silt carried down rivers following deforestation is smothering the mangrove ecosystem that serves as a nursery for these shellfish. Most coastal ecosystems are not as bountiful as they once were because of deforestation and a myriad of other assaults.

Regulation of Climate

At the local level, trees provide shade and reduce the need for fans and air conditioners during the summer.

Globally, forests ameliorate the climate because they take up carbon dioxide. The leaves of trees use carbon dioxide when they photosynthesize, and the bodies of the trees store carbon. When trees are cut and burned, carbon dioxide is released into the atmosphere. Carbon dioxide makes a significant contribution to global warming, which is expected to be stressful for many plants and animals. Only a small percentage of wildlife will be able to move northward, where the weather will be suitable for them.

Ecotourism

Almost everyone prefers to vacation in the natural beauty of an ecosystem. In the United States, nearly 100 million people enjoy vacationing in a natural setting. To do so, they spend $4 billion each year on fees, travel, lodging, and food. Many tourists want to go sport fishing, whale watching, boat riding, hiking, birdwatching, and the like.

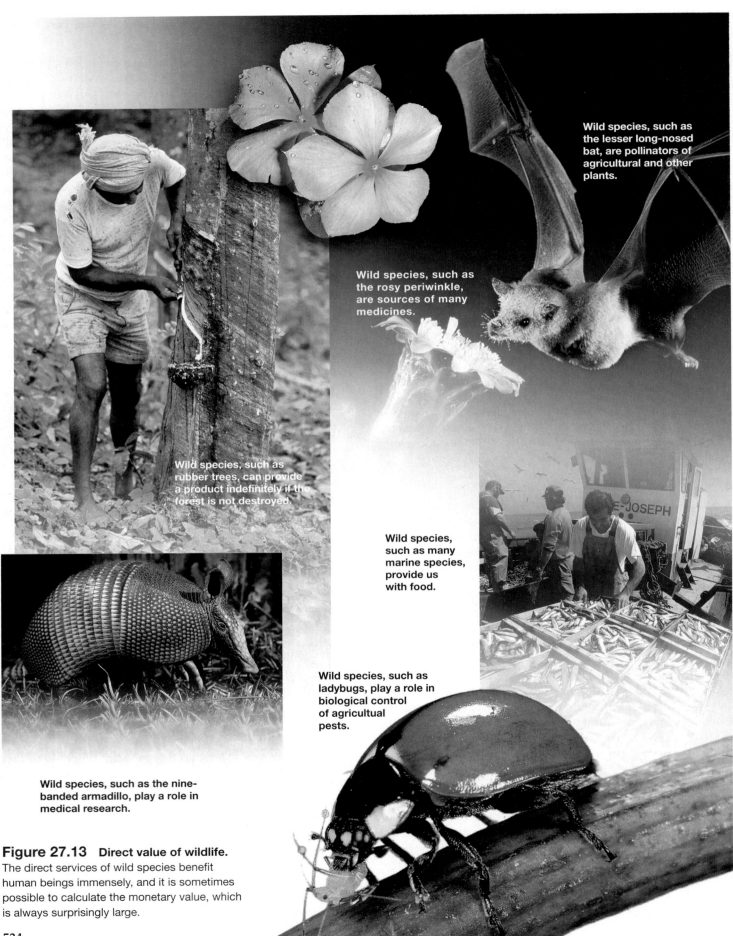

Wild species, such as the lesser long-nosed bat, are pollinators of agricultural and other plants.

Wild species, such as the rosy periwinkle, are sources of many medicines.

Wild species, such as rubber trees, can provide a product indefinitely if the forest is not destroyed.

Wild species, such as many marine species, provide us with food.

Wild species, such as ladybugs, play a role in biological control of agricultual pests.

Wild species, such as the nine-banded armadillo, play a role in medical research.

Figure 27.13   Direct value of wildlife.
The direct services of wild species benefit human beings immensely, and it is sometimes possible to calculate the monetary value, which is always surprisingly large.

Direct Value

Various individual species perform services for human beings and contribute greatly to the value we should place on biodiversity. Only some of the most obvious values are discussed here and illustrated in Figure 27.13.

Medicinal Value

Most of the prescription drugs used in the United States were originally derived from living organisms. The rosy periwinkle from Madagascar is an excellent example of a tropical plant that has provided us with useful medicines. Potent chemicals from this plant are now used to treat two forms of cancer: leukemia and Hodgkin disease. Because of these drugs, the survival rate for childhood leukemia has gone from 10% to 90%, and Hodgkin disease is usually curable. Although the value of saving a life cannot be calculated, it is still sometimes easier for us to appreciate the worth of a resource if it is explained in monetary terms. Thus, researchers tell us that, judging from the success rate in the past, an additional 328 types of drugs are yet to be found in tropical rain forests, and the value of this resource to society is probably $147 billion.

You may already know that the antibiotic penicillin is derived from a fungus and that certain species of bacteria produce the antibiotics tetracycline and streptomycin. These drugs have proven to be indispensable in the treatment of diseases, including certain sexually transmitted diseases.

Leprosy is among those diseases for which there is, as yet, no cure. The bacterium that causes leprosy will not grow in the laboratory, but scientists discovered that it grows naturally in the nine-banded armadillo. Having a source for the bacterium may make it possible to find a cure for leprosy. The blood of horseshoe crabs contains a substance called limulus amoebocyte lysate, which is used to ensure that medical devices, such as pacemakers, surgical implants, and prosthetic devices, are free of bacteria. Blood is taken from 250,000 crabs a year, and then they are returned to the sea unharmed.

Agricultural Value

Crops, such as wheat, corn, and rice, are derived from wild plants that have been modified to be high producers. The same high-yield, genetically similar strains tend to be grown worldwide. When rice crops in Africa were being devastated by a virus, researchers grew wild rice plants from thousands of seed samples until they found one that contained a gene for resistance to the virus. These wild plants were then used in a breeding program to transfer the gene into high-yield rice plants. If this variety of wild rice had become extinct before it could be discovered, rice cultivation in Africa might have collapsed.

Biological pest controls—natural predators and parasites—are often preferable to using chemical pesticides. When a rice pest, called the brown planthopper, became resistant to pesticides, farmers began to use natural brown planthopper enemies instead. The economic savings were calculated at well over $1 billion. Similarly, cotton growers in Cañete Valley, Peru, found that pesticides were no longer working against the cotton aphid because of resistance. Research identified natural predators that are now being used to an ever greater degree by cotton farmers. Again, savings have been enormous.

Most flowering plants are pollinated by animals, such as bees, wasps, butterflies, beetles, birds, and bats. The honeybee, *Apis mellifera*, has been domesticated, and it pollinates almost $10 billion worth of food crops annually in the United States. The danger of this dependency on a single species is exemplified by mites that have now wiped out more than 20% of the commercial honeybee population in the United States. Where can we get resistant bees? From the wild, of course. The value of wild pollinators to the U.S. agricultural economy has been calculated at $4.1 to $6.7 billion a year. And yet, modern agriculture often kills bees by spraying fields with pesticides.

Consumptive Use Value

We have had much success cultivating crops, keeping domesticated animals, growing trees in plantations, and so forth. But so far, aquaculture, the growing of fish and shellfish for human consumption, has contributed only minimally to human welfare—instead, most freshwater and marine harvests depend on the catching of wild animals, such as fishes (e.g., trout, cod, tuna, and flounder), crustaceans (e.g., lobsters, shrimps, and crabs), and mammals (e.g., whales). Obviously, these aquatic organisms are an invaluable biodiversity resource.

The environment provides all sorts of other products that are sold in the marketplace worldwide, including wild fruits and vegetables, skins, fibers, beeswax, and seaweed. Also, some people obtain their meat directly from the environment. In one study, researchers calculated that the economic value of wild pig in the diet of native hunters in Sarawak, East Malaysia, was approximately $40 million per year.

Similarly, many trees are still felled in the natural environment for their wood. Researchers have calculated that a species-rich forest in the Peruvian Amazon is worth far more if the forest is used for fruit and rubber production than for timber production. Fruit and the latex needed to produce rubber can be brought to market for an unlimited number of years, whereas once the trees are gone, no more timber can be harvested.

The value of biodiversity is both indirect and direct. The indirect value is associated with the many services that ecosystems perform for a very large human population. The direct value is related to medicinal value, agricultural value, and consumptive use value.

Bioethical Focus

Cyanide Fishing and Coral Reefs

Coral reefs are areas of biological abundance found in shallow, warm, tropical waters just below the surface of the water. They occur in the Caribbean and off the coasts of the Southern Hemisphere continents. The Great Barrier Reef off the coast of Australia is the largest coral reef in the world. The chief constituents of a coral reef are stony corals, animals that exist as small polyps with a calcium carbonate (limestone) exterior (Fig. 27A). Corals do not usually occur individually; rather they form colonies derived from just one individual. When the corals die off, they leave behind a hard, stony, branching limestone structure. The large number of crevices and caves of a reef provide shelter for many animals, including sponges, nudibranchs, small fish (groupers, clown fish, parrotfish, snapper, and scorpion fish), jellyfish, anemones, sea stars (including the destructive Crown of Thorns), crustaceans (like crabs, shrimp, and lobsters), turtles, sea snakes, snails, and mollusks (like octopuses, nautilus, and clams). The barracuda, moray eel, and shark are top predators in coral reefs.

Coral reefs are such incredibly diverse ecosystems that they are often referred to as the "rain forests of the sea." They are home to thousands of known species, with perhaps millions more yet to be documented. Coral reef degradation is a worldwide problem that involves overfishing for the food and aquarium trades, careless tourist divers, impacts from boat anchors and propellers, oil spills, nutrient pollution, global climate change, and an increase in coral diseases. It has been estimated that 58% of all coral reefs are being harmed by human activities. Even so, many aquarium hobbyists enjoy collecting and caring for the beautiful fish, starfish, sea anemones, and other organisms that call the reef home.

One of the most damaging methods of collecting aquarium fish from coral reefs is known as cyanide fishing (Fig. 27A). Cyanide is a poison that interferes with the mitochondrial electron transport system and effectively shuts down aerobic respiration. Reef fish can be challenging for divers to capture with handheld nets alone, since they are able to seek refuge in hard-to-reach nooks and crannies. However, spewing a cyanide solution over the fish stuns them and makes them much easier to catch. Unfortunately, cyanide dosing in open water is a tricky proposition. Many fish die immediately, and even more expire later from aftereffects of the poison. To make matters worse, the coral itself, which takes thousands of years to grow and form a reef, can succumb to cyanide. Even the divers do not always escape unscathed; they can inadvertently poison themselves.

The United States imports almost half of all marine aquarium organisms. Approximately two thirds of them come from the Philippines, where cyanide fishing began, and Indonesia, throughout which the practice has spread. Even though cyanide fishing is officially illegal, many of the people in this region live in poverty. As a result, numerous individuals feel that they must assign a lower

Figure 27A Coral reef ecosystem.
Gathering tropical fish in coral reefs with cyanide.

priority to protection of the coral reefs than the effort to earn a living.

There is hope that cyanide fishing may become a less popular way of obtaining organisms for the aquarium trade, as hobbyists and retailers become better educated about the harmful effects of this practice. The Marine Aquarium Council (MAC) is a nonprofit, international organization that certifies marine organisms as having been harvested using environmentally responsible methods. However, some scientists contend that removing fish by any means may be detrimental to the reef community, since some of the most popular aquarium fish are herbivores who keep the plants of the reef from growing too much and overwhelming the coral.

Decide Your Opinion

1. Do you think that marine aquarium hobbyists who opt to buy only MAC-certified fish are making a responsible choice? Or, do you think that stricter measures are necessary? Why or why not?
2. Should immediate human needs take precedence over preserving coral reefs? Can you think of alternatives to cyanide fishing that would help people who live near coral reefs to make a living?
3. At this time, some nations, such as the United States and Australia, have designated small "no-take" zones within their reef systems, where harvesting of reef organisms is strictly prohibited. Do you think that this is a useful step toward coral reef preservation? Can you think of any disadvantages of this approach?

27.4 Working Toward a Sustainable Society

A **sustainable** society, like a sustainable ecosystem, would be able to provide the same goods and services for future generations of human beings as it does now. At the same time, biodiversity would be preserved.

Today's Unsustainable Society

Evidence indicates that at present, human society is most likely not sustainable (Fig. 27.14). The following characteristics make the present human society unsustainable:

- A considerable proportion of land, and therefore natural ecosystems, is presently being used for human purposes (homes, agriculture, factories, etc.).
- Agriculture requires large inputs of nonrenewable fossil fuel energy, fertilizer, and pesticides, which create much pollution. More fresh water is used for agriculture than in homes.
- At least half of the agricultural yield in the United States goes toward feeding animals. According to the ten-to-one rule of thumb, it takes 10 lb of grain to grow 1 lb of meat. Therefore, it is wasteful for citizens in MDCs to eat as much meat as they do. Also, animal sewage pollutes water.

- Even though fresh water is a renewable resource, we are running out of the available supply.
- Our society primarily utilizes nonrenewable fossil fuel energy, which leads to global warming, acid rain, and smog.
- Minerals are nonrenewable, and the mining, manufacture, and use of products are responsible for much environmental pollution.

Characteristics of a Sustainable Society

A natural ecosystem can offer clues as to what a sustainable human society would be like. A natural ecosystem makes use of only renewable solar energy, and its materials cycle through the various populations back to the producer once again. It is clear that if we want to develop a sustainable society, we too should use renewable energy sources and recycle materials (Fig. 27.15).

While we are sometimes quick to realize that the growing populations of the LDCs are putting a strain on the environment, we should realize that the excessive resource consumption of the MDCs also stresses the environment. Sustainability is, more than likely, incompatible with the kinds of consumption/waste patterns currently practiced in the MDCs. Overpopulation, characteristic of the LDCs, and overconsumption, characteristic of the MDCs, account for increased pollution and also the extinction of wildlife.

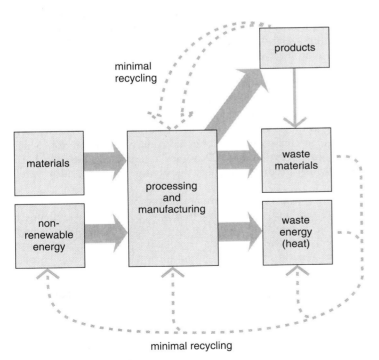

Figure 27.14   Human society at present.
At present, our "throwaway" society is characterized by a high input of energy and raw materials, a large output of waste materials and energy in the form of heat, and minimal recycling (dotted blue arrows).

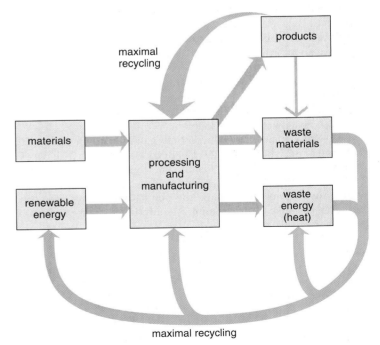

Figure 27.15   Sustainable society.
A sustainable society is characterized by the use of only renewable energy sources, reuse of heat and waste materials (solid blue arrows at bottom), and maximal recycling of products (solid blue arrows at top).

Assessing Economic Well-Being and Quality of Life

Presently, the gross national product (GNP) is a measure of the flow of money from consumers to businesses in the form of goods and services purchased. It can also be considered the total costs of all manufacturing, production, and services in the form of salaries and wages, mortgage and rent, interest and loans, taxes, and profit within and outside a country. In other words, GNP pertains solely to economic activities and does not take into consideration any activities that are socially or environmentally harmful. For example, the balance sheet would account for costs of drugs and hospital stays for lung cancer patients, but not for their pain and distress. Nor do GNP measures account for the damage done to the environment during clear-cutting of forests, strip mining, or land development.

Measures that include noneconomic indicators are probably better at revealing our quality of life than is the GNP. The Index of Sustainable Economic Welfare (ISEW) includes real per capita income, distributional equity, natural resource depletion, environmental damage, and the value of unpaid labor. Another such index is called the Genuine Progress Indicator (GPI). The ISEW and GPI both suggest that the quality of life has gone down, despite the economic improvements indicated by the GNP. While some improvements have occurred over the past several years, such as the improved life of women in many LDCs, the overall quality of life has not improved.

Ecological economists are searching for a way to measure still other values, including the following:

Use value: the actual price we pay to use or consume a resource
Option value: preserving options for the future, such as saving a wetland or a forest
Existence value: saving things we might not realize exist yet, such as flora and fauna in a tropical rain forest that one day could be the source of new drugs
Aesthetic value: appreciating an area or creature for its beauty and/or contribution to biodiversity
Cultural value: factors such as language, mythology, and history that are important for cultural identity
Scientific and educational value: valuing the knowledge of naturalists or even an experience of nature as types of rational facts

---

Today's society is not sustainable. Tomorrow's society might be sustainable if it becomes more like a natural ecosystem and begins to assign a monetary value to all kinds of environmental benefits.

Summarizing the Concepts

27.1 Human Population Growth

The present growth rate for the world's human population has decreased to 1.3%, and if it keeps on decreasing, the population could level off at 11 billion by 2050. Populations have a biotic potential for increase in size. Biotic potential is normally held in check by environmental resistance, and a population size usually levels off at the carrying capacity of the environment.

The MDCs have experienced only modest growth since 1950; their rate of growth is around 0.1%. In contrast, the LDCs have experienced a population explosion. Their growth rate peaked at 2.5% in the early 1960s, and it is now 1.6%. Although the worldwide growth rate is decreasing, the population will increase considerably because more women are entering their reproductive years than are leaving them.

27.2 Human Use of Resources and Pollution

People need a place to live, and sometimes they make poor choices. Beach erosion is common along coasts; the seas are rising, and people often fill in wetlands. Desertification is a possibility when people overuse semiarid lands and also after they remove trees from tropical rain forests, where the soil is thin and nutrient-poor.

Fresh water is available as surface water in rivers and lakes and also in underground sources called aquifers. To increase the supply of fresh water, people build dams, which may not be useful for long because of sediment buildup. Many rivers around the world now run dry and carry a heavy burden of salt. People also remove water from aquifers at a rate that cannot be sustained.

Subsidence, sinkholes, and saltwater intrusion are environmental consequences to withdrawing too much water from aquifers.

Food production has kept pace with population growth. Modern farming is characterized by use of few genetic varieties; heavy use of fertilizers, pesticides, and herbicides; generous irrigation; and excessive fuel consumption. Soil erosion and salinization are side effects of modern farming methods. The green revolution gave the LDCs hybrid plants called "high responders" that produce well as long as they have the subsidies already mentioned. Genetically engineered crops might usher in a second green revolution. Much of the grain grown in the MDCs goes to feeding domesticated animals, which produce much sewage that gets washed into waterways.

Some types of energy are nonrenewable (e.g., fossil fuels and ^{235}uranium), and some are renewable (e.g., hydropower, geothermal energy, wind, and solar energy). The burning of fossil fuels has environmental consequences. Like the panes of a greenhouse, carbon dioxide and other gases allow the sun's rays to pass through but impede the release of infrared wavelengths. It is predicted that a buildup of these "greenhouse gases" will lead to global warming. The effects of global warming could include a rise in sea level and a change in climate patterns. An effect on agriculture could follow.

With regard to renewable energy supplies, only hydropower (dams) and geothermal energy are routinely utilized. However, wind and solar energy are expected to be utilized more in the future. Some predict a solar-hydrogen revolution, in which solar energy replaces fossil fuel energy, and cars run on hydrogen fuel instead of gasoline. This would eventually do away with the environmental problems associated with using fossil fuel energy.

Minerals are a nonrenewable resource that we are using up at a rapid rate because, at present, we do not recycle at any of the steps involved in the production process. Rather, each step in the process creates waste and pollution. Some synthetic organic chemicals are involved in the production of plastics, pesticides, and herbicides as well as all sorts of other products. Ozone shield destruction is particularly associated with CFCs.

The countries of the world discard billions of tons of solid waste, some on land and some in fresh and marine waters. The sources of surface water pollution are many and varied, including human sewage and agricultural and industrial wastes.

27.3 Biodiversity

Habitat loss is the most frequent cause of extinctions followed by introduction of alien species, pollution, overexploitation, and disease. Habitat loss has occurred in all parts of the biosphere, but concern has now centered on tropical rain forests and coral reefs where biodiversity is especially high. Alien species have been introduced into foreign ecosystems because of colonization, horticulture or agriculture, and accidental transport. Among the various causes of pollution, global warming is expected to cause the most instances of extinction. Overexploitation is exemplified by commercial fishing, which is so efficient that fisheries of the world are collapsing. Wildlife is subject to an increasing number of disease-causing pathogens.

The indirect services provided by ecosystems are largely unseen but absolutely necessary to our well-being. These services include the workings of biogeochemical cycles, waste disposal, provision of fresh water, prevention of soil erosion, and regulation of climate. Many people enjoy vacationing in natural settings.

The direct value of biodiversity is exemplified by using wild species as our best source of new medicines to treat human ills and for other medical needs. Wild species have agricultural value. Domesticated plants and animals are derived from wild species, which also serve as a source of genes for the improvement of their phenotypes. Instead of pesticides, wild species can be used as biological controls, and most flowering plants make use of animal pollinators. Much of our food, particularly fish and shellfish, is still caught in the wild. Hardwood trees from natural forests supply us with lumber for various purposes, such as making furniture.

27.4 Working Toward a Sustainable Society

Our present-day society is not sustainable. Calculation of the GNP does not take into account overuse of environmental resources as it should. If we were to pattern our society after natural ecosystems, solar energy would supply our energy needs, and materials would be recycled. A new index such as the GPI would take into account nonmonetary, ecological values.

Studying the Concepts

1. Explain why today's world population is still undergoing exponential growth, even though the growth rate is decreasing. 522–23
2. Distinguish between MDCs and LDCs. Why are most LDCs, but not most MDCs, increasing in size? 522–23
3. Name three locales where humans have settled with unfortunate environmental consequences. What are those consequences? 524–25

4. What environmental problems are associated with damming rivers and taking water from aquifers? What can be done to conserve water? 525–26
5. Name four characteristics of modern farming methods and the drawbacks of each. What is happening to the soil around the world? What was the green revolution, and why might there be another one? What are the drawbacks of raising livestock? 526–27
6. What are the types of fossil fuels, and what environmental problems are associated with burning fossil fuels? 528
7. What renewable energy sources are available? Discuss the possible solar-hydrogen revolution that is expected to be under way. What are the benefits of this revolution? 528–29
8. What are minerals, and what are the drawbacks of mining them? 530
9. What hazardous wastes are being dumped into the environment? Why do some of these result in biological magnification? 530
10. Discuss the five major reasons we are losing biodiversity today. 531–32
11. Discuss the indirect and direct values of biodiversity. 533–35
12. What are the characteristics of the present unsustainable human society? Of a sustainable society? Contrast the GNP with the GPI. 537–38

Thinking Critically About the Concepts

Refer to the opening vignette on page 521, and then answer these questions.

1. What sorts of pressures could cause modern-day farmers to use the four farming practices listed on page 526?
2. What environmental reasons would you give a friend for becoming a vegetarian?
3. Do you think a solar-hydrogen revolution will occur during the lifetime of this generation? Why or why not?

Testing Your Knowledge of the Concepts

Choose the best answer for each question.

1. Exponential growth is best described by
   a. steep unrestricted growth.
   b. an S-shaped growth curve.
   c. a constant rate of growth.
   d. growth that levels off after rapid growth.
   e. Both b and d are correct.
2. When the carrying capacity of the environment is exceeded, the population will typically
   a. increase but at a slower rate.
   b. stabilize at the highest level reached.
   c. decrease.
   d. die off entirely.
3. Decreased death rate followed by decreased birthrate has occurred in
   a. MDCs.
   b. LDCs.
   c. MDCs and LDCs.
   d. neither MDCs nor LDCs.

4. Which of the following is a renewable resource?
   a. oil
   b. coal
   c. solar energy
   d. deep aquifers
   e. phosphorous

5. Renewable resources
   a. are always forthcoming compared with nonrenewable resources.
   b. supply may be inadequate for human needs.
   c. include such energy sources as wind, solar, and biomass.
   d. All of these are correct.

6. Desertification is often caused by
   a. overuse of aquifers.
   b. urban sprawl.
   c. air pollution.
   d. overgrazing.

7. Soil in the tropics is often nutrient-poor because
   a. nutrients are tied up in plants.
   b. it is mostly sand.
   c. it has a high pH.
   d. rainfall leaches out minerals.

8. Most fresh water is used for
   a. domestic purposes, such as bathing, flushing toilets, and watering lawns.
   b. domestic purposes, such as cooking and drinking.
   c. agriculture.
   d. industry.

9. Which of the following is not a major problem with the damming of rivers?
   a. increase in salinity
   b. loss of water through evaporation
   c. change in the level of the water table
   d. buildup of sediment

10. Removal of groundwater from aquifers may cause
    a. pollution.
    b. subsidence.
    c. mineral depletion.
    d. soil erosion.
    e. All of these are correct.

11. Which of the following is not a component of modern agriculture?
    a. dependency on chemical inputs
    b. frequent irrigation
    c. high fuel consumption
    d. high diversity of cultivars planted

12. Farmland becomes desertized as a result of
    a. high fertilizer input.
    b. frequent irrigation.
    c. soil erosion.
    d. deep tilling.
    e. Both b and d are correct.

13. Green revolution crop varieties are
    a. genetically diverse.
    b. high responders.
    c. drought tolerant.
    d. deep-rooted plants.

14. The raising of domestic livestock
    a. consumes large amounts of fossil fuels.
    b. leads to water pollution.
    c. is energetically wasteful.
    d. All of these are correct.

15. The best way to maintain fish supplies is to
    a. limit harvesting to the ability of fish to reproduce.
    b. do away with all the other animals that feed on fish.
    c. use larger and better kinds of nets
    d. All of these are good ways to maintain fish supplies.

For questions 16–20, match the description to the type of fuel in the key. Each answer can be used more than once. Each question may have more than one answer.

Key:

   a. nuclear power
   b. fossil fuels
   c. hydropower
   d. solar power
   e. wind power
   f. geothermal power

16. Renewable source of power

17. Waste products are harmful

18. Detrimental environmental effects

19. More available in certain geographic locations

20. Contribute(s) to global warming

21. Heavy metals are dangerous to humans because they
    a. inhibit important enzymes.
    b. cause apoptosis.
    c. reduce the body's ability to carry oxygen.
    d. break down mitochondria.

22. The Earth's ozone shield has been damaged by
    a. heavy metals.
    b. strip mining.
    c. chlorofluorocarbons.
    d. fossil fuels.

23. Which of these are a direct value of wildlife?
    a. medicinal value
    b. agricultural value
    c. consumptive use value
    d. All of these are correct.

24. Markets for endangered species is an example of
    a. habitat loss.
    b. pollution.
    c. alien species.
    d. disease.
    e. overexploitation.

25. It would be a good idea to
    a. stop using wildlife as having economic value when calculating the GNP.
    b. start considering the harm done to the environment from various commercial activities when calculating the GNP.
    c. give up the idea of searching for a way to measure values, such as aesthetic value.
    d. All of these are correct.

26. Which of the following is not a function that ecosystems can perform for humans?
    a. purification of water
    b. immobilization of pollutants
    c. reduction of soil erosion
    d. removal of excess soil nitrogen
    e. All of these are functions of an ecosystem.

27. A transition to hydrogen fuel technology will
    a. be long in coming and not likely to be of major significance.
    b. lessen many current environmental problems.
    c. not be likely since it will always be expensive and as polluting as natural gas.
    d. be of major consequence, but resource limitations for obtaining hydrogen will hinder its progress.

28. GNP measures all but
    a. total costs of all manufacturing and production.
    b. costs of services.
    c. cost of environmental degradation through waste costs.
    d. profit.
    e. All of these are correct.

29. In which of the following is biological magnification most pronounced?
    a. aquatic food chains
    b. terrestrial food chains
    c. long food chains
    d. energy pyramids
    e. Both a and c are correct.

30. Which of these results is not expected because of global warming?
    a. the inability of species to migrate to cooler climates as environmental temperatures rise
    b. the bleaching and drowning of coral reefs
    c. rise in sea levels and loss of wetlands
    d. preservation of species because cold weather causes hardships
    e. All of these results are expected.

31. Complete the following graph by labeling each bar with a cause of extinction, from the most influential to the least.

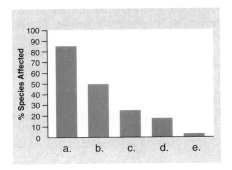

a. _____
b. _____
c. _____
d. _____
e. _____

Understanding Key Terms

alien species 531
aquifer 525
biodiversity 531
biological magnification 530
biotic potential 522
carrying capacity 522
chlorofluorocarbons (CFCs) 530
deforestation 525
desertification 524
environmental resistance 522
exponential growth 522
fossil fuel 528
greenhouse gases 528

growth rate 522
mineral 530
nonrenewable resource 524
ozone shield 530
photovoltaic (solar) cell 529
pollution 524
renewable resource 524
replacement reproduction 523
resource 524
salinization 526
saltwater intrusion 526
sinkhole 526
subsidence 526
sustainable 537

Match the key terms to these definitions.

a. _____ The ability of a society or ecosystem to maintain itself while also providing services to human beings.

b. _____ Largest number of organisms of a particular species that can be maintained indefinitely in an ecosystem.

c. _____ Gases such as carbon dioxide and methane in the atmosphere that trap heat.

d. _____ Concentration of a synthetic organic chemical as it passes along a food chain.

e. _____ Water reservoir below the Earth's surface.

Online Learning Center

www.mhhe.com/maderhuman9

The Online Learning Center provides a wealth of information fully organized and integrated by chapter. You will find practice quizzes, interactive activities, labeling exercises, flashcards, and much more that will complement your learning and understanding of human biology.

Looking at Both Sides

Each day, the Internet, media, and other people present you with opposing viewpoints on a wide range of subjects. Your ability to develop an informed opinion on an issue, and talk to others about it, is extremely important.

To expand and enhance your knowledge of a highly relevant bioethical issue, visit the "Student Edition" of the Online Learning Center. Under "Course-Wide Content," select "Looking at Both Sides." Once there, you will be asked to complete activities that will increase your understanding of a current bioethical issue related to this chapter and allow you to defend your opinion.

APPENDIX

Answer Key

This appendix contains the answers to the Testing Your Knowledge of the Concepts and Understanding Key Terms questions, which appear at the end of each chapter, and the Practice Problems and Additional Genetics Problems, which appear in Chapter 18.*

Chapter 1
Testing Your Knowledge of the Concepts
1. d; **2.** e; **3.** a; **4.** c; **5.** a; **6.** b; **7.** c; **8.** a; **9.** c; **10.** a; **11.** b; **12.** d; **13.** d; **14.** b; **15.** c; **16.** c; **17.** a; **18.** d; **19.** a; **20.** c; **21.** b; **22.** e; **23.** d

Understanding Key Terms
a. biosphere; **b.** cell; **c.** scientific theory; **d.** homeostasis; **e.** domain

Chapter 2
Testing Your Knowledge of the Concepts
1. b; **2.** c; **3.** a; **4.** b; **5.** c; **6.** e; **7.** a; **8.** b; **9.** d; **10.** a; **11.** c; **12.** a; **13.** c; **14.** d; **15.** b; **16.** b; **17.** b; **18.** d; **19.** c; **20.** a; **21.** d; **22.** e; **23.** b; **24.** c; **25.** c; **26.** e; **27.** c; **28. a.** subunits; **b.** dehydration reaction; **c.** macromolecule; **d.** hydrolysis reaction

Understanding Key Terms
a. emulsification; **b.** ion; **c.** covalent bond; **d.** hydrophilic; **e.** hydrogen bond

Chapter 3
Testing Your Knowledge of the Concepts
1. c; **2.** b; **3.** c; **4.** a; **5.** d; **6.** b; **7.** c; **8.** c; **9.** a; **10.** c; **11.** b; **12.** b; **13.** b; **14.** c; **15. a.** carbohydrate chain; **b.** glycoprotein; **c.** glycolipid; **d.** hydrophilic head; **e.** hydrophobic tails; **f.** phospholipid bilayer; **g.** filaments of the cytoskeleton; **h.** membrane protein; **i.** cholesterol; **j.** membrane protein; **16.** c; **17.** a; **18.** e; **19.** e; **20.** a; **21. a.** active site; **b.** substrates; **c.** product; **d.** enzyme; **e.** enzyme-substrate complex; **f.** enzyme. The shape of an enzyme is important to its activity because it allows an enzyme-substrate complex to form; **22.** b; **23.** c; **24.** b,d; **25.** c; **26.** b; **27.** a; **28.** a; **29.** c

Understanding Key Terms
a. coenzyme; **b.** osmosis; **c.** selectively permeable; **d.** fermentation; **e.** cellular respiration

Chapter 4
Testing Your Knowledge of the Concepts
1. d; **2.** d; **3.** b; **4.** d; **5.** c; **6.** d; **7.** d; **8.** b; **9.** b; **10.** d; **11.** a; **12.** d; **13.** c; **14.** a; **15.** b; **16.** c; **17.** c; **18.** d; **19. a.** thoracic cavity, **b.** abdominal cavity; **c.** dorsal cavity; **d.** diaphragm; **20.** e; **21.** b

Understanding Key Terms
a. ligament; **b.** epidermis; **c.** striated; **d.** homeostasis; **e.** spongy bone

Chapter 5
Testing Your Knowledge of the Concepts
1. b; **2.** a; **3.** c; **4.** b; **5.** a; **6.** c; **7.** b; **8.** b; **9.** c; **10.** c; **11.** c; **12.** d; **13.** b; **14.** e; **15.** e; **16.** d; **17.** c; **18.** c; **19.** e; **20.** e; **21.** a; **22.** b; **23. a.** jugular vein;

*Answers to the Thinking Critically About the Concepts questions can be found on the Online Learning Center at www.mhhe.com/maderhuman9.

A-1

b. pulmonary artery; **c.** superior vena cava; **d.** inferior vena cava; **e.** hepatic vein; **f.** hepatic portal vein; **g.** renal vein; **h.** iliac vein; **i.** carotid artery; **j.** pulmonary vein; **k.** aorta; **l.** mesenteric arteries; **m.** renal artery; **n.** iliac artery. See also Figure 5.11, page 86.

Understanding Key Terms
a. diastole; **b.** inferior vena cava; **c.** pulse; **d.** venule; **e.** systemic circuit

Chapter 6
Testing Your Knowledge of the Concepts
1. a; **2.** a; **3.** b; **4.** d; **5.** c; **6.** e; **7.** c; **8.** d; **9.** a; **10.** e; **11.** b; **12.** c; **13.** a; **14.** d; **15.** c; **16.** b; **17.** a; **18.** b; **19.** a; **20.** c; **21.** c; **22.** d; **23.** d; **24.** d; **25.** e; **26.** e; **27.** d; **28.** d; **29.** e; **30.** c; **31.** a; **32.** a; **33. a.** blood pressure; **b.** osmotic pressure; **c.** blood pressure; **d.** osmotic pressure

Understanding Key Terms
a. hemoglobin; **b.** formed element; **c.** plasma; **d.** osmotic pressure; **e.** prothrombin

Chapter 7
Testing Your Knowledge of the Concepts
1. d; **2.** a; **3.** b; **4.** e; **5.** c; **6.** a; **7.** b; **8.** e; **9.** d; **10.** d; **11.** d; **12.** e; **13.** c; **14.** e; **15.** b; **16.** c; **17.** d; **18.** a; **19.** c; **20.** a; **21.** b; **22.** d; **23.** Test tube 1: no digestion—no enzyme and no HCl; Test tube 2: some digestion—no HCl; Test tube 3: no digestion—no enzyme; Test tube 4: digestion—both enzyme and HCl are present; **24.** c; **25.** b; **26.** a; **27.** d; **28.** a; **29.** c; **30.** b, c; **31.** d; **32.** a; **33.** e; **34.** b, c; **35.** e; **36.** a

Understanding Key Terms
a. vitamin; **b.** lipase; **c.** lacteal; **d.** esophagus; **e.** gallbladder

Chapter 8
Testing Your Knowledge of the Concepts
1. d; **2.** d; **3.** c; **4.** d; **5.** c; **6.** b; **7.** a; **8.** b; **9.** e; **10.** b; **11.** d; **12.** f; **13.** d; **14.** a; **15.** b; **16.** e; **17.** d; **18. a.** nasal cavity; **b.** nose; **c.** pharynx; **d.** epiglottis; **e.** glottis; **f.** larynx; **g.** trachea; **h.** bronchus; **i.** bronchiole. See also Figure 8.1, page 142.

Understanding Key Terms
a. pharynx; **b.** aortic body; **c.** vocal cords; **d.** bicarbonate ion; **e.** expiration

Chapter 9
Testing Your Knowledge of the Concepts
1. c; **2.** c; **3.** d; **4.** a; **5.** c; **6.** b; **7.** d; **8.** a; **9.** d; **10.** d; **11.** a; **12.** c; **13.** d; **14.** d; **15.** c; **16.** a; **17.** c; **18.** c; **19.** f; **20.** a; **21.** c; **22.** e; **23.** b; **24.** d; **25.** g; **26.** b; **27.** a, b; **28.** a, b; **29.** a; **30.** a, c; **31.** b; **32. a.** glomerular capsule; **b.** glomerulus; **c.** efferent arteriole; **d.** afferent arteriole; **e.** proximal convoluted tubule; **f.** renal artery; **g.** renal vein; **h.** descending limb; **i.** ascending limb; **j.** loop of the nephron; **k.** peritubular capillary network; **l.** distal convoluted tubule; **m.** collecting duct; **33.** a; **34.** e

Understanding Key Terms
a. diuretic; **b.** excretion; **c.** urethra; **d.** renal pelvis; **e.** glomerular filtrate

Chapter 10
Testing Your Knowledge of the Concepts
1. b; **2.** c; **3.** d; **4.** a; **5.** g; **6.** f; **7.** e; **8.** e; **9.** a; **10.** b; **11.** c; **12.** f; **13.** d; **14.** b; **15.** b; **16.** a; **17.** b; **18.** c; **19.** c; **20.** e; **21.** c; **22.** c; **23.** F; **24.** T; **25.** F; **26.** T; **27.** T; **28.** b; **29.** d; **30.** d; **31.** a; **32.** c; **33. a.** coxal bone; **b.** femur; **c.** patella; **d.** tibia; **e.** fibula; **f.** metatarsals; **g.** phalanges; **h.** tarsals; **34.** c; **35.** b; **36.** a; **37.** e; **38.** c; **39.** d

Understanding Key Terms
a. meniscus; **b.** compact bone; **c.** sinus; **d.** fontanel; **e.** osteocyte

Chapter 11
Testing Your Knowledge of the Concepts
1. a; **2.** c; **3.** b; **4.** a; **5.** c; **6.** c; **7. a.** T tubule; **b.** sarcoplasmic reticulum; **c.** myofibril **d.** Z line; **e.** sarcomere **f.** sarcolemma; **8.** e; **9.** a; **10.** d; **11.** d; **12.** b; **13.** e; **14.** a; **15.** e; **16.** e; **17.** d; **18.** e; **19.** d; **20.** a; **21.** b; **22.** c; **23.** c; **24.** a; **25.** d; **26.** b; **27.** c; **28.** a; **29.** b; **30.** a; **31.** c; **32.** b; **33.** b; **34.** a; **35.** c.

Understanding Key Terms
a. sarcomere; **b.** insertion; **c.** oxygen deficit; **d.** tetanus

Chapter 12
Testing Your Knowledge of the Concepts
1. c; **2.** b; **3.** a; **4.** c; **5.** d; **6.** c; **7.** d; **8.** b; **9.** c; **10.** e; **11.** b; **12.** c; **13.** a; **14.** a; **15.** c; **16.** d; **17.** b; **18.** c; **19.** b; **20.** d; **21.** d; **22.** c; **23. a.** sensory neuron (or fiber); **b.** interneuron; **c.** motor neuron (or fiber); **d.** sensory receptor; **e.** cell body; **f.** dendrites; **g.** axon; **h.** nucleus of Schwann cell; **i.** node of Ranvier; **j.** effector

Understanding Key Terms
a. reflex; **b.** neurotransmitter; **c.** autonomic system; **d.** ganglion; **e.** acetylcholine

Chapter 13
Testing Your Knowledge of the Concepts
1. d; **2.** e; **3.** b; **4.** c; **5.** d; **6.** d; **7.** c; **8.** b; **9.** e; **10.** d; **11.** b; **12.** c; **13.** a; **14.** e; **15.** b; **16. a.** retina—contains receptors; **b.** choroid—absorbs stray light; **c.** sclera—protects and supports eyeball; **d.** optic nerve—transmits impulses to brain; **e.** fovea centralis—makes acute vision possible; **f.** ciliary body—holds lens in place, accommodation; **g.** lens—refracts and focuses light rays; **h.** iris—regulates light entrance; **i.** pupil—admits light; **j.** cornea—refracts light rays; **17.** a; **18.** c; **19.** d; **20.** b; **21.** d; **22.** a

Understanding Key Terms
a. sensory receptor; **b.** retina; **c.** sclera; **d.** chemoreceptor; **e.** spiral organ

Chapter 14
Testing Your Knowledge of the Concepts
1. d; **2.** b; **3.** c; **4.** c; **5.** e; **6.** d; **7.** c; **8.** a; **9.** d; **10.** e; **11.** c; **12.** b; **13.** b; **14.** e; **15.** b; **16.** d; **17. a.** inhibits; **b.** inhibits; **c.** releasing hormone; **d.** stimulating hormone; **e.** target gland hormone; **18.** d; **19.** b; **20.** f; **21.** b; **22.** c; **23.** a; **24.** e; **25.** e; **26.** d

Understanding Key Terms
a. thyroid gland; **b.** diabetes mellitus; **c.** adrenocorticotropic hormone (ACTH); **d.** peptide hormone; **e.** oxytocin

Chapter 15
Testing Your Knowledge of the Concepts
1. a. seminal vesicle; **b.** ejaculatory duct; **c.** prostate gland; **d.** bulbourethral gland; **e.** anus; **f.** vas deferens; **g.** epididymis; **h.** testis;

i. scrotum; **j.** foreskin; **k.** glans penis; **l.** penis; **m.** urethra; **n.** vas deferens; **o.** urinary bladder. Path of sperm: h, g, f, n, b, m. See also Figure 15.1, page 290; **2.** c; **3.** d; **4.** c; **5.** c; **6.** b; **7.** d; **8.** c; **9.** d; **10.** d; **11.** e; **12.** c; **13.** d; **14.** c; **15.** d; **16.** a; **17.** d; **18.** d; **19.** c; **20.** a; **21.** e; **22.** c; **23.** b; **24.** d; **25.** d; **26.** b; **27.** a; **28.** c

Understanding Key Terms
a. ovulation; **b.** progesterone; **c.** semen; **d.** cervix; **e.** acrosome

Chapter 16
Testing Your Knowledge of the Concepts
1. c; **2.** b; **3.** a; **4.** c; **5.** d; **6.** d; **7.** d; **8.** b; **9.** c; **10.** b; **11.** c; **12.** c; **13.** a; **14.** e; **15.** d; **16.** d; **17.** e; **18.** e; **19. a.** chorion (contributes to forming placenta where wastes are exchanged for nutrients with the mother); **b.** amnion (protects and prevents desiccation); **c.** umbilical cord (connects developing embryo to the placenta); **d.** allantois (blood vessels become umbilical blood vessels); **e.** yolk sac (first site of blood cell formation); **20.** e; **21.** e; **22.** e; **23.** e; **24.** b; **25.** e; **26. a.** arterial duct; **b.** oval opening; **c.** venus duct; **d.** umbilical vein; **e.** umbilical arteries

Understanding Key Terms
a. lanugo; **b.** differentiation; **c.** amnion; **d.** fertilization; **e.** primary germ layer

Chapter 17
Testing Your Knowledge of the Concepts
1. a; **2.** a; **3.** b; **4.** a; **5.** c; **6.** d; **7.** c; **8.** e; **9.** a; **10.** d; **11.** b; **12.** c; **13.** d; **14.** d; **15.** d; **16.** a; **17.** b; **18.** e; **19.** d; **20.** a; **21.** c; **22.** c; **23.** b; **24.** c; **25.** c; **26.** c; **27.** c; **28.** b

Understanding Key Terms
a. homologous chromosome; **b.** cell cycle; **c.** mitotic spindle; **d.** polar body; **e.** haploid

Chapter 18
Practice Problems 1
1. a. *W*; **b.** *WS, Ws*; **c.** *T, t*; **d.** *Tg, tg*; **e.** *AB, Ab, aB, ab*; **2. a.** gamete; **b.** genotype; **c.** gamete; **d.** genotype; **3. a.** *EeSs*; **b.** *eeSS*

Practice Problems 2
1. *Ww*; **2.** 75% or 3/4; **3.** mother and father: *Ee* and *Ee*; **4.** father: *DD*; mother: *dd*; children: *Dd*

Practice Problems 3
1. Dihybrid *EeWw*; **2.** dihybrid *EeWw*; **3.** 1/16; **4.** child: *ddff*; father: *DdFf*; mother: *ddff*

Practice Problems 4
1. *AABBCC* and *aabbcc*; **2.** very light; **3.** child: *ii*, mother: $I^A i$, father: *ii*, $I^A i$, $I^B i$; **4.** baby 1 = Doe; baby 2 = Jones

Practice Problems 5
1. His mother; mother $X^B X^b$, father $X^B Y$, son $X^b Y$; **2.** 100%; none; 100%; **3.** color-blind; The husband is not the father; **4.** $ss X^b Y$; $SS X^B X^B$

Testing Your Knowledge of the Concepts
1. e; **2.** c; **3.** a; **4.** d; **5.** d; **6.** b; **7.** c; **8.** b; **9.** a; **10.** a; **11.** See Figure 18.5, page 356; **12.** a; **13.** c; **14.** d; **15.** d; **16.** c; **17.** a; **18.** d; **19.** b; **20.** c; **21.** a; **22.** e; **23.** b; **24.** d; **25.** c; **26.** b; **27.** b; **28.** c

Understanding Key Terms
a. Punnett square; **b.** allele; **c.** dominant allele; **d.** locus; **e.** genotype

Chapter 19
Testing Your Knowledge of the Concepts
1. e; **2.** e; **3.** c; **4.** c; **5.** d; **6.** b; **7.** b; **8.** e; **9.** e; **10.** d; **11.** a; **12.** c; **13.** d; **14.** c; **15.** e; **16. a.** ACU'CCU'GAA'UGC'AAA; **b.** UGA'GGA'CU-U'ACG'UUU; **17.** c; **18.** e

Understanding Key Terms
a. polyribosome; **b.** transgenic organism; **c.** template; **d.** transcription; **e.** vector

Chapter 20
Testing Your Knowledge of the Concepts
1. e; **2.** d; **3.** a; **4.** b; **5.** d; **6.** c; **7.** a; **8.** e; **9.** d; **10.** c; **11.** a; **12.** b; **13.** $X^B X^b$; **14.** e; **15.** c; **16.** b; **17.** d; **18.** d; **19.** b; **20.** autosomal recessive

Additional Genetic Problems
1. a. All sons will inherit the X^b from the mother and therefore, will be color-blind. **b.** All daughters will inherit one X^b from their mother, and therefore will not be color-blind but will be carriers. **2. a.** His mother could have had the disease, or have been a carrier for the disease. **b.** His daughter would be a carrier.; **3.** Her mother was either a carrier or a hemophiliac, and her father was a hemophiliac. **4. a.** He has either one or two dominant alleles for the disease. **b.** His father may have the disease or may be normal. **5. a., b.** Yes, if he is heterozygous and the son or daughter receives the recessive gene. **6. a.** At least one of his parents has the disease and passed one allele to him. **b.** He has one allele for the disease, and therefore could live long enough to father a child. **7.** If she is a carrier for cystic fibrosis, they could not have a child with the disease unless her husband is also a carrier. **8.** Parents are heterozygous; child is homozygous recessive. There is a 25% chance that each child would have the disease. **9.** Yes, one or both parents could be homozygous recessive.

Understanding Key Terms
a. karyotype; **b.** chorionic villi sampling; **c.** Barr body; **d.** inversion; **e.** cystic fibrosis

Chapter 21
Testing Your Knowledge of the Concepts
1. b; **2.** d; **3.** e; **4.** a; **5.** f; **6.** c; **7.** b; **8.** d; **9.** a; **10.** e; **11.** e; **12.** d; **13.** c; **14.** c; **15.** b; **16. a.** antigen-binging sites; **b.** light chain; **c.** heavy chain; **d.** v = variable regions, c = constant region; **17.** c; **18.** c; **19.** c

Understanding Key Terms
a. vaccine; **b.** complement system; **c.** antigen; **d.** apoptosis; **e.** T cell

Chapter 22
Testing Your Knowledge of the Concepts
1. d; **2.** d; **3.** d; **4.** a; **5.** a; **6.** b; **7.** b; **8.** b; **9.** d; **10.** d; **11.** b; **12.** b; **13.** a; **14.** a; **15.** d; **16.** a; **17.** a; **18.** c; **19.** d; **20.** c; **21.** e; **22.** b; **23.** e; **24.** c

Understanding Key Terms
a. bacilli; **b.** pandemic; **c.** epidemiology; **d.** eukaryotic cell; **e.** endospore

Chapter 23
Testing Your Knowledge of the Concepts
1. d; **2.** d; **3.** c; **4.** d; **5.** c; **6.** e; **7.** b; **8.** a, b, c; **9.** g; **10.** a, b; **11.** e, f; **12.** b; **13.** b; **14.** d; **15.** d; **16.** d; **17.** d; **18.** d; **19.** b; **20.** d; **21.** c; **22.** d; **23.** b; **24.** c; **25.** b; **26.** e; **27.** b; **28.** c; **29.** d; **30.** b; **31.** a; **32.** c; **33.** d; **34.** e

Understanding Key Terms
a. hepatitis; **b.** pelvic inflammatory disease (PID); **c.** retrovirus; **d.** opportunistic infection; **e.** candidal vaginitis

Chapter 24
Testing Your Knowledge of the Concepts
1. d; **2.** d; **3.** d; **4.** c; **5.** c; **6.** c; **7.** b; **8.** d; **9.** b; **10.** c; **11.** b; **12.** a; **13.** c; **14.** e; **15.** b; **16.** d; **17.** d; **18.** c; **19.** a; **20.** d; **21.** a

Understanding Key Terms
a. telomere; **b.** carcinogen; **c.** proto-oncogene; **d.** angiogenesis; **e.** metastasis

Chapter 25
Testing Your Knowledge of the Concepts
1. c; **2.** b; **3.** b; **4.** a; **5.** e; **6.** e; **7.** e; **8.** e; **9.** a; **10.** b; **11.** b; **12.** d; **13.** c; **14.** b; **15.** e; **16.** b; **17. a.** a, b, c, d; **b.** e, See also Figure 25.10, page 499; **18. a.** Chordata; **b.** class; **c.** order; **d.** Hominidae; **e.** genus; **f.** *Homo sapiens*; **19.** b; **20.** a; **21.** d; **22.** c

Understanding Key Terms
a. natural selection; **b.** adaptation; **c.** homologous structure; **d.** chemical evolution; **e.** fossil

Chapter 26
Testing Your Knowledge of the Concepts
1. d; **2.** a; **3.** b; **4.** c; **5.** c; **6.** b; **7.** e; **8.** e; **9.** c; **10.** c; **11.** b; **12. a.** producers; **b.** consumers; **c.** inorganic nutrient pool; **d.** decomposers; **13. a.** top carnivore, tertiary consumers; **b.** carnivore, secondary consumers; **c.** herbivore, primary consumers; **d.** producer, autotrophs; **14.** c; **15.** b; **16.** b; **17.** c, d; **18.** a; **19.** f; **20.** e; **21.** f; **22.** b, c, d; **23.** a, b, c; **24.** d

Understanding Key Terms
a. ecological pyramid; **b.** ecological succession; **c.** fossil fuel; **d.** nitrogen fixation; **e.** producer

Chapter 27
Testing Your Knowledge of the Concepts
1. a; **2.** c; **3.** a; **4.** c; **5.** d; **6.** d; **7.** a; **8.** c; **9.** c; **10.** b; **11.** d; **12.** c; **13.** b; **14.** d; **15.** a; **16.** c, d, e, f; **17.** a, b; **18.** a, b, c; **19.** c, d, e, f; **20.** b; **21.** a; **22.** c; **23.** d; **24.** e; **25.** b; **26.** e; **27.** b; **28.** c; **29.** e; **30.** d; **31. a.** habitat loss; **b.** alien species; **c.** pollution; **d.** overexploitation; **e.** disease

Understanding Key Terms
a. sustainable; **b.** carrying capacity; **c.** greenhouse gases; **d.** biological magnification; **e.** aquifer

GLOSSARY

A

acetylcholine (ACh) (uh-seet-ul-koh-leen) Neurotransmitter active in both the peripheral and central nervous systems.   222

acetylcholinesterase (AChE) (uh-seet-ul-koh-luh-nes-tuh-rays) Enzyme that breaks down acetylcholine bound to postsynaptic receptors within a synapse.   222

acid Molecules tending to raise the hydrogen ion concentration in a solution and to lower its pH numerically.   20

acidosis Excessive accumulation of acids in body fluids.   170

acquired immunodeficiency syndrome (AIDS) (im-yuh-noh-dih-fish-un-see) Disease caused by HIV and transmitted via body fluids; characterized by failure of the immune system.   460

acromegaly (ak-roh-meg-uh-lee) Condition resulting from an increase in growth hormone production after adult height has been achieved.   272

acrosome (ak-ruh-sohm) Cap at the anterior end of a sperm that partially covers the nucleus and contains enzymes that help the sperm penetrate the egg.   293

actin (ak-tin) One of two major proteins of muscle; makes up thin filaments in myofibrils of muscle fibers. See myosin.   202

actin filaments Cytoskeletal filaments of eukaryotic cells composed of the protein actin; also refers to the thin filaments of muscle cells.   43

action potential Electrochemical changes that take place across the axomembrane; the nerve impulse.   220

active immunity Reistance to disease due to the immune system's response to a microorganism or a vaccine.   424

active site Region on the surface of an enzyme where the substrate binds and where the reaction occurs.   48

active transport Use of a plasma membrane carrier protein and energy to move a substance into or out of a cell from lower to higher concentration.   42

acute bronchitis (brahn-ky-tis) Infection of the primary and secondary bronchi.   152

acute infection Disease characterized by rapid onset and short duration.   434

adaptation Organism's modification in structure, function, or behavior suitable to the environment.   489

Addison disease Condition resulting from a deficiency of adrenal cortex hormones; characterized by low blood glucose, weight loss, and weakness.   277

adenine (A) (ad-uh-neen) One of four nitrogen bases in nucleotides composing the structure of DNA and RNA.   30

adipose tissue (ah-duh-pohs) Connective tissue in which fat is stored.   56

ADP (adenosine diphosphate) (ah-den-ah-seen dy-fahs-fayt) Nucleotide with two phosphate groups that can accept another phosphate group and become ATP.   30

adrenal cortex (uh-dree-nul kor-teks) Outer portion of the adrenal gland; secretes mineralocorticoids, such as aldosterone, and glucocorticoids, such as cortisol.   275

adrenal gland (uh-dree-nul) An endocrine gland that lies atop a kidney; consisting of the inner adrenal medulla and the outer adrenal cortex.   275

adrenal medulla (uh-dree-nul muh-dul-uh) Inner portion of the adrenal gland; secretes the hormones epinephrine and norepinephrine.   275

adrenocorticotropic hormone (ACTH) (uh-dree-noh-kawrt-ih-koh-troh-pik) Hormone secreted by the anterior lobe of the pituitary gland that stimulates activity in the adrenal cortex.   270

afterbirth Placenta and the extraembryonic membranes, which are delivered (expelled) during the third stage of parturition.   325

agglutination (uh-gloot-un-ay-shun) Clumping of red blood cells due to a reaction between antigens on red blood cell plasma membranes and antibodies in the plasma.   106

aging Progressive changes over time, leading to loss of physiologic function and eventual death.   326

agranular leukocyte White blood cell that does not contain distinctive granules.   103

albumin (al-byoo-mun) Plasma protein of the blood having transport and osmotic functions.   99

aldosterone (al-dahs-tuh-rohn) Hormone secreted by the adrenal cortex that decreases sodium and increases potassium excretion; raises blood volume and pressure.   168, 276

alien species Nonnative species that migrate or are introduced by humans into a new ecosystem; also called exotics.   531

alkalosis Excessive accumulation of bases in body fluids.   170

allantois (uh-lan-toh-is) Extraembryonic membrane that contributes to the formation of umbilical blood vessels in humans.   311

allele (uh-leel) Alternative form of a gene; alleles occur at the same locus on homologous chromosomes.   352

allergen (al-ur-jun) Foreign substance capable of stimulating an allergic response.   426

allergy Immune response to substances that usually are not recognized as foreign.   426

all-or-none law Law that states that muscle fibers either contract maximally or not at all, and that neurons either conduct a nerve impulse completely or not at all.   206

alveolus (pl., alveoli) (al-vee-uh-lus) Air sac of a lung.   145

Alzheimer disease (AD) Brain disorder characterized by a general loss of mental abilities.   236

amino acid Organic molecule having an amino group and an acid group, which covalently bonds to produce peptide molecules.   26

amniocentesis Procedure in which a sample of amniotic fluid is removed through the abdominal wall of a pregnant woman. Fetal cells in it are cultured before doing a karyotype of the chromosomes.   390

amnion (am-nee-ahn) Extraembryonic membrane that forms an enclosing, fluid-filled sac.   311

ampulla (am-pool-uh, -pul-uh) Base of a semicircular canal in the inner ear.   261

amygdala (uh-mig-duh-luh) Portion of the limbic system that functions to add emotional overtones to memories.   230

anabolic steroid (a-nuh-bahl-ik) Synthetic steroid that mimics the effect of testosterone.   280

analogous structure Structure that has a similar function in separate lineages but differs in anatomy and ancestry.   490

anaphase Mitotic phase during which daughter chromosomes move toward the poles of the spindle.   338

anaphylactic shock Severe systemic form of allergic reaction involving bronchiolar contriction, impaired breathing, vasodilation, and a rapid drop in blood pressure with a threat of circulatory failure.   426

androgen (an-druh-jun) Male sex hormone (e.g., testosterone).   280

anemia (uh-nee-mee-uh) Inefficiency in the oxygen-carrying ability of blood due to a shortage of hemoglobin.   101

aneurysm Sac-like expansion of a blood vessel wall.   88

angina pectoris (an-jy-nuh pek-tuh-ris) Condition characterized by thoracic pain resulting from occluded coronary arteries; precedes a heart attack.   88

angiogenesis (an-jee-oh-jen-uh-sis) Formation of new blood vessels; one mechanism by which cancer spreads.   473

angioplasty (an-jee-uh-plas-tee) Surgical procedure for treating clogged arteries, in which a plastic tube is threaded through a major blood vessel toward the heart and then a balloon at the end of the tube is inflated, forcing open the vessel. A stent is then placed in the vessel.   91

anorexia nervosa (a-nuh-rek-see-uh nur-voh-suh) Eating disorder characterized by a morbid fear of gaining weight.   137

anterior pituitary (pih-too-ih-tair-ee) Portion of the pituitary gland that is controlled by the hypothalamus and produces six types of hormones, some of which control other endocrine glands.   270

anthropoid Group of primates that includes monkeys, apes, and humans.   493

antibody (an-tih-bahd-ee) Protein produced in response to the presence of an antigen; each antibody combines with a specific antigen.   103, 414

antibody-mediated immunity Specific mechanism of defense in which plasma cells derived from B cells produce antibodies that combine with antigens.   419

antibody titer Amount of antibody present in a sample of blood serum.   424

anticodon (an-tih-koh-dahn) Three-base sequence in a tRNA molecule base that pairs with a complementary codon in mRNA.   374

antidiuretic hormone (ADH) (an-tih-dy-uh-ret-ik) Hormone secreted by the posterior pituitary that increases the permeability of the collecting ducts in a kidney.   169, 270

antigen (an-tih-jun) Foreign substance, usually a protein or a polysaccharide, that stimulates the immune system to produce antibodies.   103, 414

antigen-presenting cell (APC) Cell that displays the antigen to the cells of the immune system so they can defend the body against that particular antigen.   422

anus Outlet of the digestive tract.   122

aorta (ay-or-tuh) Major systemic artery that receives blood from the left ventricle.   86

aortic body Sensory receptor in the aortic arch sensitive to the O_2, CO_2, and H^+ content of the blood.   149

apoptosis (ap-uh-toh-sis, -ahp-) Programmed cell death involving a cascade of specific cellular events leading to death and destruction of the cell.   334, 419, 472

appendicular skeleton (ap-un-dik-yuh-lur) Portion of the skeleton forming the pectoral girdles and upper extremities and the pelvic girdle and lower extremities.   190

aqueous humor (ay-kwee-us, ak-wee-) Clear, watery fluid between the cornea and lens of the eye.   250

aquifer (ahk-wuh-fur) Rock layers that contain water that is released in appreciable quantities to wells or springs.   510, 525

arteriole (ar-teer-ee-ohl) Vessel that takes blood from an artery to capillaries.   79

artery Vessel that takes blood away from the heart to arterioles; characteristically possessing thick, elastic, muscular walls.   78

articular cartilage (ar-tik-yuh-lur) Hyaline cartilaginous covering over the articulating surface of the bones of synovial joints.   178

association area One of several regions of the cerebral cortex related to memory, reasoning, judgment, and emotional feelings.   228

aster Short, radiating fibers about the centrioles at the poles of a spindle.   337

asthma (az-muh, as-) Condition in which bronchioles constrict and cause difficulty in breathing.   154, 426

astigmatism (uh-stig-muh-tiz-um) Blurred vision due to an irregular curvature of the cornea or the lens.   255

atherosclerosis (ath-uh-roh-skluh-roh-sis) Condition in which fatty substances accumulate abnormally beneath the inner linings of the arteries.   88

atom Smallest particle of an element that displays the properties of the element.   14

atomic number Number of protons within the nucleus of an atom.   14

atomic weight Weight of an atom equal to the number of protons plus the number of neutrons within the nucleus.   14

ATP (adenosine triphosphate) (uh-den-uh-seen try-fahs-fayt) Nucleotide with three phosphate groups. The breakdown of ATP into ADP + Ⓟ makes energy available for energy-requiring processes in cells.   30

atrial natriuretic hormone (ANH) (ay-tree-ul nay-tree-yoo-ret-ik) Hormone secreted by the heart that increases sodium excretion and therefore, lowers blood volume and pressure.   169, 276

atrioventricular bundle (ay-tree-oh-ven-trik-yuh-lur) Group of specialized fibers that conduct impulses from the atrioventricular node to the ventricles of the heart; also called AV bundle.   82

atrioventricular valve Valve located between the atrium and the ventricle.   80

atrium (ay-tree-um) One of the upper chambers of the heart, either the left atrium or the right atrium, that receives blood.   80

auditory canal Curved tube extending from the pinna to the tympanic membrane.   256

auditory (Eustachian) tube Extension from the middle ear to the nasopharynx that equalizes air pressure on the eardrum.   152, 256

australopithecine (aw-stray-loh-pith-uh-syn) Any of the first evolved hominids; classified into several species of *Australopithecus*.   496

autoimmune disease Disease that results when the immune system mistakenly attacks the body's own tissues.   428

autonomic system (aw-tuh-nahm-ik) Branch of the peripheral nervous system that has control over the internal organs; consists of the sympathetic and parasympathetic systems.   235

autosome (aw-tuh-sohm) Any chromosome other than the sex chromosomes.   362

autotroph Organism that can capture energy and synthesize organic nutrients from inorganic nutrients.   506

AV (atrioventricular) node Small region of neuromuscular tissue that transmits impulses received from the sinoatrial node to the ventricles.   82

axial skeleton (ak-see-ul) Portion of the skeleton that supports and protects the organs of the head, the neck, and the trunk.   186

axis Second cervical vertebra upon which the atlas rotates, allowing the head to turn.   188

axon (ak-sahn) Elongated portion of a neuron that conducts nerve impulses typically from the cell body to the synapse.   218

axon terminal Small swelling at the tip of one of many endings of the axon.   222

B

bacillus (pl., bacilli) Rod-shaped bacterium.   441

bacterial vaginosis (BV) Sexually transmitted disease caused by *Gardnerella vaginalis, Mobiluncus* spp., *Mycoplasma hominis*, and various anaerobic bacteria. Although a mild disease, it is a risk factor for obstetric infections and pelvic inflammatory disease.   459

ball-and-socket joint The most freely movable type of joint (e.g., the shoulder or hip joint).   192

Barr body Dark-staining body (discovered by M. Barr) in the nuclei of female mammals that contains a condensed, inactive X chromosome.   392

basal body Cytoplasmic structure that is located at the base of—and may organize—cilia or flagella.   46

basal nuclei (bay-sul) Subcortical nuclei deep within the white matter that serve as relay stations for motor impulses and produce dopamine to help control skeletal muscle activities.   228

base Molecules tending to lower the hydrogen ion concentration in a solution and raise the pH numerically.   20

basement membrane Layer of nonliving material that anchors epithelial tissue to underlying connective tissue.   62

basophil (bay-suh-fil) White blood cell with a granular cytoplasm; able to be stained with a basic dye.   103

B cell Lymphocyte that matures in the bone marrow and, when stimulated by the presence of a specific antigen, gives rise to antibody-producing plasma cells.   418

bicarbonate ion Ion that participates in buffering the blood; the form in which carbon dioxide is transported in the bloodstream.   150

bile Secretion of the liver that is temporarily stored and concentrated in the gallbladder before being released into the small intestine, where it emulsifies fat.   121

binary fission Bacterial reproduction into two daughter cells without the utilization of a mitotic spindle.   441

binomial name Two-part scientific name of an organism. The first part designates the genus, the second part the specific epithet.   493

biodiversity Total number of species, the variability of their genes, and the communities in which they live.   4, 531

biogeochemical cycle (by-oh-jee-oh-kem-ih-kul) Circulating pathway of elements such as carbon and nitrogen involving exchange pools, storage areas, and biotic communities.   510

biogeography Study of the geographical distribution of organisms.   490

bioinformatics Computer technologies used to study the genome.   379

biological evolution Change in life-forms that has taken place in the past and will take place in the future; includes descent from a common ancestor and adaptation to the environment.   489

biological magnification Process by which substances become more concentrated in organisms in the higher trophic levels of a food web.   530

biology Scientific study of life.   2

biomass The number of organisms multiplied by their weight.   509

biosphere (by-oh-sfeer) Zone of air, land, and water at the surface of the Earth in which living organisms are found.   2, 506

biotechnology Term that encompasses genetic engineering and other techniques that make use of natural biological systems to create a product or achieve a particular result desired by humans.   383

biotic potential Maximum reproductive rate of an organism, given unlimited resources and ideal environmental conditions. Compare with environmental resistance.   522

bipedal posture Ability to walk upright on two feet.   494

birth control method Prevents either fertilization or implantation of an embryo in the uterine lining.   301

birth control pill Oral contraceptive containing estrogen and progesterone.   301

blastocyst (blas-tuh-sist) Early stage of human embryonic development that consists of a hollow, fluid-filled ball of cells.   313

blind spot Region of the retina lacking rods or cones where the optic nerve leaves the eye.   253

blood Type of connective tissue in which cells are separated by a liquid called plasma.   58

blood pressure Force of blood pushing against the inside wall of a vessel.   84

blood transfusion Introduction of whole blood or a blood component directly into the bloodstream.   106

bone Connective tissue having protein fibers and a hard matrix of inorganic salts, notably calcium salts.   57

bone marrow transplant A cancer patient's stem cells are harvested and stored before chemotherapy beings. Then, the stored cells are returned to the patient by injection.   482

bone remodeling Ongoing mineral deposits and withdrawals from bone that adjust bone strength and maintain levels of calcium and phophorus in blood.   182

botulism (boch-oo-lizm) Form of food poisoning caused by a neurotoxin (botulin) produced by *Clostridium botulinum* serotypes A–G; sometimes found in improperly canned or preserved food.   444

brain Enlarged superior portion of the central nervous system located in the cranial cavity of the skull.   226

brainstem Portion of the brain consisting of the medulla oblongata, pons, and midbrain.   229

Braxton Hicks contraction Strong, late-term uterine contractions prior to cervical dilation; also called false labor.   324

breech birth Birth in which the baby is positioned rump first.   319

Broca's area Region of the frontal lobe that coordinates complex muscular actions of the mouth, tongue, and larynx, making speech possible.   228

bronchiole (brahng-kee-ohl) Smaller air passages in the lungs that begin at the bronchi and terminate in alveoli.   145

bronchus (pl., bronchi) (brahng-kus) One of two major divisions of the trachea leading to the lungs.   145

buffer Substance or group of substances that tend to resist pH changes of a solution, thus stabilizing its relative acidity and basicity.   21, 170

bulbourethral gland (bul-boh-yoo-ree-thrul) Either of two small structures located below the prostate gland in males; each adds secretions to semen.   291

bulimia nervosa (byoo-lee-mee-uh, -lim-ee-, nur-voh-suh) Eating disorder characterized by binge eating followed by purging via self-induced vomiting or use of a laxative.   136

bursa (bur-suh) Sac-like, fluid-filled structure, lined with synovial membrane, that occurs near a joint.   192

bursitis (bur-sy-tis) Inflammation of any of the friction-easing sacs called bursae within the knee joint.   192

C

calcitonin (kal-sih-toh-nin) Hormone secreted by the thyroid gland that increases the blood calcium level.   274

calorie Amount of heat energy required to raise the temperature of 1 gram of water 1°C.   18

cancer Malignant tumor whose nondifferentiated cells exhibit loss of contact inhibition, uncontrolled growth, and the ability to invade tissue and metastasize.   472

candidal vaginitis Vaginitis caused by *Candida albicans.*   459

candidiasis Infection caused by *Candida albicans*, commonly involving the skin, mouth, and vagina.   446

capillary (kap-uh-lair-ee) Microscopic vessel connecting arterioles to venules; exchange of substances between blood and tissue fluid occurs across their thin walls.   78

capsid Protein coat or shell that surrounds a virion's nucleic acid.   436

carbaminohemoglobin Hemoglobin carrying carbon dioxide.   150

carbohydrate Class of organic compounds that includes monosaccharides, disaccharides, and polysaccharides.   22

carbonic anhydrase (kar-bahn-ik an-hy-drays, -drayz) Enzyme in red blood cells that speeds the formation of carbonic acid from the reactants water and carbon dioxide.   150

carcinogen (kar-sin-uh-jun) Environmental agent that causes mutations leading to the development of cancer.   476

carcinogenesis (kar-suh-nuh-jen-uh-sis) Development of cancer.   473

carcinoma (kar-suh-noh-muh) Cancer arising in epithelial tissue.   56, 475

cardiac cycle One complete cycle of systole and diastole for all heart chambers.   82

cardiac muscle Striated, involuntary muscle found only in the heart.   59, 198

cardiovascular system (kar-dee-oh-vas-kyuh-lur) Organ system in which blood vessels distribute blood powered by the pumping action of the heart.   66

carnivore (kar-nuh-vor) Consumer in a food chain that eats other animals.   506

carotid body (kuh-raht-id) Structure located at the branching of the carotid arteries; contains chemoreceptors sensitive to the O_2, CO_2, and H^+ content in blood.   149

carrier Heterozygous individual who has no apparent abnormality but can pass on an allele for a recessively inherited genetic disorder.   398

carrying capacity Maximum number of individuals of any species that can be supported by a particular ecosystem on a long-term basis.   522

cartilage (kar-tul-ij, kart-lij) Connective tissue in which the cells lie within lacunae separated by a flexible proteinaceous matrix.   56, 178

cecum (see-kum) Small pouch that lies below the entrance of the small intestine and is the blind end of the large intestine.   122

cell Smallest unit that displays the properties of life; always contains cytoplasm surrounded by a plasma membrane.   2

cell body Portion of a neuron that contains a nucleus and from which dendrites and an axon extend.   218

cell cycle Repeating sequence of cellular events that consists of interphase, mitosis, and cytokinesis.   334

cell-mediated immunity Specific mechanism of defense in which T cells destroy antigen-bearing cells.   423

cell theory One of the major theories of biology; states that all organisms are made up of cells and cells come only from preexisting cells.   36

cellular respiration Metabolic reactions that use the energy primarily from carbohydrates but also from fatty acid or amino acid breakdown to produce ATP molecules.   49

cellulose (sel-yuh-lohs, -lohz) Polysaccharide that is the major complex carbohydrate in plant cell walls.   23

central nervous system (CNS) Portion of the nervous system consisting of the brain and spinal cord.   218

centriole (sen-tree-ohl) Cellular structure, existing in pairs, that possibly organizes the mitotic spindle for chromosomal movement during mitosis and meiosis.   337

centromere (sen-truh-meer) Constriction where sister chromatids of a chromosome are held together.   337

centrosome Central microtubule organizing center of cells. In animal cells, it contains two centrioles.   43, 337

cerebellum (ser-uh-bel-um) Part of the brain located posterior to the medulla oblongata and pons that coordinates skeletal muscles to produce smooth, graceful motions.   229

cerebral cortex (suh-ree-brul, ser-uh-brul kor-teks) Outer layer of cerebral hemispheres; receives sensory information and controls motor activities.   227

cerebral hemisphere One of the large, paired structures that together constitute the cerebrum of the brain.   227

cerebrospinal fluid (sair-uh-broh-spy-nul, suh-ree-broh-) Fluid found in the ventricles of the brain, in the central canal of the spinal cord, and in association with the meninges.   224

cerebrum (sair-uh-brum, suh-ree-brum) Main part of the brain consisting of two large masses, or cerebral hemispheres; the largest part of the brain in mammals.   227

cervix (sur-viks) Narrow end of the uterus, which projects into the vagina.   294

cesarean section Birth by surgical incision of the abdomen and uterus.   319

chemical evolution Increase in the complexity of chemicals over time that could have led to the first cells.   488

chemical signal Molecule that brings about a change in a cell, tissue, organ, or individual when it binds to a specific receptor.   268

chemoreceptor (kee-moh-rih-sep-tur) Sensory receptor that is sensitive to chemical stimuli—for example, receptors for taste and smell.   244

chlamydia (kluh-mid-ee-uh) Sexually transmitted disease, caused by the bacterium *Chlamydia trachomatis*; can lead to pelvic inflammatory disease.   454

chlorofluorocarbons (CFCs) (klor-oh-floor-oh-kar-buns) Organic compounds containing carbon, chlorine, and fluorine atoms. CFCs, such as Freon, can deplete the ozone shield by releasing chlorine atoms in the upper atmosphere.   530

chondrocyte Type of cell found in the lacunae of cartilage.   178

chordae tendineae (kor-dee ten-din-ee-ee) Tough bands of connective tissue that attach the papillary muscles to the atrioventricular valves within the heart.   80

chorion (kor-ee-ahn) Extraembryonic membrane that contributes to placenta formation.   311

chorionic villi (kor-ee-ahn-ik vil-eye) Tree-like extensions of the chorion that project into the maternal tissues at the placenta.   317

chorionic villi sampling (CVS) Removal of cells from the chorionic villi portion of the placenta. Karyotyping is done to determine if the fetus has a chromosomal abnormality.   390

choroid (kor-oyd) Vascular, pigmented middle layer of the eyeball.   250

chromatin (kroh-muh-tin) Network of fine threads in the nucleus that are composed of DNA and proteins.   44

chromosomal mutation Variation in regard to the normal number of chromosomes inherited or in regard to the normal sequence of alleles on a chromosome; the sequence can be inverted, translocated from a nonhomologous chromosome, deleted, or duplicated.   396

chromosome (kroh-muh-som) Chromatin condensed into a compact structure.   44

chronic bronchitis Obstructive pulmonary disorder that tends to recur; marked by inflamed airways filled with mucus and degenerative changes in the bronchi, including loss of cilia.   153

chronic infection Disease that persists over a long duration with less severe symptoms.   434

chyme (kym) Thick, semiliquid food material that passes from the stomach to the small intestine.   120

ciliary body (sil-ee-air-ee) Structure associated with the choroid layer that contains ciliary muscle and controls the shape of the lens of the eye.   250

cilium (pl., cilia) (sil-ee-um) Short, hair-like projection from the plasma membrane, occurring usually in large numbers.   46

circadian rhythm (sur-kay-dee-un) Biological rhythm with a 24-hour cycle.   282

cirrhosis (sih-roh-sis) Chronic, irreversible injury to liver tissue; commonly caused by frequent alcohol consumption.   125

citric acid cycle Cycle of reactions in mitochondria that begins with citric acid; it breaks down an acetyl group as CO_2, ATP, NADH, and $FADH_2$ are given off; also called the Krebs cycle.   49

cleavage Cell division without cytoplasmic addition or enlargement; occurs during the first stage of animal development.   311

cleavage furrow Indentation that begins the process of cleavage, by which human cells undergo cytokinesis.   339

clonal selection theory Concept that an antigen selects which lymphocyte will undergo clonal expansion and produce more lymphocytes bearing the same type of antigen receptor.   419

cloning Production of identical copies; can be either the production of identical individuals or, in genetic engineering, the production of identical copies of a gene.   380

clotting Process of blood coagulation, usually when injury occurs.   103

coccus (pl., cocci) Spherical-shaped bacterium.   441

cochlea (kohk-lee-uh, koh-klee-uh) Portion of the inner ear that resembles a snail's shell and contains the spiral organ, the sense organ for hearing.   256

cochlear canal (koh-klee-ur) Canal within the cochlea that bears the spiral organ.   257

cochlear nerve Either of two cranial nerves that carry nerve impulses from the spiral organ to the brain; also called the auditory nerve.   257

codominance Inheritance pattern in which both alleles of a gene are equally expressed.   360

codon Three-base sequence in mRNA that causes the insertion of a particular amino acid into a protein or termination of translation.   372

coelom (see-lum) Embryonic body cavity lying between the digestive tract and body wall that becomes the thoracic and abdominal cavities.   68

coenzyme (koh-en-zym) Nonprotein organic molecule that aids the action of the enzyme to which it is loosely bound.   48

collagen fiber (kahl-uh-jun) White fiber in the matrix of connective tissue; gives flexibility and strength.   56

collecting duct Duct within the kidney that receives fluid from several nephrons; the reabsorption of water occurs here.   165

colon (koh-lun) The major portion of the large intestine, consisting of the ascending colon, the transverse colon, and the descending colon.   122

colony-stimulating factor (CSF) Protein that stimulates differentiation and maturation of white blood cells.   103

color blindness Deficiency in one or more of the three kinds of cone cells responsible for color vision.   402

color vision Ability to detect the color of an object; dependent on three kinds of cone cells.   252

columnar epithelium (kuh-lum-nur ep-uh-thee-lee-um) Type of epithelial tissue with cylindrical cells.   62

community Assemblage of populations interacting with one another within the same environment.   506

compact bone Type of bone that contains osteons consisting of concentric layers of matrix and osteocytes in lacunae.   57, 178

complementary base pairing Hydrogen bonding between particular bases. In DNA, thymine (T) pairs with adenine (A), and guanine (G) pairs with cytosine (C); in RNA, uracil (U) pairs with A, and G pairs with C.   368

complement system Series of proteins in plasma that form a nonspecific defense mechanism against a microbe invasion; it complements the antigen-antibody reaction.   418

compound Substance having two or more different elements united chemically in a fixed ratio.   16

conclusion Statement made following an experiment as to whether the results support the hypothesis.   6

cone cell Photoreceptor in retina of eye that responds to bright light; detects color and provides visual acuity.   252

congenital hypothyroidism Condition resulting from improper development of the thyroid in an infant; characterized by stunted growth and mental retardation.   273

connective tissue Type of tissue that binds structures together, provides support and protection, fills spaces, stores fat, and forms blood cells; adipose tissue, cartilage, bone, and blood are types of connective tissue.   56

constipation (kahn-stuh-pay-shun) Delayed and difficult defecation caused by insufficient water in the feces.   123

consumer Organism that feeds on another organism in a food chain; primary consumers eat plants, and secondary consumers eat animals.   5, 506

contagious Highly transmissible by direct contact with infected people and their fresh secretions or excretions.   434

contraceptive (kahn-truh-sep-tiv) Medication or device used to reduce the chance of pregnancy.   301

contraceptive implant Birth control method utilizing synthetic progesterone; prevents ovulation by disrupting the ovarian cycle.   301

contraceptive injection Birth control method utilizing progesterone or estrogen and progesterone together; prevents ovulation by disrupting the ovarian cycle.   301

contraceptive vaccine Under development, this birth control method immunizes against the hormone HCG, crucial to maintaining implantation of the embryo.   302

control group Sample that goes through all the steps of an experiment but lacks the factor or is not exposed to the factor being tested; a standard against which results of an experiment are checked.   8

cornea (kor-nee-uh) Transparent, anterior portion of the outer layer of the eyeball.   250

coronary artery (kor-uh-nair-ee) Artery that supplies blood to the wall of the heart.   87

coronary bypass operation Therapy for blocked coronary arteries in which part of a blood vessel from another part of the body is grafted around the obstructed artery.   89

corpus luteum (kor-pus loot-ee-um) Yellow body that forms in the ovary from a follicle that has discharged its secondary oocyte; it secretes progesterone and some estrogen.   297

cortisol (kor-tuh-sawl) Glucocorticoid secreted by the adrenal cortex that responds to stress on a long-term basis; reduces inflammation and promotes protein and fat metabolism.   276

covalent bond (coh-vay-lent) Chemical bond in which atoms share one pair of electrons.   17

cranial nerve Nerve that arises from the brain.   232

creatine phosphate (kree-uh-teen fahs-fayt) Compound unique to muscles that contains a high-energy phosphate bond.   208

creatinine (kree-ah-tuhn-een) Nitrogenous waste; the end product of creatine phosphate metabolism.   160

Cro-Magnon (kroh-mag-nun) Common name for first fossils to be designated *Homo sapiens*.   500

crossing-over Exchange of segments between nonsister chromatids of a tetrad during meiosis.   341

cuboidal epithelium (kyoo-boyd-ul) Type of epithelial tissue with cube-shaped cells.   62

cultural eutrophication Overenrichment caused by human activities, leading to excessive bacterial growth and oxygen depletion.   511

culture Total pattern of human behavior; includes technology and the arts, and depends upon the capacity to speak and transmit knowledge.   2, 497

Cushing syndrome (koosh-ing) Condition resulting from hypersecretion of glucocorticoids; characterized by thin arms and legs and a "moon face," and accompanied by high blood glucose and sodium levels.   277

cutaneous receptor Sensory receptors for pressure and touch found in the dermis of the skin.   246

cyclic adenosine monophosphate (cAMP) (sy-klik, sih-klik) ATP-related compound that acts as the second messenger in peptide hormone transduction; it initiates activity of the metabolic machinery.   269

cyclin Protein that regularly increases and decreases in concentration during the cell cycle.   474

cystic fibrosis A generalized, autosomal recessive disorder of infants and children in which there is widespread dysfunction of the exocrine glands.   400

cystitis Inflammation of the urinary bladder.   171

cytokine (sy-tuh-kyn) Type of protein secreted by a T cell that stimulates cells of the immune system to perform their various functions.   423, 425

cytokinesis (sy-tuh-kyn-ee-sus) Division of the cytoplasm following mitosis and meiosis.   334

cytoplasm (sy-tuh-plaz-um) Contents of a cell between the nucleus and the plasma membrane that contains the organelles.   38

cytosine (C) (sy-tuh-seen) One of four nitrogen bases in nucleotides composing the structure of DNA and RNA.   30

cytoskeleton Internal framework of the cell, consisting of microtubules, actin filaments, and intermediate filaments.   38, 43

cytotoxic T cell (sy-tuh-tahk-sik) T cell that attacks and kills antigen-bearing cells.   423

D

data Facts or pieces of information collected through observation and/or experimentation.   6

daughter cell Cell that arises from a parent cell by mitosis or meiosis.   337

dead air space Volume of inspired air that cannot be exchanged with blood.   146

decomposer Organism, usually a bacterium or fungus, that breaks down organic matter into inorganic nutrients that can be recycled in the environment.   5, 506

defecation (def-ih-kay-shun) Discharge of feces from the rectum through the anus.   122

deforestation (dee-for-eh-stay-shun) Removal of trees from a forest in a way that ever reduces the size of the forest.   525

dehydration reaction Chemical reaction resulting in a covalent bond with the accompanying loss of a water molecule.   22

dehydrogenase Coenzyme that removes hydrogen atoms (electrons plus hydrogen ions) and carries electrons to the electron transport chain in mitochondria.   48

delayed allergic response Allergic response initiated at the site of the allergen by sensitized T cells, involving macrophages and regulated by cytokines.   426

deletion Change in chromosome structure in which the end of a chromosome breaks off, or two simulateneous breaks lead to the loss of an internal segment; often causes abnormalities (e.g., cri du chat syndrome).   396

denaturation (dee-nay-chuh-ray-shun) Loss of normal shape by an enzyme so that it no longer functions; caused by a less than optimal pH or temperature.   26

dendrite (den-dryt) Branched ending of a neuron that conducts signals toward the cell body.   218

dendritic cell Antigen-presenting cell of the epidermis and mucous membranes.   417

denitrification Conversion of nitrate or nitrite to nitrogen gas by bacteria in soil.   512

dense fibrous connective tissue Type of connective tissue containing many collagen fibers packed together; found in tendons and ligaments, for example.   56

dental caries (kar-eez) Tooth decay that occurs when bacteria within the mouth metabolize sugar and give off acids that erode teeth; a cavity.   117

dermis (dur-mus) Region of skin that lies beneath the epidermis.   64

desertification Denuding and degrading a once-fertile land, initiating a desert-producing cycle that feeds on itself and causes long-term changes in the soil, climate, and biota of an area.   524

detrital food chain (dih-tryt-ul) Straight-line linking of organisms according to who eats whom, beginning with detritus.   509

detrital food web (dih-tryt-ul) Complex pattern of interlocking and crisscrossing food chains, beginning with detritus.   509

detritivore Any organism that obtains most of its nutrients from the detritus in an ecosystem.   506

diabetes mellitus (dy-uh-bee-teez mel-ih-tus, muh-ly-tus) Condition characterized by a high blood glucose level and the appearance of glucose in the urine, due to a deficiency of insulin production and failure of cells to take up glucose.   279

dialysate Material that passes through the membrane in dialysis.   171

diaphragm (dy-uh-fram) Dome-shaped horizontal sheet of muscle and connective tissue that divides the thoracic cavity from the abdominal cavity.   68   Also, a birth control device consisting of a soft rubber or latex cup that fits over the cervix.   301

diarrhea (dy-uh-ree-uh) Excessively frequent bowel movements.   123

diastole (dy-as-tuh-lee) Relaxation period of a heart chamber during the cardiac cycle.   82

diastolic pressure (dy-uh-stahl-ik) Arterial blood pressure during the diastolic phase of the cardiac cycle.   84

diencephalon (dy-en-sef-uh-lahn) Portion of the brain in the region of the third ventricle that includes the thalamus and hypothalamus.   229

differentiation Cell specialization.   311

diffusion (dih-fyoo-zhun) Movement of molecules or ions from a region of higher to lower concentration; it requires no energy and stops when the distribution is equal.   41

digestive system Organ system including the mouth, esophagus, stomach, small intestine, and large intestine (colon) that receives food and digests it into nutrient molecules. Also has associated organs: teeth, tongue, salivary glands, liver, gallbladder, and pancreas.   66

dihybrid Individual that is heterozygous for two traits; shows the phenotype governed by the dominant alleles but carries the recessive alleles.   357

diploid (2n) Cell condition in which two of each type of chromosome are present in the nucleus.   337

disaccharide (dy-sak-uh-ryd) Sugar that contains two units of a monosaccharide (e.g., maltose).   23

disease Illness; state of homeostatic imbalance in which part or all of the body does not function properly.   414

distal convoluted tubule Final portion of a nephron that joins with a collecting duct; associated with tubular secretion.   165

diuretic (dy-uh-ret-ik) Drug used to counteract hypertension by causing the excretion of water.   169

DNA (deoxyribonucleic acid) Nucleic acid polymer produced from covalent bonding of nucleotide monomers that contain the sugar deoxyribose; the genetic material of nearly all organisms.   29, 368

DNA ligase (ly-gays) Enzyme that links DNA fragments; used during production of rDNA to join foreign DNA to vector DNA.   368

DNA probe Piece of single-stranded DNA that will bind to a complementary piece of DNA.   403

DNA replication Synthesis of a new DNA double helix prior to mitosis and meiosis in eukaryotic cells, and during prokaryotic fission in prokaryotic cells.   369

domain The primary taxonomic group above the kingdom level; all living organisms may be placed in one of three domains.   2

dominant allele (uh-leel) Allele that exerts its phenotypic effect in the heterozygote; it masks the expression of the recessive allele.   352

dorsal-root ganglion (gang-glee-un) Mass of sensory neuron cell bodies located in the dorsal root of a spinal nerve.   232

double helix Double spiral; describes the three-dimensional shape of DNA.   368

drug abuse Dependence on a drug, which assumes an "essential" biochemical role in the body following habituation and tolerance.   237

Duchenne muscular dystrophy Chronic progressive disease affecting the shoulder and pelvic girdles, commencing in early childhood. Characterized by increasing weakness of the muscles, followed by atrophy and a peculiar swaying gait with the legs kept wide apart. Transmitted as an X-linked trait, and affected individuals, predominantly males, rarely survive to maturity. Death is usually due to respiratory weakness or heart failure.   402

duodenum (doo-uh-dee-num) First part of the small intestine where chyme enters from the stomach.   121

duplication Change in chromosome structure in which a particular segment is present more than once in the same chromosome.   396

E

ecological pyramid Pictorial graph based on the biomass, number of organisms, or energy content of various trophic levels in a food web—from the producer to the final consumer populations.   509

ecological succession Sequential change in the relative dominance of species within an ecosystem; primary succession begins on bare rock, and secondary succession begins where soil already exists.   514

ecologist Scientist that studies the interactions of organisms with other organisms and with the physical and chemical environment.   5

ecology Study of the interactions of organisms with other organisms and with the physical and chemical environment.   506

ecosystem (ek-oh-sis-tum, ee-koh-) Biological community together with the associated abiotic environment; characterized by energy flow and chemical cycling.   506

ectopic pregnancy Implantation of the embryo in a location other than the uterus, most often in an oviduct.   315

edema (ih-dee-muh) Swelling due to tissue fluid accumulation in the intercellular spaces.   109

effector Muscle or gland that responds to stimulation.   218

egg Female gamete having the haploid number of chromosomes that is fertilized by a sperm, the male gamete.   294

elastic cartilage Type of cartilage composed of elastic fibers, allowing greater flexibility.   57

elastic fiber Yellow fiber in the matrix of connective tissue, providing flexibility.   56

electrocardiogram (ECG) (ih-lek-troh-kar-dee-uh-gram) Recording of the electrical activity associated with the heartbeat.   83

electron Negative subatomic particle, moving about in an energy level around the nucleus of an atom.   14

electron transport chain Passage of electrons along a series of membrane-bound carrier molecules from a higher to lower energy level; the energy released is used for the synthesis of ATP.   49

element Substance that cannot be broken down into substances with different properties; composed of only one type of atom.   14

embolus (em-buh-lus) Moving blood clot that is carried through the bloodstream.   88

embryo (em-bree-oh) Immature developmental stage that is not recognizable as a human being.   315

embryonic development Period of development from the second through eighth weeks.   315

embryonic disk Stage of embryonic development following the blastocyst stage that has two layers; one layer will be endoderm, and the other will be ectoderm.   315

emphysema (em-fih-see-muh) Degenerative lung disorder in which the bursting of alveolar walls reduces the total surface area for gas exchange.   153

emulsification (ih-mul-suh-fuh-kay-shun) Breaking up of fat globules into smaller droplets by the action of bile salts or any other emulsifier.   24

endemic A disease that is commonly or constantly present in a population, usually at a relatively steady, low frequency.   435

endochondral ossification Ossification that begins as hyaline cartilage that is subsequently replaced by bone tissue.   181

endocrine gland (en-duh-krin) Ductless organ that secretes (a) hormone(s) into the bloodstream.   266

endocrine system Organ system involved in the coordination of body activities; uses hormones as chemical signals secreted into the bloodstream.   67

endomembrane system A collection of membranous structures involved in transport within the cell.   45

endometrium Mucous membrane lining the interior surface of the uterus.   295

endoplasmic reticulum (ER) (en-duh-plaz-mik reh-tik-yuh-lum) System of membranous saccules and channels in the cytoplasm, often with attached ribosomes.   44

endospore Spore formed within a cell; certain bacteria form endospores.   444

environmental resistance All the limiting factors that tend to reduce population growth rates and set the maximum allowable population size or carrying capacity of an ecosystem. 522

enzyme (en-zym) Organic catalyst, usually a protein, that speeds a reaction in cells due to its particular shape. 26

eosinophil (ee-oh-sin-oh-fill) White blood cell containing cytoplasmic granules that stain with acidic dye. 103

epidemic Disease that suddenly increases in occurrence above the normal level in a given population. 435

epidemiology Study of the factors that influence the transmission and distribution of disease in human populations. 434

epidermis (ep-uh-dur-mus) Region of skin that lies above the dermis. 64

epididymis (ep-uh-did-uh-mus) Coiled tubule next to the testes where sperm mature and may be stored for a short time. 290

epiglottis (ep-uh-glaht-us) Structure that covers the glottis during the process of swallowing. 118, 144

epinephrine (ep-uh-nef-rin) Hormone secreted by the adrenal medulla in times of stress; adrenaline. 275

episiotomy (ih-pee-zee-aht-uh-mee) Surgical procedure performed during childbirth in which the opening of the vagina is enlarged to avoid tearing. 325

episodic memory Capacity of brain to store and retrieve information with regard to persons and events. 230

epithelial tissue (ep-uh-thee-lee-ul) Type of tissue that lines hollow organs and covers surfaces; also called epithelium. 62

erectile dysfunction Failure of the penis to achieve or maintain erection. 291

erythropoietin (ih-rith-roh-poy-ee-tin) Hormone, produced by the kidneys, that speeds red blood cell formation. 101, 160

esophagus (ih-sahf-uh-gus) Muscular tube for moving swallowed food from the pharynx to the stomach. 118

essential amino acids Amino acids required in the human diet because the body cannot make them. 129

essential fatty acid Fatty acid required in the human diet because the body cannot make them. 130

estrogen (es-truh-jun) Female sex hormone that helps maintain sex organs and secondary sex characteristics. 280, 298

eukaryotic cell Type of cell that has a membrane-bound nucleus and membranous organelles. 441, 489

evolution Descent of organisms from common ancestors with the development of genetic and phenotypic changes over time that make them more suited to the environment. 2

evolutionary tree Diagram that describes the evolutionary relationship of groups of organisms; a common ancestor is presumed to have been present at points of divergence. 494

excretion Removal of metabolic wastes from the body. 160

exophthalmic goiter (ek-sahf-thal-mik) Enlargement of the thyroid gland accompanied by an abnormal protrusion of the eyes. 273

experiment Artificial situation devised to test a hypothesis. 8

experimental variable Value that is expected to change as a result of an experiment; represents the factor that is being tested by the experiment. 8

expiration (ek-spuh-ray-shun) Act of expelling air from the lungs; also called exhalation. 142

expiratory reserve volume (ik-spy-ruh-tor-ee) Volume of air that can be forcibly exhaled after normal exhalation. 146

exponential growth Growth at a constant rate of increase per unit of time; can be expressed as a constant fraction or exponent. 522

external respiration Exchange of oxygen and carbon dioxide between alveoli and blood. 150

exteroceptor Sensory receptor that detects stimuli from outside the body (e.g., taste, smell, vision, hearing, and equilibrium). 244

extinction Total disappearance of a species or higher group. 4

extraembryonic membrane (ek-struh-em-bree-ahn-ik) Membrane that is not a part of the embryo but is necessary to the continued existence and health of the embryo. 311

F

facilitated transport Use of a plasma membrane carrier to move a substance into or out of a cell from higher to lower concentration; no energy required. 42

familial hypercholesterolemia (FH) Inability to remove cholesterol from the bloodstream; predisposes individual to heart attack. 401

farsighted Vision abnormality due to a shortened eyeball from front to back; light rays focus in back of retina when viewing close objects. 255

fat Organic molecule that contains glycerol and fatty acids; found in adipose tissue. 24

fatty acid Molecule that contains a hydrocarbon chain and ends with an acid group. 24

female condom Large polyurethane tube with a flexible ring that fits onto the cervix. Functions as a contraceptive and helps minimize the risk of transmitting infection. 301

fermentation Anaerobic breakdown of glucose that results in a gain of two ATP and end products, such as alcohol and lactate. 50

fertilization Union of a sperm nucleus and an egg nucleus, which creates a zygote. 310, 340

fetal development Period of development from the ninth week through birth. 319

fiber Structure resembling a thread; also, plant material that is nondigestible. 122

fibrin (fy-brun) Insoluble protein threads formed from fibrinogen during blood clotting. 104

fibrinogen (fy-brin-uh-jun) Plasma protein that is converted into fibrin threads during blood clotting. 104

fibroblast (fy-bruh-blast) Cell in connective tissues that produces fibers and other substances. 56

fibrocartilage (fy-broh-kar-tul-ij, -kart-lij) Cartilage with a matrix of strong collagenous fibers. 57

fibrous connective tissue Tissue composed mainly of closely packed collagenous fibers and found in tendons and ligaments. 178

fimbria (pl., fimbriae) (fim-bree-uh) Finger-like extension from the oviduct near the ovary. 294

first messenger Chemical signal, such as a peptide hormone, that binds to a plasma membrane receptor protein and alters the metabolism of a cell because a second messenger is activated. 269

flagellum (pl., flagella) (fluh-jel-um) Slender, long extension that propels a cell through a fluid medium. 46

floating kidney Kidney that has been dislodged from its normal position. 161

focus Bending of light rays by the cornea, lens, and humors so that they converge and create an image on the retina. 251

follicle (fahl-ih-kul) Structure in the ovary that produces a secondary oocyte and the hormones estrogen and progesterone. 297

follicle-stimulating hormone (FSH) Hormone secreted by the anterior pituitary gland that stimulates the development of an ovarian follicle in a female or the production of sperm in a male. 293

fomite An object that is not in itself harmful but is able to harbor and transmit pathogenic organisms. 435

fontanel (fahn-tun-el) Membranous region located between certain cranial bones in the skull of a fetus or infant. 186, 319

food chain Order in which one population feeds on another in an ecosystem, from detritus (detrital food chain) or producer (grazing food chain) to final consumer. 509

food poisoning General term referring to a gastrointestinal disease caused by ingesting food contaminated by pathogens or their toxins. 444

food web In ecosystems, complex pattern of interlocking and crisscrossing food chains. 509

foramen magnum (fuh-ray-mun magnum) Opening in the occipital bone of the vertebrate skull through which the spinal cord passes. 186

formed element Constituent of blood that is either cellular (red blood cells and white blood cells) or at least cellular in origin (platelets). 99

fossil Any past evidence of an organism that has been preserved in the Earth's crust. 490

fossil fuel Fuels, such as oil, coal, and natural gas, that are the result of partial decomposition of plants and animals coupled with exposure to heat and pressure for millions of years. 513, 528

fossil record History of life recorded from remains from the past. 490

fovea centralis Region of the retina consisting of densely packed cones; responsible for the greatest visual acuity. 251

G

gallbladder Organ attached to the liver that serves to store and concentrate bile. 125

gamete (ga-meet, guh-meet) Haploid sex cell; the egg or a sperm, which join in fertilization to form a zygote. 304, 340

ganglion Collection or bundle of neuron cell bodies usually outside the central nervous system. 232

gastric gland Gland within the stomach wall that secretes gastric juice. 120

gastrulation Stage of animal development during which germ layers form, at least in part, by invagination. 317

gene cloning Production of one or more copies of the same gene. 380

gene therapy Correction of a detrimental mutation by the addition of normal DNA and its insertion in a genome. 408

genetic counseling Prospective parents consult a counselor who determines the genotype of each and whether an unborn child will have a genetic disorder. 390

genetic engineering Alteration of DNA for medical or industrial purposes. 380

genetic marker Abnormality in the sequence of a base at a particular location on a chromosome, signifying a disorder. 403

genetic profile An individual's complete genotype, including any possible mutations. 406

genital herpes (jen-ih-tul hur-peez) Sexually transmitted disease caused by herpes simplex virus and sometimes accompanied by painful ulcers on the genitals. 457

genital warts Sexually transmitted disease caused by human papillomavirus, resulting in raised growths on the external genitals. 458

genomics Study of all the nucleotide sequences, including structural genes, regulatory sequences, and noncoding DNA segments, in the chromosomes of an organism. 378

genotype (jee-nuh-typ) Genes of an individual for a particular trait or traits; often designated by letters, for example, *BB* or *Aa*. 352

gerontology (jer-un-tahl-uh-jee) Study of aging. 326

gestation Period of development, from the start of the last menstrual cycle until birth; in humans, typically 280 days. 313

giardiasis Common intestinal disease caused by the parasitic protozoan *Giardia lamblia*. 448

gland Epithelial cell or group of epithelial cells that are specialized to secrete a substance. 62

glaucoma (glow-koh-muh, glaw-koh-muh) Increasing loss of field of vision; caused by blockage of the ducts that drain the aqueous humor, creating pressure buildup and nerve damage. 251

global warming Predicted increase in the Earth's temperature, due to human activities that promote the greenhouse effect. 513

glomerular capsule (gluh-mair-yuh-lur) Double-walled cup that surrounds the glomerulus at the beginning of the nephron. 165

glomerular filtrate Filtered portion of blood contained within the glomerular capsule. 167

glomerular filtration Movement of small molecules from the glomerulus into the glomerular capsule due to the action of blood pressure. 167

glomerulus (gluh-mair-uh-lus, gloh-mair-yuh-lus) Cluster; for example, the cluster of capillaries surrounded by the glomerular capsule in a nephron, where glomerular filtration takes place. 164

glottis (glaht-us) Opening for airflow in the larynx. 118, 144

glucagon (gloo-kuh-gahn) Hormone secreted by the pancreas that causes the liver to break down glycogen and raises the blood glucose level. 278

glucocorticoid (gloo-koh-kor-tih-koyd) Type of hormone secreted by the adrenal cortex that influences carbohydrate, fat, and protein metabolism; see cortisol. 275

glucose (gloo-kohs) Six-carbon sugar that organisms degrade as a source of energy during cellular respiration. 22

glycemic index (GI) Blood glucose response of a given food. 128

glycogen (gly-koh-jun) Storage polysaccharide that is composed of glucose molecules joined in a linear fashion but having numerous branches. 23

glycolysis Anaerobic breakdown of glucose that results in a gain of two ATP molecules. 49

Golgi apparatus (gohl-jee) Organelle, consisting of saccules and vesicles, that processes, packages, and distributes molecules about or from the cell. 45

gonad (goh-nad) Organ that produces gametes; the ovary produces eggs, and the testis produces sperm. 280

gonadotropic hormone (goh-nad-uh-trahp-ic, -troh-pic) Chemical signal secreted by the anterior pituitary that regulates the activity of the ovaries and testes; principally, follicle-stimulating hormone (FSH) and luteinizing hormone (LH). 270

gonadotropin-releasing hormone (GnRH) Hormone secreted by the hypothalamus that stimulates the anterior pituitary to secrete follicle-stimulating hormone (FSH) and luteinizing hormone (LH). 293

gonorrhea (gahn-nuh-ree-uh) Sexually transmitted disease caused by the bacterium *Neisseria gonorrhoeae* that can lead to pelvic inflammatory disease. 454

gout Joint inflammation caused by accumulation of uric acid. 160

Gram stain Differential staining procedure that divides bacteria into Gram-positive and Gram-negative groups based on their ability to retain crystal violet when decolorized with an organic solvent, such as ethanol. 441

granular leukocyte (gran-yuh-lur loo-kuh-syt) White blood cell with prominent granules in the cytoplasm. 103

gravitational equilibrium Maintenance of balance when the head and body are motionless.   261

gray matter Nonmyelinated axons and cell bodies in the central nervous system.   224

grazing food chain Straight-line linking of organisms according to who eats whom, beginning with a producer.   509

grazing food web Complex pattern of interlocking and crisscrossing food chains that begins with populations of autotrophs serving as producers.   509

greenhouse effect Reradiation of solar heat toward the Earth because gases, such as carbon dioxide, methane, nitrous oxide, and water vapor, allow solar energy to pass through toward the Earth but block the escape of heat back into space.   513

greenhouse gases Gases that are involved in the greenhouse effect.   528

growth Increase in the number of cells and/or the size of these cells.   311

growth factor Chemical signal that regulates mitosis and differentiation of cells that have receptors for it; important in such processes as fetal development, tissue maintenance and repair, and hematopoiesis; sometimes a contributing factor in cancer.   282, 474

growth hormone (GH) Substance secreted by the anterior pituitary; controls size of individual by promoting cell division, protein synthesis, and bone growth.   270

growth plate Cartilaginous layer within an epiphysis of a long bone that permits growth of bone to occur.   181

growth rate A percentage that reflects the difference between the number of persons in a population who are born and the number who die each year.   522

guanine (G) (gwah-neen) One of four nitrogen-containing bases in nucleotides composing the structure of DNA and RNA; pairs with cytosine.   30

H

habitat Place where an organism lives and is able to survive and reproduce.   506

hair cell Cell with stereocilia (long microvilli) that is sensitive to mechanical stimulation; mechanoreceptor for hearing and equilibrium in the inner ear.   256

hair follicle Tube-like depression in the skin in which a hair develops.   65

haploid (n) (hap-loyd) The n number of chromosomes—half the diploid number; the number characteristic of gametes, which contain only one set of chromosomes.   340

hard palate (pal-it) Bony, anterior portion of the roof of the mouth.   116

hay fever Seasonal variety of allergic reaction to a specific allergen. Characterized by sudden attacks of sneezing, swelling of nasal mucosa, and often asthmatic symptoms.   426

heart Muscular organ located in the thoracic cavity whose rhythmic contractions maintain blood circulation.   80

heart attack Damage to the myocardium due to blocked circulation in the coronary arteries; also called a myocardial infarction (MI).   88

heartburn Burning pain in the chest that occurs when part of the stomach contents escape into the esophagus.   119

heart failure Syndrome characterized by distinctive symptoms and signs resulting from disturbances in cardiac output or from increased pressure in the veins.   91

helminth Term that designates all parasitic worms.   449

helper T cell T cell that secretes cytokines that stimulate all kinds of immune system cells.   423

hemodialysis (he-moh-dy-al-uh-sus) Cleansing of blood by using an artificial membrane that causes substances to diffuse from blood into a dialysis fluid.   171

hemoglobin (Hb) (hee-muh-gloh-bun) Iron-containing pigment in red blood cells that combines with and transports oxygen.   100

hemolysis (he-mahl-uh-sus) Rupture of red blood cells accompanied by the release of hemoglobin.   101

hemophilia (he-moh-fil-ee-uh) Genetic disorder in which the affected individual is subject to uncontrollable bleeding.   104

hemorrhoids (hem-uh-royds, hem-royds) Abnormally dilated blood vessels of the rectum.   88

hepatic portal system (hih-pat-ik) Portal system that begins at capillaries servicing the small intestine and ends at capillaries in the liver.   87

hepatic portal vein Vein leading to the liver and formed by the merging blood vessels leaving the small intestine.   87

hepatic vein Vein that runs between the liver and the inferior vena cava.   87

hepatitis (hep-uh-ty-tis) Inflammation of the liver. Viral hepatitis occurs in several forms.   125, 458

herbivore (hur-buh-vor) Primary consumer in a grazing food chain; a plant eater.   506

heterotroph Organism that cannot synthesize organic molecules from inorganic nutrients, and therefore must take in organic nutrients (food).   488, 506

heterozygous Possessing unlike alleles for a particular trait.   352

hexose Six-carbon sugar.   22

hinge joint Type of joint that allows movement as a hinge does, such as the movement of the knee.   192

hippocampus (hip-uh-kam-pus) Portion of the limbic system where memories are stored.   230

histamine (his-tuh-meen, -mun) Substance, produced by basophils in blood and mast cells in connective tissue, that causes capillaries to dilate.   417

histoplasmosis Systemic fungal infection caused by *Histoplasma capsulatum* var. *capsulatum.*   446

HIV provirus Viral DNA that has been integrated into host cell DNA.   465

homeostasis (hoh-mee-oh-stay-sis) Maintenance of normal internal conditions in a cell or an organism by means of self-regulating mechanisms.   2, 70

hominid (hahm-uh-nid) Member of the family Hominidae, which contains australopithecines and humans.   494

Homo erectus (hoh-moh ih-rek-tus) Hominid who used fire and migrated out of Africa to Europe and Asia.   498

Homo habilis (hoh-moh hab-uh-lus) Hominid of 2 MYA who is believed to have been the first tool user.   497

homologous chromosome (hoh-mahl-uh-gus, huh-mahl-uh-gus) Member of a pair of chromosomes that are alike and come together in synapsis during prophase of the first meiotic division.   340

homologous structure Structure that is similar in two or more species because of common ancestry.   490

homologue Member of a homologous pair of chromosomes.   340

Homo sapiens (hoh-moh say-pe-nz) Modern humans.   499

homozygous dominant Possessing two identical alleles, such as *AA*, for a particular trait.   352

homozygous recessive Possessing two identical alleles, such as *aa*, for a particular trait.   352

hormone (hor-mohn) Chemical signal produced by one set of cells that affects a different set of cells.   122, 266

human chorionic gonadotropin (HCG) (kor-ee-ahn-ik, goh-nad-uh-trahp-in, -troh-pin) Hormone produced by the chorion that functions to maintain the uterine lining.   300, 315

human immunodeficiency virus (HIV) Virus responsible for AIDS.   460

Huntington disease Genetic disease marked by progressive deterioration of the nervous system due to deficiency of a neurotransmitter.   401

hyaline cartilage (hy-uh-lin) Cartilage whose cells lie in lacunae separated by a white, translucent matrix containing very fine collagen fibers.   57

hydrogen bond Weak bond that arises between a slightly positive hydrogen atom of one molecule and a slightly negative atom of another, or between parts of the same molecule.   18

hydrolysis reaction (hy-drahl-ih-sis re-ak-shun) Splitting of a compound by the addition of water, with the H^+ being incorporated in one fragment and the OH^- in the other.   22

hydrolytic enzyme (hy-druh-lit-ik) Enzyme that catalyzes a reaction in which the substrate is broken down by the addition of water.   126

hydrophilic (hy-druh-fil-ik) Type of molecule that interacts with water by dissolving in water and/or forming hydrogen bonds with water molecules.   19

hydrophobic (hy-druh-foh-bik) Type of molecule that does not interact with water because it is nonpolar.   19

hypertension Elevated blood pressure, particularly the diastolic pressure.   88

hypothalamic-inhibiting hormone (hy-poh-thuh-lah-mik) One of many hormones produced by the hypothalamus that inhibits the secretion of an anterior pituitary hormone.   270

hypothalamic-releasing hormone One of many hormones produced by the hypothalamus that stimulates the secretion of an anterior pituitary hormone.   270

hypothalamus (hy-poh-thal-uh-mus) Part of the brain located below the thalamus that helps regulate the internal environment of the body and produces releasing factors that control the anterior pituitary.   229, 270

hypothesis (hy-pahth-ih-sis) Supposition that is formulated after making an observation; it can be tested by obtaining more data, often by experimentation.   6

I

immediate allergic response Allergic response that occurs within seconds of contact with an allergen, caused by the attachment of the allergen to IgE antibodies.   426

immune system White blood cells and lymphatic organs that protect the body against foreign organisms and substances and also cancerous cells.   66, 414

immunity Ability of the body to protect itself from foreign substances and cells, including disease-causing agents.   414

immunization (im-yuh-nuh-zay-shun) Use of a vaccine to protect the body against specific disease-causing agents.   424

immunoglobulin (Ig) (im-yuh-noh-glahb-yuh-lin, -yoo-lin) Globular plasma protein that functions as an antibody.   420

immunosuppressive Inactivating the immune system to prevent organ rejection, usually via a drug.   428

impetigo Superficial cutaneous disease, most commonly seen in children; the most frequently diagnosed skin infection caused by *Streptococcus pyogenes*.   442

implantation Attachment and penetration of the embryo into the lining of the uterus (endometrium).   294, 315

incomplete dominance Inheritance pattern in which the offspring has an intermediate phenotype, as when a red-flowered plant and a white-flowered plant produce pink-flowered offspring.   360

incus (ing-kus) The middle of three ossicles of the ear that serve to conduct vibrations from the tympanic membrane to the oval window of the inner ear.   256

infant respiratory distress syndrome Condition in newborns, especially premature ones, in which the lungs collapse because of a lack of surfactant lining the alveoli.   145

infectious disease Any illness due to the presence of a pathogen or its products.   434

inferior vena cava (vee-nuh kay-vuh) Large vein that enters the right atrium from below and carries blood from the trunk and lower extremities.   86

infertility Inability to have as many children as desired.   304

inflammatory reaction Tissue response to injury that is characterized by redness, swelling, pain, and heat.   417

influenza virus Virus that causes an acute infection of the respiratory tract, occurring in isolated cases, epidemics, and pandemics.   437

inner cell mass An aggregation of cells at one pole of the blastocyte, which is destined to form the embryo proper.   313

inner ear Portion of the ear consisting of a vestibule, semicircular canals, and the cochlea where equilibrium is maintained and sound is transmitted.   256

insertion End of a muscle that is attached to a movable bone.   199

inspiration (in-spuh-ray-shun) Act of taking air into the lungs; also called inhalation.   142

inspiratory reserve volume (in-spy-ruh-tohr-ee) Volume of air that can be forcibly inhaled after normal inhalation.   146

insulin (in-suh-lin) Hormone secreted by the pancreas that lowers the blood glucose level by promoting the uptake of glucose by cells, and the conversion of glucose to glycogen by the liver and skeletal muscles.   278

integration Summing up of excitatory and inhibitory signals by a neuron or by some part of the brain.   223, 245

integumentary system (in-teg-yoo-men-tuh-ree, -men-tree) Organ system consisting of skin and various organs, such as hair, that are found in skin.   64

intercalated disks (in-tur-kuh-lay-tud) Region that holds adjacent cardiac muscle cells together; disks appear as dense bands at right angles to the muscle striations.   59

interferon (in-tur-feer-ahn) Antiviral agent produced by an infected cell that blocks the infection of another cell.   418

interkinesis Period of time between meiosis I and meiosis II, during which no DNA replication takes place.   342

interleukin (in-tur-loo-kun) Cytokine produced by macrophages and T cells that functions as a metabolic regulator of the immune response.   425

intermediate filament Rope-like assemblies of fibrous polypeptides in the cytoskeleton that provide support and strength to cells; so called because they are intermediate in size between actin filaments and microtubules.   43

internal respiration Exchange of oxygen and carbon dioxide between blood and tissue fluid.   150

interneuron Neuron located within the central nervous system that conveys messages between parts of the central nervous system.   218

interoceptor Sensory receptor that detects stimuli from inside the body (e.g., pressoreceptors, osmoreceptors, and chemoreceptors).   244

interphase Cell cycle stage during which growth and DNA synthesis occur when the nucleus is not actively dividing.   334

interstitial cell (in-tur-stish-ul) Hormone-secreting cell located between the seminiferous tubules of the testes.   293

intervertebral disk (in-tur-vur-tuh-brul) Layer of cartilage located between adjacent vertebrae.   188

intramembranous ossification Ossification that forms from membrane-like layers of primitive connective tissue.   180

intrauterine device (IUD) (in-truh-yoo-tur-in) Birth control device consisting of a small piece of molded plastic inserted into the uterus; believed to alter the uterine environment so that fertilization does not occur.   301

inversion Change in chromosome structure in which a segment of a chromosome is turned around 180°; this reversed sequence of genes can lead to altered gene activity and abnormalities.   396

ion (eye-un, -ahn) Charged particle that carries a negative or positive charge.   16

ionic bond (eye-ahn-ik) Chemical bond in which ions are attracted to one another by opposite charges.   16

iris (eye-ris) Muscular ring that surrounds the pupil and regulates the passage of light through this opening.   250

isotope (eye-suh-tohp) One of two or more atoms with the same atomic number but a different atomic mass due to the number of neutrons.   15

J

jaundice (jawn-dis) Yellowish tint to the skin caused by an abnormal amount of bilirubin (bile pigment) in the blood, indicating liver malfunction.   125

joint Articulation between two bones of a skeleton.   178

juxtaglomerular apparatus (juk-stuh-gluh-mer-yuh-lur) Structure located in the walls of arterioles near the glomerulus; regulates renal blood flow.   168

K

karyotype (kar-ee-uh-typ) Duplicated chromosomes arranged by pairs according to their size, shape, and general appearance.   390

kidney Organ in the urinary system that produces and excretes urine.   161

kingdom One of the categories used to classify organisms; the category above phylum.   2

L

lacteal (lak-tee-ul) Lymphatic vessel in an intestinal villus; it aids in the absorption of lipids.   121

lactose intolerance (lak-tohs) Inability to digest lactose because of an enzyme deficiency.   126

lacuna (pl., lacunae) (luh-koo-nuh, -kyoo-nuh) Small pit or hollow cavity, as in bone or cartilage, where a cell or cells are located.   56

lanugo (luh-noo-goh) Short, fine hair that is present during the later portion of fetal development.   319

large intestine Last major portion of the digestive tract, extending from the small intestine to the anus and consisting of the cecum, the colon, the rectum, and the anal canal.   122

laryngitis (lar-un-jy-tis) Infection of the larynx with accompanying hoarseness.   152

larynx (lar-ingks) Cartilaginous organ located between the pharynx and the trachea that contains the vocal cords; also called the voice box.   144

latency State of existing in a host without producing any signs of being present; some types of viruses can go through a period of latency.   436

learning Relatively permanent change in behavior that results from practice and experience.   230

lens Clear, membrane-like structure found in the eye behind the iris; brings objects into focus.   250

leptin Hormone produced by adipose tissue that acts on the hypothalamus to signal satiety.   282

leukemia (loo-kee-mee-uh) Cancer of the blood-forming tissues leading to the overproduction of abnormal white blood cells.   475

ligament (lig-uh-munt) Tough cord or band of dense fibrous connective tissue that joins bone to bone at a joint.   56, 178

limbic system Association of various brain centers, including the amygdala and hippocampus; governs learning and memory and various emotions, such as pleasure, fear, and happiness.   230

lineage Evolutionary line of descent.   494

lipase (ly-pays, ly-payz) Fat-digesting enzyme secreted by the pancreas.   124, 126

lipid (lip-id, ly-pid) Class of organic compounds that tends to be soluble only in nonpolar solvents, such as alcohol; includes fats and oils.   24

liver Large, dark red internal organ that produces urea and bile, detoxifies the blood, stores glycogen, and produces the plasma proteins, among other functions.   124

lockjaw Disease caused by the toxin of the tetanus bacterium (*Clostridium tetani*) acting on the central nervous system; characterized by painful muscular contractions.   210

locus (pl., loci) Particular site where a gene is found on a chromosome. Homologous chromosomes have corresponding gene loci.   352

long-term memory Retention of information that lasts longer than a few minutes.   230

long-term potentiation (LTP) (puh-ten-shee-ay-shun) Enhanced response at synapses within the hippocampus; likely essential to memory storage.   231

loop of the nephron (nef-rahn) Portion of the nephron lying between the proximal convoluted tubule and the distal convoluted tubule that functions in water reabsorption.   165

loose fibrous connective tissue Tissue composed mainly of fibroblasts widely separated by a matrix containing collagen and elastic fibers.   56

lumen (loo-mun) Cavity inside any tubular structure, such as the lumen of the digestive tract.   119

lung cancer Malignant growth that often begins in the bronchi.   154

lungs Paired, cone-shaped organs within the thoracic cavity; function in internal respiration and contain moist surfaces for gas exchange.   145

luteinizing hormone (LH) Hormone that controls the production of testosterone by interstitial cells in males and promotes the development of the corpus luteum in females.   293

lymph (limf) Fluid, derived from tissue fluid, that is carried in lymphatic vessels.   58, 92, 103

lymphatic organ Organ other than a lymphatic vessel that is part of the lymphatic system; includes lymph nodes, tonsils, spleen, thymus gland, and bone marrow.   414

lymphatic system (lim-fat-ik) Organ system consisting of lymphatic vessels and lymphatic organs that transports lymph and lipids, and aids the immune system.   66, 92

lymphatic vessel Vessel that carries lymph.   92

lymph node Mass of lymphatic tissue located along the course of a lymphatic vessel.   92, 415

lymphocyte (lim-fuh-syt) Specialized white blood cell that functions in specific defense; occurs in two forms—T cell and B cell.   103

lymphoma Cancer of lymphatic tissue (reticular connective tissue).   475

lysosome (ly-suh-sohm) Membrane-bound vesicle that contains hydrolytic enzymes for digesting macromolecules.   45

M

macromolecule Extremely large biological molecule; refers specifically to proteins, nucleic acids, polysaccharides, lipids, and complexes of these.   22

macrophage (mak-ruh-fayj) Large phagocytic cell derived from a monocyte that ingests microbes and debris.   417

malaria Serious infectious illness caused by the parasitic protozoan *Plasmodium*. Characterized by bouts of high fever and chills that occur at regular intervals.   447

male condom Sheath used to cover the penis during sexual intercourse; used as a contraceptive and, if latex, to minimize the risk of transmitting infection.   301

malleus (mal-ee-us) The first of three ossicles of the ear that serve to conduct vibrations from the tympanic membrane to the oval window of the inner ear.   256

maltase (mahl-tays, -tayz) Enzyme produced in the small intestine that breaks down maltose to two glucose molecules.   126

Marfan syndrome Congenital disorder of connective tissue characterized by abnormal length of the extremities.   401

mast cell Cell to which antibodies, formed in response to allergens, attach, causing it to release histamine, thus producing allergic symptoms.   417

mastoiditis (mas-toyd-eye-tis) Inflammation of the mastoid sinuses of the skull.   186

matrix (may-triks) Unstructured semifluid substance that fills the space between cells in connective tissues or inside organelles.   56

mechanoreceptor (mek-uh-noh-rih-sep-tur) Sensory receptor that responds to mechanical stimuli, such as that from pressure, sound waves, and gravity.   244

medulla oblongata (muh-dul-uh ahb-lawng-gah-tuh) Part of the brainstem that is continuous with the spinal cord; controls heartbeat, blood pressure, breathing, and other vital functions.   229

medullary cavity (muh-dul-uh-ree) Cavity within the diaphysis of a long bone containing marrow.   178

megakaryocyte (meg-uh-kar-ee-oh-syt, -uh-syt) Large cell that gives rise to blood platelets.   103

meiosis (my-oh-sis) Type of nuclear division that occurs as part of sexual reproduction in which the daughter cells receive the haploid number of chromosomes in varied combinations.   340

melanocyte Melanin-producing cell found in skin.   64

melanocyte-stimulating hormone (MSH) Substance that causes melanocytes to secrete melanin in lower vertebrates.   270

melatonin (mel-uh-toh-nun) Hormone, secreted by the pineal gland, that is involved in biorhythms.   282

membrane attack complex Group of complement proteins that form channels in a microbe's surface, thereby destroying it.   418

memory Capacity of the brain to store and retrieve information about past sensations and perceptions; essential to learning.   230

meninges (sing., meninx) (muh-nin-jeez) Protective membranous coverings about the central nervous system.   68, 224

meningitis Condition that refers to inflammation of the brain or spinal cord meninges (membranes).   68

meniscus (pl., menisci) (muh-nis-kus, -kee, -sy) Cartilaginous wedges that separate the surfaces of bones in synovial joints.   192

menopause (men-uh-pawz) Termination of the ovarian and uterine cycles in older women.   300

menstruation (men-stroo-ay-shun) Loss of blood and tissue from the uterus at the end of a uterine cycle.   298

messenger RNA (mRNA) Type of RNA formed from a DNA template that bears coded information for the amino acid sequence of a polypeptide.   370

metabolism All of the chemical reactions that occur in a cell.   48

metaphase Mitotic phase during which chromosomes are aligned at the equator of the mitotic spindle.   338

metastasis (muh-tas-tuh-sis) Spread of cancer from the place of origin throughout the body; caused by the ability of cancer cells to migrate and invade tissues.   473

microtubule (my-kro-too-byool) Small cylindrical structure that contains 13 rows of the protein tubulin around an empty central core; present in the cytoplasm, centrioles, cilia, and flagella.   43

micturition Emptying of the bladder; urination.   161

midbrain Part of the brain located below the thalamus and above the pons; contains reflex centers and tracts.   229

middle ear Portion of the ear consisting of the tympanic membrane, the oval and round windows, and the ossicles; where sound is amplified.   256

mineral Naturally occurring inorganic substance containing two or more elements; certain minerals are needed in the diet.   134, 530

mineralocorticoid (min-ur-uh-loh-kor-tih-koyd) Type of hormone secreted by the adrenal cortex that regulates water-salt balance, leading to

increases in blood volume and blood pressure.   275

mitochondrion (my-tuh-kahn-dree-un) Membrane-bound organelle in which ATP molecules are produced during the process of cellular respiration.   47

mitosis (my-toh-sis) Type of cell division in which daughter cells receive the exact chromosomal and genetic makeup of the parent cell; occurs during growth and repair.   334, 337

mitotic spindle Microtubule structure that brings about chromosomal movement during nuclear division.   337

molecular clock Mutational changes that accumulate at a presumed constant rate in regions of DNA not involved in adaptation to the environment.   494

molecule Union of two or more atoms of the same element; also, the smallest part of a compound that retains the properties of the compound.   16

monoclonal antibody One of many antibodies produced by a clone of hybridoma cells that all bind to the same antigen.   425

monocyte (mahn-uh-syt) Type of agranular white blood cell that functions as a phagocyte and an antigen-presenting cell.   103

monohybrid Individual that is heterozygous for one trait; shows the phenotype of the dominant allele but carries the recessive allele.   354

monosaccharide (mahn-uh-sak-uh-ryd) Simple sugar; a carbohydrate that cannot be decomposed by hydrolysis (e.g., glucose).   22

monosomy One less chromosome than usual.   392

morphogenesis Emergence of shape in tissues, organs, or entire embryo during development.   311

morula Spherical mass of cells resulting from cleavage during animal development, prior to the blastula stage.   313

mosaic evolution Concept that human characteristics did not evolve at the same rate; for example, some body parts are more human-like than others in early hominids.   496

motor neuron Nerve cell that conducts nerve impulses away from the central nervous system and innervates effectors (muscles and glands).   218

motor unit Motor neuron and all the muscle fibers it innervates.   206

mucous membrane (myoo-kus) Membrane lining a cavity or tube that opens to the outside of the body; also called mucosa.   68

multifactorial inheritance Inheritance pattern in which a trait is controlled by several allelic pairs; each dominant allele contributes to the phenotype in an additive and like manner.   359

multiple allele (uh-leelz) Inheritance pattern in which there are more than two alleles for a particular trait; each individual has only two of all possible alleles.   361

multiple sclerosis (MS) Disease in which the outer myelin layer of nerve fiber insulation becomes scarred, interfering with normal conduction of nerve impulses.   428

multiregional continuity hypothesis Proposal that modern humans evolved independently in at least three different places: Asia, Africa, and Europe.   499

muscle fiber Muscle cell.   198

muscle tone Continuous, partial contraction of muscle.   206

muscle twitch Contraction of a whole muscle in response to a single stimulus.   206

muscular dystrophy (mus-ku-lar dis-tro-fee) Progressive muscle weakness and atrophy caused by deficient dystrophin protein.   210

muscular system System of muscles that produces movement, both within the body and of its limbs; principal components are skeletal, smooth, and cardiac muscle.   67

muscular (contractile) tissue Type of tissue composed of fibers that can shorten and thicken.   59

mutagen (myoo-tuh-jun) Agent, such as radiation or a chemical, that brings about a mutation.   476

mutation Alteration in chromosome structure or number and also an alteration in a gene due to a change in DNA composition.   369

myalgia Muscular pain.   210

myasthenia gravis (mi-as-thee-ne-ah grav-is) Chronic disease characterized by muscles that are weak and easily fatigued. It results from the immune system's attack on neuromuscular junctions so that stimuli are not transmitted from motor neurons to muscle fibers.   210, 428

mycosis (pl., mycoses) Any disease caused by a fungus.   446

myelin sheath (my-uh-lin) White, fatty material, derived from the membrane of Schwann cells, that forms a covering for nerve fibers.   219

myocardium (my-oh-kar-dee-um) Cardiac muscle in the wall of the heart.   80

myofibril (my-uh-fy-brul) Contractile portion of muscle cells that contains a linear arrangement of sarcomeres and shortens to produce muscle contraction.   202

myogram Recording of a muscular contraction.   206

myosin (my-uh-sin) One of two major proteins of muscle; makes up thick filaments in myofibrils of muscle fibers. See actin.   202

myxedema (mik-sih-dee-muh) Condition resulting from a deficiency of thyroid hormone in an adult.   273

N

NAD (nicotinamide adenine dinucleotide) Coenzyme that functions as a carrier of electrons and hydrogen ions, especially in cellular respiration.   48

nail Protective covering of the distal part of fingers and toes.   65

nasal cavity One of two canals in the nose, separated by a septum.   143

nasopharynx (nay-zoh-far-ingks) Region of the pharynx associated with the nasal cavity.   118

natural killer (NK) cell Lymphocyte that causes an infected or cancerous cell to burst.   418

natural selection Mechanism resulting in adaptation to the environment.   492

Neanderthal (nee-an-dur-thahl, -tahl) Hominid with a sturdy build who lived during the last Ice Age in Europe and the Middle East; hunted large game and has left evidence of being culturally advanced.   500

nearsighted Vision abnormality due to an elongated eyeball from front to back; light rays focus in front of retina when viewing distant objects.   255

necrotizing fasciitis Disease that results from a severe invasive group A *Streptococcus* infection. It begins with skin reddening, swelling, pain, and cellulitis and proceeds to skin breakdown and gangrene after three to five days.   442

negative feedback Mechanism of homeostatic response in which a stimulus initiates reactions that reduce the stimulus.   72

nephron (nef-rahn) Microscopic kidney unit that regulates blood composition by glomerular filtration, tubular reabsorption, and tubular secretion.   163

nerve Bundle of long axons outside the central nervous system.   60, 232

nerve impulse Action potential (electrochemical change) traveling along a neuron.   220

nervous system Organ system consisting of the brain, spinal cord, and associated nerves that coordinates the other organ systems of the body.   67

nervous tissue Tissue that contains nerve cells (neurons), which conduct impulses, and neuroglia, which support, protect, and provide nutrients to neurons.   60

neuroglia (noo-rahg-lee-uh, noo-rohg-lee-uh) Nonconducting nerve cells that are intimately associated with neurons and function in a supportive capacity.   60, 218

neuromuscular junction Region where an axon terminal approaches a muscle fiber; the synaptic cleft separates the axon terminal from the sarcolemma of a muscle fibre.   204

neuron (noor-ahn, nyoor-) Nerve cell that characteristically has three parts: dendrites, cell body, and axon.   60, 218

neurotransmitter Chemical stored at the ends of axons that is responsible for transmission across a synapse.   222

neutron (noo-trahn) Neutral subatomic particle, located in the nucleus and having a weight of approximately one atomic mass unit.   14

neutrophil (noo-truh-fil) Granular leukocyte that is the most abundant of the white blood cells; first to respond to infection.   103

niche (nich) Role an organism plays in its community, including its habitat and its interactions with other organisms.   506

nitrification Process by which nitrogen in ammonia and organic molecules is oxidized to nitrites and nitrates by soil bacteria.   512

nitrogen fixation Process whereby free atmospheric nitrogen is converted into compounds, such as ammonium and nitrates, usually by bacteria.   512

node of Ranvier (rahn-vee-ay) Gap in the myelin sheath around a nerve fiber.   219

nondisjunction Failure of homologous chromosomes or daughter chromosomes to separate during meiosis I and meiosis II, respectively.   392

nonrenewable resource Minerals, fossil fuels, and other materials present in essentially fixed amounts (within human time scales) in our environment.   524

norepinephrine (NE) (nor-ep-uh-nef-rin) Neurotransmitter of the postganglionic fibers in the sympathetic division of the autonomic system; also, a hormone produced by the adrenal medulla.   222, 275

nuclear envelope Double membrane that surrounds the nucleus and is connected to the endoplasmic reticulum; has pores that allow substances to pass between the nucleus and the cytoplasm.   44

nuclear pore Opening in the nuclear envelope that permits the passage of proteins into the nucleus and ribosomal subunits out of the nucleus.   44

nucleoid An irregularly shaped region in the prokaryotic cell that contains its genetic material.   441

nucleolus (noo-klee-uh-lus, nyoo-) Dark-staining, spherical body in the cell nucleus that produces ribosomal subunits.   38, 44

nucleoplasm (noo-klee-uh-plaz-um) Semifluid medium of the nucleus, containing chromatin.   44

nucleotide Monomer of DNA and RNA consisting of a 5-carbon sugar bonded to a nitrogen-containing base and a phosphate group.   29

nucleus (noo-klee-us, nyoo-) (pl., nuclei) Membrane-bounded organelle that contains chromosomes and controls the structure and function of the cell.   38, 44, 229

nutrient Chemical substances in foods that are essential to the diet and contribute to good health.   128

O

obesity (oh-bee-sih-tee) Excess adipose tissue; exceeding ideal weight by more than 20%.   136

oil Substance, usually of plant origin and liquid at room temperature, formed when a glycerol molecule reacts with three fatty acid molecules.   24

oil gland Gland of the skin associated with hair follicle; secretes sebum; also called sebaceous gland.   65

olfactory cell (ahl-fak-tuh-ree, -tree, ohl-) Modified neuron that is a sensory receptor for the sense of smell.   249

omnivore (ahm-nuh-vor) Organism in a food chain that feeds on both plants and animals.   506

oncogene (ahng-koh-jeen) Cancer-causing gene.   474

oncologist Physician who specializes in one or more types of cancers.   475

oncology The study of cancer.   475

oogenesis (oh-uh-jen-uh-sis) Production of an egg in females by the process of meiosis and maturation.   294, 346

opportunistic infection Infection that has an opportunity to occur because the immune system has been weakened.   464

optic chiasma X-shaped structure on the underside of the brain formed by a partial crossing-over of optic nerve fibers.   254

optic nerve Either of two cranial nerves that carry nerve impulses from the retina of the eye to the brain, thereby contributing to the sense of sight.   251

organ Combination of two or more different tissues performing a common function.   2

organelle (or-guh-nel) Small membranous structure in the cytoplasm having a specific structure and function.   38

organic molecule Type of molecule that contains carbon and hydrogen—and often contains oxygen also.   22

origin End of a muscle that is attached to a relatively immovable bone.   199

oscilloscope (ah-sil-uh-skohp, uh-sil-) Apparatus that records changes in voltage by graphing them on a screen; used to study the nerve impulse.   220

osmosis (ahz-moh-sis, ahs-) Diffusion of water through a selectively permeable membrane.   41

osmotic pressure Measure of the tendency of water to move across a selectively permeable membrane; visible as an increase in liquid on the side of the membrane with higher solute concentration.   99

ossicle (ahs-ih-kul) One of the small bones of the middle ear—malleus, incus, and stapes.   256

ossification Formation of bone tissue.   180

osteoarthritis Disintegration of the cartilage between bones at a synovial joint.   193

osteoblast (ahs-tee-uh-blast) Bone-forming cell.   180

osteoclast (ahs-tee-uh-klast) Cell that causes erosion of bone.   180

osteocyte (ahs-tee-uh-syt) Mature bone cell located within the lacunae of bone.   178, 180

osteoporosis Condition in which bones break easily because calcium is removed from them faster than it is replaced.   134

otitis media (oh-ty-tis mee-dee-uh) Infection of the middle ear, characterized by pain and possibly by a sense of fullness, hearing loss, vertigo, and fever.   152

otolith (oh-tuh-lith) Calcium carbonate granule associated with ciliated cells in the utricle and the saccule.   261

outer ear Portion of ear consisting of the pinna and auditory canal.   256

out-of-Africa hypothesis Proposal that modern humans originated only in Africa; then migrated out of Africa and supplanted populations of early *Homo* in Asia and Europe about 100,000 years ago.   499

oval window Membrane-covered opening between the stapes and the inner ear.   256

ovarian cycle (oh-vair-ee-un) Monthly follicle changes occurring in the ovary that control the level of sex hormones in the blood and the uterine cycle.   297

ovary Female gonad that produces eggs and the female sex hormones.   280, 294

oviduct (oh-vuh-dukt) Tube that transports eggs to the uterus; also called uterine tube.   294

ovulation (ahv-yuh-lay-shun, ohv-) Release of a secondary oocyte from the ovary; if fertilization occurs, the secondary oocyte becomes an egg.   294

oxygen deficit Amount of oxygen needed to metabolize lactate, a compound that accumulates during vigorous exercise.   208

oxyhemoglobin (ahk-see-hee-muh-gloh-bin) Compound formed when oxygen combines with hemoglobin.   150

oxytocin (ahk-sih-toh-sin) Hormone released by the posterior pituitary that causes contraction of uterus and milk letdown.   270

ozone shield Accumulation of O_3, formed from oxygen in the upper atmosphere; a filtering layer that protects the Earth from ultraviolet radiation.   530

P

pacemaker See sinoatrial (SA) node.   82

pain receptor Sensory receptor that is sensitive to chemicals released by damaged tissues or excess stimuli of heat or pressure.   244

pancreas (pang-kree-us, pan-) Internal organ that produces digestive enzymes and the hormones insulin and glucagon.   124, 278

pancreatic amylase (pang-kree-at-ik am-uh-lays, -layz) Enzyme in the pancreas that digests starch to maltose.   124, 126

pancreatic islets (islets of Langerhans) Masses of cells that constitute the endocrine portion of the pancreas.   278

pandemic An increase in the occurrence of a disease within a large and geographically widespread population (often refers to a worldwide epidemic).   435

Pap test Analysis done on cervical cells for detection of cancer.   294

parasympathetic division That part of the autonomic system that is active under normal conditions; uses acetylcholine as a neurotransmitter.   235

parathyroid gland (par-uh-thy-royd) Gland embedded in the posterior surface of the thyroid gland; it produces parathyroid hormone.   274

parathyroid hormone (PTH) Hormone secreted by the four parathyroid glands that increases the blood calcium level and decreases the blood phosphate level.   274

parent cell Cell that divides so as to form daughter cells.   337

Parkinson disease Progressive deterioration of the central nervous system due to a deficiency in the neurotransmitter dopamine. 236

parturition (par-tyoo-rish-un, par-chuh-) Processes that lead to and include birth and the expulsion of the afterbirth. 324

passive immunity Protection against infection acquired by transfer of antibodies to a susceptible individual. 424

pathogen (path-uh-jun) Disease-causing agent. 58, 434

pectoral girdle (pek-tur-ul) Portion of the skeleton that provides support and attachment for an arm; consists of a scapula and a clavicle. 190

pedigree Chart showing the relationships of relatives and which ones have a particular trait. 398

pelvic girdle Portion of the skeleton to which the legs are attached; consists of the coxal bones. 191

pelvic inflammatory disease (PID) Disease state of the reproductive organs caused by a sexually transmitted disease that can result in scarring and infertility. 454

pelvis Bony ring formed by the sacrum and coxae. 191

penis External organ in males through which the urethra passes; also serves as the organ of sexual intercourse. 291

pentose (pen-tohs, -tohz) Five-carbon sugar. Deoxyribose is the pentose sugar found in DNA; ribose is a pentose sugar found in RNA. 22

pepsin (pep-sin) Enzyme secreted by gastric glands that digests proteins to peptides. 120, 126

peptidase (pep-tih-days, -dayz) Intestinal enzyme that breaks down short chains of amino acids to individual amino acids that are absorbed across the intestinal wall. 126

peptide bond Type of covalent bond that joins two amino acids. 26

peptide hormone Type of hormone that is a protein, a peptide, or derived from an amino acid. 269

peptidoglycan Unique molecule found in bacterial cell walls. 441

perception Mental awareness of sensory stimulation. 245

pericardium (pair-ih-kar-dee-um) Protective serous membrane that surrounds the heart. 80

periosteum (pair-ee-ahs-tee-um) Fibrous connective tissue covering the surface of bone. 179

peripheral nervous system (PNS) (puh-rif-ur-ul) Nerves and ganglia that lie outside the central nervous system. 218

peristalsis (pair-ih-stawl-sis) Wavelike contractions that propel substances along a tubular structure, such as the esophagus. 118

peritonitis (pair-ih-tuh-ny-tis) Generalized infection of the lining of the abdominal cavity. 68, 122

peritubular capillary network (pair-ih-too-byuh-lur) Capillary network that surrounds a nephron and functions in reabsorption during urine formation. 164

Peyer's patches Lymphatic organs located in the small intestine. 415

phagocytosis (fag-uh-sy-toh-sis) Process by which amoeboid-type cells engulf large substances, forming an intracellular vacuole. 103

pharynx (far-ingks) Portion of the digestive tract between the mouth and the esophagus that serves as a passageway for food and also for air on its way to the trachea. 117, 143

phenotype (fee-nuh-typ) Visible expression of a genotype—for example, brown eyes or attached earlobes. 352

phenylketonuria (PKU) Result of accumulation of phenylalanine, characterized by mental retardation, light pigmentation, eczema, and neurologic manifestations unless treated by a diet low in phenylalanine. 400

pheromone Chemical signal released by an organism that affects the metabolism or influences the behavior of another individual of the same species. 268

phlebitis (flih-by-tis) Inflammation of a vein. 89

phospholipid (fahs-foh-lip-id) Molecule that forms the bilayer of the cell's membranes; has a polar, hydrophilic head bonded to two nonpolar, hydrophobic tails. 25

photoreceptor Sensory receptor in retina that responds to light stimuli. 244

photovoltaic (solar) cell An energy-conversion device that captures solar energy and directly converts it to electrical current. 529

pH scale Measurement scale for hydrogen ion concentration. 20

pineal gland (pin-ee-ul, py-nee-ul) Endocrine gland located in the third ventricle of the brain; produces melatonin. 282

pinna Part of the ear that projects on the outside of the head. 256

pituitary dwarfism (pih-too-ih-tair-ee, -tyoo-) Condition in which an affected individual has normal proportions but small stature; caused by inadequate growth hormone. 272

pituitary gland Endocrine gland that lies just inferior to the hypothalamus;

consists of the anterior pituitary and posterior pituitary. 270

placenta (pluh-sen-tuh) Structure that forms from the chorion and the uterine wall and allows the embryo, and then the fetus, to acquire nutrients and rid itself of wastes. 300, 311

plaque (plak) Accumulation of soft masses of fatty material, particularly cholesterol, beneath the inner linings of the arteries. 88, 130

plasma (plaz-muh) Liquid portion of blood; contains nutrients, wastes, salts, and proteins. 99

plasma cell Cell derived from a B lymphocyte that is specialized to mass-produce antibodies. 419

plasma membrane Membrane surrounding the cytoplasm that consists of a phospholipid bilayer with embedded proteins; functions to regulate the entrance and exit of molecules from the cell. 38

plasmid (plaz-mid) Self-replicating ring of accessory DNA in the cytoplasm of bacteria. 380

platelet (thrombocyte) (playt-lit) Component of blood that is necessary to blood clotting; also called a thrombocyte. 58, 103

pleura Serous membrane that encloses the lungs. 68

pneumonectomy (noo-muh-nek-tuh-mee, nyoo-) Surgical removal of all or part of a lung. 154

pneumonia (noo-mohn-yuh, nyoo-) Infection of the lungs that causes alveoli to fill with mucus and pus. 152

polar Combination of atoms in which the electrical charge is not distributed symmetrically. 18

polar body In oogenesis, a nonfunctional product; two to three meiotic products are of this type. 347

pollution Any environmental change that adversely affects the lives and health of living things. 5, 524

polymerase chain reaction (PCR) (pahl-uh-muh-rays, -rayz) Technique that uses the enzyme DNA polymerase to produce millions of copies of a particular piece of DNA. 381

polyp (pahl-ip) Small, abnormal growth that arises from the epithelial lining. 123

polypeptide Polymer of many amino acids linked by peptide bonds. 26

polyribosome (pahl-ih-ry-buh-sohm) String of ribosomes simultaneously translating regions of the same mRNA strand during protein synthesis. 44, 374

polysaccharide (pahl-ee-sak-uh-ryd) Polymer made from sugar monomers; the polysaccharides starch and glycogen are polymers of glucose monomers.   23

pons (pahnz) Portion of the brainstem above the medulla oblongata and below the midbrain; assists the medulla oblongata in regulating the breathing rate.   229

population Organisms of the same species occupying a certain area.   506

positive feedback Mechanism in which the stimulus initiates reactions that lead to an increase in the stimulus.   73, 270

posterior pituitary Portion of the pituitary gland that stores and secretes oxytocin and antidiuretic hormone, which are produced by the hypothalamus.   270

pre-embryonic development Development of the zygote in the first week, including fertilization, the beginning of cell division, and the appearance of the chorion.   313

prefrontal area Association area in the frontal lobe that receives information from other association areas and uses it to reason and plan actions.   228

preparatory reaction Reaction that oxidizes pyruvate with the release of carbon dioxide; results in acetyl-CoA and connects glycolysis to the citric acid cycle.   49

primary germ layer Three layers (ectoderm, mesoderm, and endoderm) of embryonic cells that develop into specific tissues and organs.   317

primary motor area Area in the frontal lobe where voluntary commands begin; each section controls a part of the body.   227

primary productivity Amount of biomass produced primarily by photosynthesizers.   516

primary somatosensory area (soh-mat-uh-sens-ree, -suh-ree) Area dorsal to the central sulcus where sensory information arrives from skin and skeletal muscles.   227

primate (pry-mayt) Animal that belongs to the order Primate; includes prosimians, monkeys, apes, and humans, all of whom have adaptations for living in trees.   493

principle Theory that is generally accepted by an overwhelming number of scientists; a law.   6

prion An infectious particle that is the cause of diseases, such as scrapie in sheep, mad cow disease, and Creutzfeldt-Jakob disease in humans; it has a protein component, but no nucleic acid has yet been detected.   439

producer Photosynthetic organism at the start of a grazing food chain that makes its own food (e.g., green plants on land and algae in water).   5, 506

product Substance that forms as a result of a reaction.   48

progesterone (proh-jes-tuh-rohn) Female sex hormone that helps maintain sex organs and secondary sex characteristics.   280, 298

prokaryotic cell Type of cell that lacks a membrane-bounded nucleus and organelles.   441, 489

prolactin (PRL) (proh-lak-tin) Hormone secreted by the anterior pituitary that stimulates the production of milk from the mammary glands.   270

prophase (proh-fayz) Mitotic phase during which chromatin condenses so that chromosomes appear; chromosomes are scattered.   338

proprioceptor (proh-pree-oh-sep-tur) Sensory receptor in skeletal muscles and joints that assists the brain in knowing the position of the limbs.   246

prosimian Group of primates that includes lemur and tarsiers and may resemble the first primates to have evolved.   493

prostaglandin (prahs-tuh-glan-din) Hormone that has various and powerful local effects.   282

prostate gland (prahs-tayt) Gland located around the male urethra below the urinary bladder; adds secretions to semen.   290

protein Molecule consisting of one or more polypeptides.   26

protein-first hypothesis In chemical evolution, the proposal that protein originated before other macromolecules and allowed the formation of protocells.   488

proteomics The study of all proteins in an organism.   379

prothrombin (proh-thrahm-bin) Plasma protein that is converted to thrombin during the steps of blood clotting.   104

prothrombin activator Enzyme that catalyzes the transformation of the precursor prothrombin to the active enzyme thrombin.   104

protocell In biological evolution, a possible cell forerunner that became a cell once it could reproduce.   488

proton Positive subatomic particle, located in the nucleus and having a weight of approximately one atomic mass unit.   14

proto-oncogene (proh-toh-ahng-koh-jeen) Normal gene that can become an oncogene through mutation.   474

proximal convoluted tubule Highly coiled region of a nephron near the glomerular capsule, where tubular reabsorption takes place.   165

pubic symphysis Slightly movable cartilaginous joint between the anterior surfaces of the hip bones.   191

pulmonary artery (pool-muh-nair-ee, puul-) Blood vessel that takes blood away from the heart to the lungs.   81

pulmonary circuit Circulatory pathway that consists of the pulmonary trunk, the pulmonary arteries, and the pulmonary veins; takes O_2-poor blood from the heart to the lungs and O_2-rich blood from the lungs to the heart.   78

pulmonary fibrosis (fy-broh-sis) Accumulation of fibrous connective tissue in the lungs; caused by inhaling irritating particles, such as silica, coal dust, or asbestos.   153

pulmonary tuberculosis Tuberculosis of the lungs, caused by the bacillus *Mycobacterium tuberculosis*.   152

pulmonary vein Blood vessel that takes blood from the lungs to the heart.   81

pulse Vibration felt in arterial walls due to expansion of the aorta following ventricle contraction.   84

Punnett square (pun-ut) Grid-like device used to calculate the expected results of simple genetic crosses.   354

pupil (pyoo-pul) Opening in the center of the iris of the eye.   250

Purkinje fibers (pur-kin-jee) Specialized muscle fibers that conduct the cardiac impulse from the AV bundle into the ventricles.   82

pyelonephritis Inflammation of the kidney due to bacterial infection.   171

R

radioactive isotope Unstable form of an atom that spontaneously emits radiation in the form of radioactive particles or radiant energy.   15

reactant (re-ak-tunt) Substance that participates in a reaction.   48

recessive allele (uh-leel) Allele that exerts its phenotypic effect only in the homozygote; its expression is masked by a dominant allele.   352

recombinant DNA (rDNA) DNA that contains genes from more than one source.   380

rectum (rek-tum) Terminal end of the digestive tube between the sigmoid colon and the anus.   122

red blood cell (erythrocyte) Formed element that contains hemoglobin and carries oxygen from the lungs to the tissues; also called erythrocyte.   58, 100

red bone marrow Blood-cell-forming tissue located in the spaces within spongy bone.   178, 414

reduced hemoglobin (hee-muh-gloh-bun) Hemoglobin that is carrying hydrogen ions.   150

referred pain Pain perceived as having come from a site other than that of its actual origin.   247

reflex Automatic, involuntary response of an organism to a stimulus.   233

reflex action An action performed automatically, without conscious thought (e.g., swallowing).   118

refractory period (rih-frak-tuh-ree) Time following an action potential when a neuron is unable to conduct another nerve impulse.   220

renal artery (ree-nul) Vessel that originates from the aorta and delivers blood to the kidney.   161

renal cortex (ree-nul kor-teks) Outer portion of the kidney that appears granular.   163

renal medulla (ree-nul muh-dul-uh) Inner portion of the kidney that consists of renal pyramids.   163

renal pelvis Hollow chamber in the kidney that lies inside the renal medulla and receives freshly prepared urine from the collecting ducts.   163

renal vein (ree-nul) Vessel that takes blood from the kidney to the inferior vena cava.   161

renewable resource Resources normally replaced or replenished by natural processes; resources not depleted by moderate use. Examples include solar energy, biological resources such as forests and fisheries, biological organisms, and some biogeochemical cycles.   524

renin (ren-in) Enzyme released by kidneys that leads to the secretion of aldosterone and a rise in blood pressure.   168, 276

replacement reproduction Population in which each person is replaced by only one child.   523

reproduce To produce a new individual of the same kind.   2

reproductive system Organ system that contains male or female organs and specializes in the production of offspring.   67

residual volume Amount of air remaining in the lungs after a forceful expiration.   146

resource In economic terms, anything with potential use in creating wealth or giving satisfaction.   524

respiratory center Group of nerve cells in the medulla oblongata that sends out nerve impulses on a rhythmic basis, resulting in involuntary inspiration on an ongoing basis.   149

respiratory system Organ system consisting of the lungs and tubes that bring oxygen into the lungs and take carbon dioxide out.   67

resting potential Polarity across the plasma membrane of a resting neuron due to an unequal distribution of ions.   220

restriction enzyme Bacterial enzyme that stops viral reproduction by cleaving viral DNA; used to cut DNA at specific points during production of recombinant DNA.   380

reticular fiber (rih-tik-yuh-lur) Very thin collagen fibers in the matrix of connective tissue, highly branched and forming delicate supporting networks.   56

reticular formation (rih-tik-yuh-lur) Complex network of nerve fibers within the central nervous system that arouses the cerebrum.   229

retina (ret-n-uh, ret-nuh) Innermost layer of the eyeball that contains the rod cells and the cone cells.   251

retinal (ret-n-al, -awl) Light-absorbing molecule that is a derivative of vitamin A and a component of rhodopsin.   252

retrovirus RNA virus containing the enzyme reverse transcriptase that carries out RNA to DNA transcription.   465

rheumatic fever Autoimmune disease characterized by inflammation of the heart valves, joints, subcutaneous tissues, and central nervous system. The disease is associated with hemolytic streptococci in the body.   442

rheumatoid arthritis Persistent inflammation of synovial joints, often causing cartilage destruction, bone erosion, and joint deformities.   428

rhodopsin (roh-dahp-sun) Light-absorbing molecule in rod cells and cone cells that contains a pigment and the protein opsin.   252

ribosomal RNA (rRNA) (ry-buh-soh-mul) Type of RNA found in ribosomes where protein synthesis occurs.   370

ribosome (ry-buh-sohm) RNA and protein in two subunits; site of protein synthesis in the cytoplasm.   44

ringworm Common name for a fungal infection of the skin, even though it is not caused by a worm and is not always ring-shaped in appearance.   446

RNA (ribonucleic acid) (ry-boh-noo-klee-ik) Nucleic acid produced from covalent bonding of nucleotide monomers that contain the sugar ribose; occurs in three forms: messenger RNA, ribosomal RNA, and transfer RNA.   29, 370

RNA-first hypothesis In chemical evolution, the proposal that RNA originated before other macromolecules and allowed the formation of the first cell(s).   488

RNA polymerase (pahl-uh-muh-rays) During transcription, an enzyme that joins nucleotides complementary to a DNA template.   373

rod cell Photoreceptor in retina of eyes that responds to dim light.   252

rotational equilibrium Maintenance of balance when the head and body are suddenly moved or rotated.   261

rotator cuff Tendons that encircle and help form a socket for the humerus, and also help reinforce the shoulder joint.   190

round window Membrane-covered opening between the inner ear and the middle ear.   256

S

SA (sinoatrial) node (sy-noh-ay-tree-ul) Small region of neuromuscular tissue that initiates the heartbeat; also called the pacemaker.   82

saccule (sak-yool) Sac-like cavity in the vestibule of the inner ear; contains sensory receptors for gravitational equilibrium.   261

salinization Process in which mineral salts accumulate in the soil, killing plants; occurs when soils in dry climates are irrigated profusely.   526

salivary amylase (sal-uh-vair-ee am-uh-lays, -layz) Secreted from the salivary glands; the first enzyme to act on starch.   116, 126

salivary gland Gland associated with the mouth that secretes saliva.   116

saltwater intrusion Movement of salt water into freshwater aquifers in coastal areas where groundwater is withdrawn faster than it is replenished.   526

sarcolemma (sar-kuh-lem-uh) Plasma membrane of a muscle fiber; also forms the tubules of the T system involved in muscular contraction.   202

sarcoma Cancer that arises in muscles and connective tissues.   475

sarcomere (sar-kuh-mir) One of many units, arranged linearly within a myofibril, whose contraction produces muscle contraction.   202

sarcoplasmic reticulum (sar-kuh-plaz-mik rih-tik-yuh-lum) Smooth endoplasmic reticulum of skeletal muscle cells; surrounds the myofibrils and stores calcium ions.   202

saturated fatty acid Fatty acid molecule that lacks double bonds between the atoms of its carbon chain.   24

scarlet fever Communicable disease spread by respiratory droplets resulting from infection by a strain of *Streptococcus pyogenes*; rash-inducing toxin causes shedding of the skin.   442

scavenger Animal that specializes in the consumption of dead animals. 506

schistosomiasis Infection by a blood fluke (*Schistosoma*), often as a result of contact with contaminated water in rivers and streams. Symptoms include fever, chills, diarrhea, and cough. Infection may be chronic. 449

Schwann cell Cell that surrounds a fiber of a peripheral nerve and forms the myelin sheath. 219

science Development of concepts about the natural world, often by utilizing the scientific method. 6

scientific method Process of attaining knowledge by making observations, testing hypotheses, and coming to conclusions. 6

scientific theory Concept supported by a broad range of observations, experiments, and conclusions. 6

sclera (skleer-uh) White, fibrous, outer layer of the eyeball. 250

scoliosis Abnormal laterial (side-to-side) curvature of the vertebral column. 188

scrotum (skroh-tum) Pouch of skin that encloses the testes. 290

secondary oocyte In oogenesis, the functional product of meiosis I; becomes the egg. 347

second messenger Chemical signal such as cyclic AMP that causes the cell to respond to the first messenger—a hormone bound to a receptor protein in the plasma membrane. 269

selectively permeable Having degrees of permeability; the cell is impermeable to some substances and allows others to pass through at varying rates. 40

semantic memory Capacity of the brain to store and retrieve information with regard to words or numbers. 230

semen (see-mun) Thick, whitish fluid consisting of sperm and secretions from several glands of the male reproductive tract. 290

semicircular canal (sem-ih-sur-kyuh-lur) One of three tubular structures within the inner ear that contain sensory receptors responsible for the sense of rotational equilibrium. 256

semilunar valve (sem-ee-loo-nur) Valve resembling a half moon located between the ventricles and their attached vessels. 80

seminal vesicle (sem-uh-nul) Convoluted structure attached to the vas deferens near the base of the urinary bladder in males; adds secretions to semen. 290

seminiferous tubule (sem-uh-nif-ur-us) Long, coiled structure contained within chambers of the testis; where sperm are produced. 292

sensation Conscious awareness of a stimulus due to nerve impulses sent to the brain from a sensory receptor by way of sensory neurons. 244

sensory adaptation Phenomenon of a sensation becoming less noticeable once it has been recognized by constant repeated stimulation. 245

sensory neuron Nerve cell that transmits nerve impulses to the central nervous system after a sensory receptor has been stimulated. 218

sensory receptor Structure that receives either external or internal environmental stimuli and is a part of a sensory neuron or transmits signals to a sensory neuron. 218, 244

septum Wall between two cavities; in the human heart, a septum separates the right side from the left side. 80

serous membrane (seer-us) Membrane that covers internal organs and lines cavities without an opening to the outside of the body; also called serosa. 68

serum (seer-um) Light yellow liquid left after clotting of blood. 104

severe combined immunodeficiency disease (SCID) Congenital illness in which both antibody- and cell-mediated immunity are lacking or inadequate. 428

sex chromosome Chromosome that determines the sex of an individual; in humans, females have two X chromosomes, and males have an X and Y chromosome. 362

sex-linked Allele that occurs on the sex chromosomes but may control a trait that has nothing to do with the sex characteristics of an individual. 362

sexually transmitted disease (STD) Illness communicated primarily or exclusively through sexual contact. 453

shingles Reactivated form of chickenpox caused by the varicella-zoster virus. 438

short-term memory Retention of information for only a few minutes, such as remembering a telephone number. 230

sickle-cell disease Genetic disorder in which the affected individual has sickle-shaped red blood cells that are subject to hemolysis. 101, 400

simple goiter (goy-tur) Condition in which an enlarged thyroid produces low levels of thyroxine. 273

sinkhole Large surface crater caused by the collapse of an underground channel or cavern; often triggered by groundwater withdrawal. 526

sinus (sy-nus) Cavity or hollow space in an organ such as the skull. 186

sinusitis (sy-nuh-sy-tis) Infection of the sinuses, caused by blockage of the openings to the sinuses, and characterized by postnasal discharge and facial pain. 152

skeletal muscle Striated, voluntary muscle tissue found in muscles that move the bones. 59, 198

skeletal system System of bones, cartilage, and ligaments that works with the muscular system to protect the body and provide support for locomotion and movement. 67

skill memory Capacity of the brain to store and retrieve information necessary to perform motor activities, such as riding a bike. 230

skin Outer covering of the body; can be called the integumentary system because it contains organs such as sense organs. 64

skull Bony framework of the head, composed of cranial bones and the bones of the face. 186

sliding filament model An explanation for muscle contraction based on the movement of actin filaments in relation to myosin filaments. 202

small intestine Long, tube-like chamber of the digestive tract between the stomach and large intestine. 121

smooth (visceral) muscle Nonstriated, involuntary muscle tissue found in the walls of internal organs. 59, 198

sodium-potassium pump Carrier protein in the plasma membrane that moves sodium ions out of and potassium ions into cells; important in nerve and muscle cells. 220

soft palate (pal-it) Entirely muscular posterior portion of the roof of the mouth. 116

somatic cell (soh-mat-ik) Body cell; excludes cells that undergo meiosis and become a sperm or egg. 334

somatic system That portion of the peripheral nervous system containing motor neurons that control skeletal muscles. 233

spasm Sudden, involuntary contraction of one or more muscles. 210

sperm Male gamete having a haploid number of chromosomes and the ability to fertilize an egg, the female gamete. 293

spermatogenesis (spur-mat-uh-jen-ih-sis) Production of sperm in males by the process of meiosis and maturation. 292, 346

sphincter (sfingk-tur) Muscle that surrounds a tube and closes or opens the tube by contracting and relaxing. 118

spinal cord Part of the central nervous system; the nerve cord that is continuous with the base of the brain plus the vertebral column that protects the nerve cord. 224

spinal nerve Nerve that arises from the spinal cord.   232

spiral organ Organ in the cochlear duct of the inner ear that is responsible for hearing; also called the organ of Corti.   257

spleen Large, glandular organ located in the upper left region of the abdomen; stores and purifies blood.   92, 414

spongy bone Porous bone found at the ends of long bones where red bone marrow is sometimes located.   57, 178

sporadic occurrence Disease that occurs occasionally and at random intervals in a population.   435

sprain Injury to a ligament caused by abnormal force applied to a joint.   210

squamous epithelium (skway-mus, skwah-) Type of epithelial tissue that contains flat cells.   62

stapes (stay-peez) The last of three ossicles of the ear that serve to conduct vibrations from the tympanic membrane to the oval window of the inner ear.   256

starch Storage polysaccharide found in plants that is composed of glucose molecules joined in a linear fashion with few side chains.   23

stem cell Any undifferentiated cell that can divide and differentiate into more functionally specific cell types, such as those in red bone marrow that give rise to blood cells.   101

steroid (steer-oyd) Type of lipid molecule having a complex of four carbon rings; examples are cholesterol, progesterone, and testosterone.   25

steroid hormone Type of hormone that has a complex of four carbon rings but different side chains from other steroid hormones.   269

stimulus Change in the internal or external environment that a sensory receptor can detect, leading to nerve impulses in sensory neurons.   244

stomach Muscular sac that mixes food with gastric juices to form chyme, which enters the small intestine.   120

strain Injury to a muscle resulting from overuse or improper use.   210

strep throat Disease spread by droplets of saliva or nasal secretions and caused by *Streptococcus* spp.   442

striae gravidarum Linear, depressed, scar-like lesions occurring on the abdomen, breasts, buttocks, and thighs due to the weakening of the elastic tissues during pregnancy.   324

striated (stry-ayt-ud) Having bands; in cardiac and skeletal muscle, alternating light and dark crossbands produced by the distribution of contractile proteins.   59

stroke Condition resulting when an arteriole in the brain bursts or becomes blocked by an embolism; also called cerebrovascular accident.   88

subcutaneous layer (sub-kyoo-tay-nee-us) Tissue layer that lies just beneath the skin and contains adipose tissue.   64

subsidence Occurs when a portion of the Earth's surface gradually settles downward.   526

substrate Reactant in a reaction controlled by an enzyme.   48

superior vena cava (vee-nuh kay-vuh) Large vein that enters the right atrium from above and carries blood from the head, thorax, and upper limbs to the heart.   86

surfactant Agent that reduces the surface tension of water; in the lungs, a surfactant prevents the alveoli from collapsing.   145

sustainable Ability of a society or ecosystem to maintain itself while also providing services to human beings.   537

suture (soo-chur) Type of immovable joint articulation found between bones of the skull.   192

sweat gland Skin gland that secretes a fluid substance for evaporative cooling; also called sudoriferous gland.   65

sympathetic division The part of the autonomic system that usually promotes activities associated with emergency (fight-or-flight) situations; uses norepinephrine as a neurotransmitter.   235

synapse (sin-aps, si-naps) Junction between neurons consisting of the presynaptic (axon) membrane, the synaptic cleft, and the postsynaptic (usually dendrite) membrane.   222

synapsis (sih-nap-sis) Pairing of homologous chromosomes during prophase I of meiosis I.   340

synaptic cleft (sih-nap-tik) Small gap between presynaptic and postsynaptic membranes of a synapse.   222

syndrome Group of symptoms that appear together and tend to indicate the presence of a particular disorder.   390

synovial joint (sih-noh-vee-ul) Freely movable joint in which two bones are separated by a cavity.   192

synovial membrane Membrane that forms the inner lining of the capsule of a freely movable joint.   68, 192

syphilis (sif-uh-lis) Sexually transmitted disease caused by the bacterium *Treponema pallidum* that, if untreated, can lead to cardiac and central nervous system disorders.   456

systemic Occurring throughout the body; said of infections that invade many compartments and organs via circulation.   434

systemic circuit Blood vessels that transport blood from the left ventricle and back to the right atrium of the heart.   78

systemic lupus erythematosus (SLE) Syndrome involving the connective tissues and various organs, including kidney.   428

systole (sis-tuh-lee) Contraction period of the heart during the cardiac cycle.   82

systolic pressure (sis-tahl-ik) Arterial blood pressure during the systolic phase of the cardiac cycle.   84

T

T cell Lymphocyte that matures in the thymus. Cytotoxic T cells kill antigen-bearing cells outright; helper T cells release cytokines that stimulate other immune system cells.   418

T (transverse) tubule Membranous channel that extends inward.   202

taste bud Sense organ containing the receptors associated with the sense of taste.   248

Tay-Sachs disease Lethal genetic disease in which the newborn has a faulty lysosomal digestive enzyme.   400

technology The science or study of the practical or industrial arts.   9

tectorial membrane (tek-tor-ee-ul) Membrane that lies above and makes contact with the hair cells in the spiral organ.   257

teleological Belief that the outcome is known ahead of time because the outcome is influenced by the need to progress in a certain direction.   492

telomere (tel-uh-meer) Tip of the end of a chromosome.   472

telophase (tel-uh-fayz) Mitotic phase during which daughter chromosomes are located at each pole.   339

template (tem-plit) Pattern or guide used to make copies; parental strand of DNA serves as a guide for the production of daughter DNA strands, and DNA also serves as a guide for the production of messenger RNA.   369

tendinitis (ten-din-eye-tis) An inflammation of muscle tendons and their attachments.   210

tendon (ten-dun) Strap of fibrous connective tissue that connects skeletal muscle to bone.   56, 178, 199

testes (sing., testis) (tes-teez, tes-tus) Male gonads that produce sperm and the male sex hormones.   280, 290

test group Group exposed to the experimental variable in an experiment, rather than the control group.   8

testosterone (tes-tahs-tuh-rohn) Male sex hormone that helps maintain sexual organs and secondary sex characteristics.   280, 293

tetanus (tet-n-us) Sustained muscle contraction without relaxation. 206

tetany (tet-n-ee) Severe twitching caused by involuntary contraction of the skeletal muscles due to a calcium imbalance. 274

thalamus (thal-uh-mus) Part of the brain located in the lateral walls of the third ventricle that serves as the integrating center for sensory input; it plays a role in arousing the cerebral cortex. 229

thermoreceptor Sensory receptor that is sensitive to changes in temperature. 244

threshold Electrical potential level (voltage) at which an action potential or nerve impulse is produced. 220

thrombin (thrahm-bin) Enzyme that converts fibrinogen to fibrin threads during blood clotting. 104

thromboembolism (thrahm-boh-em-buh-liz-um) Obstruction of a blood vessel by a thrombus that has dislodged from the site of its formation. 88

thrombus (thrahm-bus) Blood clot that remains in the blood vessel where it formed. 88

thymine (T) (thy-meen) One of four nitrogen-containing bases in nucleotides composing the structure of DNA; pairs with adenine. 30

thymosin Group of peptides secreted by the thymus gland that increases production of certain types of white blood cells. 282

thymus gland Lymphatic organ, located along the trachea behind the sternum, involved in the maturation of T lymphocytes in the thymus gland. Secretes hormones called thymosins, which aid the maturation of T cells and perhaps stimulate immune cells in general. 282, 414

thyroid gland Endocrine gland in the neck that produces several important hormones, including thyroxine, triiodothyronine, and calcitonin. 273

thyroid-stimulating hormone (TSH) Substance produced by the anterior pituitary that causes the thyroid to secrete thyroxine and triiodothyronine. 270

thyroxine (T₄) (thy-rahk-sin) Hormone secreted from the thyroid gland that promotes growth and development; in general, it increases the metabolic rate in cells. 273

tidal volume Amount of air normally moved in the human body during an inspiration or expiration. 146

tissue Group of similar cells that perform a common function. 2, 56

tissue fluid Fluid that surrounds the body's cells; consists of dissolved substances that leave the blood

capillaries by filtration and diffusion. 58, 108

tonicity (toh-nis-ih-tee) Osmolarity of a solution compared with that of a cell. If the solution is isotonic to the cell, there is no net movement of water; if the solution is hypotonic, the cell gains water; and if the solution is hypertonic, the cell loses water. 41

tonsillectomy (tahn-suh-lek-tuh-mee) Surgical removal of the tonsils. 152

tonsillitis Infection of the tonsils that causes inflammation and can spread to the middle ears. 116, 152

tonsils Partially encapsulated lymph nodules located in the pharynx. 152, 415

total artificial heart (TAH) A mechanical replacement for the heart as opposed to a partial replacement. 91

toxoplasmosis Disease of animals and humans caused by the parasitic protozoan *Toxoplasma gondii.* 447

tracer Substance having an attached radioactive isotope that allows a researcher to track its whereabouts in a biological system. 15

trachea (tray-kee-uh) Passageway that conveys air from the larynx to the bronchi; also called the windpipe. 144

tracheostomy (tray-kee-ahs-tuh-mee) Creation of an artificial airway by incision of the trachea and insertion of a tube. 144

tract Bundle of myelinated axons in the central nervous system. 224

transcription Process whereby a DNA strand serves as a template for the formation of mRNA. 372

transcription activator Protein that initiates transcription by RNA polymerase and thereby starts the process that results in gene expression. 377

transfer rate Amount of a substance that moves from one component of the environment to another within a specified period of time. 511

transfer RNA (tRNA) Type of RNA that transfers a particular amino acid to a ribosome during protein synthesis; at one end, it binds to the amino acid, and at the other end it has an anticodon that binds to an mRNA codon. 370

transgenic organism Free-living organism in the environment that has a foreign gene in its cells. 383

translation Process whereby ribosomes use the sequence of codons in mRNA to produce a polypeptide with a particular sequence of amino acids. 372

translocation Movement of a chromosomal segment from one chromosome to another nonhomologous chromosome,

leading to abnormalities; e.g, Down syndrome. 397

trichinosis Infection by the *Trichinella spiralis* parasite, usually caused by eating the meat of an infected animal. Early symptoms include fever, diarrhea, nausea, and abdominal pain that progress to intense muscle and joint pain and shortness of breath. In the final stages, heart and brain function are at risk, and death is possible. 449

trichomoniasis Sexually transmitted disease caused by the parasitic protozoan *Trichomonas vaginalis.* 459

triglyceride (trih-glis-uh-ryd) Neutral fat composed of glycerol and three fatty acids. 24

triplet code Each sequence of three nucleotide bases in the DNA of genes stands for a particular amino acid. 372

trisomy One more chromosome than usual. 392

trophic level Feeding level of one or more populations in a food web. 509

trophoblast Outer cells of a blastocyte that help form the placenta and other extraembryonic membranes. 313

tropomyosin (trahp-uh-my-uh-sin, trohp-) Protein that functions with troponin to block muscle contraction until calcium ions are present. 205

troponin (troh-puh-nin) Protein that functions with tropomyosin to block muscle contraction until calcium ions are present. 205

trypsin (trip-sin) Protein-digesting enzyme secreted by the pancreas. 124, 126

tubercle Small, rounded, nodular lesion produced by *Mycobacterium tuberculosis.* 443

tuberculosis (TB) Infectious disease of humans and other animals resulting from an infection by *Mycobacterium tuberculosis* and characterized by the formation of tubercles and tissue necrosis. Infection is usually by inhalation, and the disease commonly affects the lungs (pulmonary tuberculosis), although it may occur in any part of the body. 443

tubular reabsorption Movement of primarily nutrient molecules and water from the contents of the nephron into blood at the proximal convoluted tubule. 167

tubular secretion Movement of certain molecules from blood into the distal convoluted tubule of a nephron so that they are added to urine. 167

tumor (too-mur) Cells derived from a single mutated cell that has repeatedly undergone cell division; benign tumors remain at the site of origin, and malignant tumors metastasize. 472

tumor marker test Blood test for a substance, such as a tumor antigen, that indicates a patient has cancer.   481

tumor-suppressor gene Gene that codes for a protein that ordinarily suppresses cell division; inactivity can lead to a tumor.   474

tympanic membrane (tim-pan-ik) Located between the outer and middle ear where it receives sound waves; also called the eardrum.   256

U

ulcer (ul-sur) Open sore in the lining of the stomach; frequently caused by bacterial infection.   120

umbilical cord Cord connecting the fetus to the placenta through which blood vessels pass.   317

unsaturated fatty acid Fatty acid molecule that has one or more double bonds between the atoms of its carbon chain.   24

uracil (U) (yoor-uh-sil) The base in RNA that replaces thymine found in DNA; pairs with adenine.   30, 370

urea (yoo-ree-uh) Primary nitrogenous waste of humans derived from amino acid breakdown.   160

uremia High level of urea nitrogen in the blood.   171

ureter (yoor-uh-tur) One of two tubes that take urine from the kidneys to the urinary bladder.   161

urethra (yoo-ree-thruh) Tubular structure that receives urine from the bladder and carries it to the outside of the body.   161, 290

urethritis Inflammation of the urethra.   171

uric acid (yoor-ik) Waste product of nucleotide metabolism.   160

urinary bladder Organ where urine is stored before being discharged by way of the urethra.   161

urinary system Organ system consisting of the kidneys and urinary bladder; rids the body of nitrogenous wastes and helps regulate the water-salt balance of the blood.   67

uterine cycle (yoo-tur-in, -tuh-ryn) Monthly occurring changes in the characteristics of the uterine lining (endometrium).   298

uterus (yoo-tur-us) Organ located in the female pelvis where the fetus develops; also called the womb.   294

utricle (yoo-trih-kul) Sac-like cavity in the vestibule of the inner ear that contains sensory receptors for gravitational equilibrium.   261

V

vaccine Antigens prepared in such a way that they can promote active immunity without causing disease.   424

vagina Organ that leads from the uterus to the vestibule and serves as the birth canal and organ of sexual intercourse in females.   295

valve Membranous extension of a vessel of the heart wall that opens and closes, ensuring one-way flow.   79

varicose vein (var-ih-kohs, vair-) Irregular dilation of superficial veins, seen particularly in lower legs and is due to weakened valves within the veins.   88

vas deferens (vas def-ur-unz, -uh-renz) Tube that leads from the epididymis to the urethra in males.   290

vector (vek-tur) In genetic engineering, a means to transfer foreign genetic material into a cell (e.g., a plasmid).   380, 435

vehicle Inanimate substance or medium involved in the transmission of a pathogen.   435

vein Vessel that takes blood to the heart from venules; characteristically has nonelastic walls.   78

ventilation Process of moving air into and out of the lungs; also called breathing.   142

ventricle (ven-trih-kul) Cavity in an organ, such as a lower chamber of the heart or the ventricles of the brain.   80, 224

venule (ven-yool, veen-) Vessel that takes blood from capillaries to a vein.   79

vermiform appendix Small, tubular appendage that extends outward from the cecum of the large intestine.   122, 415

vernix caseosa (vur-niks kay-see-oh-suh) Cheese-like substance covering the skin of the fetus.   319

vertebral column (vur-tuh-brul) Series of joined vertebrae that extends from the skull to the pelvis.   188

vertebrate (vur-tuh-brit, -brayt) An animal with a vertebral column.   2

vertigo (vur-tih-goh) Dizziness and a sense of rotation.   261

vestibule (ves-tuh-byool) Space or cavity at the entrance of a canal, such as the cavity that lies between the semicircular canals and the cochlea.   256

villus (pl., villi) (vil-us) Small, finger-like projection of the inner small intestinal wall.   121

virulence factor Bacterial product or mechanism that contributes to pathogenicity.   434

visual accommodation Ability of the eye to focus at different distances by changing the curvature of the lens.   251

vital capacity Maximum amount of air moved in or out of the human body with each breathing cycle.   146

vitamin Essential requirement in the diet, needed in small amounts. They are often part of coenzymes.   132

vitamin D Required for proper bone growth.   64

vitreous humor (vit-ree-us) Clear, gelatinous material between the lens of the eye and the retina.   251

vocal cord Fold of tissue within the larynx; creates vocal sounds when it vibrates.   144

vulva External genitals of the female that surround the opening of the vagina.   295

W

water (hydrologic) cycle Interdependent and continuous circulation of water from the ocean to the atmosphere, to the land, and back to the ocean.   510

Wernicke's area Brain area involved in language comprehension.   228

white blood cell (leukocyte) Type of blood cell that is transparent without staining and protects the body from invasion by foreign substances and organisms; also called a leukocyte.   58, 103

white matter Myelinated axons in the central nervous system.   224

X

xenotransplantation Use of animal organs, instead of human organs, in human transplant patients.   428

X-linked Allele located on an X chromosome, but may control a trait that has nothing to do with the sex characteristics of an individual.   362

Y

yolk sac Extraembryonic membrane that encloses the yolk of birds; in humans, it is the first site of blood cell formation.   311

Z

zygote (zy-goht) Diploid cell formed by the union of sperm and egg; the product of fertilization.   294, 310, 340

CREDITS

Text and Line Art

Chapter 2
Ecology Focus, page 21: Data from G. Tyler Miller, *Living in the Environment*, 1993, Wadsworth Publishing Company, Belmont, CA; and Lester R. Brown, *State of the World*, 1992, W. W. Norton & Company, Inc., New York, NY p. 29.

Chapter 8
Health Focus, page 155: From *The Most Often Asked Questions About Smoking Tobacco and Health and the Answers*, Revised July 1993. Copyright American Cancer Society, Inc., Atlanta, GA. Used with permission.

Chapter 15
Ecology Focus, page 303: Courtesy Dr. John M. Matter, Juniata College.

Chapter 23
Figures 23.2 and 23.6: Source: Data from Center for Disease Control and Prevention: Tracking the Hidden Epidemics, Trends in STDS in the United States 2000.

Photographs

Chapter 1
Opener: © Vol. 52/Corbis; 1.2a: © David C. Fritts/Animals Animals/Earth Scenes; 1.2b: © Vol. 124/Corbis; 1Ba: © Stephanie Maze/Corbis; 1Bb: © Corbis Royalty Free.

Chapter 2
Opener: © Epperson-Offpress/Agence Vandsytadt/Photo Researchers; 2.2: © Biomed Commun/Custom Medical Stock Photos; 2.3(top): © Hank Morgan/Rainbow; 2.3:(bottom) © Mazzlota et al./Photo Researchers, Inc.; 2.4b: © Charles M. Falco/Photo Researchers, Inc.; 2.7a: © Martin Dohrn/SPL/Photo Researchers, Inc.; 2.7b: © Comstock, Inc.; 2.7c: © Martha Cooper/Peter Arnold, Inc.; 2Aa: © Ray Pfortner/Peter Arnold, Inc.; 2A(b): © Frederica Georgia/Photo Researchers, Inc.; 2.10: © The McGraw Hill Companies, Inc./John Thoeming, photographer; 2.11: © Jeremy Burgess/SPL/Photo Researchers, Inc.; 2.12: © Don W. Fawcett/Photo Researchers, Inc.; 2.15a: © Corbis Royalty Free; 2.15b: © Corbis Royalty Free; 2C: © William Freese.

Chapter 3
Opener: Pascal Rondeau/Stone/Getty Images; 3.1(left): © Prof. P. Motta, Dept. of Anatomy, Univ. LaSapienza Rome/SPL/Photo Researchers, Inc.; 3.1(center): From Lennart Nilsson, Behold Man © 1974 Albert Bonniers Forlag and Little Brown and Company.; 3.1(right): © Fred Hossler/Visuals Unlimited; 3.2a: © David M. Phillips/Visuals Unlimited; 3.2b: © Alfred Pasieka/Photo Researchers, Inc.; 3.2c: © Warren Rosenberg/BPS; 3.3b: © Alfred Pasieka/Photo Researchers, Inc.; 3.7a-c: Dennis Kunkel/Phototake NYC; 3.10b: Courtesy Drs. J.V. Small and G. Rinnerthaler; 3.11(left): Courtesy of Ron Milligan/Scripps Research Institute; 3.11(right): © R. Bolender & D. Fawcett/Visuals Unlimited; 3.13b: © Y. Nikas/Photo Researchers, Inc.; 3.13c: © David M. Phillips/Photo Researchers, Inc.; 3.14b: © Dr. Don W. Fawcett/Visuals Unlimited; 3.17: © Tim Davis/Photo Researchers, Inc.; 3A: © Jerry Cooke/Photo Researchers, Inc.

Chapter 4
Opener: © Adam Smith Productions/Corbis; 4.2a-d, 4.5a-c: © Ed Reschke; 4Aa: © Vol. 154/Corbis; 4Ab: © Vol. 12/Corbis; 4B(top): © AP Photo/Ellcot D.

Novak; 4B(bottom): © Diana De Rosa - Press Link; 4.8(all): © Ed Reschke/Peter Arnold, Inc.; 4.10a: © John Cunningham/Visuals Unlimited; 4.10b: © Ken Greer/Visuals Unlimited; 4.10c: © James Stevenson/SPL/Photo Researchers, Inc.; 4C: © Vol. 83/PhotoDisc.

Chapter 5
Opener: © National Cancer Institute/SPL/Photo Researchers, Inc.; 5.2, 5.6b, c: © Ed Reschke; 5.13a: © Pascal Goethgheluck/SPL/Photo Researchers, Inc.; 5A(left): © Ed Reschke; 5A(right): © Biophoto Associates/Photo Researchers, Inc.; 5.14b: ABIOMED, Inc.; 5B: © Paul Hardy/CORBIS.

Chapter 6
Opener: © Tony Freeman/Photo Edit; 6.5: © Manfred Kage/Peter Arnold, Inc.; 6B: © Chris Carroll/Corbis; 6.11: © David Young-Wolff/Photo Edit.

Chapter 7
Opener: © Roger Ressmeyer/Corbis; 7.4b: © Biophoto Associates/Photo Researchers, Inc.; 7.5b: © Ed Reschke/Peter Arnold, Inc.; 7.5c: © J. James/Photo Researchers, Inc.; 7.6: © Manfred Kage/Peter Arnold, Inc.; 7.6(inset): Photo by Susumu Ito, from Charles Flickinger, *Medical Cellular Biology*, W.B. Saunders, 1979; 7.8b: © Ed Reschke; 7.14: © The McGraw-Hill Companies, Inc./Bob Coyle, photographer; 7A © F. Hache/Photo Researchers, Inc.; 7.15a: © Biophoto Associates/Photo Researchers, Inc.; 7.15b: © Ken Greer/Visuals Unlimited; 7.15c: © Biophoto Associates/Photo Researchers, Inc.; 7.17: © Carl Centineo/Medichrome/Stock Photo; 7.18: © Donna Day/Stone/Getty Images; 7.19: © Tony Freeman/PhotoEdit.

Chapter 8
Opener: © Daivd Gray/Reuters/Corbis; 8.3: © CNRI/Phototake; 8.4: © Dr. Kessel & Dr. Kardon/Tissues & Organs/Visuals Unlimited; 8.6: © Yoav Levy/Phototake; 8Aa: © Bill Aron/Photo Edit; 8.11a,b: © Martin Rotker/Martin Rotker Photography.

Chapter 9
Opener: © Dr. E. Walker/Photo Researchrs, Inc.; 9.4: (top left): © Prof. P.M. Motta & M. Castellucci/Science Photo Library/Photo Researchers, Inc.; 9.4(top right, bottom): © 1966 Academic Press, from A.B. Maunsbach, Journal of Ultrastructure and Molecular Structure Research, Vol. 15, pp 242-282. Reprinted by permission of Elsevier; 9.5a: © Gennaro/Photo Researchers, Inc.; 9.10: © SIU/Peter Arnold, Inc.; 9.11: © CNRI/Photo Researchers, Inc.

Chapter 10
Opener: © Walter Reiter/Phototake; 10.1(both, top): © Ed Reschke; 10.1(bottom): © Biophoto Associates/Photo Researchers, Inc.; 10.4: © Biophoto Associates/Photo Researchers, Inc.; 10.6: © Junebug Clark/Photo Researchers, Inc.; 10Aa: © Susan Mullane/NewSport/Corbis; 10Ab: © Michael Klein/Peter Arnold, Inc.; 10.9b: © Corbis Royalty Free; 10.14(bottom right): © Ed Reschke/Peter Arnold, Inc; 10.14(all other images): © Ed Reschke.

Chapter 11
Opener: © Stock Image/SuperStock; 11.1(all): © Ed Reschke; 11.4: Courtesy of Hugh E. Huxley; 11A: © Ronald C. Modra/Time Inc.; 11.9: © Julie Lemberger/Corbis.

Chapter 12
Opener: © Nancy Kedersha/UCLA/SPL/Photo Researchers, Inc.; 12.3b: © M.B. Bunge/Biological Photo Service; 12.4b: © Linda Bartlett; 12.6: Courtesy

of Dr. E. R. Lewis, University of California Berkeley; 12.8c: © Manfred Kage/Peter Arnold, Inc.; 12.9b: © Colin Chumbley/Science Source/Photo Researchers, Inc.; 12.14(1-4): © Marcus Raichle; 12.19: © Vol. 94/PhotoDisc; 12.20 © Corbis Royalty Free.

Chapter 13
Opener: © Mauro Fermariello/SPL/Photo Researchers, Inc.; 13.4: © Omikron/SPL/Photo Researchers, Inc.; 13.8: © Lennart Nilsson, from "The Incredible Machine"; 13.9b: © The McGraw-Hill Companies, Inc./Dennis Strete, photographer; 13.13: © P. Motta/SPL/Photo Researchers, Inc.; 13A: Robert S. Preston and Joseph E. Hawkins, Kresage Hearing Research Institute, University of Michigan.

Chapter 14
Opener: © Bob Daemmrich/Stock Boston; 14.6a: © Bob Daemmrich/Stock Boston; 14.6b: © Ewing Galloway, Inc.; 14.7a-d: From Clinical Pathological Conference, "Acromegaly, Diabetes, Hypermetabolism, Proteinura and Heart Failure", American Journal of Medicine 20 (1956) 133, with permission from Excerpta Medica, Inc.; 14.8a: © Biophoto Associates/Photo Researchers, Inc.; 14.8b: © John Paul Kay/Peter Arnold, Inc.; 14.8c: © Imagingbody.com; 14.12a: © Custom Medical Stock Photos; 14.12b: © NMSB/Custom Medical Stock Photos; 14.13: "Atlas of Pediatric Physical Diagnosis," Second Edition by Zitelli & Davis, 1992. Mosby-Wolfe Europe Limited, London, UK; 14A: © James Darell/Stone/Getty Images; 14B: © Corbis Royalty Free; 14.17: © Vol. 113/ PhotoDisc.

Chapter 15
Opener: © Dr. Yorgos Nikas/SPL/Photo Researchers, Inc.; 15.3b: © Secchi-Leaque/CNRI/SPL/Photo Researchers, Inc.; 15.7: © Ed Reschke/Peter Arnold, Inc.; 15.10: © Lennart Nilsson, from "A Child Is Born", page 68.; 15.11a-d, f: © The McGraw-Hill Companies, Inc./Bob Coyle, photographer; 15.11e: Courtesy Population Council, Karen-Tweedy Holmes.; 15A(lower left): © Index Stock; 15A(upper middle): © Norbert WU; 15A(lower middle): © Art Wolfe/Stone/Getty Images; 15A(right): © Steven Peters/Stone/Getty Images; 15B: © Sygma/Corbis.

Chapter 16
Opener(all): © Lennart Nilsson, "A CHILD IS BORN", 1990 Delacorte Press; 16.1a: © Dennis Kunkel/Phototake; 16.6: © Lennart Nilsson, A CHILD IS BORN, 1990, Delacortes Press; 16.8: © James Stevenson/SPL/Photo Researchers, Inc.; 16Bb, c: Streissguth, A.P., Landesman-Dwyer, S. Martin J.C., and Smith D.W. (1980). Teratogenic Effects of Alcohol in Humans and Laboratory Animals. *Science*: 209 (18): 353-361.; 16Bd: Courtesy Dr. Ann Streissguth, University of Washington School of Medicine, Fetal Alcohol and Drug Unit; 16.11: © Vol. 58/PhotoDisc; 16.12: © Richard Hutchings/ Photo Edit; 16C: © Bob Daemmrich/Stock Boston.

Chapter 17
Opener: © Biophoto Associates/Photo Researchers, Inc.; 17.2(inset): Courtesy Douglas R. Green/LaJolla Institute for Allergy and Immunology; 17A: © Steven L. McKnight; 17A: © Biophoto Assoc./Photo Researchers, Inc.; 17.5(late interphase, early prophase): © Ed Reschke; 17.6(late prophase): © Michael Abbey/Photo Researchers, Inc.; 17.6(metaphase, anaphase, telophase): © Ed Reschke.

Chapter 18
Opener: © Jeff Slocomb/Outline; 18.2a: © Superstock; 18.2b-f: © Michael Grecco/Stock Boston; 18.2g: Courtesy of Mary L. Drapeau; 18.2h: © The McGraw-Hill Companies, Inc./Bob Coyle, photographer; 18.8a:

INDEX

Note: Page numbers in *italics* indicate material presented in figures and tables.

Abduction, 193, *193*
Abiotic community, 506
ABO blood types, 361, *361*
Abortion, 300
Abstinence, *302*, 463
Acetabulum, *191*
Acetylcholine (ACh), 204, 222, *223*, 235
Acetylcholinesterase (AChE), 222
Achilles tendon, *200*
Acid(s), 20
    amino (*See* Amino acids)
    essential fatty, 130
    fatty, 24
        in digestion, 121
    folic, *133*
    lactic, 50
    nicotinic, *133*
    nucleic, 29–30, 436, *436*
    Omega-3, 130
    pantothenic, *133*
    pyruvic, 50
    trans-fatty, 130
    uric, 160
Acidosis, 279
Acid rain, 21, 531
Acid reflux, 119
Acquired immunity, 424–426
Acquired immunodeficiency syndrome. *See* AIDS
Acromegaly, 272, *272*
Acromion process, *190*
Acrosome, of sperm, *292*, 293, 310, *310*
Actin, 202, 205
Actin filament, *39*, 43, *43*, 46, 59, *203*
Action potential, 220, *221*
Active immunity, 424
Acute infections, 434
Acyclovir, 445, 457
Adaptation
    in evolution, 489
    in natural selection, 492
Addison disease, 277, *277*
Adduction, 193, *193*
Adductor longus, *200, 201*
Adenine (A), 30
    in DNA, 368
    in RNA, 370
Adenocarcinoma, 475

Adenosine triphosphate. *See* ATP
Adenoviruses, 483
ADH (antidiuretic hormone), 270, *271*, 284
Adhesion factors, of pathogens, 434
Adipose tissue, 56, *56, 57, 192*
    glucose in, *278*
    leptin and, 282
ADP (adenosine diphosphate), 30, *30*, 205, *209*
Adrenal cortex, 275, *275*
    in homeostasis, 284
    malfunction of, 277, *277*
Adrenal glands, *266, 267*, 275, *275*
Adrenal medulla, 275, *275*
Adrenocorticotropic hormone (ACTH), 270, *271*, 275, *275*
Adult stem cells
    in cloning, 314
    mitosis of, 346
    transplant of, 305
Afferent arteriole, *168*
AFP (alpha-fetoprotein), 481
Africa
    AIDS in, 467
    australopithecines in, 496
    early hominids in, 495
    Homo erectus in, 498
    Homo sapiens in, 499
African Americans
    lactose intolerance in, 126
    and sickle-cell disease, 400
African sleeping sickness, 448, *448*
Afterbirth, 325, *325*
Agent Orange, 421
Age structure, 523, *523*
Agglutination, 106
Aging, 309–328, *326*
    and body systems, 327–328
    hypotheses of, 326–327
Agriculture, 526–527, 535
AID (artificial insemination by donor), 304
AIDS (acquired immunodeficiency syndrome), 460–466. *See also* HIV
    drug therapy and, 466
    in HIV progression, 464, *464*

immune system and, 428
    and pneumonia, 152
    population growth and, 523
    prevalence of, 460–461, *461*
    prevention of, 463
    T lymphocytes in, 282
AIED (autoimmune inner ear disease), 258
Airborne transmission, *434*, 435
Air pollution, 147
Alagille syndrome, 397, *397*
Albumins, 99
Alcohol
    abuse of, 237–238
    behavioral effects of, *237*
    cancer caused by, 478, 484
    and cardiovascular disease, 90
    dehydration from, 284
    and digestion, 120
    in pregnancy, 322, *322*
Aldosterone, 276, 324
Algal bloom, 511, 512
Alien species, 531
Alkylating agents, in chemotherapy, 482
Allantois, 311, *311, 315*, 317
Alleles, 352, *352*, 356
Allen's lymphoma/leukemia, 482
Allergies, 426, 427, *427*
All-or-none law, 206
Alpha-fetoprotein (AFP), 481
ALS (amyotropic lateral sclerosis), 218
Alveolus, *142*, 145, *145*
Alzheimer disease (AD)
    apoptosis in, 231
    brain degeneration in, 236
    melatonin in, 281
Amino acids, 26
    in biological evolution, 490
    in diet, 129
    essential, 129
    in proteins, 371, *371*
    translation into, 372
    tRNA and, 370
Aminoglycosides, 445
Ammonium, in nitrogen cycle, 512, *512*
Amniocentesis, 390, *391*, 404
Amnion, 311, *311, 315*
Amniotic cavity, 315, *315*

Amniotic membrane, 325, *325*
Amphetamine(s)
    and cardiovascular disease, 90
    methamphetamine and, 239
Amphetamine psychosis, 239
Ampulla, *260*, 261
Amygdala, 230, *230*, 231
Amyotropic lateral sclerosis (ALS), 218
Anabolic steroids, 280, *280*, 293
Anal canal, *116*
Analogous structures, 490
Anal-rectal intercourse, 463, 466
Anandamide, marijuana and, 239
Anaphase, 338–339, *339*
Anaphase I, 342, *342*
Anaphase II, 342, *343*
Anaphylactic shock, 426
Androgen insensitivity, 268, 320
Androgens
    in endocrine system, 280
    in male reproductive system, 293
Anemia, 101
Anencephaly, 322
Aneurysm, 88
Angina pectoris, 88
Angiogenesis, 473, 483
Angioplasty, 91
Angiostatin, 483
ANH (atrial natriuretic hormone), 169, 276
Animals
    disease and, 532, *532*
    overexploitation of, 531–532
    transgenic, 384, *384*
    viral diseases of, 440
    xenotransplantation with, 428
Anorexia nervosa, 137, *137*
Anterior compartment, *250*, 250–251
Anterior pituitary, 270, *271*, 284
Anthrax, 433
Anthropoids, 493
Antiangiogenic drugs, 483
Antibacterial agents, 445

Antibiotic agents, 445
    for chlamydia, 455
    for gonorrhea, 455
    problems with, 445
    production of, 535
    resistance to, 152, 445
    for tuberculosis, 443
    types of, 445
Antibodies, 103
    in clonal selection theory,
        419, *419*
    definition of, 414
    in passive immunity,
        425, *425*
    structure of, 420, *420*
    types of, 420, *420*
Antibody-mediated
    immunity, 419
Antibody titer, 424
Anticodon, 374, *374*
Antidiuretic hormone
    (ADH), 270, *271*, 284
Antigen(s), 103
    in blood type, 361
    in clonal selection theory,
        419, *419*, 422, *422*
    definition of, 414
Antigen-antibody
    complex, 420
Antigenic drift, 437, *437*
Antigenic shift, 437, *437*
Antigen-presenting cell
    (APC), 422
Anti-inflammatory
    agents, 417
Antimetabolites, in
    chemotherapy, 482
Anti-Müllerian
    hormone, 320
Antioxidants, 132, 407
Antiretroviral drugs
    (ARVs), 467
Antitumor antibiotics, in
    chemotherapy, 482
Antivenoms, 425
Antiviral agents, 445
Anus, 122
ANWR (Arctic National
    Wildlife Refuge),
    517, *517*
Aorta, *80, 81, 86, 86,
    87, 160*
Aortic bodies, 149
APC (antigen-presenting
    cell), 422
APC gene, 348
Apes, 494, *495*
Apoptosis
    of B cells, 419, *419*
    cancer cells and, 472,
        474, 483

in cell decrease, 334,
    335, *335*
    from excitotoxicity, 231
    of T cells, 422, *422*
Appendix, *116*, 122, *123*
Aquaculture, 535
Aquatic ecosystems, 514, *514*
    and carbon cycle, 513
    and nitrogen cycle, 512
    and phosphorus cycle, 511
    primary productivity
        of, 516
Aqueous humor, *250,*
    250–251
Aquifers, 510, 525–526
Arachidonate,
    prostaglandins and, 282
Arbor vitae, 229
Arctic National Wildlife
    Refuge (ANWR),
    517, *517*
Ardipithecus ramidus, 495
*Ardipithecus ramidus
    kkadabba,* 495
Arm, bones of, 190, *190*
Arrector pili, 64
ART (assisted reproductive
    technologies), 304
Arterial duct, 318
Arterioles, 79, *79, 121, 168*
Artery(ies), 79, *79*
    blood flow in, 84–85, *85*
    brachial, *84*
    brachiocephalic, *80*
    carotid, *81, 84, 86, 87*
    clogged, treating, 89, *89*–90
    common carotid, *87*
    coronary, *87*
    dorsalis pedis, *84*
    facial, *84*
    femoral, *84*
    iliac, *86*
    mesenteric, *86*
    popliteal, *84*
    posterior tibial, *84*
    pulmonary, *80, 81, 86,
        145, 151*
Arthritis, 193
    aging and, 328
    cortisone for, 276
Artificial insemination by
    donor (AID), 304
ARVs (antiretroviral
    drugs), 467
Asbestos, 153, *153*, 477
Ascaris lumbricoides, 449
Asia
    Homo erectus in, 498
    Homo sapiens in, 499
Aspirin, prostaglandins
    and, 282

Assembly, in HIV life cycle,
    465, 466
Assisted reproductive
    technologies (ART), 304
Association areas. *See* Sensory
    association areas
Aster, 337, *337*
Asthma, *153*, 154, 426, 427
Astigmatism, 255, *255*
Astrocytes, 60, *60*
Atherosclerosis, 88
Athlete's foot, 446, *446*
Atkins's diet, 131
Atlas (bone), 188, *188*
Atom, 14, *14*
Atomic number, 14
Atomic weight, 14
ATP (adenosine
    triphosphate), 2,
    30, *30*
    and active transport, 42
    and cellular respiration,
        49, *49*
    and fermentation, 50
    and mitochondria, 47, *47*
    and muscular action,
        205, 208, *209*
Atrial natriuretic hormone
    (ANH), 169, 276
Atrioventricular bundle,
    82, *83*
Atrioventricular (AV) node,
    82, 83, *83*
Atrioventricular valves, 80, *81*
Atrium, 80, *80, 81*
Attachment
    in HIV life cycle, 465, *465*
    in virus replication,
        436, *436*
Auditory association area,
    227, 228
Auditory canal, *186*, 256, *256*
Auditory cortex, 257
Auditory tube, 152, 256, *256*
Australopithecines,
    evolution of, 496
Australopithecus afarensis,
    496, *496*
Australopithecus africanus, 496
Australopithecus boisei, 496
Australopithecus robustus, 496
Autoantibodies, 414
Autoimmune disorders,
    414, 428
Autoimmune inner ear
    disease (AIED), 258
Automobiles, electric, 529
Autonomic system,
    234, 235
Autosomal disorders, *398,*
    398–399

Autosomal dominant
    disorders, *398, 399,*
    401, *401*
Autosomal recessive
    disorders, *398,* 398–399,
    400–401, 403–405
Autosomes, 362
Autotrophs, 506
AV (atrioventricular) node,
    82, 83, *83*
Avoparcin, 449
Axillary secretions, 268
Axon, 60, *60*
    myelinated, 219, *219*
    in neuron structure, 218
    voltage of, 220
Axon terminal, 222, *222*
AZT (zidovudine), 466

Bacilli, 441
Bacteria
    antibiotic-resistant,
        445, 449
    diseases caused by,
        442–444, *444*
    as immune defenses, 417
    in nitrogen fixation, 512
    sexually transmitted
        diseases caused by,
        454–456
    structure of, 441, *441*
    transgenic, 383
Bacterial vaginosis (BV), 459
Baldness, 280
Ball-and-socket joints, 192
Barr body, 392
Barriers to entry, 417
Basal bodies, 46
Basal nuclei
    in cerebrum, 228
    in Parkinson disease, 236
Base(s), 20
    in amino acids, 372, *372*
    in DNA, 368, *368*
    sequencing, 378
Basement membrane, 62, *63*
Basilar membrane, 257, *257*
Basophils, *100*, 103
Bax protein, 474
B cell(s) (B lymphocytes)
    bone marrow and, 414
    in inflammatory
        reaction, 417
    monoclonal antibodies
        from, 425–426, *426*
    in specific immune
        defense, 418–420, *419*
B-cell receptor (BCR), 418, *419*
Beaches, 524
Beta amyloid plaques, in
    Alzheimer disease, 236

bGH (bovine growth hormone), 384
Bicarbonate ions, 150, 513
Biceps brachii, *199*, 200, *200, 201*
Bile, 121, *124*, 125
Bile canals, *124*
Bile duct, *124*
Binary fission, 441
Binomial name, 493
Biodefense, 433
Biodiversity, 531–535
    direct value of, *534*, 535
    indirect value of, 533
    loss of, *531*, 531–532
    threats to, 4
Bioethics
    AIDS/HIV medication access, 467
    alcohol use, 484
    cyanide fishing, 536
    DNA fingerprinting, 386
    fertilization, 10
    gender selection, 363
    genetically modified foods, 31
    genetic profiling, 409
    genetic selection, 305
    genetic testing, 348
    growth promoters, 449
    hormone replacement therapy, 283
    maternal health habits, 329
    oil drilling in Arctic, 517
    smoking, 155
    stem cell research, 51
    steroids, 211
    teaching evolution, 501
    tobacco use, 484
    unhealthy lifestyle choices, 93
Biogeochemical cycles, 510–513, 533
Biogeography, 490
Bioinformatics, 379
Biological evolution, 489–492
Biological magnification, 530, *530*
Biological pest control, 421
Biomass, 509
Biopsy, 481
Biosphere, 2, 4, 5, 506
Biosynthesis
    in HIV life cycle, *465*, 466
    in virus replication, 436, *436*
Biotechnology, 383, *383*
Bioterrorism, 433
Biotic community, 506, 510
Biotic potential, 522
Biotin, *133*

Bipedal posture, 494–495
Bird flu, 437, 440
Birth, 270, 324–325, *325*
Birth control methods, *301*, 301–304, *302*
Birth control pills, 301, *301*
Birth defects, prevention of, 322–323
Bladder, urinary, *160*, 161, *161, 162*
Bladder cancer, testing for, 481
Blastocyst, in pre-embryonic development, 313, *313*
Blind spot, 253, *253*
Blood, 58, *58*, 98–110
    artificial, 102
    calcium levels in, 274
    clotting of, *103*, 103–104
    compatibility of, 107
    composition of, *98*
    dissolving clots in, 89
    fetal cells in, testing, 404
    flow of, *84*, 84–87, *85, 86, 87*
        fetal, 318, *318*
    formed elements of, *100*, 100–101, *101*
    functions of, 99
    glucose levels in, 276, *278*, 278–279
    and homeostasis, 70, 110
    mercury in, effects of, 105
    passage through heart of, 81, *81*
    pH of, 21
    Rh of, 107
    sodium levels in, 276, *276*
    and stem cells, *100*
    transfusion of, 102, 106
        HIV transmitted by, 460
    volume, and kidneys, 276, *276*
    water-salt balance of, 270, 275
Blood cells, *37*, 58, *58*. See *also* Red blood cells; White blood cells
    in sickle cell disease, 400–401, *401*
    and skeletal system, 185
Blood flukes, 449
Blood pressure, *84*, 84–85, *85*
    and capillary exchange, 108
    high, 88
    and kidneys, 160, 276, *276*
    spinal cord and, 225
Blood type, *106*, 106–107
    inheritance of, 360, 361, *361*

Blood vessels, *37*, 79, *79, 86*, 86–87, *87*
    disorders of, 88–91
    for tumors, 473
Bloody show, 324
B lymphocytes. See B cell(s)
Body shape, 501
Bolus, 118, *118*
Bonds
    covalent, 17, *17*
    hydrogen, 18, 368, 369
    ionic, 16, *16*
    peptide, 26
Bone(s), 57, *57, 179, 180*. See *also* Skeletal system
    atlas, 188, *188*
    classification of, 185
    compact, 178, *179, 180, 192*
    coxal, 191, *191*
    ethmoid, *186*
    facial, 187
    fetal development of, 319
    frontal, 186, *186, 187*
    growth of, 180, 180–183, *181*
    hyoid, 187, *187*
    jawbone, *117*
    lacrimal, *186*
    nasal, *186*, 187, *187*
    occipital, 186, *186*
    palatine, *186*
    parietal, 186, *186*
    remodeling of, *182*, 182–183
    repair of fractured, 183, *183*
    sphenoid, 186, *186*, 187
    spongy, 178, *179, 180*
    structure of, 178–179, *179*
    temporal, *186*, 187
    vomer, *186*
    zygomatic, *186*, 187, *187*
Bone marrow, 212, 482. See *also* Red bone marrow; Yellow bone marrow
Booster vaccines, 424
Botox, 204
Botulism, 444, *444*
Bovine growth hormone (bGH), 384
Bovine spongiform encephalopathy, 439
Bowman's capsule, 165, *165*
Brachial artery, *84*
Brachiocephalic artery, *80*
Brain, *149*, 226–229
    auditory pathway to, 256–257
    control of respiration by, 149
    degenerative disorders of, 236

    of hominids, 495
    of primates, 493
    visual pathway to, 252–254
Brainstem, *226*, 229
Braxton Hicks contractions, 324
BRCA1 gene, 348, 476, 481
BRCA2 gene, 348, 476
Breast, in female orgasm, 295
Breast cancer, 475
    gene for (See BRCA1 gene; BRCA2 gene)
    genetic testing for, 348
    hormone replacement therapy and, 283
    monoclonal antibodies in treating, 426
    screening for, 479, *479*
Breast self-examination, 479, 480, *480*
Breathing. See Respiration
Breech birth, 319
Broca's area, 227, 228, 231, *231*
Bronchi, *142, 143*
Bronchial tree, 145
Bronchiole, *142, 143, 145*
Bronchitis, 152, 153, *153*
Bruising, 101
Brunk, Conrad G., 385
BT corn, 385
Budding, in HIV life cycle, *465*, 466
Buffers (chemical), 21, 170
Bulbourethral glands, in reproductive system, *290*, 291
Bulimia nervosa, 136, *137*
Burke, Chris, 389
Bursa, *192*
Bursitis, 192, 276
Buttocks, muscles in, *201*
BV (bacterial vaginosis), 459

Cabbage, 478
Caffeine, 169
Calcitocin, 182
Calcitonin, 274
Calcitrol, 274
Calcium, 134, *135*, 212
    blood levels of, 274, *274*
    calcitonin and, 274
    in muscular action, 205
    in synaptic transmission, 222, *222*
Calories
    definition of, 18
    restricting, aging and, 326
cAMP (cyclic adenosine monophosphate), *268*, 269
Campylobacter, 449

Canals, bile, *124*
Cancer, 471–484. *See also specific types*
  apoptosis and, 422
  and asbestos, 153
  causes of, 476–477
  cytokines in treating, 425
  diagnosis of, *479*, 479–481
  and diet, 131
  early detection of, 348
  gene therapy for, 408
  as genetic disease, 474
  genetic testing for, 348
  hormone replacement therapy and, 283
  monoclonal antibodies in treating, 426
  as mutation, 413
  prevention of, 478
  testing for, 478
  and tissue types, 56
  treatment of, 481–483
  types of, 475, *475*
Cancer cells, 472, 472–475
Candida albicans, 459, *459*, 464
Candidal vaginitis, 459, *459*
Candidiasis, 446
Cannabis abuse, 239
Cannabis delirium, 239
Cannabis psychosis, 239
Canola oil, 130
Capillaries, *64*, *79*, *79*, *108*, 108–109, *151*
  arterial end of, *108*, 109
  blood flow in, 85, *85*
  in lungs, *142*, *145*, *145*, *151*
  lymphatic, 109, *109*
  midsection of, *108*, 109
  peritubular network of, 164, *164*
  venous end of, *108*, 109
Capillary bed, 79, *79*
Capillary exchange, *108*, 108–109
Capitulum, *190*
Capsid, 436, *436*, 465
Capsules, 434, 472
Carbaminohemoglobin, 150
Carbohydrates, 22, 22–23, *128*, 128–129
  in diet, 28, 131
  metabolism of, 275
Carbon cycle, 513, *513*, 533
Carbonic anhydrase, 150
Carboniferous period, 513
Carcinoembryonic antigen (CEA), 481
Carcinogenesis, 473, *473*
Carcinogens, environmental, 476–477
Carcinoma, 56, 64, *65*, 475

Cardiac cycle. *See* Heartbeat
Cardiac veins, *80*, *81*
Cardiovascular disease
  aging and, 328
  and amphetamines, 90
  devices for treatment of, 91
  factors in, 327
  in familial hypercholesterolemia, 401
  hormone replacement therapy and, 283
  and trans fats, 130
Cardiovascular system, 66, *66*, *78*, 78–92, 98–110
  aging of, 327
  blood in, 98–110 (*See also* Blood)
  components of, *78*
  disorders of, 88–91
  features of, *84*, 84–85, *85*
  pathways of, *86*, 86–87, *87*
  prevention of disease in, 90
  syphilis and, 456
Cardioverterdefibrillator (ICD), 91
Carnivores, 506, *506*, 507, *507*
Carotid artery, *81*, *84*, *86*, *87*
Carotid bodies, 149
Carpals, *185*, 190, *190*
Carrier proteins, 42, *42*
Carriers, 398
Carrying capacity, 522
Cartilage, 56–57, *57*, 178, 189, *192*
Caspases, in apoptosis, 335
Cataracts, 251
CA-125 test, 481
CAT scan (computerized axial tomography), 481
Cavities, body, 68, *68*
CCK (cholecystokinin), 122, *122*
CD4 T lymphocytes, in HIV infection, 462–464
CEA (carcinoembryonic antigen), 481
Cecum, 122, *123*
Cell(s), 2, 36, 36–50, *39*. *See also specific cells*
  ADP and ATP in, 30
  construction of macromolecules in, 22, *22*
  differentiation of, 311, 472
  evolution of, 488, 489
  metabolism in, 48–50, 268–269
  microscopy and, 37
  movement of, 46
  respiration of, 49, *49*
  sizes of, 36

  specialization of, 377
  structure and organization of, *38*, 38–47, *39*, 334
  theory of, 36
Cell body, in neuron structure, 218
Cell cycle, 334, 334–335
  of cancer, 474
  control of, 335
Cell division, 334
Cell increase, 334
Cell-mediated immunity, 423, *423*
Cellular respiration, 49, *49*
  and exercise, 50
  and muscles, 208, *209*
Cellulose, 23
Cementum, *117*
Central canal, in spinal cord, 224, *225*
Central nervous system, 218, *218*, 224, 224–229
  myelinated axons of, 219
  nicotine and, 238
Central sulcus, 227
Centriole, *38*, *39*, 337, *337*
Centromere, 337
Centrosome, 337, *337*
Cephalosporins, 445
Cerebellum, *226*, 229
Cerebral cortex, 227
  in aging, 328
  in primates, 493
Cerebral hemispheres, 227, *227*
Cerebrospinal fluid, 224
Cerebrum, *226*, 227–228
Cervical cancer, 458, 464
Cervical cap, 301, *302*
Cervix, 325, *325*
Cesarean section, 319
CFCs (chlorofluorocarbons), 530
cGMP (cyclic guanosine monophosphate), 291
Chancre, from syphilis, 456, *456*
Chemical(s)
  in biological evolution, 490
  cancer caused by, 476–477
  pregnancy and, 322
Chemical cycling, 507, *507*
  global, 510–513
Chemical evolution, 488, *489*
Chemical signals, hormones as, 268–269
Chemistry, 14–32
  of respiration, 149
  of water, 18–19
Chemoreceptors, 244, *244*

Chemotherapy, 482, *482*
Chernobyl Power Station, 476
Chicken pox, 438, *438*
Chimpanzee, genome of, 378, *378*
Chlamydia, 323, 454, *454*
Chloride, *135*
Chloride ion channels, and cystic fibrosis, 43, 400
Chlorofluorocarbons (CFCs), 530
Cholecystokinin (CCK), 122, *122*
Cholesterol, 25, *40*. *See also* HDL (high-density lipoprotein); LDL (low-density lipoprotein)
  and cardiovascular disease, 90
  and liver, 124
  in plasma membrane, 40
Chondrocytes, 178
Chondroitin, 193
Chordae tendinae, *80*, *81*
Chorion, 311, *311*
  in embryonic development, *315*
  mesoderm and, 317
  in placenta, 318
  in pre-embryonic development, 313
Chorionic villi, *315*, 317
Chorionic villi sampling (CVS), 390, *391*, 404
Choroid, 250, *250*
Chromatin, *39*, 44, *44*
  activated, 377, *377*
  in chromosome organization, 336, *336*
Chromosomal disorders. *See* Genetic disorders
Chromosomes
  abnormalities in, 323
  decondensation of, 377, *377*
  homologous, 340, 341, *341*, 344
  karyotyping, 390, *391*
  in meiosis, 340, *341*, 341–342, 344, 346
  in mitosis, 335, 337, 344
  mutation of, 396–397
  number of, changes in, 392–395
  organization of, 336, *336*
Chronic infections, 434
Chylomicrons, 121
Chyme, 120
Cilia, *38*, 46, *46*
Ciliary body, 250, *250*
Ciliary muscle, 251, *251*
Circadian rhythms, 282

Circuit, 86–87, *87*
pulmonary, 78, *78,* 86, *86*
systemic, 86–87
Circumduction, 193, *193*
Cirrhosis, 125, 237
Citric acid cycle, 49, *49,* 50
Clavicle, *185,* 190, *190*
Cleavage
in development before birth, 311
in pre-embryonic development, *313*
Cleavage (viral), in HIV life cycle, *465,* 466
Cleavage furrow, 339
Cleft, synaptic, *204*
Climate, regulation of, 533
Clitoris. *See* Glans clitoris
Clonal selection theory
for B cells, 419, *419*
for T cells, 422, *422*
Cloning, 314, *314, 380,* 380–381
Clostridium botulinum, 444, *444*
Clotting, 103–104, *103*
Coal, 528
Cocaine
abuse of, 238–239
and cardiovascular disease, 90
Cocci, 441
Coccyx, 188, *188*
Cochlea, *256,* 256–257, *257*
Cochlear canal, 257, *257*
Cochlear implants, 258
Cochlear nerve, 257, *257*
Codominance, 360
Codons, 372, *372,* 374
Coelom, 68
Coenzymes, 48, *48,* 132
Cognitive skills, aging and, 328
Coitus interruptus, *302*
Cold, common, 439
Cold receptors, 247
Coliform bacteria, 122, 432, *432*
Collagen fibers, 56, *56, 57,* 65
Colon, *116,* 122
Colon cancer
genetic testing for, 348
and polyps, 122
prevention of, 23
screening for, 480
Colony-stimulating factors, *416, 417, 417*
Color blindness, 255, *362,* 362–363, 402
Colorectal cancer, 475
Color vision, 252

Columnar epithelium, 62, *63*
Common carotid artery, *87*
Common cold, 439
Common descent, 490
Community, 506
Competition for limited resources, 492
Complementary base pairing, 368, 370
Complement system, 418, *418*
Compounds, 16–17
Computerized axial tomography (CAT) scan, 481
Conclusion, 6
Condoms, 301, *301, 302,* 463
Conduction deafness, 258
Cone cells, 251, 252, *252,* 253, *253,* 493
Congenital defects, 322–323
Connective tissue, *56,* 56–58, *58,* 178, *192*
Constipation, 123
Consumers (ecological), 5, 506, 507, *507*
Contagious diseases, 434
Continuous variation, of phenotypes, 359
Contraceptive implants, 301, *301, 302*
Contraceptive injections, 301, *301, 302*
Contraceptive vaccines, 302
Contractions, in birth, 324, 325
Control group, 8
Convergent evolution, 490
Coordination, aging and, 328
Copper, *135*
Coracoid process, *190*
Coral reefs, 516, 531, 536, *536*
Cords, vocal, 144, *144*
Corn, genetically engineered, 385
Cornea, 250, *250*
Corona radiata, 310, *310*
Coronary artery, *87*
Coronary bypass, 89, *89*
Corpus luteum
in embryonic development, 315
in ovarian cycle, *296,* 297
Cortex, renal, 163, *163, 169*
Cortisol, 276
Cortisone, 210, 275
Covalent bond, 17, *17*
Coxal bone, 191, *191*
Crabs (pubic lice), 459, *459*
Crack abuse, 238
Crack babies, 322
Cranberry juice, 162

Cranial nerves, 232, *232*
Craniosacral portion. *See* Parasympathetic division
Cranium, *185, 186, 186*
Creatine phosphate, 208, *209*
Creatinine, 160
Cretinism, 273, *273*
Creutzfeldt-Jakob disease, 439
Cri du chat syndrome, 396
Criminals, DNA fingerprinting and, 386
Cristae, 47, *47*
Cro-Magnons, 500, *500*
Crossing-over, 341, *341*
Cross-linking, aging and, 326–327
Cry9C protein, 385
Cryptosporidium, 448
Cuboidal epithelium, 62, *63*
Cultural eutrophication, 511
Culture
of Cro-Magnon, 500
of *Homo habilis,* 497
of Neanderthals, 500
Cunnilingus, 463
Cushing syndrome, 277, *277*
Cutaneous receptors, 246–247
CVS (chorionic villi sampling), 390, *391,* 404
Cyanide fishing, 536, *536*
Cyclic adenosine monophosphate (cAMP), *268,* 269
Cyclic guanosine monophosphate (cGMP), 291
Cyclin, 335, 474
Cyclin D, 474
Cystic fibrosis, 43, 400, *400,* 408
Cystitis, 171
Cytokines
in clonal expansion, 419, *419*
from helper T cells, 423
in immunity, 425
Cytokinesis, 334, 335, 339
Cytoplasm, 38, *39*
division of, 339
gene expression regulation in, 377
Cytosine (C), 30
in DNA, 368
in RNA, 370
Cytoskeleton, 38, *38,* 43, *43*
Cytotoxic T cells, 422, *422,* 423, 425

Dams, 525
Dandruff, 64

Dart, Raymond, 496
Darwin, Charles, 490
Data, 6, *8*
Daughter cells
in meiosis, 340, 342, *343,* 344
in mitosis, 336, 337, 344
DDT, 421
Deafness, 258
Decomposers, 5, 506, *506, 507,* 533
Deductive reasoning, 7
Defecation, 122
Defibrillation, 83
Deforestation, 525, *525*
Degenerative brain disorders, 236
Dehydration, from alcohol, 284
Dehydration reaction, 22
Dehydrogenase, 48
Delayed allergic response, 426
Deletion, 396, *396*
Deltoid, 200, *200, 201*
Deltoid tuberosity, *190*
Dementia, hormone replacement therapy and, 283
Denaturation, 26
Dendrite, 60, *60,* 218
Dendritic cells, in inflammatory response, *416,* 417
Denitrification, 512
Dental caries, 117
Dentin, *117*
Deoxyribonucleic acid. *See* DNA
Depo-Provera, *301*
Depression (anatomical motion), 193
Dermatitis, *132*
Dermis, 64–65
DES (diethylstilbestrol), 322
Desert, 514
Desertification, *524,* 524–525
Detrital food chain, *508,* 509
Detrital food web, *508,* 509
Detrivores, 506, 507, *507*
Development, human, 309–328
after birth, *326,* 326–328
before birth, 311–320
embryonic, *312, 315,* 315–317
fertilization, 310, *310*
fetal, *312,* 319, *319*
pre-embryonic, *312, 313, 313*
of sex organs, 320, *321*
stages of, 313–317

DHT (dihydrotestos-terone), 320
Diabetes, 42, 69, 324
Diabetes insipidus, 270
Diabetes mellitus, 279
Dialysis, 171, *171*
Diaphragm, *80, 116, 142, 148, 149*
Diaphragm (contraceptive), 301, *301, 302*
Diarrhea, 123
Diastole, 82, *82*
Diastolic pressure, 84, *84,* 85
Diencephalon, *226,* 229
Diet. *See also* Eating disorders; Food; Nutrition
  in aging, 327
  and anemia, 101
  cancer and, 477
  and cardiovascular disease, 90
  fats in, 25, 28
  fish in, 105
  importance of balanced, 28, *28*
  low carbohydrate, 131
  meat in, 129
  milk in, 126
  and minerals, 134–135
Diethylstilbestrol (DES), 322
Differentiation
  cancer cells and, 472
  in development before birth, 311
Diffusion, 41, *41, 42*
Digestion, *127*
Digestive enzymes, 126, *127*
Digestive system, 66, *66, 116,* 116–127
  lower portion of, 120–125
  and nutrition, 128–135
  upper portion of, 116–119
Digestive tract, wall of, 119, *119*
Digits, 190
Dihybrid cross, 357, *357*
Dihydrotestosterone (DHT), 320
Diploid (2n) number, 337, 340
Direct contact transmission, *434,* 434–435
Disaccharide, 23
Disease. *See also* Pathogens
  bacterial, 441–444, *444*
  biodiversity loss from, 532, *532*
  categories of, 435
  definition of, 413, 414
  fungal, 446, *446, 448*
  genetic testing for, 305
  genome study and, 378

helminth, 449
  infectious, 434
  nonspecific defenses against, 417–418
  protozoan, 447–448, *448*
  specific defenses against, 418–423
  systemic, 434
  viral, *435,* 436–439
Disks, intercalated, 59
Distal convoluted tubule, *168*
Diuretics, 169
DNA (deoxyribonucleic acid)
  in biological evolution, 490
  in cell evolution, 489
  chemistry of, *29,* 29–30
  in chromosome organization, 336
  as evidence, 367
  and radiation, 15
  repair of, 335
  replication of, 369, *369*
    chromosomes in, 336
    and gene cloning, *380,* 380–381, *381*
    meiosis and mitosis and, 344
  vs. RNA, *370*
  sequence of, 378
  steroid hormones and, 269
  structure of, 368, *368*
  synthesis of, 334
  technology using, 380–384
  testing, 403
  in vaccines, 466
  viral, 436, *436*
DNA chips, 403, *403,* 406
DNA fingerprinting, 382, *382,* 386
DNA ligase, 380–381
DNA polymerase, 369, 381
DNA probes, 403, *403*
Dolly (sheep), 314
Dominance, incomplete, 360
Dominant allele, 352, *352*
  in autosomal disorders, *398,* 399, 401, *401*
  in sex-linked disorders, 399
L-Dopa, for Parkinson disease, 236
Dopamine
  in drug abuse, 237, 238
  in Parkinson disease, 236
Dorsalis pedis artery, *84*
Dorsal root, 232, *232*
Dorsal-root ganglia, 232, *232*
Double helix, *29,* 368, *368*
Douche, as birth control, 302
Douglas, Kirk, 351
Douglas, Michael, 351

Down syndrome, 389, 393, *393*
  karyotype of, 390, *391*
  translocation and, 397
  as trisomy, 392
Drinking water, 525
Droplets, in pathogen transmission, *434,* 434–435
Drug(s) (illegal)
  abuse of, 237–239
  HIV transmission and, 463
  neurotransmitters and, 223, *237*
  performance-enhancing, 211
    and cardiovascular disease, 90
  in pregnancy, 322, *322*
Drug(s) (prescription)
  biodiversity and, 535
  bioengineering, 384
  for HIV, 466, 467
  nerve deafness from, 258
  pregnancy and, 322
  tailoring, 407
Drug resistance
  of antibiotic agents, 152, 445
  of bacteria, 445, 449
  multidrug, 482
  of viruses, 461
Dubois, Eugene, 498
Duchenne muscular dystrophy, 402
Duct
  bile, *124*
  common hepatic, *124*
  pancreatic, *116, 124*
Duodenum, *116, 122, 124*
Duplication, 396, *396*
Dwarfism, pituitary, 272
Dystrophin, 402

Ear
  anatomy of, *256,* 256–257
  in embryonic development, 317, *317*
  functions of, *261*
Ear, middle, 152
Earlobes, alleles for, 352, *352*
Earth, primitive, 488
Earwax, 256, 258
Eating disorders, 136–137. *See also* Diet; Food
Ebola virus, 440
ECG (electrocardiogram), 83, *83*
Ecoestrogens, 303

Ecological pyramids, 509, *509,* 527
Ecological succession, 514
Ecology
  endocrine-disrupting contaminants, 303
  global, 505–517
  pesticides, 421
  scope of, 506–507
Economic well-being, 538
Ecosystems, 5, 506
  chemical cycling in, 507, *507*
  energy flow in, 507, *507*
  global, 514–516
  organization of, *5*
  primary productivity of, 516, *516*
Ecotourism, 533
Ecstasy, 239
Ectoderm, *315, 316,* 317
Ectopic pregnancy, 315
EDCs (endocrine-disrupting contaminants), 303, *303*
Edema, 109
Effacement, in birth, 325
Effectors, 218
Efferent arteriole, *168*
Egg
  anatomy of, 310
  in female reproductive system, 294
  gene therapy for, 407
  genetic testing of, 404–405, *405*
  in IVF, 304
  in meiosis, 347, *347*
EIS (Epidemic Intelligence Service), 433
Ejaculation, 291
Elastic cartilage, 57
Elastic fiber, *56, 57,* 65
Elbow, bones of, 190, *190*
Electrocardiogram (ECG), 83, *83*
Electron, 14, *14,* 17
Electron microscopes, 37, *37*
Electron transport chain, 49, *49*
Elements, 14, *14*
Elevation, 193
Elongation, in polypeptide synthesis, 374, *375*
Embolus, 88
Embryo
  gender selection of, 363
  gene therapy for, 407
  genetic testing of, 304, 404–405, *405*
Embryonic cells, cell cycle of, 335

Embryonic development, *312, 315*, 315–317
Embryonic disk, 315, *315*
Embryonic stem cells, in cloning, 314, *314*
Emergency contraception, 302
Emphysema, *153*, 153–154
Emulsification, 24
Enamel, tooth, *117*
Encephalitis
    from measles, 439
    toxoplasmic, AIDS deaths from, 464
Endemic disease, 435
Endocardium, *81*
Endocrine-disrupting contaminants (EDCs), 303, *303*
Endocrine glands, 266–269, *267*
Endocrine system, 67, *67*, 265–284
    adrenal glands in, *266, 267, 275, 275*
    and homeostasis, 70, 284
    hypothalamus in, *266, 267*, 270–272, *271*
    and nervous system, 284
    vs. nervous system, 266, *266*
    ovaries in, *266, 267*, 280
    pancreas in, *266, 267*, 278–279
    parathyroid glands in, *266, 267*, 274
    pineal gland in, *266, 267*, 282
    pituitary gland in, *266, 267*, 270–272
    pollutants and, 303
    and reproductive system, 284
    testes in, *266, 267*, 280
    thymus gland in, *266, 267*, 282
    thyroid gland in, *266, 267*, 273–274
Endocrine tissue, 278
Endocytosis, *42*, 43
Endoderm, *315, 316*, 317
Endometrial cancer, hormone replacement therapy and, 283
Endometriosis, infertility from, 304
Endometrium, 295, *299*
Endoplasmic reticulum (ER), *38*, 44, *44*, 45, *45*
Endoplasmic reticulum, rough, *38, 39, 44, 45, 45*

Endoplasmic reticulum, smooth, *38, 39, 44, 45, 45*
Endorphins, heroin and, 239
Endospores, 444
Endostatin, 483
Energy, 528–529, *529*
Energy flow, 507, *507*, 509
Enterococcus, 449
Entry, in HIV life cycle, 465, *465*
Envelope, viral, 436, *436*
Environmental influences
    on chromosomal structure, 396
    on multifactorial inheritance, 360, *360*
Environmental Protection Agency (EPA), 303, 530
Environmental resistance, 522
Environmental toxins, as EDC, 303
Enzyme(s), 26, 48, *48*
    digestive, 126, *127*
    in DNA replication, 369
    function of, 371
    in gene expression, 377
    hydrolytic, 126
    in polymerase chain reaction, 381
    in recombinant DNA, 380–381
    in transcription, 373
Enzyme cascade, *268*, 269
Eosinophils, *100*, 103
EPA (Environmental Protection Agency), 303, 530
Epicondyle, *191*
Epidemic, 435
Epidemic Intelligence Service (EIS), 433
Epidemiology, 434–435
Epidermal growth factor, 282
Epidermis, 64, *64*
Epididymis, 290, *290*
Epigenic layer, 379
Epiglottis, 118, *118, 142, 143*, 144
Epinephrine, 275, *275*
Epiphysis, *179, 180*
Episiotomy, 325
Episodic memory, 230
Epithelial tissue, 56, 62, *62, 63*
Epithelium, cuboidal, 62, *63*
Epstein-Barr virus, cancer caused by, 477
Equilibrium, *260*, 261
ER (endoplasmic reticulum), *38*, 44, *44, 45, 45*
Erectile dysfunction, 291

Erythroblasts, *100*
Erythrocytes. *See* Red blood cells
Erythromycin, 445
Erythroprotein, 101, *101*, 160
Esophagus, *116, 118*, 118–119, *143*
Estrogen, 25, 182
    in embryonic development, 318
    in endocrine system, 280
    in oral contraceptives, 301
    in ovarian cycle, 297, *297*
    in pregnancy, 300, 324, *324*
    in reproductive system, 300
    in uterine cycle, 298
Ethmoid bone, *186*
Eukaryotic cells
    DNA passed in, 336
    evolution of, 489
    vs. prokaryotic cells, 441
Europe
    Homo erectus in, 498
    Homo sapiens in, 499
Eustachian tube, 152
Eversion, 193, *193*
Evolution, 2, 487–501
    of australopithecines, 496
    biological, 489–492
    chemical, 488, *489*
    DNA in study of, 381
    of humans, *497*, 497–501
    mosaic, 496
    teaching, 501
    theory of, 6
Evolutionary tree, 494, *494*
Exchange pool, 510
Excitatory neurotransmitters, 222
Excitotoxicity, hippocampus in, 231
Exercise, 207, *207*
    in aging, 327
    and cardiovascular disease, 90
    and cellular respiration, 50
    and diabetes, 69
    and osteoporosis, 184
Exocrine glands, 266
Exocrine tissue, 278
Exocytosis, *42*, 43
Exons, 373, *373*
Exophthalmic goiter, 273
Experiments, 8–9
Expiration, 149
Expiratory reserve volume, 146
Exponential population growth, 522
Extension, 192, *193*
Extensor carpi, *200, 201*

Extensor digitorum, 200, *200, 201*
Extensor digitorum longus, *200, 201*
External oblique, *200, 201*
Exteroceptors, 244, *244*
Extinction, 4
Extraembryonic membranes, 311, *311*
Ex vivo gene therapy, 408, *408*
Eye
    abnormalities of, 255, *255*
    anatomy of, *250*, 250–254
    in embryonic development, 317, *317*
    gonorrhea infection in, 455, *455*
Eyestrain, 251

Face, hominid, 495
Facial artery, *84*
Facial bones, 187
Factor IX, 402
Factor VIII, 402
FAD (flavinadenine dinucleotide), 49, *49*
Fallopian tubes. *See* Oviducts
False-labor, 324
Familial hypercholesterolemia (FH), 401, *402*, 408
Family pedigrees, *398*, 398–399, *399*
Fanconi's anemia, 305
Farming, 526–527
Farsightedness, 255, *255*
FAS (fetal alcohol syndrome), 238, 322, *322, 323*
Fascia, *199*
Fascicle, *199*
Fats, 24, *24*, 130
    cancer and, 477
    in diet, 28, 130
    fake, 130
    metabolism of, 275
Feedback
    in endocrine system, 266, 270
    negative, *72*, 72–73, *73*
    positive, 73
Fellatio, 463
Female condom, 301, *301, 302*
Femoral artery, *84*
Femoral vein, *87*
Femur, *185, 191, 191, 192*
Fermentation, 50, 208, *209*
Fertility treatments, 1

Fertilization, 300, 310, *310*
  chromosomes and, 340
  in pre-embryonic
    development, *313*
Fertilizer, 512, 526
Fetal alcohol syndrome
    (FAS), 238, 322, *322, 323*
Fetal cannabis syndrome, 239
Fetal cells, testing, 404
Fetal circulation, 318, *318*
Fetal development,
    312, 319, *319*
Fetus
  blood type of,
    vs. mother, 107
  genetic testing of, 404, *404*
FH (familial
    hypercholesterolemia),
    401, *402,* 408
Fiber(s)
  collagen, 56, *56, 57,* 65
  elastic, *56, 57,* 65
  motor, 232
  nerve, 232
  parasympathetic
    preganglionic, *234*
  Purkinje, 82, *83*
  reticular, *56*
  sensory, 232
  spindle, 337, *337*
  sympathetic
    preganglionic, *234*
Fiber, dietary, 122, 123, 478
Fibrillin, 401
Fibrinogen, 104, *104*
Fibroblast, *56, 57*
Fibrocartilage, 57
Fibrosis, pulmonary, *153*
Fibula, *185,* 191, *191*
Filament, actin, *39, 43, 43,*
    46, 59
Filament, intermediate,
    43, 43
Fimbria, 294, *294*
Finches, natural selection
    among, 492
Fingerprints, 64
First division, in meiosis, 342
First messenger, *268, 269*
Fish
  in diet, 105
  overexploitation of,
    532, 532
Flagella, *38, 46, 46*
  of bacteria, 434
  of sperm, 293, 310, *310*
Flavinadenine dinucleotide
    (FAD), 49, *49*
Flexible sigmoidoscopy, 480
Flexion, 192, *193*
Flexor carpi, *200, 201*

Flexor digitorum, *200, 201*
Flexor digitorum longus, *201*
Fluid, tissue, *70,* 92
Fluid-mosaic model, 40
Focus, in vision, 251, *251*
Folacin, *133*
Folic acid, *133,* 322
Follicles, in ovarian cycle,
    296, 297
Follicle-stimulating hormone
    (FSH), 293, 297, *297*
Follicular phase, of ovarian
    cycle, 297
Fomites, *434,* 435
Fontanels, 186, 319
Food. *See also* Diet; Digestive
    system; Eating disorders
  genetically modified,
    31, 384, 385
  microbial, 432
  minerals in, *135*
  as resource, 526–527
  vitamins in, *133*
Food chains, 509
Food poisoning, 444, *444*
Food web, *508,* 509
Foramen magnum, 186, *186*
Foreskin, 291
Forests, 21, 514
Formulas, molecular, 17
Fossil, 490
Fossil fuels, 513, 528
Fossil record, 490, *491*
Fovea centralis, *250,* 251
Fraternal twins, 313
Free radicals, 132, 326
Freshwater, provision of, 533
Frontal bone, 186, *186, 187*
Frontalis, *200, 200, 201*
Frontal lobe, 227, *227*
FSH (follicle-stimulating
    hormone), 293,
    297, 297
Fuel consumption, 526
Fungi, diseases caused by,
    446, *446,* 448
Fungicides, 445
Fusion, in HIV life cycle,
    465, *465*

GABA neurotransmitter, 237
Gallbladder, *116, 124,* 125
Galloping gangrene,
    442, *442*
Gamete, 304, 340, 341, *341*
Gamete intrafallopian
    transfer (GIFT), 304
Gametogenesis
  alleles in, 353
  meiosis in, 346, 356, *356*
Gammagard, 425

Gamma rays, in cancer
    treatment, 481
Ganglia, 232
Ganglion cells, in retina,
    253, *253*
Gangrene, galloping,
    442, *442*
Gardnerella vaginalis, 459, *459*
Gart gene, 393, *393*
Gases, in primitive
    atmosphere, 488
Gas exchange
  and homeostasis, 150
  in lungs, 78, *78,* 145, *145*
Gastric glands, 120, *120*
Gastrin, 122, *122*
Gastrocnemius, *200, 201*
Gastrulation, 317
Gehrig, Lou, 218
Gel electrophoresis, 382, *382*
Gender
  choosing, 363
  and hemophilia, 104
Gene(s)
  in aging, 326
  in Alzheimer disease, 236
  cancer and, 474, 476
  cloning, *380,* 380–381
Gene expression,
    371–387, *376*
  overview of, 372
  regulation of, 377
  transcription in, 373, *373*
  translation in, 374,
    374, 375
Gene pharming, 384
Gene therapy, 408, *408*
  for cancer, 483
  for cardiovascular
    disease, 89
  gene cloning in, 380
  pre-embryonic, 407
Genetically modified foods,
    31, 527
Genetic code, 372
Genetic counseling, 389–409
  for chromosomal
    disorders, 390–397
  future, *406,* 406–408
  present, 398–405
Genetic disorders, 400–402
  chromosomal
    abnormalities and,
    390, 390–397
  gender choice and, 363
  sex-linked inheritance
    of, 362
  testing for, 403–405
Genetic engineering, 380
Genetic markers, 403, *403*
Genetic profile, 406, *406,* 409

Genetic testing
  for cancer, 348, 481
  of eggs, 304
  genetic selection and, 305
Genital herpes, 438, 453,
    457, *457*
Genitals, female, 295, *295*
Genital tract, 294–295
Genital warts, 458
Genomes
  comparisons of, 378, *378*
  future uses of, 407
  of HIV, 465
  three-dimensionality
    of, 379
  viral, 436
Genomics, 378–379
Genotype, 352, 363
Genotypic ratio, 354
Geothermal energy, 528
Gerontology, 326
GH (growth hormone),
    182, 270, *271, 272, 272*
Giantism, 272, *272*
Giardiasis, 448, *448*
GIFT (gamete intrafallopian
    transfer), 304
Giraffes, evolution of,
    492, 492
Girdles, pectoral, 190
Glands, 62
  adrenal, *266, 267, 275, 275*
  bulbourethral, *290,* 291
  endocrine, 266–269, *267*
  exocrine, 266
  gastric, 120, *120*
  oil, 417
  parathyroid, *266, 267,* 274
  pineal, 229, *266, 267,* 282
  pituitary, *266, 267,*
    270–272, 280
  salivary, 116
  sweat, *64,* 65, 172
  tear, 143
  thymus, *92*
    in endocrine system,
      266, 267, 282
    in immune system,
      414, *415*
  thyroid, *15, 266, 267,*
    273–274
Glans clitoris, 295, *295*
  in female orgasm, 295
  fetal development
    of, *321*
Glans penis, 291, *291*
Glaucoma, 251
Glenoid cavity, 190, *190*
Global ecology, 505–517
Global warming, 513, 528,
    531, 533

Glomerular capsule, 165, *165*, *168*
Glomerular filtration, *166*, 167
Glomerulus, *168*
Glottis, 118, *118, 142, 143*
Glucagon, 278, *278*
Glucocorticoids, 275, *275, 276*
Glucosamine chondroitin, 193
Glucose, 22, *22*
  blood levels of, 276, *278*, 278–279, *279*
  and diabetes, 69
  in diabetes mellitus, 279, *279*
  and homeostasis, 70
  and liver, 124
Glutamate, 231, 237
Glutamines, 401
Gluteus maximus, 200, *200, 201*
Gluteus medius, *200, 201*
Glycemic index, 128
Glycogen, 23, *23*, 124, *202*
Glycolipid, 40, *40*
Glycolysis, 49, *49*
Glycoprotein, 40, *40*
GM-CSF (granulocyte and macrophage colony-stimulating factor), 282
GNP (gross national product), 538
GnRH (gonadotropin-releasing hormone), 293, 297, *297*
Goblet cell, *63, 121, 123*
Goiters, 273, *273*
Golgi apparatus, *38, 39, 45, 45*
Gonadotropic hormones, 270, *271*, 304
Gonadotropin-releasing hormone (GnRH), 293, 297, *297*
Gonads, *267*, 280. *See also* Ovaries; Testes
Gonorrhea, 454–455, *455*
  adhesion factors of, 434
  in pregnancy, 323
  treatment of, 445
Gonorrhea proctitis, 455
Gout, *160*
Graafian follicle. *See* Vesicular follicle
Gracile australopithecines, 496
Gram stain, 441, *441*
Granulocyte and macrophage colony-stimulating factor (GM-CSF), 282
Grasslands, 514

Graves' disease, 273, 414
Gravitational equilibrium, *260*, 261
Gray matter
  in central nervous system, 224
  in cerebrum, 228
  in spinal cord, 224, *225*
Grazing food chain, *508*, 509
Grazing food web, *508, 509*
Great Barrier Reef, 536
Greater trochanter, *191*
Greater tubercle, *190*
Great saphenous veins, *87*
Greenhouse effect, 513, 528
Green revolutions, 526–527
Griseofulvin, 445
Gross national product (GNP), 538
Ground substance, *56*
Groundwater mining, 510
Growth, 2
  in development before birth, 311
  mitosis in, 346
Growth factors, 268, 282, 472, 474
  epidermal, 282
  inhibitory, 472
  nerve, 282
  platelet-derived, 282
  stimulatory, 472
  vescular endothelial, 408
Growth hormone (GH), 182, 270, *271, 272, 272*
Growth plate, 181, *181*
Growth promoters, 449
Growth rate, 522
G_0 stage, 335
G_1 stage, *334*, 334–335
G_2 stage, *334*, 334–335
Guanine (G), 30
  in DNA, 368
  in RNA, 370
Gummas, 456, *456*
Gums, *117*

HAART (highly active antiretroviral therapy), 466
Habitat, 506
Habitat loss, 531
Hair, testosterone and, 293
Hair cells, of basiliar membrane, 257, *257*, 258, *259*
Hair follicle, *64*, 65
Hamstring, *200, 201*
Hand, bones of, 190, *190*
H antigen (hemagglutinin antigen), 437, *437*

Haploid (n) number, 340
Haplotypes, 378
HapMap project, 378, *379*
Harkin, Tom, 93
HAV (hepatitus A virus), 458
Hay fever, 426
Hazardous waste, 530, *530*
HBV (hepatitis B), 458
HCG. *See* Human chorionic gonadotropin
HCl (hydrochloric acid), and digestion, 120
HCV (hepatitis C), 458
HDL (high-density lipoprotein), 90, 130
HDN (hemolytic disease of newborn), 107
Head, muscles of, *201*
Hearing, 256, 256–257, *257*
Hearing loss, 258
Heart, *80*, 80–83. *See also* Cardiovascular system
  artificial, 91, *91*
  disorders of, 91
  in embryonic development, 317
  muscle in, 59, *59*
  passage of blood through, 81, *81*
  transplants, 91
Heart attack, 88, 90
Heartbeat, *82*, 82–83
Heartburn, 119
Heart disease. *See* Cardiovascular disease
Heart failure, 91
Height, multifactorial inheritance of, 359
Helminths
  diseases caused by, 449
  treatments for, 445
Helper T cells, 422, 423, 460, 462–464
Hemagglutinin (H antigen), 437, *437*
Hematoma, 183, *183*
Hemodialysis, *171*, 171
Hemoglobin, 26, 100, *100*, 150
Hemolysis, 101
Hemolytic disease of newborn (HDN), 107
Hemophilia, 104, *104*, 402
Hemorrhoids, 88
Hepatic duct, common, *124*
Hepatic portal system, 87, *87*, 125
Hepatic portal vein, *87*
Hepatic vein, *86, 87*
Hepatitis, 125, 458

Hepatitis B
  cancer caused by, 477
  vaccine against, 424
Herbicides
  cancer caused by, 477
  as EDCs, 303
  food supply and, 526
Herbivores, 506, *506*
Herceptin, 426
Heredity. *See* Gene(s); Inheritance
Hermaphroditism, 320
Heroin, 237, 239
Herpes, 323, 438, *438*
Herpes simplex virus type 1 (HSV-1), 438, 457, *457*
Herpes simplex virus type 2 (HSV-2), 438, 457, *457*
Herpes zoster, 438, *438*
Heterosexual community, AIDS in, 460
Heterotroph, 488, 506, 507, *507*
Heterozygous genotypes, 352, 355
HEV (hepatitis E), 458
Hexosaminidase A (Hex A), 400
Hexose, 22
Hibernation, melatonin in, 281
High-density lipoprotein (HDL), 90, 130
Higher mental functions, 230–231
Highly active antiretroviral therapy (HAART), 466
High responder plants, 526–527
Hip, bones of, 191
Hippocampus, *230*, 230–231
Histamine
  in allergies, 426
  in asthma, 427
  in inflammatory response, *416*, 417
Histones, 336, *336*
Histoplasmosis, 446, *446*
HIV (human immunodeficiency virus). *See also* AIDS
  drug-resistant, 461
  hepatitis B and, 458
  life cycle of, 465, *465*
  origin of, 460
  phases of infection, *462*, 462–464
  in pregnancy, 323, 466
  prevalence of, 460–461, *461*

HIV—*Cont.*
  prevention of, 463
  structure of, 465
  T cells in, 423
  transmission of,
    460, 460–461
  treatment for, 466, 467
HIV-1B, 461
HIV-1C, 461
HIV provirus, 465
HLA types, 268
Hodgkin's lymphoma,
    475, 482
Homeostasis, 2, 70–73
  and blood, 110
  and endocrine system,
    70, 284
  and gas exchange, 150
  and glucose, 70
  interoceptors in, 244
  and muscular system, 212
  negative feedback in,
    72–73
  and nervous system,
    70, 284
  positive feedback in, 73
  sensory receptors in, 245
  and urinary system, 171
Hominids, evolution of,
    494–495
Homo erectus, 498, *498*
Homo habilis, 497
Homologous structures, 490
Homologues, 340, 341, *341*
  alignment of, 341, *341*
  alleles and, 356
  instructions carried by, 341
  in meiosis I, 344
Homo sapiens, 499, *499*
Homosexual community,
    AIDS in, 460, 463
Homozygous dominant
    genotypes, 352
Homozygous genotypes, 355
Homozygous recessive
    genotypes, 352
Honeybees, 535
Hormone(s), 121, 266, *267*.
    See also Endocrine
    system
  actions of, 268–269
  adrenocorticotropic, 270,
    271, 275, *275*
  antidiuretic, 270, *271*, 284
  anti-Müllerian, 320
  atrial natriuretic, 169, 276
  bovine growth, 384
  as chemical signals,
    268–269
  decline in, aging
    and, 326

follicle-stimulating,
    293, 297, *297*
  gonadotropic, 270,
    271, 304
  growth, 182, 270, *271*,
    272, *272*
  hypothalamic-
    inhibiting, 270
  hypothalamic-
    releasing, 270
  local, 268
  luteinizing, 293, 297, *297*
  in male fetal
    development, 320
  melanocyte-
    stimulating, 270
  parathyroid, 182, 266, 274
  peptide, *268*, 269, 324, *324*
  regulation of
    in females, *297*, 297–300
    in males, 293, *293*
  steroid, 269, *269*
  thyroid, 269
  thyroid-stimulating,
    270, *271*
Hormone replacement
    therapy (HRT), 283,
    300, 478
Horse antibodies, 425
HPVs (human
    papillomaviruses),
    458, 477
HRT (hormone replacement
    therapy), 283, 300, 478
HSV-1 (herpes simplex virus
    type 1), 438, 457, *457*
HSV-2 (herpes simplex virus
    type 2), 438, 457, *457*
HTLV-1 (human T-cell
    lymphotropic virus), 477
Human(s)
  and carbon cycle, 513
  classification of, *493*
  ecological impact of, 516
  evolution of, *497*, 497–501
  life cycle of, *346*, 346–347
  and nitrogen cycle, 512
  and phosphorus cycle, 511
  population growth of,
    522, 522–523
  as primates, *493*, 493–495
  species of, 501
  and water cycle, 510
Human chorionic
    gonadotropin (HCG)
  in embryonic
    development, 315
  in pregnancy, 300
  vaccine against, 302
Human immunodeficiency
    virus. *See* HIV

Human papillomaviruses
    (HPVs), 458, 477
Human T-cell lymphotropic
    virus (HTLV-1), 477
Humerus, *185*, 190, *190*, *199*
Hunger, 282
Hunting, 532
Huntingtin protein, 401
Huntington disease,
    401, *401*, 403, 404
Hyaline cartilage, 57, *57*,
    189, *192*
Hybridoma cells, 426
Hydrocephalus, 224
Hydrochloric acid. *See* HCl
Hydrogen bonds, 18, *18*,
    368, 369
Hydrogen fuel, 529
Hydrologic cycle, 510, *510*
Hydrolysis reaction, 22
Hydrolytic enzymes, 126
Hydrophilic, 19
Hydrophobic, 19
Hydropower, 528
Hymen, 295
Hyoid bone, 187, *187*
Hypertension, 88
Hyperthyroidism, 273, 414
Hypertonic, 41, *41*
Hyperventilation, 150
Hypoglycemia, 279
Hypophysis. *See* Pituitary
    gland
Hypothalamic-inhibiting
    hormones, 270
Hypothalamic-releasing
    hormones, 270
Hypothalamus, 229
  adrenal glands and,
    275, *275*
  in endocrine system, 266,
    267, 270–272, *271*
  gonads and, 280
  in homeostasis, 284
  hormones in, 268
  leptin and, 282
  in neuroendocrine
    system, 284
  in ovarian cycle,
    297, *297*
  reproductive system
    and, 284
Hypothesis, 6
Hypothyroidism, 273
Hypotonic, 41, *41*

ICD (cardioverterde-
    fibrillator), 91
ICSI (intracytoplasmic
    sperm injection), 304
Identical twins, 313

Identification, DNA used for,
    382, *382*, 386
IgA antibodies, 420, *420*
IgD antibodies, 420, *420*
IgE antibodies, 420, *420*,
    426, 427
IgG antibodies, 420, *420*
IgM antibodies, 420, *420*
Ileum, *123*
Iliac artery, *86*
Iliac vein, *86*, *87*
Iliopsoas, *200*, *201*
Ilium, *185*, *191*
Imagining procedures, for
    cancer diagnosis, 481
Immediate allergic
    response, 426
Immune complexes, 420
Immune system, 66, *66*,
    414–415
  aging and, 326
  diseases of, 428
  nonspecific defenses of,
    417–418
  pesticides and, 421
  side effects from, 426–428
  specific defenses of,
    418–423
  thymus in, 414
Immunity, 414
  acquired, 424–426
  active, 424
  passive, 424
Immunization, 424, *424*
Immunoglobulins (Igs).
    See Antibodies
Immunosuppression,
    421, 428
Immunotherapy, 483, *483*
Impetigo, 442, *442*
Implantation
  in embryonic
    development, 315
  emergency contraception
    and, 302
  in pregnancy, 294, 300, *300*
Incisors, *117*
Incomplete dominance,
    360, *360*
Incompletely dominant
    disorders, 401
Incus, 256, *256*
Index of Sustainable
    Economic Welfare
    (ISW), 538
Inductive reasoning, 7
Infant respiratory distress
    syndrome, 145
Infectious diseases, 434
Inferior vena cava, *80*, *86*, *86*,
    87, *160*

Infertility, 290, 304, 455
Inflammation, glucocorticoids for, 276
Inflammatory reaction, *416*, 417–418
Influenza, 437, *437*
Inheritance, 353, *353*
    codominance, 360
    incomplete dominance, 360, *360*
    multifactorial, *359*, 359–360
    multiple allele, 361
    one-trait, *354*, 354–355, *355*
    pedigrees for, *398*, 398–399, *399*
    sex-linked, *362*, 362–363
    two-trait, *356*, 356–358, *357*, *358*
    unusual patterns in, 399
Inhibitory growth factors, 472
Inhibitory neurotransmitters, 222
Initiation
    in carcinogenesis, 473, *473*
    in polypeptide synthesis, 374, *375*
Inner cell mass, in pre-embryonic development, 313, *313*
Inner ear, 256, *256*
Insects, 421, 440
Inspiration, *148*, 148–149
Inspiratory reserve volume, 146
Insulin
    in blood glucose levels, *278*, 278–279
    and diabetes, 69
    in diabetes mellitus, 279
    and liver, 124
Integrase, 465
Integration (synaptic), 223, *223*
    in aging, 328
    in association areas, 228
    in retina, 253
    by sensory receptors, 245
Integration (viral), in HIV life cycle, 465, *465*
Integumentary system, *64*, 64–65, 66, *66*
Intelligent-design theory, 501
Intercalated disks, 59
Intercostal muscles, *149*
Intercostal nerves, *149*
Interferons, 418, 425
Interkinesis, 342, *342*
Interleukins, 425
Intermediate filaments, 43, *43*
Internal clock, 281
Internal jugular vein, *87*

Interneuron, 218
Interoceptors, 244
Interphase, *334*, 334–335, 338, *338*
Interstitial cells, 293
Intervertebral disks, 188, *188*
Intestine, large, *116*, 122–123, 432, *432*
Intestine, small, *116*, 121, *121*
Intracytoplasmic sperm injection (ICSI), 304
Intrauterine device (IUD), 301, *301*, *302*
Intrauterine insemination (IUI), 304
Intravenous drug use, AIDS and, 463
Introns, 373, *373*
Invasive factors, of pathogens, 434
Inversion, 193, *193*, 396, 397, *397*
Inversion, thermal, 147
In vitro fertilization (IVF), 304, 404
In vivo gene therapy, 408
Iodine, 134, *135*, 273
Ionic bond, 16, *16*
Ions, 16, *16*, 19
Iris, 250, *250*
Iron, 134, *135*
Irrigation, 526
Ischium, *185*
Isotopes, 15
ISW (Index of Sustainable Economic Welfare), 538
IUD (intrauterine device), 301, *301*, *302*
IUI (intrauterine insemination), 304

Jacobs syndrome, 392, 395
Jaundice, 125
Jawbone, *117*
Johnson, Ben, *211*
Joints, 178, *192*, 192–193
Jugular vein, *86*, *87*
Juxtaglomerate apparatus, 168, *168*

Kaposi's sarcoma, AIDS deaths from, 464
Kaposi's sarcoma-associated herpesvirus (KSHV), 477
Karyotype, 390, *391*
Keratin, 64
Ketonuria, 279
Kidneys, *160*, 160–173, *162*.
    See also Urinary system
    aging of, 327
    aldosterone and, 276

    disorders of, 171
    functions of, 160
    and pH regulation, 170, *170*
    regulatory functions of, 168–170, 172
    replacement of, 171
    structure of, 163–165
    water in, *168*, 168
Kingdom, 2, *3*
Kinocilium, *260*, 261
Klinefelter syndrome, 394, *394*, 395
Knee, 191, 192, *192*
Knee-jerk reflex, 246
Koplik spots, 439
Krause end bulbs, 247, *247*
KSHV (Kaposi's sacroma-associated herpesvirus), 477
Kuru, 439
Kwashiorkor, 527
Kyphosis, 188

Labia majora, 295, *295*, 320, *321*
Labia minora, 295, *295*, 320, *321*
Lacrimal bone, *186*
Lacteal, *121*
Lactic acid, 50
Lactose intolerance, 126
Lacunae, 56, *57*
Lamarck, Jean-Baptiste, 492
Lampbrush chromosomes, 377, *377*
Land, *524*, 524–525, *525*
Language
    brain in, 231
    Homo habilis and, 497
Lanugo, 319
Large intestine, *116*, 122–123, 432, *432*
Laryngitis, 152
Laryngopharynx, *143*
Larynx, *118*, *142*, *143*, 144, 187, *187*
LASIK (laser-assisted in situ keratomileusis) eye surgery, 243, 255
Latency, 436, *436*, 438, 457
Lateral epicondyle, *191*
Lateral malleolus, *191*
Lateral sulcus, *227*
Latissiumus dorsi, *200*, *201*
Laws of thermodynamics, 507
LDCs (less-developed countries), 522, 523, *523*, 537
LDL (low-density lipoprotein), 90, 130

Lead, pregnancy and, 322
Learning, limbic system and, 230–231
Left brain, in language and speech, 231
Left optic tract, 254
Left ventricular assist device (LVAD), 91
Leg
    bones of, 191
    muscles of, *201*
Lens, 250, *250*, 251, *251*
Leprosy, 535
Leptin, 282, 304
Less-developed countries (LDCs), 522, 523, *523*, 537
Lesser trochanter, *191*
Leukemia, 56, 475
    AIDS deaths and, 460
    treatment for, 482, 535
Leukocytes, *98*, *100*, 103.
    See also White blood cells
LH (luteinizing hormone), 293, 297, *297*
Life, origin of, 488–489
Life cycle, 346, *346*–347
Life span
    genetically increasing, 407
    male *vs.* female, 328
Ligaments, 56, 178
Limb buds, in embryonic development, 317, *317*
Limbic system, 230, *230*
    drug abuse and, 237
    olfactory bulbs and, 249
Limestone, 513
Limited resources, competition for, 492
Limulus amoebocyte lysate, 535
Lineage, 494
Lipase, 124, 126
Lipids, 24–25, 130, *130*
Lipopolysaccharides, in bacteria, 441
Liver, *116*, 122, 124, *124*
    aging of, 327
    alcohol metabolized by, 237
    in diabetes mellitus, 279
    disorders of, 125
    functions of, *125*
    glucose in, *278*
Livestock, 527
Lobule, *145*, 292
Local hormones, 268
Loci, of alleles, 352
Lockjaw, 210
Longitudinal fissure, 227

Long-term memory, 230–231
Long-term potentiation (LTP), 231
Lordosis, 188
Lou Gehrig's disease, 218
Low-carbohydrate diet, 131
Low-density lipoprotein (LDL), 90, 130
Low sperm count, 304
LTP (long-term potentiation), 231
Lucy (australopithecine), 496, 496
Lumen, 119, 119
Lung cancer, 154, 475, 477
Lungs, 80, 142, 143, 145, 148
  gas exchange in, 78, 78, 145, 145
Luteal phase, of ovarian cycle, 297
Luteinizing hormone (LH), 293, 297, 297
LVAD (left ventricular assist device), 91
Lyme disease, discovery of, 7, 7
Lymph, 92, 103, 109
Lymphatic capillaries, 109, 109
Lymphatic organs, 414–415, 415
Lymphatic system, 66, 66, 92, 92
Lymph nodes, 92, 92
  in immune system, 415, 415, 417
Lymph nodule, 121
Lymphocytes, 100, 103. See also B cell(s); T cell(s)
  in immunity, 414–415, 415, 418–423
  pesticides and, 421
  thymus and, 282
Lymphoma, 475, 482
Lysosome, 38, 39, 45, 45, 400

Macromolecules, 22, 22, 40, 488, 489
Macrophages, 416, 417, 417
Mad cow disease, 439
Magnesium, 134, 135
Magnetic resonance imaging (MRI), 481
Major histocompatibility complex (MHC), 422
Malaria, 424, 447, 447
Male condom, 301, 301, 302
Male pseudohermaphroditism, 320
Malleus, 256, 256–257

Maltase, 126
Mammography, 479, 479
Mandible, 185, 186, 187, 187
Manganese, 134, 135
Manubrium, 189
Marfan syndrome, 401
Marijuana abuse, 239
Masseter, 200
Mast cell, 56, 416, 417
Mastoditis, 186
Matrix, 47, 47, 57
Maturation, in virus replication, 436, 436
Mature mRNA, 373, 373
Maxilla, 185, 186, 187, 187
MDCs (more-developed countries), 522–523, 523, 537
MDMA (methylenedioxymethamphetamine), 239
Measles, 439, 439
Meat, 129
Mechanoreceptors, 244, 244
  for equilibrium, 260, 261
  for hearing, 257
Medecins sans Frontieres (MSF), 467
Medial epicondyle, 191
Medial malleolus, 191
Medications. See Drug(s) (prescription)
Medulla, renal, 163, 169
Medulla oblongata, 229
  and heartbeat, 83
  in homeostasis, 284
Megakaryoblasts, 100
Megakaryocytes, 100, 103
Meiosis, 340, 340–343
  in gametogenesis, 356, 356
  in life cycle, 346, 346
  in males, 346
  vs. mitosis, 344, 344, 345
  mutation during, 396
  nondisjunction in, 392, 392
  stages of, 341–342
Meiosis I, 340, 341–342, 342
Meiosis II, 340, 342, 343
Meissner corpuscles, 247, 247
Melacine, 483
Melanin, 64
Melanocytes, 64, 64
Melanocyte-stimulating hormone (MSH), 270
Melanoma, 64, 65, 479, 479, 483
Melatonin, 229, 281, 281, 282
Membrane
  amniotic, 325, 325
  basement, 62, 63
  basilar, 257, 257

extraembryonic, 311, 311
  mucous, 68
  otolithic, 260, 261
  peridontal, 117
  plasma (See Plasma membrane)
  postsynaptic, 222, 222
  presynaptic, 222, 222
  synovial, 68, 192
  tectorial, 257, 257
  tympanic, 256, 256–257
Membrane attack complex, 418, 418
Memory
  limbic system and, 230–231
  smell and, 249
Memory cells
  in active immunity, 424
  B cells, 419, 419
  T cells, 423, 423
Meninges, 68, 224, 225
Meningitis, 68
Menopause, 283, 300, 328
Menstruation
  prostaglandins in, 282
  in uterine cycle, 298
Mental retardation, Gart gene and, 393, 393
Mercury, 105
Merkel disks, 247, 247
Mesenteric artery, 86
Mesenteric vein, 87
Mesoderm, 315, 316, 317
Messenger RNA (mRNA), 370
  in gene expression, 377
  processing of, 373, 373
  steroid hormones and, 269
  transcription of, 373, 373
  in translation, 374, 374, 375
Metabolism, aging and, 328
Metacarpals, 185, 190, 190
Metaphase, 338, 339
Metaphase I, 341, 341, 342, 342
Metaphase II, 342, 343
Metastasis, 154, 473
Metatarsals, 185, 191, 191
Metcalfe, Dean D., 385
Methamphetamine abuse, 239
Methicillin-resistant staph aureus (MRSA), 442
Methylenedioxymethamphetamine (MDMA), 239
MHC (major histocompatibility complex), 422
Microbes, 432–435
Microflora, 432, 432
Microglia, 60, 60
Microsatellites, 481
Microscopes, electron, 37, 37
Microtubule, 39, 43, 43

Microturition, 161
Microvilli, 43, 63, 121, 248
Midbrain, 229
Middle ear, 152, 256, 256
Mifepristone (RU-486), 302
Milk, 126, 132
Miller, Stanley, 488
Mineralocorticoids, 275, 275, 276
Minerals
  in diet, 134–135
  as resource, 530
  and skeletal system, 185
Mitochondria, 38, 39, 47, 47, 204
  mutated, 399
  of sperm, 293, 310
Mitochondrial hypothesis of aging, 326
Mitosis, 334, 337, 337–339
  in life cycle, 346, 346
  vs. meiosis, 344, 344, 345
Mitotic inhibitors, in chemotherapy, 482
Mitotic (M) stage, 335
Molars, 117
Molecular clock, 494
Molecular formulas, 17
Molecules, 16–17
  diffusion of, 41, 41
  hydrophilic, 19
  hydrophobic, 19
  in life, 22
  organic, 22
  polar, 18
  in primitive earth, 488
Monoclonal antibodies, 425–426, 426, 483, 483
Monoculture, 526
Monocytes, 100, 103, 416, 417
Monohybrids, 354, 354
Monosaccharide, 22
Monosomy, 392
Montagut, Jacques, 305
More-developed countries (MDCs), 522–523, 523, 537
Morning-after pills, 302
Morphine, heroin and, 239
Morphogenesis, in development before birth, 311
Morula, in pre-embryonic development, 313, 313
Mosaic evolution, 496
Motion sickness, 261
Motor fibers, 232
Motor impulses, 229
Motor neurons, 218

Motor speech area. *See* Broca's area
Motor unit, 206
Mouth, *116, 117, 143*
MRI (magnetic resonance imaging), 481
mRNA. *See* Messenger RNA
MRSA (methicillin-resistant staph aureus), 442
MS (multiple sclerosis), 219, 428
MSF (Medecins sans Frontieres), 467
MSH (melanocyte-stimulating hormone), 270
M (mitotic) stage, 335
Mucosa, 119, *119*
Mucous, 68
    in cystic fibrosis, 400
    in the stomach, 120
Mucous membranes, 68
Müllerian ducts, 320, *321*
Multidrug resistance, 482
Multifactorial inheritance, *359,* 359–360, 406
Multiple allele inheritance, 361
Multiple sclerosis (MS), 219, 428
Multiregional continuity hypothesis, 499, *499*
Muscles, 198–213, *200*
    action of, 199, *199, 201, 202*–209, *209*
    cardiac, 59, *59,* 198, *198*
    chemistry of, 205
    ciliary, 251, *251*
    fibers, 202, *203,* 206
    functions of, 198
    glucose in, *278*
    insertion of, 199
    intercostal, *149*
    origin of, 199
    proprioceptors in, 246, *246*
    skeletal, 59, *59, 192*
    smooth, 59, *59,* 198, *198*
    spasms in, 210
    straining, 210
    tone of, 206
    twitching of, 206
    types of, 198, *198*
Muscle spindle, 246, *246*
Muscular dystrophy, 210, 402, *402*
Muscularis, 119, *119*
Muscular system, 67, *67,* 199–213
Muscular tissue, 56, 59, *59*
Mutagen, 476

Mutation
    in cancer cells, 413, 472, 474
    of chromosomes, 396–397
    in DNA, 369
Myalgia, 210
Myasthenia gravis, 210, 428
Mycobacterium tuberculosis, 464
Mycoses, 446
Myelin, 60, *60,* 219
Myelin sheath, 219, *219*
Myeloblasts, *100*
Myocardial infarction, 88
Myocardium, 80, *81*
Myofibrils, 202, *202, 203, 204*
Myofilaments, 202, *202*
Myoglobin, *202*
Myogram, 206
Myosin, 202, 205
Myosin filaments, 59, *203*
Myxedema, 273, *273*

NAD (nicotinamide adenine dinucleotide), 48
Nails, 65
N antigen (neuraminidase), 437, *437*
Nares, *143*
Nasal bone, *186, 187, 187*
Nasal cavity, *142, 143, 143*
Nash, Jack and Lisa, 305
Nasopharynx, 118, *118*
Natriuresis, 276
Natural family planning, *302*
Natural killer cells (NKs), 418
Natural selection, 492, *492*
NE. *See* Norepinephrine
Neanderthals, 500, *500*
Nearsightedness, 255, *255*
Neck muscles, *201*
Necrotizing fasciitis, 442, *442*
Negative feedback, *72,* 72–73, *73,* 266
Neisseria gonorrhoeae, 454
Nephrons, 163, *163, 164,* 164–165
    anatomy of, 164, *164*
    parts of, 165, *165*
Nerve(s)
    action of, in muscles, 205
    cochlear, 257, *257*
    cranial, 232, *232*
    intercostal, *149*
    optic, *250,* 251, 253, 254, *254*
    in peripheral nervous system, 232
    phrenic, *149*
    spinal, 232, *232*
    vagus, 232, *232*
Nerve deafness, 258
Nerve fibers, in peripheral nervous system, 232

Nerve growth factor, 282
Nerve impulse, 220
    in sensation, 245
    in spinal cord, 225
Nervous system, *218,* 218–239. *See also* Central nervous system; Peripheral nervous system
    drug abuse and, *237,* 237–239
    in embryonic development, 317
    vs. endocrine system, 266, *266*
    functions of, 60, 67, *67*
    and heartbeat, 83
    HIV infection and, 464
    and homeostasis, 70
    organization of, 218, *218*
    syphilis and, 456
Nervous tissue, 56, 60, *60*
    in nervous system, 218–223
    regeneration of, 61
Neural tube, in embryonic development, 317
Neuraminidase (N antigen), 437, *437*
Neuroendocrine system, 284
Neurofibrillary tangles, in Alzheimer disease, 236
Neuroglia, 60, *60,* 218, 219
Neuromuscular junction, 203, *203*
Neuron(s), 60, *60*
    in Alzheimer disease, 236
    in nervous system, 218
    types of, *219*
Neurotransmitter(s), *204,* 222, *222, 223*
    drugs and, 237, *237*
Neutron(s), 14, *14*
Neutrophils, *100, 103,* 416, 417
Niacin, *133*
Niche, 506
Nicotinamide adenine dinucleotide (NAD), 48
Nicotine abuse, 238
Nicotinic acid, *133*
Nitrates, in nitrogen cycle, 512
Nitrification, 512
Nitrite, in nitrogen cycle, 512
Nitrite-cured foods, 478
Nitrogen, in DNA. *See* Base(s)
Nitrogen cycle, 512, *512*
Nitrogen fixation, 512, *512*
Nitrosoureas, in chemotherapy, 482
NKs (natural killer cells), 418

Nociceptors. *See* Pain receptors
Nodes of Ranvier, 219, *219*
Noise, nerve deafness from, 258, *259*
Nondisjunction, 392, *392*
Non-Hodgkin's lymphoma, 475
Nonrenewable resources, 524, 528
Nonspecific immune defenses, 417–418
Norepinephrine (NE), 222, 223
    adrenal production of, 275, *275*
    in autonomic system, 235
Nose, 142, 143, 317, *317*
Nostril, *142*
Nuclear envelope, 39, 44, *44*
Nuclear pore, *39*
Nuclear power, 528
Nuclear radiation, cancer caused by, 476
Nucleic acids, 29–30, 436, *436. See also* DNA; RNA
Nucleoid, of bacteria, 441
Nucleolus, 38, *38, 39,* 44, *44*
Nucleosome, 336
Nucleotides, 29
    in DNA, 368
    in polymerase chain reaction, 381
    in RNA, 370
    translation of, 372
Nucleus, 38, *38, 39,* 44, *44*
    of cancer cells, 472
    of egg, *310*
    gene expression regulation in, 377
    of sperm, 310, *310*
    steroid hormones and, 269
Number, atomic, 14
Nursing, oxytocin in, 270
Nutrient cycling, microbes in, 432, *432*
Nutrition, 128–135, 359. *See also* Diet; Food

Obesity, 136
    cancer caused by, 478
    and cardiovascular disease, 90
Occipital bone, 186, *186*
Occipitalis, *201*
Occipital lobe, 227, *227,* 254
Occupational hazards, cancer and, 478

Oil
  bacteria for cleanup of, 383, *383*
  vs. coal, 528
  drilling for, 517
Oil glands, 417
Oils, 24, 130
Olfactory bulb, 249, *249*
Olfactory cells, 249, *249*
Oligodendrocytes, 60, *60*
Olive oil, 130
Olympics, 211
Omega-3 fatty acids, 130
Omnivores, 506
Oncogenes, 474, *474*
Oncology, 475
One-trait inheritance, *354*, 354–355, *355*
Oocyte, in ovarian cycle, *296*
Oogenesis
  in female reproductive system, 294
  meiosis in, 346, 347, *347*
Opportunistic infection, 464
Opposable thumb, 493
Opsin, 252, *252*
Optic chiasma, 254, *254*
Optic nerve, *250*, 251, 253, 254, *254*
Optic tract, 254, *254*
Oral cancer, 471, 477
Oral contraceptives, 301, *301*, *302*, 454
Oral thrush, 446, 464
Orbicularis oculi, *200*, 201
Orbicularis oris, *200*
Orca whales, 532
Organ, definition of, 2
Organelles, 38, 339
Organic chemicals, cancer caused by, 476–477
Organic molecules, 22
Organ of Corti.
  See Spiral organ
Organ rejection, 428
Organ systems, 2, *66*, 66–67, *67*
Organ transplantation, 428
Orgasm
  in females, 295
  in males, 291
Origin of life, 488–489, 501
Oropharynx, *143*
Orrorin tugenesis, 495
Oscilloscope, nerve impulse studied with, 220
Osmoreceptors, 244
Osmosis, 41, *41*
Osmotic pressure, 41
  and blood, 99
  in capillary exchange, 108

Ossicles, 256, *256*
Ossification, 180–181, *180*, 319
Osteoarthritis, 193
Osteoblasts, *179*, 180, 183
Osteoclasts, 180
Osteocytes, 178, *179*, 180
Osteoporosis, 134, 182, 184
  factors in, 327, 328
  hormone replacement therapy and, 283
Otitis media, 152, 258
Otolith(s), *260*, 261
Otolithic membrane, *260*, 261
Otosclerosis, 258
Outer ear, 256, *256*
Out-of-Africa hypothesis, 499, *499*, 500
Oval opening, 318, *318*
Oval window, 256, *256*
Ovarian cancer
  genetic testing for, 348
  hormone replacement therapy and, 283
  treatment for, 482
Ovarian cycle, *296*, 297, *299*
Ovaries
  in endocrine system, *266*, *267*, 280
  in female reproductive system, 294, *294*
  fetal development of, 320, *321*
  in menopause, 300
  removal of, 295
Overconsumption, 537
Overexertion, 207
Overexploitation, 531–532
Overpopulation, 537
Oviducts
  in female reproductive system, 294, *294*
  fetal development of, 320, *321*
Ovulation
  in female reproductive system, 294
  in ovarian cycle, *296*, 297
  in pre-embryonic development, *313*
Oxygen deficit, 208
Oxyhemoglobin, 100, *100*, 150
Oxytocin, 270, *271*, 284, 324
Ozone depletion, 531
Ozone shield, 530

p53, 335, 474, 483
Pacemakers, 82
Pacinian corpuscles, 247, *247*
Paget's disease, 182
Pain receptors, 244, 247

Palate, hard, 116, *117*, *118*, *143*
Palate, soft, 116, *117*, *118*, *143*
Palatine bone, *186*
Pancreas, *116*, *122*, *124*
  and diabetes, 69
  in diabetes mellitus, 279
  in endocrine system, *266*, *267*, 278–279
Pancreatic amylase, 124, 126
Pancreatic duct, *116*, *124*
Pancreatic islets, 278, 279
Pandemic, 435, 437
Pantothenic acid, *133*
Pap test, 294, 479
Parasites, 431–449
Parasympathetic division, 235, *235*
Parasympathetic preganglionic fibers, 234
Parathyroid glands, *266*, *267*, 274
Parathyroid hormone (PTH), 182, 266, 274
Parent cells, 337, 340
Parietal bone, 186, *186*
Parietal lobe, 227, *227*
Parkinson disease, 236
Parturition, 324, 325, *325*
Passive immunity, 424, 425, *425*
Passive smoking, cancer caused by, 477, 484
Patagonian hare, 490, *490*
Patella, *185*, 191, *191*, *192*
Patellar ligament, *192*
Pathogens, 431–449. *See also* Bacteria; Virus(es)
  inflammation from, *416*, 417
  study of, 434–435
  transmission of, 434–435
  in vaccines, 424
  virulence factors of, 434
PCBs (polychlorinated biphenyls), 303
PCR (polymerase chain reaction), 381, *381*, 382, *382*
PCT (proximal convoluted tubule), 165, *165*
Pectoral girdles, 190
Pectoralis major, *200*, 201
Pedigrees, *398*, 398–399, *399*
Pelvic girdle, 191, *191*
Pelvic inflammatory disease (PID)
  from chlamydia, 454
  from gonorrhea, 454–455
  infertility from, 304
Pelvis, renal, 163, *163*

Penetration, in virus replication, 436, *436*
Penicillin, 445
Penis, *162*
  fetal development of, *321*
  in orgasm, 291
  in reproductive system, 290, *290*
Pentose, 22, 368, *368*
Pepsin, 120, 126
Peptidases, 126
Peptide bond, 26
Peptide hormones, *268*, 269, 324, *324*
Peptidoglycan, in bacteria, 441, *441*
Perception, 245, *245*
Pericardium, 80, *80*
Periodontal membrane, *117*
Periosteum, 179, *179*
Peripheral nervous system, 218, *218*, 232–235
  myelin sheaths in, 219
  neurotransmitters in, 222
  nicotine and, 238
Peristalsis, 118
  in heroin dependence, 237
  in urinary system, 161
Peritonitis, 68, 122
Peritubular capillary network, 164, *164*, *165*
Permeability, selective, 40, *40*
Peroneus longus, *200*, 201
Peroxisome, *39*
Pest control, 421, 535
Pesticides, 303, 421, 526, 530
PET (positron emission tomography), *15*
Peyer's patches, in immune system, 415
p16 gene, 481
pH, 20, *20*
  of blood, 21
  regulation of, by kidneys, 160, 170
  of stomach, 120
Phagocytosis, 43, 103
Phalanges, *185*, 190, *190*, 191, *191*
Pharynx, *116*, *118*, *142*, *143*
  and digestion, 117–118
  and respiration, 143
Phenotype, 352
  continuous variation of, 359
  human, 501
Phenotypic ratio, 354
Phenylalanine
  in phenylketonuria, 400
  production of, 383

Phenylketonuria (PKU), 400, 403
Pheromones, 268
Phlebitis, 89
Phosphate, in DNA, 368, *368*
Phospholipids, 25, *25*, 40, *40*
Phosphoric acid, in DNA. *See* Phosphate, in DNA
Phosphorus, 134, *135*
Phosphorus cycle, 511, *511*
Photoreceptors, 244, *244*
   in eye, 252, *252*
   in retina, 251
Photosynthesis
   bioengineering, 384
   in biosphere, 506
   in carbon cycle, 513
Photovoltaic cell, 529
Phrenic nerve, *149*
Phthalate esters, as EDCs, 303
Phthirus pubis, 459, *459*
Physical drug dependence, 237
PID. *See* Pelvic inflammatory disease
Pig, xenotransplantation with, 428
Pigment, in photoreceptors, 252
Pineal gland, 229, *266*, *267*, 282
Pinna, 256, *256*
Pinocytosis, 43
Pitch, in hearing, 257
Pituitary dwarfism, 272
Pituitary gland
   in endocrine system, *266*, *267*, 270–272
   gonads and, 280
PKU (phenylketonuria), 400, 403
Placenta, 318, *318*
   in birth, 325, *325*
   formation of, 295, 300, 311, 318
Plants
   transgenic, 384
   transgenic bacteria used for, 383
Plaque, 88, *90*, 130, 236
Plasma, *98*, 99. *See also* Blood
   proteins, 99
   solutes in, *99*
Plasma cells, from B cells, 418–419, *419*
Plasma membrane, 38, *38*, *39*, *40*, 40–43
   of egg, 310, *310*
   hormone receptors in, *268*
   peptide hormone receptors in, 269
   of sensory receptors, 245

Plasmids, 380
Plastics, as EDCs, 303
Platelet-derived growth factor, 282
Platelets, *98*, 103
Pleura, 145, 148
PMS (premenstrual syndrome), 298
Pneumococcus, capsule of, 434
Pneumocystis jiroveci, 464
Pneumonectomy, 154
Pneumonia, 152
   AIDS deaths from, 464
   streptococci in, 442
Podocyte, *168*
Polar body, 347, *347*, 405
Pollination, 535
Pollinators, 303, 477
Pollution, 524–530
   and acid rain, 21
   in air, 147
   biodiversity loss from, 531
   definition of, 5, 524
Polychlorinated biphenyls (PCBs), 303
Polymerase chain reaction (PCR), 381, *381*, 382, *382*
Polynucleotides, in DNA, 368
Polypeptide, 26, 377
Polypeptide chains, in antibodies, 420
Polypeptide synthesis, 374, *375*
Polyps, colon, 123, 480
Polyribosome, *39*, 374, *375*
Polysaccharides, 23
Polyspermy, 310
Poly-X females, 395
Pons, 229
Popliteal artery, *84*
Population, 4, 506
   growth of, human, *522*, 522–523
Positive feedback, 73, 270
Positron emission tomography (PET), *15*
Posterior compartment, *250*, 251
Posterior pituitary, 270, *271*
Posterior tibial artery, *84*
Postsynaptic membrane, 222, *222*
Posttranscriptional control, 377
Posttranslational control, 377
Potassium, 134, *135*
   in axion action potential, 220
   in axion resting potential, 220
Potassium gates, 220

p53 protein, in cell cycle, 335, 474, 483
Pre-embryonic development, *312*, 313, *313*
Prefrontal area, *227*, 228, 230–231
Pregnancy, 300, 324–325
   bacterial vaginosis in, 459
   and blood types, 107
   chlamydia in, 454
   congenital defects and, 322–323
   detecting, 426
   drug abuse during, 238–239, *239*
   health habits during, 329
   herpes in, 457
   HIV in, 323
   HIV treatment in, 466
   reproductive organs in, 295
   sexually transmitted diseases in, 323
   trichomoniasis in, 459
Premature birth, 319
Premenstrual syndrome (PMS), 298
Premolars, *117*
Premotor area, *227*, 228
Preparatory reaction, 49, *49*
Pressoreceptors, 244
Pressure, blood, *84*, 84–85, *85*
Pressure, osmotic, 41
Presynaptic membrane, 222, *222*
Preven, 302
Primary auditory area, *227*, 227, 231, *231*
Primary follicle, *296*, 297
Primary germ layers, *316*, 317
Primary lymphatic organs, 414, *415*
Primary motor area, *227*, 227, 228, 231, *231*
Primary mRNA, 373, *373*
Primary olfactory area, 227
Primary oocyte, 347, *347*
Primary productivity, 516, *516*
Primary somatosensory area, *227*, 227, 228
Primary spermatocytes, 346, *347*
Primary succession, 514
Primary taste areas, 227, *227*
Primary visual area, 227, *227*
Primates
   characteristics of, 493
   evolutionary tree of, 494, *494*
   humans as, *493*, 493–495
Primers, in polymerase chain reaction, 381

Prions, 439
PRL (prolactin), 270, *271*
Probability, in genetics, 355
Processing, in aging, 327
Processing centers, 228
Producers, 5, 506, *506*
Products, 48, *48*
Progesterone
   in embryonic development, 318
   in emergency contraception, 302
   in endocrine system, 280
   in oral contraceptives, 301
   in ovarian cycle, 297, *297*
   in pregnancy, 300, 324, *324*
   in reproductive system, 300
   in uterine cycle, 298
Progression, in carcinogenesis, 473, *473*
Prokaryotic cells, 441, 489
Prolactin (PRL), 270, *271*
Proliferative phase, of uterine cycle, 298, *299*
Promotion, in carcinogenesis, 473, *473*
Pronation, 193
Prophase, 338, *338*
Prophase I, 341, 342, *342*
Prophase II, 342, *343*
Proprioceptors, 244, 246
Prosecution, for pregnancy behaviors, 329
Prosimians, 493, 494, *494*
Prostaglandins, 268, 282, 298, 302
Prostate, 162, *162*, 290, *290*
Prostate cancer, 475
Prostate-specific antigen (PSA) test, 481
Prostatitis, 162, *162*
Protease, 465
Protease inhibitors, 466
Protein(s), 26, *27*. *See also* Enzyme(s)
   as allergens, 385
   carrier, 42, *42*
   complementary, *129*
   cross-linking, aging and, 326–327
   in diet and nutrition, 129, 527
   function of, 371
   metabolism of, 275
   in primitive evolution, 488, 489
   self, 418, 422
   structure of, 371, *371*
   study of, 379
   testing for, 403

Proteinaceous infectious particles, 439
Protein-coding sequences, 379
Protein-first hypothesis, 488, 489
Protein synthesis
  RNA in, 370
  steroid hormones in, 269
  in translation, 372
Proteomics, 379, 406
Prothrombin, 104, *104*
Prothrombin activator, 104, *104*
Protocell, 488
Protons, 14, *14*
Proto-oncogenes, 474, *474*, 481
Protoplasts, 384
Protozoans, diseases caused by, 447–448, *448*
Proximal convoluted tubule (PCT), 165, *165*
PSA (prostate-specific antigen) test, 481
Pseudostratification, 144
Psychological drug dependence, 237
PTH (parathyroid hormone), 182, 266, 274
Puberty, 280
  endocrine system in, 265
  female, 300
  melatonin in, 282
  testosterone in, 280
  and voice, 144
Pubic lice, 459, *459*
Pubic symphysis, 191
Pubis, *185*
Pulmonary arteries, 80, 81, 86, 145, 151
Pulmonary arteriole, *142, 145*
Pulmonary circuit, 78, *78*, 86, *86*
Pulmonary embolisms, 283
Pulmonary tuberculosis, 152, *153*, 445
Pulmonary valves, in pregnancy, 324
Pulmonary veins, 80, 81, 86, *145, 151*
Pulmonary venule, *142, 145*
Pulse, 84, *84*
Punnett square, 354, *354*, 355
Pupil, 250, *250*
Purine, mental retardation and, 393
Purine bases, 368
Purkinje fibers, 82, *83*
Pus, 417
P wave, 83, *83*

Pyelonephritis, 171
Pyramids, renal, 163, *163*
Pyrimidine bases, 368
Pyruvic acid, 50

Quadriceps femoris, 192, *200, 201*
Quadriceps tendon, *192*
Quality of life, 283, 538
Quinine, 445

Radial artery, *84*
Radiation, 15
  cancer caused by, 476, 478
  in cancer treatment, 481
Radioactive scan, 481
Radius, *185*, 190, *190*
Radon gas, cancer caused by, 476
Rapid plasma reagin (RPR), 456
RAS (reticular activating system), 229, *229*, 245
Ras oncogene, 474, 481
RB gene, 476
RB (retinoblastoma) protein, 474
Reactants, 48, *48*
Reassortment, of viruses, 437, *437*
Receptive field, of ganglion cells, 253
Recessive allele, 352, *352*
  in autosomal disorders, *398*, 398–399, *400*, 400–401, *401*
  in sex-linked disorders, 399, *399*, 402
Recombinant DNA technology, 380–381
Rectum, 122, *123*, 162
Rectus abdominis, 200, *200, 201*
Red blood cells, *100*, 100–101, *101*
Red bone marrow, 92, *92*, 212
  in immune system, 414, *415*
  transplantation of, 482
Red pulp, 414
Reduced hemoglobin, 150
Reeve, Christopher, 61
Referred pain, 247
Reflex(es), 233, *233*, 284, 317
Reflex arcs, 225, 233, *233*
Refractory period
  action potential and, 220
  in female orgasm, 295
  in male orgasm, 291
Release, in virus replication, 436, *436*
Renal artery, *86, 160, 163*

Renal cortex, 163, *163, 169*
Renal medulla, 163
Renal pelvis, 163, *163*
Renal pyramids, 163, *163*
Renal vein, *163*
Renewable resources, 524, 528–529, *529*
Renin, 168, 276, *276*
Replacement reproduction, 523
Replication
  of cancer cells, 472
  of DNA, 30
  of viruses, 436, *436*
Reproduction, 2, 341
Reproductive cloning, 314, *314*
Reproductive control, *301*, 301–304, *302*
Reproductive system, 67, *67*, 289–304
  aging of, 328
  control of, 284
  female, *294*, 294–295, *295, 296*
  and urinary system, 295
  fetal development of, 320
  male, *290*, 290–293, *291, 292, 293*
Reservoir, 510
Residual volume, 146
Resources
  energy, 528–529, *529*
  food, 526–527
  human use of, *524*, 524–530
  land, *524*, 524–525, *525*
  minerals, 530
  water, *525*, 525–526
Respiration, 146–149, *151*
  and air pollution, 147
  and blood flow, 85
  cellular (See Cellular respiration)
  control of, 149
  external, 150, *151*
  and health, 152–154
  internal, 150, *151*
  in pregnancy, 324
Respiratory center, *149*, 170
Respiratory system, *66, 67*, *142*, 142–155
  action of, 146–149
  aging of, 327
  disorders of, 152–154
  gas exchange in, 150, *151*
  immune defenses in, 417
  lower, 144–145
  and smoking, 154–155
  upper, 142–144

Respiratory tract, 142–145, 152–153
Respiratory volume, 146, *146*
Resting potential, 220, *221*
Restriction enzyme, 380–381
RET gene, 476, 481
Reticular activating system (RAS), 229, *229*, 245
Reticular fiber, *56*
Reticular formation, 229, *229*
Retina, 251, 253, *253*
Retinal, 252, *252*
Retinoblastoma protein (RB), 474
Retroviruses, 408, *408*, 465
  cancer caused by, 477
  in cancer treatment, 483
Reverse transcriptase, 465, 466
Reverse transcription, in HIV life cycle, 465, *465*
Rh, 107. *See also* Blood
Rh antibodies, in pregnancy, 323
Rheumatic fever, 442
Rheumatoid arthritis, 428
Rhinoviruses, 439
Rhodopsin, 252, *252*
Rib cage, 148, *148*, 189, *189*
Riboflavin, *133*
Ribosomal RNA (rRNA), 44, 370
Ribosome, *38, 39*, 44, *44*, 374
Ribozyme, 373
Ribs, *185*, 189, *189*
Rickets, 132, *132*, 182, *182*
Right brain, in language and speech, 231
Right optic tract, 254
Ringworm, 446
RNA (ribonucleic acid)
  chemistry of, *29*, 29–30
  vs. DNA, *370*
  function of, 370
  of HIV, 465
  messenger (mRNA), 370
    in gene expression, 377
    processing of, 373, *373*
    steroid hormones and, 269
    transcription of, 373, *373*
    in translation, 374, *374, 375*
  in primitive evolution, 488
  ribosomal (rRNA), 44, 370
  structure of, 370, *370*
  transfer (tRNA), 370, 374, *374, 375*
  viral, 436
RNA-first hypothesis, 488, 489
RNA polymerase, 373, *373*

Robust australo-pithecines, 496
Rod cells, 251, 252, *252*, 253, *253*, 493
Root canal, *117*
Root hair plexus, 247, *247*
Rotation, 193, *193*
Rotational equilibrium, *260*, 261
Rotator cuff, 190
Round window, 256, *256*
Roundworm, 449
RPR (rapid plasma reagin), 456
rRNA (ribosomal RNA), 44, 370
RU-486 (mifepristone), 302
Rubella, in pregnancy, 322
Rubeola virus, 439, *439*
Ruffini endings, 247, *247*

Saccule, *260*, 261
Sacrum, *185*
SAD (seasonal affective disorder), 281
Sahelanthropus tchaensis, 495
Salinization, 526
Saliva, 116
Salivary amylase, 116, 126
Salivary glands, 116
Salmonella, 444, 449
Salt
 in bile, 125
 in blood, 99
 in bone, 57
 in kidneys, *169*
 vs. water, in blood, 160, 270, 275
Salt-cured foods, 478
Saltwater intrusion, 526
SA node, 82, 83, *83*
Saphenous veins, great, 87
Sarcolemma, 202, *202*, *203*, *204*
Sarcoma, 56, 475
Sarcomeres, 202, *203*
Sarcoplasm, *202*, *203*
Sarcoplasmic reticulum, 202, *202*, *203*
SARS (severe acute respiratory syndrome), 431, 440
Sartorius, *200*, *201*
Satiety, 282
Scanning electron microscope (SEM), *37*, *37*
Scapula, *185*, 190, *190*
Scarlet fever, 442
Scavengers, 506, 507
Schistosomiasis, 449

Schwann cells, 219, *219*
SCID (severe combined immunodeficiency), 408, 428
Science, 6–9
Scientific method, 6, 6–9
Scientific theories, 501
Sclera, 250, *250*
SCN (suprachiasmatic nucleus), 281
Scoliosis, 188
Scrapie, 439
Scrotum
 fetal development of, 320, *321*
 in reproductive system, 290, *290*
Seasonal affective disorder (SAD), 281
Seasonal changes, melatonin and, 281
Secondary follicle, *296*, 297
Secondary lymphatic organs, 414–415, *415*
Secondary oocyte, 347, *347*. *See also* Egg
Secondary spermatocytes, 346, *347*
Secondary succession, 514
Second division, in meiosis, 342, *342*
Second messenger, *268*, 269
Secretase enzyme, beta amyloid plaques and, 236
Secretin, 122, *122*
Secretory phase, of uterine cycle, 298, *299*
Selective permeability, 40, *40*
Selenium, *135*
Self proteins, 418, 422
SEM (scanning electron microscope), *37*, *37*
Semantic memory, 230
Semen
 HIV transmission by, 466
 in reproductive system, 290
Semiarid lands, 524–525
Semicircular canals, 256, *256*, *260*, 261
Semiconservative replication, 369
Semilunar valves, 80
Seminal vesicles, 290, *290*
Seminiferous tubule, *292*, 292–293
Sensations, 244–245, *245*

Senses, 243–261
 aging of, 328
 in embryonic development, 317, *317*
 equilibrium, 261
 hearing, *256*, 256–257, *257*
 smell, 249, *249*
 taste, 248, *248*
 vision, 250, 250–255
Sensory adaptation, 245
Sensory association areas, 227, 228, 230–231
Sensory fibers, 232
Sensory neurons, 218
Sensory receptors, 244–245
 in neuron structure, 218
 in sensation, 245
 in skin, 65
Sensory speech area. *See* Wernicke's area
Septum, 80
Serosa, 119, *119*
Serum, 104, *104*
Serum sickness, 425
Severe acute respiratory syndrome (SARS), 431, 440
Severe combined immunodeficiency (SCID), 408, 428
Sewage, 530
Sex chromosomes, 362, 392, 394–395, *395*
Sex drive, cocaine and, 238
Sex-linked disorders, 399, *399*
Sex-linked dominant disorders, 399
Sex-linked inheritance, *362*, 362–363
Sex-linked recessive disorders, 399, *399*, 402, *402*
Sex organs, fetal development of, 320, *321*
Sexually transmitted diseases (STDs). *See also* AIDS
 bacterial, 454–456
 definition of, 453
 pregnancy and, 323, 463
 prevention of, 453
 and urinary tract infections, 162
 viral, 457–458
Shingles, 438, *438*
Short-term memory, 230
Shoulder, 190, *190*
Sickle-cell disease, 101, 400, *401*

Sildenafil (Viagra), 291
Simple goiter, 273, *273*
Sinus, *143*
Sinusitis, 152
Sinusoid, *124*
Sister chromatids, 335, 337
Skeletal system, 67, *67*, 178–193, *185*. *See also* Bone(s)
 functions of, 185
Skeleton, *185*, 185–193
 appendicular, 190–191
 axial, 186–189
 axial *vs.* appendicular, 185
Skill memory, 230
Skin, *64*, 64–65, *65*
 accessory organs of, 65
 aging of, 327
 cancers of, 56
 cutaneous receptors in, 246–247
 and vitamin D, 132
Skin cancer, 56, 64, 65, 476
Skin color, multifactorial inheritance of, 359
Skull, *186*, 186–187
SLE (systemic lupus erythematosus), 428
Sleep, melatonin and, 281, 282
Small intestine, *116*, 121, *121*
Smell, 249, *249*
Smog, 147
Smoked foods, 478
Smokeless tobacco, 471, 484
Smoking, 90, 144, 155. *See also* Passive smoking
 bans on, 155
 cancer caused by, 477, *477*, 478, 484
 and lung cancer, 154
 in pregnancy, 322, *322*
Social responsibility, and science, 9
Society, sustainable, *537*, 537–538
Sodium, 134–135, *135*, 276, *276*
 in axion action potential, 220
 in axion resting potential, 220
Sodium gates, 220
Sodium-potassium pump, 220
Soil erosion, 526, 533
Solar energy
 in ecosystem, 507, *507*
 electricity from, 529
 in sustainable society, 537
Somatic cells, division of, 334

Somatic system, 233
Somatosensory association area, *227*, 228
Soy, 129
Spasms, muscle, 210
Specialization, of cells, 377
Species, 2
  extinction of, 4
  human, 501
Specific immune defenses, 418–423
Speech
  brain in, 231
  in *Homo habilis*, 497
Sperm
  anatomy of, *292*, *293*, 310
  infertility issues with, 304
  in male orgasm, 291
  production of, 292
  in reproductive system, 290
  sorting, 304, 363
Spermatids, 292, 346, *347*
Spermatogenesis, 292, *292*, 346, *347*
Spermicide, 301, *301*, *302*
Sphenoid bone, 186, *186*, 187
Sphincters, 118
Sphygmomanometer, 84, *84*
Spikes, viral, 436, *436*
Spina bifida, 322, 404
Spinal cord, 224–225, *225*, 233, *233*
Spinal ganglia, herpes and, 438
Spinal nerves, 232, *232*
Spindle (mitotic), 337, *337*, 339
Spindle fibers, 337, *337*
Spine. *See* Vertebral column
Spinous process, 189, *189*
Spiral organ, 257, *257*
Spirometer, 146, *146*
Spleen, 92, *92*, 414, *415*
Splicing, of mRNA, 373, *373*
Sporadic occurrences, of infectious disease, 435
Squamous epithelium, 62, *63*
SRY gene, 320, 394
S stage, *334*, 334–335
Stapes, *256*, 256–257
Staph infections, 442
Starch, 23, *23*
StarLink, 385
STDs. *See* Sexually transmitted diseases
Stem cells, 51, *56*
  and blood, *100*
  in cloning, 314, *314*
  in gene therapy, 408, *408*
  mitosis of, 346
  and nerve regeneration, 61

transplantation of, 482
transplant of, 305
Stereoscopic vision, 493
Sterility, from chlamydia, 323
Sternocleidomastoid, 200, *200*, *201*
Sternum, *185*, 189, *189*
Steroid hormones, 269, *269*
Steroids, 25, *25*, 211
Stimulatory growth factors, 472
Stimulus, 244
Stomach, *116*, 120, *120*, *122*
Strain, 210
Strep infections, 442, *442*
Stress
  adrenal glands and, 275, *275*
  in herpes replication, 438
Stretch marks, 324
Striae gravidarum, 324
Strip mining, 530
Stroke, 88
Styloid process, *186*
Subclavian artery, *87*
Subclavian vein, *87*
Subcutaneous layer, of skin, 65
Submucosa, 119, *119*
Subsidence, 526
Substrate, 48, *48*
Sugar, 128
  in DNA, 368, *368*
  reducing intake of, *129*
  in RNA, 370
Sulci (sulcus), 227, *227*
Sulfur, 134, *135*
Sun, cancer caused by, 478
Superior vena cava, *80*, *81*, 86, *86*, *87*
Supination, 193
Supplements, pregnancy and, 322
Suprachiasmatic nucleus (SCN), 281
Surface antigens, 440
Surface tension, and lungs, 145
Surfactant, 145
Surgery, for cancer, 481
Surrogate mothers, 304
Survival mechanisms, of pathogens, 434
Sustainable society, *537*, 537–538
Sutures (anatomical), 192
Sweat glands, *64*, 65, 172
Swine flu, 437
Sympathetic division, 235, *235*

Sympathetic preganglionic fibers, 234
Synapse, 222, 222–223
Synapsis, 340, 341, *341*
Synaptic cleft, *204*, 222, *222*
Synaptic integration, 223, *223*
Syndrome, 390, *390*
Synovial joints, 192–193
Synovial membrane, 68, 192
Synthetic organic chemicals, 530, 531
Syphilis, 456, *456*
Systemic circuit, 86–87, *87*
Systemic disease, invasive factors and, 434
Systemic lupus erythematosus (SLE), 428
Systole, 82, *82*
Systolic pressure, 84, *84*, 85

TAH (total artificial heart), 91, *91*
Talus, *191*
Target cells, for hormones, 268, *268*
Tarsals, *185*, 191, *191*
Taste, 248, *248*
Taste buds, 248, *248*
Tau protein, in Alzheimer disease, 236
Taxol, 482
Tay-Sachs disease, 400, *400*, 403, 404
T cell(s) (T lymphocytes). *See also* Helper T cells
  in inflammatory reaction, 417
  in specific immune defense, 418, 422–423, *423*
  in thymus gland, 282, 414
  types of, 423
T-cell receptor (TCR), 422, *422*
Tear glands, 143
Technology, definition, 9
Tectorial membrane, 257, *257*
Teeth, 117, *117*
  aging of, 327
  anatomy of, 117, *117*
  early hominid, 495
Teleology, 492
Telomerase, 472, 481
Telomeres, 472
Telophase, 339, *339*
Telophase I, 342, *342*
Telophase II, 342, *343*
TEM (transmission electron microscope), 37, *37*
Temperature, body, 73, *73*, 212
  sperm and, 292, 304

Temperature receptors, 247, *247*
Template, in DNA replication, 369
Temporal artery, *84*
Temporal bone, *186*, *187*
Temporal lobe, 227, *227*
Tendinitis, 210
Tendons, 56, 178, *199*
Teratogens, pregnancy and, 322
Termination, in polypeptide synthesis, 374, *375*
Terrestrial ecosystems, 514, *515*
Testes
  in endocrine system, *266*, *267*, 280
  fetal development of, 319, 320, *321*
  hormonal control of, 293, *293*
  infertility issues with, 304
  in reproductive system, 290, *290*, *292*, 292–293
Testicle self-examination, 480, *480*
Testicular cancer, treatment for, 482
Testosterone, 25
  in endocrine system, 280
  in male fetal development, 320
  in male reproductive system, 293
Tetanus, 206
Tetany, 274
Tetracyclines, 445
Thalamus, 229, 254
Thalidomide, 323
THC (tetrahydrocannabinol), 239
Theory, scientific, 6, 501
Therapeutic cloning, 314, *314*
Thermal inversion, 147
Thermodynamics, laws of, 507
Thermoreceptors, 244
Thiamine, *133*
Thoracic duct, *92*
Threshold, in action potential, 220
Thrombocytes, *100*, 103
Thrombocytopenia, 104
Thromboembolism, 88
Thrombus, 88
Thrush, 446, 464
Thumb, 493
Thymine, 30
Thymine (T), in DNA, 368

Thymosins, 282, 414
Thymus gland, *92*
    in endocrine system, *266, 267*, 282
    in immune system, 414, *415*
Thyroid cancer, 476
Thyroid gland, *15*
    in endocrine system, *266, 267*, 273–274
Thyroid hormones, steroid hormones and, 269
Thyroid-stimulating hormone (TSH), 270, *271*
Thyroxine (T$_4$), 273
Tibia, *185, 191, 192*
Tibial artery, posterior, *84*
Tibialis anterior, *200, 201*
Tibial tuberosity, *191*
Tidal volume, 146
Tineas, 446
Tissue(s), 2, 56–63
    adipose, 56, *56, 57, 192*
        glucose in, *278*
        leptin and, 282
    and cancer, 56
    connective, *56*, 56–58, *58, 178, 192*
    definition of, 56
    endocrine, 278
    epithelial, 56, 62, *62, 63*
    exchange in, 78, *78*
    exocrine, 278
    muscular, 56, 59, *59*
    nervous, 56, 60, *60*
        in nervous system, 218–223
        regeneration of, 61
    rejection of, 428
Tissue fluid, 70
    and capillary exchange, 108
    and lymphatic system, 92
T lymphocytes. *See* T cell(s)
Tobacco smoke. *See* Smoking
Tomatoes, genetically modified, 31
Tongue, *116, 117, 143*
Tonicity, 41, *41*
Tonsillitis, 116, 152
Tonsils, *92*, 116, *117, 118, 143, 143*
    in immune system, 415
Tools, of *Homo habilis*, 497
Total artificial heart (TAH), 91, *91*
Touch, sensory receptors for, 246–247
Toxins
    environmental, 303
    of pathogens, 434
Toxoplasmosis, 447

Toxoplasmic encephalitis, AIDS deaths from, 464
t-PA, 89
Tracer, 15
Trachea, *15, 118, 142, 143*, 144–145
    blockage of, 144–145
Tracts, in central nervous system, 224
Trade-related aspects of intellectual property rights (TRIPS), 467
Transcription, 372, *372, 373, 373*
Transcription, reverse, in HIV life cycle, 465, *465*
Transcription activators, 377
Transcriptional control, 377
Transfer rate, 511
Transfer RNA (tRNA), 370, 374, *374, 375*
Transfusions, blood, 102
Transgenic animals, 384, *384*
Transgenic bacteria, 383
Transgenic organisms, 380, 383–384
Transgenic plants, 384, 527
Translation, 372, *372*, 374, *374, 375*
Translational control, 377
Translocation, 397, *397*
Transmission, of pathogens, 434
Transmission electron microscope (TEM), 37, *37*
Transport, active, *42*, 42–43
Transport, facilitated, 42, *42*
Transport, in aging, 327
Transverse process, 189, *189*
Trapezius, *200, 201*
Trawling, 532
Treponema pallidum, 456
Triceps brachii, *199, 201*
Trichinosis, 449
Trichomonas vaginalis, 459, *459*
Trichomoniasis, 459, *459*
Triiodothyronine (T$_3$), 273
Triplet code, 372, *372*, 376
TRIPS (trade-related aspects of intellectual property rights), 467
Trisomy, 392
tRNA (transfer RNA), 370, 374, *374, 375*
Trochanter, *191*
Trochlea, *190*
Trophic levels, 509

Trophoblast
    in embryonic development, 315, *315*
    in pre-embryonic development, 313, *313*
Tropical rain forest, 525, *525*
Tropomyosin, 205
Troponin, 205
Trypanosoma brucei, 448, *448*
Trypsin, 124, 126
TSH (thyroid-stimulating hormone), 270, *271*
T tubule, 202, *202, 203*
Tubal ligation, *302*
Tube, auditory, 152
Tubercle, 443, *443*
Tubercle, greater, *190*
Tuberculin skin test, 426, 443
Tuberculosis, 443, *443*
    AIDS deaths from, 464
    pulmonary, 152, *153*
Tubular reabsorption, *166*, 167
Tubular secretion, *166*, 167
Tumor, cancerous, 472, *473*
Tumor angiogenesis factor, 282
Tumor marker tests, 481
Tumor-suppressor genes, 474, *474*, 481
Turner syndrome, 392, 394, *394*
T wave, 83, *83*
Twins, 313
Two-trait inheritance, 356, 356–358, *357, 358*
Tympanic canal, 257, *257*
Tympanic membrane, *256*, 256–257
Type 1 diabetes, 279
Type 2 diabetes, 279

Ulcer, 120, *120*
Ulna, *185*, 190, *190, 199*
Ultrasound, 404, *404*, 481
Ultraviolet radiation
    cancer caused by, 476
    dark skin and, 501
Umbilical arteries, 318, *318*
Umbilical cord
    adult stem cells from, 305
    in birth, 325
    in embryonic development, 315, 317, 318, *318*
Umbilical vein, 318, *318*
Uracil (U), 30, 370
Urea, 124, 160
Uremia, 171

Ureters, *160*, 161, *162*, 163
Urethra, *160*, 161, *161, 162*
    in male orgasm, 291
    in reproductive system, 290, *290*
Urethritis, 171
Urinary system, 66, 67, *160*, 160–173, *172. See also* Kidneys
    functions of, 160
    and homeostasis, 171
    and reproductive system, in females, 295
Urinary tract, in females *vs.* males, *162*
Urinary tract infections, 162
Urination, 161, *166*
Urine
    in diabetes mellitus, 279
    formation of, 167
Urogenital groove, 320, *321*
Uterine cycle, 295, 298, *299*
    in menopause, 300
    vs. ovarian cycle, *299*
Uterine tubes. *See* Oviducts
Uterus, *162*
    in female reproductive system, 294, *294*
    fetal development of, 320, *321*
    in pregnancy, 295, 324
    removal of, 295
Utricle, *260*, 261
Uvula, 117, *117, 118, 143*

Vaccines, 424
    for cancer, 483
    contraceptive, 302
    DNA, 466
    for HCG, 302
    for hepatitis B, 458
    for HIV, 466
    for HPV, 458
Vacuole, *38, 39*
Vagina, *162*
    in female reproductive system, 295
    fetal development of, 320, *321*
    infections of, 459, *459*
Vaginitis, 459, *459*
Vagus nerve, 232, *232*
Valacyclovir, 457
Valtrex (valacyclovir), 457
Valves
    atrioventricular, 80, *81*
    semilunar, 80, *81*
Vancomycin-resistant enterococci (VRE), 449
Variable, 8

Variation, in natural selection, 492
Varicella-zoster virus, 438, 438
Varicose veins, 88
Vas deferens
  in male orgasm, 291
  in reproductive system, 290, 290
Vasectomy, 302
Vector-borne transmission, 434, 435
Vector DNA, 380–381
Vegetables, 478
VEGF (vescular endothelial growth factor), 408
Vehicle transmission, 434, 435
Veins, 79, 79
  blood flow in, 85, 85
  cardiac, 80, 81
  femoral, 87
  great saphenous, 87
  hepatic, 86, 87
  hepatic portal, 87
  iliac, 86, 87
  internal jugular, 87
  jugular, 86, 87
  mesenteric, 87
  pulmonary, 80, 81, 86, 145, 151
  renal, 86, 87, 163
  subclavian, 87
  umbilical, 318, 318
  varicose, 88
Vena cavae, 80, 81, 86, 86
Venous duct, 318, 318
Ventilation, 142
Ventral root, 232, 232
Ventricles, 80, 80, 81
  brain, 224, 226, 226
Ventricular fibrillation, 83, 83
Venules, 79, 79, 121
Vermiform appendix, in immune system, 415
Vernix Caseosa, 319
Vertebrae, 188, 188
Vertebral canal, 189

Vertebral column, 185, 188, 188
Vertebrates, 2, 3
Vertigo, 261
Vescular endothelial growth factor (VEGF), 408
Vesicle, 38, 39
Vesicular follicle, 296, 297
Vessels. See Blood vessels
Vestibular canal, 257, 257
Viagra (sildenafil), 291
Victoria, Queen of England, 402
Villi, 121, 121
Viral load, of HIV infection, 462
Virulence factors, 434
Virus(es), 436–439
  cancer caused by, 477
  drug-resistant, 461
  emerging, 440, 440
  infections caused by, 435, 437–439
  replication of, 436, 436
  sexually transmitted diseases caused by, 457–458
  structure of, 436
Vision, 250, 250–255
  color, 252
  in equilibrium, 261
  pathway to brain for, 252–254
  photoreceptors in, 244, 252, 252
  of primates, 493
Visual accommodation, 251
Visual association area, 227, 228
Visual cortex, 254
Vital capacity, 146
Vitamin A, 124, 132, 133
  in cancer prevention, 478
  pregnancy and, 322
Vitamin B_1, 133
Vitamin B_2, 133

Vitamin B_6, 133
Vitamin B_{12}, 124, 133
Vitamin C, 132, 133, 478
Vitamin D, 64, 124, 132, 133, 134, 160, 182, 184
Vitamin E, 124, 132, 133
Vitamin K, 104, 122, 124, 133
Vitamins, 132, 133
Vitreous humor, 251
Vocal cords, 144, 144
Voice
  pitch of, 144
  in puberty, 144
Voltage, of axon, 220
Volume, in hearing, 257
Volume, respiratory, 146, 146
Vomer bone, 186
Vortex mixing, 384
VRE (vancomycin-resistant enterococci), 449
Vulva, 295, 295

Warmth receptors, 247
Waste disposal, by decomposers, 533
Water, 18–19
  conservation of, 526
  provision of, 533
  reabsorption of, 168
  as resource, 525, 525–526
Water cycle, 510, 510
Weight, body
  in female infertility, 304
  genetic predisposition and, 488
  in pregnancy, 324
Wernicke's area, 227, 228, 231, 231
West Nile virus, 440
White blood cells, 103, 103
White matter
  in central nervous system, 224
  in cerebrum, 228
  in spinal cord, 224–225, 225

White pulp, 414
Whitfield, Arthur Lee, 367
Williams syndrome, 396, 396
Windpipe. See Trachea
Wind power, 528–529, 529
Wolffian ducts, 320, 321
Women's Health Initiative, 283

Xenotransplantation, 428
Xiphoid process, 189, 189
X-linked alleles, 362, 362–363, 399, 399
X-linked recessive disorders, 402, 402
X-ray treatment
  cancer caused by, 476
  in cancer treatment, 481, 482
  in pregnancy, 322
XX male syndrome, 320
XY female syndrome, 320

Yeast, 432, 446
Yellow bone marrow, 178, 212
Y-linked alleles, 362, 399
Yolk sac, 311, 311, 315, 315

Zidovudine (AZT), 466
Zinc, 134, 135
Zona pellucida, of egg, 310, 310
Zovirax (acyclovir), 457
Zygomatic bone, 186, 187, 187
Zygomaticus, 200
Zygote, 310
  chromosomes of, 340
  oviducts and, 294